POST OFFICE DIRECTORY.

LIST OF POST OFFICES

IN

THE UNITED STATES

ARRANGED ALPHABETICALLY AND GIVING THE SALARIES OF THE POSTMASTERS.

ALSO

AN APPENDIX

CONTAINING THE NAMES OF POST OFFICES ARRANGED BY STATES AND COUNTIES,

WITH

MONEY-ORDER OFFICES,

AND

OTHER POSTAL INFORMATION

REVISED AND CORRECTED BY THE POST OFFICE DEPARTMENT, TO SEPTEMBER 1, 1870.

WASHINGTON.
GOVERNMENT PRINTING OFFICE.
1870.

OFFICERS OF THE DEPARTMENT.

POSTMASTER GENERAL.
JOHN A. J. CRESWELL, of Maryland.

CHIEF CLERK POST OFFICE DEPARTMENT.
E. L. CHILDS, of New Hampshire.

APPOINTMENT OFFICE.

FIRST ASSISTANT POSTMASTER GENERAL.
JAMES W. MARSHALL, of New Jersey.

CHIEF CLERK.
JAMES H. MARR, of Maryland.

CONTRACT OFFICE.

SECOND ASSISTANT POSTMASTER GENERAL.
GILES A. SMITH, of Illinois.

CHIEF CLERK.
JOHN L. FRENCH, of Ohio.

FINANCE OFFICE.

THIRD ASSISTANT POSTMASTER GENERAL.
WILLIAM H. H. TERRELL, of Indiana.

CHIEF CLERK.
WILLIAM M. IRELAND, of Pennsylvania

CHIEF OF DIVISION, DEAD-LETTER OFFICE.
CHARLES LYMAN, of Vermont.

SUPERINTENDENT OF THE MONEY-ORDER OFFICE.
C. F. MACDONALD, of Massachusetts.

SUPERINTENDENT OF THE OFFICE OF FOREIGN MAILS.
JOSEPH H. BLACKFAN, of New Jersey.

SUPERINTENDENT OF RAILWAY MAIL SERVICE.
GEORGE B. ARMSTRONG, of Illinois.

SUPERINTENDENT OF BLANK AGENCY.
N. A. GRAY, of Ohio

TOPOGRAPHER.
WALTER L. NICHOLSON, of District of Columbia.

SUPERINTENDENT OF POST OFFICE BUILDING AND DISBURSING CLERK.
FRANK A. MACARTNEY, of Pennsylvania.

AUDITOR OF THE TREASURY FOR THE POST OFFICE DEPARTMENT.
JACOB J. MARTIN, of Alabama.

CHIEF CLERK.
J. M. McGREW, of Ohio.

ORGANIZATION OF THE DEPARTMENT.

The direction and management of the Post Office Department are assigned by the Constitution and laws to the Postmaster General. That its business may be the more conveniently arranged and prepared for its final action, it is distributed among several bureaus, as follows: The Appointment Office, in charge of the First Assistant Postmaster General; the Contract Office, including the Inspection Division, in charge of the Second Assistant Postmaster General; the Finance Office, in charge of the Third Assistant Postmaster General; and the Money-order Office, and the office of Foreign Mails, each in charge of its superintendent.

APPOINTMENT OFFICE.—The First Assistant Postmaster General: To this office is assigned all business which relates to the establishment and discontinuance of post offices, changes of sites and names, appointment and removal of postmasters, route and local agents, and the giving of instructions to postmasters; also, the readjustment of postmasters' salaries, once in two years, under the act approved 1st July, 1864, and in special cases, as much oftener as may be deemed necessary. All applications for allowances, in post offices of the first and second classes, for rent, fuel, lights, and clerks, and all applications for allowances at separating offices, are examined in this office, and submitted to the Postmaster General for his decision. Postmarking and rating stamps, letter balances, blanks, wrapping paper, and twine are also furnished from this office.

CONTRACT OFFICE.—The Second Assistant Postmaster General: To this office is assigned the business of arranging the mail service of the United States, and placing the same under contract, embracing all correspondence and proceedings respecting the frequency of trips, mode of conveyance, and times of departures and arrivals on all the routes; the course of the mails between the different sections of the country, the points of mail distribution, and the regulations for the government of the domestic mail service of the United States. It prepares the advertisements for mail proposals, receives the bids, and has charge of the annual and occasional mail lettings, and the adjustment and execution of the contracts. All applications for the establishment or alteration of mail arrangements, and for mail messengers, should be sent to this office. All claims should be submitted to it for transportation service not under contract. From this office all postmasters at the ends of routes receive the statement of mail arrangements prescribed for the respective routes, and to it application should be made for mail bags, locks, and keys. It reports weekly to the Auditor all contracts executed, and all orders affecting the accounts for mail transportation; prepares the statistical exhibits of the mail service, and the reports to Congress of the mail lettings, giving a statement of each bid; also, of the contracts made, the new service originated, the curtailments ordered, and the additional allowances granted within the year.

[INSPECTION DIVISION.]—This division, formerly a distinct office, is now merged in and made part of the Contract Office. To this division is assigned the duty of receiving and examining the registers of the arrivals and departures of the mails, certificates of the service of route agents, and reports of mail failures; noting the delinquencies of contractors, and preparing cases thereon for the action of the Postmaster General; furnishing blanks for mail registers, reports of mail failures, and other duties which may be necessary to secure a faithful and exact performance of all mail contracts and service.

All cases of mail depredation, or violation of law by private expresses, or by the forging or illegal use of postage stamps, are under the supervision of this office, and should be reported to it.

All communications respecting lost money, lost letters, mail depredations, or other violations of law, should be directed "Contract Office, Inspection Division, Post Office Department."

All registers of the arrivals and departures of the mails, certificates of the service of route agents, and clerks in railway post offices, reports of mail failures, applications for blank registers, and reports of failures, and all complaints against contractors for irregular or imperfect service, should be directed "Contract Office, Inspection Division, Post Office Department."

[TOPOGRAPHICAL DIVISION.]—The Topographical Division of the department, attached to the Contract Office, consisting of the Topographer of the department and assistants, is charged with the preparation of the post-route maps and diagrams, and with the keeping up of the geographical information requisite for the various branches of the postal service.

Communications for this division (including contributions of maps and diagrams, which, for their general utility, are earnestly requested) should be directed "Second Assistant Postmaster General, Topographer, Post Office Department."

FINANCE OFFICE.—The Third Assistant Postmaster General: To this office is assigned the issuing of warrants and drafts in payment of balances reported by the Auditor to be due to mail contractors and other persons, and the superintendence of the rendition by postmasters of their quarterly returns of postages. It has charge of the DEAD-LETTER OFFICE, and of the issuing of postage stamps and stamped envelopes for the prepayment of postage.

To the Third Assistant Postmaster General postmasters at draft offices should direct their letters reporting quarterly the net proceeds of their offices, and those at depositing offices their certificates of deposit; to him should also be directed the weekly and monthly returns of the depositaries of the department, as well as all applications and receipts for postage stamps and stamped envelopes, and for dead letters.

MONEY-ORDER OFFICE.—To this office is assigned the general supervision and control of the postal money-order system throughout the United States.

OFFICE OF FOREIGN MAILS.—To this office is assigned the supervision of the ocean mail-steamship lines, and foreign postal arrangements.

TO THE AUDITOR FOR THE POST OFFICE DEPARTMENT postmasters should address their quarterly accounts and all correspondence in relation thereto.

POST ROADS.

Post roads, by law, are—1. Those roads of the country which are declared post roads by various acts of Congress. 2. All waters on which steamboats regularly pass from port to port. 3. The navigable canals of the several States for the time during which the mail may be carried thereon. 4. All railroads and plank roads in the United States. 5. Those roads on which the Postmaster General causes the mail to be carried from the nearest post offices, on legally declared post roads, to court-houses not otherwise provided with the mail. 6. All roads to special offices. 7. And such as are established by the Postmaster General as post routes under the tenth section of the act of March 3, 1851, in cities and towns where the postmasters are appointed by the President of the United States.

The general authority to establish post roads is not vested in the Postmaster General, nor can he extend or lengthen those already established. He can only place mail service on such roads as have been declared post roads by act of Congress, and for the expense of which appropriation has been made.

MAIL CONTRACTS.

The Union is divided into four Mail Contract Sections. A letting for one of these sections occurs every year, and contracts are made at such lettings for four consecutive years, commencing on the first day of July.

The sections and their current contract terms are—

1. Maine, New Hampshire, Vermont, Massachusetts, Rhode Island, Connecticut, and New York; current term to end 30th June, 1873.
2. New Jersey, Pennsylvania, Delaware, Maryland, (including District of Columbia,) and Ohio; current term to end 30th June, 1872.
3. West Virginia, Virginia, North Carolina, South Carolina, Georgia, Florida, Alabama, Mississippi, Louisiana, Texas, Arkansas, and Indian Territory; current term to end 30th June, 1871.
4. Tennessee, Kentucky, Missouri, Iowa, Illinois, Indiana, Michigan, Wisconsin, Minnesota, Dakota, Nebraska, Kansas, Colorado, New Mexico, Arizona, Utah, Montana, Idaho, Washington, Oregon, California, Nevada, Alaska, and Wyoming; current term to end 30th June, 1874.

LIST OF POST OFFICES IN THE UNITED STATES.

ABBREVIATION OF NAMES OF STATES AND TERRITORIES.

Ala ...... Alabama.
Alaska ... Alaska Ter.
Ariz .. ... Arizona Ter.
Ark...... Arkansas.
Cal ...... California.
Colo ..... Colorado Ter.
Conn .... Connecticut.
Dak ..... Dakota Ter.
Del ...... Delaware.
D. C...... Dist. of Columbia.
Fla ...... Florida.
Ga....... Georgia.
Idaho.... Idaho Ter.
Ill .... Illinois.
Ind ...... Indiana.
Ind. T.... Indian Ter.
Iowa .. .. Iowa.
Kans.... Kansas.
Ky...... Kentucky.
La ...... Louisiana.
Me...... Maine.
Md...... Maryland.
Mass .... Massachusetts.
Mich .... Michigan.
Minn.... Minnesota.
Miss .. .. Mississippi.
Mo...... Missouri.
Mont.... Montana Ter.
Nebr .... Nebraska.
Nev ..... Nevada.
N. H .... New Hampshire.
N. J..... New Jersey.
N. Mex.. New Mexico Ter.
N. Y..... New York.
N. C..... North Carolina.
Ohio .... Ohio.
Oreg .... Oregon.
Pa ...... Pennsylvania.
R. I..... Rhode Island.
S. C..... South Carolina.
Tenn.... Tennessee.
Tex ..... Texas.
Utah..... Utah Ter.
Vt ...... Vermont.
Va ...... Virginia.
Wash ... Washington Ter.
W. Va... West Virginia.
Wis ..... Wisconsin.
Wyo.... Wyoming Ter.

EXPLANATIONS.

The name of the office is given first, then the county, and last the State or Territory. Offices having a (*) affixed, denote money-order offices.

Those printed in SMALL CAPITAL letters designate the capitals of the States and Territories.

Those printed in *italics*, with a small *c. h.* in parentheses, indicate the county seats.

Those printed in *italics*, with a large *C. H.*, form a part of the name of the office, and also indicate the county seats.

LIST

OF

POST OFFICES IN THE UNITED STATES,

(ARRANGED ALPHABETICALLY,)

WITH THE SALARIES OF THE POSTMASTERS.

Post office	Salary
AARONSBURGH, Centre, Pa	$120
Aaron's Run, Montgomery, Ky	16
Abbeville, (*c. h.*,) Henry, Ala	180
Abbeville, (*c. h.*,) Wilcox, Ga	10
Abbeville, (*c. h.*,) Vermillion, La	100
Abbeville, Lafayette, Miss	50
Abbeville C. H., Abbeville, S. C	630
Abbeyville, Medina, Ohio	12
Abbot, Piscataquis, Me	34
Abbottsburgh, Bladen, N. C	24
Abbott's Creek, Davidson, N. C	27
Abbottstown, Adams, Pa	67
Abbot Village, Piscataquis, Me	70
Abb's Valley, Tazewell, Va	7
Abbyville, Mecklenburgh, Va	25
Aberdeen, Ohio, Ind	24
Aberdeen, Harford, Md	240
Aberdeen,* (*c. h.*,) Monroe, Miss	650
Aberdeen, Brown, Ohio	170
Aberdeen, Smith, Texas	12
Aberdeen Junction, Monroe, Miss	12
Aberfoil, Bullock, Ala	6
Abernathy, Perry, Mo	16
Abilene, (*c. h.*,) Dickinson, Kans	350
Abingdon,* Knox, Ill	900
Abingdon, Jefferson, Iowa	95
Abingdon, Harford, Md	91
Abingdon,* Washington, Va	1,100
Abington, Windham, Conn	130
Abington, Wayne, Ind	40
Abington, Plymouth, Mass	550
Abington, Montgomery, Pa	81
Abiqui, Rio Arriba, N. Mex	12
Aboite, Allen, Ind	12
Absecom,* Atlantic, N. J	330
Abscota, Calhoun, Mich	25
Academia, Juniata, Pa	160
Academy, Ontario, N. Y	25
Academy, Pocahontas, W. Va	48
Acasto, Clarke, Mo	22
Accident, Alleghany, Md	41
Accokeek, Prince George's, Md	12
Accokeek, Stafford, Va	15
Accomack C. H., Accomack, Va	130

Post office	Salary
Accord, Ulster, N. Y	$140
Accotink, Fairfax, Va	73
Ackermanville, Northampton, Pa	35
Ackerville, Washington, Wis	41
Ackley,* Hardin, Iowa	1,000
Acme, Grand Traverse, Mich	26
Acomb, McLennan, Tex	12
Acorn Hill, Frederick, Va	9
Acra, Greene, N. Y	110
Acton, Marion, Ind	170
Acton, York, Me	44
Acton, Middlesex, Mass	180
Acton, Hood, Texas	12
Acushnet, Bristol, Mass	210
Acworth, Cobb, Ga	280
Acworth, Sullivan, N. H	140
Ada, Kent, Mich	320
Ada, Choctaw, Miss	12
Ada, Ray, Mo	72
Ada,* Hardin, Ohio	640
Ada, Sheboygan, Wis	13
Adair, McDonough, Ill	37
Adairsville, Bartow, Ga	230
Adairville, Logan, Ky	130
Adaline, Marshall, W. Va	1
Adams, Wilcox, Ga	6
Adams, Adams, Ill	82
Adams, Decatur, Ind	120
Adams, Berkshire, Mass	1,100
Adams, Mower, Minn	100
Adams, Jefferson, N. Y	1,100
Adams, Seneca, Ohio	20
Adams, Armstrong, Pa	41
Adams, Walworth, Wis	16
Adams' Basin, Monroe, N. Y	130
Adamsburgh, Jefferson, Ark	10
Adamsburgh, Westmoreland, Pa	53
Adams Centre, Jefferson, N. Y	350
Adams Centre, Adams, Wis	12
Adams' Mills, Pulaski, Ky	24
Adams' Mills, Muskingum, Ohio	58
Adams Peak, Pottawatomie, Kans	12
Adams' Ridge, Defiance, Ohio	8
Adams' Run, Colleton, S. C	74

* Money-order office.

Post office	
Adams' Station, Albany, N. Y	$12
Adams' Station, Robertson, Tenn	10
Adamstown, Frederick, Md	180
Adamstown, Lancaster, Pa	50
Adamsville, Bradley, Ark	10
Adamsville, Kent, Del	16
Adamsville, Franklin, Mass	22
Adamsville, Cass, Mich	110
Adamsviile, Washington, N. Y	39
Adamsville, Muskingum, Ohio	140
Adamsville, Crawford, Pa	100
Adamsville, Newport, R. I	82
Adamsville, McNairy, Tenn	41
Adamsville, Beaver, Utah	10
Adamsville, Harrison, W. Va	16
Adario, Richland, Ohio	31
Addams' Tavern, Berks, Pa	2
Addison, Du Page, Ill	140
Addison, Humboldt, Iowa	9
Addison, Lenawee, Mich	170
Addison, Steuben, N. Y	1,200
Addison, Gallia, Ohio	30
Addison, Somerset, Pa	260
Addison, Addison, Vt	52
Addison, Washington, Wis	33
Addison Hill, Steuben, N. Y	76
Addison Point, Washington, Me	190
Adel,* (c. h.,) Dallas, Iowa	580
Adelante, Napa, Cal	12
Adelescat, Union, Dak	15
Adeline, Ogle, Ill	96
Adell, Sheboygan, Wis	53
Adelphi, Polk, Iowa	13
Adelphi, Ross, Ohio	140
Adena, Jefferson, Ohio	26
Adkins' Mills, Wayne, W. Va	12
Adrian, Hancock, Ill	12
Adrian,* (c. h.,) Lenawee, Mich	2,800
Adrian, Steuben, N. Y	57
Adrian, Seneca, Ohio	120
Adrian, Armstrong, Pa	12
Adriance, Dutchess, N. Y	77
Advance, Indiana, Pa	12
Adyeville, Perry, Ind	15
Aeriel, Marion, S. C	12
Aetna, Newaygo, Mich	12
Afton, Scott, Ind	12
Afton,* (c. h.,) Union, Iowa	820
Afton, Washington, Minn	130
Afton, Chenango, N. Y	290
Afton, Clermont, Ohio	46
Afton, Nelson, Va	120
Afton, Rock, Wis	68
Agatha, Vinton, Ohio	89
Agawam, Hampden, Mass	120
Agency City,* Wapello, Iowa	350
Agnew's Mills, Venango, Pa	41
Agricola, Mahaska, Iowa	17
Agricultural College, Prince George's, Md	12
Agricultural College, Centre, Pa	140
Ahnapee, Kewaunee, Wis	140
Ai, Fulton, Ohio	48
Aid, Lawrence, Ohio	25
Aiden Lair, Essex, N. Y	12
Aiken, Barnwell, S. C	1,100
Aiken, Bell, Tex	$12
Ainsworth, Washington, Iowa	240
Ainsworth Station, Cook, Ill	54
Airey's, Dorchester, Md	11
Air Hill, Montgomery, Ohio	20
Air Line, Hart, Ga	25
Air Mount, Yalabusha, Miss	16
Airy Dale, Huntingdon, Pa	16
Aken, Richland, Wis	11
Akersville, Fulton, Pa	8
Akin, Franklin, Ill	9
Akron, Peoria, Ill	21
Akron, Fulton, Ind	83
Akron, Tuscola, Mich	17
Akron, Harrison, Mo	12
Akron, Erie, N. Y	350
Akron,* (c. h.,) Summit, Ohio	2,600
Akron, Lancaster, Pa	80
Alabama, Genesee, N. Y	120
Alabama, Houston, Tex	26
Alabama, Polk, Wis	12
Alabaster, Iosco, Mich	36
Alafia, Hillsborough, Fla	12
Alameda, Alameda, Cal	99
Alamo, Contra Costa, Cal	33
Alamo, Montgomery, Ind	59
Alamo, Kalamazoo, Mich	18
Alanthus Grove, Gentry, Mo	5
Alanthus Hill, Hancock, Tenn	12
Alaska, Morgan, Ind	25
Alaska, Kent, Mich	180
Alaska, Kewaunee, Wis	12
Alba, Fillmore, Minn	10
Alba, Jasper, Mo	10
Alba, Bradford, Pa	110
Albanville, Monroe, Wis	18
Albany, (c. h.,) Dougherty, Ga	1,700
Albany, Whitesides, Ill	330
Albany, Delaware, Ind	39
Albany, Davis, Iowa	14
Albany, Nemaha, Kans	97
Albany,* (c. h.,) Clinton, Ky	60
Albany, Oxford, Me	48
Albany,* (c. h.,) Gentry, Mo	280
ALBANY,* (c. h.,) Albany, N. Y	4,000
Albany, Tuscarawas, Ohio	15
Albany,* (c. h.,) Linn, Oreg	600
Albany, Berks, Pa	12
Albany, Henry, Tenn	12
Albany, Orleans, Vt	140
Albany, Green, Wis	370
Albany Centre, Orleans, Vt	12
Albemarle, Assumption, La	12
Albemarle, (c. h.,) Stanly, N. C	81
Albert Lea,* (c. h.,) Freeborn, Minn	760
Alberton, Howard, Md	90
Alberton's, Duplin, N. C	12
Albia,* (c. h.,) Monroe, Iowa	1,200
Albion, Mendocino, Cal	25
Albion,* (c. h.,) Edwards, Ill	330
Albion, (c. h.,) Noble, Ind	340
Albion, Marshall, Iowa	240
Albion, Kennebec, Me	91
Albion,* Calhoun, Mich	2,200
Albion, Wright, Minn	11
Albion,* (c. h.,) Orleans, N. Y	2,500

* Money-order office.

Albion, Ashland, Ohio	$36
Albion,* Erie, Pa	290
Albion, Providence, R. I	78
Albion, Dane, Wis	200
Albrightsville, Carbon, Pa	14
Albuquerque, (*c. h.*,) Bernalillo, N. Mex	970
Alburgh, Grand Isle, Vt	170
Alburgh Centre, Grand Isle, Vt	76
Alburgh Springs, Grand Isle, Vt	180
Alburtis, Lehigh, Pa	160
Alcona, Alcona, Mich	25
Alcony, Miami, Ohio	12
Alden, McHenry, Ill	110
Alden, Hardin, Iowa	260
Alden, Freeborn, Minn	16
Alden, Erie, N. Y	290
Alden, Polk, Wis	12
Alden Centre, Erie, N. Y	12
Alden's Corners, Dane, Wis	27
Aldenville, Wayne, Pa	72
Alder Brook, Franklin, N. Y	10
Alder Creek, Oneida, N. Y	93
Alderley, Dodge, Wis	110
Aldie, Loudoun, Va	160
Aledo,* (*c. h.*,) Mercer, Ill	860
Aleman, Socorro, N. Mex	12
Aleppo, Greene, Pa	12
Alert, Decatur, Ind	12
Alert, Butler, Ohio	12
Alexander, Morgan, Ill	120
Alexander, Washington, Me	77
Alexander, Genesee, N. Y	210
Alexandria, Merced, Cal	12
Alexandria, Madison, Ind	200
Alexandria, Campbell, Ky	130
Alexandria,* (*c. h.*,) Rapides, La	950
Alexandria, (*c. h.*,) Douglas, Minn	420
Alexandria, Clarke, Mo	330
Alexandria, Grafton, N. H	98
Alexandria, Jefferson, N. Y	220
Alexandria, Licking, Ohio	200
Alexandria, Huntingdon, Pa	320
Alexandria, De Kalb, Tenn	130
Alexandria,* (*c. h.*,) Alexandria, Va	2,700
Alfonte, Madison, Ind	27
Alford, Berkshire, Mass	80
Alfordsville, Daviess, Ind	71
Alfred,* (*c. h.*,) York, Me	540
Alfred, Allegany, N. Y	160
Alfred, Meigs, Ohio	35
Alfred Centre.,* Allegany, N. Y	420
Algansee, Branch, Mich	10
Algiers, Orleans, La	270
Algodon, Ionia, Mich	10
Algodones, Santa Aña, N. Mex	12
Algona,* (*c. h.*,) Kossuth, Iowa	550
Algonac, St. Clair, Mich	250
Algonquin, McHenry, Ill	140
Algonquin, Carroll, Ohio	17
Alhambra, Madison, Ill	58
Alhambra, Trempealeau, Wis	8
Alice, Oceana, Mich	17
Alice, Cedar, Mo	12
Aliceton, Boyle, Ky	34
Alida, Davis, Kans	10
Alkire's Mills, Lewis, W. Va	$10
Allamakee, Allamakee, Iowa	13
Allamuchy, Warren, N. J	140
Allandale, Banks, Ga	4
Allard's Corners, Orange, N. J	25
Allatoona, Bartow, Ga	68
Allbright, Preston, W. Va	13
Allegan,* (*c. h.*,) Allegan, Mich	1,900
Allegany, Cattaraugus, N. Y	460
Alleghany, Sierra, Cal	88
Alleghany Spring, Montgomery, Va	210
Alleghany Station, Alleghany, Va	12
Allegheny,* Allegheny, Pa	3,100
Allegheny Bridge, McKean, Pa	51
Allemance, Guilford, N. C	6
Alleman's, Clearfield, Pa	12
Allen, Miami, Ind	52
Allen, Lyon, Kans	15
Allen, Hillsdale, Mich	300
Allen, Allegany, N. Y	12
Allen, Cumberland, Pa	110
Allen Centre, Allegany, N. Y	18
Allendale, Wabash, Ill	24
Allendale, Green, Ky	30
Allendale, Ottawa, Mich	17
Allendale, Worth, Mo	77
Allendale, Bergen, N. J	12
Allendale, Barnwell, S. C	65
Allenport, Washington, Pa	38
Allen's, Richmond, Ga	10
Allen's, Eaton, Mich	12
Allen's, Miami, Ohio	48
Allen's Creek, Amherst, Va	120
Allen's Factory, Marion, Ala	10
Allen's Fork, Jackson, W. Va	5
Allen's Fresh, Charles, Md	42
Allen's Grove, Scott, Iowa	31
Allen's Grove, Walworth, Wis	160
Allen's Hill, Ontario, N. Y	200
Allen Springs, Allen, Ky	12
Allen's Springs, Pope, Ill	14
Allen's Station, Steuben, N. Y	13
Allen's Store, Prentiss, Miss	5
Allenstown, Merrimack, N. H	24
Allensville, Todd, Ky	150
Allensville, Person, N. C	6
Allensville, Vinton, Ohio	44
Allensville, Mifflin, Pa	94
Allenton, Wilcox, Ala	67
Allenton, St. Louis, Mo	61
Allenton, Washington, R. I	70
Allentown, Monmouth, N. J	300
Allentown,* (*c. h.*,) Lehigh, Pa	2,600
Allenville, Cape Girardeau, Mo	12
Alleyton, Colorado, Tex	100
Alliance,* Stark, Ohio	2,300
Allis Hollow, Bradford, Pa	13
Allison, Dubuque, Iowa	31
Alloa, Columbia, Wis	34
Allowaystown, Salem, N. J	170
Allston, Middlesex, Mass	310
Alma, Marion, Ill	100
Alma, Whitley, Ind	12
Alma, (*c. h.*,) Wabaunsee, Kans	120
Alma, Gratiot, Mich	400
Alma, Allegany, N. Y	15

* Money-order office.

Alma, Ross, Ohio	$12
Alma, Rusk, Tex	10
Alma, Weber, Utah	12
Alma, Page, Va	31
Alma, (c. h.,) Buffalo, Wis	390
Alma City, Waseca, Minn	65
Almeda, Newton, Mo	18
Almena, Van Buren, Mich	34
Almira, Benzie, Mich	37
Almond, Randolph, Ala	17
Almond, Allegany, N. Y	430
Almond, Portage, Wis	92
Almont, Lapeer, Mich	770
Almoral, Delaware, Iowa	18
Alna, Lincoln, Me	73
Alonzaville, Shenandoah, Va	12
Alpena, (c. h.,)* Alpena, Mich	1,000
Alpha, Scott, Ind	50
Alpha, Clinton, Ky	12
Alpha, Grundy, Mo	41
Alpha, Greene, Ohio	80
Alpharetta, (c. h.,) Milton, Ga	67
Alpine, Talladega, Ala	120
Alpine, Clark, Ark	16
Alpine, Chattooga, Ga	12
Alpine, Fayette, Ind	12
Alpine, Wapello, Iowa	28
Alpine, Kent, Mich	30
Alpine, Schuyler, N. Y	92
Alpine, York, Pa	12
Alpine City, Utah, Utah	27
Alpine Depot, Morgan, W. Va	21
Alps, Rensselaer, N. Y	16
Alquina, Fayette, Ind	10
Alsace, Berks, Pa	8
Alstead, Cheshire, N. H	280
Alstead Centre, Cheshire, N. H	23
Altamont, Shelby, Iowa	12
Altamont, Alleghany, Md	63
Altamont, (c. h.,) Grundy, Tenn	63
Alta Vista, Daviess, Mo	190
Alta Vista, Russell, Va	6
Altay, Schuyler, N. Y	96
Altenburgh, Perry, Mo	100
Altha, Stoddard, Mo	12
Alto, Howard, Ind	19
Alto, Kent, Mich	8
Alto, Franklin, Tenn	22
Alto, Cherokee, Tex	41
Alton,* Madison, Ill	2,700
Alton, Crawford, Ind	89
Alton, Penobscot, Me	30
Alton, Kent, Mich	21
Alton, (c. h.,) Oregon, Mo	29
Alton, Belknap, N. H	270
Alton, Wayne, N. Y	120
Alton, Franklin, Ohio	73
Alton, McKean, Pa	100
Altona,* Knox, Ill	990
Altona, Marshall, Ky	12
Altona, Bates, Mo	59
Altona, Clinton, N. Y	50
Alton Bay, Belknap, N. H	12
Alton Junction, Madison, Ill	38
Altoona, Polk, Iowa	140
Altoona, Wilson, Kans	12
Altoona,* Blair, Pa	$2,800
Alum Bank, Bedford, Pa	55
Alum Creek, Delaware, Ohio	13
Alum Creek, Bastrop, Tex	15
Alum Rock, Clarion, Pa	9
Alum Springs, Rockbridge, Va	22
Alva, Aroostook, Me	55
Alvarado, Alameda, Cal	70
Alvarado, Steuben, Ind	12
Alvarado, Johnson, Tex	15
Alverson, Ingham, Mich	12
Alvira, Union, Pa	20
Alviso, Santa Clara, Cal	45
Alvon, Greenbrier, W. Va	12
Amador City, Amador, Cal	76
Amadore, Sanilac, Mich	12
Amagansett, Suffolk, N. Y	96
Amanda, Fairfield, Ohio	240
Amandaville, Hart, Ga	4
Amandaville, Cumberland, Ky	14
Amazonia, Andrew, Mo	77
Amber, Mason, Mich	12
Amber, Martin, Minn	5
Amber, Onondaga, N. Y	39
Amberson's Valley, Franklin, Pa	25
Amboy,* Lee, Ill	1,400
Amboy, Miami, Ind	63
Amboy, Jasper, Iowa	12
Amboy, Hillsdale, Mich	22
Amboy, Ashtabula, Ohio	84
Amboy Centre, Oswego, N. Y	41
Ambrose, Indiana, Pa	12
Amelia, Clermont, Ohio	180
Amelia, C. H., Amelia, Va	310
Amenia, Dutchess, N. Y	760
Amenia Union, Dutchess, N. Y	150
America, Wabash, Ind	24
America City, Nemaha, Kans	68
American Fork, Utah, Utah	130
American Ranch, Shasta, Cal	20
Americus, (c. h.,)* Sumter, Ga	2,000
Americus, Tippecanoe, Ind	36
Americus, Lyon, Kans	170
Americus, (c. h.,) Jackson, Miss	15
Americus, Montgomery, Mo	12
Ames, Story, Iowa	780
Ames, Montgomery, N. Y	85
Amesbury, Essex, Mass	1,400
Amesville, Athens, Ohio	260
Amherst, Hancock, Me	24
Amherst,* Hampshire, Mass	2,300
Amherst, Fillmore, Minn	12
Amherst, (c. h.,) Hillsborough, N. H	420
Amherst, Lorain, Ohio	80
Amherst, Portage, Wis	95
Amherst C. H., Amherst, Va	250
Amish, Johnson, Iowa	27
Amissville, Rappahannock, Va	78
Amite City, (c. h.,) Tangipahoa, La	440
Amity, Clark, Ark	24
Amity, Livingston, Ill	16
Amity, Johnson, Ind	50
Amity, Scott, Iowa	54
Amity, Aroostook, Me	19
Amity, Orange, N. Y	38
Amity, Yam Hill, Oreg	61

* Money-order office.

Amity, Washington, Pa	$40
Amity Hill, Iredell, N. C	16
Amityville, Suffolk, N. Y	170
Amo, Hendricks, Ind	150
Amoskeag, Hillsborough, N. H	32
Amsden, Montcalm, Mich	22
Amsterdam, Cass, Ind	20
Amsterdam,* Montgomery, N. Y	2,200
Amsterdam, Jefferson, Ohio	80
Amsterdam, Botetourt, Va	100
Anacostia, Washington, D. C	80
Anaheim, Los Angeles, Cal	220
Anahuac, Chambers, Tex	12
Analomink, Monroe, Pa	51
*Anamosa,** (*c. h.*,) Jones, Iowa	990
Anandale, Dutchess, N. Y	200
Anandale, Butler, Pa	16
Anawauk, Le Sueur, Minn	8
Anchorage, Buffalo, Wis	23
Ancona, Livingston, Ill	89
Ancora, Camden, N. J	12
Ancram, Columbia, N. Y	120
Ancram Centre, Columbia, N. Y	12
Ancram Lead Mines, Columbia, N. Y	22
Andalusia, Sanford, Ala	28
Andalusia, Rock Island, Ill	200
Andalusia, Bucks, Pa	170
Anderson, Mendocino, Cal	24
*Anderson,** (*c. h.*,) Madison, Ind	1,200
Anderson, Pope, Minn	16
Anderson, Alcorn, Miss	12
Anderson, Clinton, Mo	31
Anderson, Ross, Ohio	48
Anderson, (*c. h.*,) Grimes, Tex	320
Anderson, Burnett, Wis	10
*Anderson, C. H.,** Anderson, S. C	730
Andersonburgh, Perry, Pa	65
Anderson's Mills, Butler, Pa	19
Anderson's Mills, Pickens, S. C	12
Anderson's Store, Caswell, N. C	12
Andersonville, Pickens, Ala	12
Andersonville, Sumter, Ga	76
Andersonville, Franklin, Ind	70
Andes, Delaware, N. Y	360
Andover, Tolland, Conn	190
Andover, Henry, Ill	540
Andover, Oxford, Me	230
Andover,* Essex, Mass	2,300
Andover, Merrimack, N. H	210
Andover, Sussex, N. J	200
Andover,* Allegany, N. Y	520
Andover, Ashtabula, Ohio	170
Andover, Windsor, Vt	52
Andrew, (*c. h.*,) Jackson, Iowa	510
Andrew Chapel, Madison, Tenn	16
Andrew Johnson, Martin, Minn	15
Andrews, Morrow, Ohio	37
Andrews, Spottsylvania, Va	90
Andrusville, Franklin, N. Y	100
Andy, Monongalia, W. Va	4
Angelica, (*c. h.*,) Allegany, N. Y	860
Angelica, Shawanaw, Wis	28
Angel's Camp, Calaveras, Cal	160
Angerona, Jackson, W. Va	15
Angola, Sussex, Del	12
*Angola,** (*c. h.*,) Steuben, Ind	480
Angola, Erie, N. Y	$310
Angola, Clermont, Ohio	9
Anita, Cass, Iowa	78
Anna,* Union, Ill	620
Anna, Shelby, Ohio	150
Annapolis, Crawford, Ill	29
Annapolis, Parke, Ind	140
ANNAPOLIS,* (*c. h.*,) Anne Arundel, Md	2,400
Annapolis, Jefferson, Ohio	42
Annapolis Junction, Anne Arundel, Md	240
*Ann Arbor,** (*c. h.*,) Washtenaw, Mich	3,500
Annaton, Grant, Wis	49
Annawan, Henry, Ill	430
Annieville, Clay, Iowa	12
Annin Creek, McKean, Pa	11
Annisquam, Essex, Mass	160
Annville,* Lebanon, Pa	430
Anoka, Cass, Ind	14
*Anoka,** (*c. h.*,) Anoka, Minn	650
Anson, Somerset, Me	73
Ansonia, New Haven, Conn	1,400
Ansonia, Darke, Ohio	88
Ansonville, Anson, N. C	31
Ansonville, Clearfield, Pa	140
Antelope, Yolo, Cal	10
Antelope, Charles Mix, Dak	12
Antelope, Marion, Kans	12
Antelope, Jefferson, Nebr	12
Antes Fort, Lycoming, Pa	110
Antestown, Blair, Pa	140
Anthony, Delaware, Ind	7
Anthony, Hunterdon, N. J	16
Anthony, Kent, R. I	200
Anthony House, Nevada, Cal	12
Antioch, Pickens, Ala	6
Antioch,* Contra Costa, Cal	560
Antioch, Troup, Ga	230
Antioch, Lake, Ill	110
Antioch, Huntingdon, Ind	270
Antioch, Washington, Ky	24
Antioch, Alcorn, Miss	20
Antioch, Robeson, N. C	12
Antioch, Monroe, Ohio	59
Antioch, York, S. C	6
Antioch, Gibson, Tenn	12
Antioch, Lavaca, Tex	15
Antoine, Clark, Ark	62
Antreville, Abbeville, S. C	18
Antrim, Watonwan, Minn	15
Antrim, Hillsborough, N. H	320
Antrim, Guernsey, Ohio	90
Antrim City, Antrim, Mich	76
Antwerp, Jefferson. N. Y	570
Antwerp,* Paulding, Ohio	290
Apache Pass, Pima, Ariz	12
Apalachicola, (*c. h.*,) Franklin, Fla	370
Apalachin, Tioga, N. Y	130
Aplington, Butler, Iowa	200
Apollo, Armstrong, Pa	330
Apopka, Orange, Fla	12
Appanoose, Hancock, Ill	37
Appanoose, Franklin, Kans	12
Apperson's, Charles City, Va	12

* Money-order office.

Post office	
Applebachsville, Bucks, Pa	$58
Apple Creek, Wayne, Ohio	190
Applegate, Jackson, Oreg	24
Apple Grove, Marion, Ala	12
Apple Grove, Meigs, Ohio	23
Apple Grove, York, Pa	25
Apple Grove, Louisa, Va	12
Apple River, Jo. Daviess, Ill	360
Appleton, Bourbon, Kans	67
Appleton, Knox, Me	100
Appleton, Cape Girardeau, Mo	110
Appleton, Licking, Ohio	54
Appleton, Lawrence, Tenn	7
Appleton,* (*c. h.*,) Outagamie, Wis	2,200
Applewood, Caroline, Va	15
Appling, (*c. h.*,) Columbia, Ga	20
Appomattox, C. H., Appomattox, Va	22
Aptos, Santa Cruz, Cal	12
Apulia, Onondaga, N. Y	85
Aquasco, Prince George's, Md	86
Aquashicola, Carbon, Pa	21
Aquilla, Franklin, Ga	12
Aquone, Macon, N. C	12
Arabia, Lawrence, Ohio	44
Arago,* Richardson, Nebr	260
Aransas, Bee, Texas	12
Ararat, Susquehanna, Pa	41
Ararat, Patrick, Va	5
Arba, Randolph, Ind	45
Arbela, Scotland, Mo	25
Arbor Hill, Adair, Iowa	28
Arbor Hill, Augusta, Va	27
Arbor Vitae, Bullock, Ala	17
Arbuckle, Mason, W. Va	92
Arcade,* Wyoming, N. Y	370
Arcadia, Morgan, Ill	56
Arcadia, Hamilton, Ind	150
Arcadia, Crawford, Kans	76
Arcadia, Bienville, La	18
Arcadia, Wayne, N. Y	210
Arcadia, Davidson, N. C	10
Arcadia, Hancock, Ohio	110
Arcadia, Washington, R. I	38
Arcadia, Sullivan, Tenn	36
Arcadia, Trempealeau, Wis	90
Arcana, Grant, Ind	12
Arcanum, Darke, Ohio	240
Arcata, Humboldt, Cal	180
Archbald, Luzerne, Pa	290
Archbold, Fulton, Ohio	240
Archer, Alachua, Fla	33
Archer, Harrison, Ohio	12
Archerville, Campbell, Tenn	12
Arch Spring, Blair, Pa	54
Arcola,* Douglas, Ill	720
Arcola, Allen, Ind	62
Arcola, Monona, Iowa	12
Arcola, St. Helena, La	74
Arcola, Bergen, N. J	12
Arcola, Loudoun, Va	61
Arena, Iowa, Wis	270
Arenac, Bay, Mich	180
Arendahl, Fillmore, Minn	120
Arendtsville, Adams, Pa	86
Arenzville, Cass, Ill	130
Argenta, Lander, Nev	12
Argentine, Genesee, Mich	$59
Argo, Jefferson, Ala	12
Argo, Carroll, Ill	28
Argo, Lucas, Iowa	8
Argo, Winona, Minn	25
Argo, Crawford, Mo	6
Argos, Marshall, Ind	230
Argus, Crenshaw, Ala	12
Argusville, Schoharie, N. Y	91
Argyle, Winnebago, Ill	37
Argyle, Penobscot, Me	19
Argyle, Washington, N. Y	430
Argyle, La Fayette, Wis	180
Arica, DeKalb, Mo	12
Ariel, Wayne, Pa	30
Arington, Atchison, Kans	12
Arion, Cloud, Kans	12
Arizona, Burt, Nebr	39
Arizona City,* Yuma, Ariz	360
Arizonia, Claiborne, La	12
Arkabutla, De Soto, Miss	12
Arkada, Mason, Wash	3
Arkadelphia, Walker, Ala	12
Arkadelphia,* (*c. h.*,) Clark, Ark	480
Arkansas City, Cowley, Kans	12
Arkansas Post, Arkansas, Ark	21
Arkansaw, Pepin, Wis	14
Arkdale, Adams, Wis	59
Arkport, Steuben, N. Y	460
Arkwright Summit, Chautauqua, N. Y	15
Arland, Jackson, Mich	32
Arlington,* Bureau, Ill	400
Arlington, Middlesex, Mass	760
Arlington, Van Buren, Mich	22
Arlington, Sibley, Minn	12
Arlington, Phelps, Mo	740
Arlington, Hancock, Ohio	38
Arlington, Wayne, Pa	12
Arlington, Bennington, Vt	350
Arlington, Alexandria, Va	38
Armada, Macomb, Mich	370
Armagh, Indiana, Pa	160
Armenia, Juneau, Wis	14
Armiesburgh, Parke, Ind	27
Armington, Tazewell, Ill	50
Armonk, Westchester, N. Y	99
Armstrong, Vanderburgh, Ind	7
Armstrong's Corners, Fond du Lac, Wis	11
Armstrong's Grove, Emmett, Iowa	10
Armstrong's Mills, Belmont, Ohio	20
Armuchee, Floyd, Ga	12
Arnaudville, St. Landry, La	15
Arnettsville, Monongalia, W. Va	34
Arney, Owen, Ind	68
Arneytown, Burlington, N. J	5
Arnheim, Brown, Ohio	32
Arno, (*c. h.*,) Douglas, Mo	25
Arnoldsburgh, Calhoun, W. Va	12
Arnold's Mills, Pickens, S. C	4
Arnold's Store, Anne Arundel, Md	8
Arnold's Store, Bedford, Tenn	12
Arnoldsville, Buchanan, Mo	21
Arnoldton, Campbell, Va	18
Arnot, Tioga, Pa	200

* Money-order office.

Aroma, Kankakee, Ill	$68
Aroma, Dickinson, Kans	13
Arrington, Nelson, Va	160
Arrow Rock, Saline, Mo	560
Arroyo, Elk, Pa	25
Arroyo Grande, San Luis Obispo, Cal	12
Artesia, Lowndes, Miss	190
Arthursburgh, Dutchess, N. Y	75
Arvonia, Osage, Kans	12
Asbury, La Salle, Ill	100
Asbury, Warren, N. J	150
Ascension, Sullivan, Ind	80
Ascutneyville, Windsor, Vt	140
Ashaway, Washington, R. I	280
Ashborough, Clay, Ind	19
Ashborough, (*c. h.*,) Randolph, N. C	260
Ashburn, Pike, Mo	2
Ashburnham, Worcester, Mass	670
Ashburnham Depot, Worcester, Mass	470
Ashby, Middlesex, Mass	240
Ashbysburgh, Hopkins, Ky	4
Ashby's Mills, Montgomery, Ind	46
Ash Creek, Oktibbeha, Miss	12
Ashepoo, Colleton, S. C	12
Asherville, Mitchell, Kan	12
Asheville,* (*c. h.*) Buncombe, N. C	900
Ashfield, Franklin, Mass	340
Ash Flat, Lawrence, Ark	8
Ashford, Windham, Conn	120
Ashford, Cattaraugus, N. Y	72
Ashford, Fond du Lac, Wis	19
Ash Grove, Iroquois, Ill	51
Ash Grove Tippecanoe, Ind	14
Ash Grove, Greene, Mo	100
Ashippen, Watonwan, Minn	12
Ashippun, Dodge, Wis	21
Ashkum, Iroquois, Ill	78
Ashland, (*c. h.*,) Clay, Ala	12
Ashland, Cass, Ill	140
Ashland, Henry, Ind	57
Ashland, Wapello, Iowa	61
Ashland, Boyd, Ky	460
Ashland, Aroostook, Me	79
Ashland, Middlesex, Mass	490
Ashland, Newaygo, Mich	28
Ashland, Dodge, Minn	12
Ashland, Boone, Mo	130
Ashland, (*c. h.*,) Saunders, Nebr	350
Ashland, Grafton, N. H	530
Ashland, Greene, N. Y	99
Ashland,* (*c. h.*,) Ashland, Ohio	1,700
Ashland,* Schuylkill, Pa	2,100
Ashland, Hanover, Va	340
Ashland City, (*c.h.*,) Cheatham, Tenn	20
Ashland Mills, Jackson, Oreg	120
Ashley,* Washington, Ill	910
Ashley, Kent, Mich	24
Ashley, Pike, Mo	230
Ashley, Delaware, Ohio	240
Ashley Falls, Berkshire, Mass	150
Ashley Mills, Pulaski, Ark	12
Ashleyville, Hampden, Mass	25
Ashlick, Randolph, W. Va	1
Ashmore, Coles, Ill	180
Ashport, Lauderdale, Tenn	$12
Ash Ridge, Massac, Ill	8
Ash Ridge, Brown, Ohio	20
Ashtabula,* Ashtabula, Ohio	2 000
Ashton, Lee, Ill	530
Ashton, Clarke, Mo	23
Ashton, Providence, R. I	220
Ashton, Dane, Wis	74
Ashuelot, Cheshire, N. H	180
Ashville, (*c. h.*,) St. Clair, Ala	96
Ashwood, Tensas, La	25
Askeaton, Brown, Wis	12
Askew, Phillips, Ark	19
Aspen Hill, Giles, Tenn	51
Aspen Well, Charlotte, Va	17
Asper, Livingston, Mo	12
Aspin Grove, Rockingham, N. C	12
Aspinwall, Nemaha, Nebr	240
Aspinwall, Bradford, Pa	27
Assabet, Middlesex, Mass	410
Assamoosick, Southampton, Va	12
Assumption, Christian, Ill	420
Assumption, (*c. h.*,) Assumption, La	60
Assyria, Barry, Mich	22
Astoria, Fulton, Ill	200
Astoria, Wright, Mo	16
Astoria, Queens, N. Y	840
Astoria,* (*c. h.*,) Clatsop, Oreg	530
Asylum, Bradford, Pa	29
Atalissa, Muscatine, Iowa	230
Atalla, Etowah, Ala	12
Atchison,* (*c. h.*,) Atchison, Kans	3,200
Atchison, Washington, Pa	14
Atco, Camden, N. J	160
Athalia, Lawrence, Ohio	44
Athens,* (*c. h.*,) Limestone, Ala	540
Athens,* Clarke, Ga	2,500
Athens, Menard, Ill	220
Athens, Fayette, Ky	39
Athens, Claiborne, La	18
Athens, Somerset, Me	220
Athens, Calhoun, Mich	120
Athens, Monroe, Miss	12
Athens, Clarke, Mo	110
Athens, Richardson, Nebr	26
Athens, Greene, N. Y	240
Athens,* (*c. h.*,) Athens, Ohio	1,200
Athens, Bradford, Pa	740
Athens,* McMinn, Tenn	520
Athens, (*c. h.*,) Henderson, Tex	44
Athens, Windham, Vt	37
Athensville, Greene, Ill	40
Athlone, Monroe, Mich	61
Athol, Worcester, Mass	610
Athol, Warren, N. Y	24
Athol. Jackson, Wis	12
Athol Depot, Worcester, Mass	1,100
Atkinson, Henry, Ill	380
Atkinson, Piscataquis, Me	55
Atkinson, Rockingham, N. H	65
Atkinson Depot, Rockingham, N. H.	110
Atkinson's Mills, Mifflin, Pa	14
Atkinsonville, Owen, Ind	12
Atlanta, Columbia, Ark	12
Atlanta, San Joaquin, Cal	18
ATLANTA,* (*c. h.*,) Fulton, Ga	4,000

* Money-order office.

Atlanta, Alturas, Idaho	$49
Atlanta,* Logan, Ill	1,000
Atlanta, Buchanan, Iowa	3
Atlanta, Winn, La	12
Atlanta, Macon, Mo	140
Atlanta, Pickaway, Ohio	25
Atlantic,* Cass, Iowa	1,100
Atlantic City,* Atlantic, N. J	1,400
Atlantic City, Sweet Water, Wyo	12
Atlanticville, Suffolk, N. Y	19
Atlas, Pike, Ill	19
Atlas, Genesee, Mich	82
Atlas, Belmont, Ohio	28
Atlee's Station, Hanover, Va	12
Atoka, Choctaw Nation, Ind. T	12
Atoy, Cherokee, Tex	12
Attanam, Yakima, Wash	12
Attica,* Fountain, Ind	1,200
Attica, Marion, Iowa	84
Attica, Saunders, Nebr	12
Attica, Wyoming, N. Y	1,100
Attica,* Seneca, Ohio	250
Attica, Green, Wis	54
Attila, Williamson, Ill	14
Attleborough, Bristol, Mass	1,000
Attleborough, Bucks, Pa	300
Attlebury, Dutchess, N. Y	28
Atwater, Kandiyohi, Minn	12
Atwater, Portage, Ohio	210
Atwater Centre, Portage, Ohio	12
Atwood, Kosciusko, Ind	130
Atwood, Antrim, Mich	12
Atwood, Armstrong, Pa	13
Aubrey, Johnson, Kans	72
Auburn,* Lee, Ala	500
Auburn, Arkansas, Ark	20
*Auburn,** (*c. h.*,) Placer, Cal	410
Auburn, Gwinnett, Ga	12
Auburn, Sangamon, Ill	340
*Auburn,** (*c. h.*,) De Kalb, Ind	450
Auburn, Mahaska, Iowa	8
Auburn, Shawnee, Kans	100
Auburn,* Logan, Ky	330
*Auburn,** (*c. h.*,) Androscoggin, Me	2,000
Auburn, Worcester, Mass	100
Auburn, Lincoln, Mo	92
Auburn, Rockingham, N. H	110
Auburn, Salem, N. J	30
*Auburn,** (*c. h.*,) Cayuga, N. Y	4,000
Auburn, Wake, N. C	15
Auburn, Geauga, Ohio	130
Auburn, Baker, Oreg	110
Auburn, Schuylkill, Pa	130
Auburn, Cannon, Tenn	12
Auburn Centre, Susquehanna, Pa	44
Auburn Dale, Middlesex, Mass	470
Auburn Four Corners, Susquehanna, Pa	58
Audenried, Carbon, Pa	420
Aughwick Mills, Huntingdon, Pa	24
Auglaize, Van Wert, Ohio	13
Au Gres, Bay, Mich	18
Augusta, (*c. h.*,) Woodruff, Ark	320
*Augusta,** (*c. h.*,) Richmond, Ga	4,000
Augusta, Hancock, Ill	470
Augusta, Des Moines, Iowa	82
Augusta, Butler, Kans	$62
Augusta, Bracken, Ky	440
AUGUSTA,* (*c. h.*,) Kennebec	3,000
Augusta, Kalamazoo, Mich	450
Augusta, (*c. h.*,) Perry, Miss	16
Augusta, St. Charles, Mo	110
Augusta, Oneida, N. Y	80
Augusta, Carroll, Ohio	160
Augusta, Northumberland, Pa	21
Augusta, Houston, Tex	14
Augusta, Eau Claire, Wis	430
Augusta Station, Marion, Ind	63
Auman's Hill, Montgomery, N. C	15
Aumsville, Marion, Oreg	25
Auraria, Lumpkin, Ga	21
Aurelia, Cherokee, Iowa	12
Aurelius, Ingham, Mich	60
Aurelius, Cayuga, N. Y	62
Auriesville, Montgomery, N. Y	26
Aurora, Etowah, Ala	10
Aurora,* Kane, Ill	3,800
Aurora,* Dearborn, Ind	1,600
Aurora, Keokuk, Iowa	10
Aurora, Marshall, Ky	16
Aurora, Hancock, Me	30
Aurora, Steele, Minn	12
Aurora, Wright, Mo	12
*Aurora,** (*c. h.*,) Esmeralda, Nev	500
Aurora, Cayuga, N. Y	690
Aurora, Portage, Ohio	210
Aurora, Washington, Wis	25
Aurorahville, Waushara, Wis	94
Aurora Mills, Marion, Oreg	45
Au Sable, Iosco, Mich	360
Au Sable Forks, Essex, N. Y	370
Austen, Preston, W. Va	25
Austerlitz, Kent, Mich	65
Austerlitz, Columbia, N. Y	54
Austin, Prairie, Ark	150
Austin, Cook, Ill	40
Austin, Scott, Ind	140
Austin, Oakland, Mich	20
*Austin,** (*c. h.*,) Mower, Minn	1,900
Austin, (*c. h.*,) Tunica, Miss	39
Austin, Cass, Mo	230
*Austin,** (*c. h.*,) Lander, Nev	2,000
Austin, Wilson, Tenn	25
AUSTIN,* (*c. h.*,) Travis, Texas	3,100
Austinburgh, Ashtabula, Ohio	290
Austin's Mills, Hawkins, Tenn	20
Austinville, Bradford, Pa	57
Australia, Bolivar, Miss	16
Autaugaville, Autauga, Ala	24
Ava, Jackson, Ill	20
Ava, Oneida, N. Y	50
Ava, Noble, Ohio	23
Ava, Buchanan, Va	12
Avalanche, Vernon, Wis	20
Averill's Station, Midland, Mich	160
Avery, Jo Daviess, Ill	13
Avery, Berrien, Mich	100
Averysborough, Harnett, N. C	9
Avery's Creek, Buncombe, N. C	6
Avilla, Noble, Ind	120
Avilla, Jasper, Mo	120
Aviston, Clinton, Ill	110

* Money-order office.

Post office	Amount
Avoca, Lawrence, Ala	$10
Avoca, Lawrence, Ind	12
Avoca, Pottawattomie, Iowa	12
Avoca, Jefferson, Mo	31
Avoca, Cass, Nebr	5
Avoca, Steuben, N. Y	360
Avoca, Iowa, Wis	340
Avola, Vernon, Mo	8
Avon, Hartford, Conn	130
Avon, Fulton, Ill	440
Avon, Polk, Iowa	19
Avon, Coffey, Kans	18
Avon, Franklin, Me	41
Avon, St. Genevieve, Mo	6
Avon, Livingston, N. Y	880
Avon, Lorain, Ohio	140
Avon, Lebanon, Pa	39
Avon Centre, Rock, Wis	19
Avondale, Chester, Pa	310
Avondale, Polk, Wis	17
Avonia, Erie, Pa	12
Avon Lake, Lorain, Ohio	20
Aydelott, Benton, Ind	6
Ayer's Hill, Potter, Pa	5
Ayer's Point, Washington, Ill	74
Ayer's Village, Essex, Mass	12
Ayersville, Putnam, Mo	12
Ayersville, Stokes, N. C	8
Ayersville, Defiance, Ohio	16
Aylett's, King William, Va	150
Ayr, Goodhue, Minn	13
Azalia, Bartholomew, Ind	23
Aztalan, Jefferson, Wis	59

B.

Post office	Amount
BABCOCK HILL, Oneida, N. Y	18
Babylon, Hampshire, Mass	21
Babylon, Suffolk, N. Y	480
Bacchus, Hopkins, Tex	12
Bachelor's Hall, Pittsylvania, Va	24
Bachelor's Retreat, Oconee, S. C	21
Bach Grove, Wright, Iowa	16
Bachman, Montgomery, Ohio	30
Bachman's Mills, Carroll, Md	10
Back Creek Valley, Frederick, Va	37
Backville, Brown, Minn	7
Bacon, Coshocton, Ohio	20
Bacon Creek, Hart, Ky	110
Bacon Hill, Saratoga, N. Y	49
Baden, Keokuk, Iowa	71
Baden, St. Louis, Mo	130
Baden, Gage, Nebr	12
Baden, Beaver, Pa	94
Baden Baden, Bond, Ill	21
Badger, Portage, Wis	29
Badger Hill, Tama, Iowa	25
Badito, (*c. h.*,) Huerfano, Colo	32
Bad River, Gratiot, Mich	40
Bagdad, Shelby, Ky	140
Bagdad, Smith, Tenn	9
Bagdad, Williamson, Tex	25
Baggettsville, Robertson, Tenn	12
Bahala, Copiah, Miss	24
Bailey Hollow, Luzerne, Pa	100
Bailey's Creek, Osage, Mo	8
Bailey's Harbor, Door, Wis	$72
Bailey's Mill, Leon, Fla	140
Bailey's Mills, Belmont, Ohio	12
Bailey's Store, Shelby, Ky	12
Baileyville, Ogle, Ill	170
Baileyville, Washington, Me	9
*Bainbridge,** (*c. h.*,) Decatur, Ga	1,100
Bainbridge, Williamson, Ill	16
Bainbridge, Putnam, Ind	310
Bainbridge, Christian, Ky	35
Bainbridge, Berrien, Mich	49
Bainbridge, Clinton, Mo	12
Bainbridge, Chenango, N. Y	640
Bainbridge,* Ross, Ohio	330
Bainbridge, Lancaster, Pa	210
Bairdstown, Oglethorpe, Ga	110
Bairdstown, Sullivan, Mo	15
Baiting Hollow, Suffolk, N. Y	58
Baker, Jefferson, Iowa	12
Baker, St. Clair, Mo	12
*Baker City,** (*c. h.*,) Baker, Oreg	320
Baker's Basin, Mercer, N. J	20
Bakersfield, Kern, Cal	30
Bakersfield, Franklin, Vt	210
Baker's Gap, Johnson, Tenn	12
Baker's Grove, Barton, Mo	8
Baker's Run, Hardy, W. Va	120
Bakerstown, Allegheny, Pa	85
Bakersville, Litchfield, Conn	62
Bakersville, Washington, Md	35
Bakersville, (*c. h.*,) Mitchell, N. C	5
Bakersville, Coshocton, Ohio	59
Bakersville, Somerset, Pa	23
Balaka, Randolph, Ind	14
Balbec, Jay, Ind	40
Balcony Falls, Rockbridge, Va	60
Bald Creek, Yancey, N. C	6
Bald Eagle, York, Pa	8
Bald Hill, Clearfield, Pa	7
Bald Knob, Taney, Mo	12
Bald Knob, Boone, W. Va	6
Bald Mount, Luzerne, Pa	39
Bald Mountain, Gilpin, Colo	730
Baldwin, St. Mary's, La	12
Baldwin, Butler, Pa	33
Baldwin City,* Douglas, Kans	400
Baldwin's Mills, Jackson, Mich	88
Baldwin's Mills, Waupacca, Wis	12
Baldwinsville, Edgar, Ill	12
Baldwinsville, Worcester, Mass	250
Baldwinsville, Onondaga, N. Y	1,200
Baldwyn, Lee, Miss	250
Ballard's Falls, Washington, Kans	12
Ballard Vale, Essex, Mass	240
Ballardsville, Boone, W. Va	11
Ball Camp, Knox, Tenn	14
Ballena, San Diego, Cal	12
Ball Play, Etowah, Ala	12
Ball Play, Monroe, Tenn	12
Ball's Pond, Fairfield, Conn	21
*Ballston,** (*c. h.*,) Saratoga, N. Y	1,800
Ballston Centre, Saratoga, N. Y	30
Ballstown, Ripley, Ind	20
Ballsville, Powhatan, Va	53
Ballwin, St. Louis, Mo	35
Ballyclough, Dubuque, Iowa	7

* Money-order office.

Office	Amount
Balm, Blount, Ala	$12
Balm, Mercer, Pa	55
Balmoral, Otter Tail, Minn	12
Baltic, New London, Conn	560
Baltimore,* Baltimore, Md	4,000
Baltimore, Barry, Mich	38
Baltimore, Fairfield, Ohio	150
Bamberg, Barnwell, S. C	320
Bamberg, Sheboygan, Wis	8
Bancroft, Aroostook, Me	21
Bancroft, Berkshire, Mass	49
Bancroft, Freeborn, Minn	18
Bancroft, Daviess, Mo	92
Bandera, (*c. h.,*) Bandera, Tex	42
Bangall, Dutchess, N. Y	170
Bangor, Butte, Cal	26
Bangor, Marshall, Iowa	120
Bangor, Morgan, Ky	12
*Bangor,** (*c. h.,*) Penobscot, Me	4,000
Bangor, Van Buren, Mich	100
Bangor, Franklin, N. Y	120
Bangor, Northampton, Pa	12
Bangor, La Crosse, Wis	330
Bank Lick, Kenton, Ky	12
Banks, Faribault, Minn	46
Bankston, Saline, Ill	13
Bankston, Dubuque, Iowa	3
Bankston, Choctaw, Miss	39
Banksville, Fairfield, Conn	28
Banksville, Banks, Ga	11
*Bannack City,** (*c. h.,*) Beaver Head, Mont	340
Banner, Jackson, Kans	4
Banner, Calhoun, Miss	15
Banner, Fond du Lac, Wis	24
Bannerville, Snyder, Pa	44
Banquete, Nueces, Tex	8
Banta, San Joaquin, Cal	12
Bantam, Clermont, Ohio	82
Bantam Falls, Litchfield, Conn	180
Baptistown, Hunterdon, N. J	49
Baptist Valley, Tazewell, Va	12
*Baraboo,** (*c. h.,*) Sauk, Wis	1,500
Baraga, Houghton, Mich	23
Barber, Faribault, Minn	75
Barber's Mills, Wells, Ind	15
Barbersville, Jefferson, Ind	16
Barbour's Mills, Lycoming, Pa	30
Barboursville, (*c. h.,*) Knox, Ky	200
Barbourville, Delaware, N. Y	27
Barclay, Black Hawk, Iowa	13
Barclay, Bradford, Pa	250
Bardolph, McDonough, Ill	240
*Bardstown,** (*c. h.,*) Nelson, Ky	960
Bardstown Junction, Bullitt, Ky	24
Bardwell's Ferry, Franklin, Mass	17
Bareville, Lancaster, Pa	64
Barfield, Mississippi, Ark	45
Bargaintown, Atlantic, N. J	30
Bargersville, Johnson, Ind	20
Barhamsville, New Kent, Va	42
Baring, Washington, Me	110
Bark Camp Mills, Whitley, Ky	3
Barkersville, Saratoga, N. Y	42
Barkesdale, Halifax, Va	17
Barkeyville, Venango, Pa	12

Office	Amount
Barkhamsted, Litchfield, Conn	$71
Barlow, Washington, Ohio	110
Bar Mills, York, Me	110
Barnard, Linn, Kans	12
Barnard, Piscataquis, Me	14
Barnard, Charlevoix, Mich	21
Barnard, Windsor, Vt	160
Barnard's, Armstrong, Pa	18
Barnardsville, Roane, Tenn	10
Barnegat, Ocean, N. J	130
Barnerville, Schoharie, N. Y	56
Barnes, Richland, Ohio	16
Barnes' Corners, Lewis, N. Y	60
Barnes' Cross Roads, Dale, Ala	13
Barnes' Store, Tishemingo, Miss	13
Barneston, Chester, Pa	23
Barnesville, Pike, Ga	460
Barnesville, Bourbon, Kans	58
Barnesville, Montgomery, Md	44
Barnesville, Clinton, Mo	33
Barnesville,* Belmont, Ohio	1,000
Barnesville, Schuylkill, Pa	53
Barnesville, Charlotte, Va	160
Barnet, Caledonia, Vt	340
Barnhart's Mills, Butler, Pa	69
Barnsborough, Gloucester, N. J	36
Barnstable, (*c. h.,*) Barnstable, Mass	680
Barnstead, Belknap, N. H	56
Barnum, Adams, Wis	31
Barnumton, Camden, Mo	9
Barnwell, Barnwell, S. C	320
Barracksville, Marion, W. Va	71
Barre, Worcester, Mass	1,000
Barre, Washington, Vt	550
Barre Centre, Orleans, N. Y	97
Barre Forge, Huntingdon, Pa	68
Barre Mills, La Crosse, Wis	62
Barren, Harrison, Ind	19
Barren Creek Springs, Wicomico, Md	49
Barren Hill, Montgomery, Pa	56
Barren Plain, Robertson, Tenn	17
Barren Springs, Fentress, Tenn	12
Barre Plains, Worcester, Mass	29
Barret's Station, St. Louis, Mo	19
Barrett, Marshall, Kans	45
Barrettsville, Hampshire, W. Va	14
Barreville, McHenry, Ill	79
Barrington, Strafford, N. H	72
Barrington, Yates, N. Y	39
Barrington, Bristol, R. I	25
Barrington Centre, Bristol, R. I	94
Barrington Station, Cook, Ill	410
Barrittsville, Dawson, Ga	12
Barron, (*c. h.,*) Barron, Wis	12
Barr's Store, Macoupin, Ill	25
Barry, Pike, Ill	570
Barry, Frederick, Md	87
Barry, Clay, Mo	130
Barry, Cuyahoga, Ohio	8
Barry, Schuylkill, Pa	19
Barrytown, Dutchess, N. Y	320
Barryville, Delaware, Iowa	20
Barryville, Barry, Mich	14
Barryville, Sullivan, N. Y	110
Barryville, Stark, Ohio	25
Bart, Lancaster, Pa	94

* Money-order office.

Post office	
Bartholomew, Drew, Ark	$8
Bartlett, Fremont, Iowa	60
Bartlett, Carroll, N. H	27
Bartlett, Washington, Ohio	120
Bartlett, Shelby, Tenn	130
Barton, Colbert, Ala	68
Barton, Alleghany, Md	360
Barton. Newaygo, Mich	7
Barton, Barton, Mo	12
Barton, Tioga, N. Y	130
Barton, Anderson, Tex	4
Barton,* Orleans, Vt	460
Barton, Washington, Wis	170
Bartonia, Randolph, Ind	28
Barton Landing, Orleans, Vt	260
Bartonsville, Monroe, Pa	27
Bartonsville, Windham, Vt	110
Bartow, Jefferson, Ga	120
Bartramville, Lawrence, Ohio	8
Bartville, Lancaster, Pa	20
Basco, Hancock, Ill	66
Bascom, Seneca, Ohio	23
Base Lake, Washtenaw, Mich	47
Base Line, Crawford, Kans	12
Basham's Gap, Morgan, Ala	29
Bashan, Meigs, Ohio	14
Basil, Fairfield, Ohio	110
Basin Spring, Williamson, Tenn	7
Basking Ridge, Somerset, N. J	210
Basnettsville, Marion, W. Va	16
Bassett's Mill, El Paso, Colo	26
Bassett's Station, Kenosha, Wis	65
Bass Lake, Faribault, Minn	26
Bass Station, Jackson, Ala	12
Bass Wood, Richland, Wis	18
Bastinville, Hickman, Tenn	8
Bastrop, (*c. h.*,) Morehouse, La	400
Bastrop, (*c. h.*,) Bastrop, Tex	800
Bastross, Lycoming, Pa	12
Batavia, Solano, Cal	12
Batavia,* Kane, Ill	1,600
Batavia, Branch, Mich	14
Batavia,* (*c. h.*,) Genesee, N. Y	2,500
Batavia, (*c. h.*,) Clermont, Ohio	400
Batchellerville, Saratoga, N. Y	92
Batchelor's Rest, Pendleton, Ky	12
Bateham, Sullivan, Ind	4
Bates, Sangamon, Ill	39
Bates, Osceola, Mich	12
Batesville,* (*c. h.*,) Independence, Ark	580
Batesville, Ripley, Ind	170
Batesville, Panola, Miss	120
Batesville, Noble, Ohio	120
Batesville, Spartanburgh, S. C	10
Batesville, Albemarle, Va	12
Bath, Placer, Cal	71
Bath, Mason, Ill	420
Bath,* (*c. h.*,) Sagadahoc, Me	2,600
Bath, Clinton, Mich	64
Bath, Grafton, N. H	300
Bath,* (*c. h.*,) Steuben, N. Y	2,200
Bath, Beaufort, N. C	5
Bath, Summit, Ohio	41
Bath, Northampton, Pa	280
Bath, Edgefield, S. C	51
Bath, C. H., Bath, Va	$220
Bath Alum, Bath, Va	66
Baton Rouge,* (*c. h.*,) East Baton Rouge, La	2,100
Batten's Mills, Gilmer, W. Va	12
Battenville, Washington, N. Y	24
Battleborough, Edgecombe, N. C	310
Battle Creek, Tehama, Cal	12
Battle Creek,* Calhoun, Mich	3,500
Battle Creek, Madison, Nebr	12
Battle Creek Mines, Marion, Tenn	12
Battle Ground, Tippecanoe, Ind	260
Battle Mountain, Humboldt, Nev	12
Baughman, Wayne, Ohio	68
Baugh's Station, Logan, Ky	6
Baumstown, Berks, Pa	25
Bavington, Washington, Pa	40
Baxter Springs,* Cherokee, Kans	990
Bay, Gasconade, Mo	80
Bayard, Columbiana, Ohio	94
Bayborough, Horry, S. C	12
Bay City, Pope, Ill	53
Bay City,* (*c. h.*,) Bay, Mich	3,000
Bay City, Pierce, Wis	52
Bayfield, (*c. h.*,) Bayfield, Wis	90
Bay Hill, Walworth, Wis	9
Bay Hundred, Talbot, Md	20
Bay Minette, Baldwin, Ala	12
Baynesville, Westmoreland, Va	16
Bayonne, Hudson, N. J	50
Bayou Barbary, Livingston, La	10
Bayou Boeuf, St. Landry, La	10
Bayou Chicot, St. Landry, La	18
Bayou Goula, Iberville, La	50
Bayou Tunica, West Feliciana, La	61
Bay Port, Hernando, Fla	4
Bay Ridge, Kings, N. Y	32
Bay River, Craven, N. C	25
Bay Settlement, Brown, Wis	12
Bay Shore, Suffolk, N. Y	280
Bay Side, Queens, N. Y	10
Bay Springs, Prentiss, Miss	22
Bay View, Cecil, Md	74
Bay View, Essex, Mass	12
Bay View, Northampton, Va	26
Bayview, Milwaukee, Wis	12
Bayville, Ocean, N. J	12
Bazaar, Chase, Kans	16
Bazetta, Trumbull, Ohio	300
Beach Haven, Luzerne, Pa	120
Beach Pond, Wayne, Pa	75
Beach Ridge, Niagara, N. Y	23
Beacon, Ogle, Ill	12
Beacon, Mahaska, Iowa	170
Beacon Falls, New Haven, Conn	230
Bealeton, Fauquier, Va	74
Beall's Mills, Gilmer, W. Va	12
Beallsville, Montgomery, Md	66
Beallsville, Monroe, Ohio	110
Beallsville, Washington, Pa	140
Beamsville, Darke, Ohio	11
Bean Blossom, Brown, Ind	30
Bean's Corners, Franklin, Me	55
Bean's Station, Grainger, Tenn	110
Beantown, Charles, Md	35
Bear, Richland, Wis	15

* Money-order office.

Post Office	Compensation
Bear Branch, Ohio, Ind	$21
Bear Branch, Richmond, N. C	10
Bear Canyon, Douglas, Colo	15
Bear Creek, Henry, Ga	24
Bear Creek, Jay, Ind	29
Bear Creek, Hinds, Miss	12
Bear Creek, Cedar, Mo	12
Bear Creek, Luzerne, Pa	30
Bear Creek, Waupaca, Wis	19
Beard's Station, Oldham, Ky	72
*Beardstown,** (*c. h.,*) Cass, Ill	1,000
Beardstown, Perry, Tenn	19
Bear Gap, Northumberland, Pa	18
Bear Grove, Guthrie, Iowa	45
Bear Lake, Manistee, Mich	65
Bear Lake, Warren, Pa	100
Bear Lake Mills, Van Buren, Mich	20
Bear River, Emmett, Mich	10
Bearsville, Ulster, N. Y	35
Beartown, Deer Lodge, Mont	12
Beartown, Lancaster, Pa	24
Bear Valley, Mariposa, Cal	110
Bear Valley, Wabashaw, Minn	33
Bear Valley, Richland, Wis	32
Bear Wallow, Henderson, N. C	19
Beasley's Fork, Adams, Ohio	7
*Beatrice,** (*c. h.,*) Gage, Nebr	620
Beattie's Ford, Lincoln, N. C	38
Beatty,* Westmoreland, Pa	310
Beattyville, Lee, Ky	49
Beatyestown, Warren, N. J	48
Beaty's Mills, Marion, W. Va	8
Beauford, Blue Earth, Minn	8
Beaufort, Franklin, Mo	40
Beaufort, (*c. h.,*) Carteret, N. C	700
*Beaufort,** (*c. h.,*) Beaufort, S. C	1,000
Beaumont, (*c. h.,*) Jefferson, Tex	120
Beaver, Winona, Minn	68
Beaver, Douglas, Mo	4
Beaver, Pike, Ohio	23
Beaver, Clackamas, Oreg	12
*Beaver,** (*c. h.,*) Beaver, Pa	720
Beaver, Anderson, Tex	12
Beaver, (*c. h.,*) Beaver, Utah	180
Beaver, Thurston, Wash	3
Beaver Bay, (*c. h.,*) Lake, Minn	50
Beaver Brook, Sullivan, N. Y	8
Beaver Centre, Crawford, Pa	40
Beaver City, Newton, Ind	16
Beaver Creek, Dale, Ala	16
Beaver Creek, Pueblo, Colo	16
Beaver Creek, Bond, Ill	83
Beaver Creek, Washington, Md	19
Beaver Creek, Gratiot, Mich	15
Beaver Creek, Jefferson, Tenn	12
Beaver Crossing, Seward, Nebr	38
Beaver Dam, Kosciusko, Ind	18
Beaver Dam, Ohio, Ky	8
Beaver Dam, Union, N. C	5
Beaver Dam, Allen, Ohio	61
Beaver Dam,* Dodge, Wis	1,600
Beaver Dam Depot, Hanover, Va	65
Beaver Dams, Schuyler, N. Y	23
Beaver Falls, (*c. h.,*) Renville, Minn	99
Beaver Falls, Lewis, N. Y	12
Beaver Falls, Beaver, Pa	950
Beaver Head Rock, Madison, Mont	$12
Beaver Kill, Sullivan, N. Y	15
Beaver Meadows, Carbon, Pa	230
Beaver Pond, Lexington, S. C	3
Beaver Ridge, Knox, Tenn	5
Beaver Run, Sussex, N. J	12
Beaver Springs, Snyder, Pa	64
Beaverton, Sanford, Ala	5
Beavertown, Snyder, Pa	50
Beaver Valley, St. Clair, Ala	8
Beaver Valley, New Castle, Del	62
Beaver Valley, Columbia, Pa	34
Beaverville, Iroquis, Ill	8
Bechtelsville, Berks, Pa	22
Beckersville, Berks, Pa	17
Becket, Berkshire, Mass	380
Becket Centre, Berkshire, Mass	24
Beckett's Store, Pickaway, Ohio	53
Beckleysville, Baltimore, Md	21
Beck's Creek, Shelby, Ill	9
Beck's Grove, Brown, Ind	12
Beck's Mills, Washington, Ind	4
Beck's Mills, Holmes, Ohio	12
Beck's Mills, Washington, Pa	21
Beckville, Panola, Tex	12
Beckwith, Plumas, Cal	12
Beddington, Washington, Me	6
Bedford, Pike, Ill	28
*Bedford,** (*c. h.,*) Lawrence, Ind	840
*Bedford,** (*c. h.,*) Taylor, Iowa	420
Bedford, (*c. h.,*) Trimble, Ky	140
Bedford, Middlesex, Mass	220
Bedford, Calhoun, Mich	110
Bedford, Livingston, Mo	58
Bedford, Hillsborough, N. H	71
Bedford, (*c. h.,*) Westchester, N. Y	190
Bedford, Cuyahoga, Ohio	400
Bedford, (*c. h.,**) Bedford, Pa	1,200
Bedford, Bedford, Tenn	12
Bedford Springs, Bedford, Pa	27
Bedford Station, Westchester, N. Y	210
Bedias, Grimes, Tex	10
Bedminster, Bucks, Pa	8
Bed Rock, Klamath, Cal	12
Beebe Plain, Orleans, Vt	160
Bee Branch, Van Buren, Ark	5
Bee Caves, Travis, Tex	12
Beech, Licking, Ohio	14
Beech Creek, Ashley, Ark	12
Beech Creek, Clinton, Pa	210
Beecher, Will, Ill	12
Beech Fork, Washington, Ky	18
Beech Grove, Rush, Ind	120
Beech Grove, Coffee, Tenn	20
Beech Hill, Mason, W. Va	12
Beechland, Washington, Ky	12
Beech Spring, Lee, Va	29
Beech Wood, Sullivan, N. Y	10
Beech Wood, Cameron, Pa	160
Beech Wood, Sheboygan, Wis	24
Beech Woods, Newton, Ark	12
Beechy Mire, Union, Ind	27
Bee Creek, Pike, Ill	16
Bee Creek, Bledsoe, Tenn	12
Beekman, Dutchess, N. Y	81
Beekmantown, Clinton, N. Y	25

* Money-order office.

Beeler's Station, Marshall, W. Va	$10
Bee Lick, Lincoln, Ky	12
Beemerville, Sussex, N. J	25
Bee Ridge, Knox, Mo	39
Beers, Allegheny, Pa	18
Beersheba Springs, Grundy, Tenn	12
Beesley's Point, Cape May, N. J	81
Bee Spring, Edmonson, Ky	7
Beetown, Grant, Wis	130
Beetrace, Appanoose, Iowa	21
Beeville, (c. h.,) Bee, Tex	8
Belair, Richmond, Ga	74
Bel Air, (c. h.,) Harford, Md	470
Belair, Lancaster, S. C	12
Belbend, Luzerne, Pa	53
Belcher, Washington, N. Y	34
Belchertown, Hampshire, Mass	850
Belden, Wabash, Ind	38
Belden, Broome, N. Y	12
Beldenville, Pierce, Wis	11
Belew Creek Mills, Forsyth, N. C	12
Belew's Creek, Jefferson, Mo	16
Belfast, Lee, Iowa	15
Belfast, (c. h.,)* Waldo, Me	2,300
Belfast, Baltimore, Md	7
Belfast, Allegany, N. Y	280
Belfast, Clermont, Ohio	19
Belfast, Northampton, Pa	54
Belfast Mills, Russell, Va	12
Belgium, Ozaukee, Wis	59
Belgrade, Kennebec, Me	210
Belgrade, Washington, Mo	12
Belgrade Mills, Kennebec, Me	78
Belinda, Lucas, Iowa	10
Belington, Barbour, W. Va	53
Belknap, Armstrong, Pa	15
Bell, Highland, Ohio	12
Bell Air, Crawford, Ill	40
Bell Air, Cooper, Mo	40
Bell Air, Hardin, Tenn	12
Bellaire,* Belmont, Ohio	1,400
Bellasylva, Wyoming, Pa	13
Bellbrook, Greene, Ohio	110
Bellbuckle, Bedford, Tenn	85
Bell Center, Crawford, Wis	60
Belle Air, Johnson, Iowa	28
Belle Centre, Logan, Ohio	220
Belle Creek, Goodhue, Minn	30
Belle Creek, Washington, Nebr	12
Bellefontaine, Choctaw, Miss	44
Bellefontaine, St. Louis, Mo	40
Bellfontaine, (c. h.,)* Logan, Ohio	2,100
Bellefonte, Jackson, Ala	80
Bellefonte, (c. h.,)* Centre, Pa	1,900
Belle Fountain, Mahaska, Iowa	73
Bellefountain, Columbia, Wis	16
Belle Grove, Greenwood, Kans	12
Belle Haven, Accomack, Va	68
Belle Isle, Onondaga, N. Y	130
Bellemont, Warren, Iowa	12
Bellemonte, Lancaster, Pa	69
Belle Plain, Cumberland, N. J	23
Belle Plaine,* Benton, Iowa	910
Belle Plaine,* Scott, Minn	250
Belle Plaine, Shawanaw, Wis	70
Belle Point, Delaware, Ohio	16
Belle Prairie, Hamilton, Ill	$31
Belle Prairie, Morrison, Minn	23
Belle River, St. Clair, Mich	38
Belle Union, Putnam, Ind	12
Belle Vale, West Baton Rouge, La	12
Belle Valley, Erie, Pa	16
Belle Vernon, Wyandot, Ohio	38
Belle Vernon, Fayette, Pa	230
Belleview, Calhoun, Ill	30
Belleview, Iron, Mo	10
Belleview, Davidson, Tenn	41
Belleview, Rusk, Tex	24
Belleville, Conecuh, Ala	17
Belleville, (c. h.,)* St. Clair, Ill	2,300
Belleville, Hendricks, Ind	81
Belleville, Republic, Kans	12
Belleville, Wayne, Mich	180
Belleville, Fillmore, Minn	9
Belleville, Essex, N. J	380
Belleville, Jefferson, N. Y	320
Belleville,* Richland, Ohio	490
Belleville, Mifflin, Pa	120
Belleville, Wood, W. Va	81
Belleville, Dane, Wis	110
Bellevoir, Chatham, N. C	4
Bellevue, Dallas, Ala	39
Bellevue,* Jackson, Iowa	570
Bellevue, (c. h.,) Bossier, La	100
Bellevue,* Eaton, Mich	410
Bellevue, (c. h.,) Sarpy, Nebr	200
Bellevue,* Huron, Ohio	1,100
Bellevue, Yam Hill, Oreg	21
Bellevue, Washington, Utah	20
Bellevue, Bedford, Va	45
Bell Factory, Madison, Ala	44
Bellfair Mills, Stafford, Va	12
Bellingham, Norfolk, Mass	72
Bellmore, Parke, Ind	65
Bellona, Yates, N. Y	170
Bellota, San Joaquin, Cal	12
Bellows Falls,* Windham, Vt	1,200
Bell Plain, Marshall, Ill	53
Bellport, Suffolk, N. Y	220
Bell's Cross-Roads, Louisa, Va	10
Bell's Depot, Haywood, Tenn	370
Bell's Landing, Monroe, Ala	12
Bell's Mills, Jefferson, Pa	20
Bell's Store, Columbia, Ark	14
Bell's Valley, Rockbridge, Va	12
Bellton, Marshall, W. Va	70
Belltown, Monroe, Tenn	6
Bellvale, Orange, N. Y	92
Bellview, Lebanon, Pa	12
Bellville, Hamilton, Fla	7
Bellville, (c. h.,) Austin, Tex	180
Bellwood, Wilson, Tenn	12
Belmond, Wright, Iowa	130
Belmont, Crawford, Ark	9
Belmont, San Mateo, Cal	16
Belmont, Woodson, Kans	15
Belmont, Bullitt, Ky	100
Belmont, Waldo, Me	37
Belmont, Middlesex, Mass	230
Belmont, Kent, Mich	12
Belmont, Mississippi, Mo	12
Belmont, (c. h.,) Nye, Nev	520

* Money-order office.

Office	Amount
Belmont, Belknap, N. H	$180
Belmont, (c. h.,) Allegany, N. Y	580
Belmont, Belmont, Ohio	140
Belmont, Gonzales, Tex	120
Belmont, La Fayette, Wis	170
Belmore, Putnam, Ohio	86
Beloit, Mitchell, Kans	12
Beloit, Mahoning, Ohio	150
Beloit,* Rock, Wis	2,800
Belpassi, Marion, Oreg	93
Belpre, Washington, Ohio	280
Belton, Anderson, S. C	68
Belton, (c. h.,) Bell, Tex	400
Beltsville, Prince George's, Md	200
Belvidere, (c. h.,)* Boone, Ill	2,300
Belvidere, Monona, Iowa	12
Belvidere, (c. h.,)* Warren, N. J	1,000
Belvidere, Allegany, N. Y	190
Belvidere, Perquimons, N. C	36
Belvidere, Lamoille, Vt	23
Belvidere Corners, Lamoille, Vt	2
Belvoir, Douglas, Kans	12
Belvoir, Vernon, Mo	12
Bem, Green, Wis	25
Bement,* Piatt, Ill	610
Bemus Heights, Saratoga, N. Y	75
Bemus Point, Chautauqua, N. Y	110
Benaja, Rockingham, N. C	12
Benbow, Marion, Mo	39
Bendersville, Adams, Pa	160
Benela, Calhoun, Miss	27
Benevola, Washington, Md	33
Benezett, Elk, Pa	57
Benford's Store, Somerset, Pa	28
Ben Franklin, Lamar, Tex	8
Bengal, Clinton, Mich	5
Benham's Store, Ripley, Ind	15
Benicia,* Solano, Cal	950
Benjamin, Lewis, Mo	12
Ben Lomond, Sevier, Ark	79
Bennet's Corners, Madison, N. Y	48
Bennett, Allegheny, Pa	72
Bennett's Bayou, Fulton, Ark	5
Bennettsburgh, Schuyler, N. Y	38
Bennett's Corners, Medina, Ohio	27
Bennett's Creek, Steuben, N. Y	17
Bennett's Landing, Tunica, Miss	12
Bennett's Mills, Ocean, N. J	18
Bennett's River, Fulton, Ark	5
Bennett's Station, Sumter, Ala	12
Bennett's Switch, Miami, Ind	49
Bennettstown, Christian, Ky	24
Bennettsville, Etowah, Ala	12
Bennettsville, Clarke, Ind	25
Bennettsville, Chenango, N. Y	58
Bennettsville, (c. h.,) Marlborough, S. C	800
Bennington, Edwards, Ill	12
Bennington, Switzerland, Ind	55
Bennington, Ottawa, Kans	21
Bennington, Shiawassee, Mich	84
Bennington, Hillsborough, N. H	170
Bennington, Wyoming, N. Y	46
Bennington, Morrow, Ohio	84
Bennington, (c. h.,)* Bennington, Vt	1,900
Bennington Centre, Bennington, Vt	230
Bennington Furnace, Blair, Pa	$48
Benona, Oceana, Mich	93
Bensalem, Bucks, Pa	12
Benson, Franklin, Ky	12
Benson, Chippewa, Minn	12
Benson, Hamilton, N. Y	14
Benson, Rutland, Vt	260
Benson Centre, Hamilton, N. Y	15
Benson Grove, Winnebago, Iowa	3
Benson Landing, Rutland, Vt	48
Ben's Run, Tyler, W. Va	11
Bent Branch, Pike, Ky	12
Bent Creek, Appomattox, Va	13
Bentivoglio, Albemarle, Va	75
Bentley's Springs, Baltimore, Md	67
Bentleyville, Washington, Pa	70
Bently, Hancock, Ill	120
Bently Creek, Bradford, Pa	51
Bent Mountain, Roanoke, Va	12
Benton, Lowndes, Ala	180
Benton, (c. h.,) Saline, Ark	87
Benton, Mono, Cal	31
Benton, Columbia, Fla	12
Benton, (c. h.,) Franklin, Ill	350
Benton, Elkhart, Ind	69
Benton Mills, Iowa	23
Benton, (c. h.,) Marshall, Ky	70
Benton, Bossier, La	12
Benton, Kennebec, Me	85
Benton, Washtenaw, Mich	8
Benton, Carver, Minn	36
Benton, Yazoo, Miss	100
Benton, Scott, Mo	30
Benton, Saunders, Nebr	14
Benton, Grafton, N. H	43
Benton, Holmes, Ohio	65
Benton, Columbia, Pa	49
Benton, (c. h.,) Polk, Tenn	89
Benton, La Fayette, Wis	86
Benton Centre, Benton, Iowa	12
Benton Centre, Yates, N. Y	110
Benton City, Audrian, Mo	12
Benton Harbor,* Berrien, Mich	1,200
Benton Ridge, Hancock, Ohio	40
Benton's Ferry, Livingston, La	10
Benton's Ferry, Marion, W. Va	69
Benton's Port, Van Buren, Iowa	300
Bentonville, (c. h.,) Benton, Ark	290
Bentonville, Fayette, Ind	77
Bentonville, Adams, Ohio	72
Bentonville, Warren, Va	12
Bent's Fort, Bent, Colo	40
Benvenue, Dauphin, Pa	53
Benville, Jennings, Ind	23
Benwood, Marshall, W. Va	140
Benzonia, (c. h.,) Benzie, Mich	190
Beowawe, Lander, Nev	12
Berdan, Greene, Ill	57
Berea, Franklin, Kans	22
Berea, Madison, Ky	110
Berea,* Cuyahoga, Ohio	1,200
Bergen, McLeod, Minn	6
Bergen, Hudson, N. J	730
Bergen,* Genesee, N. Y	500
Bergen Point, Hudson, N. J	250
Berger, Franklin, Mo	120

* Money-order office.

Post Office	
Berger's Store, Pittsylvania, Va	$20
Bergholtz, Niagara, N. Y	50
Berkeley Springs, (*c. h.*,) Morgan, W. Va	360
Berkey, Lucas, Ohio	11
Berkley, Madison, Ala	11
Berkley, Bristol, Mass	30
Berkley's, Somerset, Pa	12
Berkshire, Berkshire, Mass	82
Berkshire, Tioga, N. Y	140
Berkshire, Delaware, Ohio	51
Berkshire, Franklin, Vt	79
Berlin, Hartford, Conn	320
Berlin, Sangamon, Ill	170
Berlin, Clinton, Ind	20
Berlin, Hardin, Iowa	25
Berlin, Bracken, Ky	37
Berlin, Worcester, Md	390
Berlin,* Worcester, Mass	81
Berlin, Ottawa, Mich	260
Berlin, Steele, Minn	37
Berlin, Camden, N. J	100
Berlin, Rensselaer, N. Y	220
Berlin, Holmes, Ohio	79
Berlin, Somerset, Pa	300
Berlin, Marshall, Tenn	13
Berlin, Washington, Tex	57
Berlin, Washington, Vt	58
Berlin, Southampton, Va	29
Berlin,* Green Lake, Wis	1,700
Berlin Centre, Mahoning, Ohio	63
Berlin Centre, Wayne, Pa	14
Berlin Cross Roads, Jackson, Ohio	150
Berlin Falls, Coos, N. H	220
Berlin Heights, Erie, Ohio	290
Berlin Station, Erie, Ohio	75
Berlinsville, Northampton, Pa	18
Berlinville, Erie, Ohio	44
Bermudian, Adams, Pa	23
Bernadotte, Fulton, Ill	71
Bernalillo, Bernalillo, N. Mex	20
Bernard, Brunswick, N. C	12
Bernard Station, Wharton, Tex	12
Bernardston, Franklin, Mass	510
Berne, Camden, Ga	12
Berne, Dodge, Minn	10
Berne, Albany, N. Y	96
Berne, Noble, Ohio	65
Bernhard's Bay, Oswego, N. Y	92
Bernville, Berks, Pa	170
Berrien Centre, Berrien, Mich	17
Berrien Springs,* (*c. h.*,) Berrien, Mich	540
Berros Creek, San Luis Obispo, Cal	12
Berry, Sangamon, Ill	12
Berry Hill, Rockingham, N. C	12
Berrysburgh, Dauphin, Pa	160
Berry's Lick, Butler, Ky	14
Berry's Mill, Franklin, Me	59
Berry's Station, Harrison, Ky	90
Berrysville, Highland, Ohio	68
Berryton, Cass, Ill	16
Berryvale, Siskiyou, Cal	12
Berryville, Carroll, Ark	24
Berryville, Wayne, Ky	21
Berryville, (*c. h.*,) Clarke, Va	540
Bertram, Linn, Iowa	25
Bertrand, Berrien, Mich	$39
Bertrandville, La Fayette, La	12
Berville, St. Clair, Mich	24
Berwick, Warren, Ill	110
Berwick, York, Me	12
Berwick, Seneca, Ohio	98
Berwick, Columbia, Pa	650
Berzelia, Columbia, Ga	85
Beta, Fulton, Ohio	4
Bethalto, Madison, Ill	230
Bethania, Forsyth, N. C	38
Bethany, New Haven, Conn	22
Bethany, Jefferson, Ga	36
Bethany, Parke, Ind	14
Bethany,* (*c. h.*,) Harrison, Mo	430
Bethany, Genesee, N. Y	49
Bethany, Butler, Ohio	100
Bethany, Wayne, Pa	83
Bethany, York, S. C	2
Bethany,* Brooke, W. Va	420
Bethel, Fairfield, Conn	710
Bethel, Morgan, Ill	74
Bethel, Wayne, Ind	26
Bethel, Fayette, Iowa	33
Bethel, Marion, Kans	12
Bethel, Bath, Ky	90
Bethel,* Oxford, Me	730
Bethel, Branch, Mich	16
Bethel, Anoka, Minn	13
Bethel, Shelby, Mo	90
Bethel, Sullivan, N. Y	100
Bethel, Clermont, Ohio	210
Bethel, Polk, Oreg	30
Bethel, Berks, Pa	65
Bethel, Giles, Tenn	12
Bethel, Anderson, Tex	6
Bethel, Windsor, Vt	580
Bethel Corners, Cayuga, N. Y	22
Bethel Springs, McNairy, Tenn	120
Bethesda, Belmont, Ohio	48
Bethesda, Lancaster, Pa	21
Bethesda, Williamson, Tenn	15
Bethlehem, Litchfield, Conn	130
Bethlehem, Clarke, Ind	31
Bethlehem, Wayne, Iowa	46
Bethlehem, Henry, Ky	12
Bethlehem, Caroline, Md	28
Bethlehem, Grafton, N. H	300
Bethlehem, Hunterdon, N. J	67
Bethlehem,* Northampton, Pa	2,200
Bethlehem, Clarendon, S. C	5
Bethlehem Centre, Albany, N. Y	7
Bethpage, McDonald, Mo	10
Betsey Lake, Grand Traverse, Mich	16
Bettsville, Seneca, Ohio	45
Beulah, (*c. h.*,) Bolivar, Miss	12
Beulah, Johnson, N. C	5
Beulahville, King William, Va	12
Bevans, Sussex, N. J	7
Beverly, Adams, Ill	78
Beverly, Christian, Ky	12
Beverly, Essex, Mass	1,600
Beverly, Macon, Mo	12
Beverly, Burlington, N. J	570
Beverly,* Washington, Ohio	410
Beverly, (*c. h.*,) Randolph, W. Va	120

* Money-order office.

Beverly Farms, Essex, Mass	$230
Beverly Station, Platte, Mo	12
Bevier, Macon, Mo	170
Bevis Tavern, Hamilton, Ohio	33
Bewleyville, Breckinridge, Ky	130
Bible Grove, Clay, Ill	24
Bible Grove, Scotland, Mo	13
Bickley's Mills, Russell, Va	6
Bicknell, Knox, Ind	23
Biddeford,* York, Me	2,500
Biddeford Pool, York, Me	70
Bidwell's Bar, Butte, Cal	34
Biehle, Perry, Mo	21
Big Bar, Trinity, Cal	13
Big Beaver, Oakland, Mich	71
Big Bend, Polk, Ark	5
Big Bend, Avoyelles, La	25
Big Bend, Venango, Pa	23
Big Bend, Calhoun, W. Va	12
Big Bend, Waukesha, Wis	39
Big Brook, Oneida, N. Y	3
Big Buffalo, Harrison, W. Va	2
Big Cane, St. Landry, La	78
Big Clear Creek, Greenbrier, W. Va.	8
Big Clifty, Grayson, Ky	37
Big Coon, Jackson, Ala	12
Big Cove Tannery, Fulton, Pa	40
Big Creek, Geneva, Ala	22
Big Creek, Greene, Ark	30
Big Creek, Forsyth, Ga	40
Big Creek, Mecosta, Mich	29
Big Creek, Texas, Mo	16
Big Creek, Steuben, N. Y	12
Big Creek, Edgefield, S. C	4
Big Creek, Cocke, Tenn	12
Big Creek, Monroe, Wis	28
Big Dry Creek, Fresno, Cal	12
Bigelow, Holt, Mo	12
Big Falls, Alamance, N. C	17
Big Flats, Chemung, N. Y	230
Big Flats, Adams, Wis	12
Big Foot Prairie, McHenry, Ill	52
Big Fork, Polk, Ark	8
Big Grove, Pottawattomie, Iowa	45
Biggsville, Henderson, Ill	400
Big Hill, Labette, Kans	45
Big Hill, Madison, Ky	17
Big Hollow, Greene, N. Y	9
Big Indian, Cass, Ind	12
Big Island, Bedford, Va	130
Big Labette, Neosho, Kans	12
Big Lake, Sherburne, Minn	66
Bigler, Adams, Pa	29
Big Lick, Stanly, N. C	5
Big Lick,* Roanoke, Va	360
Big Meadows, Plumas, Cal	12
Big Mound, Lee, Iowa	35
Big Muddy, Franklin, Ill	19
Big Neck, Adams, Ill	23
Big Oak Flat, Tuolumne, Cal	96
Big Patch, Grant, Wis	45
Big Pine, Inyo, Cal	12
Big Plain, Madison, Ohio	30
Big Pond, Sanford, Ala	12
Big Pond, Bradford, Pa	12
Big Prairie, Newaygo, Mich	12
Big Prairie, Wayne, Ohio	$84
Big Rapids, (c. h.,)* Mecosta, Mich	960
Big Reedy, Edmonson, Ky	12
Big Renox, Cumberland, Ky	5
Big River, Pierce, Wis	12
Big River Mills, St. Francois, Mo	31
Big Rock, Kane, Ill	47
Big Rock, Scott, Iowa	42
Big Rock, Harlan, Ky	2
Big Run, Athens, Ohio	83
Big Run, Jefferson, Pa	61
Big Sandy, Benton, Tenn	44
Big Savanna, Dawson, Ga	21
Big Sioux, Union, Dak	12
Big Skin Creek, Lewis, W. Va	20
Big Spring, Shelby, Ill	23
Big Spring, Breckinridge, Ky	110
Big Spring, Ottawa, Mich	19
Big Spring, Fillmore, Minn	31
Big Spring, Montgomery, Mo	20
Big Spring, Jackson, N. C	12
Big Spring, Cumberland, Pa	46
Big Spring, Meigs, Tenn	13
Big Spring, Adams, Wis	46
Big Spring Depot, Montgomery, Va.	65
Big Springs, Douglas, Kans	65
Big Springs, Chickasaw, Miss	12
Big Springs, Logan, Ohio	30
Big Stone Gap, Wise, Va	7
Big Sycamore, Clay, W. Va	4
Big Thompson, Larimer, Colo	58
Big Timber, Riley, Kans	13
Big Tree, Greene, Pa	12
Big Tree Corners, Erie, N. Y	21
Big Trees, Calaveras, Cal	12
Big Woods, Wright, Minn	48
Bijou Basin, El Paso, Colo	9
Billerica, Middlesex, Mass	330
Billings, Dutchess, N. Y	12
Billingsly, Washington, Ark	19
Billingsville, Union, Ind	38
Biloxi, Harrison, Miss	250
Bingamon, Marion, W. Va	12
Bingham, Somerset, Me	170
Bingham, Monroe, Ohio	12
Bingham Canyon, Salt Lake, Utah	12
Bingham Centre, Potter, Pa	4
Bingham's Mills, Tioga, N. Y	12
Binghamton, Solano, Cal	99
Binghamton, (c. h.,)* Broome, N. Y	3,400
Binghamton, Ontagamie, Wis	31
Binkley's Bridge, Lancaster, Pa	14
Birchardville, Susquehanna, Pa	9
Birch Cooley, Renville, Minn	21
Birch Lick, Jackson, Ky	12
Birch River, Nicholas, W. Va	12
Birch Run, Saginaw, Mich	89
Birch Run Ville, Chester, Pa	12
Birch Tree, Shannon, Mo	12
Birch Wood, Hamilton, Tenn	42
Bird Hill, Carroll, Md	11
Birdsall, Allegany, N. Y	3
Birdsborough, Berks, Pa	380
Bird's Bridge, Will, Ill	12
Birdseye, Dubois, Ind	3
Bird's Run, Guernsey, Ohio	20

* Money-order office.

Post office	Amount
Birdston, Navarro, Tex	$8
Birdsville, Livingston, Ky	33
Birk's City, Daviess, Ky	13
Birmingham, Schuyler, Ill	27
Birmingham, Miami, Ind	12
Birmingham,* Van Buren, Iowa	320
Birmingham, Marshall, Ky	100
Birmingham, Oakland, Mich	550
Birmingham, Burlington, N. J	10
Birmingham, Erie, Ohio	240
Birmingham, Huntingdon, Pa	200
Biscayne, (*c. h.*,) Dade, Fla	3
Bishop Creek, Mono, Cal	81
Bishop Hill, Henry, Ill	370
Bishop's Head, Dorchester, Md	15
Bishop's Station, Mason, Ill	12
Bishop's Store, Pulaski, Ga	12
Bishop Street, Jefferson, N. Y	12
Bishopville, Worcester, Md	12
Bishopville, Morgan, Ohio	25
Bishopville, Sumter, S. C	89
Bismarck, Wabaunsee, Kans	12
Bismarck, St. Francois, Mo	77
Bismarck, Cuming, Nebr	12
Bissell's, Geauga, Ohio	78
Bitter Creek, Carbon, Wyo	12
Biven's Grove, Marshall, Iowa	10
Black Ash, Crawford, Pa	12
Black Bear, Klamath, Cal	12
Blackberry, Kane, Ill	12
Blackberry Ridge, Oceana, Mich	24
Blackberry Station, Kane, Ill	430
Black Bird, New Castle, Del	37
Black Brook, Clinton, N. Y	130
Black Brook, Polk, Wis	12
Black Creek, Allegany, N. Y	160
Black Creek, Wilson, N. C	44
Black Creek, Holmes, Ohio	34
Black Creek, Luzerne, Pa	8
Black Diamond, Contra Costa, Cal	12
Black Earth, Dane, Wis	540
Blackfish, Crittenden, Ark	12
Blackfoot City, Deer Lodge, Mont	340
Black Fork, Tucker, W. Va	4
Black Hawk, Carroll, Miss	71
Black Hawk, Beaver, Pa	25
Black Hawk, Sauk, Wis	58
Black Hawk Mills, Posey, Ind	24
Black Hawk Point, Gilpin, Colo	1,600
Black Horse, Harford, Md	43
Black Horse, Chester, Pa	52
Blackinton, Berkshire, Mass	240
Black Jack, Scott, Ark	10
Black Jack, Douglas, Kans	92
Black Jack, Hocking, Ohio	18
Black Jack, Robertson, Tenn	19
Black Jack Grove, Hopkins, Tex	6
Black Jack Springs, Fayette, Tex	16
Black Lake, Muskegon, Mich	50
Blackleysville, Wayne, Ohio	20
Black Lick, Franklin, Ohio	72
Black Lick Station, Indiana, Pa	85
Blackman's Mills, Sampson, N. C	3
Black Mingo, Williamsburgh, S. C	73
Black Oak, Caldwell, Mo	22
Black Oak, Hopkins, Tex	10

Post office	Amount
Black Oak Point, Hickory, Mo	$16
Black Oak Ridge, Daviess, Ind	33
Black Point, Marin, Cal	15
Black River, Jefferson, N. Y	100
Black River, Lorain, Ohio	59
Black River, King, Wash	12
Black River Chapel, New Hanover, N. C	6
Black River Falls,* (*c. h.*,) Jackson, Wis	1,200
Black Rock, Fairfield, Conn	90
Black Rock, Baltimore, Md	7
Black Rock, Grant, W. Va	14
Blacks and Whites, Nottoway, Va	220
Blacksburgh, Montgomery, Va	250
Black's Gap, Franklin, Pa	12
Blackshear,* (*c. h.*,) Pierce, Ga	12
Black's Mills, Monmouth, N. J	79
Black Springs, Montgomery, Ark	12
Black Stocks, Chester, S. C	98
Blackstone, Livingston, Ill	12
Blackstone, Worcester, Mass	880
Blacksville, Monongalia, W. Va	38
Black Swamp, Sandusky, Ohio	22
Black's Wells, Choctaw, Miss	8
Blackville, (*c. h.*,) Barnwell, S. C	380
Black Walnut, Ogle, Ill	24
Black Walnut, Palo Alto, Iowa	11
Black Walnut, Wyoming, Pa	13
Black Walnut, Halifax, Va	69
Black Water, Morgan, Ky	12
Blackwater, Sussex, Del	33
Blackwell's Station, St. Francois, Mo	40
Blackwoodtown, Camden, N. J	140
Bladenborough, Bladen, N. C	15
Bladensburgh, Wapello, Iowa	12
Bladensburgh, Prince George's, Md	170
Bladensburgh, Knox, Ohio	64
Bladen Springs, Choctaw, Ala	86
Blain, Perry, Pa	120
Blaine, Lawrence, Ky	7
Blain's Cross Roads, Grainger, Tenn	24
Blair, Randolph, Ill	34
Blair, Barry, Mich	14
Blair, (*c. h.*,) Washington, Nebr	510
Blair, Hancock, W. Va	9
Blairsburgh, Hamilton, Iowa	23
Blairstown,* Benton, Iowa	870
Blairstown, Warren, N. J	430
Blairsville, (*c. h.*,) Union, Ga	99
Blairsville, Williamson, Ill	5
Blairsville, Posey, Ind	30
Blairsville,* Indiana, Pa	840
Blairsville, York, S. C	4
Blakeley, Scott, Minn	67
Blakeley, Kitsap, Wash	10
Blakely, (*c. h.*,) Early, Ga	190
Blakely, Stokes, N. C	4
Blakesburgh, Wapello, Iowa	180
Blake's Ferry, Randolph, Ala	10
Blakeville, Black Hawk, Iowa	10
Blakeville, Cheshire, N. H	63
Blanchard, Piscataquis, Me	23
Blanchard, Centre, Pa	12
Blanchardville, La Fayette, Wis	58

* Money-order office.

Blanchester, Clinton, Ohio	$330
Blanco, (c. h.,) Blanco, Tex	47
Bland C. H., Bland, Va	10
Blandinsville,* McDonough, Ill	390
Blandon, Berks, Pa	83
Blandville, (c. h.,) Ballard, Ky	140
Blanford, Hampden, Mass	130
Blanket Hill, Armstrong, Pa	7
Blauveltville, Rockland, N. Y	71
Blawenburgh, Somerset, N. J	67
Bleakwood, Newton, Tex	12
Bledsoe, Crittenden, Ark	12
Bleecker, Fulton, N. Y	100
Blendon, Ottawa, Mich	62
Bliss, Miller, Mo	12
Blissfield, Lenawee, Mich	420
Bliven's Mills, McHenry, Ill	40
Blockville, Chautauqua, N. Y	22
Blodget Mills, Cortland, N. Y	73
Blodgett, Scott, Mo	12
Bloody Run, Bedford, Pa	380
Bloom, Cook, Ill	140
Bloom, Wood, Ohio	38
Bloom Centre, Logan, Ohio	38
Bloomer, Sebastian, Ark	7
Bloomer Centre, Montcalm, Mich	20
Bloomery, Hampshire, W. Va	25
Bloomfield, Sonoma, Cal	160
Bloomfield, Hartford, Conn	170
Bloomfield, Edgar, Ill	100
Bloomfield, (c. h.,)* Greene, Ind	290
Bloomfield, (c. h.,)* Davis, Iowa	900
Bloomfield, Nelson, Ky	75
Bloomfield, (c. h.,) Stoddard, Mo	250
Bloomfield,* Essex, N. J	810
Bloomfield, Morrow, Ohio	39
Bloomfield, Crawford, Pa	28
Bloomfield, Essex, Vt	6
Bloomfield, Loudoun, Va	39
Bloomfield, Walworth, Wis	140
Bloomingburgh, Sullivan, N. Y	180
Bloomingburgh, Fayette, Ohio	150
Bloomingdale, Du Page, Ill	180
Bloomingdale, Parke, Ind	140
Bloomingdale, Van Buren, Mich	72
Bloomingdale, Passaic, N. J	100
Bloomingdale, Essex, N. Y	110
Bloomingdale, Jefferson, Ohio	87
Bloomingdale, Luzerne, Pa	12
Bloomingdale, Vernon, Wis	80
Blooming Grove, Franklin, Ind	59
Blooming Grove, Linn, Kans	220
Blooming Grove, Waseca, Minn	26
Blooming Grove, Orange, N. Y	340
Blooming Grove, Dane, Wis	21
Bloomingport, Randolph, Ind	33
Blooming Prairie, Steele, Minn	12
Blooming Rose, Phelps, Mo	9
Bloomingsburgh, Fulton, Ind	20
Bloomington, Benton, Ark	12
Bloomington, (c. h.,)* McLean, Ill	4,000
Bloomington, (c. h.,)* Monroe, Ind	1,500
Bloomington, Alleghany, Md	200
Bloomington, Hennepin, Minn	36
Bloomington, Macon, Mo	55
Bloomington, Clinton, Ohio	68
Bloomington, Clearfield, Pa	$12
Bloomington, Tipton, Tenn	31
Bloomington, Rich, Utah	12
Bloomington, Grant, Wis	290
Bloomington Ferry, Hennepin, Minn	39
Blooming Valley, Crawford, Pa	110
Bloomingville, Erie, Ohio	14
Bloomsburgh, (c. h.,)* Columbia, Pa	1,600
Bloomsburgh, Halifax, Va	24
Bloomsbury, Hunterdon, N. J	170
Bloomsdale, St. Genevieve, Mo	12
Bloom Switch, Scioto, Ohio	12
Bloomville, Delaware, N. Y	85
Bloomville, Seneca, Ohio	110
Bloserville, Cumberland, Pa	22
Blossburgh,* Tioga, Pa	600
Blossom Hill, Princess Anne, Va	4
Blossom Prairie, Lamar, Tex	12
Blossvale, Oneida, N. Y	41
Blount's Ferry, Columbia, Fla	10
Blount Springs, Blount, Ala	40
Blountsville, (c. h.,) Blount, Ala	35
Blountsville, Henry, Ind	72
Blountsville, (c. h.,) Sullivan, Tenn	130
Blowing Rock, Watauga, N. C	12
Blue Ball, Butler, Ohio	31
Blue Ball, Lancaster, Pa	33
Blue Bell, Montgomery, Pa	54
Blue Canyon, Placer, Cal	31
Blue Creek, Franklin, Ind	11
Blue Creek, Adams, Ohio	23
Blue Eagle, Clay, Mo	12
Blue Earth City, (c. h.,)* Faribault, Minn	610
Blue Eye, Stone, Mo	12
Blue Grass, Vermilion, Ill	79
Blue Grass, Fulton, Ind	15
Blue Grass, Scott, Iowa	130
Blue Hill, Hancock, Me	280
Blue Hill Falls, Hancock, Me	45
Blue Island, Cook, Ill	440
Blue Island, (c. h.,) Saline, Nebr	12
Blue Knob, Blair, Pa	12
Blue Lake, Muskegon, Mich	7
Blue Lick, Franklin, Ala	12
Blue Lick, Clarke, Ind	24
Blue Lick, Allen, Ohio	13
Blue Lick Springs, Nicholas, Ky	73
Blue Mill, Jackson, Mo	20
Blue Mound, Livingston, Mo	12
Blue Mound, Dane, Wis	20
Blue Mounds, Linn, Kans	4
Blue Mountain, Calhoun, Ala	66
Blue Mountain, Izard, Ark	21
Blue Mountain, Northampton, Pa	25
Blue Point, Poweshiek, Iowa	4
Blue Point, Suffolk, N. Y	120
Blue Pond, Cherokee, Ala	5
Blue Rapids, Marshall, Kans	12
Blue Ridge, Shelby, Ind	24
Blue Ridge, Harrison, Mo	23
Blue Ridge, Henderson, N. C	28
Blue Ridge, Botetourt, Va	66
Blue River, Grant, Wis	75
Blue Rock, Muskingum, Ohio	57

* Money-order office.

Blue Rock, Chester, Pa	$91
Blue Spring, Gordon, Ga	12
Blue Springs, Volusia, Fla	8
Blue Springs, Jackson, Mo	24
Blue Springs, Gage, Nebr	6
Blue Stone, Tazewell, Va	22
Blue Sulphur Springs, Greenbrier, W. Va	33
Blue Valley, York, Nebr	12
Blue Wing, Granville, N. C	13
Bluff, Fayette, Tex	61
Bluff City, Livingston, Mo	8
Bluff Creek, Johnson, Ind	17
Bluff Dale, Greene, Ill	12
Bluff Point, Jay, Ind	30
Bluff Point, Yates, N. Y	23
Bluff Point, Hickman, Tenn	12
Bluff Spring, Clay, Ala	13
Bluff Spring, Talbot, Ga	10
Bluff Springs, Escambia, Fla	12
Bluffton, Yell, Ark	12
*Bluffton,** (*c. h.,*) Wells, Ind	560
Bluffton, Winneshiek, Iowa	47
Bluffton, Muskegon, Mich	77
Bluffton, Montgomery, Mo	59
Bluffton,* Allen, Ohio	230
Bluffton, Beaufort, S. C	57
Blumfield, Saginaw, Mich	19
Blumfield Junction, Saginaw, Mich	38
Blytheville, Jasper, Mo	29
Boalsburgh, Centre, Pa	120
Boardman, Mahoning, Ohio	42
Boardman, St. Croix, Wis	24
Boar's Head, Rockingham, N. H	12
Boatland, Fentress, Tenn	10
Boaz, Graves, Ky	12
Boaz, Richland, Wis	16
Bodenham, Giles, Tenn	15
Bodinesville, Lycoming, Pa	29
Body Camp, Bedford, Va	7
Boerne (*c. h.,*) Kendall, Tex	71
Boeuf Creek, Franklin, Mo	17
Boggstown, Shelby, Ind	71
Boggsville, Roane, W. Va	3
Boggy Depot, Choctaw N., Ind. T	20
Bogue, Columbus, N. C	20
Bogue Chitto, Lincoln, Miss	38
Bohemia, La Crosse, Wis	50
Bohon, Mercer, Ky	17
Boiling Springs, Cumberland, Pa	87
Boilston, Henderson, N. C	12
Bois Brule, Perry, Mo	12
Bois D'Arc, Greene, Mo	12
BOISE CITY,* (*c. h.,*) Ada, Idaho	1,800
Boistfort, Lewis, Wash	11
Boke's Creek, Union, Ohio	28
Bolckow, Andrew, Mo	12
Bold Spring, Franklin, Ga	19
Boles, Scott, Ark	12
Boles, Franklin, Mo	77
Bolinas, Marin, Cal	48
Bolington, Loudoun, Va	22
Bolivar, Frederick, Md	28
Bolivar, Bolivar, Miss	68
*Bolivar,** (*c. h.,*) Polk, Mo	280
Bolivar, Allegany, N. Y	120
Bolivar, Tuscarawas, Ohio	$170
Bolivar, Westmoreland, Pa	89
*Bolivar,** (*c. h.,*) Hardeman, Tenn	450
Bolling's Landing, Buckingham, Va	12
Bolster's Mills, Cumberland, Me	63
Bolton, Tolland, Conn	59
Bolton, Worcester, Mass	150
Bolton, Harrison, Mo	12
Bolton, Warren, N. Y	99
Bolton, Brunswick, N. C	12
Bolton, Chittenden, Vt	17
Bolton's Depot, Hinds, Miss	340
Boltonville, Cobb, Ga	15
Boltonville, Iowa, Iowa	12
Boltonville, Orange, Vt	56
Boltonville, Washington, Wis	69
Bolt's Fork, Boyd, Ky	6
Boman's Bluff, Henderson, N. C	1
Bombay, Franklin, N. Y	78
Bon Accord, Johnston, Iowa	19
Bonaparte,* Van Buren, Iowa	410
Bon Aqua, Hickman, Tenn	6
Bonbrook, Franklin, Va	23
Bonchea, St. Croix, Wis	17
Bond's Station, Shelby, Tenn	12
Bond's Village, Hampden, Mass	140
Bonduel, Shawanaw, Wis	42
Bondville, Bennington, Vt	88
Bone Camp, Madison, N. C	4
Bone Cave, Van Buren, Tenn	7
Bone Creek, Ritchie, W. Va	12
Bone Gap, Edwards, Ill	32
Bonfil's Station, St. Louis, Mo	16
Bonham, (*c. h.,*) Fannin, Tex	590
Bonhomme, (*c. h.,*) Bonhomme, Dak	22
Bonhomme, St. Louis, Mo	4
Bonn, Washington, Ohio	33
Bonneau's Depot, Charleston, S. C	120
Bonner, Jackson, La	16
Bonnet Carre, St. John Baptist, La	20
Bonnie Brook, Butler, Pa	11
Bonny Eagle, Cumberland, Me	45
Bono, Douglas, Ill	12
Bono, Lawrence, Ind	10
Bono, Washington, Nebr	7
Bonsack's Roanoke, Va	220
Bontear, St. Francois, Mo	12
Bonus, Boone, Ill	24
Bonwell, Edgar, Ill	23
Booker's Mills, Tyler, W. Va	12
Boone, Boone, Ark	12
Boone, Dallas, Iowa	59
Boone, (*c. h.,*) Watauga, N. C	26
Boone Furnace, Carter, Ky	12
*Boonesborough,** (*c. h.,*) Boone, Iowa	1,200
Boone's Mill, Franklin, Va	24
Booneville, Scott, Ark	13
Booneville, Pueblo, Colo	150
Booneville, (*c. h.,*) Owsley, Ky	110
Booneville, (*c. h.,*) Prentiss, Miss	250
Booneville, Yadkin, N. C	9
Booneville, Clinton, Pa	12
Booneville, Lincoln, Tenn	12
Boon Grove, Porter, Ind	14
Boon Hill, Johnston, N. C	36
Boonsborough, Washington, Ark	220

* Money-order office.

Boonsborough, Washington, Md	$320
Boon's Creek, Washington, Tenn	10
Boon Spring, Clinton, Iowa	7
Boonton,* Morris, N. J	880
*Boonville,** (*c. h.,*) Warrick, Ind	290
*Boonville,** (*c. h.,*) Cooper, Mo	2,000
Boonville,* Oneida, N. Y	1,100
Boot, Richland, Ill	12
Booth Bay, Lincoln, Me	310
Boothby Hill, Harford, Md	12
Booth Corner, Delaware, Pa	17
Boothsville, Marion, W. Va	84
Bordentown,* Burlington, N. J	1,900
Border Plains, Webster, Iowa	40
Bordley, Union, Ky	11
Bordoville, Franklin, Vt	26
Borodino, Onondaga, N. Y	69
Boscawen, Merrimack, N. H	210
Boscobel, Westchester, N. Y	58
Boscobel,* Grant, Wis	1,000
Bosqueville, McLennan, Tex	12
Bossardsville, Monroe, Pa	25
Bostick, Jefferson, Ga	40
Bostick's Mills, Richmond, N. C	19
Boston, Thomas, Ga	180
Boston, Wayne, Ind	46
Boston, Nelson, Ky	30
BOSTON,* (*c. h.,*) Suffolk, Mass	4,000
Boston, Erie, N. Y	130
Boston, Allegheny, Pa	C9
Boston, (*c. h.,*) Bowie, Tex	160
Boston, Culpeper, Va	22
Boston Corner, Columbia, N. Y	120
Boston Mills, Linn, Oreg	12
Boston Station, Pendleton, Ky	110
Boston Store, Montgomery, Ind	29
Bostwick Lake, Kent, Mich	21
Boswell, Mahoning, Ohio	17
Boswell's, Fluvanna, Va	150
Botany, Shelby, Iowa	20
Botavia, Jefferson, Iowa	230
Botetourt Springs, Roanoke, Va	100
Botland, Nelson, Ky	12
Bouckville, Madison, N. Y	150
Boulder, (*c. h.,*) Boulder, Colo	220
Boulder Valley, Jefferson, Mont	100
Boundary, Jay, Ind	26
Boundbrook, Somerset, N. J	510
Bounty Land, Oconee, S. C	12
Bourbon, Marshall, Ind	400
Bourbon, Crawford, Mo	33
Bourbonnais Grove, Kankakee, Ill	87
Bourneville, Ross, Ohio	120
Boutonville, Westchester, N. Y	19
Boutte, St. Charles, La	140
Bovina, Tama, Iowa	14
Bovina, Warren, Miss	28
Bovina, Delaware, N. Y	27
Bovina Valley, Delaware, N. Y	51
Bovine, Gibson, Ind	10
Bow, Merrimack, N. H	12
Bowdoin, Sagadahoc, Me	15
Bowdoin Centre, Sagadahoc, Me	36
Bowdoinham, Sagadahoc, Me	510
Bowdon, Carroll, Ga	85
Bowen, Grenada, Miss	12
Bowensburgh, Hancock, Ill	$290
Bowen's Corners, Oswego, N. Y	15
Bowen's Mills, Barry, Mich	35
Bowen's Prairie, Jones, Iowa	29
Bowenville, Carroll, Ga	23
Bowenville, Fauquier, Va	140
Bower, Clearfield, Pa	36
Bower Hill, Washington, Pa	17
Bower's City, Carroll, Mo	12
Bower's Mills, Lawrence, Mo	14
Bower's Station, Berks, Pa	46
Bowerston, Harrison, Ohio	100
Bowersville, Hart, Ga	5
Bowersville, Greene, Ohio	87
Bowerville, Jefferson, Nebr	12
Bowling Brook, St. Genevieve, Mo	12
Bowling Green, Fayette, Ill	3
*Bowling Green,** (*c. h.,*) Clay, Ind	330
*Bowling Green,** (*c. h.,*) Warren, Ky	2,000
Bowling Green, (*c. h.,*) Pike, Mo	300
Bowling Green,* Wood, Ohio	450
Bowling Green, (*c. h.,*) Caroline, Va	240
Bowlusville, Clark, Ohio	60
Bowman's Creek, Wyoming, Pa	31
Bowman's Mills, Rockingham, Va	48
Bowmansville, Erie, N. Y	84
Bowmansville, Lancaster, Pa	27
Bowne, Kent, Mich	41
Boxborough, Middlesex, Mass	36
Boxford, Essex, Mass	120
Boxford, DeKalb, Mo	12
Boxley, Hamilton, Ind	100
Box Spring, Talbot, Ga	25
Boxville, Union, Ky	10
Boyd, Dallas, Mo	5
Boyd Lake, Piscataquis, Me	12
Boyd's Corner, Putnam, N. Y	16
Boyd's Landing, Hardin, Tenn	12
Boyd's Mill, Wise, Tex	12
Boyd's Mills, Coshocton, Ohio	26
Boyd's Station, Harrison, Ky	140
Boyd's Switch, Jackson, Ala	12
Boydston's Mills, Kosciusko, Ind	21
Boydsville, Graves, Ky	38
Boydton, (*c. h.,*) Mecklenburgh, Va	300
Boyer River, Crawford, Iowa	47
Boyerstown, Berks, Pa	230
Boykin's Depot, Southampton, Va	130
Boylan's Grove, Butler, Iowa	66
Boyler's Mill, Morgan, Mo	18
Boyleston, Henry, Iowa	12
Boylston, Worcester, Mass	53
Boylston Centre, Worcester, Mass	69
Boylston Centre, Oswego, N. Y	12
Boyne, Charlevoix, Mich	12
Boynton, Tazewell, Ill	36
Bozeman, (*c. h.,*) Gallatin, Mont	590
Bozrah, New London, Conn	110
Bozrahville, New London, Conn	140
Braceville, Grundy, Ill	230
Braceville, Trumbull, Ohio	86
Bracken, Huntingdon, Ind	12
Brackney, Susquehanna, Pa	28
Braddock's Field, Allegheny, Pa	320
Braddyville, Page, Iowa	95
Braden's Knobs, Bledsoe, Tenn	13

* Money-order office.

Post office	Amount
Braden Station, Fayette, Tenn	$12
Bradenville, Westmoreland, Pa	62
Bradford, Stark, Ill	150
Bradford, Harrison, Ind	20
Bradford, Chickasaw, Iowa	236
Bradford, Bracken, Ky	24
Bradford, Penobscot, Me	120
Bradford, Essex, Mass	380
Bradford, Merrimack, N. H	340
Bradford, Steuben, N. Y	120
Bradford, Miami, Ohio	12
Bradford, McKean, Pa	250
Bradford,* Orange, Vt	1,000
Bradford Centre, Orange, Vt	17
Bradford Springs, Sumter, S. C	12
Bradfordsville, Marion, Ky	45
Bradley, Bradley, Ark	16
Bradley, Jackson, Ill	18
Bradley, Allegan, Mich	90
Bradleyville, Taney, Mo	1
Bradrickville, Lawrence, Ohio	12
Bradshaw, Giles, Tenn	12
Bradtville, Grant, Wis	19
Brady, Kalamazoo, Mich	300
Brady, Indiana, Pa	190
Brady's, Richland, Wis	11
Brady's Bend, Armstrong, Pa	560
Brady's Mill, Alleghany, Md	71
Bradyville, Adams, Ohio	20
Bradyville, Cannon, Tenn	12
Brafford's Store, Knox, Ky	12
Braggs, Lowndes, Ala	12
Braggville, Middlesex, Mass	58
Braidwood, Will, Ill	220
Brainard's, Warren, N. J	110
Brainerd, Rensselaer, N. Y	110
Braintree, Norfolk, Mass	170
Braintree, Orange, Vt	83
Braman's Corners, Schenectady, N. Y	39
Bramlette, Gallatin, Ky	28
Branch, Paulding, Ga	12
Branch, Manitowoc, Wis	10
Branch Dale, Schuylkill, Pa	110
Branch Junction, Westmoreland, Pa	59
Branchport, Yates, N. Y	200
Branch Shore, Monmouth, N. J	270
Branch's Store, Duplin, N. C	12
Branchville, St. Clair, Ala	13
Branchville, Drew, Ark	51
Branchville, Prince George's, Md	20
Branchville, Sussex, N. J	250
Branchville, Orangeburgh, S. C	130
Branchville, Southampton, Va	38
Brandenburgh, (*c. h.*,) Meade, Ky	96
Brandon, DeKalb, Ala	12
Brandon, Buchanan, Iowa	51
Brandon, Oakland, Mich	20
Brandon, Douglas, Minn	12
Brandon,* (*c. h.*,) Rankin, Miss	610
Brandon, Knox, Ohio	50
Brandon,* Rutland, Vt	1,400
Brandon, Prince George, Va	100
Brandon, Fond du Lac, Wis	370
Brandon Church, Prince George, Va	14
Brandonville, Schuylkill, Pa	37

Post office	Amount
Brandonville, Preston, W. Va	$89
Brandt, Miami, Ohio	57
Brandtwood, Starke, Ind	16
Brandy Camp, Elk, Pa	12
Brandy Station, Culpeper, Va	64
Brandywine, Prince George's, Md	41
Brandywine Manor, Chester, Pa	62
Brandywine Summit, Delaware, Pa	64
Branford, New Haven, Conn	830
Branson, San Diego, Cal	12
Brant, Erie, N. Y	93
Brant, Calumet, Wis	19
Brantford, Sherburne, Minn	16
Brantingham, Lewis, N. Y	12
Brashear, St. Mary's, La	84
Brasher Falls, St. Lawrence, N. Y	300
Brasher Iron Works, St. Lawrence, N. Y	56
Brassfield, Wake, N. C	12
Bratsberg, Fillmore, Minn	120
Brattleborough,* Windham, Vt	2,300
Bratton, Nemaha, Nebr	12
Bratton's Mills, Robertson, Ky	8
Braxton C. H., Braxton, W. Va	62
Bray's Mills, Bartholomew, Ind	10
Brazil,* Clay, Ind	1,000
Brazito, Cole, Mo	20
Brazos Santiago, Cameron, Texas	120
Brazoria, (*c. h.*,) Brazoria, Texas	180
Breakabeen, Schoharie, N. Y	80
Breakneck, Butler, Pa	78
Breathedsville, Washington, Md	89
Breaux Bridge, St. Martin's, La	64
Breckinridge, (*c. h.*,) Summit, Colo	40
Breckinridge, Caldwell, Mo	290
Breckinridge, Vernon, Wis	21
Breckville, Madison, Wis	12
Breeding's, Adair, Ky	16
Breedsville, Van Buren, Mich	190
Breese, Greene, Ill	56
Breesport, Chemung, N. Y	120
Breinigsville, Lehigh, Pa	63
Bremen, Randolph, Ill	42
Bremen, Marshall, Ind	160
Bremen, Muhlenburgh, Ky	43
Bremen, Fairfield, Ohio	220
Bremo Bluff, Fluvanna, Va	82
Bremond, Robertson, Texas	310
Brenford, Kent, Del	22
Brenham,* (*c. h.*,) Washington, Tex	2,800
Brentsville, (*c. h.*,) Prince William, Va	40
Brentwood, Rockingham, N. H	66
Brentwood, Suffolk, N. Y	77
Brentwood, Williamson, Tenn	90
Bretzville, Dubois, Ind	11
Brevard, (*c. h.*,) Transylvania, N. C	20
Brewer, Penobscot, Me	420
Brewer's Mills, Marshall, Ky	26
Brewersville, Jennings, Ind	38
Brewerton, Onondaga, N. Y	170
Brewerton, Laurens, S. C	4
Brewer Village, Penobscot, Me	180
Brewerville, Randolph, Ill	12
Brewster, Barnstable, Mass	230
Brewster's Station, Putnam, N. Y	980

* Money-order office.

Brewton, Escambia, Ala	$12
Brick Church, Guilford, N. C	3
Brick Church, Giles, Tenn	46
Brickerville, Lancaster, Pa	32
Brickland, Lunenburgh, Va	13
Brick Meeting House, Cecil, Md	150
Brick Mill, Blount, Tenn	12
Bricksburgh, Ocean, N. J	690
Bricksville, Cuyahoga, Ohio	140
Brickton, Cook, Ill	10
Brickville, Merced, Cal	12
Bridgeborough, Burlington, N. J	60
Bridge Creek, Carroll, Mo	12
Bridge Creek, Wasco, Oreg	12
Bridgehampton, Suffolk, N. Y	370
Bridgeport, Jackson, Ala	140
Bridgeport, (*c. h.*,) Mono, Cal	10
Bridgeport,* Fairfield, Conn	4,000
Bridgeport, Lawrence, Ill	340
Bridgeport, Marion, Ind	120
Bridgeport, Jackson, Iowa	12
Bridgeport, Franklin, Ky	60
Bridgeport, Frederick, Md	13
Bridgeport, Warren, Mo	12
Bridgeport, Gloucester, N. J	130
Bridgeport, Madison, N. Y	61
Bridgeport, Belmont, Ohio	870
Bridgeport, Polk, Oreg	22
Bridgeport, Montgomery, Pa	220
Bridgeport, Cocke, Tenn	12
Bridgeport, Harrison, W. Va	160
Bridgeport, Crawford, Wis	66
Bridgeport Centre, Saginaw, Mich	110
Bridger Station, Uintah, Wyo	12
Bridgeton, Parke, Ind	30
Bridgeton,* Cumberland, Me	630
Bridgeton, Newaygo, Mich	49
Bridgeton, St. Louis, Mo	110
Bridgeton,* (*c. h.*,) Cumberland, N. J	2,000
Bridgetown, Caroline, Md	8
Bridge Valley, Bucks, Pa	43
Bridgeville, Pickens, Ala	88
Bridgeville, Sussex, Del	350
Bridgeville, Gratiot, Mich	53
Bridgeville, Warren, N. J	91
Bridgeville, Sullivan, N. Y	45
Bridgeville, Muskingum, Ohio	31
Bridgewater, Litchfield, Conn	200
Bridgewater, Aroostook, Me	99
Bridgewater,* Plymouth, Mass	1,100
Bridgewater, Grafton, N. H	52
Bridgewater, Oneida, N. Y	180
Bridgewater, Burke, N. C	25
Bridgewater, Williams, Ohio	18
Bridgewater, Bucks, Pa	91
Bridgewater, Windsor, Vt	220
Bridgewater, Rockingham, Va	330
Bridle Creek, Grayson, Va	10
Bridport, Addison, Vt	230
Briensburgh, Marshall, Ky	12
Brier Creek, Columbia, Pa	12
Brierfield, Bibb, Ala	200
Brier Hill, St. Lawrence, N. Y	91
Briggsville, Luzerne, Pa	23
Briggsville, Marquette, Wis	67
Brigham City, (*c. h.*,) Box Elder, Utah	400
Bright, Dearborn, Indiana	$18
Brighton, Sacramento, Cal	71
Brighton, Macoupin, Ill	940
Brighton, La Grange, Ind	15
Brighton,* Washington, Iowa	290
Brighton, Somerset, Maine	36
Brighton, Montgomery, Md	55
Brighton,* Middlesex, Mass	1,000
Brighton, Livingston, Mich	330
Brighton, Polk, Mo	18
Brighton, Monroe, N. Y	230
Brighton, Lorain, Ohio	44
Brighton, Beaufort, S. C	14
Brighton, Kenosha, Wis	14
Brighton Station, Lincoln, Tenn	8
Bright Star, Hopkins, Tex	210
Brightwood, Washington, D. C	25
Brillion, Calumet, Wis	13
Brimfield,* Peoria, Ill	340
Brimfield, Noble, Ind	200
Brimfield, Hampden, Mass	360
Brimfield, Portage, Ohio	44
Brindletown, Burke, N. C	10
Brinkerton, Clarion, Pa	19
Brinkley, Monroe, Ark	12
Brinkleyville, Halifax, N. C	12
Brinley's Station, Preble, Ohio	54
Brinsonville, Burke, Ga	12
Brinton, Champaign, Ohio	12
Brinton, Allegheny, Pa	12
Briscoe, Sullivan, N. Y	12
Briscoe Run, Wood, W. Va	11
Bristersburgh, Fauquier, Va	21
Bristoe Station, Prince William, Va	64
Bristol,* Hartford, Conn	1,400
Bristol, (*c. h.*,) Liberty, Fla	20
Bristol, Kendall, Ill	170
Bristol, Elkhart, Ind	570
Bristol, Worth, Iowa	74
Bristol, Lincoln, Me	140
Bristol, Anne Arundel, Md	100
Bristol,* Grafton, N. H	690
Bristol, Ontario, N. Y	110
Bristol, Morgan, Ohio	22
Bristol,* Bucks, Pa	1,800
Bristol,* (*c. h.*,) Bristol, R. I	1,500
Bristol,* Sullivan, Tenn	910
Bristol, Addison, Vt	460
Bristol, Kenosha, Wis	140
Bristol Centre, Ontario, N. Y	81
Bristol Station, Kendall, Ill	210
Bristolville, Trumbull, Ohio	120
Bristoria, Greene, Pa	12
Bristow Station, Warren, Ky	120
British Hollow, Grant, Wis	83
Brittain, Rutherford, N. C	7
Brittain's, Pulaski, Mo	12
Britton, Woodruff, Ark	12
Britton's Neck, Marion, S. C	19
Britt's Landing, Perry, Tenn	37
Broadalbin, Fulton, N. Y	340
Broad Axe, Montgomery, Pa	20
Broad Brook, Hartford, Conn	250
Broad Creek, Queen Anne, Md	83
Broad Creek Neck, Talbot, Md	10
Broad Ford, Fayette, Pa	160

* Money-order office.

Post office	Compensation
Broadford, Smyth, Va	$19
Broadhead, Rockcastle, Ky	12
Broad Mountain, Schuylkill, Pa	41
Broad Ripple, Marion, Ind	13
Broad Run, Frederick, Md	14
Broad Run Station, Fauquier, Va	74
Broad Shoals, Polk, Tenn	5
Broad Top, Huntingdon, Pa	140
Broadway, Warren, N. J	75
Broadway, Union, Ohio	100
Broadway Depot, Rockingham, Va	110
Broadwell, Logan, Ill	99
Broadwell, Harrison, Ky	17
Brock, Darke, Ohio	7
Brockett's Bridge, Fulton, N. Y	150
Brockport,* Monroe, N. Y	1,900
Brocktown, Pike, Ark	4
Brockway, St. Clair, Mich	110
Brockway, Stearns, Minn	10
Brockway Centre, St. Clair, Mich	88
Brockway's Mills, Piscataquis, Me	20
Brockwayville, Jefferson, Pa	200
Brocton, Chautauqua, N. Y	410
Brodbecks, York, Pa	9
Brodhead, Allegheny, Pa	25
Brodhead,* Green, Wis	810
Brodheadsville, Monroe, Pa	44
Brodie's Landing, Decatur, Tenn	12
Broken Arrow, St. Clair, Ala	11
Brokenburgh, Spottsylvania, Va	17
Broken Straw, Chautauqua, N. Y	63
Broken Sword, Crawford, Ohio	43
Bronson, Levy, Fla	12
Bronson's Prairie, Branch, Mich	540
Bronxville, Westchester, N. Y	190
Brook, Newton, Ind	47
Brookdale, Susquehanna, Pa	39
Brookeland, Sabine, Tex	5
Brookfield, Fairfield, Conn	300
Brookfield, Shelby, Ind	51
Brookfield, Clinton, Iowa	49
Brookfield, Worcester, Mass	610
Brookfield, Eaton, Mich	21
Brookfield,* Linn, Mo	1,400
Brookfield, Carroll, N. H	23
Brookfield, Madison, N. Y	250
Brookfield, Trumbull, Ohio	200
Brookfield, Tioga, Pa	14
Brookfield, Orange, Vt	180
Brookfield Centre, Fairfield, Conn	100
Brookfield Centre, Waukesha, Wis.	65
Brookhaven,* (*c. h.*,) Lincoln, Miss	940
Brookland, Potter, Pa	42
Brooklandville, Baltimore, Md	24
Brooklin, Hancock, Me	130
Brookline, Jackson, La	16
Brookline, Norfolk, Mass	1,900
Brookline, Hillsborough, N. H	130
Brooklyn, Conecuh, Ala	38
Brooklyn, Alameda, Cal	280
Brooklyn, (*c. h.*,) Windham, Conn	590
Brooklyn, Schuyler, Ill	44
Brooklyn, Morgan, Ind	88
Brooklyn,* Poweshiek, Iowa	500
Brooklyn, Linn, Kans	22
Brooklyn, Butler, Ky	12
Brooklyn, Anne Arundel, Md	$18
Brooklyn,* Jackson, Mich	380
Brooklyn, Hennepin, Minn	29
Brooklyn, Harrison, Mo	35
Brooklyn,* (*c. h.*,) Kings, N. Y	4,000
Brooklyn, Cuyahoga, Ohio	140
Brooklyn, Susquehanna, Pa	170
Brooklyn, Halifax, Va	16
Brooklyn, Green, Wis	140
Brooklyn Village, Cuyahoga, Ohio.	120
Brook Neal, Campbell, Va	29
Brooks, Waldo, Me	180
Brooks' Grove, Livingston, N. Y	46
Brookside, Osceola, Mich	16
Brookside, Morris, N. J	89
Brookston, White, Ind	360
Brooks' Vale, New Haven, Conn	35
Brooksville, Blount, Ala	12
Brooksville, Hancock, Me	53
Brooksville, Addison, Vt	96
Brook Vale, Prince William, Va	12
Brookville, Ogle, Ill	60
Brookville,* (*c. h.*,) Franklin, Ind	760
Brookville, Jefferson, Iowa	30
Brookville, Saline, Kans	12
Brookville, (*c. h.*,) Bracken, Ky	110
Brookville, Montgomery, Md	150
Brookville, Noxubee, Miss	320
Brookville, Granville, N. C	7
Brookville, Montgomery, Ohio	53
Brookville,* (*c. h.*,) Jefferson, Pa	1,000
Brookville, St. Croix, Wis	150
Broomall, Delaware, Pa	12
Broome Centre, Schoharie, N. Y	28
Broomtown, Cherokee, Ala	7
Brosley, Cass, Mo	12
Brotherton, St. Louis, Mo	8
Brothertown, Calumet, Wis	49
Brotzmanville, Warren, N. J	1
Brower, Berks, Pa	31
Brower's Mills, Randolph, N. C	11
Browne Hill, Wythe, Va	39
Brownfield, Oxford, Me	200
Brownhelm, Lorain, Ohio	88
Brown Hill, Crawford, Pa	9
Browning, Schuyler, Ill	25
Browning, Carroll, Iowa	12
Browningsville, Bracken, Ky	12
Brownington, Butler, Pa	24
Brownington, Orleans, Vt	75
Brownsborough, Madison, Ala	91
Brownsborough, Oldham, Ky	52
Brownsborough, Washington, Tenn.	24
Brownsborough, Henderson, Texas	12
Brownsburgh, Hendricks, Ind	150
Brownsburgh, Bucks, Pa	58
Brownsburgh, Rockbridge, Va	180
Brown's Corners, Huntington, Ind	12
Brown's Cove, Albemarle, Va	8
Brown's Creek, Harrison, W. Va	17
Brownsdale, Butler, Pa	15
Brown's Mills, Davis, Iowa	12
Brown's Mills, Muskegon, Mich	12
Brown's Mills, Burlington, N. J	6
Brown's Mills, Washington, Ohio	31
Brown's Mills, Franklin, Pa	54

* Money-order office.

Brownsport Furnace, Decatur, Tenn	$12
Brown's Station, Preble, Ohio	12
Brown's Store, Northumberland, Va	12
Brownstown, Fayette, Ill	12
Brownstown,* (*c. h.*,) Jackson, Ind	360
Brownstown, Wayne, Mich	210
Brown's Valley, Yuba, Cal	160
Brown's Valley, Montgomery, Ind	29
Brownsville, Yuba, Cal	20
Brownsville, Paulding, Ga	12
Brownsville, Union, Ind	110
Brownsville, (*c. h.*,) Edmonson, Ky	24
Brownsville, Piscataquis, Me	170
Brownsville, Washington, Md	57
Brownsville, Cass, Mich	74
Brownsville, Houston, Minn	340
Brownsville, Saline, Mo	320
Brownsville, Granville, N. C	5
Brownsville, Licking, Ohio	140
Brownsville, Linn, Oreg	150
Brownsville,* Fayette, Pa	1,200
Brownsville, Marlborough, S. C	10
Brownsville,* (*c.h.*,) Haywood, Tenn	1,400
Brownsville,* (*c.h.*,) Cameron, Tex	3,000
Brownsville, Windsor, Vt	180
Browntown, Bradford, Pa	17
Brownville, Mitchell, Iowa	31
Brownville,* (*c. h.*,) Nemaha, Nebr	1,300
Brownville, Jefferson, N. Y	280
Brownwood, (*c. h.*,) Brown, Tex	12
Bruceport, Chehalis, Wash	39
Bruce's Lake, Fulton, Ind	23
Bruceton Mills, Preston, W. Va	72
Bruceville, Bullock, Ala	7
Bruceville, La Salle, Ill	7
Bruceville, Knox, Ind	130
Bruceville, Carroll, Md	22
Bruin, Carter, Ky	12
Bruin, Butler, Pa	40
Bruington, King and Queen, Va	22
Bruin's Cross Roads, Parke, Ind	33
Brumfield Station, Boyle, Ky	10
Brumfieldville, Berks, Pa	36
Brumley, Miller, Mo	17
Brunersburgh, Defiance, Ohio	28
Brunnerville, Lancaster, Pa	36
Brunot, Wayne, Mo	23
Brunswick,* (*c. h.*,) Glynn, Ga	440
Brunswick, Peoria, Ill	16
Brunswick, Lake, Ind	43
Brunswick,* Cumberland, Me	2,200
Brunswick, (*c. h.*,) Kanebec, Minn	33
Brunswick,* Chariton, Mo	1,200
Brunswick, Medina, Ohio	130
Brunswick, Essex, Vt	4
Brush Creek, Perry, Ala	6
Brush Creek, Butte, Cal	35
Brush Creek, Fayette, Iowa	98
Brush Creek, Laclede, Mo	75
Brush Creek, Muskingum, Ohio	12
Brush Creek, Beaver, Pa	15
Brushey, Choctaw N., Ind. T	12
Brushland, Delaware, N. Y	19
Brush Prairie, McLeod, Minn	16
Brush Run, Washington, Pa	45
Brush's Mills, Franklin, N. Y	230
Brush Valley, Indiana, Pa	$85
Brushville, Waushara, Wis	12
Brushy Creek, Anderson, S. C	6
Brushy Fork, Douglas, Ill	23
Brushy Prairie, La Grange, Ind	22
Brushy Run, Pendleton, W. Va	12
Brussels, Door, Wis	12
Bruynswick, Ulster, N. Y	34
Bryan,* (*c. h*,,) Williams, Ohio	1,500
Bryan, (*c. h.*,) Brazos, Tex	2,000
Bryan, Uintah, Wyo	380
Bryansville, York, Pa	20
Bryant, Fulton, Ill	97
Bryantown, Charles, Md	90
Bryantsburgh, Jefferson, Ind	16
Bryant's Creek, Monroe, Ind	16
Bryant's Pond, Oxford, Me	160
Bryantsville, Lawrence, Ind	16
Bryantsville, Garrard, Ky	160
Bucatunna, Wayne, Miss	65
Buchanan, (*c. h.*,) Haralson, Ga	25
Buchanan, Lawrence, Ky	21
Buchanan,* Berrien, Mich	1,200
Buchanan, Bollinger, Mo	30
Buchanan, Granville, N. C	10
Buchanan, Perry, Ohio	20
Buchanan, Allegheny, Pa	1,800
Buchanan, Botetourt, Va	190
Buck, Lancaster, Pa	40
Buck Branch, Jasper, Mo	12
Buck Creek, Bremer, Iowa	66
Buck Creek, Richland, Wis	12
Buck Eye, Yolo, Cal	75
Buckeye, Garrard, Ky	12
Buckeye Cottage, Perry, Ohio	24
Buckeye Cove, Pocahontas, W. Va	11
Buckeystown, Frederick, Md	180
Buckfield, Oxford, Me	360
Buckannon, (*c. h.*,) Upshur, W. Va	320
Buck Head, Morgan, Ga	32
Buck Head, Fairfield, S. C	12
Buck Hollow, Franklin, Vt	16
Buck Horn, Independence, Ark	18
Buck Horn, Brown, Ill	19
Buck Horn, Mahaska, Iowa	13
Buck Horn, Ohio, Ky	23
Buckhorn, Bienville, La	9
Buckhorn, Winston, Miss	8
Buckhorn, Columbia, Pa	79
Buck Horn, Pendleton, W. Va	5
Buckhorn, Adams, Wis	12
Buckingham, Hartford, Conn	56
Buckingham,* Tama, Iowa	210
Buckingham, Bucks, Pa	190
Buckingham C.H., Buckingham, Va	160
Buckinn, Madison, Ill	12
Buckland, Hartford, Conn	100
Buckland, Franklin, Mass	94
Buckland, Gates, N. C	12
Buckland, Prince William, Va	55
Buckley, Iroquois, Ill	400
Buckley, Highland, Ohio	8
Bucklin,* Linn, Mo	440
Buckluxy, Choctaw N., Ind. T	12
Buckmanville, Bucks, Pa	39
Buck Mountain, Carbon, Pa	160

* Money-order office.

Buckner's Station, Oldham, Ky	$39
Buckner's Station, Louisa, Va	12
Buck's, Columbiana, Ohio	38
Buck Shoal, Halifax, Va	12
Buckskin, Park, Colo	50
Buckskin, Gibson, Ind	15
Buck's Mills, Hancock, Me	12
Bucksport,* Hancock, Me	1,100
Bucksport Centre, Hancock, Me	35
Buck's Ranch, Plumas, Cal	12
Buckstown, Somerset, Pa	42
Bucksville, Bucks, Pa	48
Bucksville, Horry, S. C	12
Buckton, Warren, Va	12
Buck Valley, Fulton, Pa	16
Bucyrus,* (*c. h.*,) Crawford, Ohio	2,100
Buda, Bureau, Ill	540
Budd's Creek, St. Mary's, Md	16
Budd's Lake, Morris, N. J	85
Budd Town, Burlington, N. J	12
Buddville, Centre, Pa	30
Buel, Sanilac, Mich	10
Buel, Montgomery, N. Y	37
Buena, Van Wert, Ohio	10
Buena Vista, Amador, Cal	12
Buena Vista, (*c. h.*,) Marion, Ga	160
Buena Vista, Stephenson, Ill	94
Buena Vista, Clinton, Iowa	13
Buena Vista, Prince George's, Md	20
Buena Vista, Saginaw, Mich	12
Buena Vista, Chickasaw, Miss	92
Buena Vista, Steuben, N. Y	14
Buena Vista, Duplin, N. C	12
Buena Vista, Tuscarawas, Ohio	20
Buena Vista, Polk, Oregon	12
Buena Vista, Allegheny, Pa	92
Buena Vista, Greenville, S. C	12
Buena Vista, Carroll, Tenn	8
Buena Vista, Shelby, Texas	8
Buena Vista, Portage, Wis	22
Buffalo, Sangamon, Ill	100
Buffalo, Scott, Iowa	99
Buffalo, Wilson, Kans	30
Buffalo, La Rue, Ky	54
Buffalo, (*c. h.*,) Wright, Minn	26
Buffalo, (*c. h.*,) Dallas, Mo	130
Buffalo,* (*c. h.*,) Erie, N. Y	4,000
Buffalo, Guernsey, Ohio	16
Buffalo, Washington, Pa	24
Buffalo, Humphreys, Tenn	12
Buffalo, Putnam, W. Va	140
Buffalo, Buffalo, Wis	53
Buffalo Bluff, Putnam, Fla	12
Buffalo Cross Roads, Union, Pa	36
Buffalo Ford, Randolph, N. C	3
Buffalo Forge, Rockbridge, Va	21
Buffalo Fork, Kossuth, Iowa	15
Buffalo Grove, Buchanan, Iowa	23
Buffalo Mills, Bedford, Pa	6
Buffalo Mills, Rockbridge, Va	23
Buffalo Paper Mill, Cleveland, N. C	6
Buffalo Plains, Erie, N. Y	16
Buffalo Pond, Washington, Va	130
Buffalo Prairie, Rock Island, Ill	19
Buffalo Ridge, Washington, Tenn	7
Buffalo Run, Centre, Pa	21
Buffalo Shoals, Wayne, W. Va	$7
Buffalo Valley, Putnam, Tenn	12
Buffaloville, Spencer, Ind	19
Buford, Macoupin, Ill	15
Buford, Ohio, Ky	28
Buford, Highland, Ohio	49
Buford's, Bedford, Va	120
Buford's Station, Giles, Tenn	69
Buhlsville, Gentry, Mo	12
Bula, Goochland, Va	6
Bulger, Washington, Pa	37
Bullard's, Twiggs, Ga	12
Bullard's Bar, Yuba, Cal	37
Bull Creek, Georgetown, S. C	12
Bull Creek, Wood, W. Va	68
Bulliona, Alpine, Cal	55
Bullitsville, Boone, Ky	22
Bullock, Crenshaw, Ala	10
Bullock Creek, York, S. C	10
Bull Run, Knox, Tenn	33
Bull's Gap, Hawkins, Tenn	140
Bull's Head, Dutchess, N. Y	24
Bull's Mills, Christian, Mo	4
Bulltown, Braxton, W. Va	17
Bullville, Orange, N. Y	96
Bumpass, Louisa, Va	78
Bunceton, Cooper, Mo	200
Buncomb, Brown, Kans	12
Buncombe, Pettis, Mo	10
Bunker Hill, Macoupin, Ill	860
Bunker Hill, Miami, Ind	110
Bunker Hill, Lyon, Kans	12
Bunker Hill, Ingham, Mich	18
Bunker Hill, Giles, Tenn	10
Bunker Hill, Bedford, Va	4
Bunker's Hill, Grant, Wis	12
Bunner's, Marion, W. Va	12
Bunn's Bluff, Orange, Tex	10
Buras, Plaquemines, La	110
Burbank, Monongalia, Minn	18
Burbank, Wayne, Ohio	170
Burbois, Gasconade, Mo	47
Burch's, Kent, Mich	50
Burdett, Bates, Mo	12
Burdett, Schuyler, N. Y	260
Burdickville, Leelenaw, Mich	48
Bureau Junction, Bureau, Ill	84
Burem's Store, Hawkins, Tenn	12
Burford's Landing, Wilcox, Ala	12
Burfordville, Cape Girardeau, Mo	12
Burgaw Depot, New Hanover, N. C	23
Burgess, Clinton, Iowa	49
Burgess, Dinwiddie, Va	5
Burget's Corner, Clinton, Ind	16
Burgettstown, Washington, Pa	220
Burgh Hill, Trumbull, Ohio	190
Burk, Benton, Iowa	16
Burke, Franklin, N. Y	51
Burke, Caledonia, Vt	45
Burke's Garden, Tazewell, Va	69
Burke's Mills, Augusta, Va	51
Burkesville, (*c. h.*,) Cumberland, Ky	260
Burkesville, Nottaway, Va	190
Burkettsville, Frederick, Md	170
Burkeville, Newton, Tex	31
Burk's Station, Fairfax, Va	12

* Money-order office.

Post office	
Burksville, Monroe, Ill	$31
Burleson, Franklin, Ala	10
*Burlingame,** (*c. h.,*) Osage, Kans	1,300
Burlingham, Sullivan, N. Y	18
Burlingham, Meigs, Ohio	24
Burlington,* Boulder, Colo	390
Burlington, Hartford, Conn	66
Burlington, Kane, Ill	69
Burlington, Carroll, Ind	76
*Burlington,** (*c. h.,*) Des Moines, Iowa	3,400
*Burlington,** (*c. h.,*) Coffey, Kans	430
Burlington, (*c. h.,*) Boone, Ky	86
Burlington, East Baton Rouge, La	7
Burlington, Penobscot, Me	55
Burlington, Middlesex, Mass	44
Burlington, Calhoun, Mich	80
Burlington, Boone, Mo	49
Burlington,* Burlington, N. J	2,200
Burlington, Otsego, N. Y	51
Burlington, Lawrence, Ohio	91
Burlington, Bradford, Pa	130
*Burlington,** (*c. h.,*) Chittenden, Vt	3,100
Burlington, Mineral, W. Va	85
Burlington,* Racine, Wis	880
Burlington Flats, Otsego, N. Y	150
Burnersville, Barbour, W. Va	34
Burnet, (*c. h.,*) Burnet, Tex	63
Burnett, Santa Clara, Cal	10
Burnett, Vigo, Ind	12
Burnett, Dodge, Wis	16
Burnett's Creek, White, Ind	160
Burnett Station, Dodge, Wis	200
Burnettsville, Somerset, Md	81
Burney's Mills, Randolph, N. C	12
Burnhamsville, Todd, Minn	12
Burnham Village, Waldo, Me	120
Burning Springs,* Wirt, W. Va	350
Burnip's Corners, Allegan, Mich	40
Burns, Henry, Ill	28
Burns, Shiawassee, Mich	14
Burns, Allegany, N. Y	79
Burns, La Crosse, Wis	47
Burnside, Hartford, Conn	190
Burnside, Hancock, Ill	250
Burnside, Clinton, Ind	12
Burnside, Lapeer, Mich	84
Burnside, Orange, N. Y	12
Burnside, Clearfield, Pa	64
Burnside, Buffalo, Wis	27
Burns' Mills, Bedford, Pa	12
Burns' Station, Dickson, Tenn	67
Burnsville, Dallas, Ala	12
Burnsville, Bartholomew, Ind	29
Burnsville, Tishemingo, Miss	150
Burnsville, (*c. h.,*) Yancey, N. C	44
Burnt Cabins, Fulton, Pa	83
Burnt Chimney, Rutherford, N. C	15
Burnt Corn, Monroe, Ala	12
Burnt Hills, Saratoga, N. Y	110
Burnt Ordinary, James City, Va	56
Burnt Prairie, White, Ill	92
Burnt Ranch, Trinity, Cal	12
Burntville, Brunswick, Va	9
Burr, Vernon, Wis	12
Burrageville, Worcester, Mass	54
Burrell, Westmoreland, Pa	53

Post office	
Burrillville, Providence, R. I	$160
Burritt, Winnebago, Ill	4
Burr Oak, Winneshiek, Iowa	130
Burr Oak,* St. Joseph, Mich	650
Burr Oak, Harrison, Mo	12
Burr Oak, Otoe, Nebr	12
Burr Oak, La Crosse, Wis	40
Burrows, Carroll, Ind	60
Burr's Mills, Jefferson, N. Y	8
Burrsville, Caroline, Md	25
Burrville, Litchfield, Conn	110
Bursonville, Bucks, Pa	12
Burton, Adams, Ill	72
Burton, Geauga, Ohio	270
Burton, Washington, Tex	12
Burton, Wetzel, W. Va	74
Burtonsville, Montgomery, N. Y	87
Burtville, Potter, Pa	12
Burwood, San Joaquin, Cal	14
Busaco, Miami, Ind	28
Bushberg, Jefferson, Mo	12
Bush Hill, Randolph, N. C	65
Bushkill, Pike, Pa	92
Bush Kiln Centre, Northampton, Pa	18
Bushnell,* McDonough, Ill	1,100
Bushnell Centre, Montcalm, Mich	21
Bushnell's Basin, Monroe, N. Y	17
Bushnellsville, Greene, N. Y	20
Bush's Store, Laurel, Ky	7
Bushville, Sullivan, N. Y	18
Bushy Fork, Person, N. C	5
Businessburgh, Belmont, Ohio	16
Buskirk's Bridge, Washington, N. Y	120
Busseron, Knox, Ind	19
Busseyville, Jefferson, Wis	44
Busti, Howard, Iowa	45
Busti, Chautauqua, N. Y	180
Butler, (*c. h.,*) Choctaw, Ala	94
Butler, (*c. h.,*) Taylor, Ga	280
Butler, Montgomery, Ill	390
Butler, De Kalb, Ind	460
Butler, Keokuk, Iowa	20
Butler, Washington, Kans	12
Butler, Pendleton, Ky	110
Butler, Baltimore, Md	24
Butler, Branch, Mich	21
*Butler,** (*c. h.,*) Bates, Mo	1,200
Butler, Johnson, Nebr	7
Butler, Richland, Ohio	150
*Butler,** (*c. h.,*) Butler, Pa	1,000
Butler, Johnson, Tenn	4
Butler, Freestone, Tex	20
Butler, Milwaukee, Wis	42
Butler Centre, (*c. h.,*) Butler, Iowa	88
Butler's Landing, Jackson, Tenn	23
Butler Springs, Butler, Ala	12
Butlersville, Allen, Ky	7
Butlerville, Jennings, Ind	180
Butlerville, Tama, Iowa	82
Butlerville, Warren, Ohio	53
Butte City, Deer Lodge, Mont	120
Butte Creek, Clackamas, Oreg	10
Butte des Morts, Winnebago, Wis	55
Butternuts, Otsego, N. Y	510
Butternut Valley, Blue Earth, Minn	24
Butte Valley, Butte, Cal	35

* Money-order office.

Butte Valley, Huerfano, Colo	$12
Butteville, Marion, Oreg	55
Buttsville, Grundy, Mo	12
Butztown, Northampton, Pa	21
Buxton, Clinton, Ill	14
Buxton, York, Me	38
Buxton Centre, York, Me	110
Buyerstown, Lancaster, Pa	44
Byersville, Livingston, N. Y	13
Byfield, Essex, Mass	98
Byhalia, Marshall, Miss	75
Byhalia, Union, Ohio	6
Byington, Pike, Ohio	21
Bynumville, Chariton, Mo	17
Byram, Hinds, Miss	16
Byrd's Springs, Jefferson, Ark	12
Byrne, Putnam, Tenn	9
Byrneville, Harrison, Ind	11
Byromville, Dooly, Ga	20
Byron, Houston, Ga	57
Byron, Ogle, Ill	210
Byron, Woodson, Kans	12
Byron, Oxford, Me	8
Byron, Shiawassee, Mich	270
Byron, Olmsted, Minn	150
Byron, Osage, Mo	13
Byron, Genesee, N. Y	180
Byron, Greene, Ohio	21
Byron, Fond du Lac, Wis	38
Byron Centre, Kent, Mich	47

C.

CABELL, C. H., Cabell, W. Va	130
Caberey, Kankakee, Ill	14
Cabin Creek, Lewis, Ky	22
Cabinet, Montgomery, Pa	160
Cabin Hill, Delaware, N. Y	21
Cabin Point, Surry, Va	57
Cable, Champaign, Ohio	77
Cable City, Deer Lodge, Mont	12
Cabot, Washington, Vt	320
Cacapon Depot, Morgan, W. Va	35
Cacey's Station, Fulton, Ky	20
Cache Creek, Yolo, Cal	49
Cadaretta, Choctaw, Miss	17
Caddo Grove, Johnson, Tex	12
Cade's Cove, Blount, Tenn	3
Cadet, Washington, Mo	28
Cadiz, Henry, Ind	99
*Cadiz,** (*c. h.,*) Trigg, Ky	450
Cadiz, Cattaraugus, N. Y	57
*Cadiz,** (*c. h.,*) Harrison, Ohio	1,000
Cadiz, Green, Wis	28
Cadosia Valley, Delaware, N. Y	37
Cadron, Conway, Ark	3
Cadwallader, Tuscarawas, Ohio	65
Cady, Macomb, Mich	33
Cady's Falls, Lamoille, Vt	63
Cady's Tunnel, Bath, Va	120
Cadyville, Clinton, N. Y	62
Cageville, Haywood, Tenn	16
Cahaba, Dallas, Ala	150
Cahoka, Clarke, Mo	77
Cahto, Mendocino, Cal	180
Cainesville, Harrison, Mo	99
Cain's, Gwinnett, Ga	$18
Cain's, Lancaster, Pa	84
Cain's Store, Pulaski, Ky	7
Cainsville, Wilson, Tenn	15
Cainville, Rock, Wis	24
Ca Ira, Cumberland, Va	49
Cairo, Thomas, Ga	130
*Cairo,** (*c. h.,*) Alexander, Ill	3,600
Cairo, Putnam, Ind	23
Cairo, Louisa, Iowa	66
Cairo, Henderson, Ky	35
Cairo, Randolph, Mo	55
Cairo, Greene, N. Y	250
Cairo, Stark, Ohio	11
Cairo, Ritchie, W. Va	180
Calahaln, Davie, N. C	9
Calais,* Washington, Me	2,400
Calais, Monroe, Ohio	71
Calais, Washington, Vt	60
Calamine, La Fayette, Wis	72
Calcutta, Columbiana, Ohio	53
Caldwell, Appanoose, Iowa	16
Caldwell, Essex, N. J	200
Caldwell, (*c. h.,*) Warren, N. Y	720
Caldwell, Orange, N. C	12
*Caldwell,** (*c. h.,*) Noble, Ohio	220
Caldwell, (*c. h.,*) Burleson, Tex	40
Caldwell Prairie, Racine, Wis	43
Caldwell's Store, Leon, Tex	20
Caleb's Valley, Stewart, Tenn	12
Caledonia, (*c. h.,*) Pulaski, Ill	43
Caledonia, Ringgold, Iowa	32
Caledonia, Kent, Mich	40
*Caledonia,** (*c. h.,*) Houston, Minn	190
Caledonia, Lowndes, Miss	24
Caledonia, Washington, Mo	190
Caledonia, Livingston, N. Y	330
Caledonia, Marion, Ohio	220
Caledonia, Elk, Pa	69
Caledonia, Rusk, Tex	12
Caledonia, Goochland, Va	12
Caledonia Centre, Racine, Wis	39
Caledonia Station, Boone, Ill	170
Caledonia Station, Kent, Mich	12
Calera, Shelby, Ala	12
Caler's Hill, Jackson, N. C.	12
Calf Creek, Searcy, Ark	12
Calhoun, Lowndes, Ala	21
Calhoun, Columbia, Ark	24
Calhoun, (*c. h.,*) Gordon, Ga	550
Calhoun, Richland, Ill	100
Calhoun, Harrison, Iowa	18
Calhoun, (*c. h.,*) McLean, Ky	180
Calhoun, Madison, Miss	16
Calhoun, Henry, Mo	270
Calhoun, Transylvania, N. C	18
Calhoun, Barbour, W. Va	17
Calhoun's Mills, Abbeville, S. C	13
Calico, Johnson, Ark	12
California, Campbell, Ky	58
California, Branch, Mich	56
*California,** (*c. h.,*) Moniteau, Mo	920
California, Hamilton, Ohio	170
California, Washington, Pa	140
Calistoga, Napa, Cal	26
Calla, Pawnee, Nebr	12

* Money-order office.

Post office	Compensation
Callaghan's, Alleghany, Va	$58
Callahan, Nassau, Fla	15
Callahan's Ranch, Siskiyou, Cal	13
Callanan's Corners, Albany, N. Y	12
Calland's, Pittsylvania, Va	13
Callao, La Porte, Ind	25
Callao, Macon, Mo	170
Callaway, Josh Bell, Ky	4
Callensburgh, Clarion, Pa	140
Callicoon, Sullivan, N. Y	84
Callicoon Depot, Sullivan, N. Y	170
Calliope, (*c. h.*,) Sioux, Iowa	12
Calloway, Upshur, Tex	20
Calmar,* Winnishiek, Iowa	580
Calmus, Clinton, Iowa	210
Caln, Chester, Pa	57
Calno, Warren, N. J	4
Caloma, Marion, Iowa	40
Calumet, Cook, Ill	120
Calumet, Houghton, Mich	1,400
Calumet Village, Fond du Lac, Wis	82
Calvary, Decatur, Ga	12
Calvary, Morgan, Ohio	12
Calvary, Fond du Lac, Wis	12
Calvert,* Robertson, Tex	2,000
Calverton, Suffolk, N. Y	32
Calverton Mills, Baltimore, Md	20
Calvert's, St. Francis, Ark	12
Calvin, Cass, Mich	10
Calvin, Huntingdon, Pa	13
Calvin's Corners, Crawford, Pa	12
Calvy, Franklin, Mo	14
Camac, Warren, Ga	12
Camackville, Lee, Iowa	12
Camanche, Calaveras, Cal	47
Camanche, Clinton, Iowa	270
Camargo, Douglas, Ill	200
Camargo, Lancaster, Pa	18
Camas Valley, Douglas, Oreg	12
Camba, Jackson, Ohio	54
Cambra, Luzerne, Pa	62
Cambria, San Luis Obispo, Cal	39
Cambria, Wayne, Iowa	13
Cambria, Niagara, N. Y	75
Cambria, Cambria, Pa	12
Cambria,* Columbia, Wis	560
Cambria Mills, Hillsdale, Mich	140
Cambridge, Dallas, Ala	12
Cambridge,* (*c. h.*,) Henry, Ill	640
Cambridge, Story, Iowa	110
Cambridge, Somerset, Me	56
Cambridge,* (*c. h.*,) Dorchester, Md	610
Cambridge,* Middlesex, Mass	2,200
Cambridge, Lenawee, Mich	26
Cambridge, Isanti, Minn	32
Cambridge, Saline, Mo	180
Cambridge,* Washington, N. Y	1,000
Cambridge,* (*c. h.*,) Guernsey, Ohio	1,100
Cambridge, Lancaster, Pa	44
Cambridge, Lamoille, Vt	240
Cambridge, Dane, Wis	240
Cambridgeborough, Crawford, Pa	240
Cambridge City,* Wayne, Ind	1,200
Cambridgeport,* Middlesex, Mass	2,200
Cambridgeport, Windham, Vt	140
Camden, (*c. h.*,) Wilcox, Ala	630
Camden,* (*c. h.*,) Ouachita, Ark	$1,200
Camden, Kent, Del	400
Camden, Schuyler, Ill	10
Camden, Carroll, Ind	200
Camden,* Knox, Me	940
Camden, Hillsdale, Mich	200
Camden, Madison, Miss	12
Camden, Ray, Mo	200
Camden, Seward, Nebr	83
Camden,* (*c. h.*,) Camden, N. J	2,500
Camden, Oneida, N. Y	1,300
Camden, Preble, Ohio	340
Camden,* (*c. h.*,) Kershaw, S. C	750
Camden, (*c. h.*,) Benton, Tenn	230
Camden C. H., Camden, N. C.	23
Camden Mills, Rock Island, Ill	250
Camden Point, Platte, Mo	60
Cameron, Scriven, Ga	12
Cameron, Warren, Ill	180
Cameron,* Clinton, Mo	930
Cameron, Steuben, N. Y	100
Cameron, New Hanover, N. C	23
Cameron, Monroe, Ohio	24
Cameron, Cameron, Pa	200
Cameron, (*c. h.*,) Milam, Tex	300
Cameron, Marshall, W. Va	290
Cameron Mills, Steuben, N. Y	67
Camilla, (*c. h.*,) Mitchell, Ga	140
Camillus, Onondaga, N. Y	280
Campbell, Coles, Ill	56
Campbell, Ionia, Mich	40
Campbell C. H., Campbell, Va	82
Campbell Hall, Orange, N. Y	12
Campbell's Bridge, Marion, S. C	17
Campbellsburgh, Washington, Ind	140
Campbellsburgh, Henry, Ky	120
Campbell's Mills, Windham, Conn	6
Campbell's Station, Knox, Tenn	29
Campbellstown, Preble, Ohio	34
Campbellsville, (*c. h.*,) Taylor, Ky	240
Campbellsville, Giles, Tenn	19
Campbellton, Jackson, Fla	24
Campbellton, (*c. h.*,) Campbell, Ga	53
Campbellton, Franklin, Mo	10
Campbelltown, Steuben, N. Y	250
Campbelltown, Lebanon, Pa	110
Campbellville, Sullivan, Pa	7
Camp Call, Cleveland, N. C	6
Camp Creek, Lancaster, Nebr	18
Camp Creek, Greene, Tenn	12
Camp Elkwater, Randolph, W. Va	1
Campello, Plymouth, Mass	360
Camp Grant, Humboldt, Cal	16
Camp Grove, Stark, Ill	92
Camp Halleck, Elko, Nev	130
Camp Hill, Cumberland, Pa	120
Camp Izard, Marion, Fla	6
Camp McDermitt, Humboldt, Nev	100
Camp Melvin, Bexar, Tex	12
Campobello, Spartanburgh, S. C	94
Campo Seco, Calaveras, Cal	96
Camp Point,* Adams, Ill	510
Camp Ridge, Williamsburgh, S. C	8
Camp Run, Crawford, Ohio	11
Camp Stanton, De Kalb, Ala	12
Camp Stockton, Presidio, Tex	400

* Money-order office.

Campti, Natchitoches, La	$14
Campton, Coweta, Ga	12
Campton, Kane, Ill	64
Campton, Delaware, Iowa	13
Campton, (*c. h.*,) Wolfe, Ky	12
Campton, Grafton, N. H	80
Campton Village, Grafton, N. H	270
Camptonville,* Yuba, Cal	240
Camptown, Bradford, Pa	130
Campville, Litchfield, Conn	29
Campville, Tioga, N. Y	74
Camp Watson, Grant, Oreg	12
Can, Huron, Mich	12
Cana, Jennings, Ind	12
Canaan, Litchfield, Conn	420
Canaan, Jefferson, Ind	20
Canaan, Somerset, Me	240
Canaan, Gasconade, Mo	21
Canaan, Grafton, N. H	220
Canaan, Columbia, N. Y	55
Canaan, Wayne, Ohio	76
Canaan, Wayne, Pa	72
Canaan, Essex, Vt	80
Canaan Centre, Columbia, N. Y	73
Canaan Four Corners, Columbia, N. Y	310
Canaan Valley, Litchfield, Conn	29
Canaanville, Athens, Ohio	48
Canada Road, Somerset, Me	12
Canadensis, Monroe, Pa	100
Canadice, Ontario, N. Y	53
Canajoharie, Montgomery, N. Y	1,300
Canal, Warrick, Ind	31
Canal, Venango, Pa	19
Canal Dover, Tuscarawas, Ohio	430
Canal Fulton, Stark, Ohio	390
Canal Lewisville, Coshocton, Ohio	28
Canal Winchester,* Franklin, Ohio	240
Canandaigua, Lenawee, Mich	120
Canandaigua,* (*c. h.*,) Ontario, N. Y	2,700
Canarsie, Kings, N. Y	32
Canaseraga, Allegany, N. Y	330
Canastota, Madison, N. Y	1,200
Candia, Rockingham, N. H	150
Candia Village, Rockingham, N. H	110
Candor, Tioga, N. Y	690
Candor, Washington, Pa	58
Caneadea, Allegany, N. Y	170
Cane Creek, Conway, Ark	17
Cane Creek, Walker, Ga	12
Cane Creek, Butler, Mo	16
Cane Creek, Chatham, N. C	12
Cane Hill, Cedar, Mo	10
Cane Ridge, Claiborne, La	12
Cane Spring Depot, Bullitt, Ky	31
Cane Valley, Adair, Ky	22
Caney, Ouachita, Ark	39
Caney, Howard, Kans	12
Caney, Ozark, Mo	12
Caney, Matagorda, Tex	63
Caney Branch, Green, Tenn	23
Caney Spring, Marshall, Tenn	25
Caneyville, Grayson, Ky	16
Canfield, Fillmore, Minn	6
Canfield,* (*c. h.*,) Mahoning, Ohio	570
Canisteo, Steuben, N. Y	410
Cannelton,* (*c. h.*,) Perry, Ind	$610
Cannelton, Kanawha, W. Va	40
Cannon City, Rice, Minn	48
Cannon River Falls, Goodhue, Minn	340
Cannonsburgh, Boyd, Ky	7
Cannonsburgh, Kent, Mich	74
Cannonsburgh, Hancock, Ohio	42
Cannonsburgh,* Washington, Pa	750
Cannon's Mill, Columbiana, Ohio	20
Cannon's Station, Fairfield, Conn	12
Cannon's Store, Sevier, Tenn	10
Cannonsville, Delaware, N. Y	180
Canoe, Winnishiek, Iowa	19
Canoe Camp, Tioga, Pa	12
Canoe Creek, Blair, Pa	45
Canoe Ridge, Jefferson, Pa	26
Canoe Station, Escambia, Ala	12
Canoga, Seneca, N. Y	110
Canoochee, Emanuel, Ga	21
Canoper, Adams, Ind	10
Canterbury, Windham, Conn	130
Canterbury, Kent, Del	130
Canterbury, Merrimack, N. H	120
Canton, Lawrence, Ark	5
Canton, Hartford, Conn	47
Canton, (*c. h.*,) Lincoln, Dak	120
Canton, (*c. h.*,) Cherokee, Ga	79
Canton,* Fulton, Ill	2,400
Canton, Washington, Ind	75
Canton, Jackson, Iowa	46
Canton, Trigg, Ky	92
Canton, Oxford, Me	230
Canton,* Norfolk, Mass	1,200
Canton, Wayne, Mich	58
Canton,* (*c. h.*,) Madison, Miss	2,000
Canton,* Lewis, Mo	1,000
Canton, Stanton, Nebr	14
Canton, Salem, N. J	22
Canton,* (*c. h.*,) St. Lawrence, N. Y	1,600
Canton,* (*c. h.*,) Stark, Ohio	2,600
Canton, Bradford, Pa	570
Canton, (*c. h.*,) Van Zandt, Tex	58
Canton, Marion, W. Va	10
Canton Centre, Hartford, Conn	98
Canton Point, Oxford, Me	43
Cantrelle, St. James, La	54
Cantrell's × Roads, McMinn, Tenn	17
Canville, Neosho, Kans	36
Cany Hollow, Lee, Va	12
Canyon City, (*c. h.*,) Fremont, Colo	160
Canyon City,* (*c. h.*,) Grant, Oreg	630
Canyon Ferry, Meagher, Mont	32
Capac, St. Clair, Mich	110
Cap Au Gris, Lincoln, Mo	35
Capay, Yolo, Cal	20
Cape Elizabeth Depot, Cumberland, Me	66
Cape Girardeau,* Cape Girardeau, Mo	1,400
Capell's Mills, Richmond, N. C	12
Cape May,* Cape May, N. J	2,000
Cape May C. H., Cape May, N. J	250
Cape Neddick, York, Me	120
Cape Porpoise, York, Me	80
Caperville, Northampton, Va	40
Cape Vincent,* Jefferson, N. Y	860

* Money-order office.

Capioma, Nemaha, Kans	$43
Capistrano, Los Angeles, Cal	7
Caplinger's Mills, Cedar, Mo	12
Capon Bridge, Hampshire, W. Va	72
Capon Springs, Hampshire, W. Va	25
Cappelu, St. Charles, Mo	12
Capper's Spring, Frederick, Va	5
Capp's Creek, Newton, Mo	24
Capron, Boone, Ill	240
Captina, Belmont, Ohio	18
Carbon, Webster, Iowa	12
Carbon, Carbon, Pa	30
Carbon, Carbon, Wyo	12
Carbon Cliff, Rock Island, Ill	83
Carbondale,* Jackson, Ill	1,400
Carbondale, Osage, Kans	12
Carbondale,* Luzerne, Pa	1,200
Carbon Hill, Johnson, Mo	12
Carbonvale, Kanawha, W. Va	41
Cardiff, Mitchell, Iowa	8
Cardiff, Onondaga, N. Y	81
Cardington,* Morrow, Ohio	980
Cardville, Washington, Pa	12
Carey,* Wyandot, Ohio	560
Caribou, Aroostook, Me	100
Carimona, Fillmore, Minn	52
Carl, Adams, Iowa	16
Carleton, Muskegon, Mich	12
Carlin, Lander, Nev	230
*Carlinville,** (*c. h.,*) Macoupin, Ill	220
Carlisle,* Sullivan, Ind	290
Carlisle, Warren, Iowa	69
Carlisle, (*c. h.,*) Nicholas, Ky	440
Carlisle, Middlesex, Mass	55
Carlisle, Eaton, Mich	15
Carlisle, Schoharie, N. Y	77
*Carlisle,** (*c. h.,*) Cumberland, Pa	2,500
Carlisle Springs, Cumberland, Pa	28
Carlisle Station, Warren, Ohio	140
Carlstadt, Bergen, N. J	130
Carlton, Orleans, N. Y	110
Carlton, Kewaunee, Wis	34
Carlton's Store, King and Queen, Va	10
*Carlyle,** (*c. h.,*) Clinton, Ill	630
Carlyle, Allen, Kans	87
Carmel, Hamilton, Ind	160
Carmel, Penobscot, Me	150
*Carmel,** (*c. h.,*) Putnam, N. Y	490
Carmel, Highland, Ohio	13
*Carmi,** (*c. h.,*) White, Ill	380
Carmichael's, Greene, Pa	180
Carnero, Saguache, Colo	12
Carnesville, (*c. h.,*) Franklin, Ga	62
Carney, Wyoming, Pa	12
*Caro,** (*c. h.,*) Tuscola, Mich	420
Carolina, Marion, S. C	12
Carolina, Falls, Tex	12
Carolina Mills, Washington, R. I	150
Carolina Seminary, Greene, N. C	10
Caroline, Jefferson, Nebr	12
Caroline, Tompkins, N. Y	37
Caroline Centre, Tompkins, N. Y	41
Caroline Depot, Tompkins, N. Y	58
Carondelet, St. Louis, Mo	690
Carpenter, Lycoming, Pa	12
Carpenteria, Santa Barbara, Cal	$12
Carpenter's Eddy, Delaware, N. Y	12
Carpenter's Store, Clinton, Mo	10
Carpentersville, Kane, Ill	200
Carpentersville, Putnam, Ind	71
Carpentersville, Warren, N. J	38
Carpenterville, Shannon, Mo	12
Carriage Point, Chickasaw N., Ind. Ter	12
Carrick, Allegheny, Pa	29
Carrick's Ford, Tucker, W. Va	12
Carritunk, Somerset, Me	21
Carrizo, (*c, h.,*) Zapata, Tex	12
Carroll, Carroll, Ind	34
Carroll, Penobscot, Me	55
Carroll, Baltimore, Md	37
Carroll, Coos, N. H	11
Carroll, Fairfield, Ohio	130
Carroll, Clinton, Pa	7
Carroll, Madison, Tenn	12
Carroll City, Carroll, Iowa	440
Carrollton, (*c. h.,*) Pickens, Ala	110
Carrollton, (*c. h.,*) Carroll, Ark	50
Carrollton, (*c. h.,*) Carroll, Ga	200
*Carrollton,** (*c. h.,*) Greene, Ill	1,300
Carrollton, Hancock, Ind	36
Carrollton, (*c. h.,*) Carroll, Iowa	65
*Carrolton,** (*c. h.,*) Carroll, Ky	520
Carrollton, (*c. h.,*) Jefferson, La	120
Carrollton, Carroll, Md	19
Carrollton, Saginaw, Mich	130
Carrollton, Fillmore, Minn	10
Carrollton, (*c. h.,*) Carroll, Miss	360
*Carrollton,** (*c. h.,*) Carroll, Mo	1,500
Carrollton, Cattaraugus, N. Y	12
*Carrollton,** (*c. h.,*) Carroll, Ohio	460
Carrollton, Upshur, Tex	6
Carrollton Station, Montgomery, Ohio	70
Carrolltown, Cambria, Pa	200
Carr's, Lewis, Ky	30
Carrsville, Livingston, Ky	86
Carrsville, Isle of Wight, Va	67
Carrville, Washington, Tenn	12
Carryall, Paulding, Ohio	13
Carson, Jefferson, Ark	12
Carson, Huerfano, Colo	12
Carson, Brown, Kans	42
Carson, Huron, Ohio	8
Carson City, Montcalm, Mich	48
CARSON CITY,* (*c. h.,*) Ormsby, Nev	1,600
Carson's Landing, Bolivar, Miss	18
Carter, Uintah, Wyo	60
Carter Camp, Potter, Pa	19
Carter Hill, Erie, Pa	9
Carter's Bridge, Albemarle, Va	21
Cartersburgh, Hendricks, Ind.	37
Cartersburgh, Pittsylvania, Va	12
Carter's Creek Station, Maury, Tenn	12
Carter's Depot, Carter, Tenn	56
Carter's Furnace, Carter, Tenn	12
Carter's Mills, Moore, N. C	15
Carter's Mills, Patrick, Va	12
Carter's Store, Randolph, Ala	12
*Cartersville,** (*c. h.,*) Bartow, Ga	1,200

* Money-order office.

Cartersville, Tishemingo, Miss	$46
Cartersville Parker, Tex	22
Cartersville, Cumberland, Va	150
Carthage, Tuscaloosa, Ala	15
Carthage,* (*c. h.*,) Hancock, Ill	1,200
Carthage, Rush, Ind	180
Carthage, Campbell, Ky	15
Carthage, (*c. h.*,) Leake, Miss	150
Carthage,* (*c. h.*,) Jasper, Mo	1,400
Carthage,* Jefferson, N. Y	1,000
Carthage, (*c. h.*,) Moore, N. C	80
Carthage, Hamilton, Ohio	220
Carthage, (*c. h.*,) Smith, Tenn	230
Carthage, (*c. h.*,) Panola, Tex	130
Carthage Landing, Dutchess, N. Y	150
Carthagena, Mercer, Ohio	47
Caruthersville, Pemiscot, Mo	10
Carver, Plymouth, Mass	14
Carver,* Carver, Minn	490
Carver's Harbor, Knox, Me	260
Carversville, Bucks, Pa	150
Carverton, Luzerne, Pa	3
Cary, Wake, N. C	18
Cary Station, McHenry, Ill	94
Carysville, Champaign, Ohio	30
Caryville, Norfolk, Mass	75
Caryville, Campbell, Tenn	12
Casady's Corner, Boone, Iowa	54
Casanova, Fauquier, Va	46
Casa, Perry, Ark	12
Cascade,* Dubuque, Iowa	880
Cascade, Kent, Mich	60
Cascade, Olmsted, Minn	14
Cascade, Pittsylvania, Va	35
Cascade, Sheboygan, Wis	140
Cascades, (*c. h.*,) Skamania, Wash	22
Cascade Valley, Broome, N. Y	14
Casco, Cumberland, Me	78
Casco, St. Clair, Mich	17
Casco, Kewaunee, Wis	21
Case, Laclede, Mo	10
Caseville, Huron, Mich	37
Casey, Clark, Ill	160
Casey, Adair, Iowa	230
Casey Creek, Adair, Ky	15
Caseyville, St. Clair, Ill	130
Caseyville, Union, Ky	270
Cash Creek, Lake, Colo	12
Casher's Valley, Jackson, N. C	9
Cashtown, Adams, Pa	69
Caskaid, Putnam, Ohio	11
Casky's Station, Christian, Ky	47
Casnovia, Kent, Mich	140
Cass, Franklin, Ark	5
Cass, Du Page, Ill	27
Cass, Hillsdale, Mich	21
Cass, Venango, Pa	57
Cassadaga, Chautauqua, N. Y	100
Cassandra, Walker, Ga	12
Cass Bridge, Saginaw, Mich	9
Cass City, Tuscola, Mich	65
Casscoe, Arkansas, Ark	12
Cassel, Wright, Minn	14
Cassella, Lake, Ind	12
Cassell Prairie, Sauk, Wis	10
Casselman, Somerset, Pa	12
Cassity's Mills, Rowan, Ky	$4
Cassopolis,* (*c. h.*,) Cass, Mich	820
Cass Station, Bartow, Ga	99
Casstown, Miami, Ohio	99
Cassville, Bartow, Ga	79
Cassville, Howard, Ind	31
Cassville, (*c. h.*,) Barry, Mo	98
Cassville, Ocean, N. J	25
Cassville, Oneida, N. Y	210
Cassville, Harrison, Ohio	35
Cassville, Huntingdon, Pa	150
Cassville, Monongalia, W. Va	36
Cassville, Grant, Wis	260
Castalia, Winneshiek, Iowa	160
Castalia, Nash, N. C	18
Castalia, Erie, Ohio	150
Castalian Springs, Sumner, Tenn	81
Castana, Monona, Iowa	57
Castania Grove, Lincoln, N. C	9
Castile, Wyoming, N. Y	640
Castine, Hancock, Me	550
Castine, Darke, Ohio	33
Castle, Randolph, Ind	12
Castle, Andrew, Mo	12
Castleberry, Conecuh, Ala	12
Castle Craig, Campbell, Va	37
Castle Creek, Broome, N. Y	67
Castle Fin, York, Pa	46
Castle Garden, Blue Earth, Minn	5
Castle Grove, Jones, Iowa	12
Castle Hayne, New Hanover, N. C	12
Castle Hill, Aroostook, Me	30
Castleman's Ferry, Clarke, Va	16
Castle Rock, Dakota, Minn	43
Castle Rock, Osage, Mo	24
Castle Rock, Cowlitz, Wash	18
Castle Rock, Grant, Wis	75
Castleton, Stark, Ill	12
Castleton, Marion, Ind	55
Castleton, Rensselaer, N. Y	380
Castleton,* Rutland, Vt	780
Castleton, Culpeper, Va	17
Castleville, Buchanan, Iowa	8
Castor, Bollinger, Mo	12
Castroville, Monterey, Cal	520
Castroville, (*c. h.*,) Medina, Tex	87
Caswell, La Fayette, Miss	12
Catalpa Grove, Greene, Ky	12
Catalpa Grove, Marshall, Tenn	12
Cataract, Owen, Ind	20
Cataract, Monroe, Wis	76
Catasauqua, Lehigh, Pa	1,500
Catatonk, Tioga, N. Y	98
Cataula, Harris, Ga	26
Catawba, Pendleton, Ky	32
Catawba, Clark, Ohio	69
Catawba, Roanoke, Va	16
Catawba Island, Ottawa, Ohio	21
Catawba Station, Catawba, N. C	170
Catawissa, Franklin, Mo	120
Catawissa, Columbia, Pa	500
Cat Creek, Lowndes, Ga	12
Catfish, Edgar, Ill	12
Catfish, Clarion, Pa	12
Catfish, Marion, S. C	12
Catharine, Schuyler, N. Y	120

* Money-order office.

Catharine Lake, Onslow, N. C	$7
Cathey's Creek, Transylvania, N. C.	2
Cathlamet, (*c. h.*,) Wahkiakum, Wash	12
Catlett, Fauquier, Va	150
Catlettsburgh,* Boyd, Ky	500
Catlin, Vermilion, Ill	180
Catlin, Parke, Ind	65
Cato, Crawford, Kans	150
Cato, Montcalm, Mich	43
Cato, Rankin, Miss	30
Cato, Cayuga, N. Y	130
Cato, Manitowoc, Wis	24
Catocton Furnace, Frederick, Md	55
Caton, Steuben, N. Y	69
Catonsville, Baltimore, Md	300
Catskill,* (*c. h.*,) Greene, N. Y	2,200
Catskill Station, Columbia, N. Y	44
Cat Spring, Austin, Tex	67
Cattaraugus, Cattaraugus, N. Y	210
Caudle Mills, Anson, N. C	12
Caughdenoy, Oswego, N. Y	43
Cave, Franklin, Ill	23
Cave, White, Tenn	32
Cave City, Barren, Ky	200
Cave Creek, Newton, Ark	8
Cave in Rock, Hardin, Ill	45
Cavendish, Windsor, Vt	400
Cave Pump, Camden, Mo	8
Caverna, Hart, Ky	230
Cave Spring, Floyd, Ga	310
Cave Spring, Carter, Tenn	16
Cave Spring, Roanoke, Va	10
Cave Spring Station, Logan, Ky	12
Cavetown, Washington, Md	35
Cavettsville, Westmoreland, Pa	35
Cawker City, Mitchell, Kans	12
Cayo Largo, Monroe, Fla	12
Cayuga, Livingston, Ill	110
Cayuga, Cayuga, N. Y	220
Cayuse, Umatilla, Oreg	12
Cayuta, Schuyler, N. Y	49
Cayutaville, Schuyler, N. Y	12
Cazenovia,* Madison, N. Y	1,500
Cazenovia, Richland, Wis	79
Cecil, Paulding, Ohio	140
Cecilton, Cecil, Md	360
Cedar, Fayette, Tex	19
Cedar Bluff, Cherokee, Ala	170
Cedar Bluff, Johnson, Ill	20
Cedar Bluff, Cedar, Iowa	40
Cedar Bluff, Tazewell, Va	8
Cedar Bluffs, Saunders, Nebr	78
Cedarburgh, Ozaukee, Wis	240
Cedar Bush, Davidson, N. C	1
Cedar Chapel, Hardeman, Tenn	10
Cedar City, Callaway, Mo	120
Cedar City, Iron, Utah	200
Cedar Creek, Dorchester, Md	4
Cedar Creek, Barry, Mich	19
Cedar Creek, Ocean, N. J	74
Cedar Creek, Cumberland, N. C	12
Cedar Creek, Greene, Tenn	13
Cedar Creek, Bastrop, Tex	11
Cedar Creek, Frederick, Va	5
Cedar Creek, Washington, Wis	73
Cedar Creek Landing, Perry, Tenn	12
Cedar Dale, Sanilac, Mich	$13
Cedar Falls,* Black Hawk, Iowa	2,200
Cedar Falls, Dunn, Wis	59
Cedar Fork, Menomonee, Mich	24
Cedar Fork, Union, Tenn	12
Cedar Fork, Caroline, Va	23
Cedar Grove, Jefferson, Ala	5
Cedar Grove, Walker, Ga	56
Cedar Grove, Franklin, Ind	58
Cedar Grove, Orange, N. C	10
Cedar Grove, Kaufman, Tex	24
Cedar Grove, Sheboygan, Wis	96
Cedar Grove Mills, Rockbridge, Va	28
Cedar Hill, Jefferson, Mo	12
Cedar Hill, Albany, N. Y	31
Cedar Hill, Anson, N. C	36
Cedar Hill, Fairfield, Ohio	23
Cedar Hill, Robertson, Tenn	74
Cedar Hill, Dallas, Tex	58
Cedar Junction, Missoula, Mont	12
Cedar Keys, Levy, Fla	10
Cedar Lake, Lake, Ind	35
Cedar Lake, Scott, Minn	6
Cedar Lake, Atlantic, N. J	12
Cedar Lake, Herkimer, N. Y	51
Cedar Lake, Waushara, Wis	52
Cedar Lane, Greene, Tenn	12
Cedar Mills, Renville, Minn	12
Cedar Mills, Adams, Ohio	12
Cedar Mountain, Transylvania, N. C	15
Cedar Plains, Morgan, Ala	6
Cedar Point, Chase, Kans	12
Cedar Point, Page, Va	15
Cedar Rapids,* Linn, Iowa	2,500
Cedar Rock, Franklin, N. C	12
Cedar Run, Grand Traverse, Mich	12
Cedar Run, Lycoming, Pa	34
Cedar Springs, Cherokee, Ala	12
Cedar Springs, Kent, Mich	370
Cedar Springs, Clinton, Pa	53
Cedartown, (*c. h.*,) Polk, Ga	160
Cedar Tree, Hernando, Fla	3
Cedar Vale, Howard, Kans	12
Cedar Valley, Black Hawk, Iowa	32
Cedar Valley, Wayne, Ohio	24
Cedar Valley, Utah, Utah	13
Cedarville, Siskiyou, Cal	12
Cedarville, Stephenson, Ill	140
Cedarville, Allen, Ind	28
Cedarville, Martin, Minn	7
Cedarville, Dade, Mo	12
Cedarville, Cumberland, N. J	84
Cedarville, Herkimer, N. Y	110
Cedarville, Greene, Ohio	400
Cedarville, Chehalis, Wash	6
Cedron, Clermont, Ohio	14
Celestine, Dubois, Ind	12
Celina, Perry, Ind	12
Celina,* (*c. h.*,) Mercer, Ohio	400
Celina, Jackson, Tenn	39
Cementville, Clarke, Ind	12
Centenary, Buckingham, Va	6
Center, Shelby, Tex	61
Center, Monongalia, W. Va	3
Center, Rock, Wis	44
Center Mills, Montgomery, Va	12

* Money-order office.

Post office	
*Centerville,** (*c. h.,*) Appanoose, Iowa	$640
Centerville, Davis, Utah	34
Central, St. Louis, Mo	110
Central, Columbia, Pa	8
Central Bridge, Schoharie, N. Y	170
*Central City,** (*c. h.,*) Gilpin, Colo	4,000
Central City, Marion, Ill	88
Central City, Linn, Iowa	80
Central City, Anderson, Kans	16
Central City, Putnam, Mo	16
Central City, Grant, N. Mex	12
Central College, Franklin, Ohio	83
Central Falls, Providence, R. I	1,100
Central House, Butte, Cal	29
Centralia,* Marion, Ill	2,200
Centralia, Nemaha, Kans	220
Centralia, Boone, Mo	290
Centralia, Columbia, Pa	250
Centralia, Wood, Wis	230
Central Institute, Coosa, Ala	15
Central Lake, Antrim, Mich	15
Central Park, Queens, N. Y	110
Central Plains, Fluvanna, Va	51
Central Point, Caroline, Va	37
Central Square, Oswego, N. Y	200
Central Station, Doddridge, W. Va	86
Central Village, Windham, Conn	240
Central Village, Bristol, Mass	39
Centre, (*c. h.,*) Cherokee, Ala	72
Centre, Schuyler, Ill	10
Centre, Howard, Ind	60
Centre, Page, Iowa	27
Centre, Metcalfe, Ky	21
Centre, Eaton, Mich	17
Centre, Texas, Mo	4
Centre, Guilford, N. C	27
Centre, Montgomery, Ohio	74
Centre, Perry, Pa	58
Centre Barnstead, Belknap, N. H	96
Centre Belpre, Washington, Ohio	46
Centre Bend, Morgan, Ohio	8
Centre Berlin, Rensselaer, N. Y	14
Centre Bridge, Bucks, Pa	60
Centre Brook, Middlesex, Conn	190
Centre Brunswick, Rensselaer, N. Y	36
Centreburgh, Knox, Ohio	70
Centre Cambridge, Washington, N. Y	61
Centre Canisteo, Steuben, N. Y	21
Centre Conway, Carroll, N. H	44
Centre Creek, Martin, Minn	16
Centre Creek, Jasper, Mo	140
Centre Cross, Essex, Va	12
Centredale, Providence, R. I	75
Centre Effingham, Carroll, N. H	120
Centrefield, Oldham, Ky	8
Centrefield, Highland, Ohio	28
Centre Groton, New London, Conn	30
Centre Grove, Person, N. C	4
Centre Hall, Centre, Pa	150
Centre Harbor, Belknap, N. H	420
Centre Hill, White, Ark	17
Centre Hill, Hartford, Conn	69
Centre Hill, Centre, Pa	71
Centre Lebanon, York, Me	19
Centre Lincolnville, Waldo, Me	34
Centre Lisle, Broome, N. Y	130

Post office	
Centre Lovell, Oxford, Me	$63
Centre Mills, Centre, Pa	69
Centre Montville, Waldo, Me	20
Centre Moreland, Wyoming, Pa	41
Centre Moriches, Suffolk, N. Y	170
Centre Ossipee, Carroll, N. H	100
Centre Point, Sevier, Ark	71
Centre Point, Knox, Ill	17
Centre Point, Clay, Ind	100
Centre Point, Linn, Iowa	220
Centre Point, Monroe, Ky	13
Centreport, Suffolk, N. Y	73
Centreport, Berks, Pa	24
Centre Road Station, Crawford, Pa	160
Centre Rutland, Rutland, Vt	640
Centre Sandwich, Carroll, N. H	290
Centre Sidney, Kennebec, Me	40
Centre Square, Switzerland, Ind	34
Centre Square, Montgomery, Pa	37
Centre Star, Lauderdale, Ala	12
Centre Strafford, Strafford, N. H	35
Centreton, Morgan, Ind	79
Centreton, Salem, N. J	37
Centreton, Huron, Ohio	140
Centre Town, Cole, Mo	80
Centretown, Mercer, Pa	27
Centre Valley, Hendricks, Ind	50
Centre Valley, Cass, Nebr	6
Centre Valley, Otsego, N. Y	18
Centre Valley, Lehigh, Pa	92
Centre View, Johnson, Mo	140
Centre View, Monroe, Ohio	20
Centre Village, Charlton, Ga	21
Centre Village, Broome, N. Y	100
Centre Village, Delaware, Ohio	40
Centreville, (*c. h.,*) Bibb, Ala	30
Centreville, Montgomery, Ark	12
Centreville, Alameda, Cal	200
Centreville, Lake, Colo	12
Centreville, New Castle, Del	100
Centreville, Boise, Idaho	38
Centreville, Piatt, Ill	12
Centreville, (*c. h.,*) Wayne, Ind	590
Centreville, Linn, Kans	18
Centreville, Bourbon, Ky	62
Centreville, St. Mary's, La	140
*Centreville,** (*c. h.,*) Queen Anne, Md	550
Centreville, Barnstable, Mass	180
Centreville, (*c. h.,*) St. Joseph, Mich	690
Centreville, Anoka, Minn	23
Centreville, Amite, Miss	12
Centreville, (*c. h.,*) Reynolds, Mo	16
Centreville, Lancaster, Nebr	14
Centreville, Hunterdon, N. J	36
Centreville, Allegany, N. Y	100
Centreville, Montgomery, Ohio	96
Centreville, Washington, Oreg	18
Centreville, Crawford, Pa	200
Centreville, Kent, R. I	360
Centreville, (*c. h.,*) Hickman, Tenn	72
Centreville, (*c. h.,*) Leon, Tex	80
Centreville, Fairfax, Va	58
Centreville Station, St. Clair, Ill	62
Centre White Creek, Washington, N. Y	44
Centropolis, Franklin, Kans	71

* Money-order office.

CHA	
Ceralvo, Ohio, Ky	$16
Ceredo, Wayne, W. Va	57
Ceres, Clayton, Iowa	52
Ceres, Allegany, N. Y	140
Ceresco, Calhoun, Mich	190
Ceresco, Lyon, Minn	12
Ceresco, Saunders, Nebr	12
Cerro Gordo, Inyo, Cal	12
Cerro Gordo, (*c. h.*,) Holmes, Fla	6
Cerro Gordo,* Piatt, Ill	880
Cerro Gordo, Randolph, Ind	24
Cerro Gordo, Columbus, N. C	24
Cerro Gordo, Hardin, Tenn	12
Cerulean Springs, Trigg, Ky	12
Cessford, Cedar, Iowa	10
Ceylon, Greene, Pa	12
Chadd's Ford, Delaware, Pa	240
Chadwick's Mills, Oneida, N. Y	58
Chagrin Falls,* Cuyahoga, Ohio	660
Chain Lake Centre, Martin, Minn	43
Chain of Rocks, Lincoln, Mo	12
Chalk Bluff, Marion, Ala	15
Chalk Level, St. Clair, Mo	18
Chalk Level, Harnett, N. C	2
Chalk Level, Pittsylvania, Va	44
Chalk Spring, Santa Rosa, Fla	12
Chalmers, White, Ind	54
Chalybeate, Johnson, Mo	12
Chalybeate Springs, Meriwether, Ga	6
Chalybes, Litchfield, Conn	100
Chamberlain, Allen, Ind	10
Chambers C. H.,* Chambers, Ala	410
Chambersburgh, Pike, Ill	37
Chambersburgh, Orange, Ind	30
Chambersburgh, Clarke, Mo	16
Chambersburgh, Montgomery, Ohio	12
Chambersburgh,* (*c. h.*,) Franklin, Pa	2,400
Chambers Creek, Ellis, Texas	24
Chambers' Valley, Carroll, Va	14
Chambersville, Calhoun, Ark	24
Chambersville, New Castle, Del	9
Chambersville, Indiana, Pa	41
Chamblissburgh, Bedford, Va	13
Chamois, Osage, Mo	190
Champagnolle, Union, Ark	12
Champaign,* Champaign, Ill	2,300
Champion, Jefferson, N. Y	65
Champlain, Clinton, N. Y	930
Champlin, Hennepin, Minn	49
Chanceford, York, Pa	59
Chandaller, Keokuk, Iowa	16
Chandler's Valley, Warren, Pa	55
Chandlersville, Muskingum, Ohio	98
Chandlerville, Cass, Ill	280
Chaneysville, Bedford, Pa	15
Changewater, Warren, N. J	49
Channahatchee, Elmore, Ala	6
Channahon, Will, Ill	170
Chantilly, Lincoln, Mo	12
Chantilly, Fairfax, Va	36
Chapel, Howell, Mo	12
Chapel Hill, Campbell, Ga	6
Chapel Hill, La Fayette, Mo	75
Chapel Hill, Monmouth, N. J	31
Chapel Hill,* Orange, N. C	520

CHA	
Chapel Hill, Perry, Ohio	$26
Chapel Hill, Marshall, Tenn	89
Chapel Hill, Washington, Tex	250
Chapel Hill, Fluvanna, Va	59
Chapin, Morgan, Ill	110
Chapin, Franklin, Iowa	19
Chapinville, Ontario, N. Y	41
Chapinville, Crawford, Pa	7
Chaplin, Windham, Conn	93
Chaplin, Nelson, Ky	29
Chapman, Merrick, Nebr	12
Chapman, Snyder, Pa	27
Chapman Quarries, Northampton, Pa	88
Chapman's Creek, Dickinson, Kans	72
Chapmanville, Logan, W. Va	4
Chappaqua, Westchester, N. Y	230
Chappell's Bridge, Newberry, S. C	5
Chaptico, St. Mary's, Md	91
Chardon,* (*c. h.*,) Geauga, Ohio	600
Chariton,* (*c. h.*,) Lucas, Iowa	1,500
Charlemont, Franklin, Mass	300
Charlemont, Bedford, Va	11
Charles City,* (*c. h.*,) Floyd, Iowa	1,500
Charles City C. H., Charles City, Va	12
Charles River Village, Norfolk, Mass	53
Charleston, Franklin, Ark	20
Charleston, Yola, Cal	3
Charleston,* (*c. h.*,) Coles, Ill	2,200
Charleston, Lee, Iowa	73
Charleston, Penobscot, Me	1[illegible]
Charleston, (*c. h.*,) Tallahatchee, Miss	256
Charleston, (*c. h.*,) Mississippi, Mo	320
Charleston, Montgomery, N. Y	35
Charleston, Tioga, Pa	25
Charleston,* (*c. h.*,) Charleston, S. C	4,000
Charleston, Bradley, Tenn	240
Charleston, Hopkins, Tex	12
Charleston Four Corners, Montgomery, N. Y	100
Charlestown,* (*c. h.*,) Clarke, Ind	630
Charlestown, Cecil, Md	81
Charlestown,* Middlesex, Mass	2,300
Charlestown,* Sullivan, N. H	770
Charlestown, Portage, Ohio	64
Charlestown, Luzerne, Pa	25
Charlestown, Washington, R. I	16
Charlestown,* Jefferson, W. Va	920
Charlestown, Calumet, Wis	42
Charlesville, Bedford, Pa	16
Charlevoix, (*c. h.*,) Charlevoix, Mich	160
Charlie Hope, Brunswick, Va	34
Charloe, Paulding, Ohio	28
Charlotte, Clinton, Iowa	56
Charlotte, Washington, Me	38
Charlotte,* (*c. h.*,) Eaton, Mich	1,600
Charlotte, Monroe, N. Y	220
Charlotte,* (*c. h.*,) Mecklenburgh, N. C	2,500
Charlotte, (*c. h.*,) Dickson, Tenn	100
Charlotte, Chittenden, Vt	170
Charlotte C. H., Charlotte, Va	360
Charlotteburgh, Passaic, N. J	12
Charlotte Centre, Chautauqua, N. Y	20
Charlotte Hall, St. Mary's, Md	140
Charlottesville, Hancock, Ind	120

* Money-order office.

*Charlottesville,** (*c. h.,*) Albemarle, Va	$2,400
Charlotteville, Schoharie, N. Y	150
Charlton, Worcester, Mass	120
Charlton, Saratoga, N. Y	190
Charlton City, Worcester, Mass	89
Charlton Depot, Worcester, Mass	220
Chartiers, Allegheny, Pa	16
Chase, Johnson, Iowa	13
Chaseburgh, Vernon, Wis	53
Chase's Mills, St. Lawrence, N. Y	12
Chase's Mills, Tioga, Pa	12
Chaseville, Otsego, N. Y	82
Chaska, (*c. h.,*) Carver, Minn	230
Chatata, Bradley, Tenn	60
Chatawa, Pike, Miss	230
Chateaugay, Franklin, N. Y	700
Chateaugay Lake, Franklin, N. Y	31
Chatfield,* Fillmore, Minn	760
Chatfield, Crawford, Ohio	54
Chatfield, Navarro, Tex	8
Chatham, Sangamon, Ill	270
Chatham, Buchanan, Iowa	48
Chatham, Barnstable, Mass	510
Chatham, Wright, Minn	23
Chatham, Morris, N. J	220
Chatham, Columbia, N. Y	160
Chatham, Licking, Ohio	38
Chatham, Chester, Pa	130
Chatham Centre, Columbia, N. Y	100
Chatham Centre, Medina, Ohio	160
Chatham Hill, Smyth, Va	51
Chatham Port, Barnstable, Mass	80
Chatham Run, Clinton, Pa	66
Chatham Valley, Tioga, Pa	13
Chatham Village, Columbia, N. Y	860
Chatsworth,* Livingston, Ill	1,100
Chattahoochee, Gadsden, Fla	77
Chattan, Adams, Ill	46
Chattanooga,* Hamilton, Tenn	2,600
Chatterton, King George, Va	38
Chattoogaville, Chattooga, Ga	6
Chaumont, Jefferson, N. Y	270
Chauncey, Tippecanoe, Ind	39
Chauncey, Athens, Ohio	55
Chazy, Clinton, N. Y	120
Cheat Mountain, Randolph, W. Va	12
Chebanse, Iroquois, Ill	520
Chebeague Island, Cumberland, Me	38
Cheboygan, (*c. h.,*) Cheboygan, Mich	120
Checo, Cherokee, Kans	12
Cheektowaga, Erie, N. Y	42
Cheesland, Angelina, Tex	5
Chehalis Point, Chehalis, Wash	15
Chellis, Woodson, Kans	9
Chelmsford, Middlesex, Mass	170
Chelsea, Tama, Iowa	160
Chelsea, Butler, Kans	12
Chelsea,* Suffolk, Mass	2,700
Chelsea, Washtenaw, Mich	660
Chelsea, Delaware, Pa	18
*Chelsea**, (*c. h.,*) Orange, Vt	870
Cheltenham, St. Louis, Mo	23
Cheltenham, Montgomery, Pa	140
Chemung, McHenry, Ill	95
Chemung, Chemung, N. Y	$210
Chemung Centre, Chemung, N. Y	12
Chenango, Lawrence, Pa	8
Chenango, Brazoria, Tex	12
Chenango Forks, Broome, N. Y	200
Cheneyville, Rapides, La	45
Chengwatana, (*c. h.,*) Pine, Minn	40
Chenoa,* McLean, Ill	1,100
Chepachet, Providence, R. I	160
Chepstow, Washington, Kans	12
Chepultepec, Blount, Ala	2
Chequist, Davis, Iowa	20
Cheraw,* Chesterfield, S. C	800
Cherino, Nacogdoches, Tex	15
Cherokee, Colbert, Ala	130
Cherokee, Butte, Cal	56
Cherokee, (*c. h.,*) Cherokee, Iowa	35
Cherokee, Crawford, Kans	12
Cherokee, Lawrence, Ky	12
Cherokee, San Saba, Tex	12
Cherokee Mills, Cherokee, Ga	12
Cherokee Mound, Cherokee, Kans	12
Cherry Box, Shelby, Mo	23
Cherry Camp, Harrison, W. Va	160
Cherry Creek, Arapahoe, Colo	12
Cherry Creek, Woodson, Kans	12
Cherry Creek, Pontotoc, Miss	22
Cherry Creek, Chautauqua, N. Y	120
Cherryfield, Transylvania, N. C	5
Cherry Flats, Tioga, Pa	35
Cherry Fork, Adams, Ohio	92
Cherry Grove, Saline, Ark	10
Cherry Grove, Fillmore, Minn	26
Cherry Grove, Schuyler, Mo	48
Cherry Grove, Platte, Nebr	12
Cherry Grove, Hamilton, Ohio	61
Cherry Grove, Washington, Tenn	4
Cherry Grove, Rockingham, Va	21
Cherry Hill, Cecil, Md	93
Cherry Hill, Erie, Pa	48
Cherry Lane, Alleghany, N. C	4
Cherry Lane, King William, Va	12
Cherry Point City, Edgar, Ill	15
Cherry Ridge, Wayne, Pa	31
Cherry Run Depot, Morgan, W. Va	41
Cherry Spring, Gillespie, Tex	6
Cherrystone, Northampton, Va	140
Cherry Tree, Venango, Pa	65
Cherry Valley,* Winnebago, Ill	460
Cherry Valley, Worcester, Mass	220
Cherry Valley, Otsego, N. Y	630
Cherry Valley, Ashtabula, Ohio	92
Cherry Valley, Washington, Pa	20
Cherryville, Montgomery, Kans	12
Cherryville, Crawford, Mo	24
Cherryville, Hunterdon, N. J	19
Cherryville, Gaston, N. C	74
Cherryville, Northampton, Pa	70
Chesaning, Saginaw, Mich	350
Chesapeake, Lawrence, Mo	34
Chesapeake City,* Cecil, Md	540
Cheshire,* New Haven, Conn	580
Cheshire, Berkshire, Mass	410
Cheshire, Allegan, Mich	8
Cheshire, Ontario, N. Y	67
Cheshire, Gallia, Ohio	150

* Money-order office.

Post office	Amount
Chesnut Bluffs, Dyer, Tenn	$16
Chesnut Creek, (*c. h.*,) Baker, Ala	3
Chesnut Fork, Bedford, Va	8
Chesnut Grove, Shelby, Ky	4
Chesnut Grove, Lycoming, Pa	7
Chesnut Grove, Chester, S. C	35
Chesnut Hill, Washington, Ind	23
Chesnut Hill, Middlesex, Mass	12
Chesnut Level, Lancaster, Pa	83
Chesnut Mound, Smith, Tenn	8
Chesnut Ridge, St. Genevieve, Mo	12
Chesnut Ridge, Dutchess, N. Y	20
Chesnut Ridge, Yadkin, N. C	3
Chest, Clearfield, Pa	23
Chester, Jefferson, Ala	5
Chester, Desha, Ark	12
Chester, Middlesex, Conn	440
Chester,* (*c. h.*,) Randolph, Ill	630
Chester, Wayne, Ind	14
Chester, Howard, Iowa	14
Chester, Jefferson, Kans	12
Chester, Penobscot, Me	10
Chester, Hampden, Mass	300
Chester, Eaton, Mich	12
Chester, Olmsted, Minn	10
Chester, Rockingham, N. H	270
Chester, Morris, N. J	310
Chester, Orange, N. Y	580
Chester, Meigs, Ohio	50
Chester,* Delaware, Pa	2,400
Chester,* Windsor, Vt	560
Chester, Chesterfield, Va	65
Chester C. H.,* Chester, S. C	1,100
Chester Centre, Hampden, Mass	35
Chester Cross Roads, Geauga, Ohio	110
Chesterfield, New London, Conn	43
Chesterfield, Macoupin, Ill	150
Chesterfield, Madison, Ind	77
Chesterfield, Hampshire, Mass	88
Chesterfield, Cheshire, N. H	86
Chesterfield C. H., Chesterfield, S. C	20
Chesterfield C. H., Chesterfield, Va	12
Chesterfield Factory, Cheshire, N. H	110
Chester Hill,* Morgan, Ohio	200
Chester Springs, Chester, Pa	220
Chester Station, Dodge, Wis	29
Chesterton, Porter, Ind	250
Chestertown,* (*c. h.*,) Kent, Md	780
Chestertown, Warren, N. Y	320
Chester Valley, Chester, Pa	77
Chesterville, Franklin, Me	72
Chesterville, Kent, Md	200
Chesterville, Pontotoc, Miss	14
Chesterville, Morrow, Ohio	240
Chesterville, Chester, Pa	32
Chest Springs, Cambria, Pa	95
Chetco, Curry, Oreg	19
Chetopah,* Labette, Kans	610
Cheviot, Hamilton, Ohio	92
Chewalla, McNairy, Tenn	12
Chew's Landing, Camden, N. J	16
Chewsville, Washington, Md	29
CHEYENNE CITY,* (*c. h.*,) Laramie, Wyo	2,800
Cheyney, Delaware, Pa	99
Chicago,* (*c. h.*,) Cook, Ill	4,000

Post office	Amount
Chicago, Marion, Ky	$75
Chicago, Douglas, Nebr	100
Chichester, Merrimack, N. H	62
Chickamauga, Hamilton, Tenn	5
Chickamauga Station, Hamilton, Tenn	8
Chickaming, Berrien, Mich	31
Chickasabogue, Mobile, Ala	12
Chickasaw, Franklin, Ala	12
Chickasaw,* (*c. h.*,) Chickasaw, Iowa	120
Chicken Creek, Juab, Utah	49
Chickies, Lancaster, Pa	160
Chick's Springs, Greenville, S. C	6
Chico,* Butte, Cal	730
Chicopee,* Hampden, Mass	2,000
Chicopee Falls,* Hampden, Mass	1,200
Chicora, Chicot, Ark	12
Chikalah, Yell, Ark	12
Childersburgh, Talladega, Ala	230
Childress' Store, Montgomery, Va	12
Childsville, Mitchell, N. C	4
Chilesburgh, Fayette, Ky	69
Chilesburgh, Caroline, Va	12
Chilhowee, Blount, Tenn	12
Chilhowie, Johnson, Mo	12
Chili, Calaveras, Cal	25
Chili, Hancock, Ill	47
Chili, Miami, Ind	88
Chili, Monroe, N. Y	44
Chili, Coshocton, Ohio	37
Chillicothe,* Peoria, Ill	820
Chillicothe, Wapello, Iowa	78
Chillicothe,* (*c. h.*,) Livingston, Mo	2,100
Chillicothe,* (*c. h.*,) Ross, Ohio	2,400
Chillisquaque, Northumberland, Pa	50
Chilmark, Dukes, Mass	87
Chilo, Clermont, Ohio	48
Chilton,* (*c. h.*,) Calumet, Wis	290
Chiltonville, Plymouth, Mass	100
Chimney Point, Addison, Vt	19
Chimney Rock, Rutherford, N. C	10
China, Kennebec, Me	200
China, St. Clair, Mich	33
China Grove, Pike, Ala	8
China Grove, Pike, Miss	14
China Grove, Rowan, N. C	51
China Grove, Williamsburgh, S. C	16
Chincoteague, Accomack, Va	29
Chincoteague Island, Accomack, Va	9
Chinese Camp, Tuolumne, Cal	210
Chinkapin Hill, Sangamon, Ill	12
Chinkapin Roof, Jackson, Ky	12
Chinook, Pacific, Wash	12
Chipman's Point, Addison, Vt	24
Chipmonk Cooley, Vernon, Wis	12
Chippenhook Springs, Rutland, Vt	12
Chippewa, New Castle, Del	22
Chippewa, Wayne, Ohio	140
Chippewa City, (*c. h.*,) Chippewa, Minn	10
Chippewa City, Chippewa, Wis	100
Chippewa Falls,* (*c. h.*,) Chippewa, Wis	1,300
Chippewa Lake, Mecosta, Mich	12
Chisago City, (*c. h.*,) Chisago, Minn	90
Chisago Lake, Chisago, Minn	170

* Money-order office.

Chismville, Scott, Ark	$6
Chittenango, Madison, N. Y	840
Chittenango Falls, Madison, N. Y	21
Chittenango Station, Madison, N. Y	12
Chittenden, Rutland, Vt	34
Choconut, Susquehanna, Pa	18
Choconut Centre, Broome, N. Y	13
Chocoville, Sebastian, Ark	12
Choctaw Agency, Choctaw N., Ind. T	15
Choctaw Agency, Oktibbeha, Miss	96
Choctaw Bluff, Clarke, Ala	12
Choctaw Corner, Clarke, Ala	32
Choteau Creek, Bonhomme, Dak	12
Christiana, New Castle, Del	130
Christiana, Dakota, Minn	63
Christiana, Lancaster, Pa	310
Christiana, Williamson, Tenn	10
Christiana, Dane, Wis	44
Christiansburgh, Wapello, Iowa	10
Christiansburgh, Shelby, Ky	140
Christiansburgh, Champaign, Ohio	85
*Christiansburgh,** (*c. h.,*) Montgomery, Va	750
Christiansville, Mecklenburgh, Va	39
Christy's Prairie, Clay, Ind	16
Chrome, Chester, Pa	12
Chrome Hill, Harford, Md	21
Chronicle, Catawba, N. C	4
Chuckatuck, Nansemond, Va	92
Chula Depot, Amelia, Va	210
Chulafinnee, Cleburne, Ala	55
Chulahoma, Marshall, Miss	57
Chulasky, Northumberland, Pa	16
Chunkey's Station, Newton, Miss	30
Church Creek, Dorchester, Md	99
Church Grove, Knox, Tenn	3
Church Hill, Christian, Ky	12
Church Hill, Queen Anne, Md	190
Church Hill, Jefferson, Miss	14
Church Hill, Trumbull, Ohio	12
Churchill, Ottawa, Kans	21
Churchland, Norfolk, Va	10
Church's Corners, Hillsdale, Mich	12
Churchtown, Columbia, N. Y	14
Churchtown, Lancaster, Pa	63
Church View, Middlesex, Va	15
Churchville, Harford, Md	190
Churchville, Monroe, N. Y	340
Churchville, Augusta, Va	150
Churubusco, Whitley, Ind	53
Churubusco, Clinton, N. Y	94
Cicero, Hamilton, Ind	180
Cicero, Madison, Mont	12
Cicero, Onondaga, N. Y	210
Cicero, Defiance, Ohio	29
Cimarron, Mora, N. Mex	100
Cincinnati, Washington, Ark	40
Cincinnati, Appanoose, Iowa	86
Cincinnati, Pawnee, Nebr	12
*Cincinnati,** (*c. h.,*) Hamilton, Ohio	4,000
Cincinnatus, Cortland, N. Y	300
Cinnaminson, Burlington, N. J	120
Circle, Vermilion, Ill	12
Circleville, Tazewell, Ill	7
Circleville, Jackson, Kans	38
Circleville, Orange, N. Y.	23
*Circleville,** (*c. h.,*) Pickaway, Ohio	$2,000
Circleville, Williamson, Tex	19
Circleville, Loudoun, Va	22
Cisco, Placer, Cal	12
Cistern, Fayette, Tex	12
Citico, Monroe, Tenn	8
Citronelle, Mobile, Ala	40
City, Dutchess, N. Y	80
City Island, Westchester, N. Y	57
City Point, Platte, Mo	86
City Point, Prince George, Va	100
Civer, Fulton, Ill	37
Civil Bend, Daviess, Mo	25
Claiborne, Monroe, Ala	74
Claiborne, Jasper, Miss	20
Claire Springs, Cedar, Mo	29
Clairville, Sonoma, Cal	28
Clanton, Madison, Iowa	7
Claquato, (*c. h.,*) Lewis, Wash	20
Clara, Potter, Pa	10
Claremont, Richland, Ill	100
Claremont, Dodge, Minn	70
Claremont,* Sullivan, N. H	2,000
Claremont, Allegheny, Pa	20
Claremont Wharf, Surry, Va	12
Clarence,* Cedar, Iowa	670
Clarence, Calhoun, Mich	11
Clarence, Shelby, Mo	420
Clarence, Erie, N. Y	160
Clarence Centre, Erie, N. Y	120
Clarenceville, Queens, N. Y	12
Clarendon, (*c. h.,*) Monroe, Ark	420
Clarendon, Orleans, N. Y	190
Clarendon, Rutland, Vt	53
Clarendon Centre, Calhoun, Mich	10
Clarendon Springs, Rutland, Vt	180
Claridon, Geauga, Ohio	88
*Clarinda,** (*c. h.,*) Page, Iowa	760
Clarington, Monroe, Ohio	260
Clarington, Forest, Pa	20
Clarion, (*c. h.,*) Wright, Iowa	120
*Clarion,** (*c. h.,*) Clarion, Pa	730
Clark, Mercer, Pa	270
Clark Centre, Clark, Ill	20
Clarke, Wilson, Kans	11
Clarke City, Clarke, Mo	12
Clarke Station, Lake, Ind	12
Clarkestown, Lycoming, Pa	13
Clarkesville, (*c. h.,*) Habersham, Ga	130
Clark's, Coshocton, Ohio	96
Clarksborough, Gloucester, N. J	150
Clarksborough, St. Lawrence, N. Y	12
Clarksburgh, Decatur, Ind	99
Clarksburgh, Montgomery, Md	78
Clarksburgh, Marquette, Mich	230
Clarksburgh, Moniteau, Mo	120
Clarksburgh, Monmouth, N. J	45
Clarksburgh, Erie, N. Y	19
Clarksburgh, Ross, Ohio	71
Clarksburgh, Indiana, Pa	56
Clarksburgh, Carroll, Tenn	25
*Clarksburgh,** (*c. h.,*) Harrison, W. Va	1,200
Clark's Corner, Ashtabula, Ohio	12
Clark's Creek, Grant, Ky	12
Clark's Factory, Delaware, N. Y	47
Clark's Falls, New London, Conn	37

* Money-order office.

Clarksfield, Huron, Ohio	$160
Clark's Fork, Cooper, Mo	28
Clark's Fork, York, S. C	6
Clark's Green, Luzerne, Pa	92
Clark's Grove, Freeborn, Minn	47
Clark's Hill, Tippecanoe, Ind	100
Clark's Mills, Oneida, N. Y	88
Clark's Mills, Moore, N. C	12
Clark's Mills, Manitowoc, Wis	73
Clarkson, Monroe, N. Y	180
Clarkson, Columbiana, Ohio	19
Clark's Prairie, Daviess, Ind	56
Clarkston, Oakland, Mich	270
Clarkstown, (*c. h.*,) Rockland, N. Y	96
Clarksville,* (*c. h.*,) Johnson, Ark	800
Clarksville, El Dorado, Cal	40
Clarksville, Hamilton, Ind	12
Clarksville, Butler, Iowa	310
Clarksville, Howard, Md	96
Clarksville, Pike, Mo	710
Clarksville, Merrick, Nebr	12
Clarksville, Coos, N. H	8
Clarksville, Hunterdon, N. J	320
Clarksville, Albany, N. Y	59
Clarksville, Clinton, Ohio	270
Clarksville, Greene, Pa	61
Clarksville,* (*c. h.*,) Montgomery, Tenn	2,700
Clarksville, (*c. h.*,) Red River, Tex	430
Clarksville, Mecklenburgh, Va	220
Clarkton, Dunklin, Mo	12
Clarno, Green, Wis	12
Claryville, Sullivan, N. Y.	12
Claussville, Lehigh, Pa	11
Claverack, Columbia, N. Y	640
Clay, Washington, Iowa	25
Clay, Webster, Ky	8
Clay, Clarke, Mo	12
Clay, Onondaga, N. Y	89
Clay, Jackson, Ohio	84
Clay C. H., Clay, W. Va	10
Clay Bank, Oceana, Mich	12
Clay Bank, Middlesex, N. J	12
Clay Banks, Door, Wis	16
Clay Brook, Madison, Tenn	12
Clayburgh, Clinton, N. Y	36
Clay Centre, (*c. h.*,) Clay, Kans	97
Clay City, Clay, Ill	300
Clayford, Jones, Iowa	22
Clay Hill, Marengo, Ala	4
Clay Hill, Lincoln, Ga	12
Clay Hill, Wexford, Mich	12
Clay Hill, Titus, Tex	12
Clay Lick, Licking, Ohio	66
Clay Lick, Franklin, Pa	42
Clay Mills, Jones, Iowa	13
Claymont, New Castle, Del	350
Claypool, Warren, Ky	4
Clay's Grove, Lee, Iowa	65
Clay's Prairie, Edgar, Ill	12
Claysville, Marshall, Ala	5
Claysville, Washington, Ind	13
Claysville, Harrison, Ky	25
Claysville, Boone, Mo	44
Claysville, Guernsey, Ohio	74
Claysville, Washington, Pa	200
Claysville, Mineral, W. Va	$12
Clayton, (*c. h.*,) Barbour, Ala	300
Clayton, Hempstead, Ark	12
Clayton, Contra Costa, Cal	40
Clayton, Kent, Del	290
Clayton, (*c. h.*,) Rabun, Ga	47
Clayton,* Adams, Ill	590
Clayton, Hendricks, Ind	190
Clayton, Clayton, Iowa	120
Clayton, Harford, Md	46
Clayton, Lenawee, Mich	300
Clayton, Faribault, Minn	45
Clayton, Gloucester, N. J	480
Clayton, Jefferson, N. Y	490
Clayton, Johnston, N. C	90
Clayton, Montgomery, Ohio	75
Clayton, Berks, Pa	42
Claytona, Noble, Ohio	8
Clayton Centre, Jefferson, N. Y	67
Claytonville, Brown, Kans	14
Claytonville, Transylvania, N. C	4
Clay Village, Shelby, Ky	84
Clayville, Oneida, N. Y	650
Clear Branch, Washington, Tenn	1
Clear Branch, Washington, Va	15
Clear Creek, Marion, Ark	12
Clear Creek, Monroe, Ind	12
Clear Creek, Alamakee, Iowa	10
Clear Creek, Nemaha, Kans	18
Clear Creek, Chautauqua, N. Y	33
Clear Creek, Mecklenburgh, N. C	4
Clear Creek, Fairfield, Ohio	54
Clear Creek, Clackamas, Oreg	14
Clear Creek, Greene, Tenn	5
Clear Creek, Raleigh, W. Va	12
Clear Creek Falls, Winston, Ala	10
Clear Creek Landing, Alexander, Ill	20
Clearfield,* (*c. h.*,) Clearfield, Pa	1,300
Clearfield Bridge, Clearfield, Pa	18
Clear Lake, Steuben, Ind	12
Clear Lake, Cerro Gordo, Iowa	240
Clear Lake, Sherburne, Minn	16
Clear Port, Fairfield, Ohio	23
Clear Spring, Clark, Ark	12
Clear Spring, Graves, Ky	5
Clear Spring, Washington, Md	310
Clear Spring, York, Pa	40
Clear Spring, Grainger, Tenn	2
Clearville, Bedford, Pa	36
Clear Water, Antrim, Mich	18
Clear Water, Wright, Minn	280
Clear Water Harbor, Hillsborough, Fla	6
Cleaveland, Oswego, N. Y	380
Cleaveland,* (*c. h.*,) Bradley, Tenn	1,200
Cleburne, Johnson, Tex	250
Cleek's Mills, Bath, Va	11
Clemansville, Winnebago, Wis	23
Clement, Clinton, Ill	220
Clementsville, Jackson, Tenn	12
Clendenin, Kanawha, W. Va	16
Cleona, Brown, Ind	8
Cleopatra, Mercer, Mo	24
Clermont, Marion, Ind	110
Clermont,* Fayette, Iowa	460
Clermont, Columbia, N. Y	74

* Money-order office.

Clermont Mills, Harford, Md	$38
Clermontville, McKean, Pa	4
Cleveland, (*c. h.*,) White, Ga	58
Cleveland, Henry, Ill	12
Cleveland, Hancock, Ind	78
Cleveland, Fayette, Ky	24
Cleveland, Le Sueur, Minn	84
Cleveland,* (*c. h.*,) Cuyahoga, Ohio	4,000
Cleves, Hamilton, Ohio	170
Clifford, Bartholomew, Ind	62
Clifford, Lapeer, Mich	6
Clifford, Susquehanna, Pa	82
Clifton, Wilcox, Ala	58
Clifton, Iroquois, Ill	420
Clifton, Union, Ind	22
Clifton, Louisa, Iowa	170
Clifton, Washington, Kans	12
Clifton, Penobscot, Me	29
Clifton, Schuyler, Mo	18
Clifton, Nemaha, Nebr	4
Clifton, Passaic, N. J	12
Clifton, Colfax, N. Mex	12
Clifton, Monroe, N. Y	72
Clifton, Greene, Ohio	130
Clifton, Luzerne, Pa	40
Clifton, Wayne, Tenn	69
Clifton, Bosque, Tex	8
Clifton, Cache, Utah	12
Clifton, Mason, W. Va	48
Clifton, Monroe, Wis	8
Clifton Dale, Essex, Mass	78
Clifton Forge, Alleghany, Va	74
Clifton Hill, Randolph, Mo	69
Clifton Mills, Breckinridge, Ky	24
Clifton Mills, Pierce, Wis	12
Clifton Park, Saratoga, N. Y	130
Clifton Springs,* Ontario, N. Y	980
Clifton Station, Fairfax, Va	67
Clifty, Madison, Ark	10
Clifty, Decatur, Ind	97
Clifty, Todd, Ky	4
Clifty, Fayette, W. Va	12
Clifty Dale, Maries, Mo	9
Climax Prairie, Kalamazoo, Mich	150
Cline's Mills, Augusta, Va	12
Clinton, Greene, Ala	110
Clinton, (*c. h.*,) Van Buren, Ark	20
Clinton, Middlesex, Conn	630
Clinton, (*c. h.*,) Jones, Ga	80
Clinton,* (*c. h.*,) De Witt, Ill	1,100
Clinton, Vermillion, Ind	190
Clinton,* Clinton, Iowa	3,100
Clinton, Douglas, Kans	150
Clinton, (*c. h.*,) Hickman, Ky	120
Clinton,* (*c. h.*,) East Feliciana, La	710
Clinton, Kennebec, Me	210
Clinton,* Worcester, Mass	2,000
Clinton, Lenawee, Mich	640
Clinton, Hinds, Miss	290
Clinton,* (*c. h.*,) Henry, Mo	1,300
Clinton, (*c. h.*,) Stanton, Nebr	9
Clinton, Hunterdon, N. J	630
Clinton, Oneida, N. Y	2,200
Clinton, (*c. h.*,) Sampson, N. C	180
Clinton, Summit, Ohio	180
Clinton, Allegheny, Pa	84

Clinton, Laurens, S. C	$75
Clinton, (*c. h.*,) Anderson, Tenn	160
Clinton, (*c. h.*,) De Witt, Tex	210
Clinton, Ohio, W. Va	24
Clinton,* Rock, Wis	750
Clinton Corners, Dutchess, N. Y	38
Clinton Corners, Wyoming, Pa	8
Clintondale, Ulster, N. Y	55
Clinton Falls, Steele, Minn	33
Clinton Furnace, Monongalia, W. Va	12
Clinton Hollow, Dutchess, N. Y	23
Clinton Lock, Parke, Ind	12
Clinton Mills, Clinton, N. Y	64
Clinton Point, Dutchess, N. Y	24
Clinton Station, Hunterdon, N. J	160
Clinton Station, Clinton, Ohio	16
Clinton Valley, Clinton, Ohio	18
Clintonville, Kane, Ill	190
Clintonville, Bourbon, Ky	40
Clintonville, Cedar, Mo	39
Clintonville, Clinton, N. Y	250
Clintonville, Franklin, Ohio	24
Clintonville, Venango, Pa	89
Clintonville, Greenbrier, W. Va	27
Clintonville, Waupacca, Wis	47
Clio, Barbour, Ala	12
Clio, Wayne, Iowa	10
Clio, Pulaski, Ky	20
Clio, Genesee, Mich	390
Clio, Marlborough, S. C	20
Cliola, Adams, Ill	12
Clipper Gap, Placer, Cal	23
Clipper Mills, Butte, Cal	71
Clipper Mills, Gallia, Ohio	12
Clitherall, Otter Tail, Minn	10
Clockville, Madison, N. Y	240
Clokey, Washington, Pa	33
Clonmell, Lancaster, Pa	22
Clopton, Dale, Ala	12
Closter, Bergen, N. J	190
Clouser's Mills, Montgomery, Ind	5
Cloutarf, Dane, Wis	10
Cloutierville, Natchitoches, La	20
Clove, Sussex, N. J	13
Clove, Dutchess, N. Y	11
Clove Branch Junction, Dutchess, N. Y	12
Clover Bend, (*c. h.*,) Lawrence, Ark	12
Clover Bottom, Jackson, Ky	6
Clover Bottom, Franklin, Mo	12
Clover Creek, Blair, Pa	58
Cloverdale, Sonoma, Cal	90
Cloverdale, Dade, Ga	12
Cloverdale, Putnam, Ind	190
Cloverdale, Benton, Mo	8
Cloverdale, Botetourt, Va	210
Clover Dale, Doddridge, W. Va	12
Clover Depot, Halifax, Va	170
Clover Green, Spottsylvania, Va	13
Clover Hill, Hunterdon, N. J	44
Clover Hill, Blount, Tenn	12
Cloverland, Clay, Ind	62
Clover Orchard, Alamance, N. C	5
Cloverport, Breckinridge, Ky	310
Clovesville, Delaware, N. Y	23
Cloyd's Creek, Blount, Tenn	12

* Money-order office.

Post office	Compensation
Clyde, Jasper, Iowa	$46
Clyde, Cloud, Kans	110
Clyde, Wayne, N. Y	1,600
Clyde,* Sandusky, Ohio	1,200
Clyde Mills, St. Clair, Mich	16
Clyman, Dodge, Wis	41
Clymer, Chautauqua, N. Y	250
Clymore, Labette, Kans	12
Coal Bank, Thurston, Wash	6
Coal Bluff, Washington, Pa	60
Coalburgh, Trumbull, Ohio	170
Coalburgh, Kanawha, W. Va	73
Coal Centre, Linn, Kans	12
Coal City, Venango, Pa	27
Coal Creek, Boulder, Colo	8
Coal Creek, Keokuk, Iowa	69
Coal Creek, Ottawa, Kans	12
Coal Creek, Campbell, Tenn	12
Coal Dale, Perry, Ohio	20
Coal Grove, Lawrence, Ohio	44
Coalmont, Huntingdon, Pa	66
Coal River Marshes, Raleigh, W. Va	5
Coal Run, Pike, Ky	10
Coal Run, Washington, Ohio	56
Coalsmouth, Kanawha, W. Va	120
Coalton, Monroe, Iowa	14
Coalton, Boyd, Ky	110
Coal Valley, Rock Island, Ill	200
Coal Valley, Allegheny, Pa	84
Coalville, Livingston, Ill	26
Coalville, (c. h.,) Summit, Utah	91
Coalville, Lincoln, W. Va	12
Coast Fork, Lane, Oreg	12
Coast Range, Colusa, Cal	14
Coatesville, Hendricks, Ind	84
Coatesville, Chester, Pa	1,300
Coatopa, Sumter, Ala	16
Coatsburgh, Adams, Ill	98
Coatsville, Schuyler, Mo	12
Cobalt, Middlesex, Conn	130
Cobb, Randolph, Ill	31
Cobb, Iowa, Wis	20
Cobb River, Waseca, Minn	13
Cobb's Creek, Matthews, Va	12
Cobham, Warren, Pa	37
Cobham, Albermarle, Va	170
Cobleskill, Schoharie, N. Y	870
Cob Moo Sa, Oceana, Mich	10
Coburgh, Monmouth, N. J	10
Coburn's Corners, De Kalb, Ind	23
Coburn's Store, Union, N. C	12
Cocalico, Lancaster, Pa	13
Cochecton, Sullivan, N. Y	290
Cochecton Centre, Sullivan, N. Y	65
Cochessett, Plymouth, Mass	85
Cochituate, Middlesex, Mass	91
Cochran, Pulaski, Ga	12
Cochran's Mills, Armstrong, Pa	47
Cochransville, Chester, Pa	230
Cochranton, Marion, Ohio	23
Cochranton, Crawford, Pa	330
Cockeysville,* Baltimore, Md	300
Cocolamus, Juniata, Pa	32
Coddle Creek, Cabarrus, N. C	8
Codorus, York, Pa	53
Cody's Mills, Kent, Mich	79

Post office	Compensation
Coelk, Livingston, La	$12
Coe Ridge, Cuyahoga, Ohio	35
Coesse, Whitley, Ind	120
Coeymans, Albany, N. Y	260
Coeymans Hollow, Albany, N Y	86
Coffadeliah, Neshoba, Miss	6
Coffee, Clay, Ind	15
Coffee Landing, Hardin, Tenn	12
Coffee Run, Huntingdon, Pa	32
Coffeeville, (c. h.,) Yalabusha, Miss	200
Coffeeville, Upshur, Tex	60
Coffeysburgh, Daviess, Mo	12
Coffeyville, Montgomery, Kans	12
Coffin's Summit, Dutchess, N. Y	12
Cogan House, Lycoming, Pa	11
Cogan Station, Lycoming, Pa	120
Cog Hill, McMinn, Tenn	11
Cohansey, Cumberland, N. J	12
Cohasset, Norfolk, Mass	440
Cohoctah, Livingston, Mich	7
Cohocton, Steuben, N. Y	340
Cohoes,* Albany, N. Y	2,600
Coila, Washington, N. Y	110
Coinjock, Currituck, N. C	5
Coitsville, Mahoning, Ohio	24
Cokesbury, Abbeville, S. C	150
Colaparchee, Monroe, Ga	71
Colburn, Tippecanoe, Ind	50
Colchester,* New London, Conn	824
Colchester, McDonough, Ill	300
Colchester, Delaware, N. Y	16
Colchester, Chittenden, Vt	120
Cold Brook, Herkimer, N. Y	72
Coldbrook Springs, Worcester, Mass	100
Cold Creek, Bradford, Pa	12
Colden, Erie, N. Y	100
Coldenham, Orange, N. Y	200
Cold Neck, Cooper, Mo	16
Cold Spring, El Dorado, Cal	13
Cold Spring, Fairfield, Conn	74
Cold Spring, Shelby, Ill	30
Cold Spring, Campbell, Ky	77
Cold Spring, Berkshire, Mass	26
Cold Spring, Cape May, N. J	160
Cold Spring,* Putnam, N. Y	1,200
Cold Spring, Wayne, Pa	14
Cold Spring, Bledsoe, Tenn	12
Cold Spring, Polk, Tex	100
Cold Spring, Jefferson, Wis	22
Cold Spring City, Stearns, Minn	83
Cold Spring Harbor, Suffolk, N. Y	150
Cold Springs, Edgefield, S. C	6
Cold Stream, Hampshire, W. Va	6
Cold Water, Cross, Ark	25
Coldwater, Franklin, Iowa	10
Coldwater, Callaway, Ky	11
Cold Water, (c. h.,)* Branch, Mich	2,600
Coldwater, De Soto, Miss	80
Cold Water, Wayne, Mo	42
Cold Water, Monroe, N. Y	19
Cold Water, Mercer, Ohio	45
Cold Water, Doddridge, W. Va	12
Cold Well, White, Ark	10
Cold Well, Union, S. C	12
Coldwell's Store, Anderson, Ky	2

* Money-order office.

Colebrook, Litchfield, Conn	$140
Colebrook, Coos, N. H	460
Colebrook, Ashtabula, Ohio	73
Colebrook, Lebanon, Pa	12
Colebrookdale, Berks, Pa	50
Colebrook River, Litchfield, Conn	88
Cole Camp, Benton, Mo	89
Cole Creek, Fountain, Ind	17
Colegrove, McKean, Pa	25
Colegrove's Point, Sutter, Cal	12
Coleman's Depot, Randolph, Ga	12
Colemansville, Harrison, Ky	17
Colemanville, Lancaster, Pa	34
Colerain, Franklin, Mass	100
Colerain, Bertie, N. C	89
Colerain, Belmont, Ohio	75
Colerain, Lancaster, Pa	28
Colerain Forge, Huntingdon, Pa	40
Colesburgh, Delaware, Iowa	260
Colesburgh, Potter, Pa	28
Cole's Corners, De Kalb, Ind	10
Cole's Creek, Columbia, Pa	14
Cole's Ferry, Charlotte, Va	44
Colesville, Montgomery, Md	15
Colesville, Sussex, N. J	45
Colesville, Broome, N. Y	12
Colesville, Stokes, N. C	6
Coleta, Clay, Ala	5
Coleta, Whitesides, Ill	110
Coleville, Mono, Cal	22
Coleville, Bossier, La	12
Colfax, Placer, Cal	220
Colfax, Fremont, Colo	12
Colfax, Warren, Ill	16
Colfax, Clinton, Ind	130
Colfax, Jasper, Iowa	200
Colfax, (*c. h.*,) Grant, La	12
Colfax, Mason, Mich	21
Colfax, Sullivan, Mo	6
Colfax, Guilford, N. C	12
Colfax, Fairfield, Ohio	12
Colfax, Huntingdon, Pa	13
Colfax, Van Zandt, Tex	12
Colfax, Dunn, Wis	12
Collamer, Whitley, Ind	44
Collamer, Onondaga, N. Y	170
Collamer, Cuyahoga, Ohio	140
Collamer, Chester, Pa	40
College Corner, Jay, Ind	54
College Corner, Butler, Ohio	210
College Grove, Williamson, Tenn	74
College Hill, Middlesex, Mass	130
College Hill, Hamilton, Ohio	610
College Mound, Macon, Mo	80
College Point, Queens, N. Y	270
College Springs, Page, Iowa	200
Collegeville, Saline, Ark	12
Collegeville, San Joaquin, Cal	12
Collegeville, Montgomery, Pa	300
Collettsville, Caldwell, N. C	8
Colley, Sullivan, Pa	16
Collier's Mill, Ocean, N. J	10
Collierstown, Rockbridge, Va	44
Colliersville, Otsego, N. Y	140
Colliersville, Shelby, Tenn	280
Collington, Prince George's, Md	130
Collingwood, Onondaga, N. Y	$21
Collingwood, Fairfax, Va	12
Collins, Erie, N. Y	100
Collinsburgh, Bossier, La	61
Collins Centre, Erie, N. Y	120
Collins Depot, Hampden, Mass	95
Collinsville, Etowah, Ala	14
Collinsville,* Hartford, Conn	730
Collinsville,* Madison, Ill	580
Collinsville, Lewis, N. Y	56
Collinsville, Butler, Ohio	78
Collinsville, Frederick, Va	5
Collinwood, Meeker, Minn	12
Collomsville, Lycoming, Pa	50
Colman, St. Louis, Mo	12
Colmar, McDonough, Ill	40
Colo, Story, Iowa	190
Cologne, Mason, W. Va	69
Coloma, Cherokee, Ala	10
Coloma, El Dorado, Cal	100
Coloma, Parke, Ind	12
Coloma, Woodson, Kans	20
Coloma, Berrien, Mich	120
Coloma, Carroll, Mo	98
Coloma, Waushara, Wis	44
Colon, St. Joseph, Mich	290
Colona Station, Henry, Ill	150
Colony, Knox, Mo	24
Colora, Cecil, Md	130
Colorado City, (*c. h.*,) El Paso, Colo	200
Colosse, Oswego, N. Y	74
Colquit, (*c. h.*,) Miller, Ga	25
Coltharp's, Houston, Tex	8
Colton, St. Lawrence, N. Y	270
Colton, Henry, Ohio	70
Colt's Neck, Monmouth, N. J	100
Columbia, Henry, Ala	25
Columbia,* Tuolumne, Cal	540
Columbia, Tolland, Conn	98
Columbia, Monroe, Ill	230
Columbia, Fayette, Ind	48
Columbia, Marion, Iowa	50
Columbia, (*c. h.*,) Adair, Ky	280
Columbia, (*c. h.*,) Caldwell, La	120
Columbia, Washington, Me	190
Columbia, Jackson, Mich	28
Columbia, (*c. h.*,) Marion, Miss	14
Columbia, (*c. h.*,) Boone, Mo	1,400
Columbia, Coos, N. H	19
Columbia, Warren, N. J	33
Columbia, Herkimer, N. Y	23
Columbia, (*c. h.*,) Tyrrel, N. C	12
Columbia, Hamilton, Ohio	140
Columbia,* Lancaster, Pa	2,300
COLUMBIA,* (*c. h.*,) Richland, S. C	3,000
Columbia,* (*c. h.*,) Maury, Tenn	1,400
Columbia, Brazoria, Tex	210
Columbia, Fluvanna, Va	270
Columbia Centre, Licking, Ohio	67
Columbia City,* (*c. h.*,) Whitley, Ind	940
Columbia × Roads, Bradford, Pa	78
Columbia Farm, Venango, Pa	270
Columbia Furnace, Shenandoah, Va	33
Columbiana, (*c. h.*,) Shelby, Ala	300
Columbiana, Columbiana, Ohio	520
Columbian Grove, Lunenburgh, Va	12

* Money-order office.

Columbia Station, Lorain, Ohio	$70
Columbiaville, Lapeer, Mich	52
Columbus, Hempstead, Ark	25
Columbus, Madison, Fla	12
Columbus,* (*c. h.*,) Muscogee, Ga	3,600
Columbus, Adams, Ill	110
Columbus,* (*c. h.*,) Bartholomew, Ind	1,800
Columbus,* (*c. h.*,) Cherokee, Kans	73
Columbus,* Hickman, Ky	610
Columbus, St. Clair, Mich	67
Columbus,* (*c. h.*,) Lowndes, Miss	2,200
Columbus, Johnson, Mo	93
Columbus,* (*c. h.*,) Platte, Nebr	600
Columbus, Esmeralda, Nev	12
Columbus, Burlington, N. J	230
Columbus, Chenango, N. Y	95
Columbus, (*c. h.*,) Polk, N. C	45
COLUMBUS,* (*c. h.*,) Franklin, Ohio	4,000
Columbus, Warren, Pa	430
Columbus,* (*c. h.*,) Colorado, Tex	980
Columbus,* Columbia, Wis	1,300
Columbus City,* Louisa, Iowa	350
Columbus Grove,* Putnam, Ohio	570
Colusa,* (*c. h.*.) Colusa, Cal	700
Comanche, Comanche, Tex	12
Comann's Well, Sussex, Va	12
Comettsburgh, Beaver, Pa	6
Comfort, Kerr, Tex	99
Comly, Montour, Pa	12
Commack, Suffolk, N. Y	84
Commerce, Oakland, Mich	150
Commerce, Tunica, Miss	12
Commerce, (*c. h.*,) Scott, Mo	170
Commerce, Wilson, Tenn	8
Commerce Mills, Polk, Iowa	12
Commiskey, Jennings, Ind	12
Communia, Clayton, Iowa	23
Como, Whitesides, Ill	99
Como, Henry, Tenn	30
Como Depot, Panola, Miss	34
Comorn, King George, Va	120
Company's Shops, Alamance, N. C	330
Competine, Wapello, Iowa	18
Competition, Laclede, Mo	16
Compton, Los Angeles, Cal	12
Comstock, Wapello, Iowa	24
Comstock, Kalamazoo, Mich	63
Comstock's Landing, Washington, N. Y	140
Conaway, Tyler, W. Va	3
Conception, Nodaway, Mo	12
Concord, Lawrence, Ala	9
Concord, Sussex, Del	90
Concord, Gadsden, Fla	12
Concord, Pike, Ga	12
Concord, Morgan, Ill	120
Concord, Hancock, Iowa	12
Concord, Lewis, Ky	85
Concord, Somerset, Me	5
Concord,* (*c. h.*,) Middlesex, Mass	1,000
Concord, Jackson, Mich	220
Concord, Dodge, Minn	84
Concord, Calhoun, Miss	8
Concord, Callaway, Mo	92
CONCORD,* (*c. h.*,) Merrimack, N. H	3,000
Concord,* (*c. h.*,) Cabarrus, N. C	540
Concord, Lake, Ohio	$58
Concord, Franklin, Pa	56
Concord, Knox, Tenn	150
Concord, Hardin, Tex	17
Concord, Essex, Vt	45
Concord, Jefferson, Wis	61
Concord Church, Mercer, W. Va	24
Concord Depot, Campbell, Va	150
Concordia, (*c. h.*,) Cloud, Kans	12
Concordia, La Fayette, Mo	130
Concord Station, Erie, Pa	130
Concordville, Delaware, Pa	210
Concrete, De Witt, Tex	200
Condit, Delaware, Ohio	22
Conejos, (*c. h.*,) Conejos, Colo	59
Conemaugh, Cambria, Pa	130
Conerly's, Pike, Miss	8
Conestoga, Lancaster, Pa	40
Conesus, Livingston, N. Y	20
Conesus Centre, Livingston, N. Y	180
Conesville, Muscatine, Iowa	12
Conesville, Schoharie, N. Y	34
Conewango, Cattaraugus, N. Y	35
Confederate × Roads, Muskingum, Ohio	12
Confidence, Wayne, Iowa	44
Congress, Wayne, Ohio	64
Congruity, Westmoreland, Pa	38
Conklin Centre, Broome, N. Y	45
Conklingville, Saratoga, N. Y	90
Conklin Station, Broome, N. Y	12
Conlogue, Edgar, Ill	53
Conlogue, Jackson, Ind	21
Conneaut,* Ashtabula, Ohio	1,100
Conneautville,* Crawford, Pa	700
Connecticut Lake, Coos, N. H	260
Connellsville, Fayette, Pa	860
Conner's Creek, Wayne, Mich	16
Conner's Mills, Cooper, Mo	12
Connersville,* (*c. h.*,) Fayette, Ind	1,600
Connersville, Harrison, Ky	9
Connor's Mills, Floyd, Va	12
Connor's Station, Wyandotte, Kans	16
Connotton, Harrison, Ohio	79
Conn's Creek, Shelby, Ind	170
Conococheague, Washington, Md	28
Conover, Miami, Ohio	89
Conowingo, Cecil, Md	24
Conquest, Cayuga, N. Y	100
Conrad's Store, Rockingham, Va	12
Conshohocken, Montgomery, Pa	770
Constableville, Lewis, N. Y	390
Constance, Boone, Ky	12
Constantia, Oswego, N. Y	170
Constantia, Delaware, Ohio	58
Constantia Centre, Oswego, N. Y	14
Constantine, St. Joseph, Mich	1,000
Constitution, Washington, Ohio	80
Constitution, York, Pa	25
Consville, Henry, Mo	110
Content, Colorado, Tex	72
Contoocook Village, Merrimack, N. H	250
Contreras, Butler, Ohio	24
Convent, (*c. h.*,) St. James, La	370
Convis Centre, Calhoun, Mich	25

* Money-order office.

Conway, Aroostook, Me	$26
Conway, Franklin, Mass	540
Conway, Livingston, Mich	12
Conway, Leake, Miss	19
Conway, Carroll, N. H	170
Conwayborough, (*c. h.*,) Horry, S. C	2
Conway's Landing, Mendocino, Cal	12
Conyers, Newton, Ga	150
Conyersville, Henry, Tenn	18
Conyngham, Luzerne, Pa	95
Cooch's Bridge, New Castle, Del	12
Coody's Bluff, Cherokee N., Ind. T	12
Cookerly, Vigo, Ind	10
Cooksburgh, Albany, N. Y	59
Cooksburgh, Forest, Pa	12
Cook's Corners, Franklin, N. Y	17
Cook's Ford, Jefferson, Kans	18
Cook's Mills, Coles, Ill	12
Cook's Station, Newaygo, Mich	12
Cookstown, Burlington, N. J	43
Cook's Valley, Wabashaw, Minn	30
Cook's Valley, Chippewa, Wis	12
Cooksville, Howard, Md	28
Cooksville, Rock, Wis	52
Cookville, (*c. h.*,) Putnam, Tenn	99
Cool Bank, Pike, Ill	12
Coolbaugh's, Monroe, Pa	24
Cooleysville, Steele, Minn	12
Cool Spring, Ohio, Ky	6
Cool Spring, Iredell, N. C	23
Cool Spring, Jefferson, Pa	12
Coolville, Athens, Ohio	160
Cool Well, Amherst, Va	43
Coomer, Niagara, N. Y	31
Coon Creek, Anoka, Minn	12
Coon Creek, Barton, Mo	21
Coonewar, Lee, Miss	37
Coon Island, Washington, Pa	21
Coon Prairie, Vernon, Wis	190
Coon Rapids, Carroll, Iowa	10
Coon's Corners, Crawford, Pa	18
Coon Valley, Vernon, Wis	110
Cooper, Washington, Me	13
Cooper, Kalamazoo, Mich	100
Cooperdale, Cambria, Pa	12
Coopers, Franklin, Va	4
Coopersburgh, Lehigh, Pa	180
Cooper's Gap, Rutherford, N. C	2
Cooper's Hill, Osage, Mo	37
Cooper's Mills, Lincoln, Me	110
Cooper's Plains, Steuben, N. Y	130
Cooperstown, Brown, Ill	27
Cooperstown,* (*c. h.*,) Otsego, N. Y	2,000
Cooperstown, Venango, Pa	170
Cooperstown, Manitowoc, Wis	53
Coopersville, Wapello, Iowa	16
Coopersville, Ottawa, Mich	290
Coopersville, Clinton, N. Y	37
Coopertown, Robertson, Tenn	19
Coos, Coos, N. H	290
Coosa, Floyd, Ga	20
Coosawhatchie, Beaufort, S. C	12
Coote's Store, Rockingham, Va	51
Copake, Columbia, N. Y	190
Copake Iron Works, Columbia, N. Y	170
Copeland, Telfair, Ga	3

Copenhagen, Caldwell, La	$15
Copenhagen, Lewis, N. Y	570
Copenhagen, Caldwell, N. C	6
Copi, Johnson, Iowa	18
Copley, Summit, Ohio	110
Copopa, Lorain, Ohio	32
Copperas Hill, Orange, Vt	60
Copper Creek, Rock Island, Ill	6
Copper Falls Mine, Keweenaw, Mich	420
Copper Harbor, Keweenaw, Mich	140
Copper Hill, Hunterdon, N. J	52
Copper Hill, Floyd, Va	10
Copper Mines, Clay, Ala	15
Copperopolis, Calaveras, Cal	330
Copper Vale, Lassen, Cal	7
Copper Valley, Floyd, Va	5
Coquille, Coos, Oreg	12
Coral, McHenry, Ill	25
Coral, Montcalm, Mich	23
Coral City, Trempealeau, Wis	100
Coral Hill, Barren, Ky	22
Coral Hill, Elko, Nev	12
Coralville, Johnson, Iowa	12
Coram, Suffolk, N. Y	31
Corbandale, Montgomery, Tenn	71
Corbettsville, Broome, N. Y	51
Corcoran, Hennepin, Minn	12
Cordaville, Worcester, Mass	210
Cordelia, Solano, Cal	12
Cordova, Rock Island, Ill	390
Cordova, Grant, Ky	10
Cordova, Talbot, Md	12
Cordova, Le Sueur, Minn	63
Corfu,* Genesee, N. Y	290
Corinna, Penobscot, Me	240
Corinna, Wright, Minn	8
Corinna Centre, Penobscot, Me	31
Corinne, Box Elder, Utah	1,200
Corinth, Williamson, Ill	26
Corinth, Grant, Ky	63
Corinth, Penobscot, Me	31
Corinth,* (*c. h.*,) Alcorn, Miss	2,300
Corinth, Saratoga, N. Y	170
Corinth, Orange, Vt	110
Cork, Hillsborough, Fla	20
Cork, Ashtabula, Ohio	20
Cornelia, Johnson, Mo	88
Cornersville, Dorchester, Md	33
Cornersville, Giles, Tenn	290
Corn Grove, Calhoun, Ala	17
Corning, Adams, Iowa	400
Corning, Nemaha, Kans	12
Corning, Holt, Mo	12
Corning,* (*c. h.*,) Steuben, N. Y	2,400
Cornish, York, Me	230
Cornish, Sibley, Minn	12
Cornish Flat, Sullivan, N. H	210
Cornishville, Mercer, Ky	37
Cornplanter, Warren, Pa	20
Cornsville, Scott, Va	9
Cornton, Windham, Vt	72
Cornville, La Salle, Ill	12
Cornville, Somerset, Me	25
Cornwall, Litchfield, Conn	170
Cornwall, Madison, Mo	12
Cornwall, Orange, N. Y	430

* Money-order office.

Cornwall, Lebanon, Pa	$140
Cornwall, Addison, Vt	90
Cornwall Bridge, Litchfield, Conn	180
Cornwall Hollow, Litchfield, Conn	21
Cornwallis, Ritchie, W. Va	50
Cornwall Landing, Orange, N. Y	420
Cornwallville, Greene, N. Y	11
Corona, Coffey, Kans	12
*Corpus Christi,** (*c. h.,*) Nueces, Tex	1,400
Correctionville, Woodbury, Iowa	60
Corrieville, Wabash, Ill	12
Corriganville, Alleghany, Md	12
Corry,* Erie, Pa	2,800
Corsica, Morrow, Ohio	84
Corsica, Jefferson, Pa	110
Corsicana, Barry, Mo	49
Corsicana, (*c. h.,*) Navarro, Tex	310
Cortland, Jackson, Ind	15
Cortland Centre, Kent, Mich	76
*Cortland Village,** (*c. h.,*) Cortland, N. Y	2,200
Corunna, De Kalb, Ind	150
*Corunna,** (*c. h.,*) Shiawassee, Mich	860
*Corvallis,** (*c. h.,*) Benton, Oreg	600
*Corydon,** (*c. h.,*) Harrison, Ind	340
*Corydon,** (*c. h.,*) Wayne, Iowa	800
Corydon, Warren, Pa	190
Corymbo, La Porte, Ind	12
*Coshocton,** (*c. h.,*) Coshocton, Ohio	1,800
Cosmos, Renville, Minn	12
Cosmosa, Sedgwick, Kans	12
Costigon, Bath, Ky	12
Costilla, Costilla, Colo	32
Cosumne, Sacramento, Cal	35
Cote Gelee, La Fayette, La	12
Cote Sans Dessein, Callaway, Mo	16
Cotile, Rapides, La	40
Cotile Landing, Rapides, La	12
Cottage, Hardin, Iowa	49
Cottage, Cattaraugus, N. Y	38
Cottage, Huntingdon, Pa	34
Cottage Grove, Klamath, Cal	4
Cottage Grove, Douglas, Ill	31
Cottage Grove, Union, Ind	53
Cottage Grove, Washington, Minn	150
Cottage Grove, Lane, Oreg	55
Cottage Grove, Dane, Wis	48
Cottage Hill, Dubuque, Iowa	25
Cottage Hill, Muskingum, Ohio	23
Cottage Home, Lincoln, N. C	10
Cottage Inn, La Fayette, Wis	20
Cottage Mills, Chattahoochee, Ga	6
Cottageville, Jackson, W. Va	56
Cottle's Mills, Covington, Ala	12
Cottleville, St. Charles, Mo	79
Cotton Gin, Freestone, Tex	100
Cotton Gin Port, Monroe, Miss	15
Cotton Grove, Henry, Iowa	12
Cotton Hill, Sangamon, Ill	16
Cotton Hill, Fayette, W. Va	6
Cotton Plant, Woodruff, Ark	27
Cotton Plant, Marion, Fla	12
Cotton Plant, Tippah, Miss	23
Cotton Plant, Lamar, Tex	12
Cotton Valley, Greene, N. C	12
Cottonville, Marshall, Ala	6
Cottonville, Jackson, Iowa	$45
Cottonwood, Tehama, Cal	32
Cottonwood, Gallatin, Ill	12
Cottonwood, Brown, Minn	7
*Cottonwood Falls,** (*c. h.,*) Chase, Kans	180
Cottonwood Grove, Bond, Ill	40
Cottonwood Point, Pemiscot, Mo	44
Cottonwood Springs,* Lincoln, Nebr	520
Cotuit Port, Barnstable, Mass	320
Couchville, Davidson, Tenn	8
*Coudersport,** (*c. h.,*) Potter, Pa	460
Coultersville, Randolph, Ill	140
Coultersville, Butler, Pa	82
Council Bend, Crittenden, Ark	12
*Council Bluffs,** (*c. h.,*) Pottawattomie, Iowa	3,400
*Council Grove,** (*c. h.,*) Morris, Kans	450
Council Hill, Jo Daviess, Ill	50
Council Hill, Clayton, Iowa	43
Council Hill Station, Jo Daviess, Ill	84
Counover,* Winneshiek, Iowa	220
Countsville, Lexington, S. C	12
County Line, Campbell, Ga	12
County Line, Tippecanoe, Ind	12
County Line, Eaton, Mich	18
County Line, Niagara, N. Y	45
County Line, Davie, N. C	18
County Line, Lincoln, Tenn	12
County Line × Roads, Charlotte, Va	10
Coupville, Island, Wash	110
Courter, Miami, Ind	12
Courtland, Lawrence, Ala	430
Courtland, Nicollet, Minn	24
Courtland Station, De Kalb, Ill	260
Courtney, Grimes, Tex	55
Coushatta Chute, Natchitoches, La	12
Cove, Polk, Ark	12
Cove, Union, Oreg	39
Cove City, Whitfield, Ga	12
Cove Creek, Etowah, Ala	5
Cove Creek, Tazewell, Va	12
Cove Creek, Wayne, W. Va	12
Cove Dale, Hamilton, Ohio	20
Coveland, (*c. h.,*) Island, Wash	12
Covell, McLean, Ill	12
Covelo, Mendocino, Cal	12
Coventry, Tolland, Conn	130
Coventry, Chenango, N. Y	180
Coventry, Kent, R. I	180
Coventry, Orleans, Vt	210
Coventry Centre, Kent, R. I	55
Coventry Depot, Tolland, Conn	80
Coventryville, Chenango, N. Y	100
Cove Point, Calvert, Md	12
Covert, Van Buren, Mich	12
Covert, Seneca, N. Y	81
Cove Station, Huntingdon, Pa	66
Coveton, Barbour, W. Va	6
Coveville, Saratoga, N. Y	17
Covington, (*c. h.,*) Newton, Ga	720
*Covington,** (*c. h.,*) Fountain, Ind	780
*Covington,** (*c. h.,*) Kenton, Ky	3,300
Covington, (*c. h.,*) St. Tammany, La	110
Covington, Dakota, Nebr	12
Covington, Wyoming, N. Y	29
Covington, Richmond, N. C	9

* Money-order office.

Post office	Amount
Covington, Miami, Ohio	$380
Covington, Tioga, Pa	260
Covington,* (*c. h.*,) Tipton, Tenn	210
Covington, Hill, Tex	10
Covington, (*c. h.*,) Alleghany, Va	360
Covode, Indiana, Pa	59
Cowan, Delaware, Ind	12
Cowan, Union, Pa	30
Cowan, Franklin, Tenn	140
Cowanesque Valley, Tioga, Pa	33
Cowan's Ford, Mecklenburgh, N. C	12
Cowansville, Armstrong, Pa	50
Cowikee, Barbour, Ala	14
Cowle's Station, Macon, Ala	12
Cowlesville, Wyoming, N. Y	110
Cowlitz, Lewis, Wash	35
Cowpasture Bridge, Alleghany, Va	12
Cow Run, Washington, Ohio	12
Cow Skin, Douglas, Mo	4
Coxsackie, Greene, N. Y	1,100
Cox's Creek, Clayton, Iowa	48
Cox's Creek, Nelson, Ky	12
Cox's Mills, Wayne, Ind	8
Cox's Mills, Gilmer, W. Va	13
Coyleville, Butler, Pa	47
Coytee, Blount, Tenn	12
Coyville, Wilson, Kans	72
Crab Orchard, Williamson, Ill	59
Crab Orchard, Lincoln, Ky	400
Crab Orchard, Ray, Mo	45
Crab Orchard, Johnson, Nebr	23
Crab Tree, Haywood, N. C	8
Crab Tree, Westmoreland, Pa	31
Cracow, Huron, Mich	12
Craftsbury, Orleans, Vt	94
Craggie Hope, Cheatham, Tenn	12
Craig, Switzerland, Ind	14
Craig, Holt, Mo	36
Craighead, Mecklenburgh, N. C	12
Craig's Mills, Washington, Va	10
Craigsville, Orange, N. Y	28
Craigsville, Gaston, N. C	5
Craigsville, Armstrong, Pa	12
Craigsville, Lancaster, S. C	8
Craigsville, Augusta, Va	94
Crain's Creek, Moore, N. C	24
Cram's Corner, Carroll, N. H	18
Cranberry, Allen, Ohio	12
Cranberry, Venango, Pa	89
Cranberry Creek, Fulton, N. Y	26
Cranberry Forge, Mitchell, N. C	6
Cranberry Isles, Hancock, Me	51
Cranberry Plains, Carroll, Va	38
Cranberry Prairie, Mercer, Ohio	11
Cranbury, Middlesex, N. J	410
Crandall, Lorain, Ohio	28
Crandell's Corners, Washington, N. Y	43
Cranesville, Montgomery, N. Y	38
Cranesville, Preston, W. Va	2
Crantord, Union, N. J	140
Cranston Print Works, Providence, R. I	250
Crapo, Osceola, Mich	12
Crary's Mills, St. Lawrence, N. Y	110
Crawford, Russell, Ala	63

Post office	Amount
Crawford, Oglethorpe, Ga	$150
Crawford, Gallatin, Ill	6
Crawford, Crawford, Iowa	12
Crawford, Washington, Me	9
Crawford, Isabella, Mich	10
Crawford House, Coos, N. H	12
Crawford's Fork, Cass, Mo	33
Crawfordsville, Crittenden, Ark	12
Crawfordsville,* (*c. h.*,) Montgomery, Ind	2,000
Crawfordsville, Washington, Iowa	160
Crawfordsville, Crawford, Kans	240
Crawfordsville, Linn, Oreg	12
Crawfordville, (*c. h.*,) Wakulla, Fla	33
Crawfordville, (*c. h.*,) Taliaferro, Ga	250
Crawfordville, Lowndes, Miss	370
Creagerstown, Frederick, Md	35
Cream Ridge, Livingston, Mo	12
Creek Agency, Creek Nation, Ind. T	14
Creek Centre, Warren, N. Y	58
Creek Locks, Ulster, N. Y	75
Creekside, Indiana, Pa	12
Creelsborough, Russell, Ky	34
Creighton, Guernsey, Ohio	19
Cremona, Neosho, Kans	12
Crescent, Saratoga, N. Y	150
Crescent City, (*c. h.*,) Del Norte, Cal	200
Crescent City, Iroquois, Ill	65
Crescent City, Pottawattamie, Iowa	28
Crescent Hill, Bates, Mo	160
Crescent Mills, Plumas, Cal	12
Cresco,* Howard, Iowa	1,100
Cresskill, Bergen, N. J	59
Cresson, Cambria, Pa	360
Cressona, Schuylkill, Pa	330
Crestline,* Crawford, Ohio	1,300
Creston,* Ogle, Ill	610
Creston, Union, Iowa	12
Creswell, St. Clair, Ill	12
Creswell, Jefferson, Ind	12
Creswell, Keokuk, Iowa	12
Creswell, Labette, Kans	12
Creswell, Antrim, Mich	12
Creswell, Cortland, N. Y	12
Creswell, Jefferson, Ohio	12
Creswell, Lancaster, Pa	29
Creswell, Houston, Tex	12
Crete, Will, Ill	210
Crete, Saline, Nebr	12
Crete, Indiana, Pa	10
Creve Coeur, St. Louis, Mo	16
Cribb's, Westmoreland, Pa	12
Cridersville, Auglaize, Ohio	66
Crigler's Mills, Ralls, Mo	12
Criglersville, Madison, Va	27
Crisfield, Somerset, Md	120
Crisp's Cross Roads, Harrison, Ind	8
Crittenden, Franklin, Ill	16
Crittenden, Cass, Ind	7
Crittenden, Grant, Ky	120
Crittenden, Daviess, Mo	12
Crittenden, Erie, N. Y	82
Crittenden Springs, Crittenden, Ky	6
Crockett, (*c. h.*,) Houston, Tex	340
Crockett's Bluff, Arkansas, Ark	21
Croftsville, Tazewell, Va	12

* Money-order office.

Office	Compensation
Croghan, Lewis, N. Y	$66
Cromwell, Middlesex, Conn	650
Cromwell, Noble, Ind	13
Cromwell, Union, Iowa	32
Cromwell, Ohio, Ky	44
Crook, Boone, W. Va	88
Crooked Creek, Steuben, Ind	72
Crooked Creek, Stokes, N. C	10
Crooked Creek, Tioga, Pa	57
Crooked Fork, Morgan, Tenn	8
Crooked Hill, Montgomery, Pa	14
Crooked Tree, Noble, Ohio	16
Crooksville, Perry, Ohio	17
Croom, Prince George's, Md	63
Cropper's Depot, Shelby, Ky	12
Cropsey, Gage, Nebr	12
Cropseyville, Rensselaer, N. Y	40
Cropwell, St. Clair, Ala	24
Crosbyville, Chester, S. C	5
Cross, Ringgold, Iowa	20
Cross, Lyon, Kans	12
Cross Anchor, Spartanburgh, S. C	27
Cross Anchor, Greene, Tenn	12
Cross Creek Village, Washington, Pa	110
Cross Cut, Lawrence, Pa	90
Cross Fork, Clinton, Pa	16
Cross Hill, Kennebec, Me	44
Cross Hollow, Benton, Ark	12
Crossing, La Porte, Ind	190
Crossingville, Crawford, Pa	66
Cross Keys, De Kalb, Ga	56
Cross Keys, Camden, N. J	22
Cross Keys, Union, S. C	33
Cross Keys, Rockingham, Va	43
Cross Kill Mills, Berks, Pa	46
Crossland, Callaway, Ky	12
Cross Plains, Calhoun, Ala	12
Cross Plains, Ripley, Ind	18
Cross Plains, Metcalfe, Ky	12
Cross Plains, Robertson, Tenn	100
Cross Plains, Dane, Wis	190
Cross River, Westchester, N. Y	72
Cross Roads, Charles, Md	15
Cross Roads, Madison, Ohio	110
Cross Roads, York, Pa	40
Cross Timbers, Hickory, Mo	12
Cross Timbers, Ellis, Tex	12
Crossville, De Kalb, Ala	12
Crossville, Gates, N. C	12
Crossville, (*c. h.*,) Cumberland, Tenn	130
Crosswicks, Burlington, N. J	230
Crothersville, Jackson, Ind	220
Croton, Lee, Iowa	69
Croton,* Newaygo, Mich	180
Croton, Hunterdon, N. J	6
Croton, Delaware, N. Y	120
Croton, Licking, Ohio	150
Croton Falls, Westchester, N. Y	400
Croton Landing, Westchester, N. Y	260
Crouse's Store, Dutchess, N. Y	12
Crow Creek, ———, Dak	12
Crowder's Mountain, Gaston, N. C	7
Crowley, Greene, Ark	12
Crown City, Gallia, Ohio	12
Crown Point,* (*c. h.*,) Lake, Ind	580
Crown Point, Essex, N. Y	$170
Crown Point Centre, Essex, N. Y	210
Crownsville, Anne Arundel, Md	63
Crow River, Meeker, Minn	14
Crow's Landing, Stanislaus, Cal	12
Crow's Mills, Greene, Pa	6
Crowville, Warrick, Ind	12
Crow Wing, (*c. h.*,) Crow Wing, Minn	100
Croxton, Jefferson, Ohio	10
Croyden, Sullivan, N. H	83
Croyden, Morgan, Utah	75
Croyden Flat, Sullivan, N. H	23
Cruger, Woodford, Ill	76
Crum Creek, Fulton, N. Y	25
Crum Elbow, Dutchess, N. Y	22
Crumley's, Henry, Ga	12
Crumpton, Queen Anne, Md	140
Cruso, Seneca, N. Y	10
Crystal, Tama, Iowa	57
Crystal, Montcalm, Mich	64
Crystal Hill, Montgomery, Ark	8
Crystal Lake, McHenry, Ill	250
Crystal Lake, Hancock, Iowa	12
Crystal Lake, Waupaca, Wis	25
Crystal Spring, Yates, N. Y	75
Crystal Springs,* Copiah, Miss	480
Cuba, Fulton, Ill	160
Cuba, Owen, Ind	15
Cuba, Republic, Kans	12
Cuba, Crawford, Mo	200
Cuba,* Allegany, N. Y	1,300
Cuba, Rutherford, N. C	12
Cuba, Clinton, Ohio	34
Cuba, Ouachita, La	12
Cuba, Shelby, Tenn	13
Cuba Landing, Humphreys, Tenn	12
Cuba Station, Sumter, Ala	50
Cub Creek, Jefferson, Nebr	12
Cub Hill, Baltimore, Md	21
Cub Prairie, Jefferson, Ill	12
Cucamonga, San Bernardino, Cal	12
Cuckoo, Louisa, Va	43
Cuddebackville, Orange, N. Y	73
Cuffey's Cove, Mendocino, Cal	12
Cuivre, Lincoln, Mo	8
Culdrum, Morrison, Minn	17
Cullen, Herkimer, N. Y	35
Culleoka, Maury, Tenn	190
Culloden, Monroe, Ga	63
Culpeper,* (*c. h.*) Culpeper, Va	1,100
Culver's Station, Tippecanoe, Ind	83
Culverton, Hancock, Ga	140
Cumberland, Marion, Ind	97
Cumberland, Cumberland, Me	160
Cumberland,* (*c. h.*) Alleghany, Md	2,200
Cumberland, Choctaw, Miss	12
Cumberland, Guernsey, Ohio	220
Cumberland C. H., Cumberland, Va	17
Cumberland Centre, Cumberland, Me	89
Cumberland City, Clinton, Ky	28
Cumberland City, Stewart, Tenn	51
Cumberland Furnace, Dixon, Tenn	20
Cumberland Gap, Claiborne, Tenn	50
Cumberland Hill, Providence, R. I	52

* Money-order office.

Cumberland Iron Works, Stewart, Tenn	$16
Cumberland Valley, Bedford, Pa	46
Cuming City, Washington, Nebr	200
Cumming, (c. h.) Forsyth, Ga	160
Cummingsville, Goliad, Tex	12
Cummington, Hampshire, Mass	220
Cummington West Village, Hampshire, Mass	150
Cummin's Creek, Ellis, Tex	11
Cumminsville, Hamilton, Ohio	350
Cumru, Berks, Pa	7
Cunningham, Clarion, Pa	220
Cunningham's Mills, Ritchie, W. Va	2
Cunningham's Station, Floyd, Ga	12
Cunningham's Store, Person, N. C	12
Cupola, Chester, Pa	12
Curdsville, Daviess, Ky	29
Curdsville, Buckingham, Va	75
Curllsville, Clarion, Pa	150
Curl's Wharf, Henrico, Va	12
Curran, Sangamon, Ill	62
Currant Creek, Fremont, Colo	12
Curriersville, Moore, N. C	5
Currie's Store, Caddo, La	12
Currituck C. H., Currituck, N. C	29
Currohee, Habersham, Ga	12
Curry's Run, Harrison, Ky	22
Curryville, Pike, Mo	12
Curtin, Dauphin, Pa	32
Curtis' Corner, Androscoggin, Me	44
Curtis' Mills, Alamance, N. C	6
Curtisville, Tipton, Ind	46
Curtisville, Berkshire, Mass	78
Curveton, Cass, Ind	34
Curwinsville, Clearfield, Pa	430
Cush, Clearfield, Pa	6
Cushing, Tuscaloosa, Ala	12
Cushing, Knox, Me	29
Cushing, Polk, Wis	12
Cusseta, Chambers, Ala	130
Cusseta, (c. h.) Chattahoochee, Ga	96
Custar, Wood, Ohio	160
Custard's, Crawford, Pa	26
Cutchogue, Suffolk, N. Y	280
Cuthand, Red River, Tex	8
Cuthbert, (c. h.)* Randolph, Ga	660
Cutler, Washington, Me	98
Cutler, Washington, Ohio	46
Cuttingsville, Clackamas, Oreg	12
Cuttingsville, Rutland, Vt	160
Cut Off, Drew, Ark	42
Cuyahoga Falls, Summit, Ohio	970
Cuyler, Cortland, N. Y	81
Cuylerville, Livingston, N. Y	79
Cylon, St. Croix, Wis	120
Cynthiana, Posey, Ind	79
Cynthiana, (c. h.,)* Harrison, Ky	1,100
Cynthiana, Pike, Ohio	42
Cypre-mort, St. Mary's, La	12
Cypress, Monroe, Ark	20
Cypress, Perry, Tenn	10
Cypress, Kenosha, Wis	20
Cypress Creek, Desha, Ark	16
Cypress Creek, Johnson, Ill	7
Cypress Top, Harris, Tex	15
Cyruston, Lincoln, Tenn	11

D.

Dacada, Sheboygan, Wis	$47
Dacusville, Pickens, S. C	10
Dadeville, (c. h.,) Tallapoosa, Ala	290
Dadeville, Dade, Mo	75
Dagger's Springs, Botetourt, Va	12
Daggett's Mills, Tioga, Pa	26
Dagsborough, Sussex, Del	46
Dahlonega, (c. h.,) Lumpkin, Ga	170
Dahlonega, Wapello, Iowa	53
Daileyville, Karnes, Tex	12
Daingerfield, Titus, Tex	190
Dairy, Washington, Iowa	7
Dairyland, Ulster, N. Y	12
Dakota, Stephenson, Ill	120
Dakota, (c. h.,)* Dakota, Nebr	320
Dakota, Waushara, Wis	41
Dakotah, (c. h.,) Humboldt, Iowa	180
Dalby, Allamakee, Iowa	44
Dale, Spencer, Ind	83
Dale, Campbell, Ky	19
Dale, Wyoming, N. Y	28
Dale, Berks, Pa	31
Dale City, Guthrie, Iowa	85
Daleville, Dale, Ala	10
Daleville, Delaware, Ind	82
Daleville, Lauderdale, Miss	46
Daleville, Luzerne, Pa	53
Dalhoff, St. Charles, Mo	20
Dallam's Creek, Logan, Ky	4
Dallas, (c. h.,) Polk, Ark	39
Dallas, (c. h.,) Paulding, Ga	84
Dallas, Marion, Iowa	19
Dallas, Pulaski, Ky	18
Dallas, Clinton, Mich	100
Dallas, Webster, Mo	23
Dallas, (c. h.,) Gaston, N. C	89
Dallas, Highland, Ohio	58
Dallas, (c. h.,)* Polk, Oreg	180
Dallas, Luzerne, Pa	63
Dallas, Hamilton, Tenn	12
Dallas, (c. h.,)* Dallas, Tex	700
Dallas, Marshall, W. Va	93
Dallasburgh, Warren, Ohio	110
Dallas Centre, Dallas, Iowa	12
Dallas City,* Hancock, Ill	380
Dallastown, York, Pa	49
Dallies, Surry, Va	58
Dalmanutha, Guthrie, Iowa	42
Dalmatia, Northumberland, Pa	95
Dalson, Clark, Ill	18
Dalton, (c. h.,)* Whitfield, Ga	1,100
Dalton, Wayne, Ind	39
Dalton, Berkshire, Mass	360
Dalton, Chariton, Mo	12
Dalton, Coos, N. H	83
Dalton, Bladen, N. C	16
Dalton,* Wayne, Ohio	270
Dalton's Corners, Wayne, Mich	12
Damariscotta Mills, Lincoln, Me	84
Damascoville, Columbiana, Ohio	130
Damascus, Stephenson, Ill	17
Damascus, Montgomery, Md	20
Damascus, Scott, Miss	17
Damascus, Clackamas, Oreg	12
Damascus, Wayne, Pa	130

* Money-order office.

Dames' Quarter, Somerset, Md	$14
Damiansville, Clinton, Ill	16
Dana, Worcester, Mass	110
Danborough, Bucks, Pa	50
Danburgh, Wilkes, Ga	22
Danbury,* (*c. h.*,) Fairfield, Conn	2,600
Danbury, Grafton, N. H	150
Danbury, (*c. h.*,) Stokes, N. C	10
Danby, Du Page, Ill	130
Danby, Ionia, Mich	20
Danby, Tompkins, N. Y	170
Danby, Rutland, Vt	260
Danby Four Corners, Rutland, Vt	70
Dancyville, Haywood, Tenn	160
Dandridge,* (*c. h.*,) Jefferson, Tenn	240
Dane, Dane, Wis	48
Danforth, Johnson, Iowa	23
Danforth Station, Iroquois, Ill	120
Daniel's Landing, Bladen, N. C	12
Danielsville, (*c. h.*,) Madison, Ga	120
Danielsville, Northampton, Pa	91
Danielsville, Dickson, Tenn	12
Dannemora, Clinton, N. Y	310
Dansville, Ingham, Mich	320
Dansville,* Livingston, N. Y	2,200
Danube, Herkimer, N. Y	12
Danvers, McLean, Ill	220
Danvers, Essex, Mass	1,000
Danvers Centre, Essex, Mass	210
Danversport, Essex, Mass	230
Danville, Morgan, Ala	80
Danville, (*c. h.*,) Yell, Ark	87
Danville, Contra Costa, Cal	110
Danville,* (*c. h.*,) Vermilion, Ill	2,000
Danville,* (*c. h.*,) Hendricks, Ind	660
Danville, Des Moines, Iowa	210
Danville,* (*c. h.*,) Boyle, Ky	2,000
Danville, Androscoggin, Me	140
Danville, Alcorn, Miss	11
Danville, (*c. h.*,) Montgomery, Mo	240
Danville, Rockingham, N. H	36
Danville, Warren, N. J	36
Danville, Knox, Ohio	72
Danville,* (*c. h.*,) Montour, Pa	2,400
Danville, Benton, Tenn	120
Danville, Montgomery, Tex	36
Danville, Caledonia, Vt	290
Danville,* Pittsylvania, Va	1,600
Danville, Dodge, Wis	94
Darby, Delaware, Pa	310
Darby Creek, Madison, Ohio	200
Darbyville, Pickaway, Ohio	67
Darcey's Store, Montgomery, Md	46
Dardanelle,* Yell, Ark	800
Daretown, Salem, N. J	160
Darien, Fairfield, Conn	140
Darien, (*c. h.*,) MacIntosh, Ga	430
Darien, Clark, Ill	22
Darien, Kossuth, Iowa	12
Darien, Genesee, N. Y	88
Darien, Walworth, Wis	280
Darien Centre, Genesee, N. Y	110
Darien Depot, Fairfield, Conn	320
Dark Corner, Campbell, Ga	10
Darke, Darke, Ohio	14
Darkesville, Berkeley, W. Va	56
Darksville, Randolph, Mo	$24
Darlington, Montgomery, Ind	130
Darlington, St. Helena, La	20
Darlington, Harford, Md	250
Darlington, Richland, Ohio	31
Darlington, Beaver, Pa	160
Darlington,* (*c. h.*,) La Fayette, Wis	1,200
Darlington C. H.,* Darlington, S. C	650
Darlington Heights, Prince Edward, Va	3
Darnestown, Montgomery, Md	120
Darnstadt, St. Clair, Ill	54
Darrtown, Butler, Ohio	120
Dartford, (*c. h.*,) Green Lake, Wis	230
Dartmouth, Bristol, Mass	120
Darwin, Clark, Ill	29
Darwin, Meeker, Minn	10
Darysaw, Jefferson, Ark	12
Dassel, Meeker, Minn	12
Dauphin, Dauphin, Pa	260
Dauphine, Osage, Mo	80
Davenport,* (*c. h.*,) Scott, Iowa	4,000
Davenport, Delaware, N. Y	120
Davenport Centre, Delaware, N. Y	110
Davidsburgh, York, Pa	12
Davidson, Montgomery, Ohio	12
Davidson, Sullivan, Pa	8
Davidson College, Mecklenburgh, N. C	70
Davidson's Ferry, Fayette, Pa	37
Davidson's River, Transylvania, N. C	26
Davidsonville, Anne Arundel, Md	180
Davidsville, Somerset, Pa	53
Davis,* Stephenson, Ill	370
Davisborough, Washington, Ga	160
Davisburgh, Oakland, Mich	210
Davis City, Decatur, Iowa	12
Davis Corners, Adams, Wis	25
Davis Mill, Alleghany, Md	12
Davis' Mills, Bedford, Va	21
Davison, Genesee, Mich	47
Davistown, Greene, Pa	21
Davisville, Yolo, Cal	310
Davisville, Sanilac, Mich	100
Davisville, Bucks, Pa	85
Davisville, Washington, R. I	78
Davisville, Wood, W. Va	35
Dawkin's Mills, Jackson, Ohio	18
Dawn, Livingston, Mo	250
Dawn, Darke, Ohio	65
Dawson, (*c. h.*,) Terrell, Ga	650
Dawson, Sangamon, Ill	67
Dawson's Mill, Richardson, Nebr	49
Dawson's Station, Fayette, Pa	100
Dawsonville, (*c. h.*,) Dawson, Ga	84
Dawsonville, Montgomery, Md	59
Dawsonville, Greene, Va	21
Day, Saratoga, N. Y	35
Day Book, Yancey, N. C	5
Day's Store, Greene, Pa	33
Daysville, Ogle, Ill	50
Daysville, Todd, Ky	25
Daysville, Oswego, N. Y	49
Daysville, Loudoun, Va	12
Dayton, Marengo, Ala	170

* Money-order office.

Post office	Salary
Dayton, La Salle, Ill	$75
Dayton, Tippecanoe, Ind	140
Dayton, Bourbon, Kans	21
Dayton, Campbell, Ky	12
Dayton, York, Me	12
Dayton, Howard, Md	6
Dayton, Berrien, Mich	150
Dayton, Hennepin, Minn	81
Dayton, Cass, Mo	12
Dayton, (*c. h.*,) Lyon, Nev	300
Dayton, Middlesex, N. J	78
Dayton, Cattaraugus, N. Y	45
Dayton, Wake, N. C	7
Dayton,* (*c. h.*,) Montgomery, Ohio	4,000
Dayton, Yam Hill, Oreg	160
Dayton, Armstrong, Pa	170
Dayton, Rockingham, Va	41
Dayton, Green, Wis	97
Dayton City, De Kalb, Mo	12
Daytonville, Labette, Kans	12
Dayville, Grant, Oreg	7
Dead River, Somerset, Me	37
Deakyneville, New Castle, Del	37
Deal, Monmouth, N. J	66
Deal's Island, Somerset, Md	67
Dean Lake, Wright, Minn	4
Dean's Corners, Lake, Ill	35
Dean's Corners, Saratoga, N. Y	41
Deansville, Oneida, N. Y	130
Deansville, Dane, Wis	51
Dearbornville, Wayne, Mich	240
Deardorff's Mills, Tuscarawas, Ohio	7
Deatonsville, Amelia, Va	38
Deatsville, Nelson, Ky	44
Deavertown, Morgan, Ohio	80
Debello, Vernon, Wis	9
Deblois, Washington, Me	7
De Bruce, Sullivan, N. Y	15
Decapolis, Madison, Va	12
Decatur,* Morgan, Ala	740
Decatur, (*c. h.*,) De Kalb, Ga	130
Decatur,* (*c. h.*,) Macon, Ill	3,000
Decatur,* (*c. h.*,) Adams, Ind	360
Decatur, Decatur, Iowa	120
Decatur, Van Buren, Mich	1,100
Decatur, Newton, Miss	12
Decatur,* Burt, Nebr	300
Decatur, Otsego, N. Y	25
Decatur, Brown, Ohio	100
Decatur, Mifflin, Pa	10
Decatur, (*c. h.*,) Meigs, Tenn	87
Decatur, (*c. h.*,) Wise, Tex	71
Decaturville, Camden, Mo	11
Decaturville, Washington, Ohio	8
Decaturville, Decatur, Tenn	80
Decherd, Franklin, Tenn	290
Deckard, Crawford, Pa	24
Decker's Point, Indiana, Pa	34
Decker's Station, Knox, Ind	47
Deckertown, Sussex, N. J	460
Deckerville, Sanilac, Mich	8
Decorah,* (*c. h.*,) Winneshiek, Iowa	1,800
Decoria, Blue Earth, Minn	3
Decosta, Atlantic, N. J	36
Dedham, Hancock, Me	74
Dedham,* (*c. h.*,) Norfolk, Mass	1,400

Post office	Salary
Deedsville, Miami, Ind	$12
Deem, Owen, Ind	18
Deep Creek, Clay, Kans	12
Deep Creek, Anson, N. C	12
Deep Creek, Chesterfield, S. C	12
Deep Creek, Norfolk, Va	43
Deep Cut, McHenry, Ill	25
Deep Cut, Auglaize, Ohio	39
Deep Ford, Dent, Mo	11
Deep River, Middlesex, Conn	650
Deep River, Lake, Ind	30
Deep River, Poweshiek, Iowa	160
Deep River, Guilford, N. C	13
Deer Creek, Tazewell, Ill	42
Deer Creek, Carroll, Ind	32
Deer Creek, Carter, Ky	12
Deer Creek, Livingston, Mich	16
Deer Creek, Pickaway, Ohio	8
Deerfield, Lake, Ill	41
Deerfield, Randolph, Ind	12
Deerfield, Chickasaw, Iowa	21
Deerfield, Franklin, Mass	380
Deerfield, Lenawee, Mich	180
Deerfield, Steele, Minn	12
Deerfield, Vernon, Mo	12
Deerfield, Rockingham, N. H	90
Deerfield, Oneida, N. Y	81
Deerfield, Portage, Ohio	130
Deerfield, Augusta, Va	31
Deerfield, Dane, Wis	55
Deerfield Centre, Rockingham, N. H	140
Deerfield Prairie, De Kalb, Ill	19
Deerfield Street, Cumberland, N. J	62
Deerfield Village, Warren, Ohio	93
Deering, Hillsborough, N. H	37
Deer Isle, Hancock, Me	190
Deer Lick, Williams, Ohio	37
Deer Lick, Mason, W. Va	5
Deer Lodge City,* (*c. h.*,) Deer Lodge, Mont	460
Deer Park, Washington, Ala	27
Deer Park, La Salle, Ill	52
Deer Park, Alleghany, Md	150
Deer Park, Suffolk, N. Y	150
Deer Plain, Calhoun, Ill	30
Deer Ridge, Lewis, Mo	43
Deer River, Lewis, N. Y	77
Deersville, Harrison, Ohio	120
Deer Valley, Park, Colo	12
Deer Walk, Wood, W. Va	12
Defiance,* (*c. h.*,) Defiance, Ohio	1,300
Defreestville, Rensselaer, N. Y	12
De Golier, McKean, Pa	29
De Graff, Logan, Ohio	360
Deisher's Mill, Botetourt, Va	5
De Kalb, (*c. h.*,) Kemper, Miss	48
De Kalb, Buchanan, Mo	82
De Kalb, St. Lawrence, N. Y	80
De Kalb, Crawford, Ohio	20
De Kalb, Bowie, Tex	17
De Kalb Centre,* De Kalb, Ill	940
De Kalb Junction, St. Lawrence, N. Y	150
Dekorra, Columbia, Wis	24
Delafield, Waukesha, Wis	200
Delanco, Burlington, N. J	83

* Money-order office.

Delano, Wright, Minn	$12
Delano, Schuylkill, Pa	110
Delanti, Hardin, Iowa	85
De La Palma, Brown, Ohio	12
De Lassus, St. Francois, Mo	12
Delavan,* Tazewell, Ill	930
Delavan,* Walworth, Wis	1,200
Delaware, Yell, Ark	12
Delaware, Ripley, Ind	24
Delaware, Delaware, Iowa	150
Delaware,* (*c. h.*,) Delaware, Ohio	2,700
Delaware, Pike, Pa	20
Delaware City, Summit, Colo	22
Delaware City,* New Castle, Del	610
Delaware City, Leavenworth, Kans	17
Delaware Grove, Mercer, Pa	64
Delaware Station, Warren, N. J	140
Delaware Water Gap, Monroe, Pa	300
Delhi, Jersey, Ill	100
Delhi, (*c. h.*,) Delaware, Iowa	150
Delhi, Richland, La	44
Delhi,* (*c. h.*,) Delaware, N. Y	1,200
Delhi, Hamilton, Ohio	57
Delight, Greene, Pa	12
De Lisle, Darke, Ohio	28
Dell Delight, Benton, Mo	7
Dellona, Sauk, Wis	36
Dell Prairie, Adams, Wis	19
Dellville, Perry, Pa	15
Delmar, Sussex, Del	25
Delmont, Anderson, Kans	12
De Loche's Landing, Natchitoches, La	12
Delphi,* (*c. h.*,) Carroll, Ind	1,300
Delphi, Onondaga, N. Y	95
Delphos, Ottawa, Kans	20
Delphos,* Van Wert, Ohio	740
Delpsburgh, Northampton, Pa	120
Del Rey, Iroquois, Ill	52
Delroy, Wayne, Mich	12
Delta, Randolph, Ala	3
Delta, McLean, Ill	22
Delta, Parke, Ind	5
Delta, (*c. h.*,) Madison, La	72
Delta, Eaton, Mich	26
Delta, Oneida, N. Y	110
Delta,* Fulton, Ohio	450
Delta, York, Pa	52
Delta Mills, Walla Walla, Wash	90
Delton, Sauk, Wis	150
Deming, Hamilton, Ind	44
Democracy, Knox, Ohio	53
Democrat, Walker, Ala	6
Democrat, Buncombe, N. C	12
Demopolis,* (*c. h.*,) Marengo, Ala	1,200
Demos, Belmont, Ohio	38
De Mossville, Pendleton, Ky	87
Dempseytown, Venango, Pa	82
Denison, (*c. h.*,) Crawford, Iowa	440
Denison, Herkimer, N. Y	21
Denmark, Perry, Ill	32
Denmark,* Lee, Iowa	360
Denmark, Oxford, Me	140
Denmark, Tuscola, Mich	17
Denmark, Lewis, N. Y	60
Denmark, Ashtabula, Ohio	14
Denmark, Madison, Tenn	$130
Denmark, Brown, Wis	75
Dennard's Bluff, Monroe, Ala	12
Denning, Ulster, N. Y	7
Denning's, Carroll, Md	12
Dennis, Appanoose, Iowa	12
Dennis, Barnstable, Mass	170
Dennison, Clark, Ill	12
Dennison, Ottawa, Mich	39
Dennison, Tuscarawas, Ohio	12
Dennis Port, Barnstable, Mass	300
Dennisville, Cape May, N. J	170
Denny, Warren, Ill	20
Dennysville, Washington, Me	190
Dent, Hamilton, Ohio	53
Dent, Greene, Pa	5
Denton,* (*c. h.*,) Caroline, Md	260
Denton, Wayne, Mich	96
Denton, (*c. h.*,) Denton, Tex	130
Dent's Run, Elk, Pa	180
DENVER,* (*c. h.*,) Arapahoe, Colo	4,000
Denver, Hancock, Ill	110
Denver, Miami, Ind	28
Denver, Bremer, Iowa	51
Denver, Newaygo, Mich	37
Denverton, Solano, Cal	50
Denville, Morris, N. J	110
Depauville, Jefferson, N. Y	110
De Pere,* Brown, Wis	770
De Peyster, St. Lawrence, N. Y	61
Deposit, Jefferson, Ky	17
Deposit,* Broome, N. Y	970
De Pue, Bureau, Ill	36
Deputy, Jefferson, Ind	12
Derby,* New Haven, Conn	2,500
Derby, Perry, Ind	45
Derby, Orleans, Vt	330
Derby Line,* Orleans, Vt	870
Derinda, Jo Daviess, Ill	48
De Roche, Clark, Ark	5
Derry, Rockingham, N. H	380
Derry Church, Dauphin, Pa	35
Derry Depot, Rockingham, N. H	170
Derry Station Westmoreland, Pa	74
De Ruyter, Madison, N. Y	510
Des Arc, Prairie, Ark	280
Deschutes, Wasco, Oreg	12
Deselm, Kankakee, Ill	15
Deseret, Millard, Utah	6
DES MOINES,* (*c. h.*,) Polk, Iowa	4,000
De Soto, Jackson, Ill	240
De Soto,* Dallas, Iowa	350
De Soto, Johnson, Kansas	150
De Soto, Clark, Miss	180
De Soto, Jefferson, Mo	220
De Soto, Washington, Nebr	50
De Soto, Vernon, Wis	220
De Soto Front, De Soto, Miss	12
Desotoville, Choctaw, Ala	58
Des Peres, St. Louis, Mo	25
Des Plaines, Cook, Ill	110
Detour, Chippewa, Mich	12
Detroit, Sanford, Ala	10
Detroit, Pike, Ill	78
Detroit, Dickinson, Kans	240
Detroit, Somerset, Me	130

* Money-order office.

Detroit,* (*c. h.*,) Wayne, Mich	$4,000
Devall's Bluff,* (*c. h.*,) Prairie, Ark	460
De View, Woodruff, Ark	47
Dewart, Northumberland, Pa	140
De Witt, (*c. h.*,) Arkansas, Ark	120
De Witt, De Witt, Ill	80
De Witt,* (*c. h.*,) Clinton, Iowa	1,300
De Witt, Clinton, Mich	340
De Witt, Carroll, Mo	250
De Witt, Cuming, Nebr	19
De Witt, Onondaga, N. Y	57
De Wittville, Chautauqua, N. Y	87
Dexter, Perry, Ind	12
Dexter,* Dallas, Iowa	310
Dexter, Cowley, Kans	12
Dexter,* Penobscot, Me	1,100
Dexter, Washtenaw, Mich	810
Dexter, Jefferson, N. Y	210
Dexter, Meigs, Ohio	5
D'Hanis, Medina, Tex	6
Dialton, Clark, Ohio	28
Diamond, Venango, Pa	12
Diamond Bluff, Pierce, Wis	59
Diamond City, (*c. h.*,) Meagher, Mont	350
Diamond Cross, Randolph, Ill	12
Diamond Grove, Jasper, Mo	12
Diamond Hill, Anson, N. C	12
Diamond Hill, Providence, R. I	72
Diamond Lake, Lake, Ill	76
Diamond Mountain, White Pine, Nev	12
Diamond Spring, El Dorado, Cal	93
Diamond Springs, Morris, Kans	19
Diana, Lewis, N. Y	16
Diana Mills, Buckingham, Va	12
Dias Creek, Cape May, N. J	39
Dickensonville, Russell, Va	8
Dickersonville, Niagara, N. Y	14
Dickeysville, Grant, Wis	19
Dickeyville, Arostook, Me	12
Dickinson, Franklin, N. J	14
Dickinson, Cumberland, Pa	120
Dickinson, Centre, Franklin, N. Y	94
Dickinson's, Franklin, Va	8
Dickson, Colbert, Ala	90
Dickson, Dickson, Tenn	150
Dicksonburgh, Crawford, Pa	52
Dido, Choctaw, Miss	8
Diehlstadt, Scott, Mo	12
Dificult, Smith, Tenn	16
Dighton, Bristol, Mass	290
Dille's Bottom, Belmont, Ohio	20
Dillingersville, Lehigh, Pa	18
Dillon, Tazewell, Ill	37
Dillon, Phelps, Mo	23
Dillon's Run, Hampshire, W. Va	3
Dillsborough, Dearborn, Ind	160
Dillsburgh, York, Pa	120
Dilworthtown, Chester, Pa	46
Dimock, Susquehanna, Pa	84
Dimon, Leavenworth, Kans	24
Dingman's Ferry, Pike, Pa	86
Dinsmore, Shelby, Ohio	30
Dinsmore, Washington, Pa	37
Dinwiddie C. H., Dinwiddie, Va	28
Diona, Coles, Ill	12
Dirigo, Kennebec, Me	$45
Dirt Town, Chattooga, Ga	45
Disco, Macomb, Mich	89
Dismal, Sampson, N. C	12
Disputanta, Prince George, Va	12
Ditney Hill, Dubois, Ind	10
Dittmer's Store, Jefferson, Mo	12
Dividing Creek, Cumberland, N. J	47
Dividing Ridge, Pendleton, Ky	12
Dividing Ridge, Somerset, Pa	4
Dix, Jefferson, Ill	37
Dixfield, Oxford, Me	230
Dixfield Centre, Oxford, Me	42
Dix Hills, Suffolk, N. Y	48
Dixmont, Penobscot, Me	89
Dixmont, Allegheny, Pa	180
Dixmont Centre, Penobscot, Me	24
Dixon, Solano, Cal	12
Dixon, Dawson, Ga	29
Dixon,* (*c. h.*,) Lee, Ill	2,600
Dixon, Scott, Iowa	39
Dixon, (*c. h.*,) Webster, Ky	89
Dixon, Pulaski, Mo	12
Dixon, Van Wert, Ohio	35
Dixon, Wyoming, Pa	15
Dixon's Springs, Smith, Tenn	68
Dixonville, Indiana, Pa	12
Doaksville, Choctaw N., Ind. T	14
Dobb's Ferry, Westchester, N. Y	420
Dobson, (*c. h.*,) Surry, N. C	30
Doctor Town, Wayne, Ga	37
Doddsville, Schuyler, Ill	40
Dodge, Guthrie, Iowa	7
Dodge Centre, Dodge, Minn	160
Dodge City, Steele, Minn	8
Dodge's Corners, Waukesha, Wis	31
Dodgeville, Des Moines, Iowa	99
Dodgeville,* (*c. h.*,) Iowa, Wis	770
Dodsonville, Jackson, Ala	11
Dodsonville, Highland, Ohio	23
Doe Run, Chester, Pa	93
Dog Creek, Putnam, Ohio	62
Doko, Fairfield, S. C	37
Dolington, Bucks, Pa	84
Dolingville, Jefferson, Pa	12
Dolten's Station, Cook, Ill	59
Dona Ana, Dona Ana, N. Mex	12
Donald, Washington, Kans	12
Donaldson, Schuylkill, Pa	77
Donaldsonville, (*c. h.*,) Ascension, La	510
Donally's Mills, Perry, Pa	45
Donation, Huntingdon, Pa	26
Doncaster, Charles, Md	22
Donegal, Westmoreland, Pa	49
Donelson, Davidson, Tenn	71
Donersville, Burnett, Wis	12
Dongola, Union, Ill	370
Doniphan, Doniphan, Kans	230
Doniphan, (*c. h.*,) Ripley, Mo	94
Don Juan, Perry, Ind	6
Donley, Washington, Pa	12
Donnaldsville, Abbeville, S. C	93
Donnellson, Montgomery, Ill	46
Donnelsville, Clark, Ohio	69
Doolittle's Mills, Perry, Ind	12
Door Creek, Dane, Wis	97

* Money-order office.

Post office	Compensation
Door Village, La Porte, Ind	$64
Dora, Pike, Ark	12
Dora, Wabash, Ind	47
Dora, Labette, Kans	12
Doran, Mitchell, Iowa	19
Doraville, Broome, N. Y	7
Dorcheat, Columbia, Ark	12
Dorchester, Macoupin, Ill	95
Dorchester, Allamakee, Iowa	100
Dorchester, Norfolk, Mass	250
Dorchester, Grafton, N. H	32
Dorlan's Mills, Chester, Pa	12
Dormansville, Albany, N. Y	19
Dornsife, Northumberland, Pa	12
Dorr, Allegan, Mich	12
Dorrance, Luzerne, Pa	18
Dorret's Run, Hardin, Ky	7
Dorrville, Washington, R. I	36
Dorset, De Kalb, Ill	32
Dorset, Ashtabula, Ohio	25
Dorset, Bennington, Vt	200
Dorset, Monroe, Wis	13
Dorsey, Madison, Ill	34
Dorseyville, Allegheny, Pa	11
Doty's Corner, Steuben, N. Y	11
Dotyville, Fond du Lac, Wis	57
Double Bridge, Lunenburgh, Va	2
Double Bridges, Lauderdale, Tenn	12
Double Horn, Burnet, Tex	32
Double Pipe Creek, Carroll, Md	45
Double Shoal, Cleveland, N. C	6
Double Springs, Benton, Ark	12
Double Springs, Oktibbeha, Miss	58
Double Wells, Warren, Ga	380
Doud Station, Van Buren, Iowa	110
Dougherty's Station, Alameda, Cal	45
Douglas, Coffee, Ga	12
Douglas, Knox, Ill	100
Douglas, Jackson, La	8
Douglas, Allegan, Mich	110
Douglas, Gentry, Mo	13
Douglas, Rockingham, N. C	12
Douglas Centre, Clay, Iowa	12
Douglas Centre, Marquette, Wis	27
Douglas City, Trinity, Cal	39
Douglass, Worcester, Mass	66
Douglass, Fayette, Iowa	82
Douglass, Butler, Kans	83
Douglass, Montgomery, Pa	16
Douglass, Nacogdoches, Tex	20
Douglassville, Berks, Pa	310
Douglassville, Davis, Tex	24
Dousman, Waukesha, Wis	28
Dover, (*c. h.*,) Pope, Ark	24
Dover, Merced, Cal	12
DOVER,* (*c. h.*,) Kent, Del	1,200
Dover, Bureau, Ill	310
Dover, Boone, Ind	31
Dover, Lee, Iowa	69
Dover, Shawnee, Kans	11
Dover, Mason, Ky	130
Dover, (*c. h.*,) Piscataquis, Me	330
Dover, Norfolk, Mass	72
Dover, La Fayette, Mo	250
Dover,* (*c. h.*,) Strafford, N. H	2,900
Dover,* Morris, N. J	1,300

Post office	Compensation
Dover, Dutchess, N. Y	$480
Dover, Craven, N. C	14
Dover, Cuyahoga, Ohio	68
Dover, York, Pa	57
Dover, (*c. h.*,) Stewart, Tenn	180
Dover, Windham, Vt	52
Dover, Iowa, Wis	13
Dover Centre, Olmsted, Minn	74
Dover Furnace, Dutchess, N. Y	14
Dover Hill, (*c. h.*,) Martin, Ind	110
Dover Mines, Goochland, Va	59
Dover South Mills, Piscataquis, Me	22
Dove's Creek, Elbert, Ga	6
Dove's Depot, Darlington, S. C	150
Dow, Cass, Ind	12
Dowagiac,* Cass, Mich	1,700
Dowdallville, Peoria, Ill	13
Dowd's Landing, Coahoma, Miss	12
Downer's Grove, Du Page, Ill	190
Downey, Cedar, Iowa	150
Downey's Spring, Randolph, Ark	12
Down Hill, Crawford, Ind	6
Downieville,* (*c. h.*,) Sierra, Cal	800
Downing's Mills, Strafford, N. H	92
Downingsville, Grant, Ky	18
Downington, Meigs, Ohio	46
Downingtown, Chester, Pa	800
Downsville, Union, La	13
Downsville, Washington, Md	23
Downsville, Delaware, N. Y	140
Downsville, Dunn, Wis	83
Doyle, Marion, Kans	7
Doylesburgh, Franklin, Pa	18
Doyle's Mills, Juniata, Pa	12
Doylesport, Barton, Mo	12
Doylestown,* (*c. h.*,) Bucks, Pa	1,400
Doylestown, Columbia, Wis	130
Dracut, Middlesex, Mass	49
Drady's, Wayne, Ga	20
Drake, Gasconade, Mo	23
Drake's Branch, Charlotte, Va	86
Drake's Creek, Madison, Ark	12
Drake's Mills, Crawford, Pa	37
Drakestown, Morris, N. J	20
Drakesville, Davis, Iowa	170
Drakesville, Morris, N. J	110
Dranesville, Fairfax, Va	16
Draper, Salt Lake, Utah	39
Drapersville, Mecklenburgh, Va	12
Dravosburgh, Allegheny, Pa	100
Draw Bridge, Sussex, Del	59
Draw Bridge, Dorchester, Md	13
Drayton Plains, Oakland, Mich	58
Drehersville, Schuylkill, Pa	29
Dresbach, Winona, Minn	23
Dresden, Lincoln, Me	24
Dresden, Pettis, Mo	290
Dresden, Yates, N. Y	240
Dresden,* Muskingum, Ohio	680
Dresden, (*c. h.*,) Weakley, Tenn	510
Dresden, Navarro, Tex	110
Dresden Mills, Lincoln, Me	94
Dresselville, Le Sueur, Minn	20
Dresserville, Cayuga, N. Y	30
Drewersburgh, Franklin, Ind	27
Drewryville, Southampton, Va	12

* Money-order office.

Drewsville, Cheshire, N. H	$86
Dreyspring, Montgomery, Ala.	12
Driftwood, Cameron, Pa	760
Drum's, Luzerne, Pa	68
Drury, Rock Island, Ill	3
Dry Branch, Franklin, Mo	12
Dry Brook, Ulster, N. Y	7
Dry Cove, Jackson, Ala	12
Dry Creek, Lawrence, Ala	68
Dry Creek, Linn, Iowa	31
Dry Creek, Crawford, Mo	20
Dryden, Tama, Iowa	33
Dryden, Lapeer, Mich	130
Dryden, Sibley, Minn	9
Dryden, Jefferson, Nebr	12
Dryden, Tompkins, N. Y	500
Dry Fork, Barren, Ky	7
Dry Grove, Hinds, Miss	98
Dry Hill, Lauderdale, Tenn	24
Dry Mills, Cumberland, Me	20
Dry Ponds, Catawba, N. C	9
Dry Ridge, Grant, Ky	67
Dry Ridge, Hamilton, Ohio	24
Dry Run, Scott, Ky	12
Dry Run, Prentiss, Miss	5
Dry Run, Franklin, Pa	73
Drytown, Amador, Cal	100
Dryville, Berks, Pa	14
Dry Wood, Vernon, Mo	6
Duane, Franklin, N. Y	8
Duanesburgh, Schenectady, N. Y	100
Dublin, Fayette, Ala	12
Dublin, (c. h.,) Laurens, Ga	90
Dublin,* Wayne, Ind	670
Dublin, Graves, Ky	7
Dublin, Harford, Md	140
Dublin, Cheshire, N. H	160
Dublin, Franklin, Ohio	120
Dublin, Bucks, Pa	83
Dublin, Pulaski, Va	480
Dublin Mills, Fulton, Pa	17
Dubois, Pulaski, Ga	12
Dubois, Washington, Ill	160
Dubuque, (c. h.,)* Dubuque, Iowa	4,000
Duchateau, Door, Wis	9
Duck Creek, Walker, Ga	6
Duck Creek, Warren, Ill	58
Duckers, Woodford, Ky	120
Duck Hill, Carroll, Miss	28
Duck Pond, Cumberland, Me	12
Duck Port, Madison, La	12
Duck River, Hickman, Tenn	12
Ducktown,* Polk, Tenn	250
Dudley, Edgar, Ill	140
Dudley, Wapello, Iowa	12
Dudley, Worcester, Mass	200
Dudley, Wayne, N. C	90
Dudley, Huntingdon, Pa	280
Dudleytown, Jackson, Ind	43
Dudleyville, Bond, Ill	30
Duelin, Benton, Minn	12
Due West, Abbeville, S. C	150
Duff, Dubois, Ind	5
Duffield, Charles, Md	24
Duffield's, Jefferson, W. Va	180
Dugansville, Mercer, Ky	3
Dugger's Ferry, Carter, Tenn	$6
Dug Hill, Carroll, Md	17
Dug Spur, Carroll, Va	12
Dugway, Oswego, N. Y	43
Dukedom, Weakley, Tenn	43
Dulaney's Valley, Baltimore, Md	16
Du Luth, (c. h.,) St. Louis, Minn	1,000
Dumas, Tippah, Miss	6
Dumas Ferry, Anson, N. C	12
Dumfries, Prince William, Va	58
Dummerston, Windham, Vt	120
Dumontville, Fairfield, Ohio	28
Dunbar, Washington, Ohio	20
Dunbar, Fayette, Pa	140
Dunbarton, Merrimack, N. H	83
Dunbarton, Adams, Ohio	30
Dunbarton, Barnwell, S. C	19
Duncan, Monroe, Ark	12
Duncan, Stark, Ill	12
Duncan, Mercer, Ky	21
Duncan, Allegheny, Pa	130
Duncan Creek, Vernon, Mo	12
Duncannon, Perry, Pa	610
Duncanon, Stephenson, Ill	11
Duncan's Creek, Rutherford, N. C	5
Duncan's Falls, Muskingum, Ohio	98
Duncan's Mills, Sonoma, Cal	75
Duncan's Mills, Fulton, Ill	38
Duncan's Mills, Scott, Va	5
Duncan's Retreat, Kane, Utah	9
Duncansville, Blair, Pa	140
Duncombe, Webster, Iowa	12
Dundaff, Susquehanna, Pa	120
Dundarrach, Robeson, N. C	12
Dundas, Richland, Ill	23
Dundas, Rice, Minn	200
Dundas, Pulaski, Mo	18
Dundas, Vinton, Ohio	69
Dundas, Calumet, Wis	11
Dundee, Kane, Ill	400
Dundee, Monroe, Mich	200
Dundee, Franklin, Mo	68
Dundee, Yates, N. Y	830
Dundee, Tuscarawas, Ohio	47
Dundee, Fond du Lac, Wis	14
Dun Ellen, Middlesex, N. J	12
Dungannon, Columbiana, Ohio	36
Dun Glen, Humboldt, Nev	120
Dunham, Washington, Ohio	14
Dunkard, Greene, Pa	18
Dunkinsville, Adams, Ohio	21
Dunkirk, Jay. Ind	140
Dunkirk, Calvert, Md	72
Dunkirk,* Chautauqua, N. Y	2,600
Dunkirk, Hardin, Ohio	270
Dunkirk, Dane, Wis	20
Dunkle's Store, Lawrence, Mo	21
Dunlap, Harrison, Iowa	180
Dunlap, Hamilton, Ohio	32
Dunlap, (c. h.,) Sequatchie, Tenn	37
Dunlapsville, Union, Ind	49
Dunleith, Jo Daviess, Ill	420
Dunleith, Wayne, W. Va	12
Dunlevy, Warren, Ohio	19
Dunmore, Luzerne, Pa	510
Dunmore, Pocahontas, W. Va	60

* Money-order office.

Dunn, Moultrie, Ill	$1
Dunnings, Luzerne, Pa	150
Dunningsville, Washington, Pa	41
Dunnington, Hickman, Tenn	12
Dunningville, Allegan, Mich	12
Dunn's Rock, Transylvania, N. C	9
Dunn's Store, Caroline, Va	10
Dunnsville, Albany, N. Y	20
Dunnsville, Essex, Va	100
Dunnville, Dunn, Wis	17
Dunreith, Henry, Ind	170
Dunsfort, Washington, Pa	12
Dunstable, Middlesex, Mass	83
Dunton, Cook, Ill	270
Dupage, Will, Ill	20
Du Plain, Clinton, Mich	77
Duplainville, Waukesha, Wis	29
Dupont, Jefferson, Ind	200
Dupont, Putnam, Ohio	12
Dupont, Waupaca, Wis	84
Dupree's Old Store, Charlotte, Va	19
Duquoin,* Perry, Ill	1,300
Durand,* (*c. h.*,) Pepin, Wis	360
Durand Station,* Winnebago, Ill	400
Durant's Neck, Perquimons, N. C	12
Durango, Dubuque, Iowa	11
Durant,* Cedar, Iowa	360
Durant, Holmes, Miss	330
Durbin's Corners, Williams, Ohio	36
Durell, Bradford, Pa	12
Durgen's Creek, Lewis, Mo	8
Durham, Middlesex, Conn	200
Durham, Hancock, Ill	11
Durham, Androscoggin, Me	92
Durham, Strafford, N. H	170
Durham, Greene, N. Y	220
Durham, Bucks, Pa	59
Durham Centre, Middlesex, Conn	65
Durham Hill, Waukesha, Wis	13
Durham's, Orange, N. C	180
Durhamville, Oneida, N. Y	320
Durhamville, Lauderdale, Tenn	48
Durlach, Lancaster, Pa	72
Duroc, Benton, Mo	12
Dushore,* Sullivan, Pa	280
Dustin, De Kalb, Ill	14
Dutch Creek, Washington, Iowa	86
Dutche's Creek, Yell, Ark	12
Dutch Flat,* Placer, Cal	760
Dutch Hill, St. Clair, Ill	8
Dutch Hill, Crawford, Pa	8
Dutch Neck, Mercer, N. J	46
Dutchtown, Cape Girardeau, Mo	12
Dutchville, Granville, N. C	9
Dutzow, Warren, Mo	12
Duxbury, Plymouth, Mass	450
Dwaar's Kill, Ulster, N. Y	29
Dwight,* Livingston, Ill	1,200
Dyberry, Wayne, Pa	29
Dyckesville, Kewaunee, Wis	48
Dycusburgh, Crittenden, Ky	72
Dye, Martin, Ind	12
Dyer, Lake, Ind	82
Dyer Brook, Aroostook, Me	4
Dyersburgh, (*c. h.*,) Dyer, Tenn	260
Dyer's Station, Gibson, Tenn	85
Dyersville,* Dubuque, Iowa	$500
Dykeman's, Putnam, N. Y	26
Dyson's, Guernsey, Ohio	39
Dyson's Mill, Edgefield, S. C	9
Dysortville, McDowell, N. C	16

E.

Eagle, Bremer, Iowa	6
Eagle, Clinton, Mich	11
Eagle, Harrison, Mo	220
Eagle, Cass, Nebr	12
Eagle, Wyoming, N. Y	12
Eagle, Warren, Pa	8
Eagle, Waukesha, Wis	290
Eagle Bridge, Rensselaer, N. Y	81
Eagle City, Sibley, Minn	12
Eagle Corners, Richland, Wis	12
Eagle Creek, Bradley, Ark	25
Eagle Creek, Lyon, Kans	12
Eagle Creek, Clackamas, Oreg	16
Eagle Foundry, Huntingdon, Pa	13
Eagle Furnace, Roane, Tenn	10
Eagle Grove, Hart, Ga	5
Eagle Grove, Wright, Iowa	54
Eagle Harbor, Keweenaw, Mich	200
Eagle Harbor, Orleans, N. Y	160
Eagle Hill, Owen, Ky	10
Eagle Iron Works, Wythe, Va	12
Eagle Lake, Will, Ill	29
Eagle Lake, Colorado, Tex	36
Eagle Landing, Pulaski, Ark	12
Eagle Mills, Fayette, Ala	12
Eagle Mills, Rensselaer, N. Y	49
Eagle Mills, Iredell, N. C	18
Eagle Mills, Vinton, Ohio	27
Eagle Pass, (*c. h.*,) Maverick, Tex	340
Eagle Point, Ogle, Ill	38
Eagle Point, Berks, Pa	8
Eagle River, (*c. h.*,) Keweenaw, Mich	280
Eagle Rock, Oneida, Idaho	12
Eagle Rock, Wake, N. C	17
Eagle Rock, Venango, Pa	32
Eaglesfield, Clay, Ind	8
Eagle's Mere, Sullivan, Pa	6
Eagle Springs, Jefferson, Ind	12
Eagle Springs, Coryell, Tex	12
Eagle Station, Carroll, Ky	12
Eagle Tannery, Wayne, Tenn	12
Eagletown, Hamilton, Ind	23
Eagle Village, Wyoming, N. Y	91
Eagleville, Siskiyou, Cal	34
Eagleville, Tolland, Conn	100
Eagleville, Ashtabula, Ohio	75
Eagleville, Montgomery, Pa	27
Eagleville, Rutherford, Tenn	16
Eakin, Allegheny, Pa	110
Eakle's Mills, Washington, Md	43
Earle, Lucas, Iowa	12
Earle's, Muhlenburgh, Ky	13
Earlesville, Spartanburgh, S. C	12
Earley, Elk, Pa	12
Earleysville, Albemarle, Va	45
Earlham, Madison, Iowa	150
Earlobion, Obion, Tenn	12
Earlville,* La Salle, Ill	910

* Money-order office.

Earlville, Delaware, Iowa	$470
Earlville, Madison, N. Y	310
Earlville, Portage, Ohio	59
Earlville, Berks, Pa	27
Early Grove, Marshall, Miss	26
Earpsborough, Johnston, N.C	10
Eartmon, Pulaski, Ga	12
East Abington, Plymouth, Mass	520
Easta Boga, Talladega, Ala	12
East Acworth, Sullivan, N. H	14
East Albany, Orleans, Vt	41
East Alburgh, Grand Isle, Vt	120
Eastaloe, Pickens, S. C	5
East Alton, Belknap, N. H	12
East Amherst, Erie, N. Y	34
East Andover, Merrimack, N. H	160
East Arcade, Wyoming, N. Y	20
East Arlington, Bennington, Vt	150
East Ashford, Cattaraugus, N. Y	49
East Auburn, Androscoggin, Me	39
East Aurora, Erie, N. Y	230
East Avon, Livingston, N. Y	200
East Baldwin, Cumberland, Me	59
East Bangor, Penobscot, Me	21
East Barnard, Windsor, Vt	130
East Beekmantown, Clinton, N. Y	65
East Bend, Ford, Ill	12
East Bend, Yadkin, N. C	21
East Benton, Kennebec, Me	28
East Benton, Luzerne, Pa	13
East Berkshire, Tioga, N. Y	1
East Berkshire, Franklin, Vt	140
East Berlin, Hartford, Conn	260
East Berlin, Adams, Pa	110
East Berne, Albany, N. Y	38
East Bethany, Genesee, N. Y	100
East Bethel, Windsor, Vt	100
East Bethlehem, Washington, Pa	120
East Blackstone, Worcester, Mass	92
East Bloomfield, Ontario, N. Y	490
East Boston, Madison, N. Y	57
East Bowdoinham, Sagadahoc, Me	48
East Boyleston, Oswego, N. Y	12
East Bradford, Penobscot, Me	20
East Branch, Delaware, N. Y	13
East Brewster, Barnstable, Mass	94
East Bridgewater, Plymouth, Mass	470
East Bridgewater, Susquehanna, Pa	25
East Brimfield, Hampden, Mass	66
East Brook, Lawrence, Pa	53
East Brookfield, Worcester, Mass	280
East Brookfield, Orange, Vt	72
East Bucksport, Hancock, Me	10
East Burke, Caledonia, Vt	210
East Burlington, Kane, Ill	12
East Cabot, Washington, Vt	26
East Calais, Washington, Vt	91
East Cambridge, Middlesex, Mass	1,900
East Cambridge, Lamoille, Vt	12
East Canaan, Litchfield, Conn	200
East Canaan, Grafton, N. H	416
East Canton, Bradford, Pa	50
East Carmel, Columbiana, Ohio	12
East Carlton, Orleans, N. Y	120
East Castle Rock, Dakota, Minn	33
East Chain Lakes, Martin, Minn	19
East Charlemont, Franklin, Mass	$52
East Charleston, Tioga, Pa	17
East Charleston, Orleans, Vt	54
East Chatham, Columbia, N. Y	310
East Chatham, Tioga, Pa	12
East Chester, Westchester, N. Y	410
East Clarence, Erie, N. Y	34
East Clarendon, Rutland, Vt	51
East Claridon, Geauga, Ohio	68
East Clarksfield, Huron, Ohio	19
East Clarkson, Monroe, N. Y	33
East Cleveland, Cuyahoga, Ohio	390
East Cobleskill, Schoharie, N. Y	30
East Concord, Merrimack, N. H	89
East Concord, Erie, N. Y	25
East Constable, Franklin, N. Y	120
East Corinth, Penobscot, Me	270
East Corinth, Orange, Vt	190
East Cornwall, Litchfield, Conn	18
East Coventry, Chester, Pa	12
East Coventry, Orleans, Vt	48
East Craftsbury, Orleans, Vt	63
East Creek, Cape May, N. J	31
East Creek, Herkimer, N. Y	80
East Dayton, Tuscola, Mich	29
East Deering, Hillsborough, N. H	34
East De Kalb, St. Lawrence, N. Y	45
East Delavan, Walworth, Wis	12
East Dennis, Barnstable, Mass	200
East Derry, Rockingham, N. H	12
East Dickinson, Franklin, N. Y	49
East Dimock, Susquehanna, Pa	10
East Dixfield, Oxford, Me	98
East Dixmont, Penobscot, Me	40
East Dorset, Bennington, Vt	270
East Douglass, Worcester, Mass	460
East Dover, Piscataquis, Me	14
East Dover, Windham, Vt	47
East Durham, Greene, N. Y	98
East Eddington, Penobscot, Me	67
East Eden, Hancock, Me	200
East Eden, Erie, N.Y	18
East Elba, Genesee, N. Y	39
East Elma, Erie, N. Y	19
East Elmore, Lamoille, Vt	13
East Enterprise, Switzerland, Ind	66
Eastern, Franklin, Ill	2
East Evans, Erie, N. Y	30
East Exoter, Penobscot, Me	40
East Fairfield, Columbiana, Ohio	150
East Fairfield, Franklin, Vt	64
East Falmouth, Barnstable, Mass	100
East Finley, Washington, Pa	28
East Fishkill, Dutchess, N. Y	64
East Florence, Oneida, N. Y	56
Eastford, Windham, Conn	130
East Fork, Montgomery, Ill	20
East Fork, Metcalfe, Ky	9
East Foxborough, Norfolk, Mass	71
East Franklin, Franklin, Vt	120
East Freedom, Blair, Pa	86
East Freetown, Bristol, Mass	33
East Fryeburgh, Oxford, Me	16
East Gaines, Orleans, N. Y	50
East Gainesville, Wyoming, N. Y	160
East Gallatin, Gallatin, Mont	12

EAS

East Galway, Saratoga, N. Y	$22
East Genoa, Cayuga, N. Y	35
East Georgia, Franklin, Vt	59
East German, Chenango, N. Y	65
East Germantown, Wayne, Ind	180
East Gibson, Manitowoc, Wis	13
East Gilead, Branch, Mich	57
East Glastenbury, Hartford, Conn	43
East Glenville, Schenectady, N. Y	23
East Gloucester, Essex, Mass	370
East Granby, Hartford, Conn	110
East Granger, Allegany, N. Y	6
East Granville, Hampden, Mass	47
East Granville, Addison, Vt	30
East Greenbush, Rensselaer, N. Y	78
East Greene, Chenango, N. Y	79
East Greene, Erie, Pa	19
East Greensborough, Orleans, Vt	36
East Greenville, Stark, Ohio	28
East Greenwich, Washington, N. Y	85
*East Greenwich,** (*c. h.,*) Kent, R. I	1,000
East Greenwood, Muskingum, Ohio	20
East Grove, Chemung, N. Y	4
East Groveland, Livingston, N. Y	70
East Guilford, Chenango, N. Y	91
East Haddam, Middlesex, Conn	660
Eastham, Barnstable, Mass	76
East Hamburgh, Erie, N. Y	150
East Hamilton, Madison, N. Y	75
East Hampden, Penobscot, Me	90
East Hampstead, Rockingham, N. H	12
East Hampton, Middlesex, Conn	440
East Hampton,* Hampshire, Mass	2,000
East Hampton, Suffolk, N. Y	410
East Hanover, Lebanon, Pa	40
East Hardwick, Caledonia, Vt	210
East Harpswell, Cumberland, Me	75
East Hartford, Hartford, Conn	280
East Harwich, Barnstable, Mass	46
East Haven, New Haven, Conn	56
East Haven, Essex, Vt	25
East Haverhill, Essex, Mass	59
East Haverhill, Grafton, N. H	120
East Hebron, Oxford, Me	62
East Hebron, Potter, Pa	28
East Hempfield, Lancaster, Pa	55
East Hickory, Forest, Pa	58
East Highgate, Franklin, Vt	110
East Holden, Penobscot, Me	50
East Holliston, Middlesex, Mass	76
East Homer, Cortland, N. Y	38
East Homer, Potter, Pa	12
East Houndsfield, Jefferson, N. Y	27
East Hubbardton, Rutland, Vt	14
East Hutchinson, McLeod, Minn	12
East Jaffrey, Cheshire, N. H	270
East Java, Wyoming, N. Y	39
East Jewett, Greene, N. Y	9
East Kendall, Orleans, N. Y	54
East Kent, Litchfield, Conn	13
East Killingly, Windham, Conn	130
East Kingston, Rockingham, N. H	91
East Knox, Waldo, Me	87
East Lamoine, Hancock, Me	36
East Landaff, Grafton, N. H	10
East Lansing, Tompkins, N. Y	18

EAS

East Laport, Jackson, N. C	$13
East Lebanon, Grafton, N. H	77
East Lee, Berkshire, Mass	100
East Lempster, Sullivan, N. H	48
East Leon, Cattaraugus, N. Y	30
East Leroy, Calhoun, Mich	17
East Lewistown, Mahoning, Ohio	66
East Lexington, Middlesex, Mass	90
East Liberty, Logan, Ohio	30
East Liberty, Fayette, Pa	55
East Limington, York, Me	34
East Lincoln, Penobscot, Me	40
East Line, Saratoga, N. Y	54
East Litchfield, Litchfield, Conn	61
East Livermore, Androscoggin, Me	84
East Liverpool,* Columbiana, Ohio	720
East Long Meadow, Hampden, Mass	130
East Lowell, Penobscot, Me	38
East Lyme, New London, Conn	150
East McDonough, Chenango, N. Y	8
East Machias, Washington, Me	470
East Madison, Somerset, Me	97
East Madison, Carroll, N. H	29
East Maine, Broome, N. Y	9
Eastman, Crawford, Wis	44
Eastmansville, Ottawa, Mich	170
East Marion, Suffolk, N. Y	69
East Marshfield, Plymouth, Mass	130
East Masonville, Delaware, N. Y	57
East Mauch Chunk, Carbon, Pa	12
East Medway, Norfolk, Mass	180
East Melrose, Monroe, Iowa	120
East Meredith, Delaware, N. Y	12
East Meriden, Steele, Minn	4
East Middleborough, Plymouth, Mass	25
East Middlebury, Addison, Vt	110
East Milan, Monroe, Mich	12
East Monmouth, Kennebec, Me	25
East Monroe, Highland, Ohio	80
East Montpelier, Washington, Vt	74
East Montville, Waldo, Me	14
East Moriches, Suffolk, N. Y	98
East Moultonborough, Carroll, N. H	12
East Nassau, Rensselaer, N. Y	41
East New Market, Dorchester, Md	140
East Newport, Penobscot, Me	35
East New Portland, Somerset, Me	27
East New Sharon, Franklin, Me	52
East New Vineyard, Franklin, Me	6
East New York, Kings, N. Y	1,000
East Nichols, Tioga, N. Y	11
East Nodoway, Adams, Iowa	13
East Northfield, Cook, Ill	18
East Northport, Waldo, Me	31
East Northwood, Rockingham, N. H	110
East North Yarmouth, Cumberland, Me	51
East Norwalk, Huron, Ohio	58
East Norwich, Queens, N. Y	100
East Oasis, Waushara, Wis	15
Easton, Fairfield, Conn	55
Easton, Leavenworth, Kans	81
Easton, Aroostook, Me	29
*Easton,** (*c. h.,*) Talbot, Md	1,100
Easton, Bristol, Mass	180

* Money-order office.

Post office	Amount
Easton, Ionia, Mich	$26
Easton, Buchanan, Mo	160
Easton, Washington, N. Y	110
Easton, Wayne, Ohio	45
Easton,* (*c. h.*,) Northampton, Pa	3,300
Easton, Monongalia, W. Va	23
Easton, Adams, Wis	42
East Orange, Essex, N. J	180
East Orange, Schuyler, N. Y	12
East Orange, Delaware, Ohio	12
East Orange, Orange, Vt	57
East Orangeville, Wyoming, N. Y	12
East Orleans, Barnstable, Mass	110
East Orrington, Penobscot, Me	36
East Otis, Berkshire, Mass	20
East Otisfield, Cumberland, Me	67
East Otto, Cattaraugus, N. Y	170
East Palermo, Waldo, Me	40
East Palermo, Oswego, N. Y	20
East Palestine, Columbiana, Ohio	320
East Palmyra, Wayne, N. Y	91
East Parsonfield, York, Me	69
East Paw Paw, De Kalb, Ill	100
East Pembroke, Plymouth, Mass	64
East Pembroke, Merrimack, N. H	12
East Pembroke, Genesee, N. Y	150
East Penfield, Monroe, N. Y	59
East Pepperell, Middlesex, Mass	280
East Peru, Oxford, Me	18
East Pharsalia, Chenango, N. Y	57
East Pike, Wyoming, N. Y	120
East Pitcairn, St. Lawrence, N. Y	15
East Pittston, Kennebec, Me	82
East Plainfield, Sullivan, N. H	45
East Plymouth, Ashtabula, Ohio	16
East Poestenkill, Rensselaer, N. Y	20
East Point, Fulton, Ga	7
East Poland, Androscoggin, Me	71
Eastport, Fremont, Iowa	92
Eastport,* Washington, Me	2,200
Eastport, Tishemingo, Miss	40
East Porter, Niagara, N. Y	15
East Portland, Multnomah, Oreg	12
East Poultney, Rutland, Vt	180
East Prairieville, Rice, Minn	27
East Princeton, Worcester, Mass	79
East Providence, Providence, R. I	69
East Putnam, Windham, Conn	93
East Randolph, Norfolk, Mass	280
East Randolph, Cattaraugus, N. Y	350
East Randolph, Orange, Vt	140
East Raymond, Cumberland, Me	46
East Readfield, Kennebec, Me	16
East Richford, Franklin, Vt	21
East Richland, Belmont, Ohio	73
East Ridge, Clearfield, Pa	3
East Ringgold, Pickaway, Ohio	23
East River, New Haven, Conn	180
East Rochester, Strafford, N. H	150
East Rochester, Columbiana, Ohio	110
East Rockaway, Queens, N. Y	12
East Rockport, Cuyahoga, Ohio	92
East Rodman, Jefferson, N. Y	18
East Roxbury, Washington, Vt	23
East Rumford, Oxford, Me	16
East Rupert, Bennington, Vt	69
East Rush, Susquehanna, Pa	$6
East Rush Creek, Perry, Ohio	93
East Rushford, Allegany, N. Y	19
East Saginaw,* Saginaw, Mich	3,300
East Saint Louis,* St. Clair, Ill	830
East Salamanca, Cattaraugus, N. Y	12
East Salem, Washington, N. Y	33
East Salem, Juniata, Pa	36
East Salisbury, Essex, Mass	70
East Sandwich, Barnstable, Mass	22
East Sangerville, Piscataquis, Me	15
East Sandy, Venango, Pa	19
East Sandy Creek,* Oswego, N. Y	400
East Schodack, Rensselaer, N. Y	15
East Schuyler, Herkimer, N. Y	48
East Scott, Cortland, N. Y	8
East Setauket, Suffolk, N. Y	130
East Sharon, Norfolk, Mass	7
East Sharon, Potter, Pa	20
East Sharpsburgh, Blair, Pa	18
East Sheffield, Berkshire, Mass	72
East Shelburne, Franklin, Mass	10
East Shelby, Orleans, N. Y	43
East Sheldon, Franklin, Vt	22
East Smithfield, Bradford, Pa	270
East Somerville, Middlesex, Mass	540
East Springfield, Sullivan, N. H	11
East Springfield, Otsego, N. Y	120
East Springfield, Jefferson, Ohio	100
East Springfield, Erie, Pa	200
East Springhill, Bradford, Pa	24
East Stoneham, Oxford, Me	39
East Stoughton, Norfolk, Mass	290
East Stroudsburgh, Monroe, Pa	140
East Sullivan, Hancock, Me	69
East Sullivan, Cheshire, N. H	49
East Sumner, Oxford, Me	85
East Sycamore, Hamilton, Ohio	30
East Taunton, Bristol, Mass	230
East Tawas, Iosco, Mich	290
East Templeton, Worcester, Mass	340
East Thetford, Orange, Vt	61
East Thompson, Windham, Conn	10
East Thorndike, Waldo, Me	12
East Tilton, Belknap, N. H	99
East Toledo, Lucas, Ohio	460
East Townsend, Huron, Ohio	120
East Traverse Bay, Grand Traverse, Mich	16
East Troupsburgh, Steuben, N. Y	9
East Troy, Bradford, Pa	20
East Troy,* Walworth, Wis	340
East Troy Lake, Walworth, Wis	28
East Trumbull, Ashtabula, Ohio	51
East Turner, Androscoggin, Me	47
East Union, Wayne, Ohio	26
East Unity, Sullivan, N. H	12
East Varick, Seneca, N. Y	39
East Vassalborough, Kennebec, Me	190
East Venice, Cayuga, N. Y	40
Eastville,* (*c. h.*,) Northampton, Va	250
East Vincent, Chester, Pa	280
East Virgil, Cortland, N. Y	12
East Wakefield, Carroll, N. H	26
East Wales, Androscoggin, Me	7
East Wallingford, Rutland, Vt	240

* Money-order office.

East Walpole, Norfolk, Mass	$120
East Wareham, Plymouth, Mass	160
East Warren, Washington, Vt	50
East Washington, Sullivan, N. H	120
East Waterborough, York, Me	28
East Waterford, Juniata, Pa	110
East Watertown, Jefferson, N. Y	12
East Weare, Hillsborough, N. H	73
East Westmoreland, Cheshire, N. H	59
East Weymouth, Norfolk, Mass	440
East Whately, Franklin, Mass	120
East Wheatland, Will, Ill	24
East Wilson, Niagara, N. Y	19
East Wilton, Franklin, Me	250
East Windham, Cumberland, Me	14
East Windham, Greene, N. Y	14
East Windsor, Hartford, Conn	37
East Windsor, Berkshire, Mass	48
East Windsor Hill, Hartford, Conn	170
East Winthrop, Kennebec, Me	56
East Woburn, Middlesex, Mass	75
East Woodhull, Steuben, N. Y	12
East Woodstock, Windham, Conn	150
East Worcester, Otsego, N. Y	180
East Wrightstown, Brown, Wis	20
Eaton, Crawford, Ill	18
Eaton, Delaware, Ind	54
Eaton, Madison, N. Y	400
*Eaton,** (*c. h.,*) Preble, Ohio	970
Eaton, Wyoming, Pa	29
Eaton, Manitowoc, Wis	79
Eaton Centre, Carroll, N. H	47
Eaton Rapids, Eaton, Mich	790
Eatonton, (*c. h.,*) Putnam, Ga	630
Eatontown, Monmouth, N. J	300
Eatonville, Herkimer, N. Y	30
Eau Claire, Berrien, Mich	55
Eau Claire, Butler, Pa	34
*Eau Claire,** (*c. h.,*) Eau Claire, Wis	1,800
Eau Galle, Dunn, Wis	87
Eau Pleine, Portage, Wis	47
Ebenezer, Greene, Mo	23
Ebenezer, Erie, N. Y	110
Ebenezer, Preble, Ohio	20
Ebenezer, Indiana, Pa	35
*Ebensburgh,** (*c. h.,*) Cambria, Pa	950
Eberly's Mill, Cumberland, Pa	42
Echo, Armstrong, Pa	23
Echo, Macon, Tenn	12
Echo, Live Oak, Tex	10
Echo City, Summit, Utah	12
Eckley, Carroll, Ohio	8
Eckley, Luzerne, Pa	370
Eckmansville, Adams, Ohio	92
Ecleto, Karnes, Tex	10
Economy, Wayne, Ind	91
Economy, Macon, Mo	23
Economy, Beaver, Pa	67
Ecorse, Wayne, Mich	65
Eddington, Penobscot, Me	65
Eddington, Bucks, Pa	140
Eddytown, Yates, N. Y	130
Eddyville, Pope, Ill	8
Eddyville,* Wapello, Iowa	1,000
Eddyville, (*c. h.,*) Lyon, Ky	210
Eddyville, Cattaraugus, N. Y	36
Eddyville, Armstrong, Pa	$29
Eden, Lincoln, Dak	37
Eden, Effingham, Ga	57
Eden, Iroquois, Ill	12
Eden, Hancock, Ind	22
Eden, Fayette, Iowa	28
Eden, Atchison, Kans	13
Eden, Hancock, Me	24
Eden, Ingham, Mich	47
Eden, Faribault, Minn	12
Eden, Erie, N. Y	110
Eden, Randolph, N. C	33
Eden, McKean, Pa	4
Eden, Laurens, S. C	12
Eden, Lamoille, Vt	36
Eden, Fond du Lac, Wis	8
Edenburgh, Shenandoah, Va	140
Eden Mills, La Grange, Ind	9
Eden Mills, Lamoille, Vt	41
Eden Prairie, Hennepin, Minn	77
Eden's Ridge, Sullivan, Tenn	12
Edenton, Madison, Ky	9
Edenton, St. Lawrence, N. Y	14
*Edenton,** (*c. h.,*) Chowan, N. C	660
Edenton, Clermont, Ohio	36
Eden Valley, Erie, N. Y	24
Edenville, Marshall, Iowa	35
Edenville, Midland, Mich	67
Edenville, Orange, N. Y	24
Edenville, Erie, Pa	3
Edes Falls, Cumberland, Me	45
Edesville, Kent, Md	62
Edgard, (*c. h.,*) St. John Baptist, La	110
Edgar Springs, Phelps, Mo	13
*Edgartown,** (*c. h.,*) Dukes, Mass	730
Edgecomb, Lincoln, Me	60
Edgefield C. H., Edgefield, S. C	200
Edgefield Junction, Davidson, Tenn	110
Edge Hill, Reynolds, Mo	12
Edge Hill, King George, Va	72
Edgemont, Delaware, Pa	50
Edgerton, El Paso, Colo	12
Edgerton, Kent, Mich	12
Edgerton,* Williams, Ohio	510
Edgerton, Rock, Wis	340
Edgewood, Effingham, Ill	150
Edgewood, Harford, Md	110
Edgeworth, Sullivan, Tenn	13
Edgwood, Siskiyou, Cal	12
Edgwood, Bucks, Pa	70
*Edina,** (*c. h.,*) Knox, Mo	460
Edinborough, Montgomery, N. C	4
Edinborough, Erie, Pa	630
Edinburgh, Christian, Ill	55
Edinburgh,* Johnson, Ind	920
Edinburgh, Jones, Iowa	7
Edinburgh, Hillsdale, Mich	4
Edinburgh, Leake, Miss	17
Edinburgh, Grundy, Mo	81
Edinburgh, Mercer, N. J	10
Edinburgh, Saratoga, N. Y	52
Edinburgh, Portage, Ohio	150
Edinburgh, Lawrence, Pa	100
Edinburgh, (*c. h.,*) Hidalgo, Tex	26
Edington, Rock Island, Ill	120
Edisto Island, Colleton, S. C	110

* Money-order office.

Post office	
Edith, Shenandoah, Va	$9
Edmeston, Otsego, N. Y	110
*Edmonton,** (*c. h.,*) Metcalfe, Ky	88
Edna, Cass, Iowa	15
Edneyville, Henderson, N. C	5
Edom, Rockingham, Va	19
Edon, Williams, Ohio	59
Edray, Pocahontas, W. Va	21
Edsallville, Bradford, Pa	14
Edwards, Jefferson, Ky	9
Edwards, St. Lawrence, N. Y	150
Edwards, Sheboygan, Wis	40
Edwardsburgh, Cass, Mich	240
Edwards' Depot, Hinds, Miss	190
Edwardsport, Knox, Ind	110
Edwards' Station, Peoria, Ill	33
Edwardsville, (*c. h.,*) Cleburne, Ala	28
*Edwardsville,** (*c. h.,*) Madison, Ill	1,000
Edwardsville, Floyd, Ind	24
Edwardsville, Wyandotte, Kans	110
Edwardsville, St. Lawrence, N. Y	32
Edwardsville, Warren, Ohio	27
Edwina, Monroe, Ohio	4
Eel River, Humboldt, Cal	57
Eel River, Allen, Ind	23
*Effingham,** (*c. h.,*) Effingham, Ill	1,000
Effingham, Atchison, Kans	12
Effingham, Carroll, N. H	20
Effingham Falls, Carroll, N. H	74
Effingham Station, Marion, S. C	72
Effort, Monroe, Pa	16
Efird's Mills, Stanly, N. C	1
Egan Canyon, Lander, Nev	25
Eggertsville, Erie, N. Y	36
Egg Harbor, Door, Wis	17
Egg Harbor City,* Atlantic, N. J	470
Eggleston's Springs, Giles, Va	13
Egg's Point, Washington, Miss	120
Eglantine, Van Buren, Ark	12
Egypt, Effingham, Ga	30
Egypt, Chickasaw, Miss	71
Egypt, Monroe, N. Y	210
Egypt, Wharton, Tex	16
Egypt, Monroe, W. Va	10
Egypt Depot, Chatham, N. C	100
Egypt Mills, Cape Girardeau, Mo	8
Egypt Mills, Pike, Pa	12
Ehrenberg, Yuma, Ariz	12
Eighteen Mile, Pickens, S. C	8
Eight Mile Creek, Harrison, Tex	11
Eight Mile Grove, Cass, Nebr	12
Eighty-Eight, Barren, Ky	12
Eitzen, Houston, Minn	34
Ekonk, Windham, Conn	13
Ela, Lake, Ill	15
Elam, Delaware, Pa	43
Elamsville, Patrick, Va	1
Elba, (*c. h.,*) Coffee, Ala	22
Elba, Gallatin, Ill	12
Elba, Winona, Minn	37
Elba, Genesee, N. Y	180
Elbaville, Davie, N. C	12
Elberfeld, Warrick, Ind	10
Elberton, (*c. h.,*) Elbert, Ga	170
Elbinsville, Bedford, Pa	9
Elbow Spring, Barren, Ky	12

Post office	
Elbridge, Edgar, Ill	$22
Elbridge, Onondaga, N. Y	270
El Dara, Pike, Ill	83
Eldena, Lee, Ill	52
Elder's Ridge, Indiana, Pa	80
Elderton, Armstrong, Pa	130
*Eldora,** (*c. h.,*) Hardin, Iowa	870
El Dorado, (*c. h.,*) Union, Ark	210
El Dorado, El Dorado, Cal	87
El Dorado, Saline, Ill	56
El Dorado, Fayette, Iowa	61
El Dorado, (*c. h.,*) Butler, Kans	140
El Dorado, Clarke, Mo	150
El Dorado, Colfax, Nebr	12
El Dorado, Preble, Ohio	66
El Dorado, Baker, Oreg	12
El Dorado, Blair, Pa	31
El Dorado, Culpeper, Va	6
El Dorado, Fond du Lac, Wis	22
El Dorado Mills, Fond du Lac, Wis	53
Eldred, Saunders, Nebr	12
Eldred, Wayne, Pa	15
Eldredgeville, Ford, Ill	12
Eldredsville, Sullivan, Pa	32
Eldridge, Walker, Ala	9
Eleroy, Stephenson, Ill	80
Eleven Mile, Potter, Pa	12
Elgin, Jackson, Ark	44
Elgin,* Kane, Ill	2,500
Elgin, Fayette, Iowa	73
Elgin, Genesee, Mich	12
Elgin, Wabashaw, Minn	55
Elgin, Cattaraugus, N. Y	25
Elida, Winnebago, Ill	70
Elida, Allen, Ohio	88
Elimsport, Lycoming, Pa	53
Elisabeth, Marshall, Kans	12
Eliza, Mercer, Ill	1
Eliza, Houston, Tex	8
Elizabeth, Jo Daviess, Ill	270
Elizabeth, Harrison, Ind	85
*Elizabeth,** (*c. h.,*) Union, N. J	3,800
Elizabeth, Allegheny, Pa	400
*Elizabeth City,** (*c. h.,*) Pasquotank, N. C	480
Elizabeth Furnace, Augusta, Va	43
Elizabeth Port, Union, N. J	1,300
Elizabethton, (*c. h.,*) Carter, Tenn	100
Elizabethtown, (*c. h.,*) Hardin, Ill	130
Elizabethtown, Bartholomew, Ind	190
Elizabethtown, Anderson, Kans	13
*Elizabethtown,** (*c. h.,*) Hardin, Ky	1,000
Elizabethtown, (*c. h.,*) Colfax, N. Mex	600
*Elizabethtown,** (*c. h.,*) Essex, N. Y	370
Elizabethtown, (*c. h.,*) Bladen, N. C	76
Elizabethtown, Lancaster, Pa	380
Elizabethville, Pendleton, Ky	4
Elizabethville, Dauphin, Pa	95
Elizaville, Boone, Ind	46
Elizaville, Fleming, Ky	160
Elizaville, Columbia, N. Y	21
Elk, Decatur, Iowa	13
Elk, Saginaw, Mich	16
Elk, Pocahontas, W. Va	6
Elk, Manitowoc, Wis	5
*Elkader,** (*c. h.,*) Clayton, Iowa	730

* Money-order office.

Elk City, Montgomery, Kans	$12
Elk City, Barbour, W. Va	12
Elk Creek, Spencer, Ky	49
Elk Creek, Texas, Mo	12
Elk Creek, Otsego, N. Y	12
Elk Creek, Erie, Pa	68
Elk Creek, Grayson, Va	20
Elk Creek, Trempealeau, Wis	25
Elk Cross Roads, Ashe, N. C	8
Elk Dale, Chester, Pa	59
Elk Falls, (*c. h.*,) Howard, Kans	12
Elk Grove, Sacramento, Cal	41
Elk Grove, Cook, Ill	16
Elk Grove, La Fayette, Wis	37
Elkhart,* Elkhart, Ind	2,400
Elkhart, Polk, Iowa	55
Elkhart City,* Logan, Ill	510
Elk Hill Mills, Goochland, Va	12
Elkhorn, Washington, Ill	150
Elk Horn, Shelby, Iowa	12
Elkhorn, Lincoln, Kans	13
Elk Horn, Lawrence, Mo	12
Elk Horn, Polk, Oreg	12
Elk Horn,* (*c. h.*,) Walworth, Wis	960
Elkhorn City, Douglas, Nebr	40
Elk Horn Grove, Carroll, Ill	51
Elkin, Surry, N. C	41
Elkinsville, Brown, Ind	4
Elk Lake, Susquehanna, Pa	24
Elkland, Tuscola, Mich	16
Elkland, Webster, Mo	12
Elkland, Tioga, Pa	230
Elk Lick, Somerset, Pa	140
Elk Mills, McDonald, Mo	15
Elk Mills, Chester, Pa	12
Elko, (*c. h.*,) Elko, Nev	890
Elk Point, (*c. h.*,) Union, Dak	230
Elkport, Clayton, Iowa	87
Elk Rapids, (*c. h.*,) Antrim, Mich	130
Elk Ridge Landing, Howard, Md	86
Elk River, Clinton, Iowa	28
Elk River Station, Sherburne, Minn	210
Elk Run, Tioga, Pa	13
Elk Run, Fauquier, Va	5
Elk Shoals, Iredell, N. C	7
Elk Spring, Warren, Ky	1
Elkton, Crawford, Ill	14
Elkton, (*c. h.*,) Todd, Ky	430
Elkton,* (*c. h.*,) Cecil, Md	1,400
Elkton, Hickory, Mo	67
Elkton, Columbiana, Ohio	32
Elkton, Giles, Tenn	74
Elkview, Chester, Pa	80
Elkville, Jackson, Ill	69
Elkville, Wilkes, N. C	12
Ella, Pepin, Wis	12
Ellaville, (*c. h.*,) Schley, Ga	38
Elleard, St. Louis, Mo	66
Ellejoy, Blount, Tenn	10
Ellenborough, Ritchie, W. Va	140
Ellenborough, Grant, Wis	28
Ellenburgh, Clinton, N. Y	140
Ellenburgh Centre, Clinton, N. Y	190
Ellenburgh Depot, Clinton, N. Y	79
Ellendale, Sussex, Del	68
Ellendale Forge, Dauphin, Pa	20
Ellengowan, Baltimore, Md	$82
Ellenorah, Gentry, Mo	24
Ellensberg, (*c. h.*,) Curry, Oreg	38
Ellenton, Palo Alto, Iowa	12
Ellenville,* Ulster, N. Y	1,300
Ellerslie, Harris, Ga	10
Ellerslie, Alleghany, Md	12
Ellery, Chautauqua, N. Y	72
Ellicott, Erie, N. Y	24
Ellicott City,* (*c. h.*,) Howard, Md	1,100
Ellicottsville,* (*c. h.*,) Cattaraugus, N. Y	860
Ellijay, (*c. h.*,) Gilmer, Ga	59
Ellington, Tolland, Conn	220
Ellington, (*c. h.*,) Hancock, Iowa	33
Ellington, Tuscola, Mich	59
Ellington, Dodge, Minn	8
Ellington, Chautauqua, N. Y	280
Ellingwood's Corner, Waldo, Me	27
Elliot, York, Me	25
Elliota, Fillmore, Minn	110
Elliot Depot, York, Me	20
Elliott, San Joaquin, Cal	10
Elliott, Grenada, Miss	20
Elliottsburgh, Perry, Pa	55
Elliott's Cross Roads, Morgan, Ohio	16
Elliott's Mill, Panola, Miss	17
Elliottstown, Effingham, Ill	33
Elliottsville, Monroe, Mo	12
Ellis, San Joaquin, Cal	12
Ellis, Ellis, Kans	12
Ellis, Portage, Wis	12
Ellisburgh, Jefferson, N. Y	100
Ellisburgh, Potter, Pa	25
Ellisdale, Ocean, N. J	99
Ellis Grove, Randolph, Ill	38
Ellison, Warren, Ill	51
Elliston, Grant, Ky	12
Ellistown, Lee, Miss	9
Ellisville, Columbia, Fla	24
Ellisville, Fulton, Ill	110
Ellisville, (*c. h.*,) Jones, Miss	10
Ellisville, St. Louis, Mo	20
Ellisville, Kewaunee, Wis	10
Ellittsville, Monroe, Ind	190
Ellsworth, Johnson, Ark	12
Ellsworth, Litchfield, Conn	61
Ellsworth, Vigo, Ind	24
Ellsworth, Madison, Iowa	18
Ellsworth,* (*c. h.*,) Ellsworth, Kans	1,000
Ellsworth,* (*c. h.*,) Hancock, Me	1,400
Ellsworth, Nye, Nev	41
Ellsworth, Grafton, N. H	16
Ellsworth, St. Lawrence, N. Y	62
Ellsworth, Mahoning, Ohio	83
Ellsworth, (*c. h.*,) Pierce, Wis	160
Ellwood, Hopkins, Ky	6
Ellwood, Schuylkill, Pa	25
Elm, Wayne, Mich	26
Elm, Linn, Mo	12
Elm, Fayette, Pa	86
Elma, Erie, N. Y	51
Elma, Chehalis, Wash	11
Elm Bluff, Dallas, Ala	5
Elmendaro, Lyon, Kans	8
Elmer, Salem, N. J	150

* Money-order office.

Elm Flat, Chautauqua, N. Y	$16
Elm Grove, Adams, Ill	10
Elm Grove, Franklin, Mass	16
Elm Grove, Holt, Mo	55
Elm Grove, Jefferson, Nebr	12
Elm Grove, Ohio, W. Va	66
Elm Grove, Waukesha, Wis	35
Elm Hall, Gratiot, Mich	97
Elm Hill, Montgomery, Ky	12
Elmhurst, Du Page, Ill	240
Elmington, Nelson, Va	26
Elmira, Stark, Ill	72
Elmira, Eaton, Mich	6
Elmira,* (*c. h.*,) Chemung, N. Y	3,600
Elmira, Fulton, Ohio	56
Elmore, Peoria, Ill	70
Elmore, Faribault, Minn	10
Elmore, Richardson, Nebr	18
Elmore, Ottawa, Ohio	650
Elmore, Lamoille, Vt	83
Elmore, Fond du Lac, Wis	12
Elm Point, Bond, Ill	37
Elmsford, Westchester, N. Y	18
Elm Springs, Washington, Ark	44
Elm Springs, Butler, Iowa	40
Elm Store, Randolph, Ark	20
Elm Tree, Weakley, Tenn	8
Elm Wood, Carroll, Ark	12
Elmwood,* Peoria, Ill	400
Elm Wood, Saline, Mo	130
Elmwood, Cass, Nebr	44
Elo, Winnebago, Wis	45
Elon, Allamakee, Iowa	30
Elora, Lincoln, Tenn	13
El Paso, Conway, Ark	28
El Paso, El Paso, Colo	12
El Paso,* Woodford, Ill	1,600
El Paso, (*c. h.*,) El Paso, Tex	80
El Paso, Pierce, Wis	62
Elrod, Ripley, Ind	44
Elroy, Juneau, Wis	46
Elsah, Jersey, Ill	80
El Sauz, Hidalgo, Tex	12
Elsie, Clinton, Mich	250
Elsinor, McLean, Ill	12
Elsinore, Allen, Kans	22
Elston, Labette, Kans	12
Elston Station, Cole, Mo	72
Eltham, Westmoreland, Va	12
Elton, Cattaraugus, N. Y	24
Elton, Walworth, Wis	22
Elvaston, Hancock, Ill	160
Elvira, Johnson, Ill	14
Elvira, Clinton, Iowa	41
Elwell, Bradford, Pa	8
Elwin, Macon, Ill	70
Elwood, Will, Ill	220
Elwood, Madison, Ind	200
Elwood, Doniphan, Kans	140
Elwood, Steele, Minn	6
Elwood, Atlantic, N. J	270
Elwood, Suffolk, N. Y	12
Ely, Warrick, Ind	200
Elyria,* (*c. h.*,) Lorain, Ohio	1,800
Elysburgh, Northumberland, Pa	46
Elysian, Le Sueur, Minn	72
Elyton, (*c. h.*,) Jefferson, Ala	$100
Emanuel, Bonhomme, Dak	7
Emaus, Lehigh, Pa	140
Emaus, Bedford, Va	12
Embarrass, Waupaca, Wis	52
Embden, Somerset, Me	7
Embreeville, Chester, Pa	37
Embryville, Washington, Tenn	12
Emerald, Adams, Ohio	12
Emerald, Anderson, Kans	12
Emerald Grove, Rock, Wis	110
Emerson, Mills, Iowa	12
Emerson, Marion, Mo	25
Emerson, Otoe, Nebr	16
Emery, Fulton, Ohio	12
Emery, Monroe, Wis	50
Emery's Mills, York, Me	30
Emigrant Gap, Placer, Cal	10
Emigsville, York, Pa	38
Emilie, Bucks, Pa	49
Eminence, Logan, Ill	12
Eminence, Morgan, Ind	45
Eminence, Henry, Ky	640
Eminence, (*c. h.*,) Shannon, Mo	27
Eminence, Schoharie, N. Y	24
Emison Station, Knox, Ind	12
Emlenton, Venango, Pa	280
Emma, Butler, Ala	12
Emma, White, Ill	20
Emmaville, Fulton, Pa	17
Emmett, Lake, Ill	12
Emmett, Emmett, Iowa	13
Emmett, St. Clair, Mich	12
Emmett, Paulding, Ohio	15
Emmettsburgh, Deer Lodge, Mont	12
Emmettsville, Ada, Idaho	12
Emmittsburgh, (*c. h.*,) Palo Alto, Iowa	17
Emmittsburgh,* Frederick, Md	860
Emmonsburgh, Herkimer, N. Y	64
Emmorton, Harford, Md	95
Emmorton, Richmond, Va	12
Emory, Washington, Va	340
Empire, Wright, Iowa	12
Empire, Leelenaw, Mich	68
Empire, Fond du Lac, Wis	27
Empire City, Clear Creek, Colo	55
Empire City, Dakota, Minn	20
Empire City, Ormsby, Nev	140
Empire City, (*c. h.*,) Coos, Oreg	180
Empire Iron Works, Trigg, Ky	16
Empire Junction, Columbia, Wis	17
Empire Prairie, Andrew, Mo	58
Emporia,* (*c. h.*,) Lyon, Kans	1,800
Emporium,* (*c. h.*,) Cameron, Pa	890
Emuckfaw, Tallapoosa, Ala	4
Enders, Dauphin, Pa	22
Endor, Will, Ill	12
Enfield, Hartford, Conn	290
Enfield, White, Ill	83
Enfield, Penobscot, Me	92
Enfield, Hampshire, Mass	350
Enfield, Grafton, N. H	430
Enfield, Tompkins, N. Y	12
Enfield, Halifax, N. C	420
Enfield, King William, Va	11
Enfield Centre, Grafton, N. H	230

* Money-order office.

Post office	
Enfield Centre, Tompkins, N. Y	$39
Engleman's Mills, Dade, Mo	25
Englewood, Cook, Ill	25
Englewood, Bergen, N. J	580
English, Crawford, Ind	10
English Centre, Lycoming, Pa	68
English Lake, Stark, Ind	32
English Prairie, McHenry, Ill	15
English's Creek, Atlantic, N. J	52
English Settlement, Marion, Iowa	15
Englishtown, Monmouth, N. J	180
Englishville, Kent, Mich	22
Ennisville, Huntingdon, Pa	37
Enoch, Noble, Ohio	19
Enochsburgh, Franklin, Ind	50
Enola, Iredell, N. C	10
Enon, Bullock, Ala	45
Enon, Perry, Miss	7
Enon, Clark, Ohio	150
Enon College, Sumner, Tenn	26
Enon Valley, Lawrence, Pa	380
Enoree, Spartanburgh, S. C	6
Enosburgh, Franklin, Vt	100
Enosburgh Falls,* Franklin, Vt	150
Ensley, Newaygo, Mich	10
Enterline, Dauphin, Pa	21
Enterprise, Lee, Ga	12
Enterprise, Wayne, Ill	20
Enterprise, Spencer, Ind	58
Enterprise, Black Hawk, Iowa	19
Enterprise, Winona, Minn	69
Enterprise, (*c. h.*,) Clark, Miss	770
Enterprise, McDonald, Mo	19
Enterprise, Hocking, Ohio	12
Enterprise, Lancaster, Pa	260
Enterprise, Morgan, Utah	19
Enterprise, Vernon, Wis	14
Enterprise Landing, Charleston, S.C.	12
Enterprize, Volusia, Fla	92
Eola, Polk, Oreg	42
Ephraim, San Pete, Utah	500
Ephraim, Door, Wis	90
Ephratah, Fulton, N. Y	72
Ephratah, Lancaster, Pa	310
Epping, Rockingham, N. H	310
Epsom, Daviess, Ind	12
Epsom, Merrimack, N. H	120
Epworth, Dubuque, Iowa	370
Equality, Coosa, Ala	10
Equality, Gallatin, Ill	140
Equality, Saline, Nebr	12
Equality, Anderson, S. C	14
Equinunk, Wayne, Pa	170
Erastus, Banks, Ga	9
Erata, Jones, Miss	2
Ercildoun, Chester, Pa	100
Erfurt, Jefferson, Wis	57
Erie, Whitesides, Ill	120
Erie, Lawrence, Ind	16
Erie,* (*c. h.*,) Neosho, Kans	500
Erie, Monroe, Mich	170
Erie, McDonald, Mo	8
Erie,* (*c. h.*,) Erie, Pa	3,100
Erie, Roane, Tenn	18
Erieville, Madison, N. Y	80
Erin, Meriwether, Ga	10

Post office	
Erin, Washington, Kans	$16
Erin, Calhoun, Miss	9
Erin, Chemung, N. Y	6
Erin, Stewart, Tenn	12
Erin, St. Croix, Wis	41
Erin Shades, Henrico, Va	6
Errol, Coos, N. H	37
Ervin, Howard, Ind	37
Erving, Franklin, Mass	200
Erwin Centre, Steuben, N. Y	35
Erwinna, Bucks, Pa	76
Erwinsville, Cleveland, N. C	5
Escatawpa, Washington, Ala	12
Escoheag, Kent, R. I	12
Esconawba,* (*c. h.*,) Delta, Mich	790
Eskridge, Wabaunsee, Kans	12
Esofia, Vernon, Wis	12
Esopus, Ulster, N. Y	210
Esparanza, St. John's, Fla	12
Esperance, Schoharie, N. Y	300
Espy, Columbia, Pa	240
Espyville, Crawford, Pa	84
Essex,* Middlesex, Conn	720
Essex, Essex, Mass	250
Essex, Clinton, Mich	12
Essex,* Essex, N. Y	420
Essex, Chittenden, Vt	210
Essex Junction, Chittenden, Vt	250
Esteina, Saunders, Nebr	12
Estella, Ringgold, Iowa	9
Estell Flats, Carter, Ky	12
Estelville, Atlantic, N. J	25
Estherville, (*c. h.*,) Emmett, Iowa	150
Estill's Fork, Jackson, Ala	8
Estill Springs, Franklin, Tenn	55
Estillville, (*c. h.*,) Scott, Va	100
Ethel, Mercer, Ill	11
Etlah, Franklin, Mo	24
Etna, Coles, Ill	67
Etna, Penobscot, Me	48
Etna, Fillmore, Minn	48
Etna, Scotland, Mo	89
Etna, Tompkins, N. Y	150
Etna, Licking, Ohio	89
Etna, Allegheny, Pa	180
Etna, Smith, Tex	12
Etna, La Fayette, Wis	70
Etna Centre, Penobscot, Me	20
Etna Green, Kosciusko, Ind	120
Etna Mills, Siskiyou, Cal	24
Etna Mills, King William, Va	12
Etters, York, Pa	230
Ettie, Tama, Iowa	12
Ettieville, Gentry, Mo	12
Ettrick, Trempealeau, Wis	21
Euclid, Onondaga, N. Y	86
Euclid, Cuyahoga, Ohio	69
Eudora, Douglas, Kans	250
Eufaula,* Barbour, Ala	2,000
Eugene, Knox, Ill	42
Eugene, Vermillion, Ind	170
Eugene, Ringgold, Iowa	6
Eugene, Shawnee, Kans	400
Eugene City, Carroll, Mo	12
Eugene City,* (*c. h.*,) Lane, Oreg	610
Euharley, Bartow, Ga	76

* Money-order office.

Eulalia, Potter, Pa	$8
Eulia, Macon, Tenn	12
Eunice, Chicot, Ark	13
Euphemia, Preble, Ohio	49
*Eureka,** (*c. h.,*) Humboldt, Cal	610
Eureka, Woodford, Ill	930
*Eureka,** (*c. h.,*) Greenwood, Kans	230
Eureka, Clinton, Mich	75
Eureka, St. Louis, Mo	61
Eureka, Lander, Nev	12
Eureka, Sullivan, N. Y	24
Eureka, Gallia, Ohio	94
Eureka, Winnebago, Wis	330
Eustis, Franklin, Me	12
*Eutaw,** (*c. h.,*) Greene, Ala	840
Eutaw, Limestone, Tex	17
Eva, Barry, Mo	13
Evans, (*c. h.,*) Weld, Colo	130
Evans, Erie, N. Y	73
Evansburgh, Coshocton, Ohio	60
Evansburgh, Crawford, Pa	120
Evans' Landing, Harrison, Ind	12
Evans' Mills, Jefferson, N. Y	390
Evansport, Defiance, Ohio	54
Evanston,* Cook, Ill	1,600
Evanston, Uintah, Wyo	12
Evansville, Washington, Ark	52
Evansville, Randolph, Ill	80
*Evansville,** (*c. h.,*) Vanderburgh, Ind	4,000
Evansville, Douglas, Minn	65
Evansville, Columbia, Pa	25
Evansville, Preston, W. Va	80
Evansville,* Rock, Wis	790
Evanswood, Waupaca, Wis	12
Evart, Osceola, Mich	12
Eveland Grove, Mahaska, Iowa	15
Eveline, Buchanan, Mo	19
Eve Mills, Monroe, Tenn	22
Evendale, Juniata, Pa	45
Evening Shades, (*c. h.,*) Sharp, Ark	27
Everett, Cass, Mo	70
Evergreen, (*c. h.,*) Conecuh, Ala	340
Ever Green, Washington, Ark	5
Evergreen, Santa Clara, Cal	12
Evergreen, Tama, Iowa	22
Evergreen, Avoyelles, La	110
Evergreen, Appomattox, Va	48
Everittstown, Hunterdon, N. J	54
Everton, Fayette, Ind	63
Ewald, Faribault, Minn	12
Ewan's Mills, Gloucester, N. J	8
Ewing, Franklin, Ill	20
Ewing, Jackson, Ind	78
Ewing, Hocking, Ohio	21
Ewing's Corner, Hancock, Ohio	12
Ewing's Mills, Allegheny, Pa	38
Ewing's Neck, Cumberland, N. J	23
Ewington, Gallia, Ohio	50
Ewingville, Mercer, N. J	36
Excello, Macon, Mo	12
Excelsior, Pueblo, Colo	19
Excelsior, Hennepin, Minn	170
Excelsior, Morgan, Mo	25
Excelsior, Northumberland, Pa	12
Excelsior, Richland, Wis	35
Excelsior Mills, Jo Daviess, Ill	$36
Exchange, Montour, Pa	16
Exeter, Scott, Ill	140
Exeter, Penobscot, Me	130
Exeter, Monroe, Mich	8
*Exeter,** (*c. h.,*) Rockingham, N. H	1,700
Exeter, Otsego, N. Y	50
Exeter, Luzerne, Pa	14
Exeter, Washington, R. I	27
Exeter, Green, Wis	13
Exeter Mills, Penobscot, Me	20
Exeter Station, Berks, Pa	66
Exira, (*c. h.,*) Audubon, Iowa	150
Exonville, Wabaunsee, Kans	12
Experiment Mills, Monroe, Pa	75
Express Ranch, Baker, Oreg	25
Exton, Chester, Pa	70
Eyer's Grove, Columbia, Pa	10
Eyota, Olmsted, Minn	530

F

FABER'S MILLS, Nelson, Va	65
Fabius, Onondaga, N. Y	240
Fabius, Hardy, W. Va	11
Fackler, Etowah, Ala	12
Factory Point, Bennington, Vt	430
Factory Village, Franklin, Mass	12
Factoryville, Cass, Nebr	56
Factoryville, Tioga, N. Y	150
Factoryville, Wyoming, Pa	280
Fagleysville, Montgomery, Pa	25
Fairbank, Buchanan, Iowa	150
Fair Bluff, Columbus, N. C	62
Fairburn, Campbell, Ga	110
Fairbury,* Livingston, Ill	1,500
Fairbury, (*c. h.,*) Jefferson, Nebr	59
Fairchild, Eau Claire, Wis	12
Fair Dale, Oswego, N. Y	36
Fairdale, Susquehanna, Pa	65
Fair Dealing, Marshall, Ky	12
Fairfax, Linn, Iowa	260
Fairfax, Highland, Ohio	23
Fairfax, Franklin, Vt	360
Fairfax C. H., Fairfax, Va	250
Fairfield, (*c. h.,*) Fairfield, Conn	470
*Fairfield,** (*c. h.,*) Wayne, Ill	380
Fairfield, Franklin, Ind	150
*Fairfield,** (*c. h.,*) Jefferson, Iowa	1,500
Fairfield, Nelson, Ky	110
Fairfield, Somerset, Me	45
Fairfield, St. Mary's, Md	63
Fairfield, Lenawee, Mich	150
Fairfield, Benton, Mo	44
Fairfield, Herkimer, N. Y	310
Fairfield, Hyde, N. C	20
Fairfield, Greene, Ohio	150
Fairfield, Marion, Oreg	12
Fairfield, Adams, Pa	110
Fairfield, Bedford, Tenn	10
Fairfield, (*c. h.,*) Freestone, Tex	180
Fairfield, Utah, Utah	14
Fairfield, Franklin, Vt	140
Fairfield, Rockbridge, Va	71
Fairfield, Rock, Wis	22
Fairfield Centre, De Kalb, Ind	27

* Money-order office.

Fairfield Centre, Lycoming, Pa	$9
Fairfield Corners, Somerset, Me	47
Fair Garden, Sevier, Tenn	6
Fair Grove, Greene, Mo	66
Fair Grove, Tuscola, Mich	14
Fair Grove, Davidson, N. C	5
Fair Haven, New Haven, Conn	1,300
Fair Haven, Carroll, Ill	24
Fairhaven, Bristol, Mass	990
Fair Haven, St. Clair, Mich	45
Fair Haven, Stearns, Minn	76
Fair Haven, Cayuga, N. Y	86
Fair Haven, Preble, Ohio	130
Fair Haven,* Rutland, Vt	1,000
Fair Hill, Cecil, Md	65
Fair Hill, Rockingham, Va	47
Fair Hill, Marshall, W. Va	6
Fairland, Shelby, Ind	210
Fairlee, Kent, Md	35
Fairlee, Orange, Vt	140
Fairmont, (*c. h.,*) Martin, Minn	140
Fairmont, Clarke, Mo	130
*Fairmont,** (*c. h.,*) Marion, W. Va	680
Fair Mount, Gordon, Ga	59
Fairmount,* Vermilion, Ill	350
Fairmount, Grant, Ind	130
Fairmount, Leavenworth, Kans	67
Fairmount, Jefferson, Ky	51
Fairmount, Somerset, Md	12
Fair Mount, Hunterdon, N. J	23
Fair Mount, Onondaga, N. Y	31
Fairmount Springs, Luzerne, Pa	27
Fair Oaks, San Mateo, Cal	6
Fair Play, Randolph, Ala	12
Fair Play, El Dorado, Cal	12
Fair Play, (*c. h.,*) Park, Colo	540
Fair Play, Washington, Md	43
Fair Play, Polk, Mo	28
Fair Play, Jefferson, Ohio	28
Fair Play, Oconee, S. C	26
Fair Play, Grant, Wis	98
Fair Point, Goodhue, Minn	23
Fairport, Muscatine, Iowa	16
Fairport, De Kalb, Mo	12
Fairport, Monroe, N. Y	1,800
Fairport, Granville, N. C	5
Fairton, Cumberland, N. J	96
Fairview, Walker, Ala	12
Fairview, Dallas, Ark	12
Fairview, Lincoln, Dak	12
Fairview, Fulton, Ill	300
Fairview, Randolph, Ind	32
Fairview, Jones, Iowa	60
Fairview, Brown, Kans	14
Fairview, Christian, Ky	96
Fairview, Concordia, La	15
Fairview, Washington, Md	16
Fairview, Mason, Mich	18
Fairview, Fillmore, Minn	14
Fairview, St. Louis, Mo	13
Fairview, Bergen, N. J	84
Fairview, Cattaraugus, N. Y	24
Fairview, Buncombe, N. C	150
Fairview, Guernsey, Ohio	180
Fairview,* Erie, Pa	350
Fairview, Greenville, S. C	18
Fairview, Anderson, Tenn	$12
Fair View, Wilson, Tex	12
Fair View, San Pete, Utah	39
Fairview, (*c. h.,*) Hancock, W. Va	110
Fairview, Grant, Wis	58
Fairview Village, Montgomery, Pa	44
Fairville, Saline, Mo	12
Fairville, Wayne, N. Y	68
Fairville, Chester, Pa	59
Fair Water, Fond du Lac, Wis	95
Fair Weather, Adams, Ill	41
Faison's Depot, Duplin, N. C	11
Falcon, Columbia, Ark	82
Falkland, Pitt, N. C	65
Fallassburgh, Kent, Mich	20
Fall Brook, Tioga, Pa	460
Fall City, Dunn, Wis	14
Fall Creek, Marion, Ind	10
Fall Creek, Bedford, Tenn	12
Fallen Timber, Cambria, Pa	41
Falling Creek, Lenoir, N. C	12
Falling Spring, Greenbrier, W. Va	12
Falling Springs, Douglas, Mo	12
Falling Waters, Berkeley, W. Va	51
Fallowfield, Crawford, Pa	55
Fall River,* Bristol, Mass	3,400
Fall River, Columbia, Wis	210
Falls, Wyoming, Pa	85
Falls Branch, Washington, Tenn	20
Fallsburgh, Sullivan, N. Y	43
Fallsburgh, Licking, Ohio	15
Falls Church, Fairfax, Va	130
*Falls City,** (*c. h.,*) Richardson, Nebr	300
Fallsington, Bucks, Pa	60
Falls Mill, Sullivan, N. Y	12
Falls Mills, Lincoln, W. Va	5
Falls of Blaine, Lawrence, Ky	3
Falls of Rough, Grayson, Ky	16
Fallston, Harford, Md	150
Falls Village,* Litchfield, Conn	530
Falmouth, Rush, Ind	38
Falmouth, (*c. h.,*) Pendleton, Ky	330
Falmouth, Cumberland, Me	140
Falmouth, Barnstable, Mass	420
Falmouth, Lancaster, Pa	49
Falmouth, Stafford, Va	110
Falun, Saline, Kans	12
Fame, Greenwood, Kans	12
Fancy Creek, Richland, Wis	23
Fancy Farm, Graves, Ky	46
Fancy Gap, Carroll, Va	5
Fancy Grove, Bedford, Va	13
Fancy Hill, Iredell, N. C	4
Fancy Hill, Rockbridge, Va	75
Fanlight, Wetzel, W. Va	12
Fannettsburgh, Franklin, Pa	86
Fannin, Rankin, Miss	16
Farabee's Station, Washington, Ind.	14
*Faribault,** (*c. h.,*) Rice, Minn	2,300
Farina, Fayette, Ill	260
Farley, Dubuque, Iowa	270
Farley, Platte, Mo	65
Farlington, Crawford, Kans	12
Farlinville, Linn, Kans	87
Farmdale, Franklin, Ky	250
Farmer, Defiance, Ohio	93

* **Money-order office.**

Farmer City, De Witt, Ill	$530
Farmers, Rowan, Ky	11
Farmers, Sanilac, Mich	12
Farmersburgh, Clayton, Iowa	47
Farmers' Creek, Jackson, Iowa	12
Farmers' Creek, Lapeer, Mich	33
Farmers' Grove, Fillmore, Minn	12
Farmers' Grove, Southampton, Va	11
Farmers' Grove, Green, Wis	44
Farmers' Institute, Tippecanoe, Ind	32
Farmers' Mills, Putnam, N. Y	19
Farmers' Retreat, Dearborn, Ind	40
Farmers' Station, Owen, Ind	12
Farmers' Station, Clinton, Ohio	60
Farmers' Valley, Hamilton, Nebr	12
Farmers' Valley, McKean, Pa	44
Farmers' Valley, Monroe, Wis	4
Farmersville, Lowndes, Ala	12
Farmersville, Tulare, Cal	24
Farmersville, Posey, Ind	22
Farmersville, Mahaska, Iowa	10
Farmersville, (*c. h.*,) Union, La	360
Farmersville, Livingston, Mo	67
Farmersville, Cattaraugus, N. Y	70
Farmersville, Montgomery, Ohio	65
Farmersville, Lancaster, Pa	33
Farmersville, Collin, Tex	30
Farmersville, Dodge, Wis	48
Farmer Village, Seneca, N. Y	390
Farm Hill, Olmsted, Minn	24
Farmingdale, Monmouth, N. J	230
Farmingdale, Queens, N. Y	180
Farmington, Washington, Ark	19
Farmington, San Joaquin, Cal	79
Farmington, Hartford, Conn	470
Farmington, Kent, Del	120
Farmington,* Fulton, Ill	890
Farmington,* Van Buren, Iowa	410
Farmington, Atchison, Kans	12
Farmington, Graves, Ky	33
Farmington,* (*c. h.*,) Franklin, Me	1,300
Farmington, Cecil, Md	20
Farmington, Oakland, Mich	300
Farmington,* Dakota, Minn	450
Farmington, (*c. h.*,) St. Francois, Mo	260
Farmington, Strafford, N. H	550
Farmington, Ontario, N. Y	93
Farmington, Davie, N. C	58
Farmington, Trumbull, Ohio	110
Farmington, Fayette, Pa	86
Farmington, Marshall, Tenn	41
Farmington, Grayson, Tex	66
Farmington, (*c. h.*,) Davis, Utah	61
Farmington, Marion, W. Va	89
Farmington, Jefferson, Wis	41
Farmington Centre, Tioga, Pa	13
Farmington Centre, Polk, Wis	39
Farmington Falls, Franklin, Me	110
Farmington Hill, Tioga, Pa	19
Farmland, Randolph, Ind	250
Farm Ridge, La Salle, Ill	75
Farm's Village, Hartford, Conn	25
Farmsville, Woodford, Ill	16
Farmville, Pitt, N. C	55
Farmville, Henderson, Tenn	12
Farmville,* Prince Edward, Va	1,000

Farmwell, Loudoun, Va	$180
Farnham, Erie, N. Y	52
Farnham, Richmond, Va	12
Farnham × Roads, Richmond, Va	12
Farnumsville, Worcester, Mass	110
Farrandsville, Clinton, Pa	53
Farribaville, Sevier, Ark	12
Fassett, Bradford, Pa	35
Fatama, Wilcox, Ala	12
Faunsdale, Marengo, Ala	12
Fauquier White Sulphur Springs, Fauquier, Va	41
Fawn Grove, York, Pa	44
Fawn River, St. Joseph, Mich	16
Faxon, Sibley, Minn	54
Fayette, Greene, Ill	52
Fayette,* Fayette, Iowa	580
Fayette, Kennebec, Me	85
Fayette,* (*c. h.*,) Jefferson, Miss	470
Fayette,* (*c. h.*,) Howard, Mo	580
Fayette, Seneca, N. Y	110
Fayette, Allegheny, Pa	6
Fayette, La Fayette, Wis	53
Fayette C. H., Fayette, Ala	67
Fayette City, Fayette, Pa	160
Fayette Ridge, Kennebec, Me	14
Fayette Springs, Fayette, Pa	17
Fayetteville,* (*c. h.*,) Washington, Ark	750
Fayetteville, (*c. h.*,) Fayette, Ga	26
Fayetteville, St. Clair, Ill	54
Fayetteville, Lawrence, Ind	18
Fayetteville, Clay, Kans	12
Fayetteville, Johnson, Mo	80
Fayetteville, Onondaga, N. Y	800
Fayetteville, (*c. h.*,) Cumberland, N. C	1,700
Fayetteville, Brown, Ohio	110
Fayetteville, Franklin, Pa	190
Fayetteville,* (*c. h.*,) Lincoln, Tenn	660
Fayetteville, Fayette, Tex	98
Fayetteville, (*c. h.*,) Windham, Vt	200
Fayetteville, (*c. h.*,) Fayette, W. Va	73
Fayville, Worcester, Mass	130
Fearing, Washington, Ohio	20
Fearn's Springs, Winston, Miss	15
Feasterville, Bucks, Pa	66
Feasterville, Fairfield, S. C	12
Federal Hill, Hartford, Md	12
Federal Point, Putnam, Fla	12
Federalsburgh, Carroll, Md	240
Federalton, Athens, Ohio	10
Feeding Hills, Hampden, Mass	150
Feed Spring, Harrison, Ohio	10
Feesburgh, Brown, Ohio	55
Felchville, Windsor, Vt	220
Felicity,* Clermont, Ohio	250
Fellowship, Burlington, N. J	50
Fellowsville, Preston, W. Va	38
Felton, Kent, Del	300
Felts, Ingham, Mich	10
Felt's Mills, Jefferson, N. Y	86
Femme Osage, St. Charles, Mo	73
Fenner, Madison, N. Y	30
Fennimore, Grant, Wis	100
Fenns, Shelby, Ind	12

* Money-order office.

Fenn's Bridge, Jefferson, Ga	$12
Fenn's Mills, Allegan, Mich	55
Fenton, Whitesides, Ill	12
Fenton, St. Louis, Mo	25
Fenton, Wood, Ohio	10
Fentonville,* Genesee, Mich	1,000
Fentonville, Chautauqua, N. Y	29
Fentriss, Guilford, N. C	10
Ferdinand, Mercer, Ill	9
Ferdinand, Dubois, Ind	120
Fergus Falls, Otter Tail, Minn	12
Ferguson, St. Louis, Mo	12
Ferguson's Corners, Yates N. Y	12
Ferguson's Station, Logan, Ky	66
Fergusonville, Delaware, N. Y	110
Fernandez de Taos, (c. h.,) Tex., N. Mex	47
Fernandina, (c. h.,)* Nassau, Fla	1,000
Fern Creek, Jefferson, Ky	12
Ferndale, Humboldt, Cal	53
Fern Leaf, Mason, Ky	30
Fern Valley, Palo Alto, Iowa	8
Ferris, Hancock, Ill	12
Ferris, Montcalm, Mich	12
Ferrisburgh, Addison, Vt	90
Ferrona, Clinton, N. Y	12
Ferry, Mahaska, Iowa	12
Ferry Point, Norfolk, Va	23
Ferrysburgh, Ottawa, Mich	160
Ferry Village, Cumberland, Me	12
Ferryville, St. Clair, Ala	12
Ferryville, Crawford, Wis	10
Fertigs, Venango, Pa	18
Fertile, Worth, Iowa	12
Fertility, Lancaster, Pa	7
Festina, Winneshiek, Iowa	61
Fetherolffsville, Berks, Pa	16
Fetterman, Taylor, W. Va	120
Fiatt, Fulton, Ill	16
Fiddletown, Amador, Cal	120
Fidelity, Jersey, Ill	70
Fidelity, Jasper, Mo	27
Fidelity, Miami, Ohio	12
Field Bend, Pike, Pa	22
Fieldon, Jersey, Ill	70
Fieldsborough, New Castle, Del	10
Fife's, Goochland, Va	15
Fifteen Mile Grove, Tama, Iowa	38
Fig Grove, Coosa, Ala	12
Filer City, Manistee, Mich	12
Fillmore, Montgomery, Ill	20
Fillmore, Putnam, Ind	120
Fillmore, Dubuque, Iowa	9
Fillmore, Barry, Mich	63
Fillmore, Fillmore, Minn	81
Fillmore, Andrew, Mo	160
Fillmore, Monmouth, N. J	61
Fillmore, Allegany, N. Y	100
Fillmore, Washington, Ohio	18
Fillmore, Centre, Pa	37
Fillmore, Sequatchie, Tenn	2
Fillmore, Randolph, W. Va	3
Fillmore, Washington, Wis	70
Fillmore City, (c. h.,) Millard, Utah	140
Fincastle, Brown, Ohio	41
Fincastle, Campbell, Tenn	23
Fincastle, Henderson, Tex	$12
Fincastle, (c. h.,)* Botetourt, Va	390
Findley, (c. h.,)* Hancock, Ohio	1,800
Findley's Lake, Chautauqua, N. Y	35
Findley's Mills, Jackson, Ind	5
Fine, St. Lawrence, N. Y	46
Fine Creek Mills, Powhatan, Va	39
Finksburgh, Carroll, Md	65
Fink's Creek, Lewis, W. Va	12
Finley Station, Cumberland, N. J	14
Finleyville, Washington, Pa	75
Finney's Creek, Saline, Mo	12
Fir Cap, Sierra, Cal	12
Firebaugh, Fresno, Cal	20
Fire Island, Suffolk, N. Y	12
Fireplace, Suffolk, N. Y	53
Fire Prairie, Jackson, Mo	12
First Broad, Rutherford, N. C	5
First Fork, Cameron, Pa	13
Fish Creek, Steuben, Ind	13
Fish Creek, Jefferson, Mont	12
Fish Creek, Oneida, N. Y	12
Fish Creek, Door, Wis	56
Fish Dam, Wake, N. C	6
Fish Dam, Union, S. C	12
Fisher, Clarion, Pa	20
Fisherman's Bay, Sonoma, Cal	71
Fisher's, Ontario, N. Y	69
Fishersburgh, Madison, Ind	25
Fisher's Ferry, Northumberland, Pa	68
Fisher's Landing, Decatur, Tenn	12
Fisher's Point, Jackson, W. Va	9
Fishersville,* Merrimack, N. H	900
Fishersville, Augusta, Va	160
Fisherville, Jefferson, Ky	63
Fisherville, Dauphin, Pa	32
Fish Haven, Rich, Utah	8
Fish Hook, Pike, Ill	24
Fishing Creek, Dorchester, Md	8
Fishing Creek, Cape May, N. J	10
Fishing Creek, Columbia, Pa	12
Fishkill, Dutchess, N. Y	680
Fishkill on the Hudson, Dutchess, N. Y	1,200
Fishkill Plains, Dutchess, N. Y	40
Fish Lake, Elkhart, Ind	5
Fish Pond, Tallapoosa, Ala	10
Fish Springs, Inyo, Cal	12
Fiskedale, Worcester, Mass	270
Fiskeville, Providence, R. I	72
Fisk's Corners, Winnebago, Wis	10
Fitchburgh,* Worcester, Mass	3,000
Fitchburgh, Ingham, Mich	50
Fitchburgh, Dane, Wis	55
Fitchville, Huron, Ohio	98
Fithian, Vermilion, Ill	12
Fitts Hill, Franklin, Ill	23
Fitz Henry, Ogle, Ill	24
Fitz Henry, Westmoreland, Pa	49
Fitzpatrick's, Bullock, Ala	12
Fitzwatertown, Montgomery, Pa	42
Fitzwilliam, Cheshire, N. H	340
Fitzwilliam Depot, Cheshire, N. H	190
Five Corners, Miami, Ind	12
Five Corners, Cayuga, N. Y	120
Five Lakes, Lapeer, Mich	12

* Money-order office.

Post office	
Five Mile, Hale, Ala	$5
Five Mile, Brown, Ohio	20
Five Mile, Pickens, S. C	4
Five Mile House, Milwaukee, Wis	12
Five Points, Gloucester, N. J	17
Five Points, Pickaway, Ohio	23
Flackville, St. Lawrence, N. Y	28
Flagg Spring, Campbell, Ky	12
Flaggtown, Somerset, N. J	68
Flag Pond, Washington, Tenn	12
Flag Springs, Andrew, Mo	12
Flagstaff, Somerset, Me	40
Flag Station, Ogle, Ill	67
Flanders, Morris, N. J	140
Flanders, Suffolk, N. Y	12
Flat, Pike, Ohio	40
Flat Branches, Forsyth, N. C	12
Flatbrook, Columbia, N. Y	25
Flatbrookville, Sussex, N. J	28
Flatbush, Kings, N. Y	270
Flat Creek, Barry, Mo	18
Flat Creek, Montgomery, N. Y	21
Flat Creek, Bedford, Tenn	13
Flat Fork, Anson, N. C	2
Flat Fork, Roane, W. Va	2
Flat Gap, Jefferson, Tenn	10
Flatlands, Kings, N. Y	53
Flat Lick, Knox, Ky	22
Flatonia, Fayette, Tex	12
Flat River, St. Francois, Mo	12
Flat River, Orange, N. C	7
Flat Rock, Talladega, Ala	5
Flat Rock, Crawford, Ill	9
Flat Rock, Shelby, Ind	62
Flat Rock, Neosho, Kans	12
Flat Rock, Bourbon, Ky	14
Flat Rock, Henderson, N. C	44
Flat Rock, Seneca, Ohio	84
Flat Rock, Kershaw, S. C	14
Flat Rock, Lewis, Tenn	6
Flat Rock, Mason, W. Va	12
Flat Shoal, Surry, N. C	7
Flat Shoals, Meriwether, Ga	12
Flat Top, Mercer, W. Va	12
Flatwoods, Fayette, Pa	84
Flat Woods, Braxton, W. Va	15
Fleetville, Luzerne, Pa	43
Fleetwood, Berks, Pa	150
Fleming, Liberty, Ga	56
Fleming, Livingston, Mich	20
Fleming, Cayuga, N. Y	120
Fleming, Washington, Ohio	42
Fleming, Centre, Pa	200
*Flemingsburgh,** (*c. h.*,) Fleming, Ky	640
Flemingsville, Tioga, N. Y	23
Flemington, Marion, Fla	28
*Flemington,** (*c. h.*,) Hunterdon, N. J	1,200
Flemington, Columbus, N. C	12
Flemington, Clinton, Pa	130
Flemington, Taylor, W. Va	110
Flemingville, Linn, Iowa	8
Flemming's Ranch, Weld, Colo	8
Fletcher, Miami, Ohio	100
Fletcher, Franklin, Vt	77
Flint, Cherokee N., Ind. T	5
Flint, Pike, Ill	35

Post office	
Flint, Steuben, Ind	$59
Flint, Mahaska, Iowa	25
*Flint,** (*c. h.*,) Genesee, Mich	2,600
Flint, Franklin, Ohio	12
Flint Creek, Ontario, N. Y	24
Flint Factory, Madison, Ala	12
Flint Hill, St. Charles, Mo	24
Flint Hill, Rappahannock, Va	44
Flint Island, Meade, Ky	83
Flint Ridge, Lancaster, S. C	12
Flint River, Morgan, Ala	12
Flint's Mills, Washington, Ohio	23
Flint Stone, Alleghany, Md	70
Flintville, Lincoln, Tenn	19
Flintville, Brown, Wis	12
Flinty Branch, Yancey, N. C	14
Flippin, Monroe, Ky	8
Flippo's, Caroline, Va	16
Flora, Clay, Ill	610
Flora Dale, Adams, Pa	31
Floraville, St. Clair, Ill	27
Florence, (*c. h.*,) Lauderdale, Ala	930
Florence, Pima, Ariz	12
Florence, Drew, Ark	12
Florence, Stewart, Ga	12
Florence, Pike, Ill	68
Florence, Switzerland, Ind	120
Florence, Benton, Iowa	360
Florence, Boone, Ky	170
Florence, Howard, Md	12
Florence, Hampshire, Mass	680
Florence, St. Joseph, Mich	32
Florence, Morgan, Mo	34
Florence, Douglas, Nebr	100
Florence, Burlington, N. J	30
Florence, Oneida, N. Y	160
Florence, Erie, Ohio	77
Florence, Washington, Pa	95
Florence, Darlington, S. C	360
Florence, Williamson, Tex	48
Florence City, Idaho, Idaho	24
Florence Station, Stephenson, Ill	42
Florence Station, McCracken, Ky	23
Florence Station, Rutherford, Tenn	12
Florid, Putnam, Ill	56
Florida, Madison, Ind	42
Florida, Berkshire, Mass	21
Florida, Monroe, Mo	68
Florida, Orange, N. Y	370
Florida, Henry, Ohio	94
Florin, Sacramento, Cal	20
Floris, Davis, Iowa	47
Florisant, St. Louis, Mo	160
Flourtown, Montgomery, Pa	12
Flower Creek, Pendleton, Ky	33
Flower Creek, Oceana, Mich	21
Flowerfield, St. Joseph, Mich	160
Flowerville, White, Ind	16
Floyd, Floyd, Iowa	220
Floyd, Oneida, N. Y	18
Floyd C. H., Floyd, Va	160
Floyd's Creek, Adair, Mo	4
Floyd's Knobs, Floyd, Ind	35
Flukes, Botetourt, Va	45
Flushing, Genesee, Mich	440
Flushing,* Queens, N. Y	1,600

* Money-order office.

FOR	
Flushing, Belmont, Ohio	$130
Fluvanna, Chautauqua, N. Y	54
Fly Creek, Cherokee, Kans	12
Fly Creek, Otsego, N Y	160
Fly Mountain, Ulster, N. Y	180
Flynn's Lick, Jackson, Tenn	12
Fogelsville, Lehigh, Pa	68
Folk's Station, Harrison, Ohio	12
Folkville, Morgan, Ala	12
Folsom City,* Sacramento, Cal	360
Folsomdale, Wyoming, N. Y	50
Folsomville, Warrick, Ind	21
*Fonda,** (*c. h.,*) Montgomery, N. Y	980
Fond du Lac, St. Louis, Minn	10
*Fond du Lac,** (*c. h.,*) Fond du Lac, Wis	3,800
Fonta Flora, Burke, N. C	12
*Fontanelle,** (*c. h.,*) Adair, Iowa	320
Fontanelle, Washington, Nebr	150
Fontania, Miami, Kans	12
Fontenoy, Brown, Wis	12
Foote, Iowa, Iowa	17
Footville, Yadkin, N. C	12
Footville, Rock, Wis	140
Forbestown, Butte, Cal	82
Ford, Geauga, Ohio	27
Fordham, Westchester, N. Y	550
Ford's Creek, Catahoula, La	5
Ford's Depot, Dinwiddie, Va	54
Ford's Ferry, Crittenden, Ky	24
Ford's Store, Hart, Ga	4
Fordsville, Ohio, Ky	22
Fordsville, Marion, Miss	1
Fordtown, Sullivan, Tenn	8
Fordyce, Greene, Pa	16
Forest, Livingston, Ill	390
Forest, Scott, Miss	150
Forest, Clinton, N. Y	46
Forest,* Hardin, Ohio	280
Forest, Clearfield, Pa	12
Forest, Richland, Wis	39
Forest Bay, Huron, Mich	8
Forestburgh, Sullivan, N. Y	43
Forest City, St. Francis, Ark	12
Forest City, Sierra, Cal	80
Forest City, Mason, Ill	96
Forest City, (*c. h.,*) Winnebago, Iowa	160
Forest City, Muskegon, Mich	20
Forest City,* Meeker, Minn	170
Forest City,* Holt, Mo	340
Forest City, Sarpy, Nebr	100
Forest Dale, Lawrence, Ohio	12
Forest Dale, Rutland, Vt	93
Forest Depot, Bedford, Va	17
Forest Grove, Gloucester, N. J	94
Forest Grove, Washington, Oreg	190
Forest Hill,* Placer, Cal	190
Forest Hill, Decatur, Ind	71
Forest Hill, Lyon, Kans	23
Forest Hill, Harford, Md	77
Forest Hill, Gratiot, Mich	51
Forest Hill, Union, Pa	36
Forest Hill, Monroe, W. Va	20
Forest Home, Amador, Cal	80
Forest Home, Poweshiek, Iowa	16
Forest Home, Franklin, Kans	33

FOR	
Forest House, Potter, Pa	$12
Forest Lake, Washington, Minn	12
Forest Lake, Susquehanna, Pa	25
Forest Lake Centre, Susquehanna, Pa	25
Forest Mound, Wabashaw, Minn	26
Forest Oak, Montgomery, Md	43
Foreston, Ogle, Ill	740
Foreston, Howard, Iowa	26
Forest Port, Oneida, N. Y	240
Forest Station, Clayton, Ga	12
Forestville, Hartford, Conn	360
Forestville, Madison, Ind	13
Forestville, Delaware, Iowa	61
Forestville, Prince George's, Md	94
Forestville, Sanilac, Mich	70
Forestville, Fillmore, Minn	59
Forestville, Chautauqua, N. Y	610
Forestville, Wake, N. C	270
Forestville, Marion, S. C	5
Forestville, Shenandoah, Va	16
Forestville, Door, Wis	20
Forge Village, Middlesex, Mass	97
Fork, Mecosta, Mich	12
Forked River, Ocean, N. J	12
Forkland, Nottoway, Va	19
Fork Meeting House, Baltimore, Md	40
Fork Mountain, Mitchell, N. C	2
Forkner's Hill, Webster, Mo	78
Forks, Columbia, Pa	23
Forksburgh, Marion, W. Va	4
Forks of Capon, Hampshire, W. Va	12
Forks of Elkhorn, Franklin, Ky	25
Forks of Pigeon, Haywood, N. C	11
Forks of Salmon, Klamath, Cal	12
Forkston, Wyoming, Pa	25
Forksville, Ouachita, La	12
Forksville, Sullivan, Pa	51
Forksville, Mecklenburgh, Va	10
Forktown, Wicomico, Md	94
Fork Union, Fluvanna, Va	50
Forrester, Sanilac, Mich	140
Forsyth, (*c. h.,*) Monroe, Ga	770
Forsyth, (*c. h.,*) Taney, Mo	12
Forsythe, Macon, Ill	79
Fort Abercrombie, Shyenne, Dak	710
Fort Adams, Wilkinson, Miss	30
Fort Ancient, Warren, Ohio	69
Fort Ann, Washington, N. Y	520
Fort Arbuckle, Chickasaw N., Ind. T	670
Fort Atkinson, Winneshiek, Iowa	120
Fort Atkinson,* Jefferson, Wis	1,300
Fort Benton, (*c. h.,*) Choteau, Mont	380
Fort Bidwell, Siskiyou, Cal	12
Fort Blackimore, Scott, Va	6
Fort Branch,* Gibson, Ind	320
*Fort Bridger,** (*c. h.,*) Uintah, Wyo	350
Fort Browder, Barbour, Ala	20
Fort Buffington, Cherokee, Ga	6
Fort Calhoun, Washington, Nebr	170
Fort Clark, (*c. h.,*) Kinney, Tex	30
Fort Collins, Larimer, Colo	12
Fort Colville, (*c. h.,*) Stevens, Wash	130
Fort Concho, Bexar, Tex	520
Fort Covington, Franklin, N. Y	410

* Money-order office.

Fort Covington Centre, Franklin, N. Y	$12
Fort Craig, Socorro, N. Mex	290
Fort Cummings, Grant, N. Mex	150
Fort Dade, Hernando, Fla	4
Fort Davis, Presidio, Tex	260
Fort Deposit, Lowndes, Ala	160
Fort Dodge,* (*c. h.*,) Webster, Iowa	2,100
Fort Edward,* Washington, N. Y	1,600
Fort Fairfield,* Aroostook, Me	160
Fort Fred Steele, Carbon, Wyo	12
Fort Gaines, (*c. h.*,) Clay, Ga	400
Fort Garland, Costilla, Colo	110
Fort Gay, Wayne, W. Va	24
Fort George, Duval, Fla	12
Fort Gibson, Cherokee N., Ind. T	440
Fort Gratiot, St. Clair, Mich	12
Fort Griffin, Shackelford, Tex	190
Fort Halleck, Carbon, Wyo	12
Fort Hamilton,* Kings, N. Y	750
Fort Hampton, Limestone, Ala	69
Fort Harker, Ellsworth, Kans	680
Fort Henry, Randolph, Mo	23
Fort Hill, Lake, Ill	19
Fort Howard, Brown, Wis	1,000
Fort Hunter, Montgomery, N. Y	83
Fort Jennings, Putnam, Ohio	24
Fort Jesup, Sabine, La	12
Fort Jones, Siskiyou, Cal	240
Fort Kearney,* Kearney, Nebr	360
Fort Kent, Aroostook, Me	26
Fort Lamar, Madison, Ga	20
Fort Laramie, Laramie, Wyo	460
Fort Larned, Pawnee, Kans	140
Fort Leavenworth, Leavenworth, Kans	1,000
Fort Lee, Bergen, N. J	99
Fort Lemhi, Lemhi, Idaho	12
Fort Lincoln, Bourbon, Kans	120
Fort Littleton, Fulton, Pa	47
Fort Lupton, Weld, Colo	12
Fort Lyon, (*c. h.*,) Bent, Colo	470
Fort Lyon, Benton, Mo	99
Fort McKavett, Menard, Tex	390
Fort Madison,* (*c. h.*,) Lee, Iowa	2,000
Fort Mill, York, S. C	69
Fort Miller, Washington, N. Y	130
Fort Mitchell, Russell, Ala	12
Fort Montgomery, Orange, N. Y	130
Fort Motte, Orangeburgh, S. C	72
Fort Payne, De Kalb, Ala	12
Fort Pike, Orleans, La	41
Fort Plain, Warren, Iowa	68
Fort Plain,* Montgomery, N. Y	1,500
Fort Quitman, El Paso, Tex	150
Fort Randall, (*c. h.*,) Todd, Dak	450
Fort Recovery, Mercer, Ohio	210
Fort Ridgely,* Nicollet, Minn	81
Fort Riley, Davis, Kans	370
Fort Ripley, Morrison, Minn	100
Fort Ritner, Lawrence, Ind	55
Forts, Dallas, Ala	20
Fort Scott,* (*c. h.*,) Bourbon, Kans	2,600
Fort Selden, Dona Ana, N. Mex	340
Fort Seneca, Seneca, Ohio	13
Fort Shaw, Lewis and Clarke, Mont	110

Fort Sill, Choctaw N., Ind. T	$800
Fort Simcoe, Klikitat, Wash	12
Fort Smith,* Sebastian, Ark	2,400
Fort Snelling, Hennepin, Minn	130
Fort's Station, Robertson, Tenn	50
Fort Stanton, Socorro, N. Mex	150
Fort Stephens, Kemper, Miss	14
Fort Sully, Buffalo, Dak	580
Fortsville, Saratoga, N. Y	41
Fort Taylor, Hernando, Fla	5
Fort Tongass, ———, Alaska	12
Fort Totten, ———, Dak	52
Fort Union, Mora, N. Mex	1,700
Fort Valley, Houston, Ga	790
Fortville, Hancock, Ind	190
Fort Wadsworth, Deuel, Dak	12
Fort Wallace, Wallace, Kans	430
Fort Washington, Prince George's, Md	150
Fort Washita, Chickasaw N., Ind. T	51
Fort Wayne,* (*c. h.*,) Allen, Ind	4,000
Fort Willopa, Chehalis, Wash	10
Fort Worth, (*c. h.*,) Tarrant, Tex	560
Fort Wrangel, ———, Alaska	12
Forty Fort, Luzerne, Pa	4
Foster, Bracken, Ky	100
Foster, Providence, R. I	52
Foster, Fond du Lac, Wis	47
Fosterburgh, Madison, Ill	44
Foster Centre, Providence, R. I	27
Fosterdale, Sullivan, N. Y	28
Foster's, Tuscaloosa, Ala	20
Foster's Crossings, Warren, Ohio	160
Foster's Cross Roads, Bledsoe, Tenn	7
Foster's Mills, Armstrong, Pa	63
Foster's Ridge, Perry, Ind	10
Fosterville, Cayuga, N. Y	37
Fosterville, Rutherford, Tenn	76
Fosterville, Anderson, Tex	12
Fostoria,* Seneca, Ohio	850
Fostoria, Blair, Pa	43
Foundryville, Columbia, Pa	10
Fountain, El Paso, Colo	19
Fountain, Fountain, Ind	21
Fountain Bluff, Jackson, Ill	12
Fountain City,* Buffalo, Wis	310
Fountain Creek, Stephenson, Ill	12
Fountain Creek, Maury, Tenn	20
Fountaindale, Winnebago, Ill	12
Fountain Dale, Adams, Pa	26
Fountain Green, Hancock, Ill	150
Fountain Green, Harford, Md	20
Fountain Green, San Pete, Utah	61
Fountain Head, Sumner, Tenn	45
Fountain Hill, Ashley, Ark	10
Fountain Inn, Greenville, S. C	9
Fountain Run, Monroe, Ky	34
Fountain Spring, Wood, W. Va	10
Fountaintown, Shelby, Ind	64
Fourche á Renault, Washington, Mo	12
Four Corners, Huron, Ohio	74
Four Mile, Butler, Kans	12
Four Mile, Dunklin, Mo	21
Four Mile Branch, Monroe, Tenn	10
Four Mile Prairie, Perry, Ill	12
Fourth Crossing, Calaveras, Cal	20

* Money-order office.

Four Towns, Oakland, Mich	$21
Foust's Mills, Randolph, N. C	10
Fowler, Adams, Ill	120
Fowler, St. Lawrence, N. Y	41
Fowler, Trumbull, Ohio	120
Fowler's, Brooke, W. Va	37
Fowler's Knob, Nicholas, W. Va	12
Fowler's Landing, Humphreys, Tenn	16
Fowler's Mills, Geauga, Ohio	42
Fowlersville, Rice, Minn	3
Fowlersville, Columbia, Pa	29
Fowlerville, Livingston, Mich	160
Fowlerville, Livingston, N. Y	280
Fowling Creek, Caroline, Md	25
Fox, Wells, Ind	24
Fox, Ray, Mo	16
Foxborough,* Norfolk, Mass	1,100
Foxburgh, Clarion, Pa	84
Fox Creek, St. Louis, Mo	19
Foxcroft,* Piscataquis, Me	440
Fox Lake, Lake, Ill	35
Fox Lake,* Dodge, Wis	850
Fox River, Kenosha, Wis	14
Foxville, Frederick, Md	12
Framingham, Middlesex, Mass	1,000
Frampton, Lawrence, Ohio	16
Francesville, Pulaski, Ind	160
Francisco, Gibson, Ind	55
Francisco, Stokes, N. C	10
Franciscoville, Jackson, Mich	78
Francis Creek, Manitowoc, Wis	45
Francistown, Hillsborough, N. H	300
Franconia, Chisago, Minn	55
Franconia, Grafton, N. H	190
Franconia, Montgomery, Pa	3
Frank, Seneca, Ohio	12
Frankenlust, Saginaw, Mich	17
Frankenmuth, Saginaw, Mich	49
Frankford, Sussex, Del	81
Frankford, Mower, Minn	46
Frankford, Pike, Mo	200
Frankford, Greenbrier, W. Va	52
Frankfort, Franklin, Ala	69
Frankfort, Franklin, Ill	25
*Frankfort,** (*c. h.,*) Clinton, Ind	490
Frankfort, Montgomery, Iowa	12
Frankfort, Marshall, Kans	320
FRANKFORT,* (*c. h.,*) Franklin, Ky	2,400
Frankfort, Waldo, Me	190
Frankfort, Benzie, Mich	160
Frankfort, L'Eau qui Court, Nebr	13
Frankfort, Herkimer, N. Y	540
Frankfort, Ross, Ohio	210
Frankfort, Mineral, W. Va	56
Frankfort, Pepin, Wis	53
Frankfort Hill, Herkimer, N. Y	15
Frankfort Springs, Beaver, Pa	130
Frankfort Station, Will, Ill	240
Frank Hill, Winona, Minn	24
Franklin, Henry, Ala	3
Franklin, Fulton, Ark	75
Franklin, Sacramento, Cal	25
Franklin, New London, Conn	49
Franklin, (*c. h.,*) Heard, Ga	38
Franklin, Morgan, Ill	120
*Franklin,** (*c. h.,*) Johnson, Ind	1,200
Franklin, Decatur, Iowa	$39
*Franklin,** (*c. h.,*) Simpson, Ky	740
Franklin, (*c. h.,*) St. Mary's, La	750
Franklin, Hancock, Me	160
Franklin,* Norfolk, Mass	900
Franklin, Oakland, Mich	120
Franklin, Renville, Minn	11
Franklin, Howard, Mo	130
Franklin,* Merrimack, N. H	1,300
Franklin, Essex, N. J	160
Franklin, Delaware, N. Y	750
Franklin, (*c. h.,*) Macon, N. C	100
Franklin,* Warren, Ohio	570
Franklin, Lane, Oreg	19
*Franklin,** (*c. h.,*) Venango, Pa	2,800
*Franklin,** (*c. h.,*) Williamson, Tenn	870
Franklin, Cache, Utah	40
Franklin, Franklin, Vt	240
Franklin, Pierce, Wash	4
Franklin, (*c. h.,*) Pendleton, W. Va	160
Franklin, Sheboygan, Wis	12
Franklin Centre, Lee, Iowa	97
Franklin City, Norfolk, Mass	46
Franklin College, Davidson, Tenn	44
Franklin Corners, Erie, Pa	33
Franklin Crossing, Rock Island, Ill	12
Franklindale, Bradford, Pa	41
Franklin Depot, Southampton, Va	390
Franklin Falls, Franklin, N. Y	48
Franklin Furnace, Sussex, N. J	160
Franklin Furnace, Scioto, Ohio	92
Franklin Grove,* Lee, Ill	640
Franklin Grove, Page, Iowa	22
Franklin Iron Works, Oneida, N. Y	14
Franklin Mills, Des Moines, Iowa	28
Franklin's × Roads, Hardin, Ky	14
Franklin Springs, Franklin, Ga	6
Franklin Square, Columbiana, Ohio	86
Franklin Station, Coshocton, Ohio	67
Franklinton, Henry, Ky	22
Franklinton, (*c. h.,*) Washington, La	23
Franklinton, Schoharie, N. Y	62
Franklinton, Franklin, N. C	330
Franklintown, York, Pa	20
Franklinville, Carroll, Md	18
Franklinville, Gloucester, N. J	130
Franklinville, Cattaraugus, N. Y	280
Franklinville, Randolph, N. C	51
Franklinville, Huntingdon, Pa	48
Frank Pierce, Johnson, Iowa	13
Frankstown, Blair, Pa	63
Frankton, Madison, Ind	140
Franktown, (*c. h.,*) Douglas, Colo	50
Franktown, Washoe, Nev	25
Franktown, Northampton, Va	68
Frankville, Winneshiek, Iowa	100
Frankville, Alleghany, Md	11
Frankville, Howell, Mo	12
Frankville, Clark, Wis	16
Fransonia, Richland, Ill	14
Fraser, Macomb, Mich	66
Frazer, Chester, Pa	100
Frazeysburgh, Muskingum, Ohio	260
Frazier's Bottom, Putnam, W. Va	11
Frederica, Kent, Del	330
Frederica, Glynn, Ga	32

* Money-order office.

Frederica, Bremer, Iowa	$15
*Frederick,** (*c. h.,*) Frederick, Md	2,500
Frederick, Mahoning, Ohio	5
Frederick, Montgomery, Pa	43
Fredericksburgh, Washington, Ind	47
Fredericksburgh, Chickasaw, Iowa	190
Fredericksburgh, Osage, Mo	11
Fredericksburgh, Wayne, Ohio	250
Fredericksburgh, Lebanon, Pa	82
Fredericksburgh, (*c. h.,*) Gillespie, Tex	470
Fredericksburgh,* Spottsylvania, Va	2,000
Frederick's Hall, Louisa, Va	170
Fredericksville, Schuyler, Ill	92
Fredericksville, Berks, Pa	3
Fredericktown, Coffey, Kans	4
Fredericktown, Washington, Ky	24
*Fredericktown,** (*c. h.,*) Madison, Mo	370
Fredericktown,* Knox, Ohio	750
Fredericktown, Washington, Pa	65
Fredie, Butler, Mo	12
Fredon, Sussex, N. J	14
Fredonia, Chambers, Ala	37
Fredonia, Williamson, Ill	20
Fredonia, Crawford, Ind	17
Fredonia, Louisa, Iowa	91
Fredonia, (*c. h.,*) Wilson, Kans	12
Fredonia, Caldwell, Ky	33
Fredonia, Washtenaw, Mich	42
Fredonia, Licking, Ohio	68
Fredonia, Mercer, Pa	12
Fredonia,* Chautauqua, N. Y	1,700
Fredonia, Ozaukee, Wis	75
Fredric, Monroe, Iowa	120
Freeborn, Freeborn, Minn	140
Freeburgh, St. Clair. Ill	790
Freeburgh, Houston, Minn	17
Freeburgh, Stark, Ohio	30
Freeburgh, Snyder, Pa	150
Freedom, La Salle, Ill	120
Freedom, Owen, Ind	120
Freedom, Lucas, Iowa	25
Freedom, Barren, Ky	10
Freedom, Waldo, Me	140
Freedom, Carroll, Md	24
Freedom, La Fayette, Mo	91
Freedom, Carroll, N. H	84
Freedom, Portage, Ohio	89
Freedom, Beaver, Pa	170
Freedom, Washington, Tenn	170
Freedom, Outagamie, Wis	14
Freedom Centre, La Salle, Ill	18
Freedom Mills, Henry, Ohio	12
Freedom Plains, Dutchess, N. Y	31
Freedom Station, Portage, Ohio	95
*Freehold,** (*c. h.,*) Monmouth, N. J	1,500
Freehold, Greene, N. Y	48
Freehold, Warren, Pa	68
Freeland, De Kalb, Ill	65
Freeland, Baltimore, Md	85
Freelandville, Knox, Ind	70
Freeman, Franklin, Me	7
Freeman, Licking, Ohio	16
Freeman, Crawford, Wis	11
Freemansburgh, Northampton, Pa	230
Freeman's Landing, Hancock, W. Va	$58
Freemansville, Cherokee, Ga	18
Freemanton, Effingham, Ill	20
Freeo, Ouachita, Ark	31
Freeport, Sacramento, Cal	18
*Freeport,** (*c. h.,*) Stephenson, Ill	3,200
Freeport, Shelby, Ind	16
Freeport, Winneshiek, Iowa	67
Freeport, Cumberland, Me	420
Freeport, Queens, N. Y	83
Freeport, Harrison, Ohio	93
Freeport,* Armstrong, Pa	700
Freeport, Cowlitz, Wash	44
Freeshade, Middlesex, Va	10
Free Soil, Fillmore, Minn	12
Freestone, Sonoma, Cal	37
Freestone, Scioto, Ohio	120
Freetown, Jackson, Ind	24
Freetown, Bristol, Mass	210
Freetown Corners, Cortland, N. Y	52
Free Union, Albemarle, Va	29
Freeville, Tompkins, N. Y	23
Freistadt, Ozaukee, Wis	31
Frelsburgh, Colorado, Tex	110
Fremont, Steuben, Ind	230
Fremont, Mahaska, Iowa	99
Fremont, Lyon, Kans	12
Fremont, Shiawassee, Mich	26
Fremont, Freeborn, Minn	13
*Fremont,** (*c. h.,*) Dodge, Nebr	1,000
Fremont, Rockingham, N. H	59
*Fremont,** (*c. h.,*) Sandusky, Ohio	2,800
Fremont, Chester, Pa	23
Fremont, Waupaca, Wis	140
Fremont Centre, Lake, Ill	27
Fremont Centre, Newaygo, Mich	67
Fremont Centre, Sullivan, N. Y	74
French Bar, Lewis and Clarke, Mont	12
French Corral, Nevada, Cal	12
French Creek, Allamakee, Iowa	16
French Creek, Chautauqua, N. Y	21
French Creek, Mercer, Pa	13
French Creek, Upshur, W. Va	60
French Creek Church, Bladen, N. C	10
French Grove, Peoria, Ill	21
French Gulch, Shasta, Cal	68
French Gulch, Deer Lodge, Mont	12
French Hay, Hanover, Va	10
French Lake, Wright, Minn	8
French Lick, Orange, Ind	39
French Mountain, Warren, N. Y	57
Frenchton, Upshur, W. Va	11
Frenchtown, Missoula, Mont	12
Frenchtown,* Hunterdon, N. J	580
Frenchtown, Crawford, Pa	12
French Village, St. Clair, Ill	21
French Village, St. Francois, Mo	25
Frenchville, Clearfield, Pa	35
Frenchville, Trempealeau, Wis	71
Fresh Pond, Suffolk, N. Y	25
Frewsburgh, Chautauqua, N. Y	230
Frey's Bush, Montgomery, N. Y	50
Friar's Point, (*c. h.,*) Coahoma, Miss	230
Frick's Gap, Walker, Ga	7
Friedburgh, Forsyth, N. C	5

* Money-order office.

Friedensburgh, Schuylkill, Pa	$23
Friedensville, Lehigh, Pa	340
Friend Grove, Wabash, Ill	12
Friendship, Ripley, Ind	71
Friendship, Caldwell, Ky	12
Friendship, Knox, Me	72
Friendship, Anne Arundel, Md	140
Friendship, Allegany, N. Y	840
Friendship, Guilford, N. C	21
Friendship, Scioto, Ohio	18
Friendship, Clarendon, S. C	12
Friendship, Dyer, Tenn	12
Friendship, (*c. h.*,) Adams, Wis	140
Friendshipville, King George, Va	24
Friendsville, Wabash, Ill	110
Friendsville, Medina, Ohio	30
Friendsville, Susquehanna, Pa	140
Friendsville, Blount, Tenn	53
Friendswood, Hendricks, Ind	12
Fritztown, Berks, Pa	19
Frizellburgh, Carroll, Md	39
Frog Level, Newberry, S. C	88
Frohna, Perry, Mo	12
Frontenac, Goodhue, Minn	150
Frontier, Hillsdale, Mich	21
Frontier, Clinton, N. Y	59
Front Royal, (*c. h.*,) Warren, Va	370
Frost, Pocahontas, W. Va	5
Frostburgh,* Alleghany, Md	890
Frostburgh, Jefferson, Pa	27
Frost's Station, Fayette, Pa	12
Fruitland, Burlington, N. J	87
Fruitport, Muskegon, Mich	74
Frumet, Jefferson, Mo	12
Fryburgh, Auglaize, Ohio	63
Fryburgh, Clarion, Pa	59
Fryeburgh, Wright, Iowa	20
Fryeburgh, Oxford, Me	290
Fryeburgh Centre, Oxford, Me	50
Fudgy's Creek, Cabell, W. Va	12
Fulda, Spencer, Ind	34
Fulkerson, Scott, Va	4
Fullen's, Greene, Tenn	78
Fullersburgh, Du Page, Ill	68
Fuller's Point, Coles, Ill	12
Fullerville Iron Works, St. Lawrence, N. Y	85
Fullwood's Store, Mecklenburgh, N. C	5
Fulmer Valley, Allegany, N. Y	12
Fulton, Sumter, Ala	12
Fulton, Hempstead, Ark	24
Fulton,* Whitesides, Ill	1,200
Fulton, Fulton, Ind	68
Fulton, Jackson, Iowa	43
Fulton, Kalamazoo, Mich	42
Fulton, Prentiss, Miss	44
Fulton, (*c. h.*,) Callaway, Mo	940
Fulton,* Oswego, N. Y	2,200
Fulton, Davie, N. C	9
Fulton, Westmoreland, Pa	20
Fulton, Lauderdale, Tenn	64
Fulton, Refugio, Tex	12
Fulton, Rock, Wis	75
Fultonham, Schoharie, N. Y	35
Fultonham, Muskingum, Ohio	110
Fulton House, Lancaster, Pa	$22
Fulton Station, Fulton, Ky	190
Fultonville, Montgomery, N. Y	830
Funkhouser, Effingham, Ill	12
Funkstown, Washington, Md	130
Funny Louis, Catahoula, La	11
Furnessville, Porter, Ind	67
Fussville, Waukesha, Wis	64

G.

Gabilan, Monterey, Cal	12
Gadsden, (*c. h.*,) Etowah, Ala	460
Gadsden, Madison, Tenn	95
Gage's Lakes, Lake, Ill	18
Gagetown, Tuscola, Mich	12
Gahanna, Franklin, Ohio	65
Gaines, Orleans, N. Y	120
Gaines, Tioga, Pa	46
Gainesborough, (*c. h.*,) Jackson, Tenn	50
Gainesborough, Frederick, Va	21
Gaines' Cross Roads, Rappahannock, Va	18
Gaines Farm, Henry, Mo	21
Gaines Station, Genesee, Mich	200
Gainestown, Clarke, Ala	20
Gainesville, Sumter, Ala	790
Gainesville, (*c. h.*,) Greene, Ark	140
Gainesville,* (*c. h.*,) Alachua, Fla	950
Gainesville, (*c. h.*,) Hall, Ga	130
Gainesville, Kent, Mich	34
Gainesville, Hancock, Miss	18
Gainesville, (*c. h.*,) Ozark, Mo	22
Gainesville, Wyoming, N. Y	140
Gainesville, Prince William, Va	160
Gainesville Junction, Kemper, Miss	12
Gainsville, Allen, Ky	12
Gainsville, (*c. h.*,) Cooke, Tex	170
Galbraith's Store, Henry, Mo	39
Galena,* (*c. h.*,) Jo Daviess, Ill	2,900
Galena, Floyd, Ind	28
Galena, Kent, Md	290
Galena, (*c. h.*,) Stone, Mo	20
Galena, Dodge, Nebr	12
Galena, Humboldt, Nev	12
Galena, Delaware, Ohio	200
Gales, Sullivan, N. Y	7
Galesburgh,* Knox, Ill	3,200
Galesburgh, Jasper, Iowa	60
Galesburgh,* Kalamazoo, Mich	770
Galesburgh, Jasper, Mo	12
Gale's Ferry, New London, Conn	43
Gales Town, Dorchester, Md	22
Galesville, Washington, N. Y	130
Galesville, Douglas, Oreg	22
Galesville, (*c. h.*,) Trempealeau, Wis	260
Galeville Mills, Ulster, N. Y	29
Galien, Berrien, Mich	230
Galigher, Guernsey, Ohio	6
Galilee, Wayne, Pa	3
Galion, Crawford, Ohio	1,400
Galivant's Ferry, Horry, S. C	17
Gallant Green, Charles, Md	12
Gallatia, Saline, Ill	41
Gallatin, Copiah, Miss	12
Gallatin,* (*c. h.*,) Daviess, Mo	370

* Money-order office.

Gallatin, Gallatin, Mont	$110
Gallatin,* (*c. h.*,) Sumner, Tenn	830
Gallatinville, Columbia, N. Y	42
Gallaudet, Marion, Ind	12
Gallaway's Station, Osage, Mo	12
Galley Rock, Pope, Ark	12
Gallia Furnace, Gallia, Ohio	24
Gallipolis,* (*c. h.*,) Gallia, Ohio	2,000
Gallitzin, Cambria, Pa	160
Galloway, La Salle, Ill	23
Gallupville, Schoharie, N. Y	170
Galt, Sacramento, Cal	12
Galt, Whitesides, Ill	130
Galt's Mills, Amherst, Va	12
Galum, Perry, Ill	12
Galva,* Henry, Ill	2,200
Galveston, Cass, Ind	270
Galveston,* (*c. h.*,) Galveston, Tex	4,000
Galway, Saratoga, N. Y	220
Galway, Fayette, Tenn	81
Gamaliel, Monroe, Ky	12
Gambier,* Knox, Ohio	560
Gamble's, Allegheny, Pa	19
Gamble's Store, Blount, Tenn	46
Game Hill, Franklin, Ark	21
Ganges, Allegan, Mich	110
Ganges, Richland, Ohio	30
Gansevoort, Saratoga, N. Y	210
Gap, Lancaster, Pa	280
Gap Civil, (*c. h.*,) Alleghany, N. C	13
Gap Creek, Ashe, N. C	23
Gap Creek, Knox, Tenn	12
Gap Grove, Lee, Ill	60
Gap Mills, Monroe, W. Va	19
Gap Run, Carter, Tenn	6
Gapsville, Fulton, Pa	12
Garber's Mills, Washington, Tenn	9
Garden, Delta, Mich	17
Garden, Athens, Ohio	17
Garden City, Blue Earth, Minn	330
Garden Cottage, Pulaski, Ky	3
Garden Grove, Decatur, Iowa	200
Garden Grove, Ralls, Mo	12
Garden Prairie, Boone, Ill	310
Garden Prairie, Blue Earth, Minn	10
Garden Valley, Smith, Tex	12
Gardenville, Erie, N. Y	99
Gardenville, Bucks, Pa	48
Gardiner,* Kennebec, Me	2,200
Gardiner, Douglas, Oreg	43
Gardner, Grundy, Ill	570
Gardner, Johnson, Kans	110
Gardner, Worcester, Mass	900
Gardner, Noble, Ohio	12
Gardner's Corner, Beaufort, S. C	12
Gardner's Ford, Cleveland, N. C	13
Gardner's Station, Weakley, Tenn	39
Gardnersville, Pendleton, Ky	12
Gard's Point, Wabash, Ill	7
Garfield, La Salle, Ill	12
Garfield, Mahoning, Ohio	12
Garibaldi, Saguache, Colo	12
Garibaldi, Keokuk, Iowa	33
Garibaldi, Tillamook, Oreg	12
Garland, Butler, Ala	47
Garland, Penobscot, Me	140
Garland, Warren, Pa	$180
Garlandville, Jasper, Miss	37
Garman's Mills, Cambria, Pa	13
Garnavillo,* Clayton, Iowa	200
Garner, Cass, Ill	12
Garner's Station, Yalabusha, Miss	24
Garnett,* (*c. h.*,) Anderson, Kans	1,000
Garnettsville, Meade, Ky	180
Garoga, Fulton, N. Y	40
Garrattsville, Otsego, N. Y	130
Garretson's Landing, Jefferson, Ark	32
Garrett, Meade, Ky	23
Garrettsburgh, Christian, Ky	48
Garrettsville,* Portage, Ohio	1,500
Garrison Point, Walker, Ala	5
Garrison's, Putnam, N. Y	360
Garrisonville, Stafford, Va	40
Garrote, Tuolumne, Cal	20
Garry Owen, Jackson, Iowa	34
Gartsides, St. Clair, Ill	78
Gary's Store, Buckingham, Va	39
Garysville, Prince George, Va	12
Gasconade City, Gasconade, Mo	42
Gasconade Ferry, Gasconade, Mo	23
Gas Jet, Humboldt, Cal	12
Gaskill's Corners, Tioga, N. Y	10
Gasport, Niagara, N. Y	180
Gassett's Station, Windsor, Vt	70
Gaston, Sumter, Ala	28
Gaston, Lewis, W. Va	5
Gatchellville, York, Pa	16
Gates, Newton, Mo	13
Gates, Monroe, N. Y	12
Gates' Mills, Cuyahoga, Ohio	20
Gatesville, Clay, Ga	12
Gatesville, Clay, Kans	14
Gatesville, (*c. h.*,) Gates, N. C	39
Gatesville, (*c. h.*,) Coryell, Tex	30
Gatewood, Ripley, Mo	4
Gatlinburgh, Sevier, Tenn	9
Gauley Bridge, Fayette, W. Va	62
Gavers, Columbiana, Ohio	25
Gayhead, Greene, N. Y	12
Gaylesville, Cherokee, Ala	42
Gaylordsville, Litchfield, Conn	180
Gayoso, (*c. h.*,) Pemiscot, Mo	24
Gaysville, Windsor, Vt	280
Gazelle, Siskiyou, Cal	12
Geary, Doniphan, Kans	37
Geary, Clinton, Mich	12
Geary, Westmoreland, Pa	12
Gebhart's, Somerset, Pa	63
Geddes, Onondaga, N. Y	390
Geetingsville, Clinton, Ind	30
Geiger's Mills, Berks, Pa	48
Gem, Clayton, Iowa	35
General Wayne, Montgomery, Pa	12
Genesee, Waukesha, Wis	80
Genesee Depot, Waukesha, Wis	93
Genesee Fork, Potter, Pa	28
Genesee Village, Genesee, Mich	23
Geneseo,* Henry, Ill	1,900
Geneseo, Cerro Gordo, Iowa	12
Geneseo,* (*c. h.*,) Livingston, N. Y	1,600
Geneva, (*c. h.*,) Geneva, Ala	22
Geneva, Talbot, Ga	200

* Money-order office.

*Geneva,** (*c. h.,*) Kane, Ill	$860
Geneva, Franklin, Iowa	8
Geneva, Allen, Kans	88
Geneva, Lenawee, Mich	32
Geneva, Freeborn, Minn	61
Geneva,* Ontario, N. Y	3,000
Geneva, Ashtabula, Ohio	950
Geneva, Walworth, Wis	830
Genevia, Henderson, Ky	12
Genito, Powhatan, Va	140
Genoa, De Kalb, Ill	93
Genoa, Wayne, Iowa	73
Genoa, Livingston, Mich	39
Genoa, Platte, Nebr	53
Genoa, (*c. h.,*) Douglas, Nev	270
Genoa, Cayuga, N. Y	140
Genoa, Ottawa, Ohio	170
Genoa, Vernon, Wis	33
Genoa Bluff, Iowa, Iowa	49
Gentryville, Spencer, Ind	53
Gentryville, Gentry, Mo	260
George Lake, Stearns, Minn	4
George's Creek, Pickens, S. C	10
George's Mills, Sullivan, N. H	38
George's Store, Lincoln, Tenn	7
Georgesville, Franklin, Ohio	15
Georgetown, Pope, Ark	13
Georgetown,* El Dorado, Cal	350
Georgetown,* Clear Creek, Colo	2,000
Georgetown, Fairfield, Conn	200
Georgetown, (*c. h.,*) Sussex, Del	540
Georgetown,* Washington, D. C	2,500
Georgetown, Putnam, Fla	12
Georgetown, (*c. h.,*) Quitman, Ga	81
Georgetown, Vermilion, Ill	250
Georgetown, Floyd, Ind	23
Georgetown, Monroe, Iowa	48
*Georgetown,** (*c. h.,*) Scott, Ky	1,100
Georgetown, Sagadahoc, Me	12
Georgetown, Essex, Mass	590
Georgetown, Ottawa, Mich	11
Georgetown, Clay, Minn	21
Georgetown, Pettis, Mo	99
Georgetown, Lewis and Clarke, Mont	12
Georgetown, Jefferson, Nebr	12
Georgetown, Burlington, N. J	53
Georgetown, Madison, N. Y	140
Georgetown, (*c. h.,*) Brown, Ohio	470
Georgetown, Beaver, Pa	68
Georgetown, (*c. h.,*) Georgetown, S. C	1,100
Georgetown, Hamilton, Tenn	18
Georgetown, (*c. h.,*) Williamson, Tex	200
Georgetown, Lewis, W. Va	12
Georgetown, Grant, Wis	80
Georgeville, Monongalia, Minn	40
Georgeville, Ray, Mo	10
Georgia, Lawrence, Ind	19
Georgia, Franklin, Vt	85
Georgia City, Jasper, Mo	12
Georgiana, Butler, Ala	40
Georgia Plain, Franklin, Vt	36
Georgiaville, Providence, R. I	240
German, Chenango, N. Y	16
German, Darke, Ohio	50
German Gulch, Deer Lodge, Mont	12
Germania, Potter, Pa	$83
Germania, Marquette, Wis	250
Germano, Harrison, Ohio	120
German Settlement, Preston, W. Va	60
Germanton, Stokes, N. C	50
Germantown, Clinton, Ill	120
Germantown, Mason, Ky	140
Germantown, Montgomery, Md	23
Germantown,* Henry, Mo	360
Germantown, Columbia, N. Y	200
Germantown, Montgomery, Ohio	500
Germantown, Shelby, Tenn	150
Germantown, Juneau, Wis	34
German Valley, Morris, N. J	84
Germanville, Jefferson, Iowa	32
Germany, Warren, Pa	6
Gerrardstown, Berkeley, W. Va	77
Gery's, Bucks, Pa	33
Gethsemane, Nelson, Ky	39
Gettysburgh, Darke, Ohio	180
*Gettysburgh,** (*c. h.,*) Adams, Pa	1,700
Getzville, Erie, N. Y	19
Ghent, Carroll, Ky	220
Ghent, Columbia, N. Y	140
Ghent, Summit, Ohio	32
Gholson, Noxubee, Miss	200
Gholsonville, Brunswick, Va	12
Giard, Clayton, Iowa	71
Gibb's Cross Roads, Cumberland, N. C	12
Gibb's Cross Roads, Macon, Tenn	12
Gibbsville, Sheboygan, Wis	88
Gibesonville, Hocking, Ohio	29
Gibraltar, Lyons, Iowa	12
Gibraltar, Wayne, Mich	6
Gibson, (*c. h.,*) Glascock, Ga	10
Gibson, Steuben, N. Y	40
Gibson, Pike, Ohio	11
Gibson, Susquehanna, Pa	160
Gibsonburgh, Luzerne, Pa	12
Gibson's Station, Lake, Ind	41
Gibson's Station, Guernsey, Ohio	64
Gibsonville,* Sierra, Cal	100
Gibsonville, Guilford, N. C	39
Gibsonville, Russell, Va	12
Gilbert, Scott, Iowa	35
Gilbert, Monroe, Pa	19
Gilbert Hollow, Lexington, S. C	12
Gilbert's, Kane, Ill	12
Gilbertsborough, Limestone, Ala	8
Gilbert's Creek Station, Lincoln, Ky	12
Gilbert's Mills, Oswego, N. Y	43
Gilbertsville, Montgomery, Pa	60
Gilbertville, Black Hawk, Iowa	27
Gilbertville, Worcester, Mass	170
Gilbirdsport, Brown, Ill	12
Gilboa, Schoharie, N. Y	180
Gilboa, Putnam, Ohio	88
Gilchrist, Pope, Minn	61
Gilchrist's Bridge, Marion, S. C	10
Gilead, Tolland, Conn	59
Gilead, Calhoun, Ill	20
Gilead, Miami, Ind	49
Gilead, Oxford, Me	36
Gilead, Branch, Mich	52
Gilead, Lewis, Mo	31

* **Money-order office.**

Gilford, Tuscola, Mich	$12
Gilford Village, Belknap, N. H	15
Gilgal, Pike, Ill	9
Gill, Franklin, Mass	130
Gillem's Station, Dickson, Tenn	44
Gillen's Landing, Phillips, Ark	18
Gillespie, Macoupin, Ill	300
Gillespieville, Ross, Ohio	87
Gillespieville, Kanawha, W. Va	12
Gillett's Grove, Clay, Iowa	12
Gill Hall, Allegheny, Pa	12
Gillisonville, Beaufort, S. C	50
Gill's Mills, Rowan, Ky	12
Gillsville, Hall, Ga	33
Gilman, Iroquois, Ill	950
Gilman, Hamilton, N. Y	5
Gilmanton, Belknap, N. H	250
Gilmanton Iron Works, Belknap, N. H	160
Gilmantown, Buffalo, Wis	75
Gilmer, Lake, Ill	23
Gilmer, (*c. h.*,) Upshur, Tex	120
Gilmer, Uintah, Wyo	300
Gilmer's, Lowndes, Ala	12
Gilmer's Store, Guilford, N. C	4
Gilmore, Sarpy, Nebr	12
Gilmore, Tuscarawas, Ohio	54
Gilmore's Mills, Rockbridge, Va	12
Gilpin, Indiana, Pa	8
Gilroy,* Santa Clara, Cal	800
Gilson, Knox, Ill	10
Gilsum, Cheshire, N. H	130
Ginger Hill, Washington, Pa	60
Ginghamsburgh, Miami, Ohio	8
Girard, Macoupin, Ill	720
Girard,* (*c. h.*,) Crawford, Kans	240
Girard, Branch, Mich	120
Girard, Trumbull, Ohio	310
Girard,* Erie, Pa	720
Girard Manor, Schuylkill, Pa	51
Girardsville, Schuylkill, Pa	440
Girdletree Hill, Worcester, Md	12
Gird's Creek, Missoula, Mont	12
Gishe's Mills, Roanoke, Va	59
Givin, Mahaska, Iowa	19
Glade, Somerset, Pa	12
Glade Creek, Ashe, N. C	8
Glade Farms, Preston, W. Va	7
Glade Hill, Franklin, Va	9
Glade Mills, Butler, Pa	160
Gladen's Run, Bedford, Pa	12
Glades, Morgan, Tenn	4
Gladesborough, Randolph, N. C	3
Gladesborough, Carroll, Va	3
Glade Spring, Washington, Va	83
Gladesville, Preston, W. Va	5
Gladeville, Wilson, Tenn	24
Glad Tidings, Clackamas, Oreg	9
Glasco, Cloud, Kans	12
Glasco, Ulster, N. Y	84
Glasford, Peoria, Ill	110
Glasgow, New Castle, Del	36
Glasgow, Scott, Ill	53
Glasgow, Jefferson, Iowa	89
Glasgow,* (*c. h.*,) Barren, Ky	680
Glasgow, Wabashaw, Minn	6

Glasgow,* Howard, Mo	$830
Glasgow, Columbiana, Ohio	35
Glasgow Junction, Barren, Ky	80
Glassborough, Gloucester, N. J	280
Glass River, Shiawassee, Mich	19
Glass Village, Pope, Ark	6
Glastenbury, Hartford, Conn	310
Glaze City, Camden, Mo	11
Gleeson Station, Weakley, Tenn	12
Glen, Montgomery, N. Y	96
Glen Allen, Henrico, Va	20
Glenaloon, Moore, N. C	4
Glen Alta, Marion, Ga	12
Glen Arbor, Leelenaw, Mich	61
Glen Aubrey, Broome, N. Y	19
Glenbeulah, Sheboygan, Wis	200
Glenburn, Penobscot, Me	26
Glen Carbon, Schuylkill, Pa	12
Glen Castle, Broome, N. Y	61
Glencoe, Cook, Ill	21
Glencoe, Gallatin, Ky	12
Glencoe,* (*c. h.*,) McLeod, Minn	160
Glencoe, St. Louis, Mo	20
Glencoe, Belmont, Ohio	72
Glencoe, Buffalo, Wis	45
Glencoe Mills, Columbia, N. Y	17
Glen Cove, Queens, N. Y	450
Glendale, Pope, Ill	24
Glen Dale, Daviess, Ind	10
Glendale, Jefferson, Iowa	97
Glendale, Bourbon, Kans	10
Glendale, Hardin, Ky	150
Glendale, Berkshire, Mass	100
Glendale, Van Buren, Mich	22
Glendale, McLeod, Minn	12
Glendale, Cass, Nebr	17
Glendale, Hamilton, Ohio	420
Glendale, Cambria, Pa	100
Glendale, Monroe, Wis	20
Glendower, Albemarle, Va	12
Glen Easton, Marshall, W. Va	94
Glen Elder, Mitchell, Kans	12
Glenelg, Howard, Md	14
Glengary, Berkeley, W. Va	8
Glen Grove, Douglas, Colo	12
Glen Hall, Tippecanoe, Ind	40
Glenham, Dutchess, N. Y	360
Glen Haven, Leelenaw, Mich	12
Glen Haven, Cortland, N. Y	38
Glen Haven, Grant, Wis	62
Glen Hope, Clearfield, Pa	140
Glenloch, Chester, Pa	180
Glen Mills, Delaware, Pa	45
Glenmore, Ware, Ga	20
Glenmore, Oneida, N. Y	16
Glenmore, Buckingham, Va	20
Glenn, Johnson, Kans	12
Glenn, McKean, Pa	4
Glenn's, Gloucester, Va	12
Glenn Springs, Spartanburgh, S. C	36
Glenn's Valley, Marion, Ind	40
Glennville, Barbour, Ala	190
Glenora, Yates, N. Y	58
Glen Park, Wyandotte, Kans	12
Glen Riddle, Delaware, Pa	160
Glen Rock, Nemaha, Nebr	26

*Money-order office.

Glen Rock, York, Pa	$360
Glen Roy, Howard, Iowa	300
Glen Roy, Chester, Pa	19
Glensdale, Lewis, N. Y	100
Glen's Falls,* Warren, N. Y	2,200
Glen's Fork, Adair, Ky	8
Glen Union, Clinton, Pa	51
Glenville, Fairfield, Conn	24
Glenville, Harford, Md	64
Glenville, Schenectady, N. Y	76
Glenville, Cuyahoga, Ohio	70
Glenville, (*c. h.*,) Gilmer, W. Va	150
Glen Wild, Sullivan, N. Y	22
Glenwood,* (*c. h.*,) Mills, Iowa	1,200
Glenwood, Leavenworth, Kans	20
Glenwood, Aroostook, Me	33
Glenwood, (*c. h.*,) Pope, Minn	120
Glenwood, Schuyler, Mo	310
Glenwood, Sussex, N. J	40
Glenwood, Erie, N. Y	52
Glenwood, Susquehanna, Pa	120
Glidden, Carroll, Iowa	120
Globe, Caldwell, N. C	18
Globe Creek, Marshall, Tenn	10
Globe Village, Worcester, Mass	480
Gloucester,* Essex, Mass	2,700
Gloucester C. H., Gloucester, Va	170
Gloucester City, Camden, N. J	320
Glover, Orleans, Vt	210
Glover's Creek, Metcalfe, Ky	2
Glover's Gap, Marion, W. Va	34
Gloversville, Fulton, N. Y	1,600
Glymont, Charles, Md	56
Glyndon, Crawford, Pa	25
Gnadenhutten, Tuscarawas, Ohio	84
Godfrey, Madison, Ill	410
Godwinville, Bergen, N. J	140
Goff's, Ritchie, W. Va	9
Goff's Falls, Hillsborough, N. H	47
Goff's Mills, Steuben, N. Y	18
Goffstown, Hillsborough, N. H	210
GoffstownCentre, Hillsborough, N.H	83
Gogginsville, Franklin, Va	32
Goheenville, Armstrong, Pa	30
Golconda, (*c. h.*,) Pope, Ill	520
Golconda, Humboldt, Nev	12
Golden City, (*c. h.*,) Jefferson, Colo	600
Golden City, Barton, Mo	12
Golden Corners, Wayne, Ohio	28
Golden Gate, Brown, Minn	87
Golden Hill, Dorchester, Md	16
Golden Hill, Wyoming, Pa	16
Golden Lake, Waukesha, Wis	31
Golden Pond, Trigg, Ky	14
Golden Prairie, Delaware, Iowa	12
Golden Ridge, Aroostook, Me	6
Golden's Bridge, Westchester, N. Y	160
Golden Springs, Anderson, S. C	12
Golden Valley, Rutherford, N. C	5
Goldfield, Wright, Iowa	66
Gold Hill, Storey, Nev	1,700
Gold Hill, Rowan, N. C	59
Gold Hill, Buckingham, Va	29
Golding, Oceana, Mich	37
Gold Mine, Marion, Ala	12
Gold Run, Placer, Cal	200
Goldsborough, Caroline, Md	$12
Goldsborough,* (*c. h.*,) Wayne, N. C	1,100
Goldville, Tallapoosa, Ala	7
Goliad, (*c. h.*,) Goliad, Tex	230
Golindo, Falls, Tex	47
Gomber, Guernsey, Ohio	63
Gomer, Allen, Ohio	88
Gomeria, Republic, Kans	12
Gomer's Mills, Douglas, Colo	12
Gonic, Strafford, N. H	100
Gonzales,* (*c. h.*,) Gonzales, Tex	1,000
Goochland, Rock Castle, Ky	12
Goochland C. H., Goochland, Va	5
Gooch's Mill, Cooper, Mo	36
Goodale's Corner, Penobscot, Me	49
Goodall's, Hanover, Va	23
Goodfield, Meigs, Tenn	3
Goodgiou's Factory, Laurens, S. C	12
Good Ground, Suffolk, N. Y	76
Good Harbor, Leelenaw, Mich	34
Good Hope, McDonough, Ill	200
Good Hope, Leake, Miss	16
Good Hope, Fayette, Ohio	62
Good Hope, Cumberland, Pa	23
Good Hope, Milwaukee, Wis	20
Goodhue Centre, Goodhue, Minn	59
Gooding's Grove, Will, Ill	51
Good Intent, Washington, Pa	12
Goodland, Newton, Ind	290
Goodland, Lapeer, Mich	68
Goodland, Knox, Mo	22
Goodlettsville, Davidson, Tenn	100
Goodman, Holmes, Miss	320
Goodrich, Genesee, Mich	200
Good Spring, Giles, Tenn	2
Good View, Bedford, Va	5
Goodville, Lancaster, Pa	28
Goodwin's Mills, York, Me	49
Goodwynsville, Dinwiddie, Va	21
Goodyear's Bar, Sierra, Cal	16
Goole, Vernon, Wis	13
Goose Creek, Ritchie, W. Va	2
Goose Island, Alexander, Ill	16
Gopher Prairie, Wabashaw, Minn	7
Gordon, Henry, Ala	99
Gordon, Wilkinson, Ga	100
Gordon, Darke, Ohio	54
Gordon, Schuylkill, Pa	21
Gordonsville, Logan, Ky	37
Gordonsville, Freeborn, Minn	6
Gordonsville, Lancaster, Pa	69
Gordonsville, Smith, Tenn	16
Gordonsville,* Orange, Va	680
Gore, Hocking, Ohio	13
Goresville, Loudoun, Va	67
Goresville, Johnson, Ill	10
Gorham,* Cumberland, Me	660
Gorham,* Coos, N. H	700
Gorham, Ontario, N. Y	140
Gorham, Fulton, Ohio	120
Gorman's Depot, Cocke, Tenn	12
Gorsuch's Mills, Baltimore, Md	20
Goshen, Litchfield, Conn	180
Goshen, Lincoln, Ga	10
Goshen, (*c. h.*,) Elkhart, Ind	2,200
Goshen, Oldham, Ky	71

* Money-order office.

Goshen, Montgomery, Md	$20
Goshen, Hampshire, Mass	160
Goshen, Mercer, Mo	37
Goshen, Sullivan, N. H	23
Goshen, Cape May, N. J	80
*Goshen,** (*c. h.,*) Orange, N. Y	1,500
Goshen, Clermont, Ohio	200
Goshen, Lancaster, Pa	52
Goshen, Lincoln, Tenn	12
Goshen Bridge, Rockbridge, Va	250
Goshen Hill, Union, S. C	10
Goshen Springs, Rankin, Miss	8
Goshenville, Chester, Pa	22
Gosport, Clarke, Ala	4
Gosport, Owen, Ind	490
Gosport, Marion, Iowa	47
Gouge's, Grant, Ky	16
Gouglersville, Berks, Pa	4
Gouldsborough, Hancock, Me	100
Gouldsborough, Luzerne, Pa	83
Gouldsville, Washington, Vt	130
Gourley's Bridge, Greene, Tenn	12
Gouverneur,* St. Lawrence, N. Y	1,300
Govanstown, Baltimore, Md	120
Gowanda, Cattaraugus, N. Y	640
Gowdeysville, Union, S. C	25
Gowensville, Greenville, S. C	19
Gower, Du Page, Ill	12
Gower's Ferry, Cedar, Iowa	12
Graafschap, Allegan, Mich	75
Graceham, Frederick, Md	45
Gradyville, Adair, Ky	16
Graefenberg, Shelby, Ky	45
Graefenberg, Herkimer, N. Y	15
Graefenburgh, Adams, Pa	23
Grafton, Yolo, Cal	170
Grafton, Jersey, Ill	220
Grafton, Oxford, Me	10
Grafton, Worcester, Mass	710
Grafton, Monroe, Mich	17
Grafton, Grafton, N. H	140
Grafton, Rensselaer, N. Y	54
Grafton, Lorain, Ohio	78
Grafton, Windham, Vt	270
Grafton,* Taylor, W. Va	640
Grafton, Ozaukee, Wis	140
Grafton Centre, Grafton, N. H	70
Graham, Jefferson, Ind	13
Graham, Nodaway, Mo	190
Graham, (*c. h.,*) Alamance, N. C	250
Graham Lake, Noble, Minn	5
Graham's Forge, Wythe, Va	12
Graham Station, Mason, W. Va	5
Graham's Turn Out, Barnwell, S. C	140
Grahamsville, Sullivan, N. Y	60
Grahamsville, Jackson, Ohio	12
Grahamton, Clearfield, Pa	42
Grahamville, York, Pa	21
Grahamville, Beaufort, S. C	97
Grampian Hills, Clearfield, Pa	58
Granada, Nemaha, Kans	35
Granbury, (*c. h.,*) Hood, Tex	12
Granby, Hartford, Conn	240
Granby, Hampshire, Mass	150
Granby, Nicollet, Minn	20
Granby,* Newton, Mo	430
Granby, Essex, Vt	$26
Granby Centre, Oswego, N. Y	88
Grand Blanc, Genesee, Mich	190
Grand Bluff, Panola, Tex	16
Grand Cane, De Soto, La	10
Grand Chenier, Vermillion, La	15
Grand Coteau, St. Landry, La	120
Grand Detour, Ogle, Ill	200
Grand Forks, Pembina, Dak	12
Grand Glade, Crawford, Ill	12
Grand Glaze, Jackson, Ark	12
Grand Gulf, Claiborne, Miss	74
*Grand Haven,** (*c. h.,*) Ottawa, Mich	1,700
Grand Island, Colusa, Cal	50
*Grand Island Station,** (*c. h.,*) Hall, Nebr	330
Grand Isle, Grand Isle, Vt	110
Grand Junction, Greene, Iowa	61
Grand Junction, Hardeman, Tenn	150
Grand Lake, Chicot, Ark	130
Grand Lodge, Eaton, Mich	380
Grand Marsh, Adams, Wis	27
Grand Meadow, Mower, Minn	97
Grand Mound, Clinton, Iowa	140
Grand Mound, Thurston, Wash	16
Grand Portage, Lake, Minn	12
Grand Prairie, Brown, Kans	12
Grand Prairie, Lewis, Wash	18
Grand Prairie, Green Lake, Wis	21
*Grand Rapids,** (*c. h.,*) Kent, Mich	4,000
Grand Rapids,* Wood, Ohio	310
*Grand Rapids,** (*c. h.,*) Wood, Wis	670
Grand River, Buffalo, Dak	12
Grand River, Wayne, Iowa	84
Grand Ronde, Polk, Oreg	8
Grand Tower, Jackson, Ill	16
Grand Valley, Hamilton, Ohio	12
Grand View, Edgar, Ill	150
Grand View, Spencer, Ind	230
Grand View, Louisa, Iowa	170
Grand View, Hardin, Ky	12
Grand View, Washington, Ohio	72
Grandville, Kent, Mich	230
Granger, Fillmore, Minn	84
Granger, Allegany, N. Y	17
Granger, Medina, Ohio	75
Granite, (*c. h.,*) Lake, Colo	12
Granite Falls, Chippewa, Minn	10
Granite Hall, Adams, Pa	37
Graniteville, Nevada, Cal	12
Graniteville, Middlesex, Mass	130
Graniteville, Edgefield, S. C	260
Grant, Pima, Ariz	12
Grant, Park, Colo	12
Grant, Vermilion, Ill	12
Grant, Montgomery, Iowa	46
Grant, Wabaunsee, Kans	12
Grant, Boone, Ky	12
Grant, Kent, Mich	10
Grant, Faribault, Minn	3
Grant, Holt, Mo	12
Grant, Nemaha, Nebr	26
Grant, Herkimer, N. Y	43
Grant, Hardin, Ohio	12
Grant, Grant, Oreg	12
Grant, Indiana, Pa	180

* Money-order office.

Grant, Portage, Wis	$4
Grant C. H., Grant, W. Va	59
Grant Centre, Monona, Iowa	12
Grant City, Sac, Iowa	64
Grant City, (*c. h.*,) Worth, Mo	260
Grantfork, Madison, Ill	12
Grantham, Sullivan, N. H	64
Grant Isle, Aroostook, Me	12
Grantsborough, Craven, N. C	12
Grantsburgh, Johnson, Ill	13
Grantsburgh, Crawford, Ind	17
Grantsburgh, (*c. h.*,) Burnett, Wis	48
Grant's Hill, Worth, Mo	90
Grant's Lick, Campbell, Ky	16
Grant's Mills, Delaware, N. Y	1
Grant's Pass, Jackson, Oreg	19
Grantsville, Alleghany, Md	180
Grantsville, Linn, Mo	46
Grantsville, Tooele, Utah	95
Grantsville, (*c. h.*,) Calhoun, W. Va	15
Grantville, Coweta, Ga	150
Grantville, Jefferson, Kans	93
Grantville, Norfolk, Mass	200
Grantville, Dauphin, Pa	30
Granville, Putnam, Ill	200
Granville, Delaware, Ind	99
Granville, Mahaska, Iowa	54
Granville, Monroe, Mo	74
Granville, Washington, N. Y	610
Granville,* Licking, Ohio	950
Granville, Mifflin, Pa	43
Granville, Jackson, Tenn	21
Granville, Addison, Vt	47
Granville, Monongalia, W. Va	10
Granville, Milwaukee, Wis	66
Granville Centre, Bradford, Pa	53
Granville Corners, Hampden, Mass	150
Granville, Summit, Bradford, Pa	60
Grape Island, Pleasants, W. Va	15
Grapeland, Faribault, Minn	52
Grapeville, Greene, N. Y	12
Grapeville, Westmoreland, Pa	12
Grason, Andrew, Mo	16
Grasshopper Falls,*Jefferson, Kans	370
Grass Lake,* Jackson, Mich	830
Grassland, Harrison, W. Va	3
Grass Lick, Jackson, W. Va	10
Grass Valley,* Nevada, Cal	3,200
Grassy Creek, Livingston, Mo	23
Grassy Creek, Yancey, N. C	3
Grassy Pond, Spartanburgh, S. C	5
Grater's Ford, Montgomery, Pa	37
Gratiot, Licking, Ohio	71
Gratiot, La Fayette, Wis	170
Gratis, Preble, Ohio	140
Grattan, Kent, Mich	96
Gratz, Owen, Ky	16
Gratz, Dauphin, Pa	68
Gravel Hill, Buckingham, Va	63
Gravella, Conecuh, Ala	12
Gravelly Spring, Lauderdale, Ala	29
Gravel Ridge, Bradley, Ark	14
Gravel Run, Washtenaw, Mich	10
Gravel Spring, Frederick, Va	14
Gravelton, Wayne, Mo	17
Grave Run Mills, Baltimore, Md	14
Gravesend, Kings, N. Y	$70
Graves' Mill, Madison, Va	9
Graveston, Knox, Tenn	8
Gravesville, Herkimer, N. Y	44
Gravesville, Calumet, Wis	100
Gravity, Taylor, Iowa	11
Gravois Mills, Morgan, Mo	14
Gray, Cumberland, Me	200
Gray, Herkimer, N. Y	61
Gray Eagle, Buncombe, N. C	12
Gray Hawk, Jackson, Ky	3
Gray Rock, Titus, Tex	20
Graysburgh, Greene, Tenn	3
Gray's Chapel, Jackson, Ala	12
Gray's Creek, Cumberland, N. C	12
Gray's Flat, Marion, W. Va	4
Gray's Hill, Roane, Tenn	8
Gray's Landing, Greene, Pa	43
Grayson, Crittenden, Ark	5
Grayson, (*c. h.*,) Carter, Ky	82
Grayson Springs, Grayson, Ky	66
Graysonville, Stanislaus, Cal	12
Gray's Point, Lawrence, Mo	11
Graysport, Grenada, Miss	17
Gray's Summit, Franklin, Mo	140
Gray's Valley, Tioga, Pa	16
Graysville, Catoosa, Ga	40
Graysville, Sullivan, Ind	39
Graysville, Monroe, Ohio	53
Graysville, Huntingdon, Pa	120
Graytown, Bexar, Tex	8
Grayville,* White, Ill	360
Gray Willow, Kane, Ill	30
Greason, Cumberland, Pa	48
Greasy, Macoupin, Ill	4
Greasy Creek, Floyd, Va	22
Greasy Ridge, Lawrence, Ohio	34
Great Barrington,* Berkshire, Mass	1,500
Great Bend, Jefferson, N. Y	90
Great Bend, Meigs, Ohio	22
Great Bend, Susquehanna, Pa	810
Great Bend Village, Susquehanna, Pa	260
Great Bridge, Norfolk, Va	10
Great Crossings, Scott, Ky	21
Great Falls,* Strafford, N. H	2,300
Great Mills, St. Mary's, Md	120
Great Neck, Queens, N. Y	94
Great Oak, Palo Alto, Iowa	16
Great Pond, Hancock, Me	8
Great Valley, Cattaraugus, N. Y	51
Great Works, Penobscot, Me	93
Greble, Lebanon, Pa	15
Greece, Monroe, N. Y	28
Greeley, Weld, Colo	12
Greeley, Delaware, Iowa	90
Greeley, Anderson, Kans	100
Green, Licking, Ohio	10
Greenback, Jefferson, Ark	20
Green Bank, Burlington, N. J	23
Green Bank, Lancaster, Pa	8
Green Bank, Pocahontas, W. Va	32
Green Bay, Clarke, Iowa	61
Green Bay, Prince Edward, Va	39
Green Bay,* (*c. h.*,) Brown, Wis	2,500
Green Bottom, Cabell, W. Va	10

* Money-order office.

Greenbrier, Limestone, Ala	$12
Greenbrier, Conway, Ark	9
Green Brier, Orange, Ind	5
Green Brier, Monroe, Ohio	7
Greenbrier, Northumberland, Pa	21
Green Brier, Robertson, Tenn	22
Greenbush, Walker, Ga	11
Greenbush, Warren, Ill	77
Greenbush, Penobscot, Me	15
Green Bush, Alcona, Mich	12
Greenbush, Sheboygan, Wis	110
Green Camp, Marion, Ohio	44
Greencastle,* (*c. h.*,) Putnam, Ind	2,400
Greencastle, Jasper, Iowa	110
Green Castle, Warren, Ky	16
Green Castle, Sullivan, Mo	96
Green Castle, Fairfield, Ohio	32
Greencastle,* Franklin, Pa	780
Green Centre, Noble, Ind	12
Green Cove Springs, Clay, Fla	96
Green Creek, Cape May, N. J	68
Greendale, Armstrong, Pa	12
Greene, Jay, Ind	25
Greene, Androscoggin, Me	84
Greene, Chenango, N. Y	860
Greene, Lancaster, Pa	77
Greene, Kent, R. I	130
Greene Corner, Androscoggin, Me	28
Greeneville,* (*c. h.*,) Greene, Tenn	690
Greenfield, Colquitt, Ga	12
Greenfield, Greene, Ill	330
Greenfield,* (*c. h.*,) Hancock, Ind	540
Greenfield, Adair, Iowa	51
Greenfield, Penobscot, Me	10
Greenfield,* (*c. h.*,) Franklin, Mass	2,800
Greenfield, Wayne, Mich	49
Greenfield,* (*c. h.*,) Dade, Mo	370
Greenfield, Hillsborough, N. H	170
Greenfield, Ulster, N. Y	22
Greenfield,* Highland, Ohio	1,100
Greenfield, Erie, Pa	12
Greenfield, Nelson, Va	24
Greenfield, Milwaukee, Wis	24
Greenfield Centre, Saratoga, N. Y	77
Greenfield Hill, Fairfield, Conn	98
Greenfield Mills, Frederick, Md	64
Greenford, Mahoning, Ohio	130
Green Forest, Carroll, Ark	12
Green Garden, Will, Ill	38
Green Garden, Beaver, Pa	10
Green Grove, Madison, Ala	12
Green Grove, Luzerne, Pa	22
Green Hall, Jackson, Ky	6
Green Haven, Dutchess, N. Y	51
Green Hill, Lauderdale, Ala	9
Green Hill, Stewart, Ga	40
Green Hill, Warren, Ky	12
Green Hill, Wicomico, Md	13
Green Hill, Rutherford, N. C	6
Green Hill, Columbiana, Ohio	14
Green Hill, Wilson, Tenn	73
Green Hill, Campbell, Va	12
Greenhorn, Huerfano, Colo	12
Green Island, Albany, N. Y	250
Green Isle, Sibley, Minn	7
Green Lake, Monongalia, Minn	47

Green Lake, Green Lake, Wis	$41
Greenland, Fayette, Ill	40
Greenland, Ontonagon, Mich	210
Greenland, Boone, Mo	36
Greenland, Rockingham, N. H	190
Greenland, Ross, Ohio	23
Greenland, Lancaster, Pa	10
Greenland, Barnwell, S. C	12
Greenland, Grant, W. Va	54
Greenland Depot, Rockingham, N. H	41
Greenleaf, Meeker, Minn	240
Green Level, Wake, N. C	5
Green Mount, Drew, Ark	22
Green Mount, Adams, Pa	24
Greenmount, Rockingham, Va	13
Green Oak, Fulton, Ind	24
Green Oak, Livingston, Mich	23
Green Park, Perry, Pa	56
Green Plain, Southampton, Va	12
Green Point,* Kings, N. Y	2,000
Greenpoint, Bedford, Pa	12
Green Pond, Pike, Ill	12
Green Pond, Colleton, S. C	12
Greenport,* Suffolk, N. Y	900
Green Prairie, Morrison, Minn	6
Green Ridge, Pettis, Mo	69
Green Ridge, Adams, Pa	16
Green River, Henry, Ill	280
Green River, Columbia, N. Y	36
Green River, Henderson, N. C	12
Green River, Windham, Vt	49
Green River City, Sweetwater, Wyo	12
Greensborough,* (*c. h.*,) Hale, Ala	940
Greensborough, Craighead, Ark	57
Greensborough, (*c. h.*,) Greene, Ga	660
Greensborough, Henry, Ind	120
Greensborough,* Caroline, Md	320
Greensborough, (*c. h.*,) Choctaw, Miss.	70
Greensborough,* (*c. h.*,) Guilford, N. C	1,400
Greensborough, Greene, Pa	130
Greensborough, Orleans, Vt	170
Greensburgh, Clay, Ill	11
Greensburgh,* (*c. h.*,) Decatur, Ind	1,600
Greensburgh,* (*c. h.*,) Greene, Ky	500
Greensburgh, (*c. h.*,) St. Helena, La.	160
Greensburgh, Knox, Mo	46
Greensburgh, Mercer, N. J	46
Greensburgh, Trumbull, Ohio	110
Greensburgh,* (*c. h.*,) Westmoreland, Pa	1,400
Greensburgh × Roads, Sandusky, Ohio	29
Green Sea, Horry, S. C	12
Green's Fork, Wayne, Ind	150
Greenside, Webster, Iowa	12
Green's Landing, Hancock, Me	51
Greensport, St. Clair, Ala	16
Green Spring, Seneca, Ohio	330
Green Spring Furnace, Washington, Md	22
Green Spring Run, Hampshire, W. Va	19
Green Sulphur Springs, Greenbrier, W. Va	8

* Money-order office.

Office	
Greenton, La Fayette, Mo	$73
Green Top, Schuyler, Mo	150
Greentown, Howard, Ind	47
Greentown, Stark, Ohio	53
Green Tree, Allegheny, Pa	53
Green Tree, White, Tenn	2
Greenup, Cumberland, Ill	190
Greenup,* (*c. h.*,) Greenup, Ky	350
Greenvale, Jo Daviess, Ill	23
Greenvale, Dallas, Iowa	14
Green Vale, Franklin, Me	10
Greenvale, Queens, N. Y	22
Green Valley, El Dorado, Cal	57
Green Valley, Tazewell, Ill	20
Green Valley, Decatur, Iowa	12
Green Valley, Bath, Va	6
Greenview, Menard, Ill	220
Green Village, Morris, N. J	46
Green Village, Franklin, Pa	58
Greenville,* (*c. h.*,) Butler, Ala	1,200
Greenville, Washington, Ark	5
Greenville, Plumas, Cal	12
Greenville, New London, Conn	760
Greenville, (*c. h.*,) Meriwether, Ga	150
Greenville,* (*c. h.*,) Bond, Ill	780
Greenville, Floyd, Ind	84
Greenville,* (*c. h.*,) Muhlenburgh, Ky	420
Greenville, Piscataquis, Me	250
Greenville,* Montcalm, Mich	1,100
Greenville, (*c. h.*,) Washington, Miss	800
Greenville, (*c. h.*,) Wayne, Mo	10
Greenville, Hudson, N. J	130
Greenville, Greene, N. Y	220
Greenville, (*c. h.*,) Pitt, N. C	270
Greenville,* (*c. h.*,) Darke, Ohio	1,200
Greenville,* Mercer, Pa	1,600
Greenville, Providence, R. I	170
Greenville, (*c. h.*,) Hunt, Tex	770
Greenville, Augusta, Va	77
Greenville, Outagamie, Wis	13
Greenville C. H.,* Greenville, S. C	1,500
Greenway, Nelson, Va	12
Greenwich, Fairfield, Conn	710
Greenwich, Hampshire, Mass	120
Greenwich, Cumberland, N. J	270
Greenwich, Washington, N. Y	920
Greenwich Station, Huron, Ohio	200
Greenwich Village, Hampshire, Mass	110
Greenwood, Etowah, Ala	7
Greenwood, (*c. h.*,) Sebastian, Ark	31
Greenwood, El Dorado, Cal	22
Greenwood, (*c. h.*,) Charles Mix, Dak	20
Greenwood, Sussex, Del	110
Greenwood, Jackson, Fla	92
Greenwood, McHenry, Ill	48
Greenwood, Johnson, Ind	250
Greenwood, Polk, Iowa	27
Greenwood, Franklin, Kans	10
Greenwood, Caddo, La	8
Greenwood, Oxford, Me	16
Greenwood, Baltimore, Md	25
Greenwood, Middlesex, Mass	56
Greenwood, Hennepin, Minn	20
Greenwood, Carroll, Miss	450
Greenwood, Jackson, Mo	$270
Greenwood, Deer Lodge, Mont	12
Greenwood, Cass, Nebr	12
Green Wood, Bergen, N. J	12
Greenwood, Steuben, N. Y	90
Greenwood, Columbia, Pa	20
Greenwood, Abbeville, S. C	390
Greenwood, Shelby, Tenn	83
Greenwood, Doddridge, W. Va	59
Greenwood Centre, Kossuth, Iowa	12
Greenwood Depot, Albemarle, Va	91
Greenwood Furnace, Marquette, Mich	20
Greenwood Furnace, Huntingdon, Pa	57
Greenwood Iron Works, Orange, N. Y	160
Greersville, Knox, Ohio	37
Greggsville, Ohio, W. Va	16
Gregory Landing, Clarke, Mo	12
Greig, Lewis, N. Y	50
Greigsville, Livingston, N. Y	52
Grenada,* (*c. h.*,) Grenada, Miss	1,100
Greshville, Berks, Pa	16
Gretna, Jefferson, La	12
Greystone, Wilson, Kans	10
Grider, Cumberland, Ky	29
Gridley, McLean, Ill	330
Grier's Point, Perry, Pa	8
Griesemersville, Berks, Pa	12
Griffin,* (*c. h.*,) Spalding, Ga	1,700
Griffin's Corners, Delaware, N. Y	140
Griffin's Mills, Erie, N. Y	60
Griffinsville, Appanoose, Iowa	4
Griffithsville, Lincoln, W. Va	6
Grigg's Corners, Ashtabula, Ohio	12
Griggstown, Somerset, N. J	76
Griggsville,* Pike, Ill	720
Grim's Store, Upshur, W. Va	5
Grimville, Berks, Pa	31
Grinell, Grundy, Mo	12
Grinnell,* Poweshiek, Iowa	1,500
Grinnell, Wallace, Kans	12
Grinstead's Mills, Hart, Ky	12
Grinton, Will, Ill	8
Grissom's Landing, Daviess, Ky	12
Grist's Station, Columbus, N. C	22
Griswold, New London, Conn	73
Griswold, Hamilton, Ill	8
Griswold's Mills, Washington, N. Y	15
Griswoldville, Jones, Ga	52
Griswoldville, Franklin, Mass	120
Grizzly Bear House, Placer, Cal	20
Grizzly Flat, El Dorado, Cal	56
Groesbeck, Hamilton, Ohio	69
Groff's Store, Lancaster, Pa	26
Groom's Corners, Saratoga, N. Y	22
Groomsville, Tipton, Ind	12
Grooverville, Brooks, Ga	25
Grosvenor Dale, Windham, Conn	200
Groton, New London, Conn	380
Groton, Middlesex, Mass	610
Groton, Grafton, N. H	77
Groton, Tompkins, N. Y	440
Groton, Caledonia, Vt	76
Groton City, Tompkins, N. Y	34

* Money-order office.

Groton Junction,* Middlesex, Mass	$770
Grouse, Kane, Ill	29
Grove, Geauga, Ohio	22
Grove, Chatham, N. C	10
Grove, Walworth, Wis	9
Grove City, Christian, Ill	210
Grove City, Cass, Iowa	45
Grove City, Jefferson, Kans	12
Grove City, Franklin, Ohio	63
Grove Cottage, Perry, Ala	12
Grove Creek, Jones, Iowa	12
Grove Hill, (c. h.,) Clarke, Ala	55
Grove Hill, Crawford, Ohio	10
Grove Hill, Page, Va	11
Groveland, Tazewell, Ill	92
Groveland, Putnam, Ind	22
Groveland, Essex, Mass	210
Groveland, Oakland, Mich	10
Groveland, Livingston, N. Y	43
Grovenor's Corners, Schoharie, N. Y	39
Groveport, Franklin, Ohio	220
Grover, Ottawa, Kans	12
Grover Town, Stark, Ind	47
Groves, Fayette, Ind	35
Grove Station, Greenville, S. C	19
Groveton, Coos, N. H	220
Grubbtown, Grundy, Mo	12
Grubville, Franklin, Mo	27
Grundy, (c. h.,) Buchanan, Va	12
Grundy Centre, (c. h.,) Grundy, Iowa	300
Guahonga, San Diego, Cal	12
Gualala, Mendocino, Cal	85
Gubser's Mills, Campbell, Ky	12
Guenoc, Lake, Cal	20
Guerneville, Sonoma, Cal	12
Guest's Station, Wise, Va	12
Guilderland, Albany, N. Y	120
Guilderland Centre, Albany, N. Y	82
Guilderland Station, Albany, N. Y	20
Guildford, Freeborn, Minn	8
Guildhall, (c. h.,) Essex, Vt	100
Guilford,* New Haven, Conn	920
Guilford, Jo Daviess, Ill	12
Guilford, Dearborn, Ind	82
Guilford, Wilson, Kans	12
Guilford, Piscataquis, Me	190
Guilford, Nodaway, Mo	83
Guilford, Chenango, N. Y	240
Guilford, Medina, Ohio	330
Guilford, Windham, Vt	98
Guilford, Accomack, Va	17
Guilford Centre, Chenango, N. Y	44
Guilford Centre, Windham, Vt	88
Guilford Station, Loudoun, Va	45
Guiney's, Caroline, Va	200
Guionsville, Dearborn, Ind	9
Guittard Station, Marshall, Kans	15
Gulf Mills, Montgomery, Pa	44
Gulf Summit, Broome, N. Y	32
Gull Lake, Barry, Mich	33
Gully Branch, Coffee, Ga	6
Gumborough, Sussex, Del	39
Gum Branch, Onslow, N. C	10
Gum Spring, Louisa, Va	24
Gum Sulphur, Rock Castle, Ky	12
Gum Tree, Chester, Pa	67

Gundrum, Pulaski, Ind	$12
Gun Marsh, Allegan, Mich	19
Gunnison, San Pete, Utah	51
Guntersville, (c. h.,) Marshall, Ala	210
Guntown, Lee, Miss	210
Gurleysville, Madison, Ala	14
Gurleyville, Tolland, Conn	56
Gussettville, Live Oak, Tex	27
Gustavus, Trumbull, Ohio	200
Guthrie, Lawrence, Ind	1
Guthrie, Guthrie, Iowa	240
Guthrie, Todd, Ky	110
Guthrie Centre, Guthrie, Iowa	120
Guthriesville, Chester, Pa	61
Guthriesville, York, S. C	31
Guttenberg,* Clayton, Iowa	280
Guyandotte, Cabell, W. Va	200
Guymard, Orange, N. Y	83
Guy's Mills, Crawford, Pa	57
Guysville, Athens, Ohio	29
Guyton, Effingham, Ga	65
Gwynedd, Montgomery, Pa	76
Gypsum, Ontario, N. Y	45
Gypsum Creek, McPherson, Kans	9

H

Hackberry, Floyd, Iowa	12
Hackberry, Lavaca, Tex	45
Hackensack, (c. h.,) Bergen, N. J	870
Hacker's Creek, Lewis, W. Va	8
Hacker's Valley, Webster, W. Va	4
Hackettstown,* Warren, N. J	1,100
Haddam, (c. h.,) Middlesex, Conn	150
Haddam, Washington, Kans	12
Haddam Neck, Middlesex, Conn	78
Haddonfield, Camden, N. J	410
Haden's, Madison, Ala	12
Hadensville, Todd, Ky	20
Hadensville, Goochland, Va	16
Hader, Goodhue, Minn	81
Hadley, Will, Ill	58
Hadley, Warren, Ky	22
Hadley, Hampshire, Mass	420
Hadley, Lapeer, Mich	170
Hadley, Saratoga, N. Y	150
Hadley, Mercer, Pa	29
Hadley's Mills, Chatham, N. C	10
Hadley Station, Lawrence, Ill	47
Hadlock, Northampton, Va	23
Hadlyme, New London, Conn	85
Hagaman's Mills, Montgomery, N. Y	90
Hagarstown, Fayette, Ill	12
Hagedorn's Mills, Saratoga, N. Y	34
Hager's Grove, Shelby, Mo	10
Hagerstown,* Wayne, Ind	410
Hagerstown,(c. h.,)* Washington, Md	2,200
Hagersville, Bucks, Pa	52
Hagley, Cass, Ill	30
Hague, Warren, N. Y	46
Hague, Westmoreland, Va	69
Hailesborough, St. Lawrence, N. Y	17
Hailsville, Montgomery, Ala	12
Hainesburgh, Warren, N. J	70
Hainesport, Burlington, N. J	18
Hainesville, Lake, Ill	72

* Money-order office.

Hainesville, Clinton, Mo	$140
Hainesville, Sussex, N. J	42
Hainesville, Berkeley, W. Va	34
Hair's Valley, Huntingdon, Pa	12
Halcott Centre, Greene, N. Y	8
Halcottsville, Delaware, N. Y	37
Halcyon Dale, Scriven, Ga	15
Haldane, Ogle, Ill	45
Hale, Ogle, Ill	86
Hale, Trempealeau, Wis	12
Hale's Corners, Milwaukee, Wis	56
Hale's Creek, Scioto, Ohio	46
Hale's Eddy, Delaware, N. Y	110
Hale's Ford, Franklin, Va	26
Hale's Mills, Fentress, Tenn	10
Hale's Point, Lauderdale, Tenn	8
Haley's, Marion, Ala	5
Haley's Station, Bedford, Tenn	22
Half Day, Lake, Ill	98
Half Moon, Saratoga, N. Y	74
Half Moon, Centre, Pa	68
Halfmoon Bay, San Mateo, Cal	200
Half Rock, Mercer, Mo	8
Half Way, Polk, Mo	35
Half Way, Onondaga, N. Y	12
Half Way, Montgomery, Pa	12
Half Way Creek, La Crosse, Wis	100
Half Way House, Vermilion, Ill	12
Half Way Prairie, Monroe, Iowa	12
Halifax, Plymouth, Mass	160
Halifax, (*c. h.*,) Halifax, N. C	410
Halifax, Dauphin, Pa	180
Halifax, Windham, Vt	50
Halifax C. H., Halifax, Va	340
Hall, Morgan, Ind	44
Hall, York, Pa	9
Hall Centre, Wayne, N. Y	12
Halleck, Buchanan, Mo	64
Hallettsville, (*c. h.*,) Lavaca, Tex	370
Hallock, Peoria, Ill	33
Hallock's Mills, Westchester, N. Y	50
Hallowell, Kennebec, Me	1,300
Hallsa's Ferry, Nodaway, Mo	23
Hallsborough, Chesterfield, Va	18
Hall's Corners, Allen, Ind	20
Hall's Corners, Ontario, N. Y	78
Hall's Gap Station, Lincoln, Ky	12
Hall's Hill, Rutherford, Tenn	12
Hall's Mill, Bartow, Ga	38
Hallsport, Allegany, N. Y	19
Hall's Valley, Morgan, Ohio	7
Hallsville, Pike, Ala	12
Hallsville, De Witt, Ill	24
Hallsville, Boone, Mo	120
Hallsville, Montgomery, N. Y	29
Hallsville, Duplin, N. C	14
Hallsville, Ross, Ohio	57
Hallsville, Harrison, Tex	20
Halltown, Saline, Ill	12
Halltown, Jefferson, W. Va	120
Halsellville, Chester, S. C	8
Halsey Valley, Tioga, N. Y	39
Hambaugh's, Warren, Va	12
Hamburgh, Perry, Ala	15
Hamburgh,* (*c. h.*,) Ashley, Ark	250
Hamburgh, New London, Conn	130

Hamburgh, Calhoun, Ill	$99
Hamburgh, Franklin, Ind	15
Hamburgh, Fremont, Iowa	730
Hamburgh, Livingston, Mich	67
Hamburgh, Franklin, Miss	12
Hamburgh, St. Charles, Mo	21
Hamburgh, Sussex, N. J	110
Hamburgh, Erie, N. Y	20
Hamburgh, Fairfield, Ohio	5
Hamburgh, Berks, Pa	570
Hamburgh, Edgefield, S. C	41
Hamburgh, Hardin, Tenn	42
Hamburgh, Shenandoah, Va	12
Hamden, New Haven, Conn	250
Hamden, Delaware, N. Y	170
Hamer, Paulding, Ohio	11
Hamersville, Brown, Ohio	91
Hamilton, Park, Colo	55
Hamilton, (*c. h.*,) Harris, Ga	180
Hamilton,* Hancock. Ill	490
Hamilton, Steuben, Ind	80
Hamilton, Marion, Iowa	65
Hamilton, Crawford, Kans	12
Hamilton, Boone, Ky	13
Hamilton, Essex, Mass	110
Hamilton, Allegan, Mich	62
Hamilton, Fillmore, Minn	110
Hamilton, Monroe, Miss	6
Hamilton, Caldwell, Mo	1,100
Hamilton, Gallatin, Mont	90
Hamilton,* (*c. h.*,) White Pine, Nev	1,200
Hamilton,* Madison, N. Y	1,400
Hamilton, Martin, N. C	98
Hamilton,* (*c. h.*,) Butler, Ohio	3,000
Hamilton, Jefferson, Pa	59
Hamilton, Shelby, Tex	12
Hamilton, Loudoun, Va	190
Hamilton Square, Mercer, N. J	81
Hamilton Station, Scott, Minn	54
Hamlet, Mercer, Ill	97
Hamlet, Stark, Ind	38
Hamlet, Chautauqua, N. Y	98
Hamlin, McLean, Ill	16
Hamlin, Brown, Kans	15
Hamlin, Monroe, Mich	16
Hamlin, Monroe, N. Y	110
Hamlin, Lebanon, Pa	18
Hamlin, (*c. h.*,) Lincoln, W. Va	36
Hamlin, Trempealeau, Wis	13
Hamlin Grove, Audubon, Iowa	24
Hamlinton, Wayne, Pa	120
Hammersley's Fork, Clinton, Pa	50
Hammond, Tangipahoa, La	92
Hammond, Kent. Mich	12
Hammond, St. Lawrence, N. Y	150
Hammond, Barnwell, S. C	7
Hammond, Robertson, Tex	12
Hammond, St. Croix, Wis	95
Hammondsburgh, Warren, Iowa	18
Hammond's Creek, Tioga, Pa	17
Hammondsport, Steuben, N. Y	540
Hammondsville, Jefferson, Ohio	280
Hammonton,* Atlantic, N. J	700
Hammonville, Hart, Ky	31
Hamorton, Chester, Pa	100
Hampden, Penobscot, Me	180

* Money-order office.

Post office	Amount
Hampden, Geauga, Ohio	$66
Hampden Corner, Penobscot, Me	230
Hampden Sidney College, Prince Edward, Va	370
Hampshire, Kane, Ill	92
Hampshire, Maury, Tenn	33
Hampstead, Carroll, Md	61
Hampstead, Rockingham, N. H	130
Hampstead, King George, Va	35
Hampton, (*c. h.*,) Calhoun, Ark	48
Hampton, Windham, Conn	490
Hampton, Rock Island, Ill	200
Hampton,* (*c. h.*,) Franklin, Iowa	120
Hampton, Dakota, Minn	49
Hampton, Platte, Mo	16
Hampton, Rockingham, N. H	380
Hampton, Washington, N. Y	100
Hampton, Adams, Pa	58
Hampton, Carter, Tenn	12
Hampton, (*c. h.*,) Elizabeth City, Va	690
Hampton Falls, Rockingham, N. H	110
Hamptonville, Yadkin, N. C	20
Hamrick's Station, Putnam, Ind	12
Ham's Prairie, Callaway, Mo	24
Hanby's Mills, Walker, Ala	12
Hancock, Harrison, Ind	9
Hancock, Hancock, Me	88
Hancock,* Washington, Md	440
Hancock, Berkshire, Mass	120
Hancock, Houghton, Mich	1,500
Hancock, Pulaski, Mo	12
Hancock, Hillsborough, N. H	220
Hancock,* Delaware, N. Y	510
Hancock, Addison, Vt	93
Hancock, Waushara, Wis	73
Hancock's Bridge, Salem, N. J	38
Handsborough, Harrison, Miss	50
Handy, Fayette, Ala	12
Handy, Fulton, Ohio	14
Hanerville, Dane, Wis	28
Hanesville, Kent, Md	72
Haneyville, Lycoming, Pa	8
Hanford's Landing, Monroe, N. Y	35
Hanging Rock, Lawrence, Ohio	150
Hanging Rock, Hampshire, W. Va	12
Hankins, Sullivan, N. Y	130
Hanley, Ottawa, Mich	12
Hanlin Station, Washington, Pa	10
Hanly, Jessamine, Ky	37
Hannahatchee, Stewart, Ga	10
Hannahsville, Tucker, W. Va	13
Hanna Station, La Porte, Ind	110
Hannersville, Davidson, N. C	4
Hannibal,* Marion, Mo	3,400
Hannibal, Oswego, N. Y	340
Hannibal, Monroe, Ohio	150
Hannibal Centre, Oswego, N. Y	51
Hanover, Coosa, Ala	4
Hanover, New London, Conn	62
Hanover, Jo Daviess, Ill	190
Hanover, Jefferson, Ind	400
Hanover, Washington, Kans	12
Hanover, Oxford, Me	64
Hanover, Howard, Md	23
Hanover, Plymouth, Mass	290
Hanover, Jackson, Mich	47
Hanover, Jefferson, Mo	$59
Hanover,* Grafton, N. H	1,800
Hanover, Morris, N. J	68
Hanover, Licking, Ohio	82
Hanover,* York, Pa	1,000
Hanover, Rock, Wis	95
Hanover C. H., Hanover, Va	100
Hanover Centre, Grafton, N. H	46
Hanover Junction, York, Pa	160
Hanoverton, Columbiana, Ohio	110
Hanoverville, Northampton, Pa	46
Hansel's, Dearborn, Ind	12
Hansen, Oceana, Mich	14
Hanson, Hopkins, Ky	12
Hanson, Plymouth, Mass	93
Hansonville, Frederick, Md	12
Hansonville, Russell, Va	40
Happy Camp, Del Norte, Cal	26
Happy Hollow, Wapello, Iowa	12
Happy Home, Burke, N. C	12
Happy Valley, Harrison, Mo	11
Happy Valley, Carter, Tenn	10
Harbeson, Sussex, Del	12
Harbour Creek, Erie, Pa	120
Harbour's Mills, Putnam, W. Va	12
Hardeeville, Beaufort, S. C	12
Hardenburgh, Ulster, N. Y	6
Hardin, (*c. h.*,) Calhoun, Ill	93
Hardin, Clayton, Iowa	74
Hardin, Ray, Mo	27
Hardin, Shelby, Ohio	62
Hardin, (*c. h.*,) Hardin, Tex	21
Hardin City, Hardin, Iowa	21
Hardinsburgh, Washington, Ind	54
Hardinsburgh, (*c. h.*,) Breckinridge, Ky	200
Hardinsville, Crawford, Ill	21
Hardison's Mills, Maury, Tenn	12
Hardwick, Worcester, Mass	170
Hardwick, Warren, N. J	8
Hardwick, Caledonia, Vt	200
Hardwicksville, Nelson, Va	22
Hardy, Dallas, Ala	12
Hardy Station, Grenada, Miss	12
Hardyville, Mohave, Ariz	180
Hardyville, Hart, Ky	25
Hare's Corner, New Castle, Del	24
Harewood, Baltimore, Md	12
Harford, Cortland, N. Y	72
Harford, Susquehanna, Pa	300
Harford Furnace, Harford, Md	73
Harford Mills, Cortland, N. Y	54
Hark, Shelby, Ill	8
Harker's Corners, Peoria, Ill	16
Harlan, Allen, Ind	95
Harlan, (*c. h.*,) Shelby, Iowa	68
Harlan, (*c. h.*,) Harlan, Ky	16
Harlem, Winnebago, Ill	31
Harlem, Clay, Mo	190
Harlem, Delaware, Ohio	31
Harlem Spring, Carroll, Ohio	89
Harlemville, Columbia, N. Y	35
Harlensburgh, Lawrence, Pa	84
Harleysville, Montgomery, Pa	57
Harlingen, Somerset, N. J	74
Harmar, Washington, Ohio	590

* Money-order office.

HAR		HAR	
Harmarville, Allegheny, Pa	$71	Harris Lot, Charles, Md	$12
Harmon, Bracken, Ky	12	*Harrison*, (*c. h.*,) Boone, Ark	33
Harmonsburgh, Crawford, Pa	84	Harrison, Winnebago, Ill	56
Harmony, McHenry, Ill	30	Harrison, Dèlaware, Ind	12
Harmony, Clay, Ind	300	Harrison, Cumberland, Me	230
Harmony, Taylor, Iowa	11	Harrison, Dorchester, Md	24
Harmony, Owen, Ky	11	Harrison, Monongalia, Minn	96
Harmony, Somerset, Me	120	Harrison, Madison, Mont	12
Harmony, Fillmore, Minn	12	Harrison, Westchester, N. Y	60
Harmony, Washington, Mo	27	Harrison,* Hamilton, Ohio	650
Harmony, Warren, N. J	20	*Harrison*, (*c. h.*,) Hamilton, Tenn	81
Harmony, Chautauqua, N. Y	170	*Harrisonburgh*, (*c. h.*,) Catahoula, La	170
Harmony, Clark, Ohio	20	*Harrisonburgh*,* (*c. h.*,) Rockingham, Va	1,900
Harmony, Butler, Pa	130	Harrison City, Westmoreland, Pa	49
Harmony, Providence, R. I	21	Harrison Mills, Scioto, Ohio	8
Harmony, York, S. C	3	Harrison's Creek, Bladen, N. C	12
Harmony, Halifax, Va	21	Harrison's Mills, Crawford, Mo	10
Harmony, Mason, W. Va	12	Harrison Square, Norfolk, Mass	650
Harmony, Vernon, Wis	21	Harrison's Store, Shelby, Tenn	12
Harmony Centre, Susquehanna, Pa	50	Harrison Station. Tallahatchie, Miss	160
Harmony Grove, Jackson, Ga	67	Harrison Valley, Potter, Pa	37
Harmony Hill, Rusk, Tex	77	Harrisonville, Monroe, Ill	32
Harmony Village, Middlesex, Va	12	Harrisonville, Shelby, Ky	16
Harmsburgh, Armstrong, Pa	12	Harrisonville, Baltimore. Md	16
Harnedsville, Somerset, Pa	23	*Harrisonville*,* (*c. h.*,) Cass, Mo	1,000
Harnett C. H., Harnett, N. C	14	Harrisonville, Gloucester, N. J	93
Harney, Carroll, Md	27	Harrisonville, Meigs, Ohio	83
Harold, Montgomery, Ark	12	Harrisonville, Fulton, Pa	55
Harp, De Witt, Ill	12	Harris Station, Limestone, Ala	12
Harper, Logan, Ohio	38	Harris Station, Obion, Tenn	12
Harper's Ferry, Allamakee, Iowa	43	Harristown, Macon, Ill	230
Harper's Ferry, Henry, Ky	12	Harristown, Washington, Ind	53
Harper's Ferry,* Jefferson, W. Va	760	Harrisville, Randolph, Ind	15
Harpersfield, Delaware, N. Y	100	*Harrisville*, (*c. h.*,) Alcona, Mich	270
Harpersfield, Ashtabula, Ohio	62	Harrisville, Cheshire, N. H	210
Harper's Mills, Pendleton, W. Va	8	Harrisville, Lewis, N.Y	110
Harpersville, Broome, N. Y	350	Harrisville, Harrison, Ohio	150
Harpswell Centre, Cumberland, Me	37	Harrisville, Butler, Pa	170
Harreldsville, Butler, Ky	10	Harrisville, Bell, Tex	45
Harrell, Decatur, Ga	12	*Harrisville*, (*c. h.*,) Ritchie, W. Va	120
Harrell's Store, New Hanover, N. C	15	Harrisville, Marquette, Wis	57
Harrellsville, Hertford, N. C	78	Harrmann's Station, Dearborn, Ind	12
Harriettsville, Noble, Ohio	43	Harrodsburgh, Monroe, Ind	130
Harrington, Kent, Del	140	*Harrodsburgh*,* (*c. h.*,) Mercer, Ky	300
Harrington, Washington, Me	200	Harshasville, Adams, Ohio	38
Harrington, Harnett, N. C	10	Harshaville, Beaver, Pa	14
Harris, Louisa, Va	18	Harshmansville, Montgomery, Ohio	45
Harrisburgh, (*c. h.*,) Poinsett, Ark	86	*Hart*,* (*c. h.*,) Oceana, Mich	360
Harrisburgh, Alameda, Cal	13	Hartfield, Chautauqua, N. Y	50
Harrisburgh,* (*c. h.*,) Saline, Ill	270	HARTFORD,* (*c. h.*,) Hartford, Conn	4,000
Harrisburgh, Fayette, Ind	25	Hartford, Saline, Ill	3
Harrisburgh, Lyon, Kans	13	Hartford, Ohio, Ind	13
Harrisburgh, Deer Lodge, Mont	12	Hartford, Warren, Iowa	79
Harrisburgh, Lewis, N. Y	16	Hartford, Lyon, Kans	76
Harrisburgh, Franklin, Ohio	69	*Hartford*,* (*c. h.*,) Ohio, Ky	320
Harrisburgh, Linn, Oreg	150	Hartford, Oxford, Me	49
HARRISBURGH,* (*c. h.*,) Dauphin, Pa	3,600	Hartford, Van Buren, Mich	210
Harrisburgh, Harris, Tex	170	Hartford, Todd, Minn	12
Harrisburgh, Washington, Utah	28	Hartford, Putnam, Mo	17
Harris Creek, Kent, Mich	26	Hartford, Burlington, N. J	37
Harris Creek, Amherst, Va	12	Hartford, Washington, N. Y	190
Harris Depot, Cabarrus, N. C	40	Hartford, Trumbull, Ohio	98
Harris' Ferry, Wood, W. Va	24	Hartford, Windsor, Vt	490
Harris Grove, Jefferson, Ill	16	Hartford, Washington, Wis	500
Harris Grove, Harrison, Iowa	24	*Hartford City*,* (*c.h.*,) Blackford, Ind	440
Harris Hill, Erie, N. Y	20		

* Money-order office.

Hartford City, Mason, W. Va	$100
Harthegig, Mercer, Pa	40
Hartland, Hartford, Conn	72
Hartland, Worth, Iowa	21
Hartland, Somerset, Me	320
Hartland, Livingston, Mich	230
Hartland, Freeborn, Minn	15
Hartland, Niagara, N. Y	95
Hartland, Huron, Ohio	12
Hartland, Windsor, Vt	250
Hartland, Waukesha, Wis	260
Hartland Four Corners, Windsor, Vt	70
Hartleton, Union, Pa	120
Hartley, York, Pa	12
Hartleyville, Athens, Ohio	16
Hart Lot, Onondaga, N. Y	140
Hartmonsville, Mineral, W. Va	10
Hart's Corners, Westchester, N. Y	87
Hart's Falls, Rensselaer, N. Y	520
Hart's Grove, Ashtabula, Ohio	75
Hartshorn, Alamance, N. C	3
Hartstown, Crawford, Pa	170
Hartsville, Bartholomew, Ind	190
Hartsville, Berkshire, Mass	120
Hartsville, Bucks, Pa	89
Hartsville, Darlington, S. C	24
Hartsville, Sumner, Tenn	250
Hartville, (c. h.,) Wright, Mo	60
Hartville, Stark, Ohio	29
Hartwell, (c. h.,) Hart, Ga	71
Hartwell, Hamilton, Ohio	12
Hartwellville, Shiawassee, Mich	64
Hartwick, Otsego, N. Y	86
Hartwick Seminary, Otsego, N. Y	79
Hartwood, Stafford, Va	23
Harvard,* McHenry, Ill	910
Harvard, Worcester, Mass	310
Harvard, Delaware, N. Y	60
Harvey, Marquette, Mich	29
Harvey, Dane, Wis	70
Harvey's, Greene, Pa	58
Harveysburgh, Fountain, Ind	37
Harveysburgh, Warren, Ohio	260
Harvey's Mills, Jefferson, Iowa	15
Harvey's Store, Charlotte, Va	23
Harveyville, Wabaunsee, Kans	12
Harveyville, Luzerne, Pa	64
Harwich, Barnstable, Mass	370
Harwich Port, Barnstable, Mass	240
Harwinton, Litchfield, Conn	180
Harwood, Muskegon, Mich	30
Hasbrouck, Sullivan, N. Y	13
Haskell, La Porte, Ind	18
Haskell Flats, Cattaraugus, N. Y	21
Haskins, Wood, Ohio	160
Haskinsville, Greene, Ky	17
Haskinville, Steuben, N. Y	36
Hasler, Lapeer, Mich	25
Hassan, Hennepin, Minn	6
Hassan, Hancock, Ohio	67
Hastings, (c. h.,)* Barry, Mich	1,200
Hastings, (c. h.,)* Dakota, Minn	2,000
Hastings, Oswego, N. Y	82
Hastings, Richland, Ohio	16
Hastings Centre, Oswego, N. Y	35
Hastings Landing, Calhoun, Ill	12
Hastings-upon-Hudson, Westchester, N. Y	$400
Hatborough, Montgomery, Pa	160
Hatchechubbee, Russell, Ala	31
Hatcher's Station, Quitman, Ga	21
Hatch Hollow, Erie, Pa	16
Hatchsophka, Elmore, Ala	12
Hatchville, Barnstable, Mass	55
Hat Creek, Campbell, Va	8
Hatfield, Hampshire, Mass	290
Hatfield, Montgomery, Pa	99
Haubstadt, Gibson, Ind	97
Haught's Store, Dallas, Tex	8
Hauppauge, Suffolk, N. Y	49
Hausertown, Owen, Ind	48
Havana, (c. h.,)* Mason, Ill	1,100
Havana, Gentry, Mo	19
Havana,* Schuyler, N. Y	800
Havana, Huron, Ohio	170
Havanna, Hale, Ala	12
Havanna, Steele, Minn	12
Havelock, Cook, Ill	65
Havelock, Washington, Pa	83
Haverford, Delaware, Pa	38
Haverhill,* Essex, Mass	3,100
Haverhill, (c. h.,)* Grafton, N. H	520
Haverhill, Scioto, Ohio	43
Haverstraw, Rockland, N. Y	1,000
Havilah, (c. h.,) Kern, Cal	230
Haviland Hollow, Putnam, N. Y	21
Havilandsville, Harrison, Ky	27
Havre de Grace,* Harford, Md	730
Haw Branch, Onslow, N. C	5
Haw Creek, Benton, Mo	12
Hawes' Cross Roads, Washington, Tenn	14
Hawesville, (c. h.,) Hancock, Ky	160
Hawk Creek, Chippewa, Minn	26
Hawk Eye, Fayette, Iowa	12
Hawkinstown, Shenandoah, Va	12
Hawkinsville, (c. h.,) Pulaski, Ga	560
Hawkinsville, Oneida, N. Y	120
Hawkinsville, Sussex, Va	12
Hawk Point, Lincoln, Mo	17
Hawk's Nest, Fayette, W. Va	12
Hawley, Franklin, Mass	50
Hawley, Wayne, Pa	660
Hawley's Store, Sampson, N. C	8
Hawleysville, Page, Iowa	85
Hawleyton, Broome, N. Y	22
Hawleyville, Fairfield, Conn	120
Haw Ridge, Dale, Ala	37
Haw River, Alamance, N. C	83
Haw's Ford, Floyd, Ky	12
Hawthorne, Passaic, N. J	8
Hayden Row, Middlesex, Mass	62
Haydenville, Hampshire, Mass	520
Haydenville, Hocking, Ohio	12
Hayes' Store, Madison, Ala	8
Hayes' Store, Gloucester, Va	12
Hayesville, Keokuk, Iowa	190
Hayesville,* Ashland, Ohio	340
Hayesville, (c. h.,) Clay, N. C	12
Hayesville, Chester, Pa	71
Hayesville, Greene, Tenn	12
Hayfield, Crawford, Pa	66

* Money-order office.

Hayfield, Frederick, Va	$11
Hay Market, Prince William, Va	85
Hay Meadow, Wilkes, N. C	10
Haymond, Franklin, Ind	25
Haynerville, Rensselaer, N. Y	6
Haynes, Union, Tenn	12
Haynesville, Claiborne, La	12
Haynesville, Aroostook, Me	10
Hayneville, (*c. h.*,) Lowndes, Ala	220
Haynie, Mills, Iowa	20
Hays City, (*c. h.*,) Ellis, Kans	1,300
Hays' Store, Wake, N. C	6
Haystack, Surry, N. C	10
Haysville, Dubois, Ind	41
Hayward, Freeborn, Minn	10
Haywood, Alameda, Cal	80
Haywood, Chatham, N. C	33
Hazard, Cherokee, Iowa	12
Hazard, (*c. h.*,) Perry, Ky	5
Hazardville, Hartford, Conn	180
Hazelettville, Woodson, Kans	12
Hazel Green, Madison, Tenn	12
Hazel Green, Grant, Wis	310
Hazelton, Buchanan, Iowa	18
Hazelton, Shiawassee, Mich	12
Hazelwood, Rice, Minn	15
Hazen, Cass, Mo	12
Hazle Barrens, Barry, Mo	12
Hazle Dell, Cumberland, Ill	63
Hazle Green, Delaware, Iowa	30
Hazle Green, Wolfe, Ky	6
Hazle Green, Shiawassee, Mich	12
Hazle Green, Laclede, Mo	22
Hazlehurst, Appling, Ga	12
Hazlehurst,* Copiah, Miss	170
Hazle Patch, Laurel, Ky	9
Hazleton, Gibson, Ind	260
Hazleton,* Luzerne, Pa	1,600
Hazlettville, Kent, Del	18
Hazlewood, Ballard, Ky	12
Hazlewood, Webster, Mo	12
Hazlewood, Chester, S. C	12
Hazlitt, Rock Island, Ill	17
Headland, Saunders, Nebr	11
Head of Barren, Claiborne, Tenn	6
Head of Elm, Montague, Tex	12
Head Quarters, Nicholas, Ky	20
Headsville, Mineral, W. Va	12
Head Waters, Highland, Va	5
Healdsburgh,* Sonoma, Cal	560
Healdville, Rutland, Vt	88
Healing Springs, Bath, Va	30
Hearne, Robertson, Tex	12
Heart Prairie, Walworth, Wis	35
Heartwellville, Bennington, Vt	90
Heaslyville, Marshall, Kans	12
Heath, Franklin, Mass	76
Heathsville, Halifax, N. C	6
Heathsville, (*c. h.*,) Northumberland, Va	76
Hebbardsville, Henderson, Ky	45
Hebbardsville, Athens, Ohio	52
Hebbertsburgh, Cumberland, Tenn	8
Heber, (*c. h.*,) Wasatch, Utah	19
Hebron, Tolland, Conn	180
Hebron, Washington, Ga	12
Hebron, McHenry, Ill	$130
Hebron, Porter, Ind	220
Hebron, Adair, Iowa	25
Hebron, Boone, Ky	17
Hebron, Oxford, Me	58
Hebron, Nicollet, Minn	15
Hebron, Jefferson, Nebr	12
Hebron, Grafton, N. H	88
Hebron, Washington, N. Y	15
Hebron, Licking, Ohio	110
Hebron, Potter, Pa	19
Hebron, Spartanburgh, S. C	3
Hebron, Pleasants, W. Va	31
Hebron, Jefferson, Wis	93
Hebronville, Bristol, Mass	110
Hecker, Monroe, Ill	87
Hecktown, Northampton, Pa	31
Hecla, Whitley, Ind	31
Hecla Works, Oneida, N. Y	28
Hector, Jay, Ind	4
Hector, Schuyler, N. Y	41
Hedgesville, Steuben, N. Y	17
Hedgesville, Berkeley, W. Va	160
Hedwig's Hill, Mason, Tex	12
Heffren, Washington, Ind	16
Hegarty's × Roads, Clearfield, Pa	18
Hegins, Schuylkill, Pa	20
Heidlersburgh, Adams, Pa	29
Heistersburgh, Fayette, Pa	12
Helena,* (*c. h.*,) Phillips, Ark	1,700
Helena, Lake, Colo	17
Helena, Tama, Iowa	18
Helena, Mason, Ky	45
Helena, Scott, Minn	20
HELENA,* (*c. h.*,) Lewis & Clarke, Mont	4,000
Helena, Johnson, Nebr	21
Helena, St. Lawrence, N. Y	63
Helena, (*c. h.*,) Karnes, Tex	230
Helena Station, Iowa, Wis	62
Helen Furnace, Clarion, Pa	20
Helenville, Jefferson, Wis	40
Helham, Overton, Tenn	12
Hellam, York, Pa	33
Hellen, Elk, Pa	33
Heller's Corners, Allen, Ind	16
Hellertown, Northampton, Pa	280
Helmick, Coshocton, Ohio	11
Helton, Ashe, N. C	6
Heltonville, Lawrence, Ind	27
Helvetia, Waupaca, Wis	12
Hematite, Jefferson, Mo	99
Hemlock, Cambria, Pa	63
Hemlock City, Saginaw, Mich	18
Hemlock Grove, Meigs, Ohio	8
Hemlock Hollow, Wayne, Pa	12
Hemlock Lake, Livingston, N. Y	200
Hempfield, Lancaster, Pa	78
Hemphill, (*c. h.*,) Sabine, Tex	12
Hemp's Creek, Catahoula, La	5
Hempstead, Calloway, Mo	6
Hempstead,* Queens, N. Y	690
Hempstead, Austin, Tex	680
Henderson, Pike, Ala	12
Henderson, Knox, Ill	150
Henderson, Lucas, Iowa	50

* Money-order office.

Post office	
*Henderson,** (*c. h.,*) Henderson, Ky	$1,600
Henderson, Caroline, Md	24
*Henderson,** (*c. h.,*) Sibley, Minn	560
Henderson, Webster, Mo	10
Henderson, Jefferson, N. Y	210
Henderson, Granville, N. C	620
Henderson, Mercer, Pa	41
Henderson, (*c. h.,*) Rusk, Tex	430
Henderson's Mills, Marshall, Ky	20
Henderson's Springs, Sevier, Tenn	12
Henderson Station, Madison, Tenn	180
Hendersonville, (*c. h.,*) Henderson, N. C	160
Hendersonville, Sumner, Tenn	71
Hendricks, Otoe, Nebr	16
Hendricksburgh, Luzerne, Pa	430
Hendrick's Store, Bedford, Va	10
Hendrysburgh, Belmont, Ohio	110
Henley, Siskiyou, Cal	57
*Hennepin,** (*c. h.,*) Putnam, Ill	500
Henniker, Merrimack, N. H	310
Henning's Mills, Clermont, Ohio	34
Henrietta, Jackson, Mich	32
Henrietta, Monroe, N. Y	110
Henrietta, Lorain, Ohio	31
Henrietta, Richland, Wis	2
Henry,* Marshall, Ill	1,400
Henry, Ray, Mo	12
Henry, Sussex, Va	20
Henry Clay Factory, New Castle, Del	250
Henry's × Roads, Sevier, Tenn	23
Henry's Fork, Roane, W. Va	12
Henry Station, Henry, Tenn	110
Henrysville, Marshall, Ala	7
Henrysville, Logan, Ky	36
Henrysville, Monroe, Pa	39
Henryville, Clarke, Ind	150
Henryville, Lawrence, Tenn	9
Hensonville, Greene, N, Y	23
Hepler, Schuylkill, Pa	7
Hepton, Kosciusko, Ind	12
Herbert, Kemper, Miss	5
Hereford, Baltimore, Md	53
Hereford, Berks, Pa	64
*Herkimer,** (*c. h.,*) Herkimer, N. Y	1,000
Hermaan, Ripley, Ind	13
Herman, Dodge, Wis	22
*Hermann,** (*c. h.,*) Gasconade, Mo	750
Hermansville, Coos, Oreg	12
Hermitage, Mendocino, Cal	4
Hermitage, Point Coupee, La	96
Hermitage, (*c. h.,*) Hickory, Mo	150
Hermitage, Wyoming, N. Y	83
Hermitage, Mercer, Pa	320
Hermitage, Augusta, Va	20
Hermon, Knox, Ill	71
Hermon, Penobscot, Me	40
Hermon,* St. Lawrence, N. Y	410
Hermon Pond, Penobscot, Me	83
Hermosilla, Pueblo, Colo	12
Hernando, (*c. h.,*) De Soto, Miss	520
Herndon, Greene, Ark	12
Herndon, Burke, Ga	50
Herndon, Montgomery, Ill	20
Herndon, Northumberland, Pa	65

Post office	
Herndon, Fairfax, Va	$110
Herrick, Bradford, Pa	37
Herrick Centre, Susquehanna, Pa	77
Herrickville, Bradford, Pa	57
Herriman, Salt Lake, Utah	10
Herring, Allen, Ohio	150
Herrington's Corners, Chemung, N. Y	5
Herrin's Prairie, Williamson, Ill	21
Herriottsville, Washington, Pa	19
Hersey, (*c. h.,*) Osceola, Mich	270
Herseyville, Monroe, Wis	18
Hersman's, Brown, Ill	58
Hertford, (*c. h.,*) Perquimons, N. C	190
Herzhorn, Renville, Minn	10
Heshbon, Indiana, Pa	17
Hesper, Winneshiek, Iowa	210
Hesper, Douglas, Kans	12
Hesperia, Oceana, Mich	56
Hesperian, Webster, Iowa	46
Hess Road, Niagara, N. Y	39
Hessville, Harrison, W. Va	6
Hester, Marion, Mo	16
Hester Mills, Meigs, Tenn	23
Hester's Store, Person, N. C	12
Hetricks, York, Pa	25
Hetslersville, Darke, Ohio	12
Heuvelton, St. Lawrence, N. Y	210
Hewlett's, Hanover, Va	88
Heyworth, McLean, Ill	400
Hiawassee, (*c. h.,*) Towns, Ga	12
*Hiawatha,** (*c. h.,*) Brown, Kans	470
Hibbetts, Carroll, Ohio	14
Hibbsville, Appanoose, Iowa	18
Hibernia, Duval, Fla	38
Hibernia, Morris, N. J	340
Hibernia, Dutchess, N. Y	22
*Hickman,** (*c. h.,*) Fulton, Ky	860
Hickman Mills, Jackson, Mo	97
Hickman's, Tuscaloosa, Ala	9
Hickory, Benton, Ark	18
Hickory, Lake, Ill	10
Hickory, Van Buren, Iowa	160
Hickory, Newton, Miss	210
Hickory, Lucas, Ohio	8
Hickory, Washington, Pa	110
Hickory Barren, Greene, Mo	23
Hickory Branch, Posey, Ind	24
Hickory Corners, Barry, Mich	160
Hickory Corners, Niagara, N. Y	9
Hickory Corners, Northumberland, Pa	25
Hickory Creek, Fayette, Ill	15
Hickory Creek, Audrian, Mo	9
Hickory Flat, Chambers, Ala	13
Hickory Flat, Tippah, Miss	24
Hickory Fork, Gloucester, Va	83
Hickory Grove, Crawford, Ga	14
Hickory Grove, Massac, Ill	1
Hickory Grove, Graves, Ky	22
Hickory Grove, York, S. C	11
Hickory Hill, Marion, Ill	4
Hickory Hill, Cole, Mo	44
Hickory Hill, Chester, Pa	30
Hickory Hill, Davis, Tex	37
Hickory Plains, Prairie, Ark	52

* Money-order office.

Hickory Ridge, Hancock, Ill	$39
Hickory Run, Carbon, Pa	77
Hickory Springs, Texas, Mo	12
Hickory Tavern, Harford, Md	67
Hickory Tavern, Catawba, N. C	160
Hickory Town, Montgomery, Pa	14
Hickory Valley, Hardeman, Tenn	26
Hicksford, (*c. h.*,) Greenville, Va	260
Hicks' Mills, De Kalb, Ill	23
Hicks Station, Prairie, Ark	62
Hicksville, Sacramento, Cal	68
Hicksville, Queens, N. Y	150
Hicksville, Defiance, Ohio	130
Hick's Wharf, Matthews, Va	12
Hico, Benton, Ark	12
Hico, Callaway, Ky	7
Hidalgo, Jasper, Ill	11
Hiester's Mill, Berks, Pa	20
Higganum, Middlesex, Conn	84
Higginsport, Jackson, Iowa	4
Higginsport, Brown, Ohio	170
Higginsville, Vermilion, Ill	90
Higginsville, La Fayette, Mo	12
Higginsville, Oneida, N. Y	160
High Blue, Cass, Mo	18
High Bluff, Dale, Ala	12
High Bridge, Hunterdon, N. J	130
High Creek, Fremont, Iowa	12
High Falls, Geneva, Ala	12
High Falls, Ulster, N. Y	120
High Forest, Olmsted, Minn	180
Highgate, Franklin, Vt	160
Highgate Centre, Franklin, Vt	110
Highgate Springs, Franklin, Vt	92
High Grove, Nelson, Ky	38
High Grove, Maries, Mo	8
High Health, Johnson, Tenn	6
High Hill, Leake, Miss	8
High Hill, Montgomery, Mo	240
High Hill, Muskingum, Ohio	42
High Hill, Fayette, Tex	160
High Lake, Emmett, Iowa	12
High Lake, Wayne, Pa	22
Highland,* Madison, Ill	900
Highland, Clayton, Iowa	38
Highland, Doniphan, Kans	300
Highland, Lincoln, Ky	12
Highland, Somerset, Me	8
Highland, Oakland, Mich	54
Highland, Fillmore, Minn	100
Highland, Tishemingo, Miss	11
Highland, Moniteau, Mo	12
Highland, Richardson, Nebr	12
Highland, Ulster, N. Y	380
Highland, Highland, Ohio	170
Highland, Clackamas, Oreg	12
Highland, Bradford, Pa	43
Highland, Jackson, Tenn	12
Highland, Collin, Tex	44
Highland, Ritchie, W. Va	6
Highland, Iowa, Wis	170
Highland Centre, Wapello, Iowa	12
Highland Falls, Orange, N. Y	460
Highland Grove, Jones, Iowa	18
Highland Grove, Greenville, S. C	5
Highland Home, Laurens, S. C	6
Highland Mills, Orange, N. Y	$85
Highland Park, Lake, Ill	220
Highland Station, Galveston, Tex	12
Highland Town, Grundy, Ill	8
Highlandville, Winneshiek, Iowa	76
High Point, Walker, Ga	12
High Point, Mercer, Ill	20
High Point, Decatur, Iowa	20
High Point, Moniteau, Mo	110
High Point, Guilford, N. C	420
High Ridge, Fairfield, Conn	53
High Ridge, Jefferson, Mo	17
High Shoals, Gaston, N. C	23
High Spire, Dauphin, Pa	88
Hightown, Highland, Va	33
Hightstown,* Mercer, N. J	920
High View, Frederick, Va	13
Highville, Lancaster, Pa	41
Hika, Manitowoc, Wis	100
Hiko, (*c. h.*,) Lincoln, Nev	130
Hill, Grafton, N. H	230
Hill, Mercer, Pa	86
Hillabee, Clay, Ala	11
Hill Church, Berks, Pa	12
Hillegass, Montgomery, Pa	12
Hill Grove, Meade, Ky	14
Hill Grove, Darke, Ohio	69
Hill Grove, Pittsylvania, Va	45
Hillham, Dubois, Ind	16
Hillhouse, Lake, Ohio	18
Hillians' Store, Marshall, Ala	12
Hilliard's, Allegan, Mich	12
Hilliards, Franklin, Ohio	150
Hilliardston, Nash, N. C	12
Hills, Owen, Ky	4
Hills, Washington, Ohio	11
Hillsborough, Shelby, Ala	31
Hillsborough, Union, Ark	81
Hillsborough,* (*c. h.*,) Montgomery, Ill	1,100
Hillsborough, Fountain, Ind	70
Hillsborough, Henry, Iowa	100
Hillsborough, Fleming, Ky	100
Hillsborough, Caroline, Md	140
Hillsborough, (*c. h.*,) Scott, Miss	81
Hillsborough, (*c. h.*,) Jefferson, Mo	290
Hillsborough, Hillsborough, N. H	360
Hillsborough,* (*c. h.*,) Orange, N. C	670
Hillsborough,* (*c. h.*,) Highland, Ohio	1,300
Hillsborough, (*c. h.*,) Washington, Oreg	82
Hillsborough, Coffee, Tenn	12
Hillsborough, (*c. h.*,) Hill, Tex	170
Hillsborough, Loudoun, Va	96
Hillsborough,* Vernon, Wis	96
Hillsborough Bridge, Hillsborough, N. H	510
Hillsborough Centre, Hillsborough, N. H	61
Hillsdale, Mills, Iowa	12
Hillsdale, Miami, Kans	160
Hillsdale,* (*c. h.*,) Hillsdale, Mich	2,400
Hillsdale, Nemaha, Nebr	12
Hillsdale, Bergen, N. J	12
Hillsdale, Columbia, N. Y	360
Hillsdale, Guilford, N. C	13

* **Money-order office.**

Hillsdale, Indiana, Pa	$41
Hill's Ferry, Stanislaus, Cal	12
Hill's Fork, Adams, Ohio	19
Hill's Grove, Sullivan, Pa	26
Hillside, Westmoreland, Pa	58
Hill's Point, Dorchester, Md	19
Hill Spring, Morris, Kans	4
Hill Spring, Henry, Ky	60
Hill's Station, Rock Island, Ill	12
Hill's Store, Randolph, N. C	7
Hill's View, Westmoreland, Pa	6
Hillsville, Lawrence, Pa	47
Hillsville, (*c. h.*,) Carroll, Va	190
Hilltown, Bucks, Pa	33
Hill Valley, Huntingdon, Pa	36
Hilton, Tazewell, Ill	42
Hilton, Monroe, Ky	8
Himrod's, Yates, N. Y	120
Hinckley, Pine, Minn	12
Hinckley, Medina, Ohio	53
Hindsburgh, Orleans, N. Y	22
Hindsville, Madison, Ark	12
Hiner's Run, Clinton, Pa	1[illegible]0
Hinesberg, Fond du Lac, Wis	[illegible]4
Hinesburgh, Chittenden, Vt	2[illegible]0
Hine's Mills, Ohio, Ky	12
Hinesville, (*c. h.*,) Liberty, Ga	9
Hingham, Plymouth, Mass	7[illegible]0
Hingham, Sheboygan, Wis	97
Hingham Centre, Plymouth, Mass	230
Hinkleton, Lancaster, Pa	49
Hinkleville, Ballard, Ky	12
Hinmansville, Oswego, N. Y	60
Hinnaut's Mills, Johnston, N. C	12
Hinsdale, Du Page, Ill	92
Hinsdale, Berkshire, Mass	570
Hinsdale,* Cheshire, N. Y	1,700
Hinsdale, Cattaraugus, N. Y	330
Hinton, Plymouth, Iowa	12
Hiram, Oxford, Me	100
Hiram, Portage, Ohio	330
Hiramsburgh, Noble, Ohio	25
Hiseville, Barren, Ky	47
Hitchcock's Station, Washington, Ind	36
Hitesville, Union, Ky	16
Hitt, Scotland, Mo	12
Hixton, Jackson, Wis	19
Hoag's Corner, Rensselaer, N. Y	29
Hobart, Lake, Ind	180
Hobart, Delaware, N, Y	280
Hobart's Mills, Sheboygan, Wis	12
Hobbie, Luzerne, Pa	16
Hobbieville, Greene, Ind	22
Hobbs' Ferry, Giles, Va	12
Hobbs' Station, Jefferson, Ky	240
Hobbysville, Spartanburgh, S. C	2
Hoboken,* Hudson, N. J	2,300
Hochheim, De Witt, Tex	12
Hockanum, Hartford, Conn	78
Hockessin, New Castle, Del	49
Hocking, Athens, Ohio	12
Hockingport, Athens, Ohio	66
Hockley, Harris, Tex	170
Hockley, Vernon, Wis	8
Hodgdon, Aroostook, Me	64

Hodgdon's Mills, Lincoln, Me	$150
Hodgensville, (*c. h.*,) La Rue, Ky	150
Hodges, Abbeville, S. C	130
Hodge's Mill, Kendall, Tex	6
Hodge's Prairie, Sebastian, Ark	12
Hoffman's Ferry, Schenectady, N. Y.	39
Hogansburgh, Franklin, N. Y	120
Hogansville, Troup, Ga	330
Hogarth's Landing, St. John's, Fla	7
Hog Branch, St. Helena, La	5
Hog Creek, Allen, Ohio	8
Hoge, Leavenworth, Kans	43
Hogestown, Cumberland, Pa	78
Hog Island, Surry, Va	12
Hog Mountain, Hall, Ga	10
Hohokus, Bergen, N. J	200
Hokah, Houston, Minn	190
Hokendauqua, Lehigh, Pa	280
Holaday's, Adair, Iowa	15
Holbrook, Suffolk, N. Y	78
Holbrook, Greene, Pa	12
Holbrook, Ritchie, W. Va	5
Holcombe, Burke, Ga	52
Holcomb's Rock, Bedford, Va	21
Holden, Penobscot, Me	37
Holden, Worcester, Mass	330
Holden, Goodhue, Minn	120
Holden,* Johnson, Mo	1,300
Holden, Millard, Utah	22
Holiday's Cove, Hancock, W. Va	140
Holland, Shelby, Ill	6
Holland, Dubois, Ind	51
Holland, Hampden, Mass	21
Holland,* Ottawa, Mich	790
Holland, Hunterdon, N. J	20
Holland, Erie, N. Y	370
Holland, Lucas, Ohio	90
Holland, Bucks, Pa	12
Holland, Orleans, Vt	25
Holland, Brown, Wis	16
Holland Patent, Oneida, N. Y	250
Holland's Store, Anderson, S. C	12
Hollandville, Kent, Del	18
Holley, Orleans, N. Y	520
Holliday, Macoupin, Ill	1
Hollidaysburgh,* (*c. h.*,) Blair, Pa	1,800
Holling, Douglass, Kans	12
Hollingsworth, Banks, Ga	11
Hollis, York, Me	33
Hollis, Hillsborough, N. H	230
Hollis Centre, York, Me	45
Hollister, Monterey, Cal	12
Hollisterville, Wayne, Pa	120
Holliston,* Middlesex, Mass	1,000
Holloway's Store, Walker, Tex	12
Hollowayville, Bureau, Ill	37
Hollow Rock, Carroll, Tenn	10
Hollow Square, Hale, Ala	43
Hollowtown, Highland, Ohio	13
Hollowville, Columbia, N. Y	61
Holly,* Oakland, Mich	710
Holly Grove, Walker, Ala	10
Holly Grove, Madison, N. C	9
Holly Hill, Charleston, S. C	27
Holly Meadows, Tucker, W. Va	4
Holly River, Braxton, W. Va	3

* Money-order office.

Holly Springs, Dallas, Ark	$53
*Holly Springs,** (*c. h.,*) Marshall, Miss	1,600
Hollyville, Sussex, Del	5
Hollywood, Clark, Ark	12
Hollywood, St. Mary's, Md	12
Holman, Dearborn, Ind	15
Holman Station, Scott, Ind	12
Holmdel, Monmouth, N. J	110
Holmes, Boone, Ind	12
Holmes City, Douglas, Minn	12
Holmes' Hole, Dukes, Mass	690
Holmes' Mills, Jefferson, Ohio	42
Holmesville, (*c. h.,*) Appling, Ga	39
Holmesville, Avoyelles, La	20
Holmesville, Holmes, Ohio	90
Holstein, Warren, Mo	26
Holston, Washington, Va	1
Holston Furnace, Sullivan, Tenn	8
Holston Valley, Sullivan, Tenn	12
Holt, Taylor, Iowa	16
Holt, Ingham, Mich	80
Holt, Clay, Mo	12
Holt, Wood, Ohio	16
Holt, Beaver, Pa	8
Holton, Ripley, Ind	120
*Holton,** (*c. h.,*) Jackson, Kans	410
Holt's Mills, Penobscot, Me	12
Holt's Summit, Callaway, Mo	12
Holtsville, Suffolk, N. Y	63
Holy Cross, Clay, Minn	12
Holy Cross, Ozaukee, Wis	6
Holyoke,* Hampden, Mass	2,300
Home, Wayne, Ill	12
Home, Jefferson, Ind	13
Home, Van Buren, Iowa	3
Home, Newaygo, Mich	9
Home, Brown, Minn	13
Home, Indiana, Pa	60
Home, Greene, Tenn	91
Home, Trempealeau, Wis	9
Homer, (*c. h.,*) Banks, Ga	22
Homer,* Champaign, Ill	690
Homer, Rush, Ind	50
Homer, Hamilton, Iowa	120
Homer, (*c. h.,*) Claiborne, La	120
Homer, Calhoun, Mich	410
Homer, Winona, Minn	43
Homer,* Cortland, N. Y	1,300
Homer, Licking, Ohio	88
Homer, Potter, Pa	5
Homer, (*c. h.,*) Angelina, Tex	23
Homer Creek, Greenwood, Kans	4
Homerville, (*c. h.,*) Clinch, Ga	120
Homerville, Medina, Ohio	66
Homestead,* Iowa, Iowa	370
Homestead, Benzie, Mich	40
Homestead, Burt, Nebr	14
Homet's Ferry, Bradford, Pa	12
Homewood, Cook, Ill	130
Homewood, Scott, Miss	16
Homewood, Beaver, Pa	220
Homeworth, Columbiana, Ohio	190
Hominy Creek, Buncombe, N. C	59
Homowack, Ulster, N. Y	140
Honaker's Ferry, Warren, Ky	6
Honcut, Yuba, Cal	$12
Honea Path, Anderson, S. C	75
Honek, Saline, Kans	96
Honeoye, Ontario, N. Y	260
Honeoye Falls, Monroe, N. Y	470
*Honesdale,** (*c. h.,*) Wayne, Pa	2,200
Honey Brook, Chester, Pa	240
Honey Creek, Henry, Ind	34
Honey Creek, Pottawattomie, Iowa	27
Honey Creek, McDonald, Mo	37
Honey Creek, Walworth, Wis	78
Honey Grove, Juniata, Pa	21
Honey Grove, Fannin, Tex	150
Honorville, Crenshaw, Ala	8
Hood River, Wasco, Oreg	7
Hood's Fork, Johnson, Ky	5
Hood's Mills, Carroll, Md	76
Hoodsville, Monongalia, W. Va	5
Hooker, Shelby, Ill	160
Hooker, Van Buren, Mich	35
Hooker, Gage, Nebr	17
Hooker, Butler, Pa	28
Hooker, Trempealeau, Wis	6
Hooker's Station, Fairfield, Ohio	12
Hookersville, Nicholas, W. Va	3
Hookerton, Greene, N. C	56
Hookset, Merrimack, N. H	180
Hook's Point, Hamilton, Iowa	84
Hookstown, Baltimore, Md	29
Hookstown, Beaver, Pa	150
Hooktown, Nicholas, Ky	21
Hoopa Valley, Klamath, Cal	43
Hooper, Broome, N. Y	75
Hooper, Weber, Utah	12
Hooper's Valley, Tioga, N. Y	39
Hoopersville, Dorchester, Md	2
Hooppole, Ross, Ohio	6
Hoosac Tunnel, Berkshire, Mass	240
Hoosick, Rensselaer, N. Y	200
Hoosick Falls,* Rensselaer, N. Y	1,000
Hoover Hill, Randolph, N. C	7
Hooversville, Anne Arundel, Md	130
Hop Bottom, Susquehanna, Pa	180
Hope, Vermilion, Ill	12
Hope, Bartholomew, Ind	290
Hope, Knox, Me	57
Hope, Somerset, Md	6
Hope, Warren, N. J	240
Hope, Franklin, Ohio	92
Hope, Providence, R. I	55
Hope, Lavaca, Tex	12
Hope Centre, Hamilton, N. Y	7
Hope Church, Allegheny, Pa	35
Hopedale, Tazewell, Ill	120
Hopedale, Worcester, Mass	280
Hopedale, Harrison, Ohio	230
Hope Falls, Hamilton, N. Y	16
Hope Farm, Moniteau, Mo	12
Hopefield, Crawford, Kans	12
Hope Furnace, Vinton, Ohio	81
Hope Mills, Page, Va	26
Hope Ridge, Monroe, Ohio	15
Hope Station, Lexington, S. C	14
Hopeton, Merced, Cal	170
Hope Valley, Washington, R. I	170
Hopeville, Clarke, Iowa	150

* Money-order office.

Post office	
Hopeville, Grant, W. Va	$3
Hopewell, Mahaska, Iowa	40
Hopewell, Somerset, Md	12
Hopewell, Calhoun, Miss	7
Hopewell, Mercer, N. J	120
Hopewell, Ontario, N. Y	59
Hopewell, Mecklenburgh, N. C	6
Hopewell, Muskingum, Ohio	89
Hopewell, Bedford, Pa	210
Hopewell, York, S. C	6
Hopewell Academy, Warren, Mo	53
Hopewell Centre, Ontario, N. Y	56
Hopewell Centre, York, Pa	51
Hopewell Cotton Works, Chester, Pa	33
Hopewell × Roads, Harford, Md	100
Hopewell Furnace, Washington, Mo	48
Hopewell Junction, Dutchess, N. Y	12
Hopewell Springs, Monroe, Tenn	12
Hopkins, Allegan, Mich	75
Hopkins' Mill, Greene, Pa	16
Hopkins' Station, Allegan, Mich	12
Hopkins' Turnout, Richland, S. C	24
Hopkinsville,* (*c. h.*,) Christian, Ky	1,700
Hopkinsville, Warren, Ohio	25
Hopkinsville, Gonzales, Tex	22
Hopkinton,* Delaware, Iowa	370
Hopkinton,* Middlesex, Mass	600
Hopkinton, Merrimack, N. H	310
Hopkinton, St. Lawrence, N. Y	170
Hopkinton, Washington, R. I	64
Hoppenville, Montgomery, Pa	21
Hopper's Mills, Henderson, Ill	80
Hoquiam, Chehalis, Wash	10
Hord, Clay, Ill	15
Horicon, Martin, Minn	11
Horicon, Warren, N. Y	36
Horicon,* Dodge, Wis	580
Horine Station, Jefferson, Mo	20
Horn, Jasper, Iowa	9
Hornbrook, Bradford, Pa	18
Hornby, Steuben, N. Y	16
Hornellsville,* Steuben, N. Y	2,000
Hornerstown, Ocean, N. J	48
Hornitas, Mariposa, Cal	270
Horn Lake, De Soto, Miss	70
Hornsby, Macoupin, Ill	50
Horn's Mills, Carroll, N. H	25
Horntown, Accomack, Va	78
Horr's, Champaign, Ohio	12
Horr's Ranch, Stanislaus, Cal	12
Horse Cove, Macon, N. C	12
Horse Creek, Barton, Mo	20
Horse Creek, Ashe, N. C	5
Horse Creek, Greene, Tenn	24
Horse Head, Prince George's, Md	60
Horseheads, Chemung, N. Y	820
Horseley's Landing, Nelson, Va	16
Horse Pasture, Henry, Va	22
Horse Plains, Missoula, Mont	12
Horse Prairie, Beaver Head, Mont	12
Horse Shoe Bend, Boise, Idaho	12
Horse Shoe Bend, Scott, Tenn	12
Horse Shoe Bottom, Russell, Ky	12
Horse Shoe Run, Preston, W. Va	18
Horsetown, Shasta, Cal	17
Horsham, Montgomery, Pa	$95
Horton, Bremer, Iowa	110
Horton's, Indiana, Pa	30
Hortonville, Red River, Tex	12
Hortonville, Rutland, Vt	48
Hortonville, Outagamie, Wis	110
Hosensack, Lehigh, Pa	25
Hoskinsville, Noble, Ohio	10
Host, Berks, Pa	20
Hotchkissville, Litchfield, Conn	180
Hot Creek, Nye, Nev	85
Hotel, Bertie, N. C	57
Hot House, Fannin, Ga	3
Hot Springs,* Hot Spring, Ark	830
Hot Springs, Bath, Va	25
Houcksville, Carroll, Md	17
Houcktown, Hancock, Ohio	19
Houghton, Jo Daviess, Ill	25
Houghton,* (*c. h.*,) Houghton, Mich	1,900
Houghton Creek, Allegany, N. Y	10
Houghtonville, Windham, Vt	14
Houlka, Chickasaw, Miss	12
Houlton,* (*c. h.*,) Aroostook, Me	1,100
Houma,* (*c. h.*,) Terre Bonne, La	540
Housatonic, Berkshire, Mass	320
House Creek, Wilcox, Ga	14
Houserville, Centre, Pa	12
House's Springs, Jefferson, Mo	6
House's Store, Clay, Ky	10
Houseville, Lewis, N. Y	62
Houston, (*c. h.*,) Winston, Ala	10
Houston, (*c. h.*,) Suwannee, Fla	120
Houston, Heard, Ga	20
Houston, Jackson, Ind	21
Houston, Bourbon, Ky	22
Houston, Houston, Minn	350
Houston, (*c. h.*,) Chickasaw, Miss	200
Houston, (*c. h.*,) Texas, Mo	170
Houston, Shelby, Ohio	98
Houston,* (*c. h.*,) Harris, Tex	4,000
Houston Station, Kent, Del	20
Houtzdale, Clearfield, Pa	12
Howard, Conway, Ark	12
Howard, Taylor, Ga	42
Howard, Parke, Ind	20
Howard, Howard, Kans	12
Howard, Piscataquis, Me	12
Howard, Muskegon, Mich	46
Howard, Wright, Minn	47
Howard, Nemeha, Nebr	12
Howard, Warren, N. J	8
Howard, Steuben, N. Y	120
Howard, Centre, Pa	190
Howard, Bell, Tex	16
Howard Centre, Howard, Iowa	59
Howard City, Montcalm, Mich	12
Howard's Grove, Sheboygan, Wis	110
Howard's Lick, Hardy, W. Va	5
Howard's Mills, Montgomery, Ky	6
Howard's Mills, St. Clair, Mo	12
Howard Springs, Cumberland, Tenn	12
Howardsville, Jo Daviess, Ill	15
Howardsville, St. Joseph, Mich	8
Howardsville, Albemarle, Va	120
Howardville, Floyd, Iowa	9
Howell, (*c. h.*,) Livingston, Mich	970

* Money-order office.

Post office	Compensation
Howell's Depot, Orange, N. Y	$170
Howellville, Delaware, Pa	64
Howel's Cross Roads, Cherokee, Ala.	22
Howe's Cave, Schoharie, N. Y	10
Howe's Corners, Waushara, Wis	7
Howe's Mill, Dent, Mo	22
Howe's Valley, Hardin, Ky	16
Howesville, Clay, Ind	12
Howland, Penobscot, Me	28
Howland, Trumbull, Ohio	18
Howlet Hill, Onondaga, N. Y	18
Howlett, Sangamon, Ill	100
Hoyleton, Washington, Ill	89
Hubbard,* Trumbull, Ohio	510
Hubbardston, Worcester, Mass	390
Hubbardston, Ionia, Mich	410
Hubbardstown, Wayne, W. Va	12
Hubbardsville, Madison, N. Y	210
Hubbardton, Rutland, Vt	21
Hubbleton, Jefferson, Wis	44
Hubelsville, Huntingdon, Pa	13
Hubertville, Robertson, Tenn	12
Hublersburgh, Centre, Pa	68
Huckleberry, Echols, Ga	12
Huddleston, Pike, Ark	8
Hudson, McLean, Ill	200
Hudson, Black Hawk, Iowa	18
Hudson, Penobscot, Me	64
Hudson, Middlesex, Mass	910
Hudson,* Lenawee, Mich	2,100
Hudson, Bates, Mo	23
Hudson, Hillsborough, N. H	130
Hudson, Hudson, N. J	1,800
Hudson,* (*c. h.*,) Columbia, N. Y	3,000
Hudson,* Summit, Ohio	1,000
Hudson, Jefferson, Pa	19
Huason,* (*c. h.*,) St. Croix, Wis	1,200
Hudson City, Worth, Mo	18
Hudsondale, Carbon, Pa	12
Hudsonville, Breckinridge, Ky	20
Hudsonville, Marshall, Miss	46
Huerfano, Pueblo, Colo	12
Huff's Creek, Hancock, Ky	6
Hugginsville, Gentry, Mo	20
Hughes, Schuylkill, Pa	36
Hughesburgh, Habersham, Ga	12
Hughesville, Charles, Md	68
Hughesville, Saginaw, Mich	12
Hughesville, Lycoming, Pa	290
Hughesville, Loudoun, Va	17
Hughsonville, Dutchess, N. Y	160
Huguenot, Orange, N. Y	35
Hulburton, Orleans, N. Y	92
Hull, Plymouth, Mass	24
Hull Prairie, Wood, Ohio	12
Hull's, Athens, Ohio	23
Hull's Mills, Dutchess, N. Y	5
Hulmesville, Bucks, Pa	110
Hulton, Allegheny, Pa	150
Humansville, Polk, Mo	88
Humboldt, Humboldt, Iowa	10
Humboldt,* Allen, Kans	800
Humboldt, Marquette, Mich	12
Humboldt, Pulaski, Mo	280
Humboldt, Richardson, Nebr	64
Humboldt,* Gibson, Tenn	1,600
Humboldt Basin, Baker, Oreg	$64
Humburd, Clark, Wis	12
Hume, Allegany, N. Y	150
Hummell's Wharf, Snyder, Pa	12
Hummel's Store, Berks, Pa	8
Hummelstown, Dauphin, Pa	330
Humphrey, Cattaraugus, N. Y	85
Humphreysville, Columbia, N. Y	21
Humphreysville, Luzerne, Pa	28
Humphreyville, Holmes, Ohio	12
Hunlock Creek, Luzerne, Pa	22
Hunnewell, Shelby, Mo	290
Hunsucker's Store, Montgomery, N. C	12
Hunter, Boone, Ill	17
Hunter, Greene, N. Y	180
Hunter, Belmont, Ohio	41
Hunter's Bridge, Beaufort, N. C	6
Hunter's Cave, Greene, Pa	14
Hunter's Creek, Lapeer, Mich	32
Hunter's Depot, Nelson, Ky	14
Hunter's Land, Schoharie, N. Y	42
Hunter's Lodge, Fluvanna, Va	14
Hunter's Mills, Pickens, S. C	10
Hunter's Mills, Fairfax, Va	16
Hunterstown, Adams, Pa	47
Huntersville, Hardin, Ohio	36
Huntersville, Lycoming, Pa	15
Huntersville, Greenville, S. C	4
Huntersville, Rutherford, Tenn	12
Huntersville, (*c. h.*,) Pocahontas, W. Va	120
Huntertown, Allen, Ind	75
Huntingburgh, Dubois, Ind	170
Huntingdale, Henry, Mo	10
Huntingdon,* (*c.h.*,) Huntingdon, Pa.	2,100
Huntingdon, (*c. h.*,) Carroll, Tenn	300
Huntingdon Valley, Montgomery, Pa	89
Huntington, Fairfield, Conn	45
Huntington,* (*c.h.*,) Huntington, Ind.	1,600
Huntington, Hampshire, Mass	530
Huntington,* Suffolk, N. Y	990
Huntington, Lorain, Ohio	100
Huntington, Chittenden, Vt	74
Huntington Centre, Chittenden, Vt.	63
Huntingtown, Calvert, Md	58
Huntley Grove,* McHenry, Ill	290
Huntsburgh, Geauga, Ohio	96
Hunt's Corners, Cortland, N. Y	19
Hunt's Hollow, Livingston, N. Y	67
Hunt's Mills, Sussex, N. J	32
Hunt's Station, Knox, Ohio	65
Hunt's Station, Franklin, Tenn	190
Huntsville,* (*c. h.*,) Madison, Ala	2,000
Huntsville, (*c. h.*,) Madison, Ark	12
Huntsville, Douglas, Colo	12
Huntsville, Litchfield, Conn	59
Huntsville, Schuyler, Ill	84
Huntsville, Madison, Ind	35
Huntsville, Choctaw, Miss	21
Huntsville,* (*c. h.*,) Randolph, Mo	480
Huntsville, Sussex, N. J	12
Huntsville, Yadkin, N. C	62
Huntsville, Logan, Ohio	270
Huntsville, Luzerne, Pa	18

* Money-order office.

Post office	Amount
Huntsville, (*c. h.*,) Scott, Tenn	$56
Huntsville,* (*c. h.*,) Walker, Tex	640
Huntsville, Weber, Utah	26
Huntsville, Jackson, W. Va	76
Hurd, Clearfield, Pa	23
Hurdle's Mills, Person, N. C	6
Hurdtown, Morris, N. J	88
Hurffville, Camden, N. J	50
Hurlbut's Corners, Crawford, Wis	13
Hurley, Ulster, N. Y	61
Hurlock, Dorchester, Md	12
Huron, Lawrence, Ind	120
Huron, Des Moines, Iowa	30
Huron, Atchison, Kans	420
Huron, Wayne, N. Y	47
Huron, Erie, Ohio	200
Huron City, Huron, Mich	91
Huron Station, Wayne, Mich	130
Hurricane, Montgomery, Ill	38
Hurricane, Crittenden, Ky	30
Hurricane, Warren, Miss	30
Hurricane, Carroll, Mo	12
Hurricane Bridge, Putnam, W. Va	29
Hurricane Grove, Grant, Wis	20
Hurricane Switch, Maury, Tenn	12
Hurt's Cross Roads, Maury, Tenn	12
Hurtville, Russell, Ala	150
Hustisford, Dodge, Wis	220
Hustontown, Fulton, Pa	20
Hustonville, Lincoln, Ky	120
Hutchinson, McLeod, Minn	270
Hutchison's, Bourbon, Ky	54
Huth, Franklin, Ind	12
Hutsonville, Crawford, Ill	140
Hutton, Coles, Ill	14
Hutton's Switch, Alleghany, Md	43
Huttonsville, Randolph, W. Va	84
Hyannis, Barnstable, Mass	790
Hyattstown, Montgomery, Md	64
Hyattsville, Garrard, Ky	12
Hyattsville, Prince George's, Md	73
Hyco, McPherson, Kans	12
Hyco, Halifax, Va	21
Hyde Park, Cook, Ill	220
Hyde Park, Norfolk, Mass	530
Hyde Park, Wabashaw, Minn	16
Hyde Park, Dutchess, N. Y	590
Hyde Park, Luzerne, Pa	1,400
Hyde Park, Cache, Utah	24
Hyde Park, (*c. h.*,) Lamoille, Vt	320
Hydesburgh, Ralls, Mo	22
Hyde's Mills, Iowa, Wis	48
Hydesville, Humboldt, Cal	77
Hydeville, Rutland, Vt	360
Hynddale, Morgan, Ind	12
Hyndville, Schoharie, N. Y	83
Hyremansville, Lehigh, Pa	6
Hyrum, Cache, Utah	42

I.

Post office	Amount
Iamton, Montgomery, Ohio	12
Iatan, Platte, Mo	32
Iba, De Kalb, Ind	94
Iberia, Brown, Minn	12
Iberia, Morrow, Ohio	180
Iceland, Blue Earth, Minn	$8
Ichatucknee, Columbia, Fla	11
Ickesburgh, Perry, Pa	110
Iconium, Appanoose, Iowa	65
Ida, (*c. h.*,) Ida, Iowa	85
Ida, Monroe, Mich	110
Idaho, (*c. h.*,) Clear Creek, Colo	250
Idaho, Pike, Ohio	12
Idaho City,* (*c. h.*,) Boise, Idaho	1,400
Idaville, White, Ind	120
Idaville, Adams, Pa	33
Idell, Crawford, Kans	12
Iderbide, Wythe, Va	12
Ijamsville, Frederick, Md	78
Ilchester Mills, Howard, Md	61
Ilion,* Herkimer, N. Y	1,800
Illawara, Carroll, La	20
Illinois City, Rock Island, Ill	45
Illinois Grove, Marshall, Iowa	22
Illiopolis, Sangamon, Ill	280
Illyria, Fayette, Iowa	35
Imlay, Lapeer, Mich	14
Imlaystown, Monmouth, N. J	88
Imlertown, Bedford, Pa	12
Increase, Warren, Tenn	26
Independence, Autauga, Ala	1
Independence, (*c. h.*,) Inyo, Cal	180
Independence, Warren, Ind	55
Independence,* (*c. h.*,) Buchanan, Iowa	2,200
Independence, Montgomery, Kans	12
Independence, Kenton, Ky	83
Independence, Tangipahoa, La	71
Independence,* (*c. h.*,) Jackson, Mo	1,900
Independence, Allegany, N. Y	49
Independence, Caswell, N. C	10
Independence, Cuyahoga, Ohio	71
Independence, Polk, Oreg	51
Independence, Washington, Pa	81
Independence, Washington Tex	220
Independence, (*c. h.*,) Grayson, Va	170
Independent Hill, Prince William, Va	21
Indiana,* (*c. h.*,) Indiana, Pa	1,500
INDIANAPOLIS,* (*c. h.*,) Marion, Ind	4,000
Indianapolis, Mahaska, Iowa	87
Indian Bay, Monroe, Ark	120
Indian Bottom, Letcher, Ky	1
Indian Camp, Guernsey, Ohio	12
Indian Creek, Kent, Mich	33
Indian Creek, Monroe, Mo	24
Indian Creek, Fayette, Pa	14
Indian Creek, Washington, Tenn	1
Indian Creek, Monroe, W. Va	66
Indian Falls, Genesee, N. Y	40
Indian Field, Knox, Ohio	12
Indian Fields, Albany, N. Y	37
Indian Ford, Stoddard, Mo	11
Indian Ford, Rock, Wis	15
Indian Gulch, Mariposa, Cal	10
Indian Lake, Hamilton, N. Y	34
Indian Mound, Stewart, Tenn	42
Indianola, Vermilion, Ill	170
Indianola,* (*c. h.*,) Warren, Iowa	1,100
Indianola,* (*c. h.*,) Calhoun, Tex	1,500
Indian Orchard, Hampden, Mass	290

* Money-order office.

Indian Ridge, Currituck, N. C	$12
Indian River, Washington, Me	80
Indian River, Lewis, N. Y	4
Indian Run, Mercer, Pa	36
Indian Springs, Nevada, Cal	12
Indian Springs, Butts, Ga	36
Indian Springs, Campbell, Ky	4
Indian Springs, Washington, Md	24
Indian Town, Mason, Mich	17
Indian Valley, Floyd, Va	4
Indian Village, Noble, Ind	17
Industry, McDonough, Ill	170
Industry, Franklin, Me	36
Industry, Beaver, Pa	150
Industry, Austin, Tex	120
Ingall's Crossing, Oswego, N. Y	12
Ingart Grove, Ringgold, Iowa	12
Ingham, Franklin, Iowa	10
Ingham's Mills, Herkimer, N. Y	52
Inglefield, Vanderburgh, Ind	24
Ingleside, Hardin, Tenn	14
Ingomar, Issaquena, Miss	16
Ingraham, Clay, Ill	57
Ingraham, Clinton, N. Y	26
Inkermann, Hardy, W. Va	3
Inkster, Wayne, Mich	56
Inland, Cedar, Iowa	60
Inland, Benzie, Mich	39
Inland, Summit, Ohio	69
Inskip, Butte, Cal	5
Intercourse, Sumter, Ala	12
Intercourse, Lancaster, Pa	79
Inverness, Cumberland, N. C	12
Inverness, Columbiana, Ohio	12
Inwood, Marshall, Ind	160
Ioka, Keokuk, Iowa	73
Iola, Calhoun, Fla	12
Iola, Marion, Iowa	13
Iola,* (*c. h.*,) Allen, Kans	590
Iola, Columbia, Pa	18
Iola, Waupaca, Wis	75
Ion, Allamakee, Iowa	14
Iona, Cape Girardeau, Mo	12
Iona, Fairfax, Va	12
Iona Island, Rockland, N. Y	450
Ione City, Nye, Nev	65
Ione Valley,* Amador, Cal	230
Ionia, Warren, Ill	57
Ionia, Chickasaw, Iowa	12
Ionia,* (*c. h.*,) Ionia, Mich	2,200
Ionia, Dixon, Nebr	29
Ionia City, Pettis, Mo	54
Iowa Centre,* Story, Iowa	120
Iowa City, Placer, Cal	150
Iowa City,* (*c. h.*,) Johnson, Iowa	2,700
Iowa City, Crawford, Kans	12
Iowa Falls,* Hardin, Iowa	1,100
Iowa Point, Doniphan, Kans	77
Iowaville, Van Buren, Iowa	59
Ipava, Fulton, Ill	230
Ipswich, Essex, Mass	1,000
Ira, Cayuga, N. Y	100
Ira, Rutland, Vt	19
Irasburgh, (*c. h.*,) Orleans, Vt	270
Irbyville, Fulton, Ga	5
Ireland, Dubois, Ind	43
Ireland, Hampden, Mass	$39
Ireland, Lewis, W. Va	9
Ireland Corners, Albany, N. Y	5
Ireland Hill, Marion, Ala	4
Irene, Sioux, Iowa	12
Irisburgh, Henry, Va	15
Irish Grove, Atchison, Mo	61
Irishtown, Mercer, Pa	18
Irona, Talladega, Ala	12
Irona, Clinton, N. Y	48
Iron City, Iron, Utah	12
Iron Clad, Limestone, Tex	10
Iron Creek, Austin, Tex	16
Irondale,* Washington, Mo	210
Irondale, Jefferson, Ohio	370
Iron Furnace, Scioto, Ohio	120
Iron Hill, Northampton, Pa	12
Iron Hills, Jackson, Iowa	24
Iron Mountain, St. Francois, Mo	260
Iron Mountain, Rusk, Tex	12
Iron Ridge, Dodge, Wis	150
Iron Rod, Madison, Mont	12
Iron Station, Lincoln, N. C	12
Ironton,* (*c. h.*,) Iron, Mo	690
Ironton,* (*c. h.*,) Lawrence, Ohio	2,000
Ironton, Lehigh, Pa	71
Ironton, Sauk, Wis	210
Ironville, Perry, Ala	12
Ironwood, Liberty, Tex	13
Iroquois, Iroquois, Ill	99
Irvine, (*c. h.*,) Estill, Ky	270
Irvine, Warren, Pa	250
Irving, Montgomery, Ill	260
Irving,* Marshall, Kans	400
Irving, Barry, Mich	61
Irving, Monongalia, Minn	13
Irving, Chautauqua, N. Y	120
Irving, Jackson, Wis	85
Irving College, Warren, Tenn	11
Irvington, Washington, Ill	170
Irvington, Kossuth, Iowa	70
Irvington, Essex, N. J	230
Irvington, Westchester, N. Y	430
Irwin, Union, Ohio	63
Irwin's Station, Westmoreland, Pa	720
Irwinton, (*c. h.*,) Wilkinson, Ga	190
Irwinville, (*c. h.*,) Irwin, Ga	10
Isaac's Camp, Doddridge, W. Va	12
Isabella, (*c. h.*,) Worth, Ga	20
Isabella, Ozark, Mo	12
Isabella City, Isabella, Mich	12
Isadora, Worth, Mo	38
Isanti, Isanti, Minn	160
Ischua, Cattaraugus, N. Y	53
Ishpeming, Marquette, Mich	1,200
Island, Clinton, Pa	19
Island City, Owsley, Ky	3
Island City, Gentry, Mo	24
Island Creek, Jasper, Ill	7
Island Creek, Jefferson, Ohio	13
Island Falls, Aroostook, Me	36
Island Pond,* Essex, Vt	830
Isle La Motte, Grand Isle, Vt	69
Islesborough, Hocking, Ohio	20
Islip, Suffolk, N. Y	290
Issequena, Goochland, Va	10

* Money-order office.

Itasca, Anoka, Minn	$51
Italy Hill, Yates, N. Y	61
Italy Hollow, Yates, N. Y	16
Ithaca,* (*c. h.*,) Gratiot, Mich	410
Ithaca, Saunders, Nebr	12
Ithaca,* (*c. h.*,) Tompkins, N. Y	2,900
Ithaca, Darke, Ohio	47
Ithaca, Richland, Wis	13
Iuka, Marion, Ill	170
Iuka, (*c. h.*,) Tishemingo, Miss	1,500
Ivesdale, Champaign, Ill	98
Ives' Grove, Racine, Wis	39
Ivor, Southampton, Va	75
Ivy Depot, Albemarle, Va	86
Ivy Log, Union, Ga	4
Ivy Mills, Delaware, Pa	50
Ixonia Centre, Jefferson, Wis	97

J.

Jacinto, Colusa, Cal	12
Jacinto, Alcorn, Miss	39
Jacksborough, (*c. h.*,) Campbell, Tenn	78
Jacksborough, (*c. h.*,) Jack, Tex	260
Jack's Fork, Texas, Mo	12
Jackson,* (*c. h.*,) Amador, Cal	700
Jackson, (*c. h.*,) Butts, Ga	20
Jackson, Adair, Iowa	12
Jackson, Linn, Kans	10
Jackson, (*c. h.*,) Breathitt, Ky	12
Jackson, East Feliciana, La	310
Jackson, Waldo, Me	37
Jackson,* (*c. h.*,) Jackson, Mich	3,000
Jackson, (*c. h.*,) Jackson, Minn	240
JACKSON,* (*c. h.*,) Hinds, Miss	2,700
Jackson, (*c. h.*,) Cape Girardeau, Mo	370
Jackson, Dakota, Nebr	64
Jackson, Carroll, N. H	72
Jackson, (*c. h.*,) Northampton, N. C	420
Jackson,* (*c. h.*,) Jackson, Ohio	840
Jackson, Susquehanna, Pa	70
Jackson,* (*c. h.*,) Madison, Tenn	2,000
Jackson, Louisa, Va	12
Jackson, Washington, Wis	12
Jackson C. H., Jackson, W. Va	140
Jacksonborough, Butler, Ohio	31
Jacksonborough, Colleton, S. C	12
Jackson Brook, Washington, Me	12
Jacksonburgh, Wayne, Ind	32
Jackson Centre, Shelby, Ohio	35
Jackson Corners, Dutchess, N. Y	21
Jackson Corners, Monroe, Pa	8
Jackson Hall, Franklin, Pa	38
Jacksonham, Lancaster, S. C	12
Jacksonport,* (*c. h.*) Jackson, Ark	740
Jacksonport, Door, Wis	22
Jackson's Corners, Sullivan, Mo	19
Jackson's Creek, Randolph, N. C	6
Jackson's Mills, Ocean, N. J	13
Jackson Springs, Jackson, N. C	12
Jackson Station, Tipton, Ind	35
Jackson Station, Seneca, Ohio	10
Jackson Store, Conecuh, Ala	12
Jacksontown, Licking, Ohio	84
Jackson Valley, Susquehanna, Pa	9
Jacksonville, (*c. h.*,) Calhoun, Ala	500
Jacksonville,* (*c. h.*,) Duval, Fla	$3,200
Jacksonville, (*c. h.*,) Telfair, Ga	28
Jacksonville,* (*c. h.*,) Morgan, Ill	2,800
Jacksonville, Chickasaw, Iowa	63
Jacksonville, Neosho, Kans	210
Jacksonville, Shelby, Ky	12
Jacksonville, Randolph, Mo	170
Jacksonville, Burlington, N. J	15
Jacksonville, Tompkins, N. Y	210
Jacksonville,* (*c. h.*,) Jackson, Oreg	640
Jacksonville, Lehigh, Pa	39
Jacksonville, Cherokee, Tex	52
Jacksonville, Windham, Vt	170
Jacksonville, Lewis, W. Va	20
Jack's Reef, Onondaga, N. Y	40
Jacksville, Butler, Pa	15
Jacobsburgh, Belmont, Ohio	28
Jacob's Church, Shenandoah, Va	17
Jacob's Creek, Westmoreland, Pa	42
Jacob's Fork, Catawba, N. C	15
Jacobstown, Burlington, N. J	100
Jadden, Grant, Ind	8
Jaffrey, Cheshire, N. H	100
Jake's Prairie, Gasconade, Mo	32
Jake's Run, Monongalia, W. Va	12
Jalapa, Grant, Ind	39
Jalapa, Newberry, S. C	12
Jalapa, Monroe, Tenn	10
Jamaica,* (*c. h.*,) Queens, N. Y	1,000
Jamaica, Windham, Vt	280
Jamaica, Middlesex, Va	15
Jamaica Plain, Norfolk, Mass	1,000
James' Bayou, Mississippi, Mo	31
Jamesburgh, Middlesex, N. J	260
James' Creek, Huntingdon, Pa	140
James' Crossing, Jackson, Kans	13
James' Fork, Sebastian, Ark	10
Jamesport, Daviess, Mo	120
Jamesport, Suffolk, N. Y	190
James' Switch, Marion, Ind	26
Jamestown, Conecuh, Ala	6
Jamestown, Tuolumne, Cal	170
Jamestown, Boulder, Colo	23
Jamestown, Chattahoochee, Ga	23
Jamestown, Clinton, Ill	53
Jamestown, Boone, Ind	170
Jamestown, (*c, h.*,) Russell, Ky	55
Jamestown, Ottawa, Mich	58
Jamestown, Moniteau, Mo	93
Jamestown,* Chautauqua, N. Y	3,000
Jamestown, Guilford, N. C	140
Jamestown, Greene, Ohio	260
Jamestown, Mercer, Pa	420
Jamestown, Newport, R. I	61
Jamestown, (*c. h.*,) Fentress, Tenn	74
Jamestown, Grant, Wis	82
Jamesville, Onondaga, N. Y	330
Jamesville, Martin, N. C	190
Janelew, Lewis, W. Va	76
Janesville, Lassen, Cal	30
Janesville, Greenwood, Kans	31
Janesville, Waseca, Minn	220
Janesville,* (*c. h.*,) Rock, Wis	3,300
Janney's, Richland, Wis	12
Jarratt's, Sussex, Va	110
Jarrettown, Montgomery, Pa	24

* Money-order office.

Jarrett's Ford, Kanawha, W. Va	$4
Jarrettsville, Harford, Md	89
Jarrold's Valley, Raleigh, W. Va	12
Jasonville, Greene, Ind	25
Jasper, (*c. h.*,) Walker, Ala	71
Jasper, (*c. h.*,) Newton, Ark	43
Jasper, (*c. h.*,) Hamilton, Fla	20
Jasper, (*c. h.*,) Pickens, Ga	50
Jasper, (*c. h.*,) Dubois, Ind	170
Jasper, Jasper, Mo	21
Jasper, Steuben, N. Y	160
Jasper, Pike, Ohio	39
Jasper, (*c. h.*,) Marion, Tenn	200
Jasper, (*c. h.*,) Jasper, Tex	100
Jasper City, Jasper, Iowa	380
Jasper Mills, Fayette, Ohio	67
Jatt, Grant, La	10
Java, Wyoming, N. Y	47
Java, Lucas, Ohio	12
Java Village, Wyoming, N. Y	67
Jay, Franklin, Me	140
Jay, Saginaw, Mich	92
Jay, Harrison, Mo	5
Jay, Essex, N. Y	83
Jay, Orleans, Vt	44
Jayne's Store, Randolph, Ark	7
Jaynesville,* Bremer, Iowa	310
Jaynesville, Covington, Miss	8
Jaysville, Darke, Ohio	32
Jayville, Conecuh, Ala	12
Jeanerett, Iberia, La	180
Jeansville, Luzerne, Pa	280
Jeddo, Allen, Kans	8
Jeddo, St. Clair, Mich	74
Jeddo, Orleans, N. Y	140
Jeddo, Jefferson, Ohio	31
Jeddo, Luzerne, Pa	390
Jeddo, Marquette, Wis	17
Jefferson, (*c. h.*,) Jackson, Ga	170
Jefferson, Cook, Ill	170
Jefferson, Clinton, Ind	74
Jefferson,* (*c. h.*,) Greene, Iowa	990
Jefferson, Douglas, Kans	320
Jefferson, Jefferson, La	24
Jefferson, Lincoln, Me	130
Jefferson, Frederick, Md	100
Jefferson, Hillsdale, Mich	13
Jefferson, Winona, Minn	7
Jefferson, Coos, N. H	51
Jefferson, Schoharie, N. Y	190
Jefferson, (*c. h.*,) Ashe, N. C	59
Jefferson,* (*c. h.*,) Ashtabula, Ohio	830
Jefferson, Marion, Oreg	79
Jefferson, Greene, Pa	140
Jefferson, Chesterfield, S. C	10
Jefferson,* (*c. h.*,) Marion, Texas	1,800
Jefferson, Powhatan, Va	25
Jefferson,* (*c. h.*,) Jefferson, Wis	1,100
Jefferson Barracks,* St. Louis, Mo	480
JEFFERSON CITY,* (*c. h.*,) Cole, Mo	2,400
Jefferson City, Jefferson, Mont	290
Jefferson Corners, Whitesides, Ill	8
Jefferson Furnace, Clarion, Pa	37
Jefferson Lake, Le Sueur, Minn	10
Jefferson Line, Clearfield, Pa	22
Jefferson Station, York, Pa	16
Jeffersonton, Culpeper, Va	$68
Jeffersontown, Jefferson, Ky	130
Jefferson Valley, Westchester, N. Y	69
Jeffersonville, (*c. h.*,) Twiggs, Ga	56
Jeffersonville, Wayne, Ill	170
Jeffersonville*, Clarke, Ind	2,100
Jeffersonville, Lee, Iowa	20
Jeffersonville, Cowley, Kans	12
Jeffersonville, Montgomery, Ky	16
Jeffersonville, Cass, Mich	30
Jeffersonville, Sullivan, N. Y	290
Jeffersonville, Fayette, Ohio	120
Jeffersonville, Montgomery, Pa	45
Jeffersonville, Lamoille, Vt	290
Jeffress' Store, Nottaway, Va	12
Jeffrey's Creek, Marion, S. C	2
Jeffries, Clearfield, Pa	30
Jeffriesburgh, Franklin, Mo	12
Jelloway, Knox, Ohio	77
Jena, Tuscaloosa, Ala	3
Jena, Falls, Tex	8
Jenkins' Bridge, Accomack, Va	37
Jenkins' Creek, Jasper, Mo	5
Jenkins' Mills, Jefferson, Nebr	71
Jenkintown, Montgomery, Pa	310
Jenksville, Tioga, N. Y	36
Jenner's Cross Roads, Somerset, Pa	120
Jennerstown, Somerset, Pa	20
Jennersville, Chester, Pa	110
Jennieton, Iowa, Wis	21
Jennings, Hamilton, Fla	15
Jennings' Fork, Smith, Tenn	19
Jennings' Ordinary, Nottaway, Va	12
Jenningsville, Wyoming, Pa	18
Jenny, Marathon, Wis	39
Jenny Lind, Sebastian, Ark	54
Jenny Lind, Calaveras, Cal	80
Jericho, Perry, Ala	12
Jericho, Kane, Ill	27
Jericho, Henry, Ky	68
Jericho, Queens, N. Y	70
Jericho, Chittenden, Vt	190
Jericho Centre, Chittenden, Vt	94
Jerome, Howard, Ind	66
Jerome, Appanoose, Iowa	10
Jerome, Phelps, Mo	12
Jerome, Westchester, N. Y	130
Jerome, Union, Ohio	44
Jeromesville, Ashland, Ohio	65
Jersey, Oakland, Mich	10
Jersey, Licking, Ohio	78
Jersey City,* (*c. h.*,) Hudson, N. J	3,100
Jersey Mills, Lycoming, Pa	32
Jersey Shore,* Lycoming, Pa	880
Jerseytown, Columbia, Pa	17
Jerseyville,* (*c. h.*,) Jersey, Ill	1,300
Jerseyville, Monmouth, N. J	12
Jerusalem, Albany, N. Y	24
Jerusalem, Davie, N. C	73
Jerusalem, Monroe, Ohio	69
Jerusalem, (*c. h.*,) Southampton, Va	70
Jerusalem Mills, Harford, Md	41
Jessamine, Jessamine, Ky	12
Jesse's Mills, Russell, Va	12
Jesse's Store, Shelby, Ky	4
Jessup,* Buchanan, Iowa	440

* Money-order office.

Jessup's Station, Parke, Ind	$9
Jesuit's Bend, Plaquemine, La	15
Jetersville, Amelia, Va	140
Jewell, Jewell, Kans	12
Jewett, Greene, N. Y	51
Jewett, Harrison, Ohio	110
Jewett Centre, Greene, N. Y	15
Jewett City, New London, Conn	510
Jewett Mills, St. Croix, Wis	47
Jimes, Jackson, Ohio	18
Joanna Furnace, Berks, Pa	16
Jobe, Oregon, Mo	15
Jobe, Monongalia, W. Va	8
Jobstown, Burlington, N. J	62
Joe's Lick, Madison, Ky	12
Joetta, Hancock, Ill	12
Johanesburgh, Washington, Ill	12
John Day City, Grant, Oreg	12
John Day's Creek, Idaho, Idaho	12
John's Branch, Audrian, Mo	10
Johnsburgh, McHenry, Ill	24
Johnsburgh, Warren, N. Y	79
Johnsburgh, Somerset, Pa	12
Johnson, Jones, Iowa	25
Johnson, Macon, Mo	12
Johnson, Barnwell, S. C	16
Johnson,* Lemoille, Vt	370
Johnsonburgh, Warren, N. J	66
Johnson City, Washington, Tenn	280
Johnson's, Orange, N. Y	12
Johnsonsburgh, Wyoming, N. Y	62
Johnson's Corners, Summit, Ohio	34
Johnson's Creek, Carroll, Ill	10
Johnson's Creek, Niagara, N. Y	180
Johnson's Creek, Jefferson, Wis	160
Johnson's Cross Roads, Monroe, W. Va	10
Johnson's Fork, Magoffin, Ky	6
Johnson's Grove, Haywood, Tenn	12
Johnson's Mills, Marion, Ala	12
Johnson's Mills, Pitt, N. C	9
Johnson's Springs, Goochland, Va	12
Johnson's Station, Tarrant, Tex	33
Johnson's Store, Anne Arundel, Md	27
Johnsontown, Northampton, Va	48
Johnsonville, Wayne, Ill	140
Johnsonville, Rensselaer, N. Y	210
Johnsonville, Trumbull, Ohio	110
Johnsonville, Northampton, Pa	25
Johnsonville, Williamsburgh, S. C	6
Johnsonville, Humphreys, Tenn	210
Johnsonville, Sheboygan, Wis	12
Johnston's Depot, Edgefield, S. C	12
Johnston's Institute, Hays, Tex	12
Johnstown, Cumberland, Ill	31
Johnstown, Alleghany, Md	12
Johnstown, Barry, Mich	30
Johnstown, Bates, Mo	76
Johnstown,* (*c. h.*,) Fulton, N. Y	1,400
Johnstown, Licking, Ohio	100
Johnstown,* Cambria, Pa	2,500
Johnstown, Harrison, W. Va	11
Johnstown, Rock, Wis	83
Johnstown Centre, Rock, Wis	84
Johnsville, Bradley, Ark	24
Johnsville, Frederick, Md	68
Johnsville, Dutchess, N. Y	$52
Johnsville, Montgomery, Ohio	33
Joliet,* (*c. h.*,) Will, Ill	2,900
Joliett, Schuylkill, Pa	12
Jolly, Monroe, Ohio	59
Jollytown, Greene, Pa	24
Jollyville, Lee, Iowa	35
Jonas Ridge, Burke, N. C	12
Jonathan's Creek, Haywood, N. C	2
Jones' Bluff, Sumter, Ala	44
Jonesborough, Jefferson, Ala	34
Jonesborough, (*c. h.*,) Craighead, Ark	92
Jonesborough, (*c. h.*,) Clayton, Ga	330
Jonesborough, (*c. h.*,) Union, Ill	460
Jonesborough, Grant, Ind	370
Jonesborough, Washington, Me	42
Jonesborough, Tippah, Miss	30
Jonesborough, Moore, N. C	300
Jonesborough,* (*c. h.*,) Washington, Tenn	570
Jonesborough, Brunswick, Va	17
Jonesburgh, Montgomery, Mo	260
Jones' Chapel, Winston, Ala	12
Jones' Corners, Holmes, Ohio	12
Jones' Creek, Newton, Mo	12
Jones' Cross Roads, Tallapoosa, Ala	34
Jones' Mills, Meriwether, Ga	5
Jones' Mills, Westmoreland, Pa	61
Jonesport, Washington, Me	140
Jones' Springs, Berkeley, W. Va	12
Jones' Station, Dearborn, Ind	53
Jones' Station, Butler, Ohio	66
Jones' Station, Haywood, Tenn	12
Jones' Tan Yard, Callaway, Mo	20
Jonestown,* Lebanon, Pa	270
Jonesville, Bartholomew, Ind	140
Jonesville,* Hillsdale, Mich	1,200
Jonesville, Cass, Mo	18
Jonesville, Saratoga, N. Y	140
Jonesville, Yadkin, N. C	32
Jonesville, Union, S. C	27
Jonesville, Chittenden, Vt	84
Jonesville, (*c. h.*,) Lee, Va	130
Joppa Village, Plymouth, Mass	220
Jordan, Vermilion, Ill	48
Jordan, Jay, Ind	33
Jordan, Onondaga, N. Y	820
Jordan, Green, Wis	20
Jordan's Chapel, Mercer, W. Va	12
Jordan's Grove, Randolph, Ill	50
Jordan's Saline, Van Zandt, Tex	10
Jordan Spring, Montgomery, Tenn	19
Jordan Station, Fulton, Ky	99
Jordan Store, Williamson, Tenn	29
Jordan's Valley, Rutherford, Tenn	82
Jordan Valley, Baker, Oreg	12
Jordan Village, Owen, Ind	10
Jordanville, Herkimer, N. Y	110
Jo's Branch, Wyoming, W. Va	5
Josco, Livingston, Mich	10
Joseph's Mills, Tyler, W. Va	18
Joslyn, Rock Island, Ill	12
Joy, Wayne, N. Y	62
Joy Creek, Washington, Kans	12
Joyfield, Benzie, Mich	35
Joyner's Depot, Wilson, N. C	140

* Money-order office.

Juda, Green, Wis	$220
Judesville, Surry, N. C	7
Judson, White, Ark	12
Judson, Kankakee, Ill	17
Judson, Blue Earth, Minn	61
Judson, Sullivan, Mo	15
Julesburgh, Weld, Colo	50
Julian, San Diego, Cal	12
Julian Furnace, Centre, Pa	140
Julietta, Marion, Ind	23
Juliustown, Burlington, N. J	24
Jumping Branch, Mercer, W. Va	13
Junction, Pulaski, Ill	26
Junction, Madison, Mont	12
Junction, Hunterdon, N. J	210
Junction, Rensselaer, N. Y	54
Junction, Paulding, Ohio	66
Junction, Lancaster, Pa	27
Junction, Hanover, Va	12
Junction, Dane, Wis	35
Junction City, Trinity, Cal	13
Junction City, Mills, Iowa	12
Junction City,* (*c. h.*,) Davis, Kans	2,200
Junction House, Lassen, Cal	12
Juneau,* (*c. h.*,) Dodge, Wis	310
Juniata, Pueblo, Colo	12
Juniata, Perry, Pa	43
Junius, Seneca, N. Y	81
Juno, Henderson, Tenn	18
Jupiter, Madison, Ark	5

K.

Kabletown, Jefferson, W. Va	60
Kahle's, Clarion, Pa	14
Kalama, Cowlitz, Wash	1
Kalamazoo,* (*c. h.*,) Kalamazoo, Mich	3,500
Kalamo, Eaton, Mich	72
Kalida, (*c. h.*,) Putnam, Ohio	83
Kamas, Summit, Utah	12
Kanarraville, Iron, Utah	34
Kanawha C. H.,* Kanawha, W. Va	1,500
Kanawha Saline, Kanawha, W. Va	120
Kanawha Station, Wood, W. Va	36
Kandiyohi, Kandiyohi, Minn	120
Kandiyohi Station, (*c. h.*,) Kandiyohi, Minn	12
Kane, Greene, Ill	270
Kane, Campbell, Ky	24
Kane, McKean, Pa	380
Kane City, Venango, Pa	12
Kaneville, Kane, Ill	120
Kankakee,* (*c. h.*,) Kankakee, Ill	2,800
Kankakee, Starke, Ind	12
Kanona, Steuben, N. Y	97
Kanosh, Millard, Utah	32
Kansas, Walker, Ala	2
Kansas, Edgar, Ill	330
Kansas, Graves, Ky	22
Kansas, Seneca, Ohio	100
Kansas, Jefferson, Tenn	3
Kansas City,* Jackson, Mo	4,000
Kansasville, Racine, Wis	270
Kantz, Snyder, Pa	14
Kaolin, Iron, Mo	12
Kaolin, Chester, Pa	$16
Kappa, Woodford, Ill	91
Karrsville, Warren, N. J	19
Karthaus, Clearfield, Pa	30
Kasey's, Bedford, Va	6
Kaseyville, Macon, Mo	17
Kaskaskia, Randolph, Ill	82
Kasoag, Oswego, N. Y	66
Kasota, La Sueur, Minn	60
Kasson, Vanderburgh, Ind	8
Kasson, Madison, Iowa	18
Kasson,* Dodge, Minn	360
Kasson, McKean, Pa	14
Kasson, Barbour, W. Va	13
Kasson, Manitowoc, Wis	18
Katahdin Iron Works, Piscataquis, Me	23
Katonah, Westchester, N. Y	480
Kattelville, Broome, N. Y	31
Kaufman, (*c. h.*) Kaufman, Tex	220
Kaukauna, Outagamie, Wis	74
Kawkawlin, Bay, Mich	80
Kaysville, Davis, Utah	70
Kearney, Clay, Mo	170
Kearney City, (*c. h.*) Kearney, Nebr	50
Keatchie, De Soto, La	100
Keating, McKean, Pa	12
Keck's Centre, Fulton, N. Y	13
Keck's Church, Martin, Ind	23
Kedron, Fillmore, Minn	6
Keedysville, Washington, Md	110
Keefer's Corners, Albany, N. Y	3
Keefer's Store, Franklin, Pa	6
Keeler's Bay, Grand Isle, Vt	12
Keelersburgh, Wyoming, Pa	22
Keelersville, Van Buren, Mich	140
Keelville, Cherokee, Kans	12
Keene, Jessamine, Ky	91
Keene, Ionia, Mich	12
Keene,* (*c. h.*,) Cheshire, N. H	2,300
Keene, Essex, N. Y	58
Keene, Coshocton, Ohio	91
Keene, Portage, Wis	12
Keene Flats, Essex, N. Y	5
Keeney's Settlement, Cortland, N.Y	35
Keeneyville, Tioga, Pa	63
Keenville, Wayne, Ill	17
Keep Tryst, Washington, Md	12
Keepville, Erie, Pa	12
Keeseville,* Essex, N. Y	1,200
Keezletown, Rockingham, Va	25
Keith's, Noble, Ohio	27
Keithsburgh,* Mercer, Ill	540
Kekoskee, Dodge, Wis	130
Kellersville, Monroe, Pa	14
Kellerville, Dubois, Ind	12
Kelley, Mifflin, Pa	24
Kelley's Island, Erie, Ohio	280
Kelley's Mills, Lawrence, Ohio	12
Kellis' Store, Kemper, Miss	140
Kellogg's, Douglas, Oreg	5
Kelloggsville, Kent, Mich	27
Kelloggsville, Cayuga, N. Y	120
Kelloggsville, Ashtabula, Ohio	130
Kellyburgh, Lycoming, Pa	10
Kelly Point, Union, Pa	12

* Money-order office.

Kelly's Corners, Lenawee, Mich	$8
Kelly's Creek, St. Clair, Ala	12
Kelly's Station, Armstrong, Pa	78
Kellysville, Delaware, Pa	110
Kelsey, El Dorado, Cal	23
Kelso, Dearborn, Ind	16
Kelso, Sibley, Minn	4
Kelso, Lincoln, Tenn	12
Kelton, Box Elder, Utah	12
Kemblesville, Chester, Pa	130
Kemp, Kaufman, Tex	12
Kemper City, Victoria, Tex	20
Kemp's Creek, Cleburne, Ala	12
Kemptown, Frederick, Md	13
Kenansville,* (*c. h.*,) Duplin, N. C	240
Kendaia, Seneca, N. Y	72
Kendall, Kendall, Ill	46
Kendall, Van Buren, Mich	12
Kendall, Orleans, N. Y	80
Kendall, Anson, N. C	12
Kendall, Beaver, Pa	17
Kendall Creek, McKean, Pa	22
Kendall Mills, Orleans, N. Y	12
Kendall's Mills, Somerset, Me	820
Kendallville,* Noble, Ind	1,500
Kendrick's Creek, Sullivan, Tenn	12
Kenduskeag, Penobscot, Me	200
Kenesaw, Cobb, Ga	33
Kennamer Cove, Marshall, Ala	12
Kennard, Champaign, Ohio	58
Kennard, Mercer, Pa	68
Kennebunk, York, Me	640
Kennebunk Depot, York, Me	490
Kennebunk Landing, York, Me	10
Kennebunkport, York, Me	440
Kennedale, Tuscaloosa, Ala	12
Kennedy, Chautauqua, N. Y	210
Kennedy's, Brunswick, Va	25
Kennedyville, Kent, Md	210
Kennekuk, Atchison, Kans	150
Kenner, Jefferson, La	35
Kennerdell, Venango, Pa	22
Kennett, (*c. h.*,) Dunklin, Mo	61
Kennett's Square, Chester, Pa	780
Kennon, Belmont, Ohio	19
Kennonsburgh, Noble, Ohio	22
Kenockee, St. Clair, Mich	15
Kenosha,* (*c. h.*,) Kenosha, Wis	2,500
Kensico, Westchester, N. Y	60
Kensington, Hartford, Conn	230
Kensington, Oakland, Mich	53
Kensington, Rockingham, N. H	67
Kent, Litchfield, Conn	550
Kent, Stephenson, Ill	43
Kent, Jefferson, Ind	53
Kent, Newton, Mo	9
Kent, Putnam, N. Y	5
Kent,* Portage, Ohio	1,200
Kent, Indiana, Pa	110
Kentland,* (*c. h.*,) Newton, Ind	650
Kenton, Kent, Del	50
Kenton, Kenton, Ky	25
Kenton, Christian, Mo	43
Kenton,* (*c. h.*,) Hardin, Ohio	1,100
Kenton, Obion, Tenn	90
Kenton Furnace, Greenup, Ky	14
Kentontown, Robertson, Ky	$16
Kent's Hill, Kennebec, Me	370
Kentucky, Vermilion, Ill	4
Kentucky Town, Grayson, Tex	190
Kenyon, Jackson, Ark	34
Kenyon, Goodhue, Minn	100
Kenyonville, Orleans, N. Y	35
Keokuk,* Lee, Iowa	3,700
Keokuk Junction, Adams, Ill	200
Keosauqua,* (*c. h.*,) Van Buren, Iowa	490
Keowee, Oconee, S. C	12
Kerby, (*c. h.*,) Josephine, Oreg	35
Kerhonkson, Ulster, N. Y	120
Kernersville, Forsyth, N. C	36
Kerneysville, Jefferson, W. Va	150
Kernville, Kern, Cal	74
Kerr's Station, Washington, Pa	13
Kerr's Store, Clarion, Pa	57
Kerrsville, Cumberland, Pa	50
Kerrville, (*c. h.*,) Kerr, Tex	50
Kersey's, Elk, Pa	76
Kershena, Shawanaw, Wis	27
Kesler's Cross Lanes, Nicholas, W. Va	9
Kessler's, Northampton, Pa	6
Keswick Depot, Albemarle, Va	270
Ketcham, Luzerne, Pa	8
Ketchum's Corners, Saratoga, N. Y	43
Ketchumville, Tioga, N. Y	20
Kettle Creek, Potter, Pa	110
Kewanee,* Henry, Ill	1,700
Kewanee, Lauderdale, Miss	15
Kewanna, Fulton, Ind	90
Kewaskum, Washington, Wis	110
Kewaunee,* (*c. h.*,) Kewaunee, Wis	200
Keyesport, Clinton, Ill	41
Key Port,* Monmouth, N. J	740
Keysburgh, Logan, Ky	12
Keystone, Douglas, Colo	12
Keystone, Jackson, Ohio	37
Keystone, Perry, Pa	7
Keysville, Charlotte, Va	160
Keytesville,* (*c. h.*,) Chariton, Mo	340
Key West,* (*c. h.*,) Monroe, Fla	1,400
Kezar Falls, York, Me	110
Kiantone, Chautauqua, N. Y	51
Kickapoo, Peoria, Ill	110
Kickapoo, Anderson, Tex	20
Kickapoo, Vernon, Wis	12
Kickapoo City, Leavenworth, Kans	81
Kidder, Caldwell, Mo	310
Kidder's Ferry, Seneca, N. Y	25
Kiddville, Clark, Ky	24
Kiddville, Ionia, Mich	11
Kiddville, Sullivan, Mo	21
Kidron, Coweta, Ga	15
Kidwell, Tyler, W. Va	9
Kiel, Manitowoc, Wis	110
Kier, Buchanan, Iowa	15
Kilbourn, Van Buren, Iowa	20
Kilbourn City,* Columbia, Wis	1,200
Kildare, Juneau, Wis	120
Kilgore, Carroll, Ohio	60
Kilgore, Venango, Pa	8
Kilkenny, Le Sueur, Minn	36
Killawog, Broome, N. Y	95
Killbourne, Delaware, Ohio	81

* Money-order office.

Killbuck, Ogle, Ill	$22
Kill Buck, Cattaraugus, N. Y	170
Killbuck, Holmes, Ohio	37
Killian's Mills, Lincoln, N. C	10
Killinger, Dauphin, Pa	32
Killingly, Windham, Conn	340
Killingworth, Middlesex, Conn	100
Kill Mills, Warren, N. J	4
Kilmarnock, Lancaster, Va	34
Kimberton, Chester, Pa	67
Kimbolton, Guernsey, Ohio	55
Kimmel, Indiana, Pa	10
Kimmer's Stand, Cumberland, Tenn	5
Kimmswick, Jefferson, Mo	140
Kimulga, Talladega, Ala	59
Kinard's Turnout, Newberry, S. C	44
Kincheloe, Harrison, W. Va	8
Kinderhook, Van Buren, Ark	22
Kinderhook, Pike, Ill	120
Kinderhook, Branch, Mich	64
Kinderhook,* Columbia, N. Y	770
Kinderhook, Pickaway, Ohio	50
Kinderkamack, Bergen, N. J	12
King, Chattahoochee, Ga	5
King, Dubuque, Iowa	18
King City, Gentry, Mo	44
Kingfield, Franklin, Me	110
King George C. H., King George, Va	12
King of Prussia, Montgomery, Pa	71
King's, Barbour, Ala	5
King's, Athens, Ohio	31
Kingsboro, Edgecombe, N. C	7
Kingsborough, Fulton, N. Y	230
King's Bridge, Manitowoc, Wis	12
Kingsbridgeville, Westchester, N. Y	12
Kingsbury, Whitesides, Ill	38
Kingsbury, La Porte, Ind	57
Kingsbury, Piscataquis, Me	21
Kingsbury, Washington, N. Y	39
King's Cave, Harrison, Ind	12
King's Ferry, Nassau, Fla	18
King's Ferry, Cayuga, N. Y	240
King's Mountain, Gaston, N. C	10
King's Point, Dade, Mo	14
Kingsport, Sullivan, Tenn	75
King's River, Fresno, Cal	12
King's Settlement, Chenango, N. Y	10
King's Station, Gibson, Ind	44
Kingston, Autauga, Ala	16
Kingston, Fresno, Cal	67
Kingston, Bartow, Ga	420
Kingston, De Kalb, Ill	30
Kingston, Decatur, Ind	41
Kingston, Des Moines, Iowa	41
Kingston, Madison, Ky	71
Kingston, Somerset, Md	100
Kingston, Plymouth, Mass	470
Kingston, Meeker, Minn	130
Kingston, (*c. h.*,) Caldwell, Mo	300
Kingston, Rockingham, N. H	160
Kingston, Somerset, N. J	170
Kingston,* (*c. h.*,) Ulster, N. Y	2,400
Kingston, Ross, Ohio	140
Kingston, Luzerne, Pa	840
Kingston, (*c. h.*,) Washington, R. I	240
Kingston, (*c. h.*,) Roane, Tenn	390

Kingston, Green Lake, Wis	$170
Kingston Centre, Delaware, Ohio	83
Kingston Furnace, Washington, Mo	38
Kingston Mines, Peoria, Ill	83
Kingstree, (*c. h.*,) Williamsburgh, S. C	240
Kingsville, Ashtabula, Ohio	480
Kingsville, Clarion, Pa	17
Kingsville, Richland, S. C	78
King William C. H., King William, Va	53
Kingwood, Hunterdon, N. J	20
Kingwood, Somerset, Pa	20
Kingwood, (*c. h.*,) Preston, W. Va	340
Kinlock, Lawrence, Ala	6
Kinmundy, Marion, Ill	620
Kinney's Four Corners, Oswego, N. Y	17
Kinnick Kinnick, St. Croix, Wis	10
Kinsale, Westmoreland, Va	60
Kinsman's,* Trumbull, Ohio	340
Kinston, (*c. h.*,) Lenoir, N. C	630
Kintnersville, Bucks, Pa	56
Kinzer's, Lancaster, Pa	150
Kinzua, Warren, Pa	50
Kiowa, Douglas, Colo	12
Kiowa, Jefferson, Nebr	12
Kipp's Corners, Genesee, Mich	8
Kipton, Lorain, Ohio	110
Kirby, Wyandot, Ohio	60
Kirby, Greene, Pa	23
Kirbyville, Berks, Pa	3
Kirchhayn, Washington, Wis	40
Kirkersville, Licking, Ohio	100
Kirkland, Oneida, N. Y	66
Kirkmansville, Todd, Ky	33
Kirk's Cross Roads, Clinton, Ind	83
Kirk's Grove, Cherokee, Ala	5
Kirk's Mills, Lancaster, Pa	45
Kirksville, Madison, Ky	45
Kirksville,* (*c. h.*,) Adair, Mo	1,000
Kirkville, Wapello, Iowa	180
Kirkville, Onondaga, N. Y	85
Kirkwood, New Castle, Del	60
Kirkwood, St. Louis, Mo	270
Kirkwood, Camden, N. J	95
Kirkwood, Broome, N. Y	110
Kirkwood, Shelby, Ohio	58
Kirkwood, Lancaster, Pa	21
Kirkwood Centre, Broome, N. Y	13
Kirtland, Lake, Ohio	120
Kishacoquillas, Mifflin, Pa	62
Kishwaukee, Winnebago, Ill	45
Kiskiminitas, Armstrong, Pa	19
Kit Carson, (*c. h.*,) Greenwood, Colo	12
Kittaning,* (*c. h.*,) Armstrong, Pa	1,200
Kittery, York, Me	520
Kittery Depot, York, Me	120
Kittery Point, York, Me	240
Kittrell, Granville, N. C	240
Klamath, Siskiyou, Cal	12
Klecknersville, Northampton, Pa	22
Kleinfeltersville, Lebanon, Pa	12
Klikitat, Klikitat, Wash	12
Kline's Grove, Northumberland, Pa	1
Klinesville, Hunterdon, N. J	6
Klinesville, Berks, Pa	11
Klingelhoeffer Landing, Perry, Ark	14

* Money-order office.

Post office	Amount
Klingerstown, Schuylkill, Pa	$4
Knap of Reeds, Granville, N. C	11
Knapp's Creek, Crawford, Wis	12
Knauer's, Berks, Pa	9
Kniffin, Wayne, Iowa	16
Knight's Ferry, (*c. h.,*) Stanislaus, Cal	200
Knight's Mill, Berrien, Ga	12
Knight's Prairie, Hamilton, Ill	12
Knightstown, Henry, Ind	940
Knightsville, Clay, Ind	12
Knob, Beaver, Pa	6
Knob, Tazewell, Va	23
Knob Creek, Cleveland, N. C	5
Knob Fork, Wetzel, W. Va	6
Knob Lick, Metcalfe, Ky	26
Knob Lick, St. Francois, Mo	12
Knobnoster, Johnson, Mo	770
Knobsville, Fulton, Pa	25
Knobview, Crawford, Mo	41
Knott's Mills, Preston, W. Va	12
Knottsville, Daviess, Ky	37
Knottsville, Tyler, W. Va	13
Knowersville, Albany, N. Y	82
Knowlesville, Orleans, N. Y	270
Knowlton, Warren, N. J	24
Knowlton, Marathon, Wis	39
Knowlton's Landing, Desha, Ark	41
Knox, (*c. h.,*) Stark, Ind	150
Knox, Waldo, Me	80
Knox, Albany, N. Y	90
Knox, Knox, Ohio	12
Knox, Clarion, Pa	16
Knoxborough, Oneida, N. Y	160
Knox Dale, Jefferson, Pa	20
Knox Hill, Walton, Fla	14
Knoxville, Greene, Ala	27
Knoxville, Lake, Cal	89
Knoxville, (*c. h.,*) Crawford, Ga	150
*Knoxville,** (*c. h.,*) Knox, Ill	1,200
*Knoxville,** (*c. h.,*) Marion, Iowa	820
Knoxville, Pendleton, Ky	6
Knoxville, Claiborne, La	8
Knoxville, Frederick, Md	240
Knoxville, Franklin, Miss	18
Knoxville, Ray, Mo	77
Knoxville, Jefferson, Ohio	39
Knoxville, Tioga, Pa	340
*Knoxville,** (*c. h.,*) Knox, Tenn	3,400
Knoxville, Cherokee, Tex	22
Koch's, Wayne, Ohio	15
Kodiak, ———, Alaska	68
Koeltztown, Osage, Mo	23
Kohlsville, Washington, Wis	12
*Kokomo,** (*c. h.,*) Howard, Ind	1,600
Koniska, McLeod, Minn	5
Koro, Winnebago, Wis	21
Koronis, Meeker, Minn	6
Kortright, Delaware, N. Y	30
Kosciusko, (*c. h.,*) Attala, Miss	620
Koskonong, Rock, Wis	32
Kossuth, Washington, Ind	16
Kossuth, Des Moines, Iowa	120
Kossuth, Alcorn, Miss	86
Kossuth, Auglaize, Ohio	41
Kossuth, Clarion, Pa	30

Post office	Amount
Kossuth Centre, Kossuth, Iowa	$3
Koszta, Iowa, Iowa	75
Kout's Station, Porter, Ind	78
Krakow, Franklin, Mo	12
Kratzerville, Snyder, Pa	34
Kreamer, Snyder, Pa	28
Kreidersville, Northampton, Pa	34
Kresgeville, Monroe, Pa	85
Krick's Mill, Berks, Pa	2
Kroghville, Jefferson, Wis	53
Kuckville, Orleans, N. Y	39
Kulpsville, Montgomery, Pa	89
Kunckle, Luzerne, Pa	11
Kunkletown, Monroe, Pa	14
Kutztown, Berks, Pa	340
Kyger, Gallia, Ohio	20
Kylertown, Clearfield, Pa	93
Kyserike, Ulster, N. Y	83
Kyte River, Ogle, Ill	16

L.

Post office	Amount
Labaddie, Franklin, Mo	57
Labadieville, Assumption, La	13
La Bajada, Santa Aña, N. Mex	12
La Belle, Lewis, Mo	87
Labette, Labette, Kans	26
Lacelle, Clark, Iowa	12
Lacey, Drew, Ark	12
Lacey, De Kalb, Ill	12
Lacey, Muscatine, Iowa	10
Lacey Spring, Rockingham, Va	36
Lacey's Spring, Morgan, Ala	6
Laceyville, Harrison, Ohio	26
Laceyville, Wyoming, Pa	200
Lackawack, Ulster, N. Y	31
Lackawanna, Luzerne, Pa	240
Lackawaxen, Pike, Pa	42
La Clair, De Kalb, Ill	41
La Clede, Fayette, Ill	130
Laclede, Linn, Mo	430
*Lacon,** (*c. h.,*) Marshall, Ill	1,700
Lacon, Maries, Mo	9
Lacona, Warren, Iowa	12
Lacona, Jefferson, Ky	27
Laconia, Harrison, Ind	54
*Laconia,** (*c. h.,*) Belknap, N. H	1,400
La Conner, Whatcom, Wash	10
La Crescent, Houston, Minn	130
La Crosse, Izard, Ark	120
La Crosse, Hancock, Ill	12
La Crosse, La Porte, Ind	34
*La Crosse,** (*c. h.,*) La Crosse, Wis	2,400
La Cueva, Mora, N. Mex	12
La Cygne, Linn, Kans	12
Laddsburgh, Bradford, Pa	14
Ladiesburgh, Frederick, Md	24
Ladiga, Calhoun, Ala	55
Ladoga,* Montgomery, Ind	460
Ladoga, Fond du Lac, Wis	79
Ladonia, Fannin, Tex	86
Ladora, Iowa, Iowa	81
Ladore, Neosho, Kans	12
Laenna, Logan, Ill	28
La Farge, Vernon, Wis	10
La Fargeville, Jefferson, N. Y	260

* Money-order office.

La Fayette, Contra Costa, Cal	$20
La Fayette, (*c. h.*,) Walker, Ga	120
La Fayette, Stark, Ill	170
La Fayette,* (*c. h.*,) Tippecanoe, Ind	3,800
La Fayette, Linn, Iowa	45
La Fayette, Doniphan, Kans	21
La Fayette, Christian, Ky	180
La Fayette, Gratiot, Mich	65
La Fayette, Sussex, N. J	150
La Fayette, Onondaga, N. Y	78
La Fayette, Madison, Ohio	42
La Fayette,* (*c. h.*,) Yam Hill, Oreg	210
La Fayette, McKean, Pa	12
La Fayette, Washington, R. I	55
La Fayette, (*c. h.*,) Macon, Tenn	110
La Fayette, Upshur, Tex	27
La Fayette, Montgomery, Va	29
La Fayette, Chippewa, Wis	8
La Fayette Springs, La Fayette, Miss	23
La Fayetteville, Dutchess, N. Y	39
La Fontaine, Wabash, Ind	90
La Fontaine, Josh Bell, Ky	4
Laforme's Store, Braxton, W. Va	12
La Fox, Kane, Ill	96
La Grande,* (*c. h.*,) Union, Oreg	320
La Grange, Phillips, Ark	31
La Grange, Stanislaus, Cal	34
La Grange, (*c. h.*,) Troup, Ga	1,000
La Grange,* (*c. h.*,) La Grange, Ind	640
La Grange, Lucas, Iowa	57
La Grange, Morris, Kans	12
La Grange, (*c. h.*,) Oldham, Ky	350
La Grange, Penobscot, Me	100
La Grange, Cass, Mich	70
La Grange,* Lewis, Mo	500
La Grange, Wyoming, N. Y	62
La Grange, Lenoir, N. C	120
La Grange, Lorain, Ohio	190
La Grange, Wyoming, Pa	14
La Grange,* Fayette, Tenn	450
La Grange, (*c. h.*,) Fayette, Tex	850
La Grange, Grand Isle, Vt	15
La Grange, Walworth, Wis	38
La Grange Bluff, Brown, Ill	12
La Grangeville, Dutchess, N. Y	37
La Gro, Wabash, Ind	380
Laguardo, Wilson, Tenn	22
La Harpe, Hancock, Ill	430
Lahaska, Bucks, Pa	180
Laing's, Monroe, Ohio	29
Laingsburgh, Shiawassee, Mich	340
Lairdsville, Oneida, N. Y	22
Lairdsville, Lycoming, Pa	60
Lair's Station, Harrison, Ky	31
La Junta, Mora, N. Mex	12
Lake, Spencer, Ind	26
Lake, Newaygo, Mich	12
Lake, Scott, Miss	130
Lake, Washington, N. Y	43
Lake, Stark, Ohio	84
Lake, Luzerne, Pa	10
Lake Addie, McLeod, Minn	9
Lake Arthur, Calcasieu, La	12
Lake Butler, (*c. h.*,) Bradford, Fla	12
Lake Charles, (*c. h.*,) Calcasieu, La	20
Lake City, Siskiyou, Cal	$170
Lake City, (*c. h.*,) Columbia, Fla	750
Lake City, Stark, Ind	3
Lake City, (*c. h.*,) Calhoun, Iowa	91
Lake City,* Wabashaw, Minn	1,600
Lake Comfort, Hyde, N. C	5
Lake Como, Wayne, Pa	55
Lake Creek, Williamson, Ill	16
Lake Creek, Benton, Mo	24
Lake Creswell, Panola, Miss	12
Lake Crystal, Blue Earth, Minn	7
Lake Drummond, Norfolk, Va	42
Lake Five, Washington, Wis	12
Lake Forest, Lake, Ill	420
Lake Fork, Ashland, Ohio	17
Lake Fremont, Sherburne, Minn	8
Lake Grove, Suffolk, N. Y	48
Lake Harold, Meeker, Minn	80
Lake Hill, Ulster, N. Y	24
Lake Johanna, Pope, Minn	12
Lakeland, Washington, Minn	140
Lake Landing, Hyde, N. C	19
Lake Lillian, Kandiyohi, Minn	10
Lake Linden, Houghton, Mich	72
Lake Maria, Green Lake, Wis	19
Lake Mill, Van Buren, Mich	58
Lake Mills, Winnebago, Iowa	36
Lake Mills,* Jefferson, Wis	360
Lakenan, Shelby, Mo	46
Lake Pleasant, Erie, Pa	20
Lakeport, Lake, Cal	82
Lakeport, Yankton, Dak	12
Lake Port, St. Clair, Mich	110
Lakeport, Madison, N. Y	37
Lake Providence, Carroll, La	100
Lake Ridge, Lenawee, Mich	21
Lake Ridge, Tompkins, N. Y	44
Lake Road, Niagara, N. Y	16
Lake Shetik, Murray, Minn	12
Lake Sibley, Cloud, Kans	100
Lake Side, Wayne, N. Y	130
Lake Spring, Dent, Mo	24
Lake Station, Greenwood, Colo	12
Lake Station, Lake, Ind	130
Lakesville, Dorchester, Md	23
Laketon, Wabash, Ind	40
Laketon, Berrien, Mich	69
Laketown, Carver, Minn	8
Lake Traverse, Stone, Minn	13
Lake View, Cook, Ill	12
Lakeview, Montcalm, Mich	52
Lakeview, Cuming, Nebr	12
Lake View, Erie, N. Y	44
Lake Village, (*c. h.*,) Chicot, Ark	98
Lake Village, McPherson, Kans	12
Lake Village, Belknap, N. H	910
Lakeville, Sonoma, Cal	69
Lakeville, Litchfield, Conn	350
Lakeville, St. Joseph, Ind	70
Lakeville, Plymouth, Mass	120
Lakeville, Oakland, Mich	20
Lakeville, Dakota, Minn	59
Lakeville, Stoddard, Mo	17
Lakeville, Livingston, N. Y	82
Lake Washington, LeSueur, Minn	10
Lake Zurich, Lake, Ill	85

* Money-order office.

Post office	Amount
Lakin's Grove, Hamilton, Iowa	$11
Lamar, Randolph, Ala	12
Lamar, Marshall, Miss	150
Lamar,* (*c. h.*,) Barton, Mo	240
Lamar, Clinton, Pa	100
Lamar, Refugio, Tex	12
Lamar Mills, Clinton, Pa	12
Lamar's Station, Nodaway, Mo	38
Lamartine, Columbia, Ark	13
Lamartine, Carroll, Ohio	84
Lamartine, Clarion, Pa	46
Lamartine, Fond du Lac, Wis	63
Lamberton, Racine, Wis	54
Lambertville, Monroe, Mich	44
Lambertville,* Hunterdon, N. J	1,300
Lamb's, Venango, Pa	87
Lambsburgh, Carroll, Va	6
Lamb's Corners, Broome, N. Y	40
Lamb's Creek, Tioga, Pa	41
La Mine, Cooper, Mo	39
Lamira, Belmont, Ohio	54
Lamoille, Bureau, Ill	430
Lamoille, Marshall, Iowa	12
Lamoille, Winona, Minn	2
Lamoine, Hancock, Me	36
Lamont, Ottawa, Mich	190
Lamonte, Pettis, Mo	200
La Motte, Jackson, Iowa	100
Lampasas, (*c. h.*,) Lampasas, Tex	160
Lampeter, Lancaster, Pa	50
Lamson's, Onondaga, N. Y	55
Lanark, Bradley, Ark	19
Lanark, Carroll, Ill	1,100
Lanark, Lehigh, Pa	12
Lancaster, Cass, Ill	29
Lancaster, Jefferson, Ind	77
Lancaster, Keokuk, Iowa	51
Lancaster, Atchison, Kans	21
Lancaster, (*c. h.*,) Garrard, Ky	730
Lancaster, Worcester, Mass	620
Lancaster,* (*c. h.*,) Schuyler, Mo	310
Lancaster,* (*c. h.*,) Coos, N. H	1,000
Lancaster, Erie, N. Y	430
Lancaster,* (*c. h.*,) Fairfield, Ohio	2,200
Lancaster, Lane, Oreg	20
Lancaster,* (*c. h.*,) Lancaster, Pa	2,800
Lancaster, Dallas, Tex	180
Lancaster,* (*c. h.*,) Grant, Wis	790
Lancaster C. H., Lancaster, S. C	65
Lancaster C. H., Lancaster, Va	31
L'Ance, Houghton, Mich	26
Lancha Plana, Amador, Cal	25
Landaff, Grafton, N. H	37
Landenburgh, Chester, Pa	44
Lander, Frederick, Md	24
Lander, Warren, Pa	97
Landersdale, Morgan, Ind	12
Landersville, Lawrence, Ala	19
Landingville, Schuylkill, Pa	93
Landisburgh, Perry, Pa	160
Landis' Store, Berks, Pa	9
Landis Valley, Lancaster, Pa	10
Landisville, Lancaster, Pa	56
Land Mark, Howard, Mo	12
Land of Promise, Princess Anne, Va	12
Landsdale, Montgomery, Pa	250
Lane, Montgomery, Ind	$12
Lane, Franklin, Kans	60
Lanesborough, Berkshire, Mass	240
Lanesborough, Fillmore, Minn	500
Lanesborough, Anson, N. C	10
Lanesborough, Susquehanna, Pa	210
Lanesfield, Johnson, Kans	86
Lane's Prairie, Maries, Mo	32
Lanesville, Litchfield, Conn	91
Lanesville, Harrison, Ind	130
Lanesville, Floyd, Ky	18
Lanesville, Essex, Mass	210
Lanesville, King William, Va	52
Laney, Shawanaw, Wis	12
Langdon, Peoria, Ill	9
Langdon, Sullivan, N. H	34
Langford, Erie, N. Y	24
Langley, Fairfax, Va	17
Langola, Benton, Minn	20
Langston, Montcalm, Mich	12
Langsville, Meigs, Ohio	16
L'Anguille, St. Francis, Ark	12
Langworth, Stanislaus, Cal	46
Langworthy, Jones, Iowa	74
Lannon Springs, Waukesha, Wis	12
Lannsdale, Monroe, Miss	12
Lansing, Cook, Ill	64
Lansing,* Allamakee, Iowa	1,200
LANSING,* Ingham, Mich	2,600
Lansing, Mower, Minn	170
Lansing, Tioga, Pa	12
Lansingburgh,* Rensselaer, N. Y	1,500
Lansingville, Tompkins, N. Y	38
Lantz Mills, Shenandoah, Va	14
Laona, Winnebago, Ill	73
Laona, Gage, Nebr	24
Laona, Chautauqua, N. Y	120
La Paz, (*c. h.*,) Yuma, Ariz	340
Lapeer,* (*c. h.*,) Lapeer, Mich	1,100
Lapeer, Cortland, N. Y	8
Lapidum, Harford, Md	66
La Place, St. Martins, La	22
La Plata, Macon, Mo	340
La Pointe, (*c. h.*,) Ashland, Wis	14
La Porte,* Plumas, Cal	340
La Porte, (*c. h.*,) Larimer, Colo	12
La Porte,* (*c. h.*,) La Porte, Ind	2,900
La Porte, Lorain, Ohio	86
Laporte, (*c. h.*,) Sullivan, Pa	340
Laporte City, Black Hawk, Iowa	260
La Prairie, Adams, Ill	150
La Prairie Centre, Marshall, Ill	36
Lapwai, Nez Perces, Idaho	100
Laramie City, (*c. h.*,) Albany, Wyo	1,800
Laredo, (*c. h.*,) Webb, Tex	150
Larimer Mills, Sarpy, Nebr	39
Larimer's Station, Westmoreland, Pa	98
Larissa, Winston, Ala	12
Larissa, Cherokee, Tex	59
Larkinsburgh, Clay, Ill	22
Larkin's Fork, Jackson, Ala	10
Larkinsville, Jackson, Ala	130
Larone, Somerset, Me	32
Larrabee, Manitowoc, Wis	20
Larrabee's Point, Addison, Vt	12

* Money-order office.

Larry's Creek, Lycoming, Pa	$24
La Rue, Benton, Ark	12
Larue,* Marion, Ohio	230
Larwill, Whitley, Ind	290
La Salle,* La Salle, Ill	2,600
La Salle, Monroe, Mich	63
La Salle, Niagara, N. Y	88
Las Cruces, Santa Barbara, Cal	12
Las Cruces, Doña Ana, N. Mex	100
Lasellsville, Fulton, N. Y	53
Lassen, Tehama, Cal	12
Lassiter's Mills, Randolph, N. C	11
Last Chance, Lucas, Iowa	22
Las Vegas, (*c. h.,*) San Miguel, N. Mex	270
Latham, Pike, Ohio	15
Lathrop, Clinton, Mo	490
Lathrop, Susquehanna, Pa	8
Latimore, Adams, Pa	12
Latonia Springs, Kenton, Ky	16
Latrobe, El Dorado, Cal	85
Latrobe, Johnson, Nebr	10
Latrobe, Westmoreland, Pa	780
Lattas, Ross, Ohio	22
Lattasburgh, Wayne, Ohio	47
Lattner's, Dubuque, Iowa	15
Latty, Des Moines, Iowa	12
Laubach, Northampton, Pa	220
Laud, Whitley, Ind	22
Lauderdale Station, Lauderdale, Miss	350
Laughlintown, Westmoreland, Pa	59
Laura, Miami, Ohio	38
Lauraville, Baltimore, Md	22
Laurel, Sussex, Del	510
Laurel, Franklin, Ind	290
Laurel, Marshall, Iowa	12
Laurel, Clermont, Ohio	41
Laurel Bluff, Muhlenburgh, Ky	25
Laurel Bridge, Laurel, Ky	12
Laurel Creek, Clay, Ky	3
Laurel Creek, Lincoln, W. Va	12
Laurel Factory,* Prince George's, Md	380
Laurel Fork, Carroll, Va	12
Laurel Gap, Greene, Tenn	8
Laurel Grove, Pittsylvania, Va	21
Laurel Hill, Neshoba, Miss	12
Laurel Hill, Perry, Mo	16
Laurel Hill, Richmond, N. C	7
Laurel Hill, De Kalb, Tenn	12
Laurel Iron Works, Mongalia, W. Va	12
Laurel Junction, Wood, W. Va	130
Laurel Mills, Rappahannock, Va	19
Laurel Point, Monongalia, W. Va	16
Laurel Ridge, Kanawha, W. Va	12
Laurel Run, Luzerne, Pa	210
Laurel Springs, Ashe, N. C	6
Laurelton, Union, Pa	94
Laurelville, Westmoreland, Pa	22
Laurens, Otsego, N. Y	200
*Laurens C. H.,** Laurens, S. C	450
Laurens Hill, Laurens, Ga	15
Laurinburgh, Richmond, N. C	9
Laury's Station, Lehigh, Pa	60
Lavalle, Sauk, Wis	$45
Lavansville, Somerset, Pa	47
La Vega, Des Moines, Iowa	18
La Vergne, Rutherford, Tenn	120
Lavernia, Wilson, Tex	14
Lawler, Chickasaw, Iowa	300
Lawndale, Logan, Ill	52
Lawn Ridge, Marshall, Ill	190
Lawrence, McHenry, Ill	43
Lawrence, Marion, Ind	85
*Lawrence,** (*c. h.,*) Douglas, Kans	3,500
Lawrence,* Essex, Mass	4,000
Lawrence,* Van Buren, Mich	380
Lawrence, Newton, Miss	43
Lawrence, Schuyler, N. Y	15
Lawrence, Washington, Ohio	20
Lawrence, Marquette, Wis	12
*Lawrenceburgh,** (*c. h.,*) Dearborn, Ind	1,400
Lawrenceburgh, Warren, Iowa	11
Lawrenceburgh, Cloud, Kans	12
Lawrenceburgh, (*c. h.,*) Anderson, Ky	330
Lawrenceburgh, Armstrong, Pa	890
Lawrenceburgh, (*c. h.,*) Lawrence, Tenn	190
Lawrenceville, Henry, Ala	34
Lawrenceville, (*c. h.,*) Gwinnett, Ga	170
Lawrenceville, (*c. h.,*) Lawrence, Ill	290
Lawrenceville, Dearborn, Ind	25
Lawrenceville, Mercer, N. J	270
Lawrenceville, St. Lawrence, N. Y	240
Lawrenceville, Tioga, Pa	370
Lawrenceville, (*c. h.,*) Brunswick, Va	280
Lawson, Washington, Mo	12
Lawson Station, Ray, Mo	12
Lawsonville, Rockingham, N. C	3
Lawsville Centre, Susquehanna, Pa	72
Lawton, Clinch, Ga	21
Lawton,* Van Buren, Mich	620
Lawtonville, Burke, Ga	84
Lawtonville, Beaufort, S. C	20
Lawyersville, Schoharie, N. Y	13
Layman, Washington, Ohio	16
Layton, Sussex, N. J	42
Laytonia, Venango, Pa	420
Layton's Station, Fayette, Pa	59
Laytonville, Montgomery, Md	46
Lazaretto Station, Delaware, Pa	29
Leacock, Lancaster, Pa	66
Lead Hill, Marion, Ark	37
Lead Mine, Tucker, W. Va	4
Leadsville, Randolph, W. Va	31
Leadvale, Jefferson, Tenn	96
Leaksville, Rockingham, N. C	94
Leaksville, Page, Va	10
Leaman Place, Lancaster, Pa	110
Leamon Corner, Hancock, Ind	12
Leanah, Estill, Ky	12
Leasburgh, Crawford, Mo	59
Leasburgh, Doña Ana, N. Mex	20
Leasburgh, Caswell, N. C	97
Lea's Chapel, Person, N. C	12
Leasuresville, Butler, Pa	30
Leathersville, Lincoln, Ga	9
Leatherwood, Guernsey, Ohio	90

* Money-order office.

Leatherwood, Clarion, Pa	$40
*Leavenworth,** (*c. h.*,) Crawford, Ind	370
Leavenworth, Brown, Minn	29
*Leavenworth City,** (*c. h.*,) Leavenworth, Kans	4,000
Leavitt, Carroll, Ohio	37
Leavittsburgh, Trumbull, Ohio	200
Lebanon, (*c. h.*,) De Kalb, Ala	120
Lebanon, New London, Conn	180
Lebanon, Kent, Del	81
Lebanon,* St. Clair, Ill	1,000
*Lebanon,** (*c. h.*,) Boone, Ind	760
Lebanon, Van Buren, Iowa	52
*Lebanon,** (*c. h.*,) Marion, Ky	1,200
Lebanon, York, Me	47
Lebanon, (*c. h.*,) Laclede, Mo	370
Lebanon,* Grafton, N. H	1,300
Lebanon, Hunterdon, N. J	170
Lebanon, Madison, N. Y	91
*Lebanon,** (*c. h.*,) Warren, Ohio	1,700
Lebanon, Linn, Oreg	88
*Lebanon,** (*c. h.*,) Lebanon, Pa	1,600
*Lebanon,** (*c. h.*,) Wilson, Tenn	1,300
Lebanon, (*c. h.*,) Russell, Va	140
Lebanon Church, Allegheny, Pa	16
Lebanon Church, Shenandoah, Va	22
Lebanon Junction, Bullitt, Ky	98
Lebœuf, Erie, Pa	51
Le Claire,* Scott, Iowa	460
Lecompton, Douglas, Kans	110
Lecompton, Monroe, Ohio	16
Leconte's Mills, Clearfield, Pa	44
Lederachsville, Montgomery, Pa	14
Ledge Dale, Wayne, Pa	51
Ledger, Mitchell, N. C	3
Ledyard, New London, Conn	42
Ledyard, Cayuga, N. Y	83
Lee, Warrick, Ind	4
Lee, Penobscot, Me	120
Lee,* Berkshire, Mass	1,500
Lee, Strafford, N. H	51
Lee, Oneida, N. Y	27
Lee,* Athens, Ohio	230
Lee Centre, Lee, Ill	300
Lee Centre, Oneida, N. Y	180
Leechburgh, Johnston, N. C	5
Leechburgh, Armstrong, Pa	560
Leech Lake, Cass, Minn	10
Leech's Corners, Mercer, Pa	33
Leechville, Beaufort, N. C	16
Leeds, Androscoggin, Me	65
Leeds, Hampshire, Mass	220
Leeds, Greene, N. Y	320
Leeds, Washington, Utah	12
Leeds, Columbia, Wis	100
Leeds Centre, Columbia, Wis	50
Leeds Junction, Adroscoggin, Me	61
Leeds Point, Atlantic, N. J	73
Leedston, Stearns, Minn	10
Leedsville, Monmouth, N. J	25
Leedsville, Dutchess, N. Y	27
Leesburgh, Cherokee, Ala	26
Leesburgh, Lemhi, Idaho	12
Leesburgh, Kosciusko, Ind	210
Leesburgh, Harrison, Ky	63
Leesburgh, Cumberland, N. J	44
Leesburgh, Highland, Ohio	$240
Leesburgh, Mercer, Pa	46
Leesburgh, Washington, Tenn	34
*Leesburgh,** (*c. h.*,) Loudoun, Va	900
Lee's Creek, Crawford, Ark	20
Lee's Creek, Clinton, Ohio	10
Lee's Cross Roads, Cumberland, Pa	76
Leesport, Bucks, Pa	320
Lee's Summit, Jackson, Mo	790
Leesville, Middlesex, Conn	25
Leesville, Boone, Ill	6
Leesville, Lawrence, Ind	51
Leesville, Henry, Mo	61
Leesville, Schoharie, N. Y	26
Leesville, Robeson, N. C	12
Leesville, Carroll, Ohio	110
Leesville, Lexington, S. C	25
Leesville, Campbell, Va	31
Leesville Cross Roads, Crawford, Ohio	47
Leetonia, Columbiana, Ohio	460
Leetown, Jefferson, W. Va	100
Leetsdale, Allegheny, Pa	18
Lee Valley, Hawkins, Tenn	7
Le Fever Falls, Ulster, N. Y	12
Leghorn, Pottawatomie, Kans	12
Le Grand, Marshall, Iowa	300
Lehi, Jefferson, Ark	12
Lehi City, Utah, Utah	73
Lehigh Gap, Carbon, Pa	95
Lehigh Tannery, Carbon, Pa	12
Lehighton, Carbon, Pa	410
Lehigh Valley, Lehigh, Pa	33
Lehman, Luzerne, Pa	40
Leicester, Worcester, Mass	650
Leicester, Buncombe, N. C	16
Leicester, Addison, Vt	37
Leicester, Dane, Wis	81
Leidy, Clinton, Pa	18
Leighton, Franklin, Ala	20
Leighton, Mahaska, Iowa	83
Leighton, Hennepin, Minn	5
Leighton's Corners, Carroll, N. H	30
Leinbach's, Berks, Pa	22
Leipersville, Delaware, Pa	65
Leipsic, Kent, Del	100
Leipsic, Orange, Ind	36
Leipsic, Putnam, Ohio	170
Leistville, Pickaway, Ohio	35
Leitersburgh, Washington, Md	110
Leithsville, Northampton, Pa	17
Leland, La Salle, Ill	690
Leland, Leelenaw, Mich	94
Leland, Josephine, Oreg	26
Lemars, Plymouth, Iowa	12
Lemington, Essex, Vt	5
Lemon, Wyoming, Pa	21
Lemond, Steele, Minn	8
Lemont,* Cook, Ill	910
Lemont, Centre, Pa	12
Lemonweir, Juneau, Wis	49
Lempster, Sullivan, N. H	83
Lena,* Stephenson, Ill	870
Lenape, Leavenworth, Kans	12
Lenape, Chester, Pa	12
Lenexa, Johnson, Kans	20

*Money-order office.

Lenhartsville, Berks, Pa	$32
Lenni Mills, Delaware, Pa	100
Lenoir, (*c. h.*,) Caldwell, N. C	290
Lenoir's, Roane, Tenn	32
Lenora, Fillmore, Minn	120
Lenox, Kane, Ill	12
Lenox, (*c. h.*,) Berkshire, Mass	900
Lenox, Madison, N. Y	44
Lenox, Ashtabula, Ohio	84
Lenox Castle, Rockingham, N. C	23
Lenox Furnace, Berkshire, Mass	160
Lenoxville, Susquehanna, Pa	56
Lenz, Hennepin, Minn	28
Lenzburgh, St. Clair, Ill	66
Leo, White, Ga	12
Leo, Allen, Ind	78
Leo, Stanly, N. C	5
Leominster, Worcester, Mass	1,500
Leon, Crenshaw, Ala	6
Leon, Whitesides, Ill	16
Leon,* (*c. h.*,) Decatur, Iowa	520
Leon, Cattaraugus, N. Y	110
Leon, Ashtabula, Ohio	16
Leon, Madison, Va	13
Leon, Monroe, Wis	82
Leona, Bradford, Pa	58
Leona, Leon, Tex	67
Leonardsburgh, Delaware, Ohio	58
Leonardsville, Madison, N. Y	260
Leonardtown,* (*c. h.*,) St. Mary's, Md.	310
Leonardville, Monmouth, N. J	43
Leoni, Jackson, Mich	130
Leonia, Bergen, N. J	43
Leonidas, St. Joseph, Mich	180
Leon Springs, Bexar, Tex	19
Leopard, Chester, Pa	35
Leopold, Perry, Ind	37
Leota Landing, Washington, Miss	10
Leoti, Pike, Ind	8
L'Erable, Iroquois, Ill	16
Le Raysville, Jefferson, N. Y	19
Le Raysville, Bradford, Pa	260
Lê Roy, Union, Dak	12
Leroy, McLean, Ill	390
Le Roy, Lake, Ind	12
Leroy, Bremer, Iowa	20
Le Roy,* Coffey, Kans	310
Le Roy,* Mower, Minn	520
Le Roy, Barton, Mo	21
Le Roy,* Genesee, N. Y	2,200
Le Roy, Medina, Ohio	340
Le Roy, Bradford, Pa	68
Le Roy, Jackson, W. Va	29
Leroy, Dodge, Wis	33
Le Roy Station, Monroe, Wis	28
Leslie, Ingham, Mich	500
Leslie, Van Wert, Ohio	20
Lesser Cross Roads, Somerset, N. J.	67
Lester, Marion, Ill	22
Lester, Black Hawk, Iowa	21
Lester's, Giles, Tenn	25
Lester's District, Burke, Ga	120
Lesterville, Reynolds, Mo	9
Le Sueur,* (*c. h.*,) Le Sueur, Minn	540
Letart, Mason, W. Va	51
Letart Falls, Meigs, Ohio	64
Letcher, Bath, Va	$5
Letohatchee, Lowndes, Ala	20
Letsinger, Roane, Tenn	12
Letter Gap, Gilmer, W. Va	5
Letts, Louisa, Iowa	260
Lettsville, Daviess, Ind	12
Levan, Juab, Utah	12
Levanna, Cayuga, N. Y	42
Levanna, Brown, Ohio	34
Levant, Penobscot, Me	58
Levee, Montgomery, Ky	24
Level, Warren, Ohio	33
Level Land, Abbeville, S. C	5
Leverett, Franklin, Mass	250
Levering, Knox, Ohio	59
Levingood, Pendleton, Ky	26
Lewes,* Sussex, Del	460
Lewinsville, Fairfax, Va	9
Lewis, Kendall, Ill	8
Lewis, Vigo, Ind	52
Lewis,* (*c. h.*,) Cass, Iowa	480
Lewis, Essex, N. Y	92
Lewisberry, York, Pa	120
Lewisborough, Westchester, N. Y	37
Lewisburgh, Conway, Ark	140
Lewisburgh, Wayne, Iowa	32
Lewisburgh, Preble, Ohio	120
Lewisburgh,* (*c. h.*,) Union, Pa	2,100
Lewisburgh, (*c. h.*,) Marshall, Tenn	170
Lewisburgh,* (*c. h.*,) Greenbrier, W. Va	570
Lewis Centre, Delaware, Ohio	180
Lewis Creek, Shelby, Ind	23
Lewisport, Hancock, Ky	130
Lewis' Station, Escambia, Ala	7
Lewis' Store, Spottsylvania, Va	8
Lewiston, Trinity, Cal	37
Lewiston,* (*c. h.*,) Nez Perces, Idaho.	230
Lewiston, Cherokee, Kans	12
Lewiston,* Androscoggin, Me	2,700
Lewiston, Dakota, Minn	54
Lewiston, Niagara, N. Y	450
Lewiston, Columbia, Wis	19
Lewiston Station, Columbia, Wis	12
Lewistown,* (*c. h.*,) Fulton, Ill	1,000
Lewistown, Frederick, Md	44
Lewistown, Logan, Ohio	27
Lewistown,* (*c. h.*,) Mifflin, Pa	1,800
Lewistown, (*c. h.*,) La Fayette, Ark	80
Lewisville, Henry, Ind	240
Lewisville, Forsyth, N. C	9
Lewisville, Monroe, Ohio	43
Lewisville, Polk, Oreg	12
Lewisville, Chester, Pa	96
Lewisville, Denton, Tex	88
Lexington, Santa Clara, Cal	56
Lexington,* (*c. h.*,) Oglethorpe, Ga	270
Lexington, McLean, Ill	660
Lexington, (*c. h.*,) Scott, Ind	260
Lexington, Washington, Iowa	12
Lexington,* (*c. h.*,) Fayette, Ky	3,800
Lexington, Somerset, Me	20
Lexington, Middlesex, Mass	480
Lexington,* (*c. h.*,) Sanilac, Mich	620
Lexington, Le Sueur, Minn	54
Lexington, (*c. h.*,) Holmes, Miss	640

* Money-order office.

Post office	Compensation
Lexington,* (*c. h.*,) La Fayette, Mo	$1,900
Lexington, Greene, N. Y	77
Lexington, (*c. h.*,) Davidson, N. C	330
Lexington, Richland, Ohio	280
Lexington, (*c. h.*,) Henderson, Tenn	110
Lexington, Burleson, Tex	160
Lexington,* (*c. h.*,) Rockbridge, Va	2,200
Lexington C. H., Lexington, S. C	100
Leyden, Cook, Ill	69
Leyden, Franklin, Mass	39
Leyden, Lewis, N. Y	200
Leyden, Rock, Wis	14
Leyden Centre, Cook, Ill	12
Liberty, Ouachita, Ark	10
Liberty, San Joaquin, Cal	93
Liberty, Union, Dak	34
Liberty, Adams, Ill	140
Liberty,* (*c. h.*,) Union, Ind	440
Liberty, Clarke, Iowa	47
Liberty, Montgomery, Kans	12
Liberty, (*c. h.*,) Casey, Ky	45
Liberty, Waldo, Me	140
Liberty, Jackson, Mich	81
Liberty, (*c. h.*,) Amite, Miss	250
Liberty,* (*c. h.*,) Clay, Mo	890
Liberty, Pawnee, Nebr	20
Liberty, Sullivan, N. Y	200
Liberty, Montgomery, Ohio	58
Liberty, Tioga, Pa	240
Liberty, De Kalb, Tenn	57
Liberty, (*c. h.*,) Liberty, Tex	150
Liberty, Rich, Utah	4
Liberty,* (*c. h.*,) Bedford, Va	810
Liberty, Vernon, Wis	76
Liberty Centre, Warren, Iowa	15
Liberty Centre, Henry, Ohio	160
Liberty Corner, Somerset, N. J	84
Liberty Corners, Crawford, Ohio	32
Liberty Corners, Bradford, Pa	18
Liberty Falls, Sullivan, N. Y	59
Liberty Hall, Newberry, S. C	6
Liberty Hill, Dallas, Ala	26
Liberty Hill, New London, Conn	120
Liberty Hill, Pike, Ga	20
Liberty Hill, Williamson, Tex	16
Liberty Mills, Wabash, Ind	150
Liberty Mills, Orange, Va	110
Liberty Pole, Vernon, Wis	76
Liberty Prairie, Madison, Ill	12
Liberty Ridge, Grant, Wis	12
Liberty Springs, Van Buren, Ark	12
Liberty Square, Lancaster, Pa	43
Libertytown, Frederick, Md	170
Libertyville, Lake, Ill	160
Libertyville, Jefferson, Iowa	92
Libertyville, St. Francois, Mo	71
Libertyville, Sussex, N. J	21
Libertyville, Ulster, N. Y	8
Library, Allegheny, Pa	71
Lick, Fannin, Tex	12
Lick Creek, Union, Ill	13
Lick Creek, Hickman, Tenn	8
Licking, Texas, Mo	94
Licking Valley, Muskingum, Ohio	69
Lickingville, Clarion, Pa	21
Lick Run, Hamilton, Ohio	26

Post office	Compensation
Licksville, Frederick, Md	$12
Liddesdale, Columbia, Ark	15
Light Street, Columbia, Pa	100
Ligonier,* Noble, Ind	1,100
Ligonier, Vernon, Mo	12
Ligonier, Westmoreland, Pa	180
Likens, Crawford, Ohio	20
Lilesville, Anson, N. C	54
Lillard's Mills, Marshall, Tenn	20
Lillington, New Hanover, N. C	16
Lilly, Scioto, Ohio	23
Lilly Dale, Perry, Ind	10
Lilly Pond, Wright, Minn	12
Lima, Adams, Ill	96
Lima, La Grange, Ind	480
Lima, Fayette, Iowa	12
Lima, Clay, Kans	13
Lima, Washtenaw, Mich	48
Lima, Livingston, N. Y	1,600
Lima,* (*c. h.*,) Allen, Ohio	1,800
Lima, Delaware, Pa	55
Lima, Greenville, S. C	11
Lima Centre, Rock, Wis	130
Limaville, Stark, Ohio	160
Limber Lost, Adams, Ind	15
Lime Creek, Cerro Gordo, Iowa	9
Lime Hill, Bradford, Pa	26
Limekiln, Berks, Pa	12
Limeport, Lehigh, Pa	15
Limerick, Bureau, Ill	47
Limerick, York, Me	300
Limerick, Jefferson, N. Y	61
Limerick, Montgomery, Pa	82
Limerick Station, Montgomery, Pa	200
Lime Ridge, Columbia, Pa	55
Lime Ridge, Sauk, Wis	41
Lime Rock, Litchfield, Conn	200
Lime Rock, Outagamie, Wis	36
Lime Spring, Howard, Iowa	84
Limestone, Kankakee, Ill	23
Limestone, Washington, Kans	13
Limestone, Aroostook, Me	12
Limestone, Cattaraugus, N. Y	170
Limestone, Clarion, Pa	82
Limestone, Marshall, W. Va	3
Limestone Cove, Carter, Tenn	12
Limestone Springs, Spartanburgh, S. C	37
Limestone Springs, Greene, Tenn	24
Limestoneville, Montour, Pa	80
Limington, York, Me	160
Limitar, Socorro, N. Mex	18
Lincklaen, Chenango, N. Y	55
Lincoln, Talladega, Ala	12
Lincoln,* Placer, Cal	210
Lincoln, Clay, Dak	46
Lincoln, Sussex, Del	290
Lincoln,* (*c. h.*,) Logan, Ill	2,000
Lincoln, Cass, Ind	42
Lincoln, Polk, Iowa	18
Lincoln, Penobscot, Me	340
Lincoln, Middlesex, Mass	160
Lincoln, (*c. h.*,) Mason, Mich	110
Lincoln, Wabashaw, Minn	43
Lincoln, Benton, Mo	84
Lincoln, Deer Lodge, Mont	100

* Money-order office.

Office	
LINCOLN,* (*c. h.*,) Lancaster, Nebr	$1,700
Lincoln, Sussex, N. J	12
Lincoln, Wayne, N. Y	43
Lincoln, Gallia, Ohio	16
Lincoln, Polk, Oreg	7
Lincoln, Lancaster, Pa	70
Lincoln, Addison, Vt	95
Lincoln, Loudoun, Va	92
Lincoln, Kewaunee, Wis	12
Lincoln Centre, Grundy, Iowa	12
Lincoln Centre, Lincoln, Kans	12
Lincoln Centre, Penobscot, Me	160
Lincoln Centre, Polk, Wis	32
Lincoln City, Summit, Colo	20
Lincoln Falls, Sullivan, Pa	7
Lincoln Green, Johnson, Ill	9
Lincolnton, (*c. h.*,) Lincoln, Ga	35
Lincolnton, (*c. h.*,) Lincoln, N. C	360
Lincoln University, Chester, Pa	190
Lincolnville, Wabash, Ind	12
Lincolnville, Marion, Kans	8
Lincolnville, Pulaski, Ky	4
Lincolnville, Waldo, Me	170
Lincolnville, Crawford, Pa	38
Lind, Waupaca, Wis	37
Lindale, Osage, Kans	12
Lindale, Clermont, Ohio	42
Linden, Marengo, Ala	87
Linden, San Joaquin, Cal	23
Linden, Montgomery, Ind	90
Linden, Dallas, Iowa	21
Linden, Genesee, Mich	240
Linden, Brown, Minn	16
Linden, Copiah, Miss	20
Linden, Atchison, Mo	29
Linden, Union, N. J	24
Linden, Genesee, N. Y	110
Linden, Lycoming, Pa	66
Linden, (*c. h.*,) Perry, Tenn	42
Linden, (*c. h.*,) Davis, Tex	24
Linden, Warren, Va	97
Linden, Iowa, Wis	140
Linden Hall, Centre, Pa	47
Lindenville, Ashtabula, Ohio	130
Lindenwood, Ogle, Ill	97
Linder, Jasper, Ill	6
Lindersville, Adair, Mo	10
Lind Grove, Morehouse, La	12
Lindley, Grundy, Mo	130
Lindleytown, Steuben, N. Y	130
Lindly's Mills, Washington, Pa	31
Lindsborg, McPherson, Kans	12
Lindsey, (*c. h.*,) Ottawa, Kans	100
Lindsey, Sandusky, Ohio	140
Lindsey's Mill, Trigg, Ky	12
Lindseyville, Worcester, Md	16
Lindside, Monroe, W. Va	16
Line, Lyon, Kans	12
Line, Morehouse, La	12
Line Creek, Bullock, Ala	12
Line Creek, Pulaski, Ky	3
Line Creek, Laurens, S. C	12
Line Lexington, Montgomery, Pa	170
Line Mountain, Northumberland, Pa	10
Line's Hollow, Crawford, Pa	69

Office	
Lineville, Clay, Ala	$35
Lineville, Venango, Pa	16
Lineville Station, Crawford, Pa	230
Linganore, Frederick, Md	26
Linglestown, Dauphin, Pa	71
Linkinson, Franklin, N. Y	39
Linkwood, Dorchester, Md	45
Linlithgo, Columbia, N. Y	53
Linn, (*c. h.*,) Osage, Mo	150
Linn Creek, (*c. h.*,) Camden, Mo	170
Linneus, Aroostook, Me	80
Linneus,* (*c. h.*,) Linn, Mo	510
Linn Flat, Nacogdoches, Tex	12
Linn Grove, Adams, Ind	61
Linn's Valley, Kern, Cal	49
Linnville, Licking, Ohio	59
Linnwood, Osage, Mo	30
Linton, Greene, Ind	77
Linton, Des Moines, Iowa	17
Linton, Trigg, Ky	18
Linton, Jefferson, Ohio	60
Linton Mills, Coshocton, Ohio	12
Linville, Rockingham, Va	12
Linwood, Pike, Ala	12
Linwood, Carroll, Md	53
Linwood, Anoka, Minn	9
Linwood, Butler, Nebr	20
Linwood, Davidson, N. C	12
Linwood, Hamilton, Ohio	57
Linwood, Bradley, Tenn	12
Linwood, Cherokee, Tex	7
Linwood Station, Delaware, Pa	210
Lionville, Chester, Pa	130
Lisbon, Union, Ark	32
Lisbon, New London, Conn	160
Lisbon, Kendall, Ill	310
Lisbon, Noble, Ind	54
Lisbon,* Linn, Iowa	440
Lisbon, Claiborne, La	20
Lisbon, Androscoggin, Me	260
Lisbon, Howard, Md	61
Lisbon, Ottawa, Mich	160
Lisbon, Sarpy, Nebr	12
Lisbon, Grafton, N. H	500
Lisbon, St. Lawrence, N. Y	23
Lisbon, Dallas, Tex	12
Lisbon, Bedford, Va	12
Lisbon Centre, St. Lawrence, N. Y	150
Lisbon Falls, Androscoggin, Me	530
Lisburn, Cumberland, Pa	70
Liscomb, Marshall, Iowa	100
Lisha's Kill, Albany, N. Y	22
Lisle, Broome, N. Y	310
Lisle Station, Du Page, Ill	89
Litchfield,* (*c. h.*,) Litchfield, Conn	1,200
Litchfield,* Montgomery, Ill	2,000
Litchfield, Taylor, Iowa	14
Litchfield, (*c. h.*,) Grayson, Ky	210
Litchfield, Kennebec, Me	52
Litchfield,* Hillsdale, Mich	390
Litchfield, (*c. h.*,) Meeker, Minn	240
Litchfield, Herkimer, N. Y	18
Litchfield, Medina, Ohio	180
Litchfield, Bradford, Pa	37
Litchfield Corners, Kennebec, Me	150
Liter, Morgan, Ill	12

* Money-order office.

Post office	Amount
Lithgow, Dutchess, N. Y	$78
Lithonia, De Kalb, Ga	35
Lithopolis, Fairfield, Ohio	130
Litiz,* Lancaster, Pa	510
Little Black, Ripley, Mo	18
Little Britain, Lancaster, Pa	24
Little Canada, Ramsey, Minn	16
Little Cedar, Mitchell, Iowa	12
Little Chucky, Greene, Tenn	10
Little Chute, Outagamie, Wis	78
Little Compton, Carroll, Mo	19
Little Compton, Newport, R. I	240
Little Cooley, Crawford, Pa	55
Little Creek, Pike, Ky	12
Little Creek Landing, Kent, Del	50
Little Detroit, Tazewell, Ill	11
Little Doe, Johnson, Tenn	8
Little Eagle, Scott, Ky	43
Little Elk, Benton, Oreg	12
Little Falls, (*c. h.*,) Morrison, Minn	130
Little Falls, Passaic, N. J	150
Little Falls,* Herkimer, N. Y	2, 400
Little Flat, Bath, Ky	8
Little Gap, Carbon, Pa	11
Little Genesee, Allegany, N. Y	110
Little Georgetown, Berkeley, W. Va	38
Little Grant, Grant, Wis	20
Little Gunpowder, Baltimore, Md	63
Little Hickman, Jessamine, Ky	14
Little Hockhocking, Washington, Ohio	52
Little Indian, Cass, Ill	12
Little Lake, Mendocino, Cal	56
Little Lake, Adams, Wis	12
Little Lot, Hickman, Tenn	10
Little Marsh, Tioga, Pa	21
Little Meadows, Susquehanna, Pa	59
Little Mount, Spencer, Ky	14
Little Mountain, Newberry, S. C	12
Little Neck, Queens, N. Y	84
Little Oak, Crenshaw, Ala	12
Little Osage, Vernon, Mo	97
Little Otter, Braxton, W. Va	9
Little Plymouth, King and Queen, Va	36
Little Port, Clayton, Iowa	21
Little Prairie, Walworth, Wis	23
Little Prairie Ronde, Cass, Mich	51
Little Rest, Dutchess, N. Y	33
Little River, Cherokee, Ala	12
Little River, Mendocino, Cal	60
Little River, Allen, Ind	11
Little River, Horry, S. C	89
Little River, Floyd, Va	5
LITTLE ROCK,* (*c. h.*,) Pulaski, Ark	3, 400
Little Rock, Kendall, Ill	88
Little Rock, Marion, S. C	120
Little Sandusky Wyandot, Ohio	63
Little Sandy, Jefferson, Nebr	12
Little Sewall Mountain, Greenbrier, W. Va	12
Little Sioux, Harrison, Iowa	190
Little's Mills, Richmond, N. C	3
Little's Mills, Tyler, W. Va	9
Little Spring, Madison, Ark	20
Littlestown, Adams, Pa	350

Post office	Amount
Little Sturgeon, Door, Wis	$24
Little Suamico, Oconto, Wis	87
Little Sugar Loaf, Bladen, N. C	12
Littlesville, Winston, Ala	12
Little Toby, Clearfield, Pa	57
Littleton, Arapahoe, Colo	12
Littleton, Schuyler, Ill	87
Littleton, Aroostook, Me	61
Littleton, Middlesex, Mass	320
Littleton,* Grafton, N. H	1, 100
Littleton, Morris, N. J	12
Littleton, Halifax, N. C	220
Littleton, Sussex, Va	37
Little Traverse, (*c. h.*,) Emmett, Mich	29
Little Turkey, Chickasaw, Iowa	27
Little Utica, Onondaga, N. Y	45
Little Valley, Olmsted, Minn	31
Little Valley, Cattaraugus, N. Y	410
Little Warrior, Blount, Ala	12
Little Wind River, Sweetwater, Wyo	
Little Wolf, Waupaca, Wis	12
Little Yadkin, Stokes, N. C	17
Little York, Nevada, Cal	17
Little York, Warren, Ill	17
Little York, Washington, Ind	140
Little York, Meade, Ky	25
Little York, Greene, Mo	11
Little York, Hunterdon, N. J	49
Little York, Cortland, N. Y	35
Little York, Montgomery, Ohio	49
Littsville, Nodaway, Mo	43
Litwalton, Lancaster, Va	18
Litzenberg, Lehigh, Pa	12
Lively Grove, Washington, Ill	12
Lively Oaks, Lancaster, Va	32
Live Oak, San Joaquin, Cal	12
Live Oak, Suwannee, Fla	12
Live Oak Store, Livingston, La	330
Livermore, Alameda, Cal	12
Livermore, McLean, Ky	12
Livermore, Androscoggin, Me	63
Livermore, Westmoreland, Pa	130
Livermore Centre, Androscoggin, Me	240
Livermore Falls, Androscoggin, Me	47
Liverpool, Fulton, Ill	340
Liverpool, Onondaga, N. Y	24
Liverpool, Medina, Ohio	340
Liverpool, Perry, Pa	140
Livingston, (*c. h.*,) Sumter, Ala	320
Livingston, Floyd, Ga	490
Livingston, Clark, Ill	9
Livingston, Appanoose, Iowa	48
Livingston, Essex, N. J	44
Livingston, Columbia, N. Y	24
Livingston, (*c. h.*,) Overton, Tenn	74
Livingston, (*c. h.*,) Polk, Tex	95
Livingstonville, Schoharie, N. Y	200
Livonia, Washington, Ind	34
Livonia, Point Coupee, La	77
Livonia, Sherburne, Minn	12
Livonia, Putnam, Mo	9
Livonia, Livingston, N. Y	5
Livonia Station, Livingston, N. Y	140
Lizemore's, Clay, W. Va	550
Lizzard, Pocahontas, Iowa	12

* Money-order office.

8 P O

Post office	Compensation
Llano, (*c. h.*,) Llano, Tex	$40
Llewellyn, Schuylkill, Pa	69
Lloyd, Tioga, Pa	12
Lloyds, Essex, Va	21
Loachapoka, Lee, Ala	350
Loag, Chester, Pa	51
Loami, Sangamon, Ill	110
Lobachsville, Berks,Pa	12
Lobelville, Perry, Tenn	13
Lochleven, Lunenburgh, Va	20
Loch Lomond, Goochland, Va	9
Loch Sheldrake, Sullivan, N. Y	38
Lock, La Salle, Ill	12
Lock, Knox, Ohio	42
Lock Berlin, Wayne, N. Y	54
Lockbourne, Franklin, Ohio	82
Locke, Elkhart, Ind	68
Locke, Ingham, Mich	16
Locke, Cayuga, N. Y	100
Lockeford, San Joaquin, Cal	95
Locke's Mills, Oxford, Me	130
Lockhart, Lauderdale, Miss	8
Lockhart, (*c. h.*,) Caldwell, Tex	310
Lockhart's, Jackson, W. Va	12
Lockhart's Run, Wood, W. Va	4
Lockhaven,* (*c. h.*,) Clinton, Pa	2,600
Lockington, Shelby, Ohio	51
Lockland Station, Hamilton, Ohio	280
Lock No. 4, Washington, Pa	16
Lockport,* Will, Ill	1,200
Lockport, Carroll, Ind	19
Lockport, Henry, Ky	16
Lockport,* (*c. h.*,) Niagara, N. Y	4,000
Lockport, Williams, Ohio	23
Lockport Station,Westmoreland, Pa	42
Lockridge, Jefferson, Iowa	80
Locksburgh, (*c. h.*,) Sevier, Ark	12
Lock Seventeen, Tuscarawas, Ohio	78
Lock's Village, Franklin, Mass	51
Locktown, Hunterdon, N. J	19
Lockville, Chatham, N. C	12
Lockville, Fairfield, Ohio	20
Locust Bottom, Botetourt, Va	56
Locust Corner, Clermont, Ohio	30
Locust Creek, Louisa, Va	12
Locust Gap, Northumberland, Pa	12
Locust Grove, Williamson, Ill	10
Locust Grove, Atchison, Kans	13
Locust Grove, Callaway, Ky	6
Locust Grove, Kent, Md	71
Locust Grove, Clarke, Mo	6
Locust Grove, Lewis, N. Y	74
Locust Grove, Adams, Ohio	63
Locust Grove, Fulton, Pa	12
Locust Grove, Orange, Va	6
Locust Hill, Knox, Mo	28
Locust Hill, Caswell, N. C	23
Locust Hill, Washington, Pa	38
Locust Hill, Middlesex, Va	17
Locust Lane, Winneshiek, Iowa	50
Locust Lane, Indiana, Pa	36
Locust Level, Stanly, N. C	12
Locust Level, Halifax, Va	12
Locust Mills, Bracken, Ky	6
Locust Mound, Miller, Mo	62
Locust Mount, Washington, Tenn	4

Post office	Compensation
Locust Mount, Accomack, Va	$43
Locust Point, Ottawa, Ohio	18
Locust Ridge, Brown, Ohio	15
Locust Spring, Greene, Tenn	12
Locust Valley, Queens, N. Y	90
Locust Valley, Lehigh, Pa	24
Locustville, Accomack, Va	41
Lodi, Clay, Dak	12
Lodi, Coweta, Ga	5
Lodi, Wabash, Ind	11
Lodi, Choctaw, Miss	24
Lodi, Newton, Mo	12
Lodi, Dakota, Nebr	12
Lodi, Bergen, N. J	230
Lodi, Seneca, N. Y	380
Lodi, Medina, Ohio	190
Lodi, (*c. h.*,) Wilson, Tex	12
Lodi, Washington, Va	5
Lodi,* Columbia, Wis	640
Lodi Centre, Seneca, N. Y	36
Lodi Station, Kane, Ill	200
Lodore, Amelia, Va	12
Logan, Edgar, Ill	19
Logan, Dearborn, Ind	14
Logan, Harrison, Iowa	150
Logan, Dodge, Nebr	50
Logan, Schuyler, N. Y	16
Logan,* (*c. h.*,) Hocking, Ohio	550
Logan, (*c. h.*,) Cache, Utah	290
Logan C. H., Logan, W. Va	16
Logan Mills, Clinton, Pa	25
Logan's Creek, Reynolds, Mo	22
Logansport, Hamilton, Ill	9
Logansport,* (*c. h.*,) Cass, Ind	2,800
Logansport, Butler, Ky	16
Logansport, De Soto, La	10
Logan's Store, Rutherford, N. C	3
Loganville, Logan, Ohio	12
Loganville, York, Pa	20
Loganville, Sauk, Wis	190
Log Cabin, Morgan, Ohio	21
Loggy Bayou, Natchitoches, La	12
Log Town, Ouachita, La	6
Lohmansville, Washington, Minn	12
Loma, Conejos, Colo	12
Lomax, Henderson, Ill	12
Lombard, Du Page, Ill	120
Lombardville, Stark, Ill	12
Lombardville, Scioto, Ohio	12
Lombardy, Columbia, Ga	12
Lombardy Grove, Mecklenburgh, Va	21
Lomira, Dodge, Wis	55
Lonaconing,* Alleghany, Md	560
London, Shelby, Ind	80
London, (*c. h.*,) Laurel, Ky	120
London, Monroe, Mich	38
London, Nemaha, Nebr	21
London,* (*c. h.*,) Madison, Ohio	1,100
London, Mercer, Pa	31
London, Rusk, Tex	26
London Bridge, Princess Anne, Va	12
Londonderry, Rockingham, N. H	47
Londonderry, Guernsey, Ohio	55
Londonderry, Chester, Pa	10
Londonderry, Windham, Vt	150

* Money-order office.

Post office	Amount
London Grove, Chester, Pa	$97
Lone Cedar, Martin, Minn	9
Lone Cedar, Crawford, Mo	12
Lone Cedar, Jackson, W. Va	12
Lone Elm, Cooper, Mo	12
Lone Elm, Henderson, Tenn	7
Lone Jack, Jackson, Mo	130
Lone Oak, Bates, Mo	12
Lone Oak, Hunt, Tex	12
Lone Pine, Inyo, Cal	12
Lone Pine, Washington, Pa	28
Lone Pine, Bedford, Va	12
Lone Pine, Portage, Wis	23
Lone Rock, Richland, Wis	370
Lone Star, Titus, Tex	40
Lone Tree, Bureau, Ill	10
Lone Tree, Cowley, Kans	12
Lone Tree, (c. h.,) Merrick, Nebr	98
Lone Tree, Greene, Pa	12
Lone Tree, Collin, Tex	12
Lone Tree, Tyler, W. Va	12
Lonetree Lake, Brown, Minn	12
Lone Valley, Saunders, Nebr	12
Lone Well, Union, La	8
Long, Vermilion, Ill	12
Long Bottom, Meigs, Ohio	53
Long Branch, Tatnall, Ga	11
Long Branch, Monroe, Mo	35
Long Branch, Richardson, Nebr	10
Long Branch,* Monmouth, N. J	1,400
Long Branch, Franklin, Va	4
Long Creek, Decatur, Iowa	12
Long Creek Depot, Panola, Miss	12
Long Eddy, Sullivan, N. Y	260
Long Falls Creek, McLean, Ky	32
Long Glade, Augusta, Va	43
Long Green Academy, Baltimore, Md	42
Long Grove, Lake, Ill	34
Long Hill, Stearns, Minn	10
Long Hill, Morris, N. J	55
Long Island, Jackson, Ala	10
Long Island City, Queens, N. Y	690
Long Lake, Madison, Ill	12
Long Lake, Hennepin, Minn	120
Long Lake, Hamilton, N. Y	67
Long Lane, Dallas, Mo	16
Long Marsh, Queen Anne, Md	44
Long Meadow, Hampden, Mass	210
Longmire, Washington, Tenn	8
Longmire's Store, Edgefield, S. C	23
Long Pine, Anson, N. C	12
Long Plain, Bristol, Mass	80
Long Point, Livingston, Ill	150
Long Pond, Caldwell, Ky	10
Long Prairie, Wayne, Ill	38
Long Prairie, (c. h.,) Todd, Minn	12
Long Prairie, Fayette, Tex	14
Long Reach, Tyler, W. Va	50
Long Ridge, Fairfield, Conn	52
Long Ridge, Washington, N. C	2
Long Run, Jefferson, Ky	60
Long Run, Licking, Ohio	6
Long Run, Armstrong, Pa	56
Long Run Station, Doddridge, W. Va	41
Long's Mills, Stone, Mo	$12
Long's Mills, Randolph, N. C	11
Long's Stand, Crawford, Pa	12
Long Street, De Soto, La	29
Long Swamp, Berks, Pa	80
Long Tom, Lane, Oreg	9
Longton, Howard, Kans	12
Longtown, Panola, Miss	16
Long Valley, Lassen, Cal	12
Long View, Ashley, Ark	12
Long View, Christian, Ky	16
Longville, Plumas, Cal	16
Longwood, Pettis, Mo	120
Longwood, Rockbridge, Va	9
Lonsdale, Providence, R. I	820
Loogootee,* Martin, Ind	290
Lookout, Laramie, Wyo	12
Lookout Mountain, Hamilton, Tenn	210
Looney's Creek, Marion, Tenn	6
Looneyville, Erie, N. Y	33
Looniesville, McDonald, Mo	7
Loose Creek, Osage, Mo	40
Looxahoma, De Soto, Miss	12
Loramies, Shelby, Ohio	110
Loran, Stephenson, Ill	31
Lordstown, Trumbull, Ohio	34
Lord's Valley, Pike, Pa	13
Lordville, Delaware, N. Y	96
Lorentz Store, Upshur, W. Va	17
Lorettee, Houston, Minn	10
Loretto, Marion, Ky	120
Loretto, Cambria, Pa	270
Loretto, Essex, Va	79
Lorraine, Jefferson, N. Y	90
Los Alisos, Santa Barbara, Cal	12
Los Angeles, (c. h.,)* Los Angeles, Cal	2,100
Losantville, Randolph, Ind	40
Los Gatos, Santa Clara, Cal	12
Los Luceros, Rio Arriba, N. Mex	18
Los Lunas, Valencia, N. Mex	130
Los Nietos, Los Angeles, Cal	20
Lostant,* La Salle, Ill	350
Lost Branch, Lincoln, Mo	26
Lost Creek, Breathitt, Ky	8
Lost Creek, Union, Tenn	10
Lost Creek, Harrison, W. Va	31
Lostine, Cherokee, Kans	74
Lost Mountain, Cobb, Ga	6
Lost Mountain, Greene, Tenn	4
Lost River, Hardy, W. Va	13
Lost Run, Breckinridge, Ky	7
Lot, Whitley, Ky	12
Lottridge, Athens, Ohio	31
Lottsburgh, Northumberland, Va	12
Lott's Creek, Humboldt, Iowa	46
Lottsville, Warren, Pa	94
Lotus, Union, Ind	96
Lotville, Fulton, N. Y	13
Louden City, Fayette, Ill	20
Loudon, Merrimack, N. H	120
Loudon, Franklin, Pa	140
Loudon, Roane, Tenn	350
Loudon Centre, Merrimack, N. H	17
Loudon Ridge, Merrimack, N. H	57
Loudonville,* Ashland, Ohio	470

* Money-order office.

Loudsville, White, Ga	$12
Louina, Randolph, Ala	68
Louisa, (*c. h.*,) Lawrence, Ky	100
Louisa C. H., Louisa, Va	470
Louisburgh, Dallas, Mo	50
Louisburgh,* (*c. h.*,) Franklin, N. C	380
Louisiana,* Pike, Mo	1,500
Louisville, Barbour, Ala	24
Louisville, (*c. h.*,) Jefferson, Ga	170
Louisville, (*c. h.*,) Clay, Ill	280
Louisville, (*c. h.*,) Pottawatomie, Kans	160
Louisville,* (*c. h.*,) Jefferson, Ky	4,000
Louisville, Franklin, La	12
Louisville, Carroll, Md	22
Louisville, (*c. h.*,) Winston, Miss	240
Louisville, Lincoln, Mo	73
Louisville, Missoula, Mont	12
Louisville, Cass, Nebr	12
Louisville, St. Lawrence, N. Y	66
Louisville, Stark, Ohio	250
Louisville, Blount, Tenn	40
Louisville, Dunn, Wis	18
Louisville Landing, St. Lawrence, N. Y	36
Loutre, Audrian, Mo	230
Loutre Island, Montgomery, Mo	38
Lovejoy, Bureau, Ill	20
Lovejoy's Station, Clayton, Ga	28
Lovelaceville, Ballard, Ky	62
Lovelady, Caldwell, N. C	5
Loveland, Pottawattomie, Iowa	23
Loveland, Bladen, N. C	12
Loveland,* Clermont, Ohio	260
Lovell, Oxford, Me	130
Lovell's Station, Erie, Pa	24
Lovelton, Wyoming, Pa	21
Lovely Dale, Knox, Ind	16
Lovely Mount, Montgomery, Va	49
Love's Mills, Washington, Va	13
Lovett, Jennings, Ind	12
Lovett's, Adams, Ohio	22
Lovettsville, Loudoun, Va	130
Loveville, New Castle, Del	22
Loveville, Centre, Pa	16
Lovilia, Monroe, Iowa	40
Lovilla, Hamilton, Ill	27
Loving Creek, Bedford, Va	10
Lovingston, (*c. h.*,) Nelson, Va	100
Lovington, Moultrie, Ill	150
Lowden,* Cedar, Iowa	380
Lowell, La Salle, Ill	43
Lowell, Lake, Ind	170
Lowell, Henry, Iowa	53
Lowell, Cherokee, Kans	12
Lowell, Garrard, Ky	86
Lowell, Penobscot, Me	63
Lowell,* Middlesex, Mass	4,000
Lowell, Kent, Mich	1,400
Lowell, Oneida, N. Y	80
Lowell, Washington, Ohio	160
Lowell, Orleans, Vt	110
Lowell, Dodge, Wis	140
Lowell Mills, Bartholomew, Ind	22
Lowellville, Mahoning, Ohio	260
Lower Bank, Burlington, N. J	54
Lower Bartlett, Carroll, N. H	$34
Lower Bern, Berks, Pa	28
Lower Boise, Ada, Idaho	12
Lower Gilmanton, Belknap, N. H	20
Lower Heidelberg, Berks, Pa	8
Lower Lake, (*c. h.*,) Lake, Cal	170
Lower Lynxville, Crawford, Wis	34
Lower Mahantango, Schuylkill, Pa	13
Lower Marlborough, Calvert, Md	12
Lower Merion, Montgomery, Pa	43
Lower Newport, Washington, Ohio	12
Lower Peach Tree, Wilcox, Ala	24
Lower Providence, Montgomery, Pa	120
Lower Salem, Washington, Ohio	84
Lower Saucon, Northampton, Pa	7
Lower Sioux Agency, Redwood, Minn	12
Lower Squankum, Monmouth, N. J	48
Lower Valley, Hunterdon, N. J	25
Lower Waterford, Caledonia, Vt	73
Lowe's Cross Roads, Sussex, Del	22
Lowe's Station, Bourbon, Ky	24
Low Hampton, Washington, N. Y	25
Lowhill, Lehigh, Pa	16
Lowland, St. Clair, Ill	18
Lowman, Chemung, N. Y	11
Lowmansville, Lawrence, Ky	12
Low Moor, Clinton, Iowa	180
Lowndes, Wayne, Mo	12
Lowndesborough, Lowndes, Ala	87
Lowndesville, Abbeville, S. C	32
Low Point, Woodford, Ill	47
Lowry, Bedford, Va	72
Lowville, (*c. h.*,) Lewis, N. Y	1,200
Lowville, Erie, Pa	12
Lowville, Columbia, Wis	31
Loxa, Coles, Ill	57
Loyal, Carroll, Ga	12
Loyal, Clark, Wis	12
Loyal Hill, Greene, Ark	12
Loyal Oak, Summit, Ohio	12
Loyalsock, Lycoming, Pa	21
Loyalton, Sierra, Cal	61
Loyalty, Hamilton, Tenn	2
Loyal Valley, Mason, Tex	30
Loyd, Ulster, N. Y	61
Loyd, Richland, Wis	12
Loydsville, Belmont, Ohio	90
Loy's Cross Roads, Union, Tenn	6
Loysville, Perry, Pa	120
Luana, Clayton, Iowa	130
Lubec, Washington, Me	260
Lubeck, Wood, W. Va	53
Lucas, Lucas, Iowa	17
Lucas, Henry, Mo	86
Lucas, Richland, Ohio	190
Lucas, Dunn, Wis	12
Lucasville, Scioto, Ohio	78
Lucerne, Knox, Ohio	11
Lucesco, Westmoreland, Pa	66
Lucinda Furnace, Clarion, Pa	21
Luck, Polk, Wis	12
Luda, Ouachita, Ark	11
Luda, Ogle, Ill	27
Luddenville, Iroquois, Ill	12
Ludington,* Mason, Mich	400

* Money-order office.

Ludingtonville, Putnam, N. Y	$21
Ludlow, Champaign, Ill	160
Ludlow, Dubois, Ind	9
Ludlow, Allamakee, Iowa	70
Ludlow, Kenton, Ky	6
Ludlow, Hampden, Mass	120
Ludlow,* Windsor, Vt	810
Ludlow Grove, Hamilton, Ohio	12
Ludlowville, Tompkins, N. Y	210
Ludville, Pickens, Ga	12
Lumber City, Telfair, Ga	12
Lumber City, Clearfield, Pa	28
Lumberland, Sullivan, N. Y	32
Lumberman, Clark, Wis	12
Lumberport, Harrison, W. Va	42
Lumberton, Burlington, N. J	110
Lumberton, (*c. h.*,) Robeson, N. C	290
Lumberton, Clinton, Ohio	28
Lumberville, Delaware, N. Y	31
Lumberville, Bucks, Pa	130
Lumberville, Iowa, Wis	12
Lummisville, Wayne, N. Y	12
Lumpkin, (*c. h.*,) Stewart, Ga	280
Luna Landing, Chicot, Ark	60
Lundy's Lane, Erie, Pa	150
Lunenburgh, Izard, Ark	12
Lunenburgh, Worcester, Mass	240
Lunenburgh, Essex, Vt	230
Luney's Creek, Grant, W. Va	88
Luni, Wright, Iowa	20
Luray, Henry, Ind	20
Luray, (*c. h.*,) Page, Va	340
Lusby's Mill, Owen, Ky	14
Lusk, Pope, Ill	9
Lusk's Springs, Parke, Ind	6
Luthersburgh, Clearfield, Pa	180
Luther's Mills, Bradford, Pa	21
Luthersville, Meriwether, Ga	20
Lutherville, Baltimore, Md	140
Lutzton, Nodaway, Mo	20
Luverne, Rock, Minn	8
Luxemburgh, Stearns, Minn	20
Luzerne, Benton, Iowa	190
Luzerne, Warren, N. Y	220
Luzerne, Luzerne, Pa	79
Lycippus, Westmoreland, Pa	32
Lycurgus, Allamakee, Iowa	6
Lydia, Scott, Minn	11
Lydia, Darlington, S. C	17
Lykens, Dauphin, Pa	590
Lyles, Lancaster, Pa	53
Lylesford, Fairfield, S. C	12
Lyman, Pope, Ark	24
Lyman, York, Me	8
Lyman, Grafton, N. H	39
Lyme, New London, Conn	500
Lyme, Grafton, N. H	400
Lynchburgh, Jefferson, Ill	44
Lynchburgh, Nodaway, Mo	7
Lynchburgh, Highland, Ohio	230
Lynchburgh, Sumter, S. C	99
Lynchburgh, Lincoln, Tenn	83
Lynchburgh,* Campbell, Va	3,100
Lynch's Creek, Marion, S. C	14
Lynch's Lake, Williamsburgh, S. C.	33
Lynchwood, Kershaw, S. C	3

Lynd, Lyon, Minn	$18
Lyndeborough, Hillsborough, N. H	28
Lyndon, Whitesides, Ill	170
Lyndon, Osage, Kans	12
Lyndon, Aroostook, Me	20
Lyndon, Caledonia, Vt	420
Lyndon Centre, Caledonia, Vt	300
Lyndon Station, Ross, Ohio	110
Lyndonville, Orleans, N. Y	180
Lyndonville, Caledonia, Vt	370
Lynn, Randolph, Ind	73
Lynn, Warren, Iowa	40
Lynn, Greenup, Ky	22
Lynn,* Essex, Mass	2,600
Lynn, St. Clair, Mich	31
Lynn, Susquehanna, Pa	72
Lynn, Clark, Wis	4
Lynn Camp, Knox, Ky	12
Lynn Camp, Marshall, W. Va	3
Lynne, Weber, Utah	27
Lynnfield, Essex, Mass	32
Lynnfield Centre, Essex, Mass	100
Lynnport, Lehigh, Pa	12
Lynnville, Henry, Ala	12
Lynnville, Morgan, Ill	100
Lynnville, Warrick, Ind	57
Lynnville, Jasper, Iowa	150
Lynnville, Graves, Ky	70
Lynnville, Lehigh, Pa	16
Lynnville, Giles, Tenn	140
Lyon, Wabashaw, Minn	8
Lyon, Laclede, Mo	28
Lyona, Dickinson, Kans	8
Lyons, Cook, Ill	100
Lyons, Greene, Ind	12
Lyons,* Clinton, Iowa	2,200
Lyons,* Ionia, Mich	390
Lyons, Burt, Nebr	12
Lyons,* (*c. h.*,) Wayne, N. Y	2,100
Lyons, Fulton, Ohio	140
Lyons, Fayette, Tex	17
Lyons, Walworth, Wis	140
Lyonsdale, Lewis, N. Y	85
Lyon's Falls, Lewis, N. Y	120
Lyon's Mill, Clinton, Mich	29
Lyon's Station, Fayette, Ind	30
Lyon's Station, Berks, Pa	110
Lyonsville, Cook, Ill	24
Lyon Valley, Lehigh, Pa	38
Lyra, Scioto, Ohio	17
Lysander, Onondaga, N. Y	170
Lytle City, Iowa, Iowa	56

M.

McAfee, Mercer, Ky	120
McAfee Valley, Sussex, N. J	27
McAlevy's Fort, Huntingdon, Pa	98
McAllister's × Roads, Montgomery Tenn	10
McAllisterville, Juniata, Pa	200
McArthur,* (*c. h.*,) Vinton, Ohio	550
McBean Depot, Richmond, Ga	68
McBride's Mill, Watauga, N. C	4
McCainsville, Morris, N. J	12
McCall, Hancock, Ill	28

* Money-order office.

Post Office	
McCall's Ferry, York, Pa	$10
McCameron, Martin, Ind	12
McCandless, Butler, Pa	20
McCauleyville, Wilkin, Minn	14
McCleary, Noble, Ohio	28
McCleary, Beaver, Pa	6
McClelland, Franklin, N. Y	23
McClellandsville, New Castle, Del	37
McClellandtown, Fayette, Pa	49
McClellan Gulch, Deer Lodge, Mont	12
McCluney, Perry, Ohio	27
McClure, Buchanan, Va	12
McClure Settlement, Broome, N. Y	12
McComb, Hancock, Ohio	120
McConnellsburgh, (*c. h.*,) Fulton, Pa	350
McConnell's Grove, Stephenson, Ill	44
McConnellstown, Huntingdon, Pa	97
McConnellsville, Oneida, N. Y	73
McConnellsville,* (*c. h.*,) Morgan, Ohio	1,300
McCordsville, Hancock, Ind	70
McCoy's Station, Decatur, Ind	22
McCoy's Station, Jefferson, Ohio	110
McCoysville, Juniata, Pa	43
McCray's Store, Alamance, N. C	7
McCulloch's Mills, Juniata, Pa	26
McCutchanville, Vanderburgh, Ind	13
McCutchenville, Wyandot, Ohio	66
McDaniel's, Gallia, Ohio	20
McDonald, Hardin, Ohio	12
McDonald's Mill, Montgomery, Va	11
McDonaldsville, Stark, Ohio	13
McDonough, New Castle, Del	87
McDonough (*c. h.*,) Henry, Ga	140
McDonough, Chenango, N. Y	140
McDowell, Yavapai, Ariz	12
McDowell, Highland, Va	61
McElhattan, Clinton, Pa	66
McElroy, Doddridge, W. Va	4
McEwen's Station, Humphreys, Tenn	64
McEwensville, Northumberland, Pa	120
McFadden, York, Nebr	20
McFarland's, Lunenburgh, Va	12
McGaheysville, Rockingham, Va	100
McGarvey's, Clearfield, Pa	6
McGill, Paulding, Ohio	8
McGonigle's Station, Butler, Ohio	24
McGrawsville, Miami, Ind	31
McGrawville, Cortland, N. Y	310
McGregor,* Clayton, Iowa	2,100
McHenry, McHenry, Ill	250
McIndoe's Falls,* Caledonia, Vt	280
McIntire, Wilkinson, Ga	12
McIntosh, (*c. h.*,) La Fayette, Fla	12
McIntosh, Liberty, Ga	160
McKay, Ashland, Ohio	36
McKean, Erie, Pa	130
McKeansburgh, Schuylkill, Pa	12
McKean's Old Stand, Westmoreland, Pa	61
McKee, (*c. h.*,) Jackson, Ky	10
McKeen, Clark, Ill	12
McKee's Half Falls, Snyder, Pa	78
McKeesport,* Allegheny, Pa	1,000
McKenny's Mill, Rockbridge, Va	12

Post Office	
McKenzie, Carroll, Tenn	$170
McKinley, Marengo, Ala	58
McKinley's Landing, Henderson, Ky	12
McKinney, (*c. h.*,) Collin, Tex	400
McKinstry's Mills, Carroll, Md	18
McKnightstown, Adams, Pa	12
McKune's Depot, Wyoming, Pa	12
McLane, Erie, Pa	45
McLaughlin's Store, Westmoreland, Pa	22
McLean, McLean, Ill	410
McLean, Tompkins, N. Y	280
McLeansborough,* (*c. h.*,) Hamilton, Ill	260
McLean's Corners, Crawford, Pa	8
McLean's Station, Cherokee N., Ind. T	12
McLeansville, Guilford, N. C	25
McLellan's Corners, Erie, Pa	12
McLemoresville, Carroll, Tenn	59
McLeod's Station, Logan, Ky	10
McMath, Tuscaloosa, Ala	12
McMillan, Knox, Tenn	67
McMinnville, Yam Hill, Oreg	160
McMinnville,* (*c. h.*,) Warren, Tenn	930
McNairy Station, McNairy, Tenn	16
McNutt, (*c. h.*,) Sunflower, Miss	11
McPherson, Coles, Ill	22
McSherrystown, Adams, Pa	110
McSherrysville, York, Pa	90
Mc'sVille, Shelby, Tenn	12
McVeytown, Mifflin, Pa	460
McVill, Armstrong, Pa	24
McVille, Telfair, Ga	12
McWilliamstown, Chester, Pa	25
McZena, Ashland, Ohio	19
Mabbettsville, Dutchess, N. Y	85
Mabee's, Jackson, Ohio	8
Mace, Montgomery, Ind	28
Macedon, Wayne, N. Y	460
Macedon, Mercer, Ohio	50
Macedon Centre, Wayne, N. Y	120
Macedonia, Hamilton, Ill	25
Macedonia, Pottawattomie, Iowa	16
Macedonia, Bradford, Pa	17
Macedonia Depot, Summit, Ohio	120
Macfarland, Dane, Wis	130
Machias,* (*c. h.*,) Washington, Me	840
Machias, Cattaraugus, N. Y	130
Machias Port, Washington, Me	190
Machirville, Mason, W. Va	21
Mackerel Corner, Carroll, N. H	81
Mackey's Grove, Boone, Iowa	12
Mackinaw, Tazewell, Ill	210
Mackinaw,* (*c. h.*,) Mackinac, Mich	300
Mack's, Carroll, Iowa	4
Macksville, Harrison, Tex	12
Macksville, Pendleton, W. Va	12
Mackville, Washington, Ky	78
Mackville, Outagamie, Wis	19
Macomb,* (*c. h.*,) McDonough, Ill	1,500
Macomb, Macomb, Mich	39
Macomb, St. Lawrence, N. Y	92
Macomb, Grayson, Tex	15
Macon,* (*c. h.*,) Bibb, Ga	4,000
Macon,* Macon, Ill	710

* Money-order office.

Macon, Lenawee, Mich	$71
Macon, (c. h.,) Noxubee, Miss	1,000
Macon, Fayette, Tenn	110
Macon City, (c. h.,)* Macon, Mo	2,400
Macon Depot, Warren, N. C	74
Macon Station, Hale, Ala	55
Macoupin Station, Macoupin, Ill	12
Macungie, Lehigh, Pa	240
Madalin, Dutchess, N. Y	170
Madawaska, Aroostook, Me	12
Maddensville, Huntingdon, Pa	16
Madeira, Hamilton, Ohio	59
Madelia, (c. h.,) Watonwan, Minn	190
Madely, Portage, Wis	12
Madera, Clearfield, Pa	23
Madison, (c. h.,) St. Francis, Ark	230
Madison, New Haven, Conn	380
Madison, (c. h.,) Madison, Fla	170
Madison, (c. h.,)* Morgan, Ga	1,000
Madison, Richland, Ill	4
Madison, (c. h.,)* Jefferson, Ind	2,800
Madison, Jones, Iowa	30
Madison, Greenwood, Kans	43
Madison, Somerset, Me	90
Madison, Livingston, Mich	27
Madison, Mower, Minn	16
Madison, Monroe, Mo	72
Madison, Madison, Nebr	12
Madison, Carroll, N. H	82
Madison, Morris, N. J	1,000
Madison, Madison, N. Y	270
Madison, Rockingham, N. C	140
Madison,* Lake, Ohio	490
Madison, Westmoreland, Pa	81
Madison, Davidson, Tenn	140
MADISON,* *(c. h.,)* Dane, Wis	3,800
Madison C. H., Madison, Va	240
Madisonburgh, Wayne, Ohio	30
Madisonburgh, Centre, Pa	38
Madison Centre, Somerset, Me	34
Madison Mills, Fayette, Ohio	10
Madison Mills, Madison, Va	18
Madison Run Station, Orange, Va	12
Madison Station, Madison, Ala	180
Madisonville, (c. h.,)* Hopkins, Ky	350
Madisonville, St. Tammany, La	20
Madisonville, Ralls, Mo	69
Madisonville, Hamilton, Ohio	130
Madisonville, Luzerne, Pa	37
Madisonville, (c. h.,) Monroe, Tenn	270
Madisonville, (c. h.,) Madison, Tex	74
Madonaville, Monroe, Ill	18
Madrid, Franklin, Me	42
Madrid,* St. Lawrence, N. Y	380
Madrid Springs, St. Lawrence, N. Y	180
Madura, Clay, Kans	23
Maeystown, Monroe, Ill	30
Magalia, Butte, Cal	74
Magazine, Scott, Ark	16
Magee's Corners, Seneca, N. Y	22
Magnolia, (c. h.,) Columbia, Ark	190
Magnolia, Kent, Del	74
Magnolia, Putnam, Ill	250
Magnolia, Crawford, Ind	1
Magnolia, (c. h.,)* Harrison, Iowa	500
Magnolia, La Rue, Ky	16
Magnolia, Harford, Md	$120
Magnolia, Pike, Miss	48
Magnolia, Moniteau, Mo	12
Magnolia, Duplin, N. C	230
Magnolia, Stark, Ohio	57
Magnolia, Rock, Wis	50
Magnolia Centre, Lawrence, Mo	12
Magnolia Springs, Jasper, Tex	16
Maguire's Store, Washington, Ark	41
Mahalasville, Morgan, Ind	19
Mahanoy, Northumberland, Pa	28
Mahanoy City,* Schuylkill, Pa	1,800
Mahanoy Plane, Schuylkill, Pa	430
Mahomet, Champaign, Ill	230
Mahomet, Burnet, Tex	16
Mahoning, Indiana, Pa	67
Mahopac, Oakland, Mich	10
Mahopac, Putnam, N. Y	290
Mahopac Falls, Putnam, N. Y	12
Mahwah, Bergen, N. J	12
Maiden Creek, Berks, Pa	45
Maiden Rock, Pierce, Wis	120
Maidsville, Monongalia, W. Va	22
Maine, Waseca, Minn	13
Maine, Broome, N. Y	190
Maine Prairie, Solano, Cal	40
Maine Prairie, Stearns, Minn	50
Mainesburgh, Tioga, Pa	92
Mainville, Cook, Ill	11
Mainville, Warren, Ohio	130
Mainville, Columbia, Pa	23
Majenica, Huntingdon, Ind	26
Majority Point, (c. h.,) Cumberland, Ill	140
Malade City, (c. h.,) Oneida, Idaho	130
Makanda, Jackson, Ill	390
Malaga, Gloucester, N. J	130
Malaga, Monroe, Ohio	40
Malakoff, Henderson, Tex	5
Malcom,* Poweshiek, Iowa	520
Malden, Bureau, Ill	280
Malden, Middlesex, Mass	1,400
Malden, Ulster, N. Y	180
Malden Bridge, Columbia, N. Y	81
Mallet Creek, Medina, Ohio	110
Mallory, Oswego, N. Y	36
Malma, De Kalb, Ill	19
Malone, Clinton, Iowa	42
Malone, (c. h.,)* Franklin, N. Y	2,200
Malta, De Kalb, Ill	470
Malta, Saratoga, N. Y	40
Malta, Morgan, Ohio	290
Malta Bend, Saline, Mo	220
Maltaville, Saratoga, N. Y	18
Malugin Grove, Lee, Ill	100
Malvern, Carroll, Ohio	160
Mamaroneck, Westchester, N. Y	510
Manack, Lowndes, Ala	12
Manada Hill, Dauphin, Pa	19
Manahawkin, Ocean, N. J	93
Manalapan, Monmouth, N. J	87
Manamuskin, Cumberland, N. J	30
Manannah, Meeker, Minn	44
Manassas,* Prince William, Va	270
Manatawny, Berks, Pa	19
Manatee, Manatee, Fla	61

* Money-order office.

Manchaug, Worcester, Mass	$170
Manchester, Hartford, Conn	140
Manchester, Scott, Ill	240
Manchester, Dearborn, Ind	43
Manchester,* Delaware, Iowa	1,700
Manchester, (c. h.,) Clay, Ky	83
Manchester, Kennebec, Me	110
Manchester, Carroll, Md	200
Manchester, Essex, Mass	560
Manchester, Washtenaw, Mich	650
Manchester, St. Louis, Mo	77
Manchester,* Hillsborough, N. H	2,600
Manchester, Ocean, N. J	230
Manchester, Ontario, N. Y	180
Manchester, Adams, Ohio	280
Manchester, York, Pa	82
Manchester, Sumter, S. C	110
Manchester, (c. h.,) Coffee, Tenn	290
Manchester,* (c. h.,) Bennington, Vt	600
Manchester, Chesterfield, Va	200
Manchester, Green Lake, Wis	72
Manchester Bridge, Dutchess, N Y	12
Manchester Centre, Ontario, N. Y	23
Mandana, Onondaga, N. Y	18
Mandarin, Duval, Fla	59
Mandeville, St. Tammany, La	20
Mandeville, Carroll, Mo	59
Mangohick, King William, Va	16
Mangum, Richmond, N. C	18
Manhasset, Queens, N. Y	140
Manhattan, Putnam, Ind	53
Manhattan, Keokuk, Iowa	5
Manhattan,* (c. h.,) Riley, Kans	1,200
Manheim, Lancaster, Pa	360
Manilla, Rush, Ind	84
Manistee,* (c. h.,) Manistee, Mich	1,400
Manito, Mason, Ill	320
Manitowoc,* (c. h.,) Manitowoc, Wis	2,200
Manitowoc Rapids, Manitowoc, Wis	13
Mankato,* (c. h.,) Blue Earth, Minn	1,800
Manlius, Allegan, Mich	46
Manlius, Onondaga, N. Y	500
Manlius Centre, Onondaga, N. Y	64
Manlius Station, Onondaga, N. Y	110
Manlyville, Henry, Tenn	41
Mannborough, Amelia, Va	22
Manning, (c. h.,) Clarendon, S. C	110
Manningham, Butler, Ala	12
Mannington, Marion, W. Va	250
Mann's Choice, Bedford, Pa	20
Mannsville, Taylor, Ky	22
Mannsville, Jefferson, N. Y	420
Mannsville, Perry, Pa	14
Mannville, Sumter, S. C	12
Manny, (c. h.,) Sabine, La	48
Manomin, Anoka, Minn	14
Manor, Lancaster, Pa	46
Manor Dale, Westmoreland, Pa	19
Manor Hill, Huntingdon, Pa	32
Manor Kill, Schoharie, N. Y	39
Manor Station, Westmoreland, Pa	110
Manorsville, Armstrong, Pa	87
Manorville, Suffolk, N. Y	160
Manquin, King William, Va	12
Mansfield, Tolland, Conn	84
Mansfield, Piatt, Ill	12
Mansfield, Parke, Ind	$47
Mansfield, Linn, Kans	45
Mansfield, (c. h.,) De Soto, La	490
Mansfield, Bristol, Mass	410
Mansfield, Dutchess, N. Y	6
Mansfield,* (c. h.,) Richland, Ohio	2,800
Mansfield, Tioga, Pa	620
Mansfield, Tarrant, Tex	20
Mansfield Centre, Tolland, Conn	220
Mansfield Depot, Tolland, Conn	87
Mansfield Valley, Allegheny, Pa	320
Manson, Warren, N. C	100
Mansura, Avoyelles, La	34
Manteno,* Kankakee, Ill	630
Manteno, Shelby, Iowa	27
Manteo, (c. h.,) Dare, N. C	12
Manti, Fremont, Iowa	37
Manti, (c. h.,) San Pete, Utah	100
Manton, Maries, Mo	14
Manton, Providence, R. I	49
Mantorville,* (c. h.,) Dodge, Minn	510
Mantua, Gloucester, N. J	130
Mantua, Portage, Ohio	97
Mantua, Collin, Tex	12
Mantua Station, Portage, Ohio	250
Manville, Mobile, Ala	12
Manville, Jefferson, Ind	26
Manville, Providence, R. I	99
Maple, Ionia, Mich	38
Maple, Brown, Ohio	13
Maple Creek, Dodge, Nebr	12
Maple Creek, Carroll, Tenn	12
Maple Glen, Scott, Minn	41
Maple Grove, Edwards, Ill	19
Maple Grove, Aroostook, Me	20
Maple Grove, Barry, Mich	34
Maple Grove, Hennepin, Minn	5
Maple Grove, Otsego, N. Y	4
Maple Hill, Montcalm, Mich	12
Maple Hill, Oswego, N. Y	120
Maple Hill, Lycoming, Pa	12
Maple Lake, Wright, Minn	8
Maple Landing, Monona, Iowa	12
Maple Lawn, Monroe, W. Va	10
Maple Plain, Hennepin, Minn	96
Maple Rapids, Clinton, Mich	220
Maple Ridge, Isanti, Minn	12
Maple Ridge, Tioga, Pa	10
Maple River, Blue Earth, Minn	13
Maples, Allen, Ind	48
Maple's Mill, Fulton, Ill	17
Maple Springs, La Fayette, Miss	12
Maple Springs, Wilkes, N. C	6
Maple Springs, Red River, Tex	10
Maple Springs, Dunn, Wis	20
Maple Street, Niagara, N. Y	19
Maplesville, Baker, Ala	12
Mapleton, Monona, Iowa	10
Mapleton, Bourbon, Kans	120
Mapleton, Grand Traverse, Mich	16
Mapleton, Blue Earth, Minn	47
Mapleton, Stark, Ohio	68
Mapleton, Waukesha, Wis	40
Mapleton Depot, Huntingdon, Pa	190
Mapletown, Greene, Pa	17
Mapleville, Providence, R. I	140

* Money-order office.

Post office	Amount
Maplewood, Middlesex, Mass	$100
Maple Works, Clark, Wis	8
Maquoketa,* Jackson, Iowa	900
Maquon, Knox, Ill	260
Marak, Brown, Kans	12
Maramec, Phelps, Mo	75
Marathon, Lapeer, Mich	14
Marathon, Cortland, N. Y	660
Marathon, Clermont, Ohio	100
Marathon City, Marathon, Wis	12
Marble, Madison, Ark	12
Marble, Brown, Ind	4
Marble, Waupaca, Wis	6
Marble Creek, Iron, Mo	20
Marble Dale, Litchfield, Conn	57
Marblehead,* Essex, Mass	1,900
Marblehead, Ottawa, Ohio	46
Marble Hill, (*c. h.*,) Bollinger, Mo	120
Marble Ridge, Sauk, Wis	130
Marble Rock, Floyd, Iowa	96
Marble Salt Works, Cherokee N., Ind. T	12
Marbletown, Ulster, N. Y	20
Marble Valley, Coosa, Ala	6
Marbut's, Giles, Tenn	20
Marcella Falls, Lawrence, Tenn	25
Marcelline, Adams, Ill	60
Marcellon, Columbia, Wis	50
Marcellus, Cass, Mich	62
Marcellus, Onondaga, N. Y	340
Marcellus Falls, Onondaga, N. Y	110
Marchand, Indiana, Pa	61
Marco, Greene, Ind	37
Marcy, La Grange, Ind	2
Marcy, Oneida, N. Y	12
Marcy, Fairfield, Ohio	24
Marcy, Waukesha, Wis	35
Mardisville, Talladega, Ala	12
Marengo,* McHenry, Ill	1,000
Marengo, Crawford, Ind	32
Marengo,* (*c. h.*,) Iowa, Iowa	1,100
Marengo, Calhoun, Mich	120
Marengo, Wayne, N. Y	57
Marengo, Morrow, Ohio	57
Margaretta Furnace, York, Pa	35
Margarettsville, Northampton, N. C.	38
Margarettville, Delaware, N. Y	250
Mariah Hill, Spencer, Ind	26
Marianna, Phillips, Ark	13
Marianna, (*c. h.*,) Jackson, Fla	280
Maria Stein, Mercer, Ohio	24
Mariaville, Schenectady, N. Y	56
Maricopa Wells, Pima, Ariz	220
Marietta,* (*c. h.*,) Cobb, Ga	1,200
Marietta, Fulton, Ill	38
Marietta, Shelby, Ind	30
Marietta, Marshall, Iowa	95
Marietta, Onondaga, N. Y	22
Marietta,* (*c. h.*,) Washington, Ohio	2,400
Marietta,* Lancaster, Pa	860
Marietta, Greenville, S. C	13
Marietta, Crawford, Wis	8
Marilla, Erie, N. Y	110
Marindal, Yankton, Dak	12
Marine, Madison, Ill	290
Marine, Lewis, Ky	12
Marine City, * St. Clair, Mich	$430
Marine Mills, Washington, Minn	310
Mariner's Harbor, Richmond, N. Y	97
Marinette, Oconto, Wis	370
Marion,* (*c. h.*,) Perry, Ala	1,100
Marion, (*c. h.*,) Crittenden, Ark	84
Marion, Hartford, Conn	180
Marion,* (*c. h.*,) Williamson, Ill	290
Marion,* (*c. h.*,) Grant, Ind	1,300
Marion,* (*c. h.*,) Linn, Iowa	870
Marion, Douglas, Kans	12
Marion, (*c. h.*,) Crittenden, Ky	170
Marion, Union, La	12
Marion, Washington, Me	11
Marion, Plymouth, Mass	350
Marion, Livingston, Mich	7
Marion, Olmsted, Minn	80
Marion, Cole, Mo	22
Marion, Wayne, N. Y	460
Marion, (*c. h.*,) McDowell, N. C	78
Marion,* (*c. h.*,) Marion, Ohio	1,300
Marion, Franklin, Pa	62
Marion, Angelina, Tex	10
Marion,* (*c. h.*,) Smyth, Va	590
Marion C. H., Marion, S. C	580
Marion Centre, (*c. h.*,) Marion, Kans.	50
Marion Station, Lauderdale, Miss	150
Marionville, Lawrence, Mo	91
Marionville, Forest, Pa	20
Mariposa,* (*c. h.*,) Mariposa, Cal	230
Marissa, St. Clair, Ill	110
Marits, Morrow, Ohio	17
Mark, Defiance, Ohio	4
Markelsville, Perry, Pa	44
Markesan,* Green Lake, Wis	150
Market Lake, Oneida, Idaho	8
Markham Station, Fauquier, Va	160
Markle, Huntington, Ind	27
Markleeville,* Alpine, Cal	46
Markleville, Madison, Ind	24
Markleysburgh, Fayette, Pa	13
Marksborough, Warren, N. J	81
Marksville, (*c. h.*,) Avoyelles, La	170
Marksville, Page, Va	49
Mark West, Sonoma, Cal	27
Marlborough, Hartford, Conn	58
Marlborough,* Middlesex, Mass	1,600
Marlborough, Cheshire, N. H	330
Marlborough, Monmouth, N. J	100
Marlborough, Ulster, N. Y	320
Marlborough, Pitt, N. C	10
Marlborough, Stark, Ohio	130
Marlborough, Chester, Pa	12
Marlborough, Carroll, Tenn	13
Marlborough, Windham, Vt	43
Marlborough Depot, Cheshire, N. H.	120
Marlette, Sanilac, Mich	34
Marlin, (*c. h.*.) Falls, Tex	360
Marlow, Cheshire, N. H	210
Marlsville, Bladen, N. C	12
Marlton, Burlington, N. J	180
Marmiton, Bourbon, Kans	37
Marmont, Marshall, Ind	22
Maroa, *Macon, Ill	660
Marple, Delaware, Pa	64
Marquand, Madison, Mo	12

* Money-order office.

*Marquette,** *(c. h.,)* Marquette, Mich.	$2,600
Marquette, Green Lake, Wis.	120
Marriottsville, Howard, Md	77
Marron, Clearfield, Pa	10
Marrowbone, Moultrie, Ill	80
Marrowbone, Cumberland, Ky	28
Mars, Bibb, Ala	8
Mars Bluff, Marion, S. C	140
Marseilles,* La Salle, Ill	820
Marseilles, Wyandot, Ohio	91
Marsh, Chester, Pa	42
Marshall, (c. h.,) Searcy, Ark	39
*Marshall,** *(c. h.,)* Clark, Ill	630
Marshall, Henry, Iowa	130
Marshall, Bath, Ky	13
*Marshall,** *(c. h.,)* Calhoun, Mich	3,000
Marshall, (c. h.,) Saline, Mo	680
Marshall, Oneida, N. Y	40
Marshall, (c. h.,) Madison, N. C	64
Marshall, Highland, Ohio	20
Marshall, (c. h.,) Harrison, Tex	2,000
Marshall, Dane, Wis	155
Marshall College, Cabell, W. Va	11
Marshall Hall, Charles, Md	12
Marshall Prairie, Newton, Ark	13
Marshall's Creek, Monroe, Pa	42
Marshall's Ferry, Grainger, Tenn	10
Marshallsville, Macon, Ga	270
Marshallsville, Wayne, Ohio	170
Marshallton, Chester, Pa	170
*Marshalltown,** *(c. h.,)* Marshall, Iowa	2,800
Marsh Creek, Whitley, Ky	9
Marshfield, Warren, Ind	100
Marshfield, Plymouth, Mass	220
*Marshfield,** *(c. h.,)* Webster, Mo	630
Marshfield, Erie, N. Y	23
Marshfield, Athens, Ohio	190
Marshfield, Tioga, Pa	16
Marshfield, Washington, Vt	140
Mars Hill, Aroostook, Me	25
Marshland, Richmond, N. Y	48
Marshville, Oceana, Mich	12
Marshville, Montgomery, N. Y	18
Marston's Mills, Barnstable, Mass	67
Martell, Pierce, Wis	87
Martha Furnace, Centre, Pa	100
Marthasville, Warren, Mo	62
Marthaville, Natchitoches, La	8
Marticksville, Lancaster, Pa	20
Martin, Allegan, Mich	160
Martin, Green, Wis	12
Martindale, Mecklenburgh, N. C	2
Martindale Depot, Columbia, N. Y	47
*Martinez,** *(c. h.,)* Contra Costa, Cal	250
Martin's Bluff, Clark, Wash	12
Martinsburgh, Butte, Cal	12
Martinsburgh, Pike, Ill	20
Martinsburgh, Washington, Ind	57
Martinsburgh, Keokuk, Iowa	130
Martinsburgh, Monroe, Ky	12
Martinsburgh, Lewis, N. Y	270
Martinsburgh, Knox, Ohio	170
Martinsburgh, Blair, Pa	270
*Martinsburgh,** *(c. h.,)* Berkeley, W. Va	1,600
Martin's Creek, Sharpe, Ark	$12
Martin's Creek, Northampton, Pa	41
Martin's Ferry, Klamath, Cal	5
Martin's Ferry, Belmont, Ohio	430
Martin's Lime Kilns, Stokes, N. C	7
Martinstown, Putnam, Mo	13
Martinsville, Clark, Ill	250
*Martinsville,** *(c. h.,)* Morgan, Ind	850
Martinsville, Wayne, Mich	17
Martinsville, Copiah, Miss	12
Martinsville, Harrison, Mo	12
Martinsville, Adams, Nebr	12
Martinsville, Somerset, N. J	66
Martinsville, Niagara, N. Y	49
Martinsville, Clinton, Ohio	170
Martinsville, Lancaster, Pa	19
Martinsville, Nacogdoches, Tex	10
Martinsville, (c. h.,) Henry, Va	70
Martinville, Grant, Wis	33
Martville, Cayuga, N. Y	83
Martz, Clay, Ind	36
Marvel, Bates, Mo	76
Marvin, Henry, Mo	12
Marvin, Chautauqua, N. Y	21
Marydell, Caroline, Md	110
Maryland, Otsego, N. Y	95
Maryland Line, Baltimore, Md	55
Marysburgh, Le Sueur, Minn	49
*Marysville,** *(c. h.,)* Yuba, Cal	3,200
Marysville, Vermilion, Ill	8
Marysville, Marion, Iowa	18
*Marysville,** *(c. h.,)* Marshall, Kans	490
Marysville, St. Clair, Mich	68
*Marysville,** *(c. h.,)* Union, Ohio	820
Marysville, Perry, Pa	210
Marysville, Campbell, Va	40
Marytown, Fond du Lac, Wis	22
*Maryville,** *(c. h.,)* Nodaway, Mo	1,000
Maryville, (c. h.,) Blount, Tenn	300
Masardis, Aroostook, Me	29
Mascoutah,* St. Clair, Ill	480
Mashapaug, Tolland, Conn	24
Mason,* Effingham, Ill	1,160
Mason, Washington, Md	12
*Mason,** *(c. h.,)* Ingham, Mich	880
Mason, Hillsborough, N. H	92
Mason, Warren, Ohio	220
Mason, Tipton, Tenn	220
Mason, (c. h.,) Mason, Tex	160
Mason, Mason, W. Va	420
Mason and Dixon, Franklin, Pa	83
Mason City, Mason, Ill	860
*Mason City,** *(c. h.,)* Cerro Gordo, Iowa	700
Mason Creek, McLean, Ky	5
Mason's Depot, Amherst, Va	76
Masontown, Fayette, Pa	100
Masontown, Preston, W. Va	9
Mason Village, Hillsborough, N. H	360
Masonville, Delaware, Iowa	200
Masonville, Daviess, Ky	33
Masonville, Burlington, N. J	7
Masonville, Delaware, N. Y	180
Maspeth, Queens, N. Y	19
Massac Creek, Massac, Ill	12
Massack, McCracken, Ky	9

* Money-order office.

Massanatton, Page, Va	$17
Massena,* St. Lawrence, N. Y	520
Massena Centre, St. Lawrence N. Y	42
Massey's Cross Roads, Kent, Md	30
Massie's Mills, Nelson, Va	50
Massillon, Cedar, Iowa	22
Massillon,* Stark, Ohio	2,600
Mastersonville, Lancaster, Pa	20
Mastersville, McLennan, Tex	12
Masterton, Monroe, Ohio	54
Masthope, Pike, Pa	76
Mast Yard, Merrimack, N. H	55
Matagorda, (*c. h.*,) Matagorda, Tex	200
Matamoras, Pike, Pa	37
Matanzas, St. John's, Fla	12
Matawan, Monmouth, N. J	730
Matfield Green, Chase, Kans	42
Matherton, Ionia, Mich	150
Mathews, Montgomery, Ala	12
Matinicus, Knox, Me	23
Matoax, Amelia, Va	25
Mattapan, Norfolk, Mass	140
Mattapoisett, Plymouth, Mass	490
Mattawamkeag, Penobscot, Me	120
Mattawan, Van Buren, Mich	450
Matteawan,* Dutchess, N. Y	720
Matthews, (*c. h.*,) Matthews, Va	210
Matthews' Store, Howard, Md	77
Mattison, Cook, Ill	160
Mattison, Branch, Mich	35
Mattituck, Suffolk, N. Y	280
Mattoon,* Coles, Ill	2,500
Matville, Raleigh, W. Va	12
Mauch Chunk,* (*c. h.*,) Carbon, Pa	2,200
Mauckport, Harrison, Ind	87
Maumee City,* Lucas, Ohio	700
Maumelle, Pulaski, Ark	6
Maune's Store, Franklin, Mo	12
Maurertown, Shenandoah, Va	55
Mauricetown, Cumberland, N. J	160
Mauston, *Juneau, Wis	830
Maxatawny, Berks, Pa	59
Maxey, Oglethorpe, Ga	110
Maxfield, Penobscot, Me	9
Maximo, Stark, Ohio	66
Maxinkuckee, Marshall, Ind	23
Max Meadows, Wythe, Va	40
Maxville, Perry, Ohio	53
Maxville, Dyer, Tenn	13
Maxville, Buffalo, Wis	57
Maxwell, Delaware, Ohio	11
Maxwell's Creek, Mariposa, Cal	150
May, Tuscola, Mich	72
May, Martin, Minn	7
May, Lancaster, Pa	15
Mayberry, Carroll, Md	12
Mayesville, Sumter, S. C	220
Mayfield, Santa Clara, Cal	240
Mayfield, Hancock, Ga	58
Mayfield,* (*c. h.*,) Graves, Ky	470
Mayfield, Grand Traverse, Mich	12
Mayfield, Fulton, N. Y	110
Mayfield, Cuyahoga, Ohio	48
Mayhew's Station, Sacramento, Cal	12
Mayhew's Station, Lowndes, Miss	280
May Hill, Adams, Ohio	12
Maynardsville, Calhoun, Ill	$8
Maynardville, (*c. h.*,) Union, Tenn	70
Mayo Forge, Patrick, Va	21
Mayport, Duval, Fla	12
Maysfield, Milam, Tex	60
May's Landing, (*c. h.*,) Atlantic, N. J	230
May's Lick, Mason, Ky	160
May Spring, Grainger, Tenn	9
Maysville, Benton, Ark	40
Maysville, Franklin, Iowa	130
Maysville,* (*c. h.*,) Mason, Ky	2,500
Maysville,* (*c. h.*,) De Kalb, Mo	410
Maysville, Columbiana, Ohio	110
Maysville, Mercer, Pa	24
Maytown, Lancaster, Pa	130
Mayview, La Fayette, Mo	86
Mayville,* (*c. h.*,) Chautauqua, N. Y	700
Mayville,* Dodge, Wis	400
Maywood, Cook, Ill	12
Maywood, Benton, Minn	17
Mazeppa, Wabashaw, Minn	110
Mazo Manie,* Dane, Wis	620
Mazon, Grundy, Ill	42
Mead Corners, Crawford, Pa	12
Meade, Macomb, Mich	20
Meadow, Millard, Utah	4
Meadow Bluff, Greenbrier, W. Va	29
Meadow Creek, Whitley, Ky	4
Meadow Creek, Madison, Mont	15
Meadow Dale, Highland, Va	10
Meadow Gap, Huntingdon, Pa	15
Meadows of Dan, Patrick, Va	6
Meadow Valley, Plumas, Cal	38
Meadowville, Umatilla, Oreg	40
Meadowville, Barbour, W. Va	21
Mead's Basin, Passaic, N. J	60
Mead's Creek, Steuben, N. Y	10
Mead's Mills, Wayne, Mich	29
Meadville, Barry, Mich	12
Meadville, (*c. h.*,) Franklin, Miss	14
Meadville, Linn, Mo	230
Meadville,* (*c. h.*,) Crawford, Pa	3,000
Meadville, Halifax, Va	12
Meagsville, Jackson, Tenn	12
Means, Harrison, Ohio	140
Mebanesville, Alamance, N. C	260
Mecca, Trumbull, Ohio	110
Mechanicsburgh, Sangamon, Ill	130
Mechanicsburgh, Henry, Ind	94
Mechanicsburgh, Champaign, Ohio	370
Mechanicsburgh,* Cumberland, Pa	1,700
Mechanicsburgh, Bland, Va	15
Mechanic's Falls,* Androscoggin, Me	600
Mechanic's Grove, Lancaster, Pa	43
Mechanicstown, Frederick, Md	190
Mechanicstown, Carroll, Ohio	52
Mechanic's Valley, Cecil, Md	12
Mechanicsville, Vanderburgh, Ind	23
Mechanicsville,* Cedar, Iowa	500
Mechanicsville, Saratoga, N. Y	550
Mechanicsville, Ashtabula, Ohio	38
Mechanicsville, Bucks, Pa	62
Mechanicsville, Sumter, S. C	20
Mechanicsville, Rutland, Vt	230
Mechum's River, Albemarle, Va	120
Mecklenburgh, Schuyler, N. Y	210

* Money-order office.

Mecosta, Mecosta, Mich	$13
Medarysville, Pulaski, Ind	160
Mederville, Clayton, Iowa	12
Medfield, Norfolk, Mass	400
Medford, Piscataquis, Me	21
Medford, Middlesex, Mass	1,100
Medford, Steele, Minn	200
Medford, Burlington, N. J	360
Medford Centre, Piscataquis, Me	15
Media,* (*c. h.*,) Delaware, Pa	1,200
Medicine, Sullivan, Mo	12
Medicine Bow, Carbon, Wyo	12
Medina, Jefferson, Kans	100
Medina, Lenawee, Mich	160
Medina,* Orleans, N. Y	1,900
Medina,* (*c. h.*,) Medina, Ohio	790
Medina, Outagamie, Wis	100
Medo, Blue Earth, Minn	22
Medoc, Jasper, Mo	79
Medon, Madison, Tenn	120
Medora, Macoupin, Ill	60
Medora, Jackson, Ind	220
Medora, Warren, Iowa	13
Medora, Osage, Mo	140
Medusa, Albany, N. Y	48
Medway, Penobscot, Me	24
Medway,* Norfolk, Mass	500
Medway, Greene, N. Y	74
Medway, Clark, Ohio	110
Medybemps, Washington, Me	17
Meeker, Washington, Wis	12
Meeker's Grove, La Fayette, Wis	35
Meeme, Manitowoc, Wis	50
Mehoopany, Wyoming, Pa	190
Meig's Creek, Morgan, Ohio	30
Meigsville, Morgan, Ohio	45
Meinecke, San Joaquin, Cal	12
Melburn, Williams, Ohio	37
Melissa, Ozark, Mo	12
Melissadale, Butler, Pa	21
Melita, Alameda, Cal	12
Mellenbruch, Jackson, Ind	3
Mellenville, Columbia, N. Y	95
Melleray, Dubuque, Iowa	14
Mellington, Kendall, Ill	76
Mellonville, Orange, Fla	200
Mellow Valley, Clay, Ala	8
Mellwood, Prince George's, Md	12
Melmore, Seneca, Ohio	150
Meloy, Washington, Pa	12
Melpine, Muscatine, Iowa	27
Melrose, Clark, Ill	45
Melrose, Middlesex, Mass	700
Melrose, Stearns, Minn	33
Melrose, St. Louis, Mo	12
Melrose, Robeson, N. C	12
Melrose, Nacogdoches, Tex	12
Melrose, Rockingham, Va	16
Melrose, Jackson, Wis	100
Melton, Jefferson, Ark	2
Melton's Mill, Tallapoosa, Ala	12
Meltonsville, Marshall, Ala	11
Melvern, Osage, Kans	12
Melville, Chattooga, Ga	22
Melville, Leelenaw, Mich	39
Melvina, Monroe, Wis	22
Melvin Village, Carroll, N. H	$88
Memory, Taylor, Iowa	41
Memphis, Pickens, Ala	12
Memphis, Clarke, Ind	79
Memphis,* Macomb, Mich	400
Memphis,* (*c. h.*,) Scotland, Mo	350
Memphis, Onondaga, N. Y	160
Memphis, Clinton, Ohio	36
Memphis,* (*c. h.*,) Shelby, Tenn	4,000
Memphis Junction, Warren, Ky	22
Menallen, Adams, Pa	40
Menardville, (*c. h.*,) Menard, Tex	12
Menasha,* Winnebago, Wis	820
Menchville, Warwick, Va	12
Mendham, Morris, N. J	330
Mendocino,* Mendocino, Cal	380
Mendon, El Dorado, Cal	12
Mendon, Adams, Ill	120
Mendon, Worcester, Mass	120
Mendon, St. Joseph, Mich	310
Mendon, Monroe, N. Y	93
Mendon, Mercer, Ohio	40
Mendon, Westmoreland, Pa	45
Mendon, Cache, Utah	19
Mendon, Rutland, Vt	61
Mendon Centre, Monroe, N. Y	56
Mendota,* La Salle, Ill	2,700
Mendota, Labette, Kans	12
Mendota, Dakota, Minn	93
Mendota, Putnam, Mo	25
Menekaune, Oconto, Wis	250
Menlo Park, San Mateo, Cal	12
Menno, Mifflin, Pa	47
Menomonee,* (*c. h.*,) Menomonee, Mich	670
Menomonee,* (*c. h.*,) Dunn, Wis	950
Menomonee Falls, Waukesha, Wis	120
Mentor, Bremer, Iowa	14
Mentor, Lake, Ohio	260
Menzie, Franklin, Iowa	12
Mequon River, Ozaukee, Wis	140
Merced Falls, Merced, Cal	23
Mercer, Somerset, Me	120
Mercer, Mercer, Mo	8
Mercer, Mercer, Ohio	20
Mercer,* (*c. h.*,) Mercer, Pa	1,100
Mercer's Bottom, Mason, W. Va	53
Mercersburgh,* Franklin, Pa	610
Mercerville, Gallia, Ohio	19
Merchantville, Camden, N. J	20
Merchantville, Steuben, N. Y	71
Mercury, Madison, Ind	44
Mercyville, Macon, Mo	6
Meredith, Delaware, N. Y	120
Meredith, Venango, Pa	180
Meredith Centre, Belknap, N. H	46
Meredith's Tavern, Marion, W. Va	4
Meredith Village, Belknap, N. H	510
Meredosia, Morgan, Ill	270
Meriden, New Haven, Conn	1,500
Meriden, La Salle, Ill	150
Meriden, (*c. h.*,) Steele, Minn	53
Meriden,* Sullivan, N. H	560
Meridian, Sutter, Cal	20
Meridian,* (*c. h.*.) Lauderdale, Miss	1,900
Meridian, (*c. h.*,) Jefferson, Nebr	61

* Money-order office.

Meridian, Cayuga, N. Y	$390
Meridian, (*c. h.*,) Bosque, Tex	45
Meridianville, Madison, Ala	12
Mermaid, New Castle, Del	12
Mermenton, St. Landry, La	23
Meroa, Mitchell, Iowa	12
Merom, Sullivan, Ind	240
Merriam, Noble, Ind	38
Merrick, Queens, N. Y	27
Merrillsville, St. Clair, Mich	40
Merrillsville, Franklin, N. Y	12
Merrilltown, Travis, Tex	7
Merrillville, Lake, Ind	52
Merrimac, Jefferson, Iowa	10
Merrimack, Hillsborough, N. H	12
Merrimack, Sauk, Wis	69
Merrimack Point, Monroe, Ill	57
Merrimac Station, St. Louis, Mo	17
Merritt, Scott, Ill	12
Merritt's Bridge, Lexington, S. C	12
Merrittstown, Fayette, Pa	54
Merrow Station, Tolland, Conn	80
Merryall, Bradford, Pa	13
Merry Oaks, Chatham, N. C	8
Mershon's Cross Roads, Laurel, Ky	7
Merton, Steele, Minn	7
Merton, Waukesha, Wis	110
Mertztown, Berks, Pa	72
Merwinsburgh, Monroe, Pa	18
Meshack's Creek, Monroe, Ky	4
Meshannon, Centre, Pa	20
Meshoppen, Wyoming, Pa	380
Mesilla, (*c. h.*,) Doña Ana, N. Mex	120
Mesopotamia, Trumbull, Ohio	170
Messengerville, Cortland, N. Y	50
Messongo, Accomack, Va	13
Metamora,* (*c. h.*,) Woodford, Ill	580
Metamora, Franklin, Ind	170
Metamora, Lapeer, Mich	60
Metamora, Fulton, Ohio	49
Metea, Cass, Ind	15
Metedeconk, Ocean, N. J	34
Methuen, Essex, Mass	820
Metomen, Fond du Lac, Wis	53
Metropolis City,* (*c. h.*,) Massac, Ill	750
Metuchen, Middlesex, N. J	100
Metz, Steuben, Ind	93
Mexico, Miami, Ind	86
Mexico, Oxford, Me	62
Mexico,* (*c. h.*,) Audrian, Mo	1,100
Mexico, Oswego, N. Y	1,300
Mexico, Wyandot, Ohio	19
Mexico, Juniata, Pa	110
Meyer's Mills, Somerset, Pa	190
Meyerstown, Lebanon, Pa	500
Meyersville, De Witt, Tex	57
Miami, Miami, Ind	97
Miami, Saline, Mo	570
Miami, Hamilton, Ohio	59
Miamisburgh,* Montgomery, Ohio	620
Miamiville, Clermont, Ohio	94
Miami Village, Miami, Kans	6
Mianus, Fairfield, Conn	200
Micanopy, Alachua, Fla	100
Micklen, Jackson, Mo	48
Micco, Creek N., Ind. T	15
Miccosukee, Leon, Fla	$16
Michaelsville, Harford, Md	42
Micham, Leelenaw, Mich	4
Michigan Bar, Sacramento, Cal	88
Michigan Bluff, Placer, Cal	100
Michigan Centre, Jackson, Mich	35
Michigan City,* La Porte, Ind	1,400
Michigantown, Clinton, Ind	80
Michigan Valley, Osage, Kans	12
Middagh's, Northampton, Pa	32
Middle Bass, Ottawa, Ohio	44
Middleborough, Plymouth, Mass	1,100
Middlebourne, Guernsey, Ohio	120
Middlebourne, (*c. h.*,) Tyler, W. Va	74
Middle Branch, Stark, Ohio	11
Middlebrook, Montgomery, Md	16
Middlebrook, Iron, Mo	35
Middlebrook, Augusta, Va	93
Middleburgh, Clay, Fla	23
Middleburgh, Washington, Iowa	12
Middleburgh, Casey, Ky	37
Middleburgh, Carroll, Md	51
Middleburgh, Richardson, Nebr	29
Middleburgh,* Schoharie, N. Y	540
Middleburgh, Cuyahoga, Ohio	22
Middleburgh, (*c. h.*,) Snyder, Pa	130
Middleburgh, Hardeman, Tenn	12
Middleburgh, Loudoun, Va	410
Middlebury, New Haven, Conn	78
Middlebury, Elkhart, Ind	370
Middlebury, Grundy, Mo	80
Middlebury, Summit, Ohio	490
Middlebury,* (*c. h.*,) Addison, Vt	1,400
Middlebury, Iowa, Wis	30
Middlebury Centre, Tioga, Pa	9
Middlebush, Somerset, N. J	94
Middle Creek, Hancock, Ill	18
Middle Creek, Chase, Kans	6
Middle Creek, Gallatin, Mont	12
Middle Creek, Noble, Ohio	30
Middle Creek, Snyder, Pa	18
Middle Fabius, Scotland, Mo	38
Middlefield, Middlesex, Conn	320
Middlefield, Buchanan, Iowa	9
Middlefield, Hampshire, Mass	170
Middlefield, Otsego, N. Y	130
Middlefield, Geauga, Ohio	69
Middlefield Centre, Otsego, N. Y	66
Middleford, Sussex, Del	17
Middle Fork, Clinton, Ind	68
Middle Fork, Jackson, Ky	1
Middle Fork, Hocking, Ohio	11
Middle Fork, Randolph, W. Va	12
Middle Granville, Washington, N. Y	790
Middle Grove, Fulton, Ill	18
Middle Grove, Monroe, Mo	91
Middle Grove, Saratoga, N. Y	59
Middle Haddam, Middlesex, Conn	200
Middle Hope, Orange, N. Y	26
Middle Island, Suffolk, N. Y	38
Middle Lancaster, Butler, Pa	39
Middle Point, Van Wert, Ohio	72
Middleport, (*c. h.*,) Iroquois, Ill	330
Middleport, Niagara, N. Y	550
Middleport, Meigs, Ohio	540
Middleport, Schuylkill, Pa	94

* Money-order-office.

Middleport, Webster, W. Va	$5
Middle River, Banks, Ga	9
Middle River, Madison, Iowa	7
Middle Saluda, Greenville, S. C	12
Middlesex, Yates, N. Y	120
Middlesex, Washington, Vt	150
Middlesex Village, Middlesex, Mass.	57
Middle Spring, Cumberland, Pa	37
Middle Sprite, Fulton, N. Y	13
Middlesworth, Shelby, Ill	12
Middleton, Ada, Idaho	47
Middleton, Essex, Mass	170
Middleton, Strafford, N. H	6
Middleton, Washington, Oreg	12
Middleton, Rutherford, Tenn	12
Middleton, Leon, Tex	3
Middleton, Dane, Wis	35
Middleton Station, Hardeman, Tenn	110
Middletown,* (*c. h.*,) Middlesex, Conn	3,400
Middletown,* New Castle, Del	1,100
Middletown, Logan, Ill	160
Middletown, Henry, Ind	280
Middletown, Des Moines, Iowa	71
Middletown, Jefferson, Ky	74
Middletown,* Frederick, Md	570
Middletown, Ingham, Mich	10
Middletown, Montgomery, Mo	300
Middletown, Monmouth, N. J	110
Middletown,* Orange, N. Y	2,200
Middletown,* Butler, Ohio	1,300
Middletown,* Dauphin, Pa	1,100
Middletown,* Rutland, Vt	540
Middletown, Frederick, Va	190
Middletown Centre, Susquehanna, Pa	13
Middle Valley, Morris, N. J	37
Middle Valley, Wayne, Pa	79
Middleville,* Barry, Mich	480
Middleville, Sussex, N. J	15
Middleville, Herkimer, N. Y	210
Middleway, Jefferson, W. Va	130
Midland,* (*c h.*,) Midland, Mich	700
Midland, Marquette, Wis	13
Midlothian, Chesterfield, Va	160
Mid Prairie, Louisa, Iowa	16
Midville, Burke, Ga	170
Midway, Bullock, Ala	150
Midway, Hot Spring, Ark	12
Midway, Alameda, Cal	12
Midway, Fulton, Ill	37
Midway, Spencer, Ind	33
Midway, Woodford, Ky	510
Midway, Hinds, Miss	12
Midway, Boone, Mo	12
Midway, Erie, N. Y	12
Midway, Davidson, N. C	8
Midway, Guernsey, Ohio	18
Midway, Washington, Pa	96
Midway, Barnwell, S. C	110
Midway, Greene, Tenn	76
Midway, Madison, Tex	12
Midway, Wasatch, Utah	15
Mier, Wabash, Ill	50
Mier, Grant, Ind	81
Mifflin, Crawford, Ind	11
Mifflin, Ashland, Ohio	17
Mifflin, Henderson, Tenn	$55
Mifflin, Iowa, Wis	70
Mifflinburgh, Union, Pa	440
Mifflintown,* (*c. h.*,) Juniata, Pa	600
Mifflinville, Franklin, Ohio	30
Mifflinville, Columbia, Pa	52
Milam, Sabine, Tex	280
Milan, Ripley, Ind	120
Milan, Lucas, Iowa	12
Milan, Washtenaw, Mich	64
Milan,* (*c. h.*,) Sullivan, Mo	250
Milan, Coos, N. H	89
Milan, Dutchess, N. Y	25
Milan, Erie, Ohio	680
Milan, Bradford, Pa	65
Milan Depot, Gibson, Tenn	120
Milanville, Wayne, Pa	27
Milburn, Ballard, Ky	16
Mile Creek, Muskegon, Mich	12
Mile Creek, Pickens, S. C	12
Milesburgh, Centre, Pa	300
Miles Grove, Erie, Pa	100
Miles Point, Carroll, Mo	65
Miles Pond, Essex, Vt	12
Miles Station, Macoupin, Ill	91
Milestown, St. Mary's, Md	21
Mile Strip, Madison, N. Y	13
Milford, Lassen, Cal	12
Milford,* New Haven, Conn	1,200
Milford,* Kent, Del	920
Milford, Iroquois, Ill	180
Milford, Kosciusko, Ind	160
Milford, Dickinson, Iowa	12
Milford, Riley, Kans	71
Milford, Bracken, Ky	24
Milford, Penobscot, Me	97
Milford,* Worcester, Mass	2,300
Milford,* Oakland, Mich	310
Milford, Brown, Minn	10
Milford, Barton, Mo	28
Milford, (*c. h.*,) Seward, Nebr	120
Milford,* Hillsborough, N. H	1,100
Milford, Hunterdon, N. J	310
Milford, Otsego, N. Y	390
Milford,* Clermont, Ohio	670
Milford,* (*c. h.*,) Pike, Pa	360
Milford, Ellis, Tex	110
Milford, Caroline, Va	33
Milford, Jefferson, Wis	89
Milford Centre, Union, Ohio	210
Milford Mills, Chester, Pa	24
Milford Square, Bucks, Pa	77
Milfordton, Knox, Ohio	30
Mill, Fayette, Iowa	15
Millard, Adair, Mo	12
Millard, Walworth, Wis	50
Millbach, Lebanon, Pa	17
Mill Bend, Hawkins, Tenn	12
Millborough Springs, Bath, Va	44
Millbrae, San Mateo, Cal	12
Millbridge, Washington, Me	280
Mill Brook, Litchfield, Conn	16
Millbrook, Kendall, Ill	21
Millbrook, Mecosta, Mich	92
Millbrook, Warren, N. J	19
Millbrook, Dutchess, N. Y	130

* Money-order office.

Post office	Compensation
Mill Brook, Wayne, Ohio	$21
Mill Brook, Washington, Tenn	12
Millbrook, Frederick, Va	12
Millburgh, Berrien, Mich	80
Millburn, Lake, Ill	89
Millburn, Essex, N. J	330
Millburnton, Green, Tenn	3
Millbury, Worcester, Mass	1,100
Millbury, Wood, Ohio	100
Mill City, Clear Creek, Colo	110
Mill City, Humboldt, Nev	12
Mill City, Wyoming, Pa	130
Mill Creek, Izard, Ark	7
Mill Creek, Bourbon, Kans	10
Mill Creek, Calvert, Md	12
Mill Creek, Kent, Mich	16
Mill Creek, Huntingdon, Pa	170
Mill Creek, Salt Lake, Utah	12
Mill Creek, Berkeley, W. Va	71
Mill Creek, Richland, Wis	8
Milldale, Warren, Va	10
Milledgeville,* (*c. h.*,) Baldwin, Ga	1,200
Milledgeville, Carroll, Ill	190
Milledgeville, Appanoose, Iowa	11
Milledgeville, Lincoln, Ky	30
Milledgeville, Mercer, Pa	15
Milledgeville, McNairy, Tenn	12
Millen's Bay, Jefferson, N. Y	18
Miller Grove, Hopkins, Tex	8
Miller's, Lawrence, Ohio	82
Millersburgh, Mercer, Ill	120
Millersburgh, Elkhart, Ind	240
Millersburgh, Iowa, Iowa	180
Millersburgh, Bourbon, Ky	530
Millersburgh, Rice, Minn	15
Millersburg, Callaway, Mo	100
Millersburgh,* (*c. h.*,) Holmes, Ohio	910
Millersburgh,* Dauphin, Pa	900
Miller's Corners, Ontario, N. Y	86
Miller's Creek, Black Hawk, Iowa	12
Miller's Creek, Estill, Ky	19
Miller's Eddy, Armstrong, Pa	18
Miller's Falls, Franklin, Mass	130
Miller's Grove, Woodson, Kans	12
Miller's Mill, Davidson, N. C	12
Miller's Place, Suffolk, N. Y	65
Millersport, Fairfield, Ohio	64
Miller's Station, Lake, Ind	36
Miller's Station, Harrison, Ohio	12
Miller's Station, Crawford, Pa	79
Miller's Tavern, Essex, Va	12
Millerstown, Champaign, Ohio	22
Millerstown, Perry, Pa	320
Millerstown Station, Perry, Pa	25
Millersville, Russell, Ky	4
Millersville, Anne Arundel, Md	100
Millersville, Cape Girardeau, Mo	29
Millersville,* Lancaster, Pa	1,000
Millerton, (*c. h.*,) Fresno, Cal	170
Millerton, Dutchess, N. Y	520
Millerville, Douglass, Minn	12
Mill Falls, Marion, W. Va	9
Millfield, Athens, Ohio	32
Mill Ford, Cherokee, Ala	12
Mill Gap, Highland, Va	10
Mill Green, Harford, Md	20
Millgrove, Blackford, Ind	$30
Mill Grove, Poweshiek, Iowa	8
Mill Grove, Erie, N. Y	49
Mill Grove, Morgan, Ohio	11
Mill Hall, Clinton, Pa	190
Millheim, Centre, Pa	90
Millheim, Austin, Tex	20
Mill Hill, Cabarrus, N. C	12
Mill Hollow, Luzerne, Pa	8
Millhousen, Decatur, Ind	100
Millican, Brazos, Tex	300
Milligan, Tuscarawas, Ohio	6
Milliken's Bend, Madison, La	39
Millin, Burke, Ga	16
Millington, Middlesex, Conn	16
Millington, Kent, Md	220
Millington, Franklin, Mass	58
Millington, Tuscola, Mich	20
Millington, Morris, N. J	44
Millington, Albemarle, Va	25
Mill Plain, Fairfield, Conn	34
Mill Point, Sullivan, Tenn	7
Mill Point, Pocahontas, W. Va	25
Millport, Sanford, Ala	12
Millport, Washington, Ind	4
Millport, Knox, Mo	24
Mill Port, Chemung, N. Y	360
Millport, Columbiana, Ohio	68
Millport, Potter, Pa	46
Mill River, Berkshire, Mass	140
Mill River, Henderson, N. C	19
Mill Rock, Jackson, Iowa	64
Mill Run, Fayette, Pa	200
Millry, Washington, Ala	15
Mills, Jackson, Wis	12
Millsborough, Sussex, Del	79
Millsborough, Washington, Pa	100
Mills Centre, Brown, Wis	55
Mills' Corners, Jay, Ind	12
Mills' Corners, Fulton, N. Y	9
Mill Shoals, White, Ill	12
Mills' Mills, Allegany, N. Y	25
Mills' Prairie, Edwards, Ill	14
Mill Spring, St. Louis, Mo	100
Mill Spring, Jefferson, Tenn	8
Mill Springs, Wayne, Ky	24
Millstadt, St. Clair, Ill	150
Mill Station, Lapeer, Mich	10
Millstone, Somerset, N. J	260
Millstone Point, Washington, Md	21
Milltown, Chambers, Ala	53
Mill Town, Berrien, Ga	62
Milltown, Crawford, Ind	23
Milltown, Adair, Ky	16
Milltown, Washington, Me	390
Milltown, Chester, Pa	19
Millview, Sullivan, Pa	14
Mill Village, Sullivan, N. H	32
Mill Village, Erie, Pa	170
Millville, Shasta, Cal	120
Millville, Henry, Ind	80
Millville, Clayton, Iowa	61
Millville, Worcester, Mass	350
Millville, Wabashaw, Minn	8
Millville, Ray, Mo	80
Millville,* Cumberland, N. J	1,200

* Money-order office.

Millville, Orleans, N. Y	$100
Millville, Butler, Ohio	93
Millville, Cumberland, Pa	90
Millville, Spartanburgh, S. C	5
Millville, Lincoln, Tenn	22
Millville, Cache, Utah	22
Millville, Westmoreland, Va	24
Millville, Grant, Wis	36
Millville Depot, Pike, Pa	12
Millway, Lancaster, Pa	49
Millwood, Kosciusko, Ind	9
Millwood, Lincoln, Mo	62
Millwood, Knox, Ohio	70
Millwood, Westmoreland, Pa	68
Millwood, Washington, Tenn	60
Millwood, Collin, Tex	12
Millwood, Clarke, Va	130
Milmine, Piatt, Ill	80
Milner, Randolph, Ala	12
Milner, Pike, Ga	59
Milner's Corners, Hancock, Ind	12
Milnersville, Guernsey, Ohio	85
Milnesville, Augusta, Va	12
Milo, Pike, Ala	10
Milo, Bureau, Ill	44
Milo, Delaware, Iowa	12
Milo, Piscataquis, Me	190
Milo, Barry, Mich	11
Milo, Defiance, Ohio	8
Milo, Wetzel, W. Va	67
Milo Centre, Yates, N. Y	87
Milor, Sebastian, Ark	5
Milpitas, Santa Clara, Cal	84
Milquatay, San Diego, Cal	9
Milroy, Knox, Ill	16
Milroy, Rush, Ind	160
Milroy, Mifflin, Pa	290
Milton, Litchfield, Conn	86
Milton, Sussex, Del	260
Milton, (*c. h.*,) Santa Rosa, Fla	170
Milton, Pike, Ill	140
Milton, Wayne, Ind	350
Milton, Van Buren, Iowa	30
Milton, Trimble, Ky	200
Milton, Norfolk, Mass	870
Milton, Macomb, Mich	33
Milton, Randolph, Mo	50
Milton, Saunders, Nebr	12
Milton, Strafford, N. H	160
Milton, Morris, N. J	9
Milton, Ulster, N. Y	370
Milton, Caswell, N. C	210
Milton, Mahoning, Ohio	38
Milton, Northumberland, Pa	1,400
Milton, Rutherford, Tenn	12
Milton, Chittenden, Vt	360
Milton,* Rock, Wis	560
Milton Centre, Saratoga, N. Y	27
Milton Centre, Wood, Ohio	110
Milton Junction, Rock, Wis	330
Milton Mills, Strafford, N. H	220
Milton Plantation, Oxford, Me	20
Miltonsburgh, Monroe, Ohio	46
Milton Station, Coles, Ill	270
Milton Station, Mills, Iowa	12
Milton Station, Wayne, Ohio	15
Milville, Rusk, Tex	$4
Milwaukee, Clackamas, Oreg	68
Milwaukee, Luzerne, Pa	20
Milwaukee,* (*c. h.*,) Milwaukee, Wis	4,000
Mims, Barnwell, S. C	10
Mim's Store, Marion, Tex	12
Mina, Chautauqua, N. Y	47
Minaville, Montgomery, N. Y	110
Minburn, Dallas, Iowa	60
Mincy, Taney, Mo	12
Minden, Claiborne, La	250
Minden, Sanilac, Mich	58
Minden, Benton, Minn	12
Minden, Lawrence, Mo	21
Minden, Montgomery, N. Y	32
Mindoro, La Crosse, Wis	140
Mine Kill Falls, Schoharie, N. Y	12
Mine La Motte, Madison, Mo	20
Mineola, Queens, N. Y	110
Miner, La Salle, Ill	12
Mineral, Bureau, Ill	84
Mineral City, White Pine, Nev	12
Mineral Mill, Elko, Nev	12
Mineral Point, Anderson, Kans	34
Mineral Point, Washington, Mo	52
Mineral Point, Tuscarawas, Ohio	26
Mineral Point, Cambria, Pa	37
Mineral Point,* Iowa, Wis	1,700
Mineral Ridge, Boone, Iowa	210
Mineral Ridge,* Mahoning, Ohio	260
Mineral Springs, Hampstead, Ark	13
Mineral Springs, Mower, Minn	8
Mineral Springs, Schoharie, N. Y	40
Mineral Springs, Adams, Ohio	25
Miner's Delight, Sweetwater, Wyo	12
Minersville, Henry, Ill	16
Minersville, Christian, Mo	12
Minersville, Meigs, Ohio	100
Minersville,* Schuylkill, Pa	1,100
Minersville, Beaver, Utah	38
Minerva, Marshall, Iowa	17
Minerva, Mason, Ky	36
Minerva, Essex, N. Y	20
Minerva,* Stark, Ohio	500
Minetto, Oswego, N. Y	120
Mineville, Essex, N. Y	250
Mingo, Champaign, Ohio	88
Mingo Flat, Randolph, W. Va	20
Minier, Tazewell, Ill	8
Mining, Morgan, Mo	16
Minisink, Orange, N. Y	21
Minneapolis, Ottawa, Kans	41
Minneapolis,* (*c. h.*,) Hennepin, Minn	4,000
Minneola, Goodhue, Minn	14
Minnequa, Bradford, Pa	73
Minnereka, Mower, Minn	12
Minneska, Wabashaw, Minn	120
Minnesota City, Winona, Minn	45
Minnesota Junction, Dodge, Wis	180
Minnesota Lake, Faribault, Minn	110
Minnetonka, Hennepin, Minn	35
Minnetrista, Hennepin, Minn	8
Minnora, Calhoun, W. Va	3
Minonk,* Woodford, Ill	1,200
Minooka, Grundy, Ill	360
Minorsville, Scott, Ky	12

* Money-order office.

Minot, Androscoggin, Me	$110
Minster, Auglaize, Ohio	170
Minta, Indiana, Pa	55
Mint Hill, Mecklenburgh, N. C	2
Mintonville, Casey, Ky	12
Mint Spring, Augusta, Va	13
Mirabile, Caldwell, Mo	120
Miracle Run, Monongalia, W. Va	6
Miranda, Rowan, N. C	10
Miser's Station, Blount, Tenn	10
Mishawaka,* St. Joseph, Ind	1,600
Mishicot, Manitowoc, Wis	100
Mission Creek, Wabaunsee, Kans	15
Mission San José, Alameda, Cal	30
Mission Valley, Victoria, Tex	37
Mississippi City, (*c. h.*,) Harrison, Miss	140
Missoula, (*c. h.*,) Missoula, Mont	520
Missouri City, Clay, Mo	260
Missouriton, St. Charles, Mo	15
Missouri Valley,* Harrison, Iowa	670
Mitchell,* Lawrence, Ind	730
Mitchell,* (*c. h.*,) Mitchell, Iowa	280
Mitchell, Antrim, Mich	18
Mitchellsburgh, Boyle, Ky	93
Mitchell's Creek, Tioga, Pa	37
Mitchell's Mills, Indiana, Pa	37
Mitchell's Salt Works, Jefferson, Ohio	19
Mitchell's Station, Culpeper, Va	110
Mitchellsville, Saline, Ill	16
Mitchellsville, Steuben, N. Y	12
Mitchellsville, Sumner, Tenn	62
Mitchellville, Polk, Iowa	210
Mitchellville, Prince George's, Md	67
Mitchellville, Harrison, Mo	33
Mitchie, Monroe, Ill	12
Mittineague, Hampton, Mass	430
Mixersville, Franklin, Ind	24
Mixtown, Tioga, Pa	14
Moberly, Randolph, Mo	630
Mobile,* (*c. h.*,) Mobile, Ala	4,000
Mobley Pond, Scriven, Ga	15
Moccasin, Effingham, Ill	16
Mockeson, Lawrence, Tenn	12
Mock's Mill, Washington, Va	12
Mocksville, (*c. h.*,) Davie, N. C	160
Modale, Harrison, Iowa	33
Mode, Shelby, Ill	7
Model City, Cass, Mich	59
Modena, Stark, Ill	81
Modena, Mercer, Mo	13
Modena, Ulster, N. Y	38
Modena, Buffalo, Wis	33
Modest Town, Accomack, Va	85
Moe, Douglas, Minn	11
Moffatt's Creek, Augusta, Va	80
Moffettsville, Anderson, S. C	15
Moffitt's Grove, Guthrie, Iowa	1
Moffitt's Mills, Randolph, N. C	19
Moffitt's Store, Columbia, N. Y	57
Mogadore, Summit, Ohio	84
Mohave City, (*c. h.*,) Mohave, Ariz	80
Mohawk, Herkimer, N. Y	800
Mohawk Hill, Lewis, N. Y	20
Mohawk Valley, Plumas, Cal	12
Mohawk Village, Coshocton, Ohio	$80
Mohegan, Providence, R. I	130
Mohican, Ashland, Ohio	69
Mohn's Store, Berks, Pa	16
Mohontongo, Juniata, Pa	20
Mohrsville, Berks, Pa	69
Moingona,* Boone, Iowa	370
Moira, Franklin, N. Y	220
Mokelumne, San Joaquin, Cal	12
Mokelumne Hill,* (*c. h.*,) Calaveras, Cal	530
Mokena, Will, Ill	320
Moksee, (*c. h.*,) Yakima, Wash	12
Molalla, Clackamas, Oreg	12
Mole Hill, Ritchie, W. Va	10
Moline, Rock Island, Ill	2,000
Moline, Allegan, Mich	34
Molino, Escambia, Fla	110
Molino, Oswego, N. Y	14
Molino, Lincoln, Tenn	12
Molltown, Berks, Pa	8
Moluncus, Aroostook, Me	13
Momence, Kankakee, Ill	470
Mona, Mitchell, Iowa	12
Mona, Juab, Utah	18
Monagan, St. Clair, Mo	74
Monches, Waukesha, Wis	32
Monclova, Lucas, Ohio	85
Monclova, Morgan, W. Va	9
Mondamin, Harrison, Iowa	130
Mondovi, Buffalo, Wis	100
Monee, Will, Ill	460
Money Creek, Houston, Minn	68
Mongaup, Sullivan, N. Y	29
Mongaup Valley, Sullivan, N. Y	110
Mongoquinong, La Grange, Ind	74
Monhegan Island, Lincoln, Me	10
Monie, Somerset, Md	12
Monitor, Alpine, Cal	160
Monitor, Tippecanoe, Ind	34
Monitor, Marion, Oreg	12
Monk's Store, Sampson, N. C	1
Monkton, Addison, Vt	160
Monkton Mills, Baltimore, Md	120
Monkton Ridge, Addison, Vt	32
Monmouth,* (*c. h.*,) Warren, Ill	3,000
Monmouth, Adams, Ind	29
Monmouth, Jackson, Iowa	79
Monmouth, Crawford, Kans	120
Monmouth, Kennebec, Me	460
Monmouth, Polk, Oreg	96
Monmouth, Rockbridge, Va	4
Monmouth Junction, Middlesex, N. J	12
Monocacy, Montgomery, Md	12
Monocacy, Berks, Pa	84
Monon, White, Ind	140
Monona, Clayton, Iowa	150
Monongahela City,* Washington, Pa	980
Monroe, Fairfield, Conn	76
Monroe, (*c. h.*,) Walton, Ga	150
Monroe,* Jasper, Iowa	710
Monroe, (*c. h.*,*) Ouachita, La	1,000
Monroe, Waldo, Me	140
Monroe, Franklin, Mass	10

* Money-order office.

Post office	Amount
Monroe,* (*c. h.*,) Monroe, Mich	$2,100
Monroe, Perry, Miss	8
Monroe, Platte, Nebr	25
Monroe, Grafton, N. H	96
Monroe, Sussex, N. J	10
Monroe, Orange, N. Y	390
Monroe, (*c. h.*,) Union, N. C	110
Monroe, Butler, Ohio	160
Monroe, Overton, Tenn	17
Monroe,* (*c. h.*,) Green, Wis	1,500
Monroe Centre, Ogle, Ill	15
Monroe Centre, Waldo, Me	18
Monroe Centre, Grand Traverse, Mich	47
Monroe Centre, Ashtabula, Ohio	52
Monroe City, Monroe, Ill	32
Monroe City, Monroe, Mo	360
Monroe Draft, Greenbrier, W. Va	12
Monroe Forge, Lebanon, Pa	13
Monroe Furnace, Jackson, Ohio	40
Monroe Mills, Knox, Ohio	30
Monroeton, Rockingham, N. C	8
Monroeton, Bradford, Pa	180
Monroeville, (*c. h.*,) Monroe, Ala	26
Monroeville,* Allen, Ind	530
Monroeville, Salem, N. J	12
Monroeville,* Huron, Ohio	820
Monroeville, Allegheny, Pa	24
Monroe Works, Orange, N. Y	52
Monrovia, Morgan, Ind	160
Monrovia, Atchison, Kans	65
Monrovia, Frederick, Md	120
Monsey, Rockland, N. Y	120
Monson, Piscataquis, Me	160
Monson, Hampden, Mass	840
Montague, Franklin, Mass	430
Montague,* Muskegon, Mich	190
Montague, Sussex, N. J	41
Montague, Lewis, N. Y	8
Montague, (*c. h.*,) Montague, Texas	31
Montague, Essex, Va	19
Montague City, Franklin, Mass	63
Mont Alto, Franklin, Pa	59
Montana, Boone, Iowa	2100
Montana, Labette, Kans	270
Montana, Beaver Head, Mont	34
Montana, Warren, N. J	46
Montandon, Northumberland, Pa	190
Montauk, Dent, Mo	12
Montaview, Montgomery, Ky	4
Mont Clair, Essex, N. J	670
Monte, Los Angeles, Cal	77
Montello, *(*c. h.*,) Marquette, Wis	200
Monterey,* (*c. h.*,) Monterey, Cal	640
Monterey, Calhoun, Ill	31
Monterey, Pulaski, Ind	12
Monterey, Davis, Iowa	50
Monterey, Owen, Ky	58
Monterey, Berkshire, Mass	140
Monterey, Allegan, Mich	54
Monterey, Richardson, Nebr	8
Monterey, Clermont, Ohio	43
Monterey, Berks, Pa	20
Monterey, Abbeville, S. C	12
Monterey, (*c. h.*,) Highland, Va	280
Monterey, Waukesha, Wis	33
Montesano, (*c. h.*,) Chehalis, Wash	$15
Montevallo, Shelby, Ala	330
Montevallo, Vernon, Mo	20
Monte Vista, Choctaw, Miss	4
Montez, Cass, Ind	33
Montezuma, Tuolumne, Cal	20
Montezuma, Macon, Ga	610
Montezuma, Pike, Ill	18
Montezuma, Parke, Ind	170
Montezuma,*(*c. h.*,) Poweshiek, Iowa	580
Montezuma, Cayuga, N. Y	250
Montezuma, Mercer, Ohio	47
Montezuma, McNairy, Tenn	12
Montfort, Grant, Wis	150
MONTGOMERY,*(*c. h.*,) Montgomery, Ala	4,000
Montgomery, Kane, Ill	93
Montgomery, Montgomery, Kans	12
Montgomery, Trigg, Ky	17
Montgomery, Grant, La	43
Montgomery, Hampden, Mass	42
Montgomery, Le Sueur, Minn	25
Montgomery, Orange, N. Y	470
Montgomery, Montgomery, N. C	6
Montgomery, Hamilton, Ohio	110
Montgomery, (*c. h.*,) Montgomery, Tex	200
Montgomery, Franklin, Vt	62
Montgomery Centre, Franklin, Vt	72
Montgomery City, Park, Colo	20
Montgomery City,* Montgomery, Mo	350
Montgomery's Ferry, Perry, Pa	20
Montgomery Springs, Montgomery, Va	82
Montgomery Square, Montgomery, Pa	71
Montgomery's Station, Daviess, Ind	83
Montgomery Station, Lycoming, Pa	180
Monticello,* (*c. h.*,) Drew, Ark	410
Monticello, Napa, Cal	73
Monticello, (*c. h.*,) Jefferson, Fla	610
Monticello, (*c. h.*,) Jasper, Ga	140
Monticello,* (*c. h.*,) Piatt, Ill	720
Monticello,* (*c. h.*,) White, Ind	600
Monticello,* Jones, Iowa	870
Monticello, Johnson, Kans	60
Monticello, (*c. h.*,) Wayne, Ky	120
Monticello, Aroostook, Me	63
Monticello,* Wright, Minn	400
Monticello, (*c. h.*,) Lawrence, Miss	48
Monticello, (*c. h.*,) Lewis, Mo	200
Monticello,* (*c. h.*,) Sullivan, N. Y	890
Monticello, Guilford, N. C	15
Monticello, Armstrong, Pa	61
Monticello, Fairfield, S. C	34
Monticello, (*c. h.*,) Cowlitz, Wash	58
Monticello, Green, Wis	150
Montmorency, Tippecanoe, Ind	54
Montpelier, Blackford, Ind	100
Montpelier, Adair, Ky	12
Montpelier, Chickasaw, Miss	17
Montpelier, Williams, Ohio	41
Montpelier, Rich, Utah	12
MONTPELIER,* (*c. h.*,) Washington, Vt	2,400

* Money-order office.

Post office	Amount
Montpelier, Hanover, Va	$16
Montpelier, Kewaunee, Wis	24
Montra, Shelby, Ohio	58
Montreal, Nelson, Va	230
Montrose, Lee, Iowa	260
Montrose, Montgomery, Md	18
Montrose, Genesee, Mich	12
Montrose, Wright, Minn	20
Montrose, Westchester, N. Y	10
Montrose, Summit, Ohio	25
Montrose,* (*c. h.*,) Susquehanna, Pa	1,500
Montrose Depot, Susquehanna, Pa	44
Montross, (*c. h.*,) Westmoreland, Va	43
Montursville, Lycoming, Pa	270
Montvale Springs, Blount, Tenn	69
Montville, New London, Conn	150
Montville, Waldo, Me	61
Montville, Berkshire, Mass	65
Montville, Geauga, Ohio	110
Monument, El Paso, Colo	12
Monument, Pike, Ill	36
Monument, Barnstable, Mass	160
Monument House, Baltimore, Md	12
Moodna, Orange, N. Y	50
Moodus, Middlesex, Conn	420
Moodyville, Greene, Ky	12
Mooers, Clinton, N. Y	390
Mooers Forks, Clinton, N. Y	230
Mooers' Prairie, Wright, Minn	210
Moon, Allegheny, Pa	32
Mooney, Jackson, Ind	61
Moon Lake, Coahoma, Miss	12
Moons, Fayette, Ohio	18
Moon's Ranch, Tehama, Cal	5
Moorefield, Switzerland, Ind	63
Moorefield, Nicholas, Ky	74
Moorefield, Harrison, Ohio	84
Moorefield,* (*c. h.*,) Hardy, W. Va	320
Moore's, Tyler, W. Va	3
Mooresborough, Cleveland, N. C	13
Mooresburgh, Montour, Pa	25
Mooresburgh, Hawkins, Tenn	12
Moore's Creek, New Haven, N. C	12
Moore's Creek, Monroe, Wis	12
Moore's Flat, Nevada, Cal	150
Moore's Hill, Dearborn, Ind	350
Moore's Mill, Dutchess, N. Y	12
Moore's Ordinary, Prince Edward, Va	130
Moore's Prairie, Jefferson, Ill	54
Moore's Salt Works, Jefferson, Ohio	36
Moore's Station, Butte, Cal	12
Moore's Store, Jackson, Tenn	12
Moore's Store, Shenandoah, Va	20
Moorestown,* Burlington, N. J	650
Moorestown, Northampton, Pa	12
Mooresville, Limestone, Ala	140
Mooresville,* Morgan, Ind	300
Mooresville, Livingston, Mo	170
Mooresville, Monongalia, W. Va	11
Moore's Vineyard, Bartholomew, Ind	13
Mooreville, Itawamba, Miss	24
Moorhead, Allegheny, Pa	88
Moorhead, Freestone, Tex	12
Moorheadville, Erie, Pa	100
Mooringsport, Caddo, La	$12
Moorland, Wayne, Ohio	20
Moorman's River, Albemarle, Va	7
Moorton, Kent, Del	57
Moose Meadow, Tolland, Conn	32
Moose River, Somerset, Me	38
Mooshaunee, Moore, N. C	3
Moosup, Windham, Conn	340
Mora, (*c. h.*,) Mora, N. Mex	43
Moral, Shelby, Ind	11
Morales, Jackson, Tex	8
Moravia, Appanoose, Iowa	230
Moravia, Cayuga, N. Y	470
Moravia, Lawrence, Pa	59
Mordansville, Columbia, Pa	12
Moreau Station, Saratoga, N. Y	19
Moreauville, Avoyelles, La	64
Morehead, (*c. h.*,) Rowan, Ky	26
Morehead City, Carteret, N. C	300
Morehouseville, Hamilton, N. Y	59
Moreland, Pope, Ark	11
Moreland, Schuyler, N. Y	21
Moreland, Lycoming, Pa	16
Morell's Mill, Sullivan, Tenn	5
Morenci, Lenawee, Mich	590
Moresville, Delaware, N. Y	97
Moretown, Washington, Vt	150
Morgan, Lake, Cal	7
Morgan, (*c. h.*,) Calhoun, Ga	40
Morgan, Montgomery, Kans	12
Morgan, Pendleton, Ky	130
Morgan, Marquette, Mich	130
Morgan,* Ashtabula, Ohio	370
Morgan, (*c. h.*,) Morgan, Utah	150
Morgan, Orleans, Vt	36
Morganfield, (*c. h.*,) Union, Ky	290
Morgan's Fork, Franklin, Miss	12
Morgan's Glade, Preston, W. Va	16
Morgan's Mills, Union, N. C	5
Morgan Spring, Perry, Ala	12
Morgansville, Morgan, Ohio	12
Morganton, (*c. h.*,) Fannin, Ga	72
Morganton,* (*c. h.*,) Burke, N. C	350
Morgantown,* Morgan, Ind	250
Morgantown, (*c. h.*,) Butler, Ky	87
Morgantown, Berks, Pa	94
Morgantown, Blount, Tenn	33
Morgantown,* (*c. h.*,) Monongalia, W. Va	740
Morgan Valley, Wyoming, W. Va	1
Morganville, Dade, Ga	40
Morganville, Hillsdale, Mich	6
Morganville, Monmouth, N. J	12
Morganville, Genesee, N. Y	56
Morganville, Polk, Tex	12
Morganza, St. Mary's, Md	20
Morganzia, Point Coupee, La	70
Moriah, Essex, N. Y	190
Moriah Centre, Essex, N. Y	12
Morian, Schuyler, Nebr	12
Moriches, Suffolk, N. Y	51
Morley, Mecosta, Mich	12
Morley, Scott, Mo	12
Morley, St. Lawrence, N. Y	210
Mormon Island, Sacramento, Cal	43
Mormon Mills, Burnet, Tex	12

* Money-order office.

Post office	Amount
Morning Sun, Louisa, Iowa	$220
Morning Sun, Preble, Ohio	120
Mornington, Webster, Mo	9
Morning View, Kenton, Ky	53
Morning View, Belmont, Ohio	27
Moro, Monroe, Ark	10
Moro, Madison, Ill	170
Moro, Aroostook, Me	8
Moro Bay, Bradley, Ark	2
Morocco, Newton, Ind	66
Moroni, San Pete, Utah	92
Morrell, Huntingdon, Pa	12
Morrill, Jackson, Ky	13
Morrill, Waldo, Me	56
Morris, Litchfield, Conn	110
*Morris,** (*c. h.*,) Grundy, Ill	2,500
Morris, Ripley, Ind	130
Morris, Otsego, N. Y	450
Morris, Tioga, Pa	21
Morris, Hanover, Va	5
Morrisania, Westchester, N. Y	1,200
Morris Corners, Crawford, Pa	12
Morris Cross Roads, Fayette, Pa	70
Morrisdale, Clearfield, Pa	41
Morris Hill, Alleghany, Va	10
*Morrison,** (*c. h.*,) Whitesides, Ill	2,000
Morrison, Gasconade, Mo	67
Morrison, Luzerne, Pa	120
Morrison, Warren, Tenn	59
Morrison, Brown, Wis	28
Morrisonville, Clinton, N. Y	51
Morris Ridge, Harrison, Mo	12
Morris Run, Tioga, Pa	370
Morris Station, Quitman, Ga	10
Morristown, Henry, Ill	55
Morristown, Shelby, Ind	58
Morristown, Rice, Minn	100
Morristown, Cass, Mo	120
*Morristown,** (*c. h.*,) Morris, N. J	2,500
Morristown, St. Lawrence, N. Y	230
Morris Town, Moore, N. C	12
Morristown,* Belmont, Ohio	220
Morristown,* Grainger, Tenn	590
Morristown, Lamoille, Vt	57
Morrisville, Calhoun, Ala	18
*Morrisville,** (*c. h.*,) Madison, N. Y	650
Morrisville, Wake, N. C	69
Morrisville, Clinton, Ohio	24
Morrisville, Bucks, Pa	310
Morrisville, Lamoille, Vt	390
Morrisville, Fauquier, Va	18
Morrow,* Warren, Ohio	520
Morrowville, Jefferson, Ala	5
Morse's, Graves, Ky	68
Morse's Mill, Jefferson, Mo	16
Morseville, Schoharie, N. Y	12
Morsston, Sullivan, N. Y	11
Morton, Tazewell, Ill	97
Morton, Putnam, Ind	40
Morton, Scott, Miss	160
Morton, Delaware, Pa	72
Morton's Corners, Erie, N. Y	18
Mortonsville, Clinton, Ind	12
Mortonsville, Woodford, Ky	110
Mortonville, Chester, Pa	67
Morven, Anson, N. C	6
Morven, Amelia, Va	$12
Moscow, Sanford, Ala	10
Moscow, Union, Ill	26
Moscow, Rush, Ind	50
Moscow, Muscatine, Iowa	110
Moscow, Hickman, Ky	130
Moscow, Hillsdale, Mich	150
Moscow, Freeborn, Minn	21
Moscow, Livingston, N. Y	170
Moscow, Clermont, Ohio	160
Moscow, Luzerne, Pa	150
Moscow, Fayette, Tenn	50
Moscow, Polk, Tex	62
Moscow, Iowa, Wis	41
Moscow Mills, Morgan, Ohio	13
Mosel, Sheboygan, Wis	23
Moselle, Franklin, Mo	120
Moselm, Berks, Pa	14
Mosherville, Hillsdale, Mich	110
Mosherville, Saratoga, N. Y	23
Mosiertown, Crawford, Pa	67
Mosinee, Marathon, Wis	100
Moss Bluff, Liberty, Tex	12
Mossing Ford, Charlotte, Va	130
Moss Point, Jackson, Miss	12
Moss Run, Washington, Ohio	22
Mossville, Peoria, Ill	98
Mossy Creek, Jefferson, Tenn	310
Mossy Creek, Augusta, Va	12
Motier, Pendleton, Ky	10
Motley, Lancaster, Pa	12
Mott Haven, Westchester, N. Y	400
Mottomosa, Atascosa, Tex	20
Mott's Corners, Tompkins, N. Y	88
Mottville, St. Joseph, Mich	120
Mottville, Onondaga, N. Y	270
Moulton, (*c. h.*,) Lawrence, Ala	150
Moulton, Shelby, Ill	67
Moulton, Appanoose, Iowa	200
Moulton, Auglaize, Ohio	27
Moulton, Lavaca, Tex	20
Moultonborough, Carroll, N. H	25
Moultonville, Madison, Ill	16
Moultonville, Carroll, N. H	12
Moultrie, (*c. h.*,) Colquitt, Ga	10
Moultrie, Columbiana, Ohio	69
Mound City, Crittenden, Ark	12
Mound City,* Pulaski, Ill	760
*Mound City,** (*c. h.*,) Linn, Kans	650
Mounds, Vernon, Mo	12
Mound Springs, Jackson, Wis	62
Mound Station, Brown, Ill	140
Moundsville, (*c. h.*,) Marshall, W. Va	500
Mound Valley, Labette, Kans	12
Moundville, Marquette, Wis	17
Mount Adams, Arkansas, Ark	16
Mount Aerial, Allen, Ky	8
Mount Ætna, Berks, Pa	20
Mountain, Berks, Pa	12
Mountain, Morgan, Utah	10
Mountain, Monroe, Wis	15
Mountain City, Elko, Nev	12
Mountain City, Hays, Tex	200
Mountain Cove, Fayette, W. Va	24
Mountain Creek, Catawba, N. C	10

* Money-order office.

Mountain Creek, Cumberland, Pa	$20
Mountain Creek, Warren, Tenn	12
Mountain Eagle, Centre, Pa	36
Mountain Falls, Frederick, Va	12
Mountain Grove, Bath, Va	8
Mountain Hill, Harris, Ga	7
Mountain Home, Lawrence, Ala	6
Mountain Home, Bell, Tex	12
Mountain Home, Hardy, W. Va	2
Mountain House, Yam Hill, Oreg	15
Mountain Lake, Bradford, Pa	18
Mountain Ranch, Calaveras, Cal	24
Mountain Road, Halifax, Va	6
Mountain Spring, Carroll, Ark	11
Mountain Spring, Martin, Ind	16
Mountain Top, Luzerne, Pa	89
Mountain Valley, Luzerne, Pa	12
Mountain View, Santa Clara, Cal	110
Mountainville, Hunterdon, N. J	12
Mountainville, Lehigh, Pa	12
Mount Airy, Carroll, Md	180
Mount Airy, Randolph, Mo	12
Mount Airy, Surry, N. C	110
Mount Airy, Hamilton, Ohio	24
Mount Airy, Washington, Pa	41
Mount Airy, Bledsoe, Tenn	12
Mount Airy, Pittsylvania, Va	10
Mount Algor, Jackson, Iowa	57
Mount Alvis, Blount, Ala	5
Mount Andrew, Barbour, Ala	19
Mount Athos, Campbell, Va	12
Mount Auburn, Christian, Ill	180
Mount Auburn, Shelby, Ind	33
Mount Auburn, Benton, Iowa	23
Mount Auburn, Middlesex, Mass	320
Mount Ayr,* (*c. h.*,) Ringgold, Iowa	520
Mount Bethel, Northampton, Pa	130
Mount Blanchard, Hancock, Ohio	120
Mount Blanco, Meigs, Ohio	8
Mount Bullion, Mariposa, Cal	38
Mount Calm, Limestone, Tex	16
Mount Carmel, New Haven, Conn	290
Mount Carmel,* (*c. h.*,) Wabash, Ill	500
Mount Carmel, Franklin, Ind	79
Mount Carmel Fleming, Ky	72
Mount Carmel, Baltimore, Md	61
Mount Carmel, Covington, Miss	55
Mount Carmel, Clermont, Ohio	73
Mount Carmel, Northumberland, Pa	710
Mount Carmel, Wilson, Tenn	12
Mount Carmel, Halifax, Va	7
Mount Carrick, Monroe, Ohio	6
Mount Carroll,* (*c. h.*,) Carroll, Ill	1,600
Mount Chesnut, Butler, Pa	18
Mount Clemens,* (*c. h.*,) Macomb, Mich	820
Mount Clifton, Shenandoah, Va	15
Mount Clinton, Rockingham, Va	10
Mount Comfort, Hancock, Ind	17
Mount Crawford, Rockingham, Va	170
Mount Croghan, Chesterfield, S. C	12
Mount Desert, Hancock, Me	120
Mount Eaton, Wayne, Ohio	110
Mount Eden, Alameda, Cal	100
Mount Eden, Spencer, Ky	8
Mount Elba, Bradley, Ark	12
Mount Enterprise, Cedar, Mo	$12
Mount Enterprise, Rusk, Tex	89
Mount Eolia, Towns, Ga	10
Mount Ephraim, Camden, N. J	31
Mount Ephraim, Noble, Ohio	63
Mount Erie, Wayne, Ill	80
Mount Etna, Huntington, Ind	100
Mount Etna, Adams, Iowa	12
Mount Florence, Jefferson, Kans	44
Mount Freedom, Pendleton, W. Va	21
Mount Gallagher, Laurens, S. C	5
Mount Gilead, Mason, Ky	12
Mount Gilead, Montgomery, N. C	12
Mount Gilead,* (*c. h.*,) Morrow, Ohio	800
Mount Gilead, Loudoun, Va	17
Mount Healthy, Bartholomew, Ind	13
Mount Healthy, Hamilton, Ohio	140
Mount Healthy, Somerset, Pa	12
Mount Hebron, Greene, Ala	35
Mount Heron, Darke, Ohio	23
Mount Hilliard, Bullock, Ala	16
Mount Holly,* (*c. h.*,) Burlington, N. J	1,800
Mount Holly, Clermont, Ohio	37
Mount Holly, Rutland, Vt	76
Mount Holly Springs, Cumberland, Pa	310
Mount Hope, Lawrence, Ala	68
Mount Hope, Tolland, Conn	13
Mount Hope, De Kalb, Ind	5
Mount Hope, Delaware, Iowa	10
Mount Hope, Copiah, Miss	6
Mount Hope, La Fayette, Mo	50
Mount Hope, Morris, N. J	310
Mount Hope, Orange, N. Y	59
Mount Hope, Holmes, Ohio	55
Mount Hope, Lancaster, Pa	29
Mount Hope, Grant, Wis	71
Mount Horeb, Dane, Wis	85
Mount Ida, (*c. h.*,) Montgomery, Ark	44
Mount Ida, Grant, Wis	17
Mount Idaho, Nez Perces, Idaho	12
Mount Jackson, Lawrence, Pa	140
Mount Jackson, Shenandoah, Va	240
Mount Jefferson, Lee, Ala	51
Mount Joy, Scott, Iowa	26
Mount Joy,* Lancaster, Pa	750
Mount Joy, Union, S. C	12
Mount Judea, Newton, Ark	3
Mount Kisco, Westchester, N. Y	380
Mount Landing, Essex, Va	12
Mount Laurel, Burlington, N. J	38
Mount Laurel, Halifax, Va	18
Mount Lebanon, Bienville, La	29
Mount Lebanon, Columbia, N. Y	220
Mount Lebanon, Allegheny, Pa	41
Mount Liberty, Brown, Ind	13
Mount Liberty, Knox, Ohio	49
Mount Meigs, Montgomery, Ala	20
Mount Meridian, Putnam, Ind	38
Mount Meridian, Augusta, Va	45
Mount Moriah, Ouachita, Ark	12
Mount Moriah, Kent, Del	12
Mount Moriah, Brown, Ind	5
Mount Moriah, Harrison, Mo	14
Mount Morris,* Ogle, Ill	400

* Money-order office.

Mount Morris,* Livingston, N. Y	$1,400
Mount Morris, Greene, Pa	60
Mount Morris, Waushara, Wis	25
Mount Morris Station, Genesee, Mich	330
Mount Mourne, Iredell, N. C	11
Mount Murphy, Pocahontas, W. Va.	17
Mount Nebo, Miami, Kans	12
Mount Nebo, Yadkin, N. C	18
Mount Nebo, Lancaster, Pa	29
Mount Niles, St. Clair, Ala	10
Mount Olive, Coosa, Ala	12
Mount Olive, (*c. h.,*) Izard, Ark	13
Mount Olive, Macoupin, Ill	27
Mount Olive, Wayne, N. C	140
Mount Olive, Clermont, Ohio	13
Mount Olive, Shenandoah, Va	19
Mount Olivet, (*c. h.,*) Robertson, Ky.	69
Mount Orab, Brown, Ohio	30
Mount Palatine, Putnam, Ill	120
Mount Parnel, Franklin, Pa	11
Mount Parthenon, Newton, Ark	12
Mount Perry, Perry, Ohio	8
Mount Pinson, Jefferson, Ala	7
Mount Pisgah, La Grange, Ind	26
Mount Pisgah, Clermont, Ohio	60
Mount Pisgah, Overton, Tenn	7
Mount Pisgah, Monroe, Wis	38
Mount Pleasant, Monroe, Ala	12
Mount Pleasant, Carroll, Ark	60
Mount Pleasant, New Castle, Del	86
Mount Pleasant, Union, Ill	17
Mount Pleasant, Perry, Ind	12
*Mount Pleasant,** (*c. h.,*) Henry, Iowa.	2,600
Mount Pleasant, Atchison, Kans	81
Mount Pleasant, Frederick, Md	34
Mount Pleasant, (*c. h.,*) Isabella, Mich	490
Mount Pleasant, Gentry, Mo	22
Mount Pleasant, Cass, Nebr	22
Mount Pleasant, Hunterdon, N. J	80
Mount Pleasant, Cabarrus, N. C	63
Mount Pleasant, Jefferson, Ohio	370
Mount Pleasant, Westmoreland, Pa.	520
Mount Pleasant, Laurens, S. C	10
Mount Pleasant, Maury, Tenn	110
Mount Pleasant, (*c. h.,*) Titus, Tex	200
Mount Pleasant, San Pete, Utah	250
Mount Pleasant, Spottsylvania, Va.	6
Mount Pleasant Mills, Snyder, Pa	52
Mount Polk, Calhoun, Ala	12
Mount Prospect, Crawford, Ind	8
Mount Pulaski, Logan, Ill	450
Mount Read, Monroe, N. Y	27
Mount Repose, Clermont, Ohio	16
Mount Riga, Dutchess, N. Y	29
Mount Rock, Cumberland, Pa	23
Mount Roszell, Limestone, Ala	12
Mount Royal, York, Pa	12
Mount Salem, Sussex, N. J	12
Mount Salem, Putnam, W. Va	12
Mount Savage, Carter, Ky	5
Mount Savage, Alleghany, Md	390
Mount Shasta, Siskiyou, Cal	12
Mount Sherman, La Rue, Ky	18
Mount Sidney, Augusta, Va	96
Mount Sinai, Suffolk, N. Y	$33
Mount Solon, Augusta, Va	53
Mount Sterling, Choctaw, Ala	20
*Mount Sterling,** (*c. h.,*) Brown, Ill	760
Mount Sterling, Switzerland, Ind	27
Mount Sterling, Van Buren, Iowa	60
Mount Sterling, Bourbon, Kans	18
*Mount Sterling,** (*c. h.,*) Montgomery, Ky	1,200
Mount Sterling, Madison, Ohio	130
Mount Sterling, Crawford, Wis	98
Mount Storm, Grant, W. Va	10
Mount Summit, Henry, Ind	12
Mount Sumner, Jo Daviess, Ill	9
Mount Sylvan, Smith, Tex	12
Mount Tabor, Forsyth, N. C	2
Mount Tabor, Vernon, Wis	14
Mount Tirzah, Person, N. C	11
Mount Top, York, Pa	16
Mount Ulla, Rowan, N. C	15
Mount Union, Stark, Ohio	420
Mount Union, Huntingdon, Pa	370
Mount Upton, Chenango, N. Y	250
Mount Vernon, Mobile, Ala	78
Mount Vernon, Jefferson, Colo	12
Mount Vernon, (*c. h.,*) Montgomery, Ga	13
*Mount Vernon,** (*c. h.,*) Jefferson, Ill	980
*Mount Vernon,** (*c. h.,*) Posey, Ind	800
Mount Vernon,* Linn, Iowa	1,000
Mount Vernon, (*c. h.,*) Rock Castle, Ky	240
Mount Vernon, Kennebec, Me	250
Mount Vernon, Macomb, Mich	16
Mount Vernon, (*c. h.,*) Lawrence, Mo.	390
Mount Vernon, Hillsborough, N. H.	220
Mount Vernon, Westchester, N. Y	680
*Mount Vernon,** (*c. h.,*) Knox, Ohio	2,300
Mount Vernon, Chester, Pa	14
Mount Vernon, Providence, R. I	22
Mount Vernon, Monroe, Tenn	9
Mount Vernon, Dane, Wis	92
Mount Vernon Forge, Rockingham, Va	12
Mount Vernon Tannery, Frederick, Va	11
Mount Victory, Hardin, Ohio	190
Mount View, Benton, Mo	18
Mountville, Troup, Ga	12
Mountville, Effingham, Ill	37
Mountville, Lancaster, Pa	100
Mountville, Loudoun, Va	12
Mount Vinco, Buckingham, Va	7
Mount Vision, Otsego, N. Y	120
Mount Vitio, Bullitt, Ky	42
Mount Washington, Bullitt, Ky	120
Mount Washington, Baltimore, Md	150
Mount Washington, Hamilton, Ohio	150
Mount Washington, Allegheny, Pa	66
Mount Wolf, York, Pa	37
Mount Zion, Hancock, Ga	12
Mount Zion, Macon, Ill	120
Mount Zion, Van Buren, Iowa	140
Mount Zion, Grant, Ky	12

* Money-order office.

Mount Zion, Simpson, Miss	$15
Mount Zion, Lebanon, Pa	16
Mount Zion, Tipton, Tenn	12
Mount Zion, Campbell, Va	25
Mount Zion, Juneau, Wis	11
Mouse Creek, McMinn, Tenn	140
Mouse's, Grant, W. Va	6
Mouth of Indian, Monroe, W. Va	12
Mouth of Laurel, Lewis, Ky	7
Mouth of Pond, Pike, Ky	4
Mouth of Scary, Putnam, W. Va	25
Mouth of Seneca, Pendleton, W. Va	20
Mouth of Wilson, Grayson, Va	44
Mouth of Wolf, Overton, Tenn	12
Mouth Short Creek, Boone, W. Va	20
Moweaqua, Shelby, Ill	410
Mower City, Mower, Minn	65
Mowersville, Franklin, Pa	49
Mowry's Mills, Bedford, Pa	12
Mowrystown, Highland, Ohio	23
Moyer's Store, Bucks, Pa	17
Muchinippe, Logan, Ohio	6
Mud Bridge, Cabell, W. Va	16
Mud Creek, St. Clair, Ill	120
Mud Creek, Eaton, Mich	17
Muddy Creek, Lancaster, Pa	30
Muddy Creek, Preston, W Va	7
Muddy Creek Forks, York, Pa	6
Muddy Fork, Clark, Ind	12
Muddy Fork, Cleveland, N. C	5
Muddy Lake, Livingston, Mo	8
Mud Lick, Jefferson, Ind	6
Mud Lick, Monroe, Ky	22
Mud Lick, Chatham, N. C	22
Muhlenburgh, Luzerne, Pa	20
Muir, Ionia, Mich	670
Muirkirk, Prince George's, Md	160
Mukilteo, Snohomish, Wash	20
Mukwonago, Waukesha, Wis	160
Mulberry, Clinton, Ind	54
Mulberry, Wilkes, N. C	5
Mulberry, Clermont, Ohio	50
Mulberry, York, Pa	9
Mulberry, Lincoln, Tenn	80
Mulberry Corners, Geauga, Ohio	51
Mulberry Gap, Hancock, Tenn	20
Mulberry Grove, Harris, Ga	9
Mulberry Grove, Bond, Ill	140
Mulberry Grove, Crawford, Kans	12
Mule Creek, Cumberland, Ill	11
Mulford, Cook, Ill	12
Mulkeyton, Franklin, Ill	13
Mull Grove, Catawba, N. C	5
Mullica Hill, Gloucester, N. J	210
Mullin's, Baker, Ala	5
Mullin's Depot, Marion, S. C	54
Mulloy's, Robertson, Tenn	8
Mumford, Monroe, N. Y	250
Mummasburgh, Adams, Pa	24
*Muncie,** (*c. h.,*) Delaware, Ind	1,400
Muncie, Vernon, Wis	12
Muncy,* Lycoming, Pa	1,200
Muncy Bottom, Sullivan, Pa	9
Muncy Station, Lycoming, Pa	230
Mundy, Genesee, Mich	20
Munford, Talladega, Ala	94
Munfordsville, (*c. h.,*) Hart, Ky	$380
Mungen, Wood, Ohio	12
Munger's Mill, Reynolds, Mo	5
Mungerville, Shiawassee, Mich	57
Munising, Schoolcraft, Mich	82
Munnsville, Coshocton, Ohio	11
Munntown, Washington, Pa	55
Munsonville, Cheshire, N. H	73
Munster, Cambria, Pa	24
Munsville, Madison, N. Y	140
Munterville, Wapello, Iowa	12
Murdock, Warren, Ohio	70
Murdocksville, Washington, Pa	18
*Murfreesborough,** (*c. h.,*) Pike, Ark	37
Murfreesborough, Hertford, N. C	270
*Murfreesborough,** (*c. h.,*) Rutherford, Tenn	1,700
Murphey, (*c. h.,*) Cherokee, N. C	93
Murphey's Creek, Lewis, W. Va	12
Murphree's Valley, Blount, Ala	5
Murphy's, Calaveras, Cal	230
*Murphysborough,** (*c. h.,*) Jackson, Ill	650
Murphy's Mill, Wood, W. Va	14
Murphysville, Mason, Ky	18
Murray, Wells, Ind	49
Murray, Clark, Iowa	43
Murray,* (*c. h.,*) Callaway, Ky	170
Murray, Orleans, N. Y	61
Murraysville, Jackson, W. Va	31
Murrayville, Morgan, Ill	140
Murrinsville, Butler, Pa	22
Murrysville, Westmoreland, Pa	81
*Muscatine,** (*c. h.,*) Muscatine, Iowa	2,600
Muscle Fork, Chariton, Mo	12
Muscoda, Grant, Wis	300
Musconetcong, Warren, N. J	130
Muscotah, Atchison, Kans	250
Muse's Bottom, Jackson, W. Va	16
Mush Creek, Greenville, S. C	4
Muskego Centre, Waukesha, Wis	43
*Muskegon,** (*c. h.,*) Muskegon, Mich	2,500
Muskootink, Chisago, Minn	5
Musson, Iberville, La	12
Mutual, Champaign, Ohio	81
Myers, Howard, Mo	25
Myersburgh, Bradford, Pa	34
Myers Valley, Pottawatomie, Kans	12
Myersville, Vermilion, Ill	91
Myersville, Frederick, Md	95
Myersville, Williamsburgh, S. C	23
Myra, Washington, Wis	9
Myrickville, Bristol, Mass	78
Myron, Allamakee, Iowa	33
Myrtle, Knox, Mo	88
Myrtle Creek, Douglas, Oreg	20
Mystic, New London, Conn	310
Mystic Bridge,* New London, Conn	1,200
Mystic River, New London, Conn	630

N.

Naches, Houston, Tex	19
Nachusa, Lee, Ill	110
Nacogdoches, (*c. h.,*) Nacogdoches, Tex	400

*Money-order office.

Nacoochee, White, Ga	$24
Naff's, Franklin, Va	8
Nahant, Essex, Mass	370
Nahma, Delta, Mich	15
Nahunta, Wayne, N. C	12
Nail's Creek, Banks, Ga	12
Nairn, Scioto, Ohio	19
Namaqua, Larimer, Colo	41
Nanaupa, Fond du Lac, Wis	6
Nancy, Pottawatomie, Kans	12
Nanjemoy, Charles, Md	34
Nankin, Wayne, Mich	100
Nankin, Ashland, Ohio	54
Nannie, Floyd, Ga	12
Nanticoke, Wicomico, Md	12
Nanticoke, Luzerne, Pa	140
*Nantucket,** (*c. h.,*) Nantucket, Mass	2,100
Nanuet, Rockland, N. Y	240
Naomi, Walker, Ga	12
*Napa City,** (*c. h.,*) Napa, Cal	1,200
Napanock, Ulster, N. Y	350
*Naperville,** (*c. h.,*) Du Page, Ill	1,100
Naples, Scott, Ill	310
Naples, Cumberland, Me	130
Naples, Ontario, N. Y	520
*Napoleon,** (*c. h.,*) Desha, Ark	180
Napoleon, Ripley, Ind	150
Napoleon, Gallatin, Ky	20
Napoleon, Jackson, Mich	220
Napoleon, La Fayette, Mo	94
*Napoleon,** (*c. h.,*) Henry, Ohio	1,200
Napoli, Cattaraugus, N.Y	290
Narragansett, Washington, R. I	19
Narragansett Pier, Washington, R. I	290
Narraguagus, Washington, Me	500
Narrows Bridge, Daviess, Ky	8
Narrowsburgh, Sullivan, N. Y	230
Narrows Creek, Macon, Mo	12
Nash Depot, Vanderburgh, Ind	12
Nashotah Mission, Waukesha, Wis	310
Nashport Muskingum, Ohio	110
Nashua,* Chickasaw, Iowa	670
Nashua,* Hillsborough, N. H	3,200
Nashville, El Dorado, Cal	12
Nashville, (*c. h.,*) Berrien, Ga	26
*Nashville,** (*c. h.,*) Washington, Ill	650
Nashville, (*c. h.,*) Brown, Ind	140
Nashville,* Barry, Mich	320
Nashville, Barton, Mo	12
Nashville, Chautauqua, N. Y	33
Nashville, (*c. h.,*) Nash, N. C	47
Nashville, Holmes, Ohio	130
NASHVILLE,* (*c. h.,*) Davidson, Tenn	4,000
Nashville Centre, Martin, Minn	21
Nason's Mills, York, Me	12
Nasonville, Wood, Wis	14
Nassau, Nassau, Fla	12
Nassau, Rensselaer, N. Y	290
Natchez, Martin, Ind	6
*Natchez,** (*c. h.,*) Adams, Miss	3,300
Natchitoches, (*c. h.,*)Natchitoches, La	630
Natick,* Middlesex, Mass	1,500
Natick, Kent, R. I	250
National, Clayton, Iowa	81
National City, San Diego, Cal	12
National Military Asylum,* Kennebec, Me	$330
National Military Asylum,* Montgomery, Ohio	620
National Military Asylum, Milwaukee, Wis	12
Natividad, Monterey, Cal	87
Natrona, Mason, Ill	12
Natrona, Allegheny, Pa	270
Natural Bridge, Jefferson, N. Y	58
Natural Bridge, Rockbridge, Va	57
Naubuc, Hartford, Conn	52
Naugart, Marathon, Wis	38
Naugatuck,* New Haven, Conn	1,400
Naughrightville, Morris, N. J	29
Naumburgh, Lewis, N. Y	17
Nautrille, Black Hawk, Iowa	15
Nauvoo, Hancock, Ill	340
Nauvoo, Tioga, Pa	10
Navarino, Onondaga, N. Y	42
Navarre, Stark, Ohio	300
Navarro Ridge, Mendocino, Cal	12
Navasink, Monmouth, N. J	280
Navasota, Grimes, . ex	1,000
Navan, Winneshiek, Iowa	12
Navidad, Jackson, Tex	12
Nayatt Point, Bristol, R. I	120
Naylor, Lowndes, Ga	12
Nazareth,* Northampton, Pa	490
Neabsco Mills, Prince William, Va	18
Nealey's Corner, Penobscot, Me	58
Nealsville, McDowell, N. C	12
Nearman, Wyandotte, Kans	18
Neatsville, Adair, Ky	17
Neblett's Landing, Bolivar, Miss	12
Nebo, Hopkins, Ky	20
Nebo, Laclede, Mo	10
Nebraska, Scott, Ark	12
Nebraska, Jennings, Ind	98
Nebraska, Pickaway, Ohio	48
Nebraska, Forest, Pa	12
Nebraska, Jefferson, Tenn	12
Nebraska, Appomattox, Va	13
*Nebraska City,** (*c. h.,*) Otoe, Nebr	3,200
Necedah,* Juneau, Wis	320
Needham,* Norfolk, Mass	320
Needham's Station, Johnson, Ind	12
Needy, Clackamas, Oreg	44
Neely's Landing, Cape Girardeau, Mo	20
Neelysville, Morgan, Ohio	20
Neelyville, Morgan, Ill	81
Neenah, Winnebago, Wis	1,800
Neersville, Loudoun, Va	6
Neese's Store, Fayette, Tex	55
Neff, Randolph, Ind	15
Neffs, Lehigh, Pa	17
Neffs' Mills, Huntingdon, Pa	52
Neffsville, Lancaster, Pa	34
Negaunee, Marquette, Mich	1,500
Negro Foot, Hanover, Va	13
Negro Hill, White, Ark	12
Nehalem, Clatsop, Oreg	12
Neil's Creek, Jefferson. Ind	12
Neil's Creek, Steuben, N. Y	29
*Neilsville,** (*c. h.,*) Clark, Wis	460

* Money-order office.

Post office	Amount
Nekama, Winnebago, Wis	$37
Nekoma, Henry, Ill	12
Nellie, Ashley, Ark	12
Nelly's Ford, Nelson, Va	49
Nelson, Lee, Ill	63
Nelson, Vigo, Ind	12
Nelson, Kent, Mich	12
Nelson, Cheshire, N. H	58
Nelson, Madison, N. Y	80
Nelson, Portage, Ohio	56
Nelson, Tioga, Pa	130
Nelson, Hardin, Tenn	22
Nelson, Buffalo, Wis	40
Nelson Furnace, Nelson, Ky	28
Nelson Point, Plumas, Cal	12
Nelsonville, Franklin, Ala	14
Nelsonville, Charlevoix, Mich	10
Nelsonville, Marion, Mo	38
Nelsonville,* Athens, Ohio	330
Nelta Boc, Sevier, Ark	13
Nemaha City, Nemaha, Nebr	91
Nenno, Washington, Wis	33
Neodesha, Wilson, Kans	12
Neoga, Cumberland, Ill	450
Neola, Pottawattomie, Iowa	12
Neosho,* (*c. h.*,) Newton, Mo	620
Neosho, Dodge, Wis	100
Neosho Falls,* (*c. h.*,) Woodson, Kans	240
Neosho Rapids, Lyon, Kans	78
Nepaug, Litchfield, Conn	100
Neperan, Westchester, N. Y	140
Nepeuskun, Winnebago, Wis	51
Neponset,* Bureau, Ill	550
Neponset Village, Norfolk, Mass	670
Neptune, Mercer, Ohio	47
Neptune, Richland, Wis	10
Nero, Manitowoc, Wis	37
Nesbit's Station, De Soto, Miss	12
Nescopeck, Luzerne, Pa	20
Neshaminy, Bucks, Pa	28
Neshanic, Somerset, N. J	69
Neshannock Falls, Lawrence, Pa	22
Neshkoro, Marquette, Wis	28
Nesquehoning, Carbon, Pa	140
Nestocton, Tillamook, Oreg	8
Nestorville, Barbour, W. Va	6
Netarts, Tillamook, Oreg	12
Netawaka, Jackson, Kans	160
Netherland, Overton, Tenn	26
Nettle Carrier, Overton, Tenn	26
Nettle Lake, Williams, Ohio	29
Nettle Ridge, Patrick, Va	12
Nettleton, Marion, Mo	12
Nettletonville, Caldwell, Mo	12
Neuchatel, Nemaha, Kans	44
Neutral City, Cherokee, Kans	61
Nevada, Livingston, Ill	12
Nevada, Tipton, Ind	54
Nevada,* (*c. h.*,) Story, Iowa	810
Nevada, Mercer, Ky	16
Nevada, Mower, Minn	24
Nevada,* (*c. h.*,) Vernon, Mo	680
Nevada,* Wyandot, Ohio	390
Nevada City,* (*c. h.*,) Nevada, Cal	2,400
Nevada City, Madison, Mont	100
Nevada Mills, Steuben, Ind	$12
Neversink, Sullivan, N. Y	50
Neville, Winona, Minn	12
Neville, Clermont, Ohio	97
Nevin, Highland, Ohio	43
Nevinville, Adams, Iowa	53
New Alba, Winneshiek, Iowa	24
New Albany,* (*c. h.*,) Floyd, Ind	4,000
New Albany, Wilson, Kans	120
New Albany, Pontotoc, Miss	78
New Albany, Mahoning, Ohio	25
New Albany, Bradford, Pa	81
New Albion, Cattaraugus, N. Y	50
New Alexander, Columbiana, Ohio	20
New Alexandria, Jefferson, Ohio	85
New Alexandria, Westmoreland, Pa	140
New Alsace, Dearborn, Ind	40
New Alstead, Cheshire, N. H	61
New Amsterdam, Harrison, Ind	47
New Amsterdam, La Crosse, Wis	51
New Anhalt, Burleson, Tex	12
New Antioch, Clinton, Ohio	83
Newark,* New Castle, Del	660
Newark, Kendall, Ill	340
Newark, Greene, Ind	46
Newark, Worcester, Md	10
Newark, Gratiot, Mich	6
Newark, Knox, Mo	180
Newark,* (*c. h.*,) Essex, N. J	3,700
Newark,* Wayne, N. Y	1,300
Newark,* (*c. h.*,) Licking, Ohio	2,500
Newark, White, Tenn	13
Newark, Caledonia, Vt	30
Newark, Wirt, W. Va	59
Newark Valley, Tioga, N. Y	310
New Ashford, Berkshire, Mass	14
New Athens, St. Clair, Ill	240
New Athens, Harrison, Ohio	120
New Auburn, Sibley, Minn	110
Newaygo,* (*c. h.*,) Newaygo, Mich	500
New Baden, Clinton, Ill	35
New Baltimore, Wayne, Ill	2
New Baltimore, Macomb, Mich	300
New Baltimore, Greene, N. Y	240
New Baltimore, Stark, Ohio	49
New Baltimore, Somerset, Pa	14
New Baltimore, Fauquier, Va	19
New Barden, Tippah, Miss	12
New Bavaria, Henry, Ohio	43
New Bedford, Bureau, Ill	90
New Bedford,* Bristol, Mass	3,600
New Bedford, Monmouth, N. J	67
New Bedford, Coshocton, Ohio	42
New Bedford, Lawrence, Pa	74
New Bellsville, Brown, Ind	20
Newberg, Yam Hill, Oreg	12
New Berlin, Sangamon, Ill	200
New Berlin, Chenango, N. Y	690
New Berlin, Stark, Ohio	75
New Berlin, Union, Pa	270
New Berlin, Waukesha, Wis	19
New Berlin Centre, Chenango, N. Y	23
Newbern, Hale, Ala	65
Newbern, Jersey, Ill	32
Newbern, Bartholomew, Ind	22
Newbern, Marion, Iowa	77

* Money-order office.

Name	Amount
Newbern, Dyer, Tenn	$120
Newbern, (c. h.,) Pulaski, Va	190
New Berne, (c. h.,)* Craven, N. C	2,600
Newberry, Greene, Ind	75
Newberry, Lycoming, Pa	210
*Newberry C. H.,** Newberry, S. C	1,500
Newberrytown, York, Pa	37
New Bethlehem, Clarion, Pa	130
New Bloomfield, Callaway, Mo	100
New Bloomfield, (c. h.,) Perry, Pa	640
New Bloomington, Marion, Ohio	120
New Boston, Windham, Conn	72
New Boston, Mercer, Ill	590
New Boston, Lee, Iowa	15
New Boston, Berkshire, Mass	160
New Boston, Wayne, Mich	37
New Boston, Winona, Minn	50
New Boston, Macon, Mo	18
New Boston, Hillsborough, N. H	290
New Boston, Henry, Tenn	12
New Braintree, Worcester, Mass	180
New Branch, Monmouth, N. J	12
New Braunfels, (c. h.,)* Comal, Tex	630
New Bremen, Cook, Ill	110
New Bremen, Lewis, N. Y	110
New Bremen,* Auglaize, Ohio	220
New Bridge, Lumpkin, Ga	10
New Bridge, Bergen, N. J	56
New Bridge, Franklin, Pa	12
New Bridgeport, Bedford, Pa	12
New Bridgeville, York, Pa	24
New Brighton, Richmond, N. Y	550
New Brighton,* Beaver, Pa	1,200
New Brighton, Fauquier, Va	25
New Britain,* Hartford, Conn	2,500
New Britain, Bucks, Pa	72
New Britton, Hamilton, Ind	60
New Brunswick, (c. h.,)* Middlesex, N. J	2,900
New Buda, Decatur, Iowa	25
New Buena Vista, Bedford, Pa	12
New Buffalo,* Berrien, Mich	370
New Buffalo, Perry, Pa	100
Newburgh, Franklin, Ala	14
Newburgh, Izard, Ark	23
Newburgh, Macon, Ill	12
Newburgh,* Warrick, Ind	360
Newburgh, Mitchell, Iowa	73
Newburgh, Jefferson, Ky	10
Newburgh, Penobscot, Me	45
Newburgh, Charles, Md	58
Newburgh, Cass, Mich	27
Newburgh, Fillmore, Minn	110
Newburgh, Macon, Mo	12
Newburgh, (c. h.,)* Orange, N. Y	3,500
Newburgh, Cuyahoga, Ohio	980
Newburgh, Cumberland, Pa	180
Newburgh, Preston, W. Va	240
Newburgh, Washington, Mich	110
Newburgh Centre, Penobscot, Me	19
New Burlington, Delaware, Ind	26
New Burlington, Clinton, Ohio	89
Newbury, Wabaunsee, Kans	12
Newbury, Tuscola, Mich	39
Newbury, Merrimack, N. H	30
Newbury,* Orange, Vt	500

Name	Amount
Newburyport,* Essex, Mass	$3,000
New California, Union, Ohio	25
New California, Grant, Wis	21
New Cambria, Macon, Mo	370
New Canaan, Fairfield, Conn	900
New Canton, Hawkins, Tenn	15
New Canton, Buckingham, Va	150
New Carlisle,* St. Joseph, Ind	350
New Carlisle, Clark, Ohio	420
New Casco, Cumberland, Me	38
New Casco, Allegan, Mich	54
New Cassel, Fond du Lac, Wis	98
Newcastle, Placer, Cal	200
New Castle, (c. h.,)* New Castle, Del	860
Newcastle, (c. h.,)* Henry, Ind	940
Newcastle, (c. h.,) Henry, Ky	370
New Castle, Lincoln, Me	910
New Castle, Gentry, Mo	41
Newcastle, Dixon, Nebr	26
New Castle, Rockingham, N. H	110
New Castle, Westchester, N. Y	220
New Castle, Coshocton, Ohio	30
Newcastle, (c. h.,)* Lawrence, Pa	2,700
New Castle, Hardeman, Tenn	30
Newcastle, (c. h.,) Craig, Va	51
New Centreville, Oswego, N. Y	69
New Centreville, Chester, Pa	57
New Centreville, St. Croix, Wis	33
New Chambersburgh, Columbiana, Ohio	20
New Chester, Adams, Pa	28
New Chester, Adams, Wis	22
New Chicago, Neosho, Kans	12
New Church, Accomack, Va	30
New Clifton, Monroe, Wis	4
New Coeln, Milwaukee, Wis	9
New Columbia, Massac, Ill	20
New Columbia, Union, Pa	88
New Columbus, Owen, Ky	12
New Columbus, Luzerne, Pa	65
Newcomb, Champaign, Ill	24
Newcomb, Essex, N. Y	21
New Comerstown, Tuscarawas, Ohio	450
New Concord, Columbia, N. Y	45
New Concord, Muskingum, Ohio	330
New Corner, Delaware, Ind	16
New Corwin, Highland, Ohio	16
New Corydon, Jay, Ind	120
New Creek, (c. h.,) Mineral, W. Va	310
New Cumberland, Grant, Ind	72
New Cumberland, Tuscarawas, Ohio	66
New Cumberland, Cumberland, Pa	230
New Cumberland, Hancock, W. Va	130
New Dale, Wetzel, W. Va	9
New Danville, Lancaster, Pa	12
New Danville, Rusk, Tex	81
New Derry, Westmoreland, Pa	98
New Diggings, La Fayette, Wis	76
New Douglas, Madison, Ill	51
New Dorp, Richmond, N. Y	100
New Dover, Union, Ohio	52
New Dublin, Scott, Minn	23
New Dungeness, (c. h.,) Clallam, Wash	14
New Durham, Hudson, N. J	38

* Money-order office.

NEW	
New Eagle Mills, Grant, Ky	$12
New Egypt, Ocean, N. J	260
New Elizabeth, Hendricks, Ind	47
Newell, Anderson, S. C	1
Newell's Run, Washington, Ohio	23
Newellsville, Marion, Oreg	16
New England, Athens, Ohio	110
New England Village, Worcester, Mass	340
New Enterprise, Bedford, Pa	110
New Era, De Kalb, Ind	16
New Era, Bradford, Pa	8
New Eureka, Jackson, Kans	96
New Fairfield, Fairfield, Conn	32
Newfane, Niagara, N. Y	110
Newfane, Fond du Lac, Wis	18
Newfield, York, Me	56
Newfield, Gloucester, N. J	130
Newfield, Tompkins, N. Y	210
New Florence, Montgomery, Mo	340
New Florence, Westmoreland, Pa	220
New Forestville, Anson, N. C	12
Newfoundland, Elliott, Ky	12
Newfoundland, Morris, N. J	83
Newfoundland, Wayne, Pa	78
New Fountain, Medina, Tex	16
New Franken, Brown, Wis	12
New Frankfort, Saline, Mo	100
New Franklin, Wayne, Ill	16
New Franklin, Stark, Ohio	47
New Freedom, York, Pa	160
New Freeport, Greene, Pa	14
New Galilee, Beaver, Pa	250
New Garden, Wayne, Ind	110
New Garden, Ray, Mo	23
New Garden, Guilford, N. C	74
New Garden, Columbiana, Ohio	110
New Garden, Chester, Pa	20
New Garden, Russell, Va	14
New Gascony, Jefferson, Ark	20
New Genesee, Whitesides, Ill	23
New Geneva, Fayette, Pa	94
New Geneva, Jackson, W. Va	2
New Germantown, Hunterdon, N. J	160
New Germantown, Perry, Pa	74
New Glarus, Green, Wis	97
New Gloucester, Cumberland, Me	190
New Goshen, Vigo, Ind	53
New Grenada, Fulton, Pa	35
New Gretna, Burlington, N. J	85
New Guilford, Coshocton, Ohio	36
New Hackensack, Dutchess, N. Y	56
New Hagerstown, Carroll, Ohio	67
New Hamburgh, Scott, Iowa	7
New Hamburgh, Dutchess, N. Y	400
New Hamburgh, Mercer, Pa	120
New Hampden, Highland, Va	25
New Hampshire, Auglaize, Ohio	49
New Hampton, Madison, Ill	35
New Hampton, Chickasaw, Iowa	390
New Hampton, Belknap, N. H	570
New Hampton, Hunterdon, N. J	56
New Hampton, Orange, N. Y	190
New Hanover, Montgomery, Pa	96
New Harmony, Sangamon, Ill	8
New Harmony,* Posey, Ind	420

NEW	
New Harmony, Pike, Mo	$42
New Harmony, Brown, Ohio	16
New Harmony, Washington, Utah	13
New Harrisburgh, Carroll, Ohio	28
New Hartford, Litchfield, Conn	610
New Hartford, Pike, Ill	46
New Hartford, Butler, Iowa	220
New Hartford, Winona, Minn	5
New Hartford, Oneida, N.Y	400
Newharts, Northampton, Pa	11
NEW HAVEN,* (*c. h.*,) New Haven, Conn	4,000
New Haven, Gallatin, Ill	87
New Haven, Allen, Ind	340
New Haven, Nelson, Ky	150
New Haven, Macomb, Mich	180
New Haven, Franklin, Mo	290
New Haven, Oswego, N. Y	240
New Haven, Huron, Ohio	160
New Haven, Addison, Vt	230
New Haven, Mason, W. Va	91
New Haven, Adams, Wis	11
New Haven Centre, Gratiot, Mich	14
New Haven Mills, Addison, Vt	16
New Hebron, Crawford, Ill	14
New Hill, Wake, N. C	9
New Holland, Wabash, Ind	79
New Holland, Pickaway, Ohio	100
New Holland, Lancaster, Pa	240
New Holstein, Calumet, Wis	140
New Home, Montcalm, Mich	8
New Hope, Madison, Ala	6
New Hope, Wabash, Ill	12
New Hope, Nelson, Ky	16
New Hope, Caroline, Md	49
New Hope, Lincoln, Mo	170
New Hope, Cayuga, N. Y	47
New Hope, Iredell, N. C	4
New Hope, Brown, Ohio	36
New Hope, Bucks, Pa	410
New Hope, Augusta, Va	82
New Hope, Portage, Wis	50
New Hope Academy, Randolph, N. C	3
New Hope Mills, Granville, N. C	12
New House, York, S. C	6
New Hudson, Oakland, Mich	110
New Hudson, Allegany, N. Y	12
New Hurley, Ulster, N. Y	23
New Iberia,* (*c. h.*,) Iberia, La	1,200
New Idria, Fresno, Cal	88
Newington, Hartford, Conn	51
Newington, Rockingham, N. H	43
Newington Junction, Hartford, Conn	150
New Interest, Randolph, W. Va	44
New Ipswich,* Hillsborough, N. H	590
New Jasper, Greene, Ohio	20
New Jerusalem, Berks, Pa	13
New Kent C. H., New Kent, Va	80
New Kingston, Delaware, N. Y	29
New Kingstown, Cumberland, Pa	140
New Knoxville, Auglaize, Ohio	30
New Lancaster, Tipton, Ind	17
New Lancaster, Miami, Kans	56
New Lebanon, De Kalb, Ill	17

* Money-order office.

New Lebanon, Sullivan, Ind	$53
New Lebanon, Columbia, N. Y	560
New Lebanon, Montgomery, Ohio	53
New Lebanon, Mercer, Pa	110
New Lebanon Centre, Columbia, N. Y	73
New Lebanon Springs, Columbia, N. Y	270
New Lenox, Will, Ill	110
New Lenox, Berkshire, Mass	54
New Lexington, Tuscaloosa, Ala	12
*New Lexington,** (*c. h.,*) Perry, Ohio	690
New Lexington, Somerset, Pa	48
New Liberty, Pope, Ill	91
New Liberty, Scott, Iowa	18
New Liberty, Owen, Ky	210
New Light, Wake, N. C	4
New Limerick, Aroostook, Me	10
New Lisbon, Henry, Ind	77
New Lisbon, Burlington, N. J	13
New Lisbon, Otsego, N. Y	61
*New Lisbon,** (*c. h.,*) Columbiana, Ohio	1,000
*New Lisbon,** (*c. h.,*) Juneau, Wis	780
*New London,** (*c. h.,*) New London, Conn	2,900
New London, Howard, Ind	95
New London,* Henry, Iowa	350
New London, Frederick, Md	54
New London, (*c. h.,*) Monongalia, Minn	110
New London, (*c. h.,*) Ralls, Mo	160
New London,* Merrimack, N. H	320
New London, Oneida, N. Y	200
New London,* Huron, Ohio	540
New London, Chester, Pa	170
New London, Campbell, Va	43
New London, Waupaca, Wis	510
New Lyme, Ashtabula, Ohio	130
New Madison, Wabash, Ind	12
New Madison, Darke, Ohio	170
*New Madrid,** (*c. h.,*) New Madrid, Mo	330
New Mahoning, Carbon, Pa	19
Newman, Douglas, Ill	89
Newman, Jefferson, Kans	12
Newman, Sanilac, Mich	25
Newmansville, Clarion, Pa	26
New Marion, Ripley, Ind	26
New Market, Madison, Ala	68
New Market, Sebastian, Ark	12
New Market, Monroe, Ga	9
New Market, Gallatin, Ill	18
New Market, Marion, Ky	28
New Market, Frederick, Md	120
New Market, Scott, Minn	11
New Market, Platte, Mo	110
New Market, Rockingham, N. H	730
New Market, Middlesex, N. J	250
New Market, Randolph, N. C	23
New Market, Highland, Ohio	54
New Market, Abbeville, S. C	12
New Market, Jefferson, Tenn	240
New Market, Shenandoah, Va	350
New Marlborough, Berkshire, Mass	180
New Martinsburgh, Fayette, Ohio	29
New Martinsville, (*c. h.,*) Wetzel, W. Va	$140
New Maysville, Putnam, Ind	46
New Melle, St. Charles, Mo	63
New Memphis, Clinton, Ill	28
New Metamora, Washington, Ohio	170
New Michigan, Livingston, Ill	75
New Middleton, Smith, Tenn	94
New Middletown, Harrison, Ind	12
New Middletown, Mahoning, Ohio	94
New Milford,* Litchfield, Conn	1,100
New Milford, Winnebago, Ill	100
New Milford, Orange, N. Y	53
New Milford, Portage, Ohio	72
New Milford, Susquehanna, Pa	360
New Millport, Clearfield, Pa	25
New Milton, Doddridge, W. Va	7
New Minden, Washington, Ill	12
New Mollis, Outagamie, Wis	12
New Monmouth, Monmouth, N. J	86
New Moorefield, Clark, Ohio	40
New Moscow, Coshocton, Ohio	13
New Mount Pleasant, Jay, Ind	46
New Mount Pleasant, Monroe, Pa	85
New Munich, Stearns, Minn	160
Newnan, (*c. h.,*) Coweta, Ga	1,100
Newnanville, Alachua, Fla	110
New Offenburgh, St. Genevieve, Mo	33
New Ohio, Broome, N. Y	29
*New Oregon,** (*c. h.,*) Howard, Iowa	34
New Oregon, Erie, N. Y	15
NEW ORLEANS,* (*c. h.,*) Orleans, La	4,000
New Oxford, Adams, Pa	270
New Palestine, Cooper, Mo	12
New Palestine, Clermont, Ohio	26
New Paltz, Ulster, N. Y	430
New Paris, Elkhart, Ind	92
New Paris,* Preble, Ohio	280
New Paris, Bedford, Pa	46
New Petersburgh, Highland, Ohio	47
New Petersburgh, Jefferson, Pa	12
New Philadelphia, McDonough, Ill	65
New Philadelphia, Washington, Ind	150
*New Philadelphia,** (*c. h.,*) Tuscarawas, Ohio	1,300
New Pittsburgh, St. Clair, Ill	12
New Pittsburgh, Randolph, Ind	25
New Pittsburgh, Wayne, Ohio	79
New Pleasant Grove, Huntingdon, Pa	32
New Plymouth,* Vinton, Ohio	53
New Point, Decatur, Ind	12
Newport, New Castle, Del	220
Newport, Lake, Ill	8
*Newport,** (*c. h.*) Vermillion, Ind	220
Newport, Johnson, Iowa	12
Newport, Neosho, Kans	12
Newport, (*c. h.,*) Campbell, Ky	2,400
Newport, Winn, La	12
Newport, Penobscot, Me	450
Newport, Charles, Md	34
Newport, Monroe, Mich	82
Newport, Washington, Minn	65
*Newport,** (*c. h.,*) Sullivan, N. H	870

* Money-order office.

Post office	
Newport, Cumberland, N. J	$92
Newport, Herkimer, N. Y	240
Newport, Carteret, N. C	57
Newport, Washington, Ohio	130
Newport, Benton, Oreg	26
Newport,* Perry, Pa	680
NEWPORT,* (*c. h.*,) Newport, R. I	2,800
Newport, (*c. h.*,) Cocke, Tenn	200
Newport, Walker, Tex	18
Newport,* Orleans, Vt	690
Newport, Giles, Va	20
New Portage, Summit, Ohio	63
Newport Centre, Orleans, Vt	73
New Portland, Somerset, Me	120
Newport News, Warwick, Va	12
Newportville, Bucks, Pa	100
New Preston, Litchfield, Conn	230
New Prospect, Winston, Miss	51
New Prospect, Spartanburgh, S. C	11
New Prospect, Fond du Lac, Wis	7
New Providence, Pike, Ala	16
New Providence, Clarke, Ind	80
New Providence, Hardin, Iowa	130
New Providence, Osage, Mo	12
New Providence, Union, N. J	170
New Providence, Lancaster, Pa	52
New Providence, Montgomery, Tenn	140
New Republic, Monterey, Cal	12
New Richland, Waseca, Minn	12
New Richland, Logan, Ohio	21
New Richmond, Montgomery, Ind	27
New Richmond,* Clermont, Ohio	770
New Richmond, Crawford, Pa	40
New Richmond, St. Croix, Wis	140
New Ringgold, Schuylkill, Pa	150
New River, Fayette, Ala	12
New River, Ascension, La	66
New River, Huron, Mich	43
New River, Alleghany, N. C	12
New River Depot, Pulaski, Va	12
New Rochelle, Westchester, N. Y	1,100
New Rochester, Wood, Ohio	20
New Rome, Adams, Wis	16
New Ross, Montgomery, Ind	49
New Rumley, Harrison, Ohio	44
New Russia, Essex, N. Y	36
New Rutland, La Salle, Ill	480
Newry, Oxford, Me	28
Newry, Blair, Pa	130
Newry, Vernon, Wis	28
News, Calhoun, Ill	60
New Salem, Pike, Ill	120
New Salem, Rush, Ind	60
New Salem, Franklin, Mass	76
New Salem, Allegan, Mich	29
New Salem, Albany, N. Y	41
New Salem, Randolph, N. C	34
New Salem, Fairfield, Ohio	84
New Salem, Fayette, Pa	80
New Salem, Rusk, Tex	56
New Salem, Harrison, W. Va	72
New Salisbury, Harrison, Ind	18
New Santa Fé, Jackson, Mo	86
New Scandinavia, Republic, Kans	12
New Scotland, Albany, N. Y	30
New Scottsville, Beaver, Pa	$5
News Ferry, Halifax, Va	190
New Sharon, Mahaska, Iowa	170
New Sharon, Franklin, Me	330
New Sharon, Monmouth, N. J	10
New Sheffield, Beaver, Pa	42
New Shoreham, Newport, R. I	160
New Site, Tallapoosa, Ala	11
New Smyrna, Volusia, Fla	12
New Somerset, Jefferson, Ohio	12
Newson's Depot, Southampton, Va	89
New Springfield, Mahoning, Ohio	40
New Springville, Richmond, N. Y	50
New Stanton, Westmoreland, Pa	28
Newstead, Christian, Ky	24
New Stirling, Iredell, N. C	5
New Store, Buckingham, Va	74
New Texas, Allegheny, Pa	63
Newton, (*c. h.*,) Dale, Ala	65
Newton, (*c. h.*,) Baker, Ga	300
Newton, (*c. h.*,) Jasper, Ill	250
Newton,* (*c. h.*,) Jasper, Iowa	2,400
Newton,* Middlesex, Mass	1,200
Newton, Calhoun, Mich	6
Newton, Newton, Miss	86
Newton, Rockingham, N. H	87
Newton,* (*c. h.*,) Sussex, N. J	2,100
Newton, (*c. h.*,) Catawba, N. C	200
Newton, Benton, Oreg	12
Newton, (*c. h.*,) Newton, Tex	6
Newton, Cache, Utah	12
Newton, Roane, W. Va	13
Newton, Vernon, Wis	22
Newton Academy, Monroe, Ala	12
Newtonburgh, Manitowoc, Wis	39
Newton Centre, Middlesex, Mass	610
Newton Depot, Rockingham, N. H	51
Newton Factory, Newton, Ga	20
Newton Falls, Trumbull, Ohio	360
Newton Grove, Sampson, N. C	14
Newton Hamilton, Mifflin, Pa	260
Newtonia, Newton, Mo	300
Newton Lower Falls, Middlesex, Mass	330
Newton's Retreat, Tippecanoe, Ind	14
Newton Stewart, Orange, Ind	20
Newtonsville, Clermont, Ohio	22
Newton Upper Falls, Middlesex, Mass	330
Newtonville, Spencer, Ind	31
Newtonville, Buchanan, Iowa	12
Newtonville, Middlesex, Mass	610
Newtonville, Albany, N. Y	51
New Topia, Barbour, Ala	6
Newtown, El Dorado, Cal	33
Newtown, Fairfield, Conn	470
Newtown, Fountain, Ind	120
Newtown, Scott, Ky	35
Newtown, Worcester, Md	310
Newtown, Putnam, Mo	20
Newtown, Queens, N. Y	300
Newtown, Hamilton, Ohio	120
Newtown, Bucks, Pa	520
Newtown, King and Queen, Va	20
New Town Landing, Warren, Miss	12
Newtown Mills, Forest, Pa	49

* Money-order office.

Newtown Square, Delaware, Pa	$80
Newtown Stephensburgh, Frederick, Va	210
New Trenton, Franklin, Ind	92
New Trier, Dakota, Minn	100
New Tripoli, Lehigh, Pa	16
New Troy, Berrien, Mich	59
New Ulm,* (*c. h.*,) Brown, Minn	590
New Ulm, Austin, Tex	46
New Upton, Gloucester, Va	12
New Utrecht, Kings, N. Y	130
New Vernon, Morris, N. J	71
New Vernon, Mercer, Pa	40
New Vienna, Dubuque, Iowa	110
New Vienna, Clinton, Ohio	360
New Village, Warren, N. J	46
Newville, Colusa, Cal	53
Newville, De Kalb, Ind	130
Newville, Herkimer, N. Y	22
Newville, Richland, Ohio	54
Newville, Cumberland, Pa	930
Newville, Vernon, Wis	14
New Vineyard, Franklin, Me	62
New Virginia, Warren, Iowa	33
New Washington, Clarke, Ind	110
New Washington, Crawford, Ohio	140
New Washington, Clearfield, Pa	89
New Waterford, Columbiana, Ohio	120
New Waverly, Cass, Ind	68
Newway, Licking, Ohio	26
New Wells, Cape Girardeau, Mo	54
New Westville, Preble, Ohio	47
New Wilmington, Lawrence, Pa	580
New Winchester, Hendricks, Ind	43
New Windsor, Mercer, Ill	440
New Windsor, Carroll, Md	290
New Woodstock, Madison, N. Y	220
New York, Wayne, Iowa	83
New York,* (*c. h.*,) New York, N. Y	6,000
New York Mills, Oneida, N. Y	480
New Zion, Clarendon, S. C	12
Ney, De Kalb, Ill	32
Ney, Defiance, Ohio	16
Niagara Falls,* Niagara, N. Y	2,100
Niantic, New London, Conn	290
Niantic, Macon, Ill	150
Nicholas C. H., Nicholas, W. Va	45
Nicholasville,* (*c. h.*,) Jessamine, Ky	760
Nichols, Montgomery, Md	12
Nichols, Tioga, N. Y	220
Nichols, Marion, S. C	12
Nicholson, Wyoming, Pa	450
Nicholsonville, Cleveland, N. C	2
Nicholsville, Clermont, Ohio	31
Nicholville, St. Lawrence, N. Y	240
Nickleville, Venango, Pa	12
Nicojack, Marion, Tenn	84
Nicolaus, Sutter, Cal	36
Nicollet, Nicollet, Minn	30
Niconza, Miami, Ind	40
Nile, Allegany, N. Y	99
Niles, Cook, Ill	57
Niles, Van Buren, Iowa	5
Niles,* Berrien, Mich	2,600
Niles, Cayuga, N. Y	45
Niles,* Trumbull, Ohio	910

Niles, Manitowoc, Wis	$24
Niles Centre, Cook, Ill	24
Niles Valley, Tioga, Pa	50
Nilwood, Macoupin, Ill	170
Nimisila, Summit, Ohio	100
Nine Mile, Allen, Ind	18
Nine Points, Lancaster, Pa	22
Nine Times, Pickens, S. C	12
Ninety Six, Abbeville, S. C	140
Nineveh, Johnson, Ind	96
Nineveh, Adair, Mo	15
Nineveh, Broome, N. Y	240
Nineveh, Warren, Va	16
Nininger, Dakota, Minn	26
Niobrara, (*c. h.*,) L'Eau qui Court, Nebr	28
Nippenose, Lycoming, Pa	57
Nisbet, Lycoming, Pa	12
Niskayuna, Schenectady, N. Y	40
Nittany, Centre, Pa	70
Niven, Susquehanna, Pa	19
Niverville, Columbia, N. Y	180
Nixon, De Witt, Ill	15
Noah, Shelby, Ind	18
Noank, New London, Conn	290
Noble, Richland, Ill	370
Noble, Noble, Ind	150
Noble Centre, Branch, Mich	38
Noblesborough, Lincoln, Me	61
Noblestown, Allegheny, Pa	150
Noblesville,* (*c. h.*,) Hamilton, Ind	740
Nobleville, Noble, Ohio	8
Nobob, Barren, Ky	13
Nochway, Randolph, Ga	61
Nockenut, Guadalupe, Tex	5
Nodaway, Andrew, Mo	12
Nodaway Mills, Page, Iowa	12
Nohart, Richardson, Nebr	18
Nokesville, Prince William, Va	17
Nokomis,* Montgomery, Ill	800
Nolensville, Williamson, Tenn	100
Nolin, Hardin, Ky	64
Nolo, Indiana, Pa	33
Nominy Grove, Westmoreland, Va	24
Non Intervention, Lunenburgh, Va	12
Nonpariel, Knox, Ohio	38
Nooseneck Hill, Kent, R. I	19
Nora, Jo Daviess, Ill	190
Nora, Berks, Pa	20
Nora, Dane, Wis	10
Nora Springs, Floyd, Iowa	22
Norbeck, Montgomery, Md	36
Norborne, Carroll, Mo	200
Nordyk, Dallas, Iowa	12
Norfolk, Litchfield, Conn	280
Norfolk, Norfolk, Mass	150
Norfolk, (*c. h.*,) Madison, Nebr	74
Norfolk, St. Lawrence, N. Y	260
Norfolk,* (*c. h.*,) Norfolk, Va	4,000
Normal, McLean, Ill	1,500
Normanda, Tipton, Ind	12
Normandy, St. Louis, Mo	16
Normandy, Bedford, Tenn	78
Norman's Kill, Albany, N. Y	20
Normanville, Doniphan, Kans	33
Norridgewock, (*c. h.*,) Somerset, Me	350

* Money-order office.

Norris, Fulton, Ill	$91
Norris Fork, Henry, Mo	12
Norristown, Pope, Ark	12
Norristown, Carroll, Ohio	12
*Norristown,** (*c. h.*,) Montgomery, Pa	2,400
Norrisville, Harford, Md	12
Norrisville, Crawford, Pa	12
Norrisville, Caledonia, Vt	100
Norritonville, Montgomery, Pa	18
Norseland, Nicollet, Minn	100
North Abington, Plymouth, Mass	320
North Acton, York, Me	22
North Adams,* Berkshire, Mass	2,700
North Adams, Hillsdale, Mich	120
North Alfred, York, Me	27
North Amherst, Hampshire, Mass	300
North Amity, Aroostook, Me	12
*Northampton,** (*c. h.*,) Hampshire, Mass	2,400
Northampton, Fulton, N. Y	210
North Andover, Essex, Mass	310
North Andover Depot, Essex, Mass	670
North Anson, Somerset, Me	590
North Appleton, Knox, Me	42
North Argyle, Washington, N. Y	82
North Ashford, Windham, Conn	30
North Attleborough, Bristol, Mass	910
North Auburn, Androscoggin, Me	95
North Aurelius, Ingham, Mich	10
North Aurora, Kane, Ill	22
North Baldwin, Cumberland, Me	12
North Bangor, Penobscot, Me	23
North Bangor, Franklin, N. Y	170
North Barnstead, Belknap, N. H	33
North Barrier, Cabarrus, N. C	12
North Barrington, Strafford, N. H	3
North Barton, Tioga, N. Y	20
North Bass Island, Ottawa, Ohio	48
North Bay, Oneida, N. Y	130
North Bay, Door, Wis	12
North Belgrade, Kennebec, Me	35
North Bellingham, Norfolk, Mass	73
North Bend, Stark, Ind	4
North Bend, Dodge, Nebr	180
North Bend, Jackson, Wis	52
North Bennington, Bennington, Vt	680
North Benson, Shelby, Ky	44
North Benton, Mahoning, Ohio	64
North Bergen, Genesee, N. Y	56
North Berne, Fairfield, Ohio	47
North Berwick, York, Me	450
North Bethel, Oxford, Me	27
North Beverly, Essex, Mass	60
North Billerica, Middlesex, Mass	170
North Blanford, Hampden, Mass	150
North Blenheim, Schoharie, N. Y	81
North Bloomfield, Nevada, Cal	42
North Bloomfield, Ontario, N. Y	32
North Bloomfield, Trumbull, Ohio	240
North Blue Hill, Hancock, Me	34
North Boothbay, Lincoln, Me	180
Northborough, Worcester, Mass	540
North Boscawen, Merrimack, N. H	24
North Boston, Erie, N. Y	34
North Bradford, Penobscot, Me	83
North Branch, Baltimore, Md	35
North Branch, Lapeer, Mich	$120
North Branch, Isanti, Minn	17
North Branch, Hillsborough, N. H	68
North Branch, Somerset, N. J	110
North Branch, Sullivan, N. Y	50
North Branch, Jackson, Wis	12
North Branch Depot, Somerset, N. J	74
North Branford, New Haven, Conn	75
Northbridge, Worcester, Mass	190
Northbridge Centre, Worcester, Mass	130
North Bridgeton, Cumberland, Me	160
North Bridgewater,* Plymouth, Mass	1,700
North Bridgewater, Oneida, N. Y	38
North Bristol, Trumbull, Ohio	12
North Broadalbin, Fulton, N. Y	41
North Brook, Lincoln, N. C	17
North Brookfield,* Worcester, Mass	1,100
North Brookfield, Madison, N. Y	160
North Brooklin, Hancock, Me	23
North Brooksville, Hancock, Me	12
North Buckfield, Oxford, Me	18
North Bucksport, Hancock, Me	40
North Buffalo, Armstrong, Pa	12
North Byron, Kent, Mich	13
North Cambridge, Middlesex, Mass	940
North Cambridge, Lamoille, Vt	23
North Camden, Lorain, Ohio	20
North Cameron, Steuben, N. Y	8
North Canton, Hartford, Conn	19
North Canyonville, Douglas, Oreg	100
North Cape, Racine, Wis	120
North Carmel, Penobscot, Me	11
North Carver, Plymouth, Mass	42
North Castine, Hancock, Me	76
North Castle, Westchester, N. Y	20
North Cedar, Jackson, Kans	10
North Charlestown, Sullivan, N. H	140
North Chatham, Barnstable, Mass	63
North Chatham, Columbia, N. Y	86
North Chelmsford, Middlesex, Mass	240
North Chelsea, Suffolk, Mass	100
North Chemung, Chemung, N. Y	34
North Chester, Hampden, Mass	24
North Chester, Windsor, Vt	150
North Chesterville, Franklin, Me	100
North Chichester, Merrimack, N. H	64
North Chili, Monroe, N. Y	140
North Clarendon, Rutland, Vt	62
North Clarkson, Monroe, N. Y	45
North Clayton, Miami, Ohio	9
North Clayton, Crawford, Wis	12
North Clove, Dutchess, N. Y	34
North Clymer, Chautauqua, N. Y	51
North Cohasset, Norfolk, Mass	90
North Cohocton, Steuben, N. Y	200
North Colebrook, Litchfield, Conn	28
North Colesville, Broome, N. Y	14
North Columbia, Nevada, Cal	60
North Columbus, Franklin, Ohio	30
North Copake, Columbia, N. Y	130
North Conway, Carroll, N. H	700
North Cornville, Somerset, Me	39
North Cornwall, Litchfield, Conn	64

* Money-order office.

NOR	
North Cove, McDowell, N. C	$5
North Coventry, Chester, Pa	12
North Craftsbury, Orleans, Vt	180
North Creek, Phillips, Ark	16
North Creek, Warren, N. Y	44
North Cutler, Washington, Me	22
Northcutt, Linn, Mo	45
North Dana, Worcester, Mass	95
North Danville, Caledonia, Vt	63
North Dartmouth, Bristol, Mass	85
North Deer Isle, Hancock, Me	39
North Derby, Orleans, Vt	83
North Dighton, Bristol, Mass	260
North Dixmont, Penobscot, Me	78
North Dorchester, Grafton, N. H	27
North Dorset, Bennington, Vt	81
North Dover, Cuyahoga, Ohio	11
North Dunbarton, Merrimack, N. H	18
North Duxbury, Washington, Vt	39
North Eagle, Clinton, Mich	130
Northeast,* Cecil, Md	370
North East,* Erie, Pa	930
North East Centre, Dutchess, N. Y	31
North Eastham, Barnstable, Mass	59
Northeast Harbor, Hancock, Me	53
North Easton, Bristol, Mass	900
North Easton, Washington, N. Y	86
North Eaton, Lorain, Ohio	44
North Edgecomb, Lincoln, Me	82
North Egremont, Berkshire, Mass	140
Northeim, Manitowoc, Wis	36
North Elba, Essex, N. Y	20
North Elk Grove, La Fayette, Wis	24
North Ellsworth, Hancock, Me	12
North English, Iowa, Iowa	64
North Enosburgh, Franklin, Vt	17
Northern Depot, Boone, Ind	16
North Evans, Erie, N. Y	79
North Fairfax, Franklin, Vt	39
North Fairfield, Somerset, Me	25
North Fairfield, Huron, Ohio	350
North Falmouth, Barnstable, Mass	82
North Farmington, Franklin, Me	12
North Farmington, Oakland, Mich	20
North Fayette, Kennebec, Me	80
North Fayston, Washington, Vt	12
North Fenton, Broome, N. Y	63
North Ferrisburgh, Addison, Vt	160
Northfield, Litchfield, Conn	140
Northfield, Boone, Ind	25
Northfield, Des Moines, Iowa	67
Northfield, Washington, Me	12
Northfield, Franklin, Mass	480
Northfield,* Rice, Minn	1,300
Northfield, Summit, Ohio	130
Northfield,* Washington, Vt	1,200
Northfield Farms, Franklin, Mass	73
Northford, New Haven, Conn	100
North Fork, Mason, Ky	100
North Fork, Stearns, Minn	12
North Fork, Ashe, N. C	7
North Fork, Henry, Tenn	12
North Franklin, Delaware, N. Y	20
North Fryeburgh, Oxford, Me	74
North Gage, Oneida, N. Y	39
North Galway, Saratoga, N. Y	25

NOR	
North Garden, Albemarle, Va	$15
North Georgetown, Columbiana, Ohio	94
North Granby, Hartford, Conn	70
North Grantham, Sullivan, N. H	27
North Granville, Washington, N. Y	420
North Gray, Cumberland, Me	96
North Greece, Monroe, N. Y	65
North Greenfield, Saratoga, N. Y	41
North Greenfield, Logan, Ohio	12
North Greensborough, Orleans, Vt	17
North Greenwich, Washington, N. Y	58
North Grosvenor Dale, Windham, Conn	84
North Grafton, Grafton, N. H	54
North Grove, Miami, Ind	160
North Guilford, New Haven, Conn	42
North Hadley, Hampshire, Mass	190
North Hamden, Delaware, N. Y	20
North Hamlin, Monroe, N. Y	12
North Hammond, St. Lawrence, N. Y	38
North Hampton, Peoria, Ill	18
North Hampton, Rockingham, N. H	260
North Hampton, Clark, Ohio	48
North Hancock, Hancock, Me	16
North Hannibal, Oswego, N. Y	79
North Harpersfield, Delaware, N. Y	28
North Harpswell, Cumberland, Me	45
North Hartland, Niagara, N. Y	41
North Hartland, Windsor, Vt	82
North Harwich, Barnstable, Mass	52
North Hatfield, Hampshire, Mass	110
North Haven, New Haven, Conn	260
North Haven, Knox, Me	120
North Haverhill, Grafton, N. H	220
North Hebron, Washington, N. Y	17
North Hector, Schuyler, N. Y	150
North Heidelberg, Berks, Pa	9
North Hermon, Penobscot, Me	15
North Hero, (c. h.,) Grand Isle, Vt	60
North Hogan, Ripley, Ind	12
North Hoosick, Rensselaer, N. Y	140
North Hope, Butler, Pa	100
North Hudson, Essex, N. Y	38
North Huron, Wayne, N. Y	59
North Hyde Park, Lemoille, Vt	60
North Industry, Stark, Ohio	21
North Irving, Barry, Mich	31
North Isleborough, Waldo, Me	110
North Jackson, Mahoning, Ohio	90
North Jackson, Susquehanna, Pa	22
North Jasper, Steuben, N. Y	8
North Java, Wyoming, N. Y	110
North Jay, Franklin, Me	88
North Judson, Stark, Ind	110
North Kennebunk Port, York, Me	2
North Kingston, De Kalb, Ill	90
North Kingsville, Ashtabula, Ohio	190
North Kortright, Delaware, N. Y	60
North La Crosse, La Crosse, Wis	130
North Lake, Waukesha, Wis	30
North Landgrove, Bennington, Vt	69
North Lansing, Tompkins, N. Y	57
North Lawrence, St. Lawrence, N. Y	260

* Money order office.

North Lawrence, Stark, Ohio	$91
North Lebanon, York, Me	22
North Leeds, Androscoggin, Me	29
North Leeds, Columbia, Wis	61
North Leominster, Worcester, Mass	300
North Leverett, Franklin, Mass	76
North Lewisburgh, Champaign, Ohio	290
North Liberty, St. Joseph, Ind	110
North Liberty, Johnson, Iowa	58
North Liberty, Knox, Ohio	51
North Liberty, Mercer, Pa	50
North Lima, Mahoning, Ohio	60
North Limington, York, Me	29
North Lincklaen, Chenango, N. Y	12
North Linneus, Aroostook, Me	21
North Lisbon, Grafton, N. H	16
North Litchfield, Herkimer, N. Y	50
North Littleton, Grafton, N. H	19
North Livermore, Androscoggin, Me	89
North Londonderry, Rockingham, N. H	51
North Lovell, Oxford, Me	35
North Lubec, Washington, Me	12
North Lyme, New London, Conn	66
North Lyndeborough, Hillsborough, N. H	35
North McGregor, Clayton, Iowa	370
North Madison, New Haven, Conn	34
North Madison, Jefferson, Ind	290
North Madison, Somerset, Me	12
North Madison, Lake, Ohio	120
North Manchester, Hartford, Conn	360
North Manchester,* Wabash, Ind	270
North Manlius, Onondaga, N. Y	82
North Mariaville, Hancock, Me	35
North Marshfield, Plymouth, Mass	45
North Middleborough, Plymouth, Mass	180
North Middletown, Bourbon, Ky	200
North Milford, Penobscot, Me	39
North Monmouth, Kennebec, Me	110
North Monroe, Waldo, Me	12
North Monroe, Grafton, N. H	32
North Montpelier, Washington, Vt	49
North Mountain, Berkeley, W. Va	73
North Mount Pleasant, Marshall, Miss	64
North Nassau, Rensselaer, N. Y	22
North Newberg, Shiawassee, Mich	77
North Newburgh, Penobscot, Me	20
North Newbury, Geauga, Ohio	19
North New Castle, Lincoln, Me	48
North Newfield, York, Me	23
North Newport, Penobscot, Me	19
North New Portland, Somerset, Me	140
North Newry, Oxford, Me	79
North New Salem, Franklin, Mass	49
North Norfolk, Litchfield, Conn	22
North Norway, Oxford, Me	42
North Norwich, Chenango, N. Y	130
North Oakfield, Genesee, N. Y	10
North Oakland, Butler, Pa	25
North Ogden, Weber, Utah	34
North Orange, Franklin, Mass	88

North Orwell, Bradford, Pa	$40
North Oxford, Worcester, Mass	170
North Palermo, Waldo, Me	32
North Paris, Oxford, Me	150
North Parma, Monroe, N. Y	130
North Parsonfield, York, Me	54
North Pembroke, Plymouth, Mass	42
North Pembroke, Genesee, N. Y	46
North Penn, Schuylkill, Pa	14
North Penobscot, Hancock, Me	34
North Perry, Washington, Me	37
North Petersburg, Rensselaer, N. Y	36
North Pharsalia, Chenango, N. Y	12
North Pine Grove, Clarion, Pa	8
North Pitcher, Chenango, N. Y	20
North Pittston, Kennebec, Me	28
North Plains, Ionia, Mich	20
North Plato, Kane, Ill	14
North Platte, (*c. h.*,) Lincoln, Nebr	400
North Plympton, Plymouth, Mass	23
North Point, Pulaski, Ark	3
North Point, Holt, Mo	50
North Pomfret, Windsor, Vt	98
Northport, Tuscaloosa, Ala	65
Northport, Waldo, Me	100
Northport,* (*c. h.*,) Leelenaw, Mich	190
Northport, Suffolk, N. Y	310
Northport, Waupaca, Wis	62
North Powder, Union, Oreg	12
North Pownal, Cumberland, Me	54
North Pownal, Bennington, Vt	130
North Prairie, Knox, Ill	21
North Prairie, Morrison, Minn	10
North Prairie Station, Waukesha, Wis	160
North Prescott, Hampshire, Mass	100
North Raisinville, Monroe, Mich	19
North Randolph, Orange, Vt	61
North Raymond, Cumberland, Me	42
North Reading, Middlesex, Mass	160
North Reading, Schuyler, N. Y	14
North Rehoboth, Bristol, Mass	30
North Richmond, Cheshire, N. H	28
North Richmond, Ashtabula, Ohio	12
North Ridge, Niagara, N. Y	49
North Ridgeville, Lorain, Ohio	76
North Ridgeway, Orleans, N. Y	31
North River, Tuscaloosa, Ala	12
North River, Marion, Mo	12
North River, Warren, N. Y	55
North River Mills, Hampshire, W. Va	16
North Robinson, Crawford, Ohio	53
North Rome, Bradford, Pa	11
North Rose, Wayne, N. Y	22
North Royalton, Cuyahoga, Ohio	100
North Rumford, Oxford, Me	17
North Rush, Monroe, N. Y	35
North Russel, St. Lawrence, N. Y	8
North Rutland, Worcester, Mass	52
North Salem, Hendricks, Ind	96
North Salem, Linn, Mo	39
North Salem, Rockingham, N. H	30
North Salem, Westchester, N. Y	91
North Salem, Guernsey, Ohio	12
North Sanbornton, Belknap, N. H	91

* Money-order office.

Post office	Amount
North San Diego, (c. h.,) San Diego, Cal	$150
North Sandwich, Barnstable, Mass	55
North Sandwich, Carroll, N. H	120
North Sandy, Mercer, Pa	5
North Sanford, Broome, N. Y	9
North San Juan, Nevada, Cal	390
North Santee, Georgetown, S. C	12
North Scituate, Plymouth, Mass	130
North Scituate, Providence, R. I	250
North Scriba, Oswego, N. Y	52
North Searsmont, Waldo, Me	40
North Searsport, Waldo, Me	36
North Sedgwick, Hancock, Me	47
North Sewickly, Beaver, Pa	54
North Shapleigh, York, Me	44
North Sheffield, Ashtabula, Ohio	15
North Sheldon, Franklin, Vt	26
North Shenango, Crawford, Pa	89
Northside, Goochland, Va	12
North Sidney, Kennebec, Me	30
North's Landing, Switzerland, Ind	24
North's Mills, Mercer, Pa	43
North Smithfield, Bradford, Pa	9
North Solon, Cuyahoga, Ohio	39
North Somerville, Middlesex, Mass	260
North Sparta, Livingston, N. Y	22
North Spencer, Worcester, Mass	18
North Springfield, Greene, Mo	12
North Springfield, Erie, Pa	120
North Springfield, Windsor, Vt	150
North Springs, Jackson, Tenn	2
North Stamford, Fairfield, Conn	40
North Star, Gratiot, Mich	26
North Star, Atchison, Mo	58
North Star, Darke, Ohio	20
North Star, Allegheny, Pa	29
North Star, Crawford, Wis	6
North Stephentown, Rensselaer, N.Y	23
North Sterling, Cayuga, N. Y	12
North Stockholm, St. Lawrence, N. Y	160
North Stonington, New London, Conn	130
North Stoughton, Norfolk, Mass	92
North Strafford, Strafford, N. H	10
North Sudbury, Middlesex, Mass	13
North Sutton, Merrimack, N. H	90
North Swansea, Bristol, Mass	45
North Taycheedah, Fond du Lac, Wis	19
North Thetford, Orange, Vt	130
North Tisbury, Dukes, Mass	12
North Towanda, Bradford, Pa	13
North Troy, Orleans, Vt	370
North Truro, Barnstable, Mass	95
North Tunbridge, Orange, Vt	35
North Turner, Androscoggin, Me	98
North Turner Bridge, Androscoggin, Me	47
Northumberland, Coos, N. H	99
Northumberland, Saratoga, N. Y	72
Northumberland,* Northumberland, Pa	940
North Underhill, Chittenden, Vt	21
North Union, Knox, Me	54
North Uniontown, Highland, Ohio	$8
North Unity, Leelenaw, Mich	24
Northup, Gallia, Ohio	6
North Urbana, Steuben, N. Y	19
North Uxbridge, Worcester, Mass	140
North Vassalborough, Kennebec, Me	480
North Vernon, Jennings, Ind	710
North Vernon, Shiawassee, Mich	2
North Victory, Cayuga, N. Y	43
North Vienna, Kennebec, Me	38
Northville, Litchfield, Conn	51
Northville, La Salle, Ill	85
Northville, Greene, Iowa	22
Northville, Wayne, Mich	390
Northville, Fulton, N. Y	320
Northville, Erie, Pa	100
North Vineland, Cumberland, N. J	110
North Volney, Oswego, N. Y	20
North Wakefield, Carroll, N. H	59
North Waldoborough, Lincoln, Me	44
North Wales, Montgomery, Pa	160
North Walton, Delaware, N. Y	49
North Warren, Winona, Minn	8
North Washington, Chickasaw, Iowa	25
North Washington, Knox, Me	19
North Washington, Hardin, Ohio	42
North Washington, Westmoreland, Pa	45
North Waterborough, York, Me	27
North Waterford, Oxford, Me	110
North Wayne, Kennebec, Me	75
North Weare, Hillsborough, N. H	140
North West, Williams, Ohio	21
North West Bridgewater, Plymouth, Mass	13
North Western, Oneida, N. Y	130
North Wethersfield, Wyoming, N. Y	28
North Weymouth, Norfolk, Mass	250
North Wharton, Potter, Pa	12
North Whitefield, Lincoln, Me	47
North Whitehall, Lehigh, Pa	43
North Williston, Chittenden, Vt	92
North Wilmington, Middlesex, Mass	66
North Wilna, Jefferson, N. Y	34
North Wilton, Fairfield, Conn	70
North Windham, Windham, Conn	74
North Windham, Cumberland, Me	42
North Windham, Windham, Vt	79
North Windsor, Dane, Wis	54
North Winfield, Herkimer, N. Y	39
North Winterport, Waldo, Me	31
North Woburn, Middlesex, Mass	190
North Wolcott, Lamoille, Vt	52
North Wolfborough, Carroll, N. H	46
Northwood, (c. h.,) Worth, Iowa	53
Northwood, Logan, Ohio	65
Northwood Centre, Rockingham, N. H	120
Northwood Narrows, Rockingham, N. H	74
North Woodstock, Windham, Conn	160
North Woodstock, Oxford, Me	35
North Woodstock, Grafton, N. H	10
North Woodville, Penobscot, Me	8
North Yam Hill, Yam Hill, Oreg	45

* Money-order office.

North Yarmouth, Cumberland, Me	$76
Norton, Kankakee, Ill	27
Norton, Bristol, Mass	410
Norton, Delaware, Ohio	49
Norton Centre, Summit, Ohio	18
Norton Hill, Greene, N. Y	71
Norton Mills, Essex, Vt	160
Norton's Bluff, McCracken, Ky	12
Nortonville, Clarke, Iowa	12
Norval, Harnett, N. C	2
Norvell, Jackson, Mich	150
Norwalk,* Fairfield, Conn	2,400
Norwalk, Warren, Iowa	36
Norwalk, Manistee, Mich	32
Norwalk,* (*c. h.*,) Huron, Ohio	2,700
Norway, La Salle, Ill	120
Norway,* Oxford, Me	760
Norway, Goodhue, Minn	180
Norway, Herkimer, N. Y	130
Norway, Racine, Wis	31
Norway Lake, Monongalia, Minn	120
Norwegian, Watonwan, Minn	10
Norwich,* (*c. h.*,) New London, Conn	3,900
Norwich, Hampshire, Mass	30
Norwich,* (*c. h.*,) Chenango, N. Y	2,200
Norwich, Muskingum, Ohio	110
Norwich, McKean, Pa	8
Norwich, Windsor, Vt	400
Norwich Town, New London, Conn	290
Norwood, Mercer, Ill	190
Norwood, Lucas, Iowa	12
Norwood, Franklin, Kans	12
Norwood, Charlevoix, Mich	35
Norwood, Carter, Mo	12
Norwood, Bergen, N. J	10
Norwood, Stanly, N. C	24
Norwood, Hamilton, Ohio	12
Norwood, Chester, Pa	12
Norwood, Nelson, Va	340
Norwood Park, Cook, Ill	12
Nossville, Huntingdon, Pa	33
Notasulga, Macon, Ala	170
Notre Dame,* St. Joseph, Ind	1,000
Nottingham, Wells, Ind	32
Nottingham, Prince George's, Md	41
Nottingham, Rockingham, N. H	77
Nottingham, Cuyahoga, Ohio	79
Nottingham, Chester, Pa	65
Nottoway C. H., Nottoway, Va	220
Nova, Ashland, Ohio	22
Novelty, Knox, Mo	69
Novi, Oakland, Mich	74
Nuckollsville, Grayson, Va	55
Nueces, Nueces, Tex	16
Nugent's Grove, Linn, Iowa	55
Nulhegan, Essex, Vt	44
Null's Mills, Fayette, Ind	13
Numa, Parke, Ind	11
Numa, Appanoose, Iowa	26
Numidia, Columbia, Pa	59
Nunda, McHenry, Ill	240
Nunda, Freeborn, Minn	23
Nunda,* Livingston, N. Y	1,100
Nunda Station, Livingston, N. Y	320
Nunica, Ottawa, Mich	150
Nursery Hill, Dent, Mo	12
Nursery Hill, Otoe, Nebr	$80
Nuzums, Marion, W. Va	53
Nyack,* Rockland, N. Y	1,300
Nyack Turnpike, Rockland, N. Y	68
Nyce's, Pike, Pa	31

O.

Oak, Pope, Ill	12
Oak, Pulaski, Ind	23
Oak, Wayne, Mich	21
Oakalla, Iroquois, Ill	820
Oak Bower, Hart, Ga	5
Oak Creek, Milwaukee, Wis	140
Oakdale, Livingston, Ill	12
Oakdale, Jennings, Ind	10
Oakdale, Worcester, Mass	230
Oak Dale, Washington, Minn	17
Oak Dale, Hunterdon, N. J	20
Oakdale, Delaware, Pa	160
Oakdale, Rockbridge, Va	3
Oakdale Station, Suffolk, N. Y	52
Oakdale Station, Allegheny, Pa	12
Oakdam, Vanderburgh, Ind	4
Oak Farm, Brown, Ind	13
Oakfield, Audubon, Iowa	56
Oakfield, Kent, Mich	44
Oakfield, Franklin, Mo	30
Oakfield, Genesee, N. Y	330
Oakfield, Perry, Ohio	26
Oakfield, Fond du Lac, Wis	190
Oakfield Centre, Fond du Lac, Wis	110
Oak Flat, Pendleton, W. Va	16
Oakford, Howard, Ind	99
Oakford, Daviess, Ky	17
Oakford, Bucks, Pa	16
Oak Forest, Franklin, Ind	15
Oak Forest, Iredell, N. C	1
Oak Forest, Greene, Pa	14
Oak Forest, Cumberland, Va	33
Oakfuskee, Cleburne, Ala	10
Oak Glen, Steele, Minn	64
Oak Grove, Sussex, Del	12
Oak Grove, McLean, Ill	41
Oak Grove, Christian, Ky	46
Oak Grove, Prince George's, Md	35
Oak Grove, Livingston, Mich	74
Oak Grove, Anoka, Minn	9
Oak Grove, Jackson, Mo	12
Oak Grove, Hunterdon, N. J	2
Oak Grove, Union, N. C	9
Oak Grove, Marion, S. C	10
Oak Grove, Jefferson, Tenn	4
Oak Grove, Westmoreland, Va	100
Oak Grove, Dodge, Wis	100
Oak Grove Furnace, Westmoreland, Pa	14
Oak Groves, Seward, Nebr	10
Oakham, Worcester, Mass	150
Oak Harbor, Ottawa, Ohio	160
Oak Hill, Cumberland, Me	180
Oak Hill, Oakland, Mich	16
Oak Hill, Gasconade, Mo	6
Oak Hill, Greene, N. Y	120
Oak Hill, Granville, N. C	15
Oak Hill, Jackson, Ohio	330

* Money-order office.

Oak Hill, Lancaster, Pa	$65
Oak Hill, Overton, Tenn	16
Oak Hill, Travis, Tex	12
Oak Hill, Fayette, W. Va	6
Oak Hill, Jefferson, Wis	27
Oakhurst, Miller, Mo	49
Oakington, Harford, Md	12
Oakland,* Alameda, Cal	2,100
Oakland, Coles, Ill	220
Oakland, Spencer, Ind	35
Oakland, Marshall, Ky	16
Oakland, Alleghany, Md	560
Oakland, Oakland, Mich	10
Oakland, Yalabusha, Miss	70
Oakland, Laclede, Mo	16
Oakland, Burt, Nebr	33
Oakland, Livingston, N. Y	89
Oakland, Clinton, Ohio	41
Oakland, Douglas, Oreg	170
Oakland, Armstrong, Pa	82
Oakland, Fayette, Tenn	72
Oakland, Colorado, Tex	40
Oakland, (*c. h.*,) Mason, Wash	12
Oakland, Jefferson, Wis	25
Oakland City, Gibson, Ind	52
Oakland Cross Roads, Westmoreland, Pa	36
Oakland Mills, Henry, Iowa	30
Oakland Mills, Nicholas, Ky	27
Oakland Mills, Howard, Md	10
Oakland Mills, Guernsey, Ohio	12
Oakland Mills, Juniata, Pa	70
Oaklandon, Marion, Ind	38
Oakland Station, Warren, Ky	82
Oakland Valley, Franklin, Iowa	21
Oak Lawn, Shelby, Tenn	12
Oak Level, Cleburne, Ala	12
Oak Level, Henry, Va	12
Oakley, Macon, Ill	100
Oakley, Franklin, La	10
Oakley, Saginaw, Mich	57
Oakley, New Hanover, N. C	12
Oakley, Hamilton, Ohio	32
Oakley, Susquehanna, Pa	23
Oakley, Mecklenburg, Va	38
Oakley, Green, Wis	13
Oakley Depot, Charleston, S. C	89
Oak Mills, Atchison, Kans	18
Oak Orchard, Frederick, Md	14
Oak Orchard, Orleans, N. Y	17
Oak Park, Cook, Ill	220
Oak Park, Madison, Va	15
Oak Point, Clark, Ill	14
Oak Point, Van Buren, Iowa	15
Oak Point, Wilson, Tenn	8
Oak Point, Cowlitz, Wash	67
Oak Ridge, Jefferson, Ala	12
Oak Ridge, Menard, Ill	13
Oak Ridge, Winona, Minn	17
Oak Ridge, Cape Girardeau, Mo	46
Oak Ridge, Hancock, Ohio	16
Oaks, Orange, N. C	26
Oaks, Sauk, Wis	16
Oak's Corners, Ontario, N. Y	130
Oak Shade, Lancaster, Pa	13
Oak Spring, Davis, Iowa	5
Oak Spring, Rutherford, N. C	$5
Oak Springs, Anoka, Minn	10
Oak Springs, Dodge, Nebr	12
Oaksville, Otsego, N. Y	45
Oaktown, Knox, Ind	160
Oakville, Lawrence, Ala	6
Oakville, Jefferson, Ark	12
Oakville, Napa, Cal	41
Oakville, New Haven, Conn	92
Oakville, Hickman, Ky	12
Oakville, St. Mary's, Md	16
Oakville, Monroe, Mich	22
Oakville, Cumberland, Pa	110
Oakville, (*c. h.*,) Live Oak, Tex	16
Oakville, Appomattox, Va	16
Oakway, Oconee, S. C	6
Oak Well, Hawkins, Tenn	12
Oakwood, Vermilion, Ill	12
Oakwood, Linn, Kans	7
Oakwood, Oakland, Mich	74
Oakwood, Paulding, Ohio	10
Oakwood, Montgomery, Tenn	17
Oak Woods, Fleming, Ky	33
Oaky Streak, Butler, Ala	10
Oasis, Johnson, Iowa	15
Oasis, Waushara, Wis	22
Oatlands, Loudoun, Va	12
Oatmeal, Burnet, Tex	10
O'Bannon, Jefferson, Ky	120
Oberle's Corners, Carver, Minn	9
Oberlin,* Lorain, Ohio	2,400
Oblong, Crawford, Ill	60
Oblong, Dutchess, N. Y	44
O'Brien, (*c. h.*,) O'Brien, Iowa	5
Ocala, (*c. h.*,) Marion, Fla	270
Ocate, Mora, N. Mex	12
Occoquan, Prince William, Va	81
Ocean, Alleghany, Md	45
Oceana, (*c. h.*,) Wyoming, W. Va	60
Ocean Port, Monmouth, N. J	88
Ocean Springs, Jackson, Miss	92
Ocean View, Sonoma, Cal	12
Ocean View, Sussex, Del	25
Oceola, St. Joseph, Ind	30
Oceola,* (*c. h.*,) Clarke, Iowa	900
Oceola, Greene, Ky	16
Oceola, Crawford, Ohio	29
Oceola, Fond du Lac, Wis	14
Oceola Centre, Livingston, Mich	35
Ocheltree, Johnson, Kans	12
Ochesee, Calhoun, Fla	12
Ochlochnee, Thomas, Ga	12
Ocona Lufty, Jackson, N. C	5
Oconee, Washington, Ga	50
Oconee Station, Shelby, Ill	150
Oconomowoc,* Waukesha, Wis	1,100
Oconto,* (*c. h.*,) Oconto, Wis	1,000
Ocoya, Livingston, Ill	56
Ocracocke, Hyde, N. C	10
Octagon, Tippecanoe, Ind	12
Octavia, Early, Ga	12
Octoraro, Lancaster, Pa	43
Oddville, Harrison, Ky	26
Odell, Livingston, Ill	880
Odessa, New Castle, Del	370
Odessa, Schuyler, N. Y	82

* Money-order office.

Odin,* Marion, Ill $720
Odin, Vernon, Wis 5
Ofahoma, Leake, Miss 12
O'Fallon, St. Charles, Mo 140
O'Fallon Depot, St. Clair, Ill 210
Offutt's Cross Roads, Montgomery, Md 12
Ogden, Champaign, Ill 12
Ogden, Henry, Ind 83
Ogden, Dubuque, Iowa 5
Ogden, Riley, Kans 210
Ogden, Monroe, N. Y 61
Ogden, Clinton, Ohio 69
Ogden Centre, Lenawee, Mich 12
Ogden City, (*c. h.*,) Weber, Utah 190
Ogdensburgh, Sussex, N. J 61
Ogdensburgh,* St. Lawrence, N. Y 2,600
Ogdensburgh, Tioga, Pa 37
Ogdensburgh, Waupaca, Wis 52
Ogden's Landing, Ballard, Ky 12
Ogee, Blount, Ala 12
Ogeechee, Scriven, Ga 25
Ogemaw, Iosco, Mich 12
Ogle, Butler, Pa 23
Oglesby, La Salle, Ill 210
Oglethorpe, (*c. h.*,) Macon, Ga 320
Ogunquit, York, Me 80
Ohio, Bureau, Ill 54
Ohio, Madison, Iowa 18
Ohio, Herkimer, N. Y 35
Ohio Mill, Ottawa, Mich 12
Ohioville, Ulster, N. Y 64
Ohioville, Beaver, Pa 42
Ohl's Town, Trumbull, Ohio 28
Oil City,* Venango, Pa 2,600
Oil Creek, Perry, Ind 16
Oil Creek, Crawford, Pa 170
Oil Diggins, Trumbull, Ohio 12
Oil Mill Village, Hillsborough, N. H 60
Oil Rock, Wirt, W. Va 100
Oil Springs, Johnson, Ky 2
Oil Trough, Independence, Ark 12
Okaman, Waseca, Minn 48
Okaw, Washington, Ill 84
Okeana, Butler, Ohio 50
Okee, Columbia, Wis 38
Okemos, Ingham, Mich 130
Okmulkee, Creek Nation, Ind. T 12
Okolona,* Chickasaw, Miss 1,000
Okolona, Henry, Ohio 47
Okolona, Carter, Tenn 12
Okonoko, Hampshire, W. Va 12
Ola, Lucas, Iowa 9
Olamon, Penobscot, Me 85
Olathe,* (*c. h.*,) Johnson, Kans 1,300
Olcott, Niagara, N. Y 110
Old Alexandria, Lincoln, Mo 22
Old Bridge, Middlesex, N. J 68
Old Church, Hanover, Va 58
Old Creek, San Luis Obispo, Cal 12
Oldenburgh, Franklin, Ind 180
Old Forge, Luzerne, Pa 150
Old Fort, McDowell, N. C 250
Old Furnace, Gaston, N. C 3
Oldham's Cross Roads, Westmoreland, Va 15
Old Hickory, Conway, Ark $16
Old Hickory, Wayne, Ohio 40
Old Hickory, Botetourt, Va 18
Old Line, Lancaster, Pa 10
Old Mines, Washington, Mo 19
Old Mission, Winneshiek, Iowa 8
Old Mission, Grand Traverse, Mich 52
Old Monroe, Lincoln, Mo 39
Old Point Comfort,* Elizabeth City, Va 1,200
Old Richmond, Forsyth, N. C 4
Old Ripley, Bond, Ill 22
Old Store, Chesterfield, S. C 12
Old Town, Phillips, Ark 12
Old Town, Penobscot, Me 720
Old Town, Alleghany, Md 12
Old Town, Forsyth, N. C 8
Oldtown, Claiborne, Tenn 8
Old Westbury, Queens, N. Y 170
Olean, Ripley, Ind 90
Olean,* Cattaraugus, N. Y 1,400
Olema, Marin, Cal 86
Olena, Henderson, Ill 100
Olena, Huron, Ohio 81
Oleopolis, Venango, Pa 110
Oley, Berks, Pa 75
Olin, Iredell, N. C 22
Olin, Adams, Wis 16
Olio, Scott, Ark 4
Olive, Lawrence, Ill 12
Olive, Marshall, Ky 12
Olive, Clinton, Mich 12
Olive, Ulster, N. Y 50
Olive Branch, De Soto, Miss 83
Olive Branch, Lancaster, Nebr 10
Olive Branch, Union, N. C 12
Olive Branch, Clermont, Ohio 41
Olive Bridge, Ulster, N. Y 30
Oliveburgh, Jefferson, Pa 12
Olive Green, Noble, Ohio 12
Olive Hill, Wayne, Ind 26
Olive Hill, Carter, Ky 22
Olive Hill, Hardin, Tenn 12
Oliver's, Anderson, Tenn 8
Oliver's Landing, Phillips, Ark 12
Olivesburgh, Richland, Ohio 97
Olivet, Osage, Kans 12
Olivet,* Eaton, Mich 540
Olivet, Armstrong, Pa 28
Olivet, Pierce, Wis 12
Olivia, Blair, Pa 55
Olmstead, Logan, Ky 130
Olmsted, Cuyahoga, Ohio 240
Olmstedville, Essex, N. Y 92
Olney,* (*c. h.*,) Richland, Ill 2,100
Olney, Montgomery, Md 120
Olneyville, Providence, R. I 1,100
Olustee, Baker, Fla 4
Olustee Creek, Pike, Ala 31
OLYMPIA,* (*c. h.*,) Thurston, Wash 1,300
Olympian Springs, Bath, Ky 12
Olympus, Overton, Tenn 11
Olyphant, Luzerne, Pa 270
Omadi, Dakota, Nebr 12
Omaha, Putnam, Mo 12
Omaha Agency, Blackbird, Nebr 30

* Money-order office.

Omaha Barracks, Douglas, Nebr	$12
Omaha City,* (*c. h.*,) Douglas, Nebr	4,000
Omar, Jefferson, N. Y	19
Omega, Nevada, Cal	24
Omega, Marion, Ill	20
Omega, Hamilton, Ind	12
Omega, Hart, Ky	16
Omega, Pike, Ohio	95
Omega, Upshur, Tex	8
Omega, Halifax, Va	18
Omena, Leelenaw, Mich	23
Omph Ghent, Madison, Ill	14
Omro,* Winnebago, Wis	940
Onalaska, La Crosse, Wis	150
Onancock, Accomack, Va	130
Onarga,* Iroquois, Ill	1,100
Onawa City, (*c. h.*,) Monona, Iowa	450
Onberg, Indiana, Pa	12
O'Neal's Mills, Troup, Ga	8
Oneco, Windham, Conn	100
Oneco, Stephenson, Ill	29
Oneida,* Knox, Ill	790
Oneida, Kosciusko, Ind	9
Oneida,* Madison, N. Y	2,200
Oneida, Brown, Wis	11
Oneida Castle, Oneida, N. Y	200
Oneida Lake, Madison, N. Y	25
Oneida Mills, Carroll, Ohio	97
Oneida Valley, Madison, N. Y	59
Oneonta, Otsego, N. Y	840
Oneota, St. Louis, Minn	65
Onion Creek, Travis, Tex	25
Onion River, Sheboygan, Wis	23
Onisbo, Sacramento, Cal	27
Ono, Lebanon, Pa	56
Ono, Pierce, Wis	12
Onondaga, Ingham, Mich	50
Onondaga, Onondaga, N. Y	94
Onondaga Castle, Onondaga, N. Y	18
Onondaga Valley, Onondaga, N. Y	140
Onota, Schoolcraft, Mich	12
Onoville, Cattaraugus, N. Y	22
Onslow C. H., Onslow, N. C	3
Ontario, Knox, Ill	60
Ontario, La Grange, Ind	150
Ontario, Story, Iowa	69
Ontario, Jackson, Kans	6
Ontario, Wayne, N. Y	160
Ontario, Richland, Ohio	150
Ontario, Vernon, Wis	100
Ontario Centre, Wayne, N. Y	12
Ontonagon (*c. h.*,) Ontonagon, Mich	310
Onward, Cass, Ind	25
Onyx, Yell, Ark	12
Ooltewah, Hamilton, Tenn	100
Oostburgh, Sheboygan, Wis	12
Opelika, (*c. h.*,) Lee, Ala	920
Opelousas,* (*c. h.*,) St. Landry, La	730
Opequan, Lancaster, Nebr	12
Ophir Cherokee, Ga	19
Ophir, Washoe, Nev	40
O'Plain, Lake, Ill	19
Oporto, St. Joseph, Mich	20
Oppelo, Perry, Ark	14
Oppenheim, Fulton, N. Y	52
Oquawka,* (*c. h.*,) Henderson, Ill	410
Ora, Jackson, Ill	$12
Oral, Scott, Minn	63
Ora Labor, Huron, Mich	28
Oral Oaks, Lunenburgh, Va	12
Oramel, Allegany, N. Y	170
Oran, Fayette, Iowa	10
Oran, Onondaga, N. Y	45
Orange, New Haven, Conn	35
Orange, Cherokee, Ga	12
Orange, Fayette, Ind	71
Orange, Clinton, Iowa	9
Orange, Franklin, Mass	690
Orange, Ionia, Mich	12
Orange, Essex, N. J	2,500
Orange, Schuyler, N. Y	120
Orange, Mahoning, Ohio	93
Orange, Luzerne, Pa	32
Orange, (*c. h.*,) Orange, Tex	85
Orange, Orange, Vt	35
Orange, Juneau, Wis	35
Orange C. H., Orange, Va	600
Orangeburgh, Mason, Ky	47
Orangeburgh C.H., Orangeburgh, S.C	1,100
Orange Factory, Orange, N. C	15
Orange Grove, Dallas, Ala	12
Orange Lake, Orange, N. Y	12
Orange Mills, St. John's, Fla	53
Orangeport, Niagara, N. Y	70
Orange Springs, Marion, Fla	12
Orange Station, Delaware, Ohio	37
Orange Valley, Essex, N. J.	12
Orangeville, Stephenson, Ill	120
Orangeville, Orange, Ind	37
Orangeville, Baltimore, Md	12
Orangeville, Branch, Mich	31
Orangeville, Wyoming, N. Y	41
Orangeville, Trumbull, Ohio	390
Orangeville, Columbia, Pa	100
Orangeville, Fannin, Tex	15
Orangeville Mills, Barry, Mich	80
Ora Oak, Grant, Wis	12
Orbisonia, Huntingdon, Pa	130
Orchard, Mitchell, Iowa	12
Orchard Grove, Lake, Ind	38
Orcutt Creek, Bradford, Pa	31
Orcuttville, Neosho, Kans	12
Ordino, Marquette, Wis	8
Oreana, Humboldt, Nev	44
Ore Banks, Buckingham, Va	12
Orefield, Lehigh, Pa	46
Oregon, Jefferson, Ala	5
Oregon,* (*c. h.*,) Ogle, Ill	540
Oregon, Clarke, Ind	33
Oregon,* (*c. h.*,) Holt, Mo	650
Oregon, Chautauqua, N. Y	57
Oregon, Warren, Ohio	85
Oregon, Lancaster, Pa	36
Oregon, Lincoln, Tenn	11
Oregon, Dane, Wis	360
Oregon City,* (*c. h.*,) Clackamas, Oreg	820
Oregon Hill, Lycoming, Pa	12
Oregon House, Yuba, Cal	52
Oregonia, Tuscaloosa, Ala	7
Ore Hill, Litchfield, Conn	33
Orell, Jefferson, Ky	32

* Money-order office.

Post office	Compensation
Oreville, Dutchess, N. Y	$12
Orford, Tama, Iowa	330
Orford, Grafton, N. H	310
Orfordville, Grafton, N. H	75
Orfordville, Rock, Wis	270
Organ Spring, Washington, Ind	11
Orient, Adair, Iowa	21
Orient, Aroostook, Me	24
Orient, Suffolk, N. Y	270
Orihula, Winnebago, Wis	21
Orion, Pike, Ala	30
Orion, Henry, Ill	200
Orion, Kosciusko, Ind	9
Orion, Oakland, Mich	230
Orion, Henry, Mo	12
Orion, Richland, Wis	50
Oriskany, Oneida, N. Y	300
Oriskany Falls, Oneida, N. Y	390
Orizaba, Tippah, Miss	33
Orkney Springs, Shenandoah, Va	18
Orland, Cook, Ill	27
Orland,* Steuben, Ind	360
Orland, Hancock, Me	320
Orlando, (*c. h.*,) Orange, Fla	64
Orlando, Sherburne, Minn	6
Orlean, Fauquier, Va	12
Orleans, (*c. h.*,) Klamath, Cal	20
Orleans, Morgan, Ill	35
Orleans,* Orange, Ind	400
Orleans, Appanoose, Iowa	27
Orleans,* Barnstable, Mass	370
Orleans, Ionia, Mich	43
Orleans, Polk, Mo	23
Orleans, Ontario, N. Y	84
Orleans Cross Roads, Morgan, W. Va	58
Orleans Four Corners, Jefferson, N. Y	22
Ormanville, Wapello, Iowa	12
Orme's Store, Bledsoe, Tenn	20
Ormsby, Allegheny, Pa	380
Orneville, Piscataquis, Me	13
Oro, Chesterfield, S. C	26
Oro City, Placer, Cal	12
Oro City, Lake, Colo	210
Orodell, Union, Oreg	63
Oro Fino, Siskiyou, Cal	35
Orono, Penobscot, Me	510
Orono, (*c. h.*,) Sherburne, Minn	77
Oronoco, Olmsted, Minn	97
Oronoco, Amherst, Va	12
Oroville,* (*c. h.*,) Butte, Cal	1,000
Orrington, Penobscot, Me	110
Orr's Island, Cumberland, Me	42
Orrstown, Franklin, Pa	85
Orrsville, Armstrong, Pa	130
Orrville, Dallas, Ala	42
Orrville,* Wayne, Ohio	590
Orth, Montgomery, Ind	16
Ortonville, Oakland, Mich	110
Orville, Pope, Ill	7
Orwell, Oswego, N. Y	130
Orwell,* Ashtabula, Ohio	240
Orwell, Bradford, Pa	59
Orwell, Addison, Vt	280
Orwigsburgh, Schuylkill, Pa	170

Post office	Compensation
Orwin, Schuylkill, Pa	$12
Osaga, Bourbon, Kans	12
Osage, Carroll, Ark	12
Osage, Franklin, Ill	4
Osage, Mitchell, Iowa	720
Osage, Crawford, Mo	18
Osage Bluff, Cole, Mo	4
Osage City, Osage, Kans	160
Osage City, Cole, Mo	79
Osage Mills, Benton, Ark	12
Osage Mission,* Neosho, Kans	620
Osakis, Douglas, Minn	140
Osanippa, Chambers, Ala	10
Osawatomie,* Miami, Kans	360
Osborn, Rock Island, Ill	12
Osborn, Neosho, Kans	24
Osborn, De Kalb, Mo	80
Osborn,* Greene, Ohio	380
Osborne Hollow, Broome, N. Y	48
Osborne's Mills, Kanawha, W. Va	3
Osborn's Bridge, Fulton, N. Y	30
Osborn's Ford, Scott, Va	12
Osborn's Store, Issaquena, Miss	12
Oscar, Armstrong, Pa	17
Osceola, (*c. h.*,) Mississippi, Ark	83
Osceola, Stark, Ill	52
Osceola,* (*c. h.*,) St. Clair, Mo	440
Osceola, Lewis, N. Y	62
Osceola, Tioga, Pa	210
Osceola Mills, Clearfield, Pa	780
Osceola Mills, (*c. h.*,) Polk, Wis	160
Oseuma, Cherokee Nation, Ind. T	53
Osgood,* Ripley, Ind	240
Oshaukuta, Columbia, Wis	41
Oshawa, Osage, Mo	12
Oshkosh,* (*c. h.*,) Winnebago, Wis	4,000
Oshtemo, Kalamazoo, Mich	160
Oskaloosa, Clay, Ill	52
Oskaloosa,* (*c. h.*,) Mahaska, Iowa	2,200
Oskaloosa,* (*c. h.*,) Jefferson, Kans	340
Oslo, Manitowoc, Wis	18
Osman's, Adams, Ohio	24
Osnaburgh, Stark, Ohio	120
Oso, Fayette, Tex	20
Osprey, Monroe, Iowa	12
Osseo, Hillsdale, Mich	170
Osseo, Hennepin, Minn	84
Osseo, Trempealeau, Wis	93
Ossian, Wells, Ind	180
Ossian,* Winneshiek, Iowa	550
Ossian, Livingston, N. Y	24
Ossineke, Alpena, Mich	68
Ossipee, (*c. h.*,) Carroll, N. H	170
Ossipee Mills, York, Me	12
Ostend, McHenry, Ill	12
Ostend, Clearfield, Pa	12
Osterville, Barnstable, Mass	160
Osterville, Caldwell, Mo	5
Ostrander, Delaware, Ohio	100
Oswaldville, Lehigh, Pa	12
Oswayo, Potter, Pa	89
Oswego,* Kendall, Ill	500
Oswego, Kosciusko, Ind	22
Oswego,* (*c. h.*,) Labette, Kans	200
Oswego,* (*c. h.*,) Oswego, N. Y	3,800
Oswego, Clackamas, Oreg	12

* Money-order office.

Post office	Compensation
Oswego Centre, Oswego, N. Y	$12
Oswego Falls, Oswego, N. Y	180
Osyka, Pike, Miss	360
Otay, San Diego, Cal	12
Otego, Otsego, N. Y	520
Othello, Olmsted, Minn	30
Otho, Webster, Iowa	60
Otis, Hancock, Me	12
Otis, Berkshire, Mass	150
Otisco, Clarke, Ind	12
Otisco, Ionia, Mich	130
Otisco, Waseca, Minn	12
Otisco, Onondaga, N. Y	100
Otisco Valley, Onandaga, N. Y	14
Otisfield, Cumberland, Me	75
Otisville, Franklin, Iowa	110
Otisville, Genesee, Mich	150
Otisville, Orange, N. Y	350
Otley, Marion, Iowa	150
Oto, Woodbury, Iowa	3
Otoe Agency, Gage, Nebr	21
Otranto, Mitchell, Iowa	60
Otsdawa, Otsego, N. Y	12
Otsego, Fayette, Iowa	80
Otsego, Allegan, Mich	570
Otsego, Wright, Minn	16
Otsego, Ray, Mo	5
Otsego, Muskingum, Ohio	46
Otsego, Columbia, Wis	93
Otselic, Chenango, N. Y	52
*Ottawa,** (*c. h.,*) La Salle, Ill	3,400
Ottawa, Clarke, Iowa	70
*Ottawa,** (*c. h.,*) Franklin, Kans	1,700
Ottawa, Le Sueur, Minn	95
Ottawa,* Putnam, Ohio	650
Ottawa, Waukesha, Wis	20
Ottawa Lake, Monroe, Mich	52
Otter Creek, Jersey, Ill	110
Otter Creek, Jackson, Iowa	26
Otter Creek, Clay, Kans	12
Otter Creek, Jackson, Mich	18
Otter Creek, Wayne, Mo	6
Otter Creek, Rutherford, N. C	14
Otter Creek, Eau Claire, Wis	15
Otter Lake, Pottawatomie, Kans	12
Otter River, Worcester, Mass	220
Otter Tail City, Otter Tail, Minn	18
Otterville, Buchanan, Iowa	15
Otterville, Cooper, Mo	400
Otto, Fulton, Ill	20
Otto, Clarke, Ind	45
Otto, Pope, Minn	14
Otto, Cattaraugus, N. Y	280
Ottobine, Rockingham, Va	10
Ottokee, (*c. h.,*) Fulton, Ohio	120
Ottsville, Bureau, Ill	17
Ottsville, Bucks, Pa	37
*Ottumwa,** (*c. h.,*) Wapello, Iowa	2,100
Ottumwa, Coffey, Kans	140
Otway, Scioto, Ohio	12
Otwell, Pike, Ind	43
Ouaquaga, Broome, N. Y	100
Ouleout, Delaware, N. Y	24
Our Town, Sheboygan, Wis	21
Ouslie's Gap, Cabell, W. Va	12
Outlaw's Bridge, Duplin, N. C	12
Outville, Licking, Ohio	$46
Overbrook, Montgomery, Pa	160
Overisel, Allegan, Mich	60
Overfield, Barbour, W. Va	19
Overpeck's Station, Butler, Ohio	35
Overton, Pah Ute, Ariz	12
Overton, Cooper, Mo	58
Overton, Bradford, Pa	43
Ovid, Madison, Ind	17
Ovid, Taylor, Iowa	12
Ovid,* Clinton, Mich	690
Ovid, (*c. h.,*) Seneca, N. Y	730
Ovid, Franklin, Ohio	10
Ovid, Rich, Utah	12
Owaneco, Christian, Ill	20
Owasco, Sullivan, Mo	40
Owasco, Cayuga, N. Y	160
Owasco Lake, Cayuga, N. Y	11
*Owatonna,** (*c. h.,*) Steele, Minn	1,600
*Owego,** (*c. h.,*) Tioga, N. Y	2,800
Owego, Shawanaw, Wis	12
*Owensborough,** (*c. h.,*) Daviess, Ky	1,900
Owensburgh, Greene, Ind	48
Owen's Cross Roads, Madison, Ala	10
Owen's Grove, Cerro Gordo, Iowa	10
Owensville, Saline, Ark	5
Owensville, Gibson, Ind	220
Owensville, Gasconade, Mo	19
Owensville, Clermont, Ohio	120
Owensville, (*c. h.,*) Robertson, Tex	270
Owenton, (*c. h.*) Owen, Ky	120
Owing's Mills, Baltimore, Md	130
Owingsville, (*c. h.,*) Bath, Ky	120
Owl Hill, Cumberland, Tenn	10
Owl Prairie, Daviess, Ind	21
Owl Run, Fauquier, Va	46
Owosso,* Shiawassee, Mich	1,300
Oxbow, Jefferson, N. Y	160
Oxen Hill, Prince George's, Md	12
Oxford, Calhoun, Ala	370
Oxford, New Haven, Conn	120
Oxford, Newton, Ga	450
Oxford, Henry, Ill	88
*Oxford,** (*c. h.,*) Benton, Ind	270
Oxford, Johnson, Iowa	80
Oxford, Scott, Ky	15
Oxford, Oxford, Me	290
Oxford, Talbot, Md	79
Oxford, Worcester, Mass	680
Oxford, Oakland, Mich	280
Oxford, (*c. h.,*) Isanti, Minn	33
*Oxford,** (*c. h.,*) La Fayette, Miss	2,200
Oxford, Worth, Mo	44
Oxford, Warren, N. J	470
Oxford, Chenango, N. Y	1,200
Oxford, (*c. h.,*) Granville, N. C	270
Oxford,* Butler, Ohio	1,500
Oxford,* Chester, Pa	1,000
Oxford, Cache, Utah	12
Oxford, Doddridge, W. Va	14
Oxford, Marquette, Wis	96
Oxford Depot, Orange, N. Y	120
Oxford Mills, Jones, Iowa	67
Oxford Valley, Bucks, Pa	45
Oyster, Lewis, Mo	16
Oyster Bay, Queens, N. Y	430

* Money-order office.

Oysterville, (*c. h.*,) Pacific, Wash	$54
Ozark, Dale, Ala	12
Ozark, (*c. h.*,) Franklin, Ark	300
Ozark, Jackson, Iowa	14
Ozark, Allen, Kans	12
Ozark, (*c. h.*,) Christian, Mo	130
Ozark, Monroe, Ohio	22
Ozaukee,* (*c. h.*,) Ozaukee, Wis	810
Ozawkie, Jefferson, Kans	75

P.

Paces, Metcalfe, Ky	20
Pacheco, Contra Costa, Cal	320
Pacific, Franklin, Mo	290
Pacific, Franklin, N. C	54
Pacific, Columbia, Wis	18
Pacific City, Mills, Iowa	42
Packard, Vinton, Ohio	12
Packer, Jefferson, Pa	19
Pack's Ferry, Monroe, W. Va	11
Pack's Mills, Sanilac, Mich	9
Packsville, Clarendon, S. C	25
Packwaukee, Marquette, Wis	58
Pacolett Depot, Spartanburgh, S. C.	34
Pactolus, Pitt, N. C	12
Paddock's Grove, Madison, Ill	25
Paddy's Run, Butler, Ohio	60
Padonia, Brown, Kans	61
Padoria, Crawford, Ind	4
Padua, McLean, Ill	51
Paducah,* (*c. h.*,) McCracken, Ky	2,800
Page City, Page, Iowa	18
Pagetown, Morrow, Ohio	59
Pahaquarry, Warren, N. J	1
Paincourtville, Assumption, La	24
Paine's Hollow, Herkimer, N. Y	41
Paine's Point, Ogle, Ill	58
Painesville,* (*c. h.*,) Lake, Ohio	2,800
Paineville, Amelia, Va	40
Paint, Highland, Ohio	25
Paint Creek, Washtenaw, Mich	16
Paint Creek, Kanawha, W. Va	12
Painted Post, Steuben, N. Y	590
Painter Creek, Darke, Ohio	21
Painterhood, Howard, Kans	12
Paintersville, Greene, Ohio	12
Paint Lick, Garrard, Ky	72
Paint Rock, Jackson, Ala	41
Paintsville, (*c. h.*,) Johnson, Ky	59
Paint Valley, Holmes, Ohio	12
Paisley, Otoe, Nebr	12
Palatine, Cook, Ill	300
Palatine, Salem, N. J	49
Palatine, Marion, W. Va	120
Palatine Bridge, Montgomery, N. Y.	170
Palenville, Greene, N. Y	140
Palermo, Edgar, Ill	18
Palermo, Doniphan, Kans	79
Palermo, Waldo, Me	120
Palermo, Oswego, N. Y	87
Palermo, Carroll, Ohio	12
Palermo Centre, Waldo, Me	38
Palestine, Columbia, Ark	18
Palestine,* Crawford, Ill	210
Palestine, Kosciusko, Ind	57
Palestine, Johnson, Iowa	$35
Palestine, Pickaway, Ohio	20
Palestine, Lewis, Tenn	10
Palestine, (*c. h.*,) Anderson, Tex	600
Palestine, Greenbrier, W. Va	18
Palisade, Lander, Nev	12
Palisades, Rockland, N. Y	89
Pallas, Green, Mo	3
Pallas, Snyder, Pa	12
Palm, Montgomery, Pa	17
Palma, Marshall, Ky	27
Palmer, Christian, Ill	12
Palmer,* Hampden, Mass	990
Palmer's Springs, Mecklenburgh, Va	6
Palmersville, Allegheny, Pa	62
Palmetto, Pickens, Ala	7
Palmetto, Campbell, Ga	260
Palmetto, Bedford, Tenn	32
Palmyra, Macoupin, Ill	160
Palmyra, Harrison, Ind	54
Palmyra, Warren, Iowa	120
Palmyra, Somerset, Me	51
Palmyra, Lenawee, Mich	150
Palmyra,* (*c. h.*,) Marion, Mo	1,500
Palmyra, Otoe, Nebr	26
Palmyra, Burlington, N. J	77
Palmyra,* Wayne, N. Y	2,200
Palmyra, Portage, Ohio	120
Palmyra, Lebanon, Pa	240
Palmyra, (*c. h.*,) Fluvanna, Va	100
Palmyra,* Jefferson, Wis	460
Palo, Marion, Ala	12
Palo, Linn, Iowa	94
Palo, Ionia, Mich	120
Palo Alto, Louisa, Iowa	12
Palo Alto, Neosho, Kans	12
Palo Alto, Chickasaw, Miss	45
Palo Alto, Seneca, Ohio	16
Palo Alto, Schuylkill, Pa	12
Palo Alto, Lawrence, Tenn	20
Palo Alto, Highland, Va	3
Paloma, Adams, Ill	42
Palo Pinto, (*c. h.*,) Palo Pinto, Tex.	20
Palos, Cook, Ill	25
Pamelia Four Corners, Jefferson, N. Y	69
Pamlico, Craven, N. C	12
Pamplin's Depot, Appomattox, Va.	200
Pana,* Christian, Ill	1,600
Panaca, Washington, Utah	59
Panama, Lancaster, Nebr	12
Panama, Chautauqua, N. Y	230
Panamore Hill, Scriven, Ga	16
Pancoastburgh, Fayette, Ohio	41
Pandora, Johnson, Tenn	5
Pan Handle, Brooke, W. Va	38
Panoche, Fresno, Cal	12
Panola, (*c. h.*,) Panola, Miss	230
Panola Station, Woodford, Ill	120
Panora,* (*c. h.*,) Guthrie, Iowa	170
Pantego, Beaufort, N. C	44
Panther Creek, Daviess, Ky	3
Panther Creek, Yadkin, N. C	12
Panther Rock, Forest, Pa	12
Panther Springs, Jefferson, Tenn	39

* Money-order office.

Office	Amount
Panton, Addison, Vt	$24
*Paola,** (*c. h.,*) Miami, Kans	1,900
Paoli, (*c. h.,*) Orange, Ind	360
Paoli, Chester, Pa	50
Paoli, Dane, Wis	58
Papakating, Sussex, N. J	100
Papalote, Bee, Tex	12
Pa Pa Me, Oceana, Mich	6
Paper Mills, Baltimore, Md	32
Papillion, Sarpy, Nebr	12
Papinsville, Bates, Mo	270
Paraclifta, Sevier, Ark	150
Paradise, Stanislaus, Cal	200
Paradise, Coles, Ill	18
Paradise, Muhlenburgh, Ky	10
Paradise, Clay, Mo	10
Paradise, Lancaster, Pa	130
Paradise, Cache, Utah	17
Paradise Valley, Monroe, Pa	13
Paragon, Morgan, Ind	12
Paragonah, Iron, Utah	39
Paraje, Socorro, N. Mex	40
Parallel, Riley, Kans	23
Pardee, Atchison, Kans	93
Pardeeville, Columbia, Wis	160
Parham's Store, Sussex, Va	12
*Paris,** (*c. h.,*) Edgar, Ill	1,800
Paris, Jennings, Ind	130
Paris, Linn, Iowa	23
*Paris,** (*c. h.,*) Bourbon, Ky	2,000
*Paris,** (*c. h.,*) Oxford, Me	420
Paris, Mecosta, Mich	91
*Paris,** (*c. h.,*) Monroe, Mo	720
Paris, Oneida, N. Y	120
Paris, Stark, Ohio	81
Paris, Washington, Pa	84
*Paris,** (*c. h.,*) Henry, Tenn	800
*Paris,** (*c. h.,*) Lamar, Tex	400
Paris, Rich, Utah	24
Paris, Fauquier, Va	50
Paris, Kenosha, Wis	38
Parish, Oswego, N. Y	130
Parishville, St. Lawrence, N. Y	260
Parishville Centre, St. Lawrence, N. Y	22
Paris Landing, Henry, Tenn	76
Parisville, Portage, Ohio	46
Park, Greene, Ind	10
Park, Barren, Ky	19
Park, St. Joseph, Mich	10
Parker, Randolph, Ind	72
Parker, Montgomery, Kans	170
Parker's Bluff, Anderson, Tex	12
Parkersburgh, Richland, Ill	92
Parkersburgh, Montgomery, Ind	42
Parkersburgh, Butler, Iowa	460
*Parkersburgh,** (*c. h.,*) Wood, W. Va	2,200
Parker's Head, Sagadahoc, Me	110
Parker's Settlement, Posey, Ind	18
Parker's Store, Hart, Ga	12
Parker's Store, Giles, Tenn	5
Parkersville, Morris, Kans	12
Parkersville, Bates, Mo	38
Parkersville, Chester, Pa	57
Parkesburgh, Chester, Pa	640
Parkinson's Landing, Hardin, Ill	34
Park Lane, Litchfield, Conn	$24
Parkman, Piscataquis, Me	91
Parkman, Geauga, Ohio	440
Park Ridge, Bergen, N. J	12
Parks, Scott, Ark	12
Parks, Edgefield, S. C	6
Park's Corners, Boone, Ill	120
Park's Creek, Bradford, Pa	12
Park's Grove, St. Clair, Mo	30
Park's Mills, Franklin, Ohio	6
Park's Store, Jackson, Ala	12
Parksville, Boyle, Ky	82
Parksville, Sullivan, N. Y	100
Parksville, Polk, Tenn	21
Parkton, Baltimore, Md	120
Parkville, Parke, Ind	16
Parkville, St. Joseph, Mich	140
Parkville, Platte, Mo	230
Parkville, Kings, N. Y	47
Parkwood, Indiana, Pa	12
Parma,* Jackson, Mich	800
Parma, Monroe, N. Y	120
Parma, Cuyahoga, Ohio	57
Parma Centre, Monroe, N. Y	78
Parmleysville, Wayne, Ky	14
Parnassus, Westmoreland, Pa	65
Parnassus, Marlborough, S. C	10
Parnassus, Augusta, Va	35
Parowan, (*c. h.,*) Iron, Utah	130
Parrish, Franklin, Ill	10
Parrish, Des Moines, Iowa	22
Parrottsville, Cocke, Tenn	46
Parryville, Carbon, Pa	210
Parshallville, Livingston, Mich	52
Parsippany, Morris, N. J	94
Parsonfield, York, Me	39
Parson's Seminary, Travis, Tex	12
Partello, Calhoun, Mich	33
Partlow's, Spottsylvania, Va	23
Partridge, Letcher, Ky	4
Partridge Island, Delaware, N. Y	12
Pascagoula, Jackson, Miss	200
Pascoag, Providence, R. I	320
Paskack, Bergen, N. J	70
Paso Robles, San Luis Obispo, Cal	12
Passadumkeag, Penobscot, Me	85
Passaic, Passaic, N. J	1,000
Passaic Valley, Morris, N. J	47
Pass Christian, Harrison, Miss	560
Passe de Terre, Stevens, Minn	12
Passumpsic, Caledonia, Vt	190
Pastoria, Jefferson, Ark	18
Pataskala, Licking, Ohio	220
Patch Grove, Grant, Wis	160
Patchin, Erie, N. Y	29
Patchinsville, Clearfield, Pa	25
Patchogue,* Suffolk, N. Y	530
*Paterson,** (*c. h.,*) Passaic, N. J	3,000
Patesville, Hancock, Ky	7
Patmos, Mahoning, Ohio	21
Patoka, Marion, Ill	180
Patoka, Gibson, Ind	320
Patrick C. H., Patrick, Va	40
Patricksburgh, Owen, Ind	64
Patrick Springs, Patrick, Va	5
Patriot, Switzerland, Ind	290

* Money-order office.

Patriot, Decatur, Iowa	$12
Patriot, Gallia, Ohio	33
Patriot, Wayne, Tenn	12
Patroon, Shelby, Tex	12
Pattagumpus, Penobscot, Me	9
Patten, Penobscot, Me	350
Pattenburgh, Hunterdon, N. J	32
Patten's Mill, Washington, Ohio	17
Patten's Mills, Washington, N. Y	24
Patterson, Nevada, Cal	33
Patterson, Wayne, Mo	110
Patterson, Putnam, N. Y	290
Patterson, Caldwell, N. C	33
Patterson, Hardin, Ohio	180
Patterson, Juniata, Pa	300
Patterson's Bluff, Johnson, Ark	12
Patterson's Depot, Mineral, W. Va	20
Patterson's Mills, Ionia, Mich	56
Patterson's Mills, Washington, Pa	69
Patterson's Store, Alamance, N. C	7
Pattersonville, St. Mary's, La	140
Patton, Bollinger, Mo	24
Pattonsburgh, Daviess, Mo	80
Patton's Home, Rutherford, N. C	4
Pattonsville, Scott, Va	8
Pattonville, Bedford, Pa	74
Patty's Mill, Lyon, Kans	12
Patuxent, Anne Arundel, Md	80
Paul, Benton, Iowa	12
Paulding, (*c h.,*) Jasper, Miss	96
*Paulding,** (*c h.,*) Paulding, Ohio	200
Paulina, Warren, N. J	31
Paulinville, Yuba, Cal	40
Paulsborough, Gloucester, N. J	130
Paul's Cross Roads, Essex, Va	15
Paulton, Westmoreland, Pa	12
Paulville, Adair, Mo	73
Paupac, Pike, Pa	14
Pavia, Bedford, Pa	12
Pavilion, Kendall, Ill	22
Pavilion, Kalamazoo, Mich	51
Pavilion, Genesee, N. Y	91
Pavilion Centre, Genesee, N. Y	42
Pawlet, Rutland, Vt	330
Pawling, Dutchess, N. Y	400
Pawling, Chester, Pa	71
Pawnee, Sangamon, Ill	75
Pawnee, Bourbon, Kans	16
*Pawnee City,** (*c. h.,*) Pawnee, Nebr	500
Paw Paw, Miami, Ind	12
*Paw Paw,** (*c. h.,*) Van Buren, Mich	1,400
Paw Paw, Morgan, W. Va	90
Paw Paw Ford, Roane, Tenn	14
Paw Paw Grove, Lee, Ill	130
Pawselin, Wabashaw, Minn	12
Pawtucket,* Providence, R. I	3,000
Pawtuxet, Providence, R. I	100
Pawtuxett, Wakulla, Fla	6
Paxinos, Northumberland, Pa	54
*Paxton,** (*c. h.,*) Ford, Ill	1,500
Paxton, Harrison, Ky	4
Paxton, Worcester, Mass	180
Paxton, Dauphin, Pa	29
Paxton's, Sullivan, Ind	35
Paxton's Store, Pike, Mo	12
Pay Down, Maries, Mo	5
Payetteville, Ada, Idaho	$12
Payne, Paulding, Ohio	5
Payne's Corners, Trumbull, Ohio	10
Payne's Depot, Scott, Ky	21
Paynesville, Stearns, Minn	110
Paynesville, Pike, Mo	92
Paynesville, Milwaukee, Wis	25
Payneville, Meade, Ky	12
Payson, Adams, Ill	230
Payson, Utah, Utah	120
Peabody, Essex, Mass	1,700
Peace Creek, (*c. h.,*) Polk, Fla	32
Peace Dale, Washington, R. I	290
Peacham,* Caledonia, Vt	330
Peach Bottom, York, Pa	66
Peacher's Mills, Montgomery, Tenn	36
Peachland, Osage, Mo	12
Peachville, Butler, Pa	12
Peacock's Store, Columbus, N. C	34
Peakesville, Clarke, Mo	37
Peak's Hill, Calhoun, Ala	17
Peaksville, Henry, Ga	12
Peapack, Somerset, N. J	99
Pea Ridge, Caswell, N. C	12
Pearisburgh, (*c. h.,*) Giles, Va	260
Pearl, Pike, Ill	12
Pearl City, Madison, Miss	24
Pearl Creek, Wyoming, N. Y	37
Pearlington, Hancock, Miss	23
Pearson's Corner, Kent, Del	12
Peart's Eddy, Armstrong, Pa	41
Peasleeville, Clinton, N. Y	17
Pebble Creek, Dodge, Nebr	32
Pecan Point, Mississippi, Ark	50
Pecatonica,* Winnebago, Ill	770
Peck, Sanilac, Mich	84
Pecksburgh, Hendricks, Ind	26
Peck's Run, Upshur, W. Va	15
Peckville, Luzerne, Pa	64
Peconic, Suffolk, N. Y	180
Peculiar, Cass, Mo	92
Pedee, Cedar, Iowa	37
Pedee, Green, Wis	7
Peden, Kemper, Miss	12
Pedricktown, Salem, N. J	54
Pee Dee, Marion, S. C	12
Peekskill,* Westchester, N. Y	2,400
Peeled Oak, Bath, Ky	12
Peel Tree, Barbour, W. Va	49
Pee Pee, Pike, Ohio	12
Peerysville, (*c. h.,*) McDowell, W. Va	5
*Pekin,** (*c. h.,*) Tazewell, Ill	2,300
Pekin, Washington, Ind	12
Pekin, Jessamine, Ky	100
Pekin, Niagara, N. Y	180
Pekin, Montgomery, N. C	13
Pekin, Putnam, Tenn	12
Pekin, Clark, Wash	8
Pelahatchee Depot, Rankin, Miss	12
Peletier's Mills, Carteret, N. C	6
Pelham, Hampshire, Mass	11
Pelham, Hillsborough, N. H	52
Pelham, Westchester, N. Y	350
Pelham, Caswell, N. C	10
Pelham, Grundy, Tenn	13
Pella, Dearborn, Ind	12

* Money-order office.

PEN

Office	Amount
Pella,* Marion, Iowa	$1,200
Pella, Shawanaw, Wis	8
Pellonia, Massac, Ill	15
Pellville, Hancock, Ky	27
Pemaquid, Lincoln, Me	130
Pemberton, Burlington, N. J	280
Pemberton, Shelby, Ohio	73
Pemberton, Goochland, Va	45
Pemberville, Wood, Ohio	16
Pembina, (*c. h.*,) Pembina, Dak	750
Pembroke, Christian, Ky	210
Pembroke*, Washington, Me	390
Pembroke, Plymouth, Mass	59
Pembroke, Merrimack, N. H	82
Pembroke, Genesee, N. Y	130
Pembroke, Giles, Va	13
Pence's Mills, Warren, Ohio	18
Pendarvis, Wayne, Ga	12
Pendleton, Arkansas, Ark	12
Pendleton,* Madison, Ind	480
Pendleton, Henry, Ky	31
Pendleton, Warren, Mo	110
Pendleton, Niagara, N. Y	40
Pendleton, Putnam, Ohio	37
Pendleton, (*c. h.*,) Umatilla, Oreg	12
Pendleton, Anderson, S. C	380
Pendleton Centre, Niagara, N. Y	14
Pendleton Hill, Windham, Conn	30
Penfield, Greene, Ga	240
Penfield, Monroe, N. Y	220
Penfield, Lorain, Ohio	83
Penfield, Clearfield, Pa	90
Penhook, Franklin, Va	12
Penick, Marion, Ky	24
Peninsula, Summit, Ohio	140
Penllyn, Montgomery, Pa	110
Penn, Lancaster, Pa	13
Pennellville, Oswego, N. Y	28
Penn Hall, Centre, Pa	72
Penn Haven, Carbon, Pa	310
Penninger, Union, Ill	12
Pennington, Mercer, N. J	500
Pnnington, Houston, Tex	20
Pennington Point, McDonough, Ill.	21
Pennington's Mills, Pulaski, Ark	9
Penningtonville, Chester, Pa	340
Penn Line, Crawford, Pa	70
Penn Line, Keweenaw, Mich	74
Penn Run, Indiana, Pa	85
Pennsborough, Ritchie, W. Va	170
Pennsburgh, Montgomery, Pa	140
Penn's Creek, Snyder, Pa	42
Penn's Grove, Salem, N. J	130
Penn's Park, Bucks, Pa	48
Penn's Square, Montgomery, Pa	19
Penn's Station, Westmoreland, Pa	200
Penn's Store, Patrick, Va	17
Pennsville, Salem, N. J	12
Pennsville, Morgan, Ohio	110
Pennsville, Fayette, Pa	55
Pennville, Jay, Ind	230
Pennville, Sullivan, Mo	12
Penn Yan,* (*c. h.*,) Yates, N. Y	2,500
Penobscot, Hancock, Me	45
Penola, Caroline, Va	12
Pensacola,* (*c. h.*,) Escambia, Fla	1,600

PER

Office	Amount
Pensaukie, Oconto, Wis	$160
Pent Water,* Oceana, Mich	960
Pentz, Butte, Cal	34
Peoa, Summit, Utah	12
Peola Mills, Madison, Va	12
Peoli, Tuscarawas, Ohio	30
Peoria, (*c. h.*,*) Peoria, Ill	4,000
Peoria, Mahaska, Iowa	39
Peoria, Franklin, Kans	91
Peoria, Wyoming, N. Y	64
Peoria, Linn, Oreg	66
Peoria, Hill, Tex	14
Peoria City, Polk, Iowa	85
Peosta, Dubuque, Iowa	110
Peotone, Will, Ill	310
Pepacton, Delaware, N. Y	17
Pepin, Pepin, Wis	100
Pepperell, Middlesex, Mass	310
Peppertown, Franklin, Ind	28
Pepperville, Butler, Nebr	12
Pequabuck, Litchfield, Conn	85
Pequea, Lancaster, Pa	55
Peralta, Valencia, N. Mex	18
Perch Lake, Blue Earth, Minn	10
Perch River, Jefferson, N. Y.	46
Percival, Fremont, Iowa	20
Percy, Carbon, Wyo	12
Perdenales, Travis, Tex	11
Perin's Mills, Clermont, Ohio	44
Perkins' Mills, Braxton, W. Va	1
Perkinsville, Madison, Ind	47
Perkinsville, Steuben, N. Y	56
Perkinsville, Burke, N. C	3
Perkinsville,* Windsor, Vt	200
Perkinsville, Goochland, Va	15
Perkiomenville, Montgomery, Pa	20
Perote, Bullock, Ala	41
Perrine, Mercer, Pa	39
Perrineville, Monmouth, N. J	91
Perrinsville, Wayne, Mich	64
Perry, (*c. h.*,) Houston, Ga	420
Perry, Pike, Ill	470
Perry, Dallas, Iowa	250
Perry, Jefferson, Kans	230
Perry, Washington, Me	84
Perry, Shiawassee, Mich	56
Perry, Ralls, Mo	120
Perry, Wyoming, N. Y	780
Perry, Lake, Ohio	250
Perry, Forest, Pa	41
Perry, Dane, Wis	100
Perry Centre, Wyoming, N. Y	140
Perry City, Schuyler, N. Y	58
Perrydale, Polk, Oreg	12
Perrymansville, Harford, Md	200
Perryopolis, Fayette, Pa	110
Perry's Bridge, Vermillion, La	10
Perrysburgh, Miami, Ind	43
Perrysburgh, Cattaraugus, N. Y	200
Perrysburgh,* (*c. h.*,) Wood, Ohio	880
Perry's Mills, Clinton, N. Y	94
Perry Springs, Pike, Ill	7
Perrysville, Vermillion, Ind	350
Perrysville, Allegheny, Pa	81
Perrysville, Washington, R. I	14
Perryton, Licking, Ohio	36

* Money-order office.

Perryville, Perry, Ala	$12
Perryville, (c. h.,) Perry, Ark	110
Perryville, Boyle, Ky	210
Perryville, Cecil, Md	96
Perryville, (c. h.,) Perry, Mo	260
Perryville, Hunterdon, N. J	24
Perryville, Madison, N. Y	74
Perryville, Ashland, Ohio	280
Perryville, Decatur, Tenn	12
Persia, Cattaraugus, N. Y	16
Persia, Hawkins, Tenn	12
Personville, Venango, Pa	12
Personville, Limestone, Tex	8
Perth, Jefferson, Miss	12
Perth, Fulton, N. Y	42
Perth Amboy,* Middlesex, N. J	930
Peru,* La Salle, Ill	1,500
Peru, (c. h.,)* Miami, Ind	2,000
Peru, Madison, Iowa	22
Peru, Howard, Kans	12
Peru, Oldham, Ky	26
Peru, Oxford, Me	43
Peru, Berkshire, Mass	61
Peru, Nemaha, Nebr	200
Peru, Clinton, N. Y	280
Peru, Huron, Ohio	88
Peru, Bennington, Vt	49
Peru, Hardy, W. Va	5
Peru, Dunn, Wis	32
Peru Mills, Juniata, Pa	31
Peruville, Tompkins, N. Y	14
Pescadero, San Mateo, Cal	160
Peshtigo,* Oconto, Wis	380
Pesotum, Champaign, Ill	150
Petaluma,* Sonoma, Cal	1,500
Peterborough,* Hillsborough, N. H	1,000
Peterborough, Madison, N. Y	310
Petersburgh, Klamath, Cal	12
Petersburgh,* Menard, Ill	1,000
Petersburgh, (c. h.,)* Pike, Ind	350
Petersburgh, Leavenworth, Kans	18
Petersburgh, Boone, Ky	96
Petersburgh, Monroe, Mich	230
Petersburgh, Jackson, Minn	6
Petersburgh, Cape May, N. J	80
Petersburgh, Rensselaer, N. Y	75
Petersburgh, Mahoning, Ohio	140
Petersburgh, Butler, Pa	20
Petersburgh, Lincoln, Tenn	47
Petersburgh, Lavaca, Tex	22
Petersburgh, Millard, Utah	12
Petersburgh,* Dinwiddie, Va	3,900
Peter's Creek, Stokes, N. C	12
Peter's Creek, Lancaster, Pa	30
Petersham, Worcester, Mass	390
Peter's Landing, Perry, Tenn	12
Peterson, (c. h.,) Clay, Iowa	130
Peterstown, Monroe, W. Va	63
Petersville, Frederick, Md	77
Petersville, Northampton, Pa	47
Petit Jean, Yell, Ark	10
Petra, Saline, Mo	70
Petroleum Centre,* Venango, Pa	2,600
Petrolia, Humboldt, Cal	62
Petroliopolis, Los Angeles, Cal	93
Petrolium, Vernon, Wis	4
Pettis, Crawford, Pa	$9
Pettisville, Fulton, Ohio	140
Pettit, Tippecanoe, Ind	50
Pettysville, Livingston, Mich	12
Pevely, Jefferson, Mo	150
Pewamo, Ionia, Mich	300
Pewaukee, Waukesha, Wis	250
Pewee Valley, Oldham, Ky	130
Peytona, Boone, W. Va	23
Peyton's, Adams, Ill	4
Peytonsburgh, Pittsylvania, Va	10
Peytonsville, Little River, Ark	12
Peytonsville, Williamson, Tenn	49
Pharisburgh, Union, Ohio	16
Pharsalia, Chenango, N. Y	42
Pheasant Branch, Dane, Wis	29
Phelps, Lawrence, Mo	12
Phelps, Ontario, N. Y	1,100
Phelps City,* Atchison, Mo	280
Phelps Mills, Clinton, Pa	19
Phenix, Ashtabula, Ohio	8
Phenix, Kent, R. I	450
Philadelphia, Hancock, Ind	71
Philadelphia, (c. h.,) Neshoba, Miss	54
Philadelphia, Marion, Mo	58
Philadelphia, Jefferson, N. Y	240
Philadelphia, (c. h.,)* Philadelphia, Pa	4,000
Philadelphia, Monroe, Tenn	170
Philander, Gentry, Mo	18
Philanthropy, Butler, Ohio	24
Philippi, (c. h.,) Barbour, W. Va	130
Philipsburgh, Deer Lodge, Mont	43
Philipsburgh, Jefferson, Ohio	96
Philipsburgh, Centre, Pa	1,100
Philip's Mills, Indiana, Pa	84
Philipston, Clarion, Pa	58
Phillips,* Franklin, Me	420
Phillip's Bayou, Phillips, Ark	12
Phillipsburgh,* Warren, N. J	1,400
Phillip's Creek, Allegany, N. Y	18
Phillipsport, Sullivan, N. Y	220
Phillipston, Worcester, Mass	100
Phillipstown, White, Ill	62
Philmont, Columbia, N. Y	220
Philo, Champaign, Ill	250
Philo, Muskingum, Ohio	48
Philomath, Benton, Oreg	12
Philomont, Loudoun, Va	40
Philopolis, Baltimore, Md	280
Phil Sheridan, (c. h.,) Wallace, Kans	220
Phippsburgh, Sagadahoc, Me	86
Phœnicia, Ulster, N. Y	97
Phœnix, Yavapai, Ariz	12
Phœnix, Douglas, Ill	12
Phœnix, Baltimore, Md	81
Phœnix, Keweenaw, Mich	160
Phœnix, Oswego, N. Y	550
Phœnix, Jackson, Oreg	35
Phœnix, Armstrong, Pa	28
Phœnix Mills, Otsego, N. Y	12
Phœnixville, Windham, Conn	49
Phœnixville,* Chester, Pa	1,700
Piasa, Macoupin, Ill	74
Picacho, Monterey, Cal	12
Pickard's Mill, Clinton, Ind	16

* Money-order office.

Pickens C. H., Pickens, S. C	$88
Pickens Station, Holmes, Miss	34
Pickensville, Pickens, Ala	320
Pickensville, Pickens, S. C	13
Pickerel, Greene, Mo	12
Pickereltown, Logan, Ohio	60
Pickering, Chester, Pa	77
Pickerington, Fairfield, Ohio	36
Pickwick, Winona, Minn	58
Picture Rocks, Lycoming, Pa	90
Piedmont,* Mineral, W. Va	700
Piedmont, Uintah, Wyo	12
Piedmont Springs, Burke, N. C	12
Piedmont Station, Fauquier, Va	210
Piedra Blanca, San Luis Obispo, Cal	12
Pierce, Will, Ill	13
Pierce, Callaway, Mo	12
Pierce, Stark, Ohio	38
Pierce, Armstrong, Pa	26
Pierce, Kewaunee, Wis	12
Pierce City, (*c. h.*,) Shoshone, Idaho	38
Pierce City, Lawrence, Mo	12
Pierce's, Goochland, Va	11
Pierce Station, Weakley, Tenn	68
Pierceton,* Kosciusko, Ind	740
Piercetown, Anderson, S. C	12
Pierceville, (*c. h.*,) Hernando, Fla	80
Pierceville, De Kalb, Ill	17
Pierceville, Ripley, Ind	70
Pierceville, Van Buren, Iowa	24
Pierceville, Wyoming, Pa	24
Piermont, Grafton, N. H	120
Piermont, Rockland, N. Y	420
Pierpont, Ashtabula, Ohio	160
Pierrepont, St. Lawrence, N. Y	70
Pierrepont Manor, Jefferson, N. Y	160
Pierron, Madison, Ill	12
Pierson, Montcalm, Mich	72
Piffard, Livingston, N. Y	39
Pigeon Cove, Essex, Mass	220
Pigeon Creek, Butler, Ala	12
Pigeon Creek Centre, Jackson, Wis	12
Pigeon Forge, Sevier, Tenn	8
Pigeon Hill, Union, Ark	35
Pigeon River, Lake, Minn	12
Pigeon River, Haywood, N. C	21
Pigeon Run, Campbell, Va	22
Pigeon Roost, Choctaw, Miss	12
Pig River, Franklin, Va	14
Pike, Muscatine, Iowa	9
Pike,* Wyoming, N. Y	500
Pike, Bradford, Pa	13
Pike Mills, Potter, Pa	18
Pike Pond, Sullivan, N. Y	74
Pike Rapids, Morrison, Minn	2
Pike Run, Washington, Pa	41
Pike's Peak, Brown, Ind	8
Pike's Peak, Deer Lodge, Mont	12
Pike Station, Wayne, Ohio	130
Pikesville, Baltimore, Md	210
Piketon, (*c. h.*,) Pike, Ky	81
Piketon, Stoddard, Mo	43
Piketon, (*c. h.*,) Pike, Ohio	170
Pike Township, Berks, Pa	14
Pikeville, (*c. h.*,) Marion, Ala	39
Pikeville, Pike, Ind	10

Pikeville, Wayne, N. C	$22
Pikeville, Darke, Ohio	19
Pikeville, (*c. h.*,) Bledsoe, Tenn	100
Piland's Store, Ozark, Mo	12
Pilatka,* (*c. h.*,) Putnam, Fla	530
Pilcher, Belmont, Ohio	24
Pile Falls, Fayette, Pa	24
Pilgrim's Rest, Fayette, Ala	12
Pillar Point, Jefferson, N. Y	130
Pillow, Dauphin, Pa	67
Pilot, Vermilion, Ill	63
Pilot, Montgomery, Va	12
Pilot Centre, Kankakee, Ill	12
Pilot Grove, Newton, Ind	37
Pilot Grove, Lee, Iowa	68
Pilot Grove, Faribault, Minn	11
Pilot Grove, Cooper, Mo	60
Pilot Grove, Grayson, Tex	140
Pilot Hill, (*c. h.*,) Fulton, Ark	37
Pilot Hill, El Dorado, Cal	49
Pilot Hill, Washington, Tenn	14
Pilot Knob, Crawford, Ind	19
Pilot Knob, Todd, Ky	7
Pilot Knob,* Iron, Mo	280
Pilot Knob, Greene, Tenn	4
Pilot Knob, Adams, Wis	14
Pilot Mound, Boone, Iowa	21
Pilot Mound, Fillmore, Minn	61
Pilot Mountain, Stokes, N. C	8
Pilot Point, Denton, Tex	100
Pilot Rock, Cherokee, Iowa	32
Pilot Rock, Umatilla, Oreg	12
Pima Village, Yavapai, Ariz	10
Pimento, Vigo, Ind	76
Pinckney, Livingston, Mich	350
Pinckney, Warren, Mo	11
Pinckney, Lewis, N. Y	28
Pinckneyville, Clay, Ala	20
Pinckneyville, (*c. h.*,) Perry, Ill	230
Pine, Linn, Oreg	6
Pine Bend, Dakota, Minn	26
Pine Bluff,* (*c. h.*,) Jefferson, Ark	1,900
Pine Bluff, Callaway, Ky	10
Pine Bluff, Chickasaw, Miss	12
Pine Bluff, Pulaski, Mo	10
Pine Bluff, Warren, Tenn	8
Pine Bluff, Dane, Wis	38
Pine Bluff, Laramie, Wyo	12
Pine Brook, Morris, N. J	32
Pine Bush, Orange, N. Y	120
Pine City, Pine, Minn	12
Pine Creek, Butte, Cal	12
Pine Creek, Calhoun, Mich	27
Pine Creek, Laclede, Mo	12
Pine Creek, Schuyler, N. Y	18
Pine Creek, Tioga, Pa	8
Pine Flats, Indiana, Pa	32
Pine Glen, Centre, Pa	33
Pine Grove, Amador, Cal	53
Pine Grove, Clarke, Ky	45
Pine Grove, Tuscola, Mich	50
Pine Grove, Esmeralda, Nev	12
Pine Grove, Schuyler, N. Y	16
Pine Grove, Montgomery, N. C	12
Pine Grove, Gallia, Ohio	69
Pine Grove, Schuylkill, Pa	470

* Money-order office.

Pine Grove, Henderson, Tex	$5
Pine Grove, Wetzel, W. Va	13
Pine Grove, Brown, Wis	4
Pine Grove Mills, Van Buren, Mich	20
Pine Grove Mills, Centre, Pa	160
Pine Hill, Wilcox, Ala	12
Pine Hill, Ashley, Ark	12
Pine Hill, Sanilac, Mich	18
Pine Hill, Shannon, Mo	12
Pine Hill, Ulster, N. Y	56
Pine Hill, York, Pa	11
Pine Hill, Washington, R. I	6
Pine Hill, Rusk, Tex	50
Pine Hill, Jackson, Wis	21
Pine House Depot, Edgefield, S. C	12
Pine Island, Goodhue, Minn	170
Pine Island, Orange, N. Y	12
Pine Knob, Iowa, Wis	7
Pine Lake, Fulton, N. Y	12
Pine Land, Meigs, Tenn	12
Pine Level, Montgomery, Ala	33
Pine Level, Johnston, N. C	24
Pine Log, Bartow, Ga	29
Pine Meadow, Litchfield, Conn	230
Pine Mills, Muscatine, Iowa	12
Pine Mountain, Campbell, Tenn	8
Pine Plains, Dutchess, N. Y	420
Pine Ridge, Winn, La	6
Pine Ridge, Lexington, S. C	12
Pine River, Lake, Mich	12
Pine River, Washara, Wis	110
Pine Run, Genesee, Mich	140
Pine's Bridge, Westchester, N. Y	35
Pine Springs, Rowan, Ky	12
Pine Station, Clinton, Pa	34
Pine Summit, Columbia, Pa	12
Pinetown, Cherokee, Tex	10
Pine Township, Armstrong, Pa	9
Pine Tree, Chesterfield, S. C	5
Pine Tree, Upshur, Tex	12
Pine Tucky, Perry, Ala	9
Pine Valley, Yalabusha, Miss	12
Pine Valley, Chemung, N. Y	97
Pine Valley, Washington, Utah	17
Pine Village, Warren, Ind	62
Pine View, Fauquier, Va	21
Pineville, Izard, Ark	44
Pineville, Pike, Ill	12
Pineville, (*c. h.*,) Josh Bell, Ky	12
Pineville, (*c. h.*,) McDonald, Mo	92
Pineville, Mecklenburgh, N. C	54
Pineville, Bucks, Pa	50
Pine Wood, Hickman, Tenn	64
Pine Woods, Madison, N. Y	54
Piney Creek, Carroll, Md	8
Pine Creek, Alleghany, N. C	12
Piney Flats, Sullivan, Tenn	6
Piney Grove, Prince George, Va	10
Piney Point, Saint Mary's, Md	12
Pingree Grove, Kane, Ill	15
Pink Hill, Jackson, Mo	74
Pink Hill, Lenoir, N. C	10
Pinkleyville, Oregon, Mo	12
Pink Prairie, Henry, Ill	25
Pinnebog, Huron, Mich	12
Pinnellville, Jones, Miss	2
Pino, Placer, Cal	$55
Pin Oak, Wayne, Ill	26
Pin Oak, Dubuque, Iowa	20
Pin Oak, Warren, Mo	8
Pin Oak, Fayette, Tex	22
Pinos Altos, (*c. h.*,) Grant, N. Mex	37
Pinson, Madison, Tenn	88
Pinto, Iron, Utah	17
Piny, Clarion, Pa	10
Pioche, Lincoln, Nev	12
Pioneer, Greene, Ill	21
Pioneer, Deer Lodge, Mont	12
Pioneer, Williams, Ohio	190
Pioneer, Venango, Pa	660
Pioneer Mills, Cabarrus, N. C	33
Pioneerville, Boise, Idaho	12
Piper City, Ford, Ill	480
Piper's Gap, Carroll, Va	5
Pipersville, Bucks, Pa	22
Pipersville, Jefferson, Wis	38
Pipestone, Berrien, Mich	36
Piqua,* Miami, Ohio	2,500
Pireway Ferry, Columbus, N. C	12
Piscataway, Prince George's, Md	50
Pisgah, Charles, Md	9
Pisgah, Cooper, Mo	61
Pisgah, Butler, Ohio	60
Pisgah, Giles, Tenn	8
Pishon's Ferry, Kennebec, Me	62
Pitcairn, St. Lawrence, N. Y	12
Pitcher, Chenango, N. Y	150
Pitcher Springs, Chenango, N. Y	11
Pitcherville, Jo Daviess, Ill	20
Pit Hole City,* Venango, Pa	880
Pitman, Randolph, Ark	12
Pitts, Warren, Mo	10
Pittsborough, Hendricks, Ind	110
Pittsborough, (*c. h.*,) Calhoun, Miss	130
Pittsborough,* (*c. h.*,) Chatham, N. C	320
Pittsburgh, Johnson, Ark	12
Pittsburgh, Carroll, Ind	180
Pittsburgh, Van Buren, Iowa	45
Pittsburgh, Shiawassee, Mich	62
Pittsburgh, Hickory, Mo	10
Pittsburgh, Coos, N. H	16
Pittsburgh,* (*c. h.*,) Allegheny, Pa	4,000
Pittsburgh, Upshur, Tex	52
Pitt's Cross Roads, Bledsoe, Tenn	5
Pittsfield,* (*c. h.*,) Pike, Ill	1,200
Pittsfield, Somerset, Me	400
Pittsfield,* Berkshire, Mass	3,300
Pittsfield, Merrimack, N. H	470
Pittsfield, Otsego, N. Y	20
Pittsfield, Lorain, Ohio	56
Pittsfield, Warren, Pa	160
Pittsfield, Rutland, Vt	110
Pittsford, Hillsdale, Mich	140
Pittsford, Monroe, N. Y	520
Pittsford, Rutland, Vt	330
Pitt's Grove, Salem, N. J	100
Pitt's Point, Bullitt, Ky	54
Pittston, Kennebec, Me	410
Pittston, Luzerne, Pa	2,600
Pittstown, Hunterdon, N. J	87
Pittstown, Rensselaer, N. Y	230
Pittsville, Wicomico, Md	12

* Money-order office.

Post office	Amount
Pittsville, Johnson, Mo	$36
Pittsville, Venango, Pa	35
Pittsville, Fort Bend, Tex	12
Pittsylvania C. H., Pittsylvania, Va	310
Placerville,* (*c. h.*,) El Dorado, Cal	1,200
Placerville, Boise, Idaho	210
Plain, Wayne, Ohio	31
Plain, Greenville, S. C	6
Plain, Sauk, Wis	19
Plain City, Weber, Utah	40
Plainfield, Windham, Conn	270
Plainfield, Will, Ill	650
Plainfield,* Hendricks, Ind	480
Plainfield, Bremer, Iowa	130
Plainfield, Hampshire, Mass	93
Plainfield, Livingston, Mich	24
Plainfield, Sullivan, N. H	120
Plainfield,* Union, N. J	2,600
Plainfield, Coshocton, Ohio	62
Plainfield, Cumberland, Pa	370
Plainfield, Washington, Vt	150
Plainfield, Waushara, Wis	170
Plain Grove, Lawrence, Pa	56
Plainsberg, Merced, Cal	12
Plainsborough, Middlesex, N. J	16
Plains of Dura, Sumter, Ga	48
Plainsville, Luzerne, Pa	100
Plain View, Macoupin, Ill	96
Plain View,* Wabashaw, Minn	600
Plain View, King and Queen, Va	12
Plainville, Hartford, Conn	650
Plainville, Daviess, Ind	27
Plainville, Norfolk, Mass	32
Plainville, Onondaga, N. Y	85
Plainville, Hamilton, Ohio	100
Plainville, Adams, Wis	22
Plainwell, Allegan, Mich	710
Plaistow, Rockingham, N. H	270
Plane No. Four, Frederick, Md	12
Plank Road, Wayne, Mich	16
Plank Road, Onondaga, N. Y	140
Plank Road, Belmont, Ohio	42
Plank Road, York, Pa	12
Plano, Kendall, Ill	810
Plano, Collin, Tex	20
Plantation No. Fourteen, Washington, Me	3
Planter's, Phillips, Ark	12
Planter's Hall, Breckinridge, Ky	10
Plantersville, Dallas, Ala	18
Plantersville, Grimes, Tex	50
Plantersville, Lunenburgh, Va	3
Plants, Meigs, Ohio	19
Plantsville, Hartford, Conn	780
Plantsville, Morgan, Ohio	20
Plaquemine,* (*c. h.*,) Iberville, La	180
Plaquemine Brulee, St. Landry, La	12
Platea, Erie, Pa	86
Plato, Iroquois, Ill	14
Plato, Pulaski, Ky	10
Plato, McLeod, Minn	10
Plato, Texas, Mo	12
Plato, Lorain, Ohio	440
Platt, Taylor, Iowa	9
Platte, Benzie, Mich	12
Platte City, (*c. h.*,) Platte, Mo	480

Post office	Amount
Plattekill, Ulster, N. Y	$27
Platte River, Buchanan, Mo	8
Platteville, Taylor, Iowa	98
Platteville, Saunders, Nebr	12
Platteville,* Grant, Wis	1,300
Plattford, Sarpy, Nebr	14
Plattsburgh, (*c. h.*,) Clinton, Mo	600
Plattsburgh,* (*c. h.*,) Clinton, N. Y	2,500
Plattsburgh, Clark, Ohio	69
Plattsmouth,* (*c. h.*,) Cass, Nebr	1,400
Plattsville, Fairfield, Conn	12
Plattsville, Shelby, Ohio	12
Plattville, Kendall, Ill	120
Plattville, Cambria, Pa	16
Pleasant, Switzerland, Ind	56
Pleasant, Kent, Mich	27
Pleasant, Claiborne, Tenn	10
Pleasant Brook, Otsego, N. Y	61
Pleasant Corners, Franklin, Ohio	16
Pleasant Corners, Carbon, Pa	16
Pleasant Creek, Barbour, W. Va	23
Pleasant Dale, Hampshire, W. Va	29
Pleasant Farm, Miller, Mo	11
Pleasant Gap, Cherokee, Ala	29
Pleasant Gap, Bates, Mo	55
Pleasant Gap, Centre, Pa	43
Pleasant Gap, Pittsylvania, Va	5
Pleasant Green, Stark, Ill	23
Pleasant Green, Cooper, Mo	12
Pleasant Grove, Pickens, Ala	18
Pleasant Grove, Wayne, Ill	51
Pleasant Grove, Jasper, Ind	6
Pleasant Grove, Des Moines, Iowa	72
Pleasant Grove, Olmsted, Minn	92
Pleasant Grove, Morris, N. J	12
Pleasant Grove, Almance, N. C	12
Pleasant Grove, Lancaster, Pa	47
Pleasant Grove, Bedford, Tenn	12
Pleasant Grove, Utah, Utah	78
Pleasant Grove, Lunenburgh, Va	8
Pleasant Grove Creek, Sutter, Cal	12
Pleasant Hall, Franklin, Pa	18
Pleasant Hill, Dallas, Ala	50
Pleasant Hill, Franklin, Ark	12
Pleasant Hill, New Castle, Del	13
Pleasant Hill, Talbot, Ga	14
Pleasant Hill, Pike, Ill	62
Pleasant Hill, Montgomery, Ind	69
Pleasant Hill, Cedar, Iowa	26
Pleasant Hill, Mercer, Ky	20
Pleasant Hill,* Cass, Mo	1,500
Pleasant Hill, Saline, Nebr	35
Pleasant Hill, Northampton, N. C	72
Pleasant Hill, Miami, Ohio	150
Pleasant Hill, Lane, Oreg	22
Pleasant Hill, Lancaster, S. C	20
Pleasant Hill, Cumberland, Tenn	12
Pleasant Hill, Preston, W. Va	12
Pleasant Home, Owen, Ky	120
Pleasant Home, Putnam, Mo	9
Pleasant Hope, Polk, Mo	24
Pleasant Lake, Steuben, Ind	72
Pleasant Mills, Adams, Ind	35
Pleasant Mills, Atlantic, N. J	35
Pleasant Mound, Bond, Ill	61
Pleasant Mound, Montgomery, Tenn	3

* Money-order office.

Pleasant Mounds, Blue Earth, Minn	$21
Pleasant Mount, Panola, Miss	20
Pleasant Mount, Miller, Mo	70
Pleasant Mount, Wayne, Pa	200
Pleasant Oaks, Brunswick, Va	12
Pleasanton, Alameda, Cal	94
Pleasanton, Decatur, Iowa	210
Pleasanton,* Linn, Kans	460
Pleasanton, Manistee, Mich	46
Pleasanton, Prentiss, Miss	5
Pleasanton, Athens, Ohio	23
Pleasanton, (*c. h.*,) Atascosa, Tex	14
Pleasant Park, Carroll, Mo	24
Pleasant Plain, Jefferson, Iowa	81
Pleasant Plain, Warren, Ohio	93
Pleasant Plains, Sangamon, Ill	140
Pleasant Plains, Dutchess, N. Y	20
Pleasant Plains, Sullivan, Tenn	7
Pleasant Prairie, Bond, Ill	20
Pleasant Prairie, Muscatine, Iowa	28
Pleasant Prairie, Martin, Minn	7
Pleasant Prairie, Kenosha, Wis	12
Pleasant Retreat, White, Ga	11
Pleasant Retreat, Scotland, Mo	20
Pleasant Retreat, McDowell, N. C	16
Pleasant Ridge, Greene, Ala	110
Pleasant Ridge, Rock Island, Ill	18
Pleasant Ridge, Greene, Ind	12
Pleasant Ridge, Leavenworth, Kans	50
Pleasant Ridge, Daviess, Ky	17
Pleasant Ridge, Harrison, Mo	18
Pleasant Ridge, Hamilton, Ohio	76
Pleasant Ridge, Princess Anne, Va	12
Pleasant Ridge, Clark, Wis	3
Pleasant Run, Pottawatomie, Kans	12
Pleasant Run, Stanton, Nebr	16
Pleasant Run, Hunterdon, N. J	28
Pleasant Run, Hamilton, Ohio	6
Pleasant Site, Franklin, Ala	29
Pleasant Unity, Westmoreland, Pa	100
Pleasant Vale, Pike, Ill	38
Pleasant Valley, El Dorado, Cal	48
Pleasant Valley, Litchfield, Conn	110
Pleasant Valley, Jo Daviess, Ill	26
Pleasant Valley, Scott, Iowa	86
Pleasant Valley, Berrien, Mich	12
Pleasant Valley, Sherburne, Minn	14
Pleasant Valley, Wright, Mo	10
Pleasant Valley, Sussex, N. J	16
Pleasant Valley, Dutchess, N. Y	200
Pleasant Valley, Morgan, Ohio	14
Pleasant Valley, Bucks, Pa	49
Pleasant Valley, Lancaster, S. C	12
Pleasant Valley, Chittenden, Vt	33
Pleasant Valley, Fairfax, Va	21
Pleasant Valley, Monongalia, W. Va	34
Pleasant Valley, St. Croix, Wis	42
Pleasant Valley Mills, Nicholas, Ky	12
Pleasant View, Schuyler, Ill	64
Pleasant View, Madison, Iowa	12
Pleasant View, Cherokee, Kans	110
Pleasant View, Ray, Mo	16
Pleasant View, Juniata, Pa	24
Pleasant View, Cheatham, Tenn	12
Pleasantville, Sullivan, Ind	40
Pleasantville, Marion, Iowa	250
Pleasantville, Harford, Md	$61
Pleasantville, Westchester, N. Y	190
Pleasantville, Fairfield, Ohio	98
Pleasantville,* Venango, Pa	2,800
Pleasureville, Henry, Ky	91
Plenitude, Anderson, Tex	12
Plesis, Jefferson, N. Y	120
Plimpton, Holmes, Ohio	97
Pliny, Saline, Kans	12
Pliny, Greenville, S. C	12
Plover, (*c. h.*,) Portage, Wis	280
Plowden's Mills, Sumter, S. C	5
Pluckemin, Somerset, N. J	130
Plum, Venango, Pa	24
Plum Bayou, Jefferson, Ark	20
Plum City, Pierce, Wis	10
Plum Creek, Jefferson, Kans	12
Plum Creek, Caldwell, Tex	20
Plumer, Venango, Pa	210
Plum Grove, Butler, Kans	12
Plum Hill, Washington, Ill	26
Plum Hollow, Fremont, Iowa	58
Plummer's Landing, Fleming, Ky	9
Plummer's Mills, Fleming, Ky	12
Plummersville, Robeson, N. C	12
Plum River, Jo Daviess, Ill	70
Plumsteadville, Bucks, Pa	110
Plum Valley, Sierra, Cal	12
Plum Valley, Texas, Mo	9
Plumville, Indiana, Pa	77
Plunkett, Sullivan, Pa	12
Plymouth, Litchfield, Conn	430
Plymouth, Hancock, Ill	340
Plymouth,* (*c. h.*,) Marshall, Ind	1,500
Plymouth, Cerro Gordo, Iowa	38
Plymouth, Lyon, Kans	53
Plymouth, Penobscot, Me	120
Plymouth,* (*c. h.*,) Plymouth, Mass	2,600
Plymouth, Wayne, Mich	450
Plymouth,* (*c. h.*,) Grafton, N. H	1,000
Plymouth, Chenango, N. Y	92
Plymouth,* (*c. h.*,) Washington, N. C	720
Plymouth,* Richland, Ohio	580
Plymouth,* Luzerne, Pa	1,300
Plymouth, Windsor, Vt	130
Plymouth, Sheboygan, Wis	370
Plymouth Centre, (*c. h*,) Plymouth, Iowa	12
Plymouth Meeting, Montgomery, Pa	79
Plymouth Rock, Winneshiek, Iowa	26
Plympton, Plymouth, Mass	110
Plympton Station, Plymouth, Mass	54
Po, Allen, Ind	31
Poage's Mill, Roanoke, Va	10
Poast Town, Butler, Ohio	45
Pocahontas, (*c. h.*,) Randolph, Ark	260
Pocahontas, Bond, Ill	130
Pocahontas, Cape Girardeau, Mo	31
Pocahontas, Somerset, Pa	4
Pocahontas, Hardeman, Tenn	140
Pocasset, Barnstable, Mass	120
Pocataligo, Kanawha, W. Va	6
Poe, Medina, Ohio	12
Poe, Beaver, Pa	10

* Money-order office.

POM

Post Office	
Poestenkill, Rensselaer, N. Y	$31
Pohocco, Saunders, Nebr	12
Poindexter's Store, Louisa, Va	5
Point à la Hache, (*c. h.*,) Placquemines, La	92
Point Bluff, Adams, Wis	38
Point Cedar, Clark, Ark	4
Point Coupee, (*c. h.*,) Point Coupee, La	120
Point Douglass, Washington, Minn	54
Point Eastern, Caroline, Va	19
Point Hope, Grayson, Va	6
Point Isabel, Grant, Ind	13
Point Isabel, Clermont, Ohio	39
Point Isabel, Cameron, Tex	32
Point Jefferson, Morehouse, La	17
Point Lookout, St. Mary's, Md	12
Point of Rocks, Frederick, Md	230
Point of Rocks, Uintah, Wyo	80
Point of Timber, Contra Costa, Cal	12
Point Peninsula, Jefferson, N. Y	13
Point Peter, Searcy, Ark	5
Point Peter, Oglethorpe, Ga	30
Point Pleasant, Vermilion, Ill	25
Point Pleasant, Hardin, Iowa	43
Point Pleasant, Ohio, Ky	20
Point Pleasant, New Madrid, Mo	110
Point Pleasant, Ocean, N. J	39
Point Pleasant, Clermont, Ohio	39
Point Pleasant, Bucks, Pa	140
Point Pleasant, Upshur, Tex	12
Point Pleasant, (*c. h.*,) Mason, W. Va	420
Point Truth, Scott, Va	16
Pointville, Burlington, N. J	45
Pojuaque, Santa Fé, N. Mex	12
Pokagon, Cass, Mich	220
Poland, Clay, Ind	38
Poland, Androscoggin, Me	64
Poland, Herkimer, N. Y	130
Poland, Mahoning, Ohio	360
Poland Centre, Chautauqua, N. Y	35
Pole Grove, Jackson, Wis	100
Polk, Ashland, Ohio	93
Polk, Venango, Pa	75
Polk Bayou, Independence, Ark	14
Polk City, Polk, Iowa	160
Polk Patch, Warrick, Ind	41
Polk Run, Clarke, Ind	12
Polksville, Hall, Ga	11
Polkville, Smith, Miss	14
Polkville, Warren, N. J	18
Polkville, Columbia, Pa	5
Pollard, (*c. h.*,) Escambia, Ala	240
Pollinger, Madison, Mont	12
Pollock, Clarion, Pa	110
Pollocksville, Jones, N. C	49
Polo,* Ogle, Ill	1,500
Polo, Caldwell, Mo	12
Polsgrove, Carroll, Ill	16
Polsgrove's Store, Franklin, Ky	12
Pomaria, Newberry, S. C	17
Pomeroy, Calhoun, Iowa	12
Pomeroy, Wyandotte, Kans	59
Pomeroy,* (*c. h.*,) Meigs, Ohio	1,600
Pomeroy, Chester, Pa	120
Pomfret, Windham, Conn	420

POP

Post Office	
Pomfret, Windsor, Vt	$67
Pomfret Landing, Windham, Conn	96
Pomme de Terre, Grant, Minn	12
Pomona, Franklin, Kans	12
Pomona, Cumberland, Tenn	33
Pomonkey, Charles, Md	45
Pompanoosuc, Windsor, Vt	68
Pompei, Gratiot, Mich	78
Pompey, Onondaga, N. Y	200
Pompey Centre, Onondaga, N. Y	38
Pompton, Passaic, N. J	200
Pompton Plains, Morris, N. J	54
Ponama, Newaygo, Mich	22
Ponca, (*c. h.*,) Dixon, Nebr	96
Ponce de Leon, Holmes, Fla	4
Ponchatoula, Tangipahoa, La	150
Pond, St. Louis, Mo	21
Pond Creek, Campbell, Ky	4
Pond Creek Mills, Knox, Ind	4
Pond Eddy, Sullivan, N. Y	81
Ponder's Mill, Montgomery, Ala	12
Pond Grove, Benton, Ind	35
Pond Run, Scioto, Ohio	12
Pond Spring, Walker, Ga	8
Pond Spring, Williamson, Tex	8
Pond's Shop, Southampton, Va	12
Pond Valley, Howard, Iowa	12
Poney Hollow, Tompkins, N. Y	15
Ponka Agency, Todd, Dak	24
Pontiac,* (*c. h.*,) Livingston, Ill	1,500
Pontiac,* (*c. h.*,) Oakland, Mich	2,700
Pontiac, Erie, N. Y	27
Pontiac, Huron, Ohio	21
Pontiac, Kent, R. I	12
Pontoosuc, Hancock, Ill	94
Pontotoc, (*c. h.*,) Pontotoc, Miss	340
Ponville, Wilson, Tenn	12
Pool, Lapeer, Mich	14
Poole's Mill, Webster, Ky	29
Poolesville, Montgomery, Md	120
Poolsville, Warren, Ind	59
Poolville, Madison, N. Y	110
Poor Fork, Harlan, Ky	2
Poor's Mills, Waldo, Me	15
Poor Valley, Hawkins, Tenn	12
Pope's Depot, Panola, Miss	140
Pope's Mills, St. Lawrence, N. Y	24
Pope Valley, Napa, Cal	12
Poplar, Crawford, Ohio	74
Poplar Bluff, Ashley, Ark	12
Poplar Bluff, (*c. h.*,) Butler, Mo	18
Poplar Branch, Currituck, N. C	5
Poplar Creek, Choctaw, Miss	20
Poplar Flat, Lewis, Ky	15
Poplar Grove, Boone, Ill	120
Poplar Grove, Howard, Ind	41
Poplar Grove, Owen, Ky	12
Poplar Hill, McDonald, Mo	12
Poplar Hill, Anson, N. C	12
Poplar Hill, Giles, Va	61
Poplar Mount, Greenville, Va	17
Poplar Plains, Fleming, Ky	130
Poplar Ridge, Cayuga, N. Y	150
Poplar Ridge, Darke, Ohio	7
Poplar Run, Blair, Pa	12
Poplar Spring, Henderson, Tenn	5

* Money-order office.

Poplar Springs, Hall, Ga	$12
Poplar Springs, Howard, Md	150
Poquetanuck, New London, Conn	57
Poquonock, Hartford, Conn	110
Poquonock Bridge, New London, Conn	52
Porche's Prairie, Chariton, Mo	25
Portage, Kalamazoo, Mich	53
Portage, Wood, Ohio	150
Portage, Box Elder, Utah	13
Portage Centre, Hancock, Ohio	5
Portage City, * (*c. h.,*) Columbia, Wis	2,000
Portage Lake, Aroostook, Me	13
Portageville, Wyoming, N. Y	260
Port Allegheny, McKean, Pa	150
Port Allen, Louisa, Iowa	58
Port Andrew, Richland, Wis	75
Port Angeles, Clallam, Wash	76
Port Austin, (*c. h.,*) Huron, Mich	200
Port Blanchard, Luzerne, Pa	33
Port Byron, Rock Island, Ill	570
Port Byron, Cayuga, N. Y	1,100
Port Carbon, Schuylkill, Pa	530
Port Chester,* Westchester, N. Y	1,500
Port Clinton, * (*c. h.,*) Ottawa, Ohio	310
Port Clinton, Schuylkill, Pa	120
Port Colden, Warren, N. J	49
Port Conway, Prince George, Va	12
Port Crane, Broome, N. Y	26
Port Crescent, Huron, Mich	53
Port Deposit,* Cecil, Md	1,300
Port Dickinson, Broome, N. Y	69
Port Discovery, Jefferson, Wash	16
Port Edwards, Wood, Wis	37
Port Elizabeth, Cumberland, N. J	180
Porter, Oxford, Me	77
Porter, Midland, Mich	12
Porter, Jefferson, Pa	7
Porterfield, Venango, Pa	14
Porter's, Carroll, Md	14
Porter's Corners, Saratoga, N. Y	18
Porter's Cross Roads, Porter, Ind	18
Porter's Falls, Wetzel, W. Va	10
Porter's Sideling, York, Pa	22
Porter Station, Porter, Ind	100
Porter Station, Henry, Tenn	12
Portersville, DeKalb, Ala	73
Portersville, Dubois, Ind	22
Portersville, Perry, Ohio	20
Portersville, Butler, Pa	97
Portersville, Tipton, Tenn	85
Port Ewen, Ulster, N. Y	88
Port Gibson, (*c. h.,*) Claiborne, Miss	350
Port Gibson, Ontario, N. Y	74
Port Henry,* Essex, N. Y	880
Port Homer, Jefferson, Ohio	33
Port Hope, Huron, Mich	160
Port Hope, Columbia, Wis	25
Port Hudson, East Feliciana, La	90
Port Hudson, Franklin, Mo	17
Port Huron,* St. Clair, Mich	2,500
Port Jackson, Montgomery, N. Y	82
Port Jefferson,* Suffolk, N. Y	510
Port Jervis,* Orange, N. Y	2,200
Port Kennedy, Montgomery, Pa	170
Port Kent, Essex, N. Y	77

Portland, Dallas, Ala	$12
Portland, Middlesex, Conn	1,000
Portland, Whitesides, Ill	35
Portland, * (*c. h.,*) Jay, Ind	280
Portland, * (*c. h.,*) Cumberland, Me	4,000
Portland, Ionia, Mich	600
Portland, Callaway, Mo	120
Portland, Chautauqua, N. Y	140
Portland, Meigs, Ohio	73
Portland, * (*c. h.,*) Multnomah, Oreg	4,000
Portland, Northampton, Pa	210
Portland, Preston, W. Va	230
Portland Mills, Parke, Ind	130
Portlandville, Otsego, N. Y	150
Port Lavaca, Calhoun, Tex	1,200
Port Leyden, Lewis, N. Y	380
Port Louisa, Louisa, Iowa	33
Port Ludlow, Jefferson, Wash	69
Port Madison, (*c. h.,*) Kitsap, Wash	97
Port Matilda, Centre, Pa	81
Port Monmouth, Monmouth, N. J	110
Port Murry, Warren, N. J	71
Port Ontario, Oswego, N. Y	37
Port Oram, Morris, N. J	160
Port Orange, Volusia, Fla	18
Port Orchard, Kitsap, Wash	12
Port Orford, Curry, Oreg	30
Port Penn, New Castle, Del	160
Port Perry, Allegheny, Pa	170
Port Providence, Montgomery, Pa	33
Port Republic, Calvert, Md	20
Port Republic, Atlantic, N. J	160
Port Republic, Rockingham, Va	100
Port Richmond, Wapello, Iowa	16
Port Richmond, Richmond, N. Y	400
Port Royal, Henry, Ky	71
Port Royal, Juniata, Pa	400
Port Royal, Beaufort, S. C	37
Port Royal, Montgomery, Tenn	18
Port Royal, Caroline, Va	140
Port Sanilac, Sanilac, Mich	180
Port Sheldon, Ottawa, Mich	20
Portsmouth, Bay, Mich	400
Portsmouth, * (*c. h.,*) Rockingham, N. H	2,800
Portsmouth, Carteret, N. C	34
Portsmouth, * (*c. h.,*) Scioto, Ohio	2,900
Portsmouth, Newport, R. I	170
Portsmouth,* Norfolk, Va	2,400
Port Sullivan, Milam, Tex	72
Port Tobacco, (*c. h.,*) Charles, Md	320
Port Townsend, * (*c. h.,*) Jefferson, Wash	740
Port Treverton, Snyder, Pa	140
Portuguee, Shasta, Cal	12
Port Union, Butler, Ohio	15
Portville, Cattaraugus, N. Y	540
Port Washington, Queens, N. Y	97
Port Washington, Tuscarawas, Ohio	230
Port William, Clinton, Ohio	53
Port Wine, Sierra, Cal	12
Poseyville, Posey, Ind	99
Post Creek, Chemung, N. Y	14
Post Mill Village, Orange, Vt	150
Post Oak, Calhoun, Ark	12

* Money-order office.

Post Oak, Yalabusha, Miss	$6
Post Oak, Lincoln, Mo	30
Post Oak Springs, Roane, Tenn	35
Poston, Ripley, Ind	41
Postville,* Allamakee, Iowa	470
Potato Creek, Montgomery, Ind	14
Potecasi, Northampton, N. C	6
Potosi, Livingston, Ill	69
Potosi, Stevens, Minn	12
Potosi, (*c. h.*,) Washington, Mo	800
Potosi, Grant, Wis	100
Potsdam,* St. Lawrence, N. Y	2,000
Potsdam, Miami, Ohio	24
Potsdam Junction, St. Lawrence, N. Y	510
Pottamie, Ottawa, Mich	12
Potter, Yates, N. Y	83
Potter, Wood, Ohio	14
Potter Hill, Rensselaer, N. Y	14
Potter Hill, Washington, R. I	58
Pottersburgh, Union, Ohio	12
Potter's Corners, Crawford, Pa	34
Potter's Hollow, Albany, N. Y	68
Potter's Landing, Caroline, Md	69
Potter's Mills, Dale, Ala	12
Potter's Mills, Centre, Pa	100
Potter's Mills, Calumet, Wis	12
Pottersville, Cheshire, N. H	23
Pottersville, Hunterdon, N. J	47
Pottersville, Warren, N. Y	150
Potterville, Eaton, Mich	12
Potterville, Bradford, Pa	61
Pott's Grove, Northumberland, Pa	82
Pottstown,* Montgomery, Pa	2,100
Pottsville,* (*c. h.*,) Schuylkill, Pa	3,000
Poughkeepsie,* (*c. h.*,) Dutchess, N. Y	4,000
Poughquag, Dutchess, N. Y	130
Poultney, Rutland, Vt	960
Pound, Wise, Va	5
Poundridge, Westchester, N. Y	56
Powar's Store, Casey, Ky	12
Poway, San Diego, Cal	12
Powder Spring Gap, Grainger, Tenn	7
Powder Springs, Cobb, Ga	25
Powell, Delaware, Ohio	40
Powell Grove, Bowie, Tex	12
Powell's Point, Currituck, N. C	12
Powell's Station, Knox, Tenn	31
Powellton, Harrison, Tex	15
Powellton, Brunswick, Va	12
Powellville, Wicomico, Md	17
Powel's Creek, Dauphin, Pa	14
Powelton, Richmond, N. C	12
Powelton, Centre, Pa	130
Powers, Terrell, Ga	65
Powers, Jay, Ind	16
Powersville, Houston, Ga	26
Powersville, Bracken, Ky	16
Powhatan, Lawrence, Ark	67
Powhatan, Baltimore, Md	25
Powhatan, Richmond, N. C	49
Powhatan C. H., Powhatan, Va	48
Powhatan Point, Belmont, Ohio	140
Powl's Valley, Dauphin, Pa	36
Pownal, Cumberland, Me	87
Pownal, Bennington, Vt	$190
Pownal Centre, Bennington, Vt	28
Poygan, Winnebago, Wis	47
Poynett, Columbia, Wis	200
Poy Sippi, Waushara, Wis	56
Prag, Manitowoc, Wis	47
Prairie, Yolo, Cal	57
Prairie, Mower, Minn	12
Prairie, Clinton, Mo	12
Prairie, Houston, Tex	20
Prairie Bird, Adair, Mo	7
Prairie Bluff, Wilcox, Ala	18
Prairieburgh, Linn, Iowa	95
Prairie Centre, Prairie, Ark	13
Prairie Centre, La Salle, Ill	82
Prairie City, McDonough, Ill	720
Prairie City,* Jasper, Iowa	590
Prairie City, Douglas, Kans	96
Prairie City, Bates, Mo	150
Prairie City, Grant, Oreg	12
Prairie Creek, Vigo, Ind	68
Prairie Creek, Martin, Minn	10
Prairie Depot, Wood, Ohio	78
Prairie du Chien, Neosho, Kans	12
Prairie du Chien,* (*c. h.*,) Crawford, Wis	1,200
Prairie du Rocher, Randolph, Ill	95
Prairie du Sac, Sauk, Wis	430
Prairie Edge, Montgomery, Ind	18
Prairie Farm, Barron, Wis	92
Prairie Grove, Washington, Ark	12
Prairie Grove, Clarke, Iowa	41
Prairie Hall, Macon, Ill	12
Prairie Hill, Boone, Iowa	19
Prairie Hill, Chariton, Mo	12
Prairie Home, Shelby, Ill	28
Prairie Home, Cooper, Mo	18
Prairie Home, Montgomery, Tex	12
Prairie Landing, Desha, Ark	11
Prairie Lea, Caldwell, Tex	84
Prairie Mills, Muscatine, Iowa	76
Prairie Park, Nodaway, Mo	14
Prairie Plains, Grimes, Tex	51
Prairie Pond, De Kalb, Ill	30
Prairie Station, Monroe, Miss	12
Prairieton, Vigo, Ind	35
Prairie Town, Madison, Ill	46
Prairieville, Barry, Mich	150
Prairieville, Pike, Mo	39
Prairieville, Kaufman, Tex	24
Pratt, Whitesides, Ill	12
Pratt, Shelby, Ohio	140
Prattsburgh, Talbot, Ga	7
Prattsburgh,* Steuben, N. Y	590
Pratt's Corner, Franklin, Me	11
Pratt's Fork, Athens, Ohio	12
Pratt's Hollow, Madison, N. Y	95
Pratt's Junction, Worcester, Mass	41
Prattsville, Saline, Ark	6
Prattsville, Greene, N. Y	270
Prattville, (*c. h.*,) Autauga, Ala	380
Preble, Cortland, N. Y	210
Pre-emption, Mercer, Ill	110
Prentice, Morgan, Ill	75
Prentiss, Penobscot, Me	10
Prentiss Vale, McKean, Pa	19

* Money-order office.

Prescott, (c. h.,)* Yavapai, Ariz	$540
Prescott, Shelby, Ind	35
Prescott, Adams, Iowa	12
Prescott, Hampshire, Mass	42
Prescott,* Pierce, Wis	570
President, Venango, Pa	110
Presidio, Presidio, Tex	12
Presque Isle,* Aroostook, Me	350
Preston, New London, Conn	61
Preston, (c. h.,) Webster, Ga	100
Preston, Randolph, Ill	39
Preston, Caroline, Md	100
Preston, (c. h.,)* Fillmore, Minn	500
Preston, Jasper, Mo	12
Preston, Chenango, N. Y	37
Preston, Hamilton, Ohio	17
Preston, Wayne, Pa	23
Preston Bluff, Arkansas, Ark	12
Prestonburgh, (c. h.,) Floyd, Ky	56
Preston Hollow, Albany, N. Y	76
Prestonville, Cameron, Pa	20
Prestonville, Rhea, Tenn	7
Prewitt's Ferry, Desha, Ark	12
Priam, Blackford, Ind	13
Price, Mercer, Ohio	8
Price's Branch, Montgomery, Mo	41
Price's Creek, De Witt, Tex	16
Price's Landing, Scott, Mo	24
Price's Store, Rockingham, N. C	12
Pricetown, Highland, Ohio	11
Pricetown, Berks, Pa	8
Priceville, Wayne, Pa	2
Prickley Pear, Jefferson, Mont	69
Pride's Station, Colbert, Ala	12
Prillaman's, Franklin, Va	15
Primrose, Lee, Iowa	110
Primrose, Lewis, Mo	48
Primrose, Douglas, Nebr	23
Primrose, Williams, Ohio	11
Primrose, Dane, Wis	67
Prince Edward C. H., Prince Edward, Va	60
Prince Fredericktown, (c. h.,) Calvert, Md	120
Prince George C. H., Prince George, Va	42
Prince's Bay, Richmond, N. Y	52
Princess Anne, (c. h.,)* Somerset, Md	760
Princess Anne C. H., Princess Anne, Va	12
Princeton, Jackson, Ala	24
Princeton, (c. h.,) Dallas, Ark	120
Princeton, Colusa, Cal	64
Princeton, (c. h.,)* Bureau, Ill	2,400
Princeton, (c. h.,)* Gibson, Ind	1,000
Princeton, Scott, Iowa	280
Princeton, Franklin, Kans	20
Princeton, (c. h.,)* Caldwell, Ky	460
Princeton, Washington, Me	150
Princeton, Worcester, Mass	370
Princeton, (c. h.,) Mille Lacs, Minn	230
Princeton, (c. h.,)* Mercer, Mo	260
Princeton,* Mercer, N. J	2,000
Princeton, Butler, Ohio	11
Princeton, Lawrence, Pa	38
Princeton, (c. h.,) Mercer, W. Va	30
Princeton, Green Lake, Wis	$460
Princeville,* Peoria, Ill	370
Prince William, Carroll, Ind	42
Principio, Cecil, Md	48
Principio Furnace, Cecil, Md	64
Prior's Station, Polk, Ga	12
Privateer, Sumter, S. C	12
Proctor, (c. h.,) Lee, Ky	8
Proctor, Wetzel, W. Va	43
Proctor's Creek, Chesterfield, Va	12
Proctorsville, Windsor, Vt	630
Proctorville, Caldwell, Mo	12
Profile House, Grafton, N. H	17
Progress, Dauphin, Pa	17
Promise City, Wayne, Iowa	54
Prompton, Wayne, Pa	54
Prophetstown, Whitesides, Ill	250
Prospect, New Haven, Conn	150
Prospect, Madison, Ind	7
Prospect, Waldo, Me	99
Prospect, Harford, Md	42
Prospect, Oneida, N. Y	240
Prospect, Marion, Ohio	140
Prospect, Butler, Pa	130
Prospect, Burleson, Tex	10
Prospect, Prince Edward, Va	140
Prospect Ferry, Waldo, Me	170
Prospect Grove, Scotland, Mo	14
Prospect Hall, Bladen, N. C	12
Prospect Harbor, Hancock, Me	65
Prospect Hill, Linn, Iowa	20
Prospect Hill, Clay, Mo	35
Prospect Hill, Caswell, N. C	16
Prospect Hill, Fairfax, Va	8
Prospect Hill, Waukesha, Wis	59
Prospect Lake, Van Buren, Mich	18
Prospect Plains, Middlesex, N. J	66
Prospect Station, Chautauqua, N. Y	13
Prospect Station, Giles, Tenn	65
Prospect Valley, Harrison, W. Va	9
Prospectville, Montgomery, Pa	47
Prosper, Fillmore, Minn	20
Prosperity, Franklin, Ill	12
Prosperity, Madison, Ind	12
Prosperity, Lawrence, Ky	4
Prosperity, Moore, N. C	6
Prosperity, Washington, Pa	46
Protection, Erie, N. Y	62
Providence, Pickens, Ala	5
Providence, Searcy, Ark	2
Providence, Bureau, Ill	40
Providence, Webster, Ky	18
Providence, Boone, Mo	27
Providence, Saratoga, N. Y	33
Providence, Luzerne, Pa	940
PROVIDENCE,* *(c. h.,)* Providence, R. I	4,000
Providence, Cache, Utah	38
Providence Forge, New Kent, Va	36
Provincetown,* Barnstable, Mass	1,200
Proviso, Cook, Ill	30
Provo City, (c. h.,) Utah, Utah	300
Prunty's, Henry, Va	1
Pruntytown, (c. h.,) Taylor, W. Va	130
Pryorsburgh, Graves, Ky	9
Pryor's Creek, Choctaw N., Ind. T	12

* Money-order office.

Pryor's Store, Douglas, Mo	$10
*Pueblo,** (*c. h.,*) Pueblo, Colo	800
Pugh, Belmont, Ohio	39
Pughtown, Chester, Pa	100
Pulaski, Hancock, Ill	28
Pulaski, Pulaski, Ind	22
Pulaski, Davis, Iowa	16
Pulaski, Jackson, Mich	58
*Pulaski,** (*c. h.,*) Oswego, N. Y	1,100
Pulaski, Williams, Ohio	56
Pulaski, Lawrence, Pa	200
*Pulaski,** (*c. h.,*) Giles, Tenn	1,100
Pulaskiville, Morrow, Ohio	30
Pulley's Mill, Williamson, Ill	14
Pultney, Steuben, N. Y	56
Pultneyville, Wayne, N. Y	260
Pulver's Corners, Dutchess, N. Y	63
Pumphrey's Landing, Lewis, Wash	12
Pungoteague, Accomack, Va	87
Punjaub, St. Genevieve, Mo	20
Punta Arenas, Mendocino, Cal	230
Punxatawney,* Jefferson, Pa	290
Purcell, Bedford, Pa	12
Purchase Line, Indiana, Pa	12
Purdy, (*c. h.,*) McNairy, Tenn	150
Purdy Creek, Steuben, N. Y	18
Purdy's Station, Westchester, N. Y	280
Purgitsville, Hampshire, W. Va	120
Purlear's Creek, Wilkes, N. C	6
Purley, Caswell, N. C	22
Pursley, Tyler, W. Va	10
Purvis, Sullivan, N. Y	11
Pushmataha, Choctaw, Ala	12
Put in Bay, Ottawa, Ohio	250
Putnam,* Windham, Conn	400
Putnam, Fayette, Iowa	8
Putnam, Washington, N. Y	81
Putnam, Muskingum, Ohio	470
Putnamville, Putnam, Ind	110
Putney, Windham, Vt	380
Putneyville, Armstrong, Pa	47
Pylesville, Harford, Md	24
Pyrmont, Carroll, Ind	19
Pyrmont, Montgomery, Ohio	38

Q.

Quacken Kill, Rensselaer, N. Y	20
Quaker Bottom, Lawrence, Ohio	140
Quaker Hill, Vermillion, Ind	16
Quaker Hill, Dutchess, N. Y	39
Quaker Springs, Saratoga, N. Y	88
Quaker Street, Schenectady, N. Y	170
Quakertown, Union, Ind	40
Quakertown, Hunterdon, N. J	50
Quakertown, Bucks, Pa	340
Quality Valley, Butler, Ky	7
Quallatown, Jackson, N. C	5
Quantico, Wicomico, Md	71
Quarry, Marshall, Iowa	12
Quarrysville, Hawkins, Tenn	18
Quarryville, Tolland, Conn	42
Quarryville, Ulster, N. Y	22
Quarryville, Lancaster, Pa	65
Quasqueton, Buchanan, Iowa	310
Quechee, Windsor, Vt	360
Queen City, Schuyler, Mo	$13
Queens, Queens, N. Y	85
Queensbury, Warren, N. Y	36
Queenstown, Queen Anne, Md	230
Queensville, Jennings, Ind	94
Quenemo, Osage, Kans	14
Quercus Grove, Switzerland, Ind	40
Query's, Mecklenburgh, N. C	9
Quiet Dell, Harrison, W. Va	23
Quincy, (*c. h.,*) Plumas, Cal	140
Quincy, (*c. h.,*) Gadsden, Fla	600
*Quincy,** (*c. h.,*) Adams, Ill	4,000
Quincy, Owen, Ind	52
*Quincy,** (*c. h.,*) Adams, Iowa	260
Quincy, Greenwood, Kans	12
Quincy, Lewis, Ky	48
Quincy,* Norfolk, Mass	1,500
Quincy,* Branch, Mich	730
Quincy, Olmsted, Minn	18
Quincy, Hickory, Mo	50
Quincy, Logan, Ohio	240
Quincy, Franklin, Pa	91
Quincy, Gibson, Tenn	23
Quincy, Adams, Wis	35
Quincy Point, Norfolk, Mass	190
Quindaro, Wyandotte, Kans	50
Quinn, Macomb, Mich	12
Quinney, Calumet, Wis	21
Quinton, Salem, N. J	42
Quitman, Van Buren, Ark	43
Quitman, (*c. h.,*) Brooks, Ga	480
Quitman, Clark, Miss	140
Quitman, Nodaway, Mo	56
Quitman, (*c. h.,*) Wood, Tex	140
Quito, Butler, Kans	12
Quogue, Suffolk, N. Y	150
Quonochontaug, Washington, R. I	19

R.

Rabbittsville, Logan, Ky	14
Raccoon, Laurel, Ky	6
Raccoon, Washington, Pa	45
Raccoon Ford, Culpeper, Va	33
Raccoon Valley, Union, Tenn	12
Raceland, La Fourche, La	12
Racine, Newton, Mo	12
Racine, Meigs, Ohio	190
*Racine,** (*c. h.,*) Racine, Wis	3,000
Racoon, Marion, Ill	20
Racoon, Preston, W. Va	190
Radersburgh, (*c. h.,*) Jefferson, Mont	12
Radford Furnace, Pulaski, Va	12
Radfordsville, Perry, Ala	20
Radical, Madison, Ga	12
Radical City, Montgomery, Kans	12
Radnor, Delaware, Ohio	110
Radnor, Delaware, Pa	150
Raglesville, Daviess, Ind	37
Rahway,* Union, N. J	2,000
Raif Branch, Montgomery, Ala	12
Rail Road, York, Pa	120
Rail Road Flat, Calaveras, Cal	69
Rainbow, Hartford, Conn	130
Rainey Creek, Camden, Mo	12
Rainey's Creek, Coryell, Tex	12

* Money-order office.

Rainier, Columbia, Oreg	$24
Rainsborough, Highland, Ohio	50
Rainsburgh, Bedford, Pa	78
Rainsville, Warren, Ind	120
Raisin Centre, Lenawee, Mich	35
Raleigh, Saline, Ill	63
Raleigh, Rush, Ind	22
Raleigh, Union, Ky	9
Raleigh, (*c. h.*,) Smith, Miss	12
RALEIGH,* (*c. h.*,) Wake, N. C	2,500
Raleigh, Shelby, Tenn	23
Raleigh C. H., Raleigh, W. Va	50
Ralston, Lycoming, Pa	110
Ralston's Station, Weakley, Tenn	61
Ramapo Works, Rockland, N. Y	160
Ramer, Montgomery, Ala	40
Ramer, McNairy, Tenn	12
Ramey, Johnson, Mo	150
Ramsaytown, Yancey, N. C	5
Ramsey, Fayette, Ill	280
Ramsey's, Bergen, N. J	110
Rancho, Gonzales, Tex	12
Rancocas, Burlington, N. J	160
Randall, Jefferson, Ark	12
Randall, Allen, Ind	44
Randall, Hamilton, Iowa	13
Randall, Saginaw, Mich	12
Randall, Montgomery, N. Y	43
Randall, Cuyahoga, Ohio	12
Randall, Smith, Tex	12
Randall, Monongalia, W. Va	12
Randallstown, Baltimore, Md	35
Randallsville, Madison, N. Y	12
Randellsville, Christian, Ill	21
Randolph, Bibb, Ala	100
Randolph, La Fayette, Ark	12
Randolph, McLean, Ill	17
Randolph, Randolph, Ind	140
Randolph, Riley, Kans	140
Randolph, Metcalfe, Ky	20
Randolph, Norfolk, Mass	900
Randolph, Randolph, Mo	220
Randolph, Dakota, Nebr	12
Randolph, Coos, N. H	11
Randolph,* Cattaraugus, N. Y	650
Randolph, Portage, Ohio	210
Randolph, Coos, Oreg	38
Randolph, Crawford, Pa	35
Randolph, Tipton, Tenn	20
Randolph, Orange, Vt	310
Randolph Centre, Broome, N. Y	10
Randolph Centre, Columbia, Wis	27
Rangeley, Franklin, Me	14
Ranger, Perry, Ind	12
Rankin's Depot, Cocke, Tenn	12
Ransom, Hillsdale, Mich	120
Ransom, Luzerne, Pa	33
Ransom's Bridge, Nash, N. C	10
Ransomville, Niagara, N. Y	100
Rantoul,* Champaign, Ill	670
Rantoul, Calumet, Wis	12
Rapid Ann Station, Culpeper, Va	370
Rapids, Niagara, N. Y	21
Rapids, Portage, Ohio	30
Rapids City, Rock Island, Ill	44
Rappahannock Academy, Caroline, Va	12
Rapp's Mill, Rockbridge, Va	$7
Rarden, Scioto, Ohio	25
Raritan, Henderson, Ill	170
Raritan, Somerset, N. J	350
Rathboneville, Steuben, N. Y	130
Rathbun, Sheboygan, Wis	22
Rattlesnake, Lane, Oreg	21
Rauch's Gap, Clinton, Pa	30
Raught's Mills, Forest, Pa	20
Ravanna, Mercer, Mo	84
Ravena City, Los Angeles, Cal	12
Ravenna, Muskegon, Mich	71
Ravenna,* (*c. h.*,) Portage, Ohio	1,800
Raven Rock, Hunterdon, N. J	27
Raven's Eye, Fayette, W. Va	23
Raven's Nest, Washington, Va	5
Raven Stream, Scott, Minn	14
Ravenswood, Cook, Ill	17
Ravenswood, Queens, N. Y	22
Ravenswood,* Jackson, W. Va	210
Rawley Springs, Rockingham, Va	12
Rawling's Springs, (*c. h.*,) Carbon, Wyo	950
Rawling's Station, Alleghany, Md	38
Rawlingsville, De Kalb, Ala	32
Rawlinsville, Lancaster, Pa	28
Rawson, Aroostook, Me	4
Rawson, Cattaraugus, N. Y	31
Rawson, Hancock, Ohio	46
Rawsonville, Wayne, Mich	110
Rawsonville, Lorain, Ohio	220
Ray, Bedford, Tenn	12
Ray Centre, Macomb, Mich	12
Raymertown, Rensselaer, N. Y	40
Raymilton, Venango, Pa	71
Raymond, Champaign, Ill	12
Raymond, Black Hawk, Iowa	130
Raymond, Cumberland, Me	50
Raymond, Stearns, Minn	12
Raymond, (*c. h.*,) Hinds, Miss	470
Raymond, Rockingham, N. H	290
Raymond, Racine, Wis	62
Raymond City, Putnam, W. Va	59
Raymonds, Union, Ohio	130
Raymonds, Potter, Pa	18
Raymondville, St. Lawrence, N. Y	110
Raynham, Bristol, Mass	82
Raynold, Montcalm, Mich	12
Rays, Jackson, Ohio	74
Ray's Crossing, Shelby, Ind	12
Ray's Hill, Bedford, Pa	67
Raysville, Henry, Ind	160
Rayville, (*c. h.*,) Richland, La	12
Rayville, Baltimore, Md	51
Rayville, Ray, Mo	12
Raywick, Marion, Ky	41
Read, Clayton, Iowa	40
Readfield, Kennebec, Me	340
Readfield, Waupaca, Wis	16
Readfield Depot, Kennebec, Me	140
Reading, Livingston, Ill	49
Reading, Lyon, Kans	12
Reading, Middlesex, Mass	940
Reading, Hillsdale, Mich	500
Reading, Pike, Mo	12
Reading, Schuyler, N. Y	8
Reading, Hamilton, Ohio	160

* Money-order office.

Reading,* (*c. h.*,) Berks, Pa	$3,500
Reading, Windsor, Vt	49
Reading Centre, Schuyler, N. Y	65
Readington, Hunterdon, N. J	91
Readsborough, Bennington, Vt	120
Readstown, Vernon, Wis	36
Readsville, Callaway, Mo	38
Readville Station, Norfolk, Mass	320
Readyville, Rutherford, Tenn	64
Ream's Chapel, Hart, Ky	12
Ream's Station, Dinwiddie, Va	93
Reamstown, Lancaster, Pa	36
Reaville, Hunterdon, N. J	71
Rebecca, Lancaster, Nebr	38
Rebersburgh, Centre, Pa	120
Rebucks, Northumberland, Pa	8
Recklesstown, Burlington, N. J	53
Rectortown Station, Fauquier, Va	110
Rectorville, Hamilton, Ill	11
Red Apple, Marshall, Ala	12
Red Bank,* Monmouth, N. J	1,300
Red Bank, Halifax, Va	26
Red Bank Furnace, Armstrong, Pa	47
Red Banks, Marshall, Miss	12
Red Banks, Robeson, N. C	20
Red Beach, Washington, Me	64
Red Bluff, Jefferson, Ark	12
Red Bluff,* (*c. h.*,) Tehama, Cal	430
Red Bluff, Coffee, Ga	7
Red Brick, Sullivan, N. Y	10
Red Bridge, Ingham, Mich	18
Red Bud,* Randolph, Ill	410
Red Clay, Whitfield, Ga	90
Red Creek, Wayne, N. Y	290
Red Creek, Tucker, W. Va	1
Redden, Sussex, Del	12
Redding, Fairfield, Conn	110
Redding, Ringgold, Iowa	17
Redding Ridge, Fairfield, Conn	90
Red Falls, Greene, N. Y	71
Redfield, Dallas, Iowa	250
Redfield, Carver, Minn	13
Redfield, Oswego, N. Y	140
Redford, Wayne, Mich	94
Redford, Clinton, N. Y	120
Red Fork, Desha, Ark	33
Red Haw, Ashland, Ohio	47
Red Hill, Marshall, Ala	16
Red Hill, Hardin, Ky	13
Red Hill, Mitchell, N. C	2
Red Hill, Montgomery, Pa	26
Red Hook, Dutchess, N. Y	410
Red House, Morgan, Ind	12
Red House, Cattaraugus, N. Y	67
Red House, Charlotte, Va	11
Red House Shoals, Putnam, W. Va	35
Redington, Northampton, Pa	12
Red Jacket, Erie, N. Y	12
Redkey, Jay, Ind	64
Red Land, Pike, Ark	6
Redland, Montgomery, Md	16
Red Land, Pontotoc, Miss	32
Red Land, Adams, Pa	39
Red Lion, New Castle, Del	56
Red Lion, Warren, Ohio	95
Red Mound, Henderson, Tenn	12
Red Mountain, Orange, N. C	$2
Red Mountain City, Deer Lodge, Mont	12
Red Oak, Fayette, Ga	6
Red Oak, Choctaw N., Ind. T	12
Red Oak, Cedar, Iowa	61
Red Oak, Grayson, Ky	7
Red Oak, Brown, Ohio	55
Red Oak, Ellis, Tex	83
Red Oak Grove, Charlotte, Va	43
Red Oak Junction,* (*c. h.*,) Montgomery, Iowa	700
Red Plains, Yadkin, N. C	8
Red River, Kewaunee, Wis	12
Red River Iron Works, Estill, Ky	23
Red River Landing, Point Coupee, La	24
Red River Mills, Logan, Ky	12
Red Rock, Marion, Iowa	69
Red Rock, Lincoln, Kans	10
Red Rock, Columbia, N. Y	35
Red Rock, Luzerne, Pa	10
Red Rock, Bastrop, Tex	12
Red Shoals, Stokes, N. C	12
Red Stone, Cloud, Kans	12
Red Stone, Nicollet, Minn	13
Redstone, Fayette, Pa	45
Red Sulphur Springs, Monroe, W. Va	43
Red Wing,* (*c. h.*,) Goodhue, Minn	2,600
Redwood, Jefferson, N. Y	290
Redwood City, (*c. h.*,) San Mateo, Cal	360
Redwood Falls, (*c. h.*,) Redwood, Minn	250
Reed, Oceana, Mich	14
Reed Creek, Randolph, N. C	7
Reeder's Mills, Harrison, Iowa	31
Reed Island, Wythe, Va	12
Reed Level, Covington, Ala	6
Reedsburgh, Wayne, Ohio	55
Reedsburgh,* Sauk, Wis	530
Reed's Corners, Ontario, N. Y	67
Reed's Creek, Lawrence, Ark	40
Reed's Ferry, Hillsborough, N. H	110
Reed's Gap, Juniata, Pa	12
Reed's Landing, Pulaski, Ark	12
Reed's Landing, Wabashaw, Minn	350
Reed's Mills, Vinton, Ohio	290
Reedsville, Meigs, Ohio	33
Reedsville, Mifflin, Pa	220
Reedsville, Preston, W. Va	40
Reedsville, Manitowoc, Wis	48
Reedtown, Seneca, Ohio	34
Reedy, Jackson, W. Va	12
Reedy Creek, Davidson, N. C	12
Reedy Creek, Marion, S. C	11
Reedy Ripple, Wirt, W. Va	12
Reedyville, Butler, Ky	9
Reedyville, Roane, W. Va	12
Reelsville, Putnam, Ind	55
Reem's Creek, Buncombe, N. C	13
Reese Mill, Etowah, Ala	12
Reese's Mill, Boone, Ind	39
Reeseville, Chester, Pa	100
Reeseville, Dodge, Wis	80
Reeson, Chippewa, Minn	12
Reesville, Clinton, Ohio	94
Reeves' Landing, Arkansas, Ark	12

* Money-order office.

Post office	Amount
Reeves' Station, Gordon, Ga	$12
Reeves' Station, Butler, Mo	36
Reevesville, Colleton, S. C	25
Reform, Pickens, Ala	13
Reform, Jefferson, Ark	12
Reform, Callaway, Mo	13
Refugio, (*c. h.*,) Refugio, Tex	20
Reguier's Mills, Washington, Ohio	70
Rego, Orange, Ind	32
Rehoboth, Wilcox, Ala	13
Rehoboth, Bristol, Mass	48
Rehoboth, Perry, Ohio	15
Rehoboth, Edgefield, S. C	9
Rehoboth, Lunenburgh, Va	17
Rehrersburgh, Berks, Pa	71
Rei, Ripley, Ind	99
Reidenbach's Store, Lancaster, Pa	33
Reid's, Paulding, Ohio	19
Reidsburgh, Clarion, Pa	120
Reidsville, (*c. h.*,) Tatnall, Ga	20
Reidsville, Albany, N. Y	27
Reidsville, Rockingham, N. C	200
Reidsville, Spartanburgh, S. C	60
Reiffsburgh, Wells, Ind	13
Reiley, Butler, Ohio	82
Reinersville, Morgan, Ohio	33
Reinhold's Station, Lancaster, Pa	53
Reinholdsville, Lancaster, Pa	33
Reisterstown, Baltimore, Md	280
Relfe, Phelps, Mo	16
Relf's Bluff, Drew, Ark	49
Remington, Jasper, Ind	190
Remington, Allegheny, Pa	20
Remsen, Oneida, N. Y	250
Remson's Corners, Medina, Ohio	73
Renault, Monroe, Ill	47
Reno, Leavenworth, Kans	72
Reno, Pope, Minn	10
Reno, Washoe, Nev	550
Reno, Venango, Pa	190
Renovo,* Clinton, Pa	960
Renrock, Noble, Ohio	33
Rensselaer,* (*c. h.*,) Jasper, Ind	460
Rensselaer Falls, St. Lawrence, N. Y	160
Rensselaerville,* Albany, N. Y	250
Renwick, Lee, Ga	170
Repose, Haralson, Ga	12
Republic, Seneca, Ohio	270
Republic, Yadkin, N. C	9
Republican, Choctaw, Miss	12
Republican, Darke, Ohio	44
Republican City, Clay, Kans	12
Republican Grove, Halifax, Va	20
Resaca, Gordon, Ga	78
Resaca, Duplin, N. C	12
Reserve, Miami, Ind	22
Reserve, Erie, N. Y	22
Rest, Iowa, Iowa	12
Retreat, Jackson, Ind	36
Retreat, Franklin, Va	13
Retreat, Vernon, Wis	31
Reveille, Nye, Nev	5
Revilee, Scott, Ark	21
Rexford Flats, Saratoga, N. Y	110
Rexville, Ripley, Ind	12
Rexville, Steuben, N. Y	56

Post office	Amount
Reyburn, Hot Spring, Ark	$12
Reynale's Basin, Niagara, N. Y	40
Reynolds, Taylor, Ga	120
Reynolds,* White, Ind	230
Reynolds, Schuylkill, Pa	12
Reynoldsburgh, Johnson, Ill	27
Reynoldsburgh, Franklin, Ohio	240
Reynoldson, Gates, N. C	12
Reynoldsville, Schuyler, N. Y	41
Reynoldsville, Jefferson, Pa	96
Rhea, Lawrence, Ark	12
Rhea's Mills, Washington, Ark	24
Rheatown, Greene, Tenn	110
Rhine, Sheboygan, Wis	32
Rhinebeck,* Dutchess, N. Y	1,200
Rhinecliff, Dutchess, N. Y	180
Rhineland, Montgomery, Mo	28
Rialto, Chatham, N. C	5
Rice Depot, Prince Edward, Va	82
Riceford, Houston, Minn	68
Rice Lake, Dodge, Minn	32
Rice's Landing, Greene, Pa	62
Rice's Store, Westmoreland, Va	14
Riceville, Mitchell, Iowa	83
Riceville, Crawford, Pa	140
Riceville, McMinn, Tenn	150
Riceville, Pittsylvania, Va	17
Rich, Atchison, Mo	41
Richardson, St. Joseph, Ind	20
Richardson, Osage, Kans	12
Richardson's, Montgomery, Tenn	12
Richardson's Landing, Meade, Ky	12
Richardsonville, Chariton, Mo	12
Richardsonville, Edgefield, S. C	8
Richardsville, Jefferson, Pa	32
Richardsville, Culpeper, Va	20
Richborough, Bucks, Pa	140
Richburgh, Allegany, N. Y	140
Rich Creek, Logan, W. Va	4
Richfield, Adams, Ill	40
Richfield, Fayette, Iowa	17
Richfield, Genesee, Mich	52
Richfield, Hennepin, Minn	59
Richfield, Otsego, N. Y	44
Richfield, Summit, Ohio	210
Richfield, Juniata, Pa	80
Richfield, Washington, Wis	460
Richfield Springs, Otsego, N. Y	1,100
Richford, Tioga, N. Y	170
Richford, Franklin, Vt	300
Richford, Waushara, Wis	23
Rich Fountain, Osage, Mo	24
Rich Hill, Knox, Ohio	12
Richland, Sacramento, Cal	35
Richland, Union, Dak	100
Richland, Sangamon, Ill	23
Richland, Rush, Ind	53
Richland,* Keokuk, Iowa	270
Richland, Shawnee, Kans	12
Richland, Kalamazoo, Mich	240
Richland, Pulaski, Mo	12
Richland, Oswego, N. Y	65
Richland, Tazewell, Va	7
Richland Centre, Bucks, Pa	320
Richland Centre,* (*c. h.*,) Richland, Wis	680

*Money-order office.

Richland City, Richland, Wis	$46
Richland Crossing, Navarro, Tex	6
Richland Grove, Mercer, Ill	20
Richland Mill, Stafford, Va	12
Richland's, Onslow, N. C	21
Richland Station, Lebanon, Pa	98
Richland Station, Sumner, Tenn	50
Richlandtown, Bucks, Pa	48
Richland Valley, Haywood, N. C	23
Richman Falls, Raleigh, W. Va	6
Richmond, Dallas, Ala	41
Richmond, Little River, Ark	12
Richmond,* McHenry, Ill	450
Richmond,* Wayne, Ind	2,800
Richmond, Washington, Iowa	240
Richmond, Franklin, Kans	12
Richmond,* (*c. h.*,) Madison, Ky	1,100
Richmond, Madison, La	50
Richmond,* Sagadahoc, Me	830
Richmond, Berkshire, Mass	150
Richmond, Macomb, Mich	240
Richmond, Winona, Minn	15
Richmond,* (*c. h.*,) Ray, Mo	840
Richmond, Cheshire, N. H	89
Richmond,* (*c. h.*,) Richmond, N. Y	180
Richmond, Jefferson, Ohio	260
Richmond, Northampton, Pa	40
Richmond, Bedford, Tenn	12
Richmond, (*c. h.*,) Fort Bend, Tex	360
Richmond, Cache, Utah	29
Richmond, Chittenden, Vt	350
RICHMOND,* (*c. h.*,) Henrico, Va	4,000
Richmond, Walworth, Wis	64
Richmond Centre, Ashtabula, Ohio	50
Richmond Corner, Sagadahoc, Me	40
Richmond Dale, Ross, Ohio	82
Richmond Hill, Yadkin, N. C	8
Richmond Hill, Susquehanna, Pa	6
Richmond Mills, Ontario, N. Y	6
Richmond Switch, Washington, R. I	12
Richmondville, Sanilac, Mich	47
Richmondville, Schoharie, N. Y	670
Rich Patch, Alleghany, Va	6
Rich Pond Grove, Warren, Ky	48
Rich Square, Northampton, N. C	69
Rich Valley, Wabash, Ind	48
Rich Valley, Montgomery, Ky	12
Rich Valley, Dakota, Minn	24
Richview,* Washington, Ill	450
Richville, Tuscola, Mich	10
Richville, Douglas, Mo	12
Richville, St. Lawrence, N. Y	220
Richville, Addison, Vt	250
Richwood, Union, Ohio	400
Richwood, Dodge, Wis	90
Richwoods, Delaware, Ind	13
Richwoods, Washington, Mo	60
Rickardsville, Dubuque, Iowa	47
Rickoe's Bluff, Gadsden, Fla	12
Rickreall, Polk, Oreg	23
Riddicksville, Hertford, N. C	18
Riddlesburgh, Bedford, Pa	120
Riddle's Cross Roads, Butler, Pa	8
Riddlesville, Washington, Ga	12
Rider's Mills, Columbia, N. Y	70
Rider's Mills Station, Columbia, N. Y	$12
Ridge, St. Mary's, Md	26
Ridge, Carroll, Mo	12
Ridge, Livingston, N. Y	38
Ridge, Noble, Ohio	4
Ridge, Edgefield, S. C	5
Ridge, Colorado, Tex	17
Ridgebury, Fairfield, Conn	21
Ridgebury, Orange, N. Y	15
Ridgebury, Bradford, Pa	25
Ridgedale, Polk, Iowa	110
Ridge Farm, Vermilion, Ill	150
Ridgefield, Fairfield, Conn	460
Ridgefield, McHenry, Ill	150
Ridgefield Station, Fairfield, Conn	82
Ridgeland, Henry, Ohio	8
Ridgely, Caroline, Md	75
Ridge Mills, Oneida, N. Y	45
Ridge Prairie, St. Clair, Ill	110
Ridge Prairie, Saline, Mo	57
Ridge Road, Niagara, N. Y	130
Ridge Spring, Pitt, N. C	6
Ridgeview, Westmoreland, Pa	12
Ridgeville, Randolph, Ind	210
Ridgeville, Warren, Ohio	57
Ridgeville, Colleton, S. C	38
Ridgeville, Mineral, W. Va	42
Ridgeville, Monroe, Wis	33
Ridgeville Corners, Henry, Ohio	46
Ridgeway, Winneshiek, Iowa	210
Ridgeway, Osage, Kans	58
Ridgeway, Lenawee, Mich	100
Ridgeway, Winona, Minn	20
Ridgeway, Orleans, N. Y	170
Ridgeway, Warren, N. C	250
Ridgeway, Hardin, Ohio	110
Ridgeway, Fairfield, S. C	170
Ridgeway, Henry, Va	12
Ridgeway, Iowa, Wis	16
Ridgewood, Bergen, N. J	280
Ridgewood, Queens, N. Y	12
Ridgeley, Platte, Mo	68
Ridgway,* (*c. h.*,) Elk, Pa	790
Ridott, Stephenson, Ill	280
Riegelsville, Bucks, Pa	210
Rienza, Mecosta, Mich	12
Rienzi, Alcorn, Miss	290
Rifton Glen, Ulster, N. Y	66
Riga, Lenawee, Mich	120
Riga, Monroe, N. Y	60
Rigdon, Madison, Ind	62
Riggsbee's Store, Chatham, N. C	2
Rigg's Cross Roads, Williamson, Tenn	40
Riggsville, Izard, Ark	51
Riker's Hollow, Steuben, N. Y	18
Riley, McHenry, Ill	22
Riley, Vigo, Ind	17
Riley, Clinton, Mich	22
Riley Centre, Riley, Kans	12
Riley Centre, St. Clair, Mich	16
Riley's Station, Marion, Ky	26
Rileyville, Wayne, Pa	16
Rimer, Armstrong, Pa	23
Rimersburgh, Clarion, Pa	230

* Money-order office.

Rinard's Mills, Monroe, Ohio	$12
Rindge, Cheshire, N. H	210
Rinehart, Auglaize, Ohio	10
Ring, Winnebago, Wis	12
Ringgold, Cherokee, Ala	6
*Ringgold,** (*c. h.,*) Catoosa, Ga	390
Ringgold, La Grange, Ind	18
Ringgold, Ringgold, Iowa	12
Ringgold, Bienville, La	42
Ringgold, Washington, Md	51
Ringgold, Morgan, Ohio	24
Ringgold, Jefferson, Pa	25
Ringgold, Montgomery, Tenn	23
Ringgold, Pittsylvania, Va	59
Ringoes, Hunterdon, N. J	140
Ringo's Point, Adair, Mo	11
Ringtown, Schuylkill, Pa	92
Ringville, Hampshire, Mass	75
Ringwood, McHenry, Ill	75
Ringwood, Halifax, N. C	20
Ringwood Furnace, Passaic, N. J	12
Rinosa, Kankakee, Ill	2
Rio, Hart, Ky	16
Rio, Kemper, Miss	5
Rio, Columbia, Wis	430
Rio Grande, Cape May, N. J	42
Rio Grande, Gallia, Ohio	18
Rio Grande City, (*c. h.,*) Starr, Tex	170
Rio Mimbres, Grant, N. Mex	46
Rio Seco, Butte, Cal	12
Rio Vista, Solano, Cal	95
Ripley, Brown, Ill	120
Ripley, Somerset, Me	20
Ripley, (*c. h.,*) Tippah, Miss	230
Ripley, Chautauqua, N. Y	330
Ripley,* Brown, Ohio	1,000
Ripley, (*c. h.,*) Lauderdale, Tenn	200
Ripley Landing, Jackson, W. Va	35
Ripley's, Tyler, W. Va	63
Ripley's Mills, Craig, Va	21
Ripleyville, Huron, Ohio	33
Ripon, Labette, Kans	12
Ripon,* Fond du Lac, Wis	2,000
Rippey, Greene, Iowa	34
Rippon, Jefferson, W. Va	140
Rippon's Hall, York, Va	12
Ripton, Addison, Vt	78
Ripyville, Anderson, Ky	29
Risdon, St. Clair, Ill	12
Rish's Store, Lexington, S. C	9
Rising Fawn, Dade, Ga	14
Rising Sun, (*c. h.,*) Ohio, Ind	680
Rising Sun, Polk, Iowa	34
Rising Sun,* Cecil, Md	320
Rising Sun, Crawford, Wis	86
Risingville, Steuben, N. Y	12
Ritchieville, Dinwiddie, Va	14
Rittersville, Lehigh, Pa	18
River, Dane, Wis	48
River aux Vases, St. Genevieve, Mo	12
Riverdale, Clay, Kans	12
Riverdale, Westchester, N. Y	240
Riverdale, Hamilton, Ohio	66
Riverdale, Weber, Utah	40
River Edge, Bergen, N. J	12
River Falls,* Pierce, Wis	600
*Riverhead,** (*c. h.,*) Suffolk, N. Y	$1,000
River Point, Steele, Minn	8
River Point, Kent, R. I	390
River Raisin, Washtenaw, Mich	44
River Side, New Haven, Conn	34
Riverside, Clay, Dak	12
Riverside, Kane, Ill	12
Riverside, Kennebec, Me	130
Riverside, Burt, Nebr	6
Riverside, Burlington, N. J	300
Riverside, Broome, N. Y	12
Riverside, Buncombe, N. C	7
Riverside, Northumberland, Pa	12
River Side, Cocke, Tenn	12
River Styx, Medina, Ohio	73
Riversville, Amherst, Va	12
Riverton, Litchfield, Conn	230
Riverton, Wicomico, Md	13
Riverton, Mason, Mich	11
Riverton, Warren, Va	13
River Vale, Lawrence, Ind	30
River View, Jefferson, Ky	27
Rives, Richland, Ohio	55
Rives Junction, Jackson, Mich	57
Rivesville, Marion, W. Va	38
Rixeyville, Culpeper, Va	12
Rix's Mills, Muskingum, Ohio	78
Roachton, Wood, Ohio	17
Road House Station, Greene, Ill	73
Roadstown, Cumberland, N. J	100
Roadville, Charleston, S. C	14
Roan Mountain, Carter, Tenn	14
Roann, Wabash, Ind	6
Roanoke, Randolph, Ala	87
Roanoke, Huntingdon, Ind	440
Roanoke, Howard, Mo	300
Roanoke, Martin, N. C	12
Roanoke, Putnam, Ohio	160
Roan's Prairie, Grimes, Tex	12
Roaring Branch, Lycoming, Pa	100
Roaring Creek, Columbia, Pa	43
Roaring Creek, Randolph, W. Va	12
Roaring Creek, Jackson, Wis	20
Roaring Gap, Wilkes, N. C	7
Roaring Run, Botetourt, Va	47
Roaring Spring, Trigg, Ky	71
Roaring Spring, Blair, Pa	100
Robard's Station, Henderson, Ky	12
Robbinston, Washington, Me	120
Robbinsville, Mercer, N. J	27
Robbinsville, Red River, Tex	8
Rob Camp, Claiborne, Tenn	12
Robella, Allegheny, Pa	23
Roberson's Cross Roads, Bledsoe, Tenn	18
Roberts' Landing, St. Clair, Mich	29
Robertson's, Anderson, Tenn	12
Robertson's Mill, Stone, Mo	5
Robertson's Station, Harrison, Ky	32
Robertsonville, Hardin, Ky	97
Robertsonville, Calhoun, Miss	12
Robertsonville, Sullivan, N. Y	20
Robertsville, Litchfield, Conn	68
Robertsville, Stark, Ohio	32
Robertsville, Anderson, Tenn	15
Robeson, Brunswick, N. C	16

* Money-order office.

Robeson, Berks, Pa	$12
Robesonia Furnaces, Berks, Pa	140
Robeystown, Prince George's, Md	47
Robin, Benton, Iowa	21
Robin's Nest, Peoria, Ill	58
Robinson, (c. h.,) Crawford, Ill	230
Robinson, Brown, Kans	93
Robinson, Ottawa, Mich	24
Robinson, Brown, Wis	16
Robinson Creek, Pike, Ky	5
Robinson's Mills, Menard, Ill	24
Robisonville, Bedford, Pa	10
Rob Roy, Jefferson, Ark	12
Rob Roy, Fountain, Ind	44
Robtown, Pickaway, Ohio	8
Roby's Corner, Merrimack, N. H	46
Roche-a-Cri, Adams, Wis	13
Rochdale, Worcester, Mass	300
Rochelle,* Ogle, Ill	1,100
Rochelle, Madison, Va	45
Rocheport, Boone, Mo	380
Rochester, Sangamon, Ill	450
Rochester, (c. h.,)* Fulton, Ind	500
Rochester, Cedar, Iowa	80
Rochester, Neosho, Kans	12
Rochester, Butler, Ky	66
Rochester, Plymouth, Mass	120
Rochester, Oakland, Mich	330
Rochester, (c. h.,)* Olmsted, Minn	2,800
Rochester, Andrew, Mo	110
Rochester, Madison, Mont	12
Rochester, Strafford, N. H	690
Rochester, (c. h.,)* Monroe, N. Y	4,000
Rochester, Beaver, Pa	920
Rochester, Windsor, Vt	360
Rochester,* Racine, Wis	210
Rochester Depot, Lorain, Ohio	170
Rochester Mills, Wabash, Ill	27
Rock, Pope, Ill	3
Rock, Cerro Gordo, Iowa	10
Rock, Cowley, Kans	12
Rock, Plymouth, Mass	77
Rock, Schuylkill, Pa	12
Rockabema, Aroostook, Me	4
Rockaway, Morris, N. J	570
Rockaway, Queens, N. Y	54
Rock Bluff, Liberty, Fla	5
Rock Bluff, Cass, Nebr	110
Rock Bottom, Middlesex, Mass	110
Rockbridge, Greene, Ill	68
Rock Bridge, Monroe, Ky	12
Rockbridge, Ozark, Mo	12
Rockbridge, Hocking, Ohio	24
Rockbridge, Richland, Wis	30
Rockbridge Baths, Rockbridge, Va	37
Rock Butte, Douglas, Colo	9
Rock Camp, Lawrence, Ohio	10
Rock Castle, Patrick, Va	12
Rock Castle, Mason, W. Va	4
Rock Cave, Upshur, W. Va	37
Rock City, Dutchess, N. Y	64
Rock City Falls, Saratoga, N. Y	150
Rock Creek, Clark, Ark	12
Rock Creek, Butte, Cal	44
Rock Creek, Carroll, Ill	23
Rock Creek, Mitchell, Iowa	18
Rock Creek, Lyon, Kans	$12
Rock Creek, Alamance, N. C	6
Rock Dale, Dubuque, Iowa	80
Rock Dale, Owen, Ky	12
Rockdale, Chenango, N. Y	96
Rock Dale Mills, Berkshire, Mass	12
Rockdale Mills, Jefferson, Pa	69
Rock Dam, Falls, Tex	16
Rock Dell, Olmsted, Minn	52
Rock Elm, Pierce, Wis	24
Rock Elm Centre, Pierce, Wis	58
Rock Falls, Whitesides, Ill	570
Rock Falls, Huron, Mich	85
Rock Falls, Dunn, Wis	77
Rock Farm, Russell, Va	17
Rockfield, Carroll, Ind	120
Rockfield, Warren, Ky	43
Rock Fish, Duplin, N. C	3
Rockfish Depot, Nelson, Va	88
Rockford, (c. h.,) Coosa, Ala	38
Rockford, (c. h.,)* Winnebago, Ill	3,600
Rockford, Jackson, Ind	53
Rockford, Floyd, Iowa	210
Rockford, Bourbon, Kan	10
Rockford,* Kent, Mich	400
Rockford, Wright, Minn	140
Rock Ford, Lincoln, Mo	12
Rockford, Surry, N. C	20
Rockford, Blount, Tenn	40
Rockford, Harrison, W. Va	22
Rock Grove, Stephenson, Ill	72
Rock Grove City, Floyd, Iowa	54
Rock Hall, Kent, Md	65
Rock Haven, Meade, Ky	37
Rock Hill, St. Louis, Mo	28
Rock Hill, York, S. C	370
Rockhold's, Whitley, Ky	4
Rockhouse, (c. h.,) Menifee, Ky	7
Rock House, Hocking, Ohio	12
Rock House Prairie, Buchanan, Mo	46
Rockingham, (c. h.,) Richmond, N. C	300
Rockingham, Windham, Vt	80
Rock Island, (c. h.,)* Rock Island, Ill	2,800
Rock Island, Perry, Ind	12
Rock Island, White, Tenn	12
Rock Lake, Wayne, Pa	11
Rockland, New Haven, Conn	8
Rockland, Lake, Ill	38
Rockland, (c. h.,)* Knox, Me	2,500
Rockland, Ontonagon, Mich	500
Rockland, Sullivan, N. Y	69
Rockland, Venango, Pa	81
Rockland, Providence, R. I	76
Rockland Lake, Rockland, N. Y	81
Rockland Mills, Metcalfe, Ky	20
Rock Lick, Breckinridge, Ky	12
Rock Lick, Marshall, W. Va	29
Rocklin, Placer, Cal	150
Rock Mills, Randolph, Ala	46
Rock Mills, Anderson, S. C	8
Rock Mills, Rappahannock, Va	12
Rock Oak, Athens, Ohio	12
Rock Point, Jackson, Oreg	51
Rock Point, Beaver, Pa	140
Rockport, (c. h.,) Hot Spring, Ark	59
Rockport, Pike, Ill	72

* Money-order office.

Post office	Compensation
*Rockport,** (*c. h.,*) Spencer, Ind	$800
Rockport, Ohio, Ky	14
Rockport, Knox, Me	420
Rockport, Essex, Mass	740
Rockport, Copiah, Miss	10
*Rockport,** (*c. h.,*) Atchison, Mo	360
Rockport, Cuyahoga, Ohio	160
Rockport, Carbon, Pa	44
Rockport, Refugio, Tex	210
Rockport, Wood, W. Va	18
Rock Prairie, Dade, Mo	12
Rock Prairie, Rock, Wis	25
Rock Rift, Delaware, N. Y	54
Rock River, Rock, Wis	12
Rock Run, Stephenson, Ill	120
Rocksburgh, Warren, N. J	16
Rock Spring, Chickasaw N., Ind. T.	12
Rock Spring, Walker, Ga	12
Rock Spring, Washington, Mo	8
Rock Spring, Orange, N. C	12
Rock Spring, Centre, Pa	89
Rock Spring, Patrick, Va	5
Rock Springs, Cecil, Md	61
Rock Stream, Yates, N. Y	60
Rockton, Winnebago, Ill	380
Rockton, Clearfield, Pa	62
Rockton, Vernon, Wis	12
Rock Valley, Redwood, Minn	12
Rock View, Wyoming, W. Va	5
Rockville, Jefferson, Ala	40
Rockville,* Tolland, Conn	2,000
Rockville, Kankakee, Ill	24
*Rockville,** (*c. h.,*) Parke, Ind	800
Rockville, Miami, Kans	39
Rockville, Knox, Me	40
*Rockville,** (*c. h.,*) Montgomery, Md.	380
Rockville, Norfolk, Mass	100
Rockville, Stearns, Minn	4
Rockville, Chester, Pa	51
Rockville, Washington, R. I	42
Rockville, Kane, Utah	20
Rockville, Hanover, Va	12
Rockville, Grant, Wis	47
Rockville Centre, Queens, N. Y	110
Rockwall, Kaufman, Tex	140
Rockwood, Randolph, Ill	130
Rockwood, Fulton, N. Y	100
Rockwood, Roane, Tenn	95
Rocky Bar, (*c. h.,*) Alturas, Idaho	150
Rocky Brook, Washington, R. I	66
Rocky Comfort, (*c. h.,*) Little River, Ark	50
Rocky Comfort, Newton, Mo	50
Rocky Ford, Scriven, Ga	12
Rocky Ford, Pontotoc, Miss	12
Rocky Fork, Licking, Ohio	12
Rocky Gap, Bland, Va	14
Rocky Glade, Iron, Mo	12
Rocky Head, Dale, Ala	12
Rocky Hill, Hartford, Conn	140
Rocky Hill, Somerset, N. J	240
Rocky Hill, Jackson, Ohio	28
Rocky Hill, Fayette, W. Va	6
Rocky Hill Station, Edmonson, Ky.	92
Rocky Mount, Meriwether, Ga	19
Rocky Mount, Bossier, La	12

Post office	Compensation
Rocky Mount, Miller, Mo	$15
Rocky Mount, Edgecombe, N. C	410
Rocky Mount, (*c. h.,*) Franklin, Va	150
Rocky Point, New Hanover, N. C	12
Rocky River, Warren, Tenn	12
Rocky Run, McLeod, Minn	9
Rocky Run, Columbia, Wis	30
Rocky Springs, Claiborne, Miss	12
Rocky Station, Lee, Va	10
Rodman, Jefferson, N. Y	220
Rodney, Jefferson, Miss	520
Rodney, Gallia, Ohio	29
Ro Ellen, Dyer, Tenn	12
Roesburgh, Grant, Ind	10
Roesville, Queen Anne, Md	86
Rogers, Ritchie, W. Va	140
Rogersville, Lauderdale, Ala	40
Rogersville, Henry, Ind	25
Rogersville, Tuscarawas, Ohio	73
Rogersville, Greene, Pa	14
*Rogersville,** (*c. h.,*) Hawkins, Tenn.	360
Rohrersville, Washington, Md	52
Rohrsburgh, Columbia, Pa	67
Rokeby, Morgan, Ohio	40
Roland, White, Ill	39
Roland, Story, Iowa	12
Roland, Centre, Pa	30
Rolesville, Wake, N. C	21
Rolfe, (*c. h.,*) Pocahontas, Iowa	83
*Rolla,** (*c. h.,*) Phelps, Mo	1,100
Rollersville, Sandusky, Ohio	67
Rollin, Lenawee, Mich	62
Rolling Fork, Pope, Minn	12
Rolling Hill, Charlotte, Va	8
Rolling Home, Randolph, Mo	5
Rolling Prairie, Marion, Ark	64
Rolling Prairie, La Porte, Ind	220
Rolling Prairie, Dodge, Wis	140
Rolling Stone, Winona, Minn	24
Rollinsburgh, Monroe, W. Va	16
Rollo, Iosco, Mich	5
Roma, Starr, Tex	20
Romance, Vernon, Wis	4
*Rome,** (*c. h.,*) Floyd, Ga	3,200
Rome, Peoria, Ill	67
Rome, Perry, Ind	110
Rome, Henry, Iowa	76
Rome, Kennebec, Me	51
Rome, Lenawee, Mich	99
Rome, Winston, Miss	12
*Rome,** (*c. h.,*) Oneida, N. Y	2,800
Rome, Ashtabula, Ohio	61
Rome, Bradford, Pa	180
Rome, Smith, Tenn	37
Rome, Jefferson, Wis	65
Rome City, Noble, Ind	190
Romeo,* Macomb, Mich	1,100
Romeo, Greene, Tenn	8
Romine's Mills, Harrison, W. Va	31
Romney, Tippecanoe, Ind	89
Romney, (*c. h.,*) Hampshire, W. Va	330
Romulus, Tuscaloosa, Ala	6
Romulus, Wayne, Mich	28
Romulus, Seneca, N. Y	200
Romulus Centre, Seneca, N. Y	12
Rondo, La Fayette, Ark	72

* Money-order office.

Rondo, Polk, Mo	$41
Rondout,* Ulster, N. Y	2,600
Roney, Hickory, Mo	7
Ronkonkoma, Suffolk, N. Y	100
Rono, Perry, Ind	18
Rook's Creek, Livingston, Ill	14
Root, Allen, Ind	41
Root, Montgomery, N. Y	83
Root Creek, Milwaukee, Wis	23
Root River, Mower, Minn	9
Rootstown, Portage, Ohio	110
Rootville, Antrim, Mich	19
Roperville, Gage, Nebr	12
Rosalia, Butler, Kans	12
Rosaryville, Prince George's, Md	12
Rosby's Rock, Marshall, W. Va	38
Roscoe,* Winnebago, Ill	300
Roscoe, Goodhue, Minn	17
Roscoe, St. Clair, Mo	190
Roscoe, Coshocton, Ohio	290
Roscoe Centre, Goodhue, Minn	20
Roscommon, Monroe, Pa	6
Rose, Woodson, Kans	12
Rose, Oakland, Mich	24
Rose, Wayne, N. Y	240
Roseberry, Knox, Tenn	10
Roseboom, Otsego, N. Y	50
Rose Bud, White, Ark	10
Rose Bud, Pope. Ill	12
*Roseburgh,** (*c. h.,*) Douglas, Oreg	420
Roseburgh, Perry, Pa	11
Rosecrans, Lake, Ill	28
Rosecrans, Clinton, Pa	12
Rosecrans, Manitowoc, Wis	23
Rose Creek, Mower, Minn	12
Rose Creek, Jefferson, Nebr	22
Rosedale, Parke, Ind	77
Rosedale, Iberville, La	30
Rosedale, Pasquotank, N. C	12
Rosedale, Madison, Ohio	12
Rosedale, Greene, Pa	18
Rosedale, Russell, Va	23
Rosefield, Peoria, Ill	160
Rose Grove, Hamilton, Iowa	12
Rose Head, (*c. h.,*) Taylor, Fla	12
Rose Hill, Covington, Ala	6
Rose Hill, Ouachita, Ark	12
Rose Hill, Jasper, Ill	13
Rose Hill, Kosciusko, Ind	6
Rose Hill, Mercer, Ky	12
Rose Hill, Neosho, Kans	12
Rose Hill, Johnson, Mo	12
Rose Hill, Seneca, N. Y	43
Ross Hill. Darke, Ohio	27
Rose Hill, Harris, Tex	16
Rose Hill, Lee, Va	12
Rose Lake, Martin, Minn	9
Roselle, Union, N. J	12
Rosemond, Christian, Ill	300
Rose Mount, Warren, Iowa	15
Rosemount, Dakota, Minn	100
Rosendale, Andrew, Mo	12
Rosendale, Ulster, N. Y	140
Rosendale, Fond du Lac, Wis	200
Rosenhayn, Cumberland, N. J	12
Rose Point, Lawrence, Pa	46
Rose's Valley, Lycoming, Pa	$15
Rose Vale, Clay, Kans	12
Roseville, Franklin, Ark	24
Roseville, Placer, Cal	61
Roseville, Warren, Ill	270
Roseville, Parke, Ind	36
Roseville, Barren, Ky	5
Roseville, Macomb, Mich	82
Roseville, Monongalia, Minn	24
Roseville, Muskingum, Ohio	170
Rosewood, Cleburne, Ala	12
Rosewood, Harrison, Ind	12
Rosiclare, Hardin, Ill	26
Rosindale, Bladen, N. C	53
Roslin, Cumberland, N. C	12
Roslindale, Norfolk, Mass.	12
Roslyn, Queens, N. Y	310
Ross, Lake, Ind	28
Ross, Butler, Ohio	150
Ross, Anderson, Tenn	27
Ross' Corners, York, Me	22
Rosseau, Morgan, Ohio	12
Ross Fork, Oneida, Idaho	12
Ross Grove, De Kalb, Ill	17
Rossie, St. Lawrence, N. Y	130
Rossland, Monroe, Pa	2
Rosston, Armstrong, Pa	16
Rossville, Vermilion, Ill	150
Rossville, Clinton, Ind	160
Rossville, Allamakee, Iowa	88
Rossville, Shawnee, Kans	77
Rossville, Baltimore, Md	120
Rossville, Richmond, N. Y	200
Rossville, Darke, Ohio	12
Rossville, York, Pa	36
Rossville, Chester, S. C	6
Rossville, Fayette, Tenn	140
Rossville, Fayette, Tex	11
Rostraver, Westmoreland, Pa	27
Roswell, Cobb, Ga	200
Rothrock's Mills, Harrison, Ind	4
Rothsville, Lancaster, Pa	20
Rothville, Chariton, Mo	12
Roubidoux, Texas, Mo	9
Rough and Ready, Nevada, Cal	180
Rough and Ready, Anderson, Ky	54
Rough and Ready, Schuylkill, Pa	4
Rough and Ready Furnace, Stewart, Tenn	12
Rough Creek, Laurel, Ky	12
Roulette, Potter, Pa	27
Round Bottom, Monroe, Ohio	24
Round Bottom, Wayne, W. Va	12
Round Grove, Whitesides, Ill	72
Round Grove, Scott, Iowa	40
Round Head, Hardin, Ohio	54
Round Hill, Fairfield, Conn	78
Round Hill, Orange, N. C	2
Round Hill, Adams, Pa	36
Round Hill, Loudoun, Va	34
Round Island, Clinton, Pa	88
Round Knob, Putnam, W. Va	21
Round Lake, Branch, Mich	2
Round Lake, Gonzales, Tex	12
Round Mountain, Blanco, Tex	23
Round Pond, Lincoln, Me	230

* Money-order office.

Round Prairie, Todd, Minn	$10
Round Prairie, Vernon, Mo	17
Round Rock, Williamson, Tex	100
Round Top, Wilson, Tenn	8
Round Top, Fayette, Tex	180
Round Valley, Plumas, Cal	16
Rouse's Point,* Clinton, N. Y	1,000
Rouseville,* Venango, Pa	1,900
Rousseau, Brown, Wis	5
Rover, Yell, Ark	12
Rowan Mills, Rowan, N. C	1
Rowayton, Fairfield, Conn	140
Rowe, Franklin, Mass	56
Rowes, Crawford, Wis	4
Rowe's Pump, Orangeburgh, S. C	6
Rowland, Isabella, Mich	6
Rowland, Pike, Pa	62
Rowland Mills, Hunterdon, N. J	11
Rowlandsville, Cecil, Md	110
Rowlesburgh, Preston, W. Va	180
Rowletta, Pettis, Mo	130
Rowlett's Depot, Hart, Ky	24
Rowley, Essex, Mass	180
Rows, Ashland, Ohio	90
Roxabell, Ross, Ohio	110
Roxalana, Roane, W. Va	9
Roxana, Sussex, Del	32
Roxana, Eaton, Mich	12
Roxanna, Paulding, Ga	12
Roxborough, (c. h.,) Person, N. C	94
Roxbury, Litchfield, Conn	130
Roxbury, Oxford, Me	10
Roxbury, Delaware, N. Y	210
Roxbury, Morgan, Ohio	19
Roxbury, Franklin, Pa	52
Roxbury, Washington, Vt	210
Roxbury, Dane, Wis	15
Roxbury Mills, Howard, Md	18
Roxobel, Bertie, N. C	51
Roxton, Lamar, Tex	8
Royal Centre, Cass, Ind	150
Royal Oak, Talbot, Md	110
Royal Oak, Oakland, Mich	150
Royal Oak, Paulding, Ohio	37
Royalston, Worcester, Mass	160
Royalton, Boone, Ind	32
Royalton, Russell, Ky	2
Royalton, Niagara, N. Y	56
Royalton, Fairfield, Ohio	46
Royalton, Crawford, Pa	24
Royalton, Windsor, Vt	320
Royalton, Waupaca, Wis	52
Royer's Ford, Montgomery, Pa	260
Royerton, Delaware, Ind	23
Roysfield, Somerset, N. J	22
Royston, Pike, Ark	10
Rozetta, Henderson, Ill	59
Rubicon, Dodge, Wis	130
Ruby, St. Clair, Mich	50
Ruby Valley, Elko, Nev	68
Ruckersville, Elbert, Ga	23
Ruckersville, Tippah, Miss	8
Ruckersville, Green, Va	40
Ruckerville, Clark, Ky	9
Rucksville, Lehigh, Pa	27
Rudd, Floyd, Iowa	12
Ruddel's Mills, Bourbon, Ky	$34
Rudd's Mills, Monroe, Wis	12
Rudolph, Le Sueur, Minn	20
Rudyville, Hidalgo, Tex	12
Ruff Creek, Greene, Pa	17
Ruffin, Rockingham, N. C	85
Ruggles, Ashland, Ohio	51
Rulo,* Richardson, Nebr	240
Ruma, Randolph, Ill	50
Rumford, Oxford, Me	54
Rumford Centre, Oxford, Me	93
Rumford Point, Oxford, Me	58
Rummerfield Creek, Bradford, Pa	61
Rumney, Grafton, N. H	330
Rumsey, McLean, Ky	42
Rundell's, Crawford, Pa	22
Running Creek, Douglas, Colo	12
Rupert, Columbia, Pa	150
Rupert, Bennington, Vt	590
Rural, Rock Island, Ill	24
Rural, Linn, Iowa	5
Rural, Waupaca, Wis	110
Rural Dale, Grundy, Mo	31
Rural Dale, Muskingum, Ohio	80
Rural Dale, Upshur, W. Va	12
Rural Hill, Jefferson, N. Y	65
Rural Hill, Wilson, Tenn	9
Rural Retreat, Coles, Ill	12
Rural Retreat, Wythe, Va	170
Rural Ridge, Allegheny, Pa	12
Rural Shade, Navarro, Tex	20
Rural Vale, Lapeer, Mich	10
Rural Valley, Armstrong, Pa	75
Rush, Jo Daviess, Ill	20
Rush, Monroe, N. Y	99
Rush, Tuscarawas, Ohio	16
Rush, Susquehanna, Pa	78
Rushbottom, Holt, Mo	8
Rush City, Chisago, Minn	12
Rush Creek, Union, Ohio	20
Rush Creek, Navarro, Tex	32
Rushford,* Fillmore, Minn	800
Rushford, Allegany, N. Y	440
Rush Four Corners, Susquehanna, Pa	10
Rush Lake, Palo Alto, Iowa	12
Rush Lake, Otter Tail, Minn	12
Rush River, Sibley, Minn	10
Rush Run, Jefferson, Ohio	86
Rush Run, Ritchie, W. Va	12
Rushsylvania, Logan, Ohio	240
Rushtown, Northumberland, Pa	3
Rushville, (c. h.,)* Schuyler, Ill	870
Rushville, (c. h.,)* Rush, Ind	960
Rushville, Buchanan, Mo	99
Rushville, Yates, N. Y	400
Rushville, Fairfield, Ohio	110
Rushville, Susquehanna, Pa	63
Rusk, Surry, N. C	3
Rusk, (c. h.,) Cherokee, Tex	250
Russell, Lucas, Iowa	130
Russell, Hampden, Mass	170
Russell, St. Lawrence, N. Y	220
Russell, Geauga, Ohio	20
Russell, Sheboygan, Wis	20
Russell Hill, Wyoming, Pa	27

* Money-order office.

Russellsburgh, Warren, Pa	$91
Russell's Hill, Shannon, Mo	5
Russell's Mills, Parke, Ind	16
Russell's Place, Lawrence, Ohio	21
Russell's Station, Highland, Ohio	64
Russellville, (c. h.,) Franklin, Ala	72
Russellville, Pope, Ark	150
Russellville, Monroe, Ga	20
Russellville, Lawrence, Ill	59
Russellville, Putnam, Ind	84
Russellville, (c. h.,)* Logan, Ky	1,100
Russellville, Cole, Mo	28
Russellville, Brown, Ohio	100
Russellville, Chester, Pa	72
Russellville, Jefferson, Tenn	230
Russellville, Fayette, W. Va	12
Russia, Herkimer, N. Y	64
Russia, Shelby, Ohio	23
Russiaville, Howard, Ind	82
Rutersville, Fayette, Tex	110
Ruth, Texas, Mo	12
Rutherford Depot, Gibson, Tenn	310
Rutherford Park, Bergen, N. J	280
Rutherfordton, (c. h.,) Rutherford, N. C	370
Ruther Glen, Caroline, Va	94
Rutland, Humboldt, Iowa	16
Rutland, Harrison, Ky	4
Rutland, Anne Arundel, Md	41
Rutland, Worcester, Mass	160
Rutland, Martin, Minn	10
Rutland, Jefferson, N. Y	79
Rutland, Meigs, Ohio	110
Rutland, Tioga, Pa	63
Rutland, (c. h.,)* Rutland, Vt	2,400
Rutland, Dane, Wis	58
Rutledge, (c. h.,) Crenshaw, Ala	21
Rutledge, Morgan, Ga	97
Rutledge, (c. h.,) Grainger, Tenn	80
Ryan, Kewaunee, Wis	12
Ryan Creek, Winston, Ala	19
Ryan's Well, Prentiss, Miss	12
Rye, Rockingham, N. H	69
Rye, Westchester, N. Y	740
Ryegate, Caledonia, Vt	69
Ryerson's Station, Greene, Pa	38
Rye Valley, Baker, Oreg	12
Rye Valley, Smyth, Va	8
Ryland's Depot, Greenville, Va	6
Rynex's Corners, Schenectady, N. Y	10

S.

Sabattus, Androscoggin, Me	210
Sabbath Rest, Blair, Pa	52
Sabbot Island, Goochland, Va	12
Sabetha, Nemaha, Kans	34
Sabillisville, Frederick, Md	41
Sabina, Clinton, Ohio	130
Sabinal, Socorro, N. Mex	12
Sabinal, Uvalde, Tex	12
Sabine Pass, Jefferson, Tex	63
Sabinetown, Sabine, Tex	16
Sabinsville, Tioga, Pa	26
Sabula,* Jackson, Iowa	660
Saccarappa, Cumberland, Me	470
Sac City, (c. h.,) Sac, Iowa	$110
Sacket's Harbor,* Jefferson, N. Y	750
Saco,* York, Me	2,100
Sacramento. White, Ill	37
Sacramento, McLean, Ky	60
Sacramento, Wright, Mo	12
Sacramento, Schuylkill, Pa	14
SACRAMENTO CITY,* *(c. h.,)* Sacramento, Cal	4,000
Sacred Heart, Renville, Minn	8
Sadawga, Windham, Vt	71
Saddle River, Bergen, N. J	44
Saddler's Creek, Anderson, S. C	14
Sadowa, Randolph, Ill	12
Sadsburyville, Chester, Pa	44
Saegerstown, Crawford, Pa	190
Saegersville, Lehigh, Pa	26
Safe Harbor, Lancaster, Pa	82
Sagetown, Henderson, Ill	180
Sageville, (c. h.,) Hamilton, N. Y	28
Sag Harbor,* Suffolk, N. Y	1,200
Saginaw, (c. h.,)* Saginaw, Mich	2,800
Sago, Muskingum, Ohio	110
Sago, Upshur, W. Va	6
Sagone, Du Page, Ill	22
Saguache, (c. h.,) Saguache, Colo	31
Saidora, Mason, Ill	12
Saint Albans, Hancock, Ill	6
Saint Albans, Somerset, Me	230
Saint Albans, (c. h.,)* Franklin, Vt	2,400
Saint Albans Bay, Franklin, Vt	82
Saint Andrew's, Orange, N. Y	62
Saint Anna, Calumet, Wis	55
Saint Anne, Kankakee, Ill	100
Saint Annie, Pulaski, Mo	26
Saint Ansgar, Mitchell, Iowa	220
Saint Anthony's Falls,* Hennepin, Minn	1,700
Saint Aubert's, Callaway, Mo	18
Saint Augusta, Stearns, Minn	22
Saint Augustine, (c. h.,)* St. John's, Fla	950
Saint Augustine, Knox, Ill	99
Saint Augustine, Cecil, Md	42
Saint Augustine, Cambria, Pa	90
Saint Benedict, Doniphan, Kans	12
Saint Bernard, (c. h.,) St. Bernard, La	6
Saint Bernice, Vermillion, Ind	14
Saint Bethlehem, Montgomery, Tenn	12
Saint Bonifacius, Hennepin, Minn	30
Saint Bonifacius, Cambria, Pa	12
Saint Bridget, Marshall, Kans	5
Saint Catharine, Linn, Mo	280
Saint Charles, Arkansas, Ark	69
Saint Charles, Pueblo, Colo	12
Saint Charles,* Kane, Ill	900
Saint Charles, Madison, Iowa	130
Saint Charles, (c. h.,) St. Charles, La	13
Saint Charles, Saginaw, Mich	390
Saint Charles,* Winona, Minn	890
Saint Charles, (c. h.,)* St. Charles, Mo	1,700
Saint Charles, Cuming, Nebr	56
Saint Charles, Butler, Ohio	10
Saint Charles, (c. h.,) Rich, Utah	15
Saint Clair, Monona, Iowa	8

* Money-order office.

Post office	Amount
*Saint Clair,** (*c. h.,*) St. Clair, Mich	$1,000
Saint Clair, Franklin, Mo	250
Saint Clair, Columbiana, Ohio	13
Saint Clair,* Schuylkill, Pa	890
*Saint Clairsville,** (*c. h.,*) Belmont, Ohio	630
Saint Clairsville, Bedford, Pa	120
Saint Clement's Bay, St. Mary's, Md	29
Saint Cloud, Heard, Ga	10
*Saint Cloud,** (*c. h.,*) Stearns, Minn	1,700
Saint Cloud, Scott, Mo	12
Saint Cloud, Fond du Lac, Wis	12
Saint Croix Falls, Polk, Wis	270
Saint David, Fulton, Ill	37
Saint Denis, Baltimore, Md	120
Saint Deroin, Nemaha, Nebr	88
Saint Donatus, Jackson, Iowa	87
Saint Elmo, Fayette, Ill	74
Saint Elmo, Christian, Ky	10
Saint Elmo, Allegheny, Pa	10
Saint Francis, Anoka, Minn	68
Saint Francis Station, Milwaukee, Wis	330
Saint Francisville, Lawrence, Ill	46
*Saint Francisville,** (*c. h.,*) W. Feliciana, La	670
Saint Francisville, Clarke, Mo	97
Saint Frederick, Nemaha, Nebr	13
Saint Gabriel, Iberville, La	72
Saint Genevieve, (*c. h.,*) St. Genevieve, Mo	330
Saint George, Kankakee, Ill	8
Saint George, Pottawatomie, Kans	120
Saint George, Knox, Me	59
Saint George, McLeod, Minn	12
Saint George, (*c. h.,*) Washington, Utah	440
Saint George, Chittenden, Vt	150
Saint George, (*c. h.,*) Tucker, W. Va	47
Saint George's, New Castle, Del	350
Saint George's, Colleton, S. C	73
Saint Helen, (*c. h.,*) Columbia, Oreg	150
Saint Helena, Napa, Cal	290
Saint Helena, (*c. h.,*) Cedar, Nebr	62
Saint Henry, Le Sueur, Minn	12
Saint Henry's, Mercer, Ohio	38
Saint Hubertus, Le Sueur, Minn	21
Saint Inigoes, St. Mary's, Md	54
Saint Jacob, Madison, Ill	87
Saint James, (*c. h.,*) Manitou, Mich	12
Saint James, Phelps, Mo	190
Saint James, Cedar, Nebr	54
Saint James, Suffolk, N. Y	98
Saint John, Bradley, Ark	14
Saint John, Colusa, Cal	18
Saint John, Perry, Ill	120
Saint John, Lake, Ind	38
Saint John, Harrison, Iowa	32
Saint John, Putnam, Mo	42
Saint John, Hertford, N. C	6
*Saint John's,** (*c. h.,*) Clinton, Mich	1,700
Saint John's, Auglaize, Ohio	53
Saint John's, Stewart, Tenn	12
Saint Johnsburgh, Niagara, N. Y	20
*Saint Johnsbury,** (*c. h.,*) Caledonia, Vt	2,100

Post office	Amount
Saint Johnsbury Centre, Caledonia, Vt	$210
Saint Johnsbury East, Caledonia, Vt	160
Saint Johnsville, Montgomery, N.Y	720
Saint Joseph, Pah Ute, Ariz	44
Saint Joseph, Pembina, Dak	10
Saint Joseph, Vanderburgh, Ind	8
Saint Joseph,* Berrien, Mich	1,400
Saint Joseph, Stearns, Minn	180
*Saint Joseph,** (*c. h.,*) Buchanan, Mo	4,000
Saint Joseph, Susquehanna, Pa	22
Saint Joseph's, Champaign, Ill	62
Saint Joseph's, (*c. h.,*) Tensas, La	40
Saint Joseph's College, Perry, Ohio	36
Saint Joseph's Hill, Clarke, Ind	11
Saint Lawrence, Scott, Minn	39
Saint Lawrence, Jefferson, N. Y	97
Saint Lawrence, Chatham, N. C	28
Saint Lawrence, Cambria, Pa	12
Saint Lawrence, Washington, Wis	160
Saint Leger, Ozark, Mo	7
Saint Leon, Dearborn, Ind	25
Saint Leonard's, Calvert, Md	16
Saint Louis, Sierra, Cal	59
Saint Louis, Miami, Kans	15
Saint Louis, Gratiot, Mich	240
*Saint Louis,** (*c. h.,*) St. Louis, Mo	4,000
Saint Louis, Jefferson, Mont	12
Saint Louis, Marion, Oreg	30
Saint Louis Crossing, Bartholomew, Ind	65
Saint Louisville, Licking, Ohio	91
Saint Lucie, (*c. h.,*) Brevard, Fla	12
Saint Margaret's, Anne Arundel, Md	25
Saint Marie, Jasper, Ill	77
Saint Mark's, Wakulla, Fla	83
Saint Mark's, Randolph, Ill	12
Saint Martin's, Worcester, Md	17
Saint Martin's, Morgan, Mo	54
Saint Martin's, Brown, Ohio	140
Saint Martin's, Milwaukee, Wis	55
Saint Martinville, (*c. h.,*) St. Martin's, La	120
Saint Mary's, Huerfano, Colo	12
Saint Mary's, Camden, Ga	190
Saint Mary's, Vigo, Ind	150
Saint Mary's, Marion, Ky	120
Saint Mary's, St. Genevieve, Mo	100
Saint Mary's,* Auglaize, Ohio	720
Saint Mary's, Elk, Pa	850
Saint Mary's, Refugio, Tex	85
Saint Mary's, (*c.h.,*) Pleasants, W. Va	8
Saint Mary's, Monroe, Wis	34
Saint Mary's Mission, Pottawatomie, Kans	160
Saint Matthew's, Jefferson, Ky	24
Saint Matthew's, Orangeburgh, S. C	100
Saint Maurice, Decatur, Ind	19
Saint Maurice, Winn, La	8
Saint Meinrad, Spencer, Ind	54
Saint Michael's, Talbot, Md	230
Saint Michael's, Wright, Minn	25
Saint Morgan, Madison, Ill	25
Saint Nazians, Manitowoc, Wis	12
Saint Nicholas, Atchison, Kans	12
Saint Nicholas, Schuylkill, Pa	420

* Money-order office.

Saint Omer, Coles, Ill	$14
Saint Omer, Decatur, Ind	60
Saint Paris, Champaign, Ohio	310
Saint Paul, Madison, Ark	13
Saint Paul, Decatur, Ind	260
Saint Paul, Lee, Iowa	44
Saint Paul, Montgomery, Kans	12
SAINT PAUL,* (*c. h.,*) Ramsey, Minn	4,000
Saint Paul's, Robeson, N. C	12
Saint Paul's, Pickaway, Ohio	33
*Saint Peter,** (*c. h.,*) Nicollet, Minn	1,200
Saint Peter's, Franklin, Ind	24
Saint Peter's, St. Landry, La	12
Saint Peter's, St. Charles, Mo	61
Saint Peter's, Chester, Pa	39
Saint Petersburgh, Clarion, Pa	13
Saint Rose, Grant, Wis	31
Saint Sebald, Clayton, Iowa	64
Saint Stephen's Church, King and Queen, Va	50
Saint Stephen's Depot, Charleston, S. C	100
Saint Tammany's, Mecklenburgh, Va	24
Saint Thomas, (*c. h.,*) Pah Ute, Ariz	39
Saint Thomas, Cole, Mo	44
Saint Thomas, Franklin, Pa	120
Saint Vrain, Weld, Colo	10
Saint Wendell's, Posey, Ind	36
Sakeville, Randolph, Ill	17
Salado, Bell, Tex	190
Salamanca, Cattaraugus, N. Y	560
Salamonia, Jay, Ind	48
Sale Creek, Hamilton, Tenn	16
Salem, Lee, Ala	240
Salem, New London, Conn	170
Salem, Walker, Ga	12
*Salem,** (*c. h.,*) Marion, Ill	1,400
*Salem,** (*c. h.,*) Washington, Ind	750
Salem,* Henry, Iowa	490
Salem, Livingston, Ky	63
Salem, Franklin, Me	38
Salem, Dorchester, Md	17
*Salem,** (*c. h.,*) Essex, Mass	3,200
Salem, Washtenaw, Mich	24
Salem, Olmsted, Minn	37
Salem, (*c. h.,*) Dent, Mo	240
Salem, Richardson, Nebr	190
Salem, Rockingham, N. H	210
*Salem,** (*c. h.,*) Salem, N. J	1,600
Salem, (*c. h.,*) Washington, N. Y	1,000
Salem,* Forsyth, N. C	920
Salem,* Columbiana, Ohio	2,400
SALEM,* (*c. h.,*) Marion, Oreg	2,000
Salem, Snyder, Pa	12
Salem, Newton, Tex	10
*Salem,** (*c. h.,*) Roanoke, Va	950
Salem, Kenosha, Wis	190
Salem Centre, Steuben, Ind	42
Salem Centre, Westchester, N. Y	43
Salem Centre, Meigs, Ohio	18
Salem Chapel, Forsyth, N. C	3
Salem Church, Randolph, N. C	4
Salem Cross Roads, Westmoreland, Pa	270
Salem Depot, Rockingham, N. H	130
Salem Fauquier, Fauquier, Va	$210
Salesville, Guernsey, Ohio	49
Salfordville, Montgomery, Pa	49
Salina, Kankakee, Ill	12
Salina, Harrison, Ind	12
Salina, Jefferson, Iowa	110
*Salina,** (*c. h.,*) Saline, Kans	1,100
Salina, Onondaga, N. Y	780
Salina, Athens, Ohio	120
Salina, Westmoreland, Pa	37
Salinas, Monterey, Cal	150
Saline, Bienville, La	6
Saline, Washtenaw, Mich	480
Saline, Mercer, Mo	14
Saline City, Saline, Mo	12
Saline Mines, Gallatin, Ill	21
Saline Valley, Saline, Kans	12
Salineville,* Columbiana, Ohio	480
Salisbury, Litchfield, Conn	240
Salisbury, Sangamon, Ill	42
*Salisbury,** (*c. h.,*) Wicomico, Md	800
Salisbury, Essex, Mass	190
Salisbury, Chariton, Mo	530
Salisbury, Merrimack, N. H	170
Salisbury, Herkimer, N. Y	110
*Salisbury,** (*c. h.,*) Rowan, N. C	1,200
Salisbury, Lancaster, Pa	21
Salisbury, Addison, Vt	120
Salisbury Centre, Herkimer, N. Y	150
Salisbury Cove, Hancock, Me	68
Salisbury Mills, Orange, N. Y	110
Salladyburgh, Lycoming, Pa	65
Salmon Brook, Aroostook, Me	19
Salmon City, (*c. h.,*) Lemhi, Idaho	12
Salmon Falls, El Dorado, Cal	24
Salmon Falls, Strafford, N. H	500
Salmon River, Oswego, N. Y	56
Saloma, Taylor, Ky	16
Salona, Clinton, Pa	140
Sal Soda, Crenshaw, Ala	6
Salt Creek, Porter, Ind	12
Salt Creek, Perry, Ky	2
Salt Creek, Chariton, Mo	87
Salt Creek, Holmes, Ohio	24
Salt Creek, Polk, Oreg	13
Salt Creek, (*c. h.,*) Juab, Utah	200
Salt Creek, Amherst, Va	45
Saltersville, Hudson, N. J	48
Saltillo, Lee, Miss	120
Saltillo, Lancaster, Nebr	15
Saltillo, Holmes, Ohio	10
Saltillo, Huntingdon, Pa	12
Saltillo, Hardin, Tenn	41
Saltillo, Hopkins, Tex	9
Saltilloville, Washington, Ind	79
SALT LAKE CITY,* (*c. h.,*) Salt Lake, Utah	3,600
Salt Lick, Clearfield, Pa	17
Salt Lick Ridge, Braxton, W. Va	11
Salt Marsh, (*c. h.,*) Republic, Kans	34
Saltpetre Cave, Botetourt, Va	16
Salt Point, Dutchess, N. Y	76
Salt River, Isabella, Mich	130
Saltsburgh, Indiana, Pa	450
Salt Springs, Howard, Kans	14
Salt Sulphur Springs, Monroe, W. Va	77

* Money-order office.

Saltville, Washington, Va	$200
Salubria, Ada, Idaho	12
Saluda, Jefferson, Ind	24
Saluda, (*c. h.*,) Middlesex, Va	48
Saluda Oldtown, Newberry, S. C	15
Salunga, Lancaster, Pa	50
Saluria, Calhoun, Tex	50
Salvisa, Mercer, Ky	150
Salyersville, (*c. h.*,) Magoffin, Ky	37
Salzburgh, Bay, Mich	51
Samantha, Highland, Ohio	12
Samaria, Johnson, Ind	36
Sammonsville, Fulton, N. Y	27
Sampson Creek, Harrison, Mo	12
Sam's Creek, Carroll, Md	35
Samsonville, Ulster, N. Y	26
Samsonville, Jackson, Ohio	100
Samsville, Edwards, Ill	30
Samuel's Depot, Nelson, Ky	53
San Anders, Milam, Tex	9
San Andreas, Calaveras, Cal	370
San Antonio, Monterey, Cal	150
San Antonio, Socorro, N. Mex	12
San Antonio,* (*c. h.*,) Bexar, Tex	3,600
San Augustine, (*c.h.*,) San Augustine, Tex	190
San Benito, Monterey, Cal	12
San Bernadino,* (*c.h.*,) San Bernardino, Cal	460
Sanborn, Niagara, N. Y	130
Sanbornton, Belknap, N. H	120
San Buenaventura, Santa Barbara, Cal	160
Sanburn, Johnson, Ill	12
Sand Bank, Oswego, N. Y	280
Sand Beach, Huron, Mich	100
Sandborn, Knox, Ind	12
Sand Brook, Hunterdon, N. J	14
Sand Creek,* Scott, Minn	280
Sand Cut, Wayne, Pa	220
Sandefer's Store, Carroll, Ky	8
Sander's Hill, Montgomery, N. C	6
Sanderson, (*c. h.*,) Baker, Fla	12
Sanders' Store, Carteret, N. C	12
Sandersville, (*c. h.*,) Washington, Ga	390
Sand Fly, Bastrop, Tex	14
Sandford, Vigo, Ind	84
Sand Fork, Gallia, Ohio	8
Sand Fork, Gilmer, W. Va	12
Sandgate, Bennington, Vt	44
Sand Hill, Lewis, Ky	18
Sand Hill, Scotland, Mo	36
Sand Hollow, Morgan, Ohio	5
San Diego, Nueces, Tex	12
Sandisfield, Berkshire, Mass	28
Sand Lake, Lake, Ill	16
Sand Lake, Kent, Mich	12
Sand Lake, Monongalia, Minn	15
Sand Lake, Rensselaer, N. Y	210
Sandoval, Marion, Ill	460
Sandown, Rockingham, N. H	24
Sand Patch, Somerset, Pa	130
Sand Point, Volusia, Fla	12
Sand Rock, Cherokee, Ala	12
Sand Spring, Delaware, Iowa	350
Sand Springs, Webster, Mo	19
Sandstone, Jackson, Mich	$75
Sand Stone, Vernon, Mo	12
Sandt's Eddy, Northampton, Pa	12
Sandusky, Lee, Iowa	370
Sandusky, Cattaraugus, N. Y	140
Sandusky,* (*c. h.*,) Erie, Ohio	3,200
Sandusky, Sauk, Wis	81
Sandwich,* DeKalb, Ill	1,200
Sandwich,* Barnstable, Mass	960
Sandwich, Carroll, N. H	87
Sandy, Columbiana, Ohio	190
Sandy, Jackson, W. Va	23
Sandy Beach, Cumberland, Me	3
Sandy Bottom, Middlesex, Va	27
Sandy Creek, Oswego, N. Y	430
Sandy Creek, Randolph, N. C	19
Sandy Creek, Crawford, Pa	10
Sandy Cross, Oglethorpe, Ga	12
Sandy Flat, Greenville, S. C	4
Sandy Ford, Madison, Fla	20
Sandy Grove, Chatham, N. C	9
Sandy Hill, Worcester, Md	47
Sandy Hill,* (*c. h.*,) Washington, N. Y	1,100
Sandy Hill, Perry, Pa	21
Sandy Hill, Henry, Tenn	13
Sandy Hook, Fairfield, Conn	390
Sandy Hook, (*c. h.*,) Elliott, Ky	12
Sandy Hook, Harford, Md	12
Sandy Hook, Rappahannock, Va	12
Sandy Lake, Mercer, Pa	230
Sandy Level, Pittsylvania, Va	12
Sandy Mush, Buncombe, N. C	6
Sandy Point, Waldo, Me	78
Sandy Point, Brazoria, Tex	12
Sandy Spring,* Montgomery, Md	370
Sandy Springs, Grant, Ark	12
Sandyville, Warren, Iowa	120
Sandyville, Tuscarawas, Ohio	35
Sanel, Mendocino, Cal	12
San Elizario, El Paso, Tex	20
San Felipe, Santa Clara, Cal	12
San Felipe, Austin, Tex	60
Sanford, York, Me	160
Sanford, Broome, N. Y	40
Sanford's Corners, Jefferson, N. Y	50
Sanfordville, Cherokee, Kans	12
San Francisco,* (*c. h.*,) San Francisco, Cal	4,000
San Gabriel, Los Angeles, Cal	19
San Gabriel, Milam, Tex	11
Sangamon Station, Macon, Ill	41
Sangerfield, Oneida, N. Y	100
Sangerville, Piscataquis, Me	100
Sangerville, Augusta, Va	28
San Jacinto, San Diego, Cal	12
San Jacinto, Jennings, Ind	11
San Jacinto, Houston, Minn	10
San José,* (*c. h.*,) Santa Clara, Cal	3,400
San José, Mason, Ill	220
San José, San Miguel, N. Mex	12
San Juan, Monterey, Cal	350
San Juan, Rio Arriba, N. Mex	12
San Leandro, (*c. h.*,) Alameda, Cal	380
San Lorenzo, Alameda, Cal	140
San Luis, (*c. h.*,) Costilla, Colo	33

* Money-order office.

San Luis Obispo, (c. h.,) San Luis Obispo, Cal	$590
San Luis Rey, San Diego, Cal	58
San Marcial, Socorro, N. Mex	12
San Marcos, San Luis Obispo, Cal	100
San Marcos, (c. h.,) Hays, Tex	250
San Marino, Dinwiddie, Va	12
San Mateo, San Mateo, Cal	210
Sannemin, Livingston, Ill	12
San Pablo, Contra Costa, Cal	95
San Patricio, (c. h.,) San Patricio, Tex	28
San Pierre, Stark, Ind	100
San Quentin, Marin, Cal	50
San Rafael, (c. h.,)* Marin, Cal	410
San Saba, (c. h.,) San Saba, Tex	74
Santa Aña, Los Angeles, Cal	12
Santa Barbara, (c. h.,)* Santa Barbara, Cal	510
Santa Clara, Santa Clara, Cal	980
Santa Claus, Spencer, Ind	34
Santa Cruz, (c. h.,)* Santa Cruz, Cal	1,100
Santa Fé, Alexander, Ill	25
Santa Fé, Miami, Ind	29
Santa Fé, Monroe, Mo	80
SANTA FÉ, *(c. h.,)* Santa Fé, N. Mex	2,000
Santa Fé, Maury, Tenn	31
Santa Margarita, San Luis Obispo, Cal	12
Santa Maria, Santa Barbara, Cal	12
Santaquin, Utah, Utah	93
Santa Rosa, (c. h.,)* Sonoma, Cal	57
Santa Rosa, Daviess, Mo	12
Santee Agency, L'Eau qui Court, Nebr	64
Santiago, Sherburne, Minn	12
Santuck, Union, S. C	57
San Ysidro, Santa Clara, Cal	12
Sappington, Anne Arundel, Md	12
Sappington, St. Louis, Mo	27
Sarah, Blair, Pa	110
Sarahsville, Williamson, Ill	6
Sarahsville, Noble, Ohio	95
Saranac, Ionia, Mich	610
Saranac, Clinton, N. Y	180
Saranac Lake, Franklin, N. Y	75
Saratoga, Santa Clara, Cal	12
Saratoga, Randolph, Ind	28
Saratoga, Howard, Iowa	13
Saratoga, Winona, Minn	71
Saratoga Springs,* Saratoga, N. Y	3,000
Sarcoxie, Jasper, Mo	310
Sardinia, Pike, Ill	17
Sardinia, Decatur, Ind	72
Sardinia, Erie, N. Y	120
Sardinia, Brown, Ohio	73
Sardis, Mason, Ky	24
Sardis, Panola, Miss	340
Sardis, Monroe, Ohio	110
Sardis, Westmoreland, Pa	60
Sardis, Harrison, W. Va	14
Sarepta, Calhoun, Miss	57
Sargent, McKean, Pa	7
Sargentville, Buena Vista, Iowa	12
Sargentsville, Hancock, Me	62
Sartwell, McKean, Pa	16
Sarverville, Butler, Pa	$37
Sarvis Point, Webster, Mo	13
Sarvis Spring, Phelps, Mo	12
Sasabi Flat, Pima, Ariz	12
Sassafras, Kent, Md	140
Sassafras Fork, Granville, N. C	18
Satartia, Yazoo, Miss	100
Satilla Mills, Camden, Ga	12
Satsop, Chehalis, Wash	12
Satterfield, Mercer, Pa	50
Satterlee's Mills, Mecosta, Mich	12
Sattler's, Comal, Tex	12
Saturn, Whitley, Ind	15
Saugatuck, Fairfield, Conn	240
Saugatuck,* Allegan, Mich	430
Saugerties, Ulster, N. Y	1,400
Saugus, Essex, Mass	280
Saugus Centre, Essex, Mass	190
Sauk Centre,* Stearns, Minn	650
Sauk City,* Sauk, Wis	520
Sauk Rapids, (c. h.,) Benton, Minn	270
Saukville, Ozaukee, Wis	77
Saulsburgh, Huntingdon, Pa	38
Saulsbury, Hardeman, Tenn	270
Sault de Ste. Maria, (c. h.,) Chippewa, Mich	200
Saumsville, Shenandoah, Va	15
Saunders' Creek, Simpson, Miss	5
Saunders' Ferry, Garrard, Ky	12
Saundersville, Worcester, Mass	120
Saundersville, Sumner, Tenn	81
Sauquoit, Oneida, N. Y	250
Sauvie's Island, Columbia, Oreg	5
Savage, Howard, Md	75
Savanna, Carroll, Ill	510
Savannah, (c. h.,)* Chatham, Ga	4,000
Savannah, Davis, Iowa	20
Savannah, Pottawatomie, Kans	17
Savannah, (c. h.,)* Andrew, Mo	1,100
Savannah, (c. h.,) Butler, Nebr	12
Savannah, Wayne, N. Y	260
Savannah,* Ashland, Ohio	310
Savannah (c. h.,) Hardin, Tenn	160
Savannah, Red River, Tex	10
Saverton, Ralls, Mo	17
Savill, Orange, N. Y	9
Savona, Steuben, N. Y	230
Savoy, Champaign, Ill	52
Savoy, Berkshire, Mass	80
Saw Dust, Columbia, Ga	5
Saw Mill, Seneca, Ohio	13
Sawpit, Plumas, Cal	44
Sawyer, Berrien, Mich	12
Sawyer's Bar, Klamath, Cal	51
Sawyer's Mills, Lexington, S. C	12
Sawyersville, Randolph, N. C	8
Saxapahaw, Alamance, N. C	24
Saxenburgh, Butler, Pa	170
Saxeville, Waushara, Wis	68
Saxon, Henry, Ill	28
Saxon, Meigs, Ohio	20
Saxonville, Middlesex, Mass	480
Saxton, Bedford, Pa	250
Saxton's River, Windham, Vt	290
Saybrook, Middlesex, Conn	610
Saybrook, Clay, Dak	12

* Money-order office.

Saybrook,* McLean, Ill	$180
Saybrook, Ashtabula, Ohio	150
Saylorsburgh, Monroe, Pa	22
Saylorsville, Polk, Iowa	60
Sayville, Suffolk, N. Y	260
Scales Mound, Jo Daviess, Ill	220
Scalp Level, Cambria, Pa	30
Scandia, Stevens, Minn	16
Scandinavia, Waupaca, Wis	100
Scarborough, Scriven, Ga	80
Scarborough, Cumberland, Me	71
Scarborough, Westchester, N. Y	180
Scarborough, Anderson, Tenn	24
Scarlet's Mill, Berks, Pa	12
Scarsdale, Westchester, N. Y	140
Scenery Hill, Washington, Pa	230
Schellsburgh, Bedford, Pa	160
*Schenectady,** (*c. h.,*) Schenectady, N. Y	2,400
Schenevus, Otsego, N. Y	480
Schenley Station, Armstrong, Pa	33
Schererville, Lake, Ind	41
Schiller, Brown, Wis	4
Schleisingerville, Washington, Wis	210
Schleursburgh, St. Charles, Mo	14
Schlichter, Bucks, Pa	20
Schnecksville, Lehigh, Pa	39
Schneider, Schuylkill, Pa	12
Schnellville, Dubois, Ind	12
Schodack Centre, Rensselaer, N. Y	33
Schodack Depot, Rensselaer, N. Y	52
Schodack Landing, Rensselaer, N. Y	150
Schoeneck, Lancaster, Pa	44
Schoffner's Corners, Jefferson, Pa	11
*Schoharie,** (*c. h.,*) Schoharie, N. Y	960
School, White, Ill	6
Schoolcraft, Kalamazoo, Mich	610
Schooley's Mountain, Morris, N. J	280
Schooley's Station, Ross, Ohio	44
School House Station, San Mateo, Cal	12
Schraalenburgh, Bergen, N. J	46
Schroon Lake, Essex, N. Y	220
Schroon River, Essex, N. Y	78
Schultzville, Dutchess, N. Y	23
Schultzville, Luzerne, Pa	80
Schumacker's Store, St. Charles, Mo	12
Schuyler, Cass, Mo	12
*Schuyler,** (*c. h.,*) Colfax, Nebr	200
Schuyler's Falls, Clinton, N. Y	110
Schuyler's Lake, Otsego, N. Y	170
Schuylersville, Saratoga, N. Y	710
Schuylkill, Chester, Pa	71
Schuylkill Haven, Schuylkill, Pa	1,000
Schwenk's Store, Montgomery, Pa	91
Science Hill, Randolph, N. C	15
Scio, Washtenaw, Mich	8
Scio, Allegany, N. Y	330
Scio, Harrison, Ohio	220
Scio, Linn, Oreg	100
Sciola, Montgomery, Iowa	24
Sciota, McDonough, Ill	55
Sciota, Clinton, N. Y	100
Scioto, Scioto, Ohio	38
Scioto, Monroe, Pa	46
Scioto Furnace, Scioto, Ohio	69
Sciotoville, Scioto, Ohio	$110
Scipio, Jennings, Ind	110
Scipio, Anderson, Kans	45
Scipio, Cayuga, N. Y	86
Scipio, Millard, Utah	58
Scipioville, Cayuga, N. Y	110
Scitico, Hartford, Conn	98
Scituate, Plymouth, Mass	200
Scooba, Kemper, Miss	290
Scotch Bush, Montgomery, N. Y	24
Scotch Grove, Jones, Iowa	27
Scotch Hill, Clarion, Pa	36
Scotch Plains, Union, N. J	130
Scotch Ridge, Wood, Ohio	40
Scotchtown, Orange, N. Y	30
Scotia, Schenectady, N. Y	100
Scotia, Trempealeau, Wis	9
Scotland, Windham, Conn	140
Scotland, Greene, Ind	63
Scotland, Plymouth, Mass	49
Scotland, Franklin, Pa	100
Scotland Neck, Halifax, N. C	73
Scott, La Grange, Ind	41
Scott, Kenton, Ky	22
Scott, Cortland, N. Y	130
Scott, Adams, Ohio	150
Scott, Luzerne, Pa	24
Scott, Sheboygan, Wis	61
Scott Centre, Fayette, Iowa	9
Scott Land, Jefferson, Kans	5
Scott River, Siskiyou, Cal	44
Scotts, Wasco, Oreg	20
Scottsborough, (*c. h.,*) Jackson, Ala	200
Scottsburgh, Livingston, N. Y	100
Scottsburgh, Douglas, Oreg	38
Scottsburgh, Halifax, Va	79
Scott's Hill, Henderson, Tenn	16
Scottsville, Bibb, Ala	19
Scottsville, Floyd, Ind	13
Scottsville, (*c. h.,*) Allen, Ky	140
Scottsville Sullivan, Mo	79
Scottsville, Monroe, N. Y	460
Scottsville, Wyoming, Pa	18
Scottsville, Harrison, Tex	12
Scottsville,* Albemarle, Va	420
Scott Town, Lawrence, Ohio	11
Scottville, Macoupin, Ill	200
Scottville, Ashe, N. C	10
Scranton,* Luzerne, Pa	3,300
Scranton Station, Greene, Iowa	31
Screven, Appling, Ga	27
Scriba, Oswego, N. Y	120
Scroggsfield, Carroll, Ohio	24
Scuffletown, Henderson, Ky	12
Scuppernong, Washington, N. C	65
Scyene, Dallas, Tex	20
Scytheville, Merrimack, N. H	94
Seabeck, Kitsap, Wash	57
Seaboard, Northampton, N. C	62
Seabrook, Rockingham, N. H	85
Seafield, White, Ind	17
Seaford,* Sussex, Del	710
Seaford, Queens, N. Y	92
Seal, Wyandot, Ohio	16
Seal Cove, Hancock, Me	44
Seale's Station, (*c. h.,*) Russell, Ala	92

* Money-order office.

*Searcy,** (*c. h.*,) White, Ark	$410
Searight's, Fayette, Pa	40
Searsburgh, Schuyler, N. Y	120
Searsburgh, Bennington, Vt	58
Searsmont, Waldo, Me	150
Searsport,* Waldo, Me	620
Searsville, San Mateo, Cal	53
Searsville, Orange, N. Y	28
Seaton, Fayette, Iowa	13
Seattle, (*c. h.*,) King, Wash	330
Sea View, Northampton, Va	18
Seaville, Cape May, N. J	120
Sebago, Cumberland, Me	54
Sebago, Linn, Mo	5
Sebastopol, Sonoma, Cal	82
Sebec, Piscataquis, Me	83
Sebewa, Ionia, Mich	29
Sebewaing, Huron, Mich	100
Sebree, Webster, Ky	12
Sechlersville, Jackson, Wis	56
Secillia, Calhoun, Mich	10
Second Creek, Greenbrier, W. Va	47
Secor, Woodford, Ill	420
*Sedalia,** (*c. h.*,) Pettis, Mo	2,500
Sedge's Garden, Forsyth, N. C	6
Sedgewick, Decatur, Iowa	12
Sedgwick, Sedgwick, Kans	12
Sedgwick, Hancock, Me	210
Seekonk, Bristol, Mass	12
Seely Creek, Chemung, N. Y	49
Seelyville, Vigo, Ind	36
Sego, Perry, Ohio	30
Seguin, (*c. h.*,) Guadalupe, Tex	420
Seiad Valley, Siskiyou, Cal	9
Seiberlingville, Lehigh, Pa	10
Seidersville, Northampton, Pa	23
Seigfried's Bridge, Northampton, Pa	150
Seisholtzville, Berks, Pa	24
Selbysport, Alleghany, Md	20
Selbyville, Sussex, Del	45
Selden, Suffolk, N. Y	45
Selin's Grove,* Snyder, Pa	890
Selkirk, Marion, S. C	12
Sellersburgh, Clarke, Ind	96
Seller's Landing, Hardin, Ill	36
Sellersville, Bucks, Pa	310
Sell's Station, Adams, Pa	39
*Selma,** (*c. h.*,) Dallas, Ala	3,000
Selma, Drew, Ark	52
Selma, McLean, Ill	72
Selma, Delaware, Ind	150
Selma, Wayne, Iowa	59
Selma, Johnston, N. C	140
Selma, Clark, Ohio	120
Selma, Bexar, Tex	29
Selma, Alleghany, Va	41
Seminary, Ouachita, Ark	12
Sempronius, Cayuga, N. Y	32
Sempronius, Austin, Tex	12
Senatobia, De Soto, Miss	320
Seneca, La Salle, Ill	580
Seneca, Kossuth, Iowa	5
*Seneca,** (*c. h.*,), Nemaha, Kans	480
Seneca, Montgomery, Md	12
Seneca, Lenawee, Mich	16
Seneca, Newton, Mo	12
Seneca, Schuyler, N. Y	$8
Seneca, Venango, Pa	80
Seneca, Crawford, Wis	44
Seneca Castle, Ontario, N. Y	100
Seneca Falls,* Seneca, N. Y	2,800
Senecaville, Guernsey, Ohio	140
Senex, McLean, Ill	89
Sennet, Cayuga, N. Y	96
Senoia, Coweta, Ga	32
Sentinel, Juneau, Wis	18
Sentinel Prairie, Polk, Mo	22
Serbin, Bastrop, Tex	24
Serena, La Salle, Ill	10
Serena, Stafford, Va	12
Sereno, Columbia, Pa	12
Sergeant Bluffs, Woodbury, Iowa	120
Sergeantsville, Hunterdon, N. J	45
Service, Beaver, Pa	13
Setauket, Suffolk, N. Y	130
Setzler's Store, Chester, Pa	85
Sevastopol, Kosciusko, Ind	65
Seven Fountains, Shenandoah, Va	49
Seven Islands, Fluvanna, Va	25
Seven Mile, Butler, Ohio	150
Seven Mile Ford, Smyth, Va	80
Seven Mile House, Erie, Ohio	51
Seven Stars, Adams, Pa	13
Seventy-Eight, Johnson, Iowa	4
Seventy-Six, Clinton, Ky	5
Seventy-Six, Beaver, Pa	14
Seventy-Six Center, Washington, Iowa	12
Seven Valleys, York, Pa	83
Severance, Doniphan, Kans	12
Sevierville, (*c. h.*,) Sevier, Tenn	70
Seville, Fulton, Ill	29
Seville, Madison, Va	8
Sewanee, Franklin, Tenn	300
Seward, Seward, Nebr	59
Seward, Schoharie, N. Y	30
Sewee, Meigs, Tenn	21
Sewellsville, Belmont, Ohio	48
Sewicklyville, Allegheny, Pa	300
Sexton's Creek, Clay, Ky	2
Sextonville, Richland, Wis	120
Seymour, New Haven, Conn	1,000
Seymour,* Jackson, Ind	1,200
Seymour, Hart, Ky	10
Seymour, Allegany, N. Y	51
Seymour, Outagamie, Wis	12
Seymoursville, Grant, W. Va	26
Shabbonas Grove, De Kalb, Ill	160
Shabonier, Fayette, Ill	82
Shackelford, Henderson, Tex	12
Shade, Athens, Ohio	20
Shade Furnace, Somerset, Pa	9
Shade Gap, Huntingdon, Pa	150
Shade Mills, Alleghany, Md	12
Shade Valley, Juniata, Pa	12
Shadeville, Franklin, Ohio	90
Shadwell, Albemarle, Va	47
Shady, Johnson, Tenn	2
Shady Grove, Taylor, Fla	12
Shady Grove, Crittenden, Ky	12
Shady Grove, Washington, La	12
Shady Grove, Franklin, Pa	59

* Money-order office.

Shady Grove, Franklin, Va	$21
Shady Hill, Henderson, Tenn	8
Shady Plain, Armstrong, Pa	27
Shady Spring, Raleigh, W. Va	5
Shaefferstown, Lebanon, Pa	160
Shaft's Bridge, Somerset, Pa	38
Shaftsbury, Bennington, Vt	79
Shaker Village, Merrimack, N. H	71
Shakleford's, King and Queen, Va	48
Shakopee,* (*c. h.*,) Scott, Minn	710
Shaler's Mills, Knox, Ohio	81
Shalersville, Portage, Ohio	91
Shambling's Mills, Roane, W. Va	3
Shamburgh,* Venango, Pa	1,700
Shamokin,* Northumberland, Pa	1,300
Shamokin Dam, Snyder, Pa	37
Shamong, Burlington, N. J	40
Shamrock, Callaway, Mo	18
Shanandoah, Richland, Ohio	36
Shandaken, Ulster, N. Y	160
Shandsville, Pope, Ill	12
Shane, Baltimore, Md	12
Shane's Crossings, Mercer, Ohio	68
Shanesville, Tuscarawas, Ohio	180
Shanesville, Berks, Pa	19
Shanghai, Howard, Ind	12
Shanghai, Berkeley, W. Va	11
Shanksville, Somerset, Pa	35
Shannock Mills, Washington, R. I	130
Shannon,* Carroll, Ill	650
Shannon, Lee, Miss	160
Shannondale, Montgomery, Ind	7
Shannondale, Clarion, Pa	53
Shannon Hill, Goochland, Va	27
Shannonville, Montgomery, Pa	57
Shapleigh, York, Me	64
Shark River, Monmouth, N. J	55
Sharlow, Bourbon, Kans	5
Sharon, Litchfield, Conn	420
Sharon, Taliaferro, Ga	12
Sharon, Henry, Ill	23
Sharon, Delaware, Ind	16
Sharon, Warren, Iowa	18
Sharon, Norfolk, Mass	300
Sharon, Schoharie, N. Y	51
Sharon, Noble, Ohio	82
Sharon,* Mercer, Pa	2,400
Sharon, Windsor, Vt	180
Sharon, Bland, Va	25
Sharon, Chehalis, Wash	12
Sharon, Walworth, Wis	330
Sharon Centre, Schoharie, N. Y	54
Sharon Centre, Medina, Ohio	130
Sharon Centre, Potter, Pa	15
Sharon Grove, Todd, Ky	12
Sharon Springs, Schoharie, N. Y	760
Sharon Station, Dutchess, N. Y	78
Sharonville, Hamilton, Ohio	120
Sharpsburgh, Bath, Ky	270
Sharpsburgh,* Washington, Md	260
Sharpsburgh, Allegheny, Pa	290
Sharp's Chapel, Union, Tenn	9
Sharp's Cross Roads, Independence, Ark	11
Sharp's Mills, Harrison, Ind	11
Sharpsville, Tipton, Ind	190
Sharpsville, Washington, Ky	$11
Sharpsville Furnace, Mercer, Pa	600
Sharptown, Wicomico, Md	52
Sharptown, Salem, N. J	85
Shartlesville, Berks, Pa	58
Shasta,* (*c. h.*,) Shasta, Cal	540
Shattuckville, Franklin, Mass	12
Shauck's, Morrow, Ohio	81
Shaumburgh, Cook, Ill	25
Shave Head, Cass, Mich	12
Shaver's Creek, Huntingdon, Pa	260
Shavertown, Delaware, N. Y	20
Shawanaw, (*c. h.*,) Shawanaw, Wis	120
Shawangunk, Ulster, N. Y	83
Shawhan, Bourbon, Ky	70
Shaw Hill, Crawford, Wis	12
Shawnee, Johnson, Kans	260
Shawnee, Niagara, N. Y	22
Shawnee, Monroe, Pa	54
Shawnee Mission, Johnson, Kans	12
Shawnee Mound, Tippecanoe, Ind	49
Shawnee Mound, Henry, Mo	74
Shawneetown,* (*c. h.*,) Gallatin, Ill	790
Shawnee Village, Mississippi, Ark	12
Shawn's Cross Roads, Johnson, Ten	6
Shaw's Flat, Tuolumne, Cal	83
Shaw's Landing, Crawford, Pa	21
Shaw's Mills, Guilford, N. C	13
Shaw's Point, Macoupin, Ill	16
Shawsville, Clearfield, Pa	12
Shawsville, Montgomery, Va	12
Sheakleyville, Mercer, Pa	210
Shearer's Cross Roads, Westmoreland, Pa	22
Sheboygan,* (*c. h.*,) Sheboygan, Wis	1,700
Sheboygan Falls, Sheboygan, Wis	720
Shed's Corners, Madison, N. Y	34
Sheenwater, Erie, N. Y	15
Sheepscott Bridge, Lincoln, Me	97
Sheffield, Fayette, Ala	12
Sheffield, Bureau, Ill	490
Sheffield, Dubuque, Iowa	12
Sheffield, Berkshire, Mass	590
Sheffield, Lorain, Ohio	20
Sheffield, Warren, Pa	86
Sheffield, Caledonia, Vt	110
Sheffield Depot, Warren, Pa	260
Sheffield Lake, Lorain, Ohio	27
Shelbina,* Shelby, Mo	990
Shelburn, Sullivan, Ind	100
Shelburne, Franklin, Mass	82
Shelburne, Coos, N. H	78
Shelburne, Chittenden, Vt	270
Shelburne Falls,* Franklin, Mass	1,400
Shelby, Shelby, Iowa	12
Shelby, Oceana, Mich	82
Shelby, Orleans, N. Y	97
Shelby, (*c. h.*,) Cleveland, N. C	180
Shelby,* Richland, Ohio	1,100
Shelby, Austin, Tex	110
Shelby, La Crosse, Wis	8
Shelby Basin, Orleans, N. Y	20
Shelby City, Boyle, Ky	160
Shelby Iron Works, Shelby, Ala	12
Shelby Springs, Shelby, Ala	82
Shelbyville,* (*c. h.*,) Shelby, Ill	1,700

* Money-order office.

*Shelbyville,** (*c. h.,*) Shelby, Ind	$1,300
*Shelbyville,** (*c. h.,*) Shelby, Ky	1,600
Shelbyville, Blue Earth, Minn	100
Shelbyville, (*c. h.,*) Shelby, Mo	370
*Shelbyville,** (*c. h.,*) Bedford, Tenn	1,200
Shelbyville, (*c. h.,*) Shelby, Tex	31
Sheldon, Sacramento, Cal	12
Sheldon, Iroquois, Ill	250
Sheldon, Allen, Ind	12
Sheldon, Houston, Minn	35
Sheldon, Wyoming, N. Y	42
Sheldon,* Franklin, Vt	590
Sheldon, Monroe, Wis	7
Sheldon's Grove, Schuyler, Ill	30
Sheldonville, Norfolk, Mass	100
Sheldrake, Seneca, N. Y	82
Shell Mound, Sunflower, Miss	24
Shell Rock, Butler, Iowa	180
Shell Rock, Freeborn, Minn	28
Shell Rock Falls, Cerro Gordo, Iowa	56
Shellsburgh,* Benton, Iowa	470
Shelocta, Indiana, Pa	68
Shelter Island, Suffolk, N. Y	160
Shelton, Fairfield, S. C	12
Sheltonville, Forsyth, Ga	17
Shenandoah, Schuylkill, Pa	670
Shenandoah Iron Works, Page, Va	110
Shepardsville, Clinton, Mich	170
Shepherd's Store, Anne Arundel, Md	12
Shepherdstown, Belmont, Ohio	14
Shepherdstown, Cumberland, Pa	78
*Shepherdstown,** (*c. h.,*) Jefferson, W. Va	580
Shepherdsville, (*c. h.,*) Bullitt, Ky	210
Sheppardville, Wicomico, Md	16
Sherando, Augusta, Va	10
Sherborn, Middlesex, Mass	200
Sherburne,* Chenango, N. Y	920
Sherburne, Rutland, Vt	63
Sherburne Four Corners, Chenango, N. Y	12
Sherburne Mills, Fleming, Ky	72
Sherburneville, Kankakee, Ill	95
Sheridan, (*c. h.,*) Grant, Ark	12
Sheridan, Placer, Cal	21
Sheridan, La Salle, Ill	27
Sheridan, Van Buren, Iowa	34
Sheridan, Montcalm, Mich	73
Sheridan, Macon, Mo	12
Sheridan, Madison, Mont	170
Sheridan, Nemaha, Nebr	12
Sheridan, Douglas, Nev	44
Sheridan, Chautauqua, N. Y	83
Sheridan, Putnam, Ohio	15
Sheridan, Yam Hill, Oreg	12
Sheridan, Lebanon, Pa	160
Sheridan, Waupaca, Wis	14
Sheridan Coal Works, Lawrence, Ohio	8
Sherman, (*c. h.,*) Marion, Ark	12
Sherman, Fairfield, Conn	82
Sherman, Sangamon, Ill	61
Sherman, Jennings, Ind	23
Sherman, Poweshiek, Iowa	32
Sherman, Grant, Ky	$12
Sherman, Aroostook, Me	77
Sherman, (*c. h.,*) Wexford, Mich	8
Sherman, Blue Earth, Minn	10
Sherman, St. Louis, Mo	36
Sherman, Nemaha, Nebr	7
Sherman, Chautauqua, N. Y	660
Sherman, Summit, Ohio	130
Sherman, (*c. h.,*) Grayson, Tex	560
Sherman, Marathon, Wis	77
Sherman, Albany, Wyo	190
Sherman City, Cherokee, Kans	30
Sherman Mills, Aroostook, Me	67
Sherman's Dale, Perry, Pa	68
Shermantown, White Pine, Nev	12
Sherman Wells, Venango, Pa	130
Sherodsville, Carroll, Ohio	14
Sherrard, Marshall, W. Va	21
Sherrett, Armstrong, Pa	8
Sherrill's Ford, Catawba, N. C	11
Sherrill's Mount, Dubuque, Iowa	81
Sherwood, Branch, Mich	55
Sherwood, Jasper, Mo	32
Sherwood, Cayuga, N. Y	110
Sherwood, Calumet, Wis	59
Sherwood's Mills, Mason, Wash	12
Sherwood Valley, Mendocino, Cal	17
Sheshequin, Bradford, Pa	76
Shibley's Point, Adair, Mo	14
Shickshinny, Luzerne, Pa	180
Shields, Jackson, Ind	38
Shields, Belmont, Ohio	40
Shieldsborough, (*c. h.,*) Hancock, Miss	340
Shieldsville, Rice, Minn	94
Shielville, Hamilton, Ind	130
Shiloh, Marengo, Ala	20
Shiloh, St. Clair, Ill	78
Shiloh, Callaway, Ky	15
Shiloh, Cumberland, N. J	170
Shiloh, Richland, Ohio	210
Shiloh, Camden, N. C	4
Shiloh, Sumter, S. C	4
Shiloh, Montgomery, Tenn	12
Shiloh, Hunt, Tex	16
Shiloh, King George, Va	12
Shiloh Academy, Lamar, Tex	12
Shiloh Hill, Randolph, Ill	26
Shimerville, Lehigh, Pa	51
Shinbone, Fayette, Pa	12
Shin Creek, Sullivan, N. Y	19
Shingle Creek, St. Lawrence, N. Y	140
Shinglehouse, Potter, Pa	22
Shingle Springs, El Dorado, Cal	150
Shinn's Point, Johnson, Ill	14
Shinnston, Harrison, W. Va	62
Shiocton, Outagamie, Wis	43
Shipman, Macoupin, Ill	300
Shippensburgh,* Cumberland, Pa	1,200
Shippensville, Clarion, Pa	100
Shippingport, Beaver, Pa	12
Shiremantown, Cumberland, Pa	190
Shirland, Winnebago, Ill	94
Shirland, Allegheny, Pa	56
Shirley, Covington, Ala	12
Shirley, McLean, Ill	72
Shirley, Cloud, Kans	29

* Money-order office.

Shirley, Piscataquis, Me	$32
Shirley, Middlesex, Mass	72
Shirley, Erie, N. Y	23
Shirley, Tyler, W. Va	6
Shirley Mills, Piscataquis, Me	14
Shirleysburgh, Huntingdon, Pa	230
Shirley Village, Middlesex, Mass	320
Shivelton, Platte, Mo	40
Shoal Creek, Johnson, Ark	12
Shoal Creek, Livingston, Mo	12
Shoal Creek Station, Clinton, Ill	200
Shoals, Martin, Ind	310
Shoalsburgh, Newton, Mo	27
Shobe's Grove, Franklin, Iowa	12
Shockeysville, Frederick, Va	12
Shoe Heel, Robeson, N. C	280
Shoemakers, Monroe, Pa	19
Shoemakersville, Berks, Pa	130
Shoemakertown, Montgomery, Pa	190
Shoenersville, Lehigh, Pa	27
Shohola, Pike, Pa	120
Shokan, Ulster, N. Y	160
Shokokon, Henderson, Ill	59
Shoneytown, Putnam, Mo	12
Shongo, Allegany, N. Y	70
Shootman, Carroll, Mo	12
Shop Creek, Montgomery, Ill	14
Shopiere, Rock, Wis	160
Shop Spring, Wilson, Tenn	43
Shopville, Pulaski, Ky	4
Shoreham, Addison, Vt	220
Short Bend, Dent, Mo	11
Short Creek, Marshall, Ala	12
Short Creek, Grayson, Ky	33
Short Creek, Harrison, Ohio	110
Short Creek, Brooke, W. Va	31
Shorter's Depot, Macon, Ala	15
Short Falls, Merrimack, N. H	12
Short Mountain, Dauphin, Pa	11
Short Mountain, Cannon, Tenn	12
Shortsville,* Ontario, N. Y	310
Short Tract, Allegany, N. Y	97
Shoshone, Alturas, Idaho	12
Shotwell, Franklin, Mo	32
Shoustown, Allegheny, Pa	44
Shovel Mount, Burnet, Tex	12
Shreve, Wayne, Ohio	380
Shreveport, (c. h.,)* Caddo, La	2,800
Shrewsbury, Worcester, Mass	290
Shrewsbury, Monmouth, N. J	130
Shrewsbury, York, Pa	370
Shrewsbury, Rutland, Vt	62
Shrewsbury, Kanawha, W. Va	34
Shrub Oak, Westchester, N. Y	55
Shubuta, Clark, Miss	550
Shuey's Mills, Green, Wis	17
Shueyville, Johnson, Iowa	39
Shufordville, Henderson, N. C	50
Shullsburgh, La Fayette, Wis	460
Shunk, Sullivan, Pa	27
Shunpike, Columbia, N. Y	12
Shuqualak, Noxubee, Miss	270
Shushan, Washington, N. Y	190
Shutesbury, Franklin, Mass	87
Shutter's Corners, Schoharie, N. Y	21
Siam, Taylor, Iowa	41
Sibley, Sibley, Minn	$7
Sibley, Jackson, Mo	56
Sicily, Highland, Ohio	16
Sideling Hall, Fulton, Pa	12
Side View, Montgomery, Ky	24
Sidney, Champaign, Ill	260
Sidney, (c. h.,)* Fremont, Iowa	720
Sidney, Coffey, Kans	61
Sidney, Kennebec, Me	12
Sidney, Montcalm, Mich	12
Sidney, Ralls, Mo	26
Sidney, Cheyenne, Nebr	240
Sidney, Hunterdon, N. J	26
Sidney, Delaware, N. Y	18
Sidney, (c. h.,)* Shelby, Ohio	2,200
Sidney, Venango, Pa	30
Sidney Centre, Delaware, N. Y	76
Sidney Plains,* Delaware, N. Y	340
Sidonsburgh, York, Pa	43
Siegle's Store, Lincoln, N. C	8
Sierra, Vernon, Wis	6
Sierra City, Sierra, Cal	85
Sierra Valley, Sierra, Cal	71
Sigel, Clayton, Iowa	10
Sigel, Douglas, Kans	37
Sigel, Pettis, Mo	41
Sigel, Jefferson, Pa	41
Sigourney, (c. h.,)* Keokuk, Iowa	690
Sikeston, Scott, Mo	16
Siloam, Greene, Ga	12
Siloam, Oktibbeha, Miss	12
Siloam, Madison, N. Y	20
Silver Bow, Deer Lodge, Mont	12
Silver Brook, Schuylkill, Pa	57
Silver City, (c. h.,)* Owyhee, Idaho	300
Silver City, Lewis and Clarke, Mont	12
Silver City, Lyon, Nev	400
Silver Creek, Stephenson, Ill	51
Silver Creek, Chase, Kans	8
Silver Creek, Madison, Ky	62
Silver Creek, Allegan, Mich	53
Silver Creek, Wright, Minn	14
Silver Creek, Lawrence, Miss	12
Silver Creek, Cedar, Mo	3
Silver Creek, Burt, Nebr	26
Silver Creek, Chautauqua, N. Y	630
Silver Creek, Hardin, Ohio	24
Silver Creek, Schuylkill, Pa	65
Silver Glen, Merrick, Nebr	38
Silver Hill, Prince George's, Md	130
Silver Hill, Wetzel, W. Va	7
Silver Lake, Kosciusko, Ind	130
Silver Lake, Worth, Iowa	34
Silver Lake, Shawnee, Kans	12
Silver Lake, McLeod, Minn	57
Silver Lake, Perry, Mo	26
Silver Lake, Clinton, N. Y	4
Silver Lake, Susquehanna, Pa	24
Silver Mountain, (c. h.,) Alpine, Cal	130
Silver Peak, Esmeralda, Nev	12
Silver Run, Talladega, Ala	43
Silver Run, Carroll, Md	24
Silver Run, Meigs, Ohio	8
Silver Spring, Lancaster, Pa	87
Silver Spring, Wilson, Tenn	51
Silver Springs, Alcorn, Miss	18

* Money-order office.

Silver Star, Madison, Mont	$12
Silver Street, Newberry, S. C	20
Silverton, Ocean, N. J	6
Silverton, Marion, Oreg	77
Silverville, Lawrence, Ind	13
Silveyville, Solano, Cal	40
Simmon's Bluff, Wilson, Tenn	7
Simmonsville, Craig, Va	14
Simonsville, Windsor, Vt	65
Simpson, Adams, Iowa	24
Simpson's, Floyd, Va	12
Simpson's Corner, Penobscot, Me	33
Simpson's Creek, Taylor, W. Va	48
Simpson's Mills, Laurens, S. C	5
Simpson's Store, Washington, Pa	12
Simpsonville, Shelby, Ky	140
Simpsonville, Howard, Md	32
Simpsonville, Upshur, Tex	4
Simsbury, Hartford, Conn	250
Sinclairville, Chautauqua, N. Y	450
Sineath's, Charleston, S. C	12
Singer's Glen, Rockingham, Va	200
Sing Sing,* Westchester, N. Y	2,500
Sinkin, Shannon, Mo	12
Sinking Creek, Craig, Va	2
Sinking Fork, Christian, Ky	12
Sinking Spring, Highland, Ohio	38
Sinking Spring, Berks, Pa	86
Sinking Valley, Blair, Pa	100
Sink's Grove, Monroe, W. Va	26
Sinnamahoning, Cameron, Pa	170
Sinnett's Mills, Ritchie, W. Va	3
Sinsinawa Mound, Grant, Wis	99
Sioux City,* (*c. h.*,) Woodbury, Iowa	2,600
Sioux Falls, Minnehaha, Dak	55
Sioux Rapids, Buena Vista, Iowa	12
Sioux Valley, Union, Dak	36
Sipes' Mill, Fulton, Pa	12
Sipestown, Lehigh, Pa	6
Sipesville, Somerset, Pa	26
Sipsey Turnpike, Tuscaloosa, Ala	12
Sipsy Mills, Pickens, Ala	17
Sir John's Run, Morgan, W. Va	73
Sissonville, Kanawha, W. Va	7
Sisterdale, Kendall, Tex	15
Sistersville, Tyler, W. Va	200
Sitka, (*c. h.*,) ——, Alaska	240
Sitka, Martin, Ind	12
Sitka, Newaygo, Mich	12
Siuslaw, Lane, Oreg	10
Siverly, Vinton, Ohio	34
Six Corners, Ottawa, Mich	30
Six Mile, Jennings, Ind	140
Six Mile Falls, Penobscot, Me	20
Six Mile Run, Somerset, N. J	82
Six Mile Run, Bedford, Pa	190
Six Oaks, Olmsted, Minn	23
Six Points, Butler, Pa	12
Six Roads, Bedford, Pa	15
Sixteen Mile Stand, Hamilton, Ohio	36
Skaneateles,* Onondaga, N. Y	1,400
Skeel's Cross Roads, Mercer, Ohio	31
Skiddy, Morris, Kans	12
Skinner, Campbell, Ga	2
Skinner, Bay, Mich	12
Skinner, Green, Wis	20
Skinner's Eddy, Wyoming, Pa	$88
Skinquarter, Chesterfield, Va	39
Skipanon, Clatsop, Oreg	12
Skippack, Montgomery, Pa	100
Skipperville, Dale, Ala	12
Skipton, Talbot, Md	23
Skipwith's Landing, Issaquena, Miss	200
Skokomish, Mason, Wash	18
Skookumchuck, Lewis, Wash	10
Skowhegan,* Somerset, Me	1,800
Skull Valley, Yavapai, Ariz	12
Slabtown, Boone, Ind	12
Slack, Mason, Ky	13
Slack Water, Lancaster, Pa	17
Sladesburgh, Crawford, Wis	6
Sladesville, Hyde, N. C	25
Slanesville, Hampshire, W. Va	22
Slash, Grant, Ind	15
Slate, Jennings, Ind	12
Slate Creek, Josephine, Oreg	19
Slate Cut, Clarke, Ind	11
Slateford, Northampton, Pa	90
Slate Hill, Orange, N. Y	10
Slate Hill, York, Pa	85
Slate Lick, Armstrong, Pa	75
Slate Mills, Rappahannock, Va	14
Slatersville, Weber, Utah	12
Slaterville, Tompkins, N. Y	110
Slaterville, Providence, R. I	440
Slatington, Lehigh, Pa	930
Slaughter, Kent, Del	12
Slaughter, King, Wash	12
Slaughtersville, Webster, Ky	40
Sleepy Creek Bridge, Morgan, W. Va	34
Slick Rock, Barren, Ky	22
Slifer, Union, Pa	90
Sligo, Montgomery, Md	30
Sligo, Clarion, Pa	88
Slippery Ford, El Dorado, Cal	20
Slippery Rock, Butler, Pa	190
Sloan, Woodbury, Iowa	77
Sloan's Point, Adair, Mo	10
Sloan's Station, Jefferson, Ohio	120
Sloansville, Schoharie, N. Y	130
Sloatsburgh, Rockland, N. Y	110
Slocum's Grove, Muskegon, Mich	15
Slocumville, Washington, R. I	48
Small Point, Sagadahoc, Me	36
Smartt's Station, Warren, Tenn	12
Smartville, Yuba, Cal	300
Smicksburgh, Indiana, Pa	84
Smiley, Susquehanna, Pa	22
Smileytown, Spencer, Ky	29
Smith, Dade, Ga	12
Smith City, Pettis, Mo	220
Smithdale, Livingston, Ill	12
Smithdale, Amite, Miss	19
Smithfield, Fulton, Ill	12
Smithfield, Henry, Ky	130
Smithfield, Somerset, Me	84
Smithfield, Wabashaw, Minn	43
Smithfield, (*c. h.*,) Johnston, N. C	260
Smithfield, Jefferson, Ohio	310
Smithfield, Fayette, Pa	220
Smithfield, Providence, R. I	31
Smithfield, Polk, Tex	12

* Money-order office.

Post office	Compensation
Smithfield, Cache, Utah	$43
Smithfield,* (*c. h.*,) Isle of Wight, Va	460
Smithfield Summit, Bradford, Pa	14
Smith Grove, Davie, N. C	7
Smithland, Shelby, Ind	26
Smithland, Woodbury, Iowa	110
Smithland, Jackson, Kans	11
Smithland,* (*c. h.*,) Livingston, Ky	320
Smithport, (*c. h.*,) McKean, Pa	270
Smith River, Del Norte, Cal	12
Smith Road, Medina, Ohio	20
Smith's Basin, Washington, N. Y	100
Smithsborough, Tioga, N. Y	79
Smithsburgh, Washington, Md	130
Smith's Corners, Oceana, Mich	10
Smith's Creek, St. Clair, Mich	140
Smith's Creek, Washington, Va	55
Smith's Cross Roads, Rhea, Tenn	36
Smith's Ferry, Beaver, Pa	280
Smith's Ford, Cabarrus, N. C	12
Smith's Ford, Union, S. C	8
Smith's Gap, Hampshire, W. Va	16
Smith's Grove, Warren, Ky	170
Smith's Landing, Atlantic, N. J	74
Smith's Landing, Clermont, Ohio	15
Smith's Mills, Henderson, Ky	40
Smith's Mills, Passaic, N. J	8
Smith's Mills, Chautauqua, N. Y	140
Smith's Mills, Clearfield, Pa	99
Smithson's Valley, Comal, Tex	5
Smith's Ranch, Sonoma, Cal	80
Smith's Ridge, Fairfield, Conn	10
Smith's Station, Lee, Ala	66
Smith's Station, York, Pa	21
Smith's Turn Out, York, S. C	28
Smith's Valley, Johnson, Ind	12
Smithton, St. Clair, Ill	25
Smithton, Worth, Mo	12
Smithton, Doddridge, W. Va	58
Smithtown, Suffolk, N. Y	180
Smithtown Branch, Suffolk, N. Y	290
Smith Valley, Schuyler, N. Y	36
Smithville, Lawrence, Ark	120
Smithville, Peoria, Ill	50
Smithville, Monroe, Ind	93
Smithville, Caroline, Md	15
Smithville, Worcester, Mass	53
Smithville, Wayne, Mich	11
Smithville, Monroe, Miss	38
Smithville, Clay, Mo	91
Smithville, Burlington, N. J	160
Smithville, Jefferson, N. Y	120
Smithville, (*c. h.*,) Brunswick, N. C	170
Smithville, Wayne, Ohio	370
Smithville, Lancaster, Pa	20
Smithville, (*c. h.*,) De Kalb, Tenn	81
Smithville Flats, Chenango, N. Y	120
Smithville South, Queens, N. Y	20
Smitten, Indiana, Pa	10
Smoky Ordinary, Brunswick, Va	12
Smootsdell, Hendricks, Ind	34
Smyrna,* Kent, Del	1,100
Smyrna, Cobb, Ga	12
Smyrna, Clarke, Iowa	53
Smyrna, Aroostook, Me	15
Smyrna, Ionia, Mich	160
Smyrna, Chenango, N. Y	$260
Smyrna, Harrison, Ohio	63
Smyrna, Lancaster, Pa	37
Smyrna, Rutherford, Tenn	110
Smyrna Mills, Aroostook, Me	10
Snachwine, Putnam, Ill	160
Snake Root, McDowell, Va	12
Snapping Shoals, Newton, Ga	49
Snead's Ferry, Onslow, N. C	12
Snedekerville, Bradford, Pa	27
Sneedsville, (*c. h.*,) Hancock, Tenn	43
Snelling's Ranch, (*c. h.*,) Merced, Cal	200
Snibar, La Fayette, Mo	14
Snicarte, Mason, Ill	26
Snickersville, Loudoun, Va	88
Snidersville, Outagamie, Wis	23
Snipe's Store, Chatham, N. C	4
Snoddy's Mills, Fountain, Ind	10
Snohomish, (*c. h.*,) Snohomish Wash	27
Snoqualmie, King, Wash	12
Snow Camp, Alamance, N. C	36
Snow Creek, Iredell, N. C	12
Snow Creek, Smith, Tenn	12
Snow Creek, Franklin, Va	5
Snowdoun, Montgomery, Ala	6
Snow Falls, Oxford, Me	45
Snow Hill, Randolph, Ind	18
Snow Hill,* (*c. h.*,) Worcester, Md	390
Snow Hill, St. Charles, Mo	130
Snow Hill, (*c. h.*,) Greene, N. C	50
Snow Hill, Titus, Tex	24
Snow Hill, Nicholas, W. Va	5
Snow Shoe, Centre, Pa	170
Snowville, Pulaski, Va	45
Snyder, Dallas, Iowa	15
Snydersville, Monroe, Pa	23
Snydertown, Northumberland, Pa	46
Social Circle, Walton, Ga	310
Society Hill, Macon, Ala	21
Society Hill, Darlington, S. C	250
Socorro, (*c. h.*,) Socorro, N. Mex	43
Soda Bar, Palo Alto, Iowa	46
Soda Springs, Linn, Oreg	12
Soddy, Hamilton, Tenn	16
Sodorus, Champaign, Ill	230
Sodus, Berrien, Mich	61
Sodus, Wayne, N. Y	340
Sodus Centre, Wayne, N. Y	49
Sodus Point, Wayne, N. Y	110
Soldiers' Grove, Crawford, Wis	21
Soledad, Monterey, Cal	12
Solomon City, Saline, Kans	210
Solomon Rapids, Mitchell, Kans	12
Solomon's Island, Calvert, Md	12
Solon, Johnson, Iowa	180
Solon, Somerset, Me	290
Solon, Leelenaw, Mich	12
Solon, Otoe, Nebr	12
Solon, Cortland, N. Y	73
Solon, Cuyahoga, Ohio	270
Solon, White, Tenn	12
Solon Mills, McHenry, Ill	29
Solsberry, Greene, Ind	63
Solsville, Madison, N. Y	130
Somerfield, Somerset, Pa	110
Somers, Tolland, Conn	180

* Money-order office.

SOU		SOU	
Somers, Westchester, N. Y	$180	South Arkansas, Lake, Colo	$12
Somers, Kenosha, Wis	12	South Arlington, Montgomery, Ohio	13
Somerset' Saline, Ill	4	South Ashfield, Franklin, Mass	74
Somerset, Wabash, Ind	110	South Atkinson, Piscataquis, Me	39
Somerset, (*c. h.*,) Pulaski, Ky	350	South Attleborough, Bristol, Mass	110
Somerset, Bristol, Mass	380	South Auburn, Androscoggin, Me	58
Somerset, Hillsdale, Mich	45	South Auburn, Susquehanna, Pa	15
Somerset, Monroe, Mo	12	South Avon, Livingston, N. Y	21
Somerset, Niagara, N. Y	170	South Ballston, Saratoga, N. Y	73
Somerset, Perry, Ohio	400	South Bangor, Buckingham, Va	12
Somerset,* (*c. h.*,) Somerset, Pa	690	South Barnstead, Belknap, N. H	10
Somerset, Atascosa, Tex	12	South Barre, Orleans, N. Y	27
Somerset, Windham, Vt	27	South Barre, Washington, Vt	46
Somerset, St. Croix, Wis	47	South Barton, Orleans, Vt	68
Somerset Furnace, Somerset, Pa	20	South Beddington, Washington, Me	12
Somerset Mills, Somerset, Me	140	South Belmont, Waldo, Me	12
Somers' Point, Atlantic, N. J	190	South Bend, Arkansas, Ark	18
Somersville, Contra Costa, Cal	110	*South Bend*,* (*c. h.*,) St. Joseph, Ind	3,000
Somerton, Belmont, Ohio	110	South Bend, Blue Earth, Minn	350
Somerville, (*c. h.*,) Morgan, Ala	89	South Bend, Cass, Nebr	10
Somerville, Tolland, Conn	75	South Bend, Armstrong, Pa	44
Somerville, Gibson, Ind	24	South Bend, Trempealeau, Wis	60
Somerville, Lincoln, Me	41	South Berlin, Rensselaer, N. Y	32
Somerville, Middlesex, Mass	920	South Berne, Albany, N. Y	12
Somerville,* (*c. h.*,) Somerset, N. J	1,000	South Berwick,* York, Me	750
Somerville, St. Lawrence, N. Y	56	South Berwick Junction, York, Me	44
Somerville, Butler, Ohio	210	South Bethany, Bartholomew, Ind	32
Somerville, (*c. h.*,) Fayette, Tenn	720	South Bethlehem,* Northampton, Pa	610
Somerville, Fauquier, Va	13	South Bloomfield, Pickaway, Ohio	140
Somonauk, De Kalb, Ill	550	South Bloomingville, Hocking, Ohio	40
Sonestown, Sullivan, Pa	31	South Bolivar, Allegany, N. Y	14
Sonman, Cambria, Pa	47	South Bombay, Franklin, N. Y	14
Sonoma, Sonoma, Cal	260	Southborough, Worcester, Mass	360
Sonora,* (*c. h.*,) Tuolumne, Cal	1,000	South Boston, Ionia, Mich	25
Sonora, Hancock, Ill	110	South Boston Depot, Halifax, Va	160
Sonora, Hardin, Ky	180	South Bradford, Steuben, N. Y	24
Sonora, Chickasaw, Miss	12	South Braintree, Norfolk, Mass	280
Sonora, Steuben, N. Y	43	South Branch, Somerset, N. J	97
Sonora, Muskingum, Ohio	56	South Branch, Bradford, Pa	15
Sopchoppy, Wakulla, Fla	12	South Branch Depot, Hampshire, W. Va	46
Soquel, Santa Cruz, Cal	73	South Brewster, Barnstable, Mass	72
Sorghotown, Daviess, Ky	12	Southbridge,* Worcester, Mass	900
Sorrel Horse, Montgomery, Pa	35	South Bridgeton, Cumberland, Me	70
Soudersburgh, Lancaster, Pa	39	South Bristol, Lincoln, Me	46
Souder's Station, Montgomery, Pa	120	South Bristol, Ontario, N. Y	10
Sour Spring, Caldwell, Tex	22	South Britain, New Haven, Conn	210
South Abington, Plymouth, Mass	660	South Brookfield, Madison, N. Y	51
South Acton, York, Me	13	South Brooks, Waldo, Me	22
South Acton, Middlesex, Mass	210	South Brooksville, Hancock, Me	13
South Acworth, Sullivan, N. H	130	Southbury, New Haven, Conn	200
South Addison, Steuben, N. Y	53	South Butler, Butler, Ala	21
South Alabama, Genesee, N. Y	72	South Butler, Branch, Mich	8
South Albany, Orleans, Vt	50	South Butler, Wayne, N. Y	210
South Albion, Kennebec, Me	51	South Byron, Genesee, N. Y	200
South Albion, Oswego, N. Y	24	South Cabot, Washington, Vt	12
South Amboy,* Middlesex, N. J	540	South Cairo, Greene, N. Y	32
South Amenia, Dutchess, N. Y	74	South Camden, Hillsdale, Mich	12
South America, Saline, Ill	23	South Cameron, Steuben, N. Y	11
South Amesbury, Essex, Mass	150	South Canaan, Litchfield, Conn	10
South Amherst, Hampshire, Mass	83	South Carrollton, Muhlenburgh, Ky	120
Southampton, Peoria, Ill	47	South Carthage, Franklin, Me	16
Southampton, Hampshire, Mass	190	South Carver, Plymouth, Mass	120
Southampton, Suffolk, N. Y	330	South Casco, Cumberland, Me	25
Southampton Mills, Somerset, Pa	12	South Cass, Ionia, Mich	55
South Andover, Oxford, Me	110		
South Argyle, Washington, N. Y	52		

* Money-order office.

SOU

South Cedar, Jackson, Kans	$6
South Champion, Jefferson, N. Y	15
South Charleston, Clark, Ohio	450
South Charlestown, Sullivan, N. H	50
South Chatham, Barnstable, Mass	81
South Chelmsford, Middlesex, Mass	12
South Chesterville, Franklin, Me	30
South China, Kennebec, Me	93
South Colton, St. Lawrence, N. Y	69
South Cleveland, Whitley, Ind	10
South Climax, Kalamazoo, Mich	12
South Columbia, Coos, N. H	22
South Columbia, Herkimer, N. Y	14
South Corinth, Penobscot, Me	16
South Corinth, Saratoga, N. Y	100
South Cortland, Cortland, N. Y	24
South Cottonwood, Salt Lake, Utah	12
South Coventry, Tolland, Conn	270
South Creek, Beaufort, N. C	7
South Creek, Bradford, Pa	81
South Danbury, Grafton, N. H	53
South Danby, Tompkins, N. Y	15
South Dansville, Steuben, N. Y	130
South Danville, Caledonia, Vt	81
South Dartmouth, Bristol, Mass	200
South Dayton, Cattaraugus, N. Y	17
South Dedham, Norfolk, Mass	410
South Deerfield, Franklin, Mass	720
South Deerfield, Rockingham, N. H	66
South Deer Isle, Hancock, Me	110
South Dennis, Barnstable, Mass	170
South Dorset, Bennington, Vt	49
South Dover, Piscataquis, Me	53
South Dover, Dutchess, N. Y	20
South Durham, Androscroggin, Me	34
South Durham, Greene, N. Y	39
South Duxbury, Plymouth, Mass	87
South Easton, Bristol, Mass	120
South Easton, Washington, N. Y	39
South Easton, Northampton, Pa	270
South Eaton, Wyoming, Pa	27
South Edmeston, Otsego, N. Y	88
South Edwards, St. Lawrence, N. Y	34
South Egremont, Berkshire, Mass	200
South English, Keokuk, Iowa	110
Southern, Marshall, Ala	12
South Evansville, Berks, Pa	18
South Exeter, Penobscot, Me	54
Southfield, Berkshire, Mass	42
Southfield, Oakland, Mich	63
South Flint, Des Moines, Iowa	10
South Florence, Franklin, Ala	12
Southford, New Haven, Conn	130
South Fork, Owsley, Ky	5
South Foster, Providence, R. I	28
South Farmingham, Middlesex, Mass	580
South Franklin, Norfolk, Mass	42
South Freeport, Cumberland, Me	140
South Galway, Saratoga, N. Y	22
South Gardiner, Kennebec, Me	62
South Gardner,* Worcester, Mass	430
South Gaston, Halifax, N. C	82
South Gate, Franklin, Ind	15
South Georgetown, Ottawa, Mich	6

SOU

South Germantown, Washington, Wis	$21
South Gibson, Susquehanna, Pa	92
South Gilboa, Schoharie, N. Y	22
South Glastenbury, Hartford, Conn	350
South Glens Falls, Saratoga, N. Y	50
South Glover, Orleans, Vt	12
South Granby, Oswego, N. Y	25
South Granville, Washington, N. Y	20
South Greece, Monroe, N. Y	37
South Grove, De Kalb, Ill	62
South Groveland, Essex, Mass	97
South Hadley, Hampshire, Mass	900
South Hadley Falls, Hampshire, Mass	720
South Halifax, Windham, Vt	20
South Hamilton, Madison, N. Y	20
South Hampton, Gallatin, Ill	8
South Hampton, Rockingham, N.H	62
South Hancock, Hancock, Me	12
South Hannibal, Oswego, N. Y	31
South Hanover, Plymouth, Mass	110
South Hanson, Plymouth, Mass	120
South Hartford, Washington, N. Y	140
South Hartwick, Otsego, N. Y	17
South Harwich, Barnstable, Mass	110
South Haven, New Haven, Conn	12
South Haven, Van Buren, Mich	710
South Haven, Suffolk, N. Y	46
South Hermitage, Lancaster, Pa	27
South Hero, Grand Isle, Vt	20
South Hill, Bradford, Pa	17
South Hill, Mecklenburgh, Va	12
South Hinesburgh, Chittenden, Vt	13
South Hingham, Plymouth, Mass	140
South Holland, Cook, Ill	12
South Hope, Knox, Me	79
South Howard, Steuben, N. Y	10
South Hume, Whitesides, Ill	12
Southington,* Hartford, Conn	870
Southington, Trumbull, Ohio	120
South Jackson, Jackson, Mich	23
South Jefferson, Lincoln, Me	8
South Jefferson, Schoharie, N. Y	24
South Killingly, Windham, Conn	24
South Kingston, Rockingham, N. H	25
South Kirtland, Lake, Ohio	38
South Kortright, Delaware, N. Y	10
South Lancaster, Worcester, Mass	260
South Lansing, Tompkins, N. Y	63
South Lee, Berkshire, Mass	250
South Leeds, Androscoggin, Me	6
South Levant, Penobscot, Me	23
South Lewiston, Androscoggin, Me	80
South Liberty, Waldo, Me	20
South Liberty, Adams, Ohio	12
South Lima, Livingston, N. Y	62
South Limington, York, Me	78
South Litchfield, Kennebec, Me	57
South Litchfield, Bradford, Pa	27
South Livermore, Androscoggin, Me	19
South Livonia, Livingston, N. Y	66
South Londonderry, Windham, Vt	190
South Lowell, Orange, N. C	10
South Lyme, New London, Conn	25

* Money-order office.

South Lyndeborough, Hillsborough, N. H	$87
South Lyon, Oakland, Mich	72
South Malden, Middlesex, Mass	130
South Manchester, Hartford, Conn	590
South Martin, Martin, Ind	24
South Meriden, New Haven, Conn	300
South Merrimack, Hillsborough, N. H	31
South Middleborough, Plymouth, Mass	73
South Milford, La Grange, Ind	65
South Milford, Worcester, Mass	59
South Mills, Camden, N. C	82
South Milton, Strafford, N. H	10
South Moluncus, Aroostook, Me	24
South Monmouth, Kennebec, Me	9
South Montville, Waldo, Me	63
South Natick, Middlesex, Mass	320
South New Berlin, Chenango, N. Y	160
South Newburgh, Penobscot, Me	36
South Newbury, Merrimack, N. H	56
South Newbury, Geauga, Ohio	75
South Newbury, Orange, Vt	110
South Newcastle, Gallia, Ohio	16
South New Market, Rockingham, N. H	340
South Newstead, Erie, N. Y	12
South Norfolk, Litchfield, Conn	46
South Norridgewock, Somerset, Me	190
South Northfield, Cook, Ill	32
South Norwalk, Fairfield, Conn	1,600
Southold, Suffolk, N. Y	510
South Olive, Noble, Ohio	23
South Onondaga, Onondaga, N. Y	75
South Orange, Essex, N. J	770
South Orleans, Barnstable, Mass	60
South Orrington, Penobscot, Me	85
South Osborn, Outagamie, Wis	12
South Otselic, Chenango, N. Y	160
South Owego, Tioga, N. Y	10
South Oxford, Chenango, N. Y	27
South Paris, Oxford, Me	560
South Parsonfield, York, Me	38
South Pass,* Union, Ill	600
South Pass, Lancaster, Nebr	12
South Pass City, (*c. h.*,) Sweetwater, Wyo	2,000
South Peacham, Caledonia, Vt	12
South Pendleton, Hamilton, Ohio	96
South Penobscot, Hancock, Me	12
South Perry, Hocking, Ohio	37
South Plattsburgh, Clinton, N. Y	22
South Plymouth, Plymouth, Mass	47
South Plymouth, Chenango, N. Y	20
South Plymouth, Fayette, Ohio	58
South Point, Franklin, Mo	98
South Point, Gaston, N. C	10
South Point, Lawrence, Ohio	61
South Poland, Androscoggin, Me	93
South Pomfret, Windsor, Vt	59
Southport, Fairfield, Conn	250
Southport, Peoria, Ill	33
Southport, Marion, Ind	110
Southport, Lincoln, Me	63
Southport, Chemung, N. Y	25
Southport, Maury, Tenn	$12
South Portsmouth, Newport, R. I	91
South Prairie, Henderson, Ill	20
South Pultney, Steuben, N. Y	44
South Randolph, Norfolk, Mass	20
South Reading, Windsor, Vt	53
South Richland, Oswego, N. Y	55
South Ridge, Ashtabula, Ohio	40
South Riley, Clinton, Mich	12
South River, Anne Arundel, Md	62
South River, Middlesex, N. J	280
South Robbinston, Washington, Me	76
South Royalston, Worcester, Mass	270
South Royalton, Windsor, Vt	390
South Rutland, Jefferson, N. Y	51
South Ryegate, Caledonia, Vt	73
South Saginaw, Saginaw, Mich	430
South Saint George, Knox, Me	97
South Salem, Westchester, N. Y	120
South Salem, Ross, Ohio	160
South San Diego,* San Diego, Cal	370
South Sandisfield, Berkshire, Mass	29
South Sand Lake, Rensselaer, N. Y	25
South Sandwich, Barnstable, Mass	73
South Sanford, York, Me	25
South Sangerville, Piscataquis, Me	24
South Schodack, Rensselaer, N. Y	33
South Schroon, Essex, N. Y	37
South Scituate, Plymouth, Mass	130
South Scituate, Providence, R. I	58
South Scriba, Oswego, N. Y	12
South Seaville, Cape May, N. J	99
South Sebec, Piscataquis, Me	44
South Seekonk, Bristol, Mass	25
South Shaftsbury, Bennington, Vt	130
South Side, Bent, Colo	18
South Side, Richmond, N. Y	67
South Sodus, Wayne, N. Y	68
South Solon, Somerset, Me	27
South Solon, Madison, Ohio	24
South Starksborough, Addison, Vt	15
South Sterling, Wayne, Pa	57
South Stoddard, Cheshire, N. H	49
South Strafford, Orange, Vt	150
South Sudbury, Middlesex, Mass	88
South Sunapee, Sullivan, N. H	26
South Sutton, Merrimack, N. H	70
South Tamworth, Carroll, N. H	65
South Thomaston, Knox, Me	89
South Thompson, Geauga, Ohio	38
South Trenton, Oneida, N. Y	73
South Troupsburgh, Steuben, N. Y	20
South Troy, Wabashaw, Minn	24
South Union, Logan, Ky	240
South Vallejo, Solano, Cal	12
South Valley, Otsego, N. Y	66
South Vassalborough, Kennebec, Me	19
Southville, Litchfield, Conn	50
Southville, St. Lawrence, N. Y	31
South Vineland, Cumberland, N. J	290
South Walden, Caledonia, Vt	20
South Wales, Erie, N. Y	67
South Wallingford, Rutland, Vt	80
South Walpole, Norfolk, Mass	190
South Wardsborough, Windham, Vt	24

* Money-order office.

South Warren, Bradford, Pa	$14
South Warsaw, Allen, Ohio	20
South Washington, New Hanover, N. C	12
South Waterford, Oxford, Me	140
South Weare, Hillsborough, N. H	91
South Wellfleet, Barnstable, Mass	70
South West, Warren, Pa	130
South Westerlo, Albany, N. Y	67
South West Harbor, Hancock, Me	260
South Weston, Aroostook, Me	76
South West Oswego, Oswego, N. Y	80
South Westport, Bristol, Mass	20
South Weymouth, Norfolk, Mass	390
South Whitehall, Lehigh, Pa	17
South Whitley, Whitley, Ind	110
Southwick, Hampden, Mass	120
South Wilbraham, Hampden, Mass	220
South Williamstown, Berkshire, Mass	260
South Willow Creek, Lee, Ill	11
South Wilson, Niagara, N. Y	27
South Wilton, Saratoga, N. Y	10
South Windham, Windham, Conn	160
South Windham, Cumberland, Me	160
South Windham, Windham, Vt	37
South Windsor, Hartford, Conn	120
South Windsor, Kennebec, Me	46
South Winn, Penobscot, Me	11
South Wolfborough, Carroll, N. H	69
South Woodbury, Washington, Vt	77
South Woodstock, Windham, Conn	36
South Woodstock, Windsor, Vt	160
South Worcester, Otsego, N. Y	120
South Worthington, Hampshire, Mass	36
South Wright, Hillsdale, Mich	38
South Yarmouth, Barnstable, Mass	300
Spade's Depot, Ripley, Ind	52
Spadra, Los Angeles, Cal	26
Spafford, Onondaga, N. Y	36
Spafford, La Fayette, Wis	44
Spaldingville, Knox, Ind	1
Spangville, Berks, Pa	9
Spanish Bar, Clear Creek, Colo	94
Spanishburgh, Mercer, W. Va	11
Spanish Flat, El Dorado, Cal	25
Spanish Fork, Utah, Utah	77
Spanish Hollow, Wasco, Oreg	12
Spanish Ranch, Plumas, Cal	52
Spark's Hill, Hardin, Ill	10
Sparksville, Jackson, Ind	18
Sparland,* Marshall, Ill	460
Sparrow Bush, Orange, N. Y	160
Sparta, Conecuh, Ala	25
Sparta, (*c. h.*,) Hancock, Ga	590
Sparta,* Randolph, Ill	830
Sparta, Dearborn, Ind	26
Sparta, (*c. h.*,) Bienville, La	40
Sparta, Chickasaw, Miss	61
Sparta, Sussex, N. J	120
Sparta, Edgecombe, N. C	33
Sparta, Morrow, Ohio	130
Sparta, Washington, Pa	36
Sparta, (*c. h.*,) White, Tenn	260
Sparta, Caroline, Va	16
Sparta,* (*c. h.*,) Monroe, Wis	$1,800
Sparta Centre, Kent, Mich	110
Spartanburgh, Randolph, Ind	54
Spartanburgh C. H., Spartanburgh, S. C	970
Spartansburgh, Crawford, Pa	400
Sparta Station, Gallatin, Ky	12
Spavinaw, Benton, Ark	7
Speakeville, Lavaca, Tex	19
Spears, Jessamine, Ky	33
Spearsville, Brown, Ind	15
Speedsville, Tompkins, N. Y	120
Speedwell, Madison, Ky	8
Speedwell, Claiborne, Tenn	16
Speedwell, Wythe, Va	12
Speight's Bridge, Greene, N. C	13
Spencer, Will, Ill	55
Spencer,* (*c. h.*,) Owen, Ind	580
Spencer, Clay, Iowa	45
Spencer, Worcester, Mass	980
Spencer, Lawrence, Mo	12
Spencer, Tioga, N. Y	460
Spencer, Davidson, N. C	6
Spencer, Medina, Ohio	91
Spencer, (*c. h.*,) Van Buren, Tenn	36
Spencer, (*c. h.*,) Roane, W. Va	130
Spencer Brook, Isanti, Minn	27
Spencerburgh, Pike, Mo	56
Spencer Creek, Antrim, Mich	12
Spencer Grove, Benton, Iowa	8
Spencerport, Monroe, N. Y	340
Spencer's Mill, Kent, Mich	12
Spencer Springs, Tioga, N. Y	59
Spencer's Shop, Crawford, Ark	12
Spencer's Station, Guernsey, Ohio	88
Spencer's Store, Henry, Va	12
Spencertown, Columbia, N. Y	130
Spencerville, De Kalb, Ind	120
Spencerville, Montgomery, Md	17
Spencerville, Allen, Ohio	120
Speonk, Suffolk, N. Y	36
Sperry, Des Moines, Iowa	12
Sperryville, Rappahannock, Va	79
Spiceland, Henry, Ind	180
Spillville, Winneshiek, Iowa	140
Spinnerstown, Bucks, Pa	51
Spirit Lake, (*c. h.*,) Dickinson, Iowa	63
Spokan Bridge, Stevens, Wash	34
Spooner's Corners, Otsego, N. Y	16
Sporting Hill, Lancaster, Pa	18
Spotswood, Middlesex, N. J	200
Spottsylvania C. H., Spottsylvania, Va	58
Spout Spring, Appomattox, Va	140
Spout Springs, Harnett, N. C	12
Spragg's, Greene, Pa	9
Spragueville, Jackson, Iowa	69
Spraker's Basin, Montgomery, N. Y	96
Sprankle's Mills, Jefferson, Pa	23
Spread Eagle, Chester, Pa	110
Spring, Crawford, Pa	270
Spring Arbor, Jackson, Mich	41
Spring Bay, Woodford, Ill	70
Spring Bluff, Choctaw N., Ind. T	12
Spring Bluff, Adams, Wis	32
Springborough, Warren, Ohio	240

* Money-order office.

SPR	
Spring Branch, Comal, Tex	$8
Spring Brook, Jackson, Iowa	20
Spring Brook, Gratiot, Mich	25
Spring Brook, Erie, N. Y	,55
Spring Brook, Luzerne, Pa	12
Spring Church, Armstrong, Pa	30
Spring City, San Pete, Utah	130
Spring Creek, Pike, Ill	12
Spring Creek, Tama, Iowa	12
Spring Creek, Oceana, Mich	1
Spring Creek, Goodhue, Minn	23
Spring Creek, Phelps, Mo	12
Spring Creek, Johnson, Nebr	12
Spring Creek, Madison, N. C	4
Spring Creek, Warren, Pa	94
Spring Creek, Madison, Tenn	74
Spring Creek, Rockingham, Va	12
Spring Creek, Adams, Wis	28
Spring Dale, Cedar, Iowa	140
Springdale, Leavenworth, Kans	82
Springdale, Mason, Ky	8
Spring Dale, La Fayette, Miss	43
Spring Dale, Hamilton, Ohio	77
Spring Dale, Allegheny, Pa	61
Springdale, Claiborne, Tenn	12
Springdale, Kane, Utah	10
Spring Dale, Dane, Wis	15
Springerton, White, Ill	12
Springfield, (*c. h.*,) Conway, Ark	54
Springfield, Bonhomme, Dak	12
Springfield, (*c. h.*,) Effingham, Ga	27
SPRINGFIELD,* (*c. h.*,) Sangamon, Ill	4,000
Springfield, Franklin, Ind	10
Springfield, Keokuk, Iowa	110
Springfield, Linn, Kans	12
Springfield, (*c. h.*,) Washington, Ky	440
Springfield, (*c. h.*,) Livingston, La	14
Springfield, Penobscot, Me	330
Springfield,* (*c. h.*,) Hampden, Mass	4,000
Springfield, Oakland, Mich	21
Springfield,* (*c. h.*,) Greene, Mo	2,700
Springfield, Sullivan, N. H	23
Springfield, Union, N. J	140
Springfield, Otsego, N. Y	69
Springfield,* (*c. h.*,) Clark, Ohio	3,000
Springfield, Lane, Oreg	26
Springfield, Bradford, Pa	130
Springfield, (*c. h.*,) Robertson, Tenn	390
Springfield, (*c. h.*,) Limestone, Tex	190
Springfield,* Windsor, Vt	1,200
Springfield, Hampshire, W. Va	90
Springfield, Walworth, Wis	130
Springfield Centre, Otsego, N. Y	180
Springfield Furnace, Blair, Pa	36
Springfield Store, Queens, N. Y	20
Spring Forge, York, Pa	22
Spring Garden, Cherokee, Ala	12
Spring Garden, Jefferson, Ill	87
Spring Garden, Lancaster, Pa	59
Spring Garden, Pittsylvania, Va	5
Spring Green, Sauk, Wis	380
Spring Grove, Warren, Ill	43
Spring Grove, Linn, Iowa	11
Spring Grove, Houston, Minn	260
Spring Grove, Dallas, Mo	3
Spring Grove, Rowan, N. C	65

SPR	
Spring Grove, Lancaster, Pa	$12
Spring Grove, Surry, Va	12
Spring Hill, Hempstead, Ark	12
Spring Hill, Whitesides, Ill	100
Spring Hill, Decatur, Ind	26
Spring Hill, Johnson, Kans	200
Spring Hill, Barnstable, Mass	140
Spring Hill, Stearns, Minn	8
Spring Hill, Livingston, Mo	99
Spring Hill, Bradford, Pa	21
Spring Hill, Maury, Tenn	260
Spring Hill, Navarro, Tex	20
Spring Hill, Mecklenburgh, Va	9
Spring Hill Academy, Henry, Tenn	12
Spring Hill Depot, Henry, Ky	12
Springhill Furnace, Fayette, Pa	32
Spring Hills, Champaign, Ohio	70
Spring Hope, Bedford, Pa	12
Spring House, Montgomery, Pa	51
Spring House, Grainger, Tenn	6
Spring Lake, Bremer, Iowa	23
Spring Lake, Ottawa, Mich	630
Spring Lake, Williams, Ohio	28
Spring Lake, Waushara, Wis	96
Spring Meadow, Bedford, Pa	21
Spring Mills, Oakland, Mich	51
Spring Mills, Allegany, N. Y	78
Spring Mills, Richland, Ohio	22
Spring Mills, Centre, Pa	67
Spring Mills, Appomattox, Va	2
Spring Mountain, Coshocton, Ohio	48
Spring Place, (*c. h.*,) Murray, Ga	120
Spring Place, Marshall, Tenn	12
Springport, Henry, Ind	12
Springport, Henry, Ky	30
Springport, Jackson, Mich	81
Spring Prairie, Walworth, Wis	200
Spring Ridge, Caddo, La	12
Spring River Falls, Cherokee, Kans	12
Spring Run, Franklin, Pa	41
Springs, Suffolk, N. Y	32
Spring Side, Pottawatomie, Kans	12
Spring's Station, Brown, Ill	12
Spring Station, Woodford, Ky	77
Springtown, Warren, N. J	44
Springtown, Bucks, Pa	40
Springvale, Humboldt, Iowa	180
Springvale,* York, Me	350
Spring Vale, Fairfax, Va	30
Spring Valley, Colusa, Cal	21
Spring Valley, Douglas, Colo	40
Spring Valley, Marion, Ind	12
Spring Valley, Decatur, Iowa	38
Spring Valley,* Fillmore, Minn	230
Spring Valley, Adair, Mo	3
Spring Valley, Bergen, N. J	66
Spring Valley, Rockland, N. Y	430
Spring Valley, Greene, Ohio	190
Spring Valley, Grayson, Va	7
Spring Valley, Pierce, Wis	12
Springville, St. Clair, Ala	49
Springville, Coles, Ill	15
Springville, Lawrence, Ind	44
Springville, Linn, Iowa	260
Springville, Lenawee, Mich	46
Springville, Jefferson, Mont	28

* Money-order office.

STA

Springville, Erie, N. Y	$610
Springville, Wayne, Ohio	12
Springville, Multnomah, Oreg	22
Springville, Susquehanna, Pa	130
Springville, Henry, Tenn	12
Springville, Utah, Utah	120
Springville, Tazewell, Va	5
Springville, Vernon, Wis	100
Springwater, Winneshiek, Iowa	10
Springwater, Livingston, N. Y	230
Spring Water, Waushara, Wis	10
Sprout Brook, Montgomery, N. Y	130
Sprout Creek, Dutchess, N. Y	30
Spruce, Indiana, Pa	12
Spruce Creek, Huntingdon, Pa	230
Spruce Hill, Juniata, Pa	20
Spruce Hill, Highland, Va	3
Spruce Pine, Franklin, Ala	12
Sprys Landing, Kent, Md	55
Spurgeon, Pike, Ind	12
Spurlockville, Lincoln, W. Va	12
Spuyten Duyvil, Westchester, N. Y	230
Squak, King, Wash	12
Squam Village, Monmouth, N. J	200
Square Corner, Adams, Pa	23
Square Pond, Tolland, Conn	12
Squaw Creek, Boise, Idaho	12
Squaw Grove, De Kalb, Ill	66
Staatsburgh, Dutchess, N. Y	110
Staatsville, Washington, Wis	54
Stablersville, Baltimore, Md	8
Staceyville, Mitchell, Iowa	170
Stafford, Tolland, Conn	150
Stafford, Genesee, N. Y	130
Stafford, Monroe, Ohio	47
Stafford, Fort Bend, Tex	12
Stafford C. H., Stafford, Va	15
Stafford Springs,* Tolland, Conn	890
Stafford Store, Stafford, Va	21
Staffordville, Tolland, Conn	210
Staffordville, Clark, Wis	80
Stagville, Orange, N. C	12
Stahlstown, Westmoreland, Pa	24
Stairfield, Clinton, Mo	12
Stamford,* Fairfield, Conn	2,500
Stamford, Delaware, N. Y	170
Stamford, Bennington, Vt	140
Stamper's Creek, Orange, Ind	4
Stamping Ground, Scott, Ky	55
Stanard's Corners, Allegany, N. Y	13
Stanardsville, (*c. h.*,) Greene, Va	160
Stanchfield, Isanti, Minn	12
Standing Pine, Leake, Miss	2
Standing Stone, Bradford, Pa	52
Standish, Cumberland, Me	230
Stanford, McLean, Ill	12
Stanford, Monroe, Ind	52
Stanford, Marshall, Iowa	12
Stanford, (*c. h.*,) Lincoln, Ky	600
Stanfordville, Dutchess, N. Y	100
Stanhope, Sussex, N. J	340
Stanhope, Nash, N. C	7
Stanley, Morris, N. J	10
Stanley, Putnam, Ohio	11
Stanley Corners, Ontario, N. Y	110
Stanley's Creek, Gaston, N. C	12
Stanton, New Castle, Del	$140
Stanton, Montgomery, Iowa	12
Stanton, Miami, Kans	58
Stanton, (*c. h.*,) Powell, Ky	8
Stanton, (*c. h.*,) Montcalm, Mich	330
Stanton, Goodhue, Minn	25
Stanton, Hunterdon, N. J	44
Stanton, Jefferson, Pa	45
Stanton Depot, Haywood, Tenn	170
Stanton Copper Mines, Franklin, Mo	10
Stantonsburgh, Wilson, N. C	12
Stantonville, McNairy, Tenn	12
Stanwich, Fairfield, Conn	34
Stanwix, Oneida, N. Y	44
Stanwood, Cedar, Iowa	180
Stanwood, Leavenworth, Kans	12
Stapleton, Chickasaw, Iowa	9
Stapleton, Meade, Ky	13
Stapleton,* Richmond, N. Y	1,100
Stapleton, Morgan, Tenn	12
Stapleton Mills, Amherst, Va	12
Star, Rush, Ind	20
Star, Marion, Iowa	12
Star, Warren, Pa	12
Star, Lavaca, Tex	12
Star, Vernon, Wis	44
Star City, Pulaski, Ind	140
Stark, Butts, Ga	26
Stark, Somerset, Me	75
Stark, Chisago, Minn	43
Stark, Coos, N. H	58
Starke, Bradford, Fla	170
Starkesville, Lamar, Tex	4
Starkey, Yates, N. Y	91
Starksborough, Addison, Vt	110
Starkville, (*c. h.*,) Lee, Ga	46
Starkville, (*c. h.*,) Oktibbeha, Miss	220
Starkville, Herkimer, N. Y	120
Star of the West, Pike, Ark	12
Star Prairie, St. Croix, Wis	78
Starr's Point, Benton, Oreg	63
Starrville, Smith, Tex	56
Starucca, Wayne, Pa	50
State Bridge, Oneida, N. Y	97
Stateburgh, Sumter, S. C	80
State Centre, Marshall, Iowa	620
Stateley's Run, Grant, Ky	8
State Line, Columbia, Ark	12
State Line, Heard, Ga	12
State Line,* Warren, Ind	250
State Line, Berkshire, Mass	150
State Line, Freeborn, Minn	34
State Line, Franklin, Pa	55
State Line Mills, McKean, Pa	12
Statenville, Echols, Ga	93
State Road, Chemung, N. Y	6
State Road, Surry, N. C	12
Statesville,* (*c. h.*,) Iredell, N. C	450
Statesville, Wilson, Tenn	10
Station Creek, Covington, Miss	12
Station Creek, Coryell, Tex	12
Station Fifteen, Harrison, Ohio	33
Statler's Run, Monongalia, W. Va	4
Staunton, Macoupin, Ill	330
Staunton, Clay, Ind	270

* Money-order office.

Office	Compensation
Staunton, Fayette, Ohio	$32
*Staunton,** (*c. h.,*) Augusta, Va	2,400
Staunton's Mills, Somerset, Pa	39
Steamboat Rock, Hardin, Iowa	110
Steamburgh, Cattaraugus, N. Y	110
Steamburgh, Ashtabula, Ohio	16
Steamburgh, Crawford, Pa	19
Steam Corner, Fountain, Ind	19
Steam Corners, Morrow, Ohio	12
Steam Mill, Warren, Pa	50
Stebbinsville, Oceana, Mich	12
Stedman, Chautauqua, N. Y	25
Steedman's, Lexington, S. C	2
Steele Centre, Steele, Minn	6
Steele's, Rush, Ind	71
Steele's Grove, Tyler, Tex	12
Steele's Mills, Randolph, Ill	100
Steele's Tavern, Augusta, Va	85
Steeleville, Chester, Pa	30
Steelville, (*c. h.,*) Crawford, Mo	160
Steen's Prairie, Maries, Mo	8
Steep Falls, Cumberland, Me	57
Steer Creek, Gilmer, W. Va	14
Stegall's Depot, Bartow, Ga	12
*Steilacoom City,**(*c. h.,*) Pierce, Wash	370
Steinsburgh, Bucks, Pa	9
Stelapolis, Iowa, Iowa	78
Stella, Gratiot, Mich	15
Stelvidio, Darke, Ohio	22
Stembersville, Carbon, Pa	15
Stephens, Oglethorpe, Ga	60
Stephens, Boone, Mo	12
Stephensburgh, Hardin, Ky	45
Stephensburgh, Morris, N. J	43
Stephens' Chapel, Bledsoe, Tenn	2
Stephens' Mills, Steuben, N. Y	57
Stephenson's Depot, Frederick, Va	200
Stephensport, Breckinridge, Ky	51
Stephen's Store, Callaway, Mo	44
Stephensville, Wilkinson, Ga	12
Stephensville, (*c. h.,*) Erath, Tex	110
Stephensville, Outagamie, Wis	71
Stephentown, Rensselaer, N. Y	120
Stepney, Fairfield, Conn	39
Stepney Depot, Fairfield, Conn	140
Sterling, Windham, Conn	29
Sterling,* Whitesides, Ill	2,500
Sterling, Jackson, Iowa	62
Sterling, Worcester, Mass	300
Sterling, Madison, Mont	76
Sterling, Johnson, Nebr	16
Sterling, Cayuga, N. Y	160
Sterling, Wayne, Pa	67
Sterling Bush, Lewis, N. Y	11
Sterling Centre, Blue Earth, Minn	12
Sterling Hill, Windham, Conn	21
Sterling Run, Cameron, Pa	160
Sterling Valley, Cayuga, N. Y	56
Sterlingville, Jefferson, N. Y	63
Sterrettania, Erie, Pa	22
Sterrett's Gap, Perry, Pa	29
Stetson, Penobscot, Me	250
Stettin, Marathon, Wis	20
Steuben, Washington, Me	130
Steuben, Oneida, N. Y	59
Steuben, Huron, Ohio	100
*Steubenville,** (*c. h.,*) Jefferson, Ohio	2,600

Office	Compensation
Stevens, Lancaster, Pa	$40
Stevensburgh, Culpeper, Va	39
Stevenson, Jackson, Ala	210
Stevenson's Mills, Wayne, Mo	12
Stevenson's Mills, Wayne, Pa	64
Stevenson Station, Baltimore, Md	37
Stevens' Plains, Cumberland, Me	260
Stevens Point,* Portage, Wis	540
Stevenstown, Crawford, Kans	12
Stevenstown, La Crosse, Wis	66
Stevensville, Missoula, Mont	12
Stevensville, Sullivan, N. Y	67
Stevensville, Bradford, Pa	110
Stevensville, King and Queen, Va	54
Stewart, Erie, Pa	16
Stewart, Stewart, Tenn	21
Stewart, Green, Wis	64
Stewart's Run, Venango, Pa	36
Stewartstown, Coos, N. H	25
Stewartstown, York, Pa	110
Stewartstown, Monongalia, W. Va	12
Stewartsville, Posey, Ind	56
Stewartsville, Grant, Ky	8
Stewartsville,* De Kalb, Mo	370
Stewartsville, Warren, N. J	110
Stewartsville, Westmorland, Pa	40
Stewartville, Olmsted, Minn	63
Stice's Shoal, Cleveland, N. C	37
Sticklerville, Sullivan, Mo	42
Stickleyville, Lee, Va	25
Stiflesville, Crawford, Ill	34
Stiles, Davis, Iowa	83
Stiles, Oconto, Wis	70
Stilesborough, Bartow, Ga	69
Stilesville, Hendricks, Ind	140
Still Pond, Kent, Md	120
Still River, Worcester, Mass	98
Still Valley, Warren, N. J	16
Stillwater, Shasta, Cal	12
*Stillwater,** (*c. h.,*) Washington, Minn	2,000
Stillwater, Sussex, N. J	60
Stillwater, Saratoga, N. Y	430
Stillwater, Columbia, Pa	11
Stillwell, La Porte, Ind	12
Stinesville, Monroe, Ind	60
Stinesville, Lehigh, Pa	21
Stinson, Outagamie, Wis	12
Stip's Hill, Franklin, Ind	6
Stirling, Montgomery, Ga	6
Stirrup Grove, Macoupin, Ill	14
Stissing, Dutchess, N. Y	12
Stittville, Oneida, N. Y	90
Stockbridge, Henry, Ga	12
Stockbridge, Berkshire, Mass	990
Stockbridge, Ingham, Mich	100
Stockbridge, Madison, N. Y	110
Stockbridge, Windsor, Vt	98
Stockbridge, Calumet, Wis	120
Stock Creek, Scott, Va	10
Stockdale, Miami, Ind	82
Stockertown, Northampton, Pa	36
Stockholm, Sussex, N. J	39
Stockholm, St. Lawrence, N. Y	110
Stockholm, Pepin, Wis	150
Stockholm Depot, St. Lawrence, N. Y	210
Stockland, Montgomery, Mo	13

* Money-order office.

Post office	Amount
Stockport, Columbia, N. Y	$120
Stockport, Morgan, Ohio	52
Stockport Station, Delaware, N. Y	43
Stocksville, Buncombe, N. C	9
Stockton, Baldwin, Ala	12
Stockton,* (*c. h.*,) San Joaquin, Cal	3,600
Stockton, Clinch, Ga	97
Stockton, Jo Daviess, Ill	11
Stockton, Owen, Ind	11
Stockton, Waldo, Me	440
Stockton, Winona, Minn	100
Stockton,* (*c. h.*,) Cedar, Mo	450
Stockton, Hunterdon, N. J	280
Stockton, Chautaqua, N. Y	210
Stockton, Luzerne, Pa	260
Stockton, Roane, Tenn	13
Stockton, Tooele, Utah	25
Stockton, Portage, Wis	20
Stockwell,* Tippecanoe, Ind	370
Stoddard, Cheshire, N. H	110
Stoddard, Vernon, Wis	9
Stoddartsville, Luzerne, Pa	55
Stoker, Davis, Utah	100
Stokes, Oneida, N. Y	54
Stokes' Bridge, Darlington, S. C	12
Stokes' Mound, Carroll, Mo	12
Stone Arabia, Montgomery, N. Y	15
Stone Bank, Waukesha, Wis	50
Stone Bluffs, Fountain, Ind	18
Stoneborough, Mercer, Pa	150
Stone Church, Genesee, N. Y	32
Stone Church, Northampton, Pa	52
Stone Creek, Tuscarawas, Ohio	65
Stone Fort, Saline, Ill	14
Stoneham, Middlesex, Mass	1,200
Stoneham, Warren, Pa	12
Stone House, Lawrence, Ky	8
Stone House, Morgan, Mo	12
Stone House Hotel, Prince William, Va	6
Stone Lick, Clermont, Ohio	12
Stone Mills, Jefferson, N. Y	81
Stone Mountain, De Kalb, Ga	190
Stone Mountain, Carroll, Va	3
Stoner, Clarke, Ky	49
Stone Ridge, Ulster, N. Y	170
Stoner's Prairie, Dane, Wis	16
Stonersville, Carroll, Md	12
Stonersville, Berks, Pa	34
Stone's Bay, Onslow, N. C	12
Stone's Prairie, Adams, Ill	72
Stoneville, Rockingham, N. C	12
Stonewall, Scott, Ky	33
Stoney Brook, Suffolk, N. Y	240
Stoney Hill, Gasconade, Mo	13
Stoney Point, Bourbon, Ky	21
Stonington, New London, Conn	1,200
Stonington, Christian, Ill	57
Stono, St. Francois, Mo	24
Stony Bluff, Jefferson, Tenn	12
Stony Brook, Morris, N. J	12
Stony Creek, New Haven, Conn	100
Stony Creek, Washtenaw, Mich	50
Stony Creek, Somerset, Pa	41
Stony Creek, Carter, Tenn	12
Stony Creek Warehouse, Sussex, Va	98

Post office	Amount
Stony Fork, Watauga, N. C	$7
Stony Fork, Tioga, Pa	42
Stony Man, Page, Va	46
Stony Point, White, Ark	49
Stony Point, Sonoma, Cal	34
Stony Point, Jefferson, Ind	8
Stony Point, East Baton Rouge, La	20
Stony Point, Jackson, Mo	24
Stony Point, Rockland, N. Y	170
Stony Point, Alexander, N. C	12
Stony Point, Crawford, Pa	28
Stony Point, Anderson, S. C	12
Stony Point, Hawkins, Tenn	69
Stony Point, Albemarle, Va	12
Stony Point Mills, Cumberland, Va	16
Stony Ridge, Wood, Ohio	16
Stony Run, Oakland, Mich	26
Stony Run, Berks, Pa	21
Storeville, Anderson, S. C	13
Storm Lake, Buena Vista, Iowa	12
Stormville, Dutchess, N. Y	71
Stormville, Monroe, Pa	31
Storrs, Hamilton, Ohio	140
Story City, Story, Iowa	99
Stottville, Columbia, N. Y	75
Stouchsburgh, Berks, Pa	130
Stoughstown, Cumberland, Pa	19
Stoughton, Norfolk, Mass	600
Stoughton,* Dane, Wis	710
Stoutland, Camden, Mo	12
Stout's, Adams, Ohio	97
Stout's, Northampton, Pa	18
Stoutsville, Fairfield, Ohio	65
Stover, Dallas, Ark	9
Stow, Oxford, Me	37
Stow, Middlesex, Mass	120
Stowe,* Lamoille, Vt	610
Stowell's Corners, Jefferson, N. Y	11
Stoyestown, Somerset, Pa	160
Strabane, Washington, Pa	12
Strafford, Greene, Mo	12
Strafford, Strafford, N. H	82
Strafford, Orange, Vt	150
Strafford Blue Hills, Strafford, N. H	46
Strafford Corner, Strafford, N. H	32
Straight Fork, Scott, Ky	12
Strait Creek, Highland, Va	8
Strait's Corners, Tioga, N. Y	28
Strait's Lake, Oakland, Mich	6
Straitsville, Perry, Ohio	20
Stranger, Leavenworth, Kans	12
Stranger's Home, Lawrence, Ark	12
Strasburgh, Tuscarawas, Ohio	20
Strasburgh, Lancaster, Pa	400
Strasburgh, Shenandoah, Va	200
Strata, Montgomery, Ala	12
Stratford, Fairfield, Conn	990
Stratford, Coos, N. H	97
Stratford, Fulton, N. Y	93
Stratham, Rockingham, N. H	87
Stratton, Windham, Vt	19
Stratton's Falls, Delaware, N. Y	17
Strattonville, Clarion, Pa	170
Straughn's Station, Henry, Ind	36
Strausstown, Berks, Pa	43
Strawberry Plains, Jefferson, Tenn	120

*Money-order office.

Strawberry Point,* Clayton, Iowa	$410
Strawberry Valley, Yuba, Cal	55
Strawbridge, York, Pa	25
Strawtown, Hamilton, Ind	17
Streator,* La Salle, Ill	740
Street Road, Chester, Pa	340
Streetsborough, Portage, Ohio	58
Stribling Springs, Augusta, Va	51
Strickersville, Chester, Pa	97
Strickland, Isabella, Mich	12
Strickland's Ferry, Androscoggin, Me	50
Strinestown, York, Pa	12
Stringtown, Richland, Ill	10
Stringtown, Cole, Mo	13
String Town, Pickaway, Ohio	18
Stringtown, Wilson, Tenn	23
Stroderville, Cape Girardeau, Mo	12
Strode's Mills, Mifflin, Pa	58
Stronach, Manistee, Mich	36
Strong, Franklin, Me	210
Strong's Prairie, Adams, Wis	49
Strongstown, Indiana, Pa	15
Strongsville, Cuyahoga, Ohio	60
Strother, Fairfield, S. C	31
Stroudsburgh,* (*c. h.*,) Monroe, Pa	1,100
Struther's Station, Mahoning, Ohio	110
Stryker, Williams, Ohio	440
Strykersville, Wyoming, N. Y	100
Stuart, Adair, Iowa	140
Stuart's Draft, Augusta, Va	12
Stuart's Mill, Christian, Ky	16
Stuckeysville, Bedford, Pa	6
Stump Knob, Johnson, Tenn	12
Sturbridge, Worcester, Mass	200
Sturgeon, Fulton, Ind	12
Sturgeon,* Boone, Mo	400
Sturgeon Bay,* (*c. h.*,) Door, Wis	380
Sturgeonville, Brunswick, Va	12
Sturgis,* St. Joseph, Mich	1,500
Stuyvesant, Columbia, N. Y	170
Stuyvesant Falls, Columbia, N. Y	150
Suamico, Brown, Wis	70
Sublett, Adair, Mo	4
Sublette, Lee, Ill	490
Sublett's Tavern, Powhatan, Va	52
Sublimity, Pulaski, Ky	5
Sublimity, Marion, Oreg	28
Sub Rosa, Franklin, Ark	10
Sucarnoochee, Kemper, Miss	12
Success, Suffolk, N. Y	22
Suckasunny, Morris, N. J	250
Sudbury, Middlesex, Mass	120
Sudbury, Rutland, Vt	130
Sudlersville, Queen Anne, Md	50
Sudley, Anne Arundel, Md	12
Sue City, Macon, Mo	16
Suez, Mercer, Ill	77
Suffern, Rockland, N. Y	180
Suffield, Hartford, Conn	800
Suffield, Portage, Ohio	40
Suffolk, Suffolk, N. Y	100
Suffolk,* (*c. h.*,) Nansemond, Va	640
Sugar Branch, Switzerland, Ind	79
Sugar Bush, Outagamie, Wis	15
Sugar Creek, Benton, Ark	12
Sugar Creek, Vermilion, Ill	12
Sugar Creek, Hancock, Ind	$79
Sugar Creek, Jasper, Iowa	25
Sugar Creek, Gallatin, Ky	36
Sugar Creek, Claiborne, La	12
Sugar Creek, Walworth, Wis	30
Sugar Grove, Kane, Ill	33
Sugar Grove, Tippecanoe, Ind	63
Sugar Grove, Butler, Ky	43
Sugar Grove, Watauga, N. C	7
Sugar Grove, Fairfield, Ohio	83
Sugar Grove, Warren, Pa	260
Sugar Grove, Pendleton, W. Va	12
Sugar Grove, Vernon, Wis	8
Sugar Hill, Hall, Ga	12
Sugar Hill, Grafton, N. H	62
Sugar Hill, Schuyler, N. Y	12
Sugar Hill, McDowell, N. C	12
Sugar Hill, Panola, Tex	2
Sugar Lake, Crawford, Pa	11
Sugar Land, Fort Bend, Tex	30
Sugar Loaf, Sebastian, Ark	7
Sugar Loaf, Boulder, Colo	8
Sugar Loaf, Ford, Ill	12
Sugar Loaf, Orange, N. Y	83
Sugar Notch, Luzerne, Pa	200
Sugar Pine, Tuolumne, Cal	12
Sugar Run, Bradford, Pa	31
Sugartown, Chester, Pa	26
Sugartree, Guernsey, Ohio	15
Sugar Tree Ridge, Highland, Ohio	60
Sugar Valley, Gordon, Ga	15
Sugar Valley, Clinton, Pa	180
Suggsville, Clarke, Ala	53
Suisun City,* (*c. h.*,) Solano, Cal	320
Suitsville, Prince George's, Md	25
Sullivan,* (*c. h.*,) Moultrie, Ill	460
Sullivan,* (*c. h.*,) Sullivan, Ind	760
Sullivan, Hancock, Me	100
Sullivan, Franklin, Mo	180
Sullivan, Cheshire, N. H	22
Sullivan, Ashland, Ohio	110
Sullivan, Tioga, Pa	20
Sullivan, Jefferson, Wis	12
Sullivan Centre, Livingston, Ill	12
Sullivanville, Chemung, N. Y	38
Sulphur Bluff, Hopkins, Tex	21
Sulphur Fork, Henry, Ky	12
Sulphur Hill, Shelby, Ind	12
Sulphur Lick, Monroe, Ky	10
Sulphur Rock, Independence, Ark	24
Sulphur Spring, Crawford, Ohio	120
Sulphur Springs, Williamson, Ill	12
Sulphur Springs, Henry, Ind	200
Sulphur Springs, Montgomery, N. C	11
Sulphur Springs, Rhea, Tenn	82
Sulphur Springs Landing, Jefferson, Mo	73
Sulphur Well, Shelby, Tenn	65
Sumac, Bollinger, Mo	12
Summerfield, Dallas, Ala	180
Summerfield, St. Clair, Ill	300
Summerfield, Noble, Ohio	140
Summerford, Madison, Ohio	31
Summer Hill, Pike, Ill	75
Summer Hill, Cayuga, N. Y	32
Summer Hill, Cambria, Pa	94

* Money-order office.

Summers, Rockbridge, Va	$5
Summerset, Warren, Iowa	54
Summerton, Gratiot, Mich	12
Summerville, Calhoun, Ark	12
Summerville, (*c. h.*,) Chattooga, Ga	55
Summerville, Peoria, Ill	33
Summerville, Cass, Mich	59
Summerville, (*c. h.*,) Harnett, N. C	9
Summerville, Union, Oreg	43
Summerville, Jefferson, Pa	73
Summerville, Charleston, S. C	180
Summit, Blount, Ala	51
Summit, Plumas, Cal	49
Summit, Cook, Ill	18
Summit, Muscatine, Iowa	19
Summit, Jefferson, Ky	12
Summit, Washtenaw, Mich	7
Summit, Jackson, Minn	3
Summit, Pike, Miss	650
Summit, Madison, Mont	24
Summit, Union, N. J	340
Summit, Schoharie, N. Y	250
Summit, Summit, Ohio	24
Summit, Benton, Oreg	12
Summit, Cambria, Pa	82
Summit, Kent, R. I	78
Summit, Iron, Utah	40
Summit, Waukesha, Wis	61
Summit Bridge, New Castle, Del	81
Summit Hill, Carbon, Pa	600
Summit Mills, Somerset, Pa	25
Summit Point, Jefferson, W. Va	230
Summit Station, Onondaga, N. Y	84
Summit Station, Licking, Ohio	11
Summit Station, Schuylkill, Pa	22
Summitville, Madison, Ind	20
Summitville, Lee, Iowa	48
Summitville, Columbiana, Ohio	92
Summitville, Coffee, Tenn	13
Summum, Fulton, Ill	52
Sumner, Lawrence, Ill	410
Sumner, Rush, Ind	25
Sumner, Bremer, Iowa	30
Sumner, Oxford, Me	25
Sumner, Gratiot, Mich	12
Sumner, Freeborn, Minn	8
Sumnerville, Ottawa, Kans	12
Sumneytown, Montgomery, Pa	71
Sumpter, (*c. h.*,) Trinity, Tex	46
Sumption Prairie, St. Joseph, Ind	12
Sumter, Moultrie, Ill	12
Sumter, McLeod, Minn	12
Sumter C. H.,* Sumter, S. C	1,300
Sumterville, Sumter, Ala	24
Sumterville, (*c. h.*,) Sumter, Fla	51
Sun, St. Tammany, La	6
Sunapee, Sullivan, N. H	140
Sunbeam, Mercer, Ill	170
Sunbury, Livingston, Ill	19
Sunbury, Gates, N. C	18
Sunbury, Delaware, Ohio	180
Sunbury, (*c. h.*,) Northumberland, Pa	1,600
Suncliff, Indiana, Pa	14
Suncook,* Merrimack, N. H	750
Sunderland, Franklin, Mass	290
Sunderland, Bennington, Vt	$130
Sunderlandville, Calvert, Md	56
Sunderlinville, Potter, Pa	16
Sunfield, Eaton, Mich	20
Sun Hill, Wyoming, W. Va	5
Sunman, Ripley, Ind	160
Sunny Dale, Pickens, S. C	12
Sunny Side, Chicot, Ark	50
Sunny Side, Marion, Ind	12
Sunny Side, Buchanan, Iowa	44
Sunny Side, Wright, Mo	12
Sunny Side, Washington, N. C	12
Sunny Side, Allegheny, Pa	46
Sunny Side, Cumberland, Va	15
Sun Prairie,* Dane, Wis	620
Sun Rise, Bath, Va	10
Sunrise City, Chisago, Minn	81
Sun River, Lewis and Clarke, Mont	12
Sunville, Venango, Pa	46
Superior, (*c. h.*,) Douglas, Wis	510
Surgeon's Hall, Allegheny, Pa	24
Surgoinsville, Hawkins, Tenn	12
Surrency, Appling, Ga	12
Surrey, Portage, Wis	14
Surry, Hancock, Me	92
Surry, Cheshire, N. H	50
Surry C. H., Surry, Va	90
Susanville,* (*c. h.*,) Lassen, Cal	530
Suspension, Bullock, Ala	55
Suspension Bridge,* Niagara, N. Y	1,800
Susquehanna, Dauphin, Pa	52
Susquehanna Depot,* Susquehanna, Pa	1,100
Sussex, Waukesha, Wis	110
Sussex C. H., Sussex, Va	32
Sutersville, Westmoreland, Pa	53
Sutherland, Dinwiddie, Va	19
Sutherland Falls, Rutland, Vt	210
Sutherland Springs, Wilson, Tex	82
Sutter Creek, Amador, Cal	440
Sutton, Worcester, Mass	210
Sutton, Merrimack, N. H	110
Sutton, Caledonia, Vt	120
Sutton's Bay, Leelenaw, Mich	19
Sutton's Corners, Crawford, Pa	92
Sutton's Station, Robertson, Tex	130
Suwanee, Gwinnett, Ga	12
Suwannee Shoals, Columbia, Fla	16
Swain, Allegany, N. Y	66
Swainsborough, (*c. h.*,) Emanuel, Ga	12
Swale, Steuben, N. Y	8
Swampscott, Essex, Mass	630
Swan, Noble, Ind	75
Swan, Vinton, Ohio	67
Swan City, (*c. h.*,) Saline, Nebr	29
Swan Creek, Warren, Ill	57
Swan Creek, Saginaw, Mich	12
Swan Creek, Gallia, Ohio	41
Swander's Crossing, Shelby, Ohio	12
Swangstown, Cleveland, N. C	12
Swan Lake, Arkansas, Ark	25
Swan Lake, Lincoln, Dak	12
Swannano, Buncombe, N. C	9
Swann's Station, Moore, N. C	10
Swan Pond, Knox, Ky	4
Swan Quarter, (*c. h.*,) Hyde, N. C	10

* **Money-order office.**

Swan River, Morrison, Minn	$11
Swansborough, Onslow, N. C	20
Swansea, Bristol, Mass	150
Swansea, Lincoln, Minn	12
Swan's Island, Hancock, Me	85
Swansonville, Pittsylvania, Va	8
Swan Station, Erie, Pa	52
Swanton, Butler, Iowa	22
Swanton, Alleghany, Md	60
Swanton, Fulton, Ohio	160
Swanton,* Franklin, Vt	490
Swanton Centre, Franklin, Vt	21
Swanton Junction, Franklin, Vt	20
Swanville, Jefferson, Ind	24
Swanville, Waldo, Me	55
Swanzey, Cheshire, N. H	64
Swartswood, Sussex, N. J	12
Swartwout, Polk, Tex	8
Swartz Creek, Genesee, Mich	6
Swartzville, Lancaster, Pa	12
Swatara, Schuylkill, Pa	76
Swatara Station, Dauphin, Pa	96
Sweadel, (c. h.,) McPherson, Kans	12
Swede Grove, Meeker, Minn	38
Sweden, Oxford, Me	44
Sweden, Monroe, N. Y	32
Sweden, Potter, Pa	3
Sweden Valley, Potter, Pa	5
Swedesborough, Gloucester, N. J	270
Swedesburgh, Henry, Iowa	12
Swede's Forest, Redwood, Minn	12
Swedona, Mercer, Ill	220
Sweede Point, Boone, Iowa	160
Sweedlin Hill, Pendleton, W. Va	5
Sweet Air, Baltimore, Md	34
Sweet Chalybeate, Alleghany, Va	150
Sweet Home, Nodaway, Mo	21
Sweet Home, Iredell, N. C	6
Sweet Home, Lavaca, Tex	66
Sweetland, Nevada, Cal	28
Sweetland Centre, Muscatine, Iowa	16
Sweetser's, Grant, Ind	12
Sweet Springs, Monroe, W. Va	110
Sweet Valley, Luzerne, Pa	12
Sweet Water, Gwinnett, Ga	12
Sweet Water, Menard, Ill	120
Sweetwater, Esmeralda, Nev	12
Sweet Water, Monroe, Tenn	360
Sweet Wine, Hamilton, Ohio	6
Swift Creek Bridge, Craven, N. C	10
Swift Island, Montgomery, N. C	5
Swift Lake, Meeker, Minn	10
Swingleville, Washington, Tenn	10
Swit's City, Greene, Ind	12
Switzler, Monroe, Mo	12
Swoope's Depot, Augusta, Va	83
Sybertsville, Luzerne, Pa	54
Sycamore, (c. h.,)* De Kalb, Ill	1,500
Sycamore, Wyandot, Ohio	49
Sycamore, Cheatham, Tenn	19
Sycamore, Calhoun, W. Va	4
Sycamore Dale, Harrison, W. Va	18
Sycamore Grove, Putnam, W. Va	12
Sycamore Springs, Butler, Kans	7
Sydnorsville, Franklin, Va	10
Syene, Dane, Wis	28
Sykes' Mills, Elmore, Ala	$12
Sykesville, Carroll, Md	200
Sykesville, Burlington, N. J	16
Sylacauga, Talladega, Ala	12
Sylamore, Izard, Ark	7
Sylarsville, Monroe, Ark	12
Sylliman, Schuylkill, Pa	14
Sylvan, Washtenaw, Mich	59
Sylvan, Franklin, Pa	9
Sylvan, Richland, Wis	28
Sylvan Dale, Hancock, Ill	12
Sylvan Hill, Meeker, Minn	12
Sylvania, Parke, Ind	24
Sylvania, Dade, Mo	12
Sylvania, Lucas, Ohio	330
Sylvania, Bradford, Pa	86
Sylvania, Racine, Wis	27
Sylvan Lodge, Newton, Mo	12
Sylvarena, Smith, Miss	12
Sylvester, Green, Wis	39
Symco, Waupaca, Wis	29
Symmes, Hamilton, Ohio	10
Symmes' Corners, Butler, Ohio	41
Syosset, Queens, N. Y	66
Syracuse, Kosciusko, Ind	64
Syracuse,* Morgan, Mo	230
Syracuse, (c. h.,)* Onondaga, N. Y	4,000
Syracuse, Meigs, Ohio	120

T.

Taberg, Oneida, N. Y	260
Tabernacle, Tipton, Tenn	12
Taberville, St. Clair, Mo	42
Table Bluff, Humboldt, Cal	12
Table Grove, Fulton, Ill	77
Table Mountain, Pickens, S. C	5
Table Rock, Izard, Ark	12
Table Rock, Sierra, Cal	140
Table Rock, Pawnee, Nebr	53
Table Rock, Adams, Pa	14
Table Rock, Raleigh, W. Va	8
Tabo, La Fayette, Mo	89
Tabor,* Fremont, Iowa	400
Tabor, Roane, Tenn	5
Tacoma, Pierce, Wash	12
Tadmer, Montgomery, Ohio	77
Taffe, Wayne, Nebr	12
Tafton, Pike, Pa	7
Taftsville, Windsor, Vt	120
Taghkanick, Columbia, N. Y	5
Tahlequah, (c. h.,) Cherokee N., Ind. T	46
Taho, El Dorado, Cal	15
Talbotton, (c. h.,) Talbot, Ga	420
Talbott's Mills, Jefferson, Tenn	51
Talbotville, Chester, Pa	16
Talcott, Charlotte, Va	220
Talcottville, Tolland, Conn	96
Talking Rock, Pickens, Ga	28
Talladega, (c. h.,)* Talladega, Ala	1,000
TALLAHASSEE,* *(c. h.,)* Leon, Fla	2,100
Tallahoma, Lucas, Iowa	36
Tallapoosa, Haralson, Ga	12
Talleyrand, Keokuk, Iowa	140
Tallmadge, Ottawa, Mich	16

* Money-order office.

Post office	Compensation
Tallmadge, Summit, Ohio	$220
Tallman, Rockland, N. Y	27
Tallmansville, Upshur, W. Va	2
Tallula, Menard, Ill	260
Tallulah, Habersham, Ga	14
Tallulah, (*c. h.*,) Issoquena, Miss	24
Talley Cavey, Allegheny, Pa	37
Talley Ho, Granville, N. C	10
Talmage, Baldwin, Ga	30
Tama City, Tama, Iowa	1,200
Tamaqua,* Schuylkill, Pa	1,400
Tamarac, Crawford, Pa	30
Tamarack, Montcalm, Mich	12
Tamaroa, Perry, Ill	410
Tamola Station, Kemper, Miss	12
Tamorack, Will, Ill	60
Tampa,* (*c. h.*,) Hillsborough, Fla	280
Tampico, Whitesides, Ill	12
Tampico, Jackson, Ind	24
Tampico, Darke, Ohio	14
Tampico, Grainger, Tenn	21
Tamworth, Carroll, N. H	180
Tamworth Iron Works, Carroll, N. H.	110
Taneytown, Carroll, Md	230
Tangapaho, St. Helena, La	200
Tanktown, Delaware, Ohio	28
Tanners, Gilmer, W. Va	6
Tanner's Falls, Wayne, Pa	21
Tannersville, Greene, N. Y	21
Tannersville, Monroe, Pa	55
Tannery, Indiana, Pa	56
Taos, Cole, Mo	25
Tappahannock, (*c. h.*,) Essex, Va	190
Tappan, Harrison, Ohio	26
Tappantown, Rockland, N. Y	93
Tarborough,* (*c. h.*,) Edgecombe, N. C	1,200
Tardyville, Pontotoc, Miss	26
Tarentum, Allegheny, Pa	290
Tariffville, Hnrtford, Conn	190
Tarkio, Page, Iowa	32
Tarlton, Pickaway, Ohio	150
Tarrant, (*c. h.*,) Hopkins, Tex	12
Tarr Farm,* Venango, Pa	860
Tarrytown,* Westchester, N. Y	1,900
Tassinong, Porter, Ind	20
Tate Creek, Braxton, W. Va	9
Tate's Station, Montgomery, Tenn	17
Tatesville, Bedford, Pa	12
Taunton,* (*c. h.*,) Bristol, Mass	3,300
Taverner's Woods, Talbot, Md	33
Tawas City,* (*c. h.*,) Iosco, Mich	320
Tawawa, Shelby, Ohio	20
Taxahau, Lancaster, S. C	12
Taycheedah, Fond du Lac, Wis	62
Taylor, Ogle, Ill	47
Taylor, Harford, Md	40
Taylor, Cortland, N. Y	83
Taylor Centre, Wayne, Mich	10
Taylor Hill, Franklin, Ill	7
Taylor's, Sumpter, S. C	5
Taylor's Creek, St. Francis, Ark	24
Taylor's Creek, Liberty, Ga	32
Taylor's Creek, Hamilton, Ohio	26
Taylor's Depot, La Fayette, Miss	37
Taylor's Fall's, Chisago, Minn	470
Taylor's Island, Dorchester, Md	$83
Taylor's Mills, Randolph, W. Va	12
Taylor's Stand, Crawford, Pa	12
Taylor's Station, Franklin, Ohio	12
Taylor's Store, Franklin, Va	27
Taylorstown, Washington, Pa	50
Taylorstown, Loudoun, Va	56
Taylorsville, Plumas, Cal	150
Taylorsville, Bartholomew, Ind	170
Taylorsville, Fayette, Iowa	94
Taylorsville, (*c. h.*,) Spencer, Ky	190
Taylorsville, Montgomery, Ohio	20
Taylorsville, Bucks, Pa	94
Taylorsville, (*c. h.*,) Johnson, Tenn	75
Taylorsville, Hanover, Va	64
Taylorville, (*c. h.*) Christian, Ill	750
Taylorville, (*c. h.*,) Alexander, N. C	65
Taymouth, Saginaw, Mich	17
Tazewell, (*c. h.*,) Claiborne, Tenn	130
Tazewell C. H., Tazewell, Va	230
T. B., Prince George's, Md	96
Teachey's, Duplin, N. C	17
Teague's Mills, Hardeman, Tenn	12
Tebeanville, Ware, Ga	240
Tecolote, San Miguel, N. Mex	42
Tecumseh, Shawnee, Kans	60
Tecumseh, Warren, Ky	12
Tecumseh,* Lenawee, Mich	1 600
Tecumseh,* (*c. h.*,) Johnson, Nebr	280
Tedrow, Fulton, Ohio	89
Teekalet, Kitsap, Wash	140
Tehama, Tehama, Cal	120
Tehichipa, Kern, Cal	12
Tehuacana, Limestone, Tex	12
Tekamah,* (*c. h.*,) Burt, Nebr	100
Tekonsha, Calhoun, Mich	260
Telegraph City, Calaveras, Cal	61
Telford, Bucks, Pa	12
Tell City,* Perry, Ind	410
Teller's Corners, Crawford, Wis	8
Tellico Plains, Monroe, Tenn	16
Teloga Springs, Chattooga, Ga	10
Temecula, San Diego, Cal	12
Temperance, Telfair, Ga	15
Temperance Hall, De Kalb, Tenn	10
Temperance Hill, Monroe, Miss	4
Temperance Hill, Marion, S. C	12
Temperance Mount, Simpson, Ky	11
Temperanceville, Belmont, Ohio	27
Temperanceville, Allegheny, Pa	400
Temperanceville, Accomack, Va	22
Temple, Hillsborough, N. H	110
Temple, Berks, Pa	62
Temple Hill, Barren, Ky	5
Templeman's Cross Roads, Westmoreland, Va	12
Temple Mills, Franklin, Me	56
Temple of Health, Abbeville, S. C	5
Templeton, Worcester, Mass	430
Templeton, Prince George, Va	12
Templeville, Queen Anne, Md	32
Tenafly, Bergen, N. J	100
Tenallytown, Washington, D. C	31
Tenant's Harbor, Knox, Me	140
Tenhassen, Martin, Minn	39
Ten Mile, Campbell, Ky	12

* Money-order office.

Post office	
Ten Mile, Macon, Mo	$12
Ten Mile, Douglas, Oreg	12
Ten Mile, Washington, Pa	58
Ten Mile, Lincoln, W. Va	4
Ten Mile Bottom, Venango, Pa	12
Ten Mile House, Clinton, Iowa	12
Ten Mile House, Milwaukee, Wis	38
Ten Mile Stand, Meigs, Tenn	56
Tennessee, McDonough, Ill	130
Tennessee Colony, Anderson, Tex	12
Tennessee Ridge, Stewart, Tenn	20
Tennessee River Station, Stewart, Tenn	12
Tennille, Washington, Ga	140
Tensaw, Baldwin, Ala	37
Tenth Legion, Rockingham, Va	20
Terre Bonne, Terre Bonne, La	52
Terre Coupee, St. Joseph, Ind	19
Terre Haute, Henderson, Ill	160
Terre Haute,* (*c. h.*,) Vigo, Ind	4,000
Terre Haute, Decatur, Iowa	8
Terre Haute, Putnam, Mo	28
Terre Haute, Champaign, Ohio	29
Terre Hill, Lancaster, Pa	110
Terry, Hinds, Miss	370
Terry, Carroll, Tenn	9
Terrysville, Litchfield, Conn	370
Terrytown, Bradford, Pa	47
Terryville, De Witt, Tex	12
Tess Corners, Waukesha, Wis	21
Tetersburgh, Tipton, Ind	57
Teutopolis, Effingham, Ill	200
Tewkesbury, Middlesex, Mass	170
Texana, (*c. h.*,) Jackson, Tex	94
Texas, Washington, Ky	12
Texas, Oswego, N. Y	41
Texas, Henry, Ohio	89
Texas, Lycoming, Pa	16
Texas, Tucker, W. Va	2
Texas City, Saline, Ill	12
Texas Valley, Cortland, N. Y	14
Thacker's Creek, Blount, Ala	12
Thaxton's, Bedford, Va	86
Thayer, Union, Iowa	49
Thebes, Alexander, Ill	35
The Corner, Ulster, N. Y	33
The Dalles,* (*c. h.*,) Wasco, Oreg	760
The Forks, Somerset, Me	93
The Glen, Warren, N. Y	13
The Grove, Cook, Ill	59
The Grove, Caroline, Va	12
The Narrows, Crawford, Ark	3
Theological Seminary, Fairfax, Va	180
The Plains, Fauquier, Va	220
Theresa, Jefferson, N. Y	470
Theresa, Dodge, Wis	130
The Rock, Upson, Ga	22
The Rock, Mercer, W. Va	12
The Square, Cayuga, N. Y	22
Thetford, Orange, Vt	150
Thetford Centre, Genesee, Mich	3
Thetford Centre, Orange, Vt	110
Thibodeaux,* (*c. h.*,) La Fourche, La	820
Thivener, Gallia, Ohio	15
Thomas, Oceana, Mich	20
Thomas, Harrison, Mo	12

Post office	
Thomasborough, Champaign, Ill	$24
Thomas' Run, Harford, Md	33
Thomas Station, Bullock, Ala	17
Thomaston,* Litchfield, Conn	1,000
Thomaston, (*c. h.*,) Upson, Ga	170
Thomaston, Knox, Me	1,200
Thomastown, Leake, Miss	12
Thomasville, (*c. h.*,) Thomas, Ga	700
Thomasville, Oregon, Mo	97
Thomasville, Davidson, N. C	330
Thomasville, York, Pa	12
Thomasville, Cheatham, Tenn	12
Thompson, Windham, Conn	330
Thompson, Columbia, Ga	270
Thompson, Geauga, Ohio	100
Thompson, Susquehanna, Pa	130
Thompson, Washington, Wis	3
Thompson's Cross Roads, Louisa, Va	18
Thompson's River, Missoula, Mont	12
Thompson's Station, Williamson, Tenn	33
Thompsontown, Juniata, Pa	230
Thompsonville, Carroll, Ark	12
Thompsonville,* Hartford, Conn	970
Thompsonville, Pulaski, Ky	3
Thompsonville, Sullivan, N. Y	31
Thompsonville, Rockingham, N. C	4
Thompsonville, Washington, Pa	43
Thompsonville, Gonzales, Tex	12
Thompsonville, Racine, Wis	63
Thomson, Carroll, Ill	520
Thoms' Run, Greene, Pa	11
Thornburgh, Spottsylvania, Va	28
Thornbury, Chester, Pa	26
Thorndale Iron Works, Chester, Pa	120
Thorndike, Waldo, Me	12
Thorndike, Hampden, Mass	230
Thorndike, Cabell, W. Va	13
Thorn Grove, Knox, Tenn	28
Thorn Hill, Marion, Ala	10
Thorn Hill, Onondaga, N. Y	21
Thorn Hill, Grainger, Tenn	17
Thornhill, Orange, Va	20
Thornton, Cook, Ill	59
Thornton, St. Clair, Mich	36
Thornton, Grafton, N. H	20
Thornton, Delaware, Pa	16
Thornton, Taylor, W. Va	96
Thornton's Bluff, Etowah, Ala	12
Thornton's Depot, Fairfax, Va	10
Thornton's Ferry, Hillsborough, N. H	140
Thorntown,* Boone, Ind	1,000
Thornville, Lapeer, Mich	46
Thornville, Perry, Ohio	110
Three Bridges, Hunterdon, N. J	45
Three Grove, Cass, Nebr	31
Three Locusts, Marion, Ohio	24
Three Mile Bay, Jefferson, N Y	250
Three Oaks,* Berrien, Mich	340
Three Rivers, Hampden, Mass	110
Three Rivers,* St. Joseph, Mich	1,700
Three Runs, Clearfield, Pa	17
Three Springs, Hart, Ky	20
Three Springs, Huntingdon, Pa	94
Three Tons, Montgomery, Pa	50

* Money-order office.

Post office	Salary
Throopville, Cayuga, N. Y	$73
Thurlow, Delaware, Pa	77
Thurman, Warren, N. Y	25
Thurman, Gallia, Ohio	180
Thurston, Steuben, N. Y	12
Tibbatt's Cross Roads, Campbell, Ky	6
Tibby Station, Lowndes, Miss	97
Ticonderoga, Essex, N. Y	680
Ticonic, Monona, Iowa	15
Tidioute,* Warren, Pa	3,200
Tiffany, Rock, Wis	54
Tiffin, Johnson, Iowa	12
Tiffin,* (*c. h.*,) Seneca, Ohio	2,400
Tigerville, Terre Bonne, La	22
Tilden, Hancock, Me	27
Tillamook, (*c. h.*,) Tillamook, Oreg	12
Tillatoba, Yalabusha, Miss	12
Tiller's Ferry, Kershaw, S. C	2
Tilton, Whitfield, Ga	83
Tilton, Fleming, Ky	81
Tilton,* Belknap, N. H	760
Timber Cove, Sonoma, Cal	99
Timber Creek, Marshall, Iowa	23
Timber Creek, Riley, Kans	12
Timber Creek, Hunt, Tex	7
Timber Hill, Labette, Kans	12
Timber Ridge, Union, S. C	6
Timber Ridge, Greene, Tenn	12
Timber Ridge, Rockbridge, Va	11
Timberville, Dodge, Nebr	75
Timberville, Paulding, Ohio	12
Timberville, Rockingham, Va	81
Timbuctoo, Yuba, Cal	63
Time, Pike, Ill	79
Timmonsville, Darlington, S. C	240
Tindell, Grundy, Mo	12
Tingley, Union, Iowa	23
Tinker Run, Westmoreland, Pa	40
Tinmouth, Rutland, Vt	20
Tinney's Grove, Ray, Mo	49
Tinton Falls, Monmouth, N. J	45
Tioga, Neosho, Kans	160
Tioga, Tioga, Pa	540
Tioga Centre, Tioga, N. Y	77
Tioga Valley, Bradford, Pa	3
Tionesta,* (*c. h.*,) Forest, Pa	310
Tippecanoe, Harrison, Ohio	25
Tippecanoe, Fayette, Pa	35
Tippecanoe City,* Miami, Ohio	710
Tippecanoetown, Marshall, Ind	22
Tip's Branch, Pawnee, Nebr	12
Tipton,* (*c. h.*,) Tipton, Ind	580
Tipton,* (*c. h.*,) Cedar, Iowa	980
Tipton, Lenawee, Mich	26
Tipton,* Moniteau, Mo	630
Tipton, Lancaster, Nebr	12
Tipton, Blair, Pa	110
Tipton Grove, Hardin, Iowa	5
Tiptonville, Obion, Tenn	130
Tirade, Walworth, Wis	8
Tiro, Crawford, Ohio	20
Tishemingo, Chickasaw N., Ind. T	12
Tiskilwa, Bureau, Ill	670
Titusville, Ripley, Ind	14
Titusville, Mercer, N. J	160
Titusville,* Crawford, Pa	3,400
Tiverton, Newport, R. I	$80
Tiverton Four Corners, Newport, R. I	110
Tivoli, Dubuque, Iowa	25
Tivoli, Blue Earth, Minn	38
Tivoli, Dutchess, N. Y	320
Tivoli, Lycoming, Pa	38
Tobacco Stick, Dorchester, Md	33
Toboso, Licking, Ohio	43
Tobyhanna Mills, Monroe, Pa	200
Toccopola, Pontotoc, Miss	58
Todd, Huntingdon, Pa	5
Todd's, Morgan, Ohio	30
Todd's, Shelby, Tex	12
Todd's Point, Shelby, Ill	64
Todd's Point, Shelby, Ky	18
Todd's Valley, Placer, Cal	35
Toddsville, Otsego, N. Y	95
Token Creek, Dane, Wis	130
Toland's Prairie, Washington, Wis	30
Toledo,* (*c. h.*,) Tama, Iowa	1,100
Toledo, Chase, Kans	19
Toledo,* (*c. h.*,) Lucas, Ohio	3,700
Toledo, Benton, Oreg	24
Tolersville, Louisa, Va	150
Tolesborough, Lewis, Ky	23
Toleston, Lake, Ind	51
Tolland, (*c. h.*,) Tolland, Conn	360
Tolland, Hampden, Mass	45
Tolona, Champaign, Ill	620
Tomah,* Monroe, Wis	690
Tomahawk Springs, Berkeley, W. Va	18
Tomales, Marin, Cal	80
Tomb's Run, Lycoming, Pa	7
Tomhannock, Rensselaer, N. Y	48
Tomkin's Cove, Rockland, N. Y	88
Tompkins, Jackson, Mich	22
Tompkins' Corners, Chemung, N. Y	12
Tompkinsville, (*c. h.*,) Monroe, Ky	110
Tompkinsville, Richmond, N. Y	480
Tompkinsville, Luzerne, Pa	22
Tompson's Station, Audrian, Mo	36
Tom's Creek, Surry, N. C	21
Tom's River,* Ocean, N. J	540
Tonawanda,* Erie, N. Y	890
Tongaloo, Madison, Miss	12
Tonganoxie, Leavenworth, Kans	290
Tonica,* La Salle, Ill	630
Tontogany, Wood, Ohio	310
Tontzville, Miami, Kans	17
Tooele, (*c. h.*,) Tooele, Utah	55
Toolsborough, Louisa, Iowa	38
Toomsborough, Wilkinson, Ga	89
Toomsuba, Lauderdale, Miss	38
Tooner's Station, Hardeman, Tenn	10
Topeka, Mason, Ill	146
TOPEKA,* (*c. h.*,) Shawnee, Kans	3,600
Topin's Grove, Jackson, W. Va	10
Topsail Sound, New Hanover, N. C	12
Topsfield, Washington, Me	80
Topsfield, Essex, Mass	180
Topsham, Sagadahoc, Me	420
Topsham, Orange, Vt	110
Topton, Berks, Pa	35
Toquerville, (*c. h.*,) Kane, Utah	74

* Money-order office.

Torah, Stearns, Minn	$91
Torch, Athens, Ohio	28
Torch Lake, Antrim, Mich	30
Toronto, Vermillion, Ind	44
Toronto, Clinton, Iowa	45
Toronto, Woodson, Kans	12
Toronto, Miller, Mo	12
Torrance, Grenada, Miss	85
Torringford, Litchfield, Conn	25
Torrington, Litchfield, Conn	97
Toto, Stark, Ind	16
Tottonville, Richmond, N. Y	260
Touchet, Walla-Walla, Wash	12
Tough Kenamon, Chester, Pa	180
Toulon,* (*c. h.*,) Stark, Ill	570
Towanda, McLean, Ill	230
Towanda, Butler, Kans	59
Towanda,* (*c. h.*,) Bradford, Pa	2,400
Towash, Hill, Tex	12
Tower City, Schuylkill, Pa	43
Tower Hill, Shelby, Ill	200
Tower Hill, Delaware, Iowa	16
Tower Hill, Appomattox, Va	25
Towerville, Crawford, Wis	32
Towlesville, Steuben, N. Y	10
Town Bluff, Tyler, Tex	12
Town Creek, Lawrence, Ala	12
Towner's, Putnam, N. Y	130
Townesville, Granville, N. C	80
Town Hill, Luzerne, Pa	54
Town Line, Erie, N. Y	45
Town Line, Luzerne, Pa	39
Townsbury, Warren, N. J	18
Townsend, New Castle, Del	310
Townsend, Middlesex, Mass	440
Townsend, Schuyler, N. Y	38
Townsend, Sandusky, Ohio	110
Townsend Harbor, Middlesex, Mass.	120
Townsend Inlet, Cape May, N. J	96
Townsend's Mills, Gilmer, W. Va	6
Townsend Station, Huron, Ohio	110
Townsendville, Seneca, N. Y	39
Townshend, Windham, Vt	320
Townsville, Butler, Ky	12
Townville, Crawford, Pa	130
Townville, Anderson, S. C	17
Towsontown, (*c. h.*,) Baltimore, Md	450
Tracy, Barren, Ky	12
Tracy City, Marion, Tenn	12
Tracy Creek, Broome, N. Y	15
Tracy's Landing, Anne Arundel, Md.	56
Trade, Johnson, Tenn	6
Trader's Hill, (*c. h.*,) Charlton, Ga	23
Trader's Point, Marion, Ind	25
Tradersville, Madison, Ohio	10
Trafalgar, Johnson, Ind	77
Trail Ridge, Clay, Fla	12
Trail Run, Monroe, Ohio	6
Trammel, Sumner, Tenn	10
Tranquility, Appanoose, Iowa	12
Tranquility, Sussex, N. J	12
Tranquility, Adams, Ohio	53
Tranquilla, Washington, Ark	12
Transfer, Mercer, Pa	77
Transit, Sibley, Minn	9
Transit, Hamilton, Ohio	20
Transitville, Tippecanoe, Ind	$88
Trap Hill, Wilkes, N. C	13
Trappe, Talbot, Md	180
Trappe, Montgomery, Pa	210
Trask, Grant, Ind	23
Traveller's Repose, Pocahontas, W. Va	13
Traveller's Rest, Coosa, Ala	4
Traveller's Rest, Owsley, Ky	8
Traveller's Rest, Greenville, S. C	12
Travers des Sioux, Nicollet, Minn	70
Traverse City,* (*c. h.*,) Grand Traverse, Mich	810
Travis, Austin, Tex	32
Travisville, Fentress, Tenn	5
Traylorsville, Henry, Va	22
Treasure City, White Pine, Nev	1,100
Tremont, Tazewell, Ill	230
Tremont, Hancock, Me	110
Tremont, Westchester, N. Y	450
Tremont, Clark, Ohio	61
Tremont, Schuylkill, Pa	610
Trempealeau,* Trempealeau, Wis	600
Trent, Muskegon, Mich	48
Trenton, Jackson, Ala	5
Trenton, Phillips, Ark	20
Trenton, (*c. h.*,) Dade, Ga	87
Trenton,* Clinton, Ill	390
Trenton, Randolph, Ind	63
Trenton, Henry, Iowa	100
Trenton, Todd, Ky	140
Trenton, Ouachita, La	26
Trenton, Baltimore, Md	7
Trenton, Wayne, Mich	250
Trenton, Freeborn, Minn	6
Trenton, Smith, Miss	12
Trenton, (*c. h.*,) Grundy, Mo	600
TRENTON,* (*c. h.*,) Mercer, N. J	3,500
Trenton, Oneida, N. Y	250
Trenton, (*c. h.*,) Jones, N. C	25
Trenton, Butler, Ohio	170
Trenton,* (*c. h.*,) Gibson, Tenn	850
Trenton, Pierce, Wis	12
Trenton Falls, Oneida, N. Y	130
Tresckow, Carbon, Pa	120
Trevilian's Depot, Louisa, Va	250
Trevorton, Northumberland, Pa	290
Trexlertown, Lehigh, Pa	92
Trezevant, Carroll, Tenn	140
Triadelphia, Montgomery, Md	6
Triadelphia, Morgan, Ohio	15
Triadelphia, Ohio, W. Va	91
Triana, Madison, Ala	22
Triangle, Broome, N. Y	96
Tribe's Hill, Montgomery, N. Y	96
Trim Belle, Pierce, Wis	32
Trimble, Athens, Ohio	34
Trinidad, Klamath, Cal	17
Trinidad,* (*c. h.*,) Los Animas, Colo.	460
Trinity, Trinity, Cal	19
Trinity, Catahoula, La	71
Trinity Centre, Trinity, Cal	19
Trinity College,* Randolph, N. C	260
Trinity Springs, Martin, Ind	75
Trinity Station, Morgan, Ala	60
Trion, Tuscaloosa, Ala	43

* Money-order office.

Post office	Amount
Trion, Jefferson, Tenn	$7
Trion Factory, Chattooga, Ga	59
Tripoli, Bremer, Iowa	55
Triumph, La Salle, Ill	37
Triune, Williamson, Tenn	89
Trivoli, Peoria, Ill	150
Trostville, Saginaw, Mich	23
Trotwood, Montgomery, Ohio	390
Troublesome, Rockingham, N. C	7
Troup, Smith, Tex	58
Troupsburgh, Steuben, N. Y	60
Trout Creek, Meagher, Mont	50
Trout Creek, Delaware, N. Y	50
Trout River, Franklin, N. Y	90
Trout Run, Lycoming, Pa	100
Trout Run, Hardy, W. Va	7
Troutsville, Botetourt, Va	12
Troutville, Clearfield, Pa	40
Troxelville, Snyder, Pa	14
Troy,* (*c. h.*,) Pike, Ala	230
Troy,* Madison, Ill	290
Troy, Perry, Ind	180
Troy, Davis, Iowa	150
Troy,* (*c. h.*,) Doniphan, Kans	400
Troy, Woodford, Ky	12
Troy, Waldo, Me	77
Troy, Oakland, Mich	66
Troy, Winona, Minn	81
Troy, (*c. h.*,) Lincoln, Mo	360
Troy, Cheshire, N. H	260
Troy,* (*c. h.*,) Rensselaer, N. Y	4,000
Troy, (*c. h.*,) Montgomery, N. C	30
Troy,* (*c. h.*,) Miami, Ohio	1,900
Troy,* Bradford, Pa	1,200
Troy, Kershaw, S. C	12
Troy, (*c. h.*,) Obion, Tenn	130
Troy, Orleans, Vt	160
Troy, Gilmer, W. Va	20
Troy, Walworth, Wis	70
Troy Centre, Waldo, Me	24
Troy Centre, Walworth, Wis	22
Troy Grove, La Salle, Ill	120
Troy Mills, Linn, Iowa	22
Troy Mills, Adair, Mo	7
Troy Station, Obion, Tenn	20
Troy's Store, Randolph, N. C	16
Truckee, Nevada, Cal	400
Truckee Meadows, Washoe, Nev	140
Trucksville, Luzerne, Pa	46
Trumansburgh, Tompkins, N. Y	910
Trumansburgh Landing, Seneca, N. Y	19
Trumbaursville, Bucks, Pa	40
Trumbull, Fairfield, Conn	31
Trumbull, Ashtabula, Ohio	80
Trumbull Corners, Tompkins, N. Y	20
Trumbull Long Hill, Fairfield, Conn	36
Trundle's Cross Roads, Sevier, Tenn	22
Trunkeyville, Forest, Pa	12
Truro, Knox, Ill	22
Truro, Barnstable, Mass	180
Trust, Osage, Kans	12
Truxton, Bureau, Ill	9
Truxton, Lincoln, Mo	60
Truxton,* Cortland, N. Y	220
Tryon, Polk, N. C	4
Tryonville, Crawford, Pa	100

Post office	Amount
Tualitin, Washington, Oreg	$12
Tubac, Pima, Ariz	10
Tuckahoe, Cape May, N. J	220
Tuckahoe, Westchester, N. Y	210
Tuckaleechee Cove, Blount, Tenn	6
Tucker's Cross Roads, Wilson, Tenn	30
Tucker's Mills, Limestone, Tex	12
Tuckerton, Burlington, N. J	280
Tuckerton, Berks, Pa	38
TUCSON, (*c. h.*,) Pima, Ariz	620
Tuftonborough, Carroll, N. H	39
Tugalo, Oconee, S. C	12
Tug River, McDowell, W. Va	7
Tukannon, Walla-Walla, Wash	12
Tulalip, Snohomish, Wash	14
Tule, Tulare, Cal	220
Tulin, Cabarrus, N. C	12
Tulip, Dallas, Ark	97
Tullahoma,* Coffee, Tenn	500
Tullamore, Tazewell, Ill	9
Tullvania, Macon, Mo	19
Tully,* Onondaga, N. Y	350
Tully, Van Wert, Ohio	93
Tullytown, Bucks, Pa	88
Tully Valley, Onondaga, N. Y	8
Tulpehocken, Berks, Pa	25
Tumble, Hunterdon, N. J	5
Tumbling Shoals, Laurens, S. C	13
Tumwater, Thurston, Wash	100
Tunbridge, Orange, Vt	70
Tunkhannock, (*c. h.*,) Wyoming, Pa	840
Tunnel, Washington, Ohio	30
Tunnel City, Monroe, Wis	130
Tunnel Hill, Whitfield, Ga	200
Tunnel Hill, Oconee, S. C	10
Tunnelton, Lawrence, Ind	64
Tunnelton, Indiana, Pa	58
Tunnelton, Preston, W. Va	110
Tunstalls, New Kent, Va	79
Tuolumne City, Stanislaus, Cal	220
Tupelo, (*c. h.*,) Lee, Miss	440
Tupper's Plains, Meigs, Ohio	51
Tuque, Warren, Mo	10
Turbotville, Northumberland, Pa	270
Turin, Saline, Ark	6
Turin, Coweta, Ga	9
Turin,* Lewis, N. Y	410
Turkey, Monmouth, N. J	96
Turkey Cove, Lee, Va	2
Turkey Creek, Dooly, Ga	12
Turkey Creek, Steuben, Ind	41
Turkey Creek, Bourbon, Kans	110
Turkey Foot, Somerset, Pa	25
Turman's Creek, Sullivan, Ind	53
Turnback, Dade, Mo	9
Turner, Du Page, Ill	250
Turner, Androscoggin, Me	280
Turner's, Clay, Ind	12
Turner's, Orange, N. Y	190
Turnersburgh, Iredell, N. C	15
Turner's Point, Kaufman, Tex	18
Turnersport, Manistee, Mich	51
Turner's Store, Somerset, Pa	36
Turnersville, Camden, N. J	15
Turnersville, Crawford, Pa	12
Turnersville, Robertson, Tenn	16

* Money-order office.

Turnerville, Tolland, Conn	$60
Turnerville, Jasper, Miss	19
Turney's Station, Clinton, Mo	22
Turnpike, Buncombe, N. C	15
Turnwood, Ulster, N. Y	47
Turtle Creek, Allegheny, Pa	150
Turtle Point, McKean, Pa	12
Tuscaloosa,* (*c. h.*,) Tuscaloosa, Ala	1,200
Tuscarawas, Tuscarawas, Ohio	130
Tuscarora, Livingston, N. Y	65
Tuscarora, Schuylkill, Pa	87
Tuscola,* (*c. h.*,) Douglas, Ill	1,500
Tuscumbia,* (*c. h.*,) Colbert, Ala	740
Tuscumbia, (*c. h.*,) Miller, Mo	130
Tuskegee,* (*c. h.*,) Macon, Ala	650
Tusquitee, Clay, N. C	5
Tustenuggee, Columbia, Fla	12
Tustin, Waushara, Wis	14
Tuthill, Ulster, N. Y	45
Tuttle's Cross Roads, Caldwell, N. C	12
Twelve Mile, Cass, Ind	30
Twenty Mile Stand, Warren, Ohio	41
Twenty-six Mile House, Stanislaus, Cal	12
Twiggs, Pleasants, W. Va	6
Twiggsville, Twiggs, Ga	12
Twin Bridges, Madison, Mont	12
Twin Corners, Cass, Ind	12
Twin Falls, Greenwood, Kans	12
Twin Grove, Green, Wis	44
Twin Lakes, Calhoun, Iowa	16
Twin Lakes, Carlton, Minn	6
Twin Mound, Douglas, Kans	50
Twin Mountain, Coos, N. H	12
Twin River, Nye, Nev	110
Twinsburgh, Summit, Ohio	220
Twin Sisters, Blanco, Tex	10
Twin Spring, Winneshiek, Iowa	12
Twin Springs, Linn, Kans	150
Twinville, Knox, Tenn	6
Two Bayous, Ouachita, Ark	12
Two Mile Branch, Smyth, Va	12
Two Rivers, Morrison, Minn	18
Two Rivers, Manitowoc, Wis	240
Two Rocks, Sonoma, Cal	12
Two Taverns, Adams, Pa	29
Twyman's Store, Spottsylvania, Va	16
Tyaskin, Wicomico, Md	42
Tye River Depot, Nelson, Va	89
Tyler, Winnebago, Ill	24
Tyler,* (*c. h.*,) Smith, Tex	860
Tyler Mountain, Kanawha, W. Va	12
Tyler's, Brown, Kans	4
Tyler's, Clearfield, Pa	18
Tylersburgh, Clarion, Pa	74
Tyler's Port, Montgomery, Pa	74
Tylersville, Clinton, Pa	28
Tylersville, Laurens, S. C	12
Tymochtee, Wyandot, Ohio	21
Tyner, Hamilton, Tenn	27
Tyner City, Marshall, Ind	120
Tyngsborough, Middlesex, Mass	110
Tyre, Sanilac, Mich	48
Tyre, Seneca, N. Y	42
Tyringham, Berkshire, Mass	69
Tyro, Poweshiek, Iowa	3
Tyro, Marshall, Miss	$96
Tyrone, Monroe, Iowa	37
Tyrone, Livingston, Mich	29
Tyrone, Schuyler, N. Y	120
Tyrone, Coshocton, Ohio	12
Tyrone,* Blair, Pa	1,500
Tyson Furnace, Windsor, Vt	88
Tyson's Mills, Webster, Iowa	12

U.

Uchee, Russell, Ala	12
Uchee Anna, (*c. h.*,) Walton, Fla	11
Udina, Kane, Ill	53
Uhlersville, Northampton, Pa	24
Uhricksville,* Tuscarawas, Ohio	860
Uintah, Weber, Utah	12
Ukiah, (*c. h.*,) Mendocino, Cal	50
Ulah, Henry, Ill	32
Ullin, Pulaski, Ill	160
Ulman's Ridge, Miller, Mo	16
Ulster, Floyd, Iowa	18
Ulster, Bradford, Pa	140
Ulster Park, Ulster, N. Y	32
Ulsterville, Ulster, N. Y	47
Ulysses, Butler, Nebr	12
Ulysses, Potter, Pa	110
Umatilla,* Umatilla, Oreg	420
Unadilla, Livingston, Mich	160
Unadilla, Otsego, N. Y	830
Unadilla Centre, Otsego, N. Y	13
Unadilla Forks, Otsego, N. Y	200
Uncasville, New London, Conn	150
Uncle Sam, Lake, Cal	77
Underhill, Chittenden, Vt	190
Underhill Centre, Chittenden, Vt	120
Underwood, Hopkins, Ky	12
Unger's Store, Morgan, W. Va	14
Union, Greene, Ala	20
Union, Merced, Cal	64
Union, Tolland, Conn	16
Union, McHenry, Ill	180
Union, Pike, Ind	24
Union, Hardin, Iowa	62
Union, Chase, Kans	11
Union, Boone, Ky	100
Union, Knox, Me	290
Union, Cass, Mich	70
Union, Houston, Minn	16
Union, Newton, Miss	18
Union, (*c. h.*,) Franklin, Mo	290
Union, Cass, Nebr	43
Union, Carroll, N. H	220
Union, Union, N. J	45
Union, Broome, N. Y	480
Union, Montgomery, Ohio	85
Union, Union, Oreg	130
Union, York, Pa	24
Union, Salt Lake, Utah	44
Union,* (*c. h.*,) Monroe, W. Va	280
Union, Rock, Wis	60
Union Bridge, Carroll, Md	140
Unionburgh, Harrison, Iowa	19
Union Centre, Cumberland, Ill	12
Union Centre, Jackson, Iowa	20
Union Centre, Le Sueur, Minn	4

* Money-order office.

Post office	Compensation
Union Centre, Broome, N. Y	$65
Union Church, Jefferson, Miss	55
Union Church, Albany, N. Y	16
Union Church, Racine, Wis	23
Union City, Perry, Ark	12
Union City,* Randolph, Ind	1,200
Union City, Union, Iowa	28
Union City, Branch, Mich	410
Union City,* Obion, Tenn	720
Union Corner, Northumberland, Pa	10
Union Corners, Livingston, N. Y	23
Union Cross Roads, Union, La	38
Union Dale, Susquehanna, Pa	58
Union Deposit, Dauphin, Pa	100
Union Depot, Sullivan, Tenn	110
Union Falls, Clinton, N. Y	6
Union Forge, Lebanon, Pa	20
Union Grove, Whitesides, Ill	8
Union Grove, Page, Iowa	20
Union Grove, Gentry, Mo	8
Union Grove, Delaware, N. Y	12
Union Grove, Iredell, N. C	5
Union Grove,* Racine, Wis	310
Union Hall, Franklin, Va	5
Union Hill, Kankakee, Ill	21
Union Hill, Ringgold, Iowa	6
Union Lakes, Rice, Minn	15
Union Meeting House, Baltimore, Md	55
Union Mills, La Porte, Ind	36
Union Mills, Mahaska, Iowa	49
Union Mills, Carroll, Md	59
Union Mills, Tippah, Miss	12
Union Mills, Platte, Mo	17
Union Mills, Fulton, N. Y	19
Union Mills,* Erie, Pa	880
Union Mills, Fluvanna, Va	26
Union Mills, Pleasants, W. Va	12
Union Mills, Iowa, Wis	16
Union Pier, Berrien, Mich	12
Union Plains, Brown, Ohio	12
Union Point, Greene, Ga	65
Union Point, Union, Ill	6
Unionport, Jefferson, Ohio	62
Union Prairie, Allamakee, Iowa	16
Union Ridge, Brown, Ill	8
Union Ridge, Butler, Iowa	30
Union Ridge, Sullivan, Mo	7
Union Ridge, Clark, Wash	17
Union Society, Greene, N. Y	12
Union Spring, Dodge, Minn	16
Union Springs, (c. h.,) Bullock, Ala	600
Union Springs,* Cayuga, N. Y	1,300
Union Square, Oswego, N. Y	65
Union Square, Montgomery, Pa	1
Union Star, Breckinridge, Ky	34
Union Star, De Kalb, Mo	89
Union Station, Licking, Ohio	12
Union Station, Lancaster, Pa	50
Uniontown, Perry, Ala	650
Uniontown, Delaware, Iowa	14
Uniontown,* Union, Ky	360
Uniontown, Carroll, Md	230
Uniontown, Perry, Mo	23
Uniontown, Belmont, Ohio	73
Uniontown, (c. h.,)* Fayette, Pa	1,300

Post office	Compensation
Union Valley, Cortland, N. Y	$41
Union Village, Orange, Vt	120
Unionville, Hartford, Conn	650
Unionville, Monroe, Ga	10
Unionville, Monroe, Ind	12
Unionville, Appanoose, Iowa	120
Unionville, Frederick, Md	74
Unionville, Tuscola, Mich	80
Unionville, (c. h.,)* Putnam, Mo	290
Unionville, Lewis and Clarke, Mont	12
Unionville, (c. h.,) Humboldt, Nev	230
Unionville, Gloucester, N. J	43
Unionville, Orange, N. Y	260
Unionville, Lake, Ohio	170
Unionville, Chester, Pa	160
Unionville, (c. h.,)* Union, S. C	710
Unionville, Bedford, Tenn	60
Unionville, Orange, Va	9
Unionville Centre, Union, Ohio	80
Uniopolis, Auglaize, Ohio	5
Unison, Loudoun, Va	50
Unitia, Blount, Tenn	30
Unity, Alexander, Ill	9
Unity,* Waldo, Me	230
Unity, Montgomery, Md	44
Unity, Sullivan, N. H	50
Unity, Columbiana, Ohio	32
Unity, Pacific, Wash	16
Unityville, Lycoming, Pa	18
University of Virginia, Albemarle, Va	1,400
Ununda, Brown, Kans	10
Upatoie, Muscogee, Ga	14
Updegraff's, Jefferson, Ohio	14
Upland, Grant, Ind	12
Upland, Mason, W. Va	6
Uplands, Delaware, Pa	12
Upper Alton, Madison, Ill	850
Upper Aquebogue, Suffolk, N. Y	100
Upper Bern, Berks, Pa	17
Upper Black Eddy, Bucks, Pa	96
Upper Blue Licks, Fleming, Ky	8
Upper Clear Lake, Lake, Cal	47
Upperco, Baltimore, Md	38
Upper Cross Roads, Harford, Md	53
Upper Darby, Delaware, Pa	44
Upper Dublin, Montgomery, Pa	89
Upper Falls, Baltimore, Md	77
Upper Falls, Windsor, Vt	78
Upper Falls of Coal, Kanawha, W. Va	14
Upper Gloucester, Cumberland, Me	120
Upper Grove, Hancock, Iowa	81
Upper Jay, Essex, N. Y	37
Upper Lehigh, Luzerne, Pa	150
Upper Lisle, Broome, N. Y	85
Upper Madawaska, Aroostook, Me	12
Upper Mahantango, Schuylkill, Pa	20
Upper Marlborough, (c. h.,) Prince George's, Md	560
Upper Middletown, Fayette, Pa	25
Upper Providence, Delaware, Pa	10
Upper Red Hook, Dutchess, N. Y	80
Upper St. Clair, Allegheny, Pa	39
Upper Sandusky, (c. h.,)* Wyandot, Ohio	1,200

* Money-order office.

Post office	
Upper Stillwater, Penobscot, Me	$160
Upper Strasburgh, Franklin, Pa	85
Upper Tract, Pendleton, W. Va	47
Upper Trappe, Somerset, Md	28
Upper Tygart, Carter, Ky	4
Upperville, Fauquier, Va	310
Upshur, Preble, Ohio	34
Upsonville, Susquehanna, Pa	17
Upton, Van Buren, Iowa	37
Upton, Oxford, Me	48
Upton, Worcester, Mass	360
Upton, Franklin, Pa	140
Uptonville, Hardin, Ky	120
Urban, Butler, Nebr	12
Urban, Northumberland, Pa	8
Urbana, (*c. h.*,) Champaign, Ill	1,200
Urbana, Wabash, Ind	18
Urbana, Neosho, Kans	12
Urbana, Frederick, Md	63
Urbana, Dallas, Mo	45
Urbana,* (*c. h.*,) Champaign, Ohio	2,400
Urbana, Middlesex, Va	90
Urbanna, Benton, Iowa	85
Urbanna City, Monroe, Iowa	12
Urieville, Kent, Md	12
Urmeyville, Johnson, Ind	30
Ursa, Adams, Ill	24
Ursina, Somerset, Pa	12
Usquepaugh, Washington, R. I	90
Utah, Warren, Ill	18
Utah, Indiana, Pa	28
Utahville, Clearfield, Pa	41
Ute Creek, Colfax, N. Mex	12
Utica, La Salle, Ill	450
Utica, Clarke, Ind	110
Utica, Van Buren, Iowa	37
Utica,* Macomb, Mich	350
Utica, Winona, Minn	100
Utica, Hinds, Miss	86
Utica,* Livingston, Mo	290
Utica,* (*c. h.*,) Oneida, N. Y	4,000
Utica, Licking, Ohio	400
Utica, Venango, Pa	150
Utica, Dane, Wis	96
Utica Mills, Frederick, Md	23
Utsaladdy, Island, Wash	38
Uvalde, (*c. h.*,) Uvalde, Tex	110
Uwchland, Chester, Pa	38
Uxbridge,* Worcester, Mass	650

V.

Post office	
Vaca, Solano, Cal	12
Vacaville,* Solano, Cal	210
Vacherie Roads, St. James, La	12
Vaiden, Carroll, Miss	290
Vail's Cross Roads, Morrow, Ohio	38
Vail's Gate, Orange, N. Y	56
Vail's Mills, Fulton, N. Y	54
Valatie,* Columbia, N. Y	610
Valcour, Clinton, N. Y	12
Valdosta, (*c. h.*,) Lowndes, Ga	620
Valeene, Orange, Ind	21
Vale Mills, Giles, Tenn	22
Valentine, La Grange, Ind	8
Valhalla, Westchester, N. Y	58
Valhermoso Springs, Morgan, Ala	$8
Vallejo,* Solano, Cal	1,800
Valley, Washington, Iowa	29
Valley, Douglas, Nebr	12
Valley, Columbiana, Ohio	12
Valley, Clarion, Pa	12
Valley, Guadalupe, Tex	12
Valley, Vernon, Wis	12
Valley Bend, Randolph, W. Va	5
Valley Brook, Osage, Kans	12
Valley City, Harrison, Ind	22
Valley City, Neosho, Kans	12
Valley Creek, Chester, Pa	12
Valley Crucis, Watauga, N. C	4
Valley Falls, Rensselaer, N. Y	210
Valley Falls, Providence, R. I	620
Valley Falls, Spartanburgh, S. C	4
Valley Falls, Marion, W. Va	14
Valley Farm, Linn, Iowa	24
Valley Ford, Meigs, Ohio	11
Valley Forge, Chester, Pa	53
Valley Furnace, Barbour, W. Va	5
Valley Grove, Ohio, W. Va	74
Valley Head, De Kalb, Ala	73
Valley Head, Randolph, W. Va	12
Valley Junction, Hamilton, Ohio	24
Valley Mills, Marion, Ind	46
Valley Mills, Madison, N. Y	12
Valley Mills, Bosque, Tex	67
Valley Mills, Wood, W. Va	12
Valley Oak, Pulaski, Ky	15
Valley Point, Preston, W. Va	11
Valley Stream, Queens, N. Y	12
Valley Town, Cherokee, N. C	30
Vallicita, Calaveras, Cal	65
Vallonia, Jackson, Ind	65
Vallonia Springs, Broome, N. Y	22
Valmont, Boulder, Colo	78
Valparaiso,* (*c. h.*,) Porter, Ind	1,600
Valparaiso, Sullivan, Mo	34
Valton, Sauk, Wis	13
Vanatta, Licking, Ohio	35
Van Buren, (*c. h.*,) Crawford, Ark	580
Van Buren, De Kalb, Ill	16
Van Buren, Jackson, Iowa	70
Van Buren, Aroostook, Me	30
Van Buren, (*c. h.*,) Carter, Mo	5
Van Buren, Onondaga, N. Y	19
Van Buren, Hancock, Ohio	89
Van Buren, Washington, Pa	38
Van Buren Furnace, Shenandoah, Va	15
Van Camp, Columbia, Pa	18
Van Camp, Wetzel, W. Va	20
Vanceburgh, (*c. h.*,) Lewis, Ky	200
Vancefort, Allegheny, Pa	23
Vance's Ferry, Orangeburgh, S. C	28
Vanceville, Washington, Pa	18
Vancil's Point, Macoupin, Ill	12
Vancleave's, Jackson, Miss	12
Van Clevesville, Berkeley, W. Va	49
Vancouver,* (*c. h.*,) Clark, Wash	560
Vandalia, (*c. h.*,) Fayette, Ill	1,200
Vandalia, Owen, Ind	42
Vandalia, Jasper, Iowa	120
Vandalia, Cass, Mich	96

* Money-order office.

Vandalia, Cattaraugus, N. Y	$23
Vandalia, Montgomery, Ohio	94
Vanderbilt, Lander, Nev	12
Vanderburgh, Webster, Ky	21
Vandergriff's, Knox, Tenn	2
Van Deusenville, Berkshire, Mass	76
Van Dyke's Mill, Spencer, Ky	24
Van Dyne, Fond du Lac, Wis	25
Van Etten, Chemung, N. Y	8
Van Ettenville, Chemung, N. Y	98
Van Hill, Hawkins, Tenn	12
Van Hiseville, Ocean, N. J	24
Van Hook's Store, Person, N. C	10
Van Horn, Carroll, Mo	12
Van Hornesville, Herkimer, N. Y	110
Vanlue, Hancock, Ohio	90
Van Metre, Dallas, Iowa	110
Vannatterville, Lincoln, W. Va	12
Vannoy's Mill, Pike, Mo	6
Van's Valley, Delaware, Ohio	17
Van Vechten, Schenectady, N. Y	65
Vanville, Chippewa, Wis	75
Van Wert, Polk, Ga	66
Van Wert,* (*c. h.*,) Van Wert, Ohio	1,300
Van Wert, Juniata, Pa	12
Varick, Seneca, N. Y	38
Variety Mills, Nelson, Va	21
Varna, Tompkins, N. Y	58
Varnell's Station, Whitfield, Ga	87
Varysburgh, Wyoming, N. Y	100
Vasa, Goodhue, Minn	60
Vassalborough, Kennebec, Me	270
Vassar,* (*c. h.*,) Tuscola, Mich	430
Vaughnsville, Putnam, Ohio	34
Veazie, Penobscot, Me	99
Vedder, Calhoun, Ill	43
Velasco, Brazoria, Tex	25
Velp, Brown, Wis	15
Venango, Crawford, Pa	200
Venedocia, Van Wert, Ohio	15
Venedy, Washington, Ill	120
Veni, Effingham, Ill	4
Venice, Madison, Ill	120
Venice, Cayuga, N. Y	46
Venice, Erie, Ohio	18
Venice, Washington, Pa	75
Venice Centre, Cayuga, N. Y	36
Ventura, Ottawa, Mich	25
Venus, Madison, Iowa	7
Vera, Fayette, Ill	86
Vera Cruz, Wells, Ind	96
Vera Cruz, Douglas, Mo	22
Vera Cruz, Lehigh, Pa	23
Verbank, Dutchess, N. Y	47
Verdi,* Wilson, Kans	140
Verdi, Washoe, Nev	63
Verdierville, Orange, Va	39
Verdigris Falls, Greenwood, Kans	18
Verdon, Hanover, Va	58
Vergennes, Jackson, Ill	12
Vergennes, Kent, Mich	14
Vergennes,* Addison, Vt	1,200
Vermillion, (*c. h.*,) Clay, Dak	360
Vermillion, Edgar, Ill	260
Vermillion, Nemaha, Kans	12
Vermillion, Oswego, N. Y	61
Vermillion, Erie, Ohio	$410
Vermillion Lake, St. Louis, Minn	12
Vermillionville, La Salle, Ill	51
Vermillionville, (*c. h.*,) La Fayette, La	260
Vermont, Fulton, Ill	610
Vermont, Cooper, Mo	36
Vermont, Chautauqua, N. Y	52
Vermontville, Eaton, Mich	430
Vernon, Sanford, Ala	29
Vernon, Tolland, Conn	120
Vernon, Kent, Del	13
Vernon, (*c. h.*,) Washington, Fla	16
Vernon, Troup, Ga	10
Vernon,* (*c. h.*,) Jennings, Ind	550
Vernon, Van Buren, Iowa,	220
Vernon, (*c. h.*,) Jackson, La	24
Vernon, Shiawassee, Mich	390
Vernon, Dodge, Minn	30
Vernon,* Sussex, N. J	580
Vernon, Oneida, N. Y	440
Vernon, Trumbull, Ohio	48
Vernon, Marion, Oreg	10
Vernon, Wyoming, Pa	5
Vernon, Hickman, Tenn	13
Vernon, Windham, Vt	200
Vernon, Waukesha, Wis	56
Vernon Centre, Blue Earth, Minn	140
Vernon Centre, Oneida, N. Y	150
Vernon Depot, Tolland, Conn	130
Vernon Hill, Halifax, Va	19
Verona, Boone, Ky	18
Verona, Lee, Miss	310
Verona, Lawrence, Mo	83
Verona, Essex, N. J	58
Verona, Oneida, N. Y	300
Verona, Westmoreland, Pa	9
Verona, Marshall, Tenn	12
Verona, Dane, Wis	34
Verona Mills, Huron, Mich	35
Verplank, Westchester, N. Y	120
Versailles, Brown, Ill	290
Versailles,* (*c. h.*,) Ripley, Ind	220
Versailles, (*c. h.*,) Woodford, Ky	900
Versailles,* (*c. h.*,) Morgan, Mo	310
Versailles, Cattaraugus, N. Y	140
Versailles, Darke, Ohio	220
Versailles, Rutherford, Tenn	15
Vershire, Orange, Vt	140
Vervilla, Warren, Tenn	44
Vesper, Onondaga, N. Y	40
Vesta, Johnson, Nebr	40
Vestal, Broome, N. Y	30
Vestal Centre, Broome, N. Y	28
Veto, Washington, Ohio	18
Vevay,* (*c. h.*,) Switzerland, Ind	680
Vicar, Russell, Va	12
Vickery's Creek, Forsyth, Ga	58
Vickeryville, Montcalm, Mich	24
Vicksburgh, Jewell, Kans	12
Vicksburgh,* (*c. h.*,) Warren, Miss	4,000
Vicksburgh, Union, Pa	31
Vicksville, Southampton, Va	13
Victor,* Iowa, Iowa	330
Victor, Clinton, Mich	37
Victor,* Ontario, N. Y	540

* Money-order office.

Office	Amount
Victor Centre, De Kalb, Ill	$19
Victoria, Coffee, Ala	12
Victoria, Jefferson, Ark	12
Victoria, Knox, Ill	290
Victoria, (*c. h.,*) Victoria, Tex	670
Victoria Station, Jefferson, Mo	40
Victory, Mason, Mich	33
Victory, Cayuga, N. Y	120
Victory, Essex, Vt	19
Victory, Vernon, Wis	30
Victory Mills, Saratoga, N. Y	200
Vidalia, (*c. h.,*) Concordia, La	12
Vienna, (*c. h.,*) Dooly, Ga	87
*Vienna,** (*c. h.,*) Johnson, Ill	240
Vienna, Scott, Ind	140
Vienna, Marshall, Iowa	5
Vienna, Pottawatomie, Kans	40
Vienna, Clarke, Ky	10
Vienna, Jackson, La	70
Vienna, Kennebec, Me	62
Vienna, Dorchester, Md	77
Vienna, (*c. h.,*) Maries, Mo	59
Vienna, Warren, N. J	100
Vienna, Oneida, N. Y	110
Vienna, Forsyth, N. C	7
Vienna, Trumbull, Ohio	94
Vienna, Fairfax, Va	50
Vienna, Walworth, Wis	20
Vienna Cross Roads, Clark, Ohio	54
Vigo, Ross, Ohio	55
Village Creek, Allamakee, Iowa	81
Village Green, Delaware, Pa	75
Village Springs, Blount, Ala	19
Villanova, Chautauqua, N. Y	30
Villanow, Walker, Ga	25
Villa Rica, Carroll, Ga	57
Villa Ridge, Pulaski, Ill	290
Villa Platte, St. Landry, La	21
Villisca, Montgomery, Iowa	160
Villula, Russell, Ala	54
*Vincennes,** (*c. h.,*) Knox, Ind	2,500
Vincennes, Lee, Iowa	80
Vincent, St. Clair, Mich	4
Vincent, Washington, Ohio	100
Vincent, Chester, Pa	47
Vincentown, Burlington, N. J	270
Vine Grove, Hardin, Ky	24
Vine Grove, Washington, Tex	28
Vineland, Jefferson, Mo	120
Vineland,* Cumberland, N. J	2,300
Vinemount, Bollinger, Mo	12
Vine's Mills, Worth, Ga	12
Vine's Springs, Ripley, Ind	25
Vine Valley, Yates, N. Y	4
Vineyard, Bradley, Ark	12
Vineyard, Tama, Iowa	12
Vineyard Grove, Dukes, Mass	12
Vineyard Hill, Adams, Ohio	12
Vineyard Hill, Kanawha, W. Va	12
Vineyard Mills, Huntingdon, Pa	12
Viney Grove, Washington, Ark	12
Vining Station, Cobb, Ga	12
Vinland, Douglas, Kans	12
Vinland, Winnebago, Wis	23
*Vinton,** (*c. h.,*) Benton, Iowa	1,700
Vinton, Riley, Kans	12
Vinton, Gallia, Ohio	$84
Vinton Station, Vinton, Ohio	110
Viola, Mercer, Ill	140
Viola, Linn, Iowa	98
Viola, Warren, Tenn	12
Viola, Richland, Wis	51
Viola Station, Graves, Ky	47
Viona, Humboldt, Iowa	5
Virden,* Macoupin, Ill	1,300
Virgil, Greenwood, Kans	19
Virgil, Cortland, N. Y	99
Virgil City, Cedar, Mo	240
Virgin City, Kane, Utah	37
Virginia, Douglas, Colo	12
Virginia, Union, Dak	12
Virginia, Cass, Ill	660
*Virginia City,** (*c. h.,*) Madison, Mont	2,000
*Virginia City,** (*c. h.,*) Storey, Nev	4,000
Virginia Grove, Louisa, Iowa	20
Virginville, Berks, Pa	23
*Viroqua,** (*c. h.,*) Vernon, Wis	320
*Visalia,** (*c. h.,*) Tulare, Cal	690
Visalia, Kenton, Ky	44
Vischer's Ferry, Saratoga, N. Y	92
Vista, Westchester, N. Y	22
Vista Ridge, Carroll, La	12
Vistula, Elkhart, Ind	43
Vivian, Waseca, Minn	20
Voak, Yates, N. Y	16
Vogansville, Lancaster, Pa	24
Volant, Lawrence, Pa	8
Volga, Jefferson, Ind	19
Volga City, Clayton, Iowa	89
Volcano, Amador, Cal	130
Volcano,* Wood, W. Va	240
Volinia, Cass, Mich	36
Volney, Allamakee, Iowa	29
Volney, Oswego, N. Y	44
Volo, Lake, Ill	60
Volo, Bell, Tex	12
Voluntown, Windham, Conn	130
Volusia, Volusia, Fla	22
Volusia, Chautauqua, N. Y	37
Voorheesville, Albany, N. Y	25
Vosburgh, Wyoming, Pa	12
Vriesland, Ottawa, Mich	62

W.

Office	Amount
Wabash, Wayne, Ill	12
*Wabash,** (*c. h.,*) Wabash, Ind	1,800
*Wabashaw,** (*c. h.,*) Wabashaw, Minn	870
Wabaunsee, Wabaunsee, Kans	150
Wachusett Village, Worcester, Mass	49
Waco, Franklin, Ala	8
Waco, Madison, Ky	100
*Waco,** (*c. h.,*) McLennan, Tex	1,800
Waconda, Marion, Oreg	48
Waconia, Carver, Minn	37
Wacousta, Humboldt, Iowa	12
Wacousta, Clinton, Mich	76
Wadaloup, Grundy, Iowa	12
Waddam's Centre, Stephenson, Ill	12
Waddington, St. Lawrence, N. Y	380
Wade, Washington, Ohio	74

* Money-order office.

Wade's, Bedford, Va	$27
Wadesborough, Callaway, Ky	34
Wadesborough, (c. h.,) Anson, N. C	220
Wadesburgh, Cass, Mo	100
Wadestown, Monongalia, W. Va	28
Wadesville, Posey, Ind	23
Wadesville, Clarke, Va	85
Wadesville, Wood, W. Va	12
Wadhams' Mills, Essex, N. Y	89
Wading River, Burlington, N. J	32
Wading River, Suffolk, N. Y	56
Wadley's Falls, Strafford, N. H	59
Wadsworth, Washoe, Nev	470
Wadsworth,* Medina, Ohio	760
Waggoner's Ripple, Adams, Ohio	17
Wagner, Clayton, Iowa	17
Wagon Landing, Polk, Wis	24
Wagontown, Chester, Pa	90
Wagram, Licking, Ohio	16
Wahaghbonsy, Mills, Iowa	7
Wahalak Station, Hempler, Miss	27
Wahjamega, Tuscola, Mich	59
Wahoo, Saunders, Nebr	12
Wah Wah, Butler, Kans	12
Wah Wah Suk, Shawnee, Kans	12
Wailesborough, Bartholomew, Ind	46
Waite, Washington, Me	19
Waitesville, Jefferson, Wis	28
Waitsfield,* Washington, Vt	280
Wait's River, Orange, Vt	77
Wakarusa, Elkhart, Ind	94
Wakarusa, Shawnee, Kans	20
Wakatomica, Coshocton, Ohio	28
Wakefield, Richland, Ill	19
Wakefield, Clay, Kans	12
Wakefield, Carroll, Md	23
Wakefield, Middlesex, Mass	1,300
Wakefield, Carroll, N. H	160
Wakefield, Wake, N. C	1
Wakefield, Lancaster, Pa	54
Wakefield,* Washington, R. I	380
Wakefield, Outagamie, Wis	20
Wakefield Station, Sussex, Va	90
Wakeman, Huron, Ohio	340
Wakeshma, Kalamazoo, Mich	13
Walbridge, Pulaski, Ill	160
Walcott, Green, Ark	12
Walden, Orange, N. Y	460
Walden, Caledonia, Vt	32
Waldenburgh, Macomb, Mich	24
Walden's, Rappahannock, Va	12
Walden's Creek, Sevier, Tenn	1
Waldingfield, Kanawha, W. Va	12
Waldo, Alachua, Fla	42
Waldo, Waldo, Me	59
Waldo, Webster, Mo	12
Waldo, Marion, Ohio	57
Waldo, Josephine, Oreg	28
Waldoborough, Lincoln, Me	850
Waldron, (c. h.,) Scott, Ark	140
Waldron, Platte, Mo	12
Waldrop's Mill, Jefferson, Ala	2
Wales, Ogle, Ill	80
Wales, Worth, Iowa	12
Wales, Androscoggin, Me	11
Wales, Hampden, Mass	170
Wales, St. Clair, Mich	$48
Wales, Erie, N. Y	62
Wales, Gallia, Ohio	28
Wales, San Pete, Utah	12
Wales Centre, Erie, N. Y	75
Wales Station, Giles, Tenn	51
Walesville, Oneida, N. Y	67
Walhain, Kewaunee, Wis	14
Walhalla, (c. h.,) Oconee, S. C	250
Walhonding, Coshocton, Ohio	36
Walker, Centre, Pa	84
Walker, Wood, W. Va	97
Walker's, Columbia, Ark	12
Walker's Church, Appomattox, Va	18
Walker's Ford, Amherst, Va	12
Walker's Mills, Allegheny, Pa	26
Walkerstown, Forsyth, N. C	1
Walkersville, Frederick, Md	73
Walkersville, Union, N. C	8
Walkersville, Lewis, W. Va	20
Walkerton, St. Joseph, Ind	250
Walkerton, King and Queen, Va	45
Walker Valley, Ulster, N. Y	40
Walkerville, Greene, Ill	17
Wallace, Fountain, Ind	24
Wallace, Steuben, N. Y	92
Wallace, Duplin, N. C	47
Wallace, Chester, Pa	25
Wallace's Cross Roads, Anderson, Tenn	15
Wallaceton, Clearfield, Pa	12
Wallaceville, Wayne, Mich	20
Wallaceville, Venango, Pa	27
Walla Walla, (c. h.,)* Walla Walla, Wash	1,200
Walled Lake, Oakland, Mich	100
Waller, Ross, Ohio	67
Wallingford, New Haven, Conn	1,400
Wallingford, Will, Ill	25
Wallingford, Rutland, Vt	420
Walling's Ferry, Rusk, Tex	16
Wallin's Creek, Harlan, Ky	3
Wallis Run, Lycoming, Pa	4
Wallisville, (c. h.,) Chambers, Tex	12
Wallpack Centre, Sussex, N. J	8
Wall Rose, Beaver, Pa	29
Wallsville, Luzerne, Pa	23
Wallula, Walla Walla, Wash	50
Walnford, Monmouth, N. J	15
Walnut, Bureau, Ill	100
Walnut, Marshall, Ind	45
Walnut, Butler, Kans	12
Walnut, Juniata, Pa	20
Walnut Bottom, Cumberland, Pa	62
Walnut City, Appanoose, Iowa	39
Walnut Cove, Stokes, N. C	70
Walnut Creek, Contra Costa, Cal	71
Walnut Creek, Fremont, Iowa	12
Walnut Creek, Crawford, Kans	58
Walnut Creek, Buncombe, N. C	10
Walnut Creek, Holmes, Ohio	22
Walnut Creek Station, Pottawattomie, Iowa	12
Walnut Fork, Jones, Iowa	63
Walnut Grove, Blount, Ala	10
Walnut Grove, Sacramento, Cal	20

* Money-order office.

Walnut Grove, Walton, Ga	$4
Walnut Grove, Scott, Iowa	34
Walnut Grove, Caldwell, Ky	28
Walnut Grove, Martin, Minn	18
Walnut Grove, Greene, Mo	96
Walnut Grove, Morris, N. J	62
Walnut Hill, Tallapoosa, Ala	5
Walnut Hill, La Fayette, Ark	27
Walnut Hill, Marion, Ill	20
Walnut Hill, Marshall, Ind	9
Walnut Hill, Bourbon, Kans	6
Walnut Hill, Buchanan, Mo	35
Walnut Hill, Ashe, N. C	12
Walnut Hill, Sequatchie, Tenn	10
Walnut Hill, Panola, Tex	4
Walnut Hill, Lee, Va	14
Walnut Hills, Hamilton, Ohio	550
Walnut Lake, Faribault, Minn	12
Walnut Lick, Gallatin, Ky	19
Walnut Ridge, Lawrence, Ark	12
Walnut Run, Madison, Ohio	17
Walnut Shade, Taney, Mo	20
Walnut Tree, Yell, Ark	7
Walnut Valley, Warren, N. J	30
Walnut Valley, Sequatchie, Tenn	4
Walpole, Norfolk, Mass	410
Walpole, Cheshire, N. H	670
Walshville, Montgomery, Ill	120
Walterborough, (*c. h.*,) Colleton, S. C	270
Walter Hill, Rutherford, Tenn	12
Waltham, Tama, Iowa	73
Waltham, Hancock, Me	14
Waltham,* Middlesex, Mass	2,600
Waltham, Mower, Minn	10
Walthourville, Liberty, Ga	150
Walton, Cass, Ind	130
Walton, Boone, Ky	190
Walton, Delaware, N. Y	650
Walton, Roane, W. Va	21
Walton Mills, Washington, Mo	12
Walton's Ford, Habersham, Ga	12
Walts Mills, Westmoreland, Pa	10
Walworth, Wayne, N. Y	270
Walworth, Walworth, Wis	180
Wamego,* Pottawatomie, Kans	400
Wampsville, Madison, N. Y	100
Wampum, Lawrence, Pa	110
Wamsley's, Adams, Ohio	15
Wanamingа, Goodhue, Minn	190
Wanatah, Laporte, Ind	200
Waneka, Dunn, Wis	43
Wanship, Summit, Utah	65
Wapakonetta,* (*c. h.*,) Auglaize, Ohio	850
Wapella, DeWitt, Ill	270
Wapello,* (*c. h.*,) Louisa, Iowa	460
Wapping, Hartford, Conn	50
Wappinger's Falls, Dutchess, N. Y	550
Wapwallopen, Luzerne, Pa	9
Waquoit, Barnstable, Mass	95
Warananсoke, King William, Va	12
Warburgh, Callaway, Ky	4
War Creek, Hancock, Tenn	5
Ward District, Boulder, Colo	27
Wardena, Fayette, Iowa	22
Wardensville, Hardy, W. Va	63
Wardsborough, Windham, Vt	150
Ward's Corners, Buchanan, Iowa	$10
Ward's Iron Works, Johnson, Tenn	15
Wardville, Chowan, N. C	12
Ware,* Hampshire, Mass	1,400
War Eagle, Madison, Ark	12
Wareham, Plymouth, Mass	580
Warehouse Point, Hartford, Conn	380
Warfield, Lawrence, Ky	12
Warfieldburgh, Carroll, Md	21
Warfordsburgh, Fulton, Pa	38
War Gap, Hawkins, Tenn	12
Warm Fork, Oregon, Mo	12
Warminster, Bucks, Pa	31
Warminster, Nelson, Va	51
Warm Springs, Meriwether, Ga	6
Warm Springs, Madison, N. C	12
Warner, Merrimack, N. H	450
Warner's, Onondaga, N. Y	94
Warner's Landing, Vernon, Wis	10
Warner's Ranch, San Diego, Cal	12
Warnerville, Meriwether, Ga	24
Warnerville, Schoharie, N. Y	50
Warnock, Belmont, Ohio	40
Warpole, Wyandot, Ohio	12
Warren, (*c. h.*,) Bradley, Ark	180
Warren, Litchfield, Conn	95
Warren,* Jo Daviess, Ill	1,200
Warren, Huntington, Ind	190
Warren, Lee, Iowa	25
Warren, Knox, Me	300
Warren, Baltimore, Md	59
Warren, Worcester, Mass	960
Warren, Macomb, Mich	35
Warren, Marion, Mo	18
Warren, Grafton, N. H	290
Warren, Herkimer, N. Y	23
Warren,* (*c. h.*,) Trumbull, Ohio	2,400
Warren,* (*c. h.*,) Warren, Pa	2,000
Warren,* Bristol, R. I	820
Warren, Fannin, Tex	17
Warren, Washington, Vt	38
Warren, Albemarle, Va	45
Warren, Wood, W. Va	2
Warren, St. Croix, Wis	23
Warren Centre, Bradford, Pa	47
Warren Grove, Jasper, Iowa	12
Warrenham, Bradford, Pa	21
Warren Plains, Warren, N. C	33
Warrensburgh,* (*c. h.*,) Johnson, Mo	2,100
Warrensburgh,* Warren, N. Y	490
Warrensburgh, Greene, Tenn	25
Warren's Corners, Niagara, N. Y	37
Warrensville, Du Page, Ill	130
Warrensville, Cuyahoga, Ohio	49
Warrensville, Lycoming, Pa	44
Warren Tavern, Chester, Pa	130
Warrenton, Marshall, Ala	44
Warrenton, (*c. h.*,) Warren, Ga	640
Warrenton, Warren, Miss	31
Warrenton,* (*c. h.*,) Warren, Mo	790
Warrenton,* (*c. h.*,) Warren, N. C	820
Warrenton, Jefferson, Ohio	120
Warrenton,* (*c. h.*,) Fauquier, Va	1,200
Warrenville, Somerset, N. J	19
War Ridge, Hancock, Tenn	12
Warrington,* Escambia, Fla	450

* Money-order office.

Warrington, Hancock, Ind	$21
Warrington, Bucks, Pa	29
Warrior Creek, Wilkes, N. C	6
Warrior's Mark, Huntingdon, Pa	80
Warsaw, Milton, Ga	12
Warsaw,* Hancock, Ill	1,400
*Warsaw,** (*c. h.,*) Kosciusko, Ind	1,800
Warsaw, Wayne, Iowa	54
Warsaw, (*c. h.,*) Gallatin, Ky	240
Warsaw, Franklin, La	28
Warsaw, Rice, Minn	44
*Warsaw,** (*c. h.,*) Benton, Mo	490
*Warsaw,** (*c. h.,*) Wyoming, N. Y	1,400
Warsaw, Duplin, N. C	44
Warsaw, Coshocton, Ohio	35
Warsaw, Jefferson, Pa	32
Warsaw, (*c. h.,*) Richmond, Va	100
Warthen's Store, Washington, Ga	12
Wartrace Depot, Bedford, Tenn	240
Warwick, Worth, Ga	12
Warwick, Cecil, Md	130
Warwick, Franklin, Mass	200
Warwick, Orange, N. Y	820
Warwick, Chester, Pa	19
Warwick, Kent, R. I	330
Warwick C. H., Warwick, Va	11
Warwick Neck, Kent, R. I	45
Warwick's Cross Roads, Union, Tenn	85
War Woman, Rabun, Ga	12
Wasatch, Summit, Utah	340
Wasco, Wasco, Oreg	12
Waseca,* Waseca, Minn	680
Washburn, Woodford, Ill	220
Washburn, Franklin, Iowa	12
Washburn, Barry, Mo	92
Washburn, Grant, Wis	51
Washington, (*c. h.,*) Hempstead, Ark	460
Washington, Nevada, Cal	86
Washington, Litchfield, Conn	320
WASHINGTON,* (*c. h.,*) Washington, D. C	4,000
Washington, (*c. h.,*) Wilkes, Ga	680
Washington, (*c. h.,*) Idaho, Idaho	12
Washington,* Tazewell, Ill	810
*Washington,** (*c. h.,*) Daviess, Ind	1,300
*Washington,** (*c. h.,*) Washington, Iowa	1,500
Washington, (*c. h.,*) Washington, Kans	250
Washington, Mason, Ky	150
Washington, St. Landry, La	1,000
Washington, Knox, Me	93
Washington, Berkshire, Mass	58
Washington, Macomb, Mich	100
Washington, Fillmore, Minn	41
Washington,* Franklin, Mo	820
Washington, Nye, Nev	12
Washington, Sullivan, N. H	120
Washington,* Warren, N. J	1,000
Washington, Dutchess, N. Y	90
*Washington,** (*c. h.,*) Beaufort, N. C	1,200
Washington, Guernsey, Ohio	340
*Washington,** (*c. h.,*) Washington, Pa	1,800
Washington, (*c. h.,*) Rhea, Tenn	57
Washington, Washington, Tex	140
Washington, Washington, Utah	$180
Washington, Orange, Vt	130
Washington, (*c. h.,*) Rappahannock, Va	230
*Washington C. H.,** Fayette, Ohio	1,200
Washington Centre, Whitley, Ind	4
Washington Corners, Alameda, Cal	12
Washington Gulch, Deer Lodge, Mont	12
Washington Harbor, Door, Wis	54
Washington Heights, Cook, Ill	12
Washington Hollow, Dutchess, N. Y	310
Washington Mills, Oneida, N. Y	160
Washingtonville, Mahoning, Ohio	200
Washingtonville, Montour, Pa	94
Washoe City, (*c. h.,*) Washoe, Nev	440
Washta, Cherokee, Iowa	14
Wasioga, Dodge, Minn	200
Waskey's Mills, Botetourt, Va	36
Wassaic, Dutchess, N. Y	140
Wassonville, Washington, Iowa	54
Wastedo, Goodhue, Minn	120
Watab, Benton, Minn	33
Wataga, Knox, Ill	470
Watauga Falls, Watauga, N. C	2
Watauwon, Blue Earth, Minn	290
Watchemoket, Providence, R. I	110
Waterborough, York, Me	110
Waterborough Centre, York, Me	18
Waterburgh, Tompkins, N. Y	37
Waterbury,* New Haven, Conn	3,300
Waterbury, Anne Arundel, Md	51
Waterbury,* Washington, Vt	1,000
Waterbury Centre, Washington, Vt	170
Water Cure, Beaver, Pa	160
Waterford, New London, Conn	90
Waterford, Spencer, Ky	13
Waterford, Oxford, Me	140
Waterford, Oakland, Mich	180
Waterford, Dakota, Minn	23
Waterford, Marshall, Miss	77
Waterford, Saratoga, N. Y	1,200
Waterford, Washington, Ohio	68
Waterford, Erie, Pa	770
Waterford, Caledonia, Vt	96
Waterford, Loudoun, Va	220
Waterford, Racine, Wis	200
Waterford Mills, Elkhart, Ind	49
Waterford Works, Camden, N. J	88
Water Lick, Warren, Va	12
Waterloo, Lauderdale, Ala	22
Waterloo, San Joaquin, Cal	17
*Waterloo,** (*c. h.,*) Monroe, Ill	460
Waterloo,* De Kalb, Ind	730
*Waterloo,**(*c. h.,*) Black Hawk, Iowa	2,700
Waterloo, Lyon, Kans	29
Waterloo, Pulaski, Ky	22
Waterloo, Point Coupee, La	24
Waterloo, Jackson, Mich	25
Waterloo, (*c. h.,*) Clarke, Mo	110
Waterloo, Sussex, N. J	100
Waterloo, (*c. h.,*) Seneca, N. Y	2,000
Waterloo, Lawrence, Ohio	26
Waterloo, Juniata, Pa	54
Waterloo, Laurens, S. C	5
Waterloo,* Jefferson, Wis	480

* Money-order office.

Waterloo Mills, Orange, N. Y	$11
Waterman, Parke, Ind	13
Waterman's Mills, Stephenson, Ill	12
Water Mill, Suffolk, N. Y	66
Waterport, Orleans, N. Y	83
Water Proof, Tensas, La	160
Waterside, Bedford, Pa	51
Water Street, Huntingdon, Pa	61
Watersville, Carroll, Md	31
Watertown, Litchfield, Conn	440
Watertown, Rock Island, Ill	28
Watertown, Floyd, Iowa	19
Watertown,* Middlesex, Mass	1,300
Watertown, Tuscola, Mich	27
Watertown, Carver, Minn	210
*Watertown,** (*c. h.,*) Jefferson, N. Y	3,200
Watertown, Washington, Ohio	94
Watertown, Wilson, Tenn	52
Watertown,* Jefferson, Wis	2,500
Watervale, Onondaga, N. Y	22
Water Valley, Yalabusha, Miss	1,000
Water Valley, Erie, N. Y	79
Water Village, Carroll, N. H	16
Waterville, New Haven, Conn	120
Waterville, Allamakee, Iowa	73
Waterville,* Marshall, Kans.	510
Waterville,* Kennebec, Me	1,500
Waterville, Le Sueur, Minn	130
Waterville, Oneida, N. Y	890
Waterville, Lucas, Ohio	100
Waterville, Lycoming, Pa	20
Waterville, Lamoille, Vt	120
Waterville, Waukesha, Wis	27
Watervliet, Berrien, Mich	170
Watervliet Centre, Albany, N. Y	47
Wathena,* Doniphan, Kans	840
Watkins, (*c. h.,*) Schuyler, N. Y	2,000
Watkins, Union, Ohio	16
Watkinsville, (*c. h.,*) Clarke, Ga	84
Watopa, Wabashaw, Minn	4
Watrousville, Tuscola, Mich	160
Watseka,* Iroquois, Ill	1,100
Watson, Effingham, Ill	100
Watson, Prince George's, Md	12
Watson, Allegan, Mich	12
Watson, Atchison, Mo	93
Watson, Beaver Head, Mont	12
Watson, Lewis, N. Y	31
Watson Creek, Fillmore, Minn	800
Watson's Station, Seneca, Ohio	22
Watsontown,* Northumberland, Pa	430
Watsonville,* Santa Cruz, Cal	900
Watt, Indiana, Pa	12
Watterson's Ferry, Clarion, Pa	110
Wattsborough, Lunenburgh, Va	10
Wattsburgh, Erie, Pa	240
Watt's Flats, Chautauqua, N. Y	71
Wattsville, Carroll, Ohio	20
Waubeck, Linn, Iowa	65
Waubeck, Pepin, Wis	17
Waucoma, Fayette, Iowa	63
Wauconda, Lake, Ill	170
Waucousta, Fond du Lac, Wis	32
Wauhatchie, Hamilton, Tenn	12
Waukau, Winnebago, Wis	150
Waukecheon, Shawanaw, Wis	12
Waukeenah, Jefferson, Fla	$30
Waukee Station, Dallas, Iowa	12
*Waukegan,** (*c. h.,*) Lake, Ill	2,400
*Waukesha,** (*c. h.,*) Waukesha, Wis	1,900
Waukokee, Fillmore, Minn	12
*Waukon,** (*c. h.,*) Allamakee, Iowa	500
Waumandee, Buffalo, Wis	47
*Waupaca,** (*c. h.,*) Waupaca, Wis	760
Waupecong, Miami, Ind	8
Waupun,* Fond du Lac, Wis	1,900
Wauregan, Windham, Conn	230
*Wausau,** (*c. h.,*) Marathon, Wis	620
Wauseon,* Fulton, Ohio	960
Waushara, Lyon, Kans	36
Wautiska, Saunders, Nebr	12
*Wautoma,** (*c. h.,*) Waushara, Wis	330
Wauwatosa, Milwaukee, Wis	190
Wauzeka, Crawford, Wis	55
Waveland, Montgomery, Ind	240
Waveland, Pottawattomie, Iowa	12
Waveland, Shawnee, Kans	60
Waverlie, Rockingham, Va	31
Waverly, Morgan, Ill	490
Waverly, Morgan, Ind	51
*Waverly,** (*c. h.,*) Bremer, Iowa	1,500
Waverly, Caldwell, La	12
Waverly, Baltimore, Md	190
Waverly, Middlesex, Mass	85
Waverly, Van Buren, Mich	17
Waverly, Martin, Minn	11
Waverly,* La Fayette, Mo	370
Waverly,* Tioga, N. Y	1,600
Waverly, Pike, Ohio	490
Waverly, Luzerne, Pa	230
Waverly, (*c. h.,*) Humphreys, Tenn	190
Waverly, Walker, Tex	24
Waverly Hall, Harris, Ga	25
Waverly Heights, Montgomery, Pa	64
Waverly Mills, Wright, Minn	28
Waverly Station, Sussex, Va	93
Wawaka, Noble, Ind	190
Wawarsing, Ulster, N. Y	72
Wawayanda, Sussex, N. J	12
Waxahachie, (*c. h.,*) Ellis, Tex	400
Wayland, Schuyler, Ill	17
Wayland, Middlesex, Mass	190
Wayland,* Allegan, Mich	360
Wayland Depot, Steuben, N. Y	320
Waylandsburgh, Culpeper, Va	5
Wayland Springs, Lawrence, Tenn	10
Waymansville, Bartholomew, Ind	12
Waymart, Wayne, Pa	240
Wayne, Du Page, Ill	180
Wayne, Henry, Iowa	27
Wayne, Kennebec, Me	180
Wayne, Wayne, Mich	360
Wayne, Steuben, N. Y	150
Wayne, Wayne, Ohio	12
Wayne, Erie, Pa	47
Wayne, Washington, Wis	33
Wayne C. H., Wayne, W. Va	12
Wayne Centre, Wayne, N. Y	20
Wayne Centre, Crawford, Pa	4
Wayne Four Corners, Steuben, N.Y.	6
Waynesborough, (*c. h.,*) Burke, Ga	400
Waynesborough, (*c. h.,*) Wayne, Miss.	24

* Money-order office.

Waynesborough,* Franklin, Pa	$790
Waynesborough, (c. h.,) Wayne, Tenn	98
Waynesborough, Augusta, Va	390
Waynesburgh, Decatur, Ind	78
Waynesburgh, Lincoln, Ky	21
Waynesburgh, Stark, Ohio	300
Waynesburgh, (c. h.,)* Greene, Pa	1,000
Waynesfield, Auglaize, Ohio	42
Waynesville, (c. h.,) Wayne, Ga	12
Waynesville, De Witt, Ill	130
Waynesville, Bartholomew, Ind	24
Waynesville, (c. h.,)* Pulaski, Mo	88
Waynesville, (c. h.,) Haywood, N. C	80
Waynesville,* Warren, Ohio	610
Waynetown, Montgomery, Ind	130
Waynewood, Marion, Ind	12
Waynmanville, Upson, Ga	25
Wayside, Mecklenburgh, Va	12
Wayside, Brown, Wis	13
Way's Station, Bryan, Ga	12
Wayzata, Hennepin, Minn	24
Weare, Oceana, Mich	12
Weare, Hillsborough, N. H	97
Wear's Valley, Sevier, Tenn	12
Weatherford, (c. h.,) Parker, Tex	530
Weatherly, Carbon, Pa	250
Weathersfield, Windsor, Vt	59
Weathersfield Centre, Windsor, Vt	12
Weatogue, Hartford, Conn	69
Weaver's Old Stand, Westmoreland, Pa	57
Weaver's Station, Darke, Ohio	45
Weaversville, Northampton, Pa	45
Weaversville, Fauquier, Va	18
Weaverton, Wayne, Ky	18
Weaverville, (c. h.,)* Trinity, Cal	390
Webber's Falls, Cherokee Nation, Ind. T	12
Webberville, Ingham, Mich	26
Webberville, Travis, Tex	110
Webbs, Greene, Ky	6
Webb's Ford, Rutherford, N. C	13
Webb's Mills, Cumberland, Me	36
Webb's Mills, Chemung, N. Y	140
Webb's Mills, Ritchie, W. Va	7
Webb's Prairie, Franklin, Ill	11
Webbville, Lawrence, Ky	4
Webertown, Highland, Ohio	11
Webster, Hancock, Ill	52
Webster, Wayne, Ind	13
Webster, Keokuk, Iowa	48
Webster, Breckinridge, Ky	14
Webster, Androscoggin, Me	20
Webster,* Worcester, Mass	1,700
Webster, Washtenaw, Mich	19
Webster, Winston, Miss	39
Webster, Oregon, Mo	23
Webster, Merrimack, N. H	120
Webster, Monroe, N. Y	200
Webster, (c. h.,) Jackson, N. C	63
Webster, Darke, Ohio	66
Webster, Westmoreland, Pa	130
Webster, Roane, Tenn	12
Webster, Taylor, W. Va	120
Webster C. H., Webster W. Va	19
Webster City, (c. h.,)* Hamilton, Iowa	600
Webster Groves, St. Louis, Mo	$220
Webster Place, Elbert, Ga	12
Webster's Crossing, Livingston, N. Y	12
Webster's Mills, Fulton, Pa	21
Wedowee, (c. h.,) Randolph, Ala	66
Weedsport, Cayuga, N. Y	930
Weehawken, Hudson, N. J	420
Week's Mills, Kennebec, Me	75
Weeksville, Southampton, Va	12
Weelaunee, Jefferson, Fla	12
Weelaunee, Winnebago, Wis	44
Weeping Water, Cass, Nebr	140
Weesatch, Goliad, Tex	12
Weesaw, Berrien, Mich	19
Weewokaville, Talladega, Ala	6
Wegatchie, St. Lawrence, N. Y	31
Wegee, Belmont, Ohio	20
Wehoga, Calhoun, Ala	5
Weidasville, Lehigh, Pa	5
Weir's Bridge, Belknap, N. H	29
Weisburgh, Dearborn, Ind	65
Weisenburgh, Lehigh, Pa	8
Weisesburgh, Baltimore, Md	11
Weishample, Schuylkill, Pa	12
Weissport, Carbon, Pa	190
Weister, Vernon, Wis	14
Welaka, Putnam, Fla	51
Welch Glade, Webster, W. Va	4
Welch's Creek, Butler, Ky	3
Welchville, Oxford, Me	150
Weld, Weld, Colo	12
Weld, Franklin, Me	210
Weldon, Redwood, Minn	12
Weldon,* Halifax, N. C	880
Weldon, Houston, Tex	8
Well, Faribault, Minn	14
Wellborn, Suwannee, Fla	53
Weller, Monroe, Iowa	7
Wellersburgh, Somerset, Pa	65
Wellerville, Crawford, Ohio	18
Wellesley, Norfolk, Mass	300
Wellfleet,* Barnstable, Mass	550
Wellington, Piscataquis, Me	22
Wellington, La Fayette, Mo	170
Wellington, Esmeralda, Nev	12
Wellington,* Lorain, Ohio	1,300
Wells, York, Me	250
Wells, Attala, Miss	12
Wells, Elko, Nev	12
Wells, Hamilton, N. Y	68
Wells, Bradford, Pa	50
Wells, Rutland, Vt	120
Wellsborough, (c. h.,)* Tioga, Pa	1,100
Wells' Bridge, Otsego, N. Y	73
Wellsburgh, Page, Iowa	12
Wellsburgh, St. Charles, Mo	72
Wellsburgh, Chemung, N. Y	210
Wellsburgh, (c. h.,)* Brooke, W. Va	560
Wells Corner, Orange, N. Y	13
Wells Depot, York, Me	150
Wells' Mills, Appanoose, Iowa	25
Wells' Mills, Richardson, Nebr	13
Well Spring, Campbell, Tenn	14
Wells River, Orange, Vt	520
Wells Tannery, Fulton, Pa	32

* Money-order office.

Wellsville, Lenawee, Mich	$16
Wellsville, Montgomery, Mo	220
Wellsville,* Allegany, N. Y	1,400
Wellsville,* Columbiana, Ohio	1,200
Wellsville, York, Pa	96
Wellsville, Cache, Utah	360
Wellville, Nottaway, Va	62
Well Water, Buckingham, Va	5
Wellwood, Haywood, Tenn	21
Welshfield, Geauga, Ohio	89
Welsh Run, Franklin, Pa	50
Welton, Clinton, Iowa	42
Weltonville, Tioga, N. Y	19
Wendell, Franklin, Mass	50
Wendell Depot, Franklin, Mass	76
Wenham, Essex, Mass	210
Wenks, Adams, Pa	12
Wennersville, Lehigh, Pa	9
Wenona, Bay, Mich	490
Wenona Station,* Marshall, Ill	1,100
Wentworth, Mitchell, Iowa	12
Wentworth, Grafton, N. H	340
Wentworth, (*c. h.*,) Rockingham, N.C.	100
Wentworth's Location, Coos, N. H.	9
Wentzville, St. Charles, Mo	360
Weogufka, Coosa, Ala	4
Wequiock, Brown, Wis	25
Werner, Juneau, Wis	64
Wernersville, Berks, Pa	22
Wertsville, Hunterdon, N. J	63
Wescosville, Lehigh, Pa	40
Wesley, Montgomery, Ind	16
Wesley, Hickman, Ky	17
Wesley, Washington, Me	31
Wesley, Washington, Ohio	7
Wesley, Venango, Pa	22
Wesley, Austin, Tex	49
Wesleyville, Erie, Pa	130
Wesson, Copiah, Miss	140
West, Wetzel, W. Va	5
West Acton, Middlesex, Mass	260
West Addison, Steuben, N. Y	29
West Addison, Addison, Vt	23
West Albany, Wabashaw, Minn	19
West Albany, Albany, N. Y	36
West Alexander, Washington, Pa	190
West Alexandria, Preble, Ohio	210
West Almond, Allegany, N. Y	40
West Alton, Belknap, N. H	21
West Amboy, Oswego, N. Y	36
West Amesbury, Essex, Mass	430
West Andover, Merrimack, N. H	87
West Andover, Ashtabula, Ohio	120
West Appleton, Knox, Me	20
West Arlington, Bennington, Vt	51
West Ashford, Windham, Conn	59
West Athens, Somerset, Me	12
West Auburn, Androscoggin, Me	150
West Auburn, Susquehanna, Pa	20
West Avon, Hartford, Conn	27
West Baden, Orange, Ind	66
West Baldwin, Cumberland, Me	81
West Baltimore, Montgomery, Ohio.	51
West Bangor, Franklin, N. Y	94
West Bangor, York, Pa	220
West Barnet, Caledonia, Vt	85
West Barnstable, Barnstable, Mass.	$130
West Barre, Orleans, N. Y	33
West Barre, Fulton, Ohio	7
West Batavia, Genesee, N. Y	41
West Beaver, Columbiana, Ohio	11
West Becket, Berkshire, Mass	28
West Bedford, Coshocton, Ohio	64
West Bend, Palo Alto, Iowa	25
West Bend, Powell, Ky	12
West Bend,* (*c. h.*,) Washington, Wis.	480
West Bergen, Genesee, N. Y	27
West Berkshire, Franklin, Vt	140
West Berlin, Worcester, Mass	35
West Berne, Albany, N. Y	34
West Bethany, Genesee, N. Y	24
West Bethel, Oxford, Me	110
West Bingham, Potter, Pa	12
West Bloomfield, Ontario, N. Y	240
West Blue Mound, Iowa, Wis	79
West Bolton, Chittenden, Vt	33
Westborough,* Worcester, Mass	1,500
Westborough, Clinton, Ohio	130
West Bowdoin, Sagadahoc, Me	40
West Boxford, Essex, Mass	65
West Boylston, Worcester, Mass	330
West Braintree, Orange, Vt	39
West Branch, Cedar, Iowa	320
West Branch, Oneida, N. Y	66
West Branch, Richland, Wis	34
West Brattleborough, Windham, Vt.	300
West Brewster, Barnstable, Mass	60
West Bridgeton, Cumberland, Me	8
West Bridgewater, Plymouth, Mass.	310
West Bridgewater, Windsor, Vt	15
West Brighton, Monroe, N. Y	44
West Brook, Middlesex, Conn	250
West Brook, Delaware, N. Y	14
West Brook, Bladen, N. C	5
Westbrook, Blanco, Tex	6
West Brookfield, Worcester, Mass	510
West Brookfield, Stark, Ohio	310
West Brooklyn, Poweshiek, Iowa	12
West Brooksville, Hancock, Me	74
West Brookville, Sullivan, N. Y	46
West Brownsville, Washington, Pa.	76
West Brunswick, Cumberland, Me.	15
West Buena Vista, Gibson, Ind	11
West Buffalo, Williams, Ohio	44
West Burke, Caledonia, Vt	210
West Burlington, Otsego, N. Y	50
West Burlington, Bradford, Pa	59
Westbury, Cayuga, N. Y	86
West Butler, Wayne, N. Y	33
West Butte, Sutter, Cal	20
West Buxton, York, Me	230
West Cairo, Allen, Ohio	86
West Camden, Knox, Me	74
West Camden, Oneida, N. Y	83
West Camp, Ulster, N. Y	31
West Campbell, Ionia, Mich	27
West Campton, Grafton, N. H	110
West Canaan, Grafton, N. H	80
West Canaan, Madison, Ohio	21
West Candor, Tioga, N. Y	22
West Carlisle, Coshocton, Ohio	63
West Carrollton, Montgomery, Ohio	12

* Money-order office.

West Casco, Allegan, Mich	$20
West Castleton, Rutland, Vt	100
West Charleston, Penobscot, Me	32
West Charleston, Miami, Ohio	31
West Charleston, Orleans, Vt	250
West Charlotte, Chittenden, Vt	95
West Charlton, Saratoga, N. Y	70
West Chatham, Barnstable, Mass	49
West Chazy, Clinton, N. Y	210
West Chehalem, Yam Hill, Oreg	12
West Chelmsford, Middlesex, Mass	140
West Cheshire, New Haven, Conn	250
Westchester, New London, Conn	52
Westchester, Jay, Ind	38
West Chester, Wabashaw, Minn	16
West Chester, Westchester, N. Y	670
West Chester, Butler, Ohio	110
West Chester,* Chester, Pa	2,500
West Chesterfield, Hampshire, Mass	70
West Chesterfield, Cheshire, N. H	41
West Claremont, Sullivan, N. H	48
West Clarksville, Allegany, N. Y	79
West Colesville, Broome, N. Y	12
West Columbia, Mason, W. Va	96
West Concord, Merrimack, N. H	190
West Concord,* Essex, Vt	240
West Conesville, Schoharie, N. Y	23
West Constable, Franklin, N. Y	54
West Copake, Columbia, N. Y	12
West Corinna, Penobscot, Me	2
West Corinth, Orange, Vt	45
West Cornville, Somerset, Me	23
West Cornwall, Litchfield, Conn	340
West Cornwall, Addison, Vt	120
West Covington, Tioga, Pa	24
West Creek, Lake, Ind	40
West Creek, Ocean, N. J	96
West Cumberland, Cumberland, Me	62
West Damascus, Wayne, Pa	12
West Danby, Tompkins, N. Y	40
West Danvers, Essex, Mass	38
West Danville, Caledonia, Vt	77
West Davenport, Delaware, N. Y	49
West Day, Saratoga, N. Y	75
West Dayton, Webster, Iowa	200
West Decatur, Clearfield, Pa	33
West Dedham, Norfolk, Mass	120
West Deering, Hillsborough, N. H	12
West Deer Isle, Hancock, Me	12
West Dennis, Barnstable, Mass	280
West Derby, Orleans, Vt	69
West Dover, Piscataquis, Me	11
West Dover, Windham, Vt	75
West Dresden, Lincoln, Me	12
West Dryden, Tompkins, N. Y	32
West Dublin, Fulton, Pa	11
West Dudley, Worcester, Mass	58
West Dummerston, Windham, Vt	80
West Durham, Androscoggin, Me	41
West Duxbury, Plymouth, Mass	67
West Earl, Lancaster, Pa	62
West Eaton, Madison, N. Y	260
West Eau Claire,* Eau Claire, Wis	1,100
West Eden, Hancock, Me	35
West Edmeston, Otsego, N. Y	88
West Elizabeth, Allegheny, Pa	100
West Elkton, Preble, Ohio	$94
West Ellsworth, Hancock, Me	10
West Ely, Marion, Mo	26
West Embden, Somerset, Me	6
West End, Bedford, Pa	34
West Enfield, Penobscot, Me	8
West Enfield, Concord, N. H	12
West Enosburgh, Franklin, Vt	67
West Epping, Rockingham, N. H	54
Westerlo, Albany, N. Y	88
Westerly,* Washington, R. I	2,700
Western College, Linn, Iowa	190
Western Port, Alleghany, Md	260
Western Saratoga, Union, Ill	8
Western Star, Summit, Ohio	47
Westernville, Oneida, N. Y	220
Westerville, Decatur, Iowa	46
Westerville, Franklin, Ohio	440
West Exeter, Otsego, N. Y	70
West Fairfield, Westmoreland, Pa	73
West Fairlee, Orange, Vt	480
West Fairview, Cumberland, Pa	200
West Falls, Erie, N. Y	61
West Falmouth, Cumberland, Me	72
West Falmouth, Barnstable, Mass	110
West Farmingdale, Kennebec, Me	30
West Farmington, Ontario, N. Y	35
West Farmington,* Trumbull, Ohio	290
West Farms, Westchester, N. Y	430
West Fayette, Seneca, N. Y	28
Westfield, Clark, Ill	340
Westfield, Hamilton, Ind	210
Westfield, Worth, Iowa	12
Westfield, Aroostook, Me	11
Westfield,* Hampden, Mass	2,700
Westfield, Pope, Minn	12
Westfield, Union, N. J	300
Westfield,* Chautauqua, N. Y	1,400
Westfield, Stokes, N. C	12
Westfield, Morrow, Ohio	60
Westfield, Tioga, Pa	210
Westfield, Orleans, Vt	67
Westfield,* Marquette, Wis	120
West Finley, Washington, Pa	23
West Fitchburgh, Worcester, Mass	440
West Florence, Preble, Ohio	38
Westford, Windham, Conn	160
Westford, Middlesex, Mass	210
Westford, Otsego, N. Y	140
Westford, Chittenden, Vt	140
Westford, Dodge, Wis	410
West Fork, Washington, Ark	9
West Fork, Monona, Iowa	13
West Fork, Overton, Tenn	10
West Fork Furnace, Floyd, Va	13
West Fort Ann, Washington, N. Y	45
West Foxborough, Norfolk, Mass	38
West Franklin, Bradford, Pa	20
West Freedom, Clarion, Pa	42
West Freehold, Monmouth, N. J	60
West Freeman, Franklin, Me	5
West Friendship, Howard, Md	16
West Fulton, Schoharie, N. Y	44
West Galway, Fulton, N. Y	140
West Gardiner, Kennebec, Me	46
West Garland, Penobscot, Me	24

* Money-order office.

West Geneva, Van Buren, Mich	$22
West Georgia, Franklin, Vt	18
West Gloucester, Cumberland, Me	31
West Gloucester, Essex, Mass	92
West Gloucester, Providence, R. I	20
West Glover, Orleans, Vt	47
West Gorham, Cumberland, Me	66
West Goshen, Litchfield, Conn	170
West Gouldsborough, Hancock, Me	100
West Granby, Hartford, Conn	63
West Granville, Hampden, Mass	86
West Granville, Milwaukee, Wis	53
West Granville Corners, Washington, N. Y	67
West Great Works, Penobscot, Me	81
West Greece, Monroe, N. Y	67
West Greene, Erie, Pa	36
West Greenfield, Saratoga, N. Y	12
West Green Lake, Green Lake, Wis	10
West Greenwich Centre, Kent, R. I	9
West Greenwood, Crawford, Pa	14
West Groton, Middlesex, Mass	81
West Groton, Tompkins, N. Y	36
West Grove, Davis, Iowa	8
West Grove Station, Chester, Pa	350
West Halifax, Windham, Vt	55
West Hallock, Peoria, Ill	76
West Hamburgh, Erie, N. Y	13
Westham Locks, Henrico, Va	9
West Hampden, Penobscot, Me	48
West Hampstead, Rockingham, N. H	62
West Hampton, Hampshire, Mass	89
West Hampton, Suffolk, N. Y	58
West Hanover, Plymouth, Mass	80
West Hanover, Dauphin, Pa	35
West Harpswell, Cumberland, Me	73
West Hartford, Hartford, Conn	240
West Hartford, Ralls, Mo	12
West Hartford, Windsor, Vt	170
West Hartland, Hartford, Conn	43
West Harwich, Barnstable, Mass	150
West Haven, New Haven, Conn	360
West Haven, Shiawassee, Mich	12
West Haven, Rutland, Vt	32
West Haverford, Delaware, Pa	400
West Hawley, Franklin, Mass	20
West Hebron, Washington, N. Y	130
West Henniker, Merrimack, N. H	65
West Henrietta, Monroe, N. Y	100
West Hickory, Forest, Pa	16
West Hoboken, Hudson, N. J	280
West Hoosick, Rensselaer, N. Y	30
West Hope, Henry, Ohio	12
West Hopkinton, Merrimack, N. H	15
West Hurley, Ulster, N. Y	130
West Independence, Hancock, Ohio	32
West Irving, Tama, Iowa	76
West Jasper, Steuben, N. Y	5
West Jefferson,* Madison, Ohio	330
West Jersey, Stark, Ill	110
West Jordan, Salt Lake, Utah	10
West Junius, Seneca, N. Y	14
West Kendall, Orleans, N. Y	62
West Kill, Greene, N. Y	59
West Killingly,* Windham, Conn	1,500
West Kinderhook, Tipton, Ind	$8
West Kortright, Delaware, N. Y	24
West La Fayette, Coshocton, Ohio	66
West Lancaster, Fayette, Ohio	28
Westland, Hancock, Ind	14
West Laurens, Otsego, N. Y	46
West Lebanon,* Warren, Ind	290
West Lebanon, York, Me	100
West Lebanon,* Grafton, N. H	540
West Lebanon, Wayne, Ohio	57
West Lebanon, Indiana, Pa	87
West Leeds, Androscoggin, Me	26
West Lenox, Susquehanna, Pa	14
West Leroy, Calhoun, Mich	16
West Levant, Penobscot, Me	31
West Leyden, Lewis, N. Y	82
West Liberty, Howard, Ind	12
West Liberty,* Muscatine, Iowa	770
West Liberty, (*c. h.*,) Morgan, Ky	36
West Liberty, Putnam, Mo	8
West Liberty,* Logan, Ohio	830
West Liberty, Butler, Pa	28
West Liberty, Ohio, W. Va	110
West Lima, Richland, Wis	23
West Lodi, Seneca, Ohio	70
West Louisville, Daviess, Ky	12
West Lowville, Lewis, N. Y	16
West Lubec, Washington, Me	89
West Lyons, Cook, Ill	67
West Macedon,* Wayne, N. Y	620
West Magnolia, Rock, Wis	12
West Manchester, Preble, Ohio	67
West Mansfield, Bristol, Mass	72
West Mansfield, Logan, Ohio	28
West Marlborough, Windham, Vt	8
West Martinsburgh, Lewis, N. Y	59
West Medford, Middlesex, Mass	100
West Medway, Norfolk, Mass	380
West Meredith, Delaware, N. Y	12
West Meriden,* New Haven, Conn	3,300
West Middleburgh, Logan, Ohio	88
West Middlesex, Mercer, Pa	500
West Middleton, Dane, Wis	20
West Middletown, Washington, Pa	250
West Milan, Monroe, Mich	12
West Milan, Coos, N. H	85
West Milford, Passaic, N. J	55
West Milford, Harrison, W. Va	44
West Millbury, Worcester, Mass	260
West Mill Grove, Wood, Ohio	83
West Milton, Strafford, N. H	59
West Milton, Saratoga, N. Y	97
West Milton, Miami, Ohio	210
West Milton, Union, Pa	53
West Milton, Chittenden, Vt	40
West Minot, Androscoggin, Me	120
Westminster, Windham, Conn	48
Westminster,* (*c. h.*,) Carroll, Md	930
Westminster, Worcester, Mass	410
Westminster, Guilford, N. C	20
Westminster, Allen, Ohio	46
Westminster, Windham, Vt	85
Westminster Depot, Worcester, Mass	50
Westminster West, Windham, Vt	96
West Mitchell, Mitchell, Iowa	400

* Money-order office.

Post office	Amount
West Monroe, Oswego, N. Y	$93
West Monterey, Clarion, Pa	34
Westmore, Orleans, Vt	12
Westmoreland, Pottawatomie, Kans.	17
Westmoreland, Cheshire, N. H	99
Westmoreland, Oneida, N. Y	400
Westmoreland Depot, Cheshire, N. H	100
West Mount Vernon, Kennebec, Me	47
West Nanticoke, Luzerne, Pa	20
West Newark, Tioga, N. Y	17
West New Brighton, Richmond, N.Y.	590
West Newbury, Essex, Mass	230
West Newfield, York, Me	95
West Newport, Orleans, Vt	23
West Newton, Marion, Ind	76
West Newton, Middlesex, Mass	870
West Newton, Nicollet, Minn	67
West Newton, Allen, Ohio	57
West Newton, Westmoreland, Pa	590
West Norfolk, Litchfield, Conn	83
West Northfield, Cook, Ill	22
West Northfield, Franklin, Mass	160
West Norwalk, Fairfield, Conn	78
West Nottingham, Rockingham, N. H	36
West Novi, Oakland, Mich	48
West Ogden, Lenawee, Mich	18
Weston, Fairfield, Conn	110
Weston, McLean, Ill	24
Weston, Nicholas, Ky	33
Weston, Aroostook, Me	22
Weston, Middlesex, Mass	270
Weston, Lenawee, Mich	35
Weston,* Platte, Mo	940
Weston, Somerset, N. J	10
Weston, Schuyler, N. Y	47
Weston, Wood, Ohio	230
Weston, Umatilla, Oreg	12
Weston, Collin, Tex	42
Weston, Cache, Utah	12
Weston, Windsor, Vt	220
*Weston,** (*c. h.,*) Lewis, W. Va	460
Westonburgh, Crittenden, Ky	73
West Oneonta, Otsego, N. Y	75
West Ossipee, Carroll, N. H	30
West Otis, Berkshire, Mass	25
Westover, Somerset, Md	30
Westover's, Clearfield, Pa	16
West Overton, Westmoreland, Pa	20
West Paris, Oxford, Me	190
West Parsonfield, York, Me	72
West Pawlet, Rutland, Vt	150
West Pembroke, Washington, Me	130
West Penn, Schuylkill, Pa	12
West Pensaukie, Oconto, Wis	49
West Perth, Fulton, N.Y	17
West Peru, Oxford, Me	48
West Peterborough, Hillsborough, N. H	100
Westphalia, Clinton, Mich	140
Westphalia, Osage, Mo	220
West Pike, Potter, Pa	10
West Pittsfield, Somerset, Me	22
West Pittsfield, Berkshire, Mass	180
West Plains, (*c. h.,*) Howell, Mo	10

Post office	Amount
West Plattsburgh, Clinton, N. Y	$44
West Plymouth, Grafton, N. H	48
West Point, White, Ark	73
West Point, Calaveras, Cal	94
West Point, Troup, Ga	990
West Point, Hancock, Ill	46
West Point, Tippecanoe, Ind	110
West Point,* Lee, Iowa	320
West Point, Hardin, Ky	75
West Point, Lowndes, Miss	1,400
West Point, Bates, Mo	52
*West Point,** (*c. h.,*) Cuming, Nebr	220
West Point,* Orange, N. Y	1,200
West Point, Columbiana, Ohio	55
West Point, Lawrence, Tenn	5
West Point, Rio Virgin, Utah	12
West Point, King William, Va	69
West Point, Columbia, Wis	13
West Poland, Androscoggin, Me	61
Westport, Fairfield, Conn	900
Westport, Decatur, Ind	37
Westport, Oldham, Ky	100
Westport, Lincoln, Me	56
Westport, Bristol, Mass	160
Westport, Jackson, Mo	560
Westport, Cheshire, N. H	60
Westport, Essex, N. Y	430
Westport, Clatsop, Oreg	35
Westport, Clinton, Pa	200
Westport, Dane, Wis	48
Westport Point, Bristol, Mass	71
West Potsdam, St. Lawrence, N. Y	17
West Pownal, Cumberland, Me	70
West Prairie, Linn, Iowa	14
West Prairie, Dunklin, Mo	39
West Prairie, Vernon, Wis	15
West Providence, Saratoga, N. Y	9
Westralia, Montgomery, Kans	12
West Randolph,* Orange, Vt	860
West Redding, Fairfield, Conn	94
West Richfield, Summit, Ohio	180
West Richmondville, Schoharie, N. Y	35
West River, Anne Arundel, Md	230
West Rochester, Windsor, Vt	36
West Rosendale, Fond du Lac, Wis	36
West Roxbury, Norfolk, Mass	240
West Rumney, Grafton, N. H	120
West Rupert, Bennington, Vt	130
West Rush, Monroe, N. Y	47
West Rushville, Fairfield, Ohio	68
West Rutland, Worcester, Mass	44
West Rutland, Rutland, Vt	750
West Saint Paul, Dakota, Minn	170
West Salem, Edwards, Ill	81
West Salem,* Wayne, Ohio	380
West Salem, Mercer, Pa	7
West Salem, La Crosse, Wis	320
West Salisbury, Merrimack, N. H	38
West Salisbury, Addison, Vt	120
West Sand Lake, Rensselaer, N. Y	110
West Sandwich, Barnstable, Mass	98
West Schuyler, Herkimer, N. Y	46
West Scituate, Plymouth, Mass	120
West Seneca, Erie, N. Y	41
West Seneca Centre, Erie, N. Y	7

* Money-order office.

WES

West Shelby, Orleans, N. Y	$42
Westside, Crawford, Iowa	12
West's Mill, Seward, Nebr	12
West's Mills, Franklin, Me	54
West Somers, Westchester, N. Y	20
West Somerset, Niagara, N. Y	35
West Sonora, Preble, Ohio	40
West Spring Creek, Warren, Pa	35
West Springfield, Hampden, Mass	210
West Springfield, Sullivan, N. H	78
West Springfield, Erie, Pa	120
West's Station, Holmes, Miss	14
West Stafford, Tolland, Conn	80
West Stephentown, Rensselaer, N. Y	48
West Sterling, Worcester, Mass	36
West Stewartstown, Coos, N. H	72
West Stockbridge, Berkshire, Mass	540
West Stockbridge Centre, Berkshire, Mass	15
West Stockholm, St. Lawrence, N. Y	130
West Suffield, Hartford, Conn	120
West Sumner, Oxford, Me	60
West Sutton, Worcester, Mass	76
West Swanzey, Cheshire, N. H	170
West Taghkanick, Columbia, N. Y	14
West Thompson, Windsor, Conn	100
West Thornton, Grafton, N. H	110
West Tisbury, Dukes, Mass	150
West Topsham, Orange, Vt	100
West Townsend, Middlesex, Mass	290
West Townshend, Windham, Vt	100
West Town, Orange, N. Y	95
West Township, Albany, N. Y	52
West Trenton, Hancock, Me	51
West Troupsburgh, Steuben, N. Y	11
West Troy, Waldo, Me	28
West Troy, Albany, N. Y	2,400
West Union,* (*c. h.*,) Fayette, Iowa	870
West Union, Owen, Ky	6
West Union, Steuben, N. Y	11
West Union, (*c. h.*,) Adams, Ohio	230
West Union,* (*c. h.*,) Doddridge, W. Va	240
West Unity,* Williams, Ohio	380
West Upton, Worcester, Mass	220
West Valley, Cattaraugus, N. Y	20
West Valley, Armstrong, Pa	48
West Vienna, Oneida, N. Y	76
West View, Cuyahoga, Ohio	67
West View, Allegheny, Pa	10
Westville, Dale, Ala	20
Westville, New Haven, Conn	420
Westville,* La Porte, Ind	450
Westville, (*c. h.*,) Simpson, Miss	24
Westville, Gloucester, N. J	39
Westville, Otsego, N. Y	46
Westville, Champaign, Ohio	69
Westville Centre, Franklin, N. Y	48
West Vincent, Chester, Pa	77
West Walworth, Wayne, N. Y	81
West Wardsborough, Windham, Vt	73
West Wareham, Plymouth, Mass	98
West Warren, Worcester, Mass	340
West Warren, Bradford, Pa	35
West Washington, Knox, Me	41

WHE

West Waterford, Caledonia, Vt	$29
West Waterville, Kennebec, Me	600
West Webster, Monroe, N. Y	130
West Whiteland, Chester, Pa	190
West Williamsfield, Ashtabula, Ohio	96
West Willington, Tolland, Conn	140
West Wilton, Hillsborough, N. H	60
West Windham, Rockingham, N. H	22
West Windham, Bradford, Pa	19
West Windsor, Eaton, Mich	51
West Windsor, Broome, N. Y	20
West Windsor, Richland, Ohio	73
West Winfield, Herkimer, N. Y	490
West Winsted,* Litchfield, Conn	1,300
West Winterport, Waldo, Me	24
Westwood, Bergen, N. J	27
Westwood, Erie, N. Y	12
West Woodstock, Windham, Conn	110
West Woodville, Clermont, Ohio	16
West Worthington, Hampshire, Mass	35
West Wrentham, Norfolk, Mass	20
West Yarmouth, Barnstable, Mass	86
West Yorkshire, Cattaraugus, N. Y	18
West Zanesville, Muskingum, Ohio	260
Wetaug, Pulaski, Ill	21
Wet Glaze, Camden, Mo	12
Wetheredville, Baltimore, Md	33
Wethersfield, Hartford, Conn	380
Wethersfield, Henry, Ill	130
Wethersfield, Wyoming, N. Y	53
Wethersfield Springs, Wyoming, N. Y	70
Wetmore, Nemaha, Kans	140
Wetmore, Pike, Ohio	12
Wetumpka,* (*c. h.*,) Elmore, Ala	550
Wevertown, Warren, N. Y	160
We Wo Ka, Seminole N., Ind. T	52
Wexford, Wexford, Mich	43
Wexford, Allegheny, Pa	65
Weyauwega,* Waupaca, Wis	360
Weybridge Lower Falls, Addison, Vt	73
Weymouth, Norfolk, Mass	710
Weymouth, Atlantic, N. J	79
Weymouth, Medina, Ohio	74
Whalan, Fillmore, Minn	53
Whaleysville, Worcester, Md	67
Whallonsburgh, Essex, N. Y	78
Wharton, Potter, Pa	23
Wharton, (*c. h.*,) Wharton, Tex	140
Whartonsburgh, Wyandot, Ohio	89
What Cheer, Keokuk, Iowa	36
Whatcom, (*c. h.*,) Whatcom, Wash	19
Whately, Franklin, Mass	190
Wheatfield, Sangamon, Ill	2
Wheatland, Yuba, Cal	30
Wheatland, El Paso, Colo	12
Wheatland, Knox, Ind	150
Wheatland,* Clinton, Iowa	400
Wheatland, Rice, Minn	10
Wheatland, Hickory, Mo	16
Wheatland, Yam Hill, Oreg	21
Wheatland, Loudoun, Va	26
Wheatland, Kenosha, Wis	41
Wheatland Centre, Hillsdale, Mich	20

* Money-order office.

Post office	Amount
Wheatland Furnace, Mercer, Pa	$310
Wheatland Mills, Lancaster, Pa	20
Wheaton,* Du Page, Ill	760
Wheaton, Montgomery, Md	41
Wheatonville, Warrick, Ind	8
Wheat Ridge, Adams, Ohio	15
Wheatville, Miami, Ind	7
Wheatville, Genesee, N. Y	46
Wheatville, Titus, Tex	12
Wheatville, Crawford, Wis	6
Wheeler, Porter, Ind	83
Wheeler, Gratiot, Mich	12
Wheeler, Steuben, N. Y	43
Wheelersburgh, Scioto, Ohio	150
Wheeler's Grove, Pottawattomie, Iowa	10
Wheeler Station, Lawrence, Ala	12
Wheelersville, Northampton, N. C	12
Wheeling, Cook, Ill	87
Wheeling, Delaware, Ind	47
Wheeling, Marion, Iowa	31
Wheeling, Winn, La	14
Wheeling, Rice, Minn	23
Wheeling, Livingston, Mo	170
WHEELING,* (*c. h.*,) Ohio, W. Va	3, 800
Wheelock, Choctaw N., Ind. T	11
Wheelock, Robertson, Tex	37
Wheelock, Caledonia, Vt	81
Whetham, Clinton, Pa	23
Whetstone, Morrow, Ohio	17
Whetstone Agency, ———, Dak	12
Whig Valley, Holt, Mo	12
Whigville, Noble, Ohio	17
Whilden's Factory, Greenville, S. C	10
Whippany, Morris, N. J	89
Whippoorwill, Laurel, Ky	5
Whistler, Mobile, Ala	110
Whitaker's, Edgecombe, N. C	12
Whitcomb, Franklin, Ind	24
White Ash, Allegheny, Pa	160
White Bear Centre, Pope, Minn	12
White Bear Lake, Ramsey, Minn	29
White Bird, Idaho, Idaho	12
White Bluff, Dallas, Ala	12
White Bluffs, Dickson, Tenn	95
White Breast, Lucas, Iowa	4
White Church, Wyandotte, Kans	12
White Cloud, Mills, Iowa	120
White Cloud,* Doniphan, Kans	320
White Cloud, Nodaway, Mo	26
White Cottage, Muskingum, Ohio	50
White Cottage, Greene, Pa	16
White Creek, Jackson, Ind	23
White Creek, Washington, N. Y	83
White Creek, Adams, Wis	35
White Day, Monongalia, W. Va	44
White Deer Mills, Union, Pa	34
White Eyes Plains, Coshocton, Ohio	34
Whitefield, Lincoln, Me	73
Whitefield, Oktibbeha, Miss	16
Whitefield, Coos, N. H	350
Whiteford Centre, Monroe, Mich	23
White Gate, Giles, Va	12
Whitehall, Yankton, Dak	12
White Hall, Greene, Ill	750
White Hall, Owen, Ind	44
White Hall, Madison, Ky	$70
White Hall, Baltimore, Md	40
Whitehall, Muskegon, Mich	710
Whitehall, Jefferson, Mont	14
Whitehall,* Washington, N. Y	1, 900
White Hall, Bladen, N. C	12
White Hall, Montour, Pa	41
White Hall, Davis, Tex	12
White Hall, Frederick, Va	39
Whitehallville, Bucks, Pa	94
Whitehaven, Wicomico, Md	18
White Haven, Erie, N. Y	12
White Haven, Luzerne, Pa	1, 100
Whitehead's Store, Pittsylvania, Va	12
White Horn, Hawkins, Tenn	12
White Horse, Chester, Pa	12
White Horse, Greenville, S. C	12
White House, Hunterdon, N. J	100
White House, Randolph, N. C	10
White House, Lucas, Ohio	190
White House, Cumberland, Pa	53
White House, Mecklenburgh, Va	12
White House Station, Hunterdon, N. J	75
White Lake, Oakland, Mich	67
White Lake, Sullivan, N. Y	160
Whiteland, Johnson, Ind	40
Whiteley, Greene, Pa	20
Whiteleysburgh, Caroline, Md	8
White Lick, Boone, Ind	24
White Lily, Laurel, Ky	7
White Marsh, Montgomery, Pa	190
White Mills, Hardin, Ky	35
White Mills, Wayne, Pa	91
White Mound, Sauk, Wis	31
White Mountain House, Coos, N. H	10
White Oak, Montgomery, Ill	10
White Oak, Mahaska, Iowa	38
White Oak, Ingham, Mich	20
White Oak, Lancaster, Pa	8
White Oak, Hopkins, Tex	12
White Oak, Ritchie, W. Va	22
White Oak Gap, Pulaski, Ky	9
White Oak Grove, Greene, Mo	6
White Oak Springs, Barbour, Ala	14
White Oak Springs, Brown, Ill	8
White Oak Springs, Lee, Va	12
White Oak Springs, La Fayette, Wis	47
White Pigeon, Keokuk, Iowa	7
White Pigeon, St. Joseph, Mich	940
White Pine, Lycoming, Pa	45
White Plains, Calhoun, Ala	26
White Plains, Greene, Ga	16
White Plains,* (*c. h.*,) Westchester, N. Y	1, 500
White Plains, Cleveland, N. C	5
White Plains, Chesterfield, S. C	12
White Plains, Putnam, Tenn	12
White Plains, Brunswick, Va	12
White Pond, Barbour, Ala	12
White Post, Clarke, Va	57
White River, Desha, Ark	30
White River, Muskegon, Mich	61
White River, King, Wash	12
White River Junction,* Windsor, Vt	720
White Road, Forsyth, N. C	6

* Money-order office.

White Rock, Ogle, Ill	$69
White Rock, Republic, Kans	12
White Rock, Cumberland, Me	100
White Rock, Huron, Mich	92
White Rock, Hunt, Tex	48
White Rock Prairie, McDonald, Mo	12
White Sand, Lawrence, Miss	9
Whitesborough, Harrison, Iowa	19
Whitesborough, Grayson, Tex	12
Whitesburgh, Madison, Ala	12
Whitesburgh, (*c. h.*,) Letcher, Ky	12
Whitesburgh, Genesee, Mich	27
Whitesburgh, Armstrong, Pa	32
Whitesburgh, Jefferson, Tenn	110
White's Corner, Waldo, Me	20
White's Corners, Erie, N. Y	310
White's Corners, Potter, Pa	20
White's Creek, Wayne, W. Va	14
Whiteside, Marion, Tenn	190
White Shoals, Lee, Va	12
White's Mills, Logan, W. Va	12
White Springs, Hamilton, Fla	64
White's Station, Shelby, Tenn	48
White's Store, Chenango, N. Y	25
White's Store, Anson, N. C	12
White's Tannery, Monroe, Pa	78
Whitestone, Queens, N. Y	410
Whitestown, Boone, Ind	220
Whitestown, Oneida, N. Y	670
Whitestown, Butler, Pa	45
White Sulphur, Scott, Ky	6
White Sulphur, Delaware, Ohio	39
White Sulphur Springs, Jefferson, Ark	12
White Sulphur Springs, Meriwether, Ga	20
White Sulphur Springs, Catahoula, La	25
White Sulphur Springs,* Greenbrier, W. Va	170
Whitesville, Harris, Ga	43
Whitesville, Montgomery, Ind	58
Whitesville, Daviess, Ky	53
Whitesville, Andrew, Mo	100
Whitesville, Allegany, N. Y	95
Whitesville, (*c. h.*,) Columbus, N. C	180
Whitesville, Halifax, Va	8
White Swan, Charles Mix, Dak	12
Whiteville, Marion, Ark	92
Whiteville, Hardeman, Tenn	23
White Water, Pike, Ala	12
White Water, Fayette, Ga	5
White Water, Wayne, Ind	62
Whitewater,* Walworth, Wis	2,000
White Water Falls, Winona, Minn	16
White Willow, Kendall, Ill	17
Whiting, Jackson, Kans	12
Whiting, Washington, Me	46
Whiting, Ocean, N. J	25
Whiting, Addison, Vt	100
Whitingham, Windham, Vt	39
Whiting Station, Addison, Vt	110
Whitinsville, Worcester, Mass	840
Whitley C. H., Whitley, Ky	49
Whitley's Point, Moultrie, Ill	76
Whitleyville, Jackson, Tenn	8

Whitlock, Halifax, Va	$120
Whitman, Lowndes, Ala	12
Whitman, Walla Walla, Wash	12
Whitmell, Pittsylvania, Va	28
Whitmire's, Newberry, S. C	19
Whitmore Lake, Washtenaw, Mich	69
Whitney, Boulder, Colo	35
Whitney's Crossings, Allegany, N. Y	7
Whitney's Point,* Broome, N. Y	420
Whitneyville, Cass, Iowa	10
Whitneyville, Washington, Me	86
Whittington, Hot Spring, Ark	15
Whittle, Washington, Ga	12
Whittlesey, Medina, Ohio	68
Whittle's Mills, Mecklenburgh, Va	12
Wichita, (*c. h.*,) Sedgwick, Kans	12
Wick, Tyler, W. Va	10
Wickenburgh, Yavapai, Ariz	100
Wickford,* Washington, R. I	490
Wickle's Store, Macon, N. C	12
Wickliffe, Crawford, Ind	6
Wickliffe, Jackson, Iowa	27
Wickliffe, Lake, Ohio	39
Wicomico Church, Northumberland, Va	17
Wiconisco. Dauphin, Pa	160
Wiess Bluff, Jasper, Tex	54
Wilbar, Wilkes, N. C	7
Wilborn, Madison, Ill	16
Wilbraham, Hampden, Mass	660
Wilbur, Ulster, N. Y	160
Wilbur, Douglas, Oreg	12
Wilcox, Elk, Pa	490
Wilcox Wharf, Charles City, Va	74
Wildbrier, Chester, Pa	56
Wild Cat, Carroll, Ind	40
Wild Cat, Riley, Kans	12
Wild Cat, Lancaster, S. C	5
Wilderness, Spottsylvania, Va	45
Wiley, Greene, Pa	18
Wiley's Cove, Searcy, Ark	6
Wiley Station, Darke, Ohio	20
Wileysville, Steuben, N. Y	3
Wilkesbarre,* (*c. h.*,) Luzerne, Pa	2,900
Wilkesborough, (*c. h.*,) Wilkes, N. C	120
Wilkesville, Vinton, Ohio	100
Wilkins, Allegheny, Pa	560
Wilkinsburgh, Allegheny, Pa	260
Wilkinson's Shop, Amelia, Va	12
Wilkinsonville, Worcester, Mass	220
Wilkins' Run, Licking, Ohio	8
Willamette Forks, Lane, Oreg	7
Willard, Greene, Mo	38
Willard, Box Elder, Utah	70
Willard's Landing, Union, Ill	12
Willet, Cortland, N. Y	81
Willet, Indiana, Pa	30
Willet, Green, Wis	21
Willey, Preston, W. Va	20
William Penn, Montgomery, Pa	12
Williams, Hamilton, Iowa	12
Williams, Christian, Ky	25
Williams, Bay, Mich	12
Williamsburgh, Jefferson, Fla	12
Williamsburgh, Wayne, Ind	240
Williamsburgh, Wapello, Iowa	12

* Money-order office.

Williamsburgh, Franklin, Kans	$68
Williamsburgh, Piscataquis, Me	20
Williamsburgh, Dorchester, Md	36
Williamsburgh,* Hampshire, Mass	480
Williamsburgh, Grand Traverse, Mich	12
Williamsburgh, (c. h.,) Covington, Miss	24
Williamsburgh, Callaway, Mo	97
Williamsburgh,* Kings, N. Y	2,600
Williamsburgh, Iredell, N. C	11
Williamsburgh, Clermont, Ohio	200
Williamsburgh, Blair, Pa	380
Williamsburgh,* (c. h.,) James City, Va	400
Williamsburgh, Trempealeau, Wis	12
Williams Centre, Williams, Ohio	91
Williamsfield, Ashtabula, Ohio	97
Williams' Grove, Clearfield, Pa	12
Williams' Mill, Roane, Tenn	3
Williamson, Wayne, N. Y	370
Williamsport,* (c. h.,) Warren, Ind	380
Williamsport,* Washington, Md	330
Williamsport, Pickaway, Ohio	100
Williamsport,* (c. h.,) Lycoming, Pa	3,800
Williamsport, Maury, Tenn	15
Williamsport, Grant, W. Va	24
Williams' Store, Casey, Ky	32
Williamston, (c. h.,) Martin, N. C	380
Williamston, Anderson, S. C	110
Williamstown, Chickasaw, Iowa	26
Williamstown, Jefferson, Kans	43
Williamstown, (c. h.,) Grant, Ky	250
Williamstown,* Berkshire, Mass	1,000
Williamstown, Ingham, Mich	270
Williamstown, Lewis, Mo	100
Williamstown, Camden N. J	130
Williamstown, Oswego, N. Y	420
Williamstown, Hancock, Ohio	52
Williamstown, Dauphin, Pa	110
Williamstown, Orange, Vt	290
Williamstown, Wood, W. Va	50
Williamsville, Sangamon, Ill	250
Williamsville, Cass, Mich	54
Williamsville, Richardson, Nebr	12
Williamsville, Erie, N. Y	320
Williamsville, Elk, Pa	5
Williamsville, Windham, Vt	190
Williamsville, Bath, Va	6
Willimansett, Hampden, Mass	200
Willimantic,* Windham, Conn	1,800
Willington, Tolland, Conn	80
Willington, Abbeville, S. C	14
Willink, Erie, N. Y	180
Willisburgh, Washington, Ky	24
Willis Station, Fayette, Tenn	12
Williston, Erie, N. Y	25
Williston, Potter, Pa	12
Williston, Barnwell, S. C	130
Williston, Chittenden, Vt	340
Willistown Inn, Chester, Pa	22
Willmar, Kandiyohi, Minn	12
Willmathsville, Adair, Mo	30
Willoughby, Butler, Iowa	21
Willoughby, Lake, Ohio	780
Willoughby Lake, Orleans, Vt	36
Willow, Jo Daviess, Ill	$12
Willow Branch, Hancock, Ind	20
Willow Creek, Lee, Ill	55
Willow Creek, Blue Earth, Minn	8
Willow Creek, Gallatin, Mont	12
Willow Dale, Ida, Iowa	12
Willowdale, Chester, Pa	38
Willow Grove, Kent, Del	65
Willow Grove, Cumberland, N. J	12
Willow Grove, Montgomery, Pa	95
Willow Hill, Jasper, Ill	66
Willow Hole, Madison, Tex	12
Willow Island, Pleasants, W. Va	58
Willow Shade, Metcalfe, Ky	16
Willow Spring, Cook, Ill	58
Willow Spring, Russell, Va	4
Willow Springs, Douglas, Kans	12
Willow Springs, Howell, Mo	12
Willow Springs, Jackson, Oreg	24
Willow Springs, Columbia, Pa	26
Willow Street, Lancaster, Pa	68
Willow Tree, Greene, Pa	10
Willow Tree, Mason, W. Va	12
Willow Wood, Lawrence, Ohio	8
Willsborough, Essex, N. Y	230
Will's Creek, Coshocton, Ohio	10
Willseyville, Tioga, N. Y	97
Willshire, Van Wert, Ohio	110
Will's Ridge, Floyd, Va	12
Wilmarth, Elk, Pa	18
Wilmette, Cook, Ill	12
Wilmington, Walker, Ala	12
Wilmington, Union, Ark	12
Wilmington,* Los Angeles, Cal	830
Wilmington,* New Castle, Del	2,500
Wilmington,* Will, Ill	1,800
Wilmington, Dearborn, Ind	54
Wilmington, Osage, Kans	24
Wilmington, Middlesex, Mass	64
Wilmington, Houston, Minn	62
Wilmington, Essex, N. Y	46
Wilmington,* (c. h.,) New Hanover, N. C	3,200
Wilmington,* (c. h.,) Clinton, Ohio	1,200
Wilmington, Windham, Vt	420
Wilmington, Fluvanna, Va	25
Wilmore, Cambria, Pa	190
Wilmot, Noble, Ind	6
Wilmot, Merrimack, N. H	65
Wilmot, Stark, Ohio	170
Wilmot, Bradford, Pa	4
Wilmot, Kenosha, Wis	98
Wilmot Flat, Merrimack, N. H	110
Wilna, Harford, Md	21
Wilna, Jefferson, N. Y	12
Wilseyville, Defiance, Ohio	20
Wilson, Montgomery, Iowa	12
Wilson, Adair, Mo	24
Wilson, Otoe, Nebr	5
Wilson, Niagara, N. Y	190
Wilson, (c. h.,) Wilson, N. C	1,100
Wilson, Adams, Ohio	12
Wilsonburgh, Richland, Ill	14
Wilsonburgh, Harrison, W. Va	96
Wilson Creek, Tioga, N. Y	5
Wilson Grove, Fayette, Iowa	20

* Money-order office.

WIN		WIN	
Wilson's, Anderson, Tenn	$12	Windsor, Kennebec, Me	$61
Wilson's Crossing, Rockingham, N. H	54	Windsor, Berkshire, Mass	50
Wilson's Cross Roads, Hempstead, Ark	12	Windsor, Eaton, Mich	36
Wilson's Depot, Dinwiddie, Va	62	Windsor, Henry, Mo	260
Wilson's Landing, Charles City, Va	92	Windsor, Mercer, N. J	64
Wilson's Mills, Oxford, Me	7	Windsor, Broome, N. Y	230
Wilson's Mills, Johnston, N. C	12	*Windsor*, (*c. h.*,) Bertie, N. C	270
Wilson's Mills, Cuyahoga, Ohio	22	Windsor, Ashtabula, Ohio	120
Wilson's Mills, Venango, Pa	6	Windsor, York, Pa	18
Wilson's Store, Stokes, N. C	9	Windsor, Barnwell, S. C	47
Wilsonville, Shelby, Ala	120	Windsor,* Windsor, Vt	1,400
Wilsonville, Windham, Conn	65	Windsor, Dane, Wis	35
Wilsonville, Spencer, Ky	34	Windsor Castle, Berks, Pa	13
Wilsonville, Highland, Va	5	Windsor Locks,* Hartford, Conn	900
Wilton, Pike, Ark	23	Windsor Station, Isle of Wight, Va	67
Wilton, Fairfield, Conn	250	Windsorville, Hartford, Conn	74
Wilton, Franklin, Me	430	Winesburgh, Holmes, Ohio	100
Wilton,* (*c. h.*,) Waseca, Minn	220	Winfield, Columbia, Ga	6
Wilton,* Hillsborough, N. H	670	Winfield, Du Page, Ill	32
Wilton, Saratoga, N. Y	62	Winfield, Lake, Ind	26
Wilton, Granville, N. C	6	Winfield, Henry, Iowa	92
Wilton, Ellis, Tex	24	*Winfield*, (*c. h.*,) Cowley, Kans	12
Wilton, Monroe, Wis	54	*Winfield*, (*c. h.*,) Winn, La	21
Wilton Junction,* Muscatine, Iowa	910	Winfield, Carroll, Md	28
Winamac,* (*c. h.*,) Pulaski, Ind	460	Winfield, Ingham, Mich	27
Winameg, Fulton, Ohio	25	Winfield, Herkimer, N. Y	65
Winchendon,* Worcester, Mass	2,000	Winfield, Tuscarawas, Ohio	45
Winchester,* (*c. h.*,) Scott, Ill	770	Winfield, Union, Pa	98
Winchester,* (*c. h.*,) Randolph, Ind	710	Winfield, Scott, Tenn	3
Winchester, Van Buren, Iowa	96	*Winfield*, (*c. h.*,) Putnam, W. Va	98
Winchester,* (*c. h.*,) Clarke, Ky	840	Wingos Station, Graves, Ky	28
Winchester, Jefferson, Kans	40	Wing's Station, Dutchess, N. Y	180
Winchester, Middlesex, Mass	790	Winhall, Bennington, Vt	12
Winchester, Wayne, Miss	12	Winn, Penobscot, Me	160
Winchester, Clarke, Mo	100	Winn, Isabella, Mich	6
Winchester, Cheshire, N. H	610	Winnebago, Dakota, Nebr	12
Winchester, Union, N. C	6	Winnebago Agency, Blue Earth, Minn	55
Winchester, Guernsey, Ohio	72	Winnebago City,* Faribault, Minn	400
Winchester,* (*c. h.*,) Franklin, Tenn	630	Winnebago Depot, Winnebago, Ill	370
Winchester, Fayette, Tex	130	Winnebago Valley, Houston, Minn	28
Winchester,* (*c. h.*,) Frederick, Va	2,600	Winneconne, Winnebago, Wis	370
Winchester, Winnebago, Wis	110	Winnegance, Sagadahoc, Me	62
Winchester Centre, Litchfield, Conn	110	Winnemucca, Humboldt, Nev	300
Windermere, Tolland, Conn	170	Winnetka, Cook, Ill	60
Windfall, Tipton, Ind	190	Winnipauk, Fairfield, Conn	250
Wind Gap, Northampton, Pa	75	*Winnsborough*, (*c. h.*,) Franklin, La	25
Windham, Windham, Conn	230	*Winnsborough*, (*c. h.*,) Fairfield, S. C	850
Windham, Johnson, Iowa	49	Winnton, Gonzales, Tex	12
Windham, Cumberland, Me	120	Winona, Henry, Iowa	12
Windham, Rockingham, N. H	68	Winona, Trimble, Ky	16
Windham, Portage, Ohio	280	*Winona*,* (*c. h.*,) Winona, Minn	2,800
Windham, Bradford, Pa	57	Winona, Carroll, Miss	580
Windham, Windham, Vt	82	Winona, Pitt, N. C	26
Windham Centre, Greene, N. Y	330	Winona, Columbiana, Ohio	120
Windham Centre, Bradford, Pa	28	Winooski, Sheboygan, Wis	180
Windham Depot, Rockingham, N. H	100	Winooski Falls, Chittenden, Vt	850
Windham Station, Portage, Ohio	81	Winslow, Stephenson, Ill	130
Windham Summit, Bradford, Pa	4	Winslow, Pike, Ind	56
Wind Ridge, Greene, Pa	80	Winslow, Kennebec, Me	97
Windsor, Sonoma, Cal	140	Winslow, De Kalb, Mo	12
Windsor, Hartford, Conn	380	Winslow, Camden, N. J	170
Windsor, Shelby, Ill	410	Winspear, Erie, N. Y	17
Windsor, Randolph, Ind	6	Winsted,* Litchfield, Conn	970
Windsor, Ottawa, Kans	12	Winsted Lake, McLeod, Minn	10
		Winter Harbor, Hancock, Me	41

* **Money-order office.**

Winterpock, Chesterfield, Va	$56
Winterport,* Waldo, Me	800
Winterroud, Shelby, Ind	31
Winterrowd, Effingham, Ill	12
Winterset,* (*c. h.*,) Madison, Iowa	1,300
Winter's Station, Sandusky, Ohio	52
Wintersville, Decatur, Ind	27
Wintersville, Sullivan, Mo	59
Wintersville, Jefferson, Ohio	63
Wintersville, Berks, Pa	18
Winterville, Oglethorpe, Ga	32
Winthrop, Middlesex, Conn	12
Winthrop, Buchanan, Iowa	420
Winthrop, Kennebec, Me	800
Winthrop, Suffolk, Mass	49
Winthrop, Buchanan, Mo	62
Winton, (*c. h.*,) Hertford, N. C	320
Winton Place, Hamilton, Ohio	12
Wiota, Isabella, Mich	18
Wiota, La Fayette, Wis	78
Wiretown, Ocean, N. J	59
Wirt, Jefferson, Ind	42
Wirt C. H., Wirt, W. Va	150
Wirt Centre, Allegany, N. Y	31
Wirtonia, Cherokee, Kans	100
Wiscasset,* (*c. h.*,) Lincoln, Me	840
Wiscoy, Winona, Minn	11
Wiscoy, Allegany, N. Y	110
Wisdom's Store, Harris, Ga	8
Wise C. H., Wise, Va	12
Wiseville, Accomack, Va	25
Wistar, Clinton, Pa	43
Withamsville, Clermont, Ohio	65
Witherup's, Venango, Pa	180
Witoka, Winona, Minn	40
Witt, Montgomery, Ill	12
Wittenberg, Alexander, N. C	1
Wittenberg, Somerset, Pa	28
Wittenburgh, Perry, Mo	99
Witten's, Monroe, Ohio	12
Wittman, Talbot, Md	12
Wittsburgh, (*c. h.*,) Cross, Ark	83
Witt's Foundry, Jefferson, Tenn	12
Woburn, Bond, Ill	20
Woburn,* Middlesex, Mass	1,600
Wolcott, New Haven, Conn	13
Wolcott, White, Ind	85
Wolcott, Scott, Iowa	250
Wolcott,* Wayne, N. Y	580
Wolcott, Lamoille, Vt	170
Wolcottsville, Niagara, N. Y	60
Wolcottville,* Litchfield, Conn	920
Wolcottville, La Grange, Ind	150
Wolfborough, Carroll, N. H	700
Wolfborough Centre, Carroll, N. H.	12
Wolf Branch, Coffee, Ala	12
Wolf Creek, Pike, Ark	12
Wolf Creek, Tama, Iowa	25
Wolf Creek, Meade, Ky	56
Wolf Creek, Wright, Mo	4
Wolf Creek, Cherokee, N. C	11
Wolf Creek, Mercer, Pa	62
Wolf Creek, Scott, Tenn	12
Wolf Creek, Monroe, W. Va	5
Wolfdale, Woodbury, Iowa	45
Wolf Glade, Carroll, Va	20
Wolf Hill, Albany, N. Y	$12
Wolf Island, Mississippi, Mo	16
Wolf Lake, Noble, Ind	60
Wolf Run, Lycoming, Pa	19
Wolf's Store, Centre, Pa	28
Wolf Summit, Harrison, W. Va	20
Wolfsville, Frederick, Md	34
Wolfsville, Union, N. C	5
Wolf Trap, Halifax, Va	17
Womelsdorf,* Berks, Pa	390
Wonewoc, Juneau, Wis	110
Wood, Orange, N. Y	12
Wood, Wood, Wis	14
Woodbank, Marion, Ind	12
Woodberry, Baltimore, Md	210
Woodbine, Harrison, Iowa	200
Woodbine, Carroll, Md	51
Woodbourne, Sullivan, N. Y	83
Woodbridge, San Joaquin, Cal	120
Woodbridge, Middlesex, N. J	440
Woodburn, Macoupin, Ill	120
Woodburn, Allen, Ind	31
Woodburn, Warren, Ky	130
Woodbury, Litchfield, Conn	490
Woodbury, Meriwether, Ga	25
Woodbury, Cumberland, Ill	86
Woodbury, Hancock, Ind	16
Woodbury, Butler, Ky	46
Woodbury, Washington, Minn	12
Woodbury, (*c. h.*,) Gloucester, N. J	640
Woodbury, Queens, N. Y	15
Woodbury, Wood, Ohio	51
Woodbury, Bedford, Pa	150
Woodbury, (*c. h.*,) Cannon, Tenn	140
Woodbury, Washington, Vt	28
Woodcock, Crawford, Pa	170
Woodensburgh, Baltimore, Md	49
Woodford, Bennington, Vt	28
Woodford, Barbour, W. Va	12
Woodford's, Alpine, Cal	35
Woodford's, Cumberland, Me	12
Wood Grove, Morgan, Ohio	19
Woodhaven, Queens, N. Y	120
Woodhull, Henry, Ill	620
Woodhull, Steuben, N. Y	280
Woodhull, Fond du Lac, Wis	14
Woodington, Darke, Ohio	57
Wood Lake, Montcalm, Mich	31
Woodland,* Yolo, Cal	630
Woodland, St. Joseph, Ind	6
Woodland, East Feliciana, La	12
Woodland, Barry, Mich	31
Woodland, Wabashaw, Minn	15
Woodland, Ulster, N. Y	54
Woodland, Northampton, N. C	12
Woodland, Union, Ohio	21
Woodland, Clearfield, Pa	46
Woodland, Robertson, Tex	6
Woodland, Dodge, Wis	84
Woodland Mills, Obion, Tenn	12
Woodlands, Marshall, W. Va	44
Woodlawn, Ouachita, Ark	12
Woodlawn, Cecil, Md	50
Woodlawn, Monroe, Mo	52
Wood Lawn, Westchester, N. Y	62
Woodlawn, Gaston, N. C	10

* Money-order office.

Post office	Compensation
Woodlawn, Montgomery, Tenn	$15
Wood Lawn, Carroll, Va	12
Woodman, Grant, Wis	210
Woodmansie, Burlington, N. J	8
Wood River, Hall, Nebr	22
Wood River, Burnett, Wis	19
Woodrow, Washington, Pa	4
Woodruff's, Spartanburgh, S. C	22
Woods, Panola, Tex	27
Woodsborough, Frederick, Md	110
Wood's Corners, Ionia, Mich	57
Wood's Cross Roads, Gloucester, Va	12
Woodsdale, Person, N. C	23
Wood's Falls, Clinton, N. Y	56
Woodsfield,* (*c. h.*,) Monroe, Ohio	360
Wood's Hill, Roane, Tenn	12
Wood's Hole, Barnstable, Mass	250
Woodside, San Mateo, Cal	67
Woodside, Kent, Del	12
Woodside, Sangamon, Ill	25
Woodside, Queens, N. Y	43
Woodside, St. Croix, Wis	84
Wood's Mills, St. Francois, Mo	12
Woodson, Morgan, Ill	57
Woodsonville, Hart, Ky	240
Wood's Run, Allegheny, Pa	320
Wood's Station, Butler, Ohio	35
Woodstock, Tuscaloosa, Ala	6
Woodstock, Windham, Conn	150
Woodstock, Cherokee, Ga	55
Woodstock,* (*c. h.*,) McHenry, Ill	1,300
Woodstock, Oxford, Me	16
Woodstock, Howard, Md	120
Woodstock, Lenawee, Mich	10
Woodstock, Grafton, N. H	57
Woodstock, Ulster, N. Y	79
Woodstock, Champaign, Ohio	160
Woodstock,* (*c. h.*,) Windsor, Vt	1,300
Woodstock,* (*c. h.*,) Shenandoah, Va	430
Woodstock, Richland, Wis	26
Woodstock Valley, Windham, Conn	59
Woodstown, Salem, N. J	520
Woodsville, Grafton, N. H	190
Woodsville, Mercer, N. J	16
Woodview, Morrow, Ohio	34
Woodville, Jackson, Ala	12
Woodville, Litchfield, Conn	33
Woodville, Greene, Ga	15
Woodville, Adams, Ill	36
Woodville, Winneshiek, Iowa	79
Woodville, McCracken, Ky	94
Woodville, Jackson, La	24
Woodville, Frederick, Md	24
Woodville, Penobscot, Me	10
Woodville, Middlesex, Mass	77
Woodville,* (*c. h.*,) Wilkinson, Miss	600
Woodville, Macon, Mo	23
Woodville, Jefferson, N. Y	180
Woodville, Perquimons, N. C	30
Woodville, Sandusky, Ohio	140
Woodville, Allegheny, Pa	40
Woodville, Washington, R. I	120
Woodville, Haywood, Tenn	37
Woodville, (*c. h.*,) Tyler, Tex	38
Woodville, Rappahanock, Va	83
Woodward, Centre, Pa	64

Post office	Compensation
Woodward's Hollow, Erie, N. Y	$17
Woodworth, Kenosha, Wis	69
Woodyards, Athens, Ohio	* 27
Wool, Pope, Ill	24
Wooldridge's Store, Christian, Ky	8
Woolfolk, Orange, Va	21
Woollam, Gasconade, Mo	22
Woolstock, Wright, Iowa	9
Woolwich, Sagadahoc, Me	160
Woonsocket Falls,* Providence, R. I	2,800
Wooster, Kosciusko, Ind	42
Wooster, Jefferson, Iowa	47
Wooster,* (*c. h.*,) Wayne, Ohio	2,400
Wooster Summit, Wayne, Ohio	38
Woostertown, Scott, Ind	54
Woosung, Ogle, Ill	99
Wootten, Lee, Ga	130
Worcester,* (*c. h.*,) Worcester, Mass	4,000
Worcester, Otsego, N. Y	260
Worcester, Montgomery, Pa	30
Worcester, Washington, Vt	110
Worley Furnace, Dickson, Tenn	12
Worth, Boone, Iowa	22
Worth, Tuscola, Mich	160
Worth, Winona, Minn	16
Worth, Mercer, Pa	150
Worth Centre, Jefferson, N. Y	12
Worthington, Greene, Ind	400
Worthington, Dubuque, Iowa	170
Worthington, Jefferson, Ky	12
Worthington, Hampshire, Mass	120
Worthington, Franklin, Ohio	230
Worthington, Armstrong, Pa	130
Worthington, Marion, W. Va	25
Worthville, Butts, Ga	10
Worthville, Carroll, Ky	16
Worthville, Jefferson, N. Y	44
Worthville, Jefferson, Pa	29
Wrentham, Norfolk, Mass	400
Wright, Greene, Ind	18
Wright City, Warren, Mo	200
Wright's Bluff, Clarendon, S. C	62
Wrightsborough, Gonzales, Tex	12
Wright's Corners, Dearborn, Ind	30
Wright's Corners, Niagara, N. Y	43
Wright's Dale, Lancaster, Pa	18
Wright's Ferry, Crawford, Wis	6
Wrightstown, Burlington, N. J	88
Wrightstown, Bucks, Pa	100
Wrightstown, Brown, Wis	210
Wrightsville, (*c. h.*,) Johnson, Ga	23
Wrightsville, York, Pa	370
Wrightsville, Jackson, Wis	12
Wurtemburgh, Lawrence, Pa	35
Wurtsborough, Sullivan, N. Y	190
Wyaconda, Scotland, Mo	14
Wyalusing, Bradford, Pa	150
Wyalusing, Grant, Wis	26
Wyandot, Wyandot, Ohio	36
Wyandotte, Tippecanoe, Ind	12
Wyandotte,* (*c. h.*,) Wyandotte, Kans	2,300
Wyandotte, Wayne, Mich	480
Wyanet, Bureau, Ill	560
Wyatt's Store, Mariposa, Cal	3

* Money-order office.

Post office	Amount
Wyattville, Winona, Minn	$7
Wyckoff, Bergen, N. J	12
Wye Mills, Talbot, Md	54
Wykertown, Sussex, N. J	3
Wylliesburgh, Charlotte, Va	47
Wynant, Shelby, Ohio	98
Wyantskill, Rensselaer, N. Y	46
Wynn, Franklin, Ind	19
Wyocena, Columbia, Wis	180
Wyoming, Kent, Del	230
Wyoming,* Stark, Ill	240
Wyoming,* Jones, Iowa	310
Wyoming, Marshall, Kans	10
Wyoming, Bath, Ky	20
Wyoming, Chisago, Minn	120
Wyoming, Otoe, Nebr	46
Wyoming, Wyoming, N. Y	300
Wyoming, Luzerne, Pa	350
Wyoming, Washington, R. I	200
Wyoming, Iowa, Wis	42
Wyoming, Albany, Wyo	12
Wysox, Bradford, Pa	68
Wythe Depot, Shelby, Tenn	12
Wytheville,* (*c. h.*,) Wythe, Va	1,000

X.

Post office	Amount
Xenia, Clay, Ill	500
Xenia, Miami, Ind	110
Xenia, Dallas, Iowa	50
Xenia, Bourbon, Kans	120
Xenia, Nodaway, Mo	23
Xenia, Sarpy, Nebr	12
Xenia,* (*c. h.*,) Greene, Ohio	2,800
Xenia, York, Pa	12

Y.

Post office	Amount
Yadkin College, Davidson, N. C	25
Yadkinville, (*c. h.*,) Yadkin, N. C	38
Yakima, Yakima, Wash	120
Yale, Jasper, Ill	27
Yalesville, New Haven, Conn	160
Yancy, Phelps, Mo	12
Yanceyville, (*c. h.*,) Caswell, N. C	100
Yankee Hill, Butte, Cal	20
Yankee Hollow, Jo Daviess, Ill	14
Yankee Jim's, Placer, Cal	38
Yankee Ridge, Coshocton, Ohio	1,600
Yankee Settlement, Clayton, Iowa	60
Yankee Spring, Barry, Mich	21
Yankeetown, Warrick, Ind	12
Yankeetown, Crawford, Wis	17
YANKTON,* (*c. h.*,) Yankton, Dak	1,200
Yantic, New London, Conn	180
Yaphank, Suffolk, N. Y	170
Yarborough, Floyd, Ga	14
Yardleyville, Bucks, Pa	240
Yardville, Mercer, N. J	88
Yarmouth,* Cumberland, Me	620
Yarmouth, Barnstable, Mass	120
Yarmouth Port,* Barnstable, Mass	560
Yates, Orleans, N. Y	120
Yates City, Knox, Ill	400
Yatesville, Morgan, Ill	12
Yatesville, Calhoun, Iowa	20
Yatesville, Schuylkill, Pa	$82
Yatesville, Lunenburgh, Va	15
Yatton, Washington, Iowa	36
Yazoo, Harrison, Iowa	16
Yazoo City,* (*c. h.*,) Yazoo, Miss	1,000
Yeater's Mills, Doddridge, W. Va	7
Yellow Bluff, Duval, Fla	3
Yellow Branch, Campbell, Va	14
Yellow Bud, Ross, Ohio	27
Yellow Creek, Stephenson, Ill	22
Yellow Creek, Josh Bell, Ky	12
Yellow Creek, Bedford, Pa	32
Yellow Creek, Dickson, Tenn	12
Yellow House, Berks, Pa	21
Yellow Medicine, Redwood, Minn	24
Yellow River, Gwinnett, Ga	36
Yellow Spring, Blair, Pa	100
Yellow Spring, Hampshire, W.Va	6
Yellow Springs,* Greene, Ohio	1,000
Yellow Stone, La Fayette, Wis	9
Yellow Store, Hawkins, Tenn	12
Yellville, (*c. h.*,) Marion, Ark	110
Yelm, Thurston, Wash	7
Yelverton, Hardin, Ohio	47
Yelvington, Daviess, Ky	12
Yemassee, Beaufort, S. C	12
Yew, Wayne, Mich	23
Yocony, Itawamba, Miss	6
Yocumtown, York, Pa	41
Yocumville, Klamath, Cal	12
Yohoghany, Westmoreland, Pa	180
Yokum Station, Lee, Va	4
Yolo, (*c. h.*,) Yolo, Cal	130
Yoncalla, Douglas, Oreg	16
Yongesborough, Lee, Ala	12
Yonguesville, Fairfield, S. C	78
Yonkers,* Westchester, N. Y	2,800
York, Walker, Ala	6
York, Clark, Ill	64
York, Delaware, Iowa	63
York, York, Me	270
York, Washtenaw, Mich	89
York, (*c. h.*,) York, Nebr	12
York, Livingston, N. Y	200
York, Union, Ohio	24
York,* (*c. h.*,) York, Pa	2,600
York, Dane, Wis	18
York Centre, Iowa, Iowa	5
York Centre, Steuben, Ind	24
York Collegiate Institute, Alexander, N. C	7
York Furnace, York, Pa	33
York Neck, Adams, Ill	18
York Prairie, Cedar, Iowa	12
Yorkshire, Cattaraugus, N. Y	100
Yorkshire Centre, Cattaraugus, N. Y	110
York Station, Sumter, Ala	12
York Sulphur Springs, Adams, Pa	360
Yorktown, Bureau, Ill	77
Yorktown, Delaware, Ind	110
Yorktown, Salem, N. J	57
Yorktown, Westchester, N. Y	46
Yorktown, De Witt, Tex	140
Yorktown, (*c. h.*,) York, Va	220
Yorkville, Mendocino, Cal	12
Yorkville, (*c. h.*,) Kendall, Ill	400

* Money-order office.

Yorkville, Dearborn, Ind	$32
Yorkville, Kalamazoo, Mich	22
Yorkville, Bladen, N. C	2
Yorkville, Jefferson, Ohio	68
Yorkville, (*c. h.*,) York, S. C	800
Yorkville, Gibson, Tenn	66
Yorkville, Racine, Wis	43
Yortysville, Washington, Pa	10
Yosemite, Mariposa, Cal	12
You Bet, Nevada, Cal	64
Yough, Boone, Iowa	11
Young America,* Warren, Ill	570
Young America, Carver, Minn	110
Young America, Washington, Wis	69
Young Hickory, Steuben, N. Y	8
Young Hickory, Muskingum, Ohio	21
Young Hickory, Washington, Wis	32
Young's Creek, Orange, Ind	8
Young's Creek, Whitley, Ky	12
Young's Creek, Audrian, Mo	29
Young's Cross Roads, Granville, N. C.	12
Young's Mills, Guilford, N. C	12
Young's Mills, Monroe, Ohio	12
Young's Settlement, Bastrop, Tex	16
Young's Store, Franklin, Va	2
Youngstown, Vigo, Ind	34
Youngstown, Niagara, N. Y	390
Youngstown,* Mahoning, Ohio	2,400
Youngstown, Westmoreland, Pa	130
Youngsville, Sullivan, N. Y	87
Youngsville, Adams, Ohio	34
Youngsville, Warren, Pa	290
Young Womanstown, Clinton, Pa	110
Yountville, Napa, Cal	37
Ypsilanti,* (*c. h.*,) Washtenaw, Mich.	2,700
Yreka,* (*c. h.*,) Siskiyou, Cal	820
Yuba, Grand Traverse, Mich	28
Yuba, Richland, Wis	16
Yuba City,* (*c. h.*,) Sutter, Cal	280
Yucatan, Houston, Minn	16

Z.

Zackville, Wirt, W. Va	$7
Zaleski, Vinton, Ohio	290
Zanesfield, Logan, Ohio	210
Zanesville, Montgomery, Ill	71
Zanesville, Wells, Ind	69
Zanesville,* (*c. h.*,) Muskingum, Ohio	3,200
Zanzenburgh, Kerr, Tex	12
Zebulon, (*c. h.*,) Pike, Ga	82
Zeeland, Ottawa, Mich	79
Zeiglersville, Montgomery, Pa	62
Zelienople, Butler, Pa	150
Zem Zem, Lake, Cal	12
Zena, Polk, Oreg	12
Zenas, Jennings, Ind	36
Zeno, Muskingum, Ohio	28
Zeno, York, S. C	7
Zif, Wayne, Ill	20
Zig, Adair, Mo	12
Zilwaukee, Saginaw, Mich	150
Zimmerman, Greene, Ohio	90
Zinsburgh, Madison, Ind	6
Zion, Henderson, Ky	4
Zion, Cecil, Md	98
Zion, Yadkin, N. C	6
Zion, Centre, Pa	61
Zion's, Stearns, Minn	9
Zion's Grove, Schuylkill, Pa	12
Zion's Mills, Lee, Va	6
Zionsville, Boone, Ind	370
Zoar, Cedar, Iowa	19
Zoar, Franklin, Mass	120
Zoar, Tuscarawas, Ohio	59
Zoar Station, Tuscarawas, Ohio	27
Zollarsville, Washington, Pa	63
Zumbro Falls, Wabashaw, Minn	12
Zumbrota, Goodhue, Minn	290
Zuni Station, Isle of Wight, Va	93
Zwingle, Dubuque, Iowa	28

* Money-order office.

POST OFFICES IN THE UNITED STATES.

SEPTEMBER 1, 1870.

ARRANGED BY STATES AND COUNTIES.

ALABAMA.

AUTAUGA COUNTY.

Autaugaville,
Independence,
Kingston,
Prattville, (*c. h.*)

BAKER COUNTY.

Chesnut Creek, (*c. h.*,)
Maplesville,
Mullins.

BALDWIN COUNTY.

Bay Minette,
Stockton,
Tensaw.

BARBOUR COUNTY.

Clayton, (*c. h.*,)
Clio,
Cowikee,
Eufaula,*
Fort Browder,
Glennville,
Kings,
Louisville,
Mount Andrew,
Newtopia,
White Oak Springs,
White Pond.

BIBB COUNTY.

Brierfield,
Centreville, (*c. h.*,)
Mars,
Randolph,
Scottsville.

BLOUNT COUNTY.

Balm,
Blount Springs,
Blountsville, (*c. h.*,)
Brooksville,
Chepultepec,
Little Warrior,
Mount Alvis,
Murphree's Valley,
Ogee,
Summit,
Thacker's Creek,
Village Springs,
Walnut Grove.

BULLOCK COUNTY.

Aberfoil,
Arbor Vitæ,
Bruceville,
Enon,
Fitzpatrick's,
Line Creek,
Midway,
Mount Hilliard,
Perote,
Suspension,
Thomas Station,
Union Springs, (*c. h.*)

BUTLER COUNTY.

Butler Springs,
Emma,
Garland,
Georgiana,
Greenville,* (*c. h.*,)
Manningham,
Oaky Streak,
Pigeon Creek,
South Butler.

CALHOUN COUNTY.

Blue Mountain,
Corn Grove,
Cross Plains,
Jacksonville, (*c. h.*,)
Ladiga,
Morrisville,
Mount Polk,
Oxford,
Peak's Hill,
Wehoga,
White Plains.

CHAMBERS COUNTY.

Chambers C. H.,*
Cusseta,
Fredonia,
Hickory Flat,
Milltown,
Osanippa.

CHEROKEE COUNTY.

Blue Pond,
Broomtown,
Cedar Bluff,
Cedar Springs,
Centre, (*c. h.*,)
Coloma,
Gaylesville,
Howel's × Roads,
Kirk's Grove,
Leesburgh,
Little River,
Mill Ford,
Pleasant Gap,
Ringgold,
Sand Rock,
Spring Garden.

CHOCTAW COUNTY.

Bladen Springs,
Butler, (*c. h.*,)
Desotoville,
Mount Sterling,
Pushmataha.

CLARKE COUNTY.

Choctaw Bluff,
Choctaw Corner,
Gainestown,
Gosport,
Grove Hill, (*c. h.*,)
Suggsville.

* Money-order office.

Clay County.

Ashland, (*c. h.*,)
Bluff Spring,
Coleta,
Copper Mines,
Hillabee,
Lineville,
Mellow Valley,
Pinckneyville.

Cleburne County.

Chulafinnee,
Edwardsville, (*c. h.*,)
Kemp's Creek,
Oakfuskee,
Oak Level,
Rosewood.

Coffee County.

Elba, (*c. h.*,)
Victoria,
Wolf Branch.

Colbert County.

Barton,
Cherokee,
Dickson,
Pride's Station,
Tuscumbia,* (*c. h.*)

Conecuh County.

Belleville,
Brooklyn,
Castleberry,
Evergreen, (*c. h.*,)
Gravella,
Jackson Store,
Jamestown,
Jayville,
Sparta.

Coosa County.

Central Institute,
Equality,
Fig Grove,
Hanover,
Marble Valley,
Mount Olive,
Rockford, (*c. h.*,)
Traveller's Rest,
Weogufka.

Covington County.

Cottle's Mills,
Reed Level,
Rose Hill,
Shirley.

Crenshaw County.

Argus,
Bullock,
Honorville,
Leon,
Little Oak,
New Providence,
Rutledge, (*c. h.*,)
Sal Soda.

Dale County.

Barnes' × Roads,
Beaver Creek,
Clopton,
Daleville,
Haw Ridge,
High Bluff,
Newton, (*c. h.*,)
Ozark,
Potter's Mills,
Rocky Head,
Skipperville,
Westville.

Dallas County.

Bellevue,
Burnsville,
Cahaba,
Cambridge,
Elm Bluff,
Forts,
Hardy,
Liberty Hill,

Dallas County—Continued.

Orange Grove,
Orrville,
Plantersville,
Pleasant Hill,
Portland,
Richmond,
Selma,* (*c. h.*,)
Summerfield,
White Bluff.

De Kalb County.

Brandon,
Camp Station,
Crossville,
Fort Payne,
Lebanon, (*c. h.*,)
Portersville,
Rawlingsville,
Valley Head.

Elmore County.

Channahatchie,
Hatchsophka,
Syke's Mills,
Wetumpka,* (*c. h.*)

Escambia County.

Brewton,
Canoe Station,
Lewis' Station,
Pollard, (*c. h.*)

Etowah County.

Atalla,*
Aurora,
Ball Play,
Bennettsville,
Collinsville,
Cove Creek,
Gadsden, (*c. h.*,)
Greenwood,
Rees Mill,
Thornton's Bluff.

Fayette County.

Dublin,
Eagle Mills,
Fayette C. H.,
Handy,
New River,
Newtonville,
Pilgrim's Rest,
Sheffield.

Franklin County.

Blue Lick,
Burleson,
Chickasaw,
Frankfort,
Leighton,
Nelsonville,
Newburgh,
Pleasant Site,
Russellville, (*c. h.*,)
South Florence,
Spruce Pine,
Waco.

Geneva County.

Big Creek,
Geneva, (*c. h.*,)
High Falls,

Greene County.

Clinton,
*Eutaw** (*c. h.*)
Knoxville,
Mount Hebron.
Pleasant Ridge,
Union.

Hale County.

Five Mile,
Greensborough,*(*c.h.*,)
Havanna,
Hollow Square,
Macon Station,
Newbern.

* Money-order office.

Henry County.

Abbeville, (*c. h.*,)
Columbia,
Franklin,
Gordon,
Lawrenceville,
Lynnville.

Jackson County.

Bass Station,
Bellefonte,
Big Coon,
Boyd's Switch,
Bridgeport,
Dodsonville,
Dry Cove,
Estill's Fork,
Fackler,
Gray's Chapel,
Larkin's Fork,
Larkinsville,
Long Island,
Paint Rock,
Park's Store,
Princeton,
Scottsborough, (*c. h.*,)
Stevenson,
Trenton,
Woodville.

Jefferson County.

Argo,
Cedar Grove,
Chester,
Elyton, (*c. h.*,)
Jonesborough,
Morrowville,
Mount Pinson,
Oak Ridge,
Oregon,
Rockville,
Waldrop's Mill.

Lauderdale County.

Centre Star,
Florence, (*c. h.*,)
Gravelly Spring,
Green Hill,
Rogersville,
Waterloo.

Lawrence County.

Avoca,
Concord,
Courtland,
Dry Creek,
Kinlock,
Landersville,
Moulton, (*c. h.*,)
Mountain Home,
Mount Hope,
Oakville,
Town Creek,
Wheeler Station.

Lee County.

Auburn,*
Loachapoka,
Mount Jefferson,
Opelika, (*c. h.*,)
Salem,
Smith's Station,
Yongesborough.

Limestone County.

Athens,* (*c. h.*,)
Fort Hampton,
Gilbertsborough,
Greenbrier,
Harris Station,
Mooresville,
Mount Roszell.

Lowndes County.

Benton,
Bragg's,
Calhoun,
Farmersville,
Fort Deposit,
Gilmer's,
Hayneville, (*c. h.*,)
Letohatchee,
Lowndesborough,
Manack,
Whitman.

Macon County.

Cowles' Station,
Notasulga,
Shorter's Depot,
Society Hill,
Tuskegee,* (*c. h.*,)

Madison County.

Bell Factory,
Berkley,
Brownsborough,
Flint Factory,
Green Grove,
Gurleysville,
Haden's,
Hayes' Store,
Huntsville,* (*c. h.*,)
Madison Station,
Meridianville,
New Hope,
New Market,
Owen's × Roads,
Triana,
Whitesburgh.

Marengo County.

Clay Hill,
Dayton,
Demopolis, (*c. h.*,)
Faunsdale,
Linden,
McKinley,
Shiloh.

Marion County.

Allen's Factory,
Chalk Bluff,
Gold Mine,
Haley's,
Ireland Hill,
Johnson's Mills,
Palo,
Pikeville, (*c. h.*,)
Thorn Hill.

Marshall County.

Claysville,
Cottonville,
Guntersville, (*c. h.*,)
Henrysville,
Hillian's Store,
Kennamer Cove,
Meltonsville,
Red Apple,
Red Hill,
Short Creek,
Southern,
Warrenton.

Mobile County.

Chickasabogue,
Citronelle,
Manville,
Mobile,* (*c. h.*,)
Mount Vernon,
Whistler.

Monroe County.

Bell's Landing,
Burnt Corn,
Claiborne,
Dennard's Bluff,
Monroeville, (*c. h.*,)
Mount Pleasant,
Newton Academy.

Montgomery County.

Dreyspring,
Hailsville,
Mathews,
MONTGOMERY,*(*c.h.*,)
Mount Meigs,
Pine Level,
Ponder's Mill,
Raif Branch,
Ramer,
Snowdoun,
Strata.

Morgan County.

Apple Grove,
Basham's Gap,
Cedar Plains,
Danville,

* Money-order office.

MORGAN COUNTY—Continued.

Decatur,*
Flint River,
Folkville,
Lacey's Spring,
*Somerville,** (*c. h.,*)
Trinity Station,
Valhermoso Springs.

PERRY COUNTY.

Brush Creek,
Grove Cottage,
Hamburgh,
Ironville,
Jericho,
Marion, (*c. h.,*)
Morgan Spring,
Perryville,
Pine Tucky,
Radfordsville,
Uniontown.

PICKENS COUNTY.

Andersonville,
Antioch,
Bridgeville,
Carrollton, (*c. h.,*)
Memphis,
Palmetto,
Pickensville,
Pleasant Grove,
Providence,
Reform,
Sipsy Mills.

PIKE COUNTY.

China Grove,
Hallsville,
Henderson,
Linwood,
Milo,
New Providence,
Olustee Creek,
Orion,
*Troy,** (*c. h.,*)
White Water.

RANDOLPH COUNTY.

Almond,
Blake's Ferry,
Carter's Store,
Delta,
Fair Play,
Lamar,
Louina,
Milner,
Roanoke,
Rock Mills,
Wedowee, (*c. h.*)

RUSSELL COUNTY.

Crawford,
Fort Mitchell,
Hatchechubbee,
Hurtville,
Seale's Station, (*c. h.,*)
Uchee,
Villula.

SAINT CLAIR COUNTY.

Ashville, (*c. h.,*)
Beaver Valley,
Branchville,
Broken Arrow,
Cropwell,
Ferryville,
Greensport,
Kelly's Creek,
Mount Niles,
Springville.

SANFORD COUNTY.

Andalusia,
Beaverton,
Big Pond,
Detroit,
Millport,
Moscow,
Vernon.

SHELBY COUNTY.

Calera,
Columbiana, (*c. h.,*)

SHELBY COUNTY—Continued.

Hillsborough,
Montevallo,
Shelby Iron Works,
Shelby Springs,
Wilsonville.

SUMTER COUNTY.

Bennett's Station,
Coatopa,
Cuba Station,
Fulton,
Gainesville,
Gaston,
Intercourse,
Jones' Bluff,
Livingston, (*c. h.,*)
Sumterville,
York Station.

TALLADEGA COUNTY.

Alpine,
Childersburgh,
Easta Boga,
Flat Rock,
Irona,
Kimulga,
Lincoln,
Mardisville,
Munford,
Silver Run,
Sylacauga,
*Talladega,** (*c. h.,*)
Wewokaville.

TALLAPOOSA COUNTY.

Dadeville, (*c. h.,*)
Emuckfaw,
Fish Pond,
Goldville,
Jones' × Roads,
Melton's Mill,
New Site,
Walnut Hill

TUSCALOOSA COUNTY.

Carthage,
Cushing,
Fosters',
Hickman's,
Jena,
Kennedale,
McMath,
New Lexington,
North Port,
North River,
Oregonia,
Romulus,
Sipsey Turnpike,
Trion,
Tuscaloosa, (*c. h.,*)
Woodstock.

WALKER COUNTY.

Arkadelphia,
Democrat,
Eldridge,
Fairview,
Garrison Point,
Hanby's Mills,
Holly Grove,
Jasper, (*c. h.,*)
Kansas,
Wilmington,
York.

WASHINGTON COUNTY.

Deer Park,
Escatawpa,
Millry.

WILCOX COUNTY.

Allenton,
Burford's Landing,
Camden, (*c. h.,*)
Clifton,
Fatama,
Lower Peach Tree,
Pine Hill,
Prairie Bluff,
Rehoboth.

* Money-order office.

WINSTON COUNTY.

Clear Creek Falls,
Houston, (*c. h.*,)
Jones' Chapel,

WINSTON COUNTY—Continued.

Larissa,
Littlesville,
Ryan Creek.

ALASKA TERRITORY.

Fort Tongass,
Fort Wrangel,
Kodiak,
Sitka, (*c. h.*,)

ARIZONA TERRITORY.

MOHAVE COUNTY.

Hardyville,
Mohave City, (*c. h.*)

PAH UTE COUNTY.

Overton,
Saint Joseph,
Saint Thomas, (*c. h.*)

PIMA COUNTY.

Apache Pass,
Florence,
Grant,
Maricopa Wells,

PIMA COUNTY—Continued.

Sasabi Flat,
Tubac,
TUCSON, (*c. h.*)

YAVAPAI COUNTY.

McDowell,
Phœnix,
Pima Village,
Prescott,* (*c. h.*,)
Skull Valley,
Wickenburgh.

YUMA COUNTY.

Arizona City,*
Ehrenberg,
La Paz, (*c. h.*)

ARKANSAS.

ARKANSAS COUNTY.

Arkansas Post,
Auburn,
Casscoe,
Crockett's Bluff,
De Witt, (*c. h.*,)
Mount Adams,
Pendleton,
Preston Bluff,
Reeves' Landing,
Saint Charles,
South Bend,
Swan Lake.

ASHLEY COUNTY.

Beech Creek,
Fountain Hill,
Hamburgh,* (*c. h.*,)
Long View,
Nellie,
Pine Hill,
Poplar Bluff.

BENTON COUNTY.

Bentonville, (*c. h.*,)
Bloomington,
Cross Hollow,
Double Springs,
Hickory,
Hico,
La Rue,
Maysville,
Osage Mills,
Pea Ridge,
Spavinaw,
Sugar Creek.

BOONE COUNTY.

Boone,
Harrison, (*c. h.*)

BRADLEY COUNTY.

Adamsville,
Bradley,
Eagle Creek,
Gravel Ridge,
Johnsville,
Lanark,
Moro Bay,
Mount Elba,
Saint John,
Vineyard,
Warren, (*c. h.*)

CALHOUN COUNTY.

Chambersville,
Hampton, (*c. h.*,)
Post Oak,
Summerville.

CARROLL COUNTY.

Berryville,
Carrollton, (*c. h.*,)
Elm Wood,
Green Forest,
Mountain Spring,
Mount Pleasant,
Osage,
Thompsonville.

CHICOT COUNTY.

Chicora,
Eunice,
Grand Lake,
Lake Village, (*c. h.*,)
Luna Landing,
Sunny Side.

* Money-order office.

Clark County.

Alpine,
Amity,
Antoine,
*Arkadelphia,** (c. h.,)
Clear Spring,
De Roche,
Point Cedar,
Rock Creek.

Columbia County.

Atlanta,
Bell's Store,
Calhoun,
Dorcheat,
Falcon,
Lamartine,
Liddesdale,
Magnolia, (c. h.,)
Palestine,
State Line,
Walker's.

Conway County.

Cadron,
Cane Creek,
El Paso,
Greenbrier,
Howard,
Lewisburgh,
Old Hickory,
Springfield, (c. h.)

Craighead County.

Greensborough,
Jonesborough (c., h.)

Crawford County.

Belmont,
Lee's Creek,
Spencer's Shop,
The Narrows,
Van Buren, (c. h.)

Crittenden County.

Blackfish,
Bledsoe,
Council Bend,
Crawfordsville,
Grayson,
Marion, (c. h.,)
Mound City.

Cross County.

Cold Water,
Wittsburgh, (c. h.)

Dallas County.

Fairview,
Holly Springs,
Princeton, (c. h.,)
Stover,
Tulip.

Desha County.

Chester,
Cypress Creek,
Knowlton's Landing,
*Napoleon,** (c. h.,)
Prairie Landing,
Prewitt's Ferry,
Red Fork,
White River.

Drew County.

Bartholomew,
Branchville,
Cut Off,
Florence,
Green Mount,
Lacey,
*Monticello,** (c. h.,)
Relf's Bluff,
Selma.

Franklin County.

Cass,
Charleston,
Game Hill,
Ozark, (c. h.,)
Pleasant Hill,
Roseville,
Sub Rosa.

Fulton County.

Bennett's Bayou,
Bennett's River,
Franklin,
Pilot Hill, (c. h.)

Grant County.

Sandy Springs,
Sheridan, (c. h.)

Greene County.

Big Creek,
Crowley,
Gainesville, (c. h.,)
Herndon,
Loyal Hill,
Walcott.

Hempstead County.

Clayton,
Columbus,
Fulton,
Mineral Springs,
Spring Hill,
Washington, (c. h.,)
Wilson's X Roads.

Hot Spring County.

Hot Springs,*
Midway,
Reyburn,
Rockport, (c. h.,)
Whittington.

Independence County.

*Batesville,** (c. h.,)
Buck Horn,
Oil Trough,
Polk Bayou,
Sharp's Cross Roads,
Sulphur Rock.

Izard County.

Blue Mountain,
La Crosse,
Lunenburgh,
Mill Creek,
Mount Olive, (c. h.,)
Newburgh,
Pineville,
Riggsville,
Sylamore,
Table Rock.

Jackson County.

Elgin,
Grand Glaze,
Jacksonport, (c .h.,)
Kenyon.

Jefferson County.

Adamsburgh,
Byrd's Springs,
Carson,
Darysaw,
Garretson's Landing,
Greenback,
Melton,
New Gascony,
Oakville,
Pastoria,
Pine Bluff, (c. h.,)
Plum Bayou,
Randall,
Red Bluff,
Reform,
Rob Roy,
Victoria,
White Sulphur Springs.

* Money-order office.

Johnson County.

Calico,
*Clarksville,** (*c. h.*,)
Ellsworth,
Patterson's Bluff,
Pittsburgh,
Shoal Creek.

Lafayette County.

Lewisville, (*c. h.*,)
Randolph,
Rondo,
Walnut Hill.

Lawrence County.

Ash Flat,
Canton,
Clover Bend, (*c. h.*,)
Powhatan,
Reed's Creek,
Rhea,
Smithville,
Stranger's Home,
Walnut Ridge.

Little River County.

Peytonsville,
Richmond,
Rocky Comfort, (*c. h.*)

Madison County.

Clifty,
Drake's Creek,
Hindsville,
Huntsville, (*c. h.*,)
Jupiter,
Little Spring,
Marble,
Saint Paul,
War Eagle.

Marion County.

Clear Creek,
Lead Hill,
Rolling Prairie,
Sherman, (*c. h.*,)
Whiteville,
Yellville.

Mississippi County.

Barfield,
Osceola, (*c. h.*,)
Pecan Point,
Shawnee Village.

Monroe County.

Brinkley,
Clarendon (*c. h.*,)
Cypress,
Duncan,
Indian Bay,
Moro,
Sylarsville.

Montgomery County.

Black Springs,
Centreville,
Crystal Hill,
Harold,
Mount Ida, (*c. h.*)

Newton County.

Beech Woods,
Cave Creek,
Jasper, (*c. h.*,)
Marshall Prairie,
Mount Judea,
Mount Parthenon.

Ouachita County.

*Camden,** (*c. h.*,)
Caney,
Freco,
Liberty,
Luda,
Mount Moriah,

Ouachita County—Continued.

Rose Hill,
Seminary,
Two Bayous,
Woodlawn.

Perry County.

Casa,
Klingelhoeffer Landing,
Oppello,
Perryville, (*c. h.*,)
Union City.

Phillips County.

Askew,
Gillen's Landing,
*Helena,** (*c. h.*,)
La Grange,
Marianna,
North Creek,
Old Town,
Oliver's Landing,
Phillips Bayou,
Planters,
Trenton.

Pike County.

Brocktown,
Dora,
Huddleston,
Murfreesboro', (*c. h.*,)
Red Land,
Royston,
Star of the West,
Wilton,
Wolf Creek.

Poinsett County.

Harrisburgh, (*c. h.*)

Polk County.

Big Bend,
Big Fork,
Cove,
Dallas, (*c. h.*)

Pope County.

Dover, (*c. h.*,)
Galley Rock,
Georgetown,
Glass Village,
Lyman,
Moreland,
Norristown,
Russellville.

Prairie County.

Austin,
Des Arc,
*Devall's Bluff,** (*c.h.*,)
Hickory Plains,
Hicks' Station,
Prairie Centre.

Pulaski County.

Ashley Mills,
Eagle Landing,
Little Rock,*(*c.h.*,)
Maumelle,
North Point,
Pennington's Mills,
Reed's Landing.

Randolph County.

Downey's Spring,
Elm Store,
Jayne's Store.
Pitman,
Pocahontas, (*c. h.*)

St. Francis County.

Calvert's,
Forest City,
L'Anguille,
Madison, (*c. h.*,)
Taylor's Creek.

* Money-order office.

SALINE COUNTY.

Benton, (c. h.,)
Cherry Grove,
Collegeville,
Owensville,
Prattsville,
Turin.

SCOTT COUNTY.

Black Jack,
Boles,
Booneville,
Chismville,
Magazine,
Nebraska,
Olio,
Parks,
Revilee,
Waldron, (c. h.)

SEARCY COUNTY.

Calf Creek,
Marshall, (c. h.,)
Point Peter.
Providence,
Wiley's Cove.

SEBASTIAN COUNTY.

Bloomer,
Chocoville,
Fort Smith,*
Greenwood, (c. h.,)
Hodge's Prairie,
James' Fork,
Jenny Lind,
Milor,
New Market,
Sugar Loaf.

SEVIER COUNTY.

Ben Lomond,
Centre Point,
Farribaville,
Locksburgh, (c. h.,)
Nelta Boc,
Paraclifta.

SHARP COUNTY.

Evening Shades,(c.h.,)
Martin's Creek.

UNION COUNTY.

Champagnolle,
El Dorado, (c. h.,)

UNION COUNTY—Continued.

Hillsborough,
Lisbon,
Pigeon Hill,
Wilmington.

VAN BUREN COUNTY.

Bee Branch,
Clinton, (c. h.,)
Eglantine,
Kinderhook,
Liberty Springs,
Quitman.

WASHINGTON COUNTY.

Billingsly,
Boonsborough,
Cincinnati,
Elm Springs,
Evansville,
Ever Green.
Farmington,
Fayetteville, (c. h.,)*
Greenville,
Maguire's Store,
Prairie Grove,
Rhea's Mills,
Tranquilla,
Viney Grove,
West Fork.

WHITE COUNTY.

Centre Hill,
Cold Well,
Judson,
Negro Hill,
Rose Bud.
Searcy, (c. h.,)*
Stony Point,
West Point.

WOODRUFF COUNTY.

Augusta, (c. h.,)
Britton,
Cotton Plant,
De View.

YELL COUNTY.

Bluffton,
Chikalah,
Danville, (c. h.,)
Dardanelle,*
Delaware,
Dutche's Creek,
Onyx,
Petit Jean,
Rover,
Walnut Tree.

CALIFORNIA.

ALAMEDA COUNTY.

Alameda,
Alvarado,
Brooklyn,
Centreville,
Dougherty's Stat'n,
Harrisburgh,
Haywood,
Livermore,
Melita,
Midway,
Mission San Josó,
Mount Eden,
Oakland, *
Pleasanton,
San Leandro, (c. h.,)
San Lorenzo,
Washington Corners.

ALPINE COUNTY.

Bulliona,
Carey's Mills,
Markleeville, *
Monitor,
Silver Mountain, (c.h.,)
Woodford's.

AMADOR COUNTY.

Amador City,
Buena Vista,

AMADOR COUNTY—Continued.

Drytown,
Fiddletown,
Forest Home,
Ione Valley, *
Jackson, (c. h.,)*
Lancha Plana,
Pine Grove,
Sutter Creek,
Volcano.

BUTTE COUNTY.

Bangor,
Bidwell's Bar,
Brush Creek,
Butte Valley,
Central House,
Cherokee,
Chico, *
Clipper Mills,
Forbestown,
Inskip,
Magalia,
Martinsburgh,
Moore's Station,
Oroville, (c. h.,)*
Pentz,
Pine Creek,
Rio Seco,
Rock Creek,
Yankee Hill.

* Money-order office.

Calaveras County.

Angel's Camp,
Big Trees,
Camanche,
Campo Seco,
Copperopolis,
Fourth Crossing,
Jenny Lind,
Mokelumne Hill,* (*c. h.*,)
Mountain Ranch,
Murphy's,
Railroad Flat,
San Andreas,
Telegraph City,
Vallicita,
West Point.

Colusa County.

Coast Range,
Colusa,* (*c. h.*,)
Grand Island,
Jacinto,
Newville,
Princeton,
Saint John,
Spring Valley.

Contra Costa County.

Alamo,
Antioch, *
Black Diamond,
Clayton,
Danville,
La Fayette,
Martinez,* (*c. h.*,)
Pacheco,
Point of Timber,
San Pablo,
Somersville,
Walnut Creek.

Del Norte County.

Crescent City, (*c. h.*,)
Happy Camp,
Smith River.

El Dorado County.

Clarksville,
Cold Spring,
Coloma,
Diamond Spring,
El Dorado,
Fair Play,
Georgetown, *
Green Valley,
Greenwood,
Grizzly Flats,
Indian Diggings,
Kelsey,
Latrobe,
Mendon,
Nashville,
Newton,
Pilot Hill,
Placerville,* (*c. h.*,)
Pleasant Valley,
Salmon Falls,
Shingle Springs,
Slippery Ford,
Spanish Flat,
Taho.

Fresno County.

Big Dry Creek,
Firebaugh,
King's River,
Kingston,
Millerton, (*c. h.*,)
New Idria,
Panoche.

Humboldt County.

Arcata,
Camp Grant,
Eel River,
Eureka,* (*c. h.*,)
Ferndale,
Gas Jet,
Hydesville,
Petrolia,
Table Bluff.

Inyo County.

Big Pine,
Cerro Gordo,
Fish Springs,
Independence, (*c. h.*,)
Lone Pine.

Kern County.

Bakersfield,
Havilah, (*c. h.*,)
Kernville,
Linn's Valley,
Tehichipa.

Klamath County.

Bed Rock,
Black Bear,
Cottage Grove,
Forks of Salmon,
Hoopa Valley,
Martin's Ferry,
Orleans, (*c. h.*,)
Petersburgh,
Sawyer's Bar,
Trinidad,
Yocumville.

Lake County.

Guenoc,
Knoxville,
Lakeport,
Lower Lake, (*c. h.*,)
Morgan,
Uncle Sam,
Upper Clear Lake,
Zem Zem.

Lassen County.

Copper Vale,
Janesville,
Junction House,
Long Valley,
Milford,
Susanville,* (*c. h.*)

Los Angeles County.

Anaheim,
Capistrano,
Compton,
Los Angeles,* (*c. h.*,)
Los Nietos,
Monte,
Petroliopolis,
Ravena City,
San Gabriel,
Santa Ana,
Spadra,
Wilmington.*

Marin County.

Black Point,
Bolinas,
Olema,
San Quentin,
San Rafael,* (*c. h.*,)
Tomales.

Mariposa County.

Bear Valley,
Hornitas,
Indian Gulch,
Mariposa,* (*c. h.*,)
Maxwell's Creek,
Mount Bullion,
Wyatt's Store,
Yo Semite.

Mendocino County.

Albion,
Anderson,
Cahto,
Calpella,
Conway's Landing,
Covelo,
Cuffey's Cove,
Gualala,
Hermitage,
Little Lake,
Little River,
Mendocino,*
Navarro Ridge,
Punta Arenas,
Sanel,
Sherwood Valley,
Ukiah, (*c. h.*,)
Yorkville.

Merced County.

Alexandria,
Brickville,
Dover,
Hopeton,
Merced Falls,
Plainsberg,
Snelling's Ranch,(*c.h.*,)
Union.

* Money-order office.

MONO COUNTY.

Benton,
Bishop Creek,
Bridgeport, (*c. h.*,)
Coleville.

MONTEREY COUNTY.

Castroville,
Gabilon,
Hollister,
Monterey,* (*c. h.*,)
Natividad,
New Republic,
Picacho,
Salinas,
San Antonio,
San Benito,
San Juan,
Soledad.

NAPA COUNTY.

Adelante,
Calistoga,
Monticello,
Napa City,* (*c. h.*,)
Oakville,
Pope Valley,
Saint Helena,
Yountville.

NEVADA COUNTY.

Anthony House,
French Corral,
Graniteville,
Grass Valley,*
Indian Springs,
Little York,
Moore's Flat,
Nevada City,* (*c. h.*,)
North Bloomfield,
North Columbia,
North San Juan,
Omega,
Patterson,
Rough and Ready,
Sweetland,
Truckee,
Washington,
You Bet.

PLACER COUNTY.

Auburn,* (*c. h.*,)
Bath,
Blue Canyon,
Cisco,
Clipper Gap,
Colfax,
Dutch Flat,*
Emigrant Gap,
Forest Hill,*
Gold Run,
Grizzly Bear House,
Iowa City,
Lincoln,*
Michigan Bluff,
Newcastle,
Oro City,
Pino,
Rocklin,
Roseville,
Sheridan,
Todd's Valley,
Yankee Jim's.

PLUMAS COUNTY.

Beckwith,
Big Meadows,
Buck's Ranch,
Crescent Mills,
Greenville,
La Porte,*
Longville,
Meadow Valley,
Mohawk Valley,
Nelson Point,
Quincy, (*c. h.*,)
Round Valley,
Sawpit,
Spanish Ranch,
Summit,
Taylorsville.

SACRAMENTO COUNTY.

Brighton,
Cosumne,
Elk Grove,
Florin,
Folsom City,*
Franklin,
Freeport,
Galt,
Hicksville,
Mayhew's Station,
Michigan Bar,
Mormon Island,
Onisbo,
Richland,

SACRAMENTO COUNTY—Continued.

SACRAMENTO CITY,* (*c. h.*)
Sheldon,
Walnut Grove.

SAN BERNARDINO COUNTY.

Cucamonga,
San Bernardino,* (*c.h.*)

SAN DIEGO COUNTY.

Ballena,
Branson,
Guahonga,
Julian,
Milquatay,
National City,
Otay,
Poway,
San Diego, (*c. h.*,)
San Jacinto,
San Luis Rey,
South San Diego,*
Temecula,
Warner's Ranch.

SAN FRANCISCO COUNTY.

San Francisco,* (*c. h.*)

SAN JOAQUIN COUNTY.

Atlanta,
Banta,
Bellota,
Burwood,
Collegeville,
Elliott,
Ellis,
Farmington,
Liberty,
Linden,
Live Oak,
Lockeford,
Meinecke,
Mokelumne,
Stockton,* (*c. h.*,)
Waterloo,
Woodbridge.

SAN LUIS OBISPO COUNTY

Arroyo Grande,
Berros Creek,
Cambria,
Old Creek,
Paso Robles,
Piedra Blanca,
San Luis Obispo, (*c.h.*,)
San Marcos,
Santa Margarita.

SAN MATEO COUNTY.

Belmont,
Fair Oaks,
Halfmoon Bay,
Menlo Park,
Millbrae,
Pescadero,
Redwood City, (*c. h.*,)
San Mateo,
School-house Station,
Searsville,
Woodside.

SANTA BARBARA COUNTY.

Carpenteria,
Las Cruces,
Los Alisos,
Santa Barbara,* (*c.h.*,)
San Buenaventura,
Santa Maria.

SANTA CLARA COUNTY.

Alviso,
Burnett,
Gilroy,*
Lexington,
Los Gatos,
Mayfield,
Milpitas,
Mountain View,
San Felipe,
San José,* (*c. h.*,)
Santa Clara,
San Ysidro,
Saratoga.

* Money-order office.

Santa Cruz County.

Aptos,
Santa Cruz,* (*c. h.*,)
Soquel,
Watsonville.*

Shasta County.

American Ranch,
French Gulch,
Horsetown,
Millville,
Portuguee,
Shasta,* (*c. h.*,)
Stillwater.

Sierra County.

Alleghany,
Downieville,* (*c. h.*,)
Fir Cap,
Forest City,
Gibsonville,*
Goodyear's Bar,
Loyalton,
Plum Valley,
Port Wine,
Saint Louis,
Sierra City,
Sierra Valley,
Table Rock.

Siskiyou County.

Berryvale,
Callahan's Ranch,
Cedarville,
Eagleville,
Edgwood,
Etna Mills,
Fort Bidwell,
Fort Jones,
Gazelle,
Henley,
Klamath,
Lake City,
Mount Shasta,
Oro Fino,
Scott River,
Seiad Valley,
Yreka, (*c. h.*)

Solano County.

Batavia,
Benicia,*
Binghamton,
Cordelia,
Denverton,
Dixon,
Maine Prairie,
Rio Vista,
Silveyville,
South Vallejo,
Suisun City,* (*c. h.*,)
Vaca,
Vacaville,*
Vallejo.*

Sonoma County.

Bloomfield,
Clairville,
Cloverdale,
Duncan's Mills,
Fisherman's Bay,
Freestone,
Guerneville,
Healdsburgh,*
Lakeville,
Mark West,
Ocean View,
Petaluma,*
Santa Rosa,* (*c. h.*,)
Sebastopol,
Smith's Ranch,
Sonoma,
Stony Point,
Timber Cove,
Two Rocks,
Windsor.

Stanislaus County.

Crow's Landing,
Graysonville,
Hill's Ferry,
Horr's Ranch,
Knight's Ferry, (*c. h.*,)
La Grange,
Langworth,
Paradise,
Tuolumne City,
Twenty-six-Mile House.

Sutter County.

Colegrove's Point,
Meridian,
Nicolaus,
Pleasant Grove Cr'k.
West Butte,
Yuba City, (*c. h.*)

Tehama County.

Battle Creek,
Cottonwood,
Lassen,
Moon's Ranch,
Red Bluff,* (*c. h.*,)
Tehama.

Trinity County.

Big Bar,
Burnt Ranch,
Douglas City,
Junction City,
Lewiston,
Trinity,
Trinity Centre,
Weaverville,* (*c. h.*)

Tulare County.

Farmersville,
Tule,
Visalia,* (*c. h.*)

Tuolumne County.

Big Oak Flat,
Chinese Camp,
Columbia,*
Garrote,
Jamestown,
Montezuma,
Shaw's Flat,
Sonora,* (*c. h.*,)
Sugar Pine.

Yolo County.

Antelope,
Buck Eye,
Cache Creek,
Capay,
Charleston,
Davisville,
Grafton,
Prarie,
Woodland,
Yolo,* (*c. h.*)

Yuba County.

Brown's Valley,
Brownsville,
Bullard's Bar,
Camptonville,*
Honcut,
Marysville,* (*c. h.*,)
Oregon House,
Paulinville,
Smartville,
Strawberry Valley,
Timbuctoo,
Wheatland.

COLORADO TERRITORY.

Arapahoe County.

Cherry Creek,
DENVER,* (*c. h.*,)
Littleton.

Bent County.

Bent's Fort,
Fort Lyon, (*c. h.*,)
South Side.

*Money-order office.

BOULDER COUNTY.

Boulder, (*c. h.*,)
Burlington,*
Coal Creek,
Jamestown,
Sugar Loaf,
Valmont,
Ward District,
Whitney.

CLEAR CREEK COUNTY

Empire City,
Georgetown,*
Idaho, (*c. h.*,)
Mill City,
Spanish Bar.

CONEJOS COUNTY.

Concjos, (*c. h.*,)
Loma.

COSTILLA COUNTY.

Costilla,
Fort Garland,
San Luis, (*c. h.*)

DOUGLAS COUNTY.

Bear Canyon,
Franktown, (*c. h.*,)
Glen Grove,
Gomer's Mills,
Huntsville,
Keystone,
Kiowa,
Rock Butte,
Running Creek,
Spring Valley,
Virginia.

EL PASO COUNTY.

Bassett's Mill,
Bijou Basin,
Colorado City, (*c. h.*,)
Edgerton,
El Paso,
Fountain,
Monument,
Wheatland.

FREMONT COUNTY.

Canyon City, (*c. h.*,)
Colfax,
Currant Creek.

GILPIN COUNTY.

Bald Mountain,
Black Hawk Point,
Central City,* (*c. h.*)

GREENWOOD COUNTY.

Kit Carson, (*c. h.*,)
Lake Station.

HUERFANO COUNTY.

Badito, (*c. h.*,)
Butte Valley,

HUERFANO COUNTY—Continued.

Carson,
Greenhorn,
Saint Mary's.

JEFFERSON COUNTY.

Golden City, (*c. h.*,)
Mount Vernon.

LAKE COUNTY.

Cash Creek,
Centreville,
Granite, (*c. h.*,)
Helena,
Oro City,
South Arkansas.

LARIMER COUNTY.

Big Thompson,
Fort Collins,
La Porte, (*c. h.*,)
Namaqua.

LAS ANIMAS COUNTY.

Trinidad,* (*c. h.*)

PARK COUNTY.

Buckskin,
Deer Valley,
Fair Play, (*c. h.*,)
Grant,
Hamilton,
Montgomery City.

PUEBLO COUNTY.

Beaver Creek,
Booneville,
Excelsior,
Hermosilla,
Huerfano,
Juniata,
Pueblo,* (*c. h.*,)
Saint Charles.

SAGUACHE COUNTY.

Carnero,
Garibaldi,
Saguache, (*c. h.*)

SUMMIT COUNTY.

Breckinridge, (*c. h.*,)
Delaware City,
Lincoln City.

WELD COUNTY.

Evans, (*c. h.*,)
Flemming's Ranch,
Fort Lupton,
Greeley,
Julesburgh,
Saint Vrain,
Weld.

CONNECTICUT.

FAIRFIELD COUNTY.

Ball's Pond,
Banksville,
Bethel,
Black Rock,
Bridgeport,*
Brookfield,
Brookfield Centre,
Cannon's Station,
Cold Spring,
Danbury,* (*c. h.*,)
Darien,
Darien Depot,

FAIRFIELD COUNTY—Continued.

Easton,
Fairfield, (*c. h.*,)
Georgetown,
Glenville,
Greenfield Hill,
Greenwich,
Hawleyville,
High Ridge,
Huntington,
Long Ridge,
Mianus,
Mill Plain,

* Money-order office.

FAIRFIELD COUNTY—Continued.

Monroe,
New Canaan,
New Fairfield,
Newtown,
North Stamford,
North Wilton,
Norwalk,*
Plattsville,
Redding,
Redding Ridge,
Ridgebury,
Ridgefield,
Ridgefield Station,
Round Hill,
Rowayton,
Sandy Hook,
Saugatuck,
Sherman,
Smith's Ridge,
South Norwalk,
Southport,
Stamford,*
Stanwich,
Stepney,
Stepney Depot,
Stratford,
Trumbull,
Trumbull L'g Hill,
West Norwalk,
Weston,
Westport,
West Redding,
Wilton,
Winnipauk.

HARTFORD COUNTY.

Avon,
Berlin,
Bloomfield,
Bristol,*
Broad Brook,
Buckingham,
Buckland,
Burlington,
Burnside,
Canton,
Canton Centre,
Centre Hill,
Collinsville,*
East Berlin,
East Glastenbury,
East Granby,
East Hartford,
East Windsor,
East Windsor Hill,
Enfield,
Farmington,
Farm's Village,
Forestville,
Glastenbury,
Granby,
HARTFORD,* (*c. h.*,)
Hartland,
Hazardville,
Hockanum,
Kensington,
Manchester,
Marion,
Marlborough,
Naubuc,
New Britain,*
Newington,
Newington Junct'n,
North Canton,
North Granby,
North Manchester,
Plainville,
Plantsville,
Poquonock,
Rainbow,
Rocky Hill,
Scitico,
Simsbury,
South Glastenbury,
Southington,*
South Manchester,
South Windsor,
Suffield,
Tariffville,
Thompsonville,*
Unionville,
Wapping,
Warehouse Point,
Weatogue,
West Avon,
West Granby,
West Hartford,
West Hartland,
West Suffield,
Wethersfield,
Windsor,
Windsor Locks,*
Windsorville.

LITCHFIELD COUNTY.

Bakersville,
Bantam Falls,
Barkhamsted,
Bethlehem,
Bridgewater,
Burrville
Campville,
Canaan,
Canaan Valley,
Chalybes,
Colebrook,
Colebrook River,
Cornwall,
Cornwall Bridge,
Cornwall Hollow,
East Canaan,

LITCHFIELD COUNTY—Continued.

East Cornwall,
East Kent,
East Litchfield,
Ellsworth,
Falls Village,*
Gaylordsville,
Goshen,
Harwinton,
Hotchkissville,
Huntsville,
Kent,
Lakeville,
Lanesville,
Lime Rock,
Litchfield, (*c. h.*,)
Marble Dale,
Mill Brook,
Milton,
Morris,
Nepaug,
New Hartford,
New Milford,*
New Preston,
Norfolk,
North Colebrook,
North Cornwall,
Northfield,
North Norfolk,
Northville,
Ore Hill,
Park Lane,
Pequabuck,
Pine Meadow,
Pleasant Valley,
Plymouth,
Riverton,
Robertsville,
Roxbury,
Salisbury,
Sharon,
South Canaan,
South Norfolk,
Southville,
Terrysville,
Thomaston,*
Torringford,
Torrington,
Warren,
Washington,
Watertown,
West Cornwall,
West Goshen,
West Norfolk,
West Winsted,*
Winchester Centre,
Winsted,*
Wolcottville,*
Woodbury,
Woodville.

MIDDLESEX COUNTY.

Centre Brook,
Chester,
Clinton,
Cobalt,
Cromwell,
Deep River,
Durham,
Durham Centre,
East Haddam,
East Hampton,
Essex,*
Haddam, (*c. h.*,)
Haddam Neck,
Higganum,
Killingworth,
Leesville,
Middlefield,
Middle Haddam,
Middletown,* (*c. h.*,)
Millington,
Moodus,
Portland,
Saybrook,
Westbrook,
Winthrop.

NEW HAVEN COUNTY.

Ansonia,
Beacon Falls,
Bethany,
Branford,
Brook's Vale,
Cheshire,*
Derby,*
East Haven,
East River,
Fair Haven,
Guilford,*
Hamden,
Madison,
Meriden,
Middlebury,
Milford,*
Mount Carmel,
Naugatuck,*
NEW HAVEN,*(*c. h.*,)
North Branford,
Northford,
North Guilford,
North Haven,
North Madison,
Oakville,
Orange,
Oxford,
Prospect,
River Side,
Rockland,
Seymour,
South Britain,

* Money-order office.

NEW HAVEN COUNTY—Continued.

Southbury,
Southford,
South Haven,
South Meriden,
Stony Creek,
Wallingford,
Waterbury,*
Waterville,
West Cheshire,
West Haven,
West Meriden,*
Westville,
Wolcott,
Yalesville.

NEW LONDON COUNTY.

Baltic,
Bozrah,
Bozrahville,
Centre Groton,
Chesterfield,
Clark's Falls,
Colchester,*
East Lyme,
Franklin,
Gale's Ferry,
Greenville,
Griswold,
Groton,
Hadlyme,
Hamburgh,
Hanover,
Jewett City,
Lebanon,
Ledyard,
Liberty Hill,
Lisbon,
Lyme,
Montville,
Mystic,
Mystic Bridge,*
Mystic River,
*New London,** (*c. h.,*)
Niantic,
Noank,
North Lyme,
North Stonington,
*Norwich,** (*c. h.,*)
Norwich Town,
Poquetanuck,
Poquonock Bridge,
Preston,
Salem,
South Lyme,
Stonington,
Uncasville,
Waterford,
Westchester,
Yantic.

TOLLAND COUNTY.

Andover,
Bolton,
Columbia,
Coventry,
Coventry Depot,
Eagleville,
Ellington,
Gilead,
Gurleyville,
Hebron,
Mansfield,
Mansfield Centre,

TOLLAND COUNTY—Continued.

Mansfield Depot,
Mashapaug,
Merrow Station,
Moose Meadow,
Mount Hope,
Quarryville,
Rockville,*
Somers,
Somerville,
South Coventry,
Square Pond,
Stafford,
Stafford Springs,*
Staffordville,
Talcottville,
Tolland, (*c. h.,*)
Turnerville,
Union,
Vernon,
Vernon Depot,
West Stafford,
West Willington,
Willington,
Windermere.

WINDHAM COUNTY.

Abington,
Ashford,
Brooklyn, (*c. h.,*)
Campbell's Mills,
Canterbury,
Central Village,
Chaplin,
Eastford,
East Killingly,
East Putnam,
East Thompson,
East Woodstock,
Ekonk,
Grosvenor Dale,
Hampton,
Killingly,
Moosup,
New Boston,
North Ashford,
North Grosvenor Dale,
North Windham,
North Woodstock,
Oneco,
Pendleton Hill,
Phœnixville,
Plainfield,
Pomfret,
Pomfret Landing,
Putnam,*
Scotland,
South Killingly,
South Windham,
South Woodstock,
Sterling,
Sterling Hill,
Thompson,
Voluntown,
Wauregan,
West Ashford,
Westford,
West Killingly,*
Westminster,
West Thompson,
West Woodstock,
Willimantic,*
Wilsonville,
Windham,
Woodstock,
Woodstock Valley.

DAKOTA TERRITORY.

BONHOMME COUNTY.

Bonhomme, (*c. h.,*)
Chouteau Creek,
Emanuel,
Springfield.

BUFFALO COUNTY.

Fort Sully,
Grand River.

CHARLES MIX COUNTY.

Antelope,
Greenwood, (*c. h.,*)
White Swan.

CLAY COUNTY.

Lincoln,
Riverside,
Saybrook,
Vermillion, (*c. h.,*)

DEUEL COUNTY.

Fort Wadsworth.

LINCOLN COUNTY.

Canton, (*c. h.,*)
Eden,
Fairview,
Swan Lake.

MINNEHAHA COUNTY.

Sioux Falls.

PEMBINA COUNTY.

Grand Forks,
Pembina, (*c. h.,*)
Saint Joseph.

* Money-order office.

SHYENNE COUNTY.

Fort Abercrombie.

TODD COUNTY.

Fort Randall, (*c. h.*,) Ponka Agency.

UNION COUNTY.

Adelescat,
Big Sioux,
Elk Point, (*c. h.*,)
Liberty,

UNION COUNTY—Continued.

Richland,
Sioux Valley,
Virginia.

YANKTON COUNTY.

Lakeport,
Marindal,
Whitehall,
YANKTON,* (*c. h.*)

COUNTIES UNKNOWN.

Crow Creek,
Fort Totten,
Whetstone Agency.

DELAWARE.

KENT COUNTY.

Adamsville.
Brenford,
Camden,
Canterbury,
Clayton,
DOVER,* (*c. h.*,)
Farmington,
Felton Station,
Frederica,
Harrington,
Hazlettville,
Hollandville,
Houston Station,
Kenton,
Lebanon,
Leipsic,
Little Creek Landing,
Magnolia,
Milford, *
Moorton,
Mount Moriah,
Pearson's Corner,
Slaughter,
Smyrna,*
Vernon,
Willow Grove,
Woodside,
Wyoming.

NEW CASTLE COUNTY.

Beaver Valley,
Black Bird,
Centreville,
Chambersville,
Chippewa,
Christiana,
Claymont,
Cooch's Bridge,
Deakyneville,
Delaware City,*
Fieldsborough,
Glasgow,
Hare's Corner,
Henry Clay Factory,
Hockessin,
Kirkwood,

NEW CASTLE COUNTY—Continued.

Loveville,
McClellandsville,
McDonough,
Mermaid,
Middletown, *
Mount Pleasant,
Newark, *
New Castle,* (*c. h.*,)
Newport,
Odessa,
Pleasant Hill,
Port Penn,
Red Lion,
Saint George's,
Stanton,
Summit Bridge,
Townsend,
Wilmington, *

SUSSEX COUNTY.

Angola,
Black Water,
Bridgeville,
Concord,
Dagsborough,
Delmar,
Draw Bridge,
Ellendale,
Frankford,
Georgetown, (*c. h.*,)
Greenwood,
Gumborough,
Harbeson,
Hollyville,
Laurel,
Lewes, *
Lincoln,
Lowe's Cross Roads,
Middleford,
Millsborough,
Milton,
Ocean View,
Redden,
Roxana,
Seaford, *
Selbyville,
Tunnell's Store.

DISTRICT OF COLUMBIA.

WASHINGTON COUNTY.

Anacostia,
Brightwood,
Georgetown,*
Tenallytown,
WASHINGTON* (*c. h.*)

FLORIDA.

ALACHUA COUNTY.

Archer,
Gainesville,* (*c. h.*,)
Micanopy,
Newnanville,
Waldo.

BAKER COUNTY.

Olustee,
Sanderson, (*c. h.*)

BRADFORD COUNTY.

Lake Butler (*c. h.*) Starke.

* Money-order office.

BREVARD COUNTY.

Saint Lucie, (*c. h.*)

CALHOUN COUNTY.

Iola, Ochesee.

CLAY COUNTY.

Green Cove Springs, Trail Ridge.
Middleburgh.

COLUMBIA COUNTY.

Benton, *Lake City*, (*c. h.*,)
Blount's Ferry, Suwannee Shoals,
Ellisville, Tustenuggee.
Ichatucknee,

DADE COUNTY.

Biscayne, (*c. h.*)

DUVAL COUNTY.

Fort George, Mandarin,
Hibernia, Mayport,
Jacksonville,* (*c. h.*,) Yellow Bluff.

ESCAMBIA COUNTY.

Bluff Springs, *Pensacola*,* (*c. h.*,)
Molino, Warrington.*

FRANKLIN COUNTY.

Apalachicola, (*c. h.*)

GADSDEN COUNTY.

Chattahoochee, *Quincy*, (*c. h.*,)
Concord, Rickoe's Bluff.

HAMILTON COUNTY.

Bellville, Jennings,
Jasper, (*c. h.*,) White Springs.

HERNANDO COUNTY.

Bay Port, Fort Taylor,
Cedar Tree, *Pierceville*, (*c. h.*)
Fort Dade,

HILLSBOROUGH COUNTY.

Alafia, Cork,
Clear Water Harbor, *Tampa*,* (*c. h.*,)

HOLMES COUNTY.

Cerro Gordo, (*c. h.*,) Ponce de Leon.

JACKSON COUNTY.

Campbellton, *Marianna*, (*c. h.*)
Greenwood,

JEFFERSON COUNTY.

Monticello, (*c. h.*,) Weelaunee,
Waukeenah, Williamsburgh.

LA FAYETTE COUNTY.

McIntosh, (*c. h.*)

LEON COUNTY.

Bailey's Mill, TALLAHASSEE,* (*c. h.*)
Miccosukee,

LEVY COUNTY.

Bronson, Cedar Keys.

LIBERTY COUNTY.

Blue Creek, Rock Bluff.
Bristol, (*c. h.*,)

MADISON COUNTY.

Columbus, Sandy Ford.
Madison, (*c. h.*,)

MANATEE COUNTY.

Manatee.

MARION COUNTY.

Camp Izard, *Ocala*, (*c. h.*,)
Cotton Plant, Orange Springs.
Flemington,

MONROE COUNTY.

Cayo Largo, *Key West*,* (*c. h.*)

NASSAU COUNTY.

Callahan, King's Ferry,
Fernandina,* (*c. h.*,) Nassau.

ORANGE COUNTY.

Apopka, *Orlando*, (*c. h.*)
Mellonville,

POLK COUNTY.

Peace Creek, (*c. h.*)

PUTNAM COUNTY.

Buffalo Bluff, *Pilatka*, (*c. h.*,)
Federal Point, Welaka.
Georgetown,

ST. JOHN'S COUNTY.

Esparanza, Orange Mills,
Hogarth's Landing, *St. Augustine*,* (*c. h.*)
Matanzas,

* Money-order office.

SANTA ROSA COUNTY.

Chalk Spring, *Milton*, (*c. h.*)

SUMTER COUNTY.

Sumterville, (*c. h.*)

SUWANNEE COUNTY.

Houston, (*c. h.*,) Live Oak, Suwannee, Wellborn.

TAYLOR COUNTY.

Rose Head, (*c. h.*)

VOLUSIA COUNTY.

Blue Springs, *Enterprize*, (*c. h.*,) New Smyrna, Palmetto, Port Orange, Sand Point, Volusia.

WAKULLA COUNTY.

Crawfordville, (*c. h.*,) Pautuxett, Saint Marks, Sopchoppy.

WALTON COUNTY.

Knox Hill, *Uchee Anna*, (*c. h.*)

WASHINGTON COUNTY.

Vernon, (*c. h.*)

GEORGIA.

APPLING COUNTY.

Hazlehurst, *Holmesville*, (*c. h.*,) Screven, Surrency.

BAKER COUNTY.

Newton, (*c. h.*)

BALDWIN COUNTY.

Milledgeville,* (*c. h.*,) Talmage.

BANKS COUNTY.

Allandale, Banksville, Erastus, Hollingsworth, *Homer*, (*c. h.*,) Middle River, Nail's Creek.

BARTOW COUNTY.

Adairsville, Allatoona, *Cartersville*,* (*c. h.*,) Cass Station, Cassville, Euharley, Hall's Mill, Kingston, Pine Log, Stegall's Depot, Stilesborough.

BERRIEN COUNTY.

Knight's Mill, Milltown, *Nashville*, (*c. h.*)

BIBB COUNTY.

Macon,* (*c. h.*)

BROOKS COUNTY.

Grooverville, *Quitman*, (*c. h.*)

BRYAN COUNTY.

Way's Station.

BURKE COUNTY.

Brinsonville, Herndon, Holcombe, Lawtonville, Lester's District, Midville, Millin, *Waynesborough*, (*c. h.*)

BUTTS COUNTY.

Indian Springs, *Jackson*, (*c. h.*,) Stark, Worthville.

CALHOUN COUNTY.

Morgan, (*c. h.*)

CAMDEN COUNTY.

Berne, Saint Mary's, Satilla Mills.

CAMPBELL COUNTY.

Campbellton, (*c. h.*,) Chapel Hill, County Line, Dark Corner, Fairburn, Palmetto, Skinner.

CARROLL COUNTY.

Bowdon, Bowenville, *Carrollton*, (*c. h.*,) Loyal, Villa Rica.

CATOOSA COUNTY.

Graysville, *Ringgold*,* (*c. h.*)

CHARLTON COUNTY.

Centre Village, *Trader's Hill*, (*c. h.*)

CHATHAM COUNTY.

*Savannah** (*c. h.*)

* Money-order office.

Chattahoochee County.

Cottage Mills, *Cusseta*, (c. h.,) Jamestown, King.

Chattooga County.

Alpine, Chattoogaville, Dirt Town, Melville, *Summerville*, (c. h.,) Teloga Springs, Trion Factory.

Cherokee County.

Canton, (c. h.,) Cherokee Mills, Fort Buffington, Freemansville, Ophir, Orange, Woodstock.

Clarke County.

Athens,* *Watkinsville*, (c. h.)

Clay County.

Fort Gaines, (c. h.,) Gatesville.

Clayton County.

Forest Station, *Jonesborough*, (c. h.,) Lovejoy's Station.

Clinch County.

Homerville, (c. h.,) Lawton, Stockton.

Cobb County.

Acworth, Big Shanty, Boltonville, Kenesaw, Lost Mountain, *Marietta*,* (c. h.,) Powder Springs, Roswell, Smyrna, Vining Station.

Coffee County.

Douglas, Gully Branch, Red Bluff.

Colquitt County.

Greenfield, *Moultrie*, (c. h.)

Columbia County.

Appling, (c. h.,) Berzelia, Lombardy, Saw Dust, Thompson, Winfield.

Coweta County.

Campton, Grantville, Kidron, Lodi, *Newnan*, (c. h.,) Senoia, Turin.

Crawford County.

Hickory Grove, *Knoxville*, (c. h.)

Dade County.

Cloverdale, Morganville, Rising Fawn, Smith, *Trenton*, (c. h.)

Dawson County.

Barrittsville, Big Savanna, *Dawsonville*, (c. h.,) Dixon.

Decatur County.

Bainbridge,* (c. h.,) Calvary, Harrell.

De Kalb County.

Cross Keys, *Decatur*, (c. h.,) Lithonia, Stone Mountain.

Dooly County.

Byromville, Turkey Creek, *Vienna*, (c. h.)

Dougherty County.

Albany,* (c. h.)

Early County.

Blakely, (c. h.,) Octavia.

Echols County.

Huckleberry, *Statenville*, (c. h.)

Effingham County.

Eden, Egypt, Guyton, *Springfield*, (c. h.)

Elbert County.

Dove's Creek, *Elberton*, (c. h.,) Ruckersville, Webster Place.

Emanuel County.

Canoochee, *Swainsborough*, (c. h.)

Fannin County.

Hot House, *Morganton*, (c. h.)

Fayette County.

Fayetteville, (c. h.,) Red Oak, White Water.

Floyd County.

Armuchee, Cave Spring, Coosa, Cunningham's St'n, Livingston, Nannie, *Rome*,* (c. h.) Yarborough.

* Money-order office.

FORSYTH COUNTY.

Big Creek,
Cumming, (*c. h.*,)
Sheltonville,
Vickery's Creek.

FRANKLIN COUNTY.

Aquilla,
Bold Spring,
Carnesville, (*c. h.*,)
Franklin Springs.

FULTON COUNTY.

ATLANTA,* (*c. h.*,)
East Point,
Irbyville.

GILMER COUNTY.

Ellijay, (*c. h.*)

GLASCOCK COUNTY.

Gibson, (*c. h.*)

GLYNN COUNTY.

Brunswick,* (*c. h.*,)
Frederica.

GORDON COUNTY.

Blue Spring,
Calhoun, (*c. h.*,)
Fairmount,
Reeves' Station,
Resaca,
Sugar Valley.

GREENE COUNTY.

Greenesborough,(*c.h.*,)
Penfield,
Siloam,
Union Point,
White Plains,
Woodville.

GWINNETT COUNTY.

Auburn,
Cain's,
Lawrenceville, (*c. h.*,)
Suwanee,
Sweet Water,
Yellow River.

HABERSHAM COUNTY.

Clarkesville, (*c. h.*,)
Currohee,
Hughesburgh,
Tallulah,
Walton's Ford.

HALL COUNTY.

Gainesville, (*c. h.*,)
Gillsville,
Hog Mountain,
Polksville,
Poplar Springs,
Sugar Hill.

HANCOCK COUNTY.

Culverton,
Mayfield,
Mount Zion,
Sparta, (*c. h.*)

HARALSON COUNTY.

Buchanan, (*c. h.*,)
Repose,
Tallapoosa.

HART COUNTY.

Air Line,
Amandaville,
Bowersville,
Eagle Grove,
Ford's Store,
Hartwell, (*c. h.*,)
Oak Bower,
Parker's Store.

HARRIS COUNTY.

Cataula,
Ellerslie,
Hamilton, (*c.h.*,)
Mountain Hill,
Mulberry Grove,
Waverly Hall,
Whitesville,
Wisdom's Store.

HEARD COUNTY.

Franklin, (*c. h.*,)
Houston,
Saint Cloud,
State Line.

HENRY COUNTY.

Bear Creek,
Crumley's,
McDonough, (*c. h.*)
Peaksville,
Stockbridge.

HOUSTON COUNTY.

Byron,
Fort Valley,
Perry, (*c. h.*,)
Powersville.

IRWIN COUNTY.

Irwinville, (*c. h.*)

JACKSON COUNTY.

Harmony Grove,
Jefferson, (*c. h.*)

JASPER COUNTY.

Monticello, (*c. h.*)

JEFFERSON COUNTY.

Bartow,
Bethany,
Bostick,
Fenn's Bridge,
Louisville, (*c. h.*)

JOHNSON COUNTY.

Wrightsville, (*c. h.*)

JONES COUNTY.

Clinton, (*c. h.*,)
Griswoldville.

LAURENS COUNTY.

Dublin, (*c. h.*,)
Laurens Hill.

LEE COUNTY.

Renwick,
Starkville, (*c. h.*)
Wootten.

LIBERTY COUNTY.

Fleming,
Hinesville, (*c. h.*,)
McIntosh,
Taylor's Creek,
Walthourville.

* Money-order office.

Lincoln County.

Clay Hill,
Goshen,
Leathersville,
Lincolnton, (*c. h.*)

Lowndes County.

Cat Creek,
Naylor,
Valdosta, (*c. h.*)

Lumpkin County.

Auraria,
Dahlonega, (*c. h.*,)
New Bridge.

Mac Intosh County.

Darien, (*c. h.*)

Macon County.

Marshallsville,
Montezuma,
Oglethorpe, (*c. h.*)

Madison County.

Danielsville, (*c. h.*,)
Fort Lamar,
Radical.

Marion County.

Buena Vista, (*c. h.*,)
Glen Alta.

Meriwether County.

Chalybeate Springs,
Erin,
Flat Shoals,
Greenville, (*c. h.*,)
Jones' Mills,
Luthersville,
Rocky Mount,
Warm Springs,
Warnerville,
White Sulphur Springs,
Woodbury.

Miller County.

Colquit, (*c. h.*)

Milton County.

Alpharetta, (*c. h.*,)
Warsaw.

Mitchell County.

Camilla, (*c. h.*)

Monroe County.

Colaparchee,
Culloden,
Forsyth, (*c. h.*,)
New Market,
Russellville,
Unionville.

Montgomery County.

Mount Vernon, (*c. h.*,)
Stirling.

Morgan County.

Buck Head,
Madison,* (*c. h.*)
Rutledge.

Murray County.

Spring Place, (*c. h.*)

Muscogee County.

Columbus,* (*c. h.*,)
Upatoie.

Newton County.

Conyers,
Covington, (*c. h.*,)
Newton Factory,
Oxford,
Snapping Shoals.

Oglethorpe County.

Bairdstown,
Crawford,
Lexington,* (*c. h.*,)
Maxey,
Point Peter,
Sandy Cross,
Stephens,
Winterville.

Paulding County.

Branch,
Brownsville,
Dallas, (*c. h.*,)
Ludville,
Roxanna.

Pickens County.

Jasper, (*c. h.*,)
Talking Rock.

Pierce County.

Blackshear, (*c. h.*)

Pike County.

Barnesville,
Concord,
Liberty Hill,
Milner,
Zebulon, (*c. h.*)

Polk County.

Cedartown, (*c. h.*,)
Prior's Station,
Van Wert.

Pulaski County.

Bishop's Store,
Cochran,
Dubois,
Eartmon.
Hawkinsville, (*c. h.*)

Putnam County.

Eactonton, (*c. h.*)

Quitman County.

Georgetown, (*c. h.*,)
Hatcher's Station,
Morris Station.

Rabun County.

Clayton, (*c. h.*,)
War Woman.

Randolph County.

Coleman's Depot,
Cuthbert,* (*c. h.*,)
Nochway.

* Money-order office.

RICHMOND COUNTY.

Allen's,
Augusta,* (*c. h.*,)
Belair,
McBean Depot.

SCHLEY COUNTY.

Ellaville, (*c. h.*)

SCRIVEN COUNTY.

Cameron,
Halcyon Dale,
Mobley Pond,
Ogeechee,
Panamore Hill,
Rocky Ford,
Scarborough.

SPALDING COUNTY.

*Griffin**, (*c. h.*)

STEWART COUNTY.

Florence,
Green Hill,
Hannahatchee,
Lumpkin, (*c. h.*)

SUMTER COUNTY.

Americus,* (*c. h.*,)
Andersonville,
Plains of Dura.

TALBOT COUNTY.

Bluff Spring,
Box Spring,
Geneva,
Pleasant Hill,
Prattsburgh,
Talbotton, (*c. h.*)

TALIAFERRO COUNTY.

Crawfordville, (*c. h.*,)
Sharon.

TATNALL COUNTY.

Long Branch,
Reidsville, (*c. h.*)

TAYLOR COUNTY.

Butler, (*c. h.*,)
Howard,
Reynolds.

TELFAIR COUNTY.

Copeland,
Jacksonville, (*c. h.*,)
Lumber City,
McVille,
Temperance.

TERRELL COUNTY.

Dawson, (*c. h.*,)
Powers.

THOMAS COUNTY.

Boston,
Cairo,
Ochlochnee,
Thomasville, (*c. h.*)

TOWNS COUNTY.

Hiawassee, (*c. h.*,)
Mount Eolia.

TROUP COUNTY.

Antioch,
Hogansville,
La Grange, (*c. h.*,)
Mountville,
O'Neal's Mills,
Vernon,
West Point.

TWIGGS COUNTY.

Bullard's,
Jeffersonville, (*c. h.*,)
Pace's Station,
Twiggsville.

UNION COUNTY.

Blairsville, (*c. h.*,)
Ivy Log.

UPSON COUNTY.

The Rock,
Thomaston, (*c. h.*,)
Waynmanville.

WALKER COUNTY.

Cane Creek,
Cassandra,
Cedar Grove,
Duck Creek,
Frick's Gap,
Greenbush,
High Point,
La Fayette, (*c. h.*,)
Naomi,
Pond Spring,
Rock Spring,
Salem,
Villanow.

WALTON COUNTY.

Monroe, (*c. h.*,)
Social Circle,
Walnut Grove.

WARE COUNTY.

Glenmore,
Tebeanville.

WARREN COUNTY.

Camac,
Double Wells,
Warrenton, (*c. h.*,)

WASHINGTON COUNTY.

Davisborough,
Hebron,
Oconee,
Riddlesville,
Sandersville, (*c. h.*,)
Tennille,
Warthen's Store,
Whittle.

WAYNE COUNTY.

Doctor Town,
Drady's,
Pendarvis,
Waynesville, (*c. h.*)

WEBSTER COUNTY.

Preston, (*c. h.*)

WHITE COUNTY.

Cleveland, (*c. h.*,)
Leo,
Loudsville
Nacoochee,
Pleasant Retreat.

* Money-order office.

WHITFIELD COUNTY.

Cove City,
Dalton,* (*c. h.*,)
Red Clay,
Tilton,
Tunnel Hill,
Varnell's Station.

WILCOX COUNTY.

Abbeville, (*c. h.*,)
Adams,
House Creek.

WILKES COUNTY.

Danburgh,
Washington, (*c. h.*)

WILKINSON COUNTY.

Gordon,
Irwinton, (*c. h.*,)
McIntire,
Stephensville,
Toomsborough.

WORTH COUNTY.

Isabella, (*c. h.*,)
Vine's Mills,
Warwick.

IDAHO TERRITORY.

ADA COUNTY.

BOISE CITY,* (*c. h.*,)
Lower Boise,
Middleton,
Payetteville.

ALTURAS COUNTY.

Atlanta,
Rocky Bar, (*c. h.*,)
Shoshone.

BOISE COUNTY.

Centreville,
Idaho City,* (*c. h.*,)
Pioneerville,
Placerville.

IDAHO COUNTY.

Florence City,* (*c. h.*,)
John Day's Creek.
White Bird.

LEMHI COUNTY.

Fort Lemhi,
Leesburgh,
Salmon City, (*c. h.*)

NEZ PERCES COUNTY.

Lapwai,
Lewiston,* (*c. h.*)

ONEIDA COUNTY.

Eagle Rock,
Malade City, (*c. h.*,)
Market Lake,
Ross Fork.

OWYHEE COUNTY.

Silver City,* (*c. h.*)

SHOSHONE COUNTY.

Pierce City, (*c. h.*)

ILLINOIS.

ADAMS COUNTY.

Adams,
Beverly,
Big Neck,
Burton,
Camp Point,*
Chattan,
Clayton,*
Cliola,
Coatsburgh,
Columbus,
Elm Grove,
Fair Weather,
Fowler,
Keokuk Junction,
La Prairie,
Liberty,
Lima,
Marcelline,
Mendon,
Paloma,
Payson,
Peyton's,
Quincy,* (*c. h.*,)
Richfield,
Stones' Prairie,
Ursa,
Woodville,
York Neck.

ALEXANDER COUNTY.

Cairo,* (*c. h.*,)
Clear Creek Landing,
Goose Island,
Santa Fé,
Thebes,
Unity.

BOND COUNTY.

Baden Baden,
Beaver Creek,
Cottonwood Grove,
Dudleyville,
Elm Point,
Greenville,* (*c. h.*,)
Mulberry Grove,
Old Ripley,
Pleasant Mound,
Pleasant Prairie,
Pocahontas,
Woburn.

BOONE COUNTY.

Belvidere,* (*c. h.*,)
Bonus,
Caledonia Station,
Capron,
Garden Prairie,
Hunter,
Leesville,
Park's Corners,
Poplar Grove.

BROWN COUNTY.

Buck Horn,
Cooperstown,
Gilbirdsport,
Hersman's,
La Grange Bluff,
Mound Station,
Mount Sterling,*(*c.h.*,)
Ripley,
Spring's Station,
Union Ridge,
Versailles,
White Oak Springs.

* Money-order office.

Bureau County.

Arlington,*
Buda,
Bureau Junction,
De Pue,
Dover,
Hollowayville,
Lamoille,
Limerick,
Lone Tree,
Lovejoy,
Malden,
Milo,
Mineral,
Neponset,*
New Bedford,
Ohio,
Ottsville,
*Princeton,** (*c. h.,*)
Providence,
Sheffield,
Tiskilwa,
Truxton,
Walnut,
Wyanet,
Yorktown.

Calhoun County.

Belleview,
Deer Plain,
Gilead,
Hamburgh,
Hardin, (*c. h.,*)
Hastings Landing,
Maynardsville,
Monterey,
News,
Vedder.

Carroll County.

Argo,
Elk Horn Grove,
Fair Haven,
Johnson's Creek,
Lanark,
Milledgeville,
*Mount Carroll,**(*c.h.,*)
Polsgrove,
Rock Creek,
Savanna,
Shannon,*
Thomson.

Cass County.

Arenzville,
Ashland,
*Beardstown,** (*c. h.,*)
Berryton,
Chandlerville,
Hagley.
Lancaster,
Little Indian,
Virginia.

Champaign County.

Champaign,*
Homer,*
Ivesdale,
Ludlow,
Mahomet,
Newcomb,
Ogden,
Pesotum,
Philo,
Rantoul,*
Raymond,
Saint Joseph's,
Savoy,
Sidney,
Sodorus,
Thomasborough,
Tolona,
Urbana, (*c. h.*)

Christian County.

Assumption,
Edinburgh,
Grove City,
Mount Auburn,
Owaneco,
Palmer,
Pana,*
Randellsville,
Rosemond,
Stonington,
Taylorville, (*c. h.*)

Clark County.

Casey,
Clark Centre,
Dalson,
Darien,
Darwin,
Livingston,
McKeen,
*Marshall,** (*c. h.,*)
Martinsville,
Melrose,
Oak Point,
Westfield,
York.

Clay County.

Bible Grove,
Clay City,
Flora,
Greensburgh,
Hord,
Ingraham,
Larkinsburgh,
Louisville, (*c. h.,*)
Oskaloosa,
Xenia.

Clinton County.

Aviston,
Buxton,
*Carlyle,** (*c. h.,*)
Clement,
Damiansville,
Germantown,
Jamestown,
Keyesport,
New Baden,
New Memphis,
Shoal Creek Station,
Trenton.*

Coles County.

Ashmore,
Campbell,
*Charleston,** (*c. h.,*)
Diona,
Etna,
Fuller's Point,
Hutton,
Loxa,
McPherson,
Mattoon,*
Milton Station,
Oakland,
Paradise,
Rural Retreat,
Saint Omer,
Springville.

Cook County.

Ainsworth Station,
Austin,
Barrington Station,
Bloom,
Blue Island,
Brickton,
Calumet,
*Chicago,** (*c. h.,*)
Des Plaines,
Dolten's Station,
Dunton,
East Northfield,
Elk Grove,
Englewood,
Evanston,*
Glencoe,
Havelock,
Homewood,
Hyde Park,
Jefferson,
Lake View,
Lansing,
Lemont,
Leyden,
Leyden Centre,
Lyons,
Lyonsville,
Mainville,
Mattison,
Maywood,
Mulford,
New Bremen,
Niles,
Niles Centre,
Norwood Park,
Oak Park,
Orland,
Palatine,
Palos,
Proviso,
Ravenswood,
Shaumburgh,
South Holland,
South Northfield,
Summit,
The Grove,
Thornton,
Washington Heights,
West Lyons,
West Northfield,
Wheeling,
Willow Spring,
Wilmette,
Winnetka.

Crawford County.

Annapolis,
Bell Air,
Eaton,
Elkton,
Flat Rock,
Grand Glade,
Hardinsville,
Hutsonville,
New Hebron,
Oblong,
Palestine,*
Robinson, (*c. h.,*)
Stiflesville.

* Money-order office.

CUMBERLAND COUNTY.

Greenup,
Hazle Dell,
Johnstown,
Majority Point, (*c.h.*,)
Mule Creek,
Neoga,
Union Centre,
Woodbury.

DE KALB COUNTY.

Courtland Station,
Deerfield Prairie,
De Kalb Centre,*
Dorset,
Dustin,
East Paw Paw,
Freeland,
Genoa,
Hick's Mills,
Kingston,
Lacey,
La Clair,
Malma,
Malta,
New Lebanon,
Ney,
North Kingston,
Pierceville,
Prairie Pond,
Ross Grove,
Sandwich,*
Shabbonas Grove,
Somonauk,
South Grove,
Squaw Grove,
Sycamore,* (*c. h.*,)
Van Buren,
Victor Centre.

DE WITT COUNTY.

Clinton,* (*c. h.*,)
De Witt,
Farmer City,
Hallsville,
Harp,
Nixon,
Wapella,
Waynesville,

DOUGLAS COUNTY.

Arcola,*
Bono,
Brushy Fork,
Camargo,
Cottage Grove,
Newman,
Tuscola,* (*c. h.*)

DU PAGE COUNTY.

Addison,
Bloomingdale,
Cass,
Danby,
Downer's Grove,
Elmhurst,
Fullersburgh,
Gower,
Hinsdale,
Lisle Station,
Lombard,
Naperville,* (*c. h.*,)
Sagone,
Turner,
Warrensville,
Wayne,
Wheaton,*
Winfield.

EDGAR COUNTY.

Baldwinsville,
Bloomfield,
Bonwell,
Catfish,
Cherry Point City,
Conlogue,
Dudley,
Elbridge,
Grand View,
Kansas,
Logan,
Palermo,
Paris,* (*c. h.*,)
Vermillion.

EDWARDS COUNTY.

Albion,* (*c. h.*,)
Bennington,
Bone Gap,
Maple Grove,
Mills Prairie,
Samsville,
West Salem.

EFFINGHAM COUNTY.

Edgewood,
Effingham,* (*c. h.*,)
Elliottstown,
Freemanton,
Funkhouser,
Mason,*
Moccasin,
Mountville,
Teutopolis,
Veni,
Watson,

FAYETTE COUNTY.

Bowling Green,
Brownstown,
Farina,
Greenland,
Hickory Creek,
La Clede,
Louden City,
Ramsey,
Saint Elmo,
Shabonier,
Vandalia,* (*c. h.*,)
Vera.

FORD COUNTY.

East Bend,
Eldredgeville,
Paxton,* (*c. h.*,)
Piper City,
Sugar Loaf.

FRANKLIN COUNTY.

Akin,
Benton, (*c. h.*,)
Big Muddy,
Cave,
Crittenden,
Eastern,
Ewing,
Fitt's Hill,
Frankfort,
Mulkeyton,
Osage,
Parrish,
Prosperity,
Taylor Hill,
Webb's Prairie.

FULTON COUNTY.

Astoria,
Avon,
Bernadotte,
Bryant,
Canton,*
Civer,
Cuba,
Duncan's Mills,
Ellisville,
Fairview,
Farmington,*
Fiatt,
Ipava,
Lewistown,* (*c. h.*,)
Liverpool,
Maple's Mill,
Marietta,
Middle Grove,
Midway,
Norris,
Otto,
Saint David,
Seville,
Smithfield,
Summum,
Table Grove,
Vermont.

GALLATIN COUNTY.

Cottonwood,
Crawford,
Elba,
Equality,
New Haven,
New Market,
Saline Mines,
Shawneetown,* (*c. h.*,)
South Hampton.

GREENE COUNTY.

Athensville,
Berdan,
Bluff Dale,
Breese,
Carrollton,* (*c. h.*,)
Fayette,
Greenfield,
Kane,
Negro Lick,
Pioneer,
Road House Station,
Rockbridge,
Walkerville,
White Hall.

* Money-order office.

Grundy County.

Braceville,
Gardner,
Highland Town,
Mazon,
Minooka,
*Morris,** (*c. h.*)

Hamilton County.

Belle Prairie,
Knight's Prairie,
Griswold,
Logansport,
Lovilla,
Macedonia,
*McLeansboro',** (*c. h.*,)
Rectorville.

Hancock County.

Adrian,
Appanoose,
Augusta,
Basco,
Bently,
Bowensburgh,
Burnside,
*Carthage,** (*c. h.*,)
Chili,
Dallas City,*
Denver,
Durham,
Elvaston,
Ferris,
Fountain Green,
Hamilton,*
Hickory Ridge,
Joetta,
La Crosse,
La Harpe,*
McCall,
Middle Creek,
Nauvoo,
Plymouth,
Pontoosuc,
Pulaski,
Saint Albans,
Sonora,
Sylvan Dale,
Warsaw.*
Webster,
West Point.

Hardin County.

Cave in Rock,
Elizabethtown, (*c. h.*,)
Parkinson's Land'g,
Rosiclare,
Seller's Landing,
Spark's Hill.

Henderson County.

Biggsville,
Hopper's Mills,
Lomax,
Olena,
*Oquawka,** (*c. h.*,)
Raritan,
Rozetta,
Sagetown,
Shokokon,
South Prairie,
Terre Haute.

Henry County.

Andover,
Annawan,
Atkinson,
Bishop Hill,
Burns,
*Cambridge,** (*c. h.*,)
Cleveland,
Colona Station,
Galva,*
Geneseo,*
Green River,
Kewanee,*
Minersville,
Morristown,
Nekoma,
Orion,
Oxford,
Pink Prairie,
Saxon,
Sharon,
Ulah,
Wethersfield,
Woodhull.

Iroquois County.

Ash Grove,
Ashkum,
Beaverville,
Buckley,
Chebanse,
Clifton,

Iroquois County—Continued.

Crescent City,
Danforth Station,
Del Rey,
Eden,
Gilman,
Iroquois,
L'Erable,
Luddenville,
Middleport, (*c. h.*,)
Milford,
Oakalla,
Onarga,*
Plato,
Sheldon,
Watseka.

Jackson County.

Ava,
Bradley,
Carbondale,*
De Soto,
Elkville,
Fountain Bluff,
Grand Tower,
Hat Island,
Makauda,
*Murphysboro',** (*c. h.*,)
Ora,
Vergennes,
Worthington.

Jasper County.

Hidalgo,
Island Creek,
Linder,
*Newton** (*c. h.*,)
Rose Hill,
Saint Marie,
Willow Hill,
Yale.

Jefferson County.

Cub Prairie,
Dix,
Lynchburgh,
Harris Grove,
Moore's Prairie,
*Mount Vernon,** (*c.h.*,)
Spring Garden.

Jersey County.

Delhi,
Elsah,
Fidelity,
Fieldon,
Grafton,
*Jerseyville,** (*c. h.*,)
Newbern,
Otter Creek.

Jo Daviess County.

Apple River,
Avery,
Council Hill,
Council Hill Station,
Derinda,
Dunleith,
Elizabeth,
Excelsior Mills,
*Galena,** (*c. h.*,)
Greenvale,
Guilford,
Hanover,
Houghton,
Howardsville,
Mount Sumner,
Nora,
Pitcherville,
Pleasant Valley,
Plum River,
Rush,
Scales Mound,
Stockton,
Warren,*
Willow,
Yankee Hollow.

Johnson County.

Cedar Bluff,
Cypress Creek,
Elvira,
Goreville,
Grantsburgh,
Lincoln Green,
Reynoldsburgh,
Sanburn,
Shinn's Point,
*Vienna,** (*c. h.*)

* Money-order office.

Kane County.

Aurora,*
Batavia,*
Big Rock,
Blackberry,
Blackberry Station,
Burlington,
Campton,
Carpentersville,
Clintonville,
Dundee,
East Burlington,
Elgin,*
*Geneva**, (*c. h.*,)
Gilbert's,
Gray Willow,
Grouse,
Hampshire,
Jericho,
Kaneville,
Lafox,
Lodi Station,
Montgomery,
North Aurora,
North Plato,
Pingree Grove,
Saint Charles,*
Sugar Grove,
Udina.

Kankakee County.

Aroma,
Bourbonnais Grove,
Caberay,
Deselm,
Judson,
Kankakee,* (*c. h.*,)
Limestone,
Manteno,*
Momence,
Norton,
Rinosa,
Rockville,
Saint Anne,
Saint George,
Salina,
Sherburneville,
Union Hill.

Kendall County.

Bristol,
Bristol Station,
Kendall,
Lewis,
Lisbon,
Little Rock,
Mellington,
Millbrook,
Newark,
Oswego,*
Pavilion,
Plano,
Plattville,
White Willow,
Yorkville, (*c. h.*)

Knox County.

Abingdon,*
Altona,*
Centre Point,
Douglas,
Eugene,
Galesburgh,*
Gilson,
Henderson,
Hermon,
Knoxville,* (*c. h.*,)
Maquon,
Milroy,
North Prairie,
Oneida,*
Ontario,
Saint Augustine,
Truro,
Victoria,
Wataga,
Yates City.

Lake County.

Antioch,
Dean's Corners,
Deerfield,
Diamond Lake,
Ela,
Emmett,
Fort Hill,
Fox Lake,
Fremont Centre,
Gage's Lakes,
Gilmer,
Hainesville,
Half Day,
Hickory,
Highland Park,
Lake Forrest,
Lake Zurich,
Libertyville,
Long Grove,
Millburn,
Newport,
O'Plain,
Rockland,
Rosecrans,
Sand Lake,
Volo,
Wauconda,
Waukegan,* (*c. h.*)

La Salle County.

Asbury,
Bruceville,
Cornville,
Dayton,
Deer Park,
Earlville,*
Farm Ridge,
Freedom,
Freedom Centre,
Galloway,
Garfield,
La Salle,*
Leland,
Lock,
Lostant,*
Lowell,
Marseilles,*
Mendota,*
Meriden,
Miner,
New Rutland,
Northville,
Norway,
Oglesby,
Ottawa,* (*c. h.*,)
Peru,*
Prairie Centre,
Seneca,
Serena,
Sheridan,
Streator,*
Tonica,*
Triumph,
Troy Grove,
Utica,
Vermillionville.

Lawrence County.

Bridgeport,
Hadley Statton,
Lawrenceville, (*c. h.*,)
Olive,
Russellville,
Saint Francisville,
Sumner.

Lee County.

Amboy,*
Ashton,
Dixon,* (*c. h.*,)
Eldena,
Franklin Grove,*
Gap Grove,
Lee Centre,
Malugin Grove,
Nachusa,
Nelson,
Paw Paw Grove,
South Willow Creek,
Sublette,
Willow Creek.

Livingston County.

Amity,
Ancona,
Blackstone,
Cayuga,
Chatsworth,*
Coalville,
Dwight,*
Fairbury,*
Forest,
Long Point,
Nevada,
New Michigan,
Oakdale,
Ocoya,
Odell,
Pontiac,* (*c. h.*,)
Potosi,
Reading,
Rook's Creek,
Sannemin,
Smithdale,
Sullivan Centre,
Sunbury.

Logan County.

Atlanta,*
Broadwell,
Elkhart City,*
Eminence,
Laenna,
Lawndale,
Lincoln,* (*c. h.*,)
Middletown,
Mount Pulaski.

McDonough County.

Adair,
Bardolph,
Blandinsville,*
Bushnell,*
Colchester,
Colmar,
Good Hope,
Industry,
Macomb,* (*c. h.*,)
New Philadelphia,
Pennington Point,
Prairie City,
Sciota,
Tennessee.

* Money-order office.

McHenry County.

Alden,
Algonquin,
Barreville,
Big Foot Prairie,
Bliven's Mills,
Cary Station,
Chemung,
Coral,
Crystal Lake,
Deep Cut,
English Prairie,
Greenwood,
Harmony,
Harvard,*
Hebron,
Huntley Grove,*
Johnsburgh,
Lawrence,
McHenry,
Marengo,*
Nunda,
Ostend,
Richmond,*
Ridgefield,
Riley,
Ringwood,
Solon Mills,
Union,
Woodstock,* (*c. h.*)

McLean County.

Bloomington, (*c. h.*,)
Chenoa,*
Covell,
Danvers,
Delta,
Elsinor,
Gridley,
Hamlin,
Heyworth,
Hudson,
Le Roy,
Lexington,
McLean,
Normal,
Oak Grove,
Padua,
Randolph,
Saybrook,*
Selma,
Senex,
Shirley,
Stanford,
Towanda,
Weston.

Macon County.

Decatur,* (*c. h.*,)
Elwin,
Forsythe,
Harristown,
Macon,*
Maroa,*
Mount Zion,
Niantic,
Oakley,
Prairie Hall,
Sangamon Station.

Macoupin County.

Barr's Store,
Brighton,
Buford,
Bunker Hill,
Carlinville,* (*c. h.*,)
Chesterfield,
Dorchester,
Gillespie,
Girard,
Greasy,
Holliday,
Hornsby,
Macoupin Station,
Medora,
Miles' Station,
Mount Olive,
Nilwood,
Palmyra,
Piasa,
Plain View,
Scottville,
Shaw's Point,
Shipman,
Staunton,
Stirrup Grove,
Vancil's Point,
Virden,*
Woodburn.

Madison County.

Alhambra,
Alton,*
Alton Junction,
Bethalto,
Buckinn,
Collinsville,*
Dorsey,
Edwardsville,* (*c. h.*,)
Fosterburgh,
Godfrey,
Grantfork,
Highland,*

Madison County—Continued.

Liberty Prairie,
Long Lake,
Marine,
Moro,
Moultonville,
New Douglas,
New Hampton,
Omph Ghent,
Paddock's Grove,
Pierron,
Prairie Town,
Saint Jacob,
Saint Morgan,
Troy,*
Upper Alton,*
Venice,
Wilborn.

Marion County.

Alma,
Central City,
Centralia,*
Hickory Hill,
Iuka,
Kinmundy,
Lester,
Odin,*
Omega,
Patoka,
Racoon,
Salem,* (*c. h.*,)
Sandoval,
Walnut Hill.

Marshall County.

Bell Plain,
Henry,*
Lacon,* (*c. h.*,)
La Prairie Centre,
Lawn Ridge,
Sparland,*
Wenona Station.*

Mason County.

Bath,
Bishop's Station,
Forest City,
Havana,* (*c. h.*,)
Manito,
Mason City,
Natrona,
Saidora,
San José,
Snicarte,
Topeka.

Massac County.

Ash Ridge,
Hickory Grove,
Massac Creek,
Metropolis City,*(*c.h.*,)
New Columbia,
Pellonia.

Menard County.

Athens,
Greenview,
Oak Ridge,
Petersburgh,* (*c. h.*,)
Robinson's Mills,
Sweet Water,
Tallula.

Mercer County.

Aledo,* (*c. h.*,)
Eliza,
Ethel,
Ferdinand,
Hamlet,
High Point,
Keithsburgh,*
Millersburgh,
New Boston,
New Windsor,
Norwood,
Pre-emption,
Richland Grove,
Suez,
Sunbeam,
Swedona,
Viola.

Monroe County.

Burksville,
Columbia,
Harrisonville,
Hecker,

* Money-order office.

MONROE COUNTY—Continued.

Madonaville,
Maeystown,
Merrimack Point,
Mitchie,
Monroe City,
Renault,
Waterloo,* (c. h.)

MONTGOMERY COUNTY.

Butler,
Donnellson,
East Fork,
Fillmore,
Herndon,
Hillsborough,* (c. h.,)
Hurricane,
Irving,
Litchfield,*
Nokomis,*
Shop Creek,
Walshville,
White Oak,
Witt,
Zanesville.

MORGAN COUNTY.

Alexander,
Arcadia,
Bethel,
Chapin,
Concord,
Franklin,
Jacksonville,* (c. h.,)
Liter,
Lynnville,
Meredosia,
Murrayville,
Neelyville,
Orleans,
Prentice,
Waverly,
Woodson,
Yatesville.

MOULTRIE COUNTY.

Dunn,
Lovington,
Marrowbone,
Sullivan,* (c. h.,)
Sumter,
Whitley's Point.

OGLE COUNTY.

Adeline,
Baileyville,
Beacon,
Black Walnut,
Brookville,
Byron,
Crescent,*
Daysville,
Eagle Point,
Fitz Henry,
Flag Station,
Foreston,
Grand Detour,
Haldane,
Hale,
Killbuck,
Kyte River,
Lindenwood,
Luda,
Monroe Centre,
Mount Morris,*
Oregon,* (c. h.,)
Paine's Point,
Polo,*
Rochelle,*
Taylor,
Wales,
White Rock,
Woosung.

PEORIA COUNTY.

Akron,
Brimfield,*
Brunswick,
Chillicothe,*
Dowdallville,
Edward's Station,
Elmore,
Elmwood,*
French Grove,
Glasford,
Hallock,
Harker's Corners,
Kickapoo,
Kingston Mines,
Langdon,
Mossville,
North Hampton,
Peoria,* (c. h.,)
Princeville,*
Robin's Nest,
Rome,
Rosefield,
Smithville,
Southampton,
Southport,
Summerville,
Trivoli,
West Hallock.

PERRY COUNTY.

Denmark,
Duquoin,*
Four Mile Prairie,
Galum,
Pinckneyville, (c. h.,)
Pleasant Shade,
St. John,
Tamaroa.

PIATT COUNTY.

Bement,*
Centreville,
Cerro Gordo,*
Milmine,
Monticello,* (c. h.)

PIKE COUNTY.

Atlas,
Barry,
Bedford,
Bee Creek,
Chambersburgh,
Detroit,
El Dara,
Fish Hook,
Flint,
Florence,
Gilgal,
Green Pond,
Griggsville,*
Kinderhook,
Martinsburgh,
Milton,
Montezuma,
Monument,
New Hartford,
New Salem,
Pearl,
Perry,
Perry Springs,
Pineville,
Pittsfield,* (c. h.,)
Pleasant Hill,
Pleasant Vale,
Rockport,
Sardinia,
Spring Creek,
Summer Hill,
Time.

POPE COUNTY.

Allen's Springs,
Bay City,
Eddyville,
Glendale,
Golconda,* (c. h.,)
Lusk,
New Liberty,
Oak,
Orville,
Rock,
Rose Bud,
Shandsville,
Wool.

PULASKI COUNTY.

Caledonia, (c. h.,)
Grand Chain,
Junction,
Mound City,*
Ullin,
Villa Ridge,
Walbridge,
Wetaug.

PUTNAM COUNTY.

Florid,
Granville,
Hennepin,* (c. h.,)
Magnolia,
Mount Palatine,
Snachwine.

RANDOLPH COUNTY.

Blair,
Bremen,
Brewersville,
Chester,* (c. h.,)
Cobb,
Coultersville,
Diamond Cross,
Ellis Grove,
Evansville,
Jordan's Grove,
Kaskaskia,
Prairie du Rocher,
Preston,
Red Bud,*
Rockwood,
Ruma,
Sadowa,
Saint Marks,
Sakeville,
Shiloh Hill,
Sparta,*
Steele's Mills.

* Money-order office.

RICHLAND COUNTY.

Boot,
Calhoun,
Claremont,
Dundas,
Fransonia,
Madison,
Noble,
Olney,* (*c. h.*,)
Parkersburgh,
Stringtown,
Wakefield,
Wilsonburgh.

ROCK ISLAND COUNTY.

Andalusia,
Buffalo Prairie,
Camden Mills,
Carbon Cliff,
Coal Valley,
Copper Creek,
Cordova,
Drury,
Edington,
Franklin Crossing,
Hampton,
Hazlitt,
Hill's Station,
Illinois City,
Joslyn,
Moline,
Osborn,
Pleasant Ridge,
Port Byron,
Rapids City,
*Rock Island** (*c. h.*)
Rural,
Watertown.

ST. CLAIR COUNTY.

Belleville,* (*c. h.*,)
Caseyville,
Centreville Station,
Creswell,
Darnstadt,
Dutch Hill,
East St. Louis,*
Fayetteville.
Floraville,
Freeburgh,
French Village,
Gartsides,
Lebanon,*
Lenzburgh,
Lowland,
Marissa,
Mascoutah,*
Millstadt,
Mud Creek,
New Athens,
New Pittsburgh,
O'Fallon Depot,
Ridge Prairie,
Risdon,
Shiloh,
Smithton,
Summerfield.

SALINE COUNTY.

Bankston,
El Dorado,
Gallatia,
Halltown,
Harrisburgh,* (*c. h.*,)
Hartford,
Mitchellsville,
Raleigh,
Somerset,
South America,
Stone Fort,
Texas City.

SANGAMON COUNTY.

Auburn,
Bates,
Berlin,
Berry,*
Buffalo,
Chatham,
Chinkapin Hill,
Cotton Hill,
Curran,
Dawson,
Howlett,
Illiopolis,
Loami,
Mechanicsburgh,
New Berlin,
New Harmony,
Pawnee,
Pleasant Plains,
Richland,
Rochester,
Salisbury,
Sherman,
SPRINGFIELD,*(*c. h.*,)
Wheatfield,
Williamsville,
Woodside.

SCHUYLER COUNTY.

Birmingham,
Brooklyn,
Browning,
Camden,
Centre,
Doddsville,
Fredericksville,
Huntsville,
Littleton.
Pleasant View,
Rushville,* (*c. h.*,)
Sheldon's Grove,
Wayland.

SCOTT COUNTY.

Exeter,
Glasgow,
Manchester,
Merritt,
Naples,
Winchester,* (*c. h.*,)

SHELBY COUNTY.

Beck's Creek,
Big Spring,
Cold Spring,
Hark,
Holland,
Hooker,
Middlesworth,
Mode,
Moulton,
Moweaqua,
Oconee Station,
Prairie Home,
Shelbyville, (*c. h.*,)
Todd's Point,
Tower Hill,
Windsor.

STARK COUNTY.

Bradford,
Camp Grove,
Castleton,
Duncan,
Elmira,
La Fayette,
Lombardville,
Modena,
Osceola,
Pleasant Green,
Toulon,* (*c. h.*,)
West Jersey,
Wyoming.*

STEPHENSON COUNTY.

Buena Vista,
Cedarville,
Dakota,
Damascus,
Davis,*
Duncanon,
Eleroy,
Florence Station,
Freeport,* (*c. h.*,)
Kent,
Lena,*
Loran,
McConnell's Grove,
Oneco,
Orangeville,
Ridott,
Rock Grove,
Rock Run,
Silver Creek,
Waddam's Centre,
Waterman's Mills,
Winslow,
Yellow Creek.

TAZEWELL COUNTY.

Armington,
Boynton,
Circleville,
Deer Creek,
Delavan,*
Dillon,
Green Valley,
Groveland,
Hilton,
Hopedale,
Little Detroit,
Mackinaw,
Minier,
Morton,
Pekin,* (*c. h.*,)
Tremont,
Tullamore,
Washington.*

UNION COUNTY.

Anna,*
Dongola,
Jonesborough, (*c. h.*,)
Lick Creek,

* Money-order office.

UNION COUNTY—Continued.

Moscow,
Mount Pleasant,
Penninger,
South Pass,*
Union Point,
Western Saratoga,
Willard's Landing.

VERMILION COUNTY.

Blue Grass,
Catlin,
Circle,
*Danville,** (*c. h.,*)
Fairmount,
Fithian,
Georgetown,
Grant,
Half-Way House,
Higginsville,
Hope,
Indianola,
Jordan,
Kentucky,
Long,
Marysville,
Myersville,
Oakwood,
Pilot,
Point Pleasant,
Ridge Farm,
Rossville,
Sugar Creek.

WABASH COUNTY.

Armstrong,
Corrieville,
Friend Grove,
Friendsville,
Gard's Point,
Mier,
*Mount Carmel,**(*c. h.,*)
New Hope,
Rochester Mills.

WARREN COUNTY.

Berwick,
Cameron,
Colfax,
Denny,
Duck Creek,
Ellison,
Greenbush,
Ionia,
Little York,
*Monmouth,** (*c. h.,*)
Roseville,
Spring Grove,
Swan Creek,
Utah,
Young America.*

WASHINGTON COUNTY.

Ashley,*
Ayer's Point,
Dubois,
Elkhorn,
Hoyleton,
Irvington,
Johanesburgh,
Lively Grove,
*Nashville,** (*c. h.,*)
New Minden,
Okaw,
Plum Hill,
Richview,*
Venedy.

WAYNE COUNTY.

Enterprise,
*Fairfield,** (*c. h.,*)
Home,
Jeffersonville,
Johnsonville,
Keenville,
Long Prairie,
Mount Erie,
New Baltimore,
New Franklin,
Pin Oak,
Pleasant Grove,
Wabash,
Zif.

WHITE COUNTY.

Burnt Prairie,
*Carmi,** (*c. h.,*)
Emma,
Enfield,
Grayville,*
Mill Shoals,
Phillipstown,
Roland,

WHITE COUNTY—Continued.

Sacramento,
School,
Springerton.

WHITESIDES COUNTY.

Albany,
Coleta,
Como,
Erie,
Fenton,
Fulton,*
Galt,
Jefferson Corners,
Kingsbury,
Leon,
Lyndon,
*Morrison,** (*c. h.,*)
New Genesee,
Portland,
Pratt,
Prophetstown,
Rock Falls,
Round Grove
South Hume,
Spring Hill,
Sterling,*
Union Grove.

WILL COUNTY.

Beecher,
Bird's Bridge,
Braidwood,
Channahon,
Crete,
Dupage,
Eagle Lake,
East Wheatland,
Elwood,
Endor,
Frankfort Station,
Gooding's Grove,
Green Garden,
Grinton,
Hadley,
*Joliet,** (*c. h.,*)
Lockport,*
Mokena,
Monee,
New Lenox,
Peotone,
Pierce,
Plainfield,
Spencer,
Tamorack,
Wallingford,
Wilmington.*

WILLIAMSON COUNTY.

Attila,
Bainbridge,
Blairsville,
Corinth,
Crab Orchard,
Fredonia,
Herrin's Prairie,
Lake Creek,
Locust Grove,
*Marion,** (*c. h.,*)
Pulley's Mill,
Sarahsville,
Sulphur Springs.

WINNEBAGO COUNTY

Argyle,
Burritt,
Cherry Valley,*
Durand Station,*
Elida,
Fountaindale,
Harlem,
Harrison,
Kishwaukee,
Laona,
New Milford,
Pecatonica,*
*Rockford,** (*c. h.,*)
Rockton,
Roscoe,*
Shirland,
Tyler,
Winnebago Depot.

WOODFORD COUNTY.

Cruger,
El Paso,*
Eureka,
Farmsville,
Kappa,
Low Point,
*Metamora,** (*c. h.,*)
Minonk,*
Panola Station,
Secor,
Spring Bay,
Washburn.

*Money-order office.

INDIANA.

Adams County.

Canoper,
*Decatur,** (*c. h.*,)
Limber Lost,
Linn Grove,
Monmouth,
Pleasant Mills.

Allen County.

Aboite,
Arcola,
Cedarville,
Chamberlain,
Eel River,
*Fort Wayne,** (*c. h.*,)
Hall's Corners,
Harlan,
Heller's Corners,
Huntertown,
Leo,
Little River,
Maples,
Monroeville,*
New Haven,
Nine Mile,
Po,
Randall,
Root,
Sheldon,
Woodburn.

Bartholomew County.

Azalia,
Bray's Mills,
Burnsville,
Clifford,
*Columbus,** (*c. h.*,)
Elizabethtown,
Hartsville,
Hope,
Jonesville,
Lowell Mills,
Moore's Vineyard,
Mount Healthy,
Newbern,
St. Louis Crossing,
South Bethany,
Taylorsville,
Wailesborough,
Waymansville,
Waynesville.

Benton County.

Aydelott,
*Oxford,** (*c. h.*,)
Pond Grove.

Blackford County.

*Hartford City,** (*c. h.*,)
Millgrove,
Montpelier,
Priam.

Boone County.

Dover,
Elizaville,
Holmes,
Jamestown,
*Lebanon,** (*c. h.*,)
Northern Depot,
Northfield,
Reese's Mill,
Royalton,
Slabtown,
Thorntown,*
White Lick,
Whitestown,
Zionsville.

Brown County.

Bean Blossom,
Beck's Grove,
Cleona,
Elkinsville,
Marble,
Mount Liberty,
Mount Moriah,
Nashville, (*c. h.*,)
New Bellsville,
Oak Farm,
Pike's Peak,
Spearsville.

Carroll County.

Burlington,
Burrows,
Camden,
Carroll,
Deer Creek,
*Delphi,** (*c. h.*,)
Lockport,
Pittsburgh,
Prince William.
Pyrmont,
Rockfield,
Wild Cat.

Cass County.

Amsterdam,
Anoka,
Big Indian,
Crittenden,
Curveton,
Dow,
Galveston,
Lincoln,
*Logansport,** (*c. h.*,)
Metea,
Montez,
New Waverly,
Onward,
Royal Centre,
Twelve Mile,
Twin Corners,
Walton.

Clarke County.

Bennettsville,
Bethlehem,
Blue Lick,
Cementville,
*Charlestown,** (*c. h.*,)
Henryville,
Jeffersonville,*
Memphis,
Muddy Fork,
New Providence,
New Washington,
Oregon,
Otisco,
Otto,
Polk Run,
St. Joseph's Hill,
Sellersburgh,
Slate Cut,
Utica.

Clay County.

Ashborough,
*Bowling Green,**(*c.h.*,)
Brazil,*
Centre Point,
Christy's Prairie,
Cloverland,
Coffee,
Eaglesfield,
Harmony,
Howesville,
Knightsville,
Martz,
Poland,
Staunton,
Turner's.

Clinton County.

Berlin,
Burget's Corner,
Burnside,
Colfax,
*Frankfort,** (*c. h.*,)
Geetingsville,
Jefferson,
Kirk's Cross Roads,
Michigantown,
Middle Fork,
Mortonsville,
Mulberry,
Pickard's Mill,
Rossville.

Crawford County.

Alton,
Down Hill,
English,
Fredonia,
Grantsburgh,
*Leavenworth,** (*c. h.*,)
Magnolia,
Marengo,
Mifflin,
Milltown,
Mount Prospect,
Padoria,
Pilot Knob,
Wickliffe.

* Money-order office.

Daviess County.

Alfordsville, Montgomery's Sta'n,
Black Oak Ridge, Owl Prairie,
Clark's Prairie, Plainville,
Epsom, Raglesville,
Glen Dale, *Washington*,* (*c. h.*)
Lettsville,

Dearborn County.

Aurora,* Lawrenceville,
Bright, Logan,
Dillsborough, Manchester,
Farmer's Retreat, Moore's Hill,
Guilford, New Alsace,
Guionsville, Pella,
Hansel's, Saint Leon,
Harrmann's Station, Sparta,
Holman, Weisburgh,
Jones' Station, Wilmington,
Kelso, Wright's Corners,
Lawrenceburgh,* (*c. h.*,) Yorkville.

Decatur County.

Adams, New Point,
Alert, Saint Maurice,
Clarksburgh, Saint Omer,
Clifty, Saint Paul,
Forest Hill, Sardinia,
Greensburgh,* (*c. h.*,) Spring Hill,
Kingston, Waynesburgh,
McCoy's Station, Westport,
Millhousen, Wintersville.

De Kalb County.

Auburn,* (*c. h.*,) Iba,
Butler, Mount Hope,
Coburn's Corners, New Era,
Coles' Corners, Newville,
Corunna, Spencerville,
Fairfield Centre, Waterloo.*

Delaware County.

Albany, New Burlington,
Anthony, New Corner,
Cowan, Richwoods,
Daleville, Royerton,
Eaton, Selma,
Granville, Sharon,
Harrison, Wheeling,
Muncie,* (*c. h.*,) Yorktown.

Dubois County.

Birdseye, Holland,
Bretzville, Huntingburgh,
Celestine, Ireland,
Ditney Hill, *Jasper*, (*c. h.*,)
Duff, Kellerville,
Ferdinand, Ludlow,
Haysville, Portersville,
Hillham, Schnellville.

Elkhart County.

Benton, Middlebury,
Bristol, Millersburgh,
Elkhart,* New Paris,
Fish Lake, Vistula,
Goshen,* (*c. h.*,) Wakarusa,
Locke, Waterford Mills.

Fayette County.

Alpine, Groves,
Alquina, Harrisburgh,
Bentonville, Lyon's Station,
Columbia, Null's Mills,
Connersville,* (*c. h.*,) Orange.
Everton,

Floyd County

Edwardsville, Greenville,
Floyd's Knobs, *New Albany*,* (*c. h.*,)
Galena, Scottsville.
Georgetown,

Fountain County.

Attica,* Newtown,
Cole Creek, Rob Roy,
Covington,* (*c. h.*,) Snoddy's Mills,
Fountain, Steam Corner,
Harveysburgh, Stone Bluffs,
Hillsborough, Wallace,

Franklin County.

Andersonville, Mixersville,
Blooming Grove, Mount Carmel,
Blue Creek, New Trenton,
Brookville,* (*c. h.*,) Oak Forest,
Cedar Grove, Oldenburgh,
Drewersburgh, Peppertown,
Enochsburgh, Saint Peters,
Fairfield, South Gate,
Hamburgh, Springfield,
Haymond, Stip's Hill,
Huth, Whitcomb,
Laurel, Wynn.
Metamora,

Fulton County.

Akron, Green Oak,
Bloomingsburgh, Kewanna,
Blue Grass, *Rochester*,* (*c. h.*,)
Bruce's Lake, Sturgeon.
Fulton,

Gibson County.

Bovine, Oakland City,
Buckskin, Owensville,
Fort Branch,* Patoka,
Francisco, *Princeton*,* (*c. h.*,)
Haubstadt, Somerville,
Hazleton, West Buena Vista.
King's Station,

* Money-order office.

GRANT COUNTY.

Arcana, Fairmount, Jadden, Jalapa, Jonesborough, *Marion,** (c. h.,) Mier, New Cumberland, Point Isabel, Roesburgh, Slash, Sweetser's, Trask, Upland.

GREENE COUNTY.

*Bloomfield,** (c. h.,) Hobbieville, Jasonville, Linton, Lyons, Marco, Newark, Newberry, Owensburgh, Park, Pleasant Ridge, Scotland, Solsberry, Swit's City, Worthington, Wright.

HAMILTON COUNTY.

Arcadia, Boxley, Carmel, Cicero, Clarksville, Deming, Eagletown, New Britton, *Noblesville,** (c. h.,) Omega, Shielville, Strawtown, Westfield.

HANCOCK COUNTY.

Carrollton, Charlottesville, Cleveland, Eden, Fortville, *Greenfield,** (c. h.,) Leaman Corner, McCordsville, Milner's Corners, Mount Comfort, Philadelphia, Sugar Creek, Warrington, Westland, Willow Branch, Woodbury.

HARRISON COUNTY.

Barren, Bradford, Byrneville, *Corydon,** (c. h.,) Crisp's Cross Roads, Elizabeth, Evans' Landing, Hancock, King's Cave, Laconia, Lanesville, Mauckport, New Amsterdam, New Middletown, New Salisbury, Palmyra, Rosewood, Rothrock's Mills, Salina, Sharp's Mills, Valley City.

HENDRICKS COUNTY.

Amo, Belleville, Brownsburgh, Cartersburgh, Centre Valley, Clayton, Coatesville, *Danville,** (c. h.,) Friendswood, New Elizabeth, New Winchester, North Salem, Pecksburgh, Pittsborough, Plainfield,* Smootsdell, Stilesville.

HENRY COUNTY.

Ashland, Blountsville, Cadiz, Dunreith, Greensborough, Honey Creek, Knightstown, Lewisville, Luray, Mechanicsburgh, Middletown, Millville, Mount Summit, *New Castle,** (c. h.,) New Lisbon, Ogden, Raysville, Rogersville, Spiceland, Springport, Straughn's Station, Sulphur Springs.

HOWARD COUNTY.

Alto, Cassville, Centre, Ervin, Greentown, Jerome, *Kokomo,** (c. h.,) New London, Oakford, Poplar Grove, Russiaville, Shanghai, West Liberty.

HUNTINGTON COUNTY.

Antioch, Bracken, Brown's Corner, *Huntington,** (c. h.,) Majenica, Markle, Mount Etna, Roanoke, Warren.

JACKSON COUNTY.

*Brownstown,** (c. h.,) Conlogue, Cortland, Crothersville, Dudleytown, Ewing, Findley's Mills, Freetown, Houston, Medora, Mellenbruch, Mooney, Retreat, Rockford, Seymour,* Shields, Sparksville, Tampico, Vallonia, White Creek.

JASPER COUNTY.

Pleasant Grove, Remington, *Rensselaer,** (c. h.,)

JAY COUNTY.

Balbec, Bear Creek, Bluff Point, Boundary, College Corner, Dunkirk, Greene, Hector, Jordan, Mills' Corners, New Corydon, New Mt. Pleasant, Pennville, *Portland,** (c. h.,) Powers, Redkey, Salamonia, Westchester.

JEFFERSON COUNTY.

Barbersville, Bryantsburgh, Canaan, Creswell, Deputy, Dupont,

* Money-order office.

JEFFERSON COUNTY—Continued.

Eagle Springs,
Graham,
Hanover,
Home,
Kent,
Lancaster,
Madison,* (*c. h.*,)
Manville,
Mud Lick,
Neil's Creek,
North Madison,
Saluda,
Stony Point,
Swanville,
Volga,
Wirt.

JENNINGS COUNTY.

Benville,
Brewersville,
Butlerville,
Cana,
Commiskey,
Lovett,
Nebraska,
North Vernon,
Oakdale,
Paris,
Queensville,
San Jacinto,
Scipio,
Sherman,
Six Mile,
Slate,
Vernon,* (*c. h.*,)
Zenas.

JOHNSON COUNTY.

Amity,
Bargersville,
Bluff Creek,
Edinburgh,*
Franklin,* (*c. h.*,)
Greenwood,
Needham's Station,
Nineveh,
Samaria,
Smith's Valley,
Trafalgar,
Urmeyville,
Whiteland.

KNOX COUNTY.

Bicknell,
Bruceville,
Busseron,
Decker's Station,
Edwardsport,
Emison Station,
Freelandville,
Lovely Dale,
Oaktown,
Pond Creek Mills,
Sandborn,
Spaldingville,
Vincennes,* (*c. h.*,)
Wheatland.

KOSCIUSKO COUNTY.

Atwood,
Beaver Dam,
Boydston's Mills,
Etna Green,
Hepton,
Leesburgh,
Milford,
Millwood,
Oneida,
Orion,
Oswego,
Palestine,
Pierceton,*
Rose Hill,
Sevastopol,
Silver Lake,
Syracuse,
Warsaw,* (*c. h.*,)
Wooster.

LA GRANGE COUNTY.

Brighton,
Brushy Prairie,
Eden Mills,
La Grange,* (*c. h.*,)
Lima,
Marcy,
Mongoquinong,
Mount Pisgah,
Ontario,
Ringgold,
Scott,
South Milford,
Valentine,
Wolcottville.

LAKE COUNTY.

Brunswick,
Cassella,
Cedar Lake,
Clarke Station,
Crown Point,* (*c. h.*,)
Deep River,
Dyer,
Gibson's Station,
Hobart,
Lake Station,
Le Roy,
Lowell,
Merrillville,
Miller's Station,
Orchard Grove,
Ross,
Saint John,
Schererville,
Toleston,
West Creek,
Winfield.

LA PORTE COUNTY.

Callao,
Corymbo,
Crossing,
Door Village,
Hanna Station,
Haskell,
Kingsbury,
La Crosse,
La Porte,* (*c. h.*,)
Michigan City,*
Rolling Prairie,
Stillwell,
Union Mills,
Wanatah,
Westville.*

LAWRENCE COUNTY.

Avoca,
Bedford,* (*c. h.*,)
Bono,
Bryantsville,
Erie,
Fayetteville,
Fort Ritner,
Georgia,
Guthrie,
Heltonville,
Huron,
Leesville,
Mitchell,*
River Vale,
Silverville,
Springville,
Tunnelton.

MADISON COUNTY.

Alexandria,
Alfonte,
Anderson,* (*c. h.*,)
Chesterfield,
Elwood,
Fishersburgh,
Florida,
Forestville,
Frankton,
Huntsville,
Markleville,
Mercury,
Ovid,
Pendleton,*
Perkinsville,
Prospect,
Prosperity,
Rigdon,
Summitville,
Zinsburgh.

MARION COUNTY.

Acton,
Augusta Station,
Bridgeport,
Broad Ripple,
Castleton,
Clermont,
Cumberland,
Fall Creek,
Gallaudet,
Glenn's Valley,
INDIANAPOLIS,* (*c. h.*,)
James Switch,
Julietta,
Lawrence,
Oaklandon,
Southport,
Spring Valley,
Sunny Side,
Trader's Point,
Valley Mills,
Waynewood,
West Newton,
Woodbank.

* Money-order office.

Marshall County.

Argos,
Bourbon,
Bremen,
Inwood,
Marmont,
Maxinkuckee,
Plymouth,* (*c. h.*,)
Tippecanoetown,
Tyner City,
Walnut,
Walnut Hill.

Martin County.

Dover Hill,* (*c. h.*,)
Dye,
Keck's Church,
Loogootee,*
McCameron,
Mountain Spring,
Natchez,
Shoals,
Sitka,
South Martin,
Trinity Springs.

Miami County.

Allen,
Amboy,
Bennett's Switch,
Birmingham,
Bunker Hill,
Busaco,
Chili,
Courter,
Deedsville,
Denver,
Five Corners,
Gilead,
McGrawsville,
Mexico,
Miami,
Niconza,
North Grove,
Paw Paw,
Perrysburgh,
Peru,* (*c. h.*,)
Reserve,
Santa Fé,
Stockdale,
Wawpecong,
Wheatville,
Xenia.

Monroe County.

Bloomington,* (*c. h.*,)
Bryant's Creek,
Clear Creek,
Ellittsville,
Harrodsburgh,
Smithville,
Stanford,
Stinesville,
Unionville.

Montgomery County.

Alamo,
Ashby's Mills,
Boston Store,
Brown's Valley,
Clouser's Mills,
Crawfordsville,*(*c. h.*,)
Darlington,
Ladoga,*
Lane,
Linden,
Mace,
New Richmond,
New Ross,
Orth,
Parkersburgh,
Pleasant Hill,
Potato Creek,
Prairie Edge,
Shannondale,
Waveland,
Waynetown,
Wesley,
Whitesville.

Morgan County.

Alaska,
Brooklyn,
Centreton,
Eminence,
Hall,
Hyndsdale,
Landersdale,
Mahalasville,
Martinsville,* (*c. h.*,)
Monrovia,
Mooresville,
Morgantown,*
Paragon,
Red House,
Waverly.

Newton County.

Beaver City,
Brook,
Goodland,
Kentland,* (*c. h.*,)
Morocco,
Pilot Grove.

Noble County.

Albion, (*c. h.*,)
Avilla,
Brimfield,
Cromwell,
Green Centre,
Indian Village,
Kendallville,*
Ligonier,*
Lisbon,
Merriam,
Noble,
Rome City,
Swan,
Wawaka,
Wilmot,
Wolf Lake.

Ohio County.

Aberdeen,
Bear Branch,
Hartford,
Rising Sun, (*c. h.*)

Orange County.

Chambersburgh,
French Lick,
Greenbrier,
Leipsic,
Newton Stewart,
Orangeville,
Orleans,*
Paoli,* (*c. h.*,)
Rego,
Stamper's Creek,
Valeene,
West Baden,
Young's Creek.

Owen County.

Arney,
Atkinsonville,
Cataract,
Cuba,
Deem,
Farmer's Station,
Freedom,
Gosport,
Hausertown,
Jordan Village,
Patricksburgh,
Quincy,
Spencer,* (*c. h.*,)
Stockton,
Vandalia,
White Hall.

Parke County.

Annapolis,
Armiesburgh,
Bellmore,
Bethany,
Bloomingdale,
Bridgeton,
Bruin's Cross Roads,
Catlin,
Clinton Rock,
Coloma,
Delta,
Howard,
Jessup's Station,
Lusk's Springs,
Mansfield,
Montezuma,
Numa,
Parkville,
Portland Mills,
Rockville,* (*c. h.*,)
Rosedale,
Roseville,
Russell's Mills,
Sylvania,
Waterman.

Perry County.

Adyeville,
Cannelton,* (*c. h.*,)
Celina,
Derby,
Dexter,
Don Juan,
Doolittle's Mills,
Foster's Ridge,
Leopold,
Lilly Dale,
Mount Pleasant,
Oil Creek,
Ranger,
Rock Island,
Rome,
Rono,
Tell City,*
Troy.

* Money-order office.

Pike County.

Leoti,
Otwell,
Petersburgh,* (*c. h.*,)
Pikeville,
Spurgeon,
Union,
Winslow.

Porter County.

Boon Grove,
Chesterton,
Furnessville,
Hebron,
Kout's Station,
Porter's Cross Roads,
Porter Station,
Salt Creek,
Tassinong,
*Valparaiso**, (*c. h.*,)
Wheeler.

Posey County.

Black Hawk Mills,
Blairsville,
Cynthiana,
Farmersville,
Hickory Branch,
Mount Vernon,*(*c.h.*,)
New Harmony,*
Parker's Settlem'nt,
Poseyville,
Saint Wendells,
Stewartsville,
Wadesville.

Pulaski County.

Francesville,
Gundrum,
Medarysville,
Monterey,
Oak,
Pulaski,
Star City,
Winamac,* (*c. h.*,)

Putnam County.

Bainbridge,
Belle Union,
Cairo,
Carpentersville,
Cloverdale,
Fillmore,
Greencastle,* (*c. h.*,)
Groveland,
Hamrick's Station,
Manhattan,
Morton,
Mount Meridian,
New Maysville,
Putnamville,
Reelsville,
Russellville.

Randolph County.

Arba,
Balaka,
Bartonia,
Bloomingport,
Castle,
Cerro Gordo,
Deerfield,
Fairview,
Farmland,
Harrisville,
Losantville,
Lynn,
Neff,
New Pittsburgh,
Parker,
Randolph,
Ridgeville,
Saratoga,
Snow Hill,
Spartanburgh,
Trenton,
Union City,*
Winchester,* (*c. h.*,)
Windsor.

Ripley County.

Ballstown,
Batesville,
Benham's Store,
Cross Plains,
Delaware,
Elrod,
Friendship,
Hermaan,
Holton,
Milan,
Morris,
Napoleon,
New Marion,
North Hogan,

Ripley County—Continued.

Olean,
Osgood,*
Pierceville,
Poston,
Rei,
Rexville,
Spade's Depot,
Sunman,
Titusville,
Versailles,* (*c. h.*,)
Vine's Springs.

Rush County.

Beech Grove,
Carthage,
Falmouth,
Homer,
Manilla,
Milroy,
Moscow,
New Salem,
Raleigh,
Richland,
Rushville,* (*c. h.*,)
Star,
Steele's,
Sumner.

St. Joseph County.

Lakeville,
Mishawaka,*
New Carlisle,*
North Liberty,
Notre Dame,*
Oceola,
Richardson,
South Bend,* (*c. h.*,)
Sumption Prairie,
Terre Coupee,
Walkerton,
Woodland.

Scott County.

Afton,
Alpha,
Austin,
Holman Station,
Lexington,* (*c. h.*,)
Vienna,
Woostertown.

Shelby County.

Blue Ridge,
Boggstown,
Brookfield,
Conn's Creek,
Fairland,
Fenn's
Flat Rock,
Fountaintown,
Freeport,
Lewis Creek,
London,
Marietta,
Moral,
Morristown,
Mount Auburn,
Noah,
Prescott,
Ray's Crossing,
Shelbyville,* (*c. h.*,)
Smithland,
Sulphur Hill,
Winterroud.

Spencer County.

Buffaloville,
Dale,
Enterprise,
Fulda,
Gentryville,
Grand View,
Lake,
Mariah Hill,
Midway,
Newtonville,
Oakland,
Rockport,* (*c. h.*,)
Saint Meinrad,
Santa Claus.

Starke County.

Brandtwood,
English Lake,
Grover Town,
Hamlet,
Kankakee,
Knox,* (*c. h.*,)
Lake City,
North Bend,
North Judson,
San Pierre,
Toto.

* Money-order office.

STEUBEN COUNTY.

Alvarado,
Angola,* (*c. h.*,)
Clear Lake,
Crooked Creek,
Fish Creek,
Flint,
Fremont,
Hamilton,
Metz,
Nevada Mills,
Orland,*
Pleasant Lake,
Salem Centre,
Turkey Creek,
York Centre.

SULLIVAN COUNTY.

Ascension,
Bateham,
Carlisle,*
Graysville,
Merom,
New Lebanon,
Paxton's,
Pleasantville,
Shelburn,
Sullivan,* (*c. h.*,)
Turman's Creek.

SWITZERLAND COUNTY.

Bennington,
Centre Square,
Craig,
East Enterprise,
Florence,
Moorefield,
Mount Sterling,
North's Landing,
Patriot,
Pleasant,
Quercus Grove,
Sugar Branch,
Vevay,* (*c. h.*)

TIPPECANOE COUNTY.

Americus,
Ash Grove,
Battle Ground,
Chauncey,
Clark's Hill,
Colburn,
County Line,
Culver's Station,
Dayton,
Farmer's Institute,
Glen Hall,
La Fayette,* (*c. h.*,)
Monitor,
Montmorency,
Newton's Retreat,
Octagon,
Pettit,
Romney,
Shawnee Mound,
Stockwell,*
Sugar Grove,
Transitville,
West Point,
Wyandotte.

TIPTON COUNTY.

Curtisville,
Groomsville,
Jackson Station,
Nevada,
New Lancaster,
Normanda,
Sharpsville,
Tetersburgh,
Tipton,* (*c. h.*,)
West Kinderhook,
Windfall.

UNION COUNTY.

Beechy Mire,
Billingsville,
Brownsville,
Clifton,
Cottage Grove,
Dunlapsville,
Liberty,* (*c. h.*,)
Lotus,
Quakertown.

VANDERBURGH COUNTY.

Armstrong,
Evansville,* (*c. h.*,)
Inglefield,
Kasson,
McCutchanville,
Mechanicsville,

VANDERBURGH COUNTY—Continued.

Nash Depot,
Oakdam,
St. Joseph.

VERMILLION COUNTY.

Clinton,
Eugene,
Newport,* (*c. h.*,)
Perrysville,
Quaker Hill,
Saint Bernice,
Toronto.

VIGO COUNTY.

Burnett,
Cookerly,
Ellsworth,
Lewis,
Nelson,
New Goshen,
Pimento,
Prairie Creek,
Prairieton,
Riley,
Saint Mary's,
Sandford,
Seelyville,
Terre Haute,* (*c. h.*,)
Youngstown.

WABASH COUNTY.

America,
Belden,
Dora,
La Fontaine,
La Gro,
Laketon,
Liberty Mills,
Lincolnville,
Lodi,
New Holland,
New Madison,
North Manchester,*
Rich Valley,
Roann,
Somerset,
Urbana,
Wabash, (*c. h.**)

WARREN COUNTY.

Independence.
Marshfield,
Pine Village,
Poolsville,
Rainsville,
State Line, *
West Lebanon,*
Williamsport,* (*c. h.*)

WARRICK COUNTY.

Boonville,* (*c. h.*,)
Canal,
Crowville,
Elberfeld,
Ely,
Folsomville,
Lee,
Lynnville,
Newburgh,*
Polk Patch,
Wheatonville,
Yankeetown.

WASHINGTON COUNTY.

Beck's Mills,
Campbellsburgh,
Canton,
Chesnut Hill,
Claysville,
Farabee's Station,
Fredericksburgh.
Hardinsburgh,
Harristown,
Heffren,
Hitchcock's Station,
Kossuth,
Little York,
Livonia,
Martinsburgh,
Millport,
New Philadelphia,
Organ Spring,
Pekin,
Salem,* (*c. h.*,)
Saltilloville.

* Money-order office.

WAYNE COUNTY.

Abington,
Bethel,
Boston,
Cambridge City,*
Centreville, (*c. h.*,)
Chester,
Cox's Mills,
Dalton,
Dublin,*
East Germantown,
Economy,
Green's Fork,
Hagerstown,*
Jacksonburgh,
Milton,
New Garden,
Olive Hill,
Richmond,*
Webster,
White Water,
Williamsburgh.

WELLS COUNTY.

Barber's Mills,
Bluffton,* (*c. h.*,)
Fox,
Murray,
Nottingham,
Ossian,

WELLS COUNTY—Continued.

Reiffsburgh,
Vera Cruz,
Zanesville.

WHITE COUNTY.

Brookston,
Burnett's Creek,
Chalmers,
Flowerville,
Idaville,
Monon,
Monticello,* (*c. h.*,)
Reynolds,*
Seafield,
Wolcott.

WHITLEY COUNTY.

Alma,
Churubusco,
Coesse,
Collamer,
Columbia City,*(*c. h.*,)
Hecla,
Larwill,
Laud,
Saturn,
South Cleveland,
South Whitley,
Washington Centre.

INDIAN TERRITORY.

CHEROKEE NATION.

Coodey's Bluff,
Flint,
Fort Gibson,
McLean's Station,
Marble Salt Works,
Oseuma,
Tahlequah, (*c. h.*,)
Webber's Falls.

CHICKASAW NATION.

Carriage Point,
Fort Arbuckle,
Fort Washita,
Rock Spring,
Tishemingo.

CHOCTAW NATION.

Atoka,
Boggy Depot,

CHOCTAW NATION—Continued.

Brushey,
Buckluxy,
Choctaw Agency.
Doaksville,
Fort Sill,
Pryor's Creek,
Red Oak,
Spring Bluff,
Wheelock.

CREEK NATION.

Creek Agency,
Micco.
Okmulkee.

SEMINOLE NATION.

We-Wo-Ka.

IOWA.

ADAIR COUNTY.

Arbor Hill,
Casey.
Fontanelle,* (*c. h.*,)
Greenfield,
Hebron,
Holaday's,
Jackson,
Orient,
Stuart.

ADAMS COUNTY.

Carl,
Corning,
East Nodoway,
Mount Etna,
Nevinville,
Prescott,
Quincy,* (*c. h.*,)
Simpson.

ALLAMAKEE COUNTY.

Allamakee,
Clear Creek,

ALLAMAKEE COUNTY—Continued.

Dalby,
Dorchester,
Elon,
French Creek,
Harper's Ferry,
Ion,
Lansing,*
Ludlow,
Lycurgus,
Myron,
Postville,*
Rossville,
Union Prairie,
Village Creek,
Volney,
Waterville,
Waukon,* (*c. h.*)

APPANOOSE COUNTY.

Beetrace,
Caldwell,
Centerville,* (*c. h.*,)
Cincinnati,
Dennis,
Griffinsville,
Hibbsville,
Iconium,

* Money-order office.

APPANOOSE COUNTY—Continued.

Jerome,
Livingston,
Milledgeville,
Moravia,
Moulton,
Numa,
Orleans,
Tranquility,
Unionville,
Walnut City,
Wells' Mills.

AUDUBON COUNTY.

Exira, (*c. h.*,)
Hamlin Grove,
Oakfield.

BENTON COUNTY.

Belle Plaine,*
Benton Centre,
Blairstown, *
Burk,
Florence,
Luzerne,
Mount Auburn,
Paul,
Robin,
Shellsburgh,*
Spencer Grove,
Urbanna,
Vinton,* (*c. h.*)

BLACK HAWK COUNTY.

Barclay,
Blakeville,
Cedar Falls,*
Cedar Valley,
Enterprise,
Gilbertville,
Hudson,
Laporte City,
Lester,
Miller's Creek,
Nautrille,
Raymond,
Waterloo,* (*c. h.*)

BOONE COUNTY.

Boonesborough,*(*c.h.*,)
Casady's Corner,
Mackey's Grove,
Mineral Ridge,
Moingona,*
Montana,
Pilot Mound,
Prairie Hill,
Sweede Point,
Worth,
Yough.

BREMER COUNTY.

Buck Creek,
Denver,
Eagle,
Frederica,
Horton,
Jaynesville,*
Leroy,
Mentor,
Plainfield,
Spring Lake,
Sumner,
Tripoli,
Waverly,* (*c. h.*)

BUCHANAN COUNTY.

Atlanta,
Brandon,
Buffalo Grove,
Castleville,
Chatham,
Fairbank,
Hazelton,
Independence,* (*c. h.*,)
Jessup,
Kier,
Middlefield,
Newtonville,
Otterville,
Quasqueton,
Sunny Side,
Ward's Corners,
Winthrop.

BUENA VISTA COUNTY.

Sargentsville,
Sioux Rapids,
Storm Lake.

BUTLER COUNTY.

Aplington,
Boylan's Grove,
Butler Centre, (*c. h.*,)
Clarksville,
Elm Springs,
New Hartford,
Parkersburgh,
Shell Rock,
Swanton,
Union Ridge,
Willoughby.

CALHOUN COUNTY.

Lake City, (*c. h.*,)
Pomeroy,
Twin Lakes,
Yatesville.

CARROLL COUNTY.

Browning,
Carroll City,
Carrollton, (*c. h.*,)
Coon Rapids,
Glidden,
Mack's.

CASS COUNTY.

Anita,
Atlantic,*
Edna,
Grove City,
Lewis,* (*c. h.*,)
Whitneyville.

CEDAR COUNTY.

Cedar Bluff,
Cessford,
Clarence,*
Downey,
Durant,*
Gower's Ferry,
Inland,
Lowden,*
Massillon,
Mechanicsville,*
Pedee,
Pleasant Hill,
Red Oak,
Rochester,
Spring Dale,
Stanwood,
Tipton,* (*c. h.*,)
West Branch,
York Prairie,
Zoar.

CERRO GORDO COUNTY.

Clear Lake,
Geneseo,
Lime Creek,
Mason City,* (*c. h.*,)
Owen's Grove,
Plymouth,
Rock,
Shell Rock Falls

CHEROKEE COUNTY.

Aurelia,
Cherokee,* (*c. h.*,)
Hazard,
Pilot Rock,
Washta.

CHICKASAW COUNTY.

Bradford,
Chickasaw, (*c. h.*,)
Deerfield,
Fredericksburgh,
Ionia,
Jacksonville,
Lawler,
Little Turkey,
Nashua,*
New Hampton,
North Washington,
Stapleton,
Williamstown.

CLARKE COUNTY.

Green Bay,
Hopeville,
Lacelle,
Liberty,
Murray,
Nortonville,
Oceola,* (*c. h.*,)
Ottawa,
Prairie Grove,
Smyrna.

* Money-order office

Clay County.

Annieville.
Douglas Centre,
Gillett's Grove,
Peterson, (*c. h.*,)
Spencer.

Clayton County.

Ceres,
Clayton,
Communia,
Council Hill,
Cox's Creek,
Elkader,* (*c. h.*,)
Elkport,
Farmersburgh,
Garnavillo,*
Gem,
Giard,
Guttenberg,*
Hardin,
Highland,
Little Port,
Luana,
McGregor,*
Mederville,
Millville,
Monona,
National,
North McGregor,
Read,
Saint Sebald,
Sigel,
Strawberry Point,*
Volga City,
Wagner,
Yankee Settlement.

Clinton County.

Boon Spring,
Brookfield,
Buena Vista,
Burgess,
Calmus,
Camanche,
Charlotte,
Clinton,*
De Witt,* (*c. h.*,)
Elk River,
Elvira,
Grand Mound,
Low Moor,
Lyons,*
Malone,
Orange,
Ten-mile House,
Toronto,
Welton,
Wheatland.*

Crawford County.

Boyer River,
Crawford,
Denison, (*c. h.*,)
West Side.

Dallas County.

Adel,* (*c. h.*,)
Boone,
Dallas Centre,
De Soto,*
Dexter,*
Greenvale,
Linden,
Minburn,
Nordyk,
Perry,
Redfield,
Snyder,
Van Metre,
Waukee Station,
Xenia.

Davis County.

Albany,
Bloomfield,* (*c. h.*,)
Brown's Mills,
Chequist,
Drakesville,
Floris,
Monterey,
Oak Spring,
Pulaski,
Savannah,
Stiles,
Troy,
West Grove.

Decatur County.

Davis City,
Decatur,
Elk,
Franklin,

Dacatur County—Continued.

Garden Grove,
Green Valley,
High Point,
Leon,* (*c. h.*,)
Long Creek,
New Buda,
Patriot,
Pleasanton,
Sedgewick,
Spring Valley,
Terre Haute,
Westerville.

Delaware County.

Almoral,
Barryville,
Campton,
Colesburgh,
Delaware,
Delhi, (*c. h.*,)
Earlville,
Forestville,
Golden Prairie,
Greeley,
Hazle Green,
Hopkinton,*
Manchester,*
Masonville,
Milo,
Mount Hope,
Sand Spring,
Tower Hill,
Uniontown,
York.

Des Moines County.

Augusta,
Burlington,* (*c. h.*,)
Danville,
Dodgeville,
Franklin Mills,
Huron,
Kingston,
Kossuth,
Latty,
La Vega,
Linton,
Middletown,
Northfield,
Parrish,
Pleasant Grove,
South Flint,
Sperry.

Dickinson County.

Milford,
Spirit Lake, (*c. h.*)

Dubuque County.

Allison,
Ballyclough,
Bankston,
Cascade,
Cottage Hill,
Dubuque,* (*c. h.*,)
Durango,
Dyersville,*
Epworth,
Farley,
Fillmore,
King,
Lattner's,
Melleray,
New Vienna,
Ogden,
Peosta,
Pin Oak,
Rickardsville,
Rock Dale,
Sheffield,
Sherrill's Mount,
Tivoli,
Worthington,
Zwingle.

Emmett County.

Armstrong's Grove,
Emmett,
Estherville, (*c. h.*,)
High Lake.

Fayette County.

Bethel,
Brush Creek,
Clermont,*
Douglass,
Eden,
El Dorado,
Elgin,
Fayette,*
Hawk Eye,
Illyria,
Lima,
Mill,

* Money-order office.

FAYETTE COUNTY—Continued.

Oran,
Otsego,
Putnam,
Richfield,
Scott Centre,
Seaton,
Taylorsville,
Wardena,
Waucoma,
West Union,* (*c. h.*,)
Wilson Grove.

FLOYD COUNTY.

Charles City,* (*c. h.*,)
Floyd,
Hackberry,
Howardville,
Marble Rock,
Nora Springs,
Rockford,
Rock Grove City,
Rudd,
Ulster,
Watertown.

FRANKLIN COUNTY.

Chapin,
Coldwater,
Geneva,
Hampton,* (*c. h.*,)
Ingham,
Maysville,
Menzie,
Oakland Valley,
Otisville,
Shobe's Grove,
Washburn.

FREMONT COUNTY.

Bartlett,
Eastport,
Hamburgh,
High Creek,
Manti,
Percival,
Plum Hollow,
Sidney,* (*c. h.*,)
Tabor,*
Walnut Creek.

GREENE COUNTY.

Grand Junction,
Jefferson,* (*c. h.*,)
Northville,
Rippey,
Scranton Station.

GRUNDY COUNTY.

Grundy Centre, (*c. h.*,)
Lincoln Centre,
Wadiloup.

GUTHRIE COUNTY.

Bear Grove,
Dale City,
Dalmanutha,
Dodge,
Guthrie,
Guthrie Centre,
Moffitt's Grove,
Panora,* (*c. h.*)

HAMILTON COUNTY.

Blairsburgh,
Homer,
Hook's Point,
Lakin's Grove,
Randall,
Rose Grove,
Webster City,* (*c. h.*,)
Williams.

HANCOCK COUNTY.

Concord,
Crystal Lake,
Ellington, (*c. h.*,)
Upper Grove.

HARDIN COUNTY.

Ackley,*
Alden,
Berlin,
Cottage,
Delanti,
Eldora,* (*c. h.*,)
Hardin City,
Iowa Falls,*
New Providence,
Point Pleasant,
Steamboat Rock,
Tipton Grove,
Union.

HARRISON COUNTY.

Calhoun,
Dunlap,
Harris Grove,
Little Sioux,
Logan,
Magnolia,* (*c. h.*,)
Missouri Valley,*
Modale,
Mondamin,
Reeder's Mills,
Saint John,
Unionburgh,
Whitesborough,
Woodbine,
Yazoo.

HENRY COUNTY.

Boyleston,
Cotton Grove,
Hillsborough,
Lowell,
Marshall,
Mt. Pleasant,* (*c. h.*,)
New London,*
Oakland Mills,
Rome,
Salem,*
Swedesburgh,
Trenton,
Wayne,
Winfield,
Winona.

HOWARD COUNTY.

Busti,
Chester,
Cresco,*
Foreston,
Glen Roy,
Howard Centre,
Lime Spring,
New Oregon,* (*c. h.*,)
Pond Valley,
Saratoga.

HUMBOLDT COUNTY.

Addison,
Dakotah, (*c. h.*,)
Humboldt,
Lott's Creek,
Rutland,
Springvale,
Viona,
Wacousta.

IDA COUNTY.

Ida, (*c. h.*,)
Willow Dale.

IOWA COUNTY.

Boltonville,
Foote,
Genoa Bluff,
Homestead,*
Koszta,
Ladore,
Lytle City,
Marengo,* (*c. h.*,)
Millersburgh,
North English,
Rest,
Stelapolis,
Victor,*
York Centre.

JACKSON COUNTY.

Andrew, (*c. h.*,)
Bellevue,*
Bridgeport,
Canton,
Cottonville,
Farmer's Creek,
Fulton,
Garry Owen,

* Money-order office.

JACKSON COUNTY—Continued.

Higginsport,
Iron Hills,
La Motte,
Maquoketa,*
Mill Rock,
Monmouth,
Mount Algor,
Otter Creek,
Ozark,
Sabula,*
Saint Donatus,
Spragueville,
Spring Brook,
Sterling,
Union Centre,
Van Buren,
Wickliffe.

JASPER COUNTY.

Amboy,
Clyde,
Colfax,
Galesburgh,
Greencastle,
Horn,
Jasper City,
Lynnville,
Monroe,*
Newton,* (*c. h.*,)
Prairie City,*
Sugar Creek,
Vandalia,
Warren Grove.

JEFFERSON COUNTY.

Abingdon,
Baker,
Botavia,
Brookville,
Fairfield,* (*c. h.*,)
Germanville,
Glasgow,
Glendale,
Harvey's Mills,
Libertyville,
Lockridge,
Merrimac,
Pleasant Plain,
Salina,
Wooster.

JOHNSON COUNTY.

Amish,
Belle Air,
Bon Accord,
Chase,
Copi,
Coralville,
Danforth,
Frank Pierce,
Iowa City,* (*c. h.*,)
Newport,
North Liberty,
Oasis,
Oxford,
Palestine,
Seventy-eight,
Shueyville,
Solon,
Tiffin,
Windham.

JONES COUNTY.

Anamosa,* (*c. h.*,)
Bowen's Prairie,
Castle Grove,
Clayford,
Clay Mills,
Edinburgh,
Fairview,
Grove Creek,
Highland Grove,
Johnson,
Langworthy,
Madison,
Monticello,*
Oxford Mills,
Scotch Grove,
Walnut Fork,
Wyoming.*

KEOKUK COUNTY.

Aurora,
Baden,
Butler,
Chandaller,
Coal Creek,
Creswell,
Garibaldi,
Hayesville,
Ioka,
Lancaster,
Manhattan,
Martinsburgh,
Richland,*
Sigourney,* (*c. h.*,)
South English,
Springfield,
Talleyrand,
Webster,
What Cheer,
White Pigeon.

KOSSUTH COUNTY.

Algona,* (*c. h.*,)
Buffalo Fork,
Darien,
Greenwood Centre,
Irvington,
Kossuth Centre,
Seneca.

LEE COUNTY.

Belfast,
Big Mound,
Camackville,
Charleston,
Clay's Grove,
Croton,
Denmark,*
Dover,
Fort Madison,* (*c. h.*,)
Franklin Centre,
Jeffersonville,
Jollyville,
Keokuk,*
Montrose,
New Boston,
Pilot Grove,
Primrose,
Saint Paul,
Sandusky,
Summitville,
Vincennes,
Warren,
West Point.

LINN COUNTY.

Bertram,
Cedar Rapids,*
Central City,
Centre Point,
Dry Creek,
Fairfax,
Flemingville,
La Fayette,
Lisbon,*
Marion,* (*c. h.*,)
Mount Vernon,*
Nugent's Grove,
Palo,
Paris,
Prairieburgh,
Prospect Hill,
Rural,
Spring Grove,
Springville,
Troy Mills,
Valley Farm,
Viola,
Waubeck,
Western College,
West Prairie.

LOUISA COUNTY.

Cairo,
Clifton,
Columbus City,*
Fredonia,
Grand View,
Letts,
Mid Prairie,
Morning Sun,
Palo Alto,
Port Allen,
Port Louisa,
Toolsborough,
Virginia Grove,
Wapello,* (*c. h.*)

LUCAS COUNTY.

Argo,
Belinda,
Chariton,* (*c. h.*,)
Earle,
Freedom,
Henderson,
La Grange,
Last Chance,
Lucas,
Milan,
Norwood,
Ola,
Russell,
Tallahoma,
White Breast.

LYONS COUNTY.

Gibralter.

MADISON COUNTY.

Clanton,
Earlham,
Ellsworth,
Kasson,
Middle River,
Ohio,
Peru,
Pleasant View,
Saint Charles,
Venus,
Winterset,* (*c. h.*)

* Money-order office.

MAHASKA COUNTY.

Agricola,
Auburn,
Beacon,
Belle Fountain,
Buck Horn,
Eveland Grove,
Farmersville,
Ferry,
Flint,
Fremont,
Givin,
Granville,
Hopewell,
Indianapolis,
Leighton,
New Sharon,
Oskaloosa,* (*c. h.*,)
Peoria,
Union Mills,
White Oak.

MARION COUNTY.

Attica,
Caloma,
Columbia,
Dallas,
English Settlement,
Gosport,
Hamilton,
Iola,
Knoxville,* (*c. h.*,)
Marysville,
Newbern,
Otley,
Pella,*
Pleasantville,
Red Rock,
Star,
Wheeling.

MARSHALL COUNTY.

Albion,
Bangor,
Biven's Grove,
Edenville,
Illinois Grove,
Lamoille,
Laurel,
Le Grand,
Liscomb,
Marietta,
Marshalltown,* (*c. h.*,)
Minerva,
Quarry,
Stanford,
State Centre,
Timber Creek,
Vienna.

MILLS COUNTY.

Benton,
Emerson,
Glenwood,* (*c. h.*,)
Haynie,
Hillsdale,
Junction City,
Milton Station,
Pacific City,
Wahaghbonsy,
White Cloud.

MITCHELL COUNTY.

Brownville,
Cardiff,
Doran,
Little Cedar,
Meroa,
Mitchell,* (*c. h.*,)
Mona,
Newburgh,
Orchard,
Osage,
Otranto,
Riceville,
Rock Creek,
Saint Ansgar,
Staceyville,
Wentworth,
West Mitchell.

MONONA COUNTY.

Arcola,
Belvidere,
Castana,
Grant Centre,
Maple Landing,
Mapleton,
Onawa City,* (*c. h.*,)
St. Clair,
Ticonic,
West Fork.

MONROE COUNTY.

Albia,* (*c. h.*,)
Coalton,
East Melrose,
Fredric,
Georgetown,
Half Way Prairie,
Lovilia,
Osprey,
Tyrone,
Urbanna City,
Weller.

MONTGOMERY COUNTY.

Frankfort,
Grant,
Red Oak Junction,* (*c. h.*,)
Sciola,
Stanton,
Villisca,
Wilson.

MUSCATINE COUNTY.

Atalissa,
Conesville,
Fairport,
Lacey,
Melpine,
Moscow,
Muscatine,* (*c. h.*,)
Pike,
Pine Mills,
Pleasant Prairie,
Prairie Mills,
Summit,
Sweetland Centre,
West Liberty,*
Wilton Junction.*

O'BRIEN COUNTY.

O'Brien, (*c. h.*)

PAGE COUNTY.

Braddyville,
Centre,
Clarinda,* (*c. h.*,)
College Springs,
Franklin Grove,
Hawleysville,
Nodaway Mills,
Page City,
Tarkio,
Union Grove,
Wellsburgh.

PALO ALTO COUNTY.

Black Walnut,
Ellenton,
Emmittsburgh, (*c. h.*,)
Fern Valley,
Great Oak,
Rush Lake,
Soda Bar,
West Bend.

PLYMOUTH COUNTY.

Hinton,
Lemars,
Plymouth Centre,(*c. h.*)

POCAHONTAS COUNTY.

Lizzard,
Rolfe, (*c. h.*)

POLK COUNTY.

Adelphi,
Altoona,
Avon,
Commerce Mills,
DES MOINES, (*c. h.*,)
Elkhart,
Greenwood,
Lincoln,
Mitchellville,
Peoria City,
Polk City,
Ridgedale,
Rising Sun,
Saylorsville.

* Money-order office.

POTTAWATTAMIE COUNTY.

Avoca,
Big Grove,
Council Bluffs,* (*c.h.*,)
Crescent City,
Honey Creek,
Loveland,
Macedonia,
Neola,
Walnut Creek Sta'n,
Waveland,
Wheeler's Grove.

POWESHIEK COUNTY.

Blue Point,
Brooklyn,*
Deep River,
Forest Home,
Grinnell,*
Malcom,*
Mill Grove,
Montezuma,* (*c. h.*,)
Sherman,
Tyro,
West Brooklyn.

RINGGOLD COUNTY.

Caledonia,
Cross,
Estella,
Eugene,
Ingart Grove,
Mount Ayr,* (*c. h.*,)
Redding,
Ringgold,
Union Hill.

SAC COUNTY.

Grant City,
Sac City, (*c. h.*)

SCOTT COUNTY.

Allen's Grove,
Amity,
Big Rock,
Blue Grass,
Buffalo,
Davenport,* (*c. h.*,)
Dixon,
Gilbert,
Le Claire,*
Mount Joy,
New Hamburgh,
New Liberty,
Pleasant Valley,
Princeton,
Round Grove,
Walnut Grove,
Wolcott.

SHELBY COUNTY.

Altamont,
Botany,
Elk Horn,
Harlan, (*c. h.*,)
Manteno,
Shelby.

SIOUX COUNTY.

Calliope, (*c. h.*,)
Irene.

STORY COUNTY.

Ames,
Cambridge,
Colo,
Iowa Centre,
Nevada,* (*c. h.*,)
Ontario,
Roland,
Story City.

TAMA COUNTY.

Badger Hill,
Bovina,
Buckingham,*
Butlerville,
Chelsea,
Crystal,
Dryden,
Ettie,
Evergreen,
Fifteen Mile Grove,
Helena,
Orford,

TAMA COUNTY—Continued.

Spring Creek,
Tama City,
Toledo,* (*c. h.*,)
Vineyard,
Waltham,
West Irving.
Wolf Creek.

TAYLOR COUNTY.

Bedford,* (*c. h.*,)
Gravity,
Harmony,
Holt,
Memory,
Ovid,
Platt,
Platteville,
Siam.

UNION COUNTY.

Afton,* (*c. h.*,)
Creston,
Cromwell,
Thayer,
Tingley,
Union City.

VAN BUREN COUNTY.

Benton's Port,
Birmingham, *
Bonaparte,*
Doud Station,
Farmington,*
Hickory,
Home,
Iowaville,
Keosauqua,* (*c. h.*,)
Kilbourn,
Lebanon,
Milton,
Mount Sterling,
Mount Zion,
Niles,
Oak Point,
Pierceville,
Pittsburgh,
Sheridan,
Upton,
Utica,
Vernon,
Winchester.

WAPELLO COUNTY.

Agency City,*
Alpine,
Ashland,
Bladensburgh,
Blakesburgh,
Chillicothe,
Christiansburgh,
Competine,
Comstock,
Coopersville,
Dahlonega,
Dudley,
Eddyville, *
Happy Hollow,
Highland Centre,
Kirkville,
Munterville,
Ormanville,
Ottumwa,* (*c. h.*,)
Port Richmond,
Williamsburgh.

WARREN COUNTY.

Bellemont,
Carlisle,
Fort Plain,
Hammondsburgh,
Hartford,
Indianola,* (*c. h.*,)
Lacona,
Lawrenceburgh,
Liberty Centre,
Lynn,
Medora,
New Virginia,
Norwalk,
Palmyra,
Rose Mount,
Sandyville,
Sharon,
Summerset.

WASHINGTON COUNTY.

Ainsworth,
Brighton,*
Clay,
Crawfordsville,
Dairy,
Dutch Creek,

* Money-order office.

WASHINGTON COUNTY—Continued.

Lexington,
Middleburgh,
Richmond,
Seventy-six Center,
Valley,
Washington,* (*c. h.*,)
Wassonville,
Yatton.

WAYNE COUNTY.

Bethlehem,
Cambria,
Clio,
Confidence,
Corydon,* (*c. h.*,)
Genoa,
Grand River,
Kniffin,
Lewisburgh,
New York,
Promise City,
Selma,
Warsaw.

WEBSTER COUNTY.

Border Plains,
Carbon,
Duncombe,
Fort Dodge,* (*c. h.*,)
Greenside,
Hesperian,
Otho,
Tyson's Mills,
West Dayton.

WINNEBAGO COUNTY.

Benson Grove,
Forest City, (*c. h.*,)
Lake Mills.

WINNESHIEK COUNTY.

Bluffton,
Burr Oak,
Calmar,*
Canoe,

WINNESHEIK COUNTY—Continued.

Castalia,
Counover,*
Decorah,* (*c. h.*,)
Festina,
Fort Atkinson,
Frankville,
Freeport,
Hesper,
Locust Lane,
Navau,
New Alba,
Old Mission,
Ossian,*
Plymouth Rock,
Ridgeway,
Spillville,
Springwater,
Twin Spring,
Woodville.

WOODBURY COUNTY.

Correctionville,
Oto,
Sergeant Bluffs,
Sioux City,* (*c. h.*,)
Sloan,
Smithland,
Wolfdale.

WORTH COUNTY.

Bristol,
Fertile,
Hartland,
Northwood, (*c. h.*,)
Silver Lake,
Wales,
Westfield.

WRIGHT COUNTY.

Bach Grove,
Belmond,
Clarion, (*c. h.*,)
Eagle Grove,
Empire,
Fryeburgh,
Goldfield,
Luni.
Woolstock.

KANSAS.

ALLEN COUNTY.

Carlyle,
Elsinore,
Geneva,
Humboldt,*
Iola,* (*c. h.*,)
Jeddo,
Ozark.

ANDERSON COUNTY.

Central City,
Delmont,
Elizabethtown,
Emerald,
Garnett,* (*c. h.*,)
Greeley,
Mineral Point,
Scipio.

ATCHISON COUNTY.

Arington,
Atchison,* (*c. h.*,)
Eden,
Effingham,
Farmington,
Huron,
Kennekuk,
Lancaster,
Locust Grove,
Monrovia,
Mount Pleasant,
Muscotah,
Pardee,
Oak Mills,
Saint Nicholas.

BOURBON COUNTY.

Appleton,
Barnesville,
Dayton,
Fort Lincoln,
Fort Scott,* (*c. h.*,)
Glendale,
Mapleton,
Marmiton,
Mill Creek,
Mount Sterling,
Osaga,
Pawnee,
Rockford,
Sharlow,
Turkey Creek,
Walnut Hill,
Xenia.

BROWN COUNTY.

Buncomb,
Carson,
Claytonville,
Fairview,
Grand Prairie,
Hamlin,
Hiawatha,* (*c. h.*,)
Marak,
Padonia,
Robinson,
Tyler's,
Ununda.

BUTLER COUNTY.

Augusta,
Chelsea,
Douglass,
El Dorado, (*c. h.*,)
Four Mile,
Plum Grove,
Quito,
Rosalia,

* Money-order office.

Butler County—Continued.

Sycamore Springs,
Towanda,
Wah Wah,
Walnut.

Chase County.

Bazaar,
Cedar Point,
Cottonwood Falls,* (c. h.,)
Matfield Green,
Middle Creek,
Silver Creek,
Toledo,
Union.

Cherokee County.

Baxter Springs,*
Checo,
Cherokee Mound,
Columbus,* (c. h.,)
Fly Creek,
Keelville,
Lewiston,
Lostine,
Neutral City,
Pleasant View,
Sanfordville,
Sherman City,
Spring River Falls,
Wirtonia.

Clay County.

Clay Centre, (c. h.,)
Deep Creek,
Fayetteville,
Gatesville,
Lima,
Madura,
Otter Creek,
Republican City,
Riverdale,
Rosevale,
Wakefield.

Cloud County.

Arion,
Clyde,
Concordia, (c. h.,)
Glasco,
Lake Sibley,
Lawrenceburgh,
Red Stone,
Shirley.

Coffey County.

Avon,
Burlington,* (c. h.,)
Corona,
Fredericktown,
Le Roy,*
Ottumwa,
Sidney.

Cowley County.

Arkansas City,
Dexter,
Jeffersonville,
Lone Tree,
Rock,
Winfield, (c. h.)

Crawford County.

Arcadia,
Base Line,
Cato,
Cherokee,
Crawfordsville,
Farlington,
Girard,* (c. h.,)
Hamilton,
Hopefield,
Idell,
Iowa City,
Monmouth,
Mulberry Grove,
Stevenstown,
Walnut Creek.

Davis County.

Alida,
Fort Riley,
Junction City,* (c. h.)

Dickinson County.

Abilene, (c. h.,)
Aroma,
Chapman's Creek,
Detroit,
Lyona.

Doniphan County.

Doniphan,
Elwood,
Geary,
Highland,
Iowa Point,
La Fayette,
Normanville,
Palermo,
Saint Benedict,
Severance,
Troy,* (c. h.,)
Wathena,*
White Cloud.*

Douglas County.

Baldwin City,*
Belvoir,
Big Springs,
Black Jack,
Clinton,
Eudora,
Hesper,
Holling,
Jefferson,
Kanwaka,
Lawrence,* (c. h.,)
Lecompton,
Marion,
Prairie City,
Sigel,
Twin Mound,
Vinland,
Willow Springs.

Ellis County.

Ellis,
Hays City, (c. h.)

Ellsworth County.

Ellsworth,* (c. h.,)
Fort Harker.

Franklin County.

Appanoose,
Berea,
Centropolis,
Forest Home,
Greenwood,
Lane,
Norwood,
Ottawa,* (c. h.,)
Peoria,
Ponoma,
Princeton,
Richmond,
Williamsburgh.

Greenwood County.

Belle Grove,
Eureka,* (c. h.,)
Fame,
Homer Creek,
Janesville,
Madison,
Quincy,
Twin Falls,
Verdigris Falls,
Virgil.

Howard County.

Caney,
Cedar Vale,
Elk Falls, (c. h.,)
Howard,
Longton,
Painterhood,
Peru,
Salt Springs.

Jackson County.

Banner,
Circleville,
Holton,* (c. h.,)
James' Crossing,
Netawaka,
New Eureka,
North Cedar,
Ontario,
Smithland,
South Cedar,
Whiting.

* Money-order office.

JEFFERSON COUNTY.

Chester,
Cook's Ford,
Grantville,
Grasshopper Falls,*
Grove City,
Medina,
Mount Florence,
Newman,
*Oskaloosa,** (*c. h.,*)
Ozawkie,
Perry,
Plum Creek,
Scott Land,
Williamstown,
Winchester.

JEWELL COUNTY.

Jewell,
Vicksburgh.

JOHNSON COUNTY.

Aubrey,
De Soto,
Gardner,
Glenn,
Lanesfield,
Lenexa,
Monticello,
Ocheltree,
*Olathe,** (*c. h.,*)
Shawnee,
Shawnee Mission,
Spring Hill.

LABETTE COUNTY.

Big Hill,
Chetopah,*
Clymore,
Creswell,
Daytonville,
Dora,
Elston,
Labette,
Mendota,
Montana,
Mound Valley,
*Oswego,** (*c. h.,*)
Ripon,
Timber Hill.

LEAVENWORTH COUNTY.

Delaware City,
Dimon,
Easton,
Fairmount,
Fort Leavenworth,
Glenwood,
Hoge,
Kickapoo City,
*Leavenworth City,**(*c.h.,*)
Lenape,
Petersburgh,
Pleasant Ridge,
Reno,
Springdale,
Stanwood,
Stranger,
Tonganoxie.

LINCOLN COUNTY.

Elkhorn,
Lincoln Centre,
Red Rock.

LINN COUNTY.

Barnard,
Blooming Grove,
Blue Mounds,
Brooklyn,
Centreville,
Coal Centre,
Farlinville,
Jackson,
La Cygne,
Mansfield,
*Mound City,** (*c. h.,*)
Oakwood,
Pleasanton,*
Springfield,
Twin Springs.

LYON COUNTY.

Allen,
Americus,
Bunker Hill,
Cross,
Eagle Creek,
Elmendaro,

LYON COUNTY—Continued.

*Emporia,** (*c. h.,*)
Forest Hill,
Fremont,
Harrisburgh,
Hartford,
Line,
Neosho Rapids,
Patty's Mill,
Plymouth,
Reading,
Rock Creek,
Waterloo,
Waushara.

MCPHERSON COUNTY.

Gypsum Creek,
Hyco,
Lake Village,
Lindsborg,
Sweadel, (*c. h.*)

MARION COUNTY.

Antelope,
Bethel,
Doyle,
Lincolnville,
Marion Centre, (*c. h.*)

MARSHALL COUNTY.

Barrett,
Blue Rapids,
Elisabeth,
Frankfort,
Guittard Station,
Heaslyville,
Irving,*
*Marysville,** (*c. h.,*)
Saint Bridget,
Waterville,*
Wyoming.

MIAMI COUNTY.

Fontania,
Hillsdale,
Miami Village,
Mount Nebo,
New Lancaster,
Osawatomie,*
*Paola,** (*c. h.,*)
Rockville,
Saint Louis,
Stanton,
Tontzville.

MITCHELL COUNTY.

Asherville,
Beloit,
Cawker City,
Glen Elder,
Solomon Rapids.

MONTGOMERY COUNTY.

Cherryville,
Coffeyville,
Elk City,
Independence,
Liberty,
Montgomery,
Morgan,
Parker,
Radical City,
Saint Paul,
Westralia.

MORRIS COUNTY.

*Council Grove,** (*c. h.,*)
Diamond Springs,
Hill Spring,
La Grange,
Parkersville,
Skiddy.

NEMAHA COUNTY.

Albany,
America City,
Capioma,
Centralia,
Clear Creek,
Corning,
Granada,
Neuchatel,
Sabetha,
*Seneca,** (*c. h.,*)
Vermillion,
Wetmore.

* Money-order office.

Neosho County.

Big Labette.
Canville,
Cremona,
Erie,* (*c. h.*,)
Flat Rock,
Jacksonville,
Ladore,
New Chicago,
Newport,
Orcuttville,
Osage Mission,*
Osborn,
Palo Alto,
Prairie du Chien,
Rochester,
Roger's Mills,
Rose Hill,
Tioga,
Urbana,
Valley City.

Osage County.

Arvonia,
Burlingame,* (*c. h.*,)
Carbondale,
Lindale,
Lyndon,
Melvern,
Michigan Valley,
Osage City,
Olivet,
Quenemo,
Richardson,
Ridgeway,
Trust,
Valley Brook,
Wilmington.

Ottawa County.

Bennington,
Churchill,
Coal Creek,
Delphos,
Grover,
Lindsey, (*c. h.*,)
Minneapolis,
Sumnerville,
Windsor.

Pawnee County.

Fort Larned.

Pottawatomie County.

Adam's Peak,
Leghorn,
Louisville, (*c. h.*,)
Myers' Valley,
Nancy,
Otter Lake,
Pleasant Run,
Saint George,
Saint Mary's Miss'n,
Savannah,
Spring Side,
Vienna,
Wamego,*
Westmoreland.

Republic County.

Belleville,
Cuba,
Gomeria,
New Scandinavia,
Salt Marsh, (*c. h.*,)
White Rock.

Riley County.

Big Timber,
Manhattan,* (*c. h.*,)
Milford,
Ogden,
Parallel,
Randolph,
Riley Centre,
Timber Creek,
Vinton,
Wild Cat.

Saline County.

Brookville,
Falun,
Honek,
Pliny,

Saline County—Continued.

Salina,* (*c. h.*,)
Saline Valley,
Solomon City.

Sedgwick County.

Cosmosa,
Sedgwick,
Wichita, (*c. h.*)

Shawnee County.

Auburn,
Dover,
Eugene,
Richland,
Rossville,
Silver Lake,
Tecumseh,
Topeka,* (*c. h.*,)
Wah Wah Suk,
Wakarusa.
Waveland.

Wabaunsee County.

Alma, (*c. h.*,)
Bismarck,
Eskridge,
Exonville,
Grant,
Harveyville,
Mission Creek,
Newbury,
Wabaunsee.

Wallace County.

Fort Wallace,
Grinnell,
Phil Sheridan, (*c. h.*)

Washington County.

Ballard's Falls,
Butler,
Chepstow,
Clifton,
Donald,
Erin,
Haddam,
Hanover,
Joy Creek,
Limestone,
Washington, (*c. h.*)

Wilson County.

Altoona,
Buffalo,
Clarke,
Coyville,
Fredonia, (*c. h.*,)
Greystone,
Guilford,
Neodesha,
New Albany,
Verdi.*

Woodson County.

Belmont,
Byron,
Chellis,
Cherry Creek,
Coloma,
Hazelettville,
Miller's Grove,
Neosho Falls,* (*c. h.*,)
Rose,
Toronto.

Wyandotte County.

Conner's Station,
Edwardsville,
Glen Park,
Nearman,
Pomeroy,
Quindaro,
White Church,
Wyandotte,* (*c. h.*)

* Money-order office.

KENTUCKY.

ADAIR COUNTY.

Breeding's,
Cane Valley,
Casey Creek,
Columbia, (*c. h.*,)
Glen's Fork,
Gradyville,
Milltown,
Montpelier,
Neatsville.

ALLEN COUNTY.

Allen Springs,
Butlersville,
Gainsville,
Mount Aerial,
Scottsville, (*c. h.*)

ANDERSON COUNTY.

Coldwell's Store,
Lawrenceburgh, (*c. h.*,)
Ripyville,
Rough and Ready.

BALLARD COUNTY.

Blandville, (*c. h.*,)
Hazlewood,
Hinkleville,
Lovelaceville,
Milburn,
Ogden's Landing.

BARREN COUNTY.

Cave City,
Coral Hill,
Dry Fork,
Eighty-eight,
Elbow Spring,
Freedom
Glasgow,* (*c. h.*,)
Glasgow Junction,
Hiseville,
Nobob,
Park,
Roseville,
Slick Rock,
Temple Hill,
Tracy,

BATH COUNTY.

Bethel,
Costigon,
Little Flat,
Marshall,
Olympian Springs,
Owingsville, (*c. h.*,)
Peeled Oak,
Sharpsburgh,
Wyoming.

BOONE COUNTY.

Bullitsville,
Burlington, (*c. h.*,)
Constance,
Florence,
Grant,
Hamilton,
Hebron,
Petersburgh,
Union,
Verona,
Walton.

BOURBON COUNTY.

Centreville,
Clintonville,
Flat Rock,
Houston,
Hutchison's,
Lowe's Station,
Millersburgh,
North Middletown,
Paris,* (*c. h.*,)
Ruddel's Mills,
Shawhan,
Stoney Point.

BOYD COUNTY.

Ashton,
Bolt's Fork,
Cannonsburgh,
Catlettsburgh,* (*c. h.*,)
Coalton,

BOYLE COUNTY.

Aliceton,
Brumfield Station,
Danville,* (*c. h.*,)
Mitchellsburgh,
Parksville,
Perryville,
Shelby City.

BRACKEN COUNTY.

Augusta,
Berlin,
Bradford,
Brookville, (*c. h.*,)
Browningsville,
Foster,
Harmon,
Locust Mills,
Milford,
Powersville.

BREATHITT COUNTY.

Jackson, (*c. h.*,)
Lost Creek.

BRECKINRIDGE COUNTY.

Bewleyville,
Big Spring,
Clifton Mills,
Cloverport,
Hardinsburgh, (*c. h.*,)
Hudsonville,
Lost Run,
Planter's Hall,
Rock Lick,
Stephensport,
Union Star,
Webster.

BULLITT COUNTY.

Bardstown Junction,
Belmont,
Cane Spring Depot,
Lebanon Junction,
Mount Vitio,
Mount Washington,
Pitt's Point,
Shepherdsville, (*c. h.*)

BUTLER COUNTY.

Berry's Lick,
Brooklyn,
Harreldsville,
Logansport,
Morgantown, (*c. h.*,)
Quality Valley,
Reedyville,
Rochester,
Sugar Grove,
Townsville,
Welch's Creek,
Woodbury.

CALDWELL COUNTY.

Fredonia,
Friendship,
Long Pond,
Princeton,* (*c. h.*,)
Walnut Grove.

CALLAWAY COUNTY.

Coldwater,
Crossland,
Hico,
Locust Grove,
Murray,* (*c. h.*,)
Pine Bluff,
Shiloh,
Wadesborough,
Warburgh.

CAMPBELL COUNTY.

Alexandria,
California,
Carthage,
Cold Spring,
Dale,
Dayton,
Flagg Spring,
Grant's Lick,
Guber's Mills,
Indian Springs,
Kane,
Newport, (*c. h.*,)
Pond Creek,
Ten Mile,
Tibbatt's × Roads.

* Money-order office.

CARROLL COUNTY.

*Carrollton,** (*c. h.,*)
Eagle Station,
Ghent,
Sandefer's Store,
Worthville.

CARTER COUNTY.

Boone Furnace,
Bruin,
Deer Creek,
Estill Flats,
Grayson, (*c. h.,*)
Mount Savage,
Olive Hill,
Upper Tygart.

CASEY COUNTY.

Liberty, (*c. h.,*)
Middleburgh,
Mintonville,
Powar's Store,
Williams's Store,

CHRISTIAN COUNTY,

Bainbridge,
Bennettstown,
Beverly,
Casky's Station,
Church Hill,
Fairview,
Garrettsburgh,
*Hopkinsville,** (*c. h.,*)
La Fayette,
Longview,
Newstead,
Oak Grove,
Pembroke,
Saint Elmo,
Sinking Fork,
Stuart's Mill,
Williams,
Wooldridge's Store.

CLARKE COUNTY.

Kiddville,
Pine Grove,
Ruckerville,
Stoner,
Vienna,
*Winchester,** (*c. h.*)

CLAY COUNTY.

House's Store,
Laurel Creek,
Manchester, (*c. h.,*)
Sexton's Creek.

CLINTON COUNTY.

Albany, (*c. h.,*)
Alpha,
Cumberland City,
Seventy-six.

CRITTENDEN COUNTY.

Crittenden Springs,
Dycusburgh,
Ford's Ferry,
Hurricane,
Marion, (*c. h.,*)
Shady Grove,
Westonburgh.

CUMBERLAND COUNTY.

Amandaville,
Big Renox,
Burkesville, (*c. h.,*)
Grider,
Marrowbone.

DAVIESS COUNTY.

Birk's City,
Curdsville,
Grissom's Landing,
Knottsville,
Masonville,
Narrows Bridge,
Oakford,
*Owensborough,** (*c. h.,*)
Panther Creek,
Pleasant Ridge,
Sorghotown,
West Louisville,
Whitesville,
Yelvington.

EDMONSON COUNTY.

Bee Spring,
Big Reedy,
Brownsville, (*c. h.,*)
Rocky Hill Station.

ELLIOTT COUNTY.

Newfoundland,
Sandy Hook, (*c. h.*)

ESTILL COUNTY.

Irvine, (*c. h.,*)
Leanah,
Miller's Creek,
Red River Iron W'ks.

FAYETTE COUNTY.

Athens,
Chilesburgh,
Cleveland,
*Lexington,** (*c. h.*)

FLEMING COUNTY.

Elizaville,
*Flemingsburgh,** (*c.h.,*)
Hillsborough,
Mount Carmel,
Oak Woods,
Plummer's Landing,
Plummer's Mills,
Poplar Plains,
Sherburne Mills,
Tilton,
Upper Blue Licks.

FLOYD COUNTY.

Haw's Ford,
Lanesville,
Prestonsburgh, (*c. h.*)

FRANKLIN COUNTY.

Benson,
Bridgeport,
Farmdale,
Forks of Elkhorn,
FRANKFORT,* (*c. h.,*)
Polsgrove's Store.

FULTON COUNTY.

Cacey's Station,
Fulton Station,
*Hickman,** (*c. h.,*)
Jordan Station.

GALLATIN COUNTY.

Bramlette,
Glencoe,
Napoleon,
Sparta Station,
Sugar Creek,
Walnut Lick,
Warsaw, (*c. h.*)

GARRARD COUNTY.

Bryantsville,
Buckeye,
Hyattsville,
Lancaster, (*c. h.,*)
Lowell,
Paint Lick,
Saunders' Ferry.

GRANT COUNTY.

Clark's Creek,
Cordova,
Corinth,
Crittenden,
Downingsville,
Dry Ridge,
Elliston,
Gouge's,
Mount Zion,
New Eagle Mills,
Sherman,
Stateley's Run,
Stewartsville,
Williamstown, (*c. h.*)

* Money-order office.

Graves County.

Boaz,
Boydsville,
Clear Spring,
Dublin,
Fancy Farm,
Farmington,
Hickory Grove,
Kansas,
Lynnville,
*Mayfield,** (*c. h.,*)
Morse's,
Pryorsburgh,
Viola Station,
Wingo's Station.

Grayson County.

Big Clifty,
Caneyville,
Falls of Rough,
Grayson Springs,
Litchfield, (*c. h.,*)
Red Oak,
Short Creek.

Green County.

Allendale,
Catalpa Grove,
*Greensburgh,** (*c. h.,*)
Haskinsville,
Oceola,
Webbs.

Greenup County.

*Greenup,** (*c. h.,*)
Kenton Furnace,
Lynn.

Hancock County.

Hawesville, (*c. h.,*)
Huff's Creek,
Lewisport,
Patesville,
Pellville.

Hardin County.

Dorret's Run,
*Elizabethtown,**(*c. h.,*)
Franklin's × Roads,
Glendale,
Grand View,
Howe's Valley,
Nolin,
Red Hill,
Robertsonville,
Sonora,
Stephensburgh,
Uptonville,
Vine Grove,
West Point,
White Mills.

Harlan County.

Big Rock,
Harlan, (*c. h.,*)
Poor Fork,
Wallin's Creek.

Harrison County.

Berry's Station,
Boyd's Station,
Broadwell,
Claysville,
Colemansville,
Connersville,
Curry's Run,
*Cynthiana,** (*c. h.,*)
Havilandsville,
Lair's Station,
Leesburgh,
Oddville,
Paxton,
Robertson's Station,
Rutland.

Hart County.

Bacon Creek,
Caverna,
Grinstead's Mills,
Hammonville,
Hardyville,
Munfordsville, (*c. h.,*)
Omega,
Ream's Chapel,
Rio,
Rowlett's Depot,
Seymour,
Three Springs,
Woodsonville.

Henderson County.

Cairo,
Genevia,
Hebbardsville,
*Henderson,** (*c. h.,*)
McKinley's Landing,
Robard's Station,
Scuffletown,
Smith's Mills,
Zion.

Henry County.

Bethlehem,
Campbellsburgh,
Eminence,
Franklinton,
Harper's Ferry,
Hill Spring,
Jericho,
Lockport,
New Castle, (*c. h.,*)
Pendleton,
Pleasureville,
Port Royal,
Smithfield,
Spring Hill Depot,
Springport,
Sulphur Fork.

Hickman County.

Clinton, (*c. h.,*)
Columbus,*
Moscow,
Oakville,
Wesley.

Hopkins County.

Ashbysburgh,
Ellwood,
Hanson,
*Madisonville,** (*c. h.,*)
Nebo,
Underwood.

Jackson County.

Birch Lick,
Chinkapin Roof,
Clover Bottom,
Gray Hawk,
Green Hall,
McKee, (*c. h.,*)
Middle Fork,
Morrill.

Jefferson County.

Deposit,
Edwards,
Fairmount,
Fern Creek,
Fisherville,
Hobb's Station,
Jeffersontown,
Lacona,
Long Run,
*Louisville,** (*c. h.,*)
Middletown,
Newburgh,
O'Bannon,
Orell,
River View,
Summit,
Saint Matthews,
Worthington.

Jessamine County.

Hanly,
Jessamine,
Keene,
Little Hickman,
Mount Freedom,
*Nicholasville,** (*c. h.,*)
Pekin,
Spear's.

Johnson County.

Hood's Fork,
Oil Springs,
Paintsville, (*c. h.*)

Josh Bell County.

Callaway,
La Fontaine,
Pineville, (*c. h.,*)
Yellow Creek.

* Money-order office.

KENTON COUNTY.

Bank Lick,
Covington,* (*c. h.*,)
Independence,
Kenton,
Latonia Springs,
Ludlow,
Morning View,
Scott,
Visalia.

KNOX COUNTY.

Barboursville, (*c. h.*,)
Brafford's Store,
Flat Lick,
Lynn Camp,
Swan Pond.

LARUE COUNTY.

Buffalo,
Hodgensville, (*c. h.*,)
Magnolia,
Mount Sherman.

LAUREL COUNTY.

Bush's Store,
Hazle Patch,
Laurel Bridge,
London, (*c. h.*,)
Mershon's × Roads,
Raccoon,
Rough Creek,
Whippoorwill,
White Lily.

LAWRENCE COUNTY.

Blaine,
Buchanan,
Cherokee,
Falls of Blaine,
Louisa, (*c. h.*,)
Lowmansville,
Prosperity,
Stone House,
Warfield,
Webbville,

LEE COUNTY.

Beattyville,
Proctor, (*c. h.*)

LETCHER COUNTY.

Indian Bottom,
Partridge,
Whitesburgh, (*c. h.*)

LEWIS COUNTY.

Cabin Creek,
Carr's,
Concord,
Marine,
Mouth of Laurel,
Poplar Flat,
Quincy,
Sand Hill,
Tolesborough,
Vanceburgh, (*c. h.*)

LINCOLN COUNTY.

Bee Lick,
Crab Orchard,
Gilbert's Creek Station.
Hall's Gap Station,
Highland,
Hustonville,
Milledgeville,
Stanford, (*c. h.*,)
Waynesburgh.

LIVINGSTON COUNTY.

Birdsville,
Carrsville,
Salem,
Smithland,* (*c. h.*)

LOGAN COUNTY.

Adairville,
Auburn,*
Baugh's Station,
Dallam's Creek,
Ferguson's Station,
Gordonsville,
Henrysville,
Keysburgh,
McLeod's Station,
Olmstead,
Rabbittsville,
Red River Mills,
Russellville,* (*c. h.*,)
South Union.

LYON COUNTY.

Cave Spring Station,
Eddyville, (*c. h.*)

McCRACKEN COUNTY.

Florence Station,
Massack,
Norton's Bluff,
Paducah,* (*c. h.*,)
Woodville.

McLEAN COUNTY.

Calhoun, (*c. h.*,)
Livermore,
Long Falls Creek,
Mason Creek,
Rumsey,
Sacramento.

MADISON COUNTY.

Berea,
Big Hill,
Edenton,
Kingston,
Kirksville,
Richmond,* (*c. h.*,)
Silver Creek,
Speedwell,
Waco,
White Hall.

MAGOFFIN COUNTY.

Johnson's Fork,
Salyersville, (*c. h.*)

MARION COUNTY.

Bradfordsville,
Chicago,
Lebanon,* (*c. h.*,)
Loretto,
New Market,
Penick,
Raywick,
Riley's Station,
St. Mary's.

MARSHALL COUNTY.

Altona,
Aurora,
Benton, (*c. h.*,)
Birmingham,
Brewer's Mill,
Briensburgh,
Fair Dealing,
Henderson's Mill,
Oakland,
Olive,
Palma.

MASON COUNTY.

Dover,
Fern Leaf,
Germantown,
Helena,
May's Lick,
Maysville,* (*c. h.*,)
Minerva,
Mount Gilead,
Murphysville,
North Fork,
Orangeburgh,
Sardis,
Slack,
Springdale,
Washington.

* Money-order office.

Meade County.

Brandenburgh, (*c. h.*,)
Flint Island,
Garnettsville,
Garrett,
Hill Grove,
Little York,
Payneville,
Richardson's Landing,
Rock Haven,
Stapleton,
Wolf Creek.

Menifee County.

Rockhouse, (*c. h.*)

Mercer County.

Bohon,
Cornishville,
Dugansville,
Duncan,
Harrodsburgh,* (*c.h.*,)
McAfee,
Nevada,
Pleasant Hill,
Rose Hill,
Salvisa.

Metcalfe County.

Centre,
Cross Plains,
East Fork,
Edmonton, (*c. h.*,)
Glover's Creek,
Knob Lick,
Pace's,
Randolph,
Rockland Mills,
Willow Shade.

Monroe County.

Centre Point,
Flippin,
Fountain Run,
Gamaliel,
Hilton,
Martinsburgh,
Meshack's Creek,
Mud Lick,
Rock Bridge,
Sulphur Lick,
Tompkinsville, (*c. h.*)

Montgomery County.

Aaron's Run,
Elm Hill,
Howard's Mills,
Jeffersonville,
Levee,
Montaview,
Mount Sterling,* (*c.h.*,)
Rich Valley,
Side View.

Morgan County.

Bangor,
Black Water,
West Liberty, (*c. h.*)

Muhlenburgh County.

Bremen,
Earle's,
Greenville,* (*c. h.*,)
Laurel Bluff,
Paradise,
South Carrollton.

Nelson County.

Bardstown,* (*c. h.*,)
Bloomfield,
Boston,
Botland,
Chaplin,
Cox's Creek,
Deatsville,
Fairfield,
Gethsemane,
High Grove,
Hunter's Depot,
Nelson Furnace,
New Haven,
New Hope,
Samuel's Depot.

Nicholas County.

Blue Lick Springs,
Carlisle, (*c. h.*,)
Head Quarters,
Hooktown,
Moorefield,
Oakland Mills,
PleasantValley Mills,
Weston.

Ohio County.

Beaver Dam,
Buck Horn,
Buford,
Ceralvo,
Cool Spring,
Cromwell,
Fordsville,
Hartford,* (*c. h.*,)
Hines' Mills,
Point Pleasant,
Rockport.

Oldham County.

Beard's Station,
Brownsborough,
Buckner's Station,
Centrefield,
Goshen,
La Grange, (*c. h.*,)
Peru,
Pewee Valley,
Westport.

Owen County.

Eagle Hill,
Gratz,
Harmony,
Hills,
Lusby's Mill,
Monterey,
New Columbus,
Néw Liberty,
Owenton, (*c. h.*,)
Rock Dale,
Pleasant Home,
Poplar Grove,
West Union.

Owsley County.

Booneville, (*c. h.*,)
Island City,
South Fork,
Traveller's Rest.

Pendleton County.

Batchelor's Rest,
Boston Station,
Butler,
Catawba,
De Mossville,
Dividing Ridge,
Elizabethville,
Falmouth, (*c. h.*,)
Flower Creek,
Gardnersville,
Knoxville,
Levingood,
Morgan,
Motier.

Perry County.

Hazard, (*c. h.*,)
Salt Creek.

Pike County.

Bent Branch,
Coal Run,
Little Creek,
Mouth of Pond,
Piketon, (*c. h.*,)
Robinson Creek.

Powell County.

Stanton, (*c. h.*,)
West Bend.

Pulaski County.

Adams' Mills,
Cain's Store,
Clio,
Dallas,

* Money-order office.

PULASKI COUNTY—Continued.

Garden Cottage,
Lincolnville,
Line Creek,
Plato,
Shopville,
Somerset, (*c. h.*,)
Sublimity,
Thompsonville,
Valley Oak,
Waterloo,
White Oak Gap.

ROBERTSON COUNTY.

Bratton's Mills,
Kentontown,
Mount Olivet, (*c. h.*)

ROCKCASTLE COUNTY.

Broadhead,
Goochland,
Gum Sulphur,
Mount Vernon, (*c. h.*)

ROWAN COUNTY.

Cassity's Mills,
Farmers,
Gill's Mills,
Morehead, (*c. h.*,)
Pine Springs.

RUSSELL COUNTY.

Creelsborough,
Horse Shoe Bottom,
Jamestown, (*c. h.*,)
Millersville,
Royalton.

SCOTT COUNTY.

Dry Run,
Georgetown,* (*c. h.*,)
Great Crossings,
Little Eagle,
Minorsville,
Newtown,
Oxford,
Payne's Depot,
Stamping Ground,
Stonewall,
Straight Fork.
White Sulphur.

SHELBY COUNTY.

Bailey's Store,
Bagdad,
Chesnut Grove,
Christiansburgh,
Clay Village,
Cropper's Depot,
Graefenberg,
Harrisonville,
Jacksonville,
Jesse's Store,
North Benson,
Shelbyville,* (*c. h.*,)
Simpsonville,
Todd's Point.

SIMPSON COUNTY.

Franklin,* (*c. h.*,)
Temperance Mount.

SPENCER COUNTY.

Elk Creek,
Little Mount,
Mount Eden,
Smileytown,
Taylorsville, (*c. h.*,)
Van Dyke's Mill,
Waterford,
Wilsonville.

TAYLOR COUNTY.

Campbellsville, (*c. h.*,)
Mannsville,
Saloma.

TODD COUNTY.

Allensville,
Clifty,
Daysville,
Elkton, (*c. h.*,)
Guthrie,
Hadensville,
Kirkmansville,
Pilot Knob,
Sharon Grove,
Trenton.

TRIGG COUNTY.

Cadiz,* (*c. h.*,)
Canton,
Cerulean Springs,
Empire Iron Works,
Golden Pond,
Lindsey's Mill,
Linton,
Montgomery,
Roaring Spring.

TRIMBLE COUNTY.

Bedford, (*c. h.*,)
Milton,
Winona.

UNION COUNTY.

Bordley,
Boxville,
Caseyville,
Hitesville,
Lindle's Mills,
Morganfield, (*c. h.*,)
Raleigh,
Uniontown.*

WARREN COUNTY.

Bowling Green,* (*c. h.*,)
Bristow Station,
Claypool,
Elk Spring,
Green Hill,
Green Castle,
Hadley,
Honaker's Ferry,
Memphis Junction,
Oakland Station,
Rich Pond Grove,
Rockfield,
Smith's Grove,
Woodburn.

WASHINGTON COUNTY.

Antioch,
Beech Fork,
Beechland,
Fredericktown,
Mackville,
Sharpsville,
Springfield, (*c. h.*,)
Texas,
Willisburgh.

WAYNE COUNTY.

Berryville,
Mill Springs,
Monticello, (*c. h.*,)
Parmleysville
Weaverton.

WEBSTER COUNTY.

Clay,
Dixon, (*c. h.*,)
Poole's Mill,
Providence,
Sebree,
Slaughterville,
Vanderburgh.

WHITLEY COUNTY.

Bark Camp Mills,
Lot,
Marsh Creek,
Meadow Creek,
Rockhold's,
Whitley C. H.,
Young's Creek.

WOLFE COUNTY.

Campton, (*c. h.*,)
Hazle Green.

WOODFORD COUNTY.

Ducker's,
Midway,
Mortonsville,
Spring Station,
Troy,
Versailles, (*c. h.*)

* Money-order office.

LOUISIANA.

Ascension Parish.

Donaldsonville, (*c. h.,*) New River.

Assumption Parish.

Albemarle, *Assumption,* (*c. h.,*) Labadieville, Paincourtville.

Avoyelles Parish.

Big Bend, Evergreen, Holmesville, Mansura, *Marksville,* (*c. h.,*) Moreauville.

Bienville Parish.

Arcadia, Buckhorn, Mount Lebanon, Ringgold, Saline, *Sparta,* (*c. h.*)

Bossier Parish.

Bellevue, (*c. h.,*) Benton, Coleville, Collinsburgh, Rocky Mount.

Caddo Parish.

Currie's Store, Greenwood, Mooringsport, *Shreveport,** (*c. h.,*) Spring Ridge.

Calcasieu Parish.

Lake Arthur, *Lake Charles,* (*c. h.*)

Caldwell Parish.

Columbia, (*c. h.,*) Copenhagen, Waverly.

Carroll Parish.

Illawara, Lake Providence, Vista Ridge.

Catahoula Parish.

Ford's Creek, Funny Louis, *Harrisonburgh,* (*c. h.,*) Hemp's Creek, Trinity, White Sulphur Sp'gs.

Claiborne Parish.

Arizonia, Cane Ridge, Haynesville, *Homer,* (*c. h.,*) Knoxville, Lisbon, Minden, Sugar Creek.

Concordia Parish.

Fairview, *Vidalia,* (*c. h.*)

De Soto Parish.

Grand Cane, Keatchie, Logansport, Longstreet, *Mansfield,* (*c. h.*)

East Baton Rouge Parish.

Baton Rouge, (*c. h.,*) Burlington, Stony Point.

East Feliciana Parish.

*Clinton,** (*c. h.,*) Jackson, Port Hudson, Woodland.

Franklin Parish.

Louisville, Oakley, Warsaw, *Winnsborough,* (*c. h.*)

Grant Parish.

Colfax, (*c. h.,*) Jatt, Montgomery.

Iberia Parish.

Jeanerette, *New Iberia,** (*c. h.*)

Iberville Parish.

Bayou Goula, Musson, *Plaquemine,** (*c. h.,*) Rosedale. St. Gabriel.

Jackson Parish.

Bonner, Brookline, Douglas, *Vernon,* (*c. h.,*) Vienna, Woodville.

Jefferson Parish.

Carrollton, (*c. h.,*) Gretna, Jefferson, Kenner.

La Fayette Parish.

Bertrandville, Cote Gelee, *Vermillionville,* (*c. h.*)

La Fourche Parish.

Raceland, *Thibodeaux,** (*c. h.*)

Livingston Parish.

Bayou Barbary, Benton's Ferry, Coelk, Live Oak Store, *Springfield,* (*c. h.*)

* Money-order office.

MADISON PARISH.

Delta, (*c. h.*,)
Duckport,
Milliken's Bend,
Richmond.

MOREHOUSE PARISH.

Bastrop, (*c. h.*,)
Lind Grove,
Line,
Point Jefferson.

NATCHITOCHES PARISH.

Campti,
Cloutierville,
Conshatte Chute,
DeLoche's Landing,
Loggy Bayou,
Marthaville,
Natchitoches,* (*c. h.*)

ORLEANS PARISH.

Algiers,
Fort Pike,
NEW ORLEANS,* (*c. h.*)

OUACHITA PARISH.

Cuba,
Forksville,
Log Town,
Monroe,* (*c. h.*,)
Trenton.

PLAQUEMINES PARISH.

Buras,
Jesuit's Bend,
Point á la Hache, (*c. h.*)

POINT COUPEE PARISH.

Hermitage,
Livonia,
Morganzia,
Point Coupee, (*c. h.*,)
Red River Landing,
Waterloo.

RAPIDES PARISH.

Alexandria,* (*c. h.*,)
Cheneyville,
Cotile,
Cotile Landing.

RICHLAND PARISH.

Delhi,
Rayville, (*c. h.*)

SABINE PARISH.

Fort Jesup,
Manny, (*c. h.*)

SAINT BERNARD PARISH.

St. Bernard, (*c. h.*)

SAINT CHARLES PARISH.

Boutte,
St. Charles, (*c. h.*)

SAINT HELENA PARISH.

Arcola,
Darlington,
Greensburgh, (*c. h.*,)
Hog Branch,
Tangapaho.

SAINT JAMES PARISH.

Cantrelle,
Convent, (*c. h.*,)
Vacherie Roads.

SAINT JOHN BAPTIST PARISH.

Bonnet Carre,
Edgard, (*c. h.*)

SAINT LANDRY PARISH.

Arnaudville,
Bayou Bœuf,
Bayou Chicot,
Big Cane,
Grand Coteau,
Mermenton,
Opelousas,* (*c. h.*,)
Plaquemine Brulee,
Saint Peter's,
Ville Platte,
Washington.

SAINT MARTIN'S PARISH.

Breaux Bridge,
La Place,
St. Martinville, (*c. h.*)

SAINT MARY'S PARISH.

Baldwin,
Brashear,
Centreville,
Cypre-mort,
Franklin, (*c. h.*,)
Pattersonville.

SAINT TAMMANY PARISH.

Covington, (*c. h.*,)
Madisonville,
Mandeville,
Sun.

TANGIPAHOA PARISH.

Amite City, (*c. h.*,)
Hammond,
Independence,
Ponchatoula.

TENSAS PARISH.

Ashwood,
St. Joseph's, (*c. h.*,)
Water Proof.

TERRE BONNE PARISH.

Houma,* (*c. h.*,)
Terre Bonne,
Tigerville.

UNION PARISH.

Downsville,
Farmersville, (*c. h.*,)
Lone Well,
Marion,
Union Cross Roads.

VERMILLION PARISH.

Abbeville, (*c. h.*,)
Grand Chenier,
Perry's Bridge.

WASHINGTON PARISH.

Franklinton, (*c. h.*,)
Shady Grove.

WEST BATON ROUGE PARISH.

Belle Vale.

WEST FELICIANA PARISH.

Bayou Tunica,
St. Francisville,* (*c. h.*)

WINN PARISH.

Atlanta,
Newport,
Pine Ridge,
Saint Maurice,
Wheeling,
Winfield, (*c. h.*)

* Money-order office.

MAINE.

ANDROSCOGGIN COUNTY.

Auburn,* (*c. h.*,)
Curtis' Corner,
Danville,
Durham,
East Auburn,
East Livermore,
East Poland,
East Turner,
East Wales,
Greene,
Greene Corner,
Leeds,
Leeds Junction,
Lewiston,*
Lisbon,
Lisbon Falls,
Livermore,
Livermore Centre,
Livermore Falls,
Mechanics Falls,*
Minot,
North Auburn,
North Leeds,
North Livermore,
North Turner,
N. Turner Bridge,
Poland,
Sabattus,
South Auburn,
South Durham,
South Leeds,
South Lewiston,
South Livermore,
South Poland,
Strickland's Ferry,
Turner,
Wales,
Webster,
West Auburn,
West Durham,
West Leeds,
West Minot,
West Poland.

AROOSTOOK COUNTY.

Alva,
Amity,
Ashland,
Bancroft,
Bridgewater,
Caribou,
Castle Hill,
Conway,
Dickeyville,
Dyer Brook,
Easton,
Fort Fairfield,*
Fort Kent,
Glenwood,
Golden Ridge,
Grant Isle,
Haynesville,
Hodgdon,
Houlton,* (*c. h.*,)
Island Falls,
Limestone,
Linneus,
Littleton,
Lyndon,
Madawaska,
Maple Grove,
Mars Hill,
Masardis,
Moluncus,
Monticello,
Moro,
New Limerick,
North Amity,
North Linneus,
Orient,
Portage Lake,
Presque Isle,*
Rawson,
Rockabema,
Salmon Brook,
Sherman,
Sherman Mills,
Smyrna,
Smyrna Mills,
South Moluncus,
South Weston,
Upper Madawaska,
Van Buren,
Westfield,
Weston.

CUMBERLAND COUNTY.

Bolster's Mills,
Bonny Eagle,
Bridgeton,
Brunswick,*
Cape Elizabeth Depot,
Casco,
Chebeauge Island,
Cumberland,
Cumberland Centre,
Dry Mills,
Duck Pond,
East Baldwin,
East Harpswell,
E. North Yarmouth,
East Otisfield,

CUMBERLAND COUNTY—Continued.

East Raymond,
East Windham,
Edes' Falls,
Falmouth,
Ferry Village,
Freeport,
Gorham,*
Gray,
Harpswell Centre,
Harrison,
Naples,
New Casco,
New Gloucester,
North Baldwin,
North Bridgeton,
North Gray,
North Harpswell,
North Pownal,
North Raymond,
North Windham,
North Yarmouth,
Oak Hill,
Orr's Island,
Otisfield,
Portland,* (*c. h.*,)
Pownal,
Raymond,
Saccarappa,
Sandy Beach,
Scarborough,
Sebago,
South Bridgeton,
South Casco,
South Freeport,
South Windham,
Standish,
Steep Falls,
Stevens' Plains,
Upper Gloucester,
Webb's Mills,
West Baldwin,
West Bridgeton,
West Brunswick,
West Cumberland,
West Falmouth,
West Gloucester,
West Gorham,
West Harpswell,
West Pownal,
White Rock,
Windham,
Woodford's,
Yarmouth.*

FRANKLIN COUNTY.

Avon,
Bean's Corners,
Berry's Mill,
Chesterville,
East New Sharon,
East New Vineyard,
East Wilton,
Eustis,
Farmington,* (*c. h.*,)
Farmington Falls,
Freeman,
Green Vale,
Industry,
Jay,
Kingfield,
Madrid,
New Sharon,
New Vineyard,
North Chesterville,
North Farmington,
North Jay,
Phillips,*
Pratt's Corner,
Rangeley,
Salem,
South Carthage,
South Chesterville,
Strong,
Temple Mills,
Weld,
West Freeman,
Wests' Mills,
Wilton.

HANCOCK COUNTY.

Amherst,
Aurora,
Blue Hill,
Blue Hill Falls,
Brooklin,
Brooksville,
Buck's Mills,
Bucksport,
Bucksport Centre,
Castine,
Cranberry Isles,
Dedham,
Deer Isle,
East Bucksport,
East Eden,
East Lamoine,
East Sullivan,
Eden,
Ellsworth,* (*c. h.*,)
Franklin,
Gouldsborough,
Great Pond,

* Money-order office.

Hancock County—Continued.

Green's Landing,
Hancock,
Lamoine,
Mount Desert,
North Blue Hill,
North Brooklin,
North Brooksville,
North Bucksport,
North Castine,
North Deer Isle,
Northeast Harbor,
North Ellsworth,
North Hancock,
North Mariaville,
North Penobscot,
North Sedgwick,
Orland,
Otis,
Penobscot,
Prospect Harbor,
Salisbury Cove,
Sargentville,
Seal Cove,
Sedgwick,
South Brooksville,
South Hancock,
South Deer Isle,
South Penobscot,
South West Harbor,
Sullivan,
Surry,
Swan's Island,
Tilden,
Tremont,
Waltham,
West Brooksville,
West Deer Isle,
West Eden,
West Ellsworth,
West Gouldsboro'h,
West Trenton,
Winter Harbor.

Kennebec County.

Albion,
AUGUSTA,* (*c. h.*,)
Belgrade,
Belgrade Mills,
Benton,
Centre Sidney,
China,
Clinton,
Cross Hill,
Dirigo,
East Benton,
East Monmouth,
East Pittston,
East Readfield,
East Vassalborough,
East Winthrop,
Fayette,
Fayette Ridge,
Gardiner,*
Hallowell,
Kent's Hill,
Litchfield,
Litchfield Corners,
Manchester,
Monmouth,
Mount Vernon,
Nat'al Mil. Asylum,*
North Belgrade,
North Fayette,
North Monmouth,
North Pittston,
North Sidney,
North Vassalboro'h,
North Vienna,
North Wayne,
Pishon's Ferry,
Pittston,
Readfield,
Readfield Depot,
Riverside,
Rome,
Sidney,
South Albion,
South China,
South Gardiner,
South Litchfield,
South Monmouth,
South Vassalboro'h,
South Windsor,
Vassalborough,
Vienna,
Waterville,*
Wayne,
Week's Mills,
West Farmingdale,
West Gardiner,
West Mount Vernon,
West Waterville,
Windsor,
Winslow,
Winthrop.

Knox County.

Appleton,
Camden,*
Carver's Harbor,
Cushing,
Friendship,
Hope,
Matinicus,
North Appleton,
North Haven,
North Union,
North Washington,
Rockland,* (*c. h.*,)
Rockport,
Rockville,

Knox County—Continued.

Saint George,
South Hope,
South Saint George,
South Thomaston,
Tenant's Harbor,
Thomaston,
Union,
Warren,
Washington,
West Appleton,
West Camden,
West Washington.

Lincoln County.

Alna,
Booth Bay,
Bristol,
Cooper's Mills,
Damariscotta Mills,
Dresden,
Dresden Mills,
Edgecomb,
Hodgdon's Mills,
Jefferson,
Monhegan Island,
New Castle,
Noblesborough,
North Boothbay,
North Edgecomb,
North New Castle,
North Waldoboro'h,
North Whitefield,
Pemaquid,
Round Pond,
Sheepscott Bridge,
Somerville,
South Bristol,
South Jefferson,
Southport,
Waldoborough,
West Dresden,
Westport,
Whitefield,
Wiscasset,* (*c. h.*)

Oxford County.

Albany,
Andover,
Bethel,*
Brownfield,
Bryant's Pond,
Buckfield,
Byron,
Canton,
Canton Point,
Centre Lovell,
Denmark,
Dixfield,
Dixfield Centre,
East Dixfield,
East Fryeburgh,
East Hebron,
East Peru,
East Rumford,
East Stoneham,
East Sumner,
Fryeburgh,
Fryeburgh Centre,
Gilead,
Grafton,
Greenwood,
Hanover,
Hartford,
Hebron,
Hiram,
Locke's Mills,
Lovell,
Mexico,
Milton Plantation,
Newry,
North Bethel,
North Buckfield,
North Fryeburgh,
North Lovell,
North Newry,
North Norway,
North Paris,
North Rumford,
North Waterford,
North Woodstock,
Norway,*
Oxford,
Paris,* (*c. h.*,)
Peru,
Porter,
Roxbury,
Rumford,
Rumford Centre,
Rumford Point,
Snow Falls,
South Andover,
South Paris,
South Waterford,
Stow,
Sumner,
Sweden,
Upton,
Waterford,
Welchville,
West Bethel,
West Paris,
West Peru,
West Sumner,
Wilson's Mills,
Woodstock.

* Money-order office.

Penobscot County.

Alton,
Argyle,
*Bangor,** (c. h.,)
Bradford,
Brewer,
Brewer Village,
Burlington,
Carmel,
Carroll,
Charleston,
Chester,
Clifton,
Corinna,
Corinna Centre,
Corinth,
Dexter,*
Dixmont,
Dixmont Centre,
East Bangor,
East Bradford,
East Corinth,
East Dixmont,
East Eddington,
East Exeter,
East Hampden,
East Holden,
East Lincoln,
East Lowell,
East Newport,
East Orrington,
Eddington,
Enfield,
Etna,
Etna Centre,
Exeter,
Exeter Mills,
Garland,
Glenburn,
Goodale's Corner,
Great Works,
Greenbush,
Greenfield,
Hampden,
Hampden Corner,
Hermon,
Hermon Pond,
Holden,
Holt's Mills,
Howland,
Hudson,
Kenduskeag,
La Grange,
Lee,
Levant,
Lincoln,
Lincoln Centre,
Lowell,
Mattawamkeag,
Maxfield,
Medway,
Milford,
Nealey's Corner,
Newburgh,
Newburgh Centre,
Newport,
North Bangor,
North Bradford,
North Carmel,
North Dixmont,
North Hermon,
North Milford,
North Newburgh,
North Newport,
North Woodville,
Olamon,
Old Town,
Orono,
Orrington,
Passadumkeag,
Pattagumpus,
Patten,
Plymouth,
Prentiss,
Simpson's Corner,
Six Mile Falls,
South Corinth,
South Exeter,
South Levant,
South Newburgh,
South Orrington,
South Winn,
Springfield,
Stetson,
Upper Stillwater,
Veazie,
West Charleston,
West Corinna,
West Enfield,
West Garland,
West Great Works,
West Hampden,
West Levant,
West Newburgh,
Winn,
Woodville.

Piscataquis County.

Abbot,
Abbot Village,
Atkinson,
Barnard,
Blanchard,
Boyd Lake,
Brockway's Mills,
Brownsville,
Dover, (c. h.,)
Dover South Mills,
East Dover,
East Sangerville,
Foxcroft,*
Greenville,
Guilford,
Howard,
Katahdin Iron Works,
Kingsbury,

Piscataquis County—Continued.

Medford,
Medford Centre,
Milo,
Monson,
Orneville,
Parkman,
Sangerville,
Sebec,
Shirley,
Shirley Mills,
South Atkinson,
South Dover,
South Sangerville,
South Sebec,
Wellington,
West Dover,
Williamsburgh.

Sagadahoc County.

*Bath,** (c. h.,)
Bowdoin,
Bowdoin Centre,
Bowdoinham,
East Bowdoinham,
Georgetown,
Parker's Head,
Phippsburgh,
Richmond,*
Richmond Corner,
Small Point,
Topsham,
West Bowdoin,
Winnegance,
Woolwich.

Somerset County.

Anson,
Athens,
Bingham,
Brighton,
Cambridge,
Canaan,
Canada Road,
Carritunk,
Concord,
Cornville,
Dead River,
Detroit,
East Madison,
East New Portland,
Embden,
Fairfield,
Fairfield Corners,
Flagstaff,
Harmony,
Hartland,
Highland,
Kendall's Mills,
Larone,
Lexington,
Madison,
Madison Centre,
Mercer,
Moose River,
New Portland,
Norridgewock, (c. h.,)
North Anson,
North Cornville,
North Fairfield,
North New Portland,
Palmyra,
Pittsfield,
Ripley,
Saint Albans,
Skowhegan,*
Smithfield,
Solon,
Somerset Mills,
South Norridgewock,
South Solon,
Stark,
The Forks,
West Athens,
West Cornville,
West Embden,
West Pittsfield.

Waldo County.

*Belfast,** (c. h.,)
Belmont,
Brooks,
Burnham Village,
Centre Lincolnville,
Centre Montville,
East Knox,
East Montville,
East Northport,
East Palermo,
East Thorndike,
Ellingwood's Corner,
Frankfort,
Freedom,
Jackson,
Knox,
Liberty,
Lincolnville,
Monroe,
Monroe Centre,
Montville,
Morrill,
North Isleborough,
North Monroe,
North Palermo,
Northport,
North Searsmont,
North Searsport,

* Money-order office.

WALDO COUNTY—Continued.

North Winterport, Palermo, Palermo Centre, Poor's Mills, Prospect, Prospect Ferry, Sandy Point, Searsmont, Searsport,* South Belmont, South Brooks, South Liberty, South Montville, Stockton, Swanville, Thorndike, Troy, Troy Centre, Unity,* Waldo, West Troy, West Winterport, White's Corner, Winterport.*

WASHINGTON COUNTY.

Addison Point, Alexander, Baileyville, Baring, Bèddington, Calais,* Charlotte, Columbia, Cooper, Crawford, Cutler, Deblois, Dennysville, East Machias, Eastport,* Harrington, Indian River, Jackson Brook, Jonesborough, Jonesport, Lubec, *Machias*,* (*c. h.*,) Machias Port, Marion, Medybemps, Millbridge, Milltown, Narraguagus, North Cutler, Northfield, North Lubec, North Perry, Pembroke,* Perry, Plantation No. 14, Princeton, Red Beach, Robbinston, South Beddington, South Robbinston, Steuben, Topsfield, Waite, Wesley, West Lubec, West Pembroke,

WASHINGTON COUNTY—Continued.

Whiting, Whitneyville.

YORK COUNTY.

Acton, *Alfred*,* (*c. h.*,) Bar Mills, Berwick, Biddeford,* Biddeford Pool Buxton, Buxton Centre, Cape Neddick, Cape Porpoise, Centre Lebanon, Cornish, Dayton, East Limington, East Parsonfield, East Waterborough, Elliot, Elliot Depot, Emery's Mills, Goodwin's Mills, Hollis, Hollis Centre, Kennebunk, Kennebunk Depot, Kennebunk Landing, Kennebunk Port, Kezar Falls, Kittery, Kittery Depot, Kittery Point, Lebanon, Limerick, Limington, Lyman, Nason's Mills, Newfield, North Acton, North Alfred, North Berwick, North Kennebunk Port, North Lebanon, North Limington, North Newfield, North Parsonfield, North Shapleigh, North Waterborough, Ogunquit, Ossipee Mills, Parsonfield, Ross' Corners, Saco,* Sanford, Shapleigh, South Acton, South Berwick,* South Berwick Junction, South Limington, South Parsonfield, South Sanford, Springvale,* Waterborough, Waterboro'h Centre, Wells, Wells Depot, West Buxton, West Lebanon, West Newfield, West Parsonfield, York.

MARYLAND.

ALLEGHANY COUNTY.

Accident, Altamont, Barton, Bloomington, Brady's Mill, Corriganville, *Cumberland*,* (*c. h.*,) Davis Mill, Deer Park, Ellerslie, Flint Stone, Frankville, Frostburgh,* Grantsville, Hutton's Switch, Johnstown, Lonaconing,* Mount Savage, Oakland, Ocean, Old Town, Rawling's Station, Selbysport, Shade Mills, Swanton, Western Port.

ANNE ARUNDEL COUNTY.

ANNAPOLIS,* (*c. h.*,) Annapolis Junction,

ANNE ARUNDEL COUNTY—Continued.

Arnold's Store, Bristol, Brooklyn, Crownsville, Davidsonville, Friendship, Hooversville, Johnson's Store, Millersville, Patuxent, Rutland, Saint Margaret's, Sappington, Shepherd's Store, South River, Sudley, Tracy's Landing, Waterbury, West River.

BALTIMORE COUNTY.

Baltimore,* Beckleysville, Belfast, Bentley's Springs, Black Rock, Brooklandville, Butler, Calverton Mills,

* Money-order office.

Baltimore County—Continued.

Catonsville,
Carroll.
Cockeysville,*
Cub Hill,
Dulaney's Valley,
Ellengowan,
Fork Meet'g House,
Freeland,
Gorsuch's Mills,
Govanstown,
Grave Run Mills,
Greenwood,
Harewood,
Harrisonville,
Hereford,
Hookstown,
Lauraville,
Little Gunpowder,
Long Green Acad'y,
Lutherville,
Maryland Line,
Monkton Mills,
Monument House,
Mount Carmel,
Mount Washington,
North Branch,
Orangeville,
Owing's Mills,
Paper Mills,
Parkton,
Philopolis,
Phœnix,
Pikesville,
Powhatan,
Randallstown,
Rayville,
Reisterstown,
Rossville,
Saint Denis,
Shane,
Stablersville,
Stevenson Station,
Sweet Air,
Towsontown, (*c. h.*,)
Trenton,
Union Meet'g House,
Upperco,
Upper Falls,
Warren,
Waverly,
Weisesburgh,
Wetheredville,
White Hall,
Woodberry,
Woodensburgh.

Calvert County.

Cove Point,
Dunkirk,
Huntingtown,
Lower Marlborough,
Mill Creek,
Port Republic,
Prince Fredericktown, (*c. h.*,)
Saint Leonards,
Solomon's Island,
Sunderlandville.

Caroline County.

Bethlehem,
Bridgetown,
Burrsville,
Denton,* (*c. h.*,)
Federalsburgh,
Fowling Creek,
Goldsborough,
Greensborough,*
Henderson,
Hillsborough,
Marydell,
New Hope,
Potter's Landing,
Preston,
Ridgely,
Smithville,
Whiteleysburgh.

Carroll County.

Bachman's Mills,
Bird Hill,
Bruceville,
Carrollton,
Dennings,
Double Pipe Creek,
Dug Hill,
Finksburgh,
Franklinville,
Freedom,
Frizellburgh,
Hampstead,
Harney,
Hood's Mills,
Houcksville,
Linwood,
Louisville,
McKinstry's Mills,
Manchester,
Mayberry,
Middleburgh,
Mount Airy,
New Windsor,
Piney Creek,
Porters,
Sam's Creek,

Carroll County—Continued.

Silver Run,
Stonersville,
Sykesville,
Taneytown,
Union Bridge,
Union Mills,
Uniontown,
Wakefield,
Warfieldburgh,
Watersville,
Westminster,* (*c. h.*,)
Winfield,
Woodbine.

Cecil County.

Bay View,
Brick Meet'g House,
Cecilton,
Charlestown,
Cherry Hill,
Chesapeake City,*
Colora,
Conowingo,
Elkton,* (*c. h.*,)
Fair Hill,
Farmington,
Mechanics' Valley,
Northeast,*
Perryville,
Port Deposit,*
Principio,
Principio Furnace,
Rising Sun,*
Rock Springs,
Rowlandsville,
Saint Augustine,
Warwick,
Woodlawn,
Zion.

Charles County.

Allen's Fresh,
Beantown,
Bryantown,
Cross Roads,
Doncaster,
Duffield,
Gallant Green,
Glymont,
Harris' Lot,
Hughesville,
Marshall Hall,
Nanjemoy,
Newburgh,
Newport,
Pisgah,
Pomonkey,
Port Tobacco, (*c. h.*)

Dorchester County.

Airey's,
Bishop's Head,
Cambridge,* (*c. h.*,)
Cedar Creek,
Church Creek,
Cornersville,
Draw Bridge,
East New Market,
Fishing Creek,
Gales Town,
Golden Hill,
Harrison,
Hill's Point,
Hoopersville,
Hurlock,
Lakesville,
Linkwood,
Salem,
Taylor's Island,
Tobacco Stick,
Vienna,
Williamsburgh.

Frederick County.

Adamstown,
Barry,
Bolivar,
Bridgeport,*
Broad Run,
Buckeystown,
Burkettsville,
Catocton Furnace,
Creagerstown,
Emmittsburgh,*
Foxville,
Frederick,* (*c. h.*,)
Graceham,
Greenfield Mills,
Hansonville,
Ijamsville,
Jefferson,
Johnsville,
Kemptown,
Knoxville,
Ladiesburgh,
Lander,
Lewistown,
Libertytown,
Licksville,
Linganore,
Mechanicstown,
Middletown,*

* Money-order office.

FREDERICK COUNTY—Continued.

Monrovia,
Mount Pleasant,
Myersville,
New London,
New Market,
Oak Orchard,
Petersville,
Plane No. Four,
Point of Rocks,
Sabillisville,
Unionville,
Urbana,
Utica Mills,
Walkersville,
Wolfsville,
Woodsborough,
Woodville.

HARFORD COUNTY.

Aberdeen,
Abingdon,
Bel Air, (*c. h.*,)
Black Horse,
Boothby Hill,
Chrome Hill,
Churchville,
Clayton,
Clermont Mills,
Darlington,
Dublin,
Edgewood,
Emmorton,
Fallston,
Federal Hill,
Forest Hill,
Fountain Green,
Glenville,
Harford Furnace,
Havre de Grace,*
Hickory Tavern,
Hopewell × Roads,
Jarrettsville,
Jerusalem Mills,
Lapidum,
Magnolia,
Michaelsville,
Mill Green,
Norrisville,
Oakington,
Perrymansville,
Pleasantville,
Prospect,
Pylesville,
Sandy Hook,
Taylor,
Thomas' Run,
Upper × Roads,
Wilna.

HOWARD COUNTY.

Alberton,
Clarksville,
Cooksville,
Dayton,
Elk Ridge Landing,
Ellicott City,* (*c. h.*,)
Florence,
Glenelg,
Hanover,
Ilchester Mills,
Lisbon,
Marriottsville,
Matthew's Store,
Oakland Mills,
Poplar Springs,
Roxbury Mills,
Savage,
Simpsonville,
West Friendship,
Woodstock.

KENT COUNTY.

Chestertown, (*c. h.*,)
Chesterville,
Edesville,
Fairlee,
Galena,
Hanesville,
Kennedyville,
Locust Grove,
Massey's × Roads,
Millington,
Rock Hall,
Sassafras,
Spry's Landing,
Still Pond,
Urieville.

MONTGOMERY COUNTY.

Barnesville,
Beallsville,
Brighton,
Brookville,
Clarksburgh,
Colesville,
Damascus,
Darcey's Store,
Darnestown,
Dawsonville,
Forest Oak,
Germantown,

MONTGOMERY COUNTY—Continued.

Goshen,
Hyattstown,
Laytonville,
Middlebrook,
Monocacy,
Montrose,
Nichols,
Norbeck,
Offutt's × Roads,
Olney,
Poolesville,
Redland,
Rockville,* (*c. h.*)
Sandy Spring,*
Seneca,
Sligo,
Spencerville,
Triadelphia,
Unity,
Wheaton.

PRINCE GEORGE'S COUNTY.

Accokeek,
Agricultural College,
Aquasco,
Beltsville,
Bladensburgh,
Branchville,
Brandywine,
Buena Vista,
Collington,
Croom,
Forestville,
Fort Washington,
Horse Head,
Hyattsville,
Laurel Factory,*
Mellwood,
Mitchellville,
Muirkirk,
Nottingham,
Oak Grove,
Oxen Hill,
Piscataway,
Robeystown,
Rosaryville,
Silver Hill,
Suitsville,
T. B.,
Upper Marlboro, (*c.h.*,)
Watson.

QUEEN ANNE'S COUNTY.

Broad Creek,
Centreville,* (*c. h.*,)
Church Hill,
Crumpton,
Long Marsh,
Queenstown,
Roesville,
Sudlersville,
Templeville.

ST. MARY'S COUNTY.

Budd's Creek,
Chaptico,
Charlotte Hall,
Fairfield,
Great Mills,
Hollywood,
Leonardtown,* (*c. h.*,)
Milestown,
Morganza,
Oakville,
Piney Point,
Point Lookout,
Ridge,
St. Clement's Bay,
St. Inigoes.

SOMERSET COUNTY.

Burnettsville,
Crisfield,
Dames Quarter,
Deal's Island,
Fairmount,
Hope,
Hopewell,
Kingston,
Monie,
Princess Anne,* (*c. h.*,)
Upper Trappe,
Westover.

TALBOT COUNTY.

Bay Hundred,
Broad Creek Neck,
Cordova,
Easton,* (*c. h.*,)
Oxford,
Royal Oak,
Saint Michaels,
Skipton,
Taverner's Woods,
Trappe,
Wittman,
Wye Mills.

* Money-order office.

WASHINGTON COUNTY.

Bakersville,
Beaver Creek,
Benevola,
Boonsborough,
Breathedsville,
Brownsville,
Cavetown,
Chewsville,
Clear Spring,
Conococheague,
Downsville,
Eakle's Mills,
Fair Play,
Fairview,
Funkstown,
Green Spring Furnace,
Hagerstown,* (*c. h.*,)
Hancock,*
Indian Springs,
Keedysville,
Keep Tryst,
Leitersburgh,
Mason,
Millstone Point,
Ringgold,
Rohrersville,
Sharpsburgh,*
Smithsburgh,
Williamsport.*

WICOMICO COUNTY.

Barren Creek Spr'gs,
Forktown,
Green Hill,
Nanticoke,
Pittsville,
Powellville,
Quantico,
Riverton,
Salisbury,* (*c. h.*,)
Sharptown,
Sheppardsville,
Tyaskin,
Whitehaven.

WORCESTER COUNTY.

Berlin,*
Bishopville,
Girdletree Hill,
Lindseyville,
Newark,
Newtown,
Saint Martins,
Sandy Hill,
Snow Hill,* (*c. h.*,)
Whaleysville.

MASSACHUSETTS.

BARNSTABLE COUNTY.

Barnstable, (*c. h.*,)
Brewster,
Centreville,
Chatham,
Chatham Port,
Cotuit Port,
Dennis,
Dennis Port,
East Brewster,
East Dennis,
East Falmouth,
Eastham,
East Harwich,
East Orleans,
East Sandwich,
Falmouth,
Harwich,
Harwich Port,
Hatchville,
Hyannis,
Marston's Mills,
Monument,
North Chatham,
North Eastham,
North Falmouth,
North Harwich,
North Sandwich,
North Truro,
Orleans,*
Osterville,
Pocasset,
Provincetown,*
Sandwich,*
South Brewster,
South Chatham,
South Dennis,
South Harwich,
South Orleans,
South Sandwich,
South Wellfleet,
South Yarmouth,
Spring Hill,
Truro,
Waquoit,
Wellfleet,*
West Barnstable,
West Brewster,
West Chatham,
West Dennis,
West Falmouth,
West Harwich,
West Sandwich,
West Yarmouth,
Wood's Hole,
Yarmouth,
Yarmouth Port.*

BERKSHIRE COUNTY.

Adams,
Alford,
Ashley Falls,
Bancroft,
Becket,
Becket Centre,
Berkshire,
Blackinton,
Cheshire,
Cold Spring,
Curtisville,
Dalton,
East Lee,
East Otis,
East Sheffield,
East Windsor,
Florida,
Glendale,
Great Barrington,*
Hancock,

BERKSHIRE COUNTY—Continued.

Hartsville,
Hinsdale,
Hoosac Tunnel,
Housatonic,
Lanesborough,
Lee,*
Lenox, (*c. h.*,)
Lenox Furnace,
Mill River,
Monterey,
Montville,
New Ashford,
New Boston,
New Lenox,
New Marlborough,
North Adams,*
North Egremont,
Otis,
Peru,
Pittsfield,*
Richmond,
Rock Dale Mills,
Sandisfield,
Savoy,
Sheffield,
South Egremont,
Southfield,
South Lee,
South Sandisfield,
South Williamstown,
State Line,
Stockbridge,
Tyringham,
Van Deusenville,
Washington,
West Becket,
West Otis,
West Pittsfield,
West Stockbridge,
West Stockbridge Centre,
Williamstown,
Windsor.*

BRISTOL COUNTY.

Acushnet,
Attleborough,
Berkley,
Central Village,
Dartmouth,
Dighton,
East Freetown,
Easton,
East Taunton,
Fairhaven,
Fall River,*
Freetown,
Hebronville,
Long Plain,
Mansfield,
Myrickville,
New Bedford,*
North Attleborough,
North Dartmouth,
North Dighton,
North Easton,
North Rehoboth,
North Swansea,
Norton,
Raynham,
Rehoboth,
Seekonk,
Somerset,
South Attleborough,
South Dartmouth,
South Easton,
South Seekonk,

* Money-order office.

BRISTOL COUNTY—Continued.

South Westport,
Swansea,
*Taunton,** (*c. h.,*)
West Mansfield,
Westport,
Westport Point.

DUKES COUNTY.

Chilmark,
*Edgartown,** (*c. h.,*)
Holmes' Hole,
North Tisbury,
Vineyard Grove,
West Tisbury.

ESSEX COUNTY.

Amesbury,
Andover,*
Annisquam,
Ayers' Village,
Ballard Vale,
Bay View,
Beverly,
Beverly Farms,
Boxford,
Bradford,
Byfield,
Clifton Dale,
Danvers,
Danvers Centre,
Danversport,
East Gloucester,
East Haverhill,
East Salisbury,
Essex,
Georgetown,
Gloucester,*
Groveland,
Hamilton,
Haverhill,*
Ipswich,
Lanesville,
Lawrence,*
Lynn,*
Lynnfield,
Lynnfield Centre,
Manchester,
Marblehead,*
Methuen,
Middleton,
Nahant,
Newburyport,*
North Andover,
North Andover Dep't,
North Beverly,
Peabody,
Pigeon Cove,
Rockport,
Rowley,
*Salem,** (*c. h.,*)
Salisbury,
Saugus,
Saugus Centre,
South Amesbury,
South Groveland,
Swampscott,
Topsfield,
Wenham,
West Amesbury,
West Boxford,
West Danvers,
West Gloucester,
West Newbury.

FRANKLIN COUNTY.

Adamsville,
Ashfield,
Bardwell's Ferry,
Bernardstown,
Buckland,
Charlemont,
Colerain,
Conway,
Deerfield,
East Charlemont,
East Shelburne,
East Whately,
Elm Grove,
Erving,
Factory Village,
Gill,
*Greenfield,** (*c. h.,*)
Griswoldville,
Hawley,
Heath,
Leverett,
Leyden,
Lock's Village,
Miller's Falls,
Millington,
Monroe,
Montague,
Montague City,
New Salem,
Northfield,
Northfield Farms,
North Leverett,
North New Salem,
North Orange,
Orange,
Rowe,
Shattuckville,
Shelburne,
Shelburne Falls,*
Shutesbury,
South Ashfield,
South Deerfield,

FRANKLIN COUNTY—Continued.

Sunderland,
Warwick,
Wendell,
Wendell Depot,
West Hawley,
West Northfield,
Whately,
Zoar.

HAMPDEN COUNTY.

Agawam,
Ashleyville,
Blanford,
Bond's Village,
Brimfield,
Chester,
Chester Centre,
Chicopee,*
Chicopee Falls,*
Collins' Depot,
East Brimfield,
East Granville,
East Long Meadow,
Feeding Hills,
Granville Corners,
Holland,
Holyoke,*
Indian Orchard,
Ireland,
Long Meadow,
Ludlow,
Mittineague,
Monson,
Montgomery,
North Blanford,
North Chester,
Palmer,*
Russell,
Southwick,
South Wilbraham,
*Springfield,** (*c. h.,*)
Thorndike,
Three Rivers,
Tolland,
Wales,
Westfield,*
West Granville,
West Springfield,
Wilbraham,
Willimansett.

HAMPSHIRE COUNTY.

Amherst,*
Babylon,
Belchertown,
Chesterfield,
Cummington,
Cummington West Village,
East Hampton,*
Enfield,
Florence,
Goshen,
Granby,
Greenwich,
Greenwich Village,
Hadley,
Hatfield,
Haydenville,
Huntington,
Leeds,
Middlefield,
North Amherst,
*Northampton,** (*c. h.,*)
North Hadley,
North Hatfield,
North Prescott,
Norwich,
Pelham,
Plainfield,
Prescott,
Ringville,
South Amherst,
Southampton,
South Hadley,
South Hadley Falls,
South Worthington,
Ware,*
West Chesterfield,
West Hampton,
West Worthington,
Williamsburgh,*
Worthington.

MIDDLESEX COUNTY.

Acton,
Allston,
Arlington,
Ashby,
Ashland,
Assabet,
Auburn Dale,
Bedford,
Belmont,
Billerica,
Boxborough,
Braggville,
Brighton,*
Burlington,
Cambridge,*
Cambridgeport,*
Carlisle,
Charlestown,*
Chelmsford,
Chesnut Hill,
Cochituate,
College Hill,

* Money-order office.

MIDDLESEX COUNTY—Continued.

*Concord** (*c. h.*)
Dracut,
Dunstable,
East Cambridge,
East Holliston,
East Lexington,
East Pepperell,
East Somerville,
East Woburn,
Forge Village,
Framingham,
Graniteville,
Greenwood,
Groton,
Groton Junction,*
Hayden Row,
Holliston,*
Hopkinton,*
Hudson,
Lexington,
Lincoln,
Littleton,
Lowell,*
Malden,
Maplewood,
Marlborough,*
Medford,
Melrose,
Middlesex Village,
Mount Auburn,
Natick,*
Newton,*
Newton Centre,
Newton Lower Falls,
Newton Upper Falls,
Newtonville,
North Billerica,
North Cambridge,
North Chelmsford,
North Reading,
North Somerville,
North Sudbury,
North Wilmington,
North Woburn,
Pepperell,
Reading,
Rock Bottom,
Saxonville,
Sherborn,
Shirley,
Shirley Village,
Somerville,
South Acton,
South Chelmsford,
South Framingham,
South Malden,
South Natick,
South Sudbury,
Stoneham,
Stow,
Sudbury,
Tewkesbury,
Townsend,
Townsend Harbor,
Tyngsborough,
Wakefield,
Waltham,*
Watertown,*
Waverly,
Wayland,
West Acton,
West Chelmsford,
Westford,
West Groton,
West Medford,
West Newton,
Weston,
West Townsend,
Wilmington,
Winchester,
Woburn,*
Woodville.

NANTUCKET COUNTY.

*Nantucket,** (*c. h.*)

NORFOLK COUNTY.

Bellingham,
Braintree,
Brookline,
Canton,
Caryville,
Charles Riv. Village,
Cohasset,
*Dedham,** (*c. h.,*)
Dorchester,
Dover,
East Foxborough,
East Medway,
East Randolph,
East Sharon,
East Stoughton,
East Walpole,
East Weymouth.
Foxborough,*
Franklin,*
Franklin City,
Grantville,
Harrison Square.
Hyde Park,
Jamaica Plain,
Mattapan,
Medfield,
Medway,*
Milton,
Needham,*
Neponset Village,
Norfolk,
North Bellingham,
North Cohasset,
North Stoughton,

NORFOLK COUNTY—Continued.

North Weymouth,
Plainville,
Quincy,*
Quincy Point,
Randolph,
Readville Station,
Rockville,
Roslindale,
Sharon,
Sheldonville,
South Braintree,
South Dedham,
South Franklin,
South Randolph,
South Walpole,
South Weymouth,
Stoughton,
Walpole,
Wellesley,
West Dedham,
West Foxborough,
West Medway,
West Roxbury,
West Wrentham,
Weymouth,
Wrentham.

PLYMOUTH COUNTY.

Abington,
Bridgewater,*
Campello,
Carver,
Chiltonville,
Cochesett,
Duxbury,
East Abington,
East Bridgewater,
East Marshfield,
East Middleborough,
East Pembroke,
East Wareham,
Halifax,
Hanover,
Hanson,
Hingham,
Hingham Centre,
Hull,
Joppa Village,
Kingston,
Lakeville,
Marion,
Marshfield,
Mattapoisett,
Middleborough,
North Abington,
North Bridgewater,*
North Carver,
North Marshfield,
No. Middleborough,
North Pembroke,
North Plympton,
North Scituate,
N. W. Bridgewater,
Pembroke,
*Plymouth,** (*c. h.,*)
Plympton,
Plympton Station,
Rochester,
Rock,
Scituate,
Scotland,
South Abington,
South Carver,
South Duxbury,
South Hanover,
South Hanson,
South Hingham,
So. Middleborough,
South Plymouth,
South Scituate,
Wareham,
West Bridgewater,
West Duxbury,
West Hanover,
West Scituate,
West Wareham.

SUFFOLK COUNTY.

BOSTON,* (*c. h.,*)
Chelsea,*
North Chelsea,
Winthrop.

WORCESTER COUNTY.

Ashburnham,
Ashburnham Depot,
Athol,
Athol Depot,
Auburn,
Baldwinsville,
Barre,
Barre Plains,
Berlin,
Blackstone,
Bolton,
Boylston,
Boylston Centre,
Brookfield,
Burrageville,
Charlton,
Charlton City,
Charlton Depot,
Cherry Valley,
Clinton,*
Coldbrook Springs,
Cordaville,
Dana,
Douglass,

* Money-order office.

WORCESTER COUNTY—Continued.

Dudley,
East Blackstone,
East Brookfield,
Esat Douglass,
East Princeton,
East Templeton,
Farnumsville,
Fayville,
Fiskedale,
Fitchburgh,*
Gardner,
Gilbertville,
Globe Village,
Grafton,
Hardwick,
Harvard,
Holden,
Hopedale,
Hubbardston,
Lancaster,
Leicester,
Leominster,
Lunenburgh,
Manchaug,
Mendon,
Milford,*
Millbury,
Millville,
New Braintree,
New Engl'd Village,
Northborough,
Northbridge,
Northbridge Centre,
North Brookfield,*
North Dana,
North Leominster,
North Oxford,
North Rutland,
North Spencer,
North Uxbridge,
Oakdale,
Oakham,
Otter River,
Oxford,
Paxton,
Petersham,

WORCESTER COUNTY—Continued.

Phillipston,
Pratt's Junction,
Princeton,
Rochdale,
Royalston,
Rutland,
Saundersville,
Shrewsbury,
Smithville,
Southborough,
Southbridge,*
South Gardner,*
South Lancaster,
South Milford,
South Royalston,
Spencer,
Sterling,
Still River,
Sturbridge,
Sutton,
Templeton,
Upton,
Uxbridge,*
Wachusett Village,
Warren,
Webster,*
West Berlin,
Westborough,*
West Boylston,
West Brookfield,
West Dudley,
West Fitchburgh,
West Millbury,
Westminster,
Westminster Depot,
West Rutland,
West Sterling,
West Sutton,
West Upton,
West Warren,
Whitinsville,
Wilkinsonville,
Winchendon,*
Worcester,* (*c. h.*)

MICHIGAN.

ALCONA COUNTY.

Alcona,
Greenbush,
Harrisville, (*c. h.*)

ALLEGAN COUNTY.

Allegan,* (*c. h.*,)
Bradley,
Burnip's Corners,
Cheshire,
Dorr,
Douglas,
Dunningville,
Fenn's Mills,
Ganges,
Graafschap,
Gun Marsh,
Hamilton,
Hilliard's,
Hopkins,
Hopkins Station,
Manlius,
Martin,
Moline,
Monterey,
New Casco,
New Salem,
Otsego,
Overisel,
Plainwell,
Saugatuck,*
Silver Creek,
Watson,
Wayland,*
West Casco.

ALPENA COUNTY.

Alpena,* (*c. h.*,)
Ossineke.

ANTRIM COUNTY.

Antrim City,
Atwood,
Central Lake,
Clear Water,
Creswell,
Elk Rapids, (*c. h.*,)
Mitchell,
Rootville,
Spencer Creek,
Torch Lake.

BARRY COUNTY.

Assyria,
Baltimore,
Barryville,
Blair,
Bowen's Mills,
Cedar Creek,
Fillmore,
Gull Lake,
Hastings,* (*c. h.*,)
Hickory Corners,
Irving,
Johnstown,
Maple Grove,
Meadville,
Middleville,*
Milo,
Nashville,*
North Irving,
Orangeville Mills,
Prairieville,
Woodland,
Yankee Spring.

BAY COUNTY.

Arenac,
Au Gres,
Bay City,* (*c. h.*,)
Kawkawlin,
Portsmouth,
Salzburgh,
Skinner,
Wenona,
Williams.

BENZIE COUNTY.

Almira,
Benzonia, (*c. h.*,)
Frankfort,
Homestead,
Inland,
Joyfield,
Platte.

BERRIEN COUNTY.

Avery,
Bainbridge,
Benton Harbor,*
Berrien Centre,*
Berrien Springs, (*c. h.*,)
Bertrand,
Buchanan,*
Chickaming,

* Money-order office.

BERRIEN COUNTY—Continued.

Coloma,
Dayton,
Eau Claire,
Galien,
Laketon,
Millburgh,
New Buffalo,*
New Troy,
Niles,*
Pipestone,
Pleasant Valley,
Saint Joseph,*
Sawyer,
Sodus,
Three Oaks,*
Union Pier,
Watervleit,
Weesaw.

BRANCH COUNTY.

Algansee,
Batavia,
Bethel,
Bronson's Prairie,
Butler,
California,
Cold Water,* (c. h.,)
East Gilead,
Gilead,
Girard,
Kinderhook,
Mattison,
Noble Centre,
Orangeville,
Quincy,*
Round Lake,
Sherwood,
South Butler,
Union City.

CALHOUN COUNTY.

Abscota,
Albion,*
Athens,
Battle Creek,*
Bedford,
Burlington,
Ceresco,
Clarence,
Clarendon Centre,
Convis Centre,
East Leroy,
Homer,
Marengo,
Marshall,* (c. h.,)
Newton,
Partello,
Pine Creek,
Secillia,
Tekonsha,
West Leroy,

CASS COUNTY.

Adamsville,
Brownsville,
Calvin,
Cassopolis,* (c. h.,)
Dowagiac,*
Edwardsburgh,
Jeffersonville,
La Grange,
Little Prairie Ronde,
Marcellus,
Model City,
Newburgh,
Pokagon,
Shave Head,
Summerville,
Union,
Vandalia,
Volinia,
Williamsville.

CHARLEVOIX COUNTY.

Barnard,
Boyne,
Charlevoix, (c. h.,)
Nelsonville,
Norwood.

CHEBOYGAN COUNTY.

Cheboygan, (c. h.)

CHIPPEWA COUNTY.

Detour,
Sault de Ste. Marie, (c. h.)

CLINTON COUNTY.

Bath,
Bengal,
Dallas,
De Witt,
Du Plain,
Eagle,
Elsie,
Essex,
Eureka,
Geary,
Lyon's Mill,
Maple Rapids,
North Eagle,
Olive,
Ovid,*
Riley,
Saint John's,* (c. h.,)
Shepardsville,
South Riley,
Victor,
Wacousta,
Westphalia.

DELTA COUNTY.

Esconawba,* (c. h.,)
Garden,
Nahma.

EATON COUNTY.

Allen's,
Bellevue,*
Brookfield,
Carlisle,
Centre,
Charlotte,* (c. h.,)
Chester,
County Line,
Delta,
Eaton Rapids,
Elmira,
Grand Ledge,
Kalamo,
Mud Creek,
Olivet,*
Pottersville,
Roxana,
Sunfield,
Vermontville,
West Windsor,
Windsor.

EMMETT COUNTY.

Bear River,
Little Traverse, (c. h.)

GENESEE COUNTY.

Argentine,
Atlas,
Clio,
Davison,
Elgin,
Fentonville,*
Flint,* (c. h.,)
Flushing,
Gaines' Station,
Genesee Village,
Goodrich,
Grand Blanc,
Kipp's Corners,
Linden,
Montrose,
Mt. Morris Station,
Mundy,
Otisville,
Pine Run,
Richfield,
Swartz Creek,
Thetford Centre,
Whitesburgh.

GRAND TRAVERSE COUNTY.

Acme,
Betsey Lake,
Cedar Run,
East Traverse Bay,
Mapleton,
Mayfield,
Monroe Centre,
Old Mission,
Traverse City,* (c. h.,)
Williamsburgh,
Yuba.

GRATIOT COUNTY.

Alma,
Beaver Creek,
Bridgeville,
Elm Hall,
Forest Hill,
Ithaca,* (c. h.,)
La Fayette,
Newark,
New Haven Centre,
North Star,
Pompei.
Saint Louis,
Spring Brook,
Stella,
Summerton,
Sumner,
Wheeler.

* Money-order office.

Hillsdale County.

Allen,
Amboy,
Cambria Mills,
Camden,
Cass,
Church's Corners,
Edinburgh,
Frontier,
Hillsdale,* (*c. h.*,)
Jefferson,
Jonesville,*
Litchfield,*
Morganville,
Moscow,
Mosherville,
North Adams,
Osseo,
Pittsford,
Ransom,
Reading,
Somerset,
South Camden,
South Wright,
Wheatland Centre.

Houghton County.

Baraga,
Calumet,
Hancock,
Houghton,* (*c. h.*,)
Lake Linden,
L'Ance.

Huron County.

Can,
Caseville,
Cracow,
Forest Bay,
Huron City,
New River,
Ora Labor,
Pinnebog,
Port Austin, (*c. h.*,)
Port Crescent,
Port Hope,
Rock Falls,
Sand Beach,
Sebewaing,
Verona Mills,
White Rock.

Ingham County.

Alverson,
Aurelius,
Bunker Hill,
Dansville,
Eden,
Felt's,
Fitchburgh,
Holt,
LANSING,*
Leslie,
Locke,
Mason,* (*c. h.*,)
Middletown,
North Aurelius,
Okemos,
Onondaga,
Red Bridge,
Stockbridge,
Webberville,
White Oak,
Williamstown,
Winfield.

Ionia County.

Algodon,
Campbell,
Danby,
Easton,
Hubbardston,
Ionia,* (*c. h.*,)
Keene,
Kiddville,
Lyons,*
Maple,
Matherton,
Muir,
North Plains,
Orange,
Orleans,
Otisco,
Palo,
Patterson's Mills,
Pewamo,
Portland,
Saranac,
Sebewa,
Smyrna,
South Boston,
South Cass,
West Campbell,
Wood's Corners.

Iosco County.

Alabaster,
Au Sable,
East Tawas,
Ogemaw,
Rollo,
Tawas City,* (*c. h.*)

Isabella County.

Crawford,
Isabella City,
Mt. Pleasant, (*c. h.*,)
Rowland,
Salt River,
Strickland,
Winn,
Wiota.

Jackson County.

Arland,
Baldwin's Mills,
Brooklyn,*
Columbia,
Concord,
Franciscoville,
Grass Lake,*
Hanover,
Henrietta,
Jackson,* (*c. h.*,)
Leoni,
Liberty,
Michigan Centre,
Napoleon,
Norvell,
Otter Creek,
Parma,*
Pulaski,
Rives Junction,
Sandstone,
South Jackson,
Spring Arbor,
Springport,
Tompkins,
Waterloo.

Kalamazoo County.

Alamo,
Augusta,
Brady,
Climax Prairie,
Comstock,
Cooper,
Fulton,
Galesburgh,*
Kalamazoo,* (*c. h.*,)
Oshtemo,
Pavilion,
Portage,
Richland,
Schoolcraft,
South Climax,
Wakeshma,
Yorkville.

Kent County.

Ada,
Alaska,
Alpine,
Alto,
Alton,
Ashley,
Austerlitz,
Belmont,
Bostwick Lake,
Bówne,
Burch's,
Byron Centre,
Caledonia,
Caledonia Station,
Cannonsburgh,
Cascade,
Casnovia,
Cedar Springs,
Cody's Mills,
Cortland Centre,
Edgerton,
Englishville,
Fallassburgh,
Gainesville,
Grand Rapids,* (*c. h.*,)
Grandville,
Grant,
Grattan,
Hammond,
Harris' Creek,
Indian Creek,
Kelloggsville,
Lowell,
Mill Creek,
Nelson,
North Byron,
Oakfield,
Pleasant,
Rockford,*
Sand Lake,
Sparta Centre,
Spencer's Mill,
Vergennes.

Keweenaw County.

Copper Falls Mine,
Copper Harbor,
Eagle Harbor,
Eagle River, (*c. h.*,)
Penn Mine,
Phœnix.

* Money-order office.

Lake County.

Pine River.

Lapeer County.

Almont,
Burnside,
Clifford,
Columbiaville,
Dryden,
Farmer's Creek,
Five Lakes,
Goodland,
Hadley,
Hasler,
Hunter's Creek,
Imlay,
Lapeer,* (*c. h.*,)
Marathon,
Metamora,
Mill Station,
North Branch,
Pool,
Rural Vale,
Thornville.

Leelenaw County.

Burdickville,
Empire,
Glen Arbor,
Glen Haven,
Good Harbor,
Leland,
Melville,
Micham,
Northport,* (*c. h.*,)
North Unity,
Omena,
Solon,
Sutton's Bay.

Lenawee County.

Addison,
Adrian,* (*c. h.*,)
Blissfield,
Cambridge,
Canandaigua,
Clayton,
Clinton,
Deerfield,
Fairfield,
Geneva,
Hudson,*
Kelly's Corners,
Lake Ridge,
Macon,
Medina,
Morenci,
Ogden Centre,
Palmyra,
Raisin Centre,
Ridgeway,
Riga,
Rollin,
Rome,
Seneca,
Springville,
Tecumseh,*
Tipton,
Wellsville,
West Ogden,
Weston,
Woodstock.

Livingston County.

Brighton,
Cohoctah,
Conway,
Deer Creek,
Fleming,
Fowlerville,
Genoa,
Green Oak,
Hamburgh,
Hartland,
Howell, (*c. h.*,)
Josco,
Madison,
Marion,
Oak Grove,
Oceola Centre,
Parshallville,
Pettysville,
Pinckney,
Plainfield,
Tyrone,
Unadilla.

Mackinac County.

Mackinaw, (*c. h.*)

Macomb County.

Armada,
Cady,
Disco,
Fraser.
Macomb,
Meade,
Memphis,
Milton,
Mt. Clemens,* (*c. h.*,)
Mount Vernon,
New Baltimore,
New Haven,
Quinn,
Ray Centre,
Richmond,
Romeo,*
Roseville,
Utica,*
Waldenburgh,
Warren,
Washington.

Manistee County.

Bear Lake,
Filer City,
Manistee,* (*c. h.*,)
Norwalk,
Pleasanton,
Stronach,
Turnersport.

Manitou County.

St. James, (*c. h.*)

Marquette County.

Clarksburgh,
Greenwood Furnace,
Harvey,
Humboldt,
Ishpeming,
Marquette,* (*c. h.*,)
Morgan,
Negaunee.

Mason County.

Amber,
Colfax,
Fairview,
Indian Town,
Lincoln, (*c. h.*,)
Ludington,*
Riverton,
Victory.

Mecosta County.

Big Creek,
Big Rapids,* (*c. h.*,)
Chippewa Lake,
Fork,
Mecosta,
Millbrook,
Morley,
Paris,
Rienza,
Satterlee's Mills.

Menomonee County.

Cedar Fork,
Menomonee,* (*c. h.*)

Midland County.

Averill's Station,
Edenville,
Midland,* (*c. h.*,)
Porter.

Monroe County.

Athlone,
Dundee,
East Milan,
Erie,
Exeter,
Grafton,
Hamlin,
Ida,
Lambertville,
La Salle,
London,
Monroe,* (*c. h.*,)
Newport,
North Raisinville,
Oakville,
Ottawa Lake,
Petersburgh,
West Milan,
Whiteford Centre.

* Money-order office.

Montcalm County.

Amsden, Bloomer Centre, Bushnell Centre, Carson City, Cato, Coral, Crystal, Ferris, Greenville,* Howard City, Lakeview, Langston, Maple Hill, New Home, Pierson, Raynold, Sheridan, Sidney, *Stanton, (c. h.,)* Tamarack, Vickeryville, Wood Lake.

Muskegon County.

Black Lake, Blue Lake, Bluffton, Brown's Mills, Carleton, Forest City, Fruitport, Harwood, Howard, Mile Creek, Montague,* *Muskegon,* (c. h.,)* Ravenna, Slocum's Grove, Trent, Whitehall, White River.

Newaygo County.

Ætna, Ashland, Barton, Big Prairie, Bridgeton, Cook's Station, Croton,* Denver, Ensley, Fremont Centre, Home, Lake, Martinsburgh, *Newago,* (c. h.,)* Ponama, Sitka.

Oakland County.

Austin, Big Beaver, Birmingham, Brandon, Clarkston, Commerce, Davisburgh, Drayton Plains, Farmington, Four Towns, Franklin, Groveland, Highland, Holly,* Jersey, Kensington, Lakeville, Mahopac, Milford,* New Hudson, North Farmington, Novi, Oak Hill, Oakland, Oakwood, Orion, Ortonville, Oxford, *Pontiac,* (c. h.,)* Rochester, Rose, Royal Oak, Southfield, South Lyon, Springfield, Spring Mills, Stony Run, Strait's Lake, Troy, Walled Lake, Waterford, West Novi, White Lake.

Oceana County.

Alice, Benona, Blackberry Ridge, Clay Bank, Cob Moo Sa, Flower Creek, Golding, Hansen, *Hart,* (c. h.,)* Hesperia,

Oceana County—Continued.

Marshville, Pa Pa Me, Pentwater,* Reed, Shelby, Spring Creek, Smith's Corners, Stebbinsville, Thomas, Weare.

Ontonagon County.

Greenland, *Ontonagon, (c. h.,)* Rockland.

Osceola County.

Bates, Brookside, Crapo, Evarts, *Hersey, (c. h.)*

Ottawa County.

Allendale, Berlin, Big Spring, Blendon, Coopersville, Dennison, Eastmansville, Ferrysburgh, Georgetown, *Grand Haven,* (c. h.,)* Hanley, Holland* Jamestown, Lamont, Lisbon, Nunica, Ohio Mill, Port Sheldon, Pottamie, Robinson, Six Corners, South Georgetown, Spring Lake, Tallmadge, Ventura, Vriesland, Zeeland.

Saginaw County.

Birch Run, Blumfield, Blumfield Junction, Bridgeport Centre, Buena Vista, Carrollton, Cass Bridge, Chesaning, East Saginaw,* Elk, Frankenlust, Frankenmuth, Hemlock City Hughesville, Jay, Oakley, Randall, *Saginaw,* (c. h.,)* Saint Charles, South Saginaw, Swan Creek, Taymouth, Trostville, Zilwaukee.

Saint Clair County.

Algonac, Belle River, Berville, Brockway, Brockway Centre, Capac, Casco, China, Clyde Mills, Columbus, Emmett, Fair Haven, Fort Gratiot, Jeddo, Kenockee, Lake Port, Lynn, Marine City,* Marysville, Merrillsville, Port Huron,* Riley Centre, Robert's Landing, Ruby, *Saint Clair,* (c. h.,)* Smith's Creek, Thornton, Vincent, Wales.

* Money-order office.

SAINT JOSEPH COUNTY.

Burr Oak, *
Centreville, (c. h.,)
Colon,
Constantine,
Fawn River,
Florence,
Flowerfield,
Howardsville,
Leonidas,
Mendon,
Mottville,
Oporto,
Park,
Parkville,
Sturgis,*
Three Rivers, *
White Pigeon.

SANILAC COUNTY.

Amadore,
Buel,
Cedar Dale,
Davisville,
Deckerville,
Farmer's,
Forestville,
Forrester,
*Lexington,** (c. h.,)
Marlette,
Minden,
Newman,
Pack's Mills,
Peck,
Pine Hill,
Port Sanilac,
Richmondville,
Tyre.

SCHOOLCRAFT COUNTY.

Munising,
Onota.

SHIAWASSEE COUNTY.

Bennington,
Burns,
Byron,
*Corunna,** (c. h.,)
Fremont,
Glass River,
Hartwellville,
Hazelton,
Hazel Green,
Laingsburgh,
Mungerville,
North Newberg,
North Vernon,
Owosso,*
Perry,
Pittsburgh,
Vernon.
West Haven.

TUSCOLA COUNTY.

Akron,
*Caro,** (c. h.,)
Cass City,
Denmark,
East Dayton,
Elkland,
Ellington,
Fair Grove,
Gagetown,
Gilford,
May,
Millington,
Newbury,
Pine Grove,
Richville,
Unionville,
*Vassar,** (c. h.,)
Wahjamega,
Watertown,
Watrousville,
Worth.

VAN BUREN COUNTY.

Almena,
Arlington,
Bangor,
Bear Lake Mills,
Bloomingdale,
Breedsville,
Covert,
Decatur,
Glendale,
Hartford,
Hooker,
Keelersville,
Kendall,
Lake Mill,
Lawrence,*
Lawton,*
Mattawan,
*Paw Paw,** (c. h.,)
Pine Grove Mills,
Prospect Lake,
South Haven,
Waverly,
West Geneva.

WASHTENAW COUNTY.

*Ann Arbor,** (c. h.,)
Base Lake,
Benton,
Chelsea,
Dexter,
Fredonia,
Gravel Run,
Lima.
Manchester,
Milan,
Paint Creek,
River Raisin,
Salem,
Saline,
Scio,
Stony Creek,
Summit,
Sylvan,
Webster,
Whitmore Lake,
York,
Ypsilanti.*

WAYNE COUNTY.

Belleville,
Brownstown,
Canton,
Conner's Creek,
Dalton's Corners,
Dearbornville,
Delroy,
Denton,
*Detroit,** (c. h.,)
Ecorse,
Elm,
Gibraltar,
Greenfield,
Huron Station,
Inkster,
Martinsville,
Mead's Mills,
Nankin,
Northville,
Oak,
Perrinsville,
Plank Road,
Plymouth,
Rawsonville,
Redford,
Romulus,
Smithville,
Taylor Centre,
Trenton,
Wallaceville,
Wayne,
Wyandotte,
Yew.

WEXFORD COUNTY.

Clay Hill,
Sherman, (c. h.,)
Wexford.

MINNESOTA.

ANOKA COUNTY.

*Anoka,** (c. h.,)
Bethel,
Centreville,
Coon Creek,
Itaska,
Linwood,
Manomin,
Oak Grove,
Oak Springs,
Saint Francis.

BENTON COUNTY.

Duelin,
Langola,
Maywood,
Minden,
Sauk Rapids, (c. h.,)
Watab.

* Money-order office.

Blue Earth County.

Beauford,
Butternut Valley,
Castle Garden,
Decoria,
Garden City,
Garden Prairie,
Iceland,
Judson,
Lake Crystal,
Mankato,* (*c. h.*,)
Maple River,
Mapleton,
Medo,
Perch Lake,
Pleasant Mounds,
Shelbyville,
Sherman,
South Bend,
Sterling Centre,
Tivoli,
Vernon Centre,
Watauwon,
Willow Creek,
Winnebago Agency.

Brown County.

Backville,
Cottonwood,
Golden Lake,
Home,
Iberia,
Leavenworth,
Linden,
Lone Tree Lake,
Milford,
New Ulm,* (*c. h.*)

Carver County.

Benton,
Carver,*
Chaska, (*c. h.*,)
Laketown,
Oberle's Corners,
Redfield,
Waconia,
Watertown,
Young America.

Cass County.

Leech Lake.

Chippewa County.

Benson,
Chippewa City, (*c. h.*,)
Granite Falls,
Hawk Creek,
Reeson.

Chisago County.

Chisago City, (*c. h.*,)
Chisago Lake,
Franconia,
Muskootink,
Rush City,
Stark,
Sunrise City,
Taylor's Falls,
Wyoming.

Clay County.

Georgetown,
Holy Cross.

Crow Wing County.

Crow Wing, (*c. h.*)

Dakota County.

Castle Rock,
Christiana,
East Castle Rock,
Empire City,
Farmington,*
Hampton,
Hastings,* (*c. h.*,)
Lakeville,
Lewiston,
Mendota,
New Trier,
Nininger,
Pine Bend,
Rich Valley,
Rosemount,
Waterford,
West Saint Paul.

Dodge County.

Ashland,
Berne,
Claremont,
Concord,
Dodge Centre,
Ellington,
Kasson,*
Mantorville,* (*c. h.*,)
Rice Lake,
Union Spring,
Vernon,
Wasioga.

Douglas County.

Alexandria, (*c. h.*,)
Brandon,
Evansville,
Holmes City,
Millenville,
Moe,
Osakis.

Faribault County.

Banks,
Barber,
Bass Lake,
Blue Earth City,* (*c. h.*,)
Clayton,
Eden,
Elmore,
Ewald,
Grant,
Grapeland,
Minnesota Lake,
Pilot Grove,
Walnut Lake,
Well,
Winnebago City.*

Fillmore County.

Alba,
Amherst,
Arendahl,
Belleville,
Big Spring,
Bratsberg,
Canfield,
Carimona,
Carrollton,
Chatfield,*
Cherry Grove,
Elliota,
Etna,
Fairview,
Farmer's Grove,
Fillmore,
Forestville,
Free Soil,
Granger,
Hamilton,
Harmony,
Highland,
Kedron,
Lanesborough,
Lenora,
Newburgh,
Pilot Mound,
Preston,* (*c. h.*,)
Prosper,
Rushford,*
Spring Valley,*
Washington,
Watson Creek,
Waukokee,
Whalan.

Freeborn County.

Albert Lea,* (*c. h.*,)
Alden,
Bancroft,
Clark's Grove,
Freeborn,
Fremont,
Geneva,
Gordonsville,
Guildford,
Hartland,
Hayward,
Moscow,
Nunda,
Shell Rock,
State Line,
Sumner,
Trenton.

Goodhue County.

Ayr,
Belle Creek,
Cannon River Falls,
Fair Point,
Frontenac,
Goodhue Centre,
Hader,
Holden,
Kenyon,
Minneola,

* Money-order office.

GOODHUE COUNTY—Continued.

Norway,
Pine Island,
Red Wing,* (*c. h.*,)
Roscoe,
Roscoe Centre,
Spring Creek,
Stanton,
Vasa,
Wanaminga,
Wastedo,
Zumbrota.

GRANT COUNTY.

Pomme de Terre.

HENNEPIN COUNTY.

Bloomington,
Bloomington Ferry,
Brooklyn,
Champlin,
Corcoran,
Dayton,
Eden Prairie,
Excelsior,
Fort Snelling,
Greenwood,
Hassan,
Leighton,
Lenz,
Long Lake,
Maple Grove,
Maple Plain,
Minneapolis,* (*c. h.*,)
Minnetonka,
Minnetrista,
Osseo,
Richfield,
St. Anthony's Falls,*
Saint Bonifacius,
Wayzata.

HOUSTON COUNTY.

Brownsville,
Caledonia,* (*c. h.*,)
Eitzen,
Freeburgh,
Hokah,
Houston,
La Crescent,
Lorettee,
Money Creek,
Riceford,
San Jacinto,
Sheldon,
Spring Grove,
Union,
Wilmington,
Winnebago Valley,
Yucatan.

ISANTI COUNTY.

Cambridge,
Isanti,
Maple Ridge,
North Branch,
Oxford, (*c. h.*,)
Spencer Brook,
Stanchfield.

JACKSON COUNTY.

Jackson, (*c. h.*,)
Petersburgh,
Summit.

KANABEC COUNTY.

Brunswick, (*c. h.*)

KANDIYOHI COUNTY.

Atwater,
Kandiyohi,
Kandiyohi St'n, (*c. h.*,)
Lake Lillian,
Willmar.

LAKE COUNTY.

Beaver Bay, (*c. h.*,)
Grand Portage,
Pigeon River.

LE SUEUR COUNTY.

Anawauk,
Cleveland,
Cordova,
Dresselville,
Elysian,
Jefferson Lake,
Kasota,
Kilkenny,
Lake Washington,
Le Sueur,* (*c. h.*,)
Lexington,
Marysburgh,
Montgomery,
Ottawa,
Rudolph,
Saint Henry,
Saint Hubertus,
Union Centre,
Waterville.

LINCOLN COUNTY.

Swansea.

LYON COUNTY.

Ceresco,
Lynd.

MCLEOD COUNTY.

Bergen,
Brush Prairie,
E. Hutchinson,
Glencoe,* (*c. h.*,)
Glendale,
Hutchinson,
Koniska,
Lake Addie,
Plato,
Rocky Run,
Saint George,
Silver Lake,
Sumter,
Winsted Lake,

MARTIN COUNTY.

Amber,
Andrew Johnson,
Cedarville,
Centre Creek,
Chain Lake Centre,
East Chain Lakes,
Fairmont, (*c. h.*,)
Horicon,
Lone Cedar,
May,
Nashville Centre,
Pleasant Prairie,
Prairie Creek,
Rose Lake,
Rutland,
Tenhassen,
Walnut Grove,
Waverly.

MEEKER COUNTY.

Collinwood,
Crow River,
Darwin,
Dassel,
Forest City,*
Greenleaf,
Kingston,
Koronis,
Lake Harold,
Litchfield, (*c. h.*,)
Manannah,
Swede Grove,
Swift Lake,
Sylvan Hill.

MILLE LACS COUNTY.

Princeton, (*c. h.*)

MONONGALIA COUNTY.

Burbank,
Georgeville,
Green Lake,
Harrison,
Irving,
New London, (*c. h.*,)
Norway Lake,
Roseville,
Sand Lake.

* Money-order office.

Morrison County.

Belle Prairie,
Culdrum,
Fort Ripley,
Green Prairie,
Little Falls, (c. h.,)
North Prairie,
Pike Rapids,
Swan River,
Two Rivers.

Mower County.

Adams,
Austin, (c. h.)*
Frankford,
Grand Meadow,
Lansing,
Leroy,*
Madison,
Mineral Springs,
Minnereka,
Mower City,
Nevada,
Prairie,
Root River,
Rose Creek,
Waltham.

Murray County.

Lake Shetek.

Nicollet County.

Courtland,
Fort Ridgely,*
Granby,
Hebron,
Nicollet,
Norseland,
Redstone,
Saint Peter, (c. h.,)*
Travers des Sioux,
West Newton.

Noble County.

Graham Lake.

Olmsted County.

Byron,
Cascade,
Chester,
Dover Centre,
Eyota,
Farm Hill,
High Forest,
Little Valley,
Marion,
Oronoco,
Othello,
Pleasant Grove,
Quincy,
Rochester, (c. h.,)*
Rock Dell,
Salem,
Six Oaks,
Stewartville.

Otter Tail County.

Balmoral,
Clitheral,
Fergus Falls,
Otter Tail City,(c. h.,)
Rush Lake.

Pine County.

Hinckley,
Chengwatana,(c. h.,)
Pine City.

Pope County.

Anderson,
Gilchrist,
Glenwood, (c. h.,)
Lake Johanna,
Otto,
Reno,
Rolling Fork,
Westfield,
White Bear Centre.

Ramsey County.

Little Canada,
SAINT PAUL,* (c. h.,)
White Bear Lake.

Redwood County.

Lower Sioux Agency,
Redwood Falls, (c. h.,)
Rock Valley,
Swedes Forest,
Weldon,
Yellow Medicine.

Renville County.

Beaver Falls, (c. h.,)
Birch Cooley,
Cedar Mills,
Cosmos,
Franklin,
Herzhorn,
Sacred Heart.

Rice County.

Cannon City,
Dundas,
East Prairieville,
Faribault, (c. h.,)*
Fowlersville,
Hazelwood,
Millersburgh,
Morristown,
Northfield,*
Shieldsville,
Union Lakes,
Warsaw,
Wheatland,
Wheeling.

Rock County.

Luverne.

St. Louis County.

Du Luth, (c. h.,)
Fond du Lac,
Oneoto,
Vermillion Lake.

Scott County.

Belle Plaine,*
Blakeley,
Cedar Lake,
Hamilton Station,
Helena,
Lydia,
Maple Glen,
New Dublin,
New Market,
Oral,
Raven Stream,
St. Lawrence,
Sand Creek, *
Shakopee, (c. h.)*

Sherburne County.

Big Lake,
Brantford,
Clear Lake,
Elk River Station,
Lake Fremont,
Livonia,
Orlando,
Orono, (c. h.,)
Pleasant Valley,
Santiago.

Sibley County.

Arlington,
Cornish,
Dryden,
Eagle City,
Faxon,
Green Isle,
Henderson, (c. h.,)*
Kelso,
New Auburn,
Rush River,
Sibley,
Transit.

Stearns County.

Brockway,
Cold Spring City,
Fair Haven,
George Lake,
Kennebec,
Leedston,
Long Hill,
Luxemburgh,
Maine Prairie,
Melrose,
New Munich,
North Fork,

* Money-order office.

STEARNS COUNTY—Continued.

Paynesville,
Raymond,
Rockville,
Saint Augusta,
*Saint Cloud,** (*c. h.*,)
Saint Joseph,
Sauk Centre,*
Spring Hill,
Torah,
Zions.

STEELE COUNTY.

Aurora,
Berlin,
Blooming Prairie,
Clinton Falls,
Cooleysville,
Deerfield,
Dodge City,
East Meriden,
Elwood,
Havanna,
Lemond,
Medford,
Meriden, (*c. h.*,)
Merton,
Oak Glen,
Owatonna,*
River Point,
Steele Centre,

STEVENS COUNTY.

Passe de Terre,
Potosi,
Scandia.

STONE COUNTY.

Lake Traverse.

TODD COUNTY.

Burnhamsville,
Hartford,
Long Prairie, (*c. h.*,)
Round Prairie.

WABASHAW COUNTY.

Bear Valley,
Cook's Valley,
Elgin,
Forest Mound,
Glasgow,
Gopher Prairie,
Hyde Park,
Lake City, *
Lincoln,
Lyon,
Mazeppa,
Millville,
Minneska,
Pawselin,
Plainview,*
Reed's Landing,
Smithfield,
South Troy,
*Wabashaw,** (*c. h.*,)
Watopa,
West Albany,
West Chester,
Woodland,
Zumbro Falls.

WASECA COUNTY.

Alma City,
Blooming Grove,
Cobb River,
Janesville,
Maine,
New Richland,
Okaman,
Otisco,

WASECA COUNTY—Continued.

Vivian,
Waseca,*
*Wilton,** (*c. h.*,)

WASHINGTON COUNTY.

Afton,
Cottage Grove,
Forest Lake,
Lakeland,
Lohmansville,
Marine Mills,
Newport,
Oak Dale,
Point Douglas,
*Stillwater,** (*c. h.*,)
Woodbury.

WATONWAN COUNTY.

Antrim,
Ashippen,
Madelia, (*c. h.*,)
Norwegian.

WILKIN COUNTY.

McCauleyville.

WINONA COUNTY.

Argo,
Beaver,
Dresbach,
Elba,
Enterprise,
Frank Hill,
Homer,
Jefferson,
Lamoille,
Minnesota City,
Nevill,
New Boston,
New Hartford,
North Warren,
Oak Ridge,
Pickwick,
Richmond,
Ridgeway,
Rolling Stone,
Saint Charles,*
Saratoga,
Stockton,
Troy,
Utica,
White Water Falls,
*Winona,** (*c. h.*,)
Wiscoy,
Witoka,
Worth,
Wyattville.

WRIGHT COUNTY.

Albion,
Big Woods,
Buffalo, (*c. h.*,)
Cassel,
Chatham,
Clear Water,
Corrinna,
Dean Lake,
Delano,
French Lake,
Howard,
Lilly Pond,
Maple Lake,
Monticello*,
Montrose,
Mooer's Prairie,
Otsego,
Rockford,
Saint Michael's,
Silver Creek,
Waverly Mills.

MISSISSIPPI.

ADAMS COUNTY.

*Natchez,** (*c. h.*)

ALCORN COUNTY.

Anderson,
Antioch,

ALCORN COUNTY—Continued.

*Corinth,** (*c. h.*,)
Danville,
Jacinto,
Kossuth,
Rienzi,
Silver Springs.

* Money-order office

Amite County.

Centreville,
Liberty, (c. h.,)
Smithdale.

Attala County.

Kosciusko, (c. h.,)
Wells.

Bolivar County.

Australia,
Beulah, (c. h.,)
Bolivar,
Carson's Landing,
Neblett's Landing.

Calhoun County.

Banner,
Benela,
Concord,
Erin,
Hopewell,
Pittsborough, (c. h.,)
Robertsonville,
Sarepta.

Carroll County.

Black Hawk,
Carrollton, (c. h.,)
Duck Hill,
Greenwood,
Vaiden,
Winona.

Chickasaw County.

Big Springs,
Buena Vista,
Egypt,
Houlka,
Houston, (c. h.,)
Montpelier,
Okolona,*
Palo Alto,
Pine Bluff,
Sonora,
Sparta.

Choctaw County.

Ada,
Bankston,
Bellefontaine,
Black's Wells,
Cadaretta,
Cumberland,
Dido,
Greensborough, (c. h.,)
Huntsville,
Lodi,
Monte Vista,
Pigeon Roost,
Poplar Creek,
Republican.

Claiborne County.

Grand Gulf,
Port Gibson, (c. h.,)
Rocky Springs.

Clark County.

De Soto,
Enterprise, (c. h.,)
Quitman,
Shubuta.

Coahoma County.

Dowd's Landing,
Friar's Point, (c. h.,)
Moon Lake.

Copiah County.

Bahala,
Crystal Springs,*
Gallatin,
Hazlehurst,*
Linden,
Martinsville,
Mount Hope,
Pine Ridge,
Rockport,
Wesson.

Covington County.

Janesville,
Mount Carmel,
Station Creek,
Williamsburgh, (c. h.)

De Soto County.

Arkabutla,
Coldwater,
De Soto Front,
Hernando, (c. h.,)
Horn Lake,
Looxahoma,
Nesbit's Station,
Olive Branch,
Senatobia.

Franklin County.

Hamburgh,
Knoxville,
Meadville, (c. h.,)
Morgan's Fork.

Grenada County.

Bowen,
Elliott,
Graysport,
Grenada,* (c. h.,)
Hardy Station,
Torrance.

Hancock County.

Gainesville,
Pearlington,
Shieldsborough, (c. h.)

Harrison County.

Biloxi,
Handsborough,
Mississippi City, (c. h.,)
Pass Christian.

Hinds County.

Bear Creek,
Bolton's Depot,
Byram,
Clinton,
Dry Grove,
Edward's Depot,
JACKSON,* (c. h.,)
Midway,
Raymond,
Terry,
Utica.

Holmes County.

Durant,
Goodman,
Lexington, (c. h.,)
Pickens' Station,
West's Station.

Issaquena County.

Ingomar,
Osborn's Store,
Skipwith's Landing,
Tallulah, (c. h.)

Itawamba County.

Mooreville,
Yocony.

Jackson County.

Americus, (c. h.,)
Moss Point,
Ocean Springs,
Pascagoula,
Vancleave's.

Jasper County.

Claiborne,
Garlandville,
Paulding, (c. h.,)
Turnerville.

* Money-order office.

JEFFERSON COUNTY.

Church Hill, *Fayette,** (c. h.,) Perth, Rodney, Union Church.

JONES COUNTY.

Ellisville, (c. h.,) Erata, Pinnellville.

KEMPER COUNTY.

De Kalb, (c. h.,) Fort Stephens, Gainesville Junction, Herbert, Kellis' Store, Peden, Rio, Scooba, Sucarnoochee, Tamola Station, Wahalak Station.

LA FAYETTE COUNTY.

Abbeville, Caswell, La Fayette Springs, Maple Springs, *Oxford,** (c. h.,) Spring Dale, Taylor's Depot.

LAUDERDALE COUNTY.

Daleville, Kewanee, Lauderdale Station, Lockhart, Marion Station, *Meridian,** (c. h.,) Toomsuba.

LAWRENCE COUNTY.

Monticello, (c. h.,) Silver Creek, White Sand.

LEAKE COUNTY.

Carthage, (c. h.,) Conway, Edinburgh, Good Hope, High Hill, Ofahoma, Standing Pine, Thomastown.

LEE COUNTY.

Baldwyn, Coonewar, Ellistown, Guntown, Saltillo, Shannon, *Tupelo,* (c. h.,) Verona.

LINCOLN COUNTY.

Bogue Chitto, *Brookhaven,** (c. h.)

LOWNDES COUNTY.

Artesia, Caledonia, *Columbus,** (c. h.,) Crawfordville, Mayhew's Station, Tibby Station, West Point.

MADISON COUNTY.

Breckville, Calhoun, Camden, *Canton,** (c. h.,) Pearl City, Tongaloo.

MARION COUNTY.

Columbia, (c. h.,) Fordsville.

MARSHALL COUNTY.

Byhalia, Chulahoma, Early Grove, *Holly Springs,** (c. h.,) Hudsonville, Lamar, North Mt. Pleasant, Red Banks, Tyro, Waterford.

MONROE COUNTY.

*Aberdeen,** (c. h.,) Aberdeen Junction, Athens, Cotton Gin Port, Hamilton, Lannsdale, Prairie Station, Smithville, Temperance Hill.

NESHOBA COUNTY.

Coffadeliah, Laurel Hill, *Philadelphia,* (c h.)

NEWTON COUNTY.

Chunkey's Station, Decatur, Hickory, Lawrence, Newton, Union.

NOXUBEE COUNTY.

Brookville, Gholson, *Macon,* (c. h.,) Shuqualak.

OKTIBBEHA COUNTY.

Ash Creek, Choctaw Agency, Double Springs, Siloam, *Starkville,* (c. h.,) Whitefield

PANOLA COUNTY.

Batesville, Como Depot, Elliott's Mill, Lake Creswell, Long Creek Depot, Longtown, *Panola,* (c. h.,) Pleasant Mount, Pope's Depot, Sardis.

PERRY COUNTY.

Augusta, (c. h.,) Enon, Monroe.

PIKE COUNTY.

Chatawa, China Grove, Conerly's, Magnolia, Osyka, Summit.

PONTOTOC COUNTY.

Cherry Creek, Chesterville, New Albany, *Pontotoc,* (c. h.,) Red Land, Rocky Ford, Tardyville, Toccopola.

* Money-order office.

PRENTISS COUNTY.

Allen's Store,
Bay Springs,
Booneville, (*c. h.*,)
Dry Run,
Fulton,
Pleasonton,
Ryan's Well.

RANKIN COUNTY.

Brandon,* (*c. h.*,)
Cato,
Fannin,
Goshen Springs,
Pelahatchee Depot.

SCOTT COUNTY.

Damascus,
Forest,
Hillsborough, (*c. h.*,)
Homewood,
Lake,
Morton.

SIMPSON COUNTY.

Mount Zion,
Saunders' Creek,
Westville, (*c. h.*)

SMITH COUNTY.

Polkville,
Raleigh, (*c. h.*,)
Sylvarena,
Trenton.

SUN FLOWER COUNTY.

McNutt, (*c. h.*,)
Shell Mound.

TALLAHATCHEE COUNTY.

Charleston, (*c. h.*,)
Harrison Station.

TIPPAH COUNTY.

Cotton Plant,
Dumas,
Hickory Flat,
Jonesborough,
New Barden,
Orizaba,
Ripley, (*c. h.*,)
Ruckersville,
Union Mills.

TISHEMINGO COUNTY.

Barnes' Store,
Burnsville,
Cartersville,
Eastport,
Highland,
Iuka, (*c. h.*)

TUNICA COUNTY.

Austin, (*c. h.*,)
Bennett's Landing,
Commerce.

WARREN COUNTY.

Bovina,
Hurricane,
New Town Landing,
Vicksburgh,* (*c. h.*,)
Warrenton.

WASHINGTON COUNTY.

Egg's Point,
Greenville, (*c. h.*,)
Leota Landing.

WAYNE COUNTY.

Bucatunna,
Waynesborough, (*c. h.*,)
Winchester.

WILKINSON COUNTY.

Fort Adams,
Woodville,* (*c. h.*)

WINSTON COUNTY.

Buckhorn,
Fearn's Springs,
Louisville, (*c. h.*,)
New Prospect,
Rome,
Webster.

YALABUSHA COUNTY.

Air Mount,
Coffeeville, (*c. h.*,)
Garner's Station,
Oakland,
Pine Valley,
Post Oak,
Tillatoba,
Water Valley.

YAZOO COUNTY.

Benton,
Satartia,
Yazoo City,* (*c. h.*)

MISSOURI.

ADAIR COUNTY.

Floyd's Creek,
Kirksville,* (*c. h.*,)
Lindersville,
Millard,
Nineveh,
Paulville,
Prairie Bird,
Ringo's Point,
Shibley's Point,
Sloan's Point,
Spring Valley,
Sublett,
Troy Mills,
Willmathsville,
Wilson,
Zig.

ANDREW COUNTY.

Amazonia,
Bolckow,

ANDREW COUNTY—Continued.

Castle,
Empire Prairie,
Fillmore,
Flag Springs,
Grason,
Nodaway,
Rochester,
Rosendale,
Savannah,* (*c. h.*,)
Whitesville.

ATCHISON COUNTY.

Irish Grove,
Linden,
North Star.
Phelps City,*
Rich,
Rockport,* (*c. h.*,)
Watson.

* Money-order office.

Audrian County.

Benton City,
Hickory Creek,
John's Branch,
Loutre,
Mexico,* (*c. h.*,)
Tompson's Station,
Young's Creek.

Barry County.

Cassville, (*c. h.*,)
Corsicana,
Eva,
Flat Creek,
Hazle Barrens,
Washburn.

Barton County.

Baker's Grove,
Barton.
Coon Creek,
Doylesport,
Golden City,
Horse Creek,
Lamar,* (*c. h.*,)
Le Roy,
Milford,
Nashville.

Bates County.

Altona,
Burdett,
Butler,* (*c. h.*,)
Crescent Hill,
Hudson,
Johnstown,
Lone Oak,
Marvel,
Papinsville,
Parkersville,
Pleasant Gap,
Prairie City,
West Point.

Benton County.

Cloverdale,
Cole Camp,
Dell Delight,
Duroc,
Fairfield,
Fort Lyon,
Haw Creek,
Lake Creek,
Lincoln,
Mount View,
Warsaw,* (*c. h.*)

Bollinger County.

Buchanan,
Castor,
Marble Hill, (*c. h.*,)
Patton,
Sumac,
Vinemount.

Boone County.

Ashland,
Burlington,
Centralia,
Claysville,
Columbia, (*c. h.*,)
Greenland,
Hallsville,
Midway,
Providence,
Rocheport,
Stephens,
Sturgeon.*

Buchanan County.

Arnoldsville,
De Kalb,
Easton,
Eveline,
Halleck,
Platte River,
Rock House Prairie,
Rushville,
Saint Joseph,* (*c. h.*,)
Walnut Hill,
Winthrop.

Butler County.

Cane Creek,
Fredie,
Poplar Bluff, (*c. h.*,)
Reeve's Station.

Caldwell County.

Black Oak,
Breckinridge,
Hamilton,
Kidder,
Kingston, (*c. h.*,)
Mirabile,
Nettletonville,
Osterville,
Polo,
Proctorville.

Callaway County.

Cedar City,
Concord,
Cote Sans Dessein,
Fulton, (*c. h.*,)
Ham's Prairie,
Hempstead,
Holt's Summit,
Jones' Tan Yard,
Millersburgh,
New Bloomfield,
Pierce,
Portland,
Readsville,
Reform,
Saint Aubert's,
Shamrock,
Stephens' Store,
Williamsburgh.

Camden County.

Barnumton,
Cave Pump,
Decaturville,
Glaze City,
Linn Creek, (*c. h.*,)
Rainey Creek,
Stoutland,
Wet Glaze.

Cape Girardeau County.

Allenville,
Appleton,
Burfordville,
Cape Girardeau,*
Dutchtown,
Egypt Mills,
Iona,
Jackson, (*c. h.*,)
Millersville,
Neely's Landing,
New Wells,
Oak Ridge,
Pocahontas,
Stroderville.

Carroll County.

Bower's City,
Bridge Creek,
Carrollton,* (*c. h.*,)
Coloma,
De Witt,
Eugene City,
Hurricane,
Little Compton,
Mandeville,
Miles' Point,
Norborne,
Pleasant Park,
Ridge,
Shootman,
Stokes Mound,
Van Horn.

Carter County.

Norwood,
Van Buren, (*c. h.*)

Cass County.

Austin,
Brosley,
Crawford's Fork,
Dayton,
Everett,
Harrisonville,* (*c. h.*,)
Hazen,
High Blue,
Jonesville,
Morristown,
Peculiar,
Pleasant Hill,*
Schuyler,
Wadesburgh.

Cedar County.

Alice,
Bear Creek,
Cane Hill,
Caplinger's Mills,
Claire Springs,
Clintonville,
Mount Enterprise,
Silver Creek,
Stockton,* (*c. h.*,)
Virgil City.

* Money-order office

Chariton County.

Brunswick,*
Bynumville,
Dalton,
*Keytesville,** (c. h.,)
Muscle Fork,
Porche's Prairie,
Prairie Hill,
Richardsonville,
Rothville,
Salisbury,
Salt Creek.

Christian County.

Bull's Mills,
Kenton,
Minersville,
Ozark, (c. h.)

Clarke County.

Acasto,
Alexandria,
Ashton,
Athens,
Cahoka,
Chambersburgh,
Clarke City,
Clay,
El Dorado,
Fairmont,
Gregory Landing,
Locust Grove,
Peakesville,
Saint Francisville,
Waterloo, (c. h.,)
Winchester.

Clay County.

Barry,
Blue Eagle,
Harlem,
Holt,
Kearney,
*Liberty,** (c. h.,)
Missouri City,
Paradise,
Prospect Hill,
Smithville.

Clinton County.

Anderson,
Bainbridge,
Barnesville,
Cameron,*
Carpenter's Store,
Hainesville,
Lathrop,
Plattsburgh, (c. h.,)
Prairie,
Stairfield,
Turney's Station.

Cole County.

Brazito,
Centre Town,
Elston Station,
Hickory Hill,
JEFFERSON CITY,* (c. h.,)
Marion.
Osage Bluff,
Osage City,
Russellville,
St. Thomas,
Stringtown,
Taos.

Cooper County.

Bell Air,
*Boonville,** (c. h.,)
Bunceton,
Clark's Fork,
Cold Neck,
Conner's Mills,
Gooch's Mill,
La Mine,
Lone Elm,
New Palestine,
Otterville,
Overton,
Pilot Grove,
Pisgah,
Pleasant Green,
Prairie Home,
Vermont.

Crawford County.

Argo,
Bourbon,
Cherryville
Cuba,
Dry Creek,
Harrison's Mills,
Knob View,
Leasburgh,
Lone Cedar,
Osage
Steelville, (c. h.)

Dade County.

Cedarville,
Dadeville,
Engleman's Mills,
*Greenfield,** (c. h.,)
King's Point,
Rock Prairie,
Sylvania,
Turnback.

Dallas County.

Boyd,
Buffalo, (c. h.,)
Long Lane,
Louisburgh,
Spring Grove,
Urbana.

Daviess County.

Alta Vista,
Bancroft,
Civil Bend,
Coffeysburgh,
Crittenden,
*Gallatin,** (c. h.,)
Jamesport,
Pattonsburgh,
Santa Rosa.

De Kalb County.

Arica,
Boxford,
Dayton City,
Fair Port,
*Maysville,** (c. h.,)
Osborn,
Stewartsville,*
Union Star,
Winslow.

Dent County.

Deep Ford,
Howe's Mill,
Lake Spring,
Montauk,
Nursery Hill,
Salem, (c. h.,)
Short Bend.

Douglas County.

Arno, (c. h.,)
Beaver,
Cow Skin,
Falling Springs,
Pryor's Store,
Richville,
Vera Cruz.

Dunklin County.

Clarkton,
Four Mile,
Kennett, (c. h.,)
West Prairie.

Franklin County.

Beaufort,
Berger,
Bœuf Creek,
Boles,
Calvy,
Campbellton,
Catawissa,
Clover Bottom,
Dry Branch.
Dundee.
Etlah,
Gray's Summit,
Grubville,
Jeffriesburgh,
Krakow,
Labaddie,
Maune's Store,
Moselle,
New Haven,
Oakfield,
Pacific,
Port Hudson,
St. Clair,
Shotwell,
South Point,
Stanton Cop. Mines,
Sullivan,
Union, (c. h.,)
Washington.*

* Money-order office.

GASCONADE COUNTY.

Bay,
Burbois,
Canaan,
Drake,
Gasconade City,
Gasconade Ferry,
*Hermann,** (c. h.,)
Jake's Prairie,
Morrison,
Oak Hill,
Owensville,
Stoney Hill,
Woollam.

GENTRY COUNTY.

Alanthus Grove,
*Albany,** (c. h.,)
Buhlsville,
Douglas,
Ellenorah,
Ettieville,
Gentryville,
Havana,
Hugginsville,
Island City,
King City,
Mount Pleasant,
New Castle,
Philander,
Union Grove.

GREENE COUNTY.

Ash Grove,
Bois D'Arc,
Ebenezer,
Fair Grove,
Hickory Barren,
Little York,
North Springfield,
Pallas,
Pickerel,
*Springfield,** (c. h.,)
Strafford,
Walnut Grove,
White Oak Grove,
Willard.

GRUNDY COUNTY.

Alpha,
Buttsville,
Edinburgh,
Grinell,
Grubtown,
Lindley,
Middlebury,
Rural Dale,
Tindell,
Trenton, (c. h.)

HARRISON COUNTY.

Akron,
*Bethany,** (c. h.,)
Blue Ridge,
Bolton,
Brooklyn,
Burr Oak,
Cainesville,
Eagle,
Happy Valley,
Jay,
Martinsville,
Mitchellville,
Morris Ridge,
Mount Moriah,
Pleasant Ridge,
Sampson Creek,
Thomas.

HENRY COUNTY.

Calhoun,
*Clinton,** (c. h.,)
Consville,
Gaines' Farm,
Galbraith's Store,
Germantown,*
Huntingdale,
Leesville,
Lucas,
Marvin,
Norris Fork,
Orion,
Shawnee Mound,
Windsor.

HICKORY COUNTY.

Black Oak Point,
Cross Timbers,
Elkton,
Hermitage, (c. h.,)
Pittsburgh,
Quincy,
Roney,
Wheatland.

HOLT COUNTY.

Bigelow,
Corning,
Craig,
Elm Grove,
Forest City,*
Grant,
North Point,
*Oregon,** (c. h.,)
Rushbottom,
Whig Valley.

HOWARD COUNTY.

*Fayette,** (c. h.,)
Franklin,
Glasgow,*
Land Mark,
Myers,
Roanoke.

HOWELL COUNTY.

Chapel,
Frankville,
West Plains, (c. h.,)
Willow Springs.

IRON COUNTY.

Belleview,
*Ironton,** (c. h.,)
Kaolin,
Marble Creek,
Middle Brook,
Pilot Knob,*
Rocky Glade.

JACKSON COUNTY.

Blue Mill,
Blue Springs,
Fire Prairie,
Greenwood,
Hickman Mills,
*Independence,** (c. h.,)
Kansas City,*
Lee's Summit,
Lone Jack,
Micklen,
New Santa Fé,
Oak Grove,
Pink Hill,
Sibley,
Stony Point,
Westport.

JASPER COUNTY.

Alba,
Avilla,
Blytheville,
Buck Branch,
*Carthage,** (c. h.,)
Centre Creek,
Diamond Grove,
Fidelity,
Galesburgh,
Georgia City,
Jasper,
Jenkins' Creek,
Medoc,
Preston,
Sarcoxie,
Sherwood.

JEFFERSON COUNTY.

Avoca,
Belew's Creek,
Bushberg,
Cedar Hill,
De Soto,
Dittmer's Store,
Frumet,
Hanover,
Hematite,
High Ridge,
Hillsborough, (c. h.,)
Horine Station,
House's Springs,
Kimmswick,
Morse's Mill,
Pevely,
Sulphur Sp'gs L'd'g,
Victoria Station,
Vineland.

JOHNSON COUNTY.

Carbon Hill,
Centre View,
Chalybeate,
Chilhowie,
Columbus,
Cornelia,
Fayetteville,
Holden,*
Knobnoster,
Pittsville,
Ramey,
Rose Hill,
Warrensburgh, (c. h.)

* Money-order office.

Knox County.

Bee Ridge,
Colony,
Edina,* (*c. h.*,)
Goodland,
Greensburgh,
Locust Hill,
Millport,
Myrtle,
Newark,
Novelty.

Laclede County.

Brush Creek,
Case,
Competition,
Hazle Green,
Lebanon, (*c. h.*,)
Lyon,
Nebo,
Oakland,
Pine Creek.

La Fayette County.

Chapel Hill,
Concordia,
Dover,
Freedom,
Greenton,
Higginsville,
Lexington,* (*c. h.*,)
Mayview,
Mount Hope,
Napoleon,
Snibar,
Tabo,
Waverly,*
Wellington.

Lawrence County.

Bower's Mills,
Chesapeake,
Dunkle's Store,
Elk Horn,
Gray's Point,
Magnolia Centre,
Marionville,
Minden,
Mount Vernon, (*c. h.*,)
Phelps,
Pierce City,
Spencer,
Verona

Lewis County.

Benjamin,
Canton,*
Deer Ridge,
Durgen's Creek,
Gilead,
La Belle,
La Grange,*
Monticello, (*c. h.*,)
Oyster,
Primrose,
Williamstown

Lincoln County.

Auburn,
Cap au Gris,
Chain of Rocks,
Chantilly,
Cuivre,
Hawk Point,
Lost Branch,
Louisville,
Millwood,
New Hope,
Old Alexandria,
Old Monroe,
Post Oak,
Rock Ford,
Troy, (*c. h.*,)
Truxton.

Linn County.

Brookfield,*
Bucklin,*
Elm,
Grantsville,
Laclede,
Linneus,* (*c. h.*,)
Meadville,
Northcutt,
North Salem,
Saint Catherine,
Sebago.

Livingston County.

Asper,
Bedford,
Blue Mound,
Bluff City,
Chillicothe,* (*c. h.*,)
Cream Ridge,
Dawn,
Farmersville,
Grassy Creek,
Mooresville,
Muddy Lake,
Shoal Creek,
Spring Hill,
Utica,*
Wheeling.

McDonald County.

Bethpage,
Elk Mills,
Enterprise,
Erie,
Honey Creek,
Looniesville,
Pineville, (*c. h.*,)
Poplar Hill,
White Rock Prairie.

Macon County.

Atlanta,
Beverly,
Bevier,
Bloomington,
Callao,
College Mound,
Economy,
Excello,
Johnson,
Kaseyville,
La Plata,
Macon City,* (*c. h.*,)
Mercyville,
Narrows Creek,
New Boston,
Newburgh,
New Cambria,
Sheridan,
Sue City,
Ten Mile,
Tullvania,
Woodville.

Madison County.

Cornwall,
Fredericktown,* (*c. h.*,)
Marquand,
Mine La Motte.

Maries County.

Clifty Dale,
High Grove,
Lacon,
Lane's Prairie,
Manton,
Pay Down,
Steen's Prairie,
Vienna, (*c. h.*)

Marion County.

Benbow,
Emerson,
Hannibal,*
Hester,
Nelsonville,
Nettleton,
North River,
Palmyra,* (*c. h.*,)
Philadelphia,
Sharpsburgh,
Warren,
West Ely,
West Quincy.

Mercer County.

Cleopatra,
Goshen,
Half Rock,
Mercer,
Modena,
Princeton,* (*c. h.*,)
Ravanna,
Saline.

Miller County.

Bliss,
Brumley,
Locust Mound,
Oakhurst,
Pleasant Farm,
Pleasant Mount,
Rocky Mount,
Toronto,
Tuscumbia, (*c. h.*,)
Ulman's Ridge.

* Money-order office.

MISSISSIPPI COUNTY.

Belmont,
Charleston, (c. h.,)
James' Bayou.
Wolf Island.

MONITEAU COUNTY.

California,* (c. h.,)
Clarksburgh,
Highland,
High Point,
Hope Farm,
Jamestown,
Magnolia,
Tipton.*

MONROE COUNTY.

Elliottsville,
Florida,
Granville,
Indian Creek,
Long Branch,
Madison,
Middle Grove,
Monroe City,
Paris,* (c. h.,)
Santa Fé,
Somerset,
Switzler,
Woodlawn.

MONTGOMERY COUNTY.

Americus,
Big Spring,
Bluffton,
Danville, (c. h.,)
High Hill,
Jonesburgh,
Loutre Island,
Middletown,
Montgomery City,*
New Florence,
Price's Branch,
Rhineland,
Stockland,
Wellsville.

MORGAN COUNTY.

Boyler's Mill,
Excelsior,
Florence,
Gravois Mills,
Mining,
Saint Martin's,
Stone House,
Syracuse,*
Versailles,* (c. h.)

NEW MADRID COUNTY.

New Madrid,* (c. h.,)
Point Pleasant.

NEWTON COUNTY.

Almeda,
Capp's Creek,
Gates,
Granby,*
Jones' Creek,
Kent,
Lodi,
Neosho,* (c. h.,)
Newtonia,
Racine,
Rocky Comfort,
Seneca,
Shoalsburgh,
Sylvan Lodge.

NODAWAY COUNTY.

Conception,
Graham,
Guilford,
Hallsa's Ferry,
Lamar's Station,
Littsville,
Lutzton,
Lynchburgh,
Maryville,* (c. h.,)
Prairie Park,
Quitman,
Sweet Home,
White Cloud,
Xenia.

OREGON COUNTY.

Alton, (c. h.,)
Jobe,
Pinkleyville,
Thomasville,
Warm Fork,
Webster.

OSAGE COUNTY.

Bailey's Creek,
Byron,
Castle Rock,
Chamois,
Cooper's Hill,
Dauphine,
Fredericksburgh,
Gallaway's Station,
Koeltztown,
Linn, (c. h.,)
Linnwood,
Loose Creek,
Medora,
New Providence,
Oshawa.
Peachland.
Rich Fountain,
Westphalia.

OZARK COUNTY.

Caney,
Gainesville, (c. h.,)
Isabella,
Melissa,
Piland's Store,
Rockbridge,
Saint Leger.

PEMISCOT COUNTY.

Caruthersville,
Cottonwood Point,
Gayoso, (c. h.)

PERRY COUNTY.

Abernathy,
Altenburgh,
Biehle,
Bois Brule,
Frohna,
Laurel Hill,
Perryville, (c. h.,
Silver Lake,
Uniontown,
Wittenburgh.

PETTIS COUNTY.

Buncombe,
Dresden,
Georgetown,
Green Ridge,
Ionia City,
Lamonte,
Longwood,
Rowletta,
Sedalia,* (c. h.,)
Sigel,
Smith City.

PHELPS COUNTY.

Arlington,
Blooming Rose,
Dillon,
Edgar Springs,
Jerome,
Maramec,
Relfe,
Rolla,* (c. h.,)
St. James,
Sarvis Spring,
Spring Creek,
Yancey.

PIKE COUNTY.

Ashburn,
Ashley,
Bowling Green, (c. h.,)
Clarksville,
Curryville,
Frankford,
Louisiana,*
New Harmony,
Paxton's Store,
Paynesville,
Prairieville,
Reading,
Spencerburgh,
Vannoy's Mill.

PLATTE COUNTY.

Beverly Station,
Camden Point,
City Point,
Farley,
Hampton,
Iatan,
New Market.
Parkville,
Platte City, (c. h.,)
Ridgley,
Shivelton,
Union Mills,
Waldron,
Weston.*

* Money-order office.

POLK COUNTY.

*Bolivar,** (*c. h.,*)
Brighton,
Fair Play,
Half Way,
Humansville,
Orleans,
Pleasant Hope,
Rondo,
Sentinel Prairie.

PULASKI COUNTY.

Brittain's,
Dixon,
Dundas,
Hancock,
Humboldt,
Pine Bluff,
Richland,
St. Annie,
*Waynesville,** (*c. h.*)

PUTNAM COUNTY.

Ayersville,
Central City,
Hartford,
Livonia,
Martinstown,
Mendota,
Newtown,
Omaha,
Pleasant Home,
St. John,
Shoneytown,
Terre Haute,
*Unionville,** (*c. h.,*)
West Liberty.

RALLS COUNTY.

Crigler's Mills,
Garden Grove,
Hydesburgh,
Madisonville,
New London, (*c. h.,*)
Perry,
Saverton,
Sidney,
West Hartford,

RANDOLPH COUNTY.

Cairo,
Clifton Hill,
Darksville,
Fort Henry,
*Huntsville,** (*c. h.,*)
Jacksonville,
Milton,
Moberly,
Mount Airy,
Randolph,
Rolling Home.

RAY COUNTY.

Ada,
Camden,
Crab Orchard,
Fox,
Georgeville,
Hardin,
Henry,
Knoxville,
Lawson Station.
Millville,
New Garden,
Otsego,
Pleasant View,
Rayville.
*Richmond,** (*c. h.,*)
Tinney's Grove.

REYNOLDS COUNTY.

Centreville, (*c. h.,*)
Edge Hill,
Lesterville,
Logan's Creek,
Munger's Hill.

RIPLEY COUNTY.

Doniphan, (*c. h.,*)
Gatewood,
Little Black.

SAINT CHARLES COUNTY.

Augusta,
Cappelu,
Cottleville,
Dalhoff,
Femme Osage,
Flint Hill,
Hamburgh,
Missouriton,
New Melle,
O'Fallon,
*St. Charles,** (*c. h.,*)
Saint Peter's,
Schleursburgh,
Schumacker's Store,
Snow Hill,
Wellsburgh,
Wentzville.

SAINT CLAIR COUNTY.

Baker,
Chalk Level,
Howard's Mills,
Monagan,
*Osceola,** (*c. h.,*)
Park's Grove,
Roscoe,
Taberville.

SAINT FRANCOIS COUNTY.

Big River Mills,
Bismarck,
Blackwell's Station,
Bontear,
De Lassus,
Farmington, (*c. h.,*)
Flat River,
French Village,
Iron Mountain,
Knob Lick,
Libertyville,
Stono,
Wood's Mills.

SAINT GENEVIEVE COUNTY.

Avon,
Bloomsdale,
Bowling Brook,
Chesnut Ridge,
New Offenburgh,
Punjaub,
River Aux Vases,
St. Genevieve, (*c. h.,*)
Saint Mary's.

SAINT LOUIS COUNTY.

Allenton,
Baden,
Ballwin,
Barret's Station,
Bellefontaine,
Bonfil's Station,
Bonhomme,
Bridgeton,
Brotherton,
Carondelet,
Central,
Cheltenham,
Colman,
Creve Cœur,
Des Peres,
Elleard,
Ellisville,
Eureka,
Fairview,
Fenton,
Ferguson,
Florisant,
Fox Creek,
Glencoe,
Jefferson Barracks,*
Kirkwood,
Manchester,
Melrose,
Merrimac Station,
Mill Spring,
Normandy,
Pond,
Rock Hill,
*Saint Louis,** (*c. h.,*)
Sappington,
Sherman,
Webster Groves.

SALINE COUNTY.

Arrow Rock,
Brownsville,
Cambridge,
Elm Wood,
Fairville,
Finney's Creek,
Malta Bend,
Marshall, (*c. h.,*)
Miami,
New Frankfort,
Petra,
Ridge Prairie,
Saline City.

* Money-order office.

SCHUYLER COUNTY.

Cherry Grove,
Clifton,
Coatsville,
Glenwood,
Green Top,
Lancaster,* (*c. h.*,)
Queen City.

SCOTLAND COUNTY.

Arbela,
Bible Grove,
Etna,
Hitt,
Memphis,* (*c. h.*,)
Middle Fabius,
Pleasant Retreat,
Prospect Grove,
Sand Hill,
Wyaconda.

SCOTT COUNTY.

Benton,
Blodgett,
Commerce, (*c. h.*,)
Diehlstadt,
Morley,
Price's Landing,
Saint Cloud,
Sikeston.

SHANNON COUNTY.

Birch Tree,
Carpenterville,
Eminence, (*c. h.*,)
Pine Hill,
Russell's Hill,
Sinkin.

SHELBY COUNTY.

Bethel,
Cherry Box,
Clarence,
Hager's Grove,
Hunnewell,
Lakenan,
Shelbina,*
Shelbyville, (*c. h.*)

STODDARD COUNTY.

Altha,
Bloomfield, (*c. h.*,)
Indian Ford,
Lakeville,
Piketon.

STONE COUNTY.

Blue Eye,
Galena, (*c. h.*,)
Long's Mills,
Robertson's Mill.

SULLIVAN COUNTY.

Bairdstown,
Colfax,
Green Castle,
Jackson's Corners,
Judson,
Kiddville,
Medicine,
Milan,* (*c. h.*,)
Owasco,
Pennville,
Scottsville,
Sticklerville,
Union Ridge,
Valparaiso,
Wintersville.

TANEY COUNTY.

Bald Knob,
Bradleyville,
Forsyth, (*c. h.*,)
Mincy,
Walnut Shade.

TEXAS COUNTY.

Big Creek,
Centre,

TEXAS COUNTY—Continued.

Elk Creek,
Jack's Fork,
Hickory Springs,
Houston, (*c. h.*,)
Licking,
Plato,
Plum Valley,
Roubidoux,
Ruth.

VERNON COUNTY.

Avola,
Belvoir,
Deerfield,
Dry Wood,
Duncan Creek,
Ligonier,
Little Osage,
Montevallo,
Mounds,
Nevada,* (*c. h.*,)
Pleasant Run,
Round Prairie,
Sand Stone.

WARREN COUNTY.

Bridgeport,
Dutzow,
Holstein,
Hopewell Academy,
Marthasville,
Pendleton,
Pinckney,
Pin Oak,
Pitts,
Tuque,
Warrenton,* (*c. h.*,)
Wright City.

WASHINGTON COUNTY.

Belgrade,
Cadet,
Caledonia,
Fourche à Renault,
Harmony,
Hopewell Furnace,
Irondale,*
Kingston Furnace,
Lawson,
Mineral Point,
Old Mines,
Potosi, (*c. h.*,)
Richwoods,
Rock Spring,
Walton Mills.

WAYNE COUNTY.

Brunot,
Cold Water,
Gravelton,
Greenville, (*c. h.*,)
Lowndes,
Otter Creek,
Patterson,
Stevenson's Mills

WEBSTER COUNTY.

Dallas,
Elkland,
Forkner's Hill,
Hazlewood,
Henderson,
Marshfield,* (*c. h.*,)
Mornington,
Sand Springs,
Sarvis Point,
Waldo.

WORTH COUNTY.

Allendale,
Grant City, (*c. h.*,)
Grant's Hill,
Hudson City,
Isadora,
Oxford,
Smithton.

WRIGHT COUNTY.

Astoria,
Aurora,
Hartville, (*c. h.*,)
Pleasant Valley,
Sacramento,
Sunny Side,
Wolf Creek.

* Money-order office.

MONTANA TERRITORY.

Beaver Head County.

*Bannack City,** (*c. h.,*) Montana,
Horse Prairie, Watson.

Chouteau County.

Fort Benton, (*c. h.*)

Deer Lodge County.

Beartown, Blackfoot City, Butte City, *Deer Lodge City,** (*c. h.,*) Emmettsburgh, French Gulch, German Gulch, Greenwood, Harrisburgh, Lincoln, McClellan Gulch, Philipsburgh, Pike's Peak, Pioneer, Red Mountain City, Silver Bow, Washington Gulch.

Gallatin County.

Bozeman, (*c. h.,*) East Gallatin, Gallatin, Hamilton, Middle Creek.

Jefferson County.

Boulder Valley, Fish Creek, Jefferson City, Prickly Pear, *Radersburgh,* (*c. h.,*) Saint Louis, Springville, Whitehall.

Lewis and Clarke County.

Fort Shaw, French Bar, Georgetown, *Helena,** (*c. h.,*) Silver City, Sun River, Unionville.

Madison County.

Beaver Head Rock, Cicero, Harrison, Iron Rod, Junction, Meadow Creek, Nevada City, Pollinger, Rochester, Sheridan, Silver Star, Sterling, Summit, Twin Bridges, VIRGINIA CITY,* (*c. h.,*) Willow Creek.

Meagher County.

Canyon Ferry, *Diamond City,* (*c. h.,*) Trout Creek.

Missoula County.

Cedar Junction, Frenchtown, Gird's Creek, Horse Plains, Louisville, *Missoula,* (*c. h.,*)• Stevensville, Thompson's River.

NEBRASKA.

Adams County.

Martinsville.

Black Bird County.

Omaha Agency.

Burt County.

Arizona, Decatur,* Homestead, Lyons, Oakland, Riverside, Silver Creek, *Tekamah,* (*c. h.*)

Butler County.

Linwood, Pepperville, *Savannah,* (*c. h.,*) Ulysses, Urban.

Cass County.

Avoca, Centre Valley, Eagle, Eight Mile Grove, Elmwood, Factoryville, Glendale, Greenwood,

Cass County—Continued.

Louisville, Mount Pleasant, *Plattsmouth,** (*c. h.,*) Rock Bluff, South Bend, Three Grove, Union, Weeping Water.

Cedar County.

Saint Helena, (*c. h.,*) Saint James.

Cheyenne County.

Sidney.

Colfax County.

El Dorado, Morian, *Schuyler,** (*c. h.*)

Cuming County.

Bismarck, De Witt, Lakeview, Saint Charles, *West Point,** (*c. h.*)

* Money-order office.

DAKOTA COUNTY.

Covington,
*Dakota,** (c. h.,)
Jackson,
Lodi,
Omadi,
Randolph,
Winnebago.

DIXON COUNTY.

Ionia,
Newcastle,
Ponca, (c. h.)

DODGE COUNTY.

*Fremont,** (c. h.,)
Galena,
Jalapa,
Logan,
Maple Creek,
North Bend,
Oak Springs,
Pebble Creek,
Timberville.

DOUGLAS COUNTY.

Chicago,
Elkhorn City,
Florence,
Omaha Barracks,
*Omaha City,** (c. h.,)
Primrose,
Valley.

GAGE COUNTY.

Baden,
*Beatrice,** (c. h.,)
Blue Springs,
Cropsey,
Hooker,
Laona,
Otoe Agency,
Roperville.

HALL COUNTY.

*Grand Island Station,** (c. h.,)
Wood River.

HAMILTON COUNTY.

Farmers' Valley.

JEFFERSON COUNTY.

Antelope,
Bowerville,
Caroline,
Cub Creek,
Dryden,
Elm Grove,
Fairbury, (c. h.,)
Georgetown,
Hebron,
Jenkins' Mills,
Kiowa,
Little Sandy,
Meridian, (c. h.,)
Rose Creek.

JOHNSON COUNTY.

Butler,
Crab Orchard,
Helena,
Latrobe,
Spring Creek,
Sterling,
*Tecumseh,** (c. h.,)
Vesta.

KEARNEY COUNTY.

Fort Kearney,*
Kearney City, (c. h.)

L'EAU QUI COURT COUNTY.

Frankfort,
Niobrara, (c. h.,)
Santee Agency.

LANCASTER COUNTY.

Camp Creek,
Centreville,
LINCOLN,* (c. h.,)
Olive Branch,
Opequan,
Panama,
Rebecca,
Saltillo,
South Pass,
Tipton.

LINCOLN COUNTY.

Cottonwood Spr'gs,*
North Platte.

MADISON COUNTY.

Battle Creek,
Madison,
Norfolk, (c. h.)

MERRICK COUNTY.

Chapman,
Clarksville,
Lone Tree, (c. h.,)
Silver Glen.

NEMAHA COUNTY.

Aspinwall,
Bratton,
*Brownville,** (c. h.,)
Clifton,
Glen Rock,
Grant,
Hillsdale,
Howard,
London,
Nemaha City,
Peru,
Saint Deroin,
Saint Frederick,
Sheridan,
Sherman.

OTOE COUNTY.

Burr Oak,
Emerson,
Hendricks,
*Nebraska City,**(c. h.,)
Nursery Hill,
Paisley,
Palmyra,
Solon,
Wilson,
Wyoming.

PAWNEE COUNTY.

Calla,
Cincinnati,
Liberty,
*Pawnee City,** (c. h.,)
Table Rock,
Tip's Branch.

PLATTE COUNTY.

Cherry Grove,
*Columbus,** (c. h.,)
Genoa,
Monroe.

RICHARDSON COUNTY.

Arago,*
Athens,
Dawson's Mill,
Elmore,
*Falls City,** (c. h.,)
Highland,
Humboldt,
Long Branch,
Middleburgh,
Monterey,
Nohart,
Rulo,*
Salem,
Well's Mills.
Williamsville.

SALINE COUNTY.

Blue Island,
Crete,
Equality,
Pleasant Hill,
Swan City, (c. h.)

* Money-order office.

SARPY COUNTY.

Bellevue, (c. h.,)
Forest City,
Gilmore,
Larimer Mills,
Lisbon,
Papillion,
Plattford,
Xenia.

SAUNDERS COUNTY.

Ashland, (c. h.,)
Attica,
Benton,
Cedar Bluffs,
Ceresco,
Eldred,
Esteina,
Headland,
Ithaca,
Lone Valley,
Milton,
Platteville,
Pohocco,
Wahoo,
Wautisca.

SEWARD COUNTY.

Beaver Crossing,
Camden,
Milford, (c. h.,)
Oak Groves,
Seward,
West's Mill.

STANTON COUNTY.

Canton,
Clinton, (c. h.,)
Pleasant Run.

WASHINGTON COUNTY.

Belle Creek,
Blair, (c. h.,)
Bono,
Cuming City,
De Soto,
Fontanelle,
Fort Calhoun.

WAYNE COUNTY.

Taffe.

YORK COUNTY.

Blue Valley,
McFadden,
York, (c. h.)

NEVADA.

DOUGLAS COUNTY.

Genoa, (c. h.,)
Sheridan.

ELKO COUNTY.

Camp Halleck,
Coral Hill,
Elko, (c. h.,)
Mineral Hill,
Mountain City,
Ruby Valley,
Wells.

ESMERALDA COUNTY.

Aurora,* (c. h.,)
Columbus,
Pine Grove,
Silver Peak,
Sweetwater,
Wellington.

HUMBOLDT COUNTY.

Battle Mountain,
Camp McDermitt,
Dun Glen,
Galena,
Golconda,
Mill City,
Oreana,
Unionville, (c. h.,)
Winnemucca.

LANDER COUNTY.

Argenta,
Austin,* (c. h.,)
Beowawe,
Carlin,
Egan Canyon,
Eureka,
Palisade,
Vanderbilt.

LINCOLN COUNTY.

Hiko, (c. h.,)
Pioche.

LYON COUNTY.

Dayton, (c. h.,)
Silver City.

NYE COUNTY.

Belmont, (c. h.,)
Ellsworth,
Hot Creek,
Ione City,
Reveille,
Twin River,
Washington.

ORMSBY COUNTY.

CARSON CITY,*(c. h.,)
Empire City.

STOREY COUNTY.

Gold Hill,
Virginia City,* (c. h.)

WASHOE COUNTY.

Franktown,
Ophir,
Reno,
Truckee Meadows,
Verdi,
Wadsworth,
Washoe City, (c. h.)

WHITE PINE COUNTY.

Diamond Mountain,
Hamilton,* (c. h.,)
Mineral City,
Shermantown,
Treasure City.

* Money-order office.

NEW HAMPSHIRE.

Belknap County.

Alton,
Alton Bay,
Barnstead,
Belmont,
Centre Barnstead,
Centre Harbor,
East Alton,
East Tilton,
Gilford Village,
Gilmanton,
Gilmanton Iron Works,
*Laconia,** (*c. h.,*)
Lake Village,
Lower Gilmanton,
Meredith Centre,
Meredith Village,
New Hampton,
North Barnstead,
North Sanbornton,
Sanbornton,
South Barnstead,
Tilton,*
Weir's Bridge,
West Alton.

Carroll County.

Bartlett,
Brookfield,
Centre Conway,
Centre Effingham,
Centre Ossipee,
Centre Sandwich,
Conway,
Cram's Corner,
East Madison,
East Moultonboro',
East Wakefield,
Eaton Centre,
Effingham,
Effingham Falls,
Freedom,
Horn's Mills,
Jackson,
Leighton's Corners,
Lower Bartlett,
Mackerel Corner,
Madison,
Melvin Village,
Moultonborough,
Moultonville,
North Conway,
North Sandwich,
North Wakefield,
North Wolfborough.
Ossipee, (*c. h.,*)
Sandwich,
South Tamworth,
South Wolfborough,
Tamworth,
Tamworth Iron Works,
Tuftonborough,
Union,
Wakefield,
Water Village,
West Ossipee,
Wolfborough,
Wolfborough Centre.

Cheshire County.

Alstead,
Alstead Centre,
Ashuelot,
Blakeville,
Chesterfield,
Chesterfield Factory,
Drewsville,
Dublin,
East Jaffrey,
East Sullivan,
East Westmoreland,
Fitzwilliam,
Fitzwilliam Depot,
Gilsum,
Harrisville,
Hinsdale,*
Jaffrey,
*Keene,** (*c. h.,*)
Marlborough,
Marlborough Depot,
Marlow,
Munsonville,
Nelson,
New Alstead,
North Richmond,
Pottersville,
Richmond,
Rindge,
South Stoddard,
Stoddard,
Sullivan,
Surry,
Swanzey,
Troy,
Walpole,
West Chesterfield,
Westmoreland,
Westmorel'nd Depot,
Westport,
West Swanzey,
Winchester.

Coos County.

Berlin Falls,
Carroll,
Clarksville,
Colebrook,
Columbia,
Connecticut Lake,
Coos,
Crawford House,
Dalton,
Errol,
Gorham,*
Groveton,
Jefferson,
*Lancaster,** (*c. h.,*)
Milan,
Northumberland,
Pittsburgh,
Randolph,
Shelburne,
South Columbia,
Stark,
Stewartstown,
Stratford,
Twin Mountain,
Wentworth's Location,
West Milan,
West Stewartstown,
Whitefield,
White Mountain House.

Grafton County.

Alexandria,
Ashland,
Bath,
Benton,
Bethlehem,
Bridgewater,
Bristol,*
Campton,
Campton Village,
Canaan,
Danbury,
Dorchester,
East Canaan,
East Haverhill,
East Landaff,
East Lebanon,
Ellsworth,
Enfield,
Enfield Centre,
Franconia,
Grafton,
Grafton Centre,
Groton,
Hanover,*
Hanover Centre,
*Haverhill,** (*c. h.,*)
Hebron,
Hill,
Landaff,
Lebanon,*
Lisbon,
Littleton,*
Lyman,
Lyme,
Monroe,
North Dorchester,
North Groton,
North Haverhill,
North Lisbon,
North Littleton,
North Monroe,
North Woodstock,
Orford,
Orfordville,
Piermont,
*Plymouth,** (*c. h.,*)
Profile House,
Rumney,
South Danbury,
Sugar Hill,
Thornton,
Warren,
Wentworth,
West Campton,
West Canaan,
West Enfield,
West Lebanon,*
West Plymouth,
West Rumney,
West Thornton,
Woodstock,
Woodsville.

Hillsborough County.

Amherst, (*c. h.,*)
Amoskeag,
Antrim,
Bedford,
Bennington,
Brookline,
Deering,
East Deering,
East Weare,
Francistown,
Goff's Falls,
Goffstown,
Goffstown Centre,
Greenfield,
Hancock,
Hillsborough,

* Money-order office.

HILLSBOROUGH COUNTY—Continued.

Hillsborough Bridge,
Hillsboro'h Centre,
Hollis,
Hudson,
Lyndeborough,
Manchester,*
Mason,
Mason Village,
Merrimack,
Milford,*
Mount Vernon,
Nashua,*
New Boston,
New Ipswich,*
North Branch,
North Lyndeboro'h,
North Weare,
Oil Mill Village,
Pelham,
Peterborough,*
Reed's Ferry,
South Lyndeboro'h,
South Merrimack,
South Weare,
Temple,
Thornton's Ferry,
Weare,
West Deering,
West Peterborough,
West Wilton,
Wilton.*

MERRIMACK COUNTY.

Allenstown,
Andover,
Boscawen,
Bow,
Bradford,
Canterbury,
Chichester,
CONCORD,* (*c. h.*,)
Contoocook Village,
Dunbarton,
East Andover,
East Concord,
East Pembroke,
Epsom,
Fishersville,*
Franklin,*
Henniker,
Hookset,
Hopkinton,
Loudon,
Loudon Centre,
Loudon Ridge,
Mast Yard,
Newbury,
New London,*
North Boscawen,
North Chichester,
North Dunbarton,
North Sutton,
Pembroke,
Pittsfield,
Roby's Corner,
Salisbury,
Scytheville,
Shaker Village,
Short Falls,
South Newbury,
South Sutton,
Suncook,*
Sutton,
Warner,
Webster,
West Andover,
West Concord,
West Henniker,
West Hopkinton,
West Salisbury,
Wilmot,
Wilmot Flat.

ROCKINGHAM COUNTY.

Atkinson,
Atkinson Depot,
Auburn,
Boar's Head,
Brentwood,
Candia,
Candia Village,
Chester,
Danville,
Deerfield,
Deerfield Centre,
Derry,
Derry Depot,
East Derry,
East Hampstead,
East Kingston,
East Northwood,
Epping,

ROCKINGHAM COUNTY—Continued.

Exeter,* (*c. h.*,)
Fremont,
Greenland,
Greenland Depot,
Hampstead,
Hampton,
Hampton Falls,
Kensington,
Kingston,
Londonderry,
New Castle,
Newington,
New Market,
Newton,
Newton Depot,
North Hampton,
North Londonderry,
North Salem,
Northwood Centre,
N'thwood Narrows,
Nottingham,
Plaistow,
Portsmouth,* (*c. h.*,)
Raymond,
Rye,
Salem,
Salem Depot,
Sandown,
Seabrook,
South Deerfield,
South Hampton,
South Kingston,
South New Market,
Stratham,
West Epping,
West Hampstead,
West Nottingham,
West Windham,
Wilson's Crossing,
Windham,
Windham Depot.

STRAFFORD COUNTY.

Barrington,
Centre Strafford,
Dover,* (*c. h.*,)
Downing's Mills,
Durham,
East Rochester,
Farmington,
Gonic,
Great Falls,*
Lee,
Middleton,
Milton,
Milton Mills,
North Barrington,
North Strafford.
Rochester,
Salmon Falls,
South Milton,
Strafford,
Strafford Blue Hills,
Strafford Corner,
Wadley's Falls,
West Milton.

SULLIVAN COUNTY.

Acworth,
Charlestown,*
Claremont,*
Cornish Flat,
Croydon,
Croydon Flat,
East Acworth,
East Lempster,
East Plainfield,
East Springfield,
East Unity,
East Washington,
George's Mills,
Goshen,
Grantham,
Langdon,
Lempster,
Meriden,*
Mill Village,
Newport,* (*c. h.*,)
North Charlestown,
North Grantham,
Plainfield,
South Acworth,
South Charlestown,
South Sunapee,
Springfield,
Sunapee,
Unity,
Washington,
West Claremont,
West Springfield.

* Money-order office.

NEW JERSEY.

Atlantic County.

Absecom,*
Atlantic City,*
Bargaintown,
Cedar Lake,
Decosta,
Egg Harbor City,*
Elwood,
English's Creek,
Estelville.
Hammonton,*
Leeds Point,
May's Landing, (c. h.,)
Pleasant Mills,
Port Republic,
Smith's Landing,
Somers' Point,
Weymouth.

Bergen County.

Allendale,
Arcola,
Carlstadt,
Closter,
Cresskill,
Englewood,
Fairview,
Fort Lee,
Godwinville,
Green Wood,
Hackensack, (c. h.,)
Hillsdale,
Hohokus,
Kinderkamack,
Leonia,
Lodi,
Mahwah,
New Bridge,
Norwood,
Park Ridge,
Paskack,
Ramsey's,
Ridgewood,
River Edge,
Rutherford Park,
Saddle River,
Schraalenburgh,
Spring Valley,
Tenafly,
Westwood,
Wyckoff.

Burlington County.

Arneytown,
Beverly,
Birmingham,
Bordentown,*
Bridgeborough,
Brown's Mills,
Budd Town,
Burlington,*
Cinnaminson,
Columbus,
Cookstown,
Crosswicks,
Delanco,
Fellowship,
Florence,
Fruitland,
Georgetown,
Green Bank,
Hainesport,
Hartford,
Jacksonville,
Jacobstown,
Jobstown,
Juliustown,
Lower Bank,
Lumberton,
Marlton,
Masonville,
Medford,
Moorestown,*
Mount Holly,* (c. h.,)
Mount Laurel,
New Gretna,
New Lisbon,
Palmyra,
Pemberton,
Pointville,
Rancocas,
Recklesstown,
Riverside,
Shamong,
Smithville,
Sykesville,
Tuckerton,
Vincentown,
Wading River,
Woodmansie,
Wrightstown.

Camden County.

Ancora,
Atco,
Berlin,
Blackwoodtown
Camden,* (c. h.,)
Chew's Landing,

Camden County—Continued.

Cross Keys,
Gloucester City,
Haddonfield,
Hurffville,
Kirkwood,
Merchantville,
Mount Ephraim,
Turnersville,
Waterford Works,
Williamstown,
Winslow.

Cape May County.

Beesley's Point,
Cape May,*
Cape May C. H.,
Cold Spring,
Dennisville,
Dias Creek,
East Creek,
Fishing Creek,
Goshen,
Green Creek,
Petersburgh,
Rio Grande,
Seaville,
South Seaville,
Townsend Inlet,
Tuckahoe.

Cumberland County.

Belle Plain,
Bridgeton,* (c. h.,)
Cedarville,
Cohansey,
Deerfield Street,
Dividing Creek,
Ewing's Neck,
Fairton,
Finley Station,
Greenwich,
Leesburgh,
Manamuskin,
Mauricetown,
Millville,*
Newport,
North Vineland,
Port Elizabeth,
Roadstown,
Rosenhayn,
Shiloh,
South Vineland,
Vineland,*
Willow Grove.

Essex County.

Belleville,
Bloomfield,*
Caldwell,
Franklin,
East Orange,
Irvington,
Livingston,
Millburn,
Mont Clair,
Newark,* (c. h.,)
Orange,
Orange Valley,
South Orange,
Verona.

Gloucester County.

Barnsborough,
Bridgeport,
Clarksborough,
Clayton,
Ewan's Mills,
Five Points,
Forest Grove,
Franklinville,
Glassborough.
Harrisonville,
Malaga,
Mantua,
Mullica Hill,
Newfield,
Paulsborough,
Swedesborough,
Unionville,
Westville,
Woodbury, (c. h.)

Hudson County.

Bayonne
Bergen.
Bergen Point,
Greenville,
Hoboken,*
Hudson,
Jersey City,* (c. h.,)
New Durham,
Saltersville,
Weehawken,
West Hoboken.

* Money-order office.

Hunterdon County.

Anthony,
Baptistown,
Bethlehem,
Bloomsbury,
Centreville,
Cherryville,
Clarksville,
Clinton,
Clinton Station,
Clover Hill,
Copper Hill,
Croton.
Everittstown,
Fair Mount,
Flemington,* (*c. h.*,)
Frenchtown,*
High Bridge.
Holland,
Junction,
Kingwood,
Klinesville,
Lambertville,*
Lebanon,
Little York,
Locktown,
Lower Valley
Milford,
Mountainville,
Mount Pleasant,
New Germantown,
New Hampton,
Oak Dale,
Oak Grove,
Pattenburgh,
Perryville,
Pittstown,
Pleasant Run,
Potterstown,
Pottersville,
Quakertown,
Raven Rock,
Readington,
Reaville,
Ringoes,
Rowland Mills,
Sand Brook,
Sergeantsville,
Sidney,
Stanton,
Stockton,
Three Bridges,
Tumble,
Wertsville,
White House,
White House Station.

Mercer County.

Baker's Basin,
Dutch Neck,
Edinburgh,
Ewingville,
Greensburgh,
Hamilton Square,
Hightstown,*
Hopewell,
Lawrenceville,
Pennington,
Princeton,*
Robbinsville,
Titusville,
TRENTON,* (*c. h.*,)
Windsor,
Woodsville,
Yardville.

Middlesex County.

Clay Bank,
Cranbury,
Dayton,
Dun Ellen,
Jamesburgh,
Metuchen,
Monmouth Junction,
New Brunswick,* (*c. h.*,)
New Market,
Old Bridge,
Perth Amboy,*
Plainsborough,
Prospect Plains,
South Amboy,*
South River,
Spotswood,
Woodbridge.

Monmouth County.

Allentown,
Black's Mills,
Branch Shore,
Chapel Hill.
Clarksburgh,
Coburgh,
Colt's Neck,
Deal,
Eatontown,
Englishtown.
Farmingdale,
Fillmore,
Freehold,* (*c. h.*,)
Holmdel,
Imlaystown,
Jerseyville,
Key Port,*
Leedsville,
Leonardville,
Long Branch,*

Monmouth County—Continued.

Lower Squankum,
Manalapan,
Marlborough,
Mattawan,
Middletown,
Morganville,
Navasink,
New Bedford,
New Branch,
New Monmouth,
New Sharon,
Ocean Port,
Perrineville,
Port Monmouth,
Red Bank,*
Shark River,
Shrewsbury,
Squam Village,
Tinton Falls,
Turkey,
Walnford,
West Freehold.

Morris County.

Boonton,*
Brookside,
Budd's Lake,
Chatham,
Chester,
Denville,
Dover,*
Drakestown,
Drakesville,
Flanders,
German Valley,
Green Village,
Hanover,
Hibernia,
Hurdtown,
Littleton,
Long Hill,
McCainsville,
Madison,
Mendham,
Middle Valley,
Millington,
Milton,
Morristown,* (*c. h.*,)
Mount Hope,
Naughrightville,
Newfoundland,
New Vernon,
Parsippany,
Passaic Valley,
Pine Brook,
Pleasant Grove,
Pompton Plains,
Port Oram,
Rockaway,
Schooley's Mountain,
Stephensburgh,
Stanley,
Stony Brook,
Suckasunny,
Walnut Grove,
Whippany.

Ocean County.

Barnegat,
Bayville,
Bennett's Mills,
Bricksburgh,
Cassville,
Cedar Creek,
Collier's Mill,
Ellisdale,
Forked River,
Hornerstown,
Jackson's Mills,
Manahawkin,
Manchester,
Metedeconk,
New Egypt,
Point Pleasant,
Silverton,
Tom's River,* (*c. h.*,)
Vanhiseville,
West Creek,
Whiting,
Wiretown.

Passaic County.

Bloomingdale,
Charlotteburgh,
Clifton,
Hawthorne,
Little Falls,
Mead's Basin,
Passaic,
Paterson,* (*c. h.*,)
Pompton,
Ringwood Furnace.
Smith's Mills.
West Milford.

Salem County.

Allowaystown,
Auburn,
Canton,
Centreton.
Daretown.
Elmer,
Hancock's Bridge
Monroeville.

* Money-order office.

SALEM COUNTY—Continued.

Palatine,
Pedricktown,
Penn's Grove,
Pennsville,
Pitt's Grove,
Quinton,
Salem,* (*c. h.*,)
Sharptown,
Woodstown,
Yorktown.

SOMERSET COUNTY.

Basking Ridge,
Blawenburgh,
Boundbrook,
Flaggtown,
Griggstown,
Harlingen,
Kingston,
Lesser Cross Roads,
Liberty Corner,
Martinsville,
Middlebush,
Millstone,
Neshanic,
North Branch,
North Branch Depot,
Peapack,
Pluckemin,
Raritan,
Rocky Hill,
Roysfield,
Six Mile Run,
Somerville,* (*c. h.*,)
South Branch,
Warrenville,
Weston.

SUSSEX COUNTY.

Andover,
Beaver Run,
Beemerville,
Bevans,
Branchville,
Clove,
Colesville,
Deckertown,
Flatbrookville,
Franklin Furnace,
Fredon,
Glenwood,
Hainesville,
Hamburgh,
Hunt's Mills,
Huntsville,
La Fayette,
Layton,
Libertyville,
Lincoln,
McAfee Valley,
Middleville,
Monroe,
Montague,
Mount Salem,
Newton,* (*c. h.*,)
Ogdensburgh,
Papakating,
Pleasant Valley,
Sparta,
Stanhope,
Stillwater,

SUSSEX COUNTY—Continued.

Stockholm,
Swartswood,
Tranquillity,
Vernon,*
Wallpack Centre,
Waterloo,
Wawayanda,
Wykertown.

UNION COUNTY.

Cranford,
Elizabeth,* (*c. h.*,)
Elizabeth Port,
Linden,
New Providence,
Plainfield,*
Rahway,*
Roselle,
Scotch Plains,
Springfield,
Summit,
Union,
Westfield.

WARREN COUNTY.

Allamuchy,
Asbury,
Beatyestown,
Belvidere,* (*c. h.*,)
Blairstown,
Brainards,
Bridgeville,
Broadway,
Brotzmanville,
Calno,
Carpentersville,
Changewater,
Columbia,
Danville,
Delaware Station,
Hackettstown,*
Hainesburgh,
Hardwick,
Harmony,
Hope,
Howard,
Johnsonburgh.
Karrsville,
Kill Mills,
Knowlton,
Marksborough,
Millbrook,
Montana,
Mount Bethel,
Musconetcong,
New Village,
Oxford,
Pahaquarry,
Paulina,
Phillipsburgh,*
Polkville,
Port Colden,
Port Murry,
Rocksburgh,
Springtown,
Stewartsville,
Still Valley,
Townsbury,
Vienna,
Walnut Valley,
Washington.*

NEW MEXICO TERRITORY.

BERNALILLO COUNTY.

Albuquerque, (*c. h.*,)
Bernalillo.

COLFAX COUNTY.

Clifton,
Elizabethtown, (*c. h.*,)
Ute Creek.

DOÑA AÑA COUNTY.

Doña Aña,
Fort Selden,
Las Cruces,
Leasburgh,
Mesilla, (*c. h.*)

GRANT COUNTY.

Central City,
Fort Cummings,
Pinos Altos, (*c. h.*,)
Rio Mimbres.

MORA COUNTY.

Cimarron,
Fort Union,
La Cueva,
La Junta,
Mora, (*c. h.*,)
Ocate.

RIO ARRIBA COUNTY.

Abiqui,
Los Luceros,
San Juan.

SANTA AÑA COUNTY.

Algodones,
La Bajada,

SAN MIGUEL COUNTY.

Las Vegas, (*c. h.*,)
San José,
Tecolote

* Money-order office.

SANTA FÉ COUNTY.

Juana Lopez,
Pajuaque,
SANTA FÉ, (*c. h.*)

SOCORRO COUNTY.

Aleman,
Fort Craig,
Fort Stanton,
Limitar,
Paraje,
Sabinal,

SOCORRO COUNTY—Continued.

San Antonio,
San Marcial,
Socorro, (*c. h.*)

TAOS COUNTY.

Fernandez de Taos, (*c. h.*)

VALENCIA COUNTY.

Los Lunas,
Peralta.

NEW YORK.

ALBANY COUNTY.

Adams' Station,
ALBANY,* (*c. h.*,)
Berne,
Bethlehem Centre,
Callanan's Corners,
Cedar Hill,
Clarksville,
Coeymans,
Coeymans Hollow,
Cohoes,*
Cooksburgh,
Dormansville,
Dunnsville,
East Berne,
Green Island,
Guilderland,
Guilderland Centre,
Guilderland Station,
Indian Fields,
Ireland Corners,
Jerusalem,
Keefer's Corners,
Knowersville,
Knox,
Lisha's Kill,
Medusa,
New Salem,
New Scotland,
Newtonville,
Norman's Kill,
Potter's Hollow,
Preston Hollow,
Reidsville,
Rensselaerville,*
South Berne,
South Westerlo,
Union Church,
Voorheesville,
Watervliet Centre,
West Albany,
West Berne,
Westerlo,
West Township,
West Troy,
Wolf Hill.

ALLEGANY COUNTY.

Alfred,
Alfred Centre,*
Allen,
Allen Centre,
Alma,
Almond,
Andover,*
Angelica, (*c. h.*,)
Belfast,
Belmont, (*c. h.*,)
Belvidere,
Birdsall,
Black Creek,
Bolivar,
Burns,
Canaseraga,
Caneadea,
Centreville,
Ceres,
Cuba,*
East Granger,
East Rushford,
Fillmore,
Friendship,
Fulmer Valley
Granger,
Hallsport,
Houghton Creek,
Hume,
Independence,
Little Genesee,
Mills' Mills,
New Hudson,
Nile,
Oramel,
Phillips' Creek,
Richburgh,
Rushford,
Scio,
Seymour,
Shongo,
Short Tract,
South Bolivar,
Spring Mills,

ALLEGANY COUNTY—Continued.

Stanard's Corners,
Swain,
Wellsville,*
West Almond,
West Clarksville,
Whitesville,
Whitney's Crossings,
Wirt Centre,
Wiscoy.

BROOME COUNTY.

Belden,
Binghamton,* (*c. h.*,)
Cascade Valley,
Castle Creek,
Centre Lisle,
Centre Village,
Chenango Forks,
Choconut Centre,
Colesville,
Conklin Centre,
Conklin Station,
Corbettsville,
Deposit,*
Doraville,
East Maine,
Glen Aubrey,
Glen Castle,
Gulf Summit.
Harpersville,
Hawleyton,
Hooper,
Kattelville,
Killawog,
Kirkwood,
Kirkwood Centre,
Lamb's Corners,
Lisle,
McClure Settlement,
Maine,
New Ohio,
Nineveh,
North Colesville,
North Fenton,
North Sanford,
Osborne Hollow,
Ouaquaga,
Port Crane,
Port Dickinson,
Randolph Centre,
Riverside,
Sanford,
Tracy Creek,
Triangle,
Union,
Union Centre,
Upper Lisle,
Vallonia Springs,
Vestal,
Vestal Centre,
West Colesville,
West Windsor,
Whitney's Point,*
Windsor.

CATTARAUGUS COUNTY.

Allegany,
Ashford,
Cadiz,
Carrollton,
Cattaraugus,
Conewango,
Cottage,
Dayton,
East Ashford,
East Leon,
East Otto,
East Randolph,
East Salamanca,
Eddyville,
Elgin,
Ellicottsville,* (*c. h.*,)
Elton,
Fairview,
Farmersville,
Franklinville,

* Money-order office.

CATTARAUGUS COUNTY—Continued.

Gowanda,
Great Valley,
Haskell Flats,
Hinsdale,
Humphrey,
Ischua,
Kill Buck,
Leon,
Limestone,
Little Valley,
Machias,
Napoli,
New Albion,
Olean,*
Onoville,
Otto,
Perrysburgh,
Persia,
Portville,
Randolph,*
Rawson,
Red House,
Salamanca,
Sandusky,
South Dayton,
Steamburgh,
Vandalia,
Versailles,
West Valley,
West Yorkshire,
Yorkshire,
Yorkshire Centre.

CAYUGA COUNTY.

Auburn,* (*c. h.*,)
Aurelius,
Aurora,
Bethel Corners,
Cato,
Cayuga,
Conquest,
Dresserville,
East Genoa,
East Venice,
Fair Haven,
Five Corners,
Fleming,
Fosterville,
Genoa,
Ira,
Kelloggsville,
King's Ferry,
Ledyard,
Levanna,
Locke,
Martville,
Meridian,
Montezuma,
Moravia,
New Hope,
Niles,
North Sterling,
North Victory,
Owasco,
Owasco Lake,
Poplar Ridge,
Port Byron,
Scipio,
Scipioville,
Sempronius,
Sennet,
Sherwood's,
Sterling,
Sterling Valley,
Summer Hill,
The Square,
Throopsville,
Union Springs,*
Venice,
Venice Centre,
Victory,
Weedsport,
Westbury.

CHAUTAUQUA COUNTY.

Arkwright Summit,
Bemus Point,
Blockville,
Brocton,
Broken Straw,
Busti,
Cassadaga,
Charlotte Centre,
Cherry Creek,
Clear Creek,
Clymer,
De Wittville,
Dunkirk,*
Ellery,
Ellington,
Elm Flat,
Fentonville,
Findley's Lake,
Fluvanna,
Forestville,
Fredonia,*
French Creek,
Frewsburgh,
Hamlet,
Harmony,
Hartfield,
Irving,
Jamestown,*
Kennedy,
Kiantone,
Laona,
Marvin,
Mayville,* (*c. h.*,)
Mina,
Nashville,
North Clymer,

CHAUTAUQUA COUNTY—Continued.

Oregon,
Panama,
Poland Centre,
Portland,
Prospect Station,
Ripley,
Sheridan,
Sherman,
Silver Creek,
Sinclairville,
Smith's Mills,
Stedman,
Stockton,
Vermont,
Villanova,
Volusia,
Watt's Flats,
Westfield.*

CHEMUNG COUNTY.

Big Flats,
Breesport,
Chemung,
Chemung Centre,
East Grove,
Elmira,* (*c. h.*,)
Erin,
Herrington's Corners,
Horseheads,
Lowman,
Mill Port,
North Chemung,
Pine Valley,
Post Creek,
Seely Creek,
Southport,
State Road,
Sullivanville,
Tompkins' Corners,
Van Etten,
Van Ettenville,
Webb's Mills,
Wellsburgh.

CHENANGO COUNTY.

Afton,
Bainbridge,
Bennettsville,
Columbus,
Coventry,
Coventryville,
East German,
East Greene,
East Guilford,
East McDonough,
East Pharsalia,
German,
Greene,
Guilford,
Guilford Centre,
King's Settlement,
Lincklaen,
McDonough,
Mount Upton,
New Berlin,
New Berlin Centre,
North Lincklaen,
North Norwich,
North Pharsalia,
North Pitcher,
Norwich,* (*c. h.*,)
Otselic,
Oxford
Pharsalia,
Pitcher,
Pitcher Springs,
Plymouth,
Preston,
Rockdale,
Sherburne,*
Sherburne Four Corners,
Smithville Flats,
Smyrna,
South New Berlin,
South Otselic,
South Oxford,
South Plymouth,
White's Store.

CLINTON COUNTY.

Altona,
Beekmantown,
Black Brook,
Cadyville,
Champlain,
Chazy,
Churubusco,
Clayburgh,
Clinton Mills,
Clintonville,
Coopersville,
Dannemora,
East Beekmantown,
Ellenburgh,
Ellenburgh Centre,
Ellenburgh Depot,
Ferrona,
Forest,
Frontier,
Ingraham,
Irona,
Mooers,
Mooers Forks,
Morrisonville,
Peasleeville,
Perry's Mills,

*Money-order office.

Clinton County—Continued.

Peru,
Plattsburgh,* (*c. h.*,)
Redford,
Rouse's Point,*
Saranac,
Schuyler's Falls,
Sciota,
Silver Lake,
South Plattsburgh,
Union Falls,
Valcour,
West Chazy,
West Plattsburgh,
Wood's Falls.

Columbia County.

Ancram,
Ancram Centre,
Ancram Lead Mines,
Austerlitz,
Boston Corner,
Canaan,
Canaan Centre,
Canaan Four Corn's,
Cattskill Station,
Chatham,
Chatham Centre,
Chatham Village,
Churchtown,
Claverack,
Clermont,
Copake,
Copake Iron Works,
East Chatham,
Elizaville,
Flatbrook,
Gallatinville,
Germantown,
Ghent,
Glencoe Mills,
Green River,
Harlemville,
Hillsdale.
Hollowville.
Hudson,* (*c. h.*,)
Humphreysville,
Kinderhook,*
Linlithgo,
Livingston,
Malden Bridge,
Martindale Depot,
Mellenville,
Moffett's Store,
Mount Lebanon,
New Concord,
New Lebanon,
New Leb'on Centre,
New Lebanon Sp'gs,
Niverville,
North Chatham,
North Copake,
Philmont,
Red Rock,
Rider's Mills,
Rider's Mills Station,
Shunpike,
Spencertown,
Stockport,
Stottville,
Stuyvesant,
Stuyvesant Falls,
Taghkanick,
Valatie,*
West Copake,
West Taghkanick.

Cortland County.

Blodget Mills,
Cincinnatus,
Cortland Village,* (*c. h.*,)
Cresswell,
Cuyler,
East Homer,
East Scott,
East Virgil,
Freetown Corners,
Glen Haven,
Harford,
Harford Mills,
Homer,*
Hunt's Corners,
Keeney's Settlement,
Lapeer,
Little York,
McGrawville,
Marathon,
Messengerville,
Preble,
Scott,
Solon,
South Cortland,
Taylor,
Texas Valley,
Truxton,*
Union Valley,
Virgil,
Willet.

Delaware County.

Andes,
Barbourville,
Bloomville,
Bovina,
Bovina Valley,
Brushland,

Delaware County—Continued.

Cabin Hill,
Cadosia Valley,
Cannonsville,
Carpenter's Eddy,
Clark's Factory,
Clovesville,
Colchester,
Croton,
Davenport,
Davenport Centre,
Delhi,* (*c. h.*,)
Downsville,
East Branch,
East Masonville,
East Meredith,
Fergusonville,
Franklin,
Grant's Mills,
Griffin's Corners,
Halcottsville,
Hale's Eddy,
Hamden,
Hancock,*
Harpersfield,
Harvard,
Hobart,
Kortright,
Lordville,
Lumberville,
Margarettville,
Masonville,
Meredith,
Moresville,
New Kingston,
North Franklin,
North Hamden,
North Harpersfield,
North Kortright,
North Walton,
Ouleout,
Partridge Island,
Pepacton,
Rock Rift,
Roxbury,
Shavertown,
Sidney,
Sidney Centre,
Sidney Plains,*
South Kortright,
Stamford,
Stockport Station,
Stratton's Falls,
Trout Creek,
Union Grove,
Walton,
West Brook,
West Davenport,
West Kortright,
West Meredith.

Dutchess County.

Adriance,
Amenia,
Amenia Union,
Anandale,
Arthursburgh,
Attlebury,
Bangall,
Barrytown,
Beekman,
Billings,
Bull's Head,
Carthage Landing,
Chesnut Ridge,
City,
Clinton Corners,
Clinton Hollow,
Clinton Point,
Clove,
Clove Branch Junc.,
Coffin's Summit,
Crouse's Store,
Crum Elbow,
Dover,
Dover Furnace,
East Fishkill,
Fishkill,
Fishkill on the Hudson,
Fishkill Plains,
Freedom Plains,
Glenham,
Green Haven,
Hibernia,
Hopewell Junction,
Hughsonville,
Hull's Mills,
Hyde Park,
Jackson Corners,
Johnsville,
La Fayetteville,
La Grangeville,
Leedsville,
Lithgow,
Little Rest,
Mabbettsville,
Madalin,
Manchester Bridge,
Mansfield,
Matteawan,*
Milan,
Millbrook,
Millerton,
Moore's Mill,
Mount Riga,
New Hackensack,
New Hamburgh,
North Clove,
Northeast Centre,
Oblong,
Oreville,
Pawling,
Pine Plains,
Pleasant Plains,
Pleasant Valley,

* Money-order office.

DUTCHESS COUNTY—Continued.

Poughkeepsie,* (c. h.,)
Poughquag,
Pulver's Corners,
Quaker Hill,
Red Hook,
Rhinebeck,*
Rhinecliff,
Rock City,
Salt Point,
Schultzville,
Sharon Station,
South Amenia,
South Dover,
Sprout Creek,
Staatsburgh,
Stanfordville,
Stissing,
Stormville,
Tivoli,
Upper Red Hook,
Verbank,
Wappinger's Falls,
Washington,
Washington Hollow,
Wassaic,
Wing's Station.

ERIE COUNTY.

Akron,
Alden,
Alden Centre,
Angola,
Big Tree Corners,
Boston,
Bowmansville,
Brant,
Buffalo,* (c. h.,)
Buffalo Plains,
Cheektowaga,
Clarence,
Clarence Centre,
Clarksburgh,
Colden,
Collins,
Collins Centre,
Crittenden,
East Amherst,
East Aurora,
East Clarence,
East Concord,
East Eden,
East Elma,
East Evans,
East Hamburgh,
Ebenezer,
Eden,
Eden Valley,
Eggertsville,
Ellicott,
Elma,
Evans,
Farnham,
Gardenville,
Getzville,
Glenwood,
Griffin's Mills,
Hamburgh,
Harris Hill,
Holland,
Lake View,
Lancaster,
Langford,
Looneyville,
Marilla,
Marshfield,
Midway,
Mill Grove,
Morton's Corners,
New Oregon,
North Boston,
North Evans,
Patchin,
Pontiac,
Protection,
Red Jacket,
Reserve,
Sardinia,
Sheenwater,
Shirley,
South Newstead,
South Wales,
Spring Brook,
Springville,
Tonawanda,*
Town Line,
Wales,
Wales Centre,
Water Valley,
West Falls,
West Hamburgh,
West Seneca,
West Seneca Centre,
West Wood,
White Haven,
White's Corners,
Williamsville,
Willink,
Williston,
Winspear,
Woodward's Hollow.

ESSEX COUNTY.

Aiden Lair,
Au Sable Forks,
Bloomingdale,
Crown Point,
Crown Point Centre,
Elizabethtown,* (c. h.,)
Essex,*
Jay,
Keene,
Keene Flats,

ESSEX COUNTY—Continued.

Keeseville,*
Lewis,
Minerva,
Mineville,
Moriah,
Moriah Centre,
Newcomb,
New Russia,
North Elba,
North Hudson,
Olmstedville,
Port Henry,*
Port Kent,
Schroon Lake,
Schroon River,
South Schroon,
Ticonderoga,
Upper Jay,
Wadham's Mills,
Westport,
Whallonsburgh,
Willsborough,
Wilmington.

FRANKLIN COUNTY.

Alder Brook,
Andrusville,
Bangor,
Bombay,
Brush's Mills,
Burke,
Chateaugay,
Chateaugay Lake,
Cook's Corners,
Dickinson,
Dickinson Centre,
Duane,
East Constable,
East Dickinson,
Fort Covington,
Ft.Covington Centre,
Franklin Falls,
Hogansburgh,
Linkinson,
McClelland,
Malone,* (c. h.,)
Merrillsville,
Moira,
North Bangor,
Saranac Lake,
South Bombay,
Trout River,
West Bangor,
West Constable,
Westville Centre.

FULTON COUNTY.

Bleecker,
Broadalbin,
Brockett's Bridge,
Cranberry Creek,
Crum Creek,
Ephratah,
Garoga,
Gloversville,
Johnstown,* (c. h.,)
Keck's Centre,
Kingsborough,
Lasellsville,
Lotville,
Mayfield,
Middle Sprite,
Mill's Corners,
Northampton,
North Broadalbin,
Northville,
Oppenheim,
Osborn's Bridge,
Perth,
Pine Lake,
Rockwood,
Sammonsville,
Stratford,
Union Mills,
Vail's Mills,
West Galway,
West Perth.

GENESEE COUNTY.

Alabama,
Alexander,
Batavia,* (c. h.,)
Bergen,*
Bethany,
Byron,
Corfu,*
Darien,
Darien Centre,
East Bethany,
East Elba,
East Pembroke,
Elba,
Indian Falls,
Le Roy,*
Linden,
Morganville,
North Bergen,
North Oakfield,
North Pembroke,
Oakfield,
Pavilion,
Pavilion Centre,
Pembroke,
South Alabama,
South Byron,
Stafford,
Stone Church,
West Batavia,
West Bergen,
West Bethany,
Wheatville.

* Money-order office.

Greene County.

Acra,
Ashland,
Athens,
Big Hollow,
Bushnellsville,
Cairo,
Catskill,* (*c. h.*,)
Cornwallville,
Coxsackie,
Durham,
East Durham,
East Jewett,
East Windham,
Frechold,
Gayhead,
Grapeville,
Greenville,
Halcott Centre,
Hensonville,
Hunter,
Jewett,
Jewett Centre,
Leeds,
Lexington,
Medway,
New Baltimore,
Norton Hill,
Oak Hill,
Palenville,
Prattsville,
Red Falls,
South Cairo,
South Durham,
Tannersville,
Union Society,
West Kill,
Windham Centre.

Hamilton County.

Benson,
Benson Centre,
Gilman,
Hope Centre,
Hope Falls,
Indian Lake,
Long Lake,
Morehouseville,
Sageville, (*c. h.*,)
Wells.

Herkimer County.

Cedar Lake,
Cedarville,
Cold Brook,
Columbia,
Cullen,
Danube,
Denison,
East Creek,
East Schuyler,
Eatonville,
Emmonsburgh,
Fairfield,
Frankfort,
Frankfort Hill,
Graefenberg,
Grant,
Gravesville,
Gray,
Herkimer,* (*c. h.*,)
Ilion,*
Ingham's Mills,
Jordanville,
Litchfield,
Little Falls,*
Middleville,
Mohawk,
Newport,
Newville,
North Litchfield,
North Winfield,
Norway,
Ohio,
Paine's Hollow,
Poland,
Russia,
Salisbury,
Salisbury Centre,
South Columbia,
Starkville,
Van Hornesville,
Warren,
West Schuyler,
West Winfield,
Winfield.

Jefferson County.

Adams,
Adams Centre,
Alexandria,
Antwerp,
Belleville,
Bishop Street,
Black River,
Brownville,
Burr's Mills,
Cape Vincent, *
Carthage,*
Champion,
Chaumont,
Clayton,
Clayton Centre,
Depauville,
Dexter,
East Houndsfield,
East Rodman,
East Watertown,

Jefferson County—Continued.

Ellisburgh,
Evans' Mills,
Felt's Mills,
Great Bend,
Henderson,
La Fargeville,
Le Raysville,
Limerick,
Lorraine,
Mannsville,
Millen's Bay,
Natural Bridge,
North Wilna,
Omar,
Orleans Four Corners,
Oxbow,
Pamelia Four Corners,
Perch River,
Philadelphia,
Pierrepont Manor,
Pillar Point,
Plesis,
Point Peninsula,
Redwood,
Rodman,
Rural Hill,
Rutland,
Sacket's Harbor,*
Saint Lawrence,
Sanford's Corners,
Smithville,
South Champion,
South Rutland,
Sterlingville,
Stone Mills,
Stowell's Corners,
Theresa,
Three Mile Bay,
Watertown,* (*c. h.*,)
Wilna,
Woodville,
Worth Centre,
Worthville.

Kings County.

Bay Ridge,
Brooklyn,* (*c. h.*,)
Canarsie,
East New York,
Flatbush,
Flatlands,
Fort Hamilton,*
Gravesend,
Green Point,*
New Utrecht,
Parkville,
Williamsburgh.*

Lewis County.

Barnes' Corners,
Beaver Falls,
Brantingham,
Collinsville,
Constableville,
Copenhagen,
Croghan,
Deer River,
Denmark,
Diana,
Glensdale,
Greig,
Harrisburgh,
Harrisville,
Houseville,
Indian River,
Leyden,
Locust Grove,
Lowville, (*c. h.*,)
Lyonsdale,
Lyons' Falls,
Martinsburgh,
Mohawk Hill,
Montague,
Naumburgh,
New Bremen,
Osceola,
Pinckney,
Port Leyden,
Sterling Bush,
Turin,*
Watson,
West Leyden,
West Lowville,
West Martinsburgh.

Livingston County.

Avon,
Brooks' Grove,
Byersville,
Caledonia,
Conesus,
Conesus Centre,
Cuylerville,
Dansville,*
East Avon,
East Groveland,
Fowlerville,
Geneseo,* (*c. h.*,)
Greigsville,
Groveland,
Hemlock Lake,
Hunt's Hollow,
Lakeville,
Lima,

* Money-order office.

LIVINGSTON COUNTY—Continued.

Livonia,
Livonia Station,
Moscow,
Mount Morris,*
North Sparta,
Nunda,*
Nunda Station,
Oakland,
Ossian,
Piffard,
Ridge,
Scottsburgh,
South Avon,
South Lima,
South Livonia,
Springwater,
Tuscarora,
Union Corners,
Webster's Crossing,
York.

MADISON COUNTY.

Bennet's Corners,
Bouckville,
Bridgeport,
Brookfield,
Canastota,
Cazenovia,*
Chittenango,
Chittenango Falls,
Chittenango Station,
Clockville,
De Ruyter,
Earlville,
East Boston,
East Hamilton,
Eaton,
Erieville,
Fenner,
Georgetown,
Hamilton,*
Hubbardsville,
Lakeport,
Lebanon,
Lenox,
Leonardsville,
Madison,
Mile Strip,
Morrisville, (*c. h.*,)
Munsville,
Nelson,
New Woodstock,
North Brookfield,
Oneida,*
Oneida Lake,
Oneida Valley,
Perryville,
Peterborough,
Pine Woods,
Poolville,
Pratt's Hollow,
Randallsville,
Shed's Corners,
Siloam,
Solsville,
South Brookfield,
South Hamilton,
Stockbridge,
Valley Mills,
Wampsville,
West Eaton.

MONROE COUNTY.

Adams' Basin,
Brighton,
Brockport,*
Bushnell's Basin,
Charlotte,
Chili,
Churchville,
Clarkson,
Clifton,
Cold Water,
East Clarkson,
East Penfield,
Egypt,
Fairport,
Gates,
Greece,
Hamlin,
Hanford's Landing,
Henrietta,
Honeoye Falls,
Mendon,
Mendon Centre,
Mount Read,
Mumford,
North Chili,
North Clarkson,
North Greece,
North Hamlin,
North Parma,
North Rush,
Ogden,
Parma,
Parma Centre,
Penfield,
Pittsford,
Riga,
Rochester,* (*c. h.*,)
Rush,
Scottsville,
South Greece,
Spencerport,
Sweden,
Webster,
West Brighton,
West Greece,
West Henrietta,
West Rush,
West Webster.

MONTGOMERY COUNTY.

Ames,
Amsterdam,*
Auriesville,
Buel,
Burtonsville,
Canajoharie,
Charleston,
Charleston Four Corners,
Cranesville,
Flat Creek,
Fonda,* (*c. h.*,)
Fort Hunter
Fort Plain,*
Frey's Bush,
Fultonville,
Glen,
Hagaman's Mills,
Hallsville,
Marshville,
Minaville,
Minden,
Palatine Bridge,
Port Jackson,
Randall,
Root,
Saint Johnsville,
Scotch Bush,
Spraker's Basin,
Sprout Brook,
Stone Arabia,
Tribes Hill.

NEW YORK COUNTY.

New York,* (*c. h.*)

NIAGARA COUNTY.

Beach Ridge,
Bergholtz,
Cambria,
Coomer,
County Line,
Dickersonville,
East Porter,
East Wilson,
Gasport,
Hartland,
Hess Road,
Hickory Corners,
Johnson's Creek,
Lake Road,
La Salle,
Lewiston,
Lockport,* (*c. h.*,)
Maple Street,
Martinsville,
Middleport,
Newfane,
Niagara Falls,*
North Hartland,
North Ridge,
Olcott,
Orangeport,
Pekin,
Pendleton,
Pendleton Centre,
Ransomville,
Rapids,
Reynale's Basin,
Ridge Road,
Royalton,
Saint Johnsburgh,
Sanborn,
Shawnee,
Somerset,
South Wilson,
Suspension Bridge,*
Warren's Corners,
West Somerset,
Wilson,
Wolcottsville,
Wright's Corners,
Youngstown.

ONEIDA COUNTY.

Alder Creek,
Augusta,
Ava,
Babcock Hill,
Big Brook,
Blossvale,
Boonville,*
Bridgewater,
Camden,
Cassville,
Chadwick's Mills,
Clark's Mills,
Clayville,
Clinton,
Deansville,
Deerfield,
Delta,
Durhamville,
East Florence,
Fish Creek,
Florence,
Floyd,
Forest Port,
Franklin Iron Works,
Glenmore,
Hawkinsville,
Hecla Works,
Higginsville,
Holland Patent,
Kirkland,
Knoxborough,
Lairdsville,

* Money-order office.

ONEIDA COUNTY—Continued.

Lee,
Lee Centre,
Lowell,
McConnellsville,
Marcy,
Marshall,
New Hartford,
New London,
New York Mills,
North Bay,
North Bridgewater,
North Gage,
North Western,
Oneida Castle,
Oriskany,
Oriskany Falls,
Paris,
Prospect,
Remsen,
Ridge Mills,
Rome,* (*c. h.*,)
Sangerfield,
Sauquoit,
South Trenton,
Stanwix,
State Bridge,
Steuben,
Stittville,
Stokes,
Taberg,
Trenton,
Trenton Falls,
Utica,* (*c. h.*,)
Vernon,
Vernon Centre,
Verona,
Vienna,
Walesville,
Washington Mills,
Waterville,
West Branch,
West Camden,
Westernville,
Westmoreland,
West Vienna,
Whitestown.

ONONDAGA COUNTY.

Amber,
Apulia,
Baldwinsville,
Belle Isle,
Borodino,
Brewerton,
Camillus,
Cardiff,
Cicero,
Clay,
Collamer,
Collingwood,
Delphi,
De Witt,
Elbridge,
Euclid,
Fabius,
Fair Mount,
Fayetteville,
Geddes,
Half Way,
Hart Lot,
Howlet Hill,
Jack's Reef,
Jamesville,
Jordan,
Kirkville,
La Fayette,
Lamson's,
Little Utica,
Liverpool,
Lysander,
Mandana,
Manlius,
Manlius Centre,
Manlius Station,
Marcellus,
Marcellus Falls,
Marietta,
Memphis,
Mottville,
Navarino,
North Manlius,
Onondaga,
Onondaga Castle,
Onondaga Valley,
Oran,
Otisco,
Otisco Valley,
Plainville,
Plank Road,
Pompey,
Pompey Centre,
Salina,
Skaneateles,*
South Onondaga,
Spafford,
Summit Station,
Syracuse,* (*c. h.*,)
Thorn Hill,
Tully,*
Tully Valley,
Van Buren,
Vesper,
Warner's,
Watervale.

ONTARIO COUNTY.

Academy,
Allen's Hill,
Bristol,
Bristol Centre,
Canadice,
Canandaigua,* (*c. h.*,)

ONTARIO COUNTY—Continued.

Chapinville,
Cheshire,
Clifton Springs,*
East Bloomfield,
Farmington,
Fishers,
Flint Creek,
Geneva,*
Gorham,
Gypsum,
Hall's Corners,
Honeoye,
Hopewell,
Hopewell Centre,
Manchester,
Manchester Centre,
Miller's Corners,
Naples,
North Bloomfield,
Oak's Corners,
Orleans,
Phelps,
Port Gibson,
Reed's Corners,
Richmond Mills,
Seneca Castle,
Shortsville,*
South Bristol,
Stanley Corners,
Victor,*
West Bloomfield,
West Farmington.

ORANGE COUNTY.

Allard's Corners,
Amity,
Bellvale,
Blooming Grove,
Bullville,
Burnside,
Campbell Hall,
Chester,
Circleville,
Coldenham,
Cornwall,
Cornwall Landing,
Craigsville,
Cuddebackville,
Edenville,
Florida,
Fort Montgomery,
Goshen,* (*c. h.*,)
Greenwood Iron Works,
Guymard,
Highland Falls,
Highland Mills,
Howell's Depot,
Huguenot,
Johnson's,
Middle Hope,
Middletown,*
Minisink,
Monroe,
Monroe Works,
Montgomery,
Moodna,
Mount Hope,
Newburgh,* (*c. h.*,)
New Hampton,
New Milford,
Orange Lake,
Otisville,
Oxford Depot,
Pine Bush,
Pine Island,
Port Jervis,*
Ridgebury,
Saint Andrew's,
Salisbury Mills,
Savill,
Scotchtown,
Searsville,
Slate Hill,
Sparrow Bush,
Sugar Loaf,
Turner's,
Unionville,
Vail's Gate,
Walden,
Warwick,
Waterloo Mills,
Wells' Corner,
West Point,*
West Town,
Wood.

ORLEANS COUNTY.

Albion,* (*c. h.*,)
Barre Centre,
Carlton,
Clarendon,
Eagle Harbor,
East Carlton,
East Gaines,
East Kendall,
East Shelby,
Gaines,
Hindsburgh,
Holley,
Hulburton,
Jeddo,
Kendall,
Kendall Mills,
Kenyonville,
Knowlesville,
Kuckville,
Lyndonville,
Medina,*
Millville,
Murray,
North Ridgeway,

* Money-order office.

ORLEANS COUNTY—Continued.

Oak Orchard,
Ridgeway,
Shelby,
Shelby Basin,
South Barre,
Waterport,
West Barre,
West Kendall,
West Shelby,
Yates.

OSWEGO COUNTY.

Amboy Centre,
Bernhard's Bay,
Bowen's Corners,
Boylston Centre,
Butterfly,
Caughdenoy,
Central Square,
Cleaveland,
Colosse,
Constantia,
Constantia Centre,
Daysville,
Dugway,
East Boylston,
East Palermo,
East Sandy Creek,*
Fair Dale,
Fulton,*
Gilbert's Mills,
Granby Centre,
Hannibal,
Hannibal Centre,
Hastings,
Hastings Centre,
Hinmansville,
Ingalls' Crossing,
Kasoag,
Kinney's Four C'rs,
Mallory,
Maple Hill,
Mexico,
Minetto,
Molino,
New Centreville,
New Haven,
North Hannibal,
North Scriba,
North Volney,
Orwell,
*Oswego,** (c. h.,)
Oswego Centre,
Oswego Falls,
Palermo,
Parish,
Pennellville,
Phœnix,
Port Ontario,
*Pulaski,** (c. h.,)
Redfield,
Richland,
Salmon River,
Sand Bank,
Sandy Creek,
Scriba,
South Albion,
South Granby,
South Hannibal,
South Richland,
South Scriba,
South West Oswego,
Texas,
Union Square,
Vermillion,
Volney,
West Amboy,
West Monroe,
Williamstown.

OTSEGO COUNTY.

Burlington,
Burlington Flats,
Butternuts,
Centre Valley,
Chaseville,
Cherry Valley,
Colliersville,
*Cooperstown,** (c. h.,)
Decatur,
East Springfield,
East Worcester,
Edmeston,
Elk Creek,
Exeter,
Fly Creek,
Garrattsville,
Hartwick,
Hartwick Seminary,
Laurens,
Maple Grove,
Maryland,
Middlefield,
Middlefield Centre,
Milford,
Morris,
Mount Vision,
New Lisbon,
Oaksville,
Oneonta,
Otego,
Otsdawa,
Phœnix Mills,
Pittsfield,
Pleasant Brook,
Portlandville,
Richfield,
Richfield Springs,
Roseboom,
Schenevus,
Schuyler's Lake,

OTSEGO COUNTY—Continued.

South Edmeston,
South Hartwick,
South Valley,
South Worcester,
Spooner's Corners,
Springfield,
Springfield Centre,
Toddsville,
Unadilla,
Unadilla Centre,
Unadilla Forks,
Wells' Bridge,
West Burlington,
West Edmeston,
West Exeter,
Westford,
West Laurens,
West Oneonta,
Westville,
Worcester.

PUTNAM COUNTY.

Boyd's Corner,
Brewster's Station,
*Carmel,** (c. h.,)
Cold Spring,*
Dykeman's,
Farmer's Mills,
Garrison's,
Haviland Hollow,
Kent,
Ludingtonville,
Mahopac,
Mahopac Falls,
Patterson,
Towner's.

QUEENS COUNTY.

Astoria,
Bay Side,
Central Park,
Clarenceville,
College Point,
East Norwich,
East Rockaway,
Farmingdale,
Flushing,*
Freeport,
Glen Cove,
Great Neck,
Greenvale,
Hempstead,*
Hicksville,
*Jamaica,** (c. h.,)
Jericho,
Little Neck,
Locust Valley,
Long Island City,
Manhasset,
Maspeth,
Merrick,
Mineola,
Newtown,
Old Westbury,
Oyster Bay,
Port Washington,
Queens,
Ravenswood,
Ridgewood,
Rockaway,
Rockville Centre,
Roslyn,
Seaford,
Smithville South,
Springfield Store,
Syosset,
Valley Stream,
Whitestone,
Woodbury,
Woodhaven,
Woodside.

RENSSELAER COUNTY.

Alps,
Berlin,
Brainerd,
Castleton,
Centre Berlin,
Centre Brunswick,
Cropseyville,
Defreestville,
Eagle Bridge,
Eagle Mills,
East Greenbush,
East Nassau,
East Poestenkill,
East Schodack,
Grafton,
Harts Falls,
Haynerville,
Hoag's Corner,
Hoosick,
Hoosick Falls,*
Johnsonville,
Junction,
Lansingburgh,*
Nassau,
North Hoosick,
North Nassau,
North Petersburgh,
North Stephentown,
Petersburgh,
Pittstown,
Poestenkill,
Potter Hill,
Quacken Kill,
Raymertown,

* Money-order office.

RENSSELAER COUNTY—Continued.

Sand Lake,
Schodack Centre,
Schodack Depot,
Schodack Landing,
South Berlin,
South Sand Lake,
South Schodack,
Stephentown,
Tomhannock,
Troy,* (*c. h.*,)
Valley Falls,
West Hoosick,
West Sand Lake,
West Stephentown,
Wynantskill.

RICHMOND COUNTY.

Mariner's Harbor,
Marshland,
New Brighton,
New Dorp,
New Springville,
Port Richmond,
Prince's Bay,
Richmond,* (*c. h.*,)
Rossville,
South Side,
Stapleton,*
Tompkinsville,
Tottenville,
West New Brighton.

ROCKLAND COUNTY.

Blauveltville,
Clarkstown, (*c. h.*,)
Haverstraw,
Iona Island,
Monsey,
Nanuet,
Nyack,*
Nyack Turnpike,
Palisades,
Piermont,
Ramapo Works,
Rockland Lake,
Sloatsburgh,
Spring Valley,
Stony Point,
Suffern,
Tallman,
Tappantown,
Tomkin's Cove.

ST. LAWRENCE COUNTY.

Brasher Falls,
Brasher Iron Works,
Brier Hill,
Canton,* (*c. h.*,)
Chase's Mills,
Clarksborough,
Colton,
Crary's Mills,
DeKalb,
De Kalb Junction,
De Peyster,
East De Kalb,
East Pitcairn,
Edenton,
Edwards,
Edwardsville,
Ellsworth,
Fine,
Flackville,
Fowler,
Fullerville Iron Works.
Gouverneur,*
Hailesborough,
Hammond,
Helena,
Hermon,*
Heuvelton,
Hopkinton,
Lawrenceville,
Lisbon,
Lisbon Centre,
Louisville,
Louisville Landing,
Macomb,
Madrid,*
Madrid Springs,
Massena,*
Massena Centre,
Morley,
Morristown,
Nicholville,
Norfolk,
North Hammond,
North Lawrence,
North Russell,
North Stockholm,
Ogdensburgh,*
Parishville,
Parishville Centre,
Pierrepont,
Pitcairn,
Pope's Mills,
Potsdam,*
Potsdam Junction,
Raymondville,
Rensselaer Falls,
Richville,
Rossie,
Russell,
Shingle Creek,
Somerville,

ST. LAWRENCE COUNTY—Continued.

South Colton,
South Edwards,
Southville,
Stockholm,
Stockholm Depot,
Waddington,
Wegatchie,
West Potsdam,
West Stockholm.

SARATOGA COUNTY.

Bacon Hill,
Ballston,* (*c. h.*,)
Ballston Centre,
Barkersville,
Batchellerville,
Bemus' Heights,
Burnt Hills,
Charlton,
Clifton Park,
Conklingville,
Corinth,
Coveville,
Crescent,
Day,
Deans' Corners,
East Galway,
East Line,
Edinburgh,
Fortsville,
Galway,
Gansevoort,
Greenfield Centre,
Groom's Corners,
Hadley,
Hagedorn's Mills,
Half Moon,
Jonesville,
Ketchum's Corners,
Malta.
Maltaville,
Mechanicsville,
Middle Grove,
Milton Centre,
Moreau Station,
Mosherville,
North Galway,
North Greenfield,
Northumberland,
Porter's Corners,
Providence,
Quaker Springs,
Rexford Flats,
Rock City Falls,
Saratoga Springs,*
Schuylersville,
South Ballston,
South Corinth,
South Galway,
South Glens Falls,
South Wilton,
Stillwater,
Victory Mills,
Vischer's Ferry,
Waterford,
West Charlton,
West Day,
West Greenfield,
West Milton,
West Providence,
Wilton.

SCHENECTADY COUNTY.

Braman's Corners,
Duanesburgh,
East Glenville,
Glenville,
Hoffman's Ferry,
Mariaville,
Niskayuna,
Quaker Street,
Rynex's Corners,
Schenectady,* (*c. h.*,)
Scotia,
Van Vechten.

SCHOHARIE COUNTY.

Argusville,
Barnerville,
Breakabeen,
Broome Centre,
Carlisle,
Central Bridge,
Charlotteville,
Cobleskill,
Conesville,
East Cobleskill,
Eminence,
Esperance,
Franklinton,
Fultonham,
Gallupville,
Gilboa,
Grovenor's Corners
Howe's Cave,
Hunter's Land,
Hyndsville,
Jefferson.
Lawyersville,
Leesville,
Livingstonville,
Manor Kill,
Middleburgh,*
Mine Kill Falls,
Mineral Springs,
Morseville,
North Blenheim,

* Money-order office.

SCHOHARIE COUNTY—Continued.

Richmondville,
Schoharie,* (*c. h.*,)
Seward,
Sharon,
Sharon Centre,
Sharon Springs,
Shutter's Corners,
Sloansville,
South Gilboa,
South Jefferson,
Summit,
Warnerville,
West Conesville,
West Fulton,
West Richmondville.

SCHUYLER COUNTY.

Alpine,
Altay,
Beaver Dams,
Bennettsburgh,
Burdett,
Catharine,
Cayuta,
Cayutaville,
East Orange,
Havana,*
Hector,
Lawrence,
Logan,
Mecklenburgh,
Moreland,
North Hector,
North Reading,
Odessa,
Orange,
Perry City,
Pine Creek,
Pine Grove,
Reading,
Reading Centre,
Reynoldsville,
Searsburgh,
Seneca,
Smith Valley,
Sugar Hill,
Townsend,
Tyrone,
Watkins, (*c. h.*,)
Weston.

SENECA COUNTY.

Canoga,
Covert,
Cruso,
East Varick,
Farmer Village,
Fayette,
Junius,
Kendaia,
Kidder's Ferry,
Lodi,
Lodi Centre,
Magee's Corners,
Ovid, (*c. h.*,)
Romulus,
Romulus Centre,
Rose Hill,
Seneca Falls,*
Sheldrake,
Trumansburgh L'd'g,
Tyre,
Varick,
Waterloo, (*c. h.*,)
West Fayette,
West Junius.

STEUBEN COUNTY.

Addison,
Addison Hill,
Adrian,
Allen's Station,
Arkport,
Avoca,
Bath,* (*c. h.*,)
Bennett's Creek,
Big Creek,
Bradford,
Buena Vista,
Cameron,
Cameron Mills,
Campbelltown,
Canisteo,
Caton,
Centre Canisteo,
Cohocton,
Cooper's Plains,
Corning,*
Doty's Corner,
East Troupsburgh,
East Woodhull,
Erwin Centre,
Gibson,
Goff's Mills,
Greenwood,
Hammondsport,
Haskinville,
Hedgesville,
Hornby,
Hornellsville,*
Howard,
Jasper,
Kanona,
Lindleytown,
Mead's Creek,
Merchantville,

STEUBEN COUNTY—Continued.

Mitchellsville,
Neil's Creek,
North Cameron,
North Cohocton,
North Jasper,
North Urbana,
Painted Post,
Perkinsville,
Prattsburgh,*
Pultney,
Purdy Creek,
Rathboneville,
Rexville,
Riker's Hollow,
Risingville,
Savona,
Sonora,
South Addison,
South Bradford,
South Cameron,
South Dansville,
South Howard,
South Pultney,
South Troupsburgh,
Stephens' Mills,
Swale,
Thurston,
Towlesville,
Troupsburgh,
Wallace,
Wayland Depot,
Wayne,
Wayne Four Corners,
West Addison,
West Jasper,
West Troupsburgh,
West Union,
Wheeler,
Wileysville,
Woodhull,
Young Hickory.

SUFFOLK COUNTY.

Amagansett,
Amityville,
Atlanticville,
Babylon,
Baiting Hollow,
Bay Shore,
Bellport,
Blue Point,
Brentwood,
Bridgehampton,
Calverton,
Centre Moriches,
Centreport,
Cold Spring Harbor,
Commack,
Coram,
Cutchogue,
Deer Park,
Dix Hills,
East Hampton,
East Marion,
East Moriches,
East Setauket,
Elwood,
Fire Island,
Fireplace,
Flanders,
Fresh Pond,
Good Ground,
Greenport,*
Hauppauge,
Holbrook,
Holtsville,
Huntington,*
Islip,
Jamesport,
Lake Grove,
Manorville,
Mattituck,
Middle Island,
Miller's Place,
Moriches,
Mount Sinai,
Northport,
Oakdale Station,
Orient,
Patchogue,*
Peconic,
Port Jefferson,*
Quogue,
Riverhead,* (*c. h.*,)
Ronkonkoma,
Sag Harbor,*
Saint James,
Sayville,
Selden,
Setauket,
Shelter Island,
Smithtown,
Smithtown Branch,
Southampton,
South Haven,
Southold,
Speonk,
Springs,
Stoney Brook,
Success,
Suffolk,
Upper Aquebogue,
Wading River,
Water Mill,
West Hampton,
Yaphank.

SULLIVAN COUNTY.

Barryville,
Beaver Brook,
Beaver Kill,
Beech Wood,

* Money-order office.

SULLIVAN COUNTY—Continued.

Bethel,
Bloomingburgh,
Bridgeville,
Briscoe,
Burlingham,
Bushville,
Callicoon,
Callicoon Depot,
Claryville,
Cochecton,
Cochecton Centre,
De Bruce,
Eureka,
Fallsburgh,
Fall's Mill,
Forestburgh,
Fosterdale,
Fremont Centre,
Gales,
Glen Wild,
Grahamsville,
Hankins,
Hasbrouck,
Jeffersonville,
Liberty,
Liberty Falls,
Loch Sheldrake,
Long Eddy,
Lumberland,
Mongaup,
Mongaup Valley,
Monticello,* (*c. h.*,)
Morsston,
Narrowsburgh,
Neversink,
North Branch,
Parksville,
Phillipsport,
Pike Pond,
Pond Eddy,
Purvis,
Red Brick,
Robertsonville,
Rockland,
Shin Creek,
Stevensville,
Thompsonville,
West Brookville,
White Lake,
Woodbourne,
Wurtsborough,
Youngsville.

TIOGA COUNTY.

Apalachin,
Barton,
Berkshire,
Bingham's Mills,
Campville,
Candor,
Catatonk,
East Berkshire,
East Nichols,
Factoryville,
Flemingsville,
Gaskill's Corners,
Halsey Valley,
Hooper's Valley,
Jenksville,
Ketchumville,
Newark Valley,
Nichols,
North Barton,
Owego,* (*c. h.*,)
Richford,
Smithsborough,
South Owego,
Spencer,
Spencer Springs,
Strait's Corners,
Tioga Centre,
Waverly,*
Weltonville,
West Candor,
West Newark,
Willseyville,
Wilson Creek.

TOMPKINS COUNTY.

Caroline,
Caroline Centre,
Caroline Depot,
Danby,
Dryden,
East Lansing,
Enfield,
Enfield Centre,
Etna,
Freeville,
Groton,
Groton City,
Ithaca,* (*c. h.*,)
Jacksonville,
Lake Ridge,
Lansingville,
Ludlowville,
McLean,
Mott's Corners,
Newfield,
North Lansing,
Peruville,
Poney Hollow,
Slaterville,
South Danby,
South Lansing,
Speedsville,
Trumansburgh,
Trumbull Corners,
Varna,
Waterburgh,
West Danby,
West Dryden,
West Groton.

ULSTER COUNTY.

Accord,
Bearsville,
Bruynswick,
Clintondale,
Creek Locks,
Dairyland,
Denning,
Dry Brook,
Dwaar's Kill,
Ellenville,*
Esopus,
Fly Mountain,
Galeville Mills,
Glasco,
Greenfield,
Hardenburgh,
High Falls,
Highland,
Homowack,
Hurley,
Kerhonkson,
Kingston,* (*c. h.*,)
Kyserike,
Lackawack,
Lake Hill,
Le Fever Falls,
Libertyville,
Loyd,
Malden,
Marbletown,
Marlborough,
Milton,
Modena,
Napanock,
New Hurley,
New Paltz,
Ohioville,
Olive,
Olive Bridge,
Phœnicia,
Pine Hill,
Plattekill,
Port Ewen,
Quarryville,
Rifton Glen,
Rondout,*
Rosendale,
Samsonville,
Saugerties,
Shandaken,
Shawangunk,
Shokan,
Stone Ridge,
The Corner,
Turnwood,
Tuthill,
Ulster Park,
Ulsterville,
Walker Valley,
Wawarsing,
West Camp,
West Hurley,
Wilbur,
Woodland,
Woodstock.

WARREN COUNTY.

Athol,
Bolton,
Caldwell, (*c. h.*,)
Chestertown,
Creek Centre,
French Mountain,
Glens Falls,*
Hague,
Horicon,
Johnsburgh,
Luzerne,
North Creek,
North River,
Pottersville,
Queensbury,
The Glen,
Thurman,
Warrensburgh,*
Wevertown.

WASHINGTON COUNTY.

Adamsville,
Argyle,
Battenville,
Belcher,
Buskirk's Bridge,
Cambridge,*
Centre Cambridge,
Centre White Creek,
Coila,
Comstock's Landing,
Crandell's Corners,
East Greenwich,
Easton,
East Salem,
Fort Ann,
Fort Edward,*
Fort Miller,
Galesville,
Granville,
Greenwich,
Griswold's Mills,
Hampton,
Hartford,
Hebron,
Kingsbury,
Lake,
Low Hampton,
Middle Granville,
North Argyle,
North Easton,
North Granville,
North Greenwich,

* Money-order office.

WASHINGTON COUNTY—Continued.

North Hebron,
Patten's Mills,
Putnam,
Salem, (*c. h.*,)
Sandy Hill,* (*c. h.*,)
Shushan,
Smith's Basin,
South Argyle,
South Easton,
South Granville,
South Hartford,
West Fort Ann,
West Granville Corners,
West Hebron,
White Creek,
Whitehall.*

WAYNE COUNTY.

Alton,
Arcadia,
Clyde,
East Palmyra,
Fairville,
Hall Centre,
Huron,
Joy,
Lake Side,
Lincoln,
Lock Berlin,
Lummisville,
Lyons,* (*c. h.*,)
Macedon,
Macedon Centre,
Marengo,
Marion,
Newark,*
North Huron,
North Rose,
Ontario,
Ontario Centre,
Palmyra,
Pultneyville,
Red Creek,
Rose,
Savannah,
Sodus,
Sodus Centre,
Sodus Point,
South Butler,
South Sodus,
Walworth,
Wayne Centre,
West Butler,
West Macedon,*
West Walworth,
Williamson,
Wolcott.*

WESTCHESTER COUNTY.

Armonk,
Bedford, (*c. h.*,)
Bedford Station,
Boscobel,
Boutonville,
Bronxville,
Chappaqua,
City Island,
Cross River,
Croton Falls,
Croton Landing,
Dobb's Ferry,
East Chester,
Elmsford,
Fordham,
Golden's Bridge,
Hallock's Mills,
Harrison,
Hart's Corners,
Hastings upon Hudson,
Irvington,
Jefferson Valley,
Jerome,
Katonah,
Kensico,
Kingsbridgeville,
Lewisborough,
Mamaroneck,
Montrose,
Morrisania,
Mott Haven,
Mount Kisco,*
Mount Vernon,
Neperan,
New Castle,

WESTCHESTER COUNTY—Continued.

New Rochelle,
North Castle,
North Salem,
Peekskill,*
Pelham,
Pine's Bridge,
Pleasantville,
Port Chester,*
Poundridge,
Purdy's Station,
Riverdale,
Rye,
Salem Centre,
Scarborough,
Scarsdale,
Shrub Oak,
Sing Sing,*
Somers,
South Salem,
Spuyten Duyvil,
Tarrytown,*
Tremont,
Tuckahoe,
Valhalla,
Verplank,
Vista,
West Chester,
West Farms,
West Somers,
White Plains,* (*c. h.*,)
Wood Lawn,
Yonkers,*
Yorktown.

WYOMING COUNTY.

Arcade,*
Attica,
Bennington,
Castile,
Covington,
Cowlesville,
Dale,
Eagle,
Eagle Village,
East Arcade,
East Gainesville,
East Java,
East Orangeville,
East Pike,
Folsomdale,
Gainesville,
Hermitage,
Java,
Java Village,
Johnsonsburgh,
La Grange,
North Java,
North Sheldon,
North Wethersfield,
Orangeville,
Pearl Creek,
Peoria,
Perry,
Perry Centre,
Pike,*
Portageville,
Sheldon,
Strykersville,
Varysburgh,
Warsaw,* (*c. h.*,)
Wethersfield,
Wethersfield Spr'gs,
Wyoming.

YATES COUNTY.

Barrington,
Bellona,
Benton Centre,
Bluff Point,
Branchport,
Crystal Spring,
Dresden,
Dundee,
Eddytown,
Ferguson's Corners,
Glenora,
Himrod's,
Italy Hill,
Italy Hollow,
Middlesex,
Milo Centre,
Penn Yan,* (*c. h.*,)
Potter,
Rock Stream,
Rushville,
Starkey,
Vine Valley,
Voak.

NORTH CAROLINA.

ALAMANCE COUNTY.

Big Falls,
Clover Orchard,
Company's Shops,
Curtis' Mills,
McCray's Store,
Mebanesville,
Patterson's Store,
Pleasant Grove,

ALAMANCE COUNTY—Continued.

Graham, (*c. h.*,)
Hartshorn,
Haw River,
Rock Creek,
Saxapahaw,
Snow Camp.

* Money-order office.

ALEXANDER COUNTY.

Stony Point,
Taylorville, (*c. h.*,)
Wittenberg,
York Collegiate Institute.

ALLEGHANY COUNTY.

Cherry Lane,
Gap Civil, (*c. h.*,)
New River,
Piney Creek.

ANSON COUNTY.

Ansonville,
Caudle Mills,
Cedar Hill,
Deep Creek,
Diamond Hill,
Dumas Ferry,
Flat Fork,
Kendall,
Lanesborough,
Lilesville,
Long Pine,
Morven,
New Forestville,
Poplar Hill,
Wadesborough, (*c. h.*,)
White's Store.

ASHE COUNTY.

Elk Cross Roads,
Gap Creek,
Glade Creek,
Helton,
Horse Creek,
Jefferson, (*c. h.*,)
Laurel Springs,
North Fork,
Scottville,
Walnut Hill.

BEAUFORT COUNTY.

Bath,
Hunter's Bridge,
Leechville,
Pantego,
South Creek,
Washington,* (*c. h.*)

BERTIE COUNTY.

Colerain,
Hotel,
Roxobel,
Windsor, (*c. h.*)

BLADEN COUNTY.

Abbottsburgh,
Bladenborough,
Dalton,
Daniel's Landing,
Elizabethtown, (*c. h.*,)
French Creek Church,
Harrison's Creek,
Little Sugar Loaf,
Loveland,
Martsville,
Prospect Hall,
Rosindale,
West Brook,
Whitehall,
Yorkville.

BRUNSWICK COUNTY.

Bernard,
Bolton,
Robeson,
Smithville, (*c. h.*)

BUNCOMBE COUNTY.

Asheville,* (*c. h.*,)
Avery's Creek,
Democrat,
Fairview,
Gray Eagle,
Hominy Creek,
Leicester,
Reem's Creek,
Riverside,
Sandy Mush,
Stocksville,
Swannano,
Turnpike,
Walnut Creek.

BURKE COUNTY.

Bridgewater,
Brindletown,
Fonta Flora,
Happy Home,
Jonas Ridge,
Morganton,* (*c. h.*,)
Perkinsville,
Piedmont Springs.

CABARRUS COUNTY.

Coddle Creek,
Concord,* (*c. h.*,)
Harris Depot,
Mill Hill,
Mount Pleasant,
North Barrier,
Pioneer Mills,
Smith's Ford,
Tulin.

CALDWELL COUNTY.

Collettsville,
Copenhagen,
Globe,
Lenoir, (*c. h.*,)
Lovelady,
Patterson,
Tuttle's × Roads.

CAMDEN COUNTY.

Camden C. H.,
Shiloh,
South Mills.

CARTERET COUNTY.

Beaufort, (*c. h.*,)
Morehead City,
Newport,
Peletier's Mills,
Portsmouth,
Sanders' Store.

CASWELL COUNTY.

Anderson's Store,
Independence,
Leasburgh,
Locust Hill,
Milton,
Pea Ridge,
Pelham,
Prospect Hill,
Purley,
Yanceyville, (*c. h.*)

CATAWBA COUNTY.

Catawba Station,
Chronicle,
Dry Ponds,
Hickory Tavern,
Jacob's Fork,
Mountain Creek,
Mull Grove,
Newton, (*c. h.*,)
Sherrill's Ford.

CHATHAM COUNTY.

Bellevoir,
Cane Creek,
Egypt Depot,
Grove,
Hadley's Mills,
Haywood,
Lockville,
Merry Oaks,
Mud Lick,
Pittsborough,* (*c. h.*,)
Rialto,
Riggsbee's Store,
Saint Lawrence,
Sandy Grove,
Snipe's Store.

CHEROKEE COUNTY.

Murphey, (*c. h.*,)
Valley Town,
Wolf Creek.

CHOWAN COUNTY.

Edenton,* (*c. h.*,)
Wardville.

* Money-order office.

Clay County.

Hayesville, (c. h.,) Tusquitee.

Cleveland County.

Buffalo Paper Mill, Camp Call, Double Shoal, Erwinsville, Gardner's Ford, Knob Creek, Mooresborough, Muddy Fork, Nicholsonville, *Shelby*, (c. h.,) Stice's Shoal, Swangstown, White Plains.

Columbus County.

Bogue, Cerro Gordo, Fair Bluff, Flemington, Grist's Station, Peacock's Store, Pireway Ferry, *Whitesville*, (c. h.)

Craven County.

Bay River, Dover, Grantsborough, *New Berne*,* (c. h.,) Pamlico, Swift Creek Bridge.

Cumberland County.

Cedar Creek, *Fayetteville*,* (c. h.,) Gibbs' Cross Roads, Gray's Creek, Inverness, Roslin.

Currituck County.

Coinjock, *Currituck C. H.*, Indian Ridge, Poplar Branch, Powell's Point.

Dare County.

Manteo, (c. h.)

Davidson County.

Abbott's Creek, Arcadia, Cedar Bush, Fair Grove, Hannersville, *Lexington*, (c. h.,) Linwood, Midway, Miller's Mill, Reedy Creek, Spencer, Thomasville, Yadkin College.

Davie County.

Calahaln, County Line, Elbaville, Farmington, Fulton, Jerusalem, *Mocksville*, (c. h.,) Smith Grove.

Duplin County.

Alberton's, Branch's Store, Buena Vista, Faison's Depot, Hallsville, *Kenansville*,* (c. h.,) Magnolia, Outlaw's Bridge, Resaca, Rock Fish, Teachey's, Wallace, Warsaw.

Edgecombe County.

Battleborough, Kingsborough, Rocky Mount, Sparta, *Tarborough*,* (c. h.,) Whitaker's.

Forsyth County.

Belew Creek Mills, Bethania, Flat Branches, Friedburgh, Kernersville, Lewisville, Mount Tabor, Old Richmond, Old Town, Salem,* Salem Chapel, Sedges Garden, Vienna, Walkerstown White Road.

Franklin County.

Cedar Rock, Franklinton, *Louisburgh*,* (c. h.,) Pacific.

Gaston County.

Cherryville, Craigsville, Crowder's Mountain, *Dallas*, (c. h.,) High Shoals, King's Mountain, Old Furnace, South Point, Stanley's Creek, Woodlawn.

Gates County.

Buckland, Crossville, *Gatesville*, (c. h.,) Reynoldson, Sunbury.

Granville County.

Blue Wing, Brookville, Brownsville, Buchanan, Dutchville, Fairport, Henderson, Kittrell, Knap of Reeds, New Hope Mills, Oak Hill, *Oxford*, (c. h.,) Sassafras Fork, Tally Ho, Townesville, Wilton, Young's × Roads.

Greene County.

Carolina Seminary, Cotton Valley, Hookerton, *Snow Hill*, (c. h.,) Speight's Bridge.

Guilford County.

Allemance, Brick Church, Centre, Colfax, Deep River, Fentriss, Friendship, Gibsonville, Gilmer's Store, *Greensborough*,*(c. h.,) High Point, Hillsdale, Jamestown, McLeansville, Monticello, New Garden, Shaw's Mills, Westminster, Young's Mills.

* Money-order office.

Halifax County.

Brinkleyville,
Enfield,
Halifax, (*c. h.*,)
Heathsville,
Littleton,
Ringwood,
Scotland Neck,
South Gaston,
Weldon.*

Harnett County.

Averysborough,
Chalk Level,
Harnett C. H.,
Harrington,
Norval,
Spout Springs,
Summerville,

Haywood County

Crab Tree,
Forks of Pigeon,
Jonathan's Creek,
Pigeon River,
Richland Valley,
Waynesville, (*c. h.*)

Henderson County.

Bear Wallow,
Blue Ridge,
Boilston,
Boman's Bluff,
Edneyville,
Flat Rock,
Green River,
Hendersonville, (*c. h.*,)
Mill River,
Shufordville.

Hertford County.

Harrellsville,
Murfreesborough,
Riddicksville,
Saint John,
Winton, (*c. h.*)

Hyde County.

Fairfield,
Lake Comfort,
Lake Landing,
Ocracoke,
Sladesville,
Swan Quarter, (*c. h.*)

Iredell County.

Amity Hill,
Cool Spring,
Eagle Mills,
Elk Shoals,
Enola,
Fancy Hill,
Mount Mourne,
New Hope,
New Stirling,
Oak Forest,
Olin,
Snow Creek,
Statesville,* (*c. h.*,)
Sweet Home,
Turnersburgh,
Union Grove,
Williamsburgh.

Jackson County.

Big Spring,
Caler's Hill,
Casher's Valley,
East Laport,
Jackson Springs,
Ocona Lufty,
Quallatown,
Webster, (*c. h.*)

Johnston County.

Beulah,
Boon Hill,
Clayton,
Earpsborough,
Hinnaut's Mills,
Leechburgh,
Pine Level,
Selma,
Smithfield, (*c. h.*,)
Wilson's Mills.

Jones County.

Pollocksville,
Trenton, (*c. h.*)

Lenoir County.

Falling Creek,
Kinston, (*c. h.*,)
La Grange,
Pink Hill.

Lincoln County.

Beattie's Ford,
Castania Grove,
Cottage Home,
Iron Station,
Killian's Mills,
Lincolnton, (*c. h.*,)
North Brook,
Siegle's Store.

McDowell County.

Dysortville,
Marion, (*c. h.*,)
Nealsville,
North Cove,
Old Fort,
Pleasant Retreat,
Sugar Hill.

Macon County.

Aquone,
Franklin, (*c. h.*,)
Horse Cove,
Wickle's Store.

Madison County.

Bone Camp,
Holly Grove,
Marshall, (*c. h.*,)
Spring Creek,
Warm Springs.

Martin County.

Hamilton,
Jamesville,
Roanoke,
Williamston, (*c. h.*)

Mecklenburgh County.

Charlotte,* (*c. h.*,)
Clear Creek,
Cowan's Ford,
Craighead,
Davidson College,
Fullwood's Store,
Hopewell,
Martindale,
Mint Hill,
Pineville,
Query's.

Mitchell County.

Bakersville, (*c. h.*,)
Childsville,
Cranberry Forge,
Fork Mountain,
Ledger,
Red Hill.

Montgomery County.

Auman's Hill,
Edinborough,
Hunsucker's Store,
Montgomery,
Mount Gilead,
Pekin,
Pine Grove,
Sanders' Hill,
Sulphur Springs,
Swift Island,
Troy, (*c. h.*)

Moore County.

Carter's Mills,
Carthage, (*c. h.*,)
Clark's Mills,
Crain's Creek,
Curriersville,
Glenaloon,
Jonesborough,
Mooshannee,
Morris Town,
Prosperity,
Swann's Station.

* Money-order office.

NASH COUNTY.

Castalia.
Hilliardston,
Nashville, (*c. h.*,)
Ransom's Bridge,
Stanhope.

NEW HANOVER COUNTY.

Black River Chapel,
Burgaw Depot,
Cameron,
Castle Hayne,
Harrell's Store,
Lillington,
Moore's Creek,
Oakley,
Rocky Point,
South Washington,
Topsail Sound,
Wilmington,* (*c. h.*)

NORTHAMPTON COUNTY.

Jackson, (*c. h.*,)
Margarettsville,
Pleasant Hill,
Potecasi,
Rich Square,
Seaboard,
Wheelersville,
Woodland.

ONSLOW COUNTY.

Catharine Lake,
Gum Branch,
Haw Branch,
Onslow C. H.,
Richlands,
Snead's Ferry,
Stone's Bay,
Swansborough.

ORANGE COUNTY.

Caldwell,
Cedar Grove,
Chapel Hill,*
Durham's,
Flat River,
Hillsborough,* (*c. h.*,)
Oaks,
Orange Factory,
Red Mountain,
Rock Spring,
Round Hill,
South Lowell,
Stagville.

PASQUOTANK COUNTY.

Elizabeth City,* (*c. h.*,)
Rosedale.

PERQUIMONS COUNTY.

Belvidere,
Durant's Neck,
Hertford, (*c. h.*,)
Woodville.

PERSON COUNTY.

Allensville,
Bushy Fork,
Centre Grove,
Cunningham's Store,
Hester's Store.
Hurdles Mills,
Lea's Chapel,
Mount Tirzah,
Roxborough, (*c. h.*,)
Van Hook's Store,
Woodsdale.

PITT COUNTY.

Falkland,
Farmville,
Greenville, (*c. h.*,)
Johnson's Mills,
Marlborough,
Pactolus,
Ridge Spring,
Winona.

POLK COUNTY.

Columbus, (*c. h.*,)
Tryon.

RANDOLPH COUNTY.

Ashborough, (*c. h.*,)
Brower's Mills,
Buffalo Ford,
Burney's Mills,
Bush Hill,
Eden,
Foust's Mills,
Franklinville,
Gladesborough,
Hill's Store,
Hoover Hill,
Jackson's Creek,
Lassiter's Mills,
Long's Mills,
Moffit's Mills,
New Hope Academy
New Market,
New Salem,
Reed Creek,
Salem Church,
Sandy Creek,
Sawyersville,
Science Hill,
Trinity College,*
Troy's Store.
White House.

RICHMOND COUNTY.

Bear Branch,
Bostick's Mills,
Capell's Mills,
Covington,
Laurel Hill,
Laurinburgh,
Little's Mills,
Mangum,
Powelton,
Powhatan,
Rockingham, (*c. h.*)

ROBESON COUNTY.

Antioch,
Dundarrach,
Leesville,
Lumberton, (*c. h.*,)
Melrose,
Plummerville,
Red Banks,
Saint Paul's,
Shoe Heel.

ROCKINGHAM COUNTY.

Aspin Grove,
Benaja,
Berry Hill,
Douglas,
Lawsonville,
Leaksville,
Lenox Castle,
Madison,
Monroeton,
Price's Store,
Reidsville,
Ruffin,
Stoneville,
Thompsonville,
Troublesome,
Wentworth, (*c. h.*)

ROWAN COUNTY.

China Grove,
Gold Hill,
Miranda,
Mount Ulla,
Rowan Mills,
Salisbury, (*c. h.*,)
Spring Grove.

RUTHERFORD COUNTY.

Brittain,
Burnt Chimney,
Chimney Rock,
Cooper's Gap,
Cuba,
Duncan's Creek,
First Broad,
Golden Valley,
Green Hill,
Logan's Store,
Oak Spring,
Otter Creek,
Patton's Home,
Rutherfordton, (*c. h.*,)
Webb's Ford.

SAMPSON COUNTY.

Blackman's Mills,
Clinton, (*c. h.*,)
Dismal,
Hawley's Store,
Monk's Store,
Newton Grove,
Owenville.

* Money-order office.

STANLY COUNTY.

Albemarle, (c. h.,)
Big Lick,
Efird's Mills,
Leo,
Locust Level,
Norwood.

STOKES COUNTY.

Ayersville,
Blakely,
Colesville,
Crooked Creek,
Danbury, (c. h.,)
Francisco,
Germanton,
Little Yadkin,
Martin's Lime Kilns,
Peter's Creek,
Pilot Mountain,
Red Shoals,
Walnut Cove,
Westfield,
Wilson's Store.

SURREY COUNTY.

Dobson, (c. h.,)
Elkin,
Flat Shoal,
Haystack,
Judesville,
Mount Airy,
Rockford,
Rusk,
State Road,
Tom's Creek.

TRANSYLVANIA COUNTY.

Brevard, (c. h.,)
Calhoun,
Cathey's Creek,
Cedar Mountain,
Cherryfield,
Claytonville,
Davidson's River,
Dunn's Rock.

TYRREL COUNTY.

Columbia, (c. h.)

UNION COUNTY.

Beaver Dam,
Coburn's Store,
Monroe, (c. h.,)
Morgan's Mills,
Oak Grove,
Olive Branch,
Walkersville,
Winchester,
Wolfsville.

WAKE COUNTY.

Auburn,
Brassfield,
Cary,
Dayton,
Eagle Rock,
Fish Dam,
Forestville,
Green Level,
Hays' Store,
Morrisville,
New Hill,
New Light,
RALEIGH,* (c. h.,)
Rolesville,
Wakefield.

WARREN COUNTY.

Macon Depot,
Manson,
Ridgeway,
Warren Plains,
Warrenton,* (c. h.)

WASHINGTON COUNTY.

Long Ridge,
Plymouth,* (c. h.,)
Scuppernong.

WATAUGA COUNTY.

Blowing Rock,
Boone, (c. h.,)
McBride's Mill,
Stony Fork,
Sugar Grove,
Valley Crucis,
Watauga Falls.

WAYNE COUNTY.

Dudley,
Goldsborough,* (c. h.,)
Mount Olive,
Nahunta,
Pikeville.

WILKES COUNTY.

Elkville,
Hay Meadow,
Maple Springs,
Mulberry,
Purlear's Creek,
Roaring Gap,
Trap Hill,
Warrior Creek,
Wilbar,
Wilkesborough, (c. h.)

WILSON COUNTY.

Black Creek,
Joyner's Depot,
Stantonsburgh,
Wilson, (c. h.)

YADKIN COUNTY.

Booneville,
Chesnut Ridge,
East Bend,
Footville,
Hamptonville,
Huntsville,
Jonesville,
Mount Nebo,
Panther Creek,
Red Plains,
Republic,
Richmond Hill,
Yadkinville, (c. h.,)
Zion.

YANCEY COUNTY.

Bald Creek,
Burnsville, (c. h.,)
Day Book,
Flinty Branch,
Grassy Creek,
Ramsaytown.

OHIO.

ADAMS COUNTY.

Beasley's Fork,
Bentonville,
Blue Creek,
Bradyville,
Cedar Mills,
Cherry Fork,
Dunbarton,
Dunkinsville,
Eckmansville,
Emerald,
Harshasville,
Hill's Fork,

ADAMS COUNTY—Continued.

Locust Grove,
Lovett's,
Manchester,
May Hill,
Mineral Springs,
Osman's,
Scott,
South Liberty,
Stouts,
Tranquility,
Vineyard Hill,
Waggoner's Ripple,

* Money-order office.

ADAMS COUNTY—Continued.

Wamsley's,
West Union, (c. h.,)
Wheat Ridge,
Wilson,
Youngsville.

ALLEN COUNTY.

Beaver Dam,
Blue Lick,
Bluffton,*
Cranberry,
Elida,
Gomer,
Herring,
Hog Creek,
Lima,* (c. h.,)
South Warsaw,
Spencerville,
West Cairo,
Westminster,
West Newton.

ASHLAND COUNTY.

Albion,
Ashland,* (c. h.,)
Hayesville,*
Jeromesville,
Lake Fork,
Loudonville,*
McKay,
McZena,
Mifflin,
Mohican,
Nankin,
Nova,
Perryville,
Polk,
Red Haw,
Rows,
Ruggles,
Savannah,*
Sullivan.

ASHTABULA COUNTY.

Amboy,
Andover,
Ashtabula,*
Austinburgh,
Cherry Valley,
Clark's Corner,
Colebrook,
Conneaut,*
Cork,
Denmark,
Dorset,
Eagleville,
East Plymouth,
East Trumbull,
Geneva,
Grigg's Corners,
Harpersfield,
Hart's Grove,
Jefferson,* (c. h.,)
Kelloggsville,
Kingsville,
Lenox,
Leon,
Lindenville,
Mechanicsville,
Monroe Centre,
Morgan,*
New Lyme,
North Kingsville,
North Richmond,
North Sheffield,
Orwell,*
Phœnix,
Pierpont,
Richmond Centre,
Rome,
Saybrook,
South Ridge,
Steamburgh,
Trumbull,
West Andover,
West Williamsfield,
Williamsfield,
Windsor.

ATHENS COUNTY.

Amesville,
Athens,* (c. h.,)
Big Run,
Canaanville,
Chauncey,
Coolville,
Federalton,
Garden,
Guysville,
Hartleyville,
Hebbardsville,
Hocking,
Hockingport,
Hull's,
Kings,
Lee,*
Lottridge,
Marshfield,
Millfield,
Nelsonville,*
New England,
Pleasanton,
Pratt's Fork,
Rock Oak,
Salina,
Shade,
Torch,
Trimble,
Woodyards.

AUGLAIZE COUNTY.

Cridersville,
Deep Cut,
Fryburgh,
Kossuth,
Minster,
Moulton,
New Bremen,*
New Hampshire,
New Knoxville,
Rinehart,
Saint John's,
Saint Mary's,*
Uniopolis,
Wapakonetta,* (c. h.,)
Waynesfield.

BELMONT COUNTY.

Armstrong's Mills,
Atlas,
Bailey's Mills,
Barnesville,*
Bellaire,*
Belmont,
Bethesda,
Bridgeport,
Businessburgh,
Captina,
Colerain,
Demos,
Dille's Bottom,
East Richland,
Flushing,
Glencoe,
Hendrysburgh,
Hunter,
Jacobsburgh,
Kennon,
Lamira,
Loydsville,
Martin's Ferry,
Morning View,
Morristown,*
Pilcher,
Plank Road,
Powhatan Point,
Pugh,
St. Clairsville,* (c. h.,)
Sewellsville,
Shepherdstown,
Shields,
Somerton,
Temperanceville,
Uniontown,
Warnock,
Wegee.

BROWN COUNTY.

Aberdeen,
Arnheim,
Ash Ridge,
Decatur,
De La Palma,
Fayetteville,
Feesburgh,
Fincastle,
Five Mile,
Georgetown, (c. h.,)
Hamersville,
Higginsport,
Levanna,
Locust Ridge,
Maple,
Mount Orab,
New Harmony,
New Hope,
Red Oak,
Ripley,*
Russellville,
Saint Martin's,
Sardinia,
Union Plains.

BUTLER COUNTY.

Alert,
Bethany,
Blue Ball,
College Corner,
Collinsville,
Contreras,
Darrtown,
Hamilton,* (c. h.,)
Jacksonborough,
Jones' Station,
McGonigle's Station,
Middletown,*
Millville,
Monroe,
Okeana,
Overpeck's Station,
Oxford,*
Paddy's Run,
Philanthropy,
Pisgah,
Poast Town,
Port Union,
Princeton,
Reiley,
Ross,
Saint Charles,
Seven Mile,
Somerville.
Symmes' Corners.
Trenton,
West Chester,
Wood's Station.

* Money-order office.

CARROLL COUNTY.

Algonquin,
Augusta,
*Carrollton,** (*c. h.,*)
Eckley,
Harlem Springs,
Hibbett's,
Kilgore,
Lamartine,
Leavitt,
Leesville,
Malvern,
Mechanicstown,
New Hagerstown,
New Harrisburgh,
Norristown,
Oneida Mills,
Palermo,
Scroggsfield,
Sherodsville,
Wattsville.

CHAMPAIGN COUNTY.

Brinton,
Cable,
Carysville,
Christiansburgh,
Horr's,
Kennard,
Mechanicsburgh,
Millerstown,
Mingo,
Mutual,
North Lewisburgh,
Saint Paris,
Spring Hills,
Terre Haute,
*Urbana,** (*c. h.,*)
Westville,
Woodstock.

CLARK COUNTY.

Bowlusville,
Catawba,
Dialton,
Donnelsville,
Enon,
Harmony,
Medway,
New Carlisle,
New Moorefield,
North Hampton,
Plattsburgh,
Selma,
South Charleston,
*Springfield,** (*c. h.,*)
Tremont,
Vienna Cross Roads.

CLERMONT COUNTY.

Afton,
Amelia,
Angola,
Bantam,
Batavia, (*c. h.,*)
Belfast,
Bethel,
Cedron,
Chilo,
Edenton,
Felicity,*
Goshen,
Henning's Mills,
Laurel,
Lindale,
Locust Corner,
Loveland,*
Marathon,
Miamiville,
Milford*,
Monterey,
Moscow,
Mount Carmel,
Mount Holly,
Mount Olive,
Mount Pisgah,
Mount Repose,
Mulberry,
Neville,
New Palestine,
New Richmond,*
Newtonsville,
Nicholsville,
Olive Branch,
Owensville,
Perins' Mills,
Point Isabel,
Point Pleasant,
Smith's Landing,
Stone Lick,
West Woodville,
Williamsburgh,
Withamsville.

CLINTON COUNTY.

Blanchester,
Bloomington,
Clarksville,
Clinton Station
Clinton Valley,
Cuba,

CLINTON COUNTY—Continued.

Farmer's Station,
Lee's Creek,
Lumberton,
Martinsville,
Memphis,
Morrisville,
New Antioch,
New Burlington,
New Vienna,
Oakland,
Ogden,
Port William,
Reesville,
Sabina,
Westborough,
*Wilmington,** (*c. h.*)

COLUMBIANA COUNTY.

Bayard,
Bucks,
Calcutta,
Cannon's Mill,
Clarkson,
Columbiana,
Damascoville,
Dungannon,
East Carmel,
East Fairfield,
East Liverpool,*
East Palestine,
East Rochester,
Elkton,
Franklin Square,
Gavers,
Glasgow,
Green Hill,
Hanoverton,
Homeworth,
Inverness,
Leetonia,
Maysville,
Millport,
Moultrie,
New Alexander,
New Chambersb'rgh,
New Garden,
*New Lisbon,** (*c. h.,*)
New Waterford,
North Georgetown,
Saint Clair,
Salem,*
Salineville,*
Sandy,
Summitville,
Unity,
Valley,
Wellsville,*
West Beaver,
West Point,
Winona.

COSHOCTON COUNTY.

Bacon,
Bakersville,
Boyd's Mills,
Canal Lewisville,
Chili,
Clark's,
*Coshocton,** (*c. h.,*)
Evansburgh,
Franklin Station,
Helmick,
Keene,
Linton Mills,
Mohawk Village,
Munnsville,
New Bedford,
New Castle,
New Guilford,
New Moscow,
Plainfield,
Roscoe,
Spring Mountain,
Tyrone,
Wakatomika,
Walhonding,
Warsaw,
West Bedford,
West Carlisle,
West La Fayette,
White Eyes Plains
Will's Creek,
Yankee Ridge.

CRAWFORD COUNTY.

Broken Sword,
*Bucyrus,** (*c. h.,*)
Camp Run,
Chatfield,
Crestline,*
De Kalb,
Galion,
Grove Hill,
Leesville × Roads,
Liberty Corners,
Likens,
New Washington,
North Robinson,
Oceola,
Poplar,
Sulphur Spring,
Tiro,
Wellerville.

* Money-order office.

CUYAHOGA COUNTY.

Barry,
Bedford,
Berea,*
Bricksville,
Brooklyn,
Brooklyn Village,
Chagrin Falls,*
Cleveland,* (*c. h.*,)
Coe Ridge,
Collamer,
Dover,
East Cleveland,
East Rockport,
Euclid,
Gates' Mills,
Glenville,
Independence,
Mayfield,
Middleburgh,
Newburgh,
North Dover,
North Royalton,
North Solon,
Nottingham,
Olmsted,
Parma,
Randall,
Rockport,
Solon,
Strongsville,
Warrensville,
West View,
Wilson's Mills.

DARKE COUNTY.

Ansonia,
Arcanum,
Beamsville,
Brock,
Castine,
Darke,
Dawn,
De Lisle,
German,
Gettysburgh,
Gordon,
Greenville,* (*c. h.*,)
Hetslerville,
Hill Grove,
Ithaca,
Jaysville,
Mount Heron,
New Madison,
North Star,
Painter Creek,
Pikeville,
Poplar Ridge,
Republican,
Rose Hill,
Rossville,
Stelvideo,
Tampico,
Versailles,
Weaver's Station,
Webster,
Wiley Station,
Woodington.

DEFIANCE COUNTY.

Adams Ridge,
Ayersville,
Brunersburgh,
Cicero,
Defiance,* (*c. h.*,)
Evansport,
Farmer,
Hicksville,
Mark,
Milo,
Ney,
Wilseyville.

DELAWARE COUNTY.

Alum Creek,
Ashley,
Belle Point,
Berkshire,
Centre Village,
Condit,
Constantia,
Delaware,* (*c. h.*,)
East Orange,
Galena,
Harlem,
Kilbourne,
Kingston Centre,
Leonardsburgh,
Lewis Centre,
Maxwell,
Norton,
Orange Station,
Ostrander,
Powell,
Radnor,
Sunbury,
Tanktown,
Van's Valley,
White Sulphur.

ERIE COUNTY.

Berlin Heights,
Berlin Station,
Berlinville,
Birmingham,
Bloomingville,
Castalia,

ERIE COUNTY—Continued.

Florence,
Huron,
Kelley's Island,
Milan,
Sandusky,* (*c. h.*,)
Seven Mile House,
Venice,
Vermillion.

FAIRFIELD COUNTY.

Amanda,
Baltimore,
Basil,
Bremen,
Carroll,
Cedar Hill,
Clear Creek,
Clear Port,
Colfax,
Dumontville,
Green Castle,
Hamburgh,
Hooker's Station,
Lancaster,* (*c. h.*,)
Lithopolis,
Lockville,
Marcy,
Millersport,
New Salem,
North Berne,
Pickerington,
Pleasantville,
Royalton,
Rushville,
Stoutsville,
Sugar Grove,
West Rushville.

FAYETTE COUNTY.

Bloomingburgh,
Good Hope,
Jasper Mills,
Jeffersonville,
Madison Mills,
Moons,
New Martinsburgh,
Pancoastburgh,
South Plymouth,
Staunton,
Washington C. H.,*
West Lancaster.

FRANKLIN COUNTY.

Alton,
Black Lick,
Canal Winchester,*
Central College,
Clintonville,
COLUMBUS,* (*c. h.*,)
Dublin,
Flint,
Gahanna,
Georgesville,
Grove City,
Groveport,
Harrisburgh,
Hilliards,
Hope,
Lockbourne,
Mifflinville,
North Columbus,
Ovid,
Park's Mills,
Pleasant Corners,
Reynoldsburgh,
Shadeville,
Taylor's Station,
Westerville,
Worthington.

FULTON COUNTY.

Ai,
Archbold,
Beta,
Delta,*
Elmira,
Emery,
Gorham,
Handy,
Lyons,
Metamora,
Ottokee, (*c. h.*,)
Pettisville,
Swanton,
Tedrow,
Wauseon,*
West Barre,
Winameg.

GALLIA COUNTY.

Addison,
Cheshire,
Clipper Mills,
Crown City,
Eureka,
Ewington,
Gallia Furnace,
Gallipolis,* (*c. h.*,)

* Money-order office.

GALLIA COUNTY—Continued.

Kyger,
Lincoln,
McDaniel's,
Mercerville,
Northup,
Patriot,
Pine Grove,
Rio Grande,
Rodney,
Sand Fork,
South Newcastle,
Swan Creek,
Thivener,
Thurman,
Vinton,
Wales.

GEAUGA COUNTY.

Auburn,
Bissell's,
Bridge Creek,
Burton,
Chardon,* (*c. h.*,)
Chester Cross Roads,
Claridon,
East Claridon,
Ford,
Fowler's Mills,
Grove,
Hampden,
Huntsburgh,
Middlefield,
Montville,
Mulberry Corners,
North Newbury,
Parkman,
Russell,
South Newbury,
South Thompson,
Thompson,
Welshfield.

GREENE COUNTY.

Alpha,
Bellbrook,
Bowersville,
Byron,
Cedarville,
Clifton,
Fairfield,
Jamestown,
New Jasper,
Osborn,*
Paintersville,
Spring Valley,
Xenia,* (*c. h.*,)
Yellow Springs,*
Zimmerman.

GUERNSEY COUNTY.

Antrim,
Bird's Run,
Buffalo,
Cambridge,* (*c. h.*,)
Claysville,
Creighton,
Cumberland,
Dyson's,
Fairview,
Galigher,
Gibson's Station,
Gomber,
Indian Camp,
Kimbolton,
Leatherwood,
Londonderry,
Middlebourne,
Midway,
Milnersville,
North Salem,
Oakland Mills,
Salesville,
Senecaville,
Spencer's Station,
Sugartree,
Washington,
Winchester.

HAMILTON COUNTY.

Bevis' Tavern,
California,
Carthage,
Cherry Grove,
Cheviot,
Cincinnati,* (*c. h.*,)
Cleves,
College Hill,
Columbia,
Covedale,
Cumminsville,
Delhi,
Dent,
Dry Ridge,
Dunlap,
East Sycamore,
Glendale,
Groesbeck,
Grand Valley,
Harrison,*
Hartwell,
Lick Run,

HAMILTON COUNTY—Continued.

Linwood,
Lockland Station,
Ludlow Grove,
Madeira,
Madisonville,
Miami,
Montgomery,
Mount Airy,
Mount Healthy,
Mount Washington,
Newtown,
Norwood,
Oakley,
Plainville,
Pleasant Ridge,
Pleasant Run,
Preston,
Reading,
Riverdale,
Sharonville,
Sixteen Mile Stand,
South Pendleton,
Spring Dale.
Storrs,
Sweet Wine,
Symmes,
Taylor's Creek,
Transit,
Valley Junction,
Walnut Hills,
Winton Place.

HANCOCK COUNTY.

Arcadia,
Arlington,
Benton Ridge,
Cannonsburgh,
Ewing's Corner,
Findley,* (*c. h.*,)
Hassan,
Houcktown,
McComb,
Mount Blanchard,
Oak Ridge,
Portage Centre,
Rawson,
Van Buren,
Vanlue,
West Independence,
Williamstown.

HARDIN COUNTY.

Ada,*
Dunkirk,
Forest,*
Grant,
Huntersville,
Kenton,* (*c. h.*,)
McDonald,
Mount Victory,
North Washington,
Patterson,
Ridgeway,
Round Head,
Silver Creek,
Yelverton.

HARRISON COUNTY.

Archer,
Bowerston,
Cadiz,* (*c. h.*,)
Cassville,
Connotton,
Deersville,
Feed Spring,
Folk's Station,
Freeport,
Germano,
Harrisville,
Hopedale,
Jewett,
Laceyville,
Means,
Miller's Station,
Moorefield,
New Athens,
New Rumley,
Scio,
Short Creek,
Smyrna,
Station 15,
Tappan,
Tippecanoe.

HENRY COUNTY.

Colton,
Florida,
Freedom Mills,
Liberty Centre,
Napoleon,* (*c. h.*,)
New Bavaria,
Okolona,
Ridgeland,
Ridgeville Corners,
Texas,
West Hope.

* Money-order office.

Highland County.

Bell,
Berrysville,
Buckley,
Buford,
Carmel,
Centrefield,
Dallas,
Dodsonville,
East Monroe,
Fairfax,
Greenfield,*
Highland,
Hillsborough,* (*c. h.*,)
Hollowtown,
Leesburgh,
Lynchburgh,
Marshall,
Mowrystown,
Nevin,
New Corwin,
New Market,
New Petersburgh,
North Uniontown,
Paint,
Pricetown,
Rainsborough,
Russell's Station,
Samantha,
Sicily,
Sinking Spring,
Sugar Tree Ridge,
Webertown.

Hocking County.

Black Jack,
Enterprise,
Ewing,
Gibesonville,
Gore,
Haydenville,
Islesborough,
Logan,* (*c. h.*,)
Middle Fork,
Rockbridge,
Rock House,
South Bloomingville,
South Perry.

Holmes County.

Beck's Mills,
Benton,
Berlin,
Black Creek,
Holmesville,
Humphreyville,
Jones' Corners,
Killbuck,
Millersburgh,* (*c. h.*,)
Mount Hope,
Nashville,
Paint Valley,
Plimpton,
Salt Creek,
Saltillo,
Walnut Creek,
Winesburgh.

Huron County.

Bellevue,*
Carson,
Centreton,
Clarksfield,
East Clarksfield,
East Norwalk,
East Townsend,
Fitchville,
Four Corners,
Greenwich Station,
Hartland,
Havana,
Monroeville,*
New Haven,
New London,*
North Fairfield,
Norwalk,* (*c. h.*,)
Olena,
Peru,
Pontiac,
Ripleyville,
Steuben,
Townsend Station,
Wakeman.

Jackson County.

Berlin Cross Roads,
Camba,
Clay,
Dawkin's Mills,
Grahamsville,
Jackson,* (*c. h.*,)
Jimes,
Keystone,
Mabee's,
Monroe Furnace,
Oak Hill,
Ray's,
Rocky Hill,
Samsonville.

Jefferson County.

Adena,
Amsterdam,
Annapolis,
Bloomingdale,
Creswell,
Croxton,
East Springfield,
Fair Play,
Hammondsville,
Holmes' Mill,
Irondale,
Island Creek,
Jeddo,
Knoxville,
Linton,
McCoy's Station,
Mitchell's Salt Works,
Moore's Salt Works,
Mount Pleasant,
New Alexandria,
New Somerset,
Philipsburgh,
Port Homer,
Richmond,
Rush Run,
Sloan's Station,
Smithfield,
Steubenville,* (*c. h.*,)
Unionport,
Updegraffs,
Warrenton,
Wintersville,
Yorkville.

Knox County.

Bladensburgh,
Brandon,
Centreburgh,
Danville,
Democracy,
Fredericktown,*
Gambier,*
Greersville,
Hunt's Station,
Indian Field,
Jelloway,
Knox,
Levering,
Lock,
Lucerne,
Martinsburgh,
Milfordton,
Millwood,
Monroe Mills,
Mount Liberty,
*Mount Vernon** (*c. h.*,)
Nonpareil,
North Liberty,
Rich Hill,
Shaler's Mills.

Lake County.

Concord,
Hillhouse,
Kirtland,
Madison,*
Mentor,
North Madison,
Painesville,* (*c. h.*,)
Perry,
South Kirtland,
Unionville,
Wickliffe,
Willoughby.

Lawrence County.

Aid,
Arabia,
Athalia,
Bartramville,
Bradrickville,
Burlington,
Coal Grove,
Forest Dale,
Frampton,
Greasy Ridge,
Hanging Rock,
Ironton,* (*c. h.*,)
Kelley's Mills,
Miller's,
Quaker Bottom,
Rock Camp,
Russell's Place,
Scott Town,
Sheridan Coal W'ks,
South Point,
Waterloo,
Willow Wood.

Licking County.

Alexandria,
Appleton,
Beech,
Brownsville,
Chatham,
Clay Lick,
Columbia Centre,
Croton,
Etna,
Fallsburgh,
Fredonia,
Freeman,

* Money-order office.

Licking County—Continued.

Granville,*
Gratiot,
Green,
Hanover,
Hebron,
Homer,
Jacksontown,
Jersey,
Johnstown,
Kirkersville,
Linnville,
Long Run,
Newark,* (c. h.,)
New-way,
Outville,
Pataskala,
Perryton,
Rocky Fork,
Saint Louisville,
Summit Station,
Toboso,
Union Station,
Utica,
Vanatta,
Wagram,
Wilkins' Run.

Logan County.

Belle Centre,
Bellefontaine,* (c. h.,)
Big Springs,
Bloom Centre,
De Graff,
East Liberty,
Harper,
Huntsville,
Lewistown,
Loganville,
Muchinippe,
New Richland,
North Greenfield,
Northwood,
Pickereltown,
Quincy,
Rushsylvania,
West Liberty,*
West Mansfield,
West Middleburgh,
Zanesfield.

Lorain County.

Amherst,
Avon,
Avon Lake,
Black River,
Brighton,
Brownhelm,
Columbia Station,
Copopa,
Crandall,
Elyria,* (c. h.,)
Grafton,
Henrietta,
Huntington,
Kipton,
La Grange,
La Porte,
North Camden,
North Eaton,
North Ridgeville,
Oberlin,*
Penfield,
Pittsfield,
Plato,
Rawsonville,
Rochester Depot,
Sheffield,
Sheffield Lake,
Wellington.*

Lucas County.

Berkey,
East Toledo,
Hickory,
Holland,
Java,
Maumee City,*
Monclova,
Sylvania,
Toledo,* (c. h.,)
Waterville,
White House.

Madison County.

Big Plain,
Cross Roads,
Darby Creek,
La Fayette,
London,* (c. h.,)
Mount Sterling,
Rosedale,
South Solon,
Summerford,
Tradersville,
Walnut Run,
West Canaan,
West Jefferson.

Mahoning County.

Beloit,
Berlin Centre,
Boardman,
Boswell,
Canfield,* (c. h.,)
Coitsville,
East Lewistown,
Ellsworth,
Frederick,
Garfield,
Greenford,
Lowellville,
Milton,
Mineral Ridge,*
New Albany,
New Middletown,
New Springfield,
North Benton,
North Jackson,
North Lima,
Orange,
Patmos,
Petersburgh,
Poland,
Struther's Station,
Washingtonville,
Youngstown.*

Marion County.

Caledonia,
Cochranton,
Green Camp,
Larue,*
Marion,* (c. h.,)
New Bloomington,
Prospect,
Three Locusts,
Waldo.

Medina County.

Abbeyville,
Bennett's Corners,
Brunswick,
Chatham Centre,
Friendsville,
Granger,
Guilford,
Hinckley,
Homerville,
Le Roy,
Litchfield,
Liverpool,
Lodi,
Mallet Creek,
Medina,* (c. h.,)
Poe,
Remson's Corners,
River Styx,
Sharon Centre,
Smith Road,
Spencer,
Wadsworth,*
Weymouth,
Whittlesey.

Meigs County.

Alfred,
Apple Grove,
Bashan,
Burlingham,
Chester,
Dexter,
Downington,
Great Bend,
Harrisonville,
Hemlock Grove,
Langsville,
Letart Falls,
Long Bottom,
Middleport,
Minersville,
Mount Blanco,
Plants,
Pomeroy,* (c. h.,)
Portland,
Racine,
Reedsville,
Rutland,
Salem Centre,
Saxon,
Silver Run,
Syracuse,
Tupper's Plains,
Valley Ford.

Mercer County.

Carthagena,
Celina,* (c. h.,)
Cold Water,
Cranberry Prairie,
Fort Recovery,
Macedon,
Maria Stein,
Mendon,
Mercer,
Montezuma,
Neptune,
Price,
Saint Henry's,
Shane's Crossing,
Skeels × Roads.

* Money-order office.

Miami County.

Alcony,
Allen's,
Bradford,
Brandt,
Casstown,
Conover,
Covington,
Fidelity,
Fletcher,
Ginghamsburgh,
Laura,
North Clayton,
Piqua,
Pleasant Hill,
Potsdam,
Tippecanoe City,*
*Troy,** (*c. h.,*)
West Charleston,
West Milton.

Monroe County.

Antioch,
Beallsville,
Bingham,
Calais,
Cameron,
Centre View,
Clarington,
Edwina,
Graysville,
Green Brier,
Hannibal,
Hope Ridge,
Jerusalem,
Jolly,
Laing's,
Lecompton,
Lewisville,
Malaga,
Masterton,
Miltonsburgh,
Mount Carrick,
Ozark,
Rinard's Mills,
Round Bottom,
Sardis,
Stafford,
Trail Run,
Wittens,
*Woodsfield,** (*c. h.,*)
Young's Mills.

Montgomery County.

Air Hill,
Bachman,
Brookville,
Carrollton Station,
Centre,
Centreville,
Chambersburgh,
Clayton,
Davidson,
*Dayton,** (*c. h.,*)
Farmersville,
Germantown,
Harshmansville,
Iamton,
Johnsville,
Liberty,
Little York,
Miamisburgh,*
Nat'l Mil. Asylum,*
New Lebanon,
Pyrmont,
South Arlington,
Tadmer,
Taylorsville,
Trotwood,
Union,
Vandalia,
West Baltimore,
West Carrollton.

Morgan County.

Bishopville,
Bristol,
Calvary,
Centre Bend,
Chester Hill,*
Deavertown,
Elliott's × Roads,
Hall's Valley,
Log Cabin,
*McConnellsville,**
(*c. h.,*)
Malta,
Meigs' Creek,
Meigsville,
Mill Grove,
Morgansville,
Moscow Mills,
Neeleysville,
Pennsville,
Plantsville,
Pleasant Valley,
Reinersville,
Ringgold,
Rokeby,
Rosseau,
Roxbury,
Sand Hollow,
Stockport,
Todd's,
Triadelphia,
Wood Grove.

Morrow County.

Andrews,
Bennington,
Bloomfield,
Cardington,*
Chesterville,
Corsica,
Iberia,
Marengo,
Marit's,
*Mount Gilead,** (*c. h.,*)
Pagetown,
Pulaskiville,
Shauck's,
Sparta,
Steam Corners,
Vail's × Roads,
Westfield,
Whetstone,
Woodview.

Muskingum County.

Adams' Mills,
Adamsville,
Blue Rock,
Bridgeville,
Brush Creek,
Chandlersville,
Confederate × Roads
Cottage Hill,
Dresden,*
Duncan's Falls,
East Greenwood,
Frazeysburgh,
Fultonham,
High Hill,
Hopewell,
Licking Valley,
Nashport,
New Concord,
Norwich,
Otsego,
Philo,
Putnam,
Rix's Mills,
Roseville,
Rural Dale,
Sago,
Sonora,
West Zanesville,
White Cottage,
Young Hickory,
*Zanesville,** (*c. h.,*)
Zeno.

Noble County.

Ava,
Batesville,
Berne,
*Caldwell,** (*c. h.,*)
Claytona,
Crooked Tree,
Enoch,
Gardner,
Harriettsville,
Hiramsburgh,
Hoskinsville,
Keith's,
Kennonsburgh,
McCleary,
Middle Creek,
Mount Ephraim,
Nobleville,
Olive Green,
Renrock,
Ridge,
Sarahsville,
Sharon,
South Olive,
Summerfield,
Whigville.

Ottawa County.

Catawba Island,
Elmore,
Genoa,
Locust Point,
Marblehead,
Middle Bass,
North Bass Island,
Oak Harbor,
*Port Clinton,** (*c. h.,*)
Put-in Bay.

Paulding County.

Antwerp,*
Carryall,
Cecil,
Charloe,
Emmett,
Hamer,
Junction,
McGill,
Oakwood,
*Paulding,** (*c. h.,*)
Payne,
Reid's,
Royal Oak,
Timberville.

* Money-order office.

Perry County.

Buchanan,
Buckeye Cottage,
Chapel Hill,
Coal Dale,
Crooksville,
East Rush Creek,
McCluney,
Maxville,
Mount Perry,
*New Lexington,** (*c. h.,*)
Oakfield,
Portersville,
Rehoboth,
St. Joseph's College,
Sego,
Somerset,
Straitsville,
Thornville.

Pickaway County.

Atlanta,
Beckett's Store,
*Circleville,** (*c. h.,*)
Darbyville,
Deer Creek,
East Ringgold,
Five Points,
Kinderhook,
Leistville,
Nebraska,
New Holland,
Palestine,
Robtown,
Saint Paul's,
South Bloomfield,
String Town,
Tarlton,
Williamsport.

Pike County.

Beaver,
Byington,
Cynthiana,
Flat,
Gibson,
Idaho,
Jasper,
Latham,
Omega,
Pee Pee,
Piketon, (*c. h.,*)
Waverly,
Wetmore.

Portage County.

Atwater,
Atwater Centre,
Aurora,
Brimfield,
Charlestown,
Deerfield,
Earlville,
Edinburgh,
Freedom,
Freedom Station,
Garrettsville,*
Hiram,
Kent,*
Mantua,
Mantua Station,
Nelson,
New Milford,
Palmyra,
Parisville,
Randolph,
Rapids,
*Ravenna,** (*c. h.,*)
Rootstown,
Shalersville,
Streetsborough,
Suffield,
Windham,
Windham Station.

Preble County.

Brinley's Station,
Brown's Station,
Camden,
Campbellstown,
*Eaton,** (*c. h.,*)
Ebenezer,
El Dorado,
Euphemia,
Fair Haven,
Gratis,
Lewisburgh,
Morning Sun,
New Paris,*
New Westville,
Upshur,
West Alexandria,
West Elkton,
West Florence,
West Manchester,
West Sonora.

Putnam County.

Belmore,
Caskaid,
Columbus Grove,*
Dog Creek,
Dupont,
Fort Jennings,

Putnam County—Continued.

Gilboa,
Kalida, (*c. h.,*)
Leipsic,
Ottawa,*
Pendleton,
Roanoke,
Sheridan,
Stanley,
Vaughnsville.

Richland County.

Adario,
Barnes,
Belleville,*
Butler,
Darlington,
Ganges,
Hastings,
Lexington,
Lucas,
*Mansfield,** (*c. h.,*)
Newville,
Olivesburgh,
Ontario,
Plymouth,*
Rives,
Shanandoah,
Shelby,*
Shiloh,
Spring Mills,
West Windsor.

Ross County.

Adelphi,
Alma,
Anderson,
Bainbridge,*
Bourneville,
*Chillicothe,** (*c. h.,*)
Clarksburgh,
Frankfort,
Gillespieville,
Greenland,
Hallsville,
Hooppole,
Kingston,
Lattas,
Lyndon Station,
Richmond Dale,
Roxabell,
Schooley's Station,
South Salem,
Vigo,
Waller,
Yellow Bud.

Sandusky County.

Black Swamp,
Clyde,*
*Fremont,** (*c. h.,*)
Greensburgh Cross Roads,
Lindsey,
Rollersville,
Townsend,
Winter's Station,
Woodville.

Scioto County.

Bloom Switch,
Franklin Furnace,
Freestone,
Friendship,
Hale's Creek,
Harrison Mills,
Haverhill,
Iron Furnace,
Lilly,
Lombardville,
Lucasville,
Lyra,
Nairn,
Otway,
Pond Run,
*Portsmouth,** (*c. h.,*)
Rarden,
Scioto,
Scioto Furnace,
Sciotoville,
Wheelersburgh.

Seneca County.

Adams,
Adrian,
Attica,*
Bascom,
Berwick,
Bettsville,
Bloomville,
Flat Rock,
Fort Seneca,
Fostoria,*
Frank,
Green Spring,
Jackson Station,
Kansas,
Melmore,
Palo Alto,
Reedtown,
Republic,
Saw Mill,
*Tiffin,** (*c. h.,*)
Watson Station,
West Lodi.

* Money-order office.

SHELBY COUNTY.

Anna,
Dinsmore,
Hardin,
Houston,
Jackson Centre,
Kirkwood,
Lockington,
Loramie's,
Montra,
Pemberton,
Plattsville,
Pratt,
Russia,
*Sidney,** (*c. h.,*)
Swander's Crossing,
Tawawa,
Wynant.

STARK COUNTY.

Alliance,*
Barryville,
Cairo,
Canal Fulton,
*Canton,** (*c. h.,*)
East Greenville,
Freeburgh,
Greentown,
Hartville,
Lake,
Limaville,
Louisville,
McDonaldsville,
Magnolia,
Mapleton,
Marlborough,
Massillon,*
Maximo,
Middle Branch,
Minerva,*
Mount Union,
Navarre,
New Baltimore,
New Berlin,
New Franklin,
North Industry,
North Lawrence,
Osnaburgh,
Paris,
Pierce,
Robertsville,
Waynesburgh,
West Brookfield,
Wilmot.

SUMMIT COUNTY.

*Akron,** (*c. h.,*)
Bath,
Clinton,
Copley,
Cuyahoga Falls,
Ghent,
Hudson,*
Inland,
Johnson's Corners,
Loyal Oak,
Macedonia Depot,
Middlebury,
Mogadore,
Montrose,
New Portage,
Nimisila,
Northfield,
Norton Centre,
Peninsula,
Richfield,
Sherman,
Summit,
Tallmadge,
Twinsburgh,
Western Star,
West Richfield.

TRUMBULL COUNTY.

Bazetta,
Braceville,
Bristolville,
Brookfield,
Burgh Hill,
Church Hill,
Coalburgh,
Farmington,
Fowler,
Girard,
Greensburgh,
Gustavus,
Hartford,
Howland,
Hubbard,*
Johnsonville,
Kinsman's,*
Leavittsburgh,
Lordstown,
Mecca,
Mesopotamia,
Newton Falls,
Niles,*
North Bloomfield,
North Bristol,
Ohl's Town,
Oil Diggins,
Orangeville,
Payne's Corners,
Southington,
Vernon,
Vienna,
*Warren,** (*c. h.,*)
West Farmington.*

TUSCARAWAS COUNTY.

Albany,
Bolivar,
Buena Vista,
Cadwallader,
Canal Dover,
Deardorff's Mills,
Dennison,
Dundee,
Gilmore,
Gnadenhutten,
Lock Seventeen,
Milligan,
Mineral Point,
New Comerstown,
New Cumberland,
*New Philadelphia,** (*c. h.,*)
Peoli,
Port Washington,
Rogersville,
Rush,
Sandyville,
Shanesville,
Stone Creek,
Strasburgh,
Tuscarawas,
Uhricksville,*
Winfield,
Zoar,
Zoar Station.

UNION COUNTY.

Boke's Creek,
Broadway,
Byhalia,
Irwin,
Jerome,
*Marysville,** (*c. h.,*)
Milford Centre,
New California,
New Dover,
Pharisburgh,
Pottersburgh,
Raymond's
Richwood,
Rush Creek,
Unionville Centre,
Watkins,
Woodland,
York.

VAN WERT COUNTY.

Auglaize,
Buena,
Delphos,*
Dixon,
Leslie,
Middle Point,
Tully,
*Van Wert,** (*c. h.,*)
Venedocia.
Willshire.

VINTON COUNTY.

Agatha,
Allensville,
Dundas,
Eagle Mills,
Hope Furnace,
*McArthur,** (*c. h.,*)
New Plymouth,*
Packard,
Reed's Mills,
Siverly,
Swan,
Vinton Station,
Wilkesville,
Zaleski.

WARREN COUNTY.

Butlerville,
Carlisle Station,
Dallasburgh,
Deerfield Village,
Dunlevy,
Edwardsville,
Fort Ancient,
Foster's Crossings,
Franklin,*
Harveysburgh,
Hopkinsville,
Lebanon, (*c. h.,*)
Level,
Mainville,
Mason,
Morrow,*
Murdock,
Oregon,
Pence's Mills,
Pleasant Plain,
Red Lion,
Ridgeville,
Springborough,
Twenty Mile Stand.
Waynesville.*

*** Money-order office.**

Washington County.

Barlow,
Bartlett,
Belpre,
Beverly,*
Bonn,
Brown's Mills,
Centre Belpre,
Coal Run,
Constitution,
Cow Run,
Cutler,
Decaturville,
Dunbar,
Dunham,
Fearing,
Fillmore,
Fleming,
Flint's Mills,
Grand View,
Harmar,
Hills,
Lawrence,
Layman,
Little Hockhocking,
Lowell,
Lower Newport,
Lower Salem,
*Marietta,** (c. h.,)
Moss Run,
Newell's Run,
New Metamora,
Newport,
Patten's Mill,
Regnier's Mills,
Tunnel,
Veto,
Vincent,
Wade,
Waterford,
Watertown,
Wesley.

Wayne County.

Apple Creek,
Baughman,
Big Prairie,
Blackleysville,
Burbank,
Canaan,
Cedar Valley,
Chippewa,
Congress,
Dalton,*
Easton,
East Union,
Fredericksburgh,
Golden Corners,
Koch's
Lattasburgh,
Madisonburgh,
Marshallville,
Mill Brook,
Milton Station,
Moorland,
Mount Eaton,
New Pittsburgh,
Old Hickory,
Orrville,*
Pike Station,
Plain,
Reedsburgh,
Shreve,
Smithville,
Springville,
Wayne,

Wayne County—Continued.

West Lebanon,
West Salem,*
*Wooster,** (c. h.,)
Wooster Summit.

Williams County.

Bridgewater,
*Bryan,** (c. h.,)
Deer Lick,
Durbin's Corners,
Edgerton,*
Edon,
Lockport,
Melburn,
Montpelier,
Nettle Lake,
North West,
Pioneer,
Primrose,
Pulaski,
Spring Lake,
Stryker,
West Buffalo,
West Unity,*
Williams Centre.

Wood County.

Bloom,
Bowling Green,*
Custar,
Fenton,
Grand Rapids,*
Haskins,
Holt,
Hull Prairie,
Millbury,
Milton Centre,
Mungen,
New Rochester,
Pemberville,
*Perrysburgh,** (c. h.,)
Portage,
Potter,
Prairie Depot.
Roachton,
Scotch Ridge,
Stony Ridge,
Tontogany,
West Mill Grove,
Weston,
Woodbury.

Wyandot County.

Belle Vernon,
Carey,*
Kirby,
Little Sandusky,
McCutchenville,
Marseilles,
Mexico,
Nevada,*
Seal,
Sycamore,
Tymochtee,
*Upper Sandusky,** (c. h.,)
Warpole,
Whartonsburgh,
Wyandot.

OREGON.

Baker County.

Auburn,
*Baker City,** (c. h.,)
El Dorado,
Express Ranch,
Humboldt Basin,
Jordan Valley,
Rye Valley.

Benton County.

*Corvallis,** (c. h.,)
Liberty,
Little Elk,
Newport,
Newton,
Philomath,
Starr's Point,
Summit,
Toledo.

Clackamas County.

Beaver,
Butte Creek,
Clear Creek,
Cuttingsville,

Clackamas County—Continued.

Damascus,
Eagle Creek,
Glad Tidings,
Highland,
Milwaukee,
Molalla,
Needy,
*Oregon City,** (c. h.,)
Oswego.

Clatsop County.

*Astoria,** (c. h.,)
Nehalem,
Skipanon,
Westport.

Columbia County.

Rainier,
St. Helen, (c. h.,)
Sauvie's Island.

* Money-order office.

Coos County.

Coquille,
Empire City, (*c. h.*,)
Hermansville,
Randolph.

Curry County.

Chetco,
Ellensberg, (*c. h.*,)
Port Orford.

Douglas County.

Camas Valley,
Galesville,
Gardiner,
Kellogg's,
Myrtle Creek,
North Canyonville,
Oakland,
Roseburgh,* (*c. h.*,)
Scottsburgh,
Ten Mile,
Wilbur,
Yoncalla.

Grant County.

Camp Watson,
Canyon City,* (*c. h.*,)
Dayville,
Grant,
John Day City,
Prairie City.

Jackson County.

Applegate,
Ashland Mills,
Grant's Pass,
Jacksonville,* (*c. h.*,)
Phœnix,
Rock Point,
Willow Springs.

Josephine County.

Kerby, (*c. h.*,)
Leland,
Slate Creek,
Waldo.

Lane County.

Coast Fork,
Cottage Grove,
Eugene City,* (*c. h.*,)
Franklin,
Lancaster,
Long Tom,
Pleasant Hill,
Rattlesnake,
Siuslaw,
Springfield,
Willamette Forks.

Linn County.

Albany,* (*c. h.*,)
Boston Mills,
Brownsville,
Crawfordsville,
Harrisburgh,
Lebanon,
Peoria,
Pine,
Scio,
Soda Springs.

Marion County.

Aumsville,
Aurora Mills,
Belpassi,
Butteville,
Fairfield,
Jefferson,
Monitor,
Newellsville,

Marion County—Continued

Saint Louis,
SALEM,* (*c. h.*,)
Silverton,
Sublimity,
Vernon,
Waconda.

Multnomah County.

East Portland,
Portland,* (*c. h.*,)
Springville.

Polk County.

Bethel,
Bridgeport,
Buena Vista,
Dallas,* (*c. h.*,)
Elk Horn,
Eola,
Grand Ronde,
Independence,
Lewisville,
Lincoln,
Monmouth,
Perrydale,
Rickreall,
Salt Creek,
Zena.

Tillamook County.

Garibaldi,
Nestocton,
Netart's,
Tillamook, (*c. h.*)

Umatilla County.

Cayuse,
Meadowville,
Pendleton, (*c. h.*,)
Pilot Rock,
Umatilla,*
Weston.

Union County.

Cove,
La Grande,* (*c. h.*,)
North Powder,
Orodell,
Summerville,
Union.

Wasco County.

Bridge Creek,
Deschutes,
Hood River,
Scotts,
Spanish Hollow,
The Dalles,* (*c. h.*,)
Wasco.

Washington County.

Centreville,
Forest Grove,
Hillsborough, (*c. h.*,)
Middleton,
Tualitin.

Yam Hill County.

Amity,
Bellevue,
Dayton,
La Fayette,* (*c. h.*,)
McMinnville,
Mountain House,
Newberg,
North Yam Hill,
Sheridan,
West Chehalem,
Wheatland.

* Money-order office.

PENNSYLVANIA.

ADAMS COUNTY.

Abbottstown,
Arendtsville,
Bendersville,
Bermudian,
Bigler,
Cashtown,
East Berlin,
Fairfield,
Flora Dale,
Fountain Dale,
Gettysburgh,* (*c. h.*,)
Graefenburgh,
Granite Hill,
Green Mount,
Green Ridge,
Hampton,
Heidlersburgh,
Hunterstown,
Idaville,
Latimore,
Littlestown,
McKnightstown,
McSherrystown,
Menallen,
Mummasburgh,
New Chester,
New Oxford,
Red Land,
Round Hill,
Sell's Station,
Seven Stars,
Square Corner,
Table Rock,
Two Taverns,
Wenks,
York Sulphur Spr'gs.

ALLEGHENY COUNTY.

Allegheny,*
Bakerstown,
Beers,
Bennett,
Boston,
Braddock's Field,
Brinton,
Brodhead,
Buchanan,
Buena Vista,
Carrick,
Chartiers,
Claremont,
Clinton,
Coal Valley,
Dixmont,
Dorseyville,
Dravosburgh,
Duncan,
Eakin,
Elizabeth,
Etna,
Ewing's Mills,
Fayette,
Gamble's,
Gill Hall,
Green Tree,
Harmarville,
Hope Church,
Hulton,
Lebanon Church,
Leetsdale,
Library,
McKeesport,*
Mansfield Valley,
Monroeville,
Moon,
Moorhead,
Mount Lebanon,
Mount Washington,
Natrona,
New Texas.
Noblestown,
North Star,
Oakdale Station,
Ormsby,
Palmersville,
Perrysville,
Pittsburgh,* (*c. h.*,)
Port Perry,
Remington,
Robella,
Rural Ridge,
Saint Elmo,
Sewicklyville,
Sharpsburgh,
Shirland,
Shoustown,
Springdale,
Sunny Side,
Surgeon's Hall,
Talley Cavey,
Tarentum,
Temperanceville,
Turtle Creek,
Upper Saint Clair,
Vancefort,
Walker's Mills,
West Elizabeth,
West View,
Wexford,
White Ash,
Wilkins,
Wilkinsburgh,
Wood's Run,
Woodville.

ARMSTRONG COUNTY.

Adams,
Adrian,
Apollo,
Atwood,
Barnard's,
Belknap,
Blanket Hill,
Brady's Bend,
Cochran's Mills,
Cowansville,
Craigsville,
Dayton,
Echo,
Eddyville,
Elderton,
Foster's Mills,
Freeport,*
Goheenville,
Greendale,
Harmsburgh,
Kelly's Station,
Kiskiminitas,
Kittaning,* (*c. h.*,)
Lawrenceburgh,
Leechburgh,
Long Run,
McVill,
Manorsville,
Miller's Eddy,
Monticello,
North Buffalo,
Oakland,
Olivet,
Orrsville,
Oscar,
Peart's Eddy,
Phœnix,
Pierce,
Pine Township,
Putneyville,
Red Bank Furnace,
Rimer,
Rosston,
Rural Valley,
Schenley Station,
Shady Plain,
Sherrett,
Slate Lick,
South Bend,
Spring Church,
West Valley,
Whitesburgh,
Worthington.

BEAVER COUNTY.

Baden,
Beaver,* (*c. h.*,)
Beaver Falls,
Black Hawk,
Brush Creek,
Comettsburgh,
Darlington,
Economy,
Frankfort Springs,
Freedom,
Georgetown,
Green Garden,
Harshaville,
Holt,
Homewood,
Hookstown,
Industry,
Kendall,
Knob,
McCleary,
New Brighton,*
New Galilee,
New Scottsville,
New Sheffield,
North Sewickly,
Ohioville,
Poe,
Rochester,
Rock Point,
Service,
Seventy-Six,
Shippingport,
Smith's Ferry,
Wall Rose,
Water Cure.

BEDFORD COUNTY.

Alum Bank,
Bedford,* (*c. h.*,)
Bedford Springs,
Bloody Run,
Buffalo Mills,
Burns' Mills,
Chaneysville,
Charlesville,
Cherry Grove,
Clearville,
Cumberland Valley,
Dry Ridge,
Elbinsville,
Gladen's Run,
Green Point,
Hopewell,
Imlertown,
Mann's Choice,
Mowry's Mills,
New Bridgeport,

* Money-order office.

BEDFORD COUNTY—Continued.

New Buena Vista,
New Enterprise,
New Paris,
Pattonville,
Pavia,
Purcell,
Rainsburgh,
Ray's Hill,
Riddlesburgh,
Robisonville,
Saint Clairsville,
Saxton,
Schellsburgh,
Six Mile Run,
Six Roads,
Spring Hope,
Spring Meadow,
Stuckeysville,
Tatesville,
Waterside,
West End,
Woodbury,
Yellow Creek.

BERKS COUNTY.

Addams Tavern,
Albany,
Alsace,
Baumstown,
Bechtelsville,
Beckersville,
Bernville,
Bethel,
Birdsborough,
Blandon,
Bower's Station,
Boyerstown,
Brower,
Brumfieldville,
Centreport,
Clayton,
Colebrookdale,
Cross Kill Mills,
Cumru,
Dale,
Douglassville,
Dryville,
Eagle Point,
Earlville,
Exeter Station,
Fetherolffsville,
Fleetwood,
Fredericksville,
Fritztown,
Geiger's Mills,
Gouglersville,
Greshville,
Griesemersville,
Grimville,
Hamburgh,
Hereford,
Hiester's Mill,
Hill Church,
Host,
Hummel's Store,
Joanna Furnace,
Kirbyville,
Klinesville,
Knauer's,
Krick's Mill,
Kutztown,
Landis' Store,
Leesport,
Leinbach's,
Lenhartsville,
Limekiln,
Lobachsville,
Long Swamp,
Lower Bern,
Lower Heidelberg,
Lyon's Station,
Maiden Creek,
Manatawny,
Maxatawny,
Mertztown,
Mohn's Store,
Mohrsville,
Molltown,
Monocacy,
Monterey,
Morgantown,
Moselm,
Mount Ætna,
Mountain,
New Jerusalem,
Nora,
North Heidelberg,
Oley,
Pike Township,
Pricetown,
Reading,* (*c. h.*,)
Rehrersburgh,
Robeson,
Robesonia Furnaces,
Scarlet's Mill,
Seisholtzville,
Shanesville,
Shartlesville,
Shoemakersville,
Sinking Spring,
South Evansville,
Spangville,
Stonersville,
Stouchsburgh,
Stony Run,
Strausstown,
Temple,
Topton,
Tuckerton,
Tulpehocken,
Upper Bern,
Virginville,
Wernersville,
Windsor Castle,
Wintersville,
Womelsdorf,*
Yellow House.

BLAIR COUNTY.

Altoona,*
Antestown,
Arch Spring,
Bennington Furnace,
Blue Knob,
Canoe Creek,
Clover Creek,
Duncansville,
East Freedom,
East Sharpsburgh,
El Dorado,
Fostoria,
Frankstown,
Hollidaysburgh, *(*c. h.*,)
Martinsburgh,
Newry,
Olivia,
Poplar Run,
Roaring Spring,
Sabbath Rest,
Sarah,
Sinking Valley,
Springfield Furnace
Tipton,
Tyrone,*
Williamsburgh,
Yellow Spring.

BRADFORD COUNTY

Alba,
Allis Hollow,
Aspinwall,
Asylum,
Athens,
Austinville,
Barclay,
Bently Creek,
Big Pond,
Browntown,
Burlington,
Camptown,
Canton,
Cold Creek,
Columbia × Roads,
Durell,
East Canton,
East Smithfield,
East Springhill,
East Troy,
Edsallville,
Elwell,
Fassett,
Franklindale,
Granville Centre,
Granville Summit,
Herrick,
Herrickville,
Highland,
Hornet's Ferry,
Hornbrook,
Laddsburgh,
Leona,
Le Raysville,
Le Roy,
Liberty Corners,
Lime Hill,
Litchfield,
Luther's Mills,
Macedonia,
Merryall,
Milan,
Minnequa,
Monroeton,
Mountain Lake,
Myersburgh,
New Albany,
New Era,
North Orwell,
North Rome,
North Smithfield,
North Towanda,
Orcutt Creek,
Orwell,
Overton,
Park's Creek,
Pike,
Potterville,
Ridgebury,
Rome,
Rummerfield Creek,
Sheshequin,
Smithfield Summit,
Snedekerville,
South Branch,
South Creek,
South Hill,
South Litchfield,
South Warren,
Springfield,
Spring Hill,
Standing Stone,
Stevensville,
Sugar Run,
Sylvania,
Terrytown,
Tioga Valley,
Towanda,* (*c. h.*,)
Troy,*
Ulster,
Warren Centre,
Warrenham,
Wells,
West Burlington,
West Franklin,
West Warren,
West Windham,
Wilmot,
Windham,
Windham Centre,
Windham Summit,
Wyalusing,
Wysox.

* Money-order office.

BUCKS COUNTY.

Andalusia,
Applebachsville,
Attleborough,
Bedminster,
Bensalem,
Bridge Valley,
Bridgewater,
Bristol,*
Brownsburgh,
Buckingham,
Buckmanville,
Bucksville,
Bursonville,
Carversville,
Centre Bridge,
Danborough,
Davisville,
Dolington,
Doyleston,* (*c. h.*,)
Dublin,
Durham,
Eddington,
Edgwood,
Emilie,
Erwinna,
Fallsington,
Feasterville,
Gardenville,
Gery's,
Hagersville,
Hartsville,
Hilltown,
Holland,
Hulmesville,
Kintnersville,
Lahaska,
Lumberville,
Mechanicsville,
Milford Square,
Morrisville,
Moyer's Store,
Neshaming,
New Britain,
New Hope,
Newportville,
Newtown,
Oakford,
Ottsville,
Oxford Valley,
Penn's Park,
Pineville,
Pipersville,
Pleasant Valley,
Plumsteadville,
Point Pleasant,
Quakertown,
Richborough,
Richland Centre,
Richlandtown,
Riegelsville,
Schlichter,
Sellersville,
Spinnerstown,
Springtown,
Steinsburgh,
Taylorsville,
Telford,
Trumbaursville,
Tullytown,
Upper Black Eddy,
Warminster,
Warrington,
Whitehallville,
Wrightstown,
Yardleyville.

BUTLER COUNTY.

Anandale,
Anderson's Mills,
Baldwin,
Barnhart's Mills,
Bonnie Brook,
Breakneck,
Brownington,
Brownsdale,
Bruin,
Butler,* (*c. h.*,)
Coultersville,
Coyleville,
Eau Claire,
Glade Mills,
Harmony,
Harrisville,
Hooker,
Jacksville,
Leasuresville,
McCandless,
Melissadale,
Middle Lancaster,
Mount Chesnut,
Murrinsville,
North Hope,
North Oakland,
Ogle,
Peachville,
Petersburgh,
Portersville,
Prospect,
Riddle's × Roads,
Sarversville,
Saxenburgh,
Six Points,
Slippery Rock,
West Liberty,
Whitestown,
Zelienople.

CAMBRIA COUNTY.

Cambria,
Carrolltown,

CAMBRIA COUNTY—Continued.

Chest Springs,
Conemaugh,
Cooperdale,
Cresson,
Ebensburgh,* (*c. h.*,)
Fallen Timber,
Gallitzin,
Garman's Mills,
Glendale,
Hemlock,
Johnstown,*
Loretto,
Mineral Point,
Munster,
Plattville,
Saint Augustine,
Saint Bonifacius,
Saint Lawrence,
Scalp Level,
Sonman,
Summer Hill,
Summit,
Wilmore.

CAMERON COUNTY.

Beech Wood,
Cameron,
Driftwood,
Emporium,* (*c. h.*,)
First Fork,
Prestonville,
Second Fork,
Sinnamahoning,
Sterling Run.

CARBON COUNTY.

Albrightsville,
Aquashicola,
Audenried,
Beaver Meadows,
Buck Mountain,
Carbon,
East Mauch Chunk,
Hickory Run,
Hudsondale,
Lehigh Gap,
Lehigh Tannery,
Lehighton,
Little Gap,
Mauch Chunk,* (*c. h.*,)
Nesquehoning,
New Mahoning,
Parryville,
Penn Haven,
Pleasant Corners,
Rockport,
Stembersville,
Summit Hill,
Tresckow,
Weatherly,
Weissport.

CENTRE COUNTY.

Aaronsburgh,
Agricultural College,
Bellefonte,* (*c. h.*,)
Blanchard,
Boalsburgh,
Buddville,
Buffalo Run,
Centre Hall,
Centre Hill,
Centre Mills,
Fillmore,
Fleming,
Half Moon,
Houserville,
Howard,
Hublersburgh,
Julian Furnace,
Lemont,
Linden Hall,
Loveville,
Madisonburgh,
Martha Furnace,
Meshannon,
Milesburgh,
Millheim,
Mountain Eagle,
Nittany,
Penn Hall,
Philipsburgh,
Pine Glen,
Pine Grove Mills,
Pleasant Gap,
Port Matilda,
Potter's Mills,
Powelton,
Rebersburgh,
Rock Spring,
Roland,
Snow Shoe,
Spring Mills,
Walker,
Wolf's Store,
Woodward,
Zion.

* Money-order office.

CHESTER COUNTY.

Avondale,
Barneston,
Birch Run Ville,
Black Horse,
Blue Rock,
Brandywine Manor,
Caln,
Chatham,
Chester Springs,
Chester Valley,
Chesterville,
Chrome,
Coatesville,
Cochransville,
Collamer,
Cupola,
Dilworthtown,
Doe Run,
Dorlan's Mills,
Downingtown,
East Coventry,
East Vincent,
Elk Dale,
Elk Mills,
Elkview,
Embreeville,
Ercildoun,
Exton,
Fairville,
Frazer,
Frémont,
Glenloch,
Glen Roy,
Goshenville,
Gum Tree,
Guthriesville,
Hamorton,
Hayesville,
Hickory Hill,
Honey Brook,
Hopewell Cotton Works,
Jennersville,
Kaolin,
Kemblesville,
Kennett's Square,
Kimberton,
Landenburgh,
Lenape,
Leopard,
Lewisville,
Lincoln University,
Lionville,
Loag,
Londonderry,
London Grove,
McWilliamstown,
Marlborough,
Marsh,
Marshallton,
Milford Mills,
Milltown,
Mortonville,
Mount Vernon,
New Centreville,
New Garden,
New London,
North Coventry,
Norwood,
Nottingham,
Oxford,*
Paoli,
Parkersville,
Parkesburgh,
Pawling,
Penningtonville,
Phœnixville,*
Pickering,
Pomeroy,
Pughtown,
Reeseville,
Rockville,
Russellville,
Sadsburyville,
Saint Peters,
Schuylkill,
Setzler's Store,
Spread Eagle,
Steelville,
Street Road,
Strickersville,
Sugartown,
Talbotville,
Thornbury,
Thorndale Iron Works,
Tough Kenamon,
Unionville,
Uwchland,
Valley Creek,
Valley Forge,
Vincent,
Wagontown,
Wallace,
Warren Tavern,
Warwick,
West Chester,* (*c. h.*,)
West Grove Station,
West Vincent,
West Whiteland,
White Horse,
Wildbrier,
Willistown Inn,
Willowdale.

CLARION COUNTY.

Alum Rock,
Brinkerton,
Callensburgh,
Catfish,
Clarion,* (*c. h.*,)
Cunningham,
Curllsville,
Fisher,
Foxburgh,
Fryburgh,

CLARION COUNTY—Continued.

Helen Furnace,
Jefferson Furnace,
Kahle's,
Kerr's Store,
Kingsville,
Knox,
Kossuth,
Lamartine,
Leatherwood,
Lickingville,
Limestone,
Lucinda Furnace,
New Bethlehem,
Newmansville,
North Pine Grove,
Philipston,
Piny,
Pollock,
Reidsburgh,
Rimersburgh,
Saint Petersburgh,
Scotch Hill,
Shannondale,
Shippensville,
Sligo,
Strattonville,
Tylersburgh,
Valley,
Watterson's Ferry,
West Freedom,
West Monterey,

CLEARFIELD COUNTY.

Alleman's,
Ansonville,
Bald Hill,
Bloomington,
Bower,
Burnside,
Chest,
Clearfield,* (*c. h.*,)
Clearfield Bridge,
Curwinsville,
Cush,
East Ridge,
Forest,
Frenchville,
Glen Hope,
Grahamton,
Grampian Hills,
Hegarty's × Roads,
Houtzdale,
Hurd,
Jefferson Line,
Jeffries,
Karthaus,
Kylertown,
Leconte's Mills,
Little Toby,
Lumber City,
Luthersburgh,
McGarvey's,
Madera,
Marron,
Morrisdale,
New Millport,
New Washington,
Osceola Mills,
Ostend,
Patchinsville,
Penfield,
Rockton,
Salt Lick,
Shawsville,
Smith's Mills,
Three Runs,
Troutville,
Tylers,
Utahville,
Wallaceton,
West Decatur,
Westover's,
Williams Grove,
Woodland.

CLINTON COUNTY.

Beech Creek,
Booneville,
Carroll,
Cedar Springs,
Chatham Run,
Cross Fork,
Farrandsville,
Flemington,
Glen Union,
Hammersley's Fork,
Hiner's Run,
Island,
Lamar,
Lamar Mills,
Leidy,
Lockhaven,* (*c. h.*,)
Logan Mills,
McElhattan,
Mill Hall,
Phelps Mills,
Pine Station,
Rauch's Gap,
Renovo,*
Rosecrans,
Round Island,
Salona,
Sugar Valley,
Tylersville,
Westport,
Whetham,
Wistar,
Young Womanstown.

*** Money-order office.**

Columbia County.

Beaver Valley,
Benton,
Berwick,
Bloomsburgh,* (*c. h.*,)
Brier Creek,
Buckhorn,
Catawissa,
Central,
Centralia,
Cole's Creek,
Espy,
Evansville,
Eyer's Grove,
Fishing Creek,
Forks,
Foundryville,
Fowlersville,
Greenwood,
Iola,
Jerseytown,
Light Street,
Lime Ridge,
Mainville,
Mifflinville,
Millville,
Mordansville,
Numidia,
Orangeville,
Pine Summit,
Polkville,
Roaring Creek,
Rohrsburgh,
Rupert,
Sereno,
Stillwater,
Van Camp,
Willow Springs.

Crawford County.

Adamsville,
Beaver Centre,
Black Ash,
Bloomfield,
Blooming Valley,
Brown Hill,
Calvin's Corners,
Cambridgeborough,
Centre Road Station,
Centreville,
Chapinville,
Cochrantown,
Conneautville,*
Coon's Corners,
Crossingville,
Custard's,
Deckard,
Dicksonburgh,
Drake's Mills,
Dutch Hill,
Espyville,
Evansburgh,
Fallowfield,
Frenchtown,
Glyndon,
Guy's Mills,
Harmonsburgh,
Hartstown,
Hayfield,
Lincolnville,
Lines Hollow,
Lineville Station,
Little Cooley,
Long's Stand,
McLean's Corners,
Mead Corners,
Meadville,* (*c. h.*,)
Miller's Station,
Morris Corners,
Mosiertown,
New Richmond,
Norrisville,
North Shenango,
Oil Creek,
Penn Line,
Pettis,
Potter's Corners,
Randolph,
Riceville,
Royalton,
Rundells,
Saegerstown,
Sandy Creek,
Shaw's Landing,
Spartansburgh,
Spring,
Steamburgh,
Stony Point,
Sugar Lake,
Sutton's Corners,
Tamarac,
Taylor's Stand,
Titusville,*
Townville,
Tryonville,
Turnersville,
Venango,
Wayne Centre,
West Greenwood,
Woodcock.

Cumberland County.

Allen,
Big Spring,
Bloserville,
Boiling Springs,
Camp Hill,
Carlisle,* (*c. h.*)
Carlisle Springs,
Dickinson,
Eberly's Mill,
Good Hope,

Cumberland County—Continued.

Greason,
Hogestown,
Kerrsville,
Lee's Cross Roads,
Lisburn,
Mechanicsburgh,
Middle Spring,
Mountain Creek,
Mt. Holly Springs,
Mount Rock,
Newburgh,
New Cumberland,
New Kingstown,
Newville,
Oakville,
Plainfield,
Shepherdstown,*
Shippensburgh,
Shiremantown,
Stoughstown,
Walnut Bottom,
West Fairview,
White House.

Dauphin County.

Benvenue,
Berrysburgh,
Curtin,
Dauphin,
Derry Church,
Ellendale Forge,
Elizabethville,
Enders,
Enterline,
Fisherville,
Grantville,
Gratz,
Halifax,
HARRISBURGH,* (*c.h.*,)
High Spire,
Hummelstown,
Killinger,
Linglestown,
Lykens,
Manada Hill,
Middletown,*
Millersburgh,*
Paxton,
Pillow,
Powel's Creek,
Powl's Valley,
Progress,
Short Mountain,
Susquehanna,
Swatara Station,
Union Deposit,
West Hanover,
Wiconisco,
Williamstown.

Delaware County.

Booth Corner,
Brandywine Summit,
Broomall,
Chadd's Ford,
Chelsea,
Chester,*
Cheyney,
Concordville,
Darby,
Edgemont,
Elam,
Glen Mills,
Glen Riddle,
Haverford,
Howellville,
Ivy Mills,
Kellysville,
Lazaretto Station,
Leipersville,
Lenni Mills,
Lima,
Linwood Station,
Marple,
Media,* (*c. h.*,)
Morton,
Newtown Square,
Oakdale,
Radnor,
Thornton,
Thurlow,
Uplands,
Upper Darby,
Upper Providence,
Village Green,
West Haverford.

Elk County.

Arroyo,
Benezett,
Brandy Camp,
Caledonia,
Dent's Run,
Earley,
Hellen,
Kerseys,
Ridgway,* (*c. h.*,)
Saint Mary's,
Wilcox,
Williamsville,
Wilmarth.

* **Money-order office.**

Erie County.

Albion,*
Avonia,
Belle Valley,
Carter Hill,
Cherry Hill,
Concord Station,
Corry,*
East Greene,
East Springfield,
Edenville,
Edinborough,
Elk Creek,
*Erie,** (*c. h.*,)
Fairview,*
Franklin Corners,
Girard,*
Greenfield,
Harbour Creek,
Hatch Hollow,
Keepville,
Lake Pleasant,
Lebœuf,
Lovell's Station,
Lowville,
Lundy's Lane,
McKean,
McLane,
McLellan's Corners,
Miles' Grove,
Mill Village,
Moorheadville,
North East,*
North Springfield,
Northville,
Platea,
Sterrettania,
Stewart,
Swan Station,
Union Mills,*
Waterford,
Wattsburgh,
Wayne,
Wesleyville,
West Greene,
West Springfield.

Fayette County.

Belle Vernon,
Broad Ford,
Brownsville,*
Connellsville,
Davidson's Ferry,
Dawson's Station,
Dunbar,
East Liberty,
Elm,
Farmington,
Fayette City,
Fayette Springs,
Flatwoods,
Frost's Station,
Heistersburgh,
Indian Creek,
Layton's Station,
McClellandtown,
Markleysburgh,
Masontown,
Merrittstown,
Mill Run,
Morris Cross Roads,
New Geneva,
New Salem,
Pennsville,
Perryopolis,
Pile Falls,
Redstone,
Searight's,
Shinbone,
Smithfield,
Springhill Furnace,
Tippecanoe,
*Uniontown,** (*c. h.*)
Upper Middletown.

Forest County.

Clarington,
Cooksburgh,
East Hickory,
Marionville,
Nebraska,
Newtown Mills,
Panther Rock,
Perry,
Raught's Mills,
*Tionesta,** (*c. h.*,)
Trunkeyville,
West Hickory.

Franklin County.

Amberson's Valley,
Black's Gap,
Brown's Mills,
*Chambersburgh,** (*c. h.*,)
Clay Lick,
Concord,
Doylesburgh,
Dry Run,
Fannettsburgh,
Fayetteville,
Greencastle,*
Green Village,
Jackson Hall,
Keefer's Store,
Loudon,
Mason and Dixon,
Marion,
Mercersburgh,*
Mont Alto,
Mount Parnel,
Mowersville,
New Bridge,
Orrstown,

Franklin County—Continued.

Pleasant Hall,
Quincy,
Roxbury,
Saint Thomas,
Scotland,
Shady Grove,
Spring Run,
State Line,
Sylvan,
Upper Strasburgh,
Upton,
Waynesborough,*
Welsh Run.

Fulton County.

Akersville,
Big Cove Tannery,
Buck Valley,
Burnt Cabins,
Dublin Mills,
Emmaville,
Fort Littleton,
Gapsville,
Harrisonville,
Hustontown,
Knobsville,
Locust Grove,
McConnellsburgh, (*c. h.*,)
New Grenada,
Sideling Hill,
Sipe's Mill,
Warfordsburgh,
Webster's Mills,
Wells' Tannery,
West Dublin.

Greene County.

Aleppo,
Big Tree,
Bristoria,
Carmichael's,
Ceylon,
Clarksville,
Crow's Mills,
Davistown,
Day's Store,
Delight,
Dent,
Dunkard,
Fordyce,
Gray's Landing,
Greensborough,
Harvey's,
Holbrook,
Hopkins' Mills,
Hunter's Cave,
Jefferson,
Jollytown,
Kirby,
Lone Tree,
Mapletown,
Mount Morris,
New Freeport,
Oak Forest,
Rice's Landing,
Rogersville,
Rosedale,
Ruff Creek,
Ryerson's Station,
Spragg's,
Thom's Run,
*Waynesburgh,** (*c. h.*,
White Cottage,
Whiteley,
Wiley,
Willow Tree,
Wind Ridge.

Huntingdon County.

Airy Dale,
Alexandria,
Aughwick's Mills,
Barre Forge,
Birmingham,
Broad Top,
Calvin,
Cassville,
Coalmont,
Coffee Run,
Colerain Forge,
Colfax,
Cottage,
Cove Station,
Donation,
Dudley,
Eagle Foundry,
Ennisville,
Franklinville,
Graysville,
Greenwood Furnace,
Hair's Valley,
Hill Valley,
Hubelsville,
*Huntingdon,** (*c. h.*,)
James Creek,
McAlevy's Fort,
McConnellstown,
Maddensville,
Manor Hill,
Mapleton Depot,
Meadow Gap,
Mill Creek,
Morrell,
Mount Union,
Neff's Mills,
New Pleasant Grove,
Nossville,
Orbisonia,
Saltillo,
Saulsburgh,
Shade Gap,

* Money-order office.

HUNTINGDON COUNTY—Continued.

Shaver's Creek,
Shirleysburgh,
Spruce Creek,
Three Springs,
Todd,
Vineyard Mills,
Warrior's Mark,
Water Street.

INDIANA COUNTY.

Advance,
Armagh,
Ambrose,
Black Lick Station,
Blairsville,*
Brady,
Brush Valley,
Chambersville,
Clarksburgh,
Covode,
Creekside,
Crete,
Decker's Point,
Dixonville.
Ebenezer,
Elder's Ridge,
Gilpin,
Grant,
Heshbon,
Hillsdale,
Home,
Horton's,
Indiana,* (*c. h.*,)
Kent,
Kimmel,
Locust Lane,
Mahoning,
Marchand,
Minta,
Mitchell's Mills,
Nolo,
Onberg,
Parkwood,
Penn Run,
Philip's Mills,
Pine Flats,
Plumville,
Purchase Line,
Saltsburgh,
Shelocta,
Smicksburgh,
Smitten,
Spruce,
Strongstown,
Suncliff,
Tannery,
Tunnelton,
Utah,
Watt,
West Lebanon,
Willet.

JEFFERSON COUNTY.

Bell's Mills,
Big Run,
Brockwayville,
Brookville,* (*c. h.*,)
Canoe Ridge,
Cool Spring,
Corsica,
Dolingville,
Frostburgh,
Hamilton,
Hudson,
Knox Dale,
New Petersburgh,
Oliveburgh,
Packer,
Porter,
Punxatawney,*
Reynoldsville,
Richardsville,
Ringgold,
Rockdale Mills,
Schoffner's Corners,
Sigel,
Sprankle's Mills,
Stanton,
Summerville,
Warsaw,
Worthville.

JUNIATA COUNTY.

Academia,
Cocolamus,
Doyle's Mills,
East Salem.
East Waterford.
Evendale,
Honey Grove,
McAllisterville.
McCoysville,
McCulloch's Mills,
Mexico,
Mifflintown,* (*c. h.*,)
Mohontongo,
Oakland Mills,
Patterson,
Peru Mills,
Pleasant View,
Port Royal,
Reed's Gap,
Richfield,
Shade Valley,
Spruce Hill,
Thompsontown,
Van Wert,
Walnut,
Waterloo.

LANCASTER COUNTY.

Adamstown,
Akron,
Bainbridge,
Bareville,
Bart,
Bartville,
Beartown,
Bellemonte,
Bethesda,
Binkley's Bridge,
Blue Ball,
Bowmansville,
Brickerville,
Brunnerville,
Buck,
Buyerstown,
Cain's,
Camargo,
Cambridge,
Chesnut Level,
Chickies,
Christiana,
Churchtown,
Clonmell,
Cocalico,
Colemanville,
Colerain,
Columbia,*
Conestoga,
Creswell,
Durlach,
East Hempfield,
Elizabethtown,
Enterprise,
Ephratah,
Falmouth,
Farmersville,
Fertility,
Fulton House,
Gap,
Goodville,
Gordonsville,
Goshen,
Green Bank,
Greene,
Greenland,
Groff's Store,
Hempfield,
Highville,
Hinkleton,
Intercourse,
Junction,
Kinzers,
Kirk's Mills,
Kirkwood,
Lampeter,
Lancaster,* (*c. h.*,)
Landis Valley,
Landisville,
Leacock,
Leaman Place.
Liberty Square,
Lincoln,
Litiz,*
Little Britain,
Lyles,
Manheim,
Manor,
Marietta,*
Martickville,
Martinsville,
Mastersonville,
May,
Maytown,
Mechanic's Grove,
Millersville,*
Millway,
Motley,
Mount Hope,
Mount Joy,*
Mount Nebo,
Mountville,
Muddy Creek,
Neffsville,
New Danville,
New Holland,
New Providence,
Nine Points,
Oak Hill,
Oak Shade,
Octoraro,
Old Line,
Oregon,
Paradise,
Penn,
Pequea,
Peter's Creek,
Pleasant Grove,
Quarryville,
Rawlinsville,
Reamstown,
Reidenbach's Store,
Reinhold's Station,
Reinholdsville,
Rothsville,
Safe Harbor,
Salisbury,
Salunga,
Schoeneck,
Silver Spring,
Slack Water,
Smithville,
Smyrna,
Soudersburgh,
South Hermitage,
Sporting Hill,
Spring Garden,
Spring Grove,
Stevens,
Strasburgh,
Swartzville,
Terre Hill,
Union Station,
Vogansville,
Wakefield,
West Earl,
Wheatland Mills,
White Oak,
Willow Street,
Wright's Dale.

* **Money-order office.**

LAWRENCE COUNTY.

Chenango,
Cross Cut,
East Brook,
Edinburgh,
Enon Valley,
Harlensburgh,
Hillsville,
Moravia,
Mount Jackson,
Neshannock Falls,
New Bedford,
*Newcastle,** (*c. h.*,)
New Wilmington,
Plain Grove,
Princeton,
Pulaski,
Rose Point,
Volant,
Wampum,
Wurtemberg.

LEBANON COUNTY.

Annville,*
Avon,
Bellview,
Campbelltown,
Colebrook,
Cornwall,
East Hanover,
Fredericksburgh,
Greble,
Hamlin,
Jonestown,*
Kleinfeltersville,
*Lebanon,** (*c. h.*,)
Meyerstown,
Millbach,
Monroe Forge,
Mount Zion,
Ono,
Palmyra,
Richland Station,
Shaefferstown,
Sheridan,
Union Forge.

LEHIGH COUNTY.

Alburtis.
*Allentown,** (*c. h.*,)
Breinigsville,
Catasauqua,
Centre Valley,
Claussville,
Coopersburgh,
Dillingersville,
Emaus,
Fogelsville,
Friedensville,
Hokendauqua,
Hosensack,
Hyremansville,
Ironton,
Jacksonville,
Lanark,
Laury's Station,
Lehigh Valley,
Limeport,
Litzenberg,
Locust Valley,
Lowhill,
Lynnport,
Lynnville,
Lyon Valley,
Macungie,
Mountainville,
Neff's,
New Tripoli,
North Whitehall,
Orefield,
Oswaldville,
Rittersville,
Rucksville,
Saegersville,
Schnecksville,
Seiberlingville,
Shimerville,
Shoenersville,
Sipestown,
Slatington,
South Whitehall,
Stinesville,
Trexlertown,
Vera Cruz,
Weidasville,
Weisenburgh,
Wennersville,
Wescosville.

LUZERNE COUNTY.

Archbald,
Bailey Hollow,
Bald Mount,
Beach Haven,
Bear Creek,
Belbend,
Black Creek,
Bloomingdale,
Briggsville,
Cambra,
Carbondale,*
Carverton,
Charleston,
Clark's Green,
Clifton,
Conyngham,
Daleville,
Dallas,

LUZERNE COUNTY—Continued.

Dorrance,
Drum's,
Dunmore,
Dunnings,
East Benton,
Eckley,
Exeter,
Fairmount Springs,
Fleetville,
Forty Fort,
Gibsonburgh,
Gouldsborough,
Green Grove,
Harveyville,
Hazleton,*
Hendricksburgh,
Hobbie,
Humphreysville,
Hunlock Creek,
Huntsville,
Hyde Park,
Jeansville,
Jeddo,
Ketcham,
Kingston,
Kunckle,
Lackawanna,
Lake,
Laurel Run,
Lehman,
Luzerne,
Madisonville,
Mill Hollow,
Milwaukie,
Morrison,
Moscow,
Mountain Top,
Mountain Valley,
Muhlenburgh,
Nanticoke,
Nescopeck,
New Columbus,
Old Forge,
Olyphant,
Orange,
Peckville,
Pittston,
Plainsville,
Plymouth,*
Port Blanchard,
Providence,
Ransom,
Red Rock,
Schultzville,
Scott,
Scranton,*
Shickshinny,
Spring Brook,
Stockton,
Stoddartsville,
Sugar Notch,
Sweet Valley,
Sybertsville,
Tompkinsville,
Town Hill,
Town Line,
Trucksville,
Upper Lehigh,
Wallsville,
Wapwallopen,
Waverly,
West Nanticoke,
White Haven,
*Wilkesbarre,** (*c. h.*,)
Wyoming.

LYCOMING COUNTY.

Antes Fort,
Barbour's Mills,
Bastress,
Bodinesville,
Carpenter,
Cedar Run,
Chesnut Grove,
Clarkestown,
Cogan House,
Cogan Station,
Collomsville,
Elimsport,
English Centre,
Fairfield Centre,
Haneyville,
Hughesville,
Huntersville,
Jersey Mills,
Jersey Shore,*
Kellyburgh,
Lairdsville,
Larry's Creek,
Linden,
Loyalsock,
Maple Hill,
Montgomery Station,
Montoursville,
Moreland,
Muncy,*
Muncy Station,
Newberry,
Nippenose,
Nisbet,
Oregon Hill,
Picture Rocks,
Ralston,
Roaring Branch,
Rose's Valley,
Salladyburgh,
Texas,
Tivoli,
Tomb's Run,
Trout Run,
Unityville,
Wallis Run,
Warrensville,
Waterville,
White Pine,
*Williamsport,** (*c. h.*,)
Wolf Run.

* Money-order office.

McKean County.

Allegheny Bridge,
Alton,
Annin Creek,
Bradford,
Clermontville,
Colegrove,
De Golier,
Eden,
Farmer's Valley,
Glenn,
Kane,
Kasson,
Keating,
Kendall Creek,
La Fayette,
Norwich,
Port Allegheny,
Prentiss Vale,
Sargent,
Sartwell,
Smithport,* (c. h.,)
State Line Mills,
Turtle Point.

Mercer County.

Balm,
Centretown,
Clark,
Delaware Grove,
Fredonia,
French Creek,
Greenville,*
Hadley,
Harthegig,
Henderson,
Hermitage,
Hill,
Indian Run,
Irishtown,
Jamestown,
Kennard,
Leech's Corners,
Leesburgh,
London,
Maysville,
Mercer,* (c. h.,)
Milledgeville,
New Hamburgh,
New Lebanon,
New Vernon,
North Liberty,
North Sandy,
North's Mills,
Perrine,
Sandy Lake,
Satterfield,
Sharon,*
Sharpsville Furnace,
Sheakleyville,
Stoneborough,
Transfer,
West Middlesex,
West Salem,
Wheatland Furnace,
Wolf Creek,
Worth.

Mifflin County.

Allensville,
Atkinson's Mills,
Belleville,
Decatur,
Granville,
Kelley,
Kishacoquillas,
Lewistown,* (c. h.,)
McVeytown,
Menno,
Milroy,
Newton Hamilton,
Reedsville,
Strode's Mills.

Monroe County.

Analomink,
Bartonsville,
Bossardsville,
Brodheadsville,
Canadensis,
Coolbaugh's,
Delaware Water Gap,
East Stroudsburgh,
Effort,
Experiment Mills,
Gilbert,
Jackson Corners,
Henrysville,
Kellersville,
Kresgeville,
Kunkletown,
Marshall's Creek,
Merwinsburgh,
New Mt. Pleasant,
Paradise Valley,
Roscommon,
Rossland,
Saylorsburgh,
Sciota,
Shawnee,
Shoemaker's,
Snydersville,
Stormville,
Stroudsburgh,* (c. h.,)
Tannersville,
Tobyhanna Mills,
White's Tannery.

Montgomery County.

Abington,
Barren Hill,
Blue Bell,
Bridgeport,
Broad Axe,
Cabinet,
Centre Square,
Cheltenham,
Collegeville,
Conshohocken,
Crooked Hill,
Douglass,
Eagleville,
Fagleysville,
Fairview Village,
Fitzwatertown,
Flourtown,
Franconia,
Frederick,
General Wayne,
Gilbertsville,
Grater's Ford,
Gulf Mills,
Gwynedd,
Harleysville,
Half Way,
Hatborough,
Hatfield,
Hickory Town,
Hillegass,
Hoppenville,
Horsham,
Huntingdon Valley,
Jarrettown,
Jeffersonville,
Jenkintown,
King of Prussia,
Kulpsville,
Landsdale,
Lederachsville,
Limerick,
Limerick Station,
Line Lexington,
Lower Merion,
Lower Providence,
Montgomery Square,
New Hanover,
Norristown,* (c. h.,)
Norritonville,
North Wales,
Overbrook,
Palm,
Penllyn,
Pennsburgh,
Penn's Square,
Perkiomenville,
Plymouth Meeting,
Port Kennedy,
Port Providence,
Pottstown,*
Prospectville,
Red Hill,
Royer's Ford,
Salfordville,
Schwenk's Store,
Shannonville,
Shoemakertown,
Skippack,
Sorrel Horse,
Souder's Station,
Spring House,
Sumneytown,
Three Tons,
Trappe,
Tyler's Port,
Union Square,
Upper Dublin,
Waverly Heights,
White Marsh,
William Penn,
Willow Grove,
Worcester,
Zeiglersville.

Montour County.

Comly,
Danville,* (c. h.,)
Exchange,
Limestoneville,
Mooresburgh,
Washingtonville,
White Hall.

Northampton County.

Ackermanville,
Bangor,
Bath,
Belfast,
Berlinsville,
Bethlehem,*
Blue Mountain,
Bush Kiln Centre,
Butztown,
Chapman Quarries,
Cherryville,
Danielsville,
Delpsburgh,
Easton,* (c. h.,)
Freemansburgh,
Hanoverville,
Hecktown,
Hellertown,
Iron Hill,
Johnsonville,
Kessler's,
Klecknersville,
Kreidersville,
Laubach,
Leithsville,
Lower Saucon,

* Money-order office.

NORTHAMPTON COUNTY—Continued.

Martin's Creek,
Middagh's,
Moorestown,
Mount Bethel,
Nazareth,*
Newhart's,
Petersville,
Portland,
Redington,
Richmond,
Sandt's Eddy,
Seidersville,
Seigfried's Bridge,
Slateford,
South Bethlehem,*
South Easton,
Stockertown,
Stone Church,
Stouts,
Uhlersville,
Weaversville,
Wind Gap.

NORTHUMBERLAND COUNTY.

Augusta,
Bear Gap,
Chillisquaque,
Chulasky,
Dalmatia,
Dewart,
Dornsife,
Elysburgh,
Excelsior,
Fisher's Ferry,
Greenbrier,
Herndon,
Hickory Corners,
Kline's Grove,
Line Mountain,
Locust Gap,
McEwensville,
Mahanoy,
Milton,
Montandon,
Mount Carmel,
Northumberland,*
Paxinos,
Pott's Grove,
Rebuck's,
Riverside,
Rushtown,
Shamokin,*
Snydertown,
Sunbury, (*c. h.*,)
Trevorton,
Turbotville,
Union Corner,
Urban,
Watsontown.*

PERRY COUNTY.

Andersonburgh,
Blain,
Centre,
Dellville,
Donally's Mills,
Duncannon,
Elliottsburgh,
Green Park,
Grier's Point,
Ickesburgh,
Juniata,
Keystone,
Landisburgh,
Liverpool,
Loysville,
Mannsville,
Markelsville,
Marysville,
Millerstown,
Millerstown Stat'n,
Montgomery's Ferry,
New Bloomfield, (*c. h.*,)
New Buffalo,
New Germantown,
Newport,*
Roseburgh,
Sandy Hill,
Sherman's Dale,
Sterrett's Gap.

PHILADELPHIA COUNTY.

Philadelphia,* (*c. h.*)

PIKE COUNTY.

Bushkill,
Delaware,
Dingman's Ferry,
Egypt Mills,
Field Bend,
Lackawaxen,
Lord's Valley,
Masthope,
Matamoras,
Milford,* (*c. h.*,)
Millville Depot,
Nyces,
Paupac,
Rowland,
Shohola,
Tafton.

POTTER COUNTY.

Ayer's Hill,
Bingham Centre,
Brookland,
Burtville,
Carter Camp,
Clara,
Colesburgh,
Coudersport,* (*c. h.*,)
East Hebron,
East Homer,
East Sharon,
Eleven Mile,
Ellisburgh,
Eulalia,
Forest Home,
Genesee Fork,
Germania,
Harrison Valley,
Hebron,
Homer,
Kettle Creek,
Millport,
North Wharton,
Oswayo,
Pike Mills,
Raymond's,
Roulette,
Sharon Centre,
Shinglehouse,
Sunderlinville,
Sweden,
Sweden Valley,
Ulysses,
West Bingham,
West Pike,
Wharton,
White's Corners,
Williston.

SCHUYLKILL COUNTY.

Ashland,*
Auburn,
Barnesville,
Barry,
Branch Dale,
Brandonville,
Broad Mountain,
Cressona,
Delano,
Donaldson,
Drehersville,
Ellwood,
Friedensburgh,
Girard Manor,
Girardsville,
Glen Carbon,
Gordon,
Hegins,
Hepler,
Hughes,
Joliett,
Klingerstown,
Landingville,
Llewellyn,
Lower Mahantango,
McKeansburgh,
Mahanoy City,*
Mahanoy Plane,
Middleport,
Minersville,*
New Ringgold,
North Penn,
Orwigsburgh,
Orwin,
Palo Alto,
Pine Grove,
Port Carbon,
Port Clinton,
Pottsville,* (*c. h.*,)
Reynolds,
Ringtown,
Rock,
Rough and Ready,
Sacramento,
Saint Clair,*
Saint Nicholas,
Schneider,
Schuylkill Haven,
Shenandoah,
Silver Brook,
Silver Creek,
Summit Station,
Swatara,
Sylliman,
Tamaqua,*
Tower City,
Tremont,
Tuscarora,
Upper Mahantango,
Weishample,
West Penn,
Yatesville,
Zion's Grove.

SNYDER COUNTY.

Bannerville,
Beaver Springs,
Beavertown,
Chapman,
Freeburgh,
Hummell's Wharf,
Kantz,
Kratzerville,
Kreamer,
McKee's Half Falls,
Middleburgh, (*c. h.*,)
Middle Creek,
Mt. Pleasant Mills,
Pallas,
Penn's Creek,
Port Treverton,
Salem,
Selin's Grove,*
Shamokin Dam,
Troxelville.

* Money-order office.

Somerset County.

Addison,
Bakersville,
Benford's Store,
Berkley's,
Berlin,
Buckstown,
Casselman,
Davidsville,
Dividing Ridge,
Elk Lick,
Gebhart's,
Glade,
Harnedsville,
Jenner's × Roads,
Jennerstown,
Johnsburgh,
Kingwood,
Lavansville,
Meyer's Mills,
Mount Healthy,
New Baltimore,
New Lexington,
Pocahontas,
Sand Patch,
Shade Furnace,
Shaff's Bridge,
Shanksville,
Sipesville,
Somerfield,
*Somerset,** (*c. h.,*)
Somerset Furnace,
Southampton Mills,
Staunton's Mills,
Stony Creek,
Stoyestown,
Summit Mills,
Turkey Foot,
Turner's Store,
Ursina,
Wellersburgh,
Wittenberg.

Sullivan County.

Campbellville,
Colley,
Davidson,
Dushore,*
Eagle's Mere,
Eldredsville,
Forksville,
Hill's Grove,
Laporte, (*c. h.,*)
Lincoln Falls,
Millview,
Muncy Bottom,
Plunkett,
Shunk,
Sonestown.

Susquehanna County.

Ararat,
Auburn Centre,
Auburn Four Corn's,
Birchardville,
Brackney,
Brookdale,
Brooklyn,
Choconut,
Clifford,
Dimock,
Dundaff,
East Bridgewater,
East Dimock,
East Rush,
Elk Lake,
Fairdale,
Forest Lake,
Forest Lake Centre,
Friendsville,
Gibson,
Glenwood,
Great Bend,
Great Bend Village,
Harmony Centre,
Harford,
Herrick Centre,
Hop Bottom,
Jackson,
Jackson Valley,
Lanesborough,
Lathrop,
Lawsville Centre,
Lenoxville,
Little Meadows,
Lynn,
Middletown Centre,
*Montrose,** (*c. h.,*)
Montrose Depot,
New Milford,
Niven,
North Jackson,
Oakley,
Richmond Hill,
Rush,
Rush Four Corners,
Rushville,
Saint Joseph,
Silver Lake,
Smiley,
South Auburn,
South Gibson,
Springville,
Susquehanna Depot,*
Thompson,
Union Dale,
Upsonville,
West Auburn,
West Lenox.

Tioga County.

Arnot,
Blossburgh,*
Brookfield,
Canoe Camp,
Charleston,
Chase's Mills,
Chatham Valley,
Cherry Flats,
Covington,
Cowanesque Valley,
Crooked Creek,
Daggett's Mills,
East Charleston,
East Chatham,
Elkland,
Elk Run,
Fall Brook,
Farmington Centre,
Farmington Hill,
Gaines,
Gray's Valley,
Hammond's Creek,
Keeneyville,
Knoxville.
Lamb's Creek,
Lansing,
Lawrenceville,
Liberty,
Little Marsh,
Lloyd,
Mainesburgh,
Mansfield,
Maple Ridge,
Marshfield,
Middlebury Centre,
Mitchell's Creek,
Mixtown,
Morris,
Morris Run,
Nauvoo,
Nelson,
Nile's Valley,
Osceola,
Ogdensburgh,
Pine Creek,
Rutland,
Sabinsville,
Stony Fork.
Sullivan,
Tioga,
*Wellsborough,** (*c. h,*)
West Covington,
Westfield.

Union County.

Alvira,
Buffalo Cross Roads,
Cowan,
Forest Hill,
Hartleton,
Kelly Point,
Laurelton,
*Lewisburgh,** (*c. h.,*)
Mifflinburgh,
New Berlin,
New Columbia,
Slifer,
Vicksburgh,
West Milton,
White Deer Mills,
Winfield.

Venango County.

Agnew's Mills,
Barkeyville,
Big Bend,
Canal,
Cass,
Cherry Tree,
Clintonville,
Coal City,
Columbia Farm,
Cooperstown,
Cranberry,
Dempseytown,
Diamond,
Eagle Rock,
East Sandy,
Emlenton,
Fertigs,
*Franklin,** (*c. h.,*)
Kane City,
Kennerdell,
Kilgore,
Lamb's,
Laytonia,
Lineville,
Meredith,
Nickleville,
Oil City,*
Oleopolis,
Personville,
Petroleum Centre,*
Pioneer,
Pit Hole City,*
Pittsville,
Pleasantville,*
Plum,
Plumer,
Polk,
Porterfield,
President,
Raymilton,
Reno,
Rockland,
Rouseville,*
Seneca,
Shamburgh,*
Sherman Wells,
Sidney,
Stewart's Run,

* Money-order office.

VENANGO COUNTY—Continued.

Sunville,
Tarr Farm,*
Ten Mile Bottom,
Utica,
Wallaceville,
Wesley,
Wilson's Mills,
Witherup's.

WARREN COUNTY.

Bear Lake,
Chandler's Valley,
Cobham,
Columbus,
Cornplanter,
Corydon,
Eagle,
Freehold,
Garland,
Germany,
Irvine,
Kinzua,
Lander,
Lottsville,
Pittsfield,
Russellsburgh,
Sheffield,
Sheffield Depot,
South West,
Spring Creek,
Star,
Steam Mill,
Stoneham,
Sugar Grove,
Tidioute,*
Warren,* (*c. h.*,)
West Spring Creek,
Youngsville.

WASHINGTON COUNTY.

Allenport,
Amity,
Atchison,
Bavington,
Beallsville,
Beck's Mills,
Bentleyville,
Bower Hill,
Brush Run,
Buffalo,
Bulger,
Burgettstown,
California,
Candor,
Cannonsburgh,*
Cardville,
Cherry Valley,
Claysville,
Clokey,
Coal Bluff,
Coon Island,
Cross Creek Village,
Dinsmore,
Donley,
Dunningsville,
Dunsfort,
East Bethlehem,
East Finley,
Finleyville,
Florence,
Fredericktown,
Ginger Hill,
Good Intent,
Hanlin Station,
Havelock,
Herriottsville,
Hickory,
Independence,
Kerr's Station,
Lindly's Mills,
Lock No. 4,
Locust Hill,
Lone Pine,
Meloy,
Midway,
Millsborough,
Monongahela City,*
Mount Airy,
Munntown,
Murdocksville,
Paris,
Patterson's Mills,
Pike Run,
Prosperity,
Raccoon,
Scenery Hill,
Simpson's Store,
Sparta,
Strabane,
Taylorstown,
Ten Mile,
Thompsonville,
Van Buren,
Vanceville,
Venice,
Washington,* (*c. h.*,)
West Alexander,
West Brownsville,
West Finley,
West Middletown,
Woodrow,
Yortysville,
Zollarsville.

WAYNE COUNTY.

Aldenville,
Ariel,

WAYNE COUNTY—Continued.

Arlington,
Beach Pond,
Berlin Centre,
Bethany,
Canaan,
Cherry Ridge,
Cold Spring,
Damascus,
Dyberry,
Eldred,
Equinunk,
Galilee,
Hamlinton,
Hawley,
Hemlock Hollow,
High Lake,
Hollisterville,
Honesdale,* (*c. h.*,)
Lake Como,
Lodge Dale,
Middle Valley,
Milanville,
Newfoundland,
Pleasant Mount,
Preston,
Priceville,
Prompton,
Rileyville,
Rock Lake,
Sand Cut,
South Sterling,
Starucca,
Sterling,
Stevenson's Mills,
Tanner's Falls,
Waymart,
West Damascus,
White Mills.

WESTMORELAND COUNTY.

Adamsburgh,
Beatty,*
Bolivar,
Bradenville,
Branch Junction,
Burrell,
Cavettsville,
Congruity,
Crab Tree,
Cribb's,
Derry Station,
Donegal,
Fitz Henry,
Fulton,
Geary,
Grapeville,
Greensburgh,* (*c. h.*,)
Harrison City,
Hillside,
Hill's View,
Irwin's Station,
Jacob's Creek,
Jones' Mills,
Larimer's Station,
Latrobe,
Laughlintown,
Laurelville,
Ligonier,
Livermore,
Lockport Station,
Lucesco,
Lycippus,
McKean's Old Stand,
McLaughlin's Store,
Madison,
Manor Dale,
Manor Station,
Mendon,
Millwood,
Mount Pleasant,
Murrysville,
New Alexandria,
New Derry,
New Florence,
New Stanton,
North Washington,
Oak Grove Furnace,
Oakland × Roads,
Parnassus,
Paulton,
Penn's Station,
Pleasant Unity,
Ridgeview,
Rostraver,
Salem Cross Roads,
Salina,
Sardis,
Shearer's × Roads,
Stahlstown,
Stewartsville,
Sutersville,
Tinker Run,
Verona,
Walts' Mills,
Weaver's Old Stand
Webster,
West Fairfield,
West Newton,
West Overton,
Yohoghany,
Youngstown.

WYOMING COUNTY.

Bellasylva,
Black Walnut,
Bowman's Creek,
Carney,
Centre Moreland,
Clinton Corners,
Dixon,
Eaton,

* Money-order office.

WYOMING COUNTY—Continued.

Factoryville,
Falls,
Forkston,
Golden Hill,
Jenningsville,
Keelersburgh,
Laceyville,
La Grange,
Lemon,
Lovelton,
McKune's Depot,
Mehoopany,
Meshoppen,
Mill City,
Nicholson,
Pierceville,
Russell Hill,
Scottsville,
Skinner's Eddy,
South Eaton,
Tunkhannock, (*c. h.*,)
Vernon,
Vosburgh.

YORK COUNTY.

Alpine,
Apple Grove,
Bald Eagle,
Brodbeck's,
Bryansville,
Castle Fin,
Chanceford,
Clear Spring,
Codorus,
Constitution,
Cross Roads,
Dallastown,
Davidsburgh,
Delta,
Dillsburgh,
Dover,
Emigsville,
Etter's,
Fawn Grove,
Franklintown,

YORK COUNTY—Continued.

Gatchellville,
Glen Rock,
Grahamville,
Hall,
Hanover,*
Hanover Junction,
Hartley,
Hellam,
Hetricks,
Hopewell Centre,
Jefferson Station,
Lewisberry,
Loganville,
McCall's Ferry,
McSherrysville,
Manchester,
Margaretta Furnace,
Mount Royal,
Mount Top,
Mount Wolf,
Muddy Creek Forks,
Mulberry,
Newberrytown,
New Bridgeville,
New Freedom,
Peach Bottom,
Pine Hill,
Plank Road,
Porter's Sideling,
Rail Road,
Rossville,
Seven Valleys,
Shrewsbury,
Sidonsburgh,
Slate Hill,
Smith's Station,
Spring Forge,
Stewartstown,
Strawbridge,
Strinestown,
Thomasville,
Union,
Wellsville,
West Bangor,
Windsor,
Wrightsville,
Xenia,
Yocumtown,
York,* (*c. h.*,)
York Furnace.

RHODE ISLAND.

BRISTOL COUNTY.

Barrington,
Barrington Centre,
Bristol,* (*c. h.*,)
Nayatt Point,
Warren.*

KENT COUNTY.

Anthony,
Centreville,
Coventry,
Coventry Centre,
East Greenwich,* (*c.h.*)
Escoheag,
Greene,
Natick,
Nooseneck Hill,
Phœnix,
Pontiac,
River Point,
Summit,
Warwick,
Warwick Neck,
West Greenwich Centre.

NEWPORT COUNTY.

Adamsville,
Jamestown,
Little Compton,
NEWPORT,* (*c. h.*,)
New Shoreham,
Portsmouth,
South Portsmouth,
Tiverton,
Tiverton Four Corners.

PROVIDENCE COUNTY.

Albion,
Ashton,
Burrillville,
Central Falls,
Centredale,
Chepachet,
Cranston Print W'ks,
Cumberland Hill,
Diamond Hill,
East Providence,
Fiskeville,
Foster,
Foster Centre,
Georgiaville,

PROVIDENCE COUNTY—Continued.

Greenville,
Harmony,
Hope,
Lonsdale,
Manton,
Manville,
Mapleville,
Mohegan,
Mount Vernon,
North Scituate,
Olneyville,
Pascoag,
Pawtucket,*
Pawtuxet,
PROVIDENCE,* (*c. h.*,)
Rockland,
Slaterville,
Smithfield,
South Foster,
South Scituate,
Valley Falls,
Watchemoket,
West Gloucester,
Woonsocket Falls.*

WASHINGTON COUNTY.

Allenton,
Arcadia,
Ashaway,
Carolina Mills,
Charlestown,
Davisville,
Dorrville,
Exeter,
Hope Valley,
Hopkinton,
Kingston, (*c. h.*,)
La Fayette,
Narragansett,
Narragansett Pier,
Peace Dale,
Perrysville,
Pine Hill,
Potter Hill,
Quonochontaug,
Richmond Switch,
Rockville,
Rocky Brook,
Shannock Mills,
Slocumville,
Usquepaugh,
Wakefield,*
Westerly,*
Wickford,*
Woodville,
Wyoming.

* Money-order office.

SOUTH CAROLINA.

Abbeville County.

Abbeville C. H.,
Antreville,
Calhoun's Mills,
Cokesbury,
Donnaldsville,
Due West,
Greenwood,
Hodges,
Level Land,
Lowndesville,
Monterey,
New Market,
Ninety-six,
Temple of Health,
Willington.

Anderson County.

Anderson C. H.,*
Belton,
Brushy Creek,
Equality,
Golden Springs,
Holland's Store,
Honea Path,
Moffettsville,
Newell,
Pendleton,
Piercetown,
Rock Mills,
Saddler's Creek,
Stony Point,
Storeville,
Townville,
Williamston.

Barnwell County.

Aiken,
Allendale,
Bamberg,
Barnwell,
Blackville, (*c. h.*,)
Dunbarton,
Graham's Turn Out,
Greenland,
Hammond,
Johnson,
Midway,
Mims,
Williston,
Windsor.

Beaufort County.

Beaufort,* (*c. h.*,)
Bluffton,
Brighton,
Coosawhatchie,
Gardner's Corner,
Gillisonville,
Grahamville,
Hardeeville,
Lawtonville,
Port Royal,
Robertsville,
Yemassee.

Charleston County.

Bonneau's Depot,
Charleston,* (*c. h.*,)
Enterprise Landing,
Holly Hill,
Oakley Depot,
Roadville,
St. Stephen's Depot,
Sineath's,
Summerville.

Chester County.

Black Stocks,
Chesnut Grove,
Chester C. H.,*
Crosbyville,
Halsellville,
Hazlewood,
Rossville.

Chesterfield County.

Cheraw,*
Chesterfield C. H.,
Deep Creek,
Jefferson,
Mount Croghan,
Old Store,
Oro,
Pine Tree,
White Plains.

Clarendon County.

Bethlehem,
Friendship,
Manning, (*c. h.*,)
New Zion,
Packsville,
Wright's Bluff.

Colleton County.

Adam's Run,
Ashepoo,
Edisto Island,
Green Pond,
Jacksonborough,
Reevesville,
Ridgeville,
Saint George's,
Walterborough, (*c. h.*)

Darlington County.

*Darlington C. H.**
Dove's Depot,
Florence,
Hartsville,
Lydia,
Society Hill,
Stokes' Bridge,
Timmonsville.

Edgefield County.

Bath,
Big Creek,
Cold Springs,
Dyson's Mills,
Edgefield C. H.,
Graniteville,
Hamburgh,
Johnston's Depot,
Longmire's Store,
Parks,
Pine House Depot,
Rehoboth,
Richardsonville,
Ridge.

Fairfield County.

Buck Head,
Doko,
Feasterville,
Lylesford,
Monticello,
Ridgeway,
Shelton,
Strother,
Winnsborough, (*c. h.*,)
Yonguesville.

Georgetown County.

Bull Creek,
Georgetown, (*c. h.*,)
North Santee.

Greenville County.

Buena Vista,
Chick's Springs,
Fairview,
Fountain Inn,
Gowensville,
Greenville C. H.,*
Grove Station,
Highland Grove,
Huntersville,
Lima,
Marietta,
Middle Saluda,
Mush Creek,
Plain,
Pliny,
Sandy Flat,
Traveller's Rest,
Whilden's Factory,
White Horse.

Horry County.

Bayborough,
Bucksville,
Conwayborough, (*c. h.*,)
Galivant's Ferry,
Green Sea,
Little River.

* Money-order office.

Kershaw County.

Camden,* (*c. h.*,)
Flat Rock,
Lynchwood,
Tiller's Ferry,
Troy.

Lancaster County.

Belair,
Craigsville,
Flint Ridge,
Jacksonham,
Lancaster C. H.,
Pleasant Hill,
Pleasant Valley,
Taxahau,
Wild Cat.

Laurens County.

Brewerton,
Clinton,
Eden,
Goodgiou's Factory,
Highland Home,
Laurens C. H.,*
Line Creek,
Mount Gallagher,
Mount Pleasant,
Simpson's Mills,
Tumbling Shoals,
Tylersville,
Waterloo.

Lexington County.

Beaver Pond,
Countsville,
Gilbert Hollow,
Hope Station,
Leesville,
Lexington C. H.,
Merritt's Bridge,
Pine Ridge,
Rish's Store,
Sawyer's Mills,
Steedman's.

Marion County.

Aeriel,
Britton's Neck,
Campbell's Bridge,
Carolina,
Catfish,
Effingham Station,
Forestville,
Gilchrist's Bridge,
Jeffrey's Creek,
Little Rock,
Lynch's Creek,
Marion C. H.,
Mars Bluff,
Mullin's Depot,
Nichols,
Oak Grove,
Pee Dee,
Reedy Creek,
Selkirk,
Temperance Hill.

Marlborough County.

Bennettsville, (*c. h.*,)
Brownsville,
Clio,
Parnassus.

Newberry County.

Chappell's Bridge,
Frog Level,
Jalapa,
Kinard's Turnout,
Liberty Hall,
Little Mountain,
Newberry C. H.,*
Pomaria,
Saluda Oldtown,
Silver Street,
Whitmire's.

Oconee County.

Bachelor's Retreat,
Bounty Land,
Fair Play,
Keowee,
Oakway,
Tugalo,
Tunnel Hill,
Walhalla, (*c. h.*)

Orangeburgh County.

Branchville,
Fort Motte,
Orangeburgh C. H.,
Rowe's Pump,
Saint Matthews,
Vance's Ferry.

Pickens County.

Anderson's Mills,
Arnold's Mills,
Dacusville,
Eastaloe,
Eighteen Mile,
Five Mile,
George's Creek,
Hunter's Mills,
Mile Creek,
Nine Times,
Pickens C. H.,
Pickensville,
Sunny Dale,
Table Mountain.

Richland County.

COLUMBIA,* (*c. h.*,)
Hopkins Turn Out,
Kingsville.

Spartanburgh County.

Batesville,
Campobello,
Cross Anchor,
Earlesville,
Enoree,
Glenn Springs,
Grassy Pond,
Hebron,
Hobbysville,
Limestone Springs,
Millville,
New Prospect,
Pacolett Depot,
Reidsville,
Spartanburgh C. H.,
Valley Falls,
Woodruff's.

Sumter County.

Bishopville,
Bradford Springs,
Lynchburgh,
Manchester,
Mannville,
Mayesville,
Mechanicsville,
Plowden's Mills,
Privateer,
Shiloh,
Stateburgh,
Sumter C. H.,*
Taylor's.

Union County.

Cold Well,
Cross Keys,
Fish Dam,
Goshen Hill,
Gowdeysville,
Jonesville,
Mount Joy,
Santuck,
Smith's Ford,
Timber Ridge,
Unionville, (*c. h.*)

Williamsburgh County.

Black Mingo,
Camp Ridge,
China Grove,
Johnsonville,
Kingstree, (*c. h.*,)
Lynch's Lake,
Myersville.

York County.

Antioch,
Bethany,
Blairsville,
Bullock Creek,
Clark's Fork,
Fort Mill,
Guthriesville,
Harmony,
Hickory Grove,
Hopewell,
New House,
Rock Hill,
Smith's Turn Out,
Yorkville, (*c. h.*,)
Zeno.

***Money-order office.**

TENNESSEE.

Anderson County.

Clinton, (*c. h.*,)
Fairview,
Oliver's,
Robertson's,
Robertsville,
Ross,
Scarborough,
Wallace's × Roads,
Wilson's.

Bedford County.

Arnold's Store,
Bedford, (*c. h.*,)
Bellbuckle,
Fairfield,
Fall Creek,
Flat Creek,
Haley's Station,
Normandy,
Palmetto,
Pleasant Grove,
Ray,
Richmond,
Shelbyville,*
Unionville,
Wartrace Depot.

Benton County.

Big Sandy,
Camden, (*c. h.*,)
Danville.

Bledsoe County.

Bee Creek,
Braden's Knobs,
Cold Spring,
Foster's × Roads.
Mount Airy,
Orme's Store,
Pikeville, (*c. h.*,)
Pitt's × Roads,
Roberson's × Roads,
Stephen's Chapel.

Blount County.

Brick Mill,
Cade's Cove,
Chilhowee,
Clover Hill,
Cloyd's Creek,
Coytee,
Ellejoy,
Friendsville,
Gamble's Store,
Louisville,
Maryville, (*c. h.*,)
Miser's Station,
Montvale Springs,
Morgantown,
Rockford,
Tuckaleechee Cove,
Unitia.

Bradley County.

Charleston,
Chatata,
Cleveland,* (*c. h.*,)
Linwood.

Campbell County.

Archerville,
Caryville,
Coal Creek,
Fincastle,
Jacksborough, (*c. h.*,)
Pine Mountain,
Well Spring.

Cannon County.

Auburn,
Bradyville.
Short Mountain,
Woodbury, (*c. h.*)

Carroll County.

Buena Vista,
Clarksburgh,
Hollow Rock,
Huntingdon, (*c. h.*,)
McKenzie,
McLemoresville,
Maple Creek,
Marlborough,
Terry,
Trezevant.

Carter County.

Carter's Depot,
Carter's Furnace,
Cave Spring,
Dugger's Ferry.
Elizabethton, (*c. h.*,)
Gap Run,
Hampton,
Happy Valley,
Limestone Cove,
Okolona,
Roan Mountain,
Stony Creek.

Cheatham County.

Ashland City, (*c. h.*,)
Craggie Hope,
Pleasant View,
Sycamore,
Thomasville.

Claiborne County.

Cumberland Gap,
Head of Barren,
Oldtown,
Pleasant,
Rob Camp,
Speedwell,
Spring Dale,
Tazewell, (*c. h.*)

Cocke County.

Big Creek,
Bridgeport,
Gorman's Depot,
Newport, (*c. h.*,)
Parrottsville,
Rankin's Depot,
River Side.

Coffee County.

Beech Grove,
Hillsborough,
Manchester, (*c. h.*,)
Summitville,
Tullahoma.*

Cumberland County.

Crossville, (*c. h.*,)
Hebbertsburgh,
Howard Springs,
Kimmer's Stand,
Owl Hill,
Pleasant Hill,
Pomona.

Davidson County.

Belleview,
Couchville,
Donelson,
Edgefield Junction,
Franklin College,
Goodlettsville,
Madison,
NASHVILLE,* (*c. h.*)

Decatur County.

Brodie's Landing,
Brownsport Furnace,
Decaturville, (*c. h.*,)
Fisher's Landing,
Perryville.

* **Money-order office.**

De Kalb County.

Alexandria,
Laurel Hill,
Liberty,
Smithville, (*c. h.*,)
Temperance Hall.

Dickson County.

Burns' Station,
Charlotte, (*c. h.*,)
Cumberland Furn'ce,
Danielsville,
Dickson,
Gillem's Station,
White Bluffs,
Worley Furnace,
Yellow Creek.

Dyer County.

Chesnut Bluffs,
Dyersburgh, (*c. h.*,)
Friendship,
Maxville,
Newbern.

Fayette County.

Braden Station,
Galway,
La Grange,*
Macon,
Moscow,
Oakland,
Rossville,
Somerville,* (*c. h.*,)
Willis Station.

Fentress County.

Barren Springs,
Boatland,
Hale's Mills,
Jamestown, (*c. h.*,)
Travisville.

Franklin County.

Alto,
Cowan,
Decherd,
Estill Springs,
Hunt's Station,
Sewanee,
Winchester,* (*c. h.*)

Gibson County.

Antioch,
Dyer's Station,
Humboldt,*
Milan Depot,
Quincy,
Rutherford Depot,
Trenton,* (*c. h.*,)
Yorkville.

Giles County.

Aspen Hill,
Bethel,
Bodenham,
Bradshaw,
Brick Church,
Buford's Station,
Bunker Hill,
Campbellsville,
Cornersville,
Elkton,
Good Spring,
Lesters,
Lynnville,
Marbut's,
Parker's Store,
Pisgah,
Prospect Station,
Pulaski,* (*c. h.*,)
Vale Mills,
Wales Station.

Grainger County.

Bean's Station,
Blain's × Roads,
Clear Spring,
Marshall's Ferry,
May Spring,
Morristown,*
Powder Spring Gap,
Rutledge, (*c. h.*,)
Spring House,
Tampico.
Thorn Hill.

Greene County.

Camp Creek,
Caney Branch,
Cedar Creek,
Cedar Lane,
Clear Creek,
Cross Anchor,
Fullen's,
Gourley's Bridge,
Graysburgh.
Greeneville,* (*c. h.*,)
Hayesville,
Home,
Horse Creek,
Laurel Gap,
Limestone Springs,
Little Chucky,
Locust Spring,
Lost Mountain,
Midway,
Millburnton,
Pilot Knob,
Rheatown,
Romeo,
Timber Ridge,
Warrensburgh.

Grundy County.

Altamont, (*c. h.*,)
Beersheba Springs,
Pelham.

Hamilton County.

Birchwood,
Chattanooga,
Chickamauga,
Chickamauga Sta'n,
Dallas,
Georgetown,
Harrison, (*c. h.*,)
Lookout Mountain,
Loyalty,
Ooltewah,
Sale Creek,
Soddy,
Tyner,
Wauhatchie.

Hancock County.

Alanthus Hill,
Mulberry Gap,
Sneedsville, (*c. h.*,)
War Creek,
War Ridge.

Hardeman County.

Bolivar,* (*c. h.*,)
Cedar Chapel,
Grand Junction,
Hickory Valley,
Middleburgh,
Middleton Station,
New Castle,
Pocahontas,
Saulsbury,
Teague's Mills,
Tooner's Station,
Whiteville.

Hardin County.

Bell Air,
Boyd's Landing,
Cerro Gordo,
Coffee Landing,
Hamburgh,
Ingleside,
Nelson,
Olive Hill,
Saltillo,
Savannah, (*c. h.*)

Hawkins County.

Austin's Mills,
Bull's Gap,
Burem's Store,
Lee Valley,
Mill Bend,
Mooresburgh,
New Canton,
Oak Well,
Persia,
Poor Valley,
Quarrysville,
Rogersville,* (*c. h.*,)
Stony Point,
Surgoinsville,
Van Hill,
War Gap,
White Horn,
Yellow Store.

*** Money-order office.**

Haywood County.

Bell's Depot,
*Brownsville,** (*c. h.*,)
Cageville,
Dancyville,
Johnson's Grove,
Jones' Station,
Stanton Depot,
Wellwood,
Woodville.

Henderson County.

Farmville,
Juno,
Lexington, (*c. h.*,)
Lone Elm,
Mifflin,
Poplar Spring,
Red Mound,
Scott's Hill,
Shady Hill.

Henry County.

Albany,
Como,
Conyersville,
Henry Station,
Manlyville,
New Boston,
North Fork,
*Paris,** (*c. h.*)
Paris Landing,
Porter Station,
Sandy Hill,
Spring Hill Academy,
Springville.

Hickman County.

Bastinville,
Bluff Point,
Bon Aqua,
Centreville, (*c. h.*,)
Duck River,
Dunnington,
Ivy Bluff,
Lick Creek,
Little Lot,
Pine Wood,
Vernon.

Humphreys County.

Buffalo,
Cuba Landing,
Fowler's Landing,
Johnsonville,
McEwen's Station,
Waverly, (*c. h.*)

Jackson County.

Butler's Landing,
Celina,
Clementsville,
Flynn's Lick,
Gainesborough, (*c. h.*,)
Granville,
Highland,
Meagsville,
Moore's Store,
North Springs,
Whitleyville.

Jefferson County.

Beaver Creek,
*Dandridge,** (*c. h.*,)
Flat Gap,
Kansas,
Leadvale,
Mill Spring,
Mossy Creek,
Nebraska,
New Market,
Oak Grove,
Panther Springs,
Russellville,
Stony Bluff,
Strawberry Plains,
Talbott's Mills,
Trion,
Whitesburgh,
Witts' Foundry.

Johnson County.

Baker's Gap,
Butler,
High Health,
Little Doe,
Pandora,
Shady,
Shawn's Cross Roads,
Stump Knob,
Taylorsville, (*c. h.*,)
Trade,
Ward's Iron Works.

Knox County.

Ball Camp,
Beaver Ridge,
Bull Run,
Campbell's Station,
Church Grove,
Concord,
Gap Creek,
Graveston,
*Knoxville,** (*c. h.*,)
McMillan,
Powell's Station,
Roseberry,
Thorn Grove,
Twinville,
Vandergriff's.

Lauderdale County.

Ashport,
Double Bridges,
Dry Hill,
Durhamville,
Fulton,
Hale's Point,
Ripley, (*c. h.*)

Lawrence County.

Appleton,
Henryville,
Lawrenceburgh,(*c. h.*,)
Marcella Falls,
Mockeson,
Palo Alto,
Wayland Springs,
West Point.

Lewis County.

Flat Rock,
Palestine.

Lincoln County.

Booneville,
Brighton Station,
County Line,
Cyruston,
Elora,
*Fayetteville,** (*c. h.*,)
Flintville,
George's Store,
Goshen,
Kelso,
Lynchburgh,
Millville,
Molino,
Mulberry,
Oregon,
Petersburgh.

McMinn County.

*Athens,** (*c. h.*,)
Cantrell's × Roads,
Cog Hill,
Mouse Creek,
Riceville.

McNairy County.

Adamsville,
Bethel Springs,
Chewalla,
McNairy Station,
Milledgeville,
Montezuma,
Purdy, (*c. h.*,)
Ramer,
Stantonville.

Macon County.

Echo,
Eulia,
Gibb's × Roads,
La Fayette, (*c. h.*)

Madison County.

Andrew Chapel,
Carroll,
Clay Brook,
Denmark,
Gadsden,
Henderson Station,
*Jackson,** (*c. h.*,)
Medon,
Pinson,
Spring Creek.

* Money-order office.

MARION COUNTY.

Battle Creek Mines, *Jasper*, (*c. h.*,) Looney's Creek, Nicojack, Tracy City, Whiteside.

MARSHALL COUNTY.

Berlin, Caney Spring, Catalpa Grove, Chapel Hill, Farmington, Globe Creek, *Lewisburgh*, (*c. h.*,) Lillard's Mills, Spring Place, Verona.

MAURY COUNTY.

Carter's Creek Station, *Columbia*,* (*c. h.*,) Culleoka, Fountain Creek, Hampshire, Hardison's Mills, Hurricane Switch, Hurt's Cross Roads, Mount Pleasant, Santa Fé, South Port, Spring Hill, Williamsport.

MEIGS COUNTY.

Big Spring, *Decatur*, (*c. h.*,) Goodfield, Hester Mills, Pine Land, Sewee, Ten Mile Stand.

MONROE COUNTY.

Ball Play, Belltown, Citico, Eve Mills, Four Mile Branch, Hopewell Springs, Jalapa, *Madisonville*, (*c. h.*,) Mount Vernon, Philadelphia, Sweet Water, Tellico Plains.

MONTGOMERY COUNTY.

Clarksville,* (*c. h.*,) Corbandale, Jordan Springs, McAllister's × Ro'ds, New Providence, Oakwood, Peacher's Mills, Pleasant Mound, Port Royal, Richardson's, Ringgold, Saint Bethlehem, Shiloh, Tate's Station, Woodlawn.

MORGAN COUNTY.

Crooked Fork, Glades, *Montgomery*, (*c. h.*,) Stapleton.

OBION COUNTY.

Earlobion, Harris Station, Kenton, Tiptonville, *Troy*, (*c. h.*,) Troy Station, Union City,* Woodland Mills.

OVERTON COUNTY.

Helham, *Livingston*, (*c. h.*,) Monroe, Mount Pisgah, Mouth of Wolf, Netherland, Nettle Carrier, Oak Hill, Olympus, West Fork.

PERRY COUNTY.

Beardstown, Britt's Landing, Cedar Creek Landing, Cypress, *Linden*, (*c. h.*,) Lobelville, Peter's Landing.

POLK COUNTY.

Benton, (*c. h.*,) Broad Shoals, Ducktown,* Parksville.

PUTNAM COUNTY.

Buffalo Valley, Byrne, *Cookville*, (*c. h.*,) Pekin, White Plains.

RHEA COUNTY.

Prestonville, Smith's × Roads, Sulphur Springs, *Washington*, (*c. h.*)

ROANE COUNTY.

Barnardsville, Eagle Furnace, Erie, Gray's Hill, *Kingston*, (*c. h.*,) Lenoir's, Letsinger, Loudon, Paw Paw Ford, Post Oak Springs, Rockwood, Stockton, Tabor, Webster, Williams' Mill, Wood's Hill.

ROBERTSON COUNTY.

Adam's Station, Baggettsville, Barren Plain, Black Jack, Cedar Hill, Coopertown, Cross Plains, Fort's Station, Green Brier, Hubertville, Mulloy's, *Springfield*, (*c. h.*,) Turnersville.

RUTHERFORD COUNTY.

Eagleville, Florence Station, Fosterville, Hall's Hill, Huntersville, Jordan's Valley, La Vergne, Middleton, Milton, *Murfreesboro'*,* (*c. h.*,) Readyville, Smyrna, Versailles, Walter Hill.

SCOTT COUNTY.

Horse Shoe Bend, *Huntsville*, (*c. h.*,) Winfield, Wolf Creek.

SEQUATCHIE COUNTY.

Dunlap, (*c. h.*,) Fillmore, Walnut Hill, Walnut Valley.

SEVIER COUNTY.

Cannon's Store, Fair Garden, Gatlinburgh, Henderson's Spr'gs, Henry's × Roads, Pigeon Forge, *Sevierville*, (*c. h.*,) Trundle's × Roads, Walden's Creek, Wear's Valley.

* Money-order office.

Shelby County.

Bartlett,
Bond's Station,
Colliersville,
Cuba,
Germantown,
Greenwood,
Harrison's Store,
Mc's Ville,
Memphis,* (*c. h.*,)
Oak Lawn,
Raleigh, (*c. h.*,)
Sulphur Well,
White's Station,
Wythe Depot.

Smith County.

Bagdad,
Carthage, (*c. h.*,)
Chesnut Mound,
Dificult,
Dixon's Springs,
Gordonsville,
Jenning's Fork,
New Middleton,
Rome,
Snow Creek.

Stewart County.

Caleb's Valley,
Cumberland City,
Cumberland Iron Works,
Dover, (*c. h.*,)
Erin,
Indian Mound,
Rough and Ready Furnace,
Saint John's,
Stewart,
Tennessee Ridge,
Tennessee River Station.

Sullivan County.

Arcadia,
Blountsville, (*c. h.*,)
Bristol,*
Eden's Ridge,
Edgeworth,
Fordtown,
Holston Furnace,
Holston Valley,
Kendrick's Creek,
Kingsport,
Mill Point,
Morell's Mill,
Piney Flats,
Union Depot.

Sumner County.

Castalian Springs,
Enon College,
Fountain Head,
Gallatin,* (*c. h.*,)
Hartsville,
Hendersonville,
Mitchellsville,
Richland Station,
Saundersville,
Trammel.

Tipton County.

Bloomington,
Covington,* (*c. h.*,)
Mason,
Mount Zion,
Portersville,
Randolph,
Tabernacle.

Union County.

Cedar Fork,
Haynes,
Lost Creek,
Loy's Cross Roads,
Maynardville, (*c. h.*,)
Raccoon Valley,
Sharp's Chapel,
Warwick's × Roads.

Van Buren County.

Bone Cave,
Spencer, (*c. h.*)

Warren County.

Increase,
Irving College,
McMinnville,* (*c. h.*,)
Morrison,
Mountain Creek,
Pine Bluff,
Rocky River,
Smartt's Station,
Vervilla,
Viola.

Washington County.

Boon's Creek,
Brownsborough,
Buffalo Ridge,
Carrville,
Cherry Grove,
Clear Branch,
Embryville,
Falls Branch,
Flag Pond,
Freedom,
Garber's Mills,
Hawes Cross Roads,
Indian Creek,
Johnson City,
Jonesborough,* (*c. h.*,)
Leesburgh,
Locust Mount,
Longmire,
Mill Brook,
Millwood,
Pilot Hill,
Swingleville.

Wayne County.

Clifton,
Eagle Tannery,
Patriot,
Waynesboro', (*c. h.*)

Weakley County.

Dresden, (*c. h.*,)
Dukedom,
Elm Tree,
Gardner's Station,
Gleeson Station,
Pierce Station,
Ralston's Station.

White County.

Cave,
Green Tree,
Newark,
Rock Island,
Solon,
Sparta, (*c. h.*)

Williamson County.

Basin Spring,
Bethesda,
Brentwood,
Christiana,
College Grove,
Franklin,* (*c. h.*,)
Jordan's Store,
Nolensville,
Peytonsville,
Rigg's × Roads,
Thompson's Station,
Triune.

Wilson County.

Austin,
Bellwood,
Cainsville,
Commerce,
Gladeville,
Green Hill,
Laguardo,
Lebanon,* (*c. h.*,)
Mount Carmel,
Oak Point,
Ponville,
Round Top,
Rural Hill,
Shop Spring,
Silver Spring,
Simmon's Bluff,
Statesville,
Stringtown,
Tucker's × Roads,
Watertown.

* Money-order office.

TEXAS.

ANDERSON COUNTY.

Barton, Beaver, Bethel, Fosterville, Kickapoo, Parker's Bluff, *Palestine*, (*c. h.*,) Plenitude, Tennessee Colony.

ANGELINA COUNTY.

Cheesland, *Homer*, (*c. h.*,) Marion.

ATASCOSA COUNTY.

Mottomosa, *Pleasanton*, (*c. h.*,) Somerset.

AUSTIN COUNTY.

Bellville, (*c. h.*,) Cat Spring, Hempstead, Industry, Iron Creek, Millheim, New Ulm, San Felipe, Sempronius, Shelby, Travis, Wesley.

BANDERA COUNTY.

Bandera, (*c. h.*)

BASTROP COUNTY.

Alum Creek, *Bastrop*, (*c. h.*,) Cedar Creek, Red Rock, Sand Fly, Serbin, Young's Settlement.

BEE COUNTY.

Aransas, *Beeville*, (*c. h.*,) Papalote.

BELL COUNTY.

Aiken, *Belton*, (*c. h.*,) Harrisville, Howard, Mountain Home, Salado, Volo.

BEXAR COUNTY.

Camp Melvin, Fort Concho, Graytown, Leon Springs, *San Antonio*,* (*c. h.*,) Selma.

BLANCO COUNTY.

Blanco, (*c. h.*,) Round Mountain, Twin Sisters, Westbrook.

BOSQUE COUNTY.

Clifton, *Meridian*, (*c. h.*,) Valley Mills.

BOWIE COUNTY.

Boston, (*c. h.*,) De Kalb, Powell Grove.

BRAZORIA COUNTY

Brazoria, (*c. h.*,) Chenango, Columbia, Sandy Point, Velasco.

BRAZOS COUNTY.

Bryan, (*c. h.*,) Millican.

BROWN COUNTY.

Brownwood, (*c. h.*)

BURLESON COUNTY.

Caldwell, (*c. h.*,) Lexington, New Anhalt, Prospect.

BURNET COUNTY.

Burnet, (*c. h.*,) Double Horn, Mahomet, Mormon Mills, Oatmeal, Shovel Mount.

CALDWELL COUNTY.

Lockhart, (*c. h.*,) Plum Creek, Prairie Lea, Sour Spring.

CALHOUN COUNTY.

Indianola,* (*c. h.*,) Port Lavaca, Saluria.

CAMERON COUNTY.

Brazos Santiago, *Brownsville*,* (*c. h.*,) Point Isabel.

CHAMBERS COUNTY.

Anahuac, *Wallisville*, (*c. h.*)

CHEROKEE COUNTY.

Alto, Atoy, Jacksonville, Knoxville, Larissa, Linwood, Pinetown, *Rusk*, (*c. h.*)

COLLIN COUNTY.

Farmersville, Highland, Lone Tree, *McKinney*, (*c. h.*,) Mantua, Millwood, Plano, Weston.

* Money-order office.

Colorado County.

Alleyton, Frelsburgh,
*Columbus,** (*c. h.,*) Oakland,
Content, Ridge.
Eagle Lake,

Comal County.

*New Braunfels,**(*c.h.,*) Smithson's Valley,
Sattler's, Spring Branch.

Comanche County.

Comanche.

Cooke County.

Gainsville, (*c. h.*)

Coryell County.

Eagle Springs, Rainey's Creek,
Gatesville, (*c. h.,*) Station Creek.

Dallas County.

Cedar Hill, Lancaster,
*Dallas,** (*c. h.,*) Lisbon,
Haught's Store, Scyene.

Davis County.

Douglassville, *Linden,* (*c. h.,*)
Hickory Hill, White Hall.

Denton County.

Denton, (*c. h.,*) Pilot Point.
Lewisville,

De Witt County.

Clinton, (*c. h.,*) Price's Creek,
Concrete, Terryville,
Hochheim, Yorktown.
Meyersville,

Ellis County.

Chambers' Creek, Red Oak,
Cross Timbers, *Waxahachie,* (*c. h.,*)
Cummins' Creek, Wilton.
Milford,

El Paso County.

El Paso, (*c. h.,*) San Elizario.
Fort Quitman,

Erath County.

Stephensville, (*c. h.*)

Falls County.

Carolina, *Marlin,* (*c. h.,*)
Golindo, Rock Dam.
Jena,

Fannin County.

Bonham, (*c. h.,*) Lick,
Honey Grove, Orangeville,
Ladonia, Warren.

Fayette County.

Black Jack Springs, Lyons,
Bluff, Neese's Store,
Cedar, Oso,
Cistern, Pin Oak,
Fayetteville, Rossville,
Flatonia, Round Top,
High Hill, Rutersville,
La Grange, (*c. h.,*) Winchester.
Long Prairie,

Fort Bend County.

Pittsville, Stafford,
Richmond, (*c. h.,*) Sugar Land.

Freestone County.

Butler, *Fairfield,* (*c. h.,*)
Cotton Gin, Moorhead.

Galveston County.

*Galveston,** (*c. h.,*) Highland Station.

Gillespie County.

Cherry Spring, *Fredericksburgh,* (*c. h.*)

Goliad County.

Cummingsville, Weesatch.
Goliad, (*c. h.,*)

Gonzales County.

Belmont, Round Lake,
*Gonzales,** (*c. h.,*) Thompsonville,
Hopkinsville, Winnton,
Rancho, Wrightsborough.

Grayson County.

Farmington, Pilot Grove,
Kentucky Town, *Sherman,** (*c. h.,*)
Macomb, Whitesborough.

Grimes County.

Anderson, (*c. h.,*) Plantersville,
Bedias, Prairie Plains,
Courtney, Roan's Prairie.
Navasota,

Guadalupe County.

Nockenut, Valley.
Seguin, (*c. h.,*)

* Money-order office.

Hardin County.

Concord,
Hardin, (c. h.)

Harris County.

Cypress Top,
Harrisburgh,
Hockley,
Houston,* (c. h.,)
Rose Hill.

Harrison County.

Eight Mile Creek,
Hallsville,
Macksville,
Marshall, (c. h.,)
Powellton,
Scottsville.

Hays County.

Johnston's Institute,
Mountain City,
San Marcos, (c. h.)

Henderson County.

Athens, (c. h.,)
Brownsborough,
Fincastle,
Malakoff,
Pine Grove,
Shakelford.

Hidalgo County.

Edinburgh, (c. h.,)
El Sauz,
Rudyville.

Hill County.

Covington,
Hillsborough, (c. h.,)
Peoria,
Towash.

Hood County.

Acton,
Granbury, (c. h.)

Hopkins County.

Bacchus,
Black Jack Grove,
Black Oak,
Bright Star,
Charleston,
Miller Grove,
Saltillo,
Sulphur Bluff,
Tarrant, (c. h.,)
White Oak.

Houston County.

Alabama,
Augusta,
Coltharp's,
Creswell,
Crockett, (c. h.,)
Eliza,
Naches,
Pennington,
Prairie,
Weldon.

Hunt County.

Greenville, (c. h.,)
Lone Oak,
Shiloh,
Timber Creek,
White Rock.

Jack County.

Jacksborough, (c. h.)

Jackson County.

Morales,
Navidad,
Texana, (c. h.)

Jasper County.

Jasper, (c. h.,)
Magnolia Springs,
Wiess Bluff.

Jefferson County.

Beaumont, (c. h.,)
Sabine Pass.

Johnson County.

Alvarado,
Caddo Grove,
Cleburne, (c. h.)

Karnes County.

Daileyville,
Ecleto,
Helena, (c. h.)

Kaufman County.

Cedar Grove,
Kaufman, (c. h.,)
Kemp,
Prairieville,
Rockwall,
Turner's Point.

Kendall County.

Boerne, (c. h.,)
Hodge's Mill,
Sisterdale.

Kerr County.

Comfort,
Kerrville, (c. h.,)
Zanzenburgh.

Kinney County.

Fort Clark, (c. h.)

Lamar County.

Ben Franklin,
Blossom Prairie,
Cotton Plant,
Paris,* (c. h.,)
Roxton,
Shiloh Academy,
Starkesville.

Lampasas County.

Lampasas, (c. h.)

Lavaca County.

Antioch,
Hackberry,
Hallettsville, (c. h.,)
Hope,
Moulton,
Petersburgh,
Speakeville,
Star,
Sweet Home.

Leon County.

Caldwell's Store,
Centreville, (c. h.,)
Leona,
Middleton.

* Money-order office.

LIBERTY COUNTY.

Ironwood, Moss Bluff.
Liberty, (*c. h.*,)

LIMESTONE COUNTY.

Eutaw, *Springfield*, (*c. h.*,)
Iron Clad, Tehuacana,
Mount Calm, Tucker's Mills.
Personville,

LIVE OAK COUNTY.

Echo, *Oakville*, (*c. h.*)
Gussettville,

LLANO COUNTY.

Llano, (*c. h.*)

MCLENNAN COUNTY.

Acomb, Mastersville,
Bosqueville, *Waco*,* (*c. h.*)

MADISON COUNTY.

Madisonville, (*c. h.*,) Willow Hole.
Midway,

MARION COUNTY.

Jefferson,* (*c. h.*,) Mim's Store.

MASON COUNTY.

Hedwig's Hill, *Mason*, (*c. h.*)
Loyal Valley,

MATAGORDA COUNTY.

Caney, *Matagorda*, (*c. h.*)

MAVERICK COUNTY.

Eagle Pass, (*c. h.*)

MEDINA COUNTY.

Castroville, (*c. h.*,) New Fountain.
D'Hanis,

MENARD COUNTY.

Fort McKavett, *Menardville*, (*c. h.*)

MILAM COUNTY.

Cameron, (*c. h.*,) San Anders,
Maysfield, San Gabriel.
Port Sullivan,

MONTAGUE COUNTY.

Head of Elm, *Montague*, (*c. h.*)

MONTGOMERY COUNTY.

Danville, Prairie Home.
Montgomery, (*c. h.*,)

NACOGDOCHES COUNTY.

Cherino, Martinsville,
Douglass, Melrose,
Linn Flat, *Nacogdoches*, (*c. h.*)

NAVARRO COUNTY.

Birdston, Richland Crossing,
Chatfield, Rural Shade,
Corsicana, (*c. h.*,) Rush Creek,
Dresden, Spring Hill.

NEWTON COUNTY.

Bleakwood, *Newton*, (*c. h.*,)
Burkeville, Salem.

NUECES COUNTY.

Banquete, Nueces,
Corpus Christi,* (*c. h.*,) San Diego.

ORANGE COUNTY.

Bunn's Bluff, *Orange*, (*c. h.*,)

PALO PINTO COUNTY.

Palo Pinto, (*c. h.*)

PANOLA COUNTY.

Beckville, Sugar Hill,
Carthage, (*c. h.*,) Walnut Hill,
Grand Bluff, Wood's.

PARKER COUNTY.

Cartersville, *Weatherford*, (*c. h.*)

POLK COUNTY.

Cold Spring, Moscow,
Livingston, (*c. h.*,) Smithfield,
Morganville, Swartwout.

PRESIDIO COUNTY.

Camp Stockton, Presidio.
Fort Davis,

RED RIVER COUNTY.

Clarksville, (*c. h.*,) Maple Springs
Cuthand, Robbinsville,
Hortonville, Savannah.

REFUGIO COUNTY.

Fulton, Rockport,
Lamar, Saint Mary's.
Refugio, (*c. h.*,)

* Money-order office.

ROBERTSON COUNTY.

Bremond,
Calvert,*
Hammond,
Hearne,
Owensville, (*c. h.*,)
Sutton's Station,
Wheelock,
Woodland.

RUSK COUNTY.

Alma,
Belleview,
Caledonia,
Harmony Hill,
Henderson, (*c. h.*,)
Iron Mountain,
London,
Milville,
Mount Enterprise,
New Danville,
New Salem,
Pine Hill,
Walling's Ferry.

SABINE COUNTY.

Brookeland,
Hemphill, (*c. h.*,)
Milam,
Sabinetown.

SAN AUGUSTINE COUNTY.

San Augustine, (*c. h.*)

SAN PATRICIO COUNTY.

San Patricio, (*c. h.*)

SAN SABA COUNTY.

Cherokee,
San Saba, (*c. h.*)

SHACKELFORD COUNTY.

Fort Griffin.

SHELBY COUNTY.

Buena Vista,
Center,
Hamilton,
Patroon,
Shelbyville, (*c. h.*,)
Todd's.

SMITH COUNTY.

Aberdeen,
Etna,
Garden Valley,
Mount Sylvan,
Randall,
Starrville,
Troup,
Tyler,* (*c. h.*)

STARR COUNTY.

Rio Grande City,(*c.h.*,)
Roma.

TARRANT COUNTY.

Fort Worth, (*c. h.*,)
Johnson's Station
Mansfield.

TITUS COUNTY.

Clay Hill,
Daingerfield,
Gray Rock,
Lone Star,
MountPleasant,(*c. h.*,)
Snow Hill,
Wheatville.

TRAVIS COUNTY.

AUSTIN,* (*c. h.*,)
Bee Caves,
Merrilltown,
Oak Hill,
Onion Creek,
Parsons' Seminary,
Perdenales,
Webberville.

TRINITY COUNTY.

Sumpter, (*c. h.*)

TYLER COUNTY.

Steele's Grove,
Town Bluff,
Woodville, (*c. h.*)

UPSHUR COUNTY.

Calloway,
Carrollton,
Coffeeville,
Gilmer, (*c. h.*,)
La Fayette,
Omega,
Pine Tree,
Pittsburgh,
Point Pleasant,
Simpsonville.

UVALDE COUNTY.

Sabinal,
Uvalde, (*c. h.*)

VAN ZANDT COUNTY.

Canton, (*c. h.*,)
Colfax,
Jordan's Saline.

VICTORIA COUNTY.

Kemper City,
Mission Valley,
Victoria, (*c. h.*)

WALKER COUNTY.

Holloway's Store,
Huntsville,* (*c. h.*,)
Newport,
Waverly.

WASHINGTON COUNTY.

Berlin,
Brenham,* (*c. h.*,)
Burton,
Chapel Hill,
Independence,
Vine Grove,
Washington.

WEBB COUNTY.

Laredo, (*c. h.*)

WHARTON COUNTY.

Bernard Station,
Egypt,
Wharton, (*c. h.*)

WILLIAMSON COUNTY.

Bagdad,
Circleville,
Florence,
Georgetown, (*c. h.*,)
Liberty Hill,
Pond Spring,
Round Rock.

* Money-order office.

WILSON COUNTY.

Fair View,
Lavernia,
Lodi, (c. h.,)
Sutherland Springs.

WISE COUNTY.

Boyd's Mill,
Decatur, (c. h.)

WOOD COUNTY.

Quitman, (c. h.)

ZAPATA COUNTY.

Carrizo, (c. h.)

UTAH TERRITORY.

BEAVER COUNTY.

Adamsville,
Beaver, (c. h.,)
Minersville.

BOX ELDER COUNTY.

Brigham City, (c. h.,)
Corinne,
Kelton,
Portage,
Willard.

CACHE COUNTY.

Clifton,
Franklin,
Hyde Park,
Hyrum,
Logan, (c. h.,)
Mendon,
Millville,
Newton,
Oxford,
Paradise,
Providence,
Richmond,
Smithfield,
Wellsville,
Weston.

DAVIS COUNTY.

Centreville,
Farmington, (c. h.,)
Kaysville,
Stoker.

IRON COUNTY.

Cedar City,
Iron City,
Kanarraville,
Paragonah,
Parowan, (c. h.,)
Pinto,
Summit.

JUAB COUNTY.

Chicken Creek,
Levan,
Mona,
Salt Creek, (c. h.)

KANE COUNTY.

Duncan's Retreat,
Rockville,
Springdale,
Toquerville, (c. h.,)
Virgin City.

MILLARD COUNTY.

Deseret,
Fillmore City, (c. h.,)
Holden,
Kanosh,
Meadow,
Petersburgh,
Scipio.

MORGAN COUNTY.

Croydon,
Enterprise,
Morgan, (c. h.,)
Mountain.

RICH COUNTY.

Bloomington,
Fish Haven,
Liberty,
Montpelier,
Ovid,
Paris,
Saint Charles, (c. h.)

RIO VIRGEN COUNTY.

West Point.

SALT LAKE COUNTY.

Bingham Canyon,
Draper,
Herriman,
Mill Creek,
SALT LAKE CITY,* *(c. h.,)*
South Cottonwood,
Union,
West Jordan,

SAN PETE COUNTY.

Ephraim,
Fair View,
Fountain Green,
Gunnison,
Manti, (c. h.,)
Moroni,
Mount Pleasant,
Spring City,
Wales.

SUMMIT COUNTY.

Coalville, (c. h.,)
Echo City,
Kamas,
Peoa,
Wanship,
Wasatch.

TOOELE COUNTY.

Grantsville,
Stockton,
Tooele, (c. h.)

UTAH COUNTY.

Alpine City,
American Fork,
Cedar Valley,
Fairfield,
Lehi City,
Payson,
Pleasant Grove,
Provo City, (c. h.,)
Santaquin,
Spanish Fork,
Springville.

WASATCH COUNTY.

Heber, (c. h.,)
Midway.

* Money-order office.

WASHINGTON COUNTY.

Bellevue,
Harrisburgh,
Leeds,
New Harmony,
Panaca,
Pine Valley,
Saint George, (*c. h.*,)
Washington.

WEBER COUNTY.

Alma,
Hooper,
Huntsville,
Lynne,
North Ogden,
Ogden City, (*c. h.*,)
Plain City,
Riverdale,
Slatersville,
Uintah.

VERMONT.

ADDISON COUNTY.

Addison,
Bridport,
Bristol,
Brooksville,
Chimney Point,
Chipman's Point,
Cornwall,
East Granville,
East Middlebury,
Ferrisburgh,
Granville,
Hancock,
Larrabee's Point,
Leicester,
Lincoln,
Middlebury,* (*c. h.*,)
Monkton,
Monkton Ridge,
New Haven,
New Haven Mills,
North Ferrisburgh,
Orwell,
Panton,
Richville,
Ripton,
Salisbury,
Shoreham,
South Starksbor'gh,
Starksborough,
Vergennes,*
West Addison,
West Cornwall,
West Salisbury,
Weybridge Lower Falls,
Whiting,
Whiting Station.

BENNINGTON COUNTY.

Arlington,
Bennington,* (*c. h.*,)
Bennington Centre,
Bondville,
Dorset,
East Arlington,
East Dorset,
East Rupert,
Factory Point,
Heartwellville,
Manchester,* (*c. h.*,)
North Bennington,
North Dorset,
North Landgrove,
North Pownal,
Peru,
Pownal,
Pownal Centre,
Readsborough,
Rupert,
Sandgate,
Searsburgh,
Shaftsbury,
South Dorset,
South Shaftsbury,
Stamford,
Sunderland,
West Arlington,
West Rupert,
Winhall,
Woodford.

CALEDONIA COUNTY.

Barnet,
Burke,
Danville,
East Burke,
East Hardwick,
Groton,
Hardwick,
Lower Waterford,
Lyndon,
Lyndon Centre,
Lyndonville,
McIndoe's Falls,*
Newark,
Norrisville,
North Danville,
Passumpsic,
Peacham,*
Ryegate,
St. Johnsbury,* (*c. h.*,)
St. Johnsbury Centre,
St. Johnsbury East,
Sheffield,
South Danville,
South Peacham,
South Ryegate,
South Walden,

CALEDONIA COUNTY—Continued.

Sutton,
Walden,
Waterford,
West Barnet,
West Burke,
West Danville,
West Waterford,
Wheelock,

CHITTENDEN COUNTY.

Bolton,
Burlington,* (*c. h.*,)
Charlotte,
Colchester
Essex,
Essex Junction,
Hinesburgh,
Huntington,
Huntington Centre,
Jericho,
Jericho Centre,
Jonesville,
Milton,
North Underhill,
North Williston,
Pleasant Valley,
Richmond,
Saint George,
Shelburne,
South Hinesburgh,
Underhill,
Underhill Centre,
West Bolton,
West Charlotte,
Westford,
West Milton,
Williston,
Winooski Falls.

ESSEX COUNTY.

Bloomfield,
Brunswick,
Canaan,
Concord,
East Haven,
Granby,
Guildhall, (*c. h.*,)
Island Pond,*
Lemington,
Lunenburgh,
Miles Pond,
Norton Mills,
Nulhegan,
Victory,
West Concord.*

FRANKLIN COUNTY.

Bakersfield,
Berkshire,
Bordoville,
Buck Hollow,
East Berkshire,
East Fairfield,
East Franklin,
East Georgia,
East Highgate,
East Richford,
East Sheldon,
Enosburgh,
Enosburgh Falls,*
Fairfax,
Fairfield,
Fletcher,
Franklin,
Georgia,
Georgia Plain,
Highgate,
Highgate Centre,
Highgate Springs,
Montgomery,
Montgomery Centre,
North Enosburgh,
North Fairfax,
North Sheldon,
Richford,
Saint Albans,* (*c. h.*,)
Saint Albans Bay,
Sheldon,*
Swanton,*
Swanton Centre,
Swanton Junction,
West Berkshire,
West Enosburgh,
West Georgia.

* Money-order office.

Grand Isle County.

Alburgh,
Alburgh Centre,
Alburgh Springs,
East Alburgh,
Grand Isle,
Isle La Motte,
Keeler's Bay,
La Grange,
North Hero, (*c. h.*,)
South Hero.

Lamoille County.

Belvidere,
Belvidere Corners,
Cady's Falls,
Cambridge,
East Cambridge,
East Elmore,
Eden,
Eden Mills,
Elmore,
Hyde Park, (*c. h.*,)
Jeffersonville,
Johnson,*
Morristown,
Morrisville,
North Cambridge,
North Hyde Park,
North Wolcott,
Stowe, *
Waterville,
Wolcott.

Orange County.

Boltonville,
Bradford,*
Bradford Centre,
Braintree,
Brookfield,
Chelsea,* (*c. h.*,)
Copperas Hill,
Corinth,
East Brookfield,
East Corinth,
East Orange,
East Randolph,
East Thetford,
Fairlee,
Newbury,*
North Randolph,
North Thetford,
North Tunbridge,
Orange,
Post Mill Village,
Randolph,
South Newbury,
South Strafford,
Strafford,
Thetford,
Thetford Centre,
Topsham,
Tunbridge,
Union Village,
Vershire,
Wait's River,
Washington,
Wells River,
West Braintree,
West Corinth,
West Fairlee,
West Randolph,*
West Topsham,
Williamstown.

Orleans County.

Albany,
Albany Centre,
Barton,*
Barton Landing,
Beebe Plain,
Brownington,
Coventry,
Craftsbury,
Derby,
Derby Line,*
East Albany,
East Charleston,
East Coventry,
East Craftsbury,
East Greensborough,
Glover,
Greensborough,
Holland,
Irasburgh, (*c. h.*,)
Jay,
Lowell,
Morgan,
Newport,*
Newport Centre,
North Craftsbury,
North Derby,
N. Greensborough,
North Troy,
South Albany,
South Barton,
South Glover,
Troy,
West Charleston,
West Derby,
Westfield,
West Glover,
West Newport,
Wetmore,
Willoughby Lake.

Rutland County.

Benson,
Benson Landing,
Brandon,*
Castleton,*
Centre Rutland,
Chippenhook Spr'gs,
Chittenden,
Clarendon,
Clarendon Springs,
Cuttingsville,
Danby,
Danby Four Corners,
East Clarendon,
East Hubbardton,
East Poultney,
East Wallingford,
Fair Haven,*
Forest Dale,
Healdville,
Hortonville,
Hubbardton,
Hydeville,
Ira,
Mechanicsville,
Mendon,
Middletown,*
Mount Holly,
North Clarendon,
Pawlet,
Pittsfield,
Pittsford,
Poultney,
Rutland,* (*c. h.*,)
Sherburne,
Shrewsbury,
South Wallingford,
Sudbury,
Sutherland Falls,
Tinmouth,
Wallingford,
Wells,
West Castleton,
West Haven,
West Pawlet,
Rutland.

Washington County.

Barre,
Berlin,
Cabot,
Calais,
East Cabot,
East Calais,
East Montpelier,
East Roxbury,
East Warren,
Gouldsville,
Marshfield,
Middlesex,
MONTPELIER,* (*c. h.*,)
Moretown,
North Duxbury,
North Fayston,
Northfield,*
North Montpelier,
Plainfield,
Roxbury,
South Barre,
South Cabot,
South Woodbury,
Waitsfield,*
Warren,
Waterbury,*
Waterbury Centre,
Woodbury,
Worcester.

Windham County.

Athens,
Bartonsville,
Bellows Falls,*
Brattleborough,*
Cambridgeport,
Cornton,
Dover,
Dummerston,
East Dover,
Fayetteville, (*c. h.*,)
Grafton,
Green River,
Guilford,
Guilford Centre,
Halifax,
Houghtonville,
Jacksonville,
Jamaica,
Londonderry,
Marlborough,
North Windham,
Putney,
Rockingham,
Sadawga,
Saxton's River,
Somerset,
South Halifax,
South Londonderry,
S'th Wardsborough,
South Windham,
Stratton,
Townshend,
Vernon,
Wardsborough,
W. Brattleborough,
West Dover,
West Dummerston,
West Halifax,
West Marlborough,
Westminster,
Westminster West,
West Townshend,
W. Wardsborough,
Whitingham,
Williamsville,
Wilmington,
Windham.

* Money-order office.

Windsor County.

Andover,
Ascutneyville,
Barnard,
Bethel,
Bridgewater,
Brownsville.
Cavendish,
Chester,*
East Barnard,
East Bethel,
Felchville,
Gassett's Station,
Gaysville,
Hartford,
Hartland,
Hartland Four Cor's,
Ludlow,*
North Chester,
North Hartland.
North Pomfret,
North Springfield,
Norwich,
Perkinsville,*
Plymouth,
Pomfret,
Pompanoosuc,

Windor County—Continued.

Proctorsville,
Quechee,
Reading,
Rochester,
Royalton,
Sharon,
Simonsville,
South Pomfret,
South Reading,
South Royalton,
South Woodstock,
Springfield,*
Stockbridge,
Taftsville,
Tyson Furnace,
Upper Falls,
Weathersfield,
Weathersfield Centre,
West Bridgewater,
West Hartford,
Weston,
West Rochester,
White River Junc'n,*
Windsor,*
Woodstock,* (*c. h.*)

VIRGINIA.

Accomack County.

Accomack C. H.,
Belle Haven,
Chincoteague,
Chincoteague Isl'd,
Guilford,
Horntown,
Jenkins' Bridge,
Locust Mount,
Locustville,
Messongo,
Modest Town,
New Church,
Onancock,
Pungoteague,
Temperanceville,
Wiseville.

Albemarle County.

Batesville,
Bentivoglio,
Brown's Cove,
Carter's Bridge,
Charlottesville,* (*c. h.*,)
Cobham,
Earleysville,
Free Union,
Glendower,
Greenwood Depot,
Howardsville,
Ivy Depot,
Keswick Depot,
Mechum's River,
Millington,
Moorman's River,
North Garden,
Scottsville,*
Shadwell,
Stony Point,
University of Va.,
Warren.

Alexandria County.

Alexandria,* (*c. h.*,)
Arlington.

Alleghany County.

Alleghany Station,
Callaghan's,
Clifton Forge,
Covington, (*c. h.*,)
Cowpasture Bridge,
Morris Hill,
Rich Patch,
Selma,
Sweet Chalybeate.

Amelia County.

Amelia C. H.,
Chula Depot,
Deatonsville,
Jetersville,
Lodore,
Mannborough,
Matoax,
Morven,
Paineville,
Wilkinson's Shop.

Amherst County.

Allen's Creek,
Amherst C. H.,
Cool Well,
Galt's Mills,
Harris Creek,
Mason's Depot,
Oronoco,
Riversville,
Salt Creek,
Stapleton Mills,
Walker's Ford.

Appomattox County.

Appomattox C. H.,
Bent Creek,
Evergreen,
Nebraska,
Oakville,
Pamplin's Depot,
Spout Spring,
Spring Mills,
Tower Hill,
Walker's Church.

Augusta County.

Arbor Hill,
Burke's Mills,
Churchville,
Cline's Mills,
Craigsville,
Deerfield,
Elizabeth Furnace,
Fishersville,
Greenville,
Hermitage,
Long Glade,
Middlebrook,
Milnesville,
Mint Spring,
Moffatt Creek's,
Mossy Creek,
Mount Meridian,
Mount Sidney,
Mount Solon,
New Hope,
Parnassus,
Sangerville,
Sherando,
Staunton,* (*c. h.*,)
Steele's Tavern,
Stuart's Draft,
Stribling Springs,
Swoope's Depot,
Waynesborough.

Bath County.

Bath Alum,
Bath C. H.,
Cady's Tunnel,
Cleek's Mills,
Green Valley,
Healing Springs,
Hot Springs,
Letcher,
Millborough Springs,
Mountain Grove,
Sun Rise,
Williamsville.

* Money-order office.

Bedford County.

Bellevue,
Big Island,
Body Camp,
Buford's,
Bunker Hill,
Chamblissburgh,
Charlemont,
Chesnut Fork,
Davis' Mills,
Emaus,
Fancy Grove,
Forest Depot,
Good View,
Hendrick's Store,
Holcomb's Rock,
Kasey's,
Liberty,* (*c. h.*,)
Lisbon,
Lone Pine,
Loving Creek,
Lowry,
Thaxton's,
Wade's.

Bland County.

Bland C. H.,
Mechanicsburgh,
Rocky Gap,
Sharon.

Botetourt County.

Amsterdam,
Blue Ridge,
Buchanan,
Cloverdale,
Dagger's Springs,
Deisher's Mill,
Fincastle,* (*c. h.*,)
Flukes,
Locust Bottom
Old Hickory,
Roaring Run,
Saltpetre Cave,
Troutsville,
Waskey's Mills.

Brunswick County.

Burntville,
Charlie Hope,
Gholsonville,
Jonesborough,
Kennedy's,
Lawrenceville, (*c. h.*,)
Pleasant Oaks,
Powellton,
Smoky Ordinary,
Sturgeonville,
White Plains.

Buchanan County.

Ava,
Grundy, (*c. h.*,)
McClure.

Buckingham County.

Bolling's Landing,
Buckingham C. H.,
Centenary,
Curdsville,
Diana Mills,
Gary's Store,
Glenmore,
Gold Hill,
Gravel Hill,
Mount Vinco,
New Canton,
New Store,
Ore Banks,
South Bangor,
Well Water.

Campbell County.

Arnoldton,
Brook Neal,
Campbell C. H.,
Castle Craig,
Concord Depot,
Green Hill,
Hat Creek,
Leesville
Lynchburgh,*
Marysville,
Mount Athos,
Mount Zion,
New London,
Pigeon Run,
Yellow Branch.

Caroline County.

Applewood,
Bowling Green, (*c. h.*,)
Cedar Fork,
Central Point,
Chilesburgh,
Dunn's Store,
Flippo's,
Guiney's,
Milford,
Penola,
Point Eastern,
Port Royal,
Rappahannock Academy,
Ruther Glen,
Sparta,
The Grove.

Carroll County.

Chamber's Valley,
Cranberry Plains,
Dug Spur,
Fancy Gap,
Gladesborough,
Hillsville, (*c. h.*,)
Lambsburgh,
Laurel Fork,
Piper's Gap,
Stone Mountain,
Wolf Glade,
Wood Lawn.

Charles City County.

Apperson's,
Charles City C. H.,
Wilcox Wharf,
Wilson's Landing.

Charlotte County.

Aspen Wall,
Barnesville,
Charlotte C. H.,
Cole's Ferry,
County Line Cross Roads,
Drake's Branch,
Dupree's Old Store,
Harvey's Store,
Keysville,
Mossing Ford,
Red House,
Red Oak Grove,
Rolling Hill,
Talcott,
Wylliesburgh.

Chesterfield County.

Chester,
Chesterfield C. H.,
Hallsborough,
Manchester,
Midlothian,
Proctor's Creek,
Skinquarter,
Winterpock.

Clarke County.

Berryville, (*c. h.*,)
Castleman's Ferry,
Millwood,
Wadesville,
White Post.

Craig County.

New Castle, (*c. h.*,)
Ripley's Mills,
Simmonsville,
Sinking Creek.

Culpeper County.

Boston,
Brandy Station,
Castleton,
Culpeper,* (*c. h.*,)
El Dorado,
Jeffersonton,
Mitchell's Station,
Racoon Ford,
Rapid Ann Station,
Richardsville,
Rixeyville,
Stevensburgh,
Waylandsburgh.

* Money-order office.

Cumberland County.

Ca Ira,
Cartersville,
Cumberland C. H.,
Oak Forest,
Stony Point Mills,
Sunny Side.

Dinwiddie County.

Burgess,
Dinwiddie C. H.,
Ford's Depot,
Goodwynsville,
Petersburgh,*
Ream's Station,
Ritchieville,
San Marino,
Sutherland,
Wilson's Depot.

Elizabeth City County.

Hampton, (*c. h.*,)
Old Point Comfort.*

Essex County.

Centre Cross,
Dunnsville,
Lloyds,
Loretto,
Miller's Tavern,
Montague,
Mount Landing,
Paul's Cross Roads,
Tappahannock, (*c. h.*)

Fairfax County.

Accotink,
Burk's Station,
Centreville,
Chantilly,
Clifton Station,
Collingwood,
Dranesville,
Fairfax C. H.,
Falls Church,
Herndon,
Hunter's Mills,
Iona,
Langley,
Lewinsville,
Pleasant Valley,
Prospect Hill,
Spring Vale,
Theolog'l Seminary,
Thornton's Depot,
Vienna.

Fauquier County.

Bealeton,
Bowenville,
Bristersburgh,
Broad Run Station,
Casanova,
Catlett,
Elk Run,
Fauquier White Sulphur Springs,
Markham Station,
Morrisville,
New Baltimore,
New Brighton,
Orlean,
Owl Run,
Paris,
Piedmont Station,
Pine View,
Rectortown Station,
Salem Fauquier,
Somerville,
The Plains,
Upperville,
Warrenton,* (*c. h.*,)
Weaversville.

Floyd County.

Connor's Mills,
Copper Hill,
Copper Valley,
Floyd C. H.,
Greasy Creek,
Indian Valley,
Little River,
Simpson's,
West Fork Furnace,
Wills' Ridge.

Fluvanna County.

Boswell's,
Bremo Bluff,
Central Plains,
Chapel Hill,

Fluvanna County—Continued.

Columbia,
Fork Union,
Hunter's Lodge,
Palmyra, (*c. h.*,)
Seven Islands,
Union Mills,
Wilmington.

Franklin County.

Bonbrook,
Boone's Mill,
Cooper's,
Dickinson's,
Glade Hill,
Gogginsville,
Hale's Ford,
Long Branch,
Naff's,
Penhook,
Pig River,
Prillaman's,
Retreat,
Rocky Mount, (*c. h.*,)
Shady Grove,
Snow Creek,
Sydnorsville,
Taylor's Store,
Union Hall,
Young's Store.

Frederick County.

Acorn Hill,
Back Creek Valley,
Capper's Spring,
Cedar Creek,
Collinsville,
Gainesborough,
Gravel Spring,
Hayfield,
High View,
Middletown,
Millbrook,
Mountain Falls,
Mount Vernon Tannery,
Newtown Stephensburgh,
Shockeysville,
Stephenson's Depot,
White Hall,
Winchester,* (*c. h.*)

Giles County.

Eggleston's Springs,
Hobb's Ferry,
Newport,
Pearisburgh, (*c. h.*,)
Pembroke,
Poplar Hill,
White Gate.

Gloucester County.

Glenn's,
Gloucester C. H.,
Hayes' Store,
Hickory Fork,
New Upton,
Wood's Cross Roads.

Goochland County.

Bula,
Dover Mines,
Elk Hill Mills,
Fife's,
Goochland C. H.,
Hadensville,
Issequena,
Johnson's Springs,
Loch Lomond,
North Side,
Pemberton,
Perkinsville,
Pierce's,
Sabbot Island,
Shannon Hill.

Grayson County.

Bridle Creek,
Elk Creek,
Independence, (*c. h.*,)
Mouth of Wilson,
Nuckollsville,
Point Hope,
Spring Valley.

Greene County.

Dawsonville,
Ruckersville,
Stanardsville, (*c. h.*)

* Money-order office.

Greenville County.

Hicksford, (c. h.,)
Poplar Mount,
Ryland's Depot.

Halifax County.

Barkesdale,
Black Walnut,
Bloomsburgh,
Brooklyn,
Buck Shoal,
Clover Depot,
Halifax C. H.,
Harmony,
Hyco,
Locust Level,
Meadville,
Mountain Road,
Mount Carmel,
Mount Laurel,
News Ferry,
Omega,
Red Bank,
Republican Grove,
Scottsburgh,
South Boston Depot,
Vernon Hill,
Whitesville,
Whitlock,
Wolf Trap.

Hanover County.

Ashland,
Atlee's Station,
Beaver Dam Depot,
French Hay,
Goodall's,
Hanover C. H.,
Hewlett's,
Junction,
Montpelier,
Morris,
Negro Foot,
Old Church,
Rockville,
Taylorsville,
Verdon.

Henrico County.

Curl's Wharf,
Erin Shades,
Glen Allen,
RICHMOND,* (*c. h.,*)
Westham Locks.

Henry County.

Horse Pasture,
Irisburgh,
Martinsville, (c. h.,)
Oak Level,
Prunty's,
Ridgeway,
Spencer's Store,
Traylorsville.

Highland County.

Head Waters,
Hightown,
McDowell,
Meadow Dale,
Mill Gap,
Monterey, (c. h.,)
New Hampden,
Palo Alto,
Spruce Hill,
Strait Creek,
Wilsonville.

Isle of Wight County.

Carrsville,
Smithfield, (c. h.,)*
Windsor Station,
Zuni Station.

James City County.

Burnt Ordinary,
Williamsburgh, (c. h.)*

King and Queen County.

Bruington,
Carlton's Store,
Little Plymouth,
Newtown,
Plainview,
St. Stephen's Church,
Shakleford's,
Stevensville,
Walkerton.

King George County.

Chatterton,
Comorn,
Edge Hill,
Friendshipville,
Hampstead,
King George C. H.,
Port Conway,
Shiloh.

King William County.

Aylett's,
Beulahville,
Cherry Lane,
Enfield,
Etna Mills,
King William C. H.,
Lanesville,
Mangohick,
Manquin,
Waranancoke,
West Point.

Lancaster County.

Kilmarnock,
Lancaster C. H.,
Litwalton,
Lively Oaks.

Lee County.

Beech Spring,
Cany Hollow,
Jonesville, (c. h.,)
Rocky Station,
Rose Hill,
Stickleyville,
Turkey Cove,
Walnut Hill,
White Oak Springs,
White Shoals,
Yokum Station,
Zion's Mills.

Loudoun County.

Aldie,
Arcola,
Bloomfield,
Bolington,
Circleville,
Daysville,
Farmwell,
Goresville,
Guilford Station,
Hamilton,
Hillsborough,
Hughesville,
Leesburgh, (c. h.,)*
Lincoln,
Lovettsville,
Middleburgh,
Mount Gilead,
Mountville,
Neersville,
Oatlands,
Philomont,
Round Hill,
Snickersville,
Taylorstown,
Unison,
Waterford,
Wheatland.

Louisa County.

Apple Grove,
Bell's × Roads,
Buckner's Station,
Bumpass,
Cuckoo,
Fredericks Hall,
Gum Spring,
Harris,
Jackson,
Locust Creek,
Louisa C. H.,
Poindexter's Store,
Thompson's × Roads,
Tolersville,
Trevilian's Depot.

Lunenburgh County.

Brickland,
Columbian Grove,
Double Bridge,
Lochleven,
McFarland's,
Non Intervention,
Oral Oaks,
Plantersville,
Pleasant Grove,
Rehoboth,
Wattsborough,
Yatesville.

* Money-order office.

Madison County.

Criglersville, Decapolis, Graves' Mill, Leon, *Madison C. H.*, Madison Mills, Oak Park, Peola Mills, Rochelle, Seville.

Matthews County.

Cobb's Creek, Hicks' Wharf, *Matthews*, (c. h.)

Mecklenburgh County.

Abbyville, *Boydton*, (c. h.,) Christiansville, Clarksville, Drapersville, Forksville, Lombardy Grove, Oakley, Palmer's Springs, Saint Tammany's, South Hill, Spring Hill, Wayside, White House, Whittle's Mills.

Middlesex County.

Church View, Freeshade, Harmony Village, Jamaica, Locust Hill, *Saluda*, (c. h.,) Sandy Bottom, Urbana.

Montgomery County.

Alleghany Spring, Big Spring Depot, Blacksburgh, Center Mills, Childress' Store, *Christiansburgh*,*(c.h.,) La Fayette, Lovely Mount, McDonald's Mill, Montgomery Springs, Pilot, Shawsville.

Nansemond County.

Chuckatuck, *Suffolk*,* (c. h.)

Nelson County.

Afton, Arrington, Elmington, Faber's Mills, Greenfield, Greenway, Hardwicksville, Horseley's Landing, *Lovingston*, (c. h.,) Massie's Mills, Montreal, Nelly's Ford, Norwood, Rockfish Depot, Tye River Depot, Variety Mills, Warminster.

New Kent County.

Barhamsville, *New Kent C. H.*, Providence Forge, Tunstall's.

Norfolk County.

Churchland, Deep Creek, Ferry Point, Great Bridge, Lake Drummond, *Norfolk*,* (c. h.,) Portsmouth.*

Northampton County.

Bay View, Caperville, Cherrystone, *Eastville*,* (c. h.,) Franktown, Hadlock, Johnsontown, Sea View.

Northumberland County.

Brown Store, *Heathsville*, (c. h.,) Lottsburgh, Wicomico Church.

Nottoway County.

Blacks and Whites, Burkesville, Forkland, Jeffress' Store, Jennings' Ordinary, *Nottoway C. H.*, Wellville.

Orange County.

Gordonsville,* Liberty Mills, Locust Grove, Madison Run Station, *Orange C. H.*, Thornhill, Unionville, Verdierville, Woolfolk.

Page County.

Alma, Cedar Point, Grove Hill, Hope Mills, Leaksville, *Luray*, (c. h.,) Marksville, Massanutton, Shenandoah Iron Works, Stony Man.

Patrick County.

Ararat, Carter's Mills, Elamsville, Mayo Forge, Meadows of Dan, Nettle Ridge, *Patrick C. H.*, Patrick Springs, Penn's Store, Rock Castle, Rock Spring.

Pittsylvania County.

Bachelor's Hall, Berger's Store, Callands, Cartersburgh, Cascade, Chalk Level, Danville, Hill Grove, Laurel Grove, Mount Airy, Peytonsburgh, *Pittsylvania C. H.*, Pleasant Gap, Riceville, Ringgold, Sandy Level, Spring Garden, Swansonville, Whitehead's Store, Whitmell.

Powhatan County.

Ballsville, Fine Creek Mills, Genito, Jefferson, *Powhatan C. H.*, Sublett's Tavern.

* Money-order office.

PRINCE EDWARD COUNTY.

Darlington Heights,
Farmville,
Green Bay,
Hampden Sidney College,
Moore's Ordinary,
Prince Edward C. H.,
Prospect,
Rice Depot.

PRINCE GEORGE COUNTY.

Brandon,
Brandon Church,
City Point,
Disputanta,
Garysville,
Piney Grove,
Prince George C. H.,
Templeton.

PRINCESS ANNE COUNTY.

Blossom Hill,
Land of Promise,
London Bridge,
Pleasant Ridge,
Princess Anne C. H.

PRINCE WILLIAM COUNTY.

Brentsville, (*c. h.*,)
Bristoe Station,
Brook Vale,
Buckland,
Dumfries,
Gainesville,
Hay Market,
Independent Hill,
Manassas,*
Neabsco Mills,
Nokesville,
Occoquan,
Stone House Hotel.

PULASKI COUNTY.

Dublin,
Newbern, (*c. h.*,)
New River Depot,
Radford Furnace,
Snowville.

RAPPAHANNOCK COUNTY.

Amissville,
Flint Hill,
Gaines' × Roads,
Laurel Mills,
Rock Mills,
Sandy Hook,
Slate Mills,
Sperryville,
Walden's,
Washington, (*c. h.*,)
Woodville.

RICHMOND COUNTY.

Emmorton,
Farnham,
Farnham Cross R'ds,
Warsaw, (*c. h.*)

ROANOKE COUNTY.

Bent Mountain,
Big Lick,*
Bonsack's,
Botetourt Springs,
Catawba,
Cave Spring,
Gishe's Mills,
Poage's Mill,
Salem,* (*c. h.*)

ROCKBRIDGE COUNTY.

Alum Springs,
Balcony Falls,
Bell's Valley,
Brownsburgh,
Buffalo Forge,
Buffalo Mills,
Cedar Grove Mills,
Collierstown,
Fairfield,
Fancy Hill,
Gilmore's Mills,
Goshen Bridge,

ROCKBRIDGE COUNTY—Continued.

Lexington,* (*c. h.*,)
Longwood,
McKenny's Mill,
Monmouth,
Natural Bridge,
Oakdale,
Rapp's Mills,
Rockbridge Baths,
Summers,
Timber Ridge.

ROCKINGHAM COUNTY.

Bowman's Mills,
Bridgewater,
Broadway Depot,
Cherry Grove,
Coote's Store,
Conrad's Store,
Cross Keys,
Dayton,
Edom,
Fair Hill,
Greenmount,
Harrisonburgh,* (*c. h.*,)
Keezletown,
Lacey Spring,
Linville,
McGaheysville,
Melrose,
Mount Clinton,
Mount Crawford,
Mount Vernon Forge,
Ottobine,
Port Republic,
Rawley Springs,
Singer's Glen,
Spring Creek,
Tenth Legion,
Timberville,
Waverlie.

RUSSELL COUNTY.

Alta Vista,
Belfast Mills,
Bickley's Mills,
Dickensonville,
Gibsonville,
Hansonville,
Jesse's Mills,
Lebanon, (*c. h.*,)
New Garden,
Rock Farm,
Rosedale,
Vicar,
Willow Spring.

SCOTT COUNTY.

Duncan's Mills,
Estillville, (*c. h.*,)
Fort Blackimore,
Fulkerson,
Osborn's Ford,
Pattonsville,
Point Truth,
Stock Creek.

SHENANDOAH COUNTY.

Alonzaville,
Columbian Furnace,
Edenburgh,
Edith,
Forestville,
Hamburgh,
Hawkinstown,
Jacob's Church,
Lantz Mills,
Lebanon Church,
Maurertown,
Moore's Store,
Mount Clifton,
Mount Jackson,
Mount Olive,
New Market,
Orkney Springs,
Saumsville,
Seven Fountains,
Strasburgh,
Van Buren Furnace,
Woodstock,* (*c. h.*)

SMYTH COUNTY.

Broadford,
Chatham Hill,
Marion,* (*c. h.*,)
Rye Valley,
Seven Mile Ford,
Two Mile Branch.

SOUTHAMPTON COUNTY.

Assamoosick,
Berlin,
Boykin's Depot,
Branchville,

* Money-order office.

SOUTHAMPTON COUNTY—Continued.

Drewryville,
Farmer's Grove,
Franklin Depot,
Green Plain,
Ivor,
Jerusalem, (*c. h.*,)
Newsom's Depot,
Pond's Shop,
Vicksville,
Weeksville.

SPOTTSYLVANIA COUNTY.

Andrews',
Brokenburgh,
Clover Green,
Fredericksburgh,*
Lewis' Store,
Mount Pleasant,
Partlow's,
Spottsylvania C. H.,
Thornburgh,
Twyman's Store,
Wilderness.

STAFFORD COUNTY.

Accokeek,
Belfair Mills,
Falmouth,
Garrisonville,
Hartwood,
Richland Mills,
Serena,
Stafford C. H.,
Stafford Store.

SURRY COUNTY.

Cabin Point,
Claremont Wharf,
Dallies,
Hog Island,
Spring Grove,
Surry C. H.

SUSSEX COUNTY.

Coman's Well,
Hawkinsville,
Henry,
Jarratts,
Littleton,
Parham's Store,
Stony Creek Warehouse,
Sussex C. H.,
Wakefield Station,
Waverly Station.

TAZEWELL COUNTY.

Abb's Valley,
Baptist Valley,
Blue Stone,
Burke's Garden,
Cedar Bluff,
Cove Creek,
Croftsville,
Knob,
Richland,
Springville,
Tazewell C. H.

WARREN COUNTY.

Bentonville,
Buckton,
Front Royal, (*c. h.*,)
Hambaugh's,
Linden,
Milldale,
Nineveh,
Riverton,
Water Lick.

WARWICK COUNTY.

Menchville,
Newport News,
Warwick C. H.

WASHINGTON COUNTY.

Abingdon,* (*c. h.*,)
Buffalo Pond,
Clear Branch,
Craig's Mills,
Emory,
Glade Spring,
Holston,
Lodi,
Love's Mills,
Mock's Mills,
Raven's Nest,
Saltville,
Smith's Creek.

WESTMORELAND COUNTY.

Baynesville,
Eltham,
Hague,
Kinsale,
Millville,
Montross, (*c. h.*,)
Nominy Grove,
Oak Grove,
Oldham's × Roads,
Rice's Store.
Templeman's Cross Roads.

WISE COUNTY.

Big Stone Gap,
Guest's Station,
Pound,
Wise C. H.

WYTHE COUNTY.

Browne Hill,
Eagle Iron Works,
Graham's Forge,
Iderbide,
Max Meadows,
Reed Island,
Rural Retreat,
Speedwell,
Wytheville,* (*c. h.*)

YORK COUNTY.

Rippon's Hall,
Yorktown, (*c. h.*)

WASHINGTON TERRITORY.

CHEHALIS COUNTY.

Bruceport,
Cedarville,
Chehalis Point,
Elma,
Hoquiam,
Montesano, (*c. h.*,)
Satsop,
Sharon.

CLALLAM COUNTY.

New Dungeness, (*c. h.*,)
Port Angeles.

CLARKE COUNTY.

Martin's Bluff,
Pekin,
Union Ridge,
Vancouver,* (*c. h.*)

COWLITZ COUNTY.

Castle Rock,
Freeport,
Kalama,
Monticello, (*c. h.*,)
Oak Point.

* Money-order office.

ISLAND COUNTY.

Coupville,
Coveland, (c. h.,)
Utsaladdy.

JEFFERSON COUNTY.

Port Discovery,
Port Ludlow,
Port Townsend, (c. h.)*

KING COUNTY.

Black River,
Seattle, (c. h.,)
Slaughter,
Snoqualmie,
Squak,
White River.

KITSAP COUNTY.

Blakeley,
Port Madison, (c. h.,)
Port Orchard,
Seabeck,
Teekalet.

KLIKITAT COUNTY.

Klikitat.

LEWIS COUNTY.

Boistfort,
Claquato, (c. h.,)
Cowlitz,
Grand Prairie,
Pumphrey's Landing,
Skookumchuck.

MASON COUNTY.

Arkada,
Oakland, (c. h.,)
Sherwood's Mills,
Skokomish.

PACIFIC COUNTY.

Bruceport,
Chinook,
Fort Willopa,
Oysterville, (c. h.,)
Unity.

PIERCE COUNTY.

Franklin,
Steilacoom City, (c. h.,)
Tacoma.

SKAMANIA COUNTY.

Cascades, (c. h.)

SNOHOMISH COUNTY.

Mukilteo,
Snohomish, (c. h.,)
Tulalip.

STEVENS COUNTY.

Fort Colville, (c. h.,)
Spokan Bridge.

THURSTON COUNTY.

Beaver,
Coal Bank,
Grand Mound,
OLYMPIA, *(c. h.,)*
Tumwater,
Yelm.

WAUKIAKUM COUNTY.

Cathlamet, (c. h.)

WALLA WALLA COUNTY.

Delta Mills,
Touchet,
Tukannon,
Walla Walla, (c. h.,)*
Wallula,
Whitman.

WHATCOM COUNTY.

La Conner,
Whatcom, (c. h.)

YAKIMA COUNTY.

Attanam,
Fort Simcoe,
Moksee, (c. h.,)
Yakima.

WEST VIRGINIA.

BARBOUR COUNTY.

Belington,
Burnersville,
Calhoun,
Coveton.
Elk City,
Kasson,
Meadowville,
Nestorville,
Overfield,
Peel Tree,
Philippi, (c. h.,)
Pleasant Creek,
Valley Furnace,
Woodford.

BERKELEY COUNTY.

Darkesville,
Falling Waters,
Gerrardstown,
Glengary,
Hainesville,
Hedgesville,
Jones' Springs,
Little Georgetown,
Martinsburgh, (c. h.,)*
Mill Creek,
North Mountain,
Shanghai,
Tomahawk Springs,
Van Clevesville.

BOONE COUNTY.

Bald Knob,
Ballardsville, (c. h.,)
Crook,
Mouth Short Creek,
Peytona.

BRAXTON COUNTY.

Braxton C. H.,
Bulltown,
Flat Woods,
Holly River,
Laforme's Store,
Little Otter,
Perkins' Mills,
Salt Lick Ridge,
Tate Creek.

BROOKE COUNTY.

Bethany,*
Fowler's,
Pan Handle,
Short Creek,
Wellsburgh, (c. h.)*

* Money-order office.

Cabell County.

Cabell C. H.,
Fudgy's Creek,
Green Bottom,
Guyandotte,
Marshall College,
Mud Bridge,
Ouslie's Gap,
Thorndike.

Calhoun County.

Arnoldsburgh,
Big Bend,
Grantsville, (*c. h.*,)
Minnora,
Sycamore.

Clay County.

Big Sycamore,
Clay C. H.,
Lizemore's.

Doddridge County.

Central Station,
Clover Dale,
Cold Water,
Greenwood,
Isaac's Camp,
Long Run Station,
McElroy,
New Milton,
Oxford,
Smithton,
West Union,* (*c. h.*,)
Yeater's Mills.

Fayette County.

Clifty,
Cotton Hill,
Fayetteville, (*c. h.*,)
Gauley Bridge,
Hawk's Nest,
Mountain Cove,
Oak Hill,
Raven's Eye,
Rocky Hill,
Russellville.

Gilmer County.

Batten's Mills,
Beall's Mills,
Cox's Mills,
Glenville, (*c. h.*,)
Letter Gap,
Sand Fork.
Steer Creek,
Tanners,
Townsend Mills,
Troy.

Grant County.

Black Rock,
Grant C. H.,
Greenland,
Hopeville,
Luney's Creek,
Mount Storm,
Mouse's,
Seymoursville,
Williamsport.

Greenbrier County.

Alvon,
Big Clear Creek,
Blue Sulphur Sp'gs,
Clintonville,
Falling Spring,
Frankford,
Green Sulphur Sp'gs,
Lewisburgh,* (*c. h.*,)
Little Sewell M'tain,
Meadow Bluff,
Monroe Draft,
Palestine,
Second Creek.
White Sulph. Sp'gs.*

Hampshire County.

Barrettsville,
Bloomery,
Capon Bridge,
Capon Springs,
Cold Stream,
Dillon's Run,
Forks of Capon,
Green Spring Run,

Hampshire County—Continued.

Hanging Rock,
North River Mills,
Okonoko,
Pleasant Dale,
Purgitsville,
Romney, (*c. h.*,)
Slanesville,
Smith's Gap,
South Branch Depot,
Springfield,
Yellow Spring.

Hancock County.

Blair,
Fairview, (*c. h.*,)
Freeman's Landing,
Holiday's Cove,
New Cumberland.

Hardy County.

Baker's Run,
Fabius,
Howard's Lick,
Inkerman,
Lost River,
Moorfield,* (*c. h.*,)
Mountain Home,
Peru,
Trout Run,
Wardensville.

Harrison County.

Adamsville,
Big Buffalo,
Bridgeport,
Brown's Creek,
Cherry Camp,
Clarksburgh,* (*c. h.*,)
Grassland,
Hessville,
Johnstown,
Kincheloe,
Lost Creek,
Lumberport,
New Salem,
Prospect Valley,
Quiet Dell,
Rockford,
Romine's Mills,
Sardis,
Shinnston,
Sycamore Dale,
West Milford,
Wilsonburgh,
Wolf Summit.

Jackson County.

Allen's Fork,
Angerona,
Cottageville,
Fisher's Point,
Grass Lick,
Jackson C. H.,
Huntsville,
Le Roy,
Lockhart's,
Lone Cedar,
Murraysville,
Muse's Bottom,
New Geneva,
Ravenswood,*
Reedy,
Ripley Landing,
Sandy,
Topin's Grove.

Jefferson County.

Charlestown,*
Duffield's,
Halltown,
Harper's Ferry,*
Kabletown,
Kerneysville,
Leetown,
Middleway,
Rippon,
Shepherdstown,* (*c. h.*,
Summit Point.

Kanawha County.

Cannelton,
Carbonvale,
Clendenin,
Coalburgh,
Coalsmouth,
Gillespieville,
Jarrett's Ford,
Kanawha C. H.,*
Kanawha Saline,
Laurel Ridge,
Osborne's Mills,
Paint Creek,

* Money-order office.

KANAWHA COUNTY—Continued.

Pocotaligo,
Shrewsbury,
Sissonville,
Tyler Mountain,
Upper Falls of Coal,
Vineyard Hill,
Waldingfield.

LEWIS COUNTY.

Alkire's Mills,
Big Skin Creek,
Fink's Creek,
Gaston,
Georgetown,
Hacker's Creek,
Ireland,
Jacksonville,
Janelew,
Murphey's Creek,
Walkersville,
Weston,* (*c. h.*)

LINCOLN COUNTY.

Coalville,
Falls Mills,
Griffithsville,
Hamlin, (*c. h.*,)
Laurel Creek,
Spurlockville,
Ten Mile.
Vannatterville.

LOGAN COUNTY.

Chapmanville,
Logan C. H.,
Rich Creek,
White's Mills.

MCDOWELL COUNTY.

Peerysville, (*c. h.*,)
Snake Root,
Tug River.

MARION COUNTY.

Barracksville,
Basnettsville,
Beaty's Mills,
Benton's Ferry,
Bingamon,
Boothsville,
Bunner's,
Canton,
Fairmont,* (*c. h.*,)
Farmington,
Forksburgh,
Glover's Gap,
Gray's Flat,
Mannington,
Meredith's Tavern,
Mill Falls,
Nuzums.
Palatine,
Rivesville,
Valley Falls,
Worthington.

MARSHALL COUNTY.

Adaline,
Beeler's Station,
Bellton,
Benwood,
Cameron,
Dallas,
Fair Hill,
Glen Easton,
Limestone,
Lynn Camp,
Moundsville, (*c. h.*,)
Rock Lick,
Rosby's Rock,
Sherrard,
Woodlands.

MASON COUNTY.

Arbuckle,
Beech Hill,
Clifton,
Cologne.
Deer Lick,
Flat Rock,
Graham Station,
Harmony,
Hartford City,
Letart,
Machirville,
Mason,
Mercer's Bottom,
New Haven,

MASON COUNTY—Continued.

Point Pleasant, (*c. h.*,)
Rock Castle,
Upland,
West Columbia,
Willow Tree.

MERCER COUNTY.

Concord Church,
Flat Top,
Jordan's Chapel,
Jumping Branch,
Princeton, (*c. h.*,)
Spanishburgh,
The Rock.

MINERAL COUNTY.

Burlington,
Claysville,
Frankfort,
Hartmonsville,
Headsville,
New Creek, (*c. h.*,)
Patterson's Depot,
Piedmont,*
Ridgeville.

MONONGALIA COUNTY.

Andy,
Arnettsville,
Blacksville,
Cassville,
Center,
Clinton Furnace,
Easton,
Granville,
Hoodsville,
Jake's Run,
Jobe,
Laurel Iron Works,
Laurel Point,
Maidsville,
Miracle Run,
Mooresville,
Morgantown,* (*c. h.*,)
Pleasant Valley,
Randall,
Statler's Run,
Stewartstown,
Wadestown,
White Day.

MONROE COUNTY.

Egypt,
Forest Hill,
Gap Mills,
Indian Creek,
Johnson's × Roads,
Lindside,
Maple Lawn,
Monclova,
Mouth of Indian,
Pack's Ferry,
Peterstown,
Red Sulphur Springs,
Rollinsburgh,
Salt Sulphur Springs,
Sinks Grove,
Sweet Springs,
Union,* (*c. h.*,)
Wolf Creek.

MORGAN COUNTY.

Alpine Depot,
Berkeley Sp'gs, (*c. h.*,)
Cacapon Depot,
Cherry Run Depot,
Orleans × Roads,
Paw Paw,
Sir John's Run,
Sleepy Creek Bridge,
Unger's Store.

NICHOLAS COUNTY.

Birch River,
Fowler's Knob,
Hookersville,
Kesler's × Lanes,
Nicholas C. H.,
Snow Hill.

OHIO COUNTY.

Clinton,
Elm Grove,
Greggsville,
Triadelphia,
Valley Grove,
West Liberty,
WHEELING,* (*c. h.*)

* Money-order office.

PENDLETON COUNTY.

Brushy Run,
Buck Horn,
Franklin, (*c. h.*,)
Harper's Mills,
Macksville,
Mount Freedom,
Mouth of Seneca,
Oak Flat,
Sugar Grove,
Sweedlin Hill,
Upper Tract,

PLEASANTS COUNTY.

Grape Island,
Hebron,
Saint Mary's, (*c. h.*,)
Twiggs,
Union Mills,
Willow Island.

POCAHONTAS COUNTY.

Academy,
Buckeye Cove,
Dunmore,
Edray,
Elk,
Frost,
Green Bank,
Huntersville, (*c. h.*,)
Mill Point,
Mount Murphy,
Traveller's Repose.

PRESTON COUNTY.

Allbright,
Austen,
Brandonville,
Bruceton Mills,
Cranesville,
Evansville,
Fellowsville,
German Settlement,
Glade Farms,
Gladesville,
Horse Shoe Run,
Kingwood, (*c. h.*,)
Knott's Mills,
Masontown,
Morgan's Glade,
Muddy Creek,
Newburgh,
Pleasant Hill,
Portland,
Racoon,
Reedsville,
Rowlesburgh,
Tunnelton,
Valley Point,
Willey.

PUTNAM COUNTY.

Buffalo,
Frazier's Bottom,
Harbour's Mills,
Hurricane Bridge,
Mount Salem,
Mouth of Scary,
Raymond City,
Red House Shoals,
Round Knob,
Sycamore Grove,
Winfield, (*c. h.*)

RALEIGH COUNTY.

Clear Creek,
Coal River Marshes,
Jarrold's Valley,
Matville,
Raleigh C. H.,
Richman Falls,
Shady Spring,
Table Rock.

RANDOLPH COUNTY.

Ash Lick,
Beverly, (*c. h.*,)
Camp Elkwater,
Cheat Mountain,
Fillmore,
Huttonsville,
Leadsville,
Middle Fork,
Mingo Flat,
New Interest,
Roaring Creek,
Taylor's Mills,
Valley Bend,
Valley Head.

RITCHIE COUNTY.

Bone Creek,
Cairo,
Cornwallis,
Cunningham's Mills,
Ellenborough,
Goffs,
Goose Creek,
Harrisville, (*c. h.*,)
Highland,
Holbrook,
Mole Hill,
Pennsborough,
Rogers,
Rush Run,
Sinnett's Mills,
Webb's Mills,
White Oak.

ROANE COUNTY.

Boggsville,
Flat Fork,
Henry's Fork,
Newton,
Reedyville,
Roxalana,
Shambling's Mills,
Spencer, (*c. h.*,)
Walton.

TAYLOR COUNTY.

Fetterman,
Flemington,
Grafton,*
Knottsville,
Pruntytown, (*c. h.*,)
Simpson's Creek,
Thornton,
Webster.

TUCKER COUNTY.

Black Fork,
Carrick's Ford,
Hannahsville,
Holly Meadows,
Lead Mine,
Red Creek,
Saint George, (*c. h.*,)
Texas.

TYLER COUNTY.

Ben's Run,
Booker's Mills,
Conaway,
Joseph's Mills,
Kidwell,
Little's Mills,
Lone Tree,
Long Reach,
Middlebourne, (*c. h.*,)
Moore's,
Pursley,
Ripley's,
Shirley,
Sistersville,
Wick.

UPSHUR COUNTY.

Buckhannon, (*c. h.*,)
French Creek,
Frenchton,
Grim's Store,
Lorentz Store,
Peck's Run,
Rock Cave,
Rural Dale,
Sago,
Tallmansville.

WAYNE COUNTY.

Adkin's Mills,
Buffalo Shoals,
Ceredo,
Cove Creek,
Dunleith,
Fort Gay,
Hubbardstown,
Round Bottom,
Wayne C. H.,
White's Creek.

WEBSTER COUNTY.

Hacker's Valley,
Middleport,
Webster C. H.,
Welch Glade.

* Money-order office.

WETZEL COUNTY.

Burton, Fanlight, Knob Fork, Milo, New Dale, *New Martinsville,* (*c.h.,*) Pine Grove, Porter's Falls, Proctor, Silver Hill, Van Camp, West.

WIRT COUNTY.

Burning Springs,* Newark, Oil Rock, Reedy Ripple, *Wirt C. H.,* Zackville.

WOOD COUNTY.

Belleville, Briscoe Run,

WOOD COUNTY—Continued.

Bull Creek, Davisville, Deer Walk, Fountain Spring, Harris' Ferry, Kanawha Station, Laurel Junction, Lockhart's Run, Lubeck, Murphy's Mill, *Parkersburgh,** (*c. h.,*) Rockport, Valley Mills, Volcano,* Wadesville, Walker, Warren, Williamstown.

WYOMING COUNTY.

Jo's Branch. Morgan Valley, *Oceana,* (*c. h.,*) Rock View, Sun Hill.

WISCONSIN.

ADAMS COUNTY.

Adams Centre, Arkdale, Barnum, Big Flats, Big Spring, Buckhorn, Davis' Corners, Dell Prairie, Easton, *Friendship,* (*c. h.,*) Grand Marsh, Little Lake, New Chester, New Haven, New Rome, Olin, Pilot Knob, Plainville, Point Bluff, Quincy, Roche-a-Cri, Spring Bluff, Spring Creek, Strong's Prairie, White Creek.

ASHLAND COUNTY.

La Pointe, (*c. h.*)

BARRON COUNTY.

Barron, (*c. h.*)

BAYFIELD COUNTY.

Bayfield, (*c. h.*)

BROWN COUNTY.

Askeaton, Bay Settlement, Denmark, De Pere,* East Wrightstown, Flintville, Fontenoy, Fort Howard, *Green Bay,** (*c. h.,*) Mills Centre, Morrison, New Franken, Oneida, Pine Grove, Prairie Farm, Robinson, Rousseau, Schiller, Suamico, Velp, Wequiock, Wrightstown.

BUFFALO COUNTY.

Alma, (*c. h.,*) Anchorage, Buffalo, Burnside, Fountain City,* Gilmantown, Glencoe, Maxville, Modena, Mondovi, Nelson, Waumandee.

BURNETT COUNTY.

Anderson, Donersville, *Grantsburgh,* (*c. h.,*) Wood River.

CALUMET COUNTY.

Brant, Brillion, Brothertown, Charlestown, *Chilton,** (*c. h.,*) Dundas, Gravesville, New Holstein, Potter's Mills, Quinney, Rantoul, Saint Anna, Sherwood, Stockbridge.

CHIPPEWA COUNTY.

Chippewa City, *Chippewa Falls,** (*c.h.,*) Cook's Valley, La Fayette, Vanville.

CLARK COUNTY.

Frankville, Humburd, Loyal, Lumberman, Lynn, Maple Works, *Neilsville,** (*c. h.,*) Pleasant Ridge, Staffordville.

COLUMBIA COUNTY.

Alloa, Bellefountain, Cambria, * Columbus,* Dekorra, Doylestown,

* Money-order office.

Columbia County—Continued.

Empire Junction,
Fall River,
Kilbourn City,*
Leeds,
Leeds Centre,
Lewiston,
Lewiston Station,
Lodi,*
Lowville,
Marcellon,
North Leeds,
Okee,
Oshaukuta,
Otsego,
Pacific,
Pardeeville,
*Portage City,** (*c. h.*).
Port Hope,
Poynett,
Randolph Centre,
Rio,
Rocky Run,
West Point,
Wyocena.

Crawford County.

Bell Center,
Bridgeport,
Eastman,
Ferryville,
Freeman,
Hurlbut's Corners,
Knapp's Creek,
Lower Lynxville,
Marietta,
Mount Sterling,
North Clayton,
North Star,
*Prairie du Chien,** (*c. h.,*)
Rising Sun,
Rowes',
Seneca,
Shaw Hill,
Sladesburgh,
Soldier's Grove,
Teller's Corners,
Towerville,
Wauzeka,
Wheatville,
Wright's Ferry,
Yankeetown.

Dane County.

Albion,
Alden's Corners,
Ashton,
Belleville,
Black Earth,
Blooming Grove,
Blue Mound,
Cambridge,
Christiana,
Cloutarf,
Cottage Grove,
Cross Plains,
Dane,
Deansville,
Deerfield,
Door Creek,
Dunkirk,
Fitchburgh,
Hanerville,
Harvey,
Junction,
Leicester,
Macfarland,
MADISON,* (*c. h.,*)
Marshall,
Mazo Manie,*
Middleton,
Mount Horeb,
Mount Vernon,
Nora,
North Windsor,
Oregon,
Paoli,
Perry,
Pheasant Branch,
Pine Bluff,
Primrose,
River,
Roxbury,
Rutland,
Spring Dale,
Stoner's Prairie,
Stoughton,*
Sun Prairie,*
Syene,
Token Creek,
Utica,
Verona,
West Middleton,
Westport,
Windsor,
York.

Dodge County.

Alderley,
Ashippun,
Beaver Dam,*
Burnett,
Burnett Station,
Chester Station,
Clyman,
Danville,

Dodge County—Continued.

Farmersville,
Fox Lake,*
Herman,
Horicon,*
Hustisford,
Iron Ridge,
*Juneau,** (*c. h.,*)
Kekoskee,
Leroy,
Lomira,
Lowell,
Mayville,*
Minnesota Junction,
Neosho,
Oak Grove,
Reeseville,
Richwood,
Rolling Prairie,
Rubicon,
Theresa,
Westford,
Woodland.

Door County.

Bailey's Harbor,
Brussels,
Clay Banks,
Duchateau,
Egg Harbor,
Ephraim,
Fish Creek,
Forestville,
Jacksonport,
Little Sturgeon,
North Bay,
*Sturgeon Bay,** (*c. h.,*)
Washington Harbor.

Douglas County.

Superior, (*c. h.*)

Dunn County.

Cedar Falls,
Colfax,
Downsville,
Dunnville,
Eau Galle,
Fall City,
Louisville,
Lucas,
Maple Springs,
*Menomonee,** (*c. h.,*)
Peru,
Rock Falls,
Waneka.

Eau Claire County.

Augusta,
*Eau Claire,** (*c. h.,*)
Fairchild,
Otter Creek,
West Eau Claire.*

Fond du Lac County.

Armstrong's Corn'rs,
Ashford,
Banner,
Brandon,
Byron,
Calumet Village,
Calvary,
Dotyville,
Dundee,
Eden,
El Dorado,
El Dorado Mills,
Elmore,
Empire,
Fair Water,
*Fond du Lac,** (*c. h.,*)
Foster,
Hinesberg,
Ladoga,
Lamartine,
Marytown,
Metomen,
Nanaupa,
New Cassel,
Newfane,
New Prospect,
North Taycheedah,
Oakfield,
Oakfield Centre,
Osceola,
Ripon,*
Rosendale,
Saint Cloud,
Taycheedah,
Van Dyne,
Waucousta,
Waupun,*
West Rosendale,
Woodhull.

* Money-order office.

GRANT COUNTY.

Annaton,
Beetown,
Big Patch,
Bloomington,
Blue River,
Boscobel,*
Bradtville,
British Hollow,
Bunker's Hill,
Cassville,
Castle Rock,
Dickeysville,
Ellenborough,
Fair Play,
Fairview,
Fennimore,
Georgetown,
Glen Haven,
Hazel Green,
Hurricane Grove,
Jamestown,
Lancaster,* (c. h.,)
Liberty Ridge,
Little Grant,
Martinville,
Millville,
Montfort,
Mount Hope,
Mount Ida,
Muscoda,
New California,
Ora Oak,
Patch Grove,
Platteville,*
Potosi,
Rockville,
Saint Rose,
Sinsinawa Mound,
Washburn,
Woodman,
Wyalusing.

GREEN COUNTY.

Albany,
Attica,
Bem,
Brodhead,*
Brooklyn,
Cadiz,
Clarno,
Dayton,
Exeter,
Farmer's Grove,
Jordan,
Juda,
Martin,
Monroe,* (c. h.,)
Monticello,
New Glarus,
Oakley,
Pedee,
Shuey's Mills,
Skinner,
Stewart,
Sylvester,
Twin Grove,
Willet.

GREEN LAKE COUNTY.

Berlin,*
Dartford, (c. h.,)
Grand Prairie,
Green Lake,
Kingston,
Lake Maria,
Manchester,
Markesan,*
Marquette,
Princeton,
West Green Lake.

IOWA COUNTY.

Arena,
Avoca,
Cobb,
Dodgeville,* (c. h.,)
Dover,
Helena Station,
Highland,
Hyde's Mills,
Jennieton,
Linden,
Lumberville,
Middlebury,
Mifflin,
Mineral Point,*
Moscow,
Pine Knob,
Ridgeway,
Union Mills,
West Blue Mound,
Wyoming.

JACKSON COUNTY.

Athol,
Black River Falls,* (c. h.,)
Hixton,
Irving,
Melrose,
Mills,
Mound Springs,

JACKSON COUNTY—Continued.

North Bend,
North Branch,
Pigeon Creek Centre,
Pine Hill,
Pole Grove,
Roaring Creek,
Sechlersville,
Wrightsville.

JEFFERSON COUNTY.

Aztalan,
Busseyville,
Cold Spring,
Concord,
Erfurt,
Farmington,
Fort Atkinson,*
Hebron,
Helenville,
Hubbleton,
Ixonia Centre,
Jefferson,* (c. h.,)
Johnson's Creek,
Kroghville,
Lake Mills,*
Milford,
Oak Hill,
Oakland,
Palmyra,*
Pipersville,
Rome,
Sullivan,
Waitesville,
Waterloo,*
Watertown.*

JUNEAU COUNTY.

Armenia,
Elroy,
Germantown,
Kildare,
Lemonweir,
Mauston,*
Mill Haven, (c. h.,)
Mount Zion,
Necedah,*
New Lisbon,* (c. h.,)
Orange,
Sentinel,
Werner,
Wonewoc.

KENOSHA COUNTY.

Bassett's Station,
Brighton,
Bristol,
Cypress,
Fox River,
Kenosha,* (c. h.,)
Paris,
Pleasant Prairie,
Salem,
Somers,
Wheatland,
Wilmot,
Woodworth.

KEWAUNEE COUNTY.

Alaska,
Ahnapee,
Carlton,
Casco,
Dyckesville,
Ellisville,
Kewaunee,* (c. h.,)
Lincoln,
Montpelier,
Pierce,
Red River,
Ryan,
Walhain.

LA CROSSE COUNTY.

Bangor,
Barre Mills,
Bohemia,
Burns,
Burr Oak,
Half Way Creek,
La Crosse,* (c. h.,)
Mindoro,
New Amsterdam,
North La Crosse,
Onalaska,
Shelby,
Stevenstown,
West Salem.

LA FAYETTE COUNTY.

Argyle,
Belmont,
Benton,
Blanchardville,

* Money-order office.

LA FAYETTE COUNTY—Continued.

Calamine,
Cottage Inn,
Darlington,* (*c. h.*,)
Elk Grove,
Etna,
Fayette,
Gratiot,
Meeker's Grove,
New Diggings,
North Elk Grove,
Shullsburgh,
Spafford,
White Oak Springs,
Wiota,
Yellow Stone.

MANITOWOC COUNTY.

Branch,
Clark's Mills,
Cooperstown,
East Gibson,
Eaton,
Elk,
Francis Creek,
Hika,
Kasson,
Kiel,
King's Bridge,
Larrabee,
Manitowoc,* (*c. h.*,)
Manitowoc Rapids,
Meeme,
Mishicot,
Nero,
Newtonburgh,
Niles,
Northeim,
Oslo,
Prag,
Reedsville,
Rosecrans,
Saint Nazianz,
Two Rivers,
Wayside.

MARATHON COUNTY.

Jenny,
Knowlton,
Marathon City,
Mosinee,
Naugart,
Sherman,
Stettin,
Wausau,* (*c. h.*)

MARQUETTE COUNTY.

Briggsville,
Douglas Centre,
Germania,
Harrisville,
Jeddo,
Lawrence,
Midland,
Montello,* (*c. h.*,)
Moundville,
Neshkoro,
Ordino,
Oxford,
Packwaukee,
Westfield.*

MILWAUKEE COUNTY.

Bay View,
Butler,
Five Mile House,
Good Hope,
Granville,
Greenfield,
Hale's Corners,
Milwaukee,* (*c. h.*,)
Nat'l Mil'y Asylum,
New Coeln,
Oak Creek,
Paynesville,
Root Creek,
St. Francis Station,
Saint Martins,
Ten Mile House,
Wauwatosa,
West Granville.

MONROE COUNTY.

Albanville,
Big Creek,
Cataract,
Clifton,
Dorset,
Emery,
Farmer's Valley,
Glendale,
Herseyville,
Leon,
Le Roy Station,
Melvina,
Moore's Creek,
Mountain,
Mount Pisgah,
New Clifton,

MONROE COUNTY—Continued.

Ridgeville,
Rudd's Mills,
Saint Marys,
Sheldon,
Sparta,* (*c. h.*,)
Tomah,*
Tunnel City,
Wilton.

OCONTO COUNTY.

Little Suamico,
Marinette,
Menekaune,
Oconto,* (*c. h.*,)
Pensaukie.
Peshtigo,*
Stiles,
West Pensaukie.

OUTAGAMIE COUNTY.

Appleton,* (*c. h.*,)
Binghamton,
Freedom,
Greenville,
Holland,
Hortonville,
Kaukauna,
Lime Rock,
Little Chute,
Mackville,
Medina,
New Mollis,
Seymour,
Shiocton,
Snidersville,
South Osborn,
Stephensville,
Stinson,
Sugar Bush,
Wakefield.

OZAUKEE COUNTY.

Belgium,
Cedarburgh,
Fredonia,
Freistadt,
Grafton,
Holy Cross,
Mequon River,
Ozaukee,* (*c. h.*,)
Saukville.

PEPIN COUNTY.

Arkansaw,
Durand,* (*c. h.*,)
Ella,
Frankfort,
Pepin,
Stockholm,
Waubeck.

PIERCE COUNTY.

Bay City,
Beldenville,
Big River,
Clifton Mills,
Diamond Bluff,
Ellsworth, (*c. h.*,)
El Paso,
Maiden Rock,
Martell,
Olivet,
Ono,
Plum City,
Prescott,*
River Falls,*
Rock Elm,
Rock Elm Centre,
Spring Valley,
Trenton,
Trim Belle.

POLK COUNTY.

Alabama,
Alden,
Avondale,
Black Brook,
Cushing,
Farmington Centre,
Lincoln Centre,
Luck,
Osceola Mills, (*c. h.*,)
St. Croix Falls,
Wagon Landing.

* Money-order office.

PORTAGE COUNTY.

Almond,
Amherst,
Badger,
Buena Vista,
Eau Pleine,
Ellis,
Grant,
Keene,
Lone Pine,
Madely,
New Hope,
Plover, (*c. h.*,)
Stevens' Point,*
Stockton,
Surrey.

RACINE COUNTY.

Burlington,*
Caldwell Prairie,
Caledonia Centre,
Ives' Grove,
Kansasville,
Lamberton,
North Cape,
Norway,
Racine,* (*c. h.*,)
Raymond,
Rochester,*
Sylvania,
Thompsonville,
Union Church,
Union Grove,*
Waterford,
Yorkville.

RICHLAND COUNTY.

Aken,
Bass Wood,
Bear,
Bear Valley,
Boaz,
Brady's,
Buck Creek,
Cazenovia,
Eagle Corners,
Excelsior,
Fancy Creek,
Forest,
Henrietta,
Ithaca,
Janney's,
Lone Rock,
Loyd,
Mill Creek,
Neptune,
Orion,
Port Andrew,
Richland Centre,*(*c.h.*)
Richland City,
Rockbridge,
Sextonville,
Sylvan,
Viola,
West Branch,
West Lima,
Woodstock,
Yuba.

ROCK COUNTY.

Afton,
Avon Centre,
Beloit,*
Cainville,
Center,
Clinton,*
Cooksville,
Edgerton,
Emerald Grove,
Evansville,*
Fairfield,
Footville,
Fulton,
Hanover,
Indian Ford,
Janesville,* (*c. h.*,)
Johnstown,
Johnstown Centre,
Koskonong,
Leyden,
Lima Centre,
Magnolia,
Milton,*
Milton Junction,
Oxfordville,
Rock Prairie,
Rock River,
Shopiere,
Tiffany,
Union,
West Magnolia.

ST. CROIX COUNTY.

Boardman,
Bonchea,
Brookville,
Cylon,
Erin,
Hammond,
Hudson,* (*c. h.*,)
Jewett Mills,

ST. CROIX COUNTY—Continued.

Kinnick Kinnick,
New Centreville,
New Richmond,
Pleasant Valley,
Somerset,
Star Prairie,
Warren,
Woodside.

SAUK COUNTY.

Baraboo,* (*c. h.*,)
Black Hawk,
Cassell Prairie,
Dellona,
Delton,
Ironton,
Lavalle,
Lime Ridge,
Loganville,
Marble Ridge,
Merrimack,
Oaks,
Plain,
Prairie du Sac,
Reedsburgh,*
Sandusky,
Sauk City,*
Spring Green,
Valton,
White Mound.

SHAWANAW COUNTY.

Angelica,
Belle Plaine,
Bonduel,
Kershena,
Laney,
Pella,
Owego,
Shawanaw, (*c. h.*,)
Waukecheon.

SHEBOYGAN COUNTY.

Ada,
Adell,
Bamberg,
Beech Wood,
Cascade,
Cedar Grove,
Dacada,
Edwards,
Franklin,
Gibbsville,
Glenbuelah,
Greenbush,
Hingham,
Hobart's Mills,
Howard's Grove,
Johnsonville,
Mosel,
Onion River,
Oostburgh,
Our Town,
Plymouth,
Rathbun,
Rhine,
Russell,
Scott,
Sheboygan,* (*c. h.*,)
Sheboygan Falls,
Winooski.

TREMPEALEAU COUNTY.

Alhambra,
Arcadia,
Coral City,
Elk Creek,
Ettrick,
Frenchville,
Galesville, (*c. h.*,)
Hale,
Hamlin,
Home,
Hooker,
Osseo,
Scotia,
South Bend,
Trempealeau,*
Williamsburgh.

VERNON COUNTY.

Avalanche,
Bloomingdale,
Breckinridge,
Burr,
Chaseburgh,
Chipmonk Cooley,
Coon Prairie,
Coon Valley,
Debello,
De Soto,
Enterprise,
Esofia,
Genoa,
Goole,
Harmony,
Hillsborough,*
Hockley,
Kickapoo,

* Money-order office.

VERNON COUNTY—Continued.

La Farge,
Liberty,
Liberty Pole,
Mount Tabor,
Muncie,
Newry,
Newton,
Newville,
Odin,
Ontario,
Petrolium,
Readstown,
Retreat,
Rockton,
Romance,
Sierra,
Springville,
Star,
Stoddard,
Sugar Grove,
Valley,
Victory,
Viroqua,* (*c. h.*,)
Warner's Landing,
Weister,
West Prairie.

WALWORTH COUNTY.

Adams,
Allen's Grove,
Bay Hill,
Bloomfield,
Darien,
Delavan,*
East Delavan,
East Troy,*
East Troy Lake,
Elk Horn,* (*c. h.*,)
Elton,
Geneva,
Grove,
Heart Prairie,
Honey Creek,
La Grange,
Little Prairie,
Lyons,
Millard,
Richmond,
Sharon,
Springfield,
Spring Prairie,
Sugar Creek,
Tirade,
Troy,
Troy Centre,
Vienna,
Walworth,
White Water.*

WASHINGTON COUNTY.

Ackerville,
Addison,
Aurora,
Barton,
Boltonville,
Cedar Creek,
Fillmore,
Hartford,
Jackson,
Kewaskum,
Kirchayn,
Kohlsville,
Lake Five,
Meeker,
Myra,
Nenno,
Newburgh,
Richfield,
Saint Lawrence,
Schleisingerville,
South Germantown,
Staatsville,
Thompson,
Toland's Prairie,
Wayne,
West Bend,* (*c. h.*,)
Young America,
Young Hickory.

WAUKESHA COUNTY.

Big Bend,
Brookfield Centre,
Delafield,
Dodge's Corners,
Dousman,
Duplainville,
Durham Hill,
Eagle,
Elm Grove,
Fussville,
Genesce,
Genesee Depot,
Golden Lake,
Hartland,

WAUKESHA COUNTY—Continued.

Lannon Springs,
Mapleton,
Marcy,
Menomonee Falls,
Merton,
Monches,
Monterey,
Mukwonago,
Muskego Centre,
Nashotah Mission,
New Berlin,
North Lake,
North Prairie Stat'n,
Oconomowoc,*
Ottawa,
Pewaukee,
Prospect Hill,
Stone Bank,
Summit,
Sussex,
Tess Corners,
Vernon,
Waterville,
Waukesha,* (*c. h.*)

WAUPACA COUNTY.

Baldwin's Mills,
Bear Creek,
Clintonville,
Crystal Lake,
Dupont,
Embarrass,
Evanswood,
Fremont,
Helvetia,
Iola,
Lind,
Little Wolf,
Marble,
New London,
Northport,
Ogdensburgh,
Readfield,
Royalton,
Rural,
Scandinavia,
Sheridan,
Symco,
Waupaca, (*c. h.*,)
Weyauwega.

WAUSHARA COUNTY.

Aurorahville,
Brushville,
Cedar Lake,
Coloma,
Dakota,
East Oasis,
Hancock,
Howe's Corners,
Mount Morris,
Oasis,
Pine River,
Plainfield,
Poy Sippi,
Richford,
Saxeville,
Spring Lake,
Spring Water,
Tustin,
Wautoma,* (*c. h.*)

WINNEBAGO COUNTY.

Butte des Morts,
Clemansville,
Elo,
Eureka,
Fisk's Corners,
Koro,
Menasha,*
Neenah,
Nekama,
Nepeuskun,
Omro,*
Orihula,
Oshkosh,* (*c. h.*,)
Poygan,
Ring,
Vinland,
Waukau,
Weelaunee,
Winchester,
Winneconne.

WOOD COUNTY.

Centralia,
Dexterville,
Grand Rapids,* (*c.h.*,)
Nasonville,
Port Edwards,
Wood.

* Money-order office.

WYOMING TERRITORY.

ALBANY COUNTY.

Laramie, (*c. h.*,)
Sherman,
Wyoming.

CARBON COUNTY.

Carbon,
Fort Fred Steele,
Fort Halleck,
Medicine Bow,
Percy,
Rawling's Springs, (*c. h*)

LARAMIE COUNTY.

CHEYENNE CITY,* (*c. h.*,)
Fort Laramie,
Lookout,
Pine Bluff.

SWEETWATER COUNTY.

Atlantic City,
Bitter Creek,
Green River City,
Little Wind River,
Miner's Delight,
South Pass City, (*c. h.*)

UINTAH COUNTY.

Bridger Station,
Bryan,
Carter,
Evanston,
Fort Bridger, (*c. h.*,)
Gilmer,
Piedmont,
Point of Rocks.

www.ingramcontent.com/pod-product-compliance
Lightning Source LLC
LaVergne TN
LVHW020113110826
845151LV00001B/144

* 9 7 8 1 4 2 5 5 4 2 8 1 8 *